Behavior Disorders of Childhood

SIXTH EDITION

RITA WICKS-NELSON
West Virginia University Institute of Technology,
Professor Emeritus

ALLEN C. ISRAEL
University at Albany, State University of New York

UPPER SADDLE RIVER, NEW JERSEY 07458

Library of Congress Cataloging-in-Publication Data

Wicks-Nelson
  Behavior disorders of childhood / Rita Wicks-Nelson, Allen C. Israel.—6th ed.
    p. cm.
  Includes bibliographical references and index.
  ISBN 0-13-153908-6
    1. Behavior disorders in children. I. Israel, Allen C. II. Title.

RJ506.B44W534 2003
618.92′89—dc22

2005042967

Editorial Director: Leah Jewell
Executive Editor: Jennifer Gilliland
Editorial Assistant: LeeAnn Doherty
Director of Marketing: Heather Shelstad
Marketing Assistant: Irene Fraga
Assistant Managing Editor (Production): Maureen Richardson
Production Liaison: Maureen Richardson
Manufacturing Buyer: Ben Smith
Interior Design: GGS Book Services, Atlantic Highlands
Cover Design: Jose Sorreta
Cover Illustration/Photo: Creatas/Dynamic Design
Composition/Full-Service Project Management: GGS Book Services, Atlantic Highlands
Printer/Binder: Courier Corp.

Credits and acknowledgments borrowed from other sources and reproduced, with permission, in this textbook appear on appropriate page within text (or on pages 528–533).

Pearson Education, Ltd.
Pearson Education Australia PTY, Limited
Pearson Education Singapore, Pte., Ltd.
Pearson Education North Asia Ltd.
Pearson Education, Canada, Ltd.
Pearson Educación de Mexico, S.A. de C.V.
Pearson Education–Japan
Pearson Education Malaysia, Pte., Ltd.
Pearson Education, Upper Saddle River, NJ

10 9 8 7 6 5 4
ISBN 0-13-153908-6

Brief Contents

Contents

4 Research: Its Role and Methods   72

9   Attention-Deficit Hyperactivity Disorder   240

10   Language and Learning Disorders   270

14 Psychological Factors Affecting Medical Condition   400

Preface

For those interested in the well-being of children and adolescents, there is much to talk about these days. In roughly one hundred years, the study of young people has moved from relative ignorance to considerable knowledge about human development in general and disordered behavior more specifically. With much yet to be learned—and the needs of youth considerable—this is a challenging and exciting field. We are fortunate to have the opportunity to participate in it.

This sixth edition of *Behavior Disorders of Childhood* reflects the progress that continues to be made in understanding, assessing, treating, and preventing psychopathology of youth. Designed as a relatively comprehensive introduction, the text includes central issues; theoretical and methodological foundations; and the characteristics, correlates, epidemiology, developmental course, etiology, assessment, treatment, and prevention of disordered behavior. As is typically the case for a work of this kind, space limitation demands some selectivity of content.

CENTRAL THEMES

At the inception of this text, we viewed certain themes as critical to the study of problems of the young. These themes have stood the test of time, have evolved, and have become more widely and subtly recognized as essential. Indeed, their early incorporation into this text undoubtedly accounts in part for its ongoing success.

First is an emphasis on a developmental psychopathology approach as a partner to the more traditional (usual) clinical/disorder approach. The developmental psychopathology perspective assumes that disorders of young people must be viewed within a developmental context. This perspective is fully articulated in early chapters of the book and guides discussion of specific disorders in subsequent chapters.

A primary assumption is the belief that the development of normal and disturbed behavior are related and are best viewed as occurring along a dynamic pathway of growth and experience, with connections to the past and to the future. One way this proposition is reflected in the text is by the consideration of disorders across childhood and into adolescence. Taking seriously the assumption that behavioral development cannot be readily parsed by age, we employ a relatively broad time frame for discussing behavioral problems in young people.

A second theme woven throughout the text is the view that behavioral problems result from transactions among variables. With few—if any— exceptions, behavior stems from multiple influences and their continuous interactions. Biological structure and function, genetic transmission, cognition, emotion, and numerous aspects of the immediate and larger social environment play complex roles in generating and maintaining psychological and behavioral functioning.

Following from this, a third theme emphasizes that the problems of the young are intricately tied to the social and cultural contexts in which they experience life. Children and adolescents are embedded in a circle of social and environmental influences involving family, peer, school, neighborhood, societal, and cultural circumstances. Youth bring their personal attributes to these circumstances, are affected by them, and in turn, influence other people and situations. Meaningful analysis of behavioral problems thus requires the incorporation of contextual features. Such aspects as family interactions, friendships, gender, educational opportunity, poverty, ethnicity and race, and cultural values all come into play.

A fourth major theme is a bias toward the scientist-practitioner approach. Prudent and insightful thinking is required in both figuring out the puzzles of behavioral problems and applying acquired knowledge. We believe that empirical approaches and the theoretical frameworks that rely on scientific method provide the best avenue for understanding the complexity of human behavior. Research findings, a critical component of virtually all chapters of this book, thus are brought to bear on the problems experienced by youth. Facilitating the development of children and adolescents is placed front and center in this approach.

ORGANIZATION OF THE TEXT

Although we have not formally divided the chapters into broader sections, they are conceptualized as three units.

Chapters 1 through 5 present a foundation for subsequent chapters. A broad overview of the field is presented, including basic concepts, historical context, developmental influences, theoretical perspectives, research methodology, classification and diagnosis, assessment, and treatment approaches. These chapters draw heavily on the psychological literature and also recognize the multidisciplinary nature of the study and treatment of youth. We assume that readers have some background in psychology, but we have made an effort to serve those with limited background or experience.

Chapters 6 through 14 discuss major disorders. Clinical symptoms and classification, epidemiology, the developmental course of disorder, causal hypotheses, risk and prevention, assessment, and treatment are major considerations. Discussion of classification and diagnosis draws on the current DSM-IV-TR system but includes other classification systems, as well as dimensional approaches.

- Chapter 6 (anxiety) and Chapter 7 (mood disorders) focus on internalizing disorders.
- Chapter 8 (conduct problems) and Chapter 9 (attention-deficit hyperactivity disorder) discuss externalizing disorders.
- Specific and pervasive developmental problems are presented in Chapter 10 (language and learning disorders), Chapter 11 (mental retardation), and Chapter 12 (autism and schizophrenia).
- Chapter 13 (basic physical functions) and Chapter 14 (medical conditions) focus on health- and medical-related problems.

Chapter 15 rounds out and extends what has gone before. Emphasis is given to the prevention of behavioral disorders. The chapter also examines several evolving concerns regarding the development and risks to the development of the young. These focus on critical family issues, mental health services, and briefly on youth living in countries other than the United States.

The organization of individual chapters varies, of course, depending on the information and issues relevant to the specific topic. However, considerable organizational consistency exists across Chapters 6 through 14. For most disorders, classification, clinical description, epidemiology, developmental course, etiology, assessment, and treatment are discussed in that order. At the same time, flexible organization is a guiding principle so that the complexity inherent in specific chapter topics is not sacrificed.

CONTENT: HIGHLIGHTS AND UPDATES

The content of this sixth edition is updated so as to include recent research and conceptualizations. We also have been especially sensitive to specific topics that are of high current interest. Examples follow.

- Numerous developmental models of the etiology of psychopathology in general and of specific disorders are presented.
- The developmental course and outcome of major disorders are described.
- Increased attention is given to the role of culture, ethnicity, and race in psychopathology.
- Greater attention is given to the role of gender in psychopathology—both to gender differences and factors that may underlie them.
- Attention is given to neurobiological factors in the etiology of disorders, including findings from genetic and brain imaging studies.
- Examples of specific individual and family treatments are generously interwoven throughout the text.
- In updating information on pharmacological treatments, sensitivity is given to issues concerning the use of medications with children and adolescents.
- Particular consideration is given to specific problems that are especially relevant—such as child maltreatment, substance use, eating disorders, and bullying/victimization.

FEATURES: SOME OLD, SOME NEW

As will be obvious to users of the previous edition of *Behavior Disorders of Childhood*, not everything is changed in this sixth edition! Notably, we have retained the basic organization of the chapters, which appears to work well. Similarly, specific features of the book continue to emphasize for students a child-oriented, applied perspective. The text is rich in case descriptions that exemplify clinical symptoms or issues. An additional feature, the Accents, typically focuses on clinical or applied themes, for example, information on fetal alcohol syndrome and how to recognize reading disability in young people. Further, the text continues to be rich in illustrations—graphs, tables, photos, drawings—without an excessiveness that can be confusing to readers.

Some new features of the text are aimed at facilitating student learning. Key Terms in each chapter now appear in color in the text and also are listed at the end of the chapter. Summaries of the chapters are now organized according to each chapter's major heads.

The open, colorful design of the text has been enhanced. We have given thought, as we have in the past, to avoiding clutter and confusion.

The supplementary teaching and learning materials have been enhanced, as described in the following section.

SUPPLEMENTARY TEACHING AND LEARNING MATERIALS

NEW "Speaking Out" Videos. This set of nine video segments was filmed exclusively for Prentice Hall and allows students to see first-hand accounts of real patients with various disorders. The interviews were conducted by licensed clinicians and range in length from 8 to 25 minutes. Disorders include depression with deliberate self-harm, anorexia nervosa, alcoholism, autism, ADHD, conduct disorder, anxiety disorder, oppositional defiant disorder, and learning disability. The videos are available in VHS or DVD format. The Instructor's Manual for this text includes suggestions on how to integrate these videos into your class. Ask your Prentice Hall representative.

NEW Instructor's Manual with Test Item File. Susan Waldman and Mary Hughes Stone of San Francisco State University have updated and expanded the Instructor's Manual with Tests created by the author: Rita Wicks-Nelson and Allen C. Israel. The Instructor's Manual includes chapter outlines, learning objectives, lecture and discussion suggestions, classroom activities, a list of videos and online resources, and suggestions on how to integrate the "Speaking Out" video segments into your course. The Test File section has been updated to include new questions on revised text material. It includes multiple choice, true/false, short answer, and essay questions with page references to the text. New for this edition, each question has been categorized as factual, applied, or conceptual.

NEW Companion Website (www.prenhall.com/ wicks-nelson). For the first time, this textbook offers a companion website that gives students tools to study online. Developed by Andrea Rotzien of Grand Valley State University, the CW includes online quizzes with immediate scoring and feedback, links to relevant websites, Powerpoint presentations for each chapter, and more.

NEW Powerpoints. Andrea Rotzien of Grand Valley State University has developed Powerpoint presentations for each chapter, with chapter outlines, key figures and tables, and other resources to enhance your lectures. You can download the Powerpoints from the Companion Website at www.prenhall.com/ wicks-nelson.

NEW SafariX WebBooks. This new *Pearson Choice* offers students an online subscription to *Child Psychopathology, 6th Edition* at a 50 percent savings. With the SafariX WebBook, students can search the text, make notes online, print out reading assignments that incorporate lecture notes, and bookmark important passages. Ask your Prentice Hall representative for details, or visit www.safarix.com.

TestGen Testing Software. Available on one dual-platform CD-ROM, this test generating software provides instructors "best in class" features in an easy-to-use program. Create tests using the TestGen Wizard and easily select questions with drag-and-drop or point-and-click functionality. Add or modify test questions using the built-in Question Editor and print tests in a variety of formats. The program comes with full technical support.

ACKNOWLEDGMENTS

The thoughtful evaluations and suggestions of the following reviewers are much appreciated: Richard Cavasina, California University of Pennsylvania; Kristin Christodulu, SUNY Albany; Andrea Chronis, University of Maryland; Amity Currie, Marist College; Charles Fernald, University of North

Carolina–Charlotte; Kristi Lane, Winona State University; Michael Palmer, Arizona State University; Vincent Stretch, University of Southern Mississippi.

In addition, the reviews and suggestions by Dr. Aaron Sher and Dr. Marios Constantinou, regarding specific sections of this edition, are greatly appreciated. Our sincere thanks are extended to Saori Maruyama and Melissa Them for their contributions. We particularly acknowledge the multiple contributions of Meena Choi, Karen Sokolowski, and Ilana Luft to the completion of this edition. Their work in locating material, and in other ways facilitating the preparation of the manuscript, was invaluable.

And continuing thanks to Sara and Daniel for their caring and support.

Finally, we note that the order of authorship was originally decided by a flip of the coin to reflect our equal contribution. Our continuing collaboration has been one of equality and friendship.

Rita Wicks-Nelson

Allen C. Israel

Introduction

To be young is to bounce balls as high as the heavens, gobble up fairy tales, walk tightropes without falling, love friends with glee, and peer at the wondrous future.

Oh, that I should have to experience this thing called youth—with its ignorance, uselessness, aloneness, ups and downs, and unending insecurities.

The early years of life have long been described in extremes of emotions, behaviors, and encounters. In fact, most individuals who look back on their own youth admit to some of the extremes—but also to a sizable portion of more moderate experiences. And they frequently view their youth as a special time of growth and opportunity. It is against this backdrop that we embark on the study of the behavioral and psychological problems of childhood and adolescence.

This book is written for those who ask questions and are concerned about less than optimal development of children and adolescents. It addresses definitions, characteristics, origins, development, diagnosis, prevention, and amelioration of disordered behavior. We anticipate, and hope, that you will find this field of study as satisfying as we do. It is an area of study that encompasses both humanitarian concerns for young people and scientific intrigue.

Moreover, this is a particularly promising time to study behavioral and psychological disturbance. The need for increased understanding, prevention, and treatment is substantial, and is recognized in many parts of the world. At the same time, research into behavioral disturbance and human development, including that of youth, is growing by leaps and bounds, with contributions from many disciplines. As is usually true in science, increased knowledge and improved methods have led to new questions and paradoxes. This combination—new understandings, new questions, new avenues of inquiry—gives both promise and excitement to the study of the psychological problems of young people.

Defining and Identifying Disordered Behavior

Behavioral repertoires come in endless varieties, and we will examine many kinds of disorders throughout this textbook. Various labels have been applied to such problems: behavioral disturbance, psychological deficits, emotional disorder, abnormal behavior, mental illness, psychopathology, maladaptive behavior, developmental disorders, and so forth. Regardless of the label, though, there is no simple way to define or identify disordered functioning. To be sure, standards or criteria for abnormality have been developed to guide professionals in this task. These standards primarily are based on how a person is acting or what a person is saying and only rarely include a specific, known marker for disorder.

A fine line may exist between what is considered disordered and what is normal. Young people of specific ages display behaviors that may or may not be considered signs of disturbance. This was shown in a systematic, historically important investigation in which almost five hundred mothers of a sample of all six- to twelve-year-olds in Buffalo, New York, evaluated their children's behavior in detail (Lapouse & Monk, 1958). Among other things, mothers reported that 49 percent of their offspring were overactive, 48 percent lost their tempers twice weekly, and 28 percent experienced nightmares. Later studies from various countries confirmed that such behaviors are commonly reported (Cotler, 1986). Thus the questions: When are such behaviors considered problematic? and Can we distinguish problems of the "everyday" child from more serious indications of psychopathology? This dilemma is not completely

ACCENT ● ● ● ● ● ●

The Faces of Problem Behavior

Joey had been "kicked out" of preschool, where he had sat on the floor and stared, refused to talk, and hit any child who touched him. If the teacher insisted that he participate in activities, he screamed, cried, and banged his arms and legs on the floor. Similar behaviors occurred at home. In fact, Joey rarely talked or showed emotion, slept fitfully, banged his head against the wall, and rocked back and forth. (Adapted from Morgan, 1999, pp. 3–4)

Karen was a nine-year-old girl with a history of refusal to eat solid foods. Six weeks previously, she had choked on a piece of popcorn, with coughing and gagging. From that time on, she had refused to eat any solid foods and had lost about fifteen pounds. She had also developed multiple fears concerning choking. She would not brush her teeth for fear a bristle would come out and she would choke. She slept propped on pillows for fear a loose tooth would come out while she was asleep and that she would choke and suffocate. (From Chatoor, Conley, & Dickson, 1988, p. 106)

Joe, who is eight years old, has a history of multiple problems. They include chronic hyperactivity, destructive behavior, short attention span, difficulty following verbal directions, low frustration tolerance, impulsiveness, disobedience, poor interpersonal relationships, fighting, lying, stealing, running away from

school, and setting fires. His parents had discounted the importance of these behaviors, preferring to believe that little boys should be allowed to express themselves. Joe's parents had rejected the recommendation for special education placement in the first grade. His behavior worsened in the second and third grades, and after Joe exposed himself to female peers, the school forced further evaluation. (From Rapport, 1993, pp. 284–285)

Fifteen-year-old **Anne** was brought to a community mental health center by her mother, who feared Anne might be a Satanist. The previous evening, Anne had been discovered naked, chanting, and clutching a knife dripping with blood. She had begun to worship Satan and noted that praying to Satan brought her relief. . . . Anne reported that she had difficulty falling asleep because she worried about her grades and her parents' divorce. She believed she was partly responsible for the divorce. She found it hard to concentrate in school, was irritable, and had lost fifteen pounds without dieting. Anne denied any intent or plan for suicide, involvement with cults, or drug use. She no longer shops with friends, swims, or bikes, because these activities take too much energy. Anne spoke to the therapist coherently but with a slow, monotone voice. (Adapted from Morgan, 1999, pp. 35–37) solved and decisions about abnormality may sometimes appear to be quite arbitrary.

This is not to say that decisions are made thoughtlessly. Indeed, complex judgments are involved. A standard must be established for what is average, acceptable, or healthy, and judgments must be made as to whether the condition of interest falls short of the standard. Of course, dramatic differences are easy to identify. Most of us would agree that individuals who cannot learn to feed themselves, speak, or read show harmful impairments. Less dramatic instances are harder to judge. Several factors enter into judgments about psychological or behavioral disturbance, and some of these are surprisingly fluid. We will begin to look at some of the factors here, and will return to this complex issue throughout this text.

ATYPICAL AND HARMFUL BEHAVIOR

Problem behavior frequently is viewed as atypical, odd, or abnormal—all of which imply that it deviates from the average. Indeed, "ab" means "away" or "from," whereas "normal" refers to the average or standard. Abnormal thus simply means something that deviates from the average in some way. However, being atypical in itself hardly defines problem behavior. Persons who display exceptionally high intelligence, athletic skill, social competence, or musical ability are generally considered fortunate, and their "oddness" is looked upon with favor. To the contrary, the deviations we are considering are assumed to be harmful in some way to the individual.

The American Psychiatric Association (1994, 2000), for example, defines a disorder as a clinically significant behavioral or psychological pattern that occurs in an individual and is associated with distress or impairment or with increased risk of death, pain, disability, or important loss of freedom. Clearly, a disorder is viewed as "bad" for the person.

Psychopathology is frequently viewed as dysfunction that resides within an individual and interferes with adaptation, that is, with the individual fitting the circumstances of his or her life. Alternatively, though, disorder might better be viewed as an individual's reactions to circumstances—or the interface of the individual with other people or environmental conditions. The latter perspective, which is closer to our own, emphasizes that behavior is inextricably linked with the larger world in which it is embedded.

DEVELOPMENTAL STANDARDS

Age, as an index of developmental level, is always important in judging behavior, but it is especially important for children and adolescents because they change so rapidly. Judgments about behavior require developmental norms, which describe the typical rates of growth, sequences of growth, and forms of physical skills, language, cognition, emotion, and social behavior. These serve as developmental standards to evaluate the possibility that "something is wrong."

Behavior can be judged as anomalous relative to these norms in a number of ways, as indicated in Table 1–1. Delay or failure to keep up with typical developmental change indicates that something is awry. Children sometimes may "act their age" for a period of time but then fail to progress. They may also achieve developmental norms and then regress, or return, to behavior typically seen in younger children.

Several other signs are noteworthy. Behavior that meets age norms may still be judged disturbed if it occurs too frequently or infrequently, is too intense or insufficiently intense, persists over too long or too short a period of time, or is displayed in inappropriate situations. It is not unusual for a child to display fear, for example, but fearfulness may be a problem if it occurs in an excessive number of situations, is extremely intense, does not weaken over time, or occurs in harmless situations. Concern might also be expressed for the youth whose behaviors abruptly change, such as when a friendly, outgoing adolescent turns shy and solitary. And concern might be appropriate when a child displays several questionable behaviors or seems troubled by several things. All of these indications of disturbance are quantitative differences from developmental norms.

TABLE 1–1	BEHAVIORAL INDICATORS OF DISORDERS

Developmental delay
Developmental regression or deterioration
Extremely high or low frequency of behavior
Extremely high or low intensity of behavior
Behavioral difficulty persists over time
Abrupt changes in behavior
Behavior inappropriate to the situation
Several problem behaviors
Behavior qualitatively different from normal

Yet another manifestation that may signal the need for help is the display of behaviors that appear as qualitative differences from the norm. That is, the behavior—or the sequence in which it develops—is not seen at all in normal growth. For instance, most children become socially responsive to their caretakers soon after birth, but children diagnosed as autistic display unresponsive behaviors not seen in normal development (such as lack of normal eye contact). Qualitatively different behaviors frequently indicate a pervasive problem in development.

ROLE OF CULTURE AND ETHNICITY

The term culture broadly captures the idea that groups of people are organized in specific ways; live in specific environmental niches; and share specific behavioral standards, beliefs, values, and practices. Virtually all cultural groups, or societies, have in common the goals of socializing youth and facilitating their adaptation and success. But cultural groups vary in their specific goals and values, how they accomplish their goals through child rearing and other practices, and how they judge behavior.

The role of cultural norms, or standards, in judging behavior was tellingly discussed many years ago by the anthropologist Ruth Benedict. After studying widely diverse cultures, Benedict (1934b)

proposed that each society selects certain behaviors that are of value to it and socializes its members to act accordingly. Individuals who do not display these behaviors, for whatever reasons, are considered deviant by the society. Deviance is always related to cultural standards. Benedict noted, for example, that the suspiciousness in one Melanesian culture would be considered pathological in our society. These Melanesians would not leave their cooking pots for fear that others would poison their food (Benedict, 1934a). Furthermore, Melanesians who displayed the helpfulness, kindness, and cheerfulness that are viewed as positive in our society were considered abnormal in their culture.

Anthropological analyses and cross-cultural comparisons point to several facets of cultural influences. Among other things, cultural settings contribute to

- shaping normal and abnormal development;
- defining and labeling abnormality;
- conceptualizing and explaining problem behavior; and
- treating psychopathology (e.g., Harkness & Super, 2000).

Cultural standards broadly influence expectations, judgments, and beliefs about the behavior of youth. Children in the United States, for example,

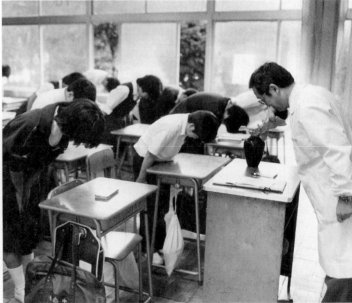

The behavior that is expected of or considered appropriate for a child varies across cultures.
(Richard Hutchings/PhotoEdit, Inc.) (Michael Heron).

are expected to show less self-control and less deference to adults compared with children in some other parts of the world (Weisz et al., 1995). Relative to some other societies, then, we might be more likely to express concern about the overcontrolled, passive child. Weisz and his colleagues (1995), in a cross-cultural study of teachers' reports of their students, found that teachers in Thailand reported more conduct problems than teachers in the United States, whereas trained observers reported just the opposite for the two student groups. The researchers suggested that Thai teachers may hold more demanding behavioral standards—and thus "see" more problems and more readily label them.

Weisz and his colleagues (1988) also showed cultural differences in the degree to which childhood problems might be judged as serious. Parents and teachers in Thailand and the United States read descriptions of child problems and then answered questions about them. As Figure 1–1 shows, the Thai adults were less worried than the adults in the United States. This finding appears consistent with the teachings of Thai Buddhism that every condition changes and that behavior does not reflect enduring personality.

The way in which problem behaviors are differentially explained was demonstrated in a study in which mothers of North African and Middle Eastern background living in Israel were interviewed about their children who were developmentally retarded (Stahl, 1991). Almost half of the mothers gave magic-religious causes for the condition. They believed in Fate, demons entering the body, an Evil Eye, and punishment from God. These mothers accordingly relied on magic-religious treatments such as burning a piece of cloth belonging to the person who cast the Evil Eye, praying, or getting help from a rabbi. All of these behaviors are consistent with the cultural beliefs of their native countries.

The above findings also suggest the advisability of examining ethnicity or race with regard to judgments about abnormality. Ethnicity denotes common customs, values, language, or traits that are associated with national origin or geographic area. Race, a distinction based on physical characteristics, can also be associated with shared customs, values, and the like. Ethnic or racial groups embedded within a heterogeneous society may hold unique beliefs and standards relative to the dominant cultural group. Such subcultural differences have been described in the United States, as might be expected in such a heterogeneous nation (García Coll & Garrido, 2000; Habenstein & Olson, 2001; Yeh et al., 2004).

GENDER AND SITUATIONAL STANDARDS

Expectations based on gender also contribute to defining problem behavior. Gender norms are among the most powerful influences on development, affecting emotions, behavior, opportunities, and choices. In most societies, males are expected to be relatively more aggressive, dominant, active, and adventurous; females to be more passive, dependent, quiet, sensitive, and emotional. These gender stereotypes play a role in judgments about normality. We would probably be less inclined to worry about the hypersensitive, shy girl and the excessively dominant boy than about their opposite-sex counterparts.

Judgments of deviance or normality of behavior also take into account situational norms—what is expected in specific social situations or settings. In the United States, energetic running may be quite acceptable on the playground, but rarely allowed in the classroom or a dental office. Norms for social interaction can be quite subtle; for example, how a

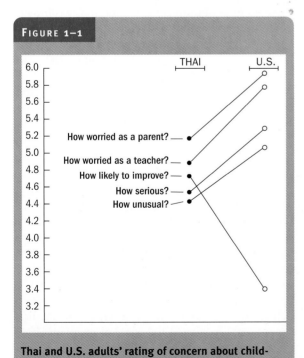

FIGURE 1–1

Thai and U.S. adults' rating of concern about childhood behavior problems.

Weisz, Suwanlet, Chaiyasit, Weiss, Walter, & Anderson, 1988.

statement is phrased could mean the difference between complimenting or insulting another person. Individuals in all cultures are expected to learn what is acceptable and to act in certain ways in certain situations. When this requirement is not met, questions may be raised about normality or competence.

ROLE OF OTHERS IN IDENTIFYING PROBLEMS

Youth, especially young children, hardly ever refer themselves for clinical evaluation, thereby declaring a problem. Rather, the feelings and beliefs of others in the immediate environment play a role in identifying problem behaviors. The labeling of a problem is likely to occur when others become concerned—for example, when parents worry about their child's social isolation or when a teacher is troubled about a child's inability to learn to read.

Referral of youth to mental health professionals may have as much or more to do with the characteristics of parents, teachers, or family physicians as with the young people themselves (Costello & Angold, 1995a; Verhulst & van der Ende, 1997). Indeed, disagreement often exists among adults as to whether a child or adolescent "has a problem." Adult attitudes, sensitivity, tolerance, and ability to cope all play a role in identifying disorders.

CHANGING VIEWS OF ABNORMALITY

Finally, judgments about abnormality are not set in stone. Examples abound. In the 1800s, masturbation was considered a sign of disturbance or a behavior that could cause insanity (Rie, 1971). Nail biting was once seen as a sign of degeneration but is viewed as quite harmless today (Anthony, 1970). More recent years have brought a loosening of gender roles and controversy about "normal" male and female behavior—a situation that is far from the idea, expressed in the late 1800s, that excessive intellectual activity, especially in young women, would lead to mental problems (Silk et al., 2000).

Many factors undoubtedly contribute to changes in judgments about abnormality. Modifications in knowledge and in cultural beliefs and values play a role. For instance, eating disorders, once found almost exclusively in Western societies, have increased worldwide in the past few decades, perhaps due to wider adoption of the modern Western preference for slender body size (Harkness & Super, 2000).

In summary, then, disordered behavior cannot simply be defined as an entity carried around within a person. It is most appropriately viewed as a judgment that a person's behavior is atypical, harmful, or unacceptable in some way—a judgment based on knowledge about development, cultural and ethnic influences, other social norms, and the characteristics of persons making the judgment.

How Common Are Behavioral Disorders of Youth?

Determining the number of individuals who experience behavioral or psychological disorders before adulthood is important because it suggests the extent to which prevention, treatment, and research are needed. However, prevalence depends on several factors, including the definition of disorder, the population examined, the method used to identify the problems, and the person who identifies the problems. Some investigations employ standardized scales or use formal criteria to achieve a clinical diagnosis. Others look for symptoms, and still others for indications of maladaptation within the social environment (Bird, 1996; Crijnen, Achenbach, & Verhulst, 1997; Fombonne, 2002).

It is thus unsurprising to find variation in reported rates of problems. For example, a summary of studies reported from 1985 to 2000 shows prevalence ranging from 5.4 to 35.5 percent of youth varying in age from 4 to 18 years (Fombonne, 2002). An estimate of 15 to 20 percent prevalence of clinic-level disorder for children and adolescents is fairly often cited (Costello & Angold, 2001; Costello et al., 2003; Weist, 1997). If we consider the number of children and adolescents who have lesser problems that may nevertheless interfere with optimal development, the picture is rather bleak.

Concern has been expressed that changing social conditions may increase the risk of disorders for young people. Although this possibility has been examined in several countries, it is difficult to draw overall conclusions due to methodological variations and issues (Achenbach, Dumenci, & Rescorla, 2003; Rutter & Smith, 1995). Further study is needed and it is important to ask about specific disorders, who is being affected, and why. For example, medical progress has facilitated the survival of infants born prematurely or with physical problems, and these infants have relatively high rates of behavioral and learning difficulties. A recent study in Scotland showed increases in emotional problems from 1987 to 1999 for adolescent females but not males (West & Sweeting, 2003). The authors suggested that elevated stress associated with changing educational expectations was a significant factor. Although stress related to social factors—such as changing expectations and family divorce—might reasonably increase psychological disorder, not all studies indicate escalating psychopathology (Achenbach et al., 2003; Sourander et al., 2004).

Recent years have seen increased interest in disturbances observed in infancy (Briggs-Gowan et al., 2001). These include various feeding and sleep disorders; disturbances in regulation of mood, soothability, and attention; and problems in establishing healthy attachments to parents or other caregivers (Lyons-Ruth, Zeanah, & Benoit, 2003). Difficulties at this time of life can be viewed as factors that increase the chance for later disorders, but they also can be considered disorders in their own right. Substantial research is needed in this area.

Overall, despite inconsistency in the data, there is little doubt that young people have substantial needs. Moreover, estimates show that most needy youth—perhaps less than one-third and as low as one-quarter—do not receive support and treatment sufficient to overcome their behavioral problems (Kestenbaum, 2000; Weist, 1997). Among the factors associated with lack of care are poverty, minority family status, rural residence, and attitudes toward mental health treatment (Logan & King, 2001).

There are several reasons for concern about this situation. Of course, no one wants to see young people suffer from the pain of anxiety, depression, or other disorders, or from lowered quality of life associated with psychological disorder (Sawyer et al., 2002). In addition, early disturbances can interfere with subsequent developmental processes, leading to an accumulation of problems. Indeed, there is growing evidence that early-occurring disorders often do not just simply go away; they may manifest themselves in unfavorable ways in adulthood. The significance of mental health problems in young people is also seen in adverse influences on families and on the broader society, as reflected in enormous health care expenditures.

How Are Developmental Level and Disorders Related?

Of interest to professionals and parents alike is whether psychological difficulties are more likely to arise, or be prevalent, during certain developmental years relative to other years. In fact, some relationship does exist between specific problems and the age at which they usually first appear or are identified. For example, the eating disorders of anorexia and bulimia, as well as schizophrenia, often first arise as adolescence approaches. Figure 1–2 depicts the age association for several disturbances. The reason for the link is sometimes obvious. Chronological age is correlated with developmental level that, in turn, makes some disorders more likely than others. Developmental speech problems thus appear when children are first acquiring language skills.

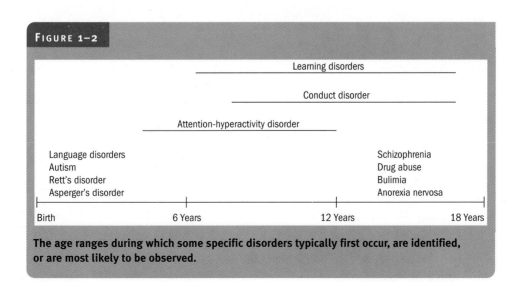

FIGURE 1–2

The age ranges during which some specific disorders typically first occur, are identified, or are most likely to be observed.

Information about developmental level and disorder is helpful in several ways. Parents might be more alert to the possibility of problems occurring at certain times in youth, adopt a "nip in the bud" strategy, and consider timely evaluation of behavior. Knowing the usual age of onset also may be important in understanding the cause, severity, or outcome of disorders (Giaconia et al., 1994). For instance, although the specific etiology of autism is not determined, its early occurrence suggests that developmental processes go awry. Or to take another example, drug abuse most often begins in adolescence, but its earlier onset is especially significant for later severe drug dependency and mental problems (Wills & Dishion, 2004).

Nevertheless, a note of caution is appropriate when considering onset of disturbances. At least for some disorders, actual onset occurs gradually, with times of worsening of symptoms and social impairment (Sandberg et al., 2001). And for some disorders, time of onset varies according to gender. Furthermore, the time at which a disorder is said to occur may depend not only on the symptom picture but also on more extraneous circumstances. Consider mental retardation, which is defined as below average intellectual functioning and adaptation that occurs by age eighteen. Although the more severe cases are identified early in life, most cases are recognized during the school years. The demands of the classroom—and school policy to evaluate intellectual performance—identify children who otherwise appeared to function adequately in their home environments. These murky issues are important because they have implications for understanding disturbances as well as for prevention and treatment.

How Are Gender and Disorders Related?

For decades, the role of gender in psychopathology in the young was neglected (Crick & Zahn-Waxler, 2003). Several fascinating findings are now emerging. Consistent over the years is the finding of gender differences in the overall rates of many disturbances, with males being more frequently affected than females (Rutter & Sroufe, 2000). Table 1–2 shows the findings for several specific disorders. But the picture actually is much more complex. Some gender differences are related to age. Depression occurs more often in females than males during adolescence but not during childhood. Problems also may be expressed differently according to gender. Males tend to display overt physical aggression but females are more likely to exhibit relational aggression by harmful gossip or rumor spreading (Zalecki & Hinshaw, 2004). Some investigators suggest that the severity of disorders may vary with gender, as may specific consequences in adulthood. It is also probable that the causes and developmental paths of disorders from infancy into adolescence are dissimilar for some, although not all, problems (Colder, Mott, & Berman, 2002; Fergusson & Horwood, 2002). Much is yet to be established regarding gender differences, and methodological issues must be considered.

TABLE 1–2 GENDER PREVALENCE FOR SOME DISORDERS OF YOUTH

PREVALENCE HIGHER FOR MALES

Mental retardation	Rumination (an eating disorder)
Reading disabilities	Encopresis
Language disabilities	Enuresis
Autism	Tourette's disorder
Asperger's disorder	Drug abuse
Childhood disintegrative disorder	Conduct disorder
Oppositional disorder	Attention-deficit hyperactivity

PREVALENCE HIGHER FOR FEMALES

Rett's disorder
Anxieties and fears
Depression
Eating disorders

Based in part on Hartung & Widiger, 1998.

METHODOLOGICAL ISSUES, TRUE DIFFERENCES

To some extent, reported gender differences may result from methodological practices. In past times, not only did a bias exist for studying males, but inferences about sex differences may have been drawn from studies that focused exclusively on one gender or the other (Rutter, Caspi, & Moffitt, 2003). Misleading gender differences can also result from females or males being more willing to report certain problems, for example, for girls to speak of emotional difficulties. Then, too, gender differences may result from a behavior being defined as it is expressed in one gender more than the other.

Gender-specific prevalence of disorders also may be an artifact of the population studied. Research often relies on clinic samples, which are biased toward boys because adults tend to seek help for children who engage in the troublesome, disruptive behavior exhibited more by boys than girls. This bias may be independent of other problems. Thus, boys with reading problems are referred over girls with reading problems—presumably because of boys' higher rates of disruptive behaviors (Shaywitz, Fletcher, & Shaywitz, 1996). Such referral bias would give misleadingly high rates of reading disorder in boys relative to girls.

The bias in clinic samples may affect gender rates in another, more indirect, way (Hartung & Widiger, 1998). When more boys are seen in mental health facilities, they become the subject of more research. This outcome leads to disorders being described in the way the symptoms are expressed in boys, which may not be identical to the symptom picture in girls. In turn, when these descriptions (criteria) are used for identifying the disorder, fewer girls will fit the symptom picture and be identified.

Although methodological issues caution us to examine research carefully, the weight of the evidence does point to real gender differences. To what might they be attributed? Here, we examine the matter broadly; subsequent chapters in this text discuss the role of gender in specific disorders.

Both biological and psychosocial influences, observed prenatally onward, might reasonably be linked to gender-specific psychopathology (Rutter, Caspi, & Moffitt, 2003). Differential biological vulnerabilities and strengths may exist. Genetic differences between the sexes are thought to play a fundamental role in gender development, for example, in the production of the sex hormones and differences in brain organization. The sex chromosomes, X and Y, are likely to be related to specific disorders in complicated ways. It is also the case that biological maturity is slower in boys, and that males have a higher death rate from the moment of conception. Gender differences, such as in the emotions, may be present early in life, which suggests biological influence on behaviors relevant to psychological disturbance.

At the same time, experience is gender related, creating increased or decreased exposure to factors associated with psychopathology. Consider the following examples. From infancy onward, boys suffer a higher rate of traumatic brain injury, which increases their risk of intellectual impairments (Anderson et al., 2001). Boys are more often physically victimized by peers, an event that is related to a variety of behavioral and emotional problems (Hanish & Guerra, 2002). Girls are more likely to have inappropriate sexual encounters. More generally, there are gender differences in friendships and interaction with parents and teachers (Rutter, Caspi, & Moffitt, 2003). Boys and girls also experience different sex-role expectations for how they should express emotion, control behavior, and the like. Worth noting, too, gender may affect responses to circumstances, that is, to chaotic environments, stress, parental psychopathology, and other conditions (Cicchetti & Sroufe, 2000; Leinonen, Solantaus, & Punamäki, 2003). We might expect all these differential experiences to potentially enter into the development of behavioral problems in complicated ways.

Further investigation of gender effects has the potential for informing us about the causes, prevention, and treatment of psychopathology. More generally, we have seen that what may appear to be simple issues regarding the psychopathology of children and adolescents often is multifaceted. Despite the complexities, progress is being made in understanding the needs of the young. This relatively recent circumstance is illuminated in the next section.

Historical Influences

Humans have long speculated on behavioral dysfunction, but early interest focused primarily on adults. Some analyses suggest that this might have been partly due to children's not being considered as very different from adults and to their having high death rates that hindered parental attachment and interest (Ariès, 1962). However, at least by the seventeenth century, children were viewed as having physical, psychological, and educational needs that required nourishment, nurturance, and instruction (Pollock, 2001). By the early eighteenth century, they were variously seen as either stained with original sin, as innately innocent and needy of protection, or as blank slates upon which experience would write. At the end of the nineteenth century recognition was given to the conceptualization of adolescence as a distinct period of transition between childhood and adulthood entailing specific change, challenge, and opportunity (Demos & Demos, 1972). Differing and often conflicting views of childhood and adolescence continue to this day, undoubtedly influencing perspectives on problem behaviors and how abnormality should be treated.

PROGRESS IN THE NINETEENTH CENTURY

The nineteenth century brought efforts to record the growth and abilities of the young, as well as progress in understanding disturbed development and behavior.

By this time, two explanations of adult mental illness already had long been recognized: demonology and somatogenesis. Demonology is the belief that abnormal behavior results from a person's being possessed or otherwise influenced by evil spirits or demons. Both adults and youth acting in unusual, bizarre, or problematic ways were often viewed as possessed by evil spirits. Closely associated with religion, demonology tended to cast suffering individuals as wicked or evil in themselves. Although demonology is still espoused in some cultures, it is largely rejected in scientifically advanced societies. Somatogenesis is the belief that mental disorder can be attributed to bodily malfunction or imbalance. It was advocated by Hippocrates, considered the father of medicine, when little was known in early Greek society about biological functioning. Although somatogenesis waxed and waned in importance, it has been a hardy hypothesis and is central in today's explanations of psychopathology. By the late nineteenth century, the dominant view of psychopathology was genetic (Costello & Angold, 2001). That is, generally it was assumed that inheritance, and degeneration that began in childhood, led to irreversible disease, which could be transmitted to the next generation. (Psychogenesis, the belief that mental problems are caused by psychological factors, developed more slowly.)

Efforts to identify and classify mental illness progressed by the late nineteenth century. Emil Kraepelin, in 1883, published a classification system in which he tried to establish a biological basis for mental disorder. Kraepelin recognized that symptoms tended to group together—to occur in syndromes—and therefore might have a common physical cause. He viewed each disorder as distinct from others in origin, symptoms, course, and outcome (Widiger & Clark, 2000). Eventually his work would be the basis of modern classification systems for mental disorders.

Although the study of youth generally lagged behind the study of adults, the first recordings of childhood behavioral disorders appeared early in the nineteenth century (Rie, 1971). By the end of the century, a few efforts had been made to classify children's disorders, and causes had been proposed. Aggression, psychoses, hyperactivity, and "masturbatory insanity" in youth were all noted, but mental retardation received by far the most attention—perhaps because it was obvious and aroused anxiety in parents (Bernstein, 1996). An optimistic remedial approach to mental retardation began in Europe and spread to the United States—although it later gave way to adverse care and institutionalization that would not be rectified for many decades.

Meanwhile, at around the turn of the twentieth century, several developments began to fundamentally alter how children and adolescents were viewed, ideas about how their development might go awry, and how they might be treated (Table 1–3). Professional and scientific activities were interwoven with progressive efforts regarding the young, females, and weak and ill members of society (Silk et al., 2000).

SIGMUND FREUD AND PSYCHOANALYTIC THEORY

One of these developments was the rise of psychoanalytic theory and its associated treatment, psychoanalysis. Sigmund Freud's theory was the first modern systematic attempt to understand mental disorders in psychological terms. As a young neurologist, Freud came to believe that certain disorders could be caused by psychological events. He was particularly interested in the idea that psychological experiences in childhood are connected to adult symptoms, which could be alleviated when patients spoke emotionally about early experiences. Such observations set Freud on a lifelong course to construct a grand theory of normal and abnormal development.

On the basis of his study of adults, Freud was convinced that unconscious, psychological childhood conflicts and crises were the keys to understanding

TABLE 1–3	SOME EARLY HISTORICAL LANDMARKS
1896	The first child clinic in the United States was established at the University of Pennsylvania by Lightner Witmer.
1905	Alfred Binet and Theophil Simon developed the first intelligence tests to identify feebleminded children.
1905	Sigmund Freud's *Three Essays on the Theory of Sexuality* described a startlingly different view of childhood development.
1908	In *A Mind That Found Itself*, Clifford Beers recounted his mental breakdown and advocated an enlightened view of mental disorders, initiating the mental hygiene and child guidance movements.
1909	G. Stanley Hall invited Sigmund Freud to Clark University in Worcester, Massachusetts, to lecture on psychoanalysis.
1909	William Healy and Grace Fernald established the Juvenile Psychopathic Institute in Chicago, which would become the model for the child guidance clinics.
1911	The Yale Clinic of Child Development was established for child development research under the guidance of Arnold Gesell.
1913	John B. Watson introduced behaviorism in his essay "Psychology as a Behaviorist Views It."
1917	William Healy and Augusta Bronner established the Judge Baker Guidance Center in Boston.
1922	The National Committee on Mental Hygiene and the Commonwealth Fund initiated a demonstration program of child guidance clinics.
1924	The American Orthopsychiatric Association was established.
1928–1929	Longitudinal studies of child development began at Berkeley and Fels Research Institute.
1935	Leo Kanner authored *Child Psychiatry*, the first child psychiatry text published in the United States.

ACCENT ●●●●●

Little Hans: A Classic Psychoanalytic Case

Freud's well-known case of "Little Hans" illustrates both the conceptualization of symptoms as arising from defense mechanisms and the phallic stage of development. The case served as a model for the psychoanalytic interpretation of childhood phobias (Freud, 1953/1909).

Hans was very affectionate toward his mother and enjoyed "cuddling" with her. When Hans was almost five, he returned from a daily walk with his nursemaid frightened, crying, and wanting to cuddle with his mother. The next day, when the mother herself took him for a walk, Hans expressed a fear of being bitten by a horse, and that evening he insisted on cuddling with his mother. He cried about having to go out the next day and expressed considerable fear concerning horses.

These worsening symptoms were interpreted by Freud as reflecting the child's conflict over the sexual impulses he had toward his mother and fear of castration by his father. Hans's ego employed three defense mechanisms to keep the unacceptable impulses unconscious or distorted. First, Hans's wish to attack his father, the rival for his mother's affection, was repressed in memory. The next step was projection of the unacceptable impulses onto the father: Hans believed that his father wished to attack him, rather than the other way around. The final step was displacement, wherein the dangerousness of the father was displaced onto the horse. According to Freud, the choice of the horse as a symbol of the father was due to numerous associations of horses with Hans's father. For example, the black muzzle and the blinders on the horse were viewed as symbolic of the father's mustache and eyeglasses. The fear Hans displaced onto the horse permitted the child's ambivalent feelings toward his father to be resolved. He could now love his father. In addition, perceiving horses as the source of anxiety allowed Hans to avoid anxiety by simply avoiding horses (Kessler, 1966).

behavior. He proposed three structures of the mind whose goals and tasks made conflict inevitable: the id, ego, and superego. The conflicts inherent in this system were viewed as unconscious. However, anxiety might be generated as a danger signal to the ego—the problem-solving part of the mind—that id impulses unacceptable to the superego were seeking to gain consciousness. To protect itself from awareness of unacceptable impulses, the ego creates defense mechanisms that distort or deny the impulses. Although defense mechanisms can be adaptive and explain everyday behavior, they may also generate psychological symptoms.

The psychoanalytic perspective rests on a psychosexual stage theory of development. As the child develops, the focus of psychological energy passes from one bodily zone to the next, leading the child through five fixed stages—oral, anal, phallic, latency, and genital. The first three stages involve particular crises that are crucial for later development. During the oral stage, the child must be weaned; during the anal stage, the child must be toilet trained; during the phallic stage, the child must resolve the crisis brought on by the desire to possess the opposite-sex parent (the Oedipal conflict for the boy, the Electra conflict for the girl). For Freud, the basic personality is laid down during these first three stages—by age six or seven—and healthy development is hindered by failure to resolve the crisis during each stage. (See Accent: "Little Hans: A Classic Psychoanalytic Case.")

In *Three Essays on the Theory of Sexuality*, published in 1905, and in his 1909 lectures at Clark University in Worcester, Massachusetts, Freud introduced his radical ideas about the importance of childhood to adult development (Evans & Koelsch, 1985; Rie, 1971). His views were controversial from the start and are criticized on several grounds. For example, they rest primarily on impressions from case studies, involve large inferences from what is observed to what is interpreted as existing, and are difficult to test. Freud's ideas nevertheless had enormous influence, in part because no other theory at that time offered as comprehensive an explanation for mental problems (Eisenberg, 2001).

Classical psychoanalytic theory has been modified by a number of workers. So-called neo-Freudians minimized the importance of sexual forces and emphasized social influences; among them is Erik Erikson, who proposed an influential theory of psychosocial development. Freud's daughter, Anna, elaborated his ideas and especially applied them to

Both Sigmund Freud (center) and his daughter Anna Freud (foreground) were influential in the development of the psychodynamic conceptualizations of childhood disorders. *(AP/Wide World Photos)*

children (Fine, 1985). By the 1930s, Freud's ideas had been widely interpreted, and they provided a framework for conceptualizing child, adolescent, and adult behavior. They helped to establish psychiatry as a major discipline in the study and treatment of childhood disorders. In 1935, Leo Kanner authored the first child psychiatry text published in the United States.

Modification of traditional psychoanalysis has continued (Gabbard, 2000). Some basic concepts have been altered, and newer forms of therapy have been employed, including briefer forms. Attempts have been made to incorporate research findings on infant and child development (Shapiro & Esman, 1992; Zeanah et al., 1989). Overall, the influence of psychoanalytic theory has waned, but among its many contributions is drawing attention to psychological causation, mental processes, anxiety and other emotions, infant and childhood experiences, and the child-parent relationship.

BEHAVIORISM AND SOCIAL LEARNING THEORY

While Freud was challenging the academic and clinical world with his innovative ideas, a rival approach stemming from psychology was introduced in the United States (Sears, 1975). Behaviorism was launched by John B. Watson's essay "Psychology as a Behaviorist Views It" (1913). Unlike Freud, Watson placed little value on describing developmental stages and on early psychological conflicts. Instead, he drew on theories of learning to emphasize that most behavior, adaptive or maladaptive, could be explained by learning experiences. Among his most quoted words are the following, which reflect his belief in the power of experience to shape children's development:

> *Give me a dozen healthy infants, well-formed, and my own specified world to bring them up in and I'll guarantee to take any one at random and train him to become any type of specialist I might select—doctor, lawyer, merchant, chief and yes, even beggar-man and thief, regardless of his talents, penchants, tendencies, abilities, vocations, and race of his ancestors. (Watson, 1930, p. 104)*

Among the models that Watson drew on was classical conditioning, described earlier by Pavlov in animal experiments that demonstrated learning that occurred through the pairing of new with old stimuli. In addition to a strong emphasis on learning and environment, Watson was committed to testing ideas by experimental methods, as were other behaviorists (Horowitz, 1992).

E. L. Thorndike (1905) made an early contribution to behaviorism by formulating the Law of Effect. Simply put, this law states that behavior is shaped by its consequences. If the consequence is satisfying, the behavior will be strengthened in the future; if the consequence is discomforting, the behavior will be weakened. Thorndike considered the Law of Effect a fundamental principle of learning and teaching; later researchers substantiated his claim. Of special note is B. F. Skinner, who is widely known for his work on operant learning—that is, for investigating and writing on the application of behavioral consequences to the shaping of behavior (Skinner, 1948; 1953; 1968). Skinner can be viewed as Watson's descendent in his emphasis on learning, the environment, and experimental methods (Horowitz, 1992).

Behaviorism, like psychoanalytic theory, thrived in the United States during the first half of

John B. Watson was a highly influential figure in the application of the behavioral perspective. *(CORBIS)*

the twentieth century. Its impact on behavioral disorders came gradually as learning principles were applied to behavior. Albert Bandura (1977) expanded the learning approach through his work on observational learning, which highlighted the roles of the social context and cognition (Grusec, 1992). His approach was a major influence.

Learning is, of course, fundamental to human functioning, and its application to many facets of problem behavior is widespread (Jacob & Pelham, 2000). Watson may have been overly simplistic about how humans develop, but learning approaches can improve the lives of youngsters experiencing emotional, cognitive, and social disorders. The explicit application of learning principles to the assessment and treatment of behavioral problems is referred to as behavior modification, or behavior therapy. Approaches that emphasize the combination of learning principles and the social context and/or cognition are referred to as social learning or cognitive-behavioral perspectives.

MENTAL HYGIENE AND CHILD GUIDANCE MOVEMENTS

The twentieth century saw another important thread being woven in different settings. Despite early interest in adult psychopathology, much remained to be learned, and treatment often consisted of custodial hospital care. The mental hygiene movement in the United States aimed to increase understanding, improve treatment, and prevent disorders from occurring at all.

In 1908, Clifford Beers wrote an autobiographical account, *A Mind That Found Itself*, telling of the insensitive and ineffective treatment he had received as a mental patient. Beers proposed reform, and he obtained support from renowned professionals, including Adolf Meyer. Offering a "commonsense" approach to studying the patient's environment and to counseling, Meyer set the course for a new professional role—the psychiatric social worker (Achenbach, 1982). Beers's efforts also led to the establishment of the National Committee for Mental Hygiene to study mental dysfunction, support treatment, and encourage prevention. Because childhood experiences were viewed as influencing adult mental health, children became the focus of investigation and guidance (Rie, 1971).

In 1896, at the University of Pennsylvania, Lightner Witmer had already set up the first child psychology clinic in the United States (McReynolds, 1987; Ross, 1972). This clinic primarily assessed and treated children who had learning difficulties. Witmer also founded the journal *Psychological Clinic* and began a hospital school for long-term observation of children. He related psychology to education, sociology, and other disciplines.

An interdisciplinary approach also was taken by psychiatrist William Healy and psychologist Grace Fernald in Chicago in 1909, when they founded the Juvenile Psychopathic Institute. The focus of the institute was on delinquent children, and its approach became the model for child guidance. Healy was convinced that antisocial behavior could be treated by psychological means, by helping youngsters adjust to the circumstances in which they lived (Santostefano, 1978). Freudian theory provided the central ideas for dealing with psychological conflicts, but it was integrated with educational, medical, and religious approaches in child guidance clinics (Costello & Angold, 2001). Healy and his wife, psychologist Augusta Bronner, opened the Judge Baker Guidance Center in Boston and the National Committee for Mental Hygiene subsequently established several other child clinics. The cases treated now included personality and emotional problems. These clinics flourished in the 1920s and 1930s.

In 1924, the child guidance movement became formally represented in the newly formed American Orthopsychiatric Association, with Healy as its first president and Bronner as its second. To this day, the association includes a variety of professionals concerned about children and adolescents.

SCIENTIFIC STUDY OF YOUTH

It was also during the early twentieth century that systematic study of youth became widespread. A central figure in this endeavor was G. Stanley Hall. Like many others of this period, Hall knew little about the development of the young, and so he collected questionnaire data about their fears, dreams, preferences, play, and other aspects of functioning (Grinder, 1967; Sears, 1975). Some questionnaires focused on the problems of youth with the goal of understanding mental disorder, crime, social disorder, and the like (White, 1992). Hall wrote extensively on children and adolescents, and he also trained students who later became leaders in the field. As president of Clark University, Hall invited Freud to lecture in 1909. He also helped establish the American Psychological Association, of which he was the first president.

G. Stanley Hall contributed to the early scientific study of youth and served as the first president of the American Psychological Association. *(Corbis/Bettmann)*

ACCENT ●●●●●

Mrs. Hillis: Improving Corn, Hogs, and Children in Iowa

The establishment of the Iowa Child Welfare Station was sparked by Mrs. Cora Bussey Hillis, who demonstrated how advocacy for children can go hand in hand with advocacy for science (Sears, 1975). Mrs. Hillis was the mother of several children, and she had also lost children. She believed that ignorance about children's development and health could be blamed for the deaths of her children.

Mrs. Hillis was aware of the much-respected agricultural station of the college in Ames, Iowa. In her mind's eye, she could see a comparable child welfare station that would be devoted to research, teaching, and dissemination of knowledge. The work of the center would focus on problems in children's development and health. Researchers would be trained, as would

professionals, to work directly with children and parents. A body of knowledge would be constructed and disseminated to the public as rapidly as possible. Mrs. Hillis had faith that if research could "improve corn and hogs it could also improve children" (p. 17).

With the consultation of Carl Emil Seashore, a psychologist and dean of the graduate school at the State University of Iowa, a proposal was written. The idea of a child center was unusual and caused bickering in the legislature. Eventually the concept was backed by labor unions, women's clubs, and other organizations. In 1917, the legislature appropriated $50,000 to open the station at the Iowa City campus, near the departments of medicine and education, where Mrs. Hillis had envisioned it.

At about the same time, an important event occurred in Europe: Alfred Binet and Theophil Simon were asked to design a test to identify children who were in need of special education (Siegler, 1992; Tuddenham, 1962). They presented children of various ages with different tasks and problems, thereby establishing age norms by which intellectual performance could be evaluated. The 1905 Binet-Simon test became the basis for the development of intelligence tests. It also encouraged professionals to search for ways to measure other psychological attributes.

Another outstanding figure was Arnold Gesell, who meticulously recorded the physical, motor, and social behavior of young children in his laboratory at Yale University (Thelen & Adolph, 1992). He charted developmental norms, relying on structured observation, naturalistic observation, and parental report. An organizing concept of his work was maturation, the intrinsic unfolding of development relatively independent of environmental influences. Gesell left an extensive film archive of infant and child behavior, as well as a record of strong advocacy for children to have optimal rearing environments.

Commencing around 1920, child study began to benefit from several longitudinal research projects

that evaluated youth as they developed over many years. Research centers existed at the universities of California, Colorado, Michigan, Minnesota, Ohio, and Washington; Fels Research Institute; Columbia Teachers College; Johns Hopkins University; and the Iowa Child Welfare Station. Knowledge about normal development began to accumulate that eventually was applied to the study of child and adolescent disorders. (See Accent: "Mrs. Hillis: Improving Corn, Hogs, and Children in Iowa.")

Current Study and Practice of Child and Adolescent Psychopathology

Today, the study and practice of child and adolescent psychopathology reflects the diverse historical theories, movements, and events that were set into motion in the early decades of the twentieth century. As we shall see in subsequent chapters of this text, some of the early occurrences are presently more significant than others. Many new influences also have come into play. Research into all areas of childhood and adolescence has reached new heights of sophistication and is being brought to bear on a multitude of questions. Both older and more recent assumptions, conceptualizations, and knowledge are giving shape to current approaches, theory, investigation, and practice.

The field of psychopathology as applied to young people is dynamic and multidisciplinary. Its primary goals are to identify, describe, and classify psychological disorder; to reveal the causes of disturbance; and to treat and prevent disorder. These goals are most central to clinical psychology and psychiatry. Nevertheless, various subspecialties of psychology, medicine, education, social work, anthropology, and other disciplines contribute important knowledge, understandings, and interests. Indeed, if we had to choose one statement to capture the essence of today's approach, the statement would emphasize diversity and complexity. It is thus at the risk of oversimplification that we highlight major themes that we believe are critical today. These will be apparent in discussions throughout this text.

- The complexity of human behavior, whether judged normal or abnormal, calls for systematic conceptualization, observation, data collection, and hypothesis testing.

- Normal and abnormal behavior go hand in hand, and we must study one in order to understand the other.

- With few, if any, exceptions, behavioral problems stem from multiple causes—psychological, sociocultural, biological—that work together. These all must be reckoned with if we are truly to understand, prevent, and ameliorate problem behavior.

- The young person displaying behavioral or psychological difficulty is best viewed as actively interacting with a changing psychological, sociocultural, and biological environment.

- Cross-cultural studies are enriching and appreciation of cultural differences is needed for complete understanding of the development and problems of youth.

- Continued efforts are needed to construct and verify treatment and prevention programs.

- Advocacy for the well-being of youth is an appropriate component of the study of psychopathology, particularly because young people may lack the maturity and social influence to advocate for themselves.

SUMMARY

DEFINING AND IDENTIFYING DISORDERED BEHAVIOR

- *Behaviors are judged as abnormal on the basis of their being atypical, harmful, and inappropriate. Standards for behavior depend on developmental, cultural, gender, and situational norms.*

- *Adult attitudes, sensitivities, and tolerance play a role in identifying disturbances in the young, and what is considered as abnormal may change over time.*

HOW COMMON ARE BEHAVIORAL DISORDERS OF YOUTH?

- *The rates of behavioral disturbances vary depending on data collection methods, populations studied, and other factors.*

- *It is generally accepted that 15 to 20 percent of youth have diagnosable behavioral disorders and that most children and adolescents do not receive adequate treatment. This situation may be worsening.*

HOW ARE DEVELOPMENTAL LEVEL AND DISORDERS RELATED?

- *Some association exists between the onset or identification of specific disorders and age/developmental level, due in part to the timing of the child's emerging abilities and environmental demands placed on the child. Onset may occur gradually, however.*

HOW ARE GENDER AND DISORDERS RELATED?

- *An overall gender difference occurs in the rates of disorder, with boys exhibiting higher rates. Some gender differences exist in the timing, severity, expression, causes, developmental paths, and consequences of behavior problems.*

- *Methodological weaknesses, including biased clinical samples, probably account in part for reported gender differences, but numerous and complex biological and psychosocial factors undoubtedly underlie true gender differences in psychopathology.*

HISTORICAL INFLUENCES

- *Early interest in psychopathology focused on adults, with causation attributed to demonology or somatogenesis.*

- *Progress in identifying and classifying mental illness was made in the nineteenth century. The study of childhood disorders generally lagged behind that of adults', but several disorders were identified, mental retardation received much attention, and biological causation held sway.*

- *The early decades of the twentieth century marked crucial influences: Psychoanalytic theory, behaviorism and social learning theory, the mental hygiene and child guidance movements, and dramatic increase in the scientific study of youth. These events and movements brought new knowledge and conceptualizations of child and adolescent disorders.*

CURRENT STUDY AND PRACTICE OF CHILD AND ADOLESCENT PSYCHOPATHOLOGY

- *The current study and practice of child and adolescent psychopathology is characterized by multidisciplinary and scientific efforts.*

- *Emphasis is given to scientific study, the relationship between normal and abnormal development, multicausality, the young person as an active developing entity, cross-cultural study, effective treatment and prevention, and advocacy.*

KEY TERMS

developmental norms *(p. 3)*

regress *(p. 3)*

quantitative differences *(p. 3)*

qualitative differences *(p. 4)*

culture *(p. 4)*

cultural norms *(p. 4)*

ethnicity, race *(p. 5)*

gender norms *(p. 5)*

situational norms *(p. 5)*

demonology *(p. 10)*

somatogenesis *(p. 10)*

psychogenesis *(p. 10)*

syndromes *(p. 10)*

psychoanalytic theory *(p. 10)*

id, ego, superego *(p. 12)*

defense mechanisms *(p. 12)*

psychosexual stage theory *(p. 12)*

classical conditioning *(p. 13)*

Law of Effect *(p. 13)*

operant learning *(p. 13)*

observational learning *(p. 13)*

behavior modification, behavior therapy *(p. 13)*

social learning perspective *(p. 13)*

cognitive-behavioral perspective *(p. 13)*

maturation *(p. 15)*

2

The Developmental Psychopathology Perspective

Parents and others are often puzzled about the reasons underlying a child's or adolescent's behavioral disturbance. For that matter, hardly a day passes without each of us wondering about many aspects of behavior. We want to know why a dependable schoolmate suddenly dropped out of class, how our father manages to be consistently sympathetic when we get into difficulties, whether a talented actor who is abusing drugs will be able to rehabilitate herself. Generally, the more usual the behavior, the fewer questions we have, and the more easily answered they seem. It is unexpected behavior that is more likely to confound us—especially when the behavior appears to be problematic or harmful in some way.

> ### Elizabeth No Obvious Explanation
>
> Elizabeth Fellows was referred to a therapist by her physician, who outlined concerns about a possible eating disorder. Elizabeth's mother, who had taken her to the physician, was worried. Not only had she heard Elizabeth vomiting in the bathroom on three occasions, but Elizabeth also had dropped all of her friends and stayed home in her bedroom. Mrs. Fellows reported that until approximately six months ago, Elizabeth seemed fairly normal to her. Since then, Elizabeth had spent more and more time by herself, dropping even Katie, with whom she had been friends since kindergarten. Elizabeth had been a straight A student; now she was earning Bs and Cs. Mrs. Fellows acknowledged that tenth grade had been a difficult one, but she felt that Elizabeth's personality was changing. Mrs. Fellows was unable to remember any single event that had occurred in the past six months that might explain her daughter's behavior.
>
> Adapted from Morgan, 1999, p. 46.

The ability to explain behavioral disorder is of critical interest to both clinicians and researchers. Although it is possible to treat and prevent disturbances without fully understanding them, increased knowledge significantly improves these efforts. Then too, as scientists, psychopathologists are committed to exploring an array of fundamental questions about behavior. In this chapter, we will present a framework for conceptualizing causation and other aspects of psychological dysfunction in young people.

Perspective and Theory

Much of today's understanding of both normal and abnormal behavior comes from applying the assumptions and methods of science. The writings of Thomas Kuhn (1962) and others have made us aware that science is not a completely objective endeavor. Like all of us, scientists must think about and deal with a complex world. To study and understand phenomena, scientists adopt a perspective—a view, an approach, or cognitive set. When a perspective is shared by investigators, it may be termed a paradigm. Paradigms typically are thought of as including assumptions and concepts—as well as ways to evaluate these. A closely related term is that of theory, which implies a formal, integrated set of propositions to explain phenomena.

There are several benefits in adopting a particular view or theory. A perspective or theory helps make sense of the puzzling and complex universe. It guides us in what kinds of questions we ask, what we select for investigation, what we decide to observe and how to observe it, and how we interpret and make sense of the information we collect. Perspective-taking strongly organizes how a problem is approached, investigated, and interpreted.

There are, of course, disadvantages in taking a perspective—all related to the fact that acting on a certain perspective usually means that we are setting limitations. When we ask certain questions, we may preclude others. When we observe some things, we do not examine others. When we choose particular methods and instruments to detect certain phenomena, we undoubtedly miss other phenomena. We limit the ways in which we might interpret and think about new information. Perspective-taking is a trade-off—albeit one that many investigators believe is, on balance, more beneficial than detrimental.

THEORIES OF PSYCHOPATHOLOGY

Because theories provide concepts and formal propositions that can be tested, they are highly valued by researchers and clinicians (Izard et al., 2002; Hinshaw, 2002). We saw in Chapter 1 that the biological, psychoanalytic, and behavior/social learning approaches to psychopathology were rooted in the early twentieth century. Currently, numerous other theoretical frameworks offer psychological explanations of child and adolescent psychopathology; they focus on emotion, self-regulation, higher level cognition, family interaction, and many other facets of psychological functioning. These theories tend to apply to circumscribed areas and are referred to as microtheories. They stand in contrast to macrotheories—grand theories, such as psychoanalytic theory, that are sometimes criticized as trying and failing to explain too much or as having outlived their usefulness for generating testable hypotheses (Cicchetti & Hinshaw, 2002; Hinshaw, 2002). Microtheories are viewed as more readily proposing specific causal links among key variables, testing specific propositions, and further developing concepts based on empirical findings.

In addition to having theories to guide the study of abnormal behavior, it is helpful to have general models that encourage us to think about and simultaneously consider the numerous factors potentially involved in psychopathology. One such approach, the vulnerability-stress model, conceptualizes the multiple causes of psychopathology as the working together of a vulnerability factor (also referred to as the diathesis) and a stress factor. For example, the vulnerability may be a child's predisposition for depression that interacts with the stress of parental divorce, which results in child problems. In this model, both vulnerability and stress are necessary, and they may be biological, psychological, or social factors.

Other models specifically incorporate several levels of explanation. Gottlieb and Halpern (2002), for example, offer a systems view of development that integrates four levels of factors. These are genetic activity, nervous system activity, behavior, and several aspects of the environment. In this and similar biopsychosocial models, development is viewed as occurring over time as the components of the system interact or transact and influence each other. Such systems perspectives are receiving increased support given that they avoid overly simplistic views of the development of problems experienced by children and adolescents.

Developmental Psychopathology Perspective: An Overview

The developmental psychopathology perspective that we heavily call upon in this textbook has rapidly become influential in the study of behavioral disorders of youth. It was forged largely by the marriage of developmental psychology and clinical child/adolescent psychology and psychiatry. Developmental psychology traditionally takes normal development as its subject matter; it is especially interested in understanding universal principles of how people grow and change during their lifetime. The primary interest of clinical psychology and psychiatry is in identifying the symptoms of behavioral disorders, understanding the causes of disorders, and alleviating the difficulties. These different disciplines began to realize that each had something to offer to and gain from the other. By the 1970s, their cooperative efforts became meaningful enough to warrant recognition and the new label of developmental psychopathology (Cicchetti, 1984; 1989).

Developmental psychopathology is interested in the origins and developmental course of disordered behavior, and in individual adaptation and success as well (Cummings, Davies, & Campbell, 2000; Sroufe, 1997). It is best viewed as an integrative or systems framework for understanding disordered behavior in relation to normal development (Cicchetti & Cohen, 1995). Rather than imposing specific theoretical explanations, it is a way of integrating various theories or approaches around a core of developmental knowledge, issues, and questions (Achenbach, 1990). As shown in Figure 2–1, these approaches—labeled microparadigms—are subsumed under developmental psychopathology.

Each microparadigm in the schema offers a view of behavioral disturbance. Each has its own assumptions, offers theoretical concepts, asks specific questions, adopts certain methods, and makes its own interpretations. Individuals working within the developmental psychopathology framework are free to adopt what they see as useful from various microparadigms and reject what is not useful. For example, although psychoanalysis is often seen, among other things, as having a shaky empirical base and including explanations inconsistent with research findings (Rutter & Sroufe, 2000), psychoanalytic concepts remain important in some explanations of psychopathology. Overall, developmental psychopathology's openness encourages integration across perspectives and disciplines, which is optimal for studying the development of both normal and abnormal behavior (Cummings et al., 2000.)

As an integrative approach, developmental psychopathology has its own assumptions, principles, and interests. In addition to the central proposition that problem behavior can be fully understood only when normal development is considered, several other assumptions inform the developmental psychopathology perspective. We turn to these after examining the concept of development.

Concept of Development

The concept of development can seem deceptively simple. If we were to ask strangers passing on the street to define the term *development*, many would surely offer *growth* as a synonym, with growth meaning not only bigger but also better. And most people would note that development requires time. However, any definition that stops here would fall far short of a full description of development.

Although many different descriptions and explanations have been proposed, there is some consensus among theorists on the essence of development (e.g., Cummings et al., 2000; Cicchetti & Schneider-Rosen, 1986; Sroufe & Rutter, 1984; Hodapp, Burack, & Zigler, 1990).

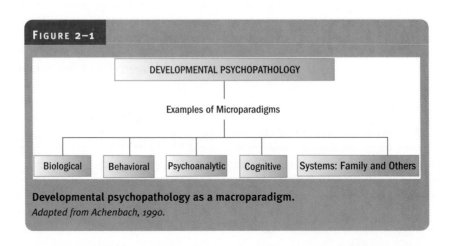

Developmental psychopathology as a macroparadigm.
Adapted from Achenbach, 1990.

- Development refers to change over the life span that results from ongoing interactions of an individual with biological, psychological, and sociocultural variables, which themselves are changing.

- Developmental change may be manifested in different ways. Behavior may change quantitatively or qualitatively; for example, a child's social responses may increase in number and also in features, or qualities.

- On a broader scale, there is a common, general course of early development of the biological, motor, physical, cognitive, emotional, and social systems. Within each system, early global structures and functions become more finely differentiated and then integrated. Integration occurs across systems as well.

- Development proceeds in a coherent pattern, so that for each person, current functioning is connected both to past and future functioning. Thus development can be thought of as proceeding along pathways of more or less complexity. In youth, developmental pathways are relatively open and flexible, but there is some narrowing of possibilities with age.

- Over the life span, developmental change may produce higher modes of functioning and the attainment of goals, but change is not inevitably positive. Physical aging in adulthood brings decrements in functioning, and maladaptive behavior can develop at any time during the life span.

With the concept of development serving as a backdrop, we now turn to five related issues central in the developmental psychopathology approach: multicausality of problem behavior, the search for causal processes, pathways of development, risk and resilience, and continuity of problems over time.

How Development Occurs: Multicausality

A fundamental assumption is that development is effected by a continuous interplay between an active, changing person engaging in a complex, changing context (Cummings et al., 2000). Part of this mix is what the individual brings to the process at any point in time.

Although this view may now seem commonsensical, there is a long history of trying to explain abnormal development in simpler ways. An example is the medical model. Here, disorders are considered as discrete entities—things, if you will—that result from specific and single biological causes within the individual. This perspective was reinforced in the early 1900s by the realization that the microorganism that caused syphilis sometimes affected the brain, thereby causing mental deterioration. On the basis of present knowledge, it is questionable at best that a single cause can account for most behavioral outcomes. (In fact, this is true for many physical illnesses; for example, biological, psychological, and social factors appear to contribute to cardiac disease.)

As an example, we can take the interplay of biology and psychosocial factors regarding children born prematurely or suffering medical complications just before or after birth (Anderson et al., 2001; Greenberg & Crnic, 1988). As a group, these children have more neurological and intellectual difficulties later in life than full-term infants; yet many do well. When infants are severely biologically damaged, the outcome is likely to be poor but most children experiencing birth complications can make enormous gains when family and cultural factors enhance development. Thus, as is now commonly acknowledged, the understanding of outcome rests on a multifactorial explanation.

Searching for Causal Processes

A full account of causation requires, however, more than identifying causal factors. Developmental psychopathologists seek to understand how causal factors work together or what the underlying processes and mechanisms might be. Thus we would want to know, for example, how the specific components of the home environment that lead to poor or optimal development of a prematurely born infant work together over time to affect the child's physical well-being, intellectual growth, social skills, and so forth. There are many ways to search for causal processes, and virtually all involve careful investigation and interpretation.

In conceptualizing causation, it is useful to make a distinction between direct and indirect causes. When a direct effect operates, variable X leads straight to the outcome. An indirect effect is operating when variable X influences one or more other variables that, in turn, lead to the outcome. Establishing indirect effects is usually more difficult, because the pathway of influence may be complex.

Consider, for example, a study that focused on the known association of children's being rejected by peers and having academic and behavioral problems (Buhs & Ladd, 2001). Evidence suggests that peer dislike may be a factor in causing academic failure

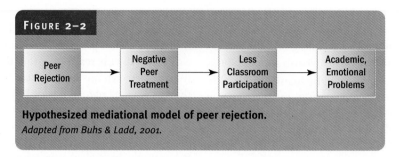

FIGURE 2–2

| Peer Rejection | → | Negative Peer Treatment | → | Less Classroom Participation | → | Academic, Emotional Problems |

Hypothesized mediational model of peer rejection.
Adapted from Buhs & Ladd, 2001.

and other problems, and it would be fruitful to know about the processes that might be involved. Does peer dislike lead directly to underachievement? Or might peer dislike operate in such a way that the rejected child is treated badly by peers and has fewer opportunities to learn—and that these mediate, or explain, the difficulties. Buhs and Ladd tested this mediational model and found partial support for it (Figure 2–2). The results suggested that peer rejection led to the child's being victimized and excluded, which led to the child's participating less in the classroom and, in turn, exhibiting academic and emotional problems.

The search for causation can also involve a moderating effect. This occurs when a factor influences the relationship between variables. For example, when children of different social class have the same experience but different outcome, social class may be a moderating factor.

Frequently, making a distinction among necessary, sufficient, and contributing causes is also useful. This distinction recognizes that the many factors that play a role in development do not play the same or equal roles. A necessary cause must be present in order for the disorder to occur; a sufficient cause can, in and of itself, be responsible for the disorder. In Down syndrome, which is characterized by mental retardation, known genetic anomalies are both necessary (they must be present) and sufficient (the occurrence of the condition does not require other factors). By contrast, in the debilitating disorder of schizophrenia, brain dysfunction is thought to be necessary but not sufficient. That is, brain abnormality underlies schizophrenia but may not always result in the disorder; other factors must also be present. It is also important to recognize that contributing causes may also operate; these are not necessary or sufficient. In some disorders, several factors may contribute by adding or multiplying their effects to reach a threshold to produce the problem.

"This is the path to adulthood. You're here."

The search for causation may encompass various levels of analysis—genetics, brain structure or function, psychological, social—and may employ various research designs. No matter what the strategy, however, one strength of the developmental psychopathology perspective is its focus on determining the mix of causal processes. We will further examine concepts and assumptions that contribute to this quest.

Pathways of Development

The developmental psychopathology perspective assumes that abnormal behavior does not appear out of the blue. It emerges gradually as child and environmental influences transact (Cummings et al., 2000). More broadly, development is characterized as involving progressive adaptations or maladaptations to changing circumstances. It can be viewed as a pathway over time, which at any point can be judged as favorable or unfavorable. Furthermore, trajectories are not cast in stone; they are viewed as open or probabilistic. New situations or circumstances, or new reactions to old circumstances, can bring about redirection. One of the tasks of developmental psychopathology is to describe pathways that may be associated with disordered behavior.

As an example of research relevant to this task, we can look at the work of Compas, Hinden, and Gerhardt (1995). From research findings, these investigators mapped five developmental trajectories across the adolescent years in terms of adaptive or maladaptive outcomes. Figure 2–3 describes

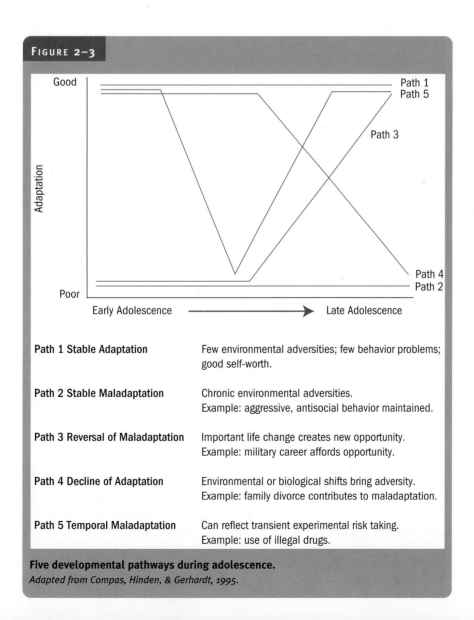

FIGURE 2-3

Path 1 Stable Adaptation	Few environmental adversities; few behavior problems; good self-worth.
Path 2 Stable Maladaptation	Chronic environmental adversities. Example: aggressive, antisocial behavior maintained.
Path 3 Reversal of Maladaptation	Important life change creates new opportunity. Example: military career affords opportunity.
Path 4 Decline of Adaptation	Environmental or biological shifts bring adversity. Example: family divorce contributes to maladaptation.
Path 5 Temporal Maladaptation	Can reflect transient experimental risk taking. Example: use of illegal drugs.

Five developmental pathways during adolescence.
Adapted from Compas, Hinden, & Gerhardt, 1995.

these pathways. Path 1 is characterized by stable adaptation, that is, positive self-worth and lack of problems. Path 2 indicates stable maladaptation. Path 3 shows maladaptation at the beginning of adolescence that turns into positive outcome. Path 4 shows adaptation at the beginning that turns into decline. Path 5 indicates a temporary decline in adolescence but a bouncing back to adaptive behavior. Compas and his colleagues identified factors that are associated with each pathway and presumably influenced the trajectories and outcomes. An obvious aspect of these pathways is that adaptation level at one time does not, in itself, predict later adaptation level. It is what occurs along the way that matters.

Equifinality and Multifinality

The dynamic and probabilistic nature of developmental pathways is recognized in the principles of equifinality and multifinality. Equifinality refers to the fact that diverse paths, or factors, can be associated with the same outcome. In other words, children can travel different pathways, or have different experiences, and yet develop the same behavioral problems (Figure 2–4). We see equifinality with regard to a number of child and adolescent disorders. One of the best established examples is the finding that different pathways exist to antisocial behavior.

The second principle, multifinality, refers to the fact that an experience may function differently depending on a host of other influences that may lead to different outcomes. Simply put, children can have many of the same kinds of experience and yet end up with different problems or no difficulties at all. A well-recognized example concerns child maltreatment. Children who are abused by adults are at risk for later behavioral disturbance, but different children display different kinds of problems or none at all.

The principles of equifinality and multifinality are a reflection of a common theme in the development of behavior: Enormous complexity usually must be addressed in terms of what is likely to happen along life's pathways. Many factors have been identified as influencing the probability that disturbance will or will not occur.

Risk and Resilience

One approach to understanding better the likelihood of a child's developing behavioral problems is to identify factors or circumstances associated with negative and positive outcomes. The concepts of risk and resilience are central to developmental psychopathology.

Risk

Risk factors, or risks, are variables that increase the chance of psychological difficulties or impairments. Table 2–1 shows one way to organize the many risk factors that have been identified by researchers. A distinction is often made between risks that originate in life events and risks that stem from the child's tendencies to respond maladaptively to life experiences. However, it is appropriate to view risk within a transactional model involving both environmental circumstance and the individual.

Figure 2–5 presents a conceptual model for the study of the relationship between life adversities (stressors) and psychopathology (Grant et al., 2003). The troublesome life experiences can be acute, occurring suddenly and perhaps disastrously (e.g., a damaging accident) or they can be chronic, persisting over time (e.g., poverty). The model proposes that stressors result in a variety of processes in the individual—biological, psychological, and

FIGURE 2–4

Equifinality

Multifinality

O U T C O M E S

Time

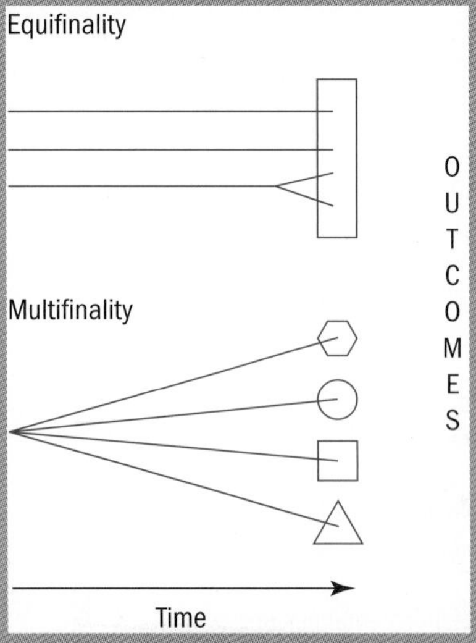

Both equifinality and multifinality operate in development.

TABLE 2–1	SOME DEVELOPMENTAL RISK FACTORS

Constitutional

Hereditary influences
Gene abnormalities
Prenatal, birth complications
Postnatal disease, damage
Inadequate health care, nutrition

Family

Poverty
Abuse, neglect
Conflict, disorganization,
  psychopathology, stress
Large family size

Emotional and Interpersonal

Psychological patterns such as low
  self-esteem, emotional immaturity,
  difficult temperament
Social incompetence
Peer rejection

Intellectual and Academic

Below average intelligence
Learning disability
Academic failure

Ecological

Neighborhood disorganization, crime
Racial, ethnic, gender injustice

Nonnormative Stressful Life Events

Early death of a parent
Outbreak of war in immediate
  environment

Based in part on Coie et al., 1993.

social—which mediate, or lead to, psychopathology. In addition, this relationship can be moderated by characteristics of the child or the environment. Child characteristics such as age, gender, or sensitivity to the environment may come into play. And features of the child's environment may have supportive or detrimental influences. This is a dynamic model in that its components have two-way influences on each other.

As this model demonstrates, researchers are interested in examining the processes or mechanisms involved in risk. It is useful to distinguish distal and proximal influences. Take, for instance, the risk factor of socioeconomic class. This is a distal variable, a description of the environment that can be considered as background, or some distance from the individual. But the impact of social class can be mediated or moderated by variables that operate in

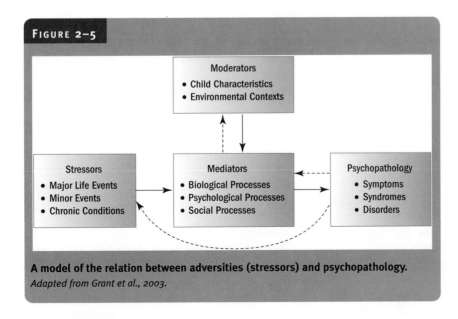

FIGURE 2–5

A model of the relation between adversities (stressors) and psychopathology.
Adapted from Grant et al., 2003.

the person's immediate context—such as diet, the quality of schools, or parental rearing style associated with social class. It is such proximal variables that are likely to tell us more about the processes of risk (e.g., Bendersky & Lewis, 1994).

Major aspects of risk. Although the processes of risk need further investigation, research has given us information on important aspects of risk. There is evidence for the following (Kopp, 1994; Lambert, 1988; Liaw & Brooks-Gunn, 1994; Rutter, 1987):

- A single risk factor may certainly have an impact, but multiple factors have been shown to be especially deleterious.

- The timing of a potential risk can make a difference. (See Accent: "The Timing of Risky Experiences.")

- Some risk factors are strongly associated with developmental problems (e.g., specific chromosome abnormalities), whereas for others the association with problems is less predictable (e.g., poverty).

- The effects of many risk factors appear to be nonspecific, a finding that is reflected in the principle of multifinality. However, some connection exists between risk factors and particular problems; for example, risks factors may be somewhat different for intellectual deficits than for behavioral difficulties.

- Risk factors may be different for the onset of a disorder than for the persistence of the disorder.

- Risk may accumulate over time to set up pathways of vulnerability; that is, the impact of a risk factor may increase the likelihood of future risks by increasing the child's vulnerability or adversely affecting the environment.

RESILIENCE

In the presence of risk, some individuals are adversely affected (are vulnerable), whereas others maintain healthy functioning, that is, they are protected. Resilience is defined by positive outcome in the face of risk or threat. It implies protection from risk factors, or the ability to withstand life's adversities (Smith & Prior, 1995).

Why do some individuals succumb, whereas others appear to rise above threat? There is a tendency to think of resilience as existing within the individual, perhaps because of the perseverance and courage that may seem to characterize children who rise above hardship. Mass media accounts of such success have sometimes described these children as quite extraordinary, as superkids. From a statistical point of view, they are extraordinary, a delight to observe. But research tells us that the bases of resilience may be quite ordinary—a finding that Masten (2001) has captured in the term *ordinary magic*. Resilience rests on well-recognized components of both individual characteristics and environmental factors. Indeed, an excessive focus on individual attributes can lead to inappropriately blaming youth for lacking the qualities to function well (Luthar & Cicchetti, 2000).

| **Ann and Amy** | **The "Ordinary Magic" of Resilience** |

Ann and Amy were from different family circumstances, and at 6 years of age, their functioning was dissimilar. Ann was from an affluent family background, with parents who had an intact marriage and optimally managed both child-rearing and emotional relations with Ann. Amy, on the other hand, was from more difficult circumstances, with a single-parent father who had experienced an acrimonious divorce. During assessment at age 6, Ann was well adjusted, whereas Amy evidenced problems in the clinical range . . . However, over the next several years, Amy was able to take advantage of her social and athletic skills to develop good social relations with classmates, and her parents (ex-spouses) learned ways to interact much more amicably in facing custody-related decisions and problems. For example, Amy's non-custodial mother gradually came to contribute faithfully to child support, even though she had remarried and had another child. An assessment conducted when both children were 10 years of age indicated that Ann, whose family circumstances had continued as stable, supportive, and positive, still scored as well-adjusted, but Amy was now also assessed as well-adjusted and above average in social competence.

Adapted from Cummings et al., 2000, p. 40.

One of the problems in investigating resilience has been how to define positive outcome (Masten, 2001). It can be defined as the absence of psychopathology or a low level of symptoms. This approach seems quite reasonable in the face of

ACCENT ● ● ● ● ●

The Timing of Risky Experiences

An important theoretical and practical concern in developmental psychopathology is to better understand when and how experiences have different influences depending on the age or developmental level of the individual. Such understanding can help prevent problematic circumstances and facilitate insight into problematic behavior.

Historically, there has been a strong interest in the proposition that early-occurring influences may be especially powerful. Research with animals indicated that early experiences can have an impact on the brain; Freud proposed that a failed infant-mother relationship carried over to later love relationships; social learning theorists suggested that early learning might be especially important because it is the basis for later learning. Such findings and theorizing led some workers to argue that the first few years of life *set* later development. Although research indicates that this extreme critical period hypothesis is unfounded for most human functioning, the timing of an event can make a difference for several reasons (Rutter, 1989b).

The nervous system may indeed be affected differently depending on its developmental status. The effects of experience also depend on the psychological processes that emerge at different ages, for example, at the age when the child develops increased ability to think adaptively about an adverse event. The impact of experience may also depend on the timing of social events. The distinction can be made between normative and nonnormative events. Normative events happen to most people at more or less predictable times: puberty occurs between ages eleven and fourteen; elementary school commences between ages five and seven. In contrast, nonnormative events, although not necessarily unusual in themselves, may occur only to certain persons, perhaps at unpredictable times and in atypical circumstances. Examples are the loss of a parent or life-threatening illness during childhood. Nonnormative events are thought to be the more stressful, partly because they are "off time" and put the individual "out of sync" with social expectations and supports.

The current view about the timing of experience holds that few, if any, events set an irretrievable path through life but that early experiences can be important (Cicchetti & Rogosch, 2002). Moreover, youth may be particularly vulnerable to certain risks at other times of life, depending on biological maturity and social demands. Notably, adolescence is marked by considerable social change as well as maturational change in the reproductive, brain, and other biological systems that may increase vulnerability for certain negative outcomes (e.g., Graber et al., 2004; Nelson et al., 2002).

---

serious threat, particularly when the threat overcomes many individuals in the same circumstance. But absence of problems may not do justice to the wellness and success achieved by some at-risk youth. Alternatively, resilience can be defined in terms of competence regarding the developmental tasks or cultural age-expectations applied to young people (Masten & Coatsworth, 1998). Here, resilience is reflected in meeting major developmental tasks and is often viewed as arising from the child's competence and adaptability. Table 2–2 provides some of these widely agreed-on developmental tasks.

Trio of Protective Factors. One of the first notable studies of resilience was conducted on the Hawaiian island of Kauai (Garmezy & Masten, 1994; Werner & Smith, 1982). The participants, who were assessed over many years, were at potential risk because of chronic adversities associated with poverty and family variables. Although most of the participants developed problems, one-third was successfully negotiating life in late adolescence. The investigators summarized the reasons for resilience in three broad categories. One category concerned the personal attributes of the youth. Family characteristics was the second category, and support from outside the family, such as from the school and church, was the third category. This trio of protection has been found in other studies as well.

TABLE 2–2	EXAMPLES OF DEVELOPMENTAL TASKS
AGE PERIOD	**TASK**
Infancy to preschool	Attachment to caregiver(s) Language Differentiation of self from environment Self-control and compliance
Middle childhood	School adjustment (attendance, appropriate conduct) Academic achievement (e.g., learning to read, do arithmetic) Getting along with peers (acceptance, making new friends) Rule-governed conduct (following rules of society for moral behavior and prosocial conduct)
Adolescence	Successful transition to secondary schooling Academic achievement (learning skills needed for higher education or work) Involvement in extracurricular activities (e.g., athletics, clubs) Forming close friendships within and across gender Forming a cohesive sense of self-identity

From Masten & Coatsworth, 1998.

Table 2–3 indicates some important factors involved in resilience. You will notice that many are the opposite of risk factors. With regard to personal characteristics, intelligence, sociability, social competence, easygoing temperament, and ability to cope with stress are among the factors that can provide protection (Compas et al., 2001; Luthar, 1993). Some have suggested that resilient children seek and receive developmentally appropriate experiences (Curtis & Cicchetti, 2003). Accordingly, in times of stress a competent boy may seek social support and be especially effective in obtaining it.

TABLE 2–3	SOME FACTORS INVOLVED IN THE RESILIENCE OF CHILDREN AND ADOLESCENTS
SOURCE	**CHARACTERISTIC**
Individual	Good intellectual functioning Appealing, sociable, easygoing disposition Self-efficacy, self-confidence, self-control Talents Faith, positive outlook
Family	Close relationship to caring parent figure Authoritative parenting: warmth, structure, high expectations Socioeconomic advantages Connections to extended supportive family networks
Extrafamilial context	Bonds to prosocial adults outside the family Connections to prosocial organizations Attending effective schools

Based on Masten & Coatsworth, 1998.

With regard to psychosocial factors, the family can be crucial in providing medical care, warmth, support, and protection from community violence (e.g., Ceballo et al., 2003). Teachers, peers, and clergy can also make a critical difference by providing support, which might foster self-worth and self-confidence. In the face of risks, good schools can foster academic achievement and positive social behaviors.

As with risk, the processes that underlie resilience need to be understood better. Some time ago, Rutter (1987) described four general ways, or mechanisms, in which young people might be protected from risk; they are applicable today (Table 2–4). Rutter viewed these protections as operating at key turning points in people's lives, when risk can be redirected. A single mechanism may have enormous effects, but the mechanisms are not mutually exclusive and can work together.

Continued research is needed in this area. Psychosocial factors are often emphasized but relatively little is known about how neurobiological systems are protected from psychosocial and other environmental risks (Curtis & Cicchetti, 2003). Knowledge about risk and resilience is critical in preventing disorder and in turning disorder around after problems begin (e.g., Buckner, Mezzacappa, & Beardslee, 2003).

Continuity and Change

Inherent in the developmental psychopathology perspective is an interest in understanding change and continuity over time. Development is defined in terms of change, and humans certainly are malleable. But there are limits to malleability and we can expect to see both change and continuity. Both are exemplified in physical aging. When someone reaches old age, the person's face is both different from and similar to its appearance at ages ten, thirty, and sixty. The same is true for psychological functioning. We can generally anticipate both change and continuity as individuals travel along life's pathways, although much is yet to be learned about the transformations along the way.

When the issue of change or continuity is applied to the study of behavioral disorders, a basic question is: Does a behavior disorder at an earlier time in life carry over to, or predict, the disorder in later life? This question is important for understanding the development of behavioral problems, and it has implications for treatment and prevention. Early difficulties are always of concern to the degree that they cause discomfort and unhappiness and close the door of opportunity for growth. When such problems continue over time in some fashion, they have even graver implications.

TABLE 2–4	RUTTER'S DESCRIPTION OF FOUR PROTECTIVE MECHANISMS
Reduction of Risk Impact The impact of risk can be reduced by providing the child with practice in coping; reducing demands of the risk factor; preparing the child for the situation; exposing the child when he/she can cognitively handle the situation; and decreasing exposure to the risk factor. **Reduction of Negative Chain Reactions** Exposure to risk often sets up a chain of reactions that perpetuates risk effects into the future. Interventions that prevent such chains are protective.	**Development of Self-Esteem and Self-Efficacy** People's concepts and feelings about their social environments, their worth, and their ability to deal with life's challenges are important. Positive development results from satisfying social relationships and success in accomplishing tasks. **Opening of Opportunities** Many events, particularly at turning points in people's lives, reduce risk by providing opportunities for adaptive growth. Examples are changes in geographic location, chance to continue one's education, shifts in family roles.

Adapted from Rutter, 1987.

What is known about the continuity of disorders? This is not an easy question to answer: Continuity would be expected to vary with the length of time being examined, different disorders, and other factors. In fact, some problems of youth appear quite transitory, others are relatively stable over time, and some are notably stable. Overall, though, we cannot assume that most children will grow out of behavior disorders or symptoms (e.g., Visser et al., 2003). Moreover, the expression of a disorder may or may not change over time. Autism is manifested over time by a relatively stable symptom presentation; that is, a fair amount of homotypic continuity is displayed. By contrast, there is a noticeable shift from childhood to adulthood in the symptom picture of attention-deficit hyperactivity disorder; here, heterotypic continuity is exhibited.

A host of questions can be asked about what variables predict continuity of problems. Do symptoms that are severe or pervasive, rather than mild and limited, forecast continuity? Is continuity more likely when a child simultaneously displays more than one disorder? Is gender related to continuity and, if so, with regard to all or only some disorders? Many of these questions are being addressed by researchers and will be discussed in later chapters on the developmental course for specific disorders.

Also being addressed are the processes responsible for change or continuity. As an example of a relevant study, we look at the work conducted by Caspi and colleagues (1987), in which the continuity of problems of eight- to ten-year-olds was traced across thirty years. The behavior examined was an ill-tempered interactional style, represented in childhood by temper tantrums (biting, kicking, striking) and verbal explosions (swearing, screaming, shouting). For males, an association was found between childhood ill-temper and adult moodiness and irritability, as well as lower levels of behavior control, dependability, and ambition. The men experienced erratic work patterns and downward occupational mobility, and they were likely to divorce. For females, childhood tantrums were related to marriage to men of low occupational status, unhappy marriage and divorce, and ill-tempered motherhood.

The researchers discussed two processes by which maladaptive behavior is maintained over time. Cumulative continuity stems from children's being channeled into environments that perpetuate the maladaptive style. The ill-tempered boy may limit opportunity by dropping out of school, thereby creating frustrating situations, to which he responds with more irritability, undercontrol, and the like. Interactional continuity originates in the transaction between the person and other people. The person acts, others respond accordingly, and the person reacts to this response. It is assumed that the coercive, ill-tempered style of the child pays off in the short run, so that it is maintained, to the detriment of the child.

Investigations into underlying processes can shed light on how maladaptive behavior is carried forward in the same or different manifestations. We would anticipate that both environmental and biological variables would play a role.

Normal Development, Problematic Outcomes: Four Examples

So far in this chapter, we have discussed core aspects of the developmental psychopathology perspective. In this section, we examine less-than-optimal outcomes within the context of normal development. We will see how normal developmental processes and behavioral disturbances go hand in hand—demonstrating the richness of the developmental psychopathology perspective. The four examples also make obvious that although it is useful to view human functioning as operating in biological, social, emotional, and cognitive domains, these domains overlap and are not independent of each other.

EARLY ATTACHMENT

Virtually all infants and their caregivers seem biologically prepared to interact in ways that foster their relationship. Most parents are remarkably sensitive in understanding their babies' signals and needs, and they respond to meet their needs and optimize social interactions. Infants, in turn, are sensitive to parental emotional-social signals. Such interactions are the basis for the special social-emotional bond called early attachment, which develops gradually and becomes evident when the child is seven to nine months of age.

Recognizing that Freudian theory gave much importance to the mother-child relationship, Bowlby (1969) emphasized that behaviors that facilitate attachment—smiling, crying, eye contact, proximity to caretakers, and the like—were "wired" into the human species to ensure that infants would be nurtured and protected by caregivers. These behaviors are viewed as an attachment system, as an organized pattern of behaviors that protects against high levels

Infants and their caregivers are predisposed to interact in ways that foster attachment.
(David Young-Wolff/PhotoEdit, Inc.)

of threat or fear in stressful situations (Lyons-Ruth et al., 2003). Among other things, Bowlby and subsequent workers were interested in whether disturbed attachment might produce poor developmental outcomes. Today, attachment theory is a dominant approach to understanding the influence of early close relationships on later psychological development (Thompson, 2000).

Early attachment has been extensively studied with a procedure developed by Ainsworth, the Strange Situation. The caregiver (usually the mother), infant, and a stranger interact in a comfortable room in a laboratory. The caregiver leaves and returns to the room several times on a predetermined schedule, while the young child's behavior is videotaped and later analyzed. Initial research indicated that many, but not all, infants could be categorized as displaying secure attachment or one of two types of insecure attachment. Securely attached infants may or may not be distressed at separation from the caretaker, they can be soothed if distressed, and upon the return of the mother they react positively and use the caretaker as a secure base from which they venture to explore the environment

(Lyons-Ruth et al., 2003). Insecurely attached infants, among other things, variously avoid contact when the caretaker returns, seek contact but show distress or anger, and are not readily soothed. The development of one pattern—or quality—of attachment over another depends on child characteristics, the broader social context, and especially parental sensitivity and appropriate response to the infant's needs (Meins et al., 2001).

Early attachment is considered significant not only because of the immediate behaviors displayed by the infant, but also because of its possible link to later behavior. Attachment experiences are hypothesized to become internalized, that is, to provide the child internal models for regulating emotion and for future relationships. Securely attached children are hypothesized to develop effective strategies for coping with stress and to have confidence in their caretakers—a trust that is applied to future relationships (Kerns, Klepac, & Cole, 1996; Sroufe et al., 1999). In fact, secure attachment has been associated with adaptive behavior in childhood and adolescence—such as competence and positive peer interactions—whereas insecure attachment appears to place children at risk for maladaptive behaviors (Dunn & McGuire, 1992; Thompson, 2000).

Disorganized/Disoriented Attachment. Research more recently has revealed a fourth pattern of attachment, referred to as disorganized/disoriented (Green & Goldwyn, 2002; Lyons-Ruth et al., 2003). This pattern appears to reflect the *lack of a consistent strategy* to organize behavior under stressful situations. Infants seem apprehensive of the caregiver, and they variously display contradictory behaviors that may be misdirected and atypical (Table 2–5). Disorganized behaviors may persist or worsen during preschool or early school age, and they are related to later emotional and behavior problems, academic problems, low self-esteem, poor peer interaction, and unusual or bizarre classroom behavior.

The disorganized/disoriented pattern is found at higher rates in conditions such as maternal depression, maternal alcohol abuse, child maltreatment, and other problematic family situations. Evidence shows that the mothers may suffer from unresolved trauma or loss and display high levels of emotion, hostile behaviors, and other undesirable parenting behaviors. The child thus may experience the parent as unavailable or threatening—and the child's behavior may become disorganized in the face of this circumstance. Nonetheless, there is a need for further research in this area as there is some evidence

TABLE 2–5	SOME INDICATIONS OF DISORGANIZED/ DISORIENTED ATTACHMENT

Infant displays contradictory behaviors, such as seeking contact with the caregiver and also avoidance of the caregiver.
Movements and expressions are undirected, misdirected, incomplete, or interrupted.
Movements and expressions are frozen or appear as in "slow-motion."
Infant appears apprehensive regarding the caregiver.
Disorganization or disorientation is obvious in disoriented wandering, confused or dazed expression, or multiple rapid changes of affect.

Adapted from Lyons-Ruth, Zeanah, & Benoit, 2003.

for biological vulnerability in these children, including genetic abnormality.

Interpreting the Findings. As interesting as the research into attachment is, caution is necessary in interpreting the results. Not all findings demonstrate a link between early attachment and later adjustment. And attachment patterns are not always stable over time; they can change from secure to insecure and vice versa. Changes in family circumstances—and their impact on parental and child behavior—likely play a role in creating instability of attachment (Thompson, 2000). Then, too, once children acquire language, parental conversation and discussion contribute to the development of their offspring's internal models of relationships. If the child's hypothesized internal working model changes over time, early attachment might well not predict later adjustment.

In addition, it should be emphasized that any link between early attachment and later adjustment is not easy to interpret. Children who have experienced secure attachment may differ in other ways from children who have experienced insecure attachments. And it may be the persistence of positive child-parent relationships—not just early attachment—that is crucial to adjustment (O'Connor, 2003). An important issue, then, is to better understand the circumstances and mechanisms that might or might not carry forward the influence of early attachment on normal and problem behavior.

TEMPERAMENT

The word temperament generally refers to basic disposition or makeup. The concept of temperament is an old one, going back to the classical Greek era. Current interest can be traced to Chess and Thomas's study of New York City children (1972; 1977). These investigators were especially interested in explaining the development of problem behaviors. They recognized environmental influences on the development of behavior, but they were struck by individual differences in how infants behaved from the first days of life. Perhaps the infants' style of behavior entered into the development of problem behavior. On the basis of parental interviews and actual observations, Chess and Thomas were able to demonstrate that young babies had distinct individual differences in temperament that were somewhat stable over time.

Chess and Thomas defined temperament in terms of nine categories of behavior on which young children varied (Table 2–6). They also identified three basic temperamental styles: easy, slow-to-warm, and difficult. The latter temperament is generally characterized by negative mood, intense reactions to stimuli, poor adaptability to new situations, and the like. Although difficult temperament has been defined somewhat variably over the years, it has been associated with social and psychological disturbance (Seifer, 2000).

Chess and Thomas avoided simplistic notions about temperament and behavioral problems. They suggested that early temperamental differences occur in the presence of parents who themselves differ in how they react to and manage their children. Parental responding, in turn, influences child reactions, which affects parental reactions, and so on—all of which occurs within the broader context of a changing environment. Chess and Thomas hypothesized that final outcome depends on goodness-of-fit, that is, how the child's temperament fits with parental characteristics and other environmental factors. The following case description demonstrates that a good match can lead to adaptation.

TABLE 2–6	THE CHESS AND THOMAS CATEGORIES OF TEMPERAMENT

1. Activity level
2. Regularity of biological functioning (e.g., eating, sleeping)
3. Approach/withdrawal to new stimuli; approach is positive, such as smiling; withdrawal is negative, such as crying
4. Adaptability to changing situations
5. Level of stimulation necessary to evoke a response
6. Intensity of reaction
7. Mood (e.g., pleasantness, friendliness)
8. Distractibility to extraneous stimuli
9. Attention span and persistence in an activity

Carl   A Case of Goodness-of-Fit

[Early] in life Carl had been one of our most extreme "difficult child" temperamental types, with intense, negative reactions to new situations and slow adaptability only after many exposures. This was true whether it was the first bath or first solid foods in infancy, the beginning of nursery school and elementary school, first birthday parties, or the first shopping trip. Each experience evoked stormy responses, with loud crying and struggling to get away. However, his parents learned to anticipate Carl's reactions, knew that if they were patient, presented only one or a few new situations at a time, and gave Carl the opportunity for repeated exposure to the new, he would finally adapt positively . . . His parents recognized that the difficulties in raising Carl were due to his temperament and not to their being "bad parents." The father even looked on his son's shrieking and turmoil as a sign of "lustiness." As a result of this positive parent-child interaction Carl never became a behavior problem even though the "difficult" child as a group is significantly at higher risk for disturbed development.

In his later childhood and high-school years Carl met very few new situations and developed an appropriately positive and self-confident image. However, the entry to college away from home suddenly confronted him simultaneously with a number of new situations . . . [This] brought him for help . . . By the end of the academic year his difficulties had disappeared . . . He was told that similar negative reactions to the new might occur in the future. His response was, "That's all right. I know how to handle them now."

Chess & Thomas, 1977, pp. 220–221.

Chess and Thomas's basic insight into temperament as a factor that enters into the transactions of development have stood the test of time. Today temperament is viewed as biologically based, with evidence for inheritance, and as somewhat stable but also malleable with development and experience. Investigators have variously revised Chess and Thomas's nine dimensions of temperament by offering additional descriptions or conceptualizations of temperament.

Behaviorally Inhibited Temperament. A group of children has been identified as displaying behaviorally inhibited temperament. When exposed to unfamiliar stimuli in infancy, they are highly reactive and appear distressed, as suggested by crying and vigorous movement. Children who display behavioral inhibition also have been shown to have biological profiles implicating cardiac reactivity, stress hormones and brain biochemicals, and activation of the frontal area of the brain (Burgess et al., 2003; Kagan, 2003). In childhood, they often are viewed as shy and socially withdrawn compared with those who were not originally highly reactive. Such behavioral inhibition is implicated in later anxiety and depression.

Only some infants who respond negatively to unfamiliar stimuli maintain this behavior over time; in one sample, one-third were fearful and inhibited in their second year (Kagan, 2003). Another study found that about 60 percent of adolescents who had been behaviorally inhibited at age two were socially anxious at age thirteen; the comparable figure for those not inhibited as toddlers was 27 percent (Kagan & Snidman, 1999). This is, of course, consistent with the view of temperament as an individual tendency that transacts with other influences and may change with experience.

Ongoing Research. Various conceptualizations of temperament have been offered during recent years. Most accounts include positive and negative emotion, approach and avoidance behaviors, activity level, and self-control (Compas, Connor-Smith, & Jaser, 2004; Frick, 2004; Rothbart, 2004). Researchers are working to establish which aspects of temperament are specifically associated with preschool, school-age, and adolescent difficulties involving shyness, social withdrawal, anxiety, depression, and aggression and other conduct problems. More generally, the ways in which components of temperament may function to increase or decrease psychopathology are being investigated, as is the relationship of temperament to experience and brain and nervous system functioning.

EMOTION AND ITS REGULATION

Although a central component of temperament, emotion is not identical to temperament and is deserving of further discussion. Three components of emotion frequently are recognized: (1) private "feelings" of sadness, joy, anger, disgust, and the like; (2) overt expressions such as smiles, scowls, and drooping shoulders; and (3) autonomic nervous system arousal and bodily reactions such as rapid heartbeat or a "nervous" stomach, as well as specific brain activity. The emotions may be viewed as relatively brief or more general mood states that vary in intensity and are experienced as positive or negative.

Human emotion is evident early in life: Infants express emotion and respond appropriately to the emotional expression of their caregivers (Harris, 1994; Izard et al., 2002). Two- and three-year-olds are able to name and talk about basic emotions and exert some control over emotional expression. Ages two to five may be particularly important because connections between emotion and cognition advance (Izard et al., 2002). During childhood further progress is made in understanding and modulating the emotions. The development of emotions is certainly shaped by the social context (Schultz et al., 2001). Families socialize their offspring by serving as models of emotional behavior, responding to the child's emotional behavior, and discussing the emotions.

The emotions enter into virtually all human experiences and serve several general functions (Lemerise & Arsenio, 2000). They are involved in human communication and in the development of sympathy for others and a conscience (Posner & Rothbart, 2000). Importantly, emotions motivate and guide individual behavior and cognition. For example, they may guide a child toward an event previously experienced with joy, or they may help decide a plan of action. Thus emotional development has broad implications.

Reactivity, Regulation, Knowledge. As we have already seen, emotional reactivity is viewed as an aspect of temperament, as influenced by biology, and as relatively stable over time. Individual differences exist in how quickly and how intensely children react to situations. Undue fear and anxiety—particularly

From their facial expressions, it appears that very young children experience basic emotions such as happiness and unhappiness. The regulation of emotion is acquired gradually, and for some children much more easily than for others.
(Courtesy of L. Wicks) (Jim Whitmer/Stock, Boston)

when they endure over time—can require professional assistance. Sadness and anger are components of depression and aggression. Indeed, the emotions play some role in most behavioral difficulties, either as a central factor (such as in extreme fears) or as a side effect (such as unhappiness resulting from academic failure). Even positive emotions such as joy and excited happiness can interfere with functioning when they are extremely intense.

All children must acquire regulation of their emotions, a task that entails learning to monitor, inhibit, and modulate the intensity and timing of emotion (Calkins & Fox, 2002). The development of effortful regulation depends on the child's physiological reactivity, external factors (such as experiences with caregivers), and the combination of these. The importance of self-regulation is demonstrated in a study that found high levels of negative emotions combined with poor regulatory skills to be associated with both low social competence and behavioral problems. Children with good regulatory skills did not have these outcomes—regardless of whether they were high or low in emotionality (Eisenberg et al., 1997).

Children's understanding of emotions is also related to developmental outcome. For example, a study by Schultz and colleagues (2001) looked at emotion knowledge and social problems/withdrawal in five- to seven-year-olds. Emotion knowledge was defined in terms of the children's ability to identify (1) emotional expressions on others' faces and (2) the emotion that would be experienced by a person in particular circumstances. As predicted, low levels of emotion knowledge were associated with social problems and withdrawal two years later. Other research demonstrates a link between the understanding of emotion and later academic or psychological problems (Fine et al., 2003; Izard et al., 2002).

Social Cognitive Processing

In contrast to feeling states that motivate and guide behavior, the cognitive domain of functioning has to do with knowing or understanding through higher order thinking processes. The study of cognitive processes is an important aspect of contemporary psychology, and the role of cognition in various disorders of young people is being vigorously pursued (Southam-Gerow & Kendall, 2002; Vasey, Dalgleish, & Silverman, 2003). Here, we only consider one aspect of cognition: social cognitive processing.

Social cognitive processing has to do with thinking about the social world. It focuses on how individuals take in, understand, and interpret social situations—and how behavior is then affected (Lemerise & Arsenio, 2000). Crick and Dodge (1994) have offered a general model of social cognitive processing. The first steps in the model involve the child's encoding, or taking in, the available social cues and then interpreting them. Interpretation includes thinking about the causes of the social situation, the intent of the persons in the situation, and so on. The child then decides on a desired outcome, selects and evaluates what responses might be appropriate, and enacts a response that might result in the desired outcome.

Of immediate interest to our discussion is the role that interpretation of social cues can play in maladaptive behavior, namely aggressive behavior. Numerous studies indicate that children and adolescents who display more than average aggression or who have been rejected by their peers tend to interpret the behavior of others as hostile. In other words, they appear to have a bias to attribute hostility to others, especially when provoked. For example, in a study in which a peer knocked down a structure that the subject children had built with blocks, aggressive children, more than nonaggressive children, perceived that the peer had acted out of hostile intent, rather than, for example, having accidentally bumped into the blocks.

Noteworthy is that although social information processing emphasizes cognition, emotion is viewed as playing an integral role (Arsenio & Lemerise, 2004; Dodge & Rabiner, 2004). Cognition and emotion may interact in various ways (cf. Lemerise & Arsenio, 2000). A child who is already emotionally aroused may be highly prone to misperceptions. For example, the arousal of negative emotions in highly aggressive boys can increase their attribution of hostile intent to others (Orobio de Castro et al., 2003). Alternatively, the perception of hostility in others can arouse feelings of negative emotions. Further, poor understanding of emotion likely plays a role in children's misperceptions of social cues (Denham et al., 2002). The research on social cognitive processing thus contributes to our understanding of how thinking and emotions are united in the interchange between individuals and their environments (Rutter & Sroufe, 2000).

Cognitive processing of the social context undoubtedly influences much human functioning. Studies show, for instance, that children's perception of their parents' interaction with them or with each other is related to parental influence on the children (Gomez et al., 2001). Specific beliefs and attributions about the world and the self appear to operate in depression, anxiety, and obesity, among other difficulties.

Inherent in all the topics we have examined—early attachment, temperament, emotion, and social cognition processing—is the assumption that development is rooted in both biological and experiential factors and their transactions with the child or adolescent. The influences of biological and environmental factors on the development of behavioral problems are further explored in Chapter 3.

SUMMARY

●●●●●○○○○

PERSPECTIVE AND THEORY

- *Perspectives or paradigms, although somewhat limiting, allow scientists to conceptualize phenomena of interest.*

- *Theory, which consists of formal propositions to explain phenomena, is highly valued because it permits the testing of hypotheses. Microtheories of psychopathology are viewed as especially constructive.*

- *The vulnerability-stress model and biopsychosocial model of psychopathology view disorder as resulting from transactions of variables. Systems models often incorporate factors that may operate at different levels of analysis.*

DEVELOPMENTAL PSYCHOPATHOLOGY PERSPECTIVE: AN OVERVIEW

- *Developmental psychopathology explores behavioral disorders with respect to several core developmental issues. It serves as an integrative framework for organizing other perspectives or theories of psychopathology.*

CONCEPT OF DEVELOPMENT

- *Development refers to change—quantitative and qualitative—over the life span that proceeds in a coherent manner along various probabilistic pathways. It is the product of multiple, transactional factors.*

HOW DEVELOPMENT OCCURS: MULTICAUSALITY

- *Development is effected by multiple influences involved in a continuous interplay between an active, changing person and a complex, changing environment.*

SEARCHING FOR CAUSAL PROCESSES

- *A major goal of developmental psychopathology is to uncover the causes of behavioral disorders. It is helpful to differentiate direct and indirect influences; mediating and moderating influences; and necessary, sufficient, and contributing causes.*

PATHWAYS OF DEVELOPMENT

- *The concept of developmental pathways is an important conceptualization. Several paths of adaptation-maladaptation through the adolescent years have been suggested by research studies.*

- *The principles of equifinality and multifinality reflect the complexity of development.*

RISK AND RESILIENCE

- *Many risk factors have been identified, both characteristics of the child and life events that cause stress. Risk is best conceptualized within a transactional model that includes moderators and mediators.*

- *Among important aspects of risk is the number of risks, timing of influences, nonspecific versus specific effects, and the accumulation of factors that set up pathways of vulnerability.*

- *Resilience is based on individual characteristics, family variables, and extra-familial psychosocial variables. Several ways have been suggested through which children may be protected from adversities.*

CONTINUITY AND CHANGE

- *A central issue about behavioral disturbance is its stability over time. Although variation in stability is observed, it cannot be assumed that most children outgrow psychopathology. Both homotypic and heterotypic continuity occur.*

- *Among the processes by which maladaptive behavior is maintained are cumulative continuity and interactional continuity.*

NORMAL DEVELOPMENT, PROBLEMATIC OUTCOMES: FOUR EXAMPLES

- *Patterns of early attachment—the socioemotional bond between infants and caregivers—have been* described. Secure attachment is associated with later positive outcome; insecure and disorganized/disoriented patterns with unfavorable outcome.

- *Temperament refers to individual disposition that is biologically based, relatively stable, and transformable with maturation and experience. Recent accounts emphasize the components of emotion, approach and avoidance, activity level, and control. Temperament can act as a risk or protective factor for behavioral problems.*

- *Emotional behavior is evident immediately at birth and develops rapidly in childhood. Emotional reactivity, regulation, and knowledge play an important role in behavioral disorders.*

- *How children and adolescents process information about social experiences underlies some maladaptive behaviors. Research demonstrates an association between aggression and a cognitive bias to view the world as hostile.*

KEY TERMS

paradigm *(p. 19)*

theory *(p. 19)*

microtheories, macrotheories *(p. 19)*

vulnerability-stress model *(p. 19)*

biopsychosocial model *(p. 19)*

medical model *(p. 21)*

direct effect, indirect effect *(p. 21)*

mediating effect *(p. 22)*

moderating effect *(p. 22)*

necessary, sufficient, contributing causes *(p. 22)*

equifinality *(p. 24)*

multifinality *(p. 24)*

risk factors *(p. 24)*

distal influences, proximal influences *(p. 25)*

resilience *(p. 26)*

critical period hypothesis *(p. 27)*

normative events, nonnormative events *(p. 27)*

homotypic continuity, heterotypic continuity *(p. 30)*

cumulative continuity *(p. 30)*

interactional continuity *(p. 30)*

attachment *(p. 30)*

Strange Situation *(p. 31)*

secure attachment *(p. 31)*

insecure attachment *(p. 31)*

disorganized/disoriented attachment *(p. 31)*

temperament *(p. 32)*

goodness-of-fit *(p. 32)*

behaviorally inhibited temperament *(p. 33)*

Influences and Risks in the Developmental Process

*... from the moment of conception develop-
ment is influenced by constitutional, economic,
social, and cultural factors. ... [These factors]
provide the set of circumstances, or context, for
development. These circumstances may, in
aggregate, generally provide normal advantage, poor advantage, or high advantage. ...
the greater the presence of poorly advantaging
circumstances, the more overall development is
put at risk; the greater the presence of highly
advantaging circumstances, the more the promise for overall development.*

(Horowitz, 2000, p. 4)

The aim of this chapter is to consider major
biological and environmental contexts of
development—with an emphasis on risks to the
behavioral and psychological well-being of youth. We
will discuss the nervous system and brain, genetics,
learning and cognition, and the social/cultural contexts of development. Basic information is provided,
with an emphasis on each aspect's role in and influence on behavioral disorders.

Brain and Nervous System

BRAIN DEVELOPMENT: BIOLOGY AND EXPERIENCE

The development of the brain and nervous system is
arguably among the most fascinating of all developmental processes. Much early growth is biologically
guided, but the influence of experience increases
over time (Grossman et al., 2003).

The nervous system begins to develop shortly
after conception when a group of cells called the neural plate thickens, folds inward, and forms the neural
tube. The rapidly developing cells migrate to fixed
locations, and much of the basic structure of the
brain is completed before birth in a more-or-less
fixed sequence. The brain contains millions of supporting cells, the glial cells, and neurons that are specialized to transmit impulses within the nervous
system and to and from other body parts. These cells
continue to become more complex, interconnected,
and functional into the adolescent years (and to a
lesser extent even later). The brain produces an excess
of neurons and connections, apparently setting itself

up to insure flexibility. Different parts of the brain develop in spurts more rapidly than others, and the pattern is related to functioning. Thus, areas that control voluntary movement grow substantially during the first year of life when the infant is gaining motor control, whereas the frontal part of the brain involved in complex thinking develops into the adolescent years, with spurts perhaps occurring at around ages 6, 10, and early adolescence (Anderson et al., 2001).

The development of the nervous system has been shown to depend, even before birth, on the interaction of biological programming and experience. Animals given the opportunity to explore object-filled, enriched environments develop more neurons and cell connections in certain brain areas than animals reared in simple environments (Hockfield & Lombroso, 1998). Experience also shapes the brain by what seems on the surface to be the opposite of growth—by pruning, or eliminating, unneeded cells and connections. For example, in animals the areas of the brain that are central to vision are shaped by pruning, which appears to require experience with patterned visual input (Grossman et al., 2003). Among the most exciting areas of investigation is the study of, and growing evidence for, a link between human experience and changes in the nervous system (e.g., Nelson et al., 2002). It is clear that biological programming, brain development, and behavior interact to produce further brain development, particularly of the higher centers of the brain (Johnson, 2000).

STRUCTURE

The brain and spinal cord together form the central nervous system. The nerves outside the central nervous system that transmit messages to and from it compose the peripheral nervous system, which has two subsystems. One is the somatic system, which involves the sensory organs and muscles and is engaged in sensing and in voluntary movement. The other, the autonomic system, helps regulate arousal and the emotions. The branches of this involuntary system either increase arousal (sympathetic system) or work to slow arousal and conserve the body's resources (parasympathetic system). The nervous system communicates within itself, and is in close communication with the endocrine system, a collection of glands that release hormones into the bloodstream.

The intact brain—a wrinkled mass crowning the spinal cord—is considered to have three major divisions. The hindbrain, which includes the cerebellum, pons, and medulla, regulates basic functions such as sleeping, breathing, heart rate, and body movements. A small area called the midbrain contains fibers that connect the hindbrain and upper brain regions. It also shares with the hindbrain net-like connections, the reticular activating system, which influences arousal states such as waking and sleeping. Sometimes the midbrain and hindbrain are called the brain stem (Figure 3–1).

The third major division, the forebrain, consists chiefly of two cerebral hemispheres, the outer surface of which is referred to as the cortex. Each hemisphere, connected to the other by the corpus callosum, has four lobes. The cerebral hemispheres are involved in a wide variety of activities, such as sensory processing, motor control, and higher mental functioning, including information processing, learning, and memory.

Situated below the cerebral hemispheres and deep in the brain are several subcortical structures. (They are variously said to be located in the lower forebrain or between the forebrain and the midbrain.) The thalamus is involved in processing and relaying information between the cerebral hemispheres and other parts of the central nervous system. The hypothalamus regulates basic urges such as hunger, thirst, and sexual activity. The multi-structured limbic system—which includes the hippocampus, amygdala, and parts of the cerebral hemispheres, thalamus, and hypothalamus—plays a central role in memory and the regulation of emotions and biological urges through its regulation of the endocrine glands and the autonomic nervous system.

NEUROTRANSMISSION

Although neurons vary in size, shape, and chemistry, they all have three major parts: dendrites, a cell body, and an axon. Communication between neurons occurs across the synapse, the small gap between the cells (the synaptic gap, or cleft). The dendrites of a neuron receive chemical messages from other neurons that result in an electric impulse being sent down the axon. When the impulse reaches the end of the axon, packets of chemicals—the neurotransmitters—are released. They cross the synaptic gap and are taken up by the receptor sites on the dendrites of the receiving neuron. The receiving neuron, in turn, generates new electrical impulses (Figure 3–2). Among the major neurotransmitters are dopamine, serotonin, and

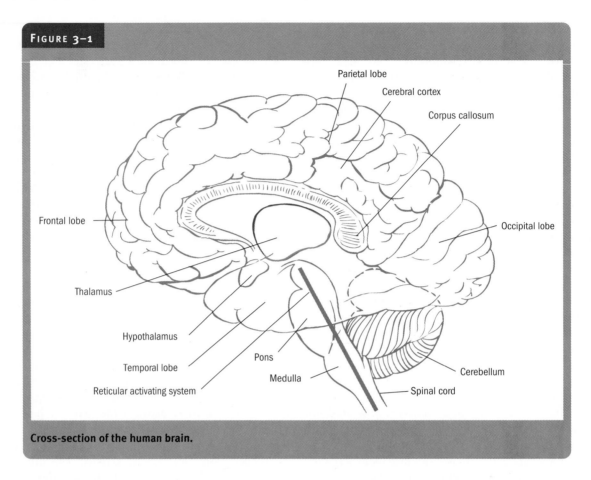

FIGURE 3-1

Cross-section of the human brain.

norepinephrine, whose role in brain functioning is being intensely investigated.

The complexity of communication is hard even to imagine. Neurons may make thousands of connections to other neurons, and there are several neurotransmitters that travel multiple pathways and can be received by different receptor sites. In addition, neurotransmitters can act to excite or inhibit neurons, that is, make them more or less likely to fire an impulse. Communication is far from helter-skelter, however. Neurons at specific locations work together, and also with neurons at other locations, to form pathways, or circuits, that are associated with different functions. The brain operates in a self-organizing manner that is flexible and open to experience (Cicchetti & Dawson, 2002).

Nervous System and Risk for Disordered Behavior

The nervous system is a major aspect of the constitutional, or organismic, factors that influence behavior. Abnormal development or functioning can result

from anomalies of the genetic processes that guide nervous system development. In this case, dysfunction can be "wired in" from the beginning. However, dysfunction can also be attributed to events that occur during pregnancy (prenatal), at about the time of birth (perinatal), or during later development (postnatal).

PRENATAL INFLUENCES

At one time, it was believed that the fetus was protected from most harmful substances, or teratogens, that might enter the mother's bloodstream. We now know that a variety of agents can interfere with brain cell formation, migration, and other developmental processes (Koger, Schettler, & Weiss, 2005). Perhaps unsurprising, the amount of exposure to a teratogen makes a difference in outcome. So does the timing of exposure during gestation; for example, early exposure especially interferes with the formation of basic brain structure.

Teratogens are associated with fetal death, malformation, low birthweight, and functional/behavioral impairments (Hogan, 1998; Singer et al., 1997).

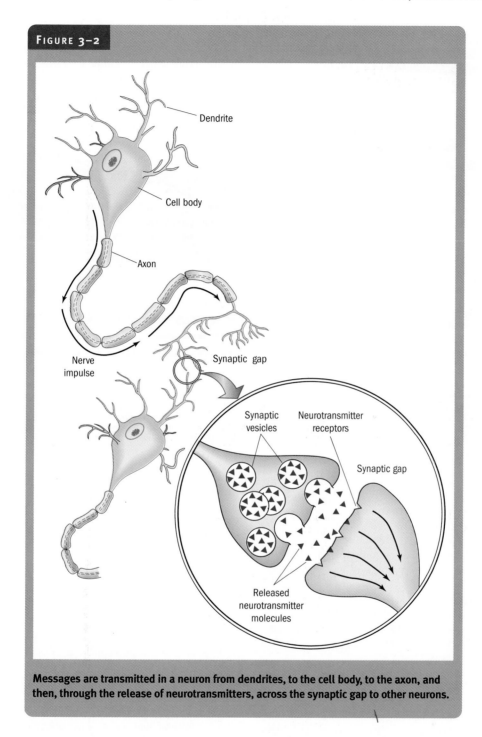

FIGURE 3-2

Messages are transmitted in a neuron from dendrites, to the cell body, to the axon, and then, through the release of neurotransmitters, across the synaptic gap to other neurons.

Potentially harmful drugs include thalidomide, alcohol, tobacco, cocaine, heroin, and methadone. (See Accent: "Fetal Alcohol Syndrome: A Preventable Tragedy.") The possible negative effects of radiation and environmental contaminants—such as lead, mercury, and polychlorinated biphenyls (PCBs)—are well known. In addition, many maternal diseases (e.g., rubella, syphilis, gonorrhea) have harmful effects, and the prenatal threat of acquired immune deficiency syndrome (AIDS) is a more recent concern (Armistead et al., 1998). Maternal stress may also be detrimental (Huizink et al., 2003). Studies of animals suggest that exposure to stress alters the biological system of the developing organism in ways that might create susceptibility to later psychopathology (Huizink, Mulder, & Buitelaar, 2004).

More generally, low birthweight, or low birthweight relative to the length of gestation, is associated with developmental risk (Saylor, Boyce, & Price, 2003). The lower the birthweight, the greater the risk. In the United States, 12 percent of infants are born prematurely (less than 37 weeks into gestation) and 7.5 percent are born with low birthweight (less than 5½ pounds). These circumstances are strongly associated with death in newborns (Field, Hernandez-Reif, & Freedman, 2004).

Although there is no doubt that prenatal threat can be consequential, research conclusions must be examined with care. Ethical considerations prohibit studies that could most clearly indicate causation— that is, experiments in which pregnant women would be intentionally exposed to potentially harmful conditions. From the uncontrolled research methods that are employed it is difficult to draw conclusions about the impact of a particular teratogen. Exposure to any one teratogen can be associated with exposure to other potentially detrimental factors (Ernst, Moolchan, & Robinson, 2001; Fried, 2002). Substance abuse, poor prenatal care, malnutrition, and other possible harmful conditions are often associated with each other (Hogan, 1998; Singer et al., 1997). In addition, many factors can influence children's development both prenatally *and* during the child's subsequent development, making it difficult to pinpoint the timing of influence (Brown et al., 2004). There are, nevertheless, research approaches that aim to circumvent interpretive difficulties (D'Onofrio et al., 2003). One of these is research with animals, which allows intentional exposure to teratogens and the testing of causal hypotheses—although generalizing the results to humans must be done cautiously.

PERINATAL AND LATER INFLUENCES

Nervous system damage also may occur during or after birth. At birth, experiences such as excessive medication given to the mother, unusual delivery,

ACCENT ● ● ● ●

Fetal Alcohol Syndrome: A Preventable Tragedy

Adverse effects from prenatal exposure to alcohol was suspected for many years before they were adequately documented. Fetal Alcohol Syndrome (FAS) is characterized by abnormal brain development and higher than average rates of numerous difficulties. The terms *alcohol-related neurodevelopmental disorder* or *alcohol-related birth defects* generally indicate less severe symptoms. Affected children are at high risk for the following attributes (American Academy of Pediatrics, 2000; Fetal Alcohol Syndrome, 2003):

- Minor facial abnormalities, such as a flat upper lip and/or narrow eye openings
- Retarded growth, both prenatally and postnatally
- Neurological signs such as impaired motor skills and an unusual gait
- A variety of birth defects of the heart, kidneys, eyes, ears, and other organs
- Intellectual deficiency, learning disabilities, and numerous cognitive impairments such as deficits in memory, abstract thinking, comprehension, and generalization

- Hyperactivity, impulsivity, oppositional behavior, and conduct problems

Although not all of the children exhibit all of these symptoms, problems can be pervasive and can persist into adulthood. And whereas educational programs and family support can be of help, the tragedy is that FAS and related conditions are completely preventable by maternal abstinence from alcohol.

FAS occurs at an estimated .2 to 1.5 per 1,000 live births in the U.S. population, and the lesser symptoms perhaps three times as often (Fetal Alcohol Syndrome, 2003). The effects of maternal alcohol use varies with several factors including amount of alcohol exposure, timing of exposure, the mother's age and health, and fetal susceptibility (American Academy of Pediatrics, 2000; Grossman et al., 2003). Prenatal harm is much more likely when alcohol intake is large, but one or more drinks a day has been associated with infant growth retardation. (One drink is defined as 1.5 ounces of distilled alcohol, 5 ounces of wine, or 12 ounces of beer.) Given the possible consequences to children, it can be argued that there is no safe level of maternal alcohol consumption.

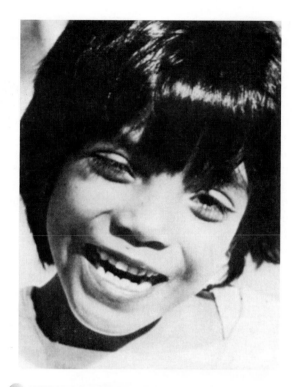

The girl pictured here is one of two daughters born to an alcoholic mother, since deceased. On the basis of history, mental deficiency, and physical findings, both daughters were diagnosed as having fetal alcohol syndrome. Several key features of the syndrome are visible in this girl, including narrow eye openings, underdeveloped-thin upper lip, flattening or absence of the usual indentation under the nose, and possible drooping of the upper eyelids. Behavioral deficits are also implicated in this syndrome.
(Courtesy of March of Dimes Birth Defects Foundation)

and anoxia (lack of oxygen) may result in neurological problems in the newborn. Postnatal damage may occur as a result of accidents, illness, malnutrition, or accidental poisoning. Exposure of children to lead, even at low levels, is an example of accidental poisoning that appears to have a negative impact on brain processes involved in attention and cognitive development.

Brain insult may occur in a limited area (e.g., an accident damages a specific brain area) or may be more general. Although the site and extent of damage help determine the nature of the difficulties, a precise description of the relationship between brain impairment and dysfunction cannot always be made.

Whenever brain damage occurs in youth, a major concern is the degree to which the resulting problems can be remediated. The plasticity, or flexibility, of the brain to recover is still controversial. On the one hand, it is argued that the young, immature nervous system is relatively adept at restoring itself or at successfully transferring functions to undamaged brain areas (Anderson et al., 2001). On the other hand, damage to the immature brain may set up a cascade of interferences with future brain development. Early or later timing of injury is only one factor affecting recovery, however. The extent, severity, and region of damage, as well as the kind and amount of environmental support and therapy provided, are among the factors to be considered.

An emphasis on plasticity can encourage efforts to develop lost or unachieved functioning, but it may have some negative consequences. Frustration for the child, parent, and teacher may result when complete plasticity is assumed but is not realized. The assumption that the young brain is highly plastic may lead also to imprecise forms of intervention. On the other hand, identification of loss and realistic expectations for recovery can lead to advances in our understanding and to improved remediation.

Genetic Context

Genetic contributions to behavioral development operate in complex ways, at both the species and the individual levels. All humans are genetically programmed to transact with the environment so as to acquire basic human abilities to physically manipulate the environment, take in and process information about the world, communicate with others, and form social and emotional attachments. At the same time, genetic processes provide much opportunity for individual characteristics to vary.

The basic genetic material is contained in all body cells. It consists of chromosomes containing DNA (deoxyribonucleic acid), functional segments of which are called genes. At conception, billions of chromosome combinations are possible for any one individual. Other genetic mechanisms result in even greater variability. Chromosomes may exchange genes, break and reattach to each other, and change by mutation, which is spontaneous alteration of the DNA molecule.

In some cases, early genetic processes produce obvious structural defects in the chromosomes or a lack or excess of the normal 23 pairs of chromosomes. These "errors" may be transmitted from parents, but numerous errors are not inherited and may influence only the specific developing embryo. In either case, the consequences can be dire, with a large minority of the abnormalities resulting in the death of the early-developing organism. Less severe outcomes can include a variety of medical syndromes, and mental retardation is commonly associated with them (Simonoff, Bolton, & Rutter, 1996). Newer methods of chromosome analysis now allow detection of quite subtle abnormalities, and both diagnosis and treatment for some of these disorders are improving.

The study of genetic influences on individual differences in behavior is known as behavior genetics. It is a research area brought to bear on understanding genetic influence on psychopathology. The tasks of behavior genetics (Plomin & Crabbe, 2000) are to

- demonstrate whether, to what extent, and how genetic influence operates in a disorder;
- discover the specific gene(s) involved in a disorder and reveal functioning at the cellular and biochemical level; and
- understand the pathways between genes and behavior.

Evidence for genetic influence has been established for many characteristics and behavioral disorders. The discovery of specific genes, the way that they function, and the way that they are linked to behavior lags behind—although enthusiastic work goes forward.

The aim of our discussion here is to introduce some of the major methods and findings of behavior genetics with a focus on behavioral disorders. Keep in mind that even today, genetic influences on behavioral characteristics are often misunderstood. Genes act only indirectly and in complex ways in guiding the biochemistry of cells. Some genes code for proteins, whereas other genes receive information from the internal and external environments to regulate the activity of coding genes. Furthermore, genes turn on and off, and they guide both change and stability. In general, then, the path between genetic endowment—the genotype—and observable characteristics of the individual—the phenotype—is much more indirect and flexible than is often believed. Genetic influences on adaptive or maladaptive behavior are critical, but they operate in conjunction with environmental influences.

SINGLE-GENE INHERITANCE

Gregor Mendel, a monk who experimented with plants in a monastery garden in Moravia in the mid-19th century, is credited with discoveries crucial to modern genetics. Among Mendel's contributions are his descriptions of the inheritance of certain characteristics that are influenced by a single gene. He correctly hypothesized that each parent carries two hereditary factors (later called genes) but passes on only one to the offspring. He noted that one form of the factor is dominant, that is, its transmission by either parent leads to the display of the trait associated with it. The other form, the recessive, displays itself only when it is transmitted by both parents. Although we know today that single-gene inheritance is far from simple, Mendel's basic descriptions have largely stood the test of time. Dominant and recessive patterns of inheritance, as well as the sex-linked pattern described later in this text, are involved in the inheritance of many human attributes and disorders. Huntington's disease is an example of a syndrome transmitted by a dominant gene; it causes death but does not show up until adulthood, when motor problems and mental deterioration become evident. Tay-Sachs disease, transmitted recessively, causes degeneration of the nervous system and death by the age of 1 to 3 years.

The preceding examples illustrate dramatic instances in which single genes lead to specific pathological syndromes. It is possible to determine such genetic influence on a specific behavioral syndrome by identifying an individual with the syndrome—the index case or the proband—and determining whether a known pattern of inheritance runs in the family. In general, the effects of such single genes are relatively predictable. Hundreds are associated with pathological syndromes, some of which involve behavioral impairment.

MULTIPLE-GENE INHERITANCE: QUANTITATIVE METHODS

Many complex human characteristics, such as intelligence and behaviors implicated in behavioral disorders, are associated with multiple genes. These genes are inherited in the usual patterns, but each of them has relatively small influence—which combine to a larger effect. The genes may vary in the size of their influence and may be interchangeable in some instances (Plomin & Crabbe, 2000). Multiple genes working together result in a range of phenotypes, varying from lesser to greater display of the characteristic (Plomin & McGuffin, 2003).

Given these considerations, it is not surprising that multigenic influence is less predictable, or more probabilistic, than single-gene inheritance. To determine multigenic effects researchers must rely on a combination of evidence from a variety of quantitative genetic methods. One of the aims of quantitative genetics is to assess heritability, the degree to which genetic influence accounts for variance in behavior among individuals in the population studied. Information about how genes work together also can be obtained, as well as the contribution of environmental influences (Rutter, 2002).

Methods. Three basic research strategies are employed with human participants: family, twin, and adoption methods (Plomin, 1994a).

Family genetic studies evaluate the likelihood of family members' displaying the same or similar behavioral problems shown by an index case. The aggregation, or clustering, of problems in families is assessed with regard to the degree of genetic relatedness. The average genetic relatedness of first-degree relatives (child-parents, siblings, fraternal twins) is 50 percent; half-siblings and other second-degree relatives are 25 percent genetically related; third-degree relatives, such as cousins, are only 12.5 percent genetically related. If genetic influence is operating, family members who are genetically more similar to the proband should be more likely to exhibit the same or related difficulties as the proband. Such a pattern does not rule out environmental influence, however, because this pattern would be expected when psychosocial transmission is operating. However, family aggregation of a behavior or trait is consistent with genetic influence.

The essence of twin studies is a comparison of identical twin resemblance (concordance) with fraternal twin resemblance. Identical, or monozygotic (MZ), twins have identical genes. Fraternal, or dizygotic (DZ), twins are, on average, only 50 percent alike genetically; in fact, they are no more alike genetically than any other two siblings. In its most basic form, the twin method points to genetic influence if there is greater concordance among identical twins than among fraternal twins. That is, genetic influence is suggested when a disorder occurs more frequently in both members of MZ twin pairs than it does in both members of DZ twin pairs (Edelbrock et al., 1995).

Adoption studies evaluate the relative contributions of genetics and environment by studying adopted and nonadopted individuals and their families. One strategy is to start with adopted children who display a particular behavior disorder and to examine rates of that disorder in members of the children's biological families compared with rates in

their adoptive families. Higher rates in the biological family are evidence for genetic influence. Another strategy is to start with biological parents who exhibit a particular disorder and to examine the rate of disorder in offspring separated from the parent in early childhood and raised in a nonrelative household. Rates of disorder in these children can then be contrasted with a number of comparison groups (e.g., siblings who were raised by the biological parent). Also, associations between risk factors, such as family conflict, and the development of behavior problems can be compared in adopted and nonadopted youngsters. Adoption strategies can thus help reveal complex relations between genetic and environmental influences (Braungart-Rieker et al., 1995).

Overall results from behavior genetic research suggest that with a few exceptions heritability for behavioral disorders or dimensions rarely exceeds 50 percent and that it is often appreciably lower (Plomin, 1994a; Rutter, 2002). This finding means that substantial variation in behavior is attributable to nongenetic influences. In fact, behavior genetic research has provided evidence for the importance of both shared and nonshared environmental influence. Shared environmental influences refer to family influences that contribute to family members' developing in similar ways (Gjone & Stevenson, 1997; O'Connor et al., 1998). Examples might be the intellectual stimulation provided in the family or exposure to environmental toxins, which similarly affect siblings and make them like each other. Nonshared environmental influences refer to influences that are different for children growing up in the same family. These effects make children in the same family different from each other. Examples might be differential treatment of siblings by the parents or differential relationships with friends or teachers. Today's researchers continue to examine the contributions of genetic, shared environmental, and nonshared environmental influences to the development of behavior (Asbury et al., 2003; Jenkins, Rasbash, & O'Conner, 2003).

We should note that all behavior genetic methods have weaknesses (Rutter & Silberg, 2002). Combinations and refinement of methods, and more sophisticated quantitative analyses, seek to address many of the shortcomings of individual methods. These advances also permit evaluation of hypothetical models of genetic transmission and of the interaction of genetic and environmental influences (Eaves et al., 1997; O'Connor et al., 1998; Plomin, 1995).

SEARCHING FOR GENES: MOLECULAR METHODS

Molecular genetics is a rapidly expanding field that seeks to discover the genes associated with a disorder, the biochemicals coded by the genes, and how these biochemicals might be involved in behavior. Research with animals is critical in these endeavors. Animals can be crossbred and their genes can be manipulated in other ways, for example, by "knocking out" gene functioning and studying the effects. In contrast, research with humans widely employs linkage analysis and association analysis (Plomin & Rutter, 1998; Plomin & McGuffin, 2003).

The aim of linkage analysis is to reveal the location of a defective gene, that is, the specific chromosome and the place on the chromosome. This strategy takes advantage of the fact that genes on the same chromosome, especially when close to each other, are transmitted to offspring together. The strategy also takes advantage of the fact that the chromosome location is known for many genetic markers (known segments of DNA that vary among individuals). Linkage analysis determines whether a specific disorder appears among family members in the same pattern as a genetic marker. If so, it can be presumed that a gene that influences the disorder is located on the same chromosome as the marker and is close to the marker. Thus the approximate genetic address for the disorder is revealed. Mapping the gene responsible for Huntington's disease was among the earliest successes of linkage analysis (Huntington's Disease Collaborative Research Group, 1993; Wexler, 1995). It required several years to locate and identify the defective gene on chromosome 4, and it is now possible to test individuals and to test prenatally for the defective gene.

Association analysis searches for genes in a different way (Plomin & McGuffin, 2003). This method tests whether a particular form of a gene (i.e., an allele) is associated with a trait in the population. The method is most appropriate when a particular gene—called a candidate gene—is suspected, based on theory or past research. Most studies compare persons exhibiting a specific disorder with matched controls. As an example, the DRD4 and the DAT1 genes have been found to be associated with attention-deficit hyperactivity disorder; both of these genes are involved in the dopamine neurotransmitter systems.

Association analysis is more suitable than linkage analysis to identify multigenes that have relatively small influence on a disorder or trait (Plomin & McGuffin, 2003). When genes with small effects are involved, it is quite possible that only some will be revealed, at least with present research methods. However, understanding how even some of the genes operate in a disorder can contribute to understanding psychopathology and can potentially facilitate treatment and prevention.

GENE-ENVIRONMENT INTERPLAY

Although we have already noted that genetic and environmental influences work hand in hand to produce traits and behaviors, it is important to examine this interplay in greater detail. We do so by turning to gene-environment interaction and gene-environment correlation.

Gene-environment interaction refers to differential sensitivity to experience due to differences in genotype (Plomin & Crabbe, 2000). An example is provided by children who carry two recessive genes for the condition called PKU (phenylketonuria). These children develop mental retardation when they digest certain foods that are harmless to youngsters who do not carry this genotype.

Gene-environment correlation refers to genetic differences in exposure to environments. Three kinds of gene-environment (GE) correlations have been described: passive, reactive, and active. Table 3–1 defines these and provides a hypothetical example of each. As children move along life's pathways, the impact of passive GE correlations may give way to the influences of reactive and active GE correlations. The importance of gene-environment correlations is that they inform us that a child's experiences are not independent of genetic influences. In fact, there is considerable evidence that genetic influences play a role in determining the experiences a person will have—and thus the risks and protections that will be encountered (Rutter & Silberg, 2002).

Learning and Cognition

Learning and cognition are inextricably intertwined with development. The abilities to learn and think not only become more advanced over time, but also facilitate other kinds of development as the child transacts with the environment. Our present discussion of this topic is introductory, and the vital role that learning and cognition play in psychopathology is woven throughout the text.

TABLE 3–1	TYPES OF GENE-ENVIRONMENT CORRELATIONS DEMONSTRATING HOW GENETIC PREDISPOSITION AND ASPECTS OF THE ENVIRONMENT ARE LINKED

PASSIVE

A family's environment is influenced by the genetic predisposition of the parents. The child experiences this environment and *also* shares the genetic predisposition of the parents. This mechanism occurs at birth and is "passive" in the sense that the child has relatively little active input.

Example: The child who has a genetic propensity for a high-activity level also experiences a high-activity family environment.

REACTIVE

A child evokes reactions from other people on the basis of her or his genetic predisposition, so that the child's genetic propensities are linked to environmental experiences.

Example: Others react to the child's high-activity level.

ACTIVE

A child, particularly as he or she grows older, selects or creates environments on the basis of his or her genetic predisposition.

Example: The child with a genetic propensity for high-activity level engages in activities requiring high activity rather than restrained, quiet activities such as reading.

Adapted from Plomin, 1994b.

CLASSICAL CONDITIONING

Pavlov focused attention on the process of classical conditioning by demonstrations that hungry dogs, which normally salivate to food, could learn to salivate to neutral stimuli presented just prior to the presentation of food. In classical conditioning, the individual learns to make a response to a stimulus that previously did not elicit the response. Many

ACCENT

Albert and Peter: Two Historic Cases

As reported by Watson and Rayner (1920), Albert, an 11-month-old child, initially showed no fear reactions to a variety of objects, including a white rat. He did, however, exhibit fear when a loud sound was produced by the striking of a steel bar. Watson and Rayner attempted to condition fear of the white rat by producing the loud clanging sound each time Albert reached for the animal. After several of these pairings, Albert reacted with crying and avoidance when the rat was presented without the noise. Thus it appeared that fear could be learned through classical conditioning. (Needless to say, there are significant ethical difficulties in conditioning fear in children, and studies such as Watson and Rayner's are unlikely today.)

The landmark study by Mary Cover Jones (1924) described the treatment of Peter, a boy nearing 3 years of age, who exhibited fear of furry objects. Jones first attempted to treat Peter by placing him with a rabbit, along with children who liked the rabbit and petted it. The treatment appeared to be working but was interrupted when Peter became ill for nearly 2 months. Just prior to his return to treatment, he was also frightened by a large dog. With Peter's fear back at its original level, Jones decided to treat Peter with a counterconditioning procedure, which involved allowing Peter to eat some of his favorite foods while the animal was moved progressively closer. In this way, the feared stimulus was associated with pleasantness. The procedure was apparently successful in reducing the boy's fears, and he was ultimately able to hold the animal by himself. Although this study has methodological weaknesses, it stimulated the development of treatments for behavioral disturbance based on the principles of classical conditioning.

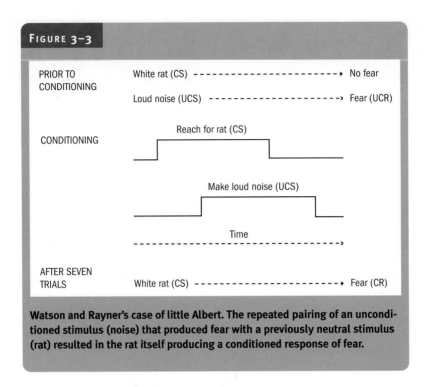

FIGURE 3-3

PRIOR TO CONDITIONING	White rat (CS) --------------------→	No fear
	Loud noise (UCS) ------------------→	Fear (UCR)

CONDITIONING

Reach for rat (CS)

Make loud noise (UCS)

Time

AFTER SEVEN TRIALS	White rat (CS) ----------------------→	Fear (CR)

Watson and Rayner's case of little Albert. The repeated pairing of an unconditioned stimulus (noise) that produced fear with a previously neutral stimulus (rat) resulted in the rat itself producing a conditioned response of fear.

aspects of this kind of learning have been described. For example, once a new response (the conditioned response) is acquired, it can generalize to similar situations and can have far-reaching effects on emotion and behavior.

Historically, two early studies based on classical conditioning had a notable impact on the application of learning to problem behavior. (See Accent: "Albert and Peter: Two Historic Cases.") The now-famous case of little Albert was an early illustration of the conditioning of fear, the process of which is illustrated in Figure 3–3. The case of Peter demonstrated that fearful responses could be eliminated by the application of classical conditioning principles.

OPERANT LEARNING

A second basic type of learning is operant learning, which was set forth in Thorndike's Law of Effect and in the work of B. F. Skinner. Operant, or instrumental, conditioning emphasizes the consequences of behavior. Behavior is acquired, strengthened or weakened, maintained or eliminated, emitted in some circumstances but not in others through reinforcement, punishment, and other learning processes (Table 3–2). Operant learning is ubiquitous; through it, knowledge is acquired and adaptive and maladaptive behaviors are shaped.

The principles of operant conditioning have been applied to a broad range of behavioral problems with regard to their etiology, maintenance, and especially treatment. The specific applications of these procedures, discussed in succeeding chapters of this book, all share the assumption that problem behavior can be changed through a learning process and that the focus of treatment should be on the consequences of behavior.

OBSERVATIONAL LEARNING

Observational learning is another fundamental way through which individuals change as a result of their experiences. A wide variety of behaviors can be acquired by observing others perform them—from jumping rope, to cooperation, to aggression, to social skills. As with other learning, observational learning can lead to both the acquisition and the removal of problem behaviors.

Early, now-classic studies by Bandura and his colleagues, as well as subsequent research, demonstrated how a problem behavior may be acquired through the observation of a model. Although observational learning may seem simple, it is actually quite complex. Children can learn new responses by watching a model; however, they are more likely to display the responses if the model had been reinforced for the behavior and are less likely to display them if the

TABLE 3–2	SOME FUNDAMENTAL OPERANT CONDITIONING PROCESSES	
TERM	**DEFINITION**	**EXAMPLE**
Positive reinforcement	A stimulus is presented following a response (*contingent* upon the response), increasing the frequency of that response.	Praise for good behavior increases the likelihood of good behavior.
Negative reinforcement	A stimulus is withdrawn contingent upon a response, and its removal increases the frequency of that response.	Removal of mother's demands following a child's tantrum increases the likelihood of tantrums.
Extinction	A weakening of a learned response is produced when the reinforcement that followed it no longer occurs.	Parents ignore bad behavior, and it decreases.
Punishment	A response is followed by either an unpleasant stimulus or the removal of a pleasant stimulus, thereby decreasing the frequency of the response.	A parent scolds a child for hitting, and the child stops hitting; food is removed from the table after a child spits, and the spitting stops.
Generalization	A response is made to a new stimulus that is different from, but similar to, the stimulus present during learning.	A child is fearful of all men with mustaches like that of a stern uncle.
Discrimination	This is the process by which a stimulus comes to signal that a certain response is likely to be followed by a particular consequence.	An adult's smile indicates that a child's request is likely to be granted.
Shaping	A desired behavior that is not in the child's repertoire is taught by rewarding responses that are increasingly similar to (*successive approximations* of) the desired response.	A mute child is taught to talk by initially reinforcing any sound, then something that sounds a little like the word, and so on.

model had been punished. As with other kinds of basic learning processes, observational learning can generalize. A child who observes another child's being scolded for shouting may become quiet in other ways (inhibition). The observation of shooting and fighting on television may lead a child to exhibit other forms of aggression, such as verbal abuse and physical roughness (disinhibition). In neither case is the exact behavior of the model imitated; rather, a class of behaviors becomes either less likely or more likely to occur because of observation of the model.

Whether imitation is specific or generalized, complex cognitive processes are required for observational learning to occur (Bandura, 1977). Such learning relies on the child's attending to the salient features of the model's behavior. The child must organize and encode this information and then remember it. The acquired behavior must then be performed when it is anticipated that it will meet with desired consequences. Thus, observational learning and the social learning perspective developed from it and other research places emphasis on cognitive processes.

COGNITIVE PROCESSES

Various approaches to cognition focus on how individuals mentally process information and think about the world. Briefly put, individuals perceive their experiences, construct concepts or schemas that represent experience, store concepts in memory, and employ their understandings to think about and act in the world. Among the many higher order mental operations involved are perception, attention, memory, and mental manipulation of information. Impairments in cognitive processes, or deficits in accumulated knowledge, play a central role in developmental disturbances such as learning disabilities, mental retardation, and attention disorders. Cognitive processes are involved, too, in the self-regulation of behavior and emotion that is implicated in numerous disturbances.

Beliefs held by young people also play a role in psychopathology. We saw in Chapter 2 that children's aggression is associated with faulty attributions regarding the causes of events. Beliefs are linked to other behaviors as well, including achievement behavior (e.g., Eccles & Wigfield, 2002). Bandura's

TABLE 3–3	COGNITIVE TERMS AND CONCEPTS

Cognitive structures. Sometimes also referred to as schema, these are the internal organization and the manner in which information is represented in memory. Anxious children and adolescents, for example, may have a dominant schema of threat and may be prone to see impending danger, loss, criticism, and the like.

Cognitive content. This refers to the specific self-talk and information that is stored in memory.

Cognitive process. This refers to how experiences are perceived and interpreted. A child's expectancy that aggressive behavior will result in getting what he or she wants is an example of a cognitive process that may characterize youngsters with conduct disorders.

Cognitive products. These are the results of structure, content, and process. Attribution and the way that the child explains the causes of behavior are examples of cognitive products. The tendency of depressed youngsters to view negative events as due to some stable characteristic of themselves (e.g., to their being stupid) is an instance.

(1997) self-efficacy model is an important model that proposes how beliefs about one's abilities and competence to carry out a task are related to developmental outcome. Such beliefs help determine the goals a person will set as well as the willingness to work and persist in attaining goals (e.g., Bandura et al., 2001).

Cognitive-Behavioral Perspective. One particular cognitive perspective—the cognitive-behavioral perspective—has contributed substantially to both the understanding and the treatment of child and adolescent problems. It incorporates behavior, cognition, affect, and social factors in understanding behavioral problems and their treatment (Kendall et al., 1997b). Behaviors are assumed to be learned and maintained by interacting systems of cognitions and external events. Cognitive factors influence whether environmental events are attended to, how events are perceived, and whether these events affect future behavior. The cognitive part of this interaction is based on the hypothesis that maladaptive cognitions are related to maladaptive behavior. As an example of support for this assumption, maladaptive thoughts and beliefs have been found among phobic and anxious children. For instance, in test situations, youngsters with test anxiety frequently report more off-task thoughts, more negative self-evaluations, and fewer positive self-evaluations (Ollendick & King, 1998). A treatment strategy for such cases is aimed at modification of the maladaptive thoughts.

One suggestion as to how the various and complex cognitive functions hypothesized to contribute to the development, maintenance, and treatment of behavioral disorders can be organized is offered by Kendall (1991; Kendall et al., 1997b). The four cognitive components—structures, content, process, products—are described in Table 3–3.

Kendall also suggests that a further way to distinguish cognitive functioning is to differentiate between cognitive deficiencies and cognitive distortions. Cognitive deficiencies refer to an absence of thinking. The lack of forethought and planning exhibited by an impulsive child is an example of a cognitive deficiency that might be targeted for intervention. Cognitive distortions are inaccurate thought processes that are dysfunctional. Depressed children's viewing themselves as less capable than their peers even though others do not hold this view is an example of cognitive distortion.

Various illustrations of the ways in which cognitive influences contribute to the development and treatment of disturbances of youth are presented throughout this book.

Sociocultural Context: An Overview

Development, whether adaptive or maladaptive, occurs within and is influenced by an elaborate sociocultural context. Although there are various ways to conceptualize this context, ecological models have grown in importance during the last decades. Ecological models typically perceive youngsters as embedded within, and interacting with, numerous

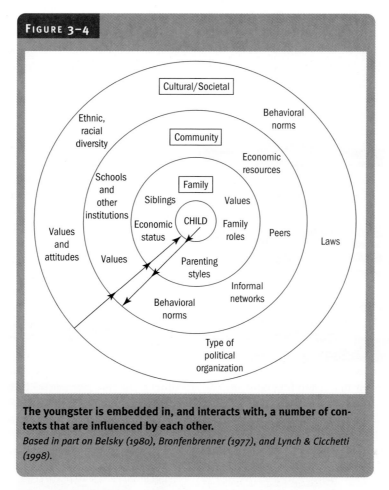

FIGURE 3–4

The youngster is embedded in, and interacts with, a number of contexts that are influenced by each other.
Based in part on Belsky (1980), Bronfenbrenner (1977), and Lynch & Cicchetti (1998).

domains of overlapping, transactional environmental influences or systems. (Ecology refers to the interrelationship of organisms and their environment.)

Figure 3–4 presents one way in which ongoing sociocultural influences can be represented. The child is surrounded by three contexts—family, community, cultural/societal—each of which consists of structures, institutions, values, rules, and other aspects that influence development. The arrows in the figure emphasize the potential interactions among the systems. Thus, for example, the youngster both is influenced by and influences peers, who may influence and be influenced by the child's parents and the school. In general, we would expect proximal contexts—the inner circles—to have relatively more direct impact on the youngster. It would also be anticipated that the importance of any one domain would vary with the developmental level of the individual, an obvious example being family influences from infancy into adolescence. This model will serve as a backdrop for discussion of select aspects of sociocultural influences on and risks to development.

Family Context, Maltreatment, and Divorce

In all societies, the family has been considered a major, if not the major, influence on the development of youth (Maccoby, 1992; Steil, 2001). Family influence is dominant during childhood at a time when developmental malleability is high, and it may endure over the entire life span. The family has daily, direct interaction with children, and it plays an important role in mediating and moderating more distal contexts. It is therefore not surprising that family interactions, structure and roles, economic status, and attitudes and values constitute a crucial context within which normal and disordered behavior develop. Poor parenting practices, parental psychopathology, and marital conflict are linked to mental health problems in childhood.

Research shows that the family is most appropriately viewed as a complex, interacting system. For example, the child's relationship with a parent may be affected by the well-being of the other parent or by the relationship between the parents (e.g., Dunn et al., 1998). Moreover, not only do parents affect children and each other, but youngsters also influence parents in subtle and not-so-subtle ways. This is not to say that the parent-child relationship is symmetrical; parents select the settings in which children develop, control access to material goods, exert physical control, and have greater power and knowledge than their children (Maccoby, 1992). Thus parents have many opportunities to influence their offspring.

PARENT-CHILD RELATIONSHIPS

Parenting Styles. The quality of the relationship between parents and their offspring, beginning with early attachment, is believed to be crucial to development and adjustment. One area of influence concerns the characteristic ways in which parents deal with and manage their offspring (Maccoby, 1992; Wood et al., 2003). Such parenting styles can be viewed as sets of attitudes, goals, and patterns of parenting practices that affect outcomes for children and adolescents. Analyses of parenting styles provide a general guideline for understanding families.

Two major dimensions have been found central to parenting styles. One dimension is degree of control, or demand; the second is degree of acceptance, or warmth. Figure 3–5 presents the four parenting styles according to these dimensions. Particular child characteristics are thought to be more or less associated with each style. It is generally agreed that the authoritative style is related to the most favorable child attributes. Authoritative parents assume control; set rules and expect their children to abide by the rules; follow through with consequences; and are simultaneously warm, accepting, and considerate of the needs of their children. The youngsters, in turn, tend to be independent, socially responsible, prosocial, and self-confident. In contrast, children of authoritarian, indulgent/permissive, and neglectful parents are thought to variously display less than optimal behaviors including aggression, withdrawal, dependence, low self-esteem, irresponsibility; antisocial behaviors; anxiety; and school problems (e.g., Steinberg et al., 1994; Wood et al., 2003).

In examining the general findings about parenting styles, it is worthwhile to consider three issues. *First*, effective parenting involves consideration of each child's needs and developmental level. What would be "controlling" for one child at one developmental level would not necessarily be controlling for others. *Second*, parenting style may in part be a response to the child's characteristics as well as other relationships and circumstances in the family. *Third*, we must consider the extent to which the analysis of parenting styles holds across cultures and situations.

FIGURE 3–5

	CONTROL	
	High	**Low**
ACCEPTANCE — High	**Authoritative** Set and enforce standards Considerate of children's needs Encourage independence, individuality	**Indulgent/Permissive** Make few demands for mature behavior Allow children to regulate themselves Tolerate children's impulses
ACCEPTANCE — Low	**Authoritarian** Strictly set rules which cannot be challenged Use fairly severe punishment	**Neglectful** Uninvolved Give little time, attention, emotional commitment to children

Patterns of parental behavior.
Based in part on Maccoby & Martin, 1983.

It has been suggested, for example, that authoritative parenting may be less appropriate when cultural values differ from those of mainstream culture in the United States, and that even in the Unites States authoritarian parenting may protect children who are reared in disadvantaged environments.

Parental Roles. Historically, the influence of mothers has received much more attention by theorists and researchers. Mothers have been considered primary to custodial care, child supervision, and child development—and have been more implicated in, and sometimes blamed for, the behavioral disturbances of their offspring. Nevertheless, recent decades have witnessed increased analysis and research directed toward fathers. Whereas the traditional contribution that fathers make as primary breadwinners continues to be recognized, greater emphasis is given to fathers as providers of care and psychological support (Cabrera et al., 2000; Coley, 2001). Fathers are likely to provide somewhat different input into child development. They are more likely to encourage independence and competition, and good fathering may be especially important to the development of healthy sexual identity in daughters (Cabrera et al., 2000; Leinonen, Solantaus, & Punamäki, 2003). Some of the influences fathers have on their families appear to work indirectly through interaction with the mother.

MALTREATMENT

Maltreatment of youth can be thought of as an extreme failure to provide adequate parenting. It can also be viewed as a failure of the larger social system to provide conditions that foster adequate parenting. Such undue failure to protect the child and/or provide positive aspects of parenting might be expected to adversely affect a wide variety of developmental processes and increase the risk for a variety of problematic outcomes.

Although child maltreatment has probably existed since the beginning of civilization, recent concern is usually dated to the early 1960s (Cicchetti & Olsen, 1990). Especially influential was an article by pediatrician C. Henry Kempe and his colleagues, in which the term *battered child syndrome* was coined (Kempe et al., 1962). Their efforts were stimulated by alarm at the large number of children at pediatric clinics with nonaccidental injuries. By 1970, all 50 states had mandated the reporting of child abuse. In 1974 the U.S. Congress passed the Child Abuse Prevention and Treatment Act (Public Law 93–247) to give national focus to the problem and to prescribe actions that the states should take. Since the late 1970s, the problem has become both a major public concern and the focus of increased research and professional attention (Cicchetti & Manly, 2001).

Unfortunately, the magnitude of the problem is appreciable. According to a report issued by the U.S. Department of Health and Human Services (2003), in 2001 there were approximately 12 to 13 victims per 1,000 children. In addition, about 25 percent of victims experience more than one type of maltreatment.

Defining Maltreatment. There is agreement that child abuse and neglect are serious and prevalent problems. What is not as clear is an agreed-on definition of what constitutes maltreatment. As described by Cicchetti and Manly (2001), several reasons exist for the difficulty in reaching definitional consensus. Maltreatment is a legal matter defined by social agencies rather than by researchers or mental health professionals. Then, too, there are no clear standards for differentiating between acceptable parental disciplinary practices and maltreatment. Standards as to what is "acceptable" practice versus "maltreatment" are likely to vary across time and culture. Further, there is disagreement as to whether maltreatment should be defined in terms of the actions of the perpetrator, the effects on the child, or a combination of the two. The question of whether parental intent should be considered is a further complication. If a child is harmed but the parent did not intend to inflict harm, is the result maltreatment? In the final analysis, agreement on a single definition that will serve all purposes may not be possible. A definition that meets the needs of a research agenda may be inappropriate in a courtroom setting, and a definition that stresses overt physical symptoms may meet medical needs but minimize psychological consequences.

When most people hear the widely used term child abuse, they assume that it refers to physical assault and serious injury. However, the general legal definition of child abuse or maltreatment that has evolved over several decades includes both the commission of injuries and acts of omission, that is, failure to care for and protect (National Institute of Mental Health, 1977). Thus, neglect needs to be addressed along with physical assault.

Four types of maltreatment are typically described in the literature: physical abuse, sexual abuse, neglect, and emotional abuse. The definitions

TABLE 3–4	DEFINITIONS OF THE MAJOR FORMS OF MALTREATMENT

1. **Physical abuse:** An act of commission by a caregiver that results or is likely to result in physical harm, including death of a child. Examples include kicking, biting, shaking, stabbing, or punching a child. Spanking is usually considered a disciplinary action but can be classified as abusive if the child is bruised or injured.
2. **Sexual abuse:** An act of commission, including intrusion or penetration, molestation with genital contact, or other forms of sexual acts in which children are used to provide sexual gratification for the perpetrator. This type of abuse also includes acts such as sexual exploitation and child pornography.
3. **Neglect:** An act of omission by a parent or caregiver that involves refusal or delay in providing health care; failure to provide basic needs such as food, clothing shelter, affection, and attention; inadequate supervision; or abandonment. This failure to act holds true for both physical and emotional neglect.
4. **Emotional abuse:** An act of commission or omission that includes rejecting, isolating, terrorizing, ignoring, or corrupting a child. Examples of emotional abuse are confinement; verbal abuse; withholding sleep, food, or shelter; exposing a child to domestic violence; allowing a child to engage in substance abuse or criminal activity; refusing to provide psychological care; and other inattention that results in harm or potential harm to a child. The abuse must be sustained and repetitive.

From English, 1998.

of the four major types of maltreatment are presented in Table 3–4 and Figure 3–6 shows the rate of each type in the United States in 2001 (U.S. Bureau of the Census, 2003). Approximately 57 percent of cases involved neglect, and 19 percent involved physical abuse.

Because the results of physical abuse may be more visible, it is probably easier to detect than other

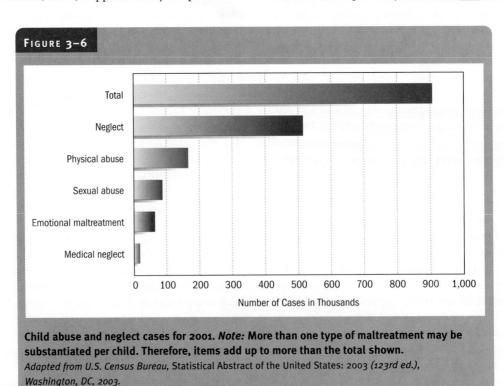

FIGURE 3–6

Number of Cases in Thousands

Child abuse and neglect cases for 2001. *Note:* More than one type of maltreatment may be substantiated per child. Therefore, items add up to more than the total shown.
Adapted from U.S. Census Bureau, Statistical Abstract of the United States: 2003 *(123rd ed.), Washington, DC, 2003.*

forms of maltreatment. However, the nature and severity of the injuries a child may suffer can vary considerably. In some cases, injuries may be intentionally inflicted, but it is more usual that they occur as the result of extreme forms of discipline and physical punishment. Moreover, whereas we can define physical abuse as a separate category from other forms of maltreatment, children likely experience it in conjunction with emotional abuse and/or neglect.

In general, sexual abuse refers to sexual experiences that occur between youth and older persons or to the sexual exploitation of the young, such as in pornographic film. Statistics suggest that sexual abuse occurs in about 10 percent of substantiated child maltreatment (U.S. Bureau of the Census, 2003). Sexual abuse of girls is more common than that of boys, and sexual abuse can vary with factors such as age of onset of abuse, the identity of the primary perpetrator (e.g., father, father figure, other relative), the number of perpetrators, the severity of the abuse, and whether the abuse was accompanied by physical violence or threats (Finkelhor, 1994; Trickett, McBride-Chang, & Putnam, 1994; Trickett et al., 2001).

Neglect, the most common form of maltreatment, refers to failure to provide for a child's basic needs. Defining a parent-child relationship as neglectful, especially in less extreme instances, clearly requires sensitivity to family and cultural values and to considerations of economic and social conditions. Neglect can involve a failure to meet physical needs—such as the need for health care or physical shelter—or can involve abandonment or inadequate supervision. Neglect may also take the form of not meeting the youngster's educational needs by allowing repeated truancy or not attending to special education needs. The child's emotional needs may also be neglected. Emotional neglect is difficult to define, however. It may include failure to insure adequate psychological care or failure to protect the youngster from witnessing harmful circumstances such as violence or substance use.

The definition of emotional (or psychological) maltreatment is probably the most difficult to agree on and the most controversial. Societal and community standards always come into play in judging "abusive" behaviors and "harmful" outcomes. Different standards for both appropriate parenting practices and valued outcomes are particularly at issue when psychological maltreatment is considered (Azar, Ferraro, & Breton, 1998; McGee & Wolfe, 1991). Emotional maltreatment is defined as persistent and extreme actions or neglect that thwart the child's basic emotional needs and that are damaging to the behavioral, cognitive, affective, or physical functioning of the child (Brassard, Hart, & Hardy, 2000; Cicchetti & Lynch, 1995). Emotional maltreatment can be seen as part of all abuse and neglect (Binggeli, Hart, & Brassard, 2001; Hart & Brassard, 1991).

Factors Contributing to Maltreatment. Conceptualizations of maltreatment recognize the complex, multiple, and interrelated determinants of the problem (Azar et al., 1998; Belsky, 1993; Cicchetti, Toth, & Maughan, 2000; Okun, Parker, & Levendosky, 1994). The following general factors are recognized as contributing to maltreatment:

- Characteristics of the abuser
- Characteristics of the child
- Parenting practices
- Parent-child interactional processes
- Social-cultural influences

The latter category includes both the immediate social environment (e.g., family employment, extended family, social networks) and the larger societal-cultural context (e.g., poverty, societal tolerance for violence).

It is impossible to even enumerate all of the specific influences that have been examined as contributing to maltreatment. Researchers continue to study not only the factors that might lead to different forms of maltreatment, but also the multiple pathways to any specific type of maltreatment. Here we highlight only some of the findings.

For the most part, parents or parent surrogates are the perpetrators of abuse. Parents who began their families at a younger age, many in their teens, are often the perpetrators (Connelly & Straus, 1992). This finding may be understood, at least in part, within the context of parenting skills. The most pervasive disturbance seen in maltreating parents concerns a variety of deficits in parenting skills (Azar & Bober, 1999). Maltreating parents tend to engage in fewer positive interactions with their child and less interaction overall; to use more coercive and negative discipline techniques; and to use fewer explanations when disciplining their child. These parents also exhibit negative attitudes toward parenting, limited child-rearing knowledge, inappropriate expectations regarding developmentally suitable behavior, lower tolerance for common demanding behavior such as infant crying, and misattributions of the child's motivation for misbehaving.

Several other characteristics of abusive parents have been noted, including difficulties in managing stress, difficulty in inhibiting impulsive behavior, social isolation from family and friends, more emotional symptoms and mood changes, and more physical health problems. High rates of substance abuse have also been reported. These factors are part of the complex influences that contribute to the development of abusive and neglectful interactions, and are also part of the youngster's more general developmental experience.

Intergenerational transmission of maltreatment has been posited. In a review of the literature, Kaufman and Zigler (1987) found that abuse is more common in the backgrounds of abusing parents. However, they also found that many parents who *had not* been abused became abusive and that some who *had* been abused did not become abusive. They estimate that on the basis of all forms of maltreatment, between 25 and 30 percent of maltreated children repeat the cycle as adults. It is generally agreed that the majority of maltreated children do not perpetuate the intergenerational cycle. What, then, is the link between generations? One suggested possibility is that a set of parenting responses, skill deficits, and "scripts" for parenting and interpersonal relations is transmitted across generations. This places the next generation at risk for disturbances in parenting, and individuals who are exposed to additional risk factors are placed in danger of becoming abusive parents themselves (Azar & Bober, 1999).

One might also ask, "Are there characteristics of the youngster that may increase the likelihood of being the target of maltreatment?" Professionals asking this question are not blaming the victim, but rather are seeking to identify children who might be at heightened risk. Research suggests that children and adolescents at highest risk are those who display behavioral and physical problems or interpersonal styles that adversely interact with parental characteristics and family stress (Bonner et al., 1992). For example, a child's early feeding problems and irritability may place increased strain on a highly stressed parent with limited parenting abilities. This may lead the caregiver to withdraw and become neglectful. Caregiver neglect may, in turn, lead to increases in dependent behavior and demands by the child (Wekerle & Wolfe, 2003).

Maltreatment also is influenced by the larger social context. A relationship between socioeconomic disadvantage and abuse and neglect has been described (English, 1998). Neglect, in particular, may be related to socioeconomic disadvantage. It is important to recognize, however, that the majority of families who experience disadvantage do not maltreat their offspring. Although it is hard to isolate the specific causal factors, reduced resources, stress, and other problems associated with socioeconomic disadvantage put the family and child at increased risk. Poverty and maltreatment may also be related due to other factors (Azar & Bober, 1999). For example, poor interpersonal and problem-solving skills in parents may lead to both economic disadvantage and problematic parenting, including maltreatment. Cultural factors, too, may play a role. Korbin and colleagues (1998), for example, found that impoverishment had a lesser impact on maltreatment in African American neighborhoods than in European American neighborhoods. This differential effect of poverty seems to have been mediated by the perceived quality of social connectedness found in the two kinds of neighborhoods. A sense of community, resources, and extended family may serve as protective factors against maltreatment.

Consequences of Maltreatment. Basic developmental processes are disrupted by maltreatment. The social and emotional support necessary for children's successful adaptations is diminished, and the formation of secure attachments is disrupted—interfering with many areas of development (Salzinger et al., 2001; Shields, Cicchetti, & Ryan, 1994). Maltreating families may also provide fewer opportunities for positive experience and growth, further compounding other failures (Cicchetti & Lynch, 1995).

Some evidence suggests that early maltreatment may be associated with neurobiological outcomes, such as dysregulation of the stress regulating system (the hypothalamic-pituitary-adrenal axis), alteration of neurotransmitter systems, and alteration of structural and functional regions of the brain (Cicchetti & Rogosch, 2001; Kaufman & Charney, 2001; Margolin & Gordis, 2000). The degree to which these neurobiological outcomes occur seems to be related to a number of factors (De Bellis, 2001) including:

- Age of onset of abuse
- Duration of abuse
- Presence of trauma-related psychological symptoms

There may also be gender-related differences in adverse brain development outcomes, with both boys and girls affected but males being more vulnerable.

The effects of maltreatment is a telling example of how adverse environments may alter basic

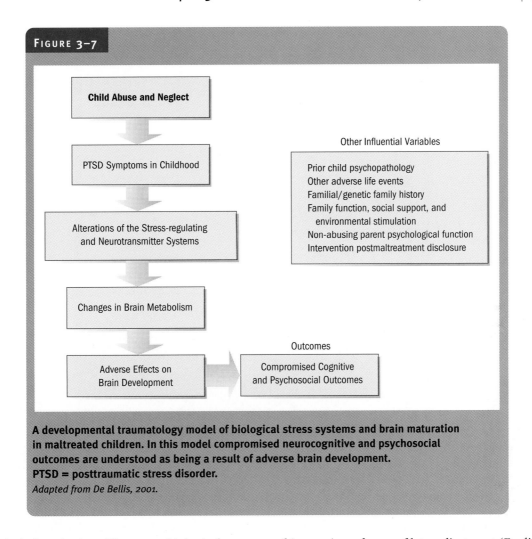

FIGURE 3-7

A developmental traumatology model of biological stress systems and brain maturation in maltreated children. In this model compromised neurocognitive and psychosocial outcomes are understood as being a result of adverse brain development.
PTSD = posttraumatic stress disorder.
Adapted from De Bellis, 2001.

biological functioning. The neurobiological outcomes may, in turn, contribute to cognitive and psychosocial difficulties observed in maltreated youngsters. De Bellis (2001) has proposed a developmental traumatology model that describes how neurobiological outcomes may underlie the variety of negative outcomes associated with abuse and neglect. In this model, maltreatment and its effects are viewed within a broad ecological-transactional model that recognizes the effects of many other variables (Figure 3–7). It is recognized that the neurobiological changes resulting from the stress of maltreatment may be positively modified by subsequent supportive caregiving environments.

Given the neurobiological outcomes and the failure of parenting that maltreatment represents, it is unsurprising that maltreatment can result in a variety of undesirable outcomes. Youngsters can experience health-related difficulties (e.g., physical injury, sexually transmitted diseases) and can manifest appreciable impairments in all early developmental domains

and in a variety of areas of later adjustment (English, 1998; Shields, Cicchetti, & Ryan, 1994; Wolfe & Birt, 1995; Yates, 2004). Problems may be serious enough to meet the diagnostic criteria for a variety of psychological disorders. The impact may also be evident at different developmental stages from infancy through adolescence and into adulthood (Kaufman & Henrich, 2000; Macfie, Cicchetti, & Toth, 2001; Stouthamer-Loeber et al., 2001; Thornberry, Ireland, & Smith, 2001). Although this is certainly a disheartening picture, it should be acknowledged that some maltreated children develop as competent individuals and that youngsters can be resilient even in the face of maltreatment (McGloin & Widom, 2001).

In general, then, the impact of maltreatment is best viewed as undermining a variety of normal developmental processes affecting areas such as cognitive functioning, self-concept, social relationships, and emotional regulation (Azar & Bober, 1999; Cicchetti & Lynch, 1995; Werkele & Wolfe, 2003). Particular outcomes may be affected by factors such

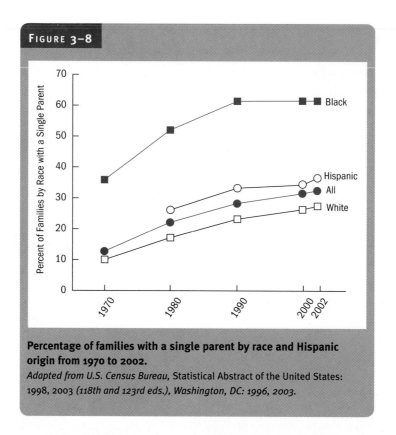

FIGURE 3–8

Percentage of families with a single parent by race and Hispanic origin from 1970 to 2002.
Adapted from U.S. Census Bureau, Statistical Abstract of the United States: 1998, 2003 *(118th and 123rd eds.), Washington, DC: 1996, 2003.*

as type and severity of maltreatment, developmental timing, and gender (Keiley et al., 2001; Manly et al., 2001; Wolfe et al., 2001). For example, research suggests that physical abuse places youngsters at particular risk for the development of externalizing and antisocial behavior problems (Jaffee et al., 2004; Lau & Weisz, 2003). Given the combination of factors that causes maltreatment, effective prevention and intervention need to address many contexts—individual, familial, community, societal—and thus include multiple components (Putnam, 2003; Scott & Crooks, 2004; Trickett et al., 1998). As we gain more precise understanding of the different types of maltreatment, we will be better able to shape interventions to fit specific needs.

CHANGES IN FAMILY STRUCTURE: DIVORCE

In research about the family, it has often been assumed that families consist of parents and children together in the home. In fact, families have always been more varied. Even so, by most standards, dramatic changes have occurred in family structure during the last decades in the United States and similar countries (Steil, 2001). Many children are living in stepfamilies of some sort. Currently over one million

children live in adopted homes, and international adoptions have become more common (Miller et al., 2000). The number of youth living in single-parent families has increased markedly during the last several decades across several ethnic/racial groups (Figure 3–8). Single-parent families make up 32 percent of all families with children, about one-fifth of these being headed by fathers (U.S. Bureau of the Census, 2003). Most youth living in nontraditional homes do well, but as a group they are at risk for emotional and behavioral difficulties.

That many marriages end in divorce is well documented. The divorce rate in the United States more than doubled between 1970 and 1981 (Guidubaldi & Perry, 1985). Although this trend has leveled off and perhaps declined in recent years, large numbers of children experience their parents' divorce (Hernandez, 1994; Sutton, 2003). Over one million youngsters a year may experience parental divorce. However compelling, this statistic does not fully capture the problem. Many children experience considerable stress prior to the divorce. Some go through periodic separation and discord in families in which divorce petitions are filed and withdrawn. Others experience more than one divorce. Divorce and subsequent reconstitution of the family are not static events but rather are a series of family transitions that modify the lives of children (Hetherington & Stanley-Hagan, 1999; Wallerstein, 1991).

Heightened Risk. Children and adolescents from divorced and remarried families are at increased risk for developing adjustment problems (Reifman et al., 2001). Those who have undergone multiple divorces are at greater risk (Grych & Fincham, 1999; Hetherington, Bridges, & Insabella, 1998). Difficulties occur in many areas of functioning. Children experience academic difficulties, behavioral problems such as noncompliance and anxiety, lower self-esteem, lower social competence, and social relationship difficulties. Adolescents exhibit some of these same problems and, in addition, are more likely to drop out of school, be unemployed, be sexually active at an earlier age, have children out of wedlock, be involved in delinquent activities and substance abuse, and associate with antisocial peers (Amato & Keith, 1991; Hetherington et al., 1998).

Although divorce can have a strong impact on the development of some young people, the adjustment differences between youngsters from divorced or remarried families and those from nondivorced families are not always large in magnitude. Moreover, the vast majority of children from divorced or remarried families function in the normal range and some experience positive outcomes. Through divorce, some youngsters move from highly conflicted and violent situations. A portion of youngsters, particularly girls who move into less stressful and more supportive circumstances, may actually experience opportunities for the development of exceptional competencies (Amato & Keith, 1991; Hetherington & Stanley-Hagan, 1999; Hetherington & Kelly, 2002). However, these findings should not lead us to ignore the clinical significance of the adjustment problems experienced by some of the youngsters (Grych & Fincham, 1999). An important question then is: What accounts for increased risk for those youngsters who do develop adjustment difficulties and for the resilience of those who do not?

Predictors of Adjustment. When considering the influence of family divorce, it is important to note that any deviation from traditional family structure has often been viewed as problematic. This perspective is, in general, not well supported. Of course, two parental figures in a good partnership generally have much to offer the child. However, the effects of family composition/parent absence are not simple and are likely modified by factors such as parent adjustment, quality of family relationships, the child's gender, and the availability of both parents to the child

(Braver, Ellman, & Fabricius, 2003; Hetherington et al., 1998; Jaffee et al., 2003). Furthermore, there are cultural and ethnic differences in how family is defined. The presence of extended family in the household, for example, is more likely among African American families than among European American families, as is an informal network of kin and friends available in a parent role (Emery & Kitzmann, 1995).

Hetherington and her colleagues (1998) suggest a model, based on a set of interrelated risks, to explain the links between divorce/remarriage and a youngster's adjustment. As Figure 3–9 shows, adjustment to marital transitions encompasses complex interactions among a large number of influences. To add to the complexity, while the process of family transitions is occurring, youngsters and the developmental tasks they face are also changing (O'Connor, 2003). In addition, ethnic and cultural influences are salient in this process, although much of what we know is based on the experiences of European American families (Hetherington & Stanley-Hagan, 1999). With such complexities in mind, we turn to an examination of some of the influences likely to affect the adjustment of children and adolescents to marital transitions.

A central aspect of the divorce process is the interaction among family members, particularly the ongoing relationship between the two parents. Indeed, the degree of marital discord prior to the divorce is considered to be a primary influence on the adjustment of children in the family. High levels of marital conflict, particularly those that involve marital violence, are problematic (Jaffee, Poisson, & Cunningham, 2001; Kelly, 2000; Margolin, 1998). Following divorce, the ongoing relationship between the parents, between each parent and the child, and between each parent and potential stepparents or significant others contribute to complicated family transitions that affect the child (Hetherington et al., 1998).

Preexisting individual characteristics is another set of influences that contribute to a youngster's adjustment. Individual attributes of adults (e.g., antisocial behavior, depression) place some parents at risk for marital discord and multiple marital transitions—thereby increasing the risk that their children will have to deal with multiple marital transitions. Individual characteristics of the youngster may also contribute to adjustment. Children with an easy temperament may be better able to cope with the disruptions associated with marital transitions. Youngsters with a difficult temperament may be more likely to elicit negative responses from their

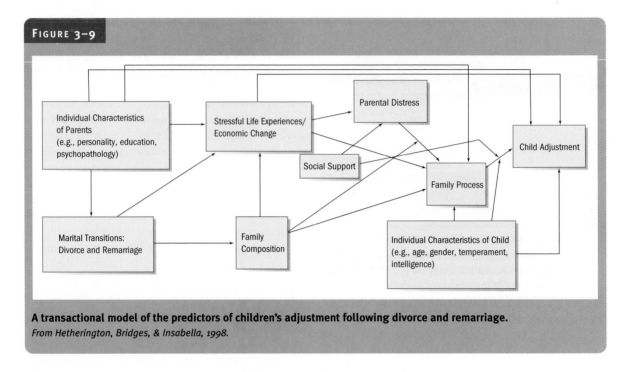

Figure 3–9

A transactional model of the predictors of children's adjustment following divorce and remarriage.
From Hetherington, Bridges, & Insabella, 1998.

stressed parents and to have greater difficulty adapting to parental negativity and marital transitions. They may be less capable of eliciting the support of other people around them (Hetherington et al., 1998). Also, a youngster's prior level of behavioral problems is likely to contribute to his or her adjustment to divorce or remarriage. Indeed, when prior level of adjustment is taken into account, differences between children due to marital transitions are greatly reduced.

The relationship between parental characteristics, child characteristics, and the ongoing divorce process is, however, complex. For example, the youngster's prior level of adjustment may have resulted in part from the marital friction that contributed to the divorce. In turn, the challenges of parenting a difficult child may have contributed to the marital difficulty and divorce. Furthermore, the parental characteristics that played a role in the divorce, as well as child behavior problems, may be influenced by common genetic contributions (Jockin, McGue, & Lykken, 1996; McGue & Lykken, 1992). Shared genes may contribute, for example, to the likelihood of parent antisocial behavior (a risk for divorce) and acting-out problems in children and adolescents.

Gender also may affect adjustment to marital transitions. Earlier reports suggested that boys were more affected by divorce and girls by remarriage. More recent studies, however, report less pronounced and less consistent gender differences. Improvements in research methodology may in part be responsible for this finding. So also may changes in custody and visitation arrangements that have possibly increased father involvement. It is likely that the impact of gender will be complex, depending on the aspect of adjustment studied, gender-related differences in patterns of development, timing of marital transitions, and other such factors (Emery & Kitzmann, 1995; Hetherington & Stanley-Hagan, 1999). Clearly, the role that individual characteristics play in adjustment to divorce is complex.

Another factor that may be involved in children's adjustment to divorce is ethnic differences. For example, black adolescents may benefit more from living in stepfamilies than white adolescents. McLanahan and Sandefur (1994) suggest that the improved income, supervision, and role models provided by some stepfathers may be more advantageous to black children because they are more likely to live in neighborhoods with fewer resources and social controls.

Finally, the divorce process may include changes in family circumstances that, although peripheral to the reasons for the marital dissolution, affect how well the family does (Amato, 2000). For example, custodial mothers and their children often experience economic decline after divorce, with many living below the poverty level. This lower standard of living and economic instability are associated with conditions that increase risk for youth, such as living in more dangerous neighborhoods and attending less adequate schools. Divorce may also result in other stressful family life changes, such as more frequent moves and changes in schools. It is thought that much of the impact of these postdivorce circumstances on the youngster's adjustment is mediated by their effect on family processes (Them, Israel, Ivanova, & Chalmers, 2003). That is, economic stress and other changes can contribute to dysfunctional family relations (e.g., conflict) and interfere with effective parenting (Hetherington et al., 1998). Within this context, however, it is important to remember that positive experiences such as good parent-child communication and supportive relationships with another adult may serve as protective factors for youngsters experiencing divorce-related events (Doyle et al., 2003; Menning, 2002).

Peer Influences

One of the many reasons that family factors affect the development of behavioral problems is their influence on the development of peer relationships. Early attachment experiences in the family are thought to serve as the basis for later interpersonal competence and peer relationships (Rudolph & Asher, 2000). Indeed, insecure attachment has been found to predict less peer acceptance, less sociability, increased aggression, and other interpersonal deficits. In contrast, secure attachment has been found to be related to peer competence and favorable peer relationships (Kerns, 1996). Parenting styles and parent-child interactions have also been found to influence the development of peer relationships. For example, parental hostility, coercion, lack of involvement, and authoritarian/restrictive parenting are associated with aggression and peer rejection (Dekovic & Janssens, 1992; Dishion, 1990).

In addition to the family, other domains of sociocultural influence affect the development of peer relationships (Fergusson & Horwood, 1999). For example, teachers can play a role in shaping peers' attitudes toward each other (White & Kistner, 1992), and neighborhood characteristics can influence the likelihood of a youngster's affiliation with deviant peers (Brody et al., 2001). Individual child characteristics—emotional, cognitive, and social— also enter into the development of peer relationships (Hay, Payne, & Chadwick, 2004).

The literature on development indicates the importance of peer relationships (Deater-Deckard, 2001; Hay et al., 2004). A youngster's peer group provides a unique developmental context that influences immediate and long-term social and cognitive growth (Dunn, 1996; Hartup, 1970, 1989; Parker et al., 1995). Areas in which peer interactions may play a unique and/or essential role include the development of sociability, intimacy, empathy, and morality; elaboration of cooperation and reciprocity; negotiation of conflict and competition; control of aggression; and socialization of sexuality and gender roles. As development proceeds, the nature of peer relationships and the characteristics of the peers in a youngster's social network are likely to grow in influence.

The multifaceted nature of peer relationships has been increasingly appreciated (Bukowski & Adams, 2005). Early research primarily focused on overall status—group acceptance and popularity. More recently, additional interest has been directed at particular peer relationships, such as that between bullies and their victims. The role of friendship and the characteristics and attitudes of a youngster's friends also have received greater attention (Deater-Deckard, 2001; Hartup, 1996). It is recognized, for example, that although popularity and having a close friend may be related, the concept of friendship is different from that of peer status or popularity (Newcomb & Bagwell, 1995). Having a close friend can serve as protection in the face of various risk factors (Criss et al., 2002). However, while a close friendship can buffer the effects of being rejected or

Peer interactions provide a unique and essential opportunity to develop certain skills.
(Courtesy of A.C. Israel)

neglected by other children, alternatively it can increase the likelihood of problematic outcomes (Bierman & Welsh, 1997; LaGreca, 1993). Take, for example, the following description of the role that friendship appears to have played in an unusual and unfortunate circumstance.

Delano   A Problematic Friendship

Delano, a 14-year-old boy, and his best friend ambushed and killed his mother on her way home. In a newspaper account, the mother was said to have had "difficulties" with her son and the family's home contained guns. Delano was described as having attention deficit disorder and learning disabilities. He had a long history of difficulties and recently had gotten into trouble with a stepbrother for wrecking a car and bringing a gun into a movie theater.

Delano was described as "a lonely and unliked kid who was the frequent victim of schoolmates' taunts, jeers, and assaults. . . . He was often teased on the bus and at school because of his appearance and abilities. . . . He got teased bad. Every day he got teased. He'd get pushed around. But he couldn't really help himself. He was kind of skinny. . . . He didn't really have that many friends."

There were actually two good friends. The first was relatively well adjusted, but Delano took a gun safety course for hunting with this friend. Delano and the second youngster described themselves as the "best of friends" and spent a great deal of time together. This friend was not as well adjusted and it was this friend with whom the murder was committed. The boys admitted to planning the ambush and it seems relatively certain that the murder would not have likely occurred if these two friends had not encouraged each other to do it.

Adapted from Hartup, 1996, p. 1.

One of the most commonly cited reasons for interest in children's peer relationships is the association with later adjustment (Parker & Asher, 1987; Realmuto, August, & Hektner, 2000; Woodward & Fergusson, 2000). Children who experience peer rejection, or those who are withdrawn and socially isolated, or those who associate with deviant peers are at risk for later adjustment difficulties (Barrera, Prelow, Dumka et al., 2002; Ladd & Troop-Gordon, 2003; Laird et al., 2001; Rubin et al., 2003). Indeed, difficult peer relationships are one of the most frequently mentioned problems in referrals to mental health centers and are reported for children with a wide variety of disorders (Deater-Deckard, 2001; Rudolph & Asher, 2000). There is a bidirectional association of peer difficulties with adjustment problems. Not only do peer difficulties contribute to the development of behavioral disorders, but youngsters with disorders are more likely to experience peer difficulties (Achenbach & Rescorla, 2001).

Whereas peer difficulties are clearly associated with behavioral problems and disorders, successful peer relations and friendships, on the other hand, may help ensure the development of social competence in the face of multiple adverse factors. They may thereby serve a preventive function and reduce the likelihood of disorder (Cicchetti, Toth, & Bush, 1988; Sroufe et al., 2000).

Community and Societal Contexts

School Influences

The school is one of the most central contexts in children's lives. The primary function of the school is to teach intellectual skills and knowledge accumulated by society. Formal education also plays a role in socializing children to societal norms and values and in shaping motivation to achieve, emotional development, mental health, and social growth (e.g., Roeser & Eccles, 2000). Unsurprisingly, success in school is related to future life success.

Both peer and teacher relationships are central in this environment. Schools are the locale for important peer interactions—for supportive friendships or the experiences of rejection and bullying. Student-teacher relationships are often crucial to young people, many of whom remember in adulthood their favored or "hated" teachers. The quality of student-teacher relationships affects adaptation. For example, in a study that followed students from sixth through eighth grade, student perception of increasing teacher support appeared causally related to student increases in self-esteem and decreases in depression (Reddy, Rhodes, & Mulhall, 2003). Among children with emotional disturbance, confidence in teacher support may buffer vulnerability to peer conflict (Little & Kobak, 2003). In general, close student-teacher relationships are associated with positive child outcomes, whereas conflicted relationships are linked with unfavorable school attitudes,

"Today we're going to learn how to deal with rejection."

classroom disengagement, and poor academic performance (Birch & Ladd, 1998).

Low socioeconomic status, academic failure, behavioral problems, and lack of family support are among the factors associated with dropping out of school or repeating a grade level (Mattison, 2000). Schools certainly do not have control over all the determinants of student success, but they can have substantial influences on academic achievement, social behavior, emotional functioning, achievement motivation, and later employment (Roeser & Eccles, 2000; Sylva, 1994). Some of these influences appear to operate directly, whereas others operate indirectly by affecting students' motivation to learn, their self-concepts with regard to learning, and their cognitions about learning (such as the belief that effort leads to achievement). It is important to note that certain qualities of school climate and practice foster scholastic and positive social behaviors, regardless of the characteristics of the students who attend them (Howlin, 1994; Rutter, 1983, 2000; Rutter & Maughan, 2002). In an ideal world, all children would have the opportunity to attend highly effective schools. Unfortunately, this is not the case. In the United States, where community taxes are crucial in supporting the educational system, large inequities exist between schools in middle- and upper-class locales and schools attended by childern of lower social class and minority background (Lott, 2002).

SOCIAL CLASS AND POVERTY

Social class, or socioeconomic status (SES), is determined by factors such as family income, educational achievement, and occupational level, which correlate with each other. Virtually all societies are stratified according to social class, and social class is marked by differences in many facets of life—environmental conditions, social interactions, values, attitudes, expectations, and opportunities.

Some youngsters from middle and upper classes certainly do develop in less than optimal ways despite their generally advantageous rearing conditions. For example, Luthar and Becker (2002) found, in an affluent community, relationships among depressive symptoms, substance use, peer attitudes, pressure for achievement, and isolation from parents. Nevertheless, the relatively higher risk associated with lower social class has led to an emphasis on the effects of poverty.

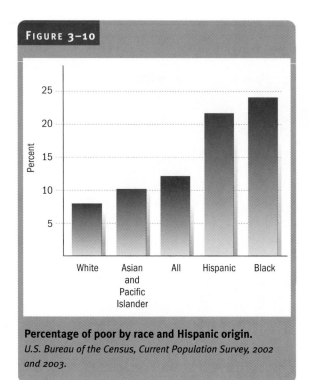

FIGURE 3–10

Percentage of poor by race and Hispanic origin.
U.S. Bureau of the Census, Current Population Survey, 2002 and 2003.

years, the young still experience higher rates of poverty than any other age group. We need to be mindful, too, that the risk of living in poverty is disproportionately high in female-headed households and families of specific ethnic/racial background. Figure 3–10 shows rates of poverty for major ethnic/racial groups. Table 3–5 indicates the degree of risk associated with poverty for several negative outcomes or experiences. For example, poor children are 1.7 times as likely to die in infancy and 2 times as likely to repeat a school grade than children in more advantageous economic circumstances.

Although it is all too easy to cite the adversities of growing up poor, it is more difficult to determine the mechanisms, pathways, and interconnectedness of the many factors involved in poverty (McLoyd, 1998). Both the physical and psychosocial environment must be considered.

Poor children are more likely to have greater exposure to unsafe levels of lead, pesticides, air pollution, inadequate water supplies, and poor sanitation (Evans, 2004). They more likely live in crowded homes, with structural defects and rodent infestation. Risks in the homes—fewer fire distinguishers, ungated stairways, and the like—are linked to childhood injuries. Homes lack not only amenities, such as washing machines, but also learning resources such as books, appropriate toys, and computers.

The family plays a crucial role in mediating the effects of poverty and social class. Parents of low SES

Despite the general economic wealth of the United States, poverty is all too common among its youth. The percentage of poverty for people under age 18 was 16.7 percent in 2002 (U.S. Bureau of the Census, Current Population Survey, 2002 and 2003). Although this rate was fortunately the lowest in several

TABLE 3–5	RISK OF POOR CHILDREN RELATIVE TO NONPOOR CHILDREN FOR SELECTED OUTCOMES/EXPERIENCES
OUTCOME	**RISK**
Infant mortality	1.7
Death during childhood (to 14 years)	1.5
Low birthweight	1.7
Lead poisoning	3.5
Developmental delay	1.3
Learning disabilities (3–17 years)	1.4
Repetition of school grade	2.0
High school dropout	2.2
Parental report of child ever having an emotional/behavioral problem for 3 or more months	1.3
Out-of-wedlock birth by female teen	3.1
Unemployed and not in school (at age 24)	1.9

Adapted from Brooks-Gunn, J., & Duncan, G. (1997, Summer/Fall). The effects of poverty on children. The Future of Children, a publication of the Center for the Future of Children, The David and Lucile Packard Foundation.

tend to have somewhat different goals for their children (Bradley & Whiteside-Mansell, 1997). In particular, they may socialize their children in ways that they believe will ensure their child's job security and acceptance by others, whereas middle-class families seem to emphasize choice, intellectual challenges, and job status. Parenting in low SES homes tends to be harsher, more punitive, and less responsive (Evans, 2004). Research suggests that higher SES is associated with parents' giving more time, effort, and verbal attention to their young children. Differences in the learning environment of the home, in turn, are related to youngsters' development (Duncan & Brooks-Gunn, 2000). The family may mediate poverty in many other ways. For example, the stress of being poor may increase the likelihood of parent-child conflict, leading to child emotional and school problems. Parents who experience poverty are themselves more likely to have health and emotional problems, which can interfere with optimal parenting and the learning environment in the home. Family separation and lower marital quality are also linked to family poverty (Evans, 2004).

We would not expect the family to mediate all of poverty's effects, of course. Peers, schools, communities, and broader cultural factors come into play. Consider, for example, some of the circumstances that may underlie the disturbing fact that disadvantaged environments are often repeated over generations. Children's lack of school achievement may be determined by many factors and may lead to less desirable jobs, unemployment, and economic stress. Economic hardship in families is linked to less access to social services and a variety of social supports. Many poor families live in poor communities; they may lack adequate childcare, psychological support, positive role models, and someone to help out in emergencies. Such an array of variables is likely to adversely influence the new generation of children, leading to an intergenerational cycle of poverty.

In discussing the impact of family income on children's achievements and verbal ability, Duncan and Brooks-Gunn (2000) point to the probable importance of poverty's *persistence, depth,* and *timing.* In one study, for example, poverty during the first 4 years of life was associated with lower intelligence at age 5 than was poverty experienced some but not all of those years. Research also suggests that the poorest of poor children have the lowest scores on intelligence tests. And the time at which poverty is experienced may have influence, with negative effects greater for early rather than later childhood.

It has also been demonstrated that poor children are exposed to multiple risks and that the accumulation of risk is related to developmental outcome (Evans, 2004). Figure 3–11 shows a striking difference in the number of cumulative risks experienced by poor and middle-class children in the third to fifth grade. Although it is reasonable to consider what role family genetics may play in poverty and its effects, the overall research suggests that the cognitive and psychosocial difficulties observed in poor children and adolescents cannot solely be accounted for by genetic influences.

NEIGHBORHOODS

All neighborhood/community contexts undoubtedly influence children and adolescents, but investigations have focused on poor urban neighborhoods. Current interest in neighborhood influences arose, in part, because poor families became increasingly clustered in urban areas during the 1970s and 1980s (Leventhal & Brooks-Gunn, 2000). Many of these communities are characterized by public housing and by a disproportionate number of families from minority ethnic/racial background. Some of the most deprived communities have been described in telling ways. The following descriptive passages are from Jonathan Kozol's *Savage Inequalities* (1991), a book that recounts the author's visit to East St. Louis, Illinois.

East St. Louis lies in the heart of the American Bottoms—the floodplain on the east side of the Mississippi River opposite St. Louis. To the east of the city lie the Illinois Bluffs. . . . Towns on the Bluffs are predominately white and do not welcome visitors from East St. Louis. (p. 9)

As [my acquaintance and I] ride past blocks and blocks of skeletal structures, some of which are still inhabited, she slows the car repeatedly at railroad crossings. . . . On the left: a blackened lot where garbage has been burning. Next to the burning garbage is a row of 12 white cabins, charred by fire. Next: a lot that holds a heap of auto tires and a mountain of tin cans. More burnt houses. More trash fires. (pp. 11–12)

Among the negative factors listed by the city's health director are the sewage running in the streets, air that has been fouled by the local

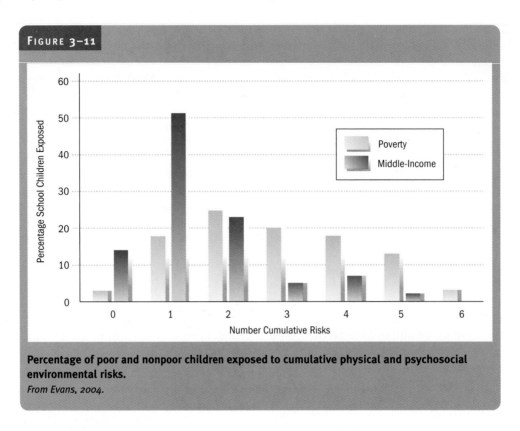

Figure 3–11

Percentage of poor and nonpoor children exposed to cumulative physical and psychosocial environmental risks.
From Evans, 2004.

plants, the high lead levels noted in the soil, poverty, lack of education, crime, dilapidated housing, insufficient health care, unemployment. (p. 20)

The problems of the streets in urban areas, as teachers often note, frequently spill over into public schools. In the public schools of East St. Louis, this is literally the case. . . . [The Post-Dispatch noted that] "East St. Louis Senior High School was awash in sewage for the second time this year.". . . The science labs at East St. Louis are 30 to 50 years outdated. . . . [The history teacher noted] "I have four girls right now in my senior home room who are pregnant or have just had babies. When I ask them why this happens, I am told, 'Well, there's no reason not to have a baby. There's not much for me in public school.' The truth is that's a pretty honest answer. A diploma from a ghetto school doesn't count for much in the United States." (pp. 23, 27, 29)

On top of all else is the very high risk of death by homicide. . . . The fear of violence is very real in East St. Louis. (p. 21)

Although separating neighborhood effects from family and other influences is difficult, there is some evidence for the independent influence of neighborhoods. Leventhal and Brooks-Gunn (2000) reviewed findings regarding child and adolescent outcomes for academic-related skills, mental health, and sexuality. The most consistent finding was that living in an affluent neighborhood provided substantial benefits to youth with regard to school readiness and achievement, especially for European American youngsters. Neighborhood effects on mental health were not as consistently found. The best evidence was for a stronger association between low-SES neighborhoods and acting out/aggressive behavior rather than problems such as depressive and withdrawn behaviors. Neighborhood effects on adolescent sexual behavior and childbearing were somewhat varied, but low social class was related to higher levels of sexual activity. In general, the strength of community influence was in the small to moderate range.

It would be helpful, of course, to understand the factors that mediate adverse community effects on children and adolescents. Drawing on research findings and on theoretical explanations, Leventhal and Brooks-Gunn (2000) offered a conceptualization of potential pathways of influence that was meant to serve as a framework for further investigation (Figure 3–12).

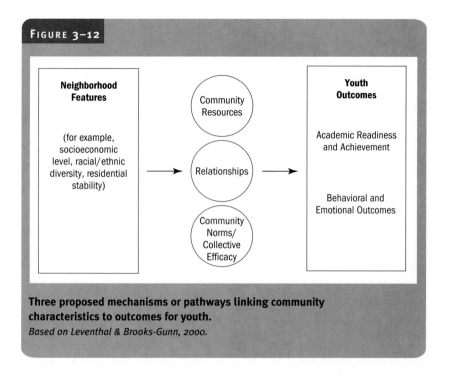

FIGURE 3–12

Three proposed mechanisms or pathways linking community characteristics to outcomes for youth.
Based on Leventhal & Brooks-Gunn, 2000.

1. The first pathway is *community resources*, which include opportunities for learning offered in schools, libraries, and museums; quality day care; medical services; and employment in the community.

2. The second pathway is *relationships*, with emphasis on the family. It includes parents' personal characteristics such as their mental health, coping skills, and physical health; parenting styles and supervision; support networks for parents; and physical and organizational features of the home such as cleanliness, safety, and regular schedules and routines.

3. The third pathway, labeled *community norms/ collective efficacy*, refers to the extent to which communities are organized to maintain behavioral norms and order. To varying degrees formal institutions or informal networks monitor or supervise the behavior of individuals and the physical risks that might exist. The neighborhood scrutinizes child and adolescent behavior, the availability of illegal substances, violence, crime, and similar activities.

Leventhal and Brooks-Gunn noted that of the three pathways, the strongest evidence was for norms/collective efficacy and that there was increasing support for the influence of relationships. Indeed, recent research describes how family functioning interfaces with characteristics of the community and can act as a risk or protective influence. For example, neighborhood disadvantage is linked to children's affiliations with deviant peers (Brody et al., 2001). Harsh/inconsistent parenting appears to encourage this association, and nurturant/involved parenting discourages it. Also demonstrated is that parents who reside in more dangerous neighborhoods tend to be more restrictive. They may cope with the adverse conditions by withdrawing from them and intensely monitoring their children. Indeed, parental monitoring can provide a protective shield (Buckner, Mezzacappa, & Beardslee, 2003; Luthar & Goldstein, 2004).

CULTURE, ETHNICITY/RACE, MINORITY STATUS

All of the contexts we have already discussed operate within a still larger cultural context. In Chapter 1, we discussed cultural influence on defining, identifying, and explaining psychopathology. Here, we look at how a society's beliefs, social structures, social roles, and ways of "doing business" more generally affect the development and lives of its youth.

The cultural context can be broadly positive or risky in that it may inadvertently foster outcomes considered detrimental even by cultural standards. For example, certain values and practices in the United States may encourage high levels of aggression and violence. A case in point concerns the exposure of youth to a high level of aggressive and violent content in media (Anderson et al., 2003; Villani, 2001). Decades of research clearly indicate that observing such television and film programming can increase aggression in children; more recent investigation indicates the same effect for video games.

Risk stemming from the cultural context may be particularly high for individuals whose ethnic/racial background is other than mainstream. Children and adolescents in many countries who belong to indigenous (native) cultural groups have higher rates of behavioral dysfunction than youth of dominant populations (Kvernmo & Heyerdahl, 1998). For instance, adolescents of American Indian background reportedly have high rates of substance abuse, disruptive behavior, and incarceration in the juvenile justice system (Hawkins, Cummins, & Marlatt, 2004; Novins et al., 1999; Novins, Beals, & Mitchell, 2001).

Several factors are likely to play a role in creating behavioral dysfunction among indigenous youth. One of these is acculturation, which refers to changes in culture resulting from different cultures coming into contact with each other (Kvernmo & Heyerdahl, 1998, 2003). Indigenous youth are thought to be at risk because cultural change is often involuntary and because prejudice and discrimination frequently exist—a situation that can create issues regarding cultural identity as well as practical problems. Certainly, indigenous people also are often socially and economically disadvantaged. For instance, the poverty rate for American Indian and Alaskan natives was almost 26 percent for the years 1998 through 2000, higher than for other ethnic/racial groups (U.S. Bureau of the Census, Current Population Survey, 1999–2001). The American Indian population also has high rates of birth, infant mortality, and unemployment relative to the general U.S. population (Beals et al., 1997).

Similar disadvantage applies to other minority groups. Economic stress—and its correlates—is felt by many of these groups. So also are prejudice, racism, and discrimination, which youngsters come to perceive relatively early in life. One 14-year-old black girl living in East St. Louis used the following

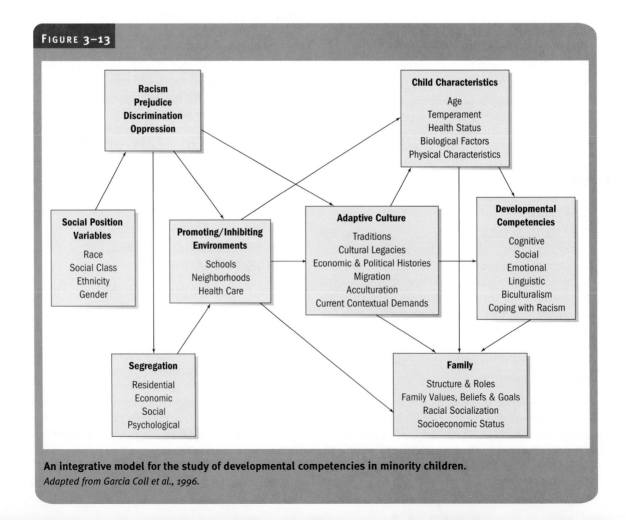

FIGURE 3–13

An integrative model for the study of developmental competencies in minority children.
Adapted from Garcia Coll et al., 1996.

words in reflecting on her experiences when, at a younger age, she had attended school in a community of mostly white people.

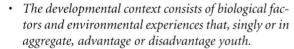

Anna   Ugliness in People's Hearts

My mother pushes me and she had wanted me to get a chance at better education. Only one other student in my class was black. I was in the fifth grade, and at that age you don't understand the ugliness in people's hearts. They wouldn't play with me. I couldn't understand it. During recess I would stand there by myself beside the fence. Then one day I got a note: "Go back to Africa."

To tell the truth, it left a sadness in my heart. Now you hear them sayin' on TV, "What's the matter with these colored people? Don't they care about their children's education?" But my mother did the best for me she knew. It was not my fault that I was not accepted by those people.

Kozol, 1991, p. 35.

Prejudice and discrimination not only reduces opportunity but has other influences. For example, negative prejudgment and stereotyping of African American students may adversely affect their academic-related performance (Steele, 1997). The discrimination and perceived experiences of racism have been shown to be associated with symptoms such as aggression, antisocial acts, and depression in African American children and adolescents (Nyborg & Curry, 2003). In general, prejudice may adversely affect the emotions, behavior, academic performance, and health of young people of minority groups (Clark et al., 1999; Compas et al., 2001). Perhaps unsurprising, among the variables that may protect these youth is the degree to which they identify with their ethnic/racial group and are reared to be proud of their heritage (Caughty et al., 2002; DuBois et al., 2002).

Some of the many variables that enter into the developmental outcome for youngsters of minority group background apply to all children whereas other variables are specific to the experiences of cultural, ethnic, and racial subgroups. Figure 3–13 depicts a developmental model for children of color, drawing attention to both general and specific variables (such as segregation and family racial socialization) that must be considered.

Finally, we should note the disadvantages often experienced by minority groups, indigenous or otherwise, in seeking and receiving treatment for behavioral problems (e.g., Sue, 2003). Efforts are being made by individuals, agencies, and professional organizations to better understand the relevant differences that may exist in the values, practices, and needs of minority groups (e.g., Belar, Nelson, & Wasik, 2003), but much remains to be done to provide sensitive and appropriate care.

SUMMARY

- *The developmental context consists of biological factors and environmental experiences that, singly or in aggregate, advantage or disadvantage youth.*

BRAIN AND NERVOUS SYSTEM

- *Early brain development—which includes cell formation, migration, connectedness, and pruning—depends on the interaction of biological programming and experience.*

- *The various parts of the nervous system and brain function as a whole, with specific areas playing primary roles in specific functions. Communication occurs through complex neurotransmission among neurons.*

NERVOUS SYSTEM AND RISK FOR DISORDERED BEHAVIOR

- *Damage to the brain can result from genetic, prenatal, and postnatal events. Numerous teratogens have* been identified; their prenatal effects depend on several variables. Fetal Alcohol Syndrome, which is readily preventable, puts children at risk for multiple abnormalities.*

- *The capacity of young people to recover from brain damage is not simple to predict. Whereas plasticity is obviously beneficial, early damage can interfere with subsequent development.*

GENETIC CONTEXT

- *Genetic influences on both typical and problematic development occur through single-gene and multigenic processes. Such influences are studied through a variety of methods, including quantitative and molecular strategies.*

- *Inheritance—as well as shared and nonshared environmental effects—have been shown for many behavioral disorders. Less is known about the specific genes involved and how they operate to affect behavior.*

- *Genetic and environmental influences collaborate with each other through gene-environment interactions and gene-environment correlations.*

LEARNING AND COGNITION

- *Through learning and cognition, children continuously take in information and think about the world. Classical conditioning, operant learning, observational learning, and higher order cognitive processes play major roles in the origins and treatment of behavioral disorder.*

SOCIOCULTURAL CONTEXT: AN OVERVIEW

- *The sociocultural context of development consists of overlapping, interacting domains of influences that include family, peers, community, societal, and cultural influences.*

FAMILY CONTEXT, MALTREATMENT, AND DIVORCE

- *Family interaction is complex, with fathers and mothers taking overlapping but not identical roles. Studies of parenting styles suggest that an authoritative, warm style fosters favorable development.*

- *Today's analyses of family life include the maltreatment of children and adolescents, the many factors that contribute to it, and its varied effects.*

- *Divorce is best conceptualized as a complex process of family transitions that heightens developmental risk. Its effects depend on multiple variables.*

PEER INFLUENCES

- *Peers influence each other in many, perhaps unique, ways through friendship and other interactions. Poor peer relationships in childhood are associated with childhood and later problem behavior.*

COMMUNITY AND SOCIETAL CONTEXTS

- *Schools are a central context for the development of youth. They teach intellectual skills and knowledge and also shape values, social and emotional behavior, motivation for learning and achievement, and mental health.*

- *Low socioeconomic status and the poverty associated with it disadvantage children in many areas of development. Poor children are exposed to multiple physical and psychosocial risks. The impact operates in part through family factors.*

- *Young people are also influenced by characteristics of the neighborhoods in which they are reared. Poor neighborhoods are a risk factor for academic performance, mental health, and other aspects of development. Neighborhood influences may operate through community resources, family relationships, and social organization to maintain order.*

- *The broad cultural context can shape behavior in ways that are maladaptive for young people. Indigenous and minority groups often experience poverty, prejudice, and discrimination, and such variables must be considered in models of the development of these youth.*

KEY TERMS

● ● ● ● ● ● ● ● ●

glial cells *(p. 38)*

neurons *(p. 38)*

central nervous system *(p. 39)*

peripheral nervous system *(p. 39)*

somatic nervous system *(p. 39)*

autonomic nervous system *(p. 39)*

sympathetic nervous system *(p. 39)*

parasympathetic nervous system *(p. 39)*

endocrine system *(p. 39)*

dendrites, cell body, axons *(p. 39)*

synapse *(p. 39)*

neurotransmitters *(p. 39)*

teratogens *(p. 40)*

Fetal Alcohol Syndrome *(p. 42)*

brain plasticity *(p. 43)*

chromosomes *(p. 43)*

DNA *(p. 43)*

genes *(p. 43)*

genetic mutation *(p. 43)*

behavior genetics *(p. 44)*

genotype *(p. 44)*

phenotype *(p. 44)*

dominant genes *(p. 44)*

recessive genes *(p. 44)*

index case, proband *(p. 44)*

heritability *(p. 45)*

family genetic studies *(p. 45)*

twin studies *(p. 45)*

concordance *(p. 45)*

monozygotic (MZ) twins *(p. 45)*

dizygotic (DZ) twins *(p. 45)*

adoption studies *(p. 45)*

shared environmental influences *(p. 45)*

nonshared environmental influences *(p. 45)*

linkage analysis *(p. 46)*

association analysis *(p. 46)*

gene-environment interaction *(p. 46)*

gene-environment correlation *(p. 46)*

self-efficacy model *(p. 50)*

cognitive-behavioral perspective *(p. 50)*

cognitive deficiencies *(p. 50)*

cognitive distortions *(p. 50)*

ecological models *(p. 50)*

parenting styles *(p. 52)*

authoritative parenting *(p. 52)*

authoritarian parenting *(p. 52)*

indulgent/permissive parenting *(p. 52)*

neglectful parenting *(p. 52)*

maltreatment *(p. 53)*

child abuse *(p. 53)*

physical abuse *(p. 54)*

sexual abuse *(p. 55)*

neglect *(p. 55)*

emotional (psychological) maltreatment *(p. 55)*

marital discord *(p. 59)*

peer relationships *(p. 61)*

socioeconomic status (SES) *(p. 63)*

acculturation *(p. 68)*

Research: Its Role and Methods

Psychology and other disciplines are committed to the view that science can provide the most complete and valid information about human functioning, behavior, and development. Although common sense tells us much about behavior, science aims to go beyond common sense to systematic, reliable, and accurate knowledge. The general purpose of science is to describe and explain phenomena.

The word *science* comes from the Latin word for "knowledge," or "to know," but refers to knowledge gained by particular methods of inquiry. We might know the world from reading literature or listening to music, but we would not consider knowledge gained in this way to be scientific knowledge. Scientific understanding derives from systematic formulation of a problem, observation and collection of data, and interpretation of findings by what is considered acceptable procedures. Despite some misgivings—and even warnings of danger—about the scientific study of humans, we have come to value what science can tell us about ourselves.

Fundamentals of Research

As we have already seen, many questions relevant to developmental psychopathology fall under the following general categories:

- What is the nature of normal and abnormal behavior?
- What demographic factors (e.g., age, gender, social class) are associated with specific disorders?
- How do behavioral disorders change over time?
- What processes or mechanisms underlie various behavioral disturbances?
- What causes psychopathology?
- What puts youngsters at risk for psychopathology, and what protects them from it?
- How can disordered behavior be effectively treated and prevented?

Of course, these general questions are transformed into countless more specific queries. To answer them, it is sometimes necessary only to describe phenomena. We can count the number of cases of depression or can describe the symptoms of disorders. At other times, it is necessary to determine the exact conditions under which a phenomenon occurs and its relationship to other variables. Often we want to determine cause-and-effect relationships to understand better and to be able to predict behavior.

We have also seen that researchers rarely, if ever, simply pose and try to answer questions in an intellectual vacuum. They are guided by already established information, concepts, perspectives or theories, and by their own inclinations. Theoretical concepts and assumptions guide research goals, choice of variables, procedures, analyses, and conclusions. But there is always at least a touch of subjectivity and creativity in the posing of research questions and in deciding how best to seek answers.

It is common to try to test specific hypotheses derived from theoretical notions. Hypothesis testing is valuable in that it tends to build knowledge systematically rather than haphazardly. Any one investigation rarely proves that a hypothesis is either correct or incorrect; instead, it provides evidence for or against the hypothesis. In turn, a hypothesis that is supported serves as evidence for the accuracy and explanatory power of the underlying theory. A failed hypothesis, in contrast, serves to disprove, limit, or redirect the theory. Together, observations and theory advance scientific understanding.

Just as researchers ask a variety of questions and pose hypotheses, they work in a variety of settings, ranging from the natural environments of the home or community to controlled laboratory settings. Similarly, different methods and strategies are used, depending on the purposes of the research—and on ethics and practicality, too. In all cases, however, careful consideration must be given to selection of participants, observation and measurement, reliability, and validity.

SELECTION OF PARTICIPANTS

For good reason, research reports require the description of the participants and the way they were selected. This information is important in judging the adequacy of investigations and interpretations of the findings.

When the purpose of research is to draw general conclusions, the ideal is to study the entire population of interest—which is rarely possible—or a representative sample of the entire population. Representativeness is best achieved by random selection of participants from the population, that is, by choosing each participant by chance. This goal may not be feasible; for example, it is impossible to randomly select a sample from all

preschoolers or *all* children with mental retardation. However, efforts can be made to approximate representativeness, and the extent to which it is achieved affects interpretation of the research results.

In the study of behavioral disorders, research participants are often drawn from clinics, hospitals, schools, and other facilities serving youngsters with problems. Such clinic populations are unlikely to represent the entire population of young people with disorders. On the one hand, they can exclude youth who have gone unnoticed or for whom help was not sought because of factors such as denial, shame, fear, or high levels of tolerance by adults. Clinic cases may also underrepresent youth whose parents cannot afford treatment. On the other hand, clinic populations can overrepresent youth who are of upper social class, who experience more serious symptoms, or who act out or otherwise disturb people. These biases have important implications. We have seen, for instance, how working with clinic populations rather than general populations, or boys rather than girls, might affect how disorders are defined (Chapter 1). The characteristics of research participants and the way that participants are chosen are critical in planning and drawing conclusions from research investigations.

OBSERVATION AND MEASUREMENT

At the heart of scientific endeavors are observation and measurement. The scientific method thus can be applied only to aspects of the world for which these processes can be used. Both observation and measurement are challenging for behavioral scientists. It is relatively simple to observe and to measure overt action, but thought and emotion, which are intricately entwined with action, are more elusive. Typically the scientist must provide an operational definition of the behavior or concept being studied. That is, some observable and measurable operation must be selected to define the behavior or concept. Aggression might be operationalized as the frequency with which children actually shove or threaten their playmates; depression might be operationalized by the degree to which an adolescent reports feelings of sadness and hopelessness.

In the attempt to tap all sources of information, behavioral scientists make many kinds of observations and measurements. They directly observe overt behavior with or without special apparatus; employ standardized tests; record physiological functioning of the brain, sensory organs, or heart; ask people to

Direct observation allows the researcher systematically to measure behavior as it is occurring.
(Courtesy of A.C. Israel)

report or rate their own behavior, feelings, and thoughts; and collect the reports of others about the subject of investigation.

Whatever the measure, it should be valid; that is, an accurate indicator of the attribute of interest. For instance, if children are asked to complete a questionnaire about their fears and anxieties, there should be good reason to believe that the questionnaire gets at what is widely meant by fear and anxiety. The observations also must be reliable, that is, the data would be similar, or consistent, if measurements were taken again under similar circumstances. Briefly put, numerous considerations and practices are required to insure objective, accurate, and dependable observation and measurement. (See Accent: "The Goodness of Measurement in Research.")

RELIABILITY OF RESEARCH FINDINGS

The concepts of reliability and validity apply to the results of research as well. The findings of a research study are assumed to report a "truth" about the

world. The scientific method assumes that "truth" repeats itself, given identical or similar conditions; consequently, it can be observed again by others. Replication of findings is thus an important component of scientific work. If the same "truth" is not reported under similar conditions, the original finding is considered unreliable or inconsistent, and therefore it remains questionable. The need for reliability, or repeatability, of results places a burden on researchers to be clear and concise as they conceptualize and conduct their study, and to communicate their findings so that others may replicate and judge their work.

VALIDITY OF RESEARCH FINDINGS

Whereas reliability refers to the consistency or repeatability of results, validity refers to the correctness, soundness, or appropriateness of scientific findings. The validity of research findings is a complex matter and in general must be judged in terms of the purpose of the research and the way that the results are used. There are several kinds of validity; we will examine two that are major components of research studies.

Internal validity refers to the extent to which explanations for phenomena are judged to be correct or sound. Or to put it in another way, it refers to the degree to which alternative explanations can be ruled out (Campbell & Stanley, 1963). The more certain we are that alternative explanations can be ruled out, the more confidence we have in the explanations we offer.

Internal validity often is specifically applied to research that aims to test causal hypotheses. As such, it concerns inferences that are made about whether one variable or factor caused another, given the conditions of the research study (Shadish, Cook, & Campbell, 2002). Closely tied to internal validity is the notion of control in research. Internal validity is maximized by research designs and procedures that build control over the variables that could affect the findings of the investigation. By controlling the procedures, the researcher limits the conditions that can explain the results. By controlling extraneous factors, the researcher optimizes the likelihood of being able to attribute the findings to specific factors. As we shall see, it is only the "true" experiment that approaches such control.

External validity asks the question of generalizability, the extent to which the results of an investigation apply to other populations and situations.

ACCENT

The Goodness of Measurement in Research

Because observations that are biased, unreliable, or invalid can be useless or misleading, investigators must always be concerned about their quality. Consider, for example, a study by Dadds and colleagues (1992), who used naturalistic observation to study childhood depression. Naturalistic observation consists of directly observing individuals in their "real world," at times simply to describe naturally occurring behavior and at other times to answer specific questions or to test hypotheses. In this study, a comparison was made of parent-child interaction in families that had a child who was clinic-referred for depression, conduct disorder, or depression/conduct disorder. The families, as well as a group of nonclinic families, were videotaped during a typical evening meal.

The videotaped behavior was then independently coded by observers who were trained to use a carefully constructed observation system, the Family Observation Schedule. This instrument provided 20 categories for parent and child behaviors—among them smiling, frowning, praising, and complaining. The reliability of measurement was then examined to determine whether the taped behaviors were coded in a consistent way by the independent coders. Such interobserver reliability is known to be generally higher when the observation schedule is optimally specific and clear. In the Dadds et al. study, interobserver reliability was checked by an additional observer, who coded one-third of the tapes. The investigation also benefited from the observers' having no knowledge of each family's clinical status, that is, the problems displayed by the children. Nor did the observers know the hypotheses being tested. Such observer "blindness" decreased the chance that the observers would be biased by such information.

All of these features of the Dadds et al. investigation—a well-constructed observation tool, observer training, a check on the reliability of the coding, and blind observation—addressed important standards for measurement in research.

Researchers are virtually always interested in generalizability, but it cannot be assumed. Findings based on European American children in the United States may or may not hold for children of Mexican American ancestry; findings from research with animals may or may not apply to humans; findings from studies conducted in the laboratory may or may not hold in the world outside the laboratory.

The question of generalizability is rarely, if ever, completely answered, although evidence increases as

"The title of my science project is 'My Little Brother: Nature or Nurture.'"

various populations, settings, and methods are used. It is ironic that attempts to increase internal validity may decrease external validity, because the former requires controls that may create situations artificial to everyday environments. This dilemma is one of several that must be taken into account in the selection of a research method.

Basic Methods of Research

There are many ways to approach and conduct research. The distinction between nonexperimental and experimental approaches is often drawn: only experimental methods include a manipulation or condition to which participants are systematically exposed. At different historical times, different approaches have been embraced more strongly than others, depending also on the discipline in which researchers were trained. Nevertheless, all research methods have strengths and weaknesses, and the choice of one over another reasonably depends on the purpose and other aspects of the research. Moreover, conclusions are especially impressive when they are based on a convergence of findings from investigations that employ different methods.

We have organized this discussion of research approaches into four basic methods that are frequently employed in investigating behavioral problems. Subsequently, general strategies that are relevant to these methods will be examined.

CASE STUDIES

The case study is a descriptive method commonly used in investigations of behavioral disorder. It focuses on an individual—describing the background, present and past life circumstances, functioning, and characteristics of the person. Case studies can tell us something about the nature, course, correlates, outcomes, and possible etiology of behavior problems.

The following is an abbreviated version of a case report of a boy who was considered at risk for a serious disorder, childhood schizophrenia.

Max Risk for Childhood Schizophrenia

Max was a seven-year-old boy when he was first referred for psychiatric evaluation by his school principal. . . . Long-standing problems such as severe rage outbursts, loss of control, aggressive behavior, and paranoid ideation had reached crisis proportions.

Max was the product of an uncomplicated pregnancy and delivery, the only child of a professional couple. There was a history of "mental illness" in the paternal grandmother and two great aunts. Max's early development was characterized by "passivity.". . . He used a bottle until age three. Verbal development was good; he spoke full sentences at one year. Toilet training was reportedly difficult. . . .

Max was clumsy and had difficulty manipulating toys, his tricycle, and his shoelaces. When he began nursery school, he was constantly in trouble with other children. . . . Max "developed a passion for animals.". . . At age five Max acquired an imaginary companion, "Casper—the man in the wall" who was ever present. Max insisted that he could see him, although no one else could. Casper's voice, he said, often told him he was a bad boy.

Max's behavior was so unmanageable during the first and second grade he was rarely able to remain in the classroom. . . . Max described animals fighting and killing people. . . . The psychologists noted a schizoid quality because of the numerous references to people from outer space, ghosts, and martians, as well as the total absence of human subjects. . . . Despite his high intelligence (IQ 130), Max was experiencing the world as hostile and dangerous. The psychologist considered Max to be at great risk for schizophrenia, paranoid type.

Cantor & Kestenbaum, 1986, pp. 627–628.

The case study continues, telling of Max's enrollment in special schools and his psychotherapy. A major focus of treatment was to reduce Max's anxiety, which was thought to cause his aggression and bizarre behaviors. Parental involvement, rewards for appropriate behavior, and medication were all employed. Despite some quite disturbed behaviors, improvement occurred, and Max eventually was able to attend a university engineering program.

The primary goal of this case report was to illustrate a therapeutic approach to treating children with severe disturbances and to emphasize that treatment must be tailored to each child's needs. Case studies can well meet such a goal, for one of their strengths is the power to illustrate. They can richly describe phenomena, even phenomena so rare that they would be difficult to study in other ways. They can provide hypotheses to be tested by other methods. The weaknesses of the case study concern reliability and validity. The descriptions of life events often go back in time, raising questions about their reliability and accuracy. When case studies go beyond description to interpretations, there are few guidelines to judge the validity of the interpretations. Generalization also is weak: Since only one person is examined, the findings cannot be generalized confidently to others. There are ways to increase reliability and validity, however (Kazdin, 1998). For example, the validity of treatment success in a case report can be increased by the use of objective rather than anecdotal measures of the client's behavior. And confidence in generalization can be facilitated by reports of several case studies demonstrating the same concept or outcome.

Despite some shortcomings, case studies have an important role in child and adolescent psychopathology. Clinicians consider them "do-able" and relevant to their concerns (Morrow-Bradley & Elliot, 1986). Case studies can thus bridge the gap that all too often exists between clinical practice and research endeavors (Kazdin, 1998).

CORRELATIONAL METHODS

The term *correlation* refers to a relationship or association between two or more factors. Correlational methods consist of a variety of research approaches that explore such relationships without exposing participants to a manipulation. The variables may be measured in the natural environment or in the laboratory in a variety of ways. Correlational studies can be extremely helpful and are widely employed in research relevant to developmental psychopathology. They are useful when initial exploration is the goal of research. Here the investigator may first want to determine whether any relationships exist among variables before specific hypotheses are advanced. Correlational studies are crucial to understanding variables that are operating in the natural environment. They can also be helpful when ethical considerations preclude manipulation. Although investigators cannot ethically expose children to abuse or poor nutrition, they can use correlational methods to study the impact of these factors on children who are unfortunately exposed to such situations in the naturally occurring environment.

Statistical procedures are employed to determine the existence of a relationship and also its nature and strength. Correlational analyses can involve many variables in complex research designs, and various ways to examine the data. Here we only examine the basic aspects of the method. In its simplest form, the question asked is, Are factors X and Y related, and, if so, in what direction are they related, and how strongly? After the selection of an appropriate sample, two scores are obtained from each participant—one a measure of variable X and the other a measure of variable Y. Statistical analysis of these scores is then performed. In this case, the Pearson product-moment coefficient, r, could be computed.

The value of Pearson r,[1] which always ranges between +1.00 and −1.00, indicates the direction and the strength of the relationship. Direction is indicated by the sign of the coefficient. A positive sign (+) means that high scores on the X variable tend to be associated with high scores on the Y variable, and that low scores on X tend to be related to low scores on Y. This relationship is referred to as a positive correlation (or direct correlation). A negative sign (−) indicates that high scores on X tend to be related to low scores on Y, and that low scores on X tend to be related to high scores on Y. This is a negative correlation (also called an indirect, or inverse, correlation).

The strength or magnitude of a correlation is reflected in the absolute value of the coefficient. The strongest relationship is expressed by an r of +1.00 or −1.00, both of which are considered perfect correlations. As the absolute value of the coefficient value decreases, the relationship becomes weaker. A coefficient of 0.00 indicates that no relationship exists at all. In this case, the scores on one variable tell us nothing about the scores on the other variable.

Suppose that an investigator explored the association of secure attachment in infancy with childhood adjustment. For each participant, the researcher obtained a measure of secure attachment in infancy and a measure of adjustment in childhood. The hypothetical data appear in Table 4–1. Pearson r for the data was calculated, and its value is .82. How would this finding be interpreted? Obviously, a correlation exists, and the positive sign indicates that children who scored higher on secure attachment tended to score higher on later adjustment. The magnitude of

[1]*Pearson r is one of several correlation coefficients that could be calculated, depending on the nature and complexity of the study. The general procedures and interpretations described here apply to other correlation coefficients.*

	VARIABLE *X* ATTACHMENT	VARIABLE *Y* CHILDHOOD ADJUSTMENT
TABLE 4–1	**DATA FROM A HYPOTHETICAL STUDY OF DEGREE OF INFANT SECURE ATTACHMENT AND CHILDHOOD ADJUSTMENT. THE PEARSON R VALUE IS +0.82, WHICH INDICATES A STRONG POSITIVE RELATIONSHIP BETWEEN THE VARIABLES.**	
CHILD	**SCORE**	**SCORE**
Daniel	2	5
Nicky	3	4
Sara	4	12
Beth	7	16
Jessica	9	10
Alia	11	22
Brent	13	18

the coefficient indicates that the relationship is strong (since 1.00 is a perfect positive relationship).

The degree to which correlational research is reliable depends mainly on the reliability of the measures used. The degree to which a study gives valid information about the relationship of the variables depends on several factors, such as the validity of the measures.

Cause and Effect. When a correlation exists, knowing a person's score on one variable allows us to predict the person's performance on the other variable. It does not, however, permit us automatically to draw a cause-and-effect conclusion. Two problems of interpretation exist.

One problem is that of directionality. If a positive correlation were found between parenting behaviors and child maladjustment, it is possible that parenting caused child maladjustment or, alternatively, that child maladjustment caused parents to behave in certain ways. The direction of causation is unclear. The directionality problem can sometimes be solved by examining the nature of the variables. For example, if a correlation between early attachment and later childhood adjustment exists, it is impossible for later adjustment to cause early secure attachment.

However, even if directionality with respect to variables *X* and *Y* is not a problem, a correlation may be caused by one or more unknown variables. Perhaps children's social competence is responsible for both the quality of their early attachment and their later social adjustment. To evaluate this possibility, social competence could be measured and a statistical technique could be applied to partial out, or hold

constant, its effects. To the extent that the correlation remains, it is not explained by social competence. As helpful as partialing techniques are in ruling out the effects of other possible causal factors, however, an investigator can never be sure that all possible causative variables have been evaluated.

Techniques such as structural equation modeling, too complex to discuss here, do permit researchers to have more confidence in their hypotheses about cause and effect. The researcher hypothesizes relationships (correlations) among the variables being studied and the direction of the correlations as well. Statistical techniques are then employed to determine how well the collected data fit the model that the researcher specified. Examples of the use of this and other methods based on correlations to address questions about behavioral disturbance appear throughout this text.

THE EXPERIMENT

The "true" experiment comes closest to meeting what are considered the most rigorous standards of the scientific method. It is the strongest method for inferring causal links between tested variables. Internal validity and experimenter control are of utmost importance. A controlled manipulation is presented to groups composed of randomly assigned participants and differences between the groups are then evaluated.

Random assignment of participants to groups is critical for interpreting group differences, because it makes it likely that any differences are not caused by prior group disparity but rather to the manipulation itself. This is a particular issue for studies of behavioral disorders because researchers often compare groups of participants who have already been classified with a diagnosis or a specific problem. Take the hypothetical experiment in which a group of children diagnosed with schizophrenia perform less well on a perception task than a group of typical youngsters. The finding would be important but caution must be taken in interpreting the results as due to schizophrenia itself. Perhaps some extraneous factor—such as the use of medication—underlies the effect. This does not mean, of course, that comparisons of diagnosed with nondiagnosed groups are worthless, but it cautions us about automatically drawing causal interpretations of the findings.

The experiment can vary in such things as the number of groups it has, the nature of the comparison groups, and the collection of data at more than one time. However, its essential features are characterized by the following:

- An explicitly stated hypothesis
- Subjects appropriately selected and randomly assigned to groups that are exposed to different conditions or manipulations, the independent variable, with at least one condition being a control group (that is, a comparison group)
- Observation and measurement of the behavior (outcome) being studied, which is the dependent variable
- Control of the procedures by the investigator

The Abecedarian Project. To illustrate the experiment, we draw on a study of the Abecedarian Project, which asked the question, Do at-risk children benefit from a child-centered, intellectually stimulating environment provided as part of a day-care service (Campbell et al., 2001; Ramey & Campbell, 1984)? Potential participants in the project were identified through prenatal clinics and the local social service department. Each family was then surveyed with the High Risk Index and families meeting a criterion score were considered at risk. The mother was interviewed and given an intelligence test, and selection was made before or soon after the birth of the participant child.

The investigators paired families according to similarity on the High Risk Index, and the children from each pair were randomly assigned to either the treatment or the control group (Ramey & Campbell, 1984). The independent variable was the provision of the educational program. All the children in the treatment group began day care by 3 months of age, and their development was tracked until they reached 54 months. The educational program included language, motor, social, and cognitive components, varying somewhat with the child's age. Control-group children did not attend the day-care center and were not exposed to the educational program. Efforts were made to otherwise equate their experiences with those of the treatment group: They were given similar nutritional supplements, pediatric care, and supportive social services. The dependent variable was standardized developmental or intelligence tests administered to all the children twice annually. The persons who conducted the tests were randomly assigned to the testing sessions.

The test results revealed that beginning at 18 months, children in the treatment group scored significantly higher than children in the control group, and this difference was statistically significant.[2] Figure 4–1 shows one way of examining the findings. It indicates that at 24, 36, and 48 months, the educationally treated children were much less likely to obtain intelligence scores at or below 85 than were the control children. The researchers concluded that the educational program resulted in intellectual benefits for the treated at-risk youngsters.[3]

Is this conclusion justified; that is, does the study have internal validity? The method by which the subjects were selected and assigned makes it unlikely that the results simply reflect group differences that existed prior to the study. Moreover, efforts were made to treat the experimental and control groups similarly except for the independent variable. To the degree that this was accomplished, it can be argued that the study is internally valid and that the results are due to the treatment. With regard to this issue, caution is appropriate, however. When research is conducted in the laboratory, it is relatively easy to control the experiences of the groups. In an experiment such as Ramey and Campbell's, the

[2]*Statistical significance refers to the probability that a finding is not due to mere chance. The accepted rule is that a significant finding would occur by chance only 5 or less times were the study repeated 100 times (p < .05.). Statistical significance tests can be applied to many kinds of research methods.*

[3]*Our present purpose in discussing the Abecedarian Project is to exemplify the experiment as a research method. However, it is worth noting that subsequent research shows that early-found benefits of the project could be observed several years later (Campbell & Ramey, 1994; Campbell et al., 2001).*

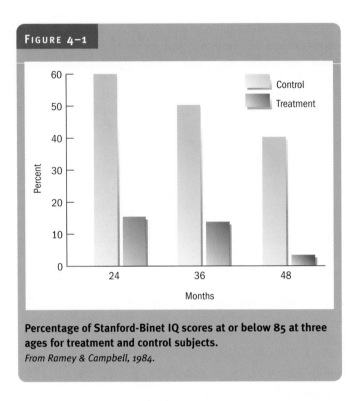

FIGURE 4–1

Percentage of Stanford-Binet IQ scores at or below 85 at three ages for treatment and control subjects.
From Ramey & Campbell, 1984.

degree of control and thus internal validity are less clear. An additional issue concerns the actual collection of data. It appears that those who gave the standardized tests may have known the group to which each child had been assigned, raising the question of bias in data collection. At the same time, possible bias of the individual testers was offset by their being randomly assigned to testing sessions.

What about external validity, or generalizability, of the findings? External validity is enhanced by the intervention's actually being conducted in a day-care center, the setting in which the program would likely be used. To the extent that other day-care settings would be similar to the original setting, external validity could be expected. Generalizability would also be anticipated when the intervention is applied to children who resemble Ramey and Campbell's original sample.

The question of generalizability of experimental results receives much attention today regarding research that evaluates the effects of treatments or prevention programs (Hinshaw, 2002a). The issue is captured by the terms efficacy and effectiveness. A treatment may be shown to work in the controlled and carefully monitored research setting (efficacy) but may be less effective or not at all effective in the real-world conditions in which it is typically provided (effectiveness). The difficulties encountered in conducting controlled experiments in real-world settings

may lead investigators to apply other research strategies. (See Accent: "Experiments of Nature.")

SINGLE-CASE EXPERIMENTAL DESIGNS

The typical experiment is conducted with groups of people and with one or more control groups serving to help rule out alternative explanations of the findings. A strategy akin to the experiment is to conduct an experiment with a single or a few individuals, provided that some control to rule out alternative explanations is employed. Such single-subject designs also are sometimes referred to as time-series methods because measures of the dependent variable are repeated across time periods.

Single-subject research appeared in the early history of psychology and other sciences (Morgan & Morgan, 2001). With careful control, internal validity is possible. External validity is not strong, because generalization from single subjects cannot be made with confidence. However, external validity can be increased by repeating the study with different subjects or in different settings.

Reversal Designs. Single-subject designs are frequently used to evaluate the influence of a clinical intervention. One way to control for the possibility of alternative explanations is to use the ABA reversal design. The problem behavior is carefully defined and measured across time periods, during which the

ACCENT ● ● ● ● ●

Experiments of Nature

Highly valued by developmental psychopathologists are what are referred to as experiments of nature or natural experiments. They are not, in fact, experiments in the methodological sense of random assignments of participants to groups exposed to manipulations or treatments. Rather, they are studies of naturally occurring events that contrast a condition of interest and a comparison condition (Shadish et al., 2002). The condition of interest may or may not be manipulatable by researchers. Nature is the basic designer, although investigators have a hand in how they go about their work.

An important example of the approach is the investigation of the effects of institutionalization on children's development. There is a lengthy history of comparing children who reside in orphanages with children who had left orphanages for their birth or adoptive homes and children who had never been institutionalized. These studies demonstrate the adverse effects of institutionalization on intellectual development, physical health, and an array of behaviors (MacLean, 2003). Lengthy institutionalization and poor quality of orphanages are associated with worse outcome, although post-orphanage settings can alter detrimental developmental paths. The research has taught us much about early adverse environments, but its nonexperimental nature leaves many questions unanswered. An unusually designed study is now underway in which children who have no other available options are being randomly assigned to leave Romanian orphanages for foster homes in which they will receive special developmental intervention (Zeanah et al., 2003). This study avoids the selection bias thought to exist in most orphanage studies, in which children selected to leave the institutions likely displayed fewer difficulties even before leaving.

Another interesting example of research that takes advantage of naturally arising events concerns the effects of poverty on behavior problems (Costello et al., 2003). The Great Smoky Mountain Study is an investigation of the development of mental disorder and the need for mental health services for youth in North Carolina. Over several years data were collected from a sample of children, 25 percent of whom were American Indian. In the middle of the 8-year study, a casino opened on the Indian reservation that equally raised the income of all the American Indian families. This allowed an analysis of the problems of children whose families moved out of poverty, remained poor, or were never poor. Youngsters whose families had moved out of poverty showed a significant decrease in symptoms, whereas no change occurred for the other children. The ex-poor children now exhibited nearly the same low rate of disorder as the never-poor, which was lower than that of the persistently poor. The effect was quite specific to oppositional and conduct problems rather than anxiety and depression. Further analysis suggested that the lessening of problems could be attributed to the family's having increased time to adequately supervise their offspring. An important aspect of this study is that the move out of poverty was not caused by characteristics of the families or the child—and so the findings could more clearly be attributed to the move from poverty itself.

The preceding examples illustrate the benefits derived from conducting experiments of nature. Similar to all research methods, this approach has both strengths and limitations (O'Connor, 2003). It is valuable in the study of psychopathology, in which it is crucial to investigate many life circumstances that cannot be readily brought into the laboratory.

---

subject is exposed to different conditions. During the first period (A), measures are taken of the behavior prior to any intervention. This baseline measure serves as a standard against which change can be evaluated. In period B, the intervention is carried out while the behavior is measured in the identical way. The intervention is then removed, and there is a return to the same condition as during baseline (A).

Figure 4–2 gives a hypothetical example of the ABA design. Appropriate play behavior occurs at low frequency during the baseline, increases during the treatment phase B, and decreases when the intervention is removed in the second A phase. In studies in which behavior improves during intervention, particularly if clinical treatment is the aim, a fourth period, during which the successful intervention is reintroduced, must be added. Typically the relevant behaviors show improvement again.

Nevertheless, the ABA design is limited in that the intervention may make reversal of the targeted behavior unlikely. For example, when treatment results in increased academic skill, the child may not

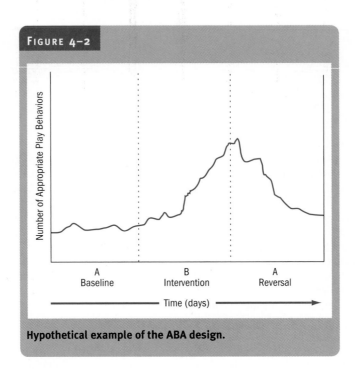

FIGURE 4–2

A
Baseline

B
Intervention

A
Reversal

Time (days)

Number of Appropriate Play Behaviors

Hypothetical example of the ABA design.

display decreases in the skill when intervention is removed. From a treatment standpoint, this is a positive outcome; from a research standpoint, there is no way to demonstrate that the intervention caused the positive behavior. The ABA design also has an ethical problem in that the researcher may hesitate to return to the baseline condition once a manipulation is associated with positive change. And again, although the manipulation may appear responsible for the change, without a return to baseline condition, a definite demonstration of its effects is lacking.

Multiple Baseline Designs. When reversal designs are inappropriate, alternative designs such as multiple baselines may be appropriate. Here, multiple baselines are recorded, which may represent different behaviors of a participant, the same behavior of a participant in different settings, the same behavior of a few different participants, and so on. Intervention is then presented to observe the effects on one of the baselines but not the others. If effects are found, they likely are due to intervention rather than extraneous factors. In this way, multiple baseline designs provide some basis for internal validity.

Consider, for example, the multiple baseline design in which two behaviors of a single child's are recorded across time. After baselines are established for both behaviors, the intervention is made for only one behavior. During the next phase, intervention is applied to the other behavior as well. A clinician may

hypothesize, say, that a child's temper tantrums and throwing of objects are maintained by adult attention to these behaviors. Withdrawal of attention would thus be expected to reduce the behaviors. Support for the hypothesis can be seen in Figure 4–3, a hypothetical graph of the frequency of both behaviors across time periods. Because behavior change follows the pattern of the treatment procedure, it is likely that withdrawal of attention and not some other variable caused the change.

In another commonly used multiple baseline design, baselines are recorded for multiple participants, and intervention follows different time lines (Gliner, Morgan, & Harmon, 2000). In such a study, Koegel, O'Dell, and Koegel (1987) evaluated the effects of a new treatment to enhance language development in children with autism. As Figure 4–4 shows, two children began the old treatment (Teaching Method I) at the same time, and individual baselines were recorded. Child 1 was then provided the new treatment, and Child 2 followed several months later. Data were recorded in the clinic for two kinds of verbal imitation (the dependent variables). Similar patterns of change for both children upon the introduction of the new treatment increase confidence that the treatment actually caused improvement, particularly in immediate imitation. Moreover, external validity is enhanced by the fact that the effect held across two persons.

There are numerous other single-case experimental designs (Hays, 1998; Kratochwill & Levin,

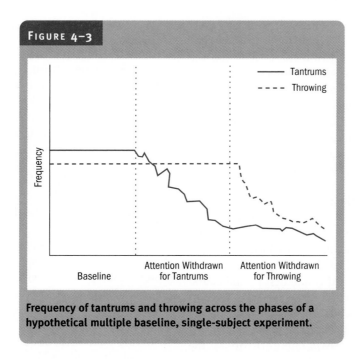

FIGURE 4-3

Frequency of tantrums and throwing across the phases of a
hypothetical multiple baseline, single-subject experiment.

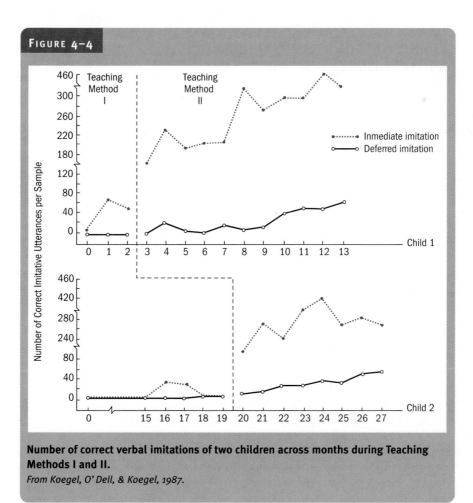

FIGURE 4-4

**Number of correct verbal imitations of two children across months during Teaching
Methods I and II.**
From Koegel, O' Dell, & Koegel, 1987.

1992). They all permit the researcher-clinician to test hypotheses while working with a single or a few subjects and, in the case of treatment, to focus on the child of immediate concern. Moreover, although control of extraneous factors is more easily effected in the laboratory, single-subject research is relatively easy to conduct in natural environments (Morgan & Morgan, 2001). As with case studies, this method has the potential of capturing actual clinic practice and thus can bridge the gap that too often exists between research and practice.

To summarize, the research methods we have discussed in this section vary in several ways, and each has weaknesses and strengths. The experiment and single-subject experiment, in which manipulation occurs in controlled situations, best meet the standards of internal validity and best permit causal inferences to be drawn. Nonetheless, the choice of research method depends on the purpose of the investigation, as well as practical and ethical considerations. Scientific endeavors are enriched by the availability of various methods.

Cross-Sectional, Longitudinal, and Sequential Strategies

Research studies that pose questions regarding development or change over time may be categorized as cross-sectional, longitudinal, or a combination of these strategies known as sequential designs.

CROSS-SECTIONAL RESEARCH

In the cross-sectional strategy, different groups of subjects are observed at one point in time, as if a snapshot were being taken. For instance, aggression displayed by fourth-, sixth-, and ninth-graders could be compared. The strategy is relatively inexpensive and efficient, and it can provide much information.

However, tracing developmental change with cross-sectional research is problematic. If the younger children displayed more aggression, it might be concluded that aggression decreases as children develop. But this conclusion may not be warranted. *Age difference* is not necessarily *age or developmental change*. Perhaps specific experiences of the age groups, due to societal changes over time, are responsible for the findings. The younger children might have watched more violent television or received more reinforcement for aggression during an era characterized by greater violence and aggression.

LONGITUDINAL RESEARCH

In the longitudinal strategy, the same subjects are evaluated over time, with repeated observations or tests. This strategy "sees" development as it occurs. One of the first such studies was Terman's investigation of intellectually gifted children, who were tested several times over many decades beginning in 1921 (Cravens, 1992; Sears, 1975). Terman's research was followed by other now-classic studies that traced the growth of intellectual, social, and physical abilities.

The longitudinal strategy is unique in its capacity to answer questions about the nature and course of development. Does an early traumatic event, such as the death of a parent, play a role in the origin of childhood psychopathology? Can early intervention prevent later problems in infants who experience prenatal difficulties? Does the nature of reading disability change from childhood to adulthood? The longitudinal method can be extremely helpful in answering these kinds of questions.

Still, the method has drawbacks. Longitudinal studies are notably expensive and require the investigators to commit themselves to a project for many years. Retaining participants over long periods of time is also difficult, and the loss of participants can bias the sample. Those who drop out may be more transient, less psychologically oriented, or less healthy than those who continue. Another problem in longitudinal research is that the repeated testing of participants may make them test-wise. Yet, efforts to change or improve the testing instruments make it difficult to compare earlier and later findings.

Finally, participants are not the only ones who change over the years; so may society. Thus, for example, if individuals were followed from birth to age 20 from 1940 to 1960, their development might be different from that of persons of the same age span followed from 1980 to 2000, because of historical variables. The 1940–1960 group would likely have had different experiences than would the 1980–2000 group (e.g., in health care, educational environments). Thus these possible generational, or cohort, effects must be considered in interpreting longitudinal studies.

SEQUENTIAL RESEARCH

To overcome some of the weaknesses of the cross-sectional and longitudinal strategies, researchers interested in developmental change can combine the two approaches in a variety of sequential designs (e.g., Farrington, 1991). Take, for example, a hypothetical

FIGURE 4–5

Age Group	Time		
	I (2000)	II (2003)	III (2006)
A	3	6	9
B	6	9	12
C	9	12	15

Schema of a sequential research design in which children of different ages are examined cross-sectionally and longitudinally.

study in which groups of children of different ages are studied over a relatively short time span. At Time I, children aged 3, 6, and 9 years are examined in a cross-sectional study. Similar examination of the same groups of children occurs again 3 years later at Time II, and again another 3 years later at Time III. Figure 4–5 depicts the study. As can be seen by reading down the columns of the figure, cross-sectional comparisons can be made at three different times. In addition, as can be seen by reading from left to right across the figure, the children (A, B, and C) are studied longitudinally over a 6-year period (2000–2006). The age range in the investigation is thus 12 years (from 3 to 15 years), although the study is completed in 6 years.

Various comparisons can provide a wealth of information from such a sequential design. To consider a simple case, if aggression were found to increase with age at Times I, II, and III (cross-sectional analyses) and also across time for each group of children (the longitudinal analyses), evidence would be strong for developmental change over the entire age range. Moreover, by comparing aggression at age 6, or 9, or 12 (as shaded in the figure), the impact of societal conditions could also be evaluated. It might be found, for example, that aggression at age 9 increased from the year 2000 to 2003 to 2006. Since only one age is involved, this increase is not developmental and likely indicates a change in societal conditions during the years under investigation. Thus, sequential designs can be powerful in separating age differences and developmental changes, while taking generational effects into consideration.

Retrospective and Prospective Strategies

We have already seen the importance of longitudinal studies in tracing development. Here, we further contrast this strategy with the retrospective strategy in the exploration of the causes, predictors, or risk factors in behavioral disorders.

Consistent with the meaning of the word *retrospective*, the retrospective strategy goes back in time. Youth are identified, some of whom display the problem of interest and others of whom serve as comparison controls. Information about their earlier characteristics and life experiences is then collected and compared. The purpose of this follow-back method is to seek hypotheses about the relationship of early variables and the later-observed characteristics. One obvious weakness of this method concerns the reliability of the data. Old records and memories of the past may be sketchy, biased, or mistaken. Another obvious limitation is that the discovery of a relationship between the past and the present does not establish causation, although it suggests possibilities. Despite these shortcomings, retrospective studies are relatively easy to conduct and are a popular approach for suggesting hypotheses about risk factors. When a comparison group is not employed, the results are not as useful.

The prospective strategy is a variation of longitudinal research that goes forward in time. Participants are selected and studied at certain time intervals; as time passes, some of the subjects may

Table 4–2	Some Commonly Used Measures in Epidemiological Research
Prevalence	Rates of a disorder in a population at a specific point in time (e.g., total number of cases or proportion of the population)
Lifetime prevalence	Number or proportion of cases of a disorder diagnosed at any time during life
Incidence	Rates of cases of a disorder diagnosed during a specified time period

show problem behaviors. The researcher then examines the data to determine what variables are linked to the occurrence of the disorder. Again, care must be taken not to assume causation from any revealed associations. Prospective studies also have the drawback of all longitudinal research (e.g., expense, loss of subjects). In addition, when researchers begin these demanding investigations, they must take educated guesses about which variables to observe along the way, and relevant variables can be missed. Another serious drawback is that the number of youth who eventually develop a disorder of interest may be quite small, so that data must be collected for large numbers of participants. Fortunately, risk researchers have found a way to increase the number of participants who may eventually display behavioral dysfunction. Youth are selected who are known to be at risk because of a factor already associated with the disorder, for example, parental psychopathology. Such prospective longitudinal research is called high-risk research. Overall, although high-risk research is difficult and expensive to conduct, it has contributed considerably to our understanding of behavioral disorders.

Epidemiology

Although epidemiological research is not a unique strategy or method of research, its history and importance in the study of psychopathology warrant special consideration. Epidemiology, which has its basis in medicine, initially focused on investigating infectious diseases. It is based on the assumption that disease or disorder can best be understood and dealt with by viewing individuals in the context of the physical and social environments in which disorder develops (Costello & Angold, 1995a). Cases of disorders are identified in large populations, or representative samples of the populations, and several kinds of data about the disorders can be collected.

A main goal of epidemiology is to establish the rates of disorders in populations, which can be measured in several ways (Table 4–2). However, the goals are much more extensive than this. Epidemiology also seeks to understand what factors or other dysfunctions are correlated with the disorder, what the causes and modes of transmission are, what groups of people are at high risk, and how the disorder can be prevented or reduced. Some epidemiologists interested in the mental health of young people are applying the developmental perspective (Costello & Angold, 2000). Briefly put, disorders are viewed from the time at which individuals are exposed to risk factors, to onset of the disorder, to the outcome of the disorder. In this and other approaches, risk might be quantified, for example, by calculating the risk for a disorder in a group that has been exposed to a specific factor compared to a group not so exposed (Tu, 2003).

Although epidemiology focuses on populations, assessment of individuals to determine disorder is a central issue. In the classic Isle of Wight study, clinicians did extensive assessments of children. (See Accent: "Epidemiology on the Isle of Wight.") But both expense and time limitations can preclude lengthy procedures. Thus, standardized structured or semistructured interviews have been increasingly employed, some of which are designed with the goal of diagnosis in mind (Regier & Burke, 2000). Although these instruments can limit the questions that might otherwise be asked by sensitive clinicians, they are more efficient and have the important benefit of facilitating comparison of the findings from different studies.

Epidemiologic research has provided important data on the rates of disorders and on factors correlated with the disorder in large populations. Identifying

ACCENT ● ● ● ● ●

Epidemiology on the Isle of Wight

Michael Rutter and his colleagues began the Isle of Wight studies in the 1960s, in a small rural island off the south coast of England (Costello & Angold, 1995a; Rutter, 1989a). These studies are among the first investigations of the prevalence of behavioral disorders in youth in large populations. Parents and teachers of all children ages 10 and 11 completed questionnaires about the children's emotional and behavioral difficulties. On the basis of cutoff scores, a high-risk group of children was identified, and prevalence for approximately 2,000 children was estimated. Parents, teachers, and the high-risk children themselves were interviewed. Diagnoses of disorders were made through a semistructured interview, conducted by psychiatrists and other clinicians. The overall prevalence rate of children deemed to have disturbances serious enough to require treatment was between 6 percent and 7 percent. Four years later, the survey was repeated with similar methods. The estimated prevalence for the 14- to 15-year-olds was now 21 percent.

Early in the 1970s, another survey compared children on the Isle of Wight with children from a poor inner-city area of London. These youngsters were 10 years of age. The methodology was somewhat different; parents but not the children were interviewed. Prevalence was estimated at 12 percent on the Isle of Wight and 25 percent in the London area.

In addition to presenting prevalence data, the studies provided valuable information about many correlates of disorders and the utilization of mental health services. In the original survey, 7 percent of the children were considered to be in need of treatment, and the overall treatment rate was 1 percent. In the 1970s study of the Isle of Wight population, 12 percent of adolescents were considered in need of treatment, and 2 percent overall were in treatment (16 percent of those with a disorder). Although prevalence data vary over time and studies, a discrepancy between the number of young people in need of treatment and the number who receive treatment has not changed.

correlates aids in formulating hypotheses about risk/causation and helps rule out specific factors. For instance, population studies have failed to show a link between autism and social class, suggesting that social class variables do not cause or put children at risk for this disorder. The epidemiology approach is committed to the prevention and reduction of disorder, and its findings contribute to social policy regarding the delivery of optimal mental health services.

Quantitative and Qualitative Strategies

Most of the research we have examined—and most research employed in studying psychopathology in youth—is quantitative, but more recently there has been increased interest in qualitative strategies. Throughout this century, psychology has been largely committed to the belief that scientific knowledge must be grounded in direct observation (Krahn, Hohn, & Kime, 1995). An integral part of this commitment is placing high value on theory-guided quantitative measurement done by objective

investigators in controlled situations. Quantitative methods are essential to the positivistic or empirical paradigm that underlies much of the scientific progress made in modern times (Eisner, 2003). The values and methods of quantitative research have earned the label of "hard" science, signifying that they follow in the footsteps of sciences such as physics and chemistry.

Advocates of qualitative approaches point to what they see as many shortcomings of quantitative methods. They also emphasize their own assumptions and values (Higgins et al., 2002; Simonton, 2003). Among these are the following:

- The qualitative approach facilitates the study of issues significant to real-world contexts.
- Events can be best understood when they are observed in natural environments rather than in contrived laboratory settings.
- Human behavior and development are best understood from a personal frame of reference when individuals have the opportunity to speak for themselves about their beliefs, attitudes, and experiences, and the meanings in their lives.

- Reported experiences should be viewed as a unified whole rather than in terms of separate variables.

Consistent with these assumptions and values, laboratory and experimental manipulations are avoided in favor of methods such as in-depth interviews, intensive case studies, and life histories (e.g., Habermas & Bluck, 2000). Diaries, letters, and other written records may be examined. Naturalistic observation is also important, with observations being recorded in narration rather than with a restrictive coding of categories. Observer participation, in which the observer engages in and becomes a part of the setting, is valued as a way to collect credible data and to optimize understanding. This overall approach is different in several ways from quantitative research (McGrath & Johnson, 2003). The methods of qualitative research are not new, of course, and they sometimes have been derided as "soft."

It is not unusual to collect large amounts of written data in qualitative research. Once collected, the narrative data are conceptualized, analyzed, and interpreted (Strauss & Corbin, 1990). This process may entail coding or categorizing statements or written observations. If so, the categories are often viewed as arising naturally from the data, not from predetermined expectations or constructed coding systems. What gets coded, how the coding is accomplished, and how data are interpreted vary with the approach and aims of the study. Quantification of data often is minimal, and statistical analysis has little, if any, role.

EXAMPLES OF QUALITATIVE RESEARCH

Examples of topics that have been examined with qualitative methods are life experiences of individuals diagnosed in childhood as learning disabled, parents' adjustment to the birth of a handicapped child, and parents' experiences regarding their child's life-threatening illness (Fiese & Bickman, 1998; Krahn et al., 1995; McNulty, 2003).

As an example of the strategy, consider a study of parents' experiences as participants in a support program called Parent to Parent (Ainbinder et al., 1998). The specific purpose of the program was to provide support for parents who have a child with disabilities, such as mental retardation or chronic illness. Each parent was matched with a supporting parent who had a child with a similar disability. The

supporting parent, who received training for the helping role, provided information and emotional support, usually by telephone. One of the ways in which the program was evaluated was through a qualitative, semistructured interview with participating parents, which explored the impact and meaning of having a supportive parent. The transcribed telephone interviews were coded and categorized according to themes that emerged from the telephone conversations. Among the themes were the way the program was helpful, reasons for program failure, availability and mutuality of support, skills and information learned by the parents, and personal growth of the parents. Here are examples of the parents' interview texts that reflect three of the themes.

Learning by the Parent
I wanted some reassurance that [our daughter] is likely to have most of the same things everybody else has, as far as you know, going to school and having friends, going out and doing things. And [our supporting parent's] daughter's involved in a lot of things. She's got a good life. And that gave me a great deal of hope about the future of our daughter, that she can have a good life, too. (p. 104)

Personal Growth (Emotional Well-Being) of the Parent
I think it really lifted my spirits. I'd get off the phone and I'd just really feel good. Even if things had been going smoothly, I felt myself even higher. And if it has been tough, if I'd had a situation that has been kind of exasperating or trying, just talking about it to somebody who understood, I feel better and I could stop beating myself up a lot. (p. 105)

Failure of the Program
And the other thing I've found with [the supporting parent], her baby is not doing very well sometimes. . . . She asks how my baby is and he has been doing very healthy, thank God. I don't want to say "doing great.". . . We don't share a lot about our children, actually, which is kind of what I would like. . . . I find the only time I really want to call her is if I have a problem because then I don't feel bad about saying "I have this problem and what do you think I should do?" (p. 106)

Overall, the data indicated that talking, sharing, comparing, and learning with others who are perceived as similar can enhance coping and adaptability. The qualitative analysis of Parent to Parent provided understanding of the strengths and weaknesses of the program in a way that other data, collected from quantitative surveys, had not provided.

WEAKNESSES AND STRENGTHS

As with other strategies, qualitative methods have weaknesses. Sample size is often small, huge amounts of data can be difficult and costly to analyze, and questions are raised about reliability and validity. At the same time, qualitative findings can increase basic knowledge, suggest hypotheses, and illustrate and enrich quantitative findings.

It also can be argued that current cultural trends are consistent with qualitative methods. The commitment to contextual research is strong, and there is high regard for applying psychological knowledge to societal problems and concerns—both of which call for community and other natural settings for research (Fabes et al., 2000; Lerner, Fisher, & Weinberg, 2000). In addition, qualitative methods have been considered more appropriate, or particularly useful, in research with ethnic minority groups and women, populations traditionally neglected by quantitative approaches (e.g., Harding, 1991; Sue, 1999).

Qualitative and quantitative strategies have often been viewed as adversarial (Rogers, 2000), and yet they are not necessarily at odds with each other and can be employed together. The qualitative procedures allow flexible, broad-scope investigation, whereas the quantitative procedures allow more traditional data collection and hypothesis testing. The data sets, obtained in different ways, can extend the scope of the findings and can serve as a check on each other, increasing confidence in them.

Ethical Issues in Research

Scientific research is enormously beneficial, but it brings concern about the welfare and rights of participants. Underlying such concern is sensitivity to individual rights—both ethical and legal—and to past documented abuse of research participants. One well-known instance in which the problem of abuse was raised involved research into the natural course of hepatitis. From the 1950s to the 1970s, children with mental retardation who resided in the Willowbrook school in the state of New York were deliberately infected with hepatitis in order to study the disease (Glantz, 1996). Abuse in social science research probably has not been as dramatic as in biomedical research, but ethical issues constantly arise.

For many years, government agencies and professional organizations have published ethical guidelines for research. Philosophical underpinnings were presented in the *Belmont Report: Ethical Principles and Guidelines for the Protection of Human Subjects of Research*, which led to the Code of Federal Regulations pertaining to human research participants (National Commission, 1979). The American Psychological Association's *Ethical Principles of Psychologists and Code of Conduct* addresses the multiple professional roles of psychologists, including that of the researcher (American Psychological Association, 2002). The Society for Research in Child Development publishes guidelines that specifically address research with youth (Table 4–3). There is considerable overlap in the guidelines set forth by different agencies and disciplines.

Following ethical guidelines is a mandate for all researchers. Although doing as mandated may seem quite simple, ethical concerns are often complex. Researchers are often advised to consult with colleagues when in doubt about an issue. Depending on the setting, research projects may also be reviewed prior to their being conducted by federally mandated Institutional Review Boards (IRBs), or by local review boards. IRBs consider such issues as the scientific soundness of the proposed research, consent of the participants, and potential harm and benefits to the participants (Glantz, 1996; Langer, 1985). Particular consideration is given to individuals requiring special protection, such as the young and those with mental disability.

VOLUNTARY INFORMED CONSENT

A fundamental ethical consideration is that individuals must be free to refuse to participate in research, given that they understand the investigation. The principle of informed consent typically requires that subjects be provided information about the investigation and give consent (often written) for their participation (Levine, 1991; Morgan, Harmon, & Gliner, 2001; Weithorn, 1987). Participants should understand the purpose of the research, procedures, risks and benefits, their role, and their option to refuse

TABLE 4–3	ETHICAL STANDARDS FOR RESEARCH WITH CHILDREN

Principle 1: Nonharmful Procedures. No research operation that may physically or psychologically harm the child should be used. The least stressful operation should be used. Doubts about harmfulness should be discussed with consultants.

Principle 2: Informed Consent. The child's consent or assent should be obtained. The child should be informed of features of the research that may affect his or her willingness to participate. In working with infants, parents should be informed. If consent would make the research impossible, it may be ethically conducted under certain circumstances; judgments should be made with institutional review boards.

Principle 3: Parental Consent. Informed consent of parents, guardians, and those acting in loci parentis (e.g., school superintendents) similarly should be obtained, preferably in writing.

Principle 4: Additional Consent. Informed consent should be obtained of persons, such as teachers, whose interaction with the child is the subject of the research.

Principle 5: Incentives. Incentives to participate in the research must be fair and not unduly exceed incentives the child normally experiences.

Principle 6: Deception. If deception or withholding information is considered essential, colleagues must agree with this judgment. Participants should be told later of the reason for the deception. Effort should be made to employ deception methods that have no known negative effects.

Principle 7: Anonymity. Permission should be gained for access to institutional records, and anonymity of information should be preserved.

Principle 8: Mutual Responsibilities. There should be clear agreement as to the responsibilities of all parties in the research. The investigator must honor all promises and commitments.

Principle 9: Jeopardy. When, in the research, information comes to the investigator's attention that may jeopardize the child's welfare, the information must be discussed with parents or guardians and experts who can arrange for assistance to the child.

Principle 10: Unforeseen Consequences. When research procedures result in unforeseen, undesirable consequences for the participant, the consequences should be corrected and the procedures redesigned.

Principle 11: Confidentiality. The identity of subjects and all information about them should be kept confidential. When confidentiality might be threatened, this possibility and methods to prevent it should be explained as part of the procedures of obtaining informed consent.

Principle 12: Informing the Participants. Immediately after data collection, any misconceptions that might have arisen should be clarified. General findings should be given the participants, appropriate to their understanding. When scientific or humane reasons justify withholding information, efforts should be made so that withholding has no damaging consequences.

Principle 13: Reporting Results. Investigators' words may carry unintended weight; thus, caution should be used in reporting results, giving advice, making evaluative statements.

Principle 14: Implications of Findings. Investigators should be mindful of the social, political, and human implications of the research, and especially careful in the presentations of findings.

Summarized from the Report from the Committee for Ethical Conduct in Child Development Research, SRCD *Newsletter (Winter 1990). Society for Research in Child Development, Inc.*

participation. Young children often cannot understand these issues, but in most situations parents must consent for their children who are not of legal age, usually age 18 (Hoagwood, 2003).

What constitutes informed consent for youth? It is suggested that adolescents be given the same information as adults and be asked to sign consent forms (e.g., Ferguson, 1978; Langer, 1985). The same procedure can be used for the school-age child, but researchers need to convey information in more concrete terms, with personal consequences spelled out. At the very least, children as young as 7 years should be asked whether they assent to participate. Miller (1998) suggests that the following information might appropriately be conveyed to the child: a general idea of what will happen ("play a game"), where it will occur ("in Mr. Smith's office"), how many people will be involved ("just you and me"), how long it will take ("about 20 minutes"), whether others will do the same thing ("lots of kids from the class will be doing this"), whether a reward will be offered ("get a little prize at the end") and the opportunity to assent ("Would you like to come?") Obviously, with infants and toddlers, informed consent is an unreasonable expectation, and parental or guardian consent is usually sufficient. Such proxy consent has problems, however, because parent and child needs are not always identical.

A component of informed consent is that it be voluntarily given. The line between voluntariness and coercion can be subtle. Take the situation in which a child may be promised rewards for participation. Does that condition meet the standards for voluntariness? Also, parents can be coerced by social and economic pressures to permit their child's participation. For example, if research participation is desired by an agency that offers therapeutic care, the parents of a child needing care may be afraid to refuse permission.

Privacy

Research may involve the participants' giving personal information. Ethically, they have the right to determine the degree to which their attitudes, behaviors, and the like can be shared with others (Morgan et al., 2001). It is often necessary that the researcher know the identity of the participant who provides specific information; however, information can be kept confidential, and participants can remain unknown in research reports.

Do No Harm and Do Good

A critical ethical principle is that no serious harm—physical, psychological, legal, or economic—be done to participants. Investigations that, for instance, engage children in aggressive acts or expose them to aggressive models raise questions of possible harm. Children also participate in research on the effects of medications, which can entail complex ethical dilemmas. Clearly, the potential for harm must be guarded against.

Moreover, ethical guidelines based on respect for each individual require that benefits be maximized. It is not always possible for individuals to benefit personally from the research that they participate in, but a risk-benefit ratio should be considered (Hoagwood, 2003). In general, when greater benefit to the participant is likely, greater risk of harm is more acceptable. Obviously this guideline has limits in that risk of serious harm is virtually never acceptable.

When a youngster participates in research, informed consent by a parent or guardian, and possibly by the youth, should be obtained. What constitutes informed consent by a youngster is a complex issue.
(Courtesy of A. C. Israel)

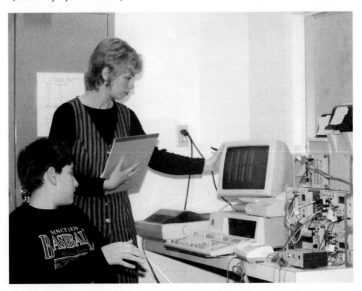

BALANCING IT ALL

In the final analysis, judgments about what is ethical often come down to balancing several factors. The individual's competence to understand and voluntarily consent, the risk of harm, and the possibility of benefit all play a crucial role in guiding ethical standards. The balancing of these factors can be demonstrated by considering informed consent and whether an investigation is of potential personal benefit to the child (Levine, 1991). For instance, parental consent may be sufficient, and the child's refusal to participate may be disregarded when the child may directly benefit and the research risk is minimal. On the other hand, the child's consent may be considered of utmost importance when benefit is unlikely and risk is greater than minimal.

The ethics of research, like other ethical concerns, can never be a completely settled matter. In fact, ongoing discussion and tension are appropriate. The prevailing emphasis on human rights and the recognition of past abuse have led to quite stringent surveillance and guidelines. Reasonable balance must be maintained, however, so that beneficial research goes forward. The need for ethical and sound research is made obvious by the fact that most of the psychosocial treatments and service programs offered to youth lack evidence to support their impact (Hoagwood, 2003).

SUMMARY

FUNDAMENTALS OF RESEARCH

- *The aim of science is to describe phenomena and offer explanations for them.*

- *Scientific knowledge is based on systematic formulation, observation, and interpretation of findings.*

- *Hypothesis testing builds knowledge systematically and is tied to the advancement of theory.*

- *The selection of research participants is critical. Random selection best ensures that a sample represents the population from which it is drawn.*

- *Observation and measurement are accomplished in various ways in various settings. The behavior or concept being studied must be operationalized. Effort must be made to achieve reliable (consistent) and valid (accurate) measurements.*

- *The assumption that events repeat themselves, given the same or similar conditions, places importance on the reliability of research findings. Also crucial is the soundness or correctness of findings. Internal validity is the degree to which alternative explanations for results can be confidently ruled out. External validity refers to generalizability of findings to other populations and settings.*

BASIC METHODS OF RESEARCH

- *Numerous research methods are employed, each suited to particular purposes and each having weaknesses and strengths. Case studies can provide compelling descriptions; correlational methods provide information about the relationships among variables;*

experimental and single-subject experimental methods most directly address causality.

- *Especially useful in studying the effects of variables that cannot be manipulated with humans are experiments of nature, which contrast naturally occurring events.*

CROSS-SECTIONAL, LONGITUDINAL, AND SEQUENTIAL STRATEGIES

- *The cross-sectional strategy examines groups of people at a particular point in time; it can examine age differences. The longitudinal strategy is more appropriate for tracing development. Sequential designs combine the longitudinal and cross-sectional strategies to permit examination of developmental change, age differences, and the influence of generational effects.*

RETROSPECTIVE AND PROSPECTIVE STRATEGIES

- *Retrospective (follow-back) studies and prospective longitudinal strategies are especially useful in identifying risk and possible causal factors. High-risk research prospectively follows the development of persons believed to be at risk for a disorder.*

EPIDEMIOLOGY

- *Epidemiology focuses on studying disorders in populations. It aims to establish the rates and distribution of disorders as well as correlates, risks, causes, course, transmission, and prevention.*

QUANTITATIVE AND QUALITATIVE STRATEGIES

- *Qualitative research places high value on individuals' perception of their experiences in their natural environments. Data are collected through in-depth interviews, life histories, and the like.*

- *The qualitative strategy and the quantitative strategy—which values control, manipulation, and quantitative measures—are often seen as adversarial but can be complementary.*

ETHICAL ISSUES IN RESEARCH

- *Ethical issues in the conduct of research are addressed by several government agencies and professional organizations. Youth and those with mental disability are viewed as requiring special protection.*

- *Central to ethical guidelines are voluntary informed consent, privacy, and assessment of risks and benefits to the participant. These and other issues must be considered by investigators and are evaluated by Institutional Review Boards.*

KEY TERMS

hypothesis testing *(p. 73)*

random selection *(p. 73)*

operational definition *(p. 73)*

validity of measurement *(p. 74)*

reliability of measurement *(p. 74)*

internal validity *(p. 74)*

control *(p. 74)*

external validity *(p. 74)*

naturalistic observation *(p. 75)*

interobserver reliability *(p. 75)*

case study *(p. 76)*

correlational methods *(p. 77)*

positive correlation *(p. 77)*

negative correlation *(p. 77)*

directionality problem *(p. 78)*

experiment *(p. 78)*

independent variable *(p. 79)*

control group *(p. 79)*

dependent variable *(p. 79)*

statistical significance *(p. 79)*

efficacy, effectiveness *(p. 80)*

single-subject designs *(p. 80)*

time-series methods *(p. 80)*

experiments of nature *(p. 81)*

cross-sectional strategy *(p. 84)*

longitudinal strategy *(p. 84)*

generational (cohort) effects *(p. 84)*

sequential designs *(p. 84)*

retrospective strategy *(p. 85)*

prospective strategy *(p. 85)*

high-risk research *(p. 86)*

observer participation *(p. 88)*

informed consent *(p. 89)*

CHAPTER 5

Classification, Assessment, and Treatment

In the next chapter we will be begin our discussion of specific problems and disorders. But before we do this, it is important to ask, "How are behavioral disorders of childhood and adolescence defined, grouped, evaluated, and treated?" In this chapter we will introduce the processes of classification, assessment, and treatment.

The terms *classification*, or *taxonomy*, and *diagnosis* are used to refer to the process of description and grouping. By classification and taxonomy we mean delineating major categories or dimensions of behavioral disorders. This can be done for either clinical or scientific purposes. Diagnosis usually refers to assigning an individual to a category of a classification system. Assessment refers to evaluating youngsters, in part to assist the processes of classification and diagnosis and, in part, to direct treatment. All of these entwined processes are intricately related to the clinical and scientific aspects of child and adolescent disorders.

Classification and Diagnosis

Classification systems are employed to systematically describe a phenomenon. Biologists have classification systems for living organisms, and physicians classify physical dysfunction. Similarly, systems exist to classify behavioral disorders. These systems describe categories or dimensions of problem behaviors. A category is a discrete grouping, for example, anxiety disorder, into which an individual is judged to fit or not fit. In contrast, the term dimension implies that a behavior is continuous and can occur to various degrees. Thus, for example, a child may exhibit high, moderate, or low levels of anxiety.

Any classification system must have clearly defined categories or dimensions. In other words, the criteria for defining a category or dimension must be explicitly stated. Clear and explicit definitions allow for good communication among professionals. Also, diagnostic groupings must be clearly discriminable from one another. It must be demonstrated, too, that a category or dimension actually exists. That is, the features used to describe a category or dimension occur together regularly—in one or more situations or as measured by one or more methods.

Classification systems must be reliable and valid. These terms were applied to research methods in Chapter 4. When applied to classification or diagnosis, the terms retain the general meanings of consistency and correctness but are used in somewhat different ways.

With regard to reliability, interrater reliability refers to whether different diagnosticians use the same category to describe a person's behavior. For example, it addresses the question, is Billy's behavior called separation anxiety by two or more professionals who observe it? Test-retest reliability asks whether the use of a category is stable over some reasonable period of time. For example, is Mary's difficulty again diagnosed as learning disability when she returns for a second evaluation?

There are also questions about the validity of diagnostic systems. To be valid a diagnosis should provide us with more information than we had when we originally defined the category. Thus diagnoses should give us information about the etiology of a disorder, the course of development that the disorder is expected to take, response to treatment, or some additional clinical features of the problem. Does the diagnosis of conduct disorder, for example, tell us something about this disorder that is different from other disorders? Does the diagnosis tell us something about what causes this problem? Does it tell us what is likely to happen to youngsters having this disorder and what treatments are likely to help? Does it tell us additional things about these young people or their backgrounds? The question of validity is thus largely one of whether we know anything we did not already know when we defined the category. Another important aspect of validity is whether our description of a disorder is accurate. Is the way we have described and classified this disorder the way it actually exists? It is often no easy matter to answer this question, as extensive clinical studies may be required.

Finally, the clinical utility of a classification system is judged by how complete and useful it is. A diagnostic system that describes all the behavioral disorders that come to the attention of clinicians in a manner that is useful to them is more likely to be employed.

THE DSM APPROACH

The most widely used classification system in the United States is the American Psychiatric Association's Diagnostic and Statistical Manual of Mental Disorders (DSM). The Tenth Revision of the International Classification of Diseases (ICD) developed by the World Health Organization (1992) is an alternative system that is widely employed. The Diagnostic Classification: 0–3 is a system developed to classify mental disorders of very young children (Zero to Three, 1995). We will focus our discussion on the DSM because it is the dominant system in the United States.

The DSM is often referred to as a clinically derived classification system. Clinically derived classification systems are based on the consensus of clinicians that certain characteristics occur together. These have been described as "top down" approaches (Achenbach, 2000). Committees of experts propose concepts of disorders and then choose diagnostic criteria for defining disorders. It is from these that the development of assessments and evaluations proceed.

The DSM is also a categorical approach to classification; a person does or does not meet the criteria for a diagnosis. Thus it is assumed that the difference between normal and pathological is one of *kind* rather than one of *degree*. This approach also suggests that distinctions can be made between *qualitatively* different types of disorders.

The DSM is an outgrowth of the original psychiatric taxonomy developed by Kraepelin in 1883. There have been a number of revisions of the DSM system. The most recent revisions are the DSM-IV and DSM-IV-TR. The DSM-IV-TR (Text Revision) was published to update information in the text material that accompanies the DSM-IV diagnostic criteria; for example, information about features that may be associated with disorders (e.g., low self-esteem or another disorder) or information regarding cultural, age and gender features, likely course of the disorder, prevalence, familial patterns, and such. However, this revision did not drop or add diagnostic categories, or change the diagnostic criteria for disorders (American Psychiatric Association, 2000).

Historically the classification of abnormal behavior focused primarily on adult disorders. Until relatively recently there was no extensive classification scheme for child and adolescent behavior disorders (Silk et al., 2000). By the 1960s, it had become obvious that a more extensive system was needed. The DSM-II, III, and III-R expanded appreciably the number of categories specific to children and adolescents. In addition, some adult diagnoses could be used for children and adolescents. These revisions and the DSM-IV also involved some changes in the organization of particular categories (American Psychiatric Association, 1968; 1980; 1987; 1994).

The Multiaxial System. The DSM is often described as a multiaxial system. In the DSM-IV-TR all disorders are classified in one of two major groups called axes.

On Axis I the clinician indicates any existing clinical disorder (e.g., Conduct Disorder) or other condition that may be a focus of treatment (for example, an academic problem). On Axis II, Mental Retardation or a Personality Disorder, if present, is indicated. These two axes represent the diagnostic categories that are the core of the DSM system. In addition to these two axes, it is recommended that each individual be evaluated in three other arenas, so that a fuller picture is created. Any current medical conditions that are relevant to understanding or treating the youngster are indicated on Axis III. Axis IV is used to indicate any psychosocial or environmental problems that may affect diagnosis, treatment, or prognosis (e.g., death of a family member, housing problems). Axis V allows the clinician to make a numerical (0 to 100) judgment of the youngster's overall level of adaptive functioning (Global Assessment of Functioning—GAF). For example, a score of

- 100 would indicate superior functioning in a wide range of activities;
- 70 might indicate some difficulty in social or school functioning, but generally good functioning;
- 50 might indicate serious impairment in social or school functioning; and
- 30 might indicate serious impairment in communication or judgment or inability to function in almost all areas.

How this multiaxial system might be used is illustrated by its application to Kevin.

Kevin | Seeking a Diagnosis

Kevin is a 9-year-old third-grader. He was brought to the clinic after his teacher repeatedly called home about his worsening behavior in school. The teacher described Kevin as likeable and friendly, but also said that, among other things, he repeatedly disrupted the class with his antics, hummed and made noises, blurted out answers, and had to be constantly reminded to stay in his seat. He was full of energy on the playground, but seemed to have few playmates and was often last to be chosen for teams. When playing games such as softball, he might be in the outfield concentrating on things in the sky or interesting pebbles on the ground. Although he seemed very bright, Kevin seldom completed his assignments in class. Despite his mother's report of considerable time and effort being spent on getting Kevin to concentrate on and complete his homework, papers sent home were seldom returned and homework was forgotten or left crumpled in his book bag.

At home Kevin is always on the go, his play is noisy and he leaves a trail of toys in his wake. Chores are left uncompleted or not done at all. Kevin's mother describes him as "the sweetest boy imaginable," but also as a "real handful." A physical examination indicates that Kevin is healthy, well nourished, and in good physical condition except for several scrapes, bruises, and healed lacerations. The only significant medical history is a broken wrist at age 3 that resulted from a fall from a high wall that Kevin had managed to climb. Kevin's birth and early development were normal, and he reached developmental milestones at a normal or early time.

To illustrate the use of the DSM-IV-TR multiaxial system, here is Kevin's diagnosis.

Axis I: Attention-Deficit/Hyperactivity Disorder, Combined Type;

Academic Problem

Axis II: No diagnosis

Axis III: None

Axis IV: Impending school expulsion

Axis V: GAF = 50 (serious impairment in schoolwork, moderate impairment in social relationships)

Adapted from Frances & Ross, 2001, pp. 8–11.

The Diagnostic Categories. Table 5–1 presents the major DSM-IV-TR diagnostic categories described as "usually first diagnosed in infancy, childhood, or adolescence." Each category is further divided into subcategories. A clinician may give a youngster any of these diagnoses, or a diagnosis from elsewhere in the DSM can be employed. Some of the other diagnostic categories that might be employed for youngsters are psychoactive substance use disorders, schizophrenia, mood disorders, anxiety disorders, eating disorders, and psychological factors affecting medical condition.

Evaluating the DSM. One of the considerations that has guided the development of the DSM is reliability. In earlier versions, disagreements between diagnosticians (interrater reliability) resulted from inadequate criteria for making a diagnosis. Thus efforts were made starting with the DSM-III to improve interrater reliability by replacing general descriptions of disorders with clear and more delineated diagnostic criteria based on a listing of

TABLE 5–1	THE DSM DISORDERS USUALLY FIRST DIAGNOSED IN INFANCY, CHILDHOOD, OR ADOLESCENCE

Mental Retardation
Learning Disorders
Motor Skills Disorder
Communication Disorders
Pervasive Developmental Disorders
  (e.g., Autistic Disorder)
Attention-Deficit and Disruptive
  Behavior Disorders

Feeding and Eating Disorders of
  Infancy or Early Childhood
Tic Disorder
Elimination Disorders
Other Disorders of Infancy, Childhood,
  or Adolescence (e.g., Separation
  Anxiety Disorder, Selective
  Mutism)

From American Psychiatric Association, 2000.

symptoms. To make a diagnosis of Separation Anxiety Disorder, for example, the following requirements must be met:

- The child must exhibit three or more of eight specific symptoms for at least 4 weeks.

- The onset of these symptoms must occur before the age of 18 (an inclusion criterion).

- The disturbance does not occur exclusively during the course of Pervasive Development Disorder, Schizophrenia, or other psychotic disorder (an exclusion criterion).

This approach has improved communication among clinicians and researchers and has increased interclinician agreement in diagnosis. As would be expected, however, reliability still varies depending on the specific disorder, the source of information (parent, child), and the child's age and sex (Nathan & Langenbucher, 1999; Rapee et al., 1994). Furthermore, evidence of higher levels of reliability has typically been obtained under research conditions in which diagnosticians are given special training and employ procedures different from those likely to be used in typical clinical practice. The reliability of typical clinicians may not be as high (Sonuga-Barke, 1998).

Over time improvements have been made in the DSM system, such as the increased use of structured diagnostic rules and greater comprehensiveness of coverage of child and adolescent disorders. Also, attempts have been made to draw on empirical data in a more consistent fashion (Widiger et al., 1991). However, substantial scientific, conceptual, and political issues remain unresolved (Follette & Houts, 1996; Kupfer, First, & Regier, 2002; Nathan & Langenbucher, 1999).

Because the DSM is the dominant classification system, it is important to mention some of these concerns. One concern is the proliferation of categories and the very comprehensiveness of the system (Houts, 2002). A related fundamental question has also been raised (Follete & Houts, 1996; Silk et al., 2000): Have we overdefined pathological behavior—have we too broadly defined children's behavior as deviant (cf. Richters & Cicchetti, 1993)? Designating common misbehaviors or various problems in academic skill areas such as reading and mathematics as mental disorders are examples of this concern.

It has also been argued that diagnostic research has focused on reliability and clarity of communication. Although this focus is clearly of importance, there is another question: Does the DSM provide an accurate representation of the nature of disorders? Whether a system is useful or helpful for clinicians is a different question from whether it is a good description of the true nature of clinically significant differences in psychological functioning (Sonuga-Barke, 1998; Waldman, Lilienfeld, & Lahey, 1995). In fact, there is still considerable concern regarding the validity of many of the DSM child and adolescent categories, even among those who are, in large part, sympathetic to the system's approach to classification (Cantwell, 1996).

Indeed, the goal of validating the DSM-defined syndromes has been elusive. For example, validity would be indicated by findings of treatments or etiologies *specific to particular syndromes*. However, as Kupfer, First, and Regier (2002) point out, many medications have been reported as being effective in treating several DSM disorders rather than being a specific treatment. Similarly, with regard to etiology, results of twin studies have challenged the assumption that separate syndromes have a different underlying genetic basis. For example, it has been found that two syndromes, generalized anxiety disorder and major depressive disorder, may share genetic risk factors (Kendler, 1996).

Another concern regarding the validity of the current DSM approach is its categorical approach. For example, research supported the validity of three subtypes of Attention-Deficit Hyperactivity Disorder (Lahey et al., 1994). However, Hudziak and his colleagues (1998) conducted structured diagnostic assessments of a large community sample of adolescent female twins. Their findings again supported the existence of the subtypes but suggested that the subtypes were best conceptualized as three dimensions (continuously distributed between clinical and nonclinical levels) rather than three disease categories. Thus, is the nature of these disorders categorical (as represented in the DSM), dimensional, or both? Researchers also point out that the practice of dichotomizing continuous symptoms to form a disorder category and a nondisorder category results in reduced statistical power and may lead to misleading research outcomes. The category versus dimension question will be a central issue as we continue to consider systems of classification (Beauchaine, 2003; Pickles & Angold, 2003; Widiger & Clark, 2000).

Another concern with the current DSM system is the problem of comorbidity. This term is used to describe the situation in which youngsters meet the criteria for more than one disorder. The use of the term is controversial and some prefer the term co-occurrence (Lilienfeld, Waldman, & Israel, 1994; Widiger & Clark, 2000). Comorbidity implies the simultaneous existence of two or more distinct disorders in the same individual. Such co-occurrence is frequently reported (see Accent: "Co-Occurrence: A Common Circumstance") and has led some to question the DSM approach to classification. Do these youngsters have multiple distinct disorders or are there other ways of understanding the existence of a wide variety of difficulties that might suggest alternative approaches to classification?

Even if one accepts the value of retaining the DSM approach, there are multiple ways to conceptualize a child's or an adolescent's meeting the diagnostic criteria for more than one disorder (Angold, Costello, & Erkanli, 1999; Carson & Rutter, 1991). It may be that many disorders have mixed patterns of symptoms. For example, mood disorders may be characterized by a mixture of depression and anxiety. Another alternative is that there are shared risk factors: Some of the same risk factors lead to the

problems used to define both disorders. Or perhaps the presence of one disorder creates an increased risk for developing the other disorder. A related idea is that the second problem is a later stage in a developmental progression in which earlier problems may or may not be retained, even as additional difficulties develop. For example, it has been suggested that for some children and adolescents, anxiety and depression are related in this kind of developmental sequence (Brady & Kendall, 1992).

These are only some of the possible hypotheses to explain "comorbidity." The issues involved in understanding co-occurrence of disorders are complex, and at present the solution to this issue remains unclear. However, the frequency of co-occurrence and the conceptual issues it raises are at the heart of how we conceptualize child and adolescent psychopathology (Jensen, Martin, & Cantwell, 1997; Lilienfeld, 2003).

Some have argued that the DSM promotes a disease/medical model that emphasizes biological etiology and treatment, and that conceptualizes disorder as being within the child rather than resulting from the interaction of the child and the environment (Silk et al., 2000; Sonuga-Barke, 1998; Sroufe, 1997). Despite its acceptance and use, the system may be considered as fundamentally inconsistent with some approaches to children's problems (Beauchaine, 2003; Scotti et al., 1996). For example, the DSM does not employ situational variability to moderate diagnostic labels. This omission may be problematic for a behavioral perspective or others in which situational factors and functional relationships are presumed to influence behavior. The DSM's de-emphasis on the context of problem behavior along with a view of disorder in terms of discrete categories rather than continuous attributes also may make it less compatible with a developmental psychopathology perspective.

The DSM approach to classification has also been criticized regarding its relative inattention to issues of age, gender, and cultural context (Achenbach, 2000; Nathan & Langenbucher, 1999; Silk et al., 2000). The DSM-IV-TR does include, in the text that accompanies each set of diagnostic criteria, a section on "Specific Culture, Age, and Gender Features" that may alert clinicians to variations associated with developmental level, gender, and culture. Nevertheless, diagnostic criteria are largely the same for both genders and all ages and cultures.

This approach may have important consequences. Achenbach (2000), for example, points out that if one applies a set of fixed cutpoints (number of

ACCENT ● ● ● ● ●

Co-Occurrence: A Common Circumstance

Children and adolescents who are evaluated by professionals in clinic or school settings often present with several different problems. These problems frequently are viewed as fitting the criteria for a number of different disorders, and thus clinicians often give these children or adolescents more than one diagnosis. How best to conceptualize these instances of co-occurrence or comorbidity is an ongoing concern. The description of Samuel illustrates this common circumstance.

Samuel   A Case of Co-Occurring Disorders

Samuel, an 11-year-old child, was referred to a clinic for attempted suicide after he had consumed a mixture of medicines, prescribed to his mother, in an attempt to kill himself. Samuel had slept at home for almost two days, when he was finally awakened by his mother and brought to the hospital.

Samuel lived in an inner-city neighborhood and since second grade had been in repeated trouble for stealing and breaking into empty homes. He had academic difficulties, was assigned to a

special reading class, and was truant from school on a number of occasions. His mother may have experienced several major depressive episodes, sometimes drank heavily, and may have relied on prostitution for income. Samuel's father had not been in contact with the mother since Samuel was born.

At his interview, Samuel appeared sad and cried at one point. He reported having severe "blue periods," the most recent of which had been continuous for the past month. During these periods he thought that he might be better off dead. Samuel also reported that he had recently started to wake up in the middle of the night and had been avoiding his usual neighborhood "gang."

Samuel was given a diagnosis of Major Depressive Disorder, and a diagnosis of Dysthymia (a milder but more chronic form of depression) was also considered. In addition he received a diagnosis of Conduct Disorder, Childhood Onset Type, and a diagnosis of Reading Disorder.

Adapted from Rapoport & Ismond, 1996.

---

symptoms needed for diagnosis) to diagnostic criteria, age and gender differences in prevalence rates for disorders may be reported. The same applies to cultural differences. We could ask, however, are these real differences in rates of disorders? As an example, DSM-IV-TR indicates that ADHD is much more frequent in males. This gender difference in diagnosis has led to the literature on ADHD being based largely on males. However, even nondeviant boys exhibit higher rates of behaviors characteristic of ADHD than do girls. Thus the gender difference in ADHD might be an artifact of higher base rates of these behaviors in boys. If these gender differences in base rates in the population were considered in setting diagnostic cutpoints, would gender differences in prevalence of ADHD still emerge? Similarly, reported declines in the rates of ADHD diagnoses

with age may also be an artifact of the age-related decline in base rates of ADHD behaviors.

Furthermore, research suggests that the potentially complex interactions of culture, context, and behavior deserve further attention. For example, Weisz and colleagues (1993), in comparing 11- through 15-year-old Kenyan, Thai, African American, and Anglo youth, describe variations in behavioral and emotional problems across various cultural groups. And Gil and colleagues (2000) found that among U.S.-born Latino adolescent males, a greater predisposition toward alcohol involvement emerges over time as traditional values of family, cohesion, and social control deteriorate. It seems clear that future diagnostic and classification systems will need to pay increasing attention to issues of cultural and developmental context (Alarcon et al., 2002; Pine et al., 2002).

Many observers accept the DSM system as a dominant reality in the present zeitgeist. A classification system, like anything else, is viewed as being influenced by the general social atmosphere within which it exists. With the various criticisms and concerns in mind, we turn to an alternative approach to classification.

EMPIRICAL APPROACHES TO CLASSIFICATION

The empirical approach to classification of behavioral problems is an alternative to the clinical approach to taxonomy. It is based on the use of statistical techniques to identify patterns of behavior that are interrelated. The general procedure is for a parent or some other respondent to indicate the presence or absence of specific behaviors in the youngster. The information from these responses is quantified in some way. For example, a "0" is marked if the child does not exhibit a certain characteristic, a "1" is given if a moderate degree of the characteristic is displayed, and a "2" is indicated if the characteristic is clearly present. Such information is obtained for a large number of youngsters. Statistical techniques such as factor analysis are then employed, and groups of items that tend to occur together are thus identified (Achenbach, 1998). These groups are referred to as factors or clusters. The term syndrome is also often employed to describe behaviors that tend to occur together, whether identified by empirical or clinical judgment procedures. Thus, rather than relying on clinicians' views as to which behaviors tend to occur together, empirical and statistical procedures are employed as the basis for developing a classification scheme.

Substantial evidence exists for two broadband syndromes, or general clusters of behaviors or characteristics. One of these clusters has been given the various labels of internalizing, overcontrolled, or anxiety-withdrawal. Descriptions such as anxious, shy, withdrawn, and depressed are some of the characteristics associated with this grouping. The second grouping has been variously labeled externalizing, undercontrolled, or conduct disorder. Fighting, temper tantrums, disobedience, and destructiveness are some of the characteristics frequently associated with this pattern.

Among the instruments used to derive the two broadband clusters just described is the Child Behavior Checklist (CBCL), which is completed by the parents of children 6 to 18 years of age (Achenbach &

Rescorla, 2001). The Teacher Report Form (TRF) is a parallel instrument completed by teachers of children 6 to 18 years old, and the Youth Self-Report (YSR) is completed by youths from 11 to 18 years of age. In addition to the two broadband syndromes labeled Internalizing and Externalizing, research with these instruments has also identified eight empirically defined, less general, or narrowband syndromes. These syndromes are described in Table 5–2. Every child who is evaluated receives a score on each of the syndromes, and a profile of syndrome scores for a particular child can be described (see Figure 5–1). This approach to classification evaluates each youngster on several dimensions.

Thus this approach to classification differs from the clinical approach of the DSM in several ways. One important difference between the two approaches is how groupings are defined and formed (empirically versus clinical consensus). A second important difference is that the empirical approach to classification views problems as dimensional rather than categorical. It suggests that differences between individuals are quantitative rather than qualitative and that the difference between normal and pathological is one of degree rather than one of kind (Achenbach, 2000).

Empirically based classifications also employ data from normative samples as a frame of reference for judging the problems of an individual youngster. For the CBCL, TRF, and YSR, for example, there are two sets of norms available against which to compare an individual child's or adolescent's scores. A youngster's scores can be compared with norms for nonreferred youngsters or with norms based on young people referred for mental health services. There are separate norms for each sex in particular age ranges, as rated by each type of informant. Thus there are separate parent informant CBCL norms for boys 6 to 11, boys 12 to 18, girls 6 to 11, and girls 12 to 18, and separate similar norms for teacher and for youth informants (Achenbach & Rescorla, 2001).

In evaluating the behavior problems of an 11-year-old boy named Jason, for example, one could compare Jason's scores on the empirically based syndromes derived from his parents' reports with two sets of norms: norms of parent reports for nonreferred 11-year-old boys and norms of parent reports for clinic-referred 11-year-old boys. Scores based on Jason's teacher's TRF could be compared with two similar sets of norms of teachers' reports for 11-year-old boys. And scores based on Jason's own YSR could be compared with norms of responses of nonreferred and clinic-referred boys his age.

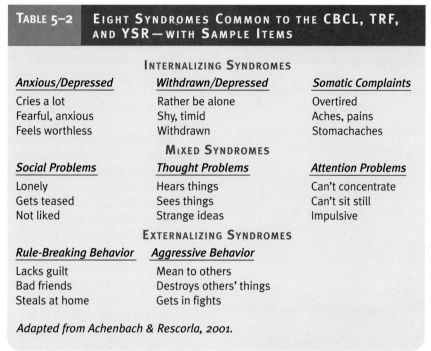

TABLE 5–2 EIGHT SYNDROMES COMMON TO THE CBCL, TRF, AND YSR—WITH SAMPLE ITEMS

INTERNALIZING SYNDROMES

Anxious/Depressed

Cries a lot
Fearful, anxious
Feels worthless

Withdrawn/Depressed

Rather be alone
Shy, timid
Withdrawn

Somatic Complaints

Overtired
Aches, pains
Stomachaches

MIXED SYNDROMES

Social Problems

Lonely
Gets teased
Not liked

Thought Problems

Hears things
Sees things
Strange ideas

Attention Problems

Can't concentrate
Can't sit still
Impulsive

EXTERNALIZING SYNDROMES

Rule-Breaking Behavior

Lacks guilt
Bad friends
Steals at home

Aggressive Behavior

Mean to others
Destroys others' things
Gets in fights

Adapted from Achenbach & Rescorla, 2001.

FIGURE 5–1

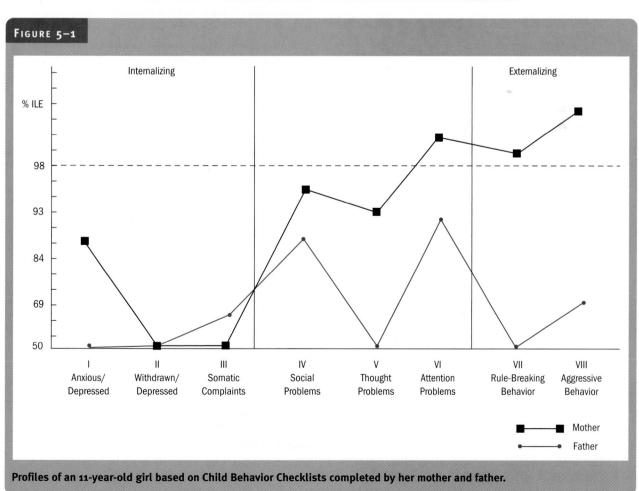

Profiles of an 11-year-old girl based on Child Behavior Checklists completed by her mother and father.

It is worth noting that, in addition to the dimensions/syndromes described above and outlined in Table 5–2, the Achenbach instruments can be scored to yield scales that correspond to some DSM categories (Achenbach, Dumenci, & Rescorla, 2003). These DSM-oriented scales are one way that the two approaches might be compared.

Reliability. Reliability studies of empirically derived systems generally indicate that problem scores are quite reliable. The pattern of reliability is both interesting and informative (Achenbach & Rescorla, 2001).

Test-retest reliability correlations from two ratings by the same informant are often in the .80 and .90 ranges. So, for example, correlation for the Total Problems score on the CBCL is .94. Interrater reliability between different informants observing the child in the same situation is also quite good, although lower than for two evaluations by the same person. The mean agreement of mothers and fathers on the CBCL problem scales is .76.

Level of interrater agreement, however, is notably lower between raters who observe youngsters in distinctly different situations. The average correlation between parents' and teachers' Total Problem Scores, for example, is .35. And youngsters' Total Problem Scores also are significantly, but modestly, related to parents' (.54) and teachers' (.21) ratings. These lower correlations may reveal something about young people's behavior, rather than just about the reliability of the approach to classification. There may be aspects of a youngster's behavior that are consistent across time and situations, but a youngster's behavior may also vary considerably with different individuals and in different situations. Also, certain attributes may be more or less evident to different individuals or to other persons as compared with the youngsters themselves (e.g., aggression versus feelings of loneliness). Such findings alert us to the possible limitations and bias of any one rater's perspective, whether obtained by responses to a particular instrument or by clinical interview (Achenbach, McConaughy, & Howell, 1987; Hay et al., 1999; Youngstrom, Loeber, & Stouthamer-Loeber, 2000). Figure 5–1 illustrates the differences in responses of a young girl's mother and father to the Child Behavior Checklist. Differing perceptions of two informants may provide important information to a clinician.

Validity. The validity of empirically derived classification systems is indicated by a variety of studies. The same broadband syndromes have emerged in a variety of studies employing different instruments, different types of informants, and different samples, suggesting that the categories reflect valid distinctions (Achenbach & Rescorla, 2001). The findings show that the syndromes are valid ones because they emerge under a variety of conditions. Cross-cultural studies that find similar syndromes add further support (Achenbach, Rescorla, & Ivanova, 2005; de Groot, Koot, & Verhulst, 1996).

Validity is also supported when differences in scores relate to other criteria. Indeed, a comparison of youngsters referred for outpatient mental health services with a sample of nonreferred young people matched for SES, age, and gender indicated that the clinical sample differed significantly from the nonreferred sample on all scores (Achenbach & Rescorla, 2001).

Also, differences between youngsters with high scores on different syndromes can address the validity of empirically identified syndromes. For example, comparison of young children with internalizing problems and those with externalizing problems has shown that they may differ with respect to the type of negative emotion they express and the style of emotion regulation and control that they exhibit (Eisenberg et al., 2001). Similarly, evidence suggests different correlates for the two syndromes *within* the externalizing domain (see Table 5–2). For example, research suggests stronger biochemical correlates and heredity and greater developmental stability for the aggressive than for the rule-breaking syndrome (Achenbach, 1998; Eley, 1997). Finally, scores on empirically derived syndromes have also been shown to predict outcomes such as future problems, use of mental health services, and police contacts (Achenbach et al., 1995; Stanger et al., 1996). Such findings support the validity of the empirical and dimensional approach to classification.

THE IMPACT OF LABELS

As we have already noted, classification and diagnosis are intended to facilitate understanding and treatment of behavior disorders. Although classification is intended as a scientific and clinical enterprise, it can be seen as a social process. The diagnostic label becomes a social status, which carries implications for how people are thought of and treated. If this impact is negative, the label actually detracts from the original purpose of categorizing—that of helping young people (Kliewer & Biklen, 1996).

Formal classification has as its stated intent the categorization of disorders, not persons. Indeed,

Cantwell, one of the creators of the current DSM approach, noted:

Any classification system classifies psychiatric disorders of childhood; it does not classify children. Thus it is correct to say, "Tommy Jones has infantile autism." It is incorrect to say "Tommy Jones, the autistic" . . . (Cantwell, 1980, p. 350).

Often ease of communication is the reason for a particular phrasing. For example, the term *autistic children* may be employed rather than repeating the phrase *children receiving the diagnosis of autism.* Thus it is realistic to expect the use of terms such as *autistic children* or *depressed children*, despite the intent to avoid misplacement of labels.

In light of such practices, it is important to be aware of the potential negative effects of the labeling process. Labels can lead to stigmatization and to even further behavioral problems and social difficulties (Milich, McAninch, & Harris, 1992). The potential negative perceptions that labels may produce is illustrated in a study by Foster and Salvia (1977). Teachers were asked to view a videotape of a boy and to rate his academic work and social behavior. The tape displayed age- and grade-appropriate behavior in all cases, but some teachers were told that the boy was learning disabled, whereas others were told that he was normal. Teachers watching the "learning disabled" boy rated him as less academically able and his behavior as more socially undesirable than did teachers watching the "normal" child.

Expectations regarding a child may be based not only on his or her actual behavior but also on biased perceptions resulting from a label. The child then may respond to others' reactions in ways that maintain or exacerbate problem behaviors. The negative expectation that may be transmitted by labels is suggested by the findings of a study by Briggs and colleagues (1994). Adults read vignettes of a 6-year-old child engaged in aggressive behavior on a school playground. The stories varied regarding the family history of the child (normal, mother dying of cancer, sexually abused). After reading the vignette, the adults completed a questionnaire about their expectations regarding the behavior of the child. Results indicated that the adults had different expectations regarding the sexually abused child; for example, that the sexually abused child would have more behavior problems and lesser achievement than either of the other two children.

Labels may not always produce negative expectations, however. Some suggest that labels provide an "explanation" for the child's problematic behavior. The adult is provided with an understanding of why the child is behaving in this manner, thus reducing the likelihood of negative reactions and creating more appropriate expectations of what a child can be expected to do. That labels do not always lead to negative expectations is illustrated in a study by Wood and Valdez-Menchaca (1996). Adults interacted with four children, one of whom had previously been diagnosed with an expressive language disorder (ELD). The adults were randomly assigned to one of two conditions: The first was a nonlabel condition in which the child with ELD was not identified, and the second was a label condition in which the child with ELD was identified. Adults in the nonlabel group ranked the child with ELD as significantly less likable, less productive, and less academically competent than the other children. Adults in the label group did not. They had observed the same inappropriate behaviors as the adults in the nonlabel group but they appeared to have been more accepting of such behavior.

Nevertheless, the use of labels may invite other difficulties. The danger of overgeneralization is one concern: It may incorrectly be assumed that all youngsters labeled with attention-deficit hyperactivity disorder, for example, are more alike than they actually are. Such an assumption readily leads to neglect of the individual child or adolescent. It is also possible that if people react to the youngster as a member of a category, then the youngster may behave in a manner consistent with the expectations of the label.

Finally, concern has been voiced that diagnostic labeling minimizes attention to the interpersonal and social context in which the child's behavior exists (Silk et al., 2000; Sroufe, 1997). Traditional diagnostic categories ignore the fact that a youngster's problems "belong" to at least one other person—the one who is identifying or reporting the problems (Algozzinne, 1977; Lilly, 1979b). As we shall see throughout this book, there is much evidence that supports the notion that how a youngster is described and viewed may reflect as much on who is doing the describing as it does on the behavior of the child or adolescent.

Many experts involved in the study and treatment of young people are concerned about the problems of categorical labels, and these experts advocate to reduce the possible harmful effects. However, categorization is embedded in our thinking and contributes to the advancement of knowledge. Completely discarding categorization is neither desirable nor possible. Thus it is important to strive to improve classification systems and at the same time to be sensitive to social factors inherent in the use of categories, the social status imparted by a label, and the impact of labels on the young person and others (Adelman, 1996; Hobbs, 1975).

Assessment

Evaluating child and adolescent problems is a complex process. By the time a youngster comes to the attention of a clinician, the presenting problem is usually, if not always, multifaceted. But because assessment is the first part of any contact, the professional's knowledge of the problem is limited. Both of these factors, as well as common sense and caution, argue that the best interests of the young person are most likely served by a comprehensive assessment of multiple facets of the youngster and his or her environment.

CONDUCTING A COMPREHENSIVE ASSESSMENT

Alicia | An Initial Assessment

The parents of 6-year-old Alicia were seeking assistance in understanding her problems and ways to help their daughter improve her adjustment at home and school and with her peers. The parents described Alicia as impulsive, moody, and having difficulty in school. The initial information provided by the parents indicated that several male relatives on the mother's side of the family were mentally retarded and that one of these relatives had recently been diagnosed with a fragile X syndrome chromosomal disorder. The clinician hypothesized that Alicia might be a fragile X carrier because females are carriers for the defective gene associated with the syndrome. Based on initial information the clinician also hypothesized that Alicia might have ADHD and a learning disability.

Information about Alicia was gathered from several sources: the parents (interview, rating scales, daily behavioral logs, observation of parent-child interactions), the teacher (rating scales, academic performance and test scores), and Alicia herself (interview, direct observation, psychoeducational testing). Information obtained during the assessment revealed that Alicia had many characteristics of females who carry the fragile X chromosome. This was discussed with the parents and referral for a genetic evaluation revealed that this was indeed the case. The assessment also indicated that Alicia met the diagnostic criteria for ADHD and that she had a learning problem.

In addition, evaluation revealed that Alicia's parents provided a structured yet stimulating environment for her. Alicia had friends, successfully engaged in age-appropriate activities, and felt loved by her parents. She also realized that her impulsive behavior created problems for herself and her family. Positive aspects of the case were Alicia's desire to please and her good social skills, warm and loving parents, and supportive home and school environments.

The assessment lead to intervention strategies that included a change in Alicia's class placement and resource support, support for the family, referral to a support group for parents of children with fragile X syndrome, behavior management techniques for the parents, and brief individual work with Alicia to help her recognize her strengths and cope with her difficulties. The clinician indicated that Alicia would likely adapt and continue to develop successfully, but further assessment and intervention might be needed as new challenges were encountered.

Adapted from Schroeder & Gordon, 2002, pp. 49–50.

As we shall see throughout our discussion, behavioral disorders in youngsters are complex, often encompassing a variety of components rather than a single problem behavior. Furthermore, these problems are typically best understood as arising out of and being maintained by multiple influences. Such influences include biological factors; various aspects of the youngster's behavioral, cognitive, and social functioning; and influences of the family and other social systems such as peers and school. Thus an assessment must be comprehensive in evaluating a variety of potential presenting problems, measuring a variety of aspects of youngsters themselves, and assessing various contexts and other individuals.

Information must be obtained from a variety of sources (e.g., the youngster, parents, teachers) to assess problems that may vary by context or be displayed differently with different individuals. A child may behave differently at home, in school, or in playing with his or her peers. Also, observers may view the same or similar behaviors differently. A mother who is depressed and experiencing a variety of life stresses may be less able to tolerate minor deviations from expected behavior. Such differences in perception may be important both in coming to understand the presenting problems and in planning interventions. Assessment thus requires the use of multiple and varied methods as well as familiarity with assessment instruments for individuals of many different ages. The process requires considerable skill and sensitivity.

Assessment may be best accomplished by a team of clinicians carefully trained in the administration and interpretation of specific procedures and instruments. It is desirable for clinicians to employ evidence-based assessment—procedures for which there is empirical evidence regarding validity (Lilienfeld, Lynn, & Lohr, 2003; McClure, Kubiszyn, & Kaslow, 2002). As we will see later in this chapter when we discuss empirically supported treatments, such evidence-based or empirically supported practice is an ongoing goal.

Because assessment is usually conducted immediately on contact with the young person or family, it demands special sensitivity to anxiety, fear, shyness, manipulativeness, and the like. If treatment ensues, assessment should be a continuous process, so that new information can be gleaned and the ongoing effects of treatment can be ascertained. In this way, the clinician remains open to nuances and can avoid rigid judgments about a multifaceted and complex phenomenon.

THE INTERVIEW

The General Clinical Interview. The general clinical interview is clearly the most common method of assessment (Watkins et al., 1995). Information on all areas of functioning is obtained by interviewing the youngster and various other people in the social environment.

Whether the youngster will be interviewed alone will probably vary with age. An older child or adolescent generally is more capable and is more likely to provide valuable information. Nevertheless, clinicians often elect to interview even the very young child in order to obtain their own impressions.

Preschool and grade school children can provide valuable information if appropriate developmental considerations are involved in tailoring the interview to the individual child (Bierman & Schwartz, 1986; Kamphaus & Frick, 1996). For example, an adultlike face-to-face interview may be intimidating for a young child, but this difficulty may be reduced if the interview is modeled after a more familiar play or school task. Alternatively, some professionals recommend that the assessment of preadolescent children begin with more structured aspects of the evaluation (e.g., rating scales, structured interviews) rather than the relatively unstructured general clinical interview (Kamphaus & Frick, 1996).

Most clinicians seek information concerning the nature of the problem, past and recent history, present conditions, feelings and perceptions, attempts to solve the problem, and expectations concerning treatment. The general clinical interview is used not only to determine the nature of the presenting problem and perhaps to help formulate a diagnosis but also to gather information that allows the clinician to conceptualize the case and to plan an appropriate therapeutic intervention.

Structured Diagnostic Interviews. The general clinical interview is usually described as open-ended or unstructured. Because such interviews are most often conducted in the context of a therapeutic interaction and are employed along with a variety of other assessment instruments, it has been difficult to evaluate reliability and validity. Structured diagnostic interviews have arisen in part to create interviews that are likely to be more reliable. They also have been developed for the more limited purpose of deriving a diagnosis based on a particular classification scheme, such as the DSM, or for use in research or in screening large populations for the prevalence of disorders. These interviews can be conducted with the youngster and/or parent(s). The Anxiety Disorders Interview for Children (ADIS-IV; Silverman & Albano, 1997), the Diagnostic Interview for Children and Adolescents (DICA; Reich, 2000), and the Schedule for Affective Disorders and Schizophrenia for School-Age Children (K-SADS; Ambrosini, 2000) are examples of these diagnostic interviews.

In the unstructured general clinical interview, there are no particular questions that the clinician must ask, no designated format, and no stipulated method to record information. That is not to say that there are no guidelines or agreed-on procedures for conducting an effective interview. Indeed, there is an extensive literature on effective interviewing

(Cox & Rutter, 1985; Nietzel, Bernstein, & Milich, 1994). However, unstructured interviews are intended to give the clinician great latitude. In contrast, structured diagnostic interviews consist of a set of questions that the interviewer asks the youngster. In addition, rules are provided for how the interview is to be conducted, and explicit guidelines are provided for how the youngster's responses are to be recorded and scored (McClellan & Werry, 2000).

PROBLEM CHECKLISTS AND SELF-REPORT INSTRUMENTS

Problem checklists and rating scales were described in our discussion of classification (pp. 101–102). There are a wide variety of these instruments. Some are for general use—such as the Child Behavior Checklist (Achenbach & Rescorla, 2001), the Personality Inventory for Children (Wirt et al., 2001), and the Behavior Assessment System for Children (Reynolds & Kamphaus, 1992; 2002). Others are used with particular populations. The Conners Parent Rating Scale-Revised (Conners et al., 1998b), for instance, can be used when attention-deficit hyperactivity disorder needs to be assessed. A considerable empirical literature suggests that these instruments may be valuable tools for clinicians and researchers (Frick & Kamphaus, 2001).

For example, the parent-reported problems and competencies of youth assessed at intake into mental health services and demographically matched nonreferred youngsters were compared (Achenbach & Rescorla, 2001). Checklist scores clearly discriminated between the clinic and nonreferred children regarding both behavior problems and social competencies. Figure 5–2 illustrates the differences between clinic and nonreferred children.

A general rating scale may thus help a clinician judge the child's adjustment against norms for referred and nonreferred populations. This procedure can help in evaluating the appropriateness of the referral. Once a particular presenting problem is identified, the use of a more specific rating scale might also be part of the clinician's assessment strategy.

Furthermore, rating scales completed by different informants may help the clinician gain a fuller appreciation of the clinical picture and of potential situational aspects of the child's problem. For example, the Teacher Report Form can supplement a parent's report on the Child Behavior Checklist (CBCL). The CBCL, TRF, and YSR in the Achenbach instruments make it possible to compare multiple informants' reports about the child with respect to a common set of problem items and dimensions. When two or more respondents using

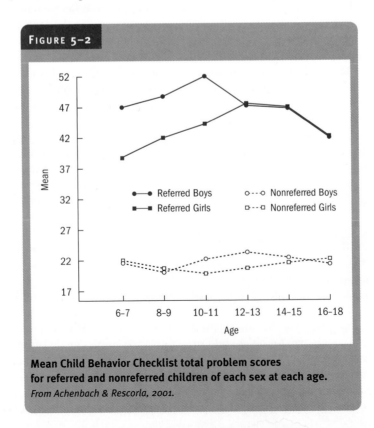

FIGURE 5-2

Mean Child Behavior Checklist total problem scores for referred and nonreferred children of each sex at each age.
From Achenbach & Rescorla, 2001.

these instruments describe a child, a statistic can be computed indicating the degree of agreement. This degree of agreement for a particular child can then be compared with the degree of agreement between comparable informants for a large representative sample. Thus it is possible to know whether the degree of agreement between Tommy's mother and his teacher is less than, similar to, or greater than the average mother-teacher agreement about boys in Tommy's age range.

In addition, the clinician or researcher may also draw on a wide variety of self-report measures to assess the youth's own report (Reynolds, 1993). Here, too, there are general measures and there are also self-report measures to assess specific problems such as anxiety and depression. Instruments also are available to assess constructs related to adjustment such as self-control and self-concept (Connell, 1985; Harter, 1985; Kovacs, 1992; Reynolds & Richmond, 1985). Many of these measures will be described in later chapters that focus on particular child and adolescent problems.

Parents and other adults can also be asked to complete self-report instruments about themselves. These instruments may assess specific problems, for example, a parent's own anxiety or depression. However, a wide variety of aspects of adult functioning can be important. For instance, the feelings, attitudes, and beliefs of adults, particularly with respect to the child or adolescent, may be assessed (e.g., the Parenting Stress Index—Abidin, 1995); or aspects of the family environment may be measured (e.g., the Family Environment Scale—Moos & Moos, 1994; and the Parent-Adolescent Relationship Questionnaire—Robin, Koepke, & Moye, 1990). Such assessment can provide important information about the social environment and factors that may contribute to problem behavior. The use of such measures is consistent with conceptualizing the presenting problem as complex and existing in a social context.

Observational Assessment

Early attempts to observe children's behavior made use of diaries or continuous observations and narrations that were deliberately nonselective (Wright, 1960). From this tradition evolved observations of a more focused, pinpointed set of behaviors that could be reliably coded by observers (Bijou et al., 1969).

More recent observational methods have most often come from workers with a behavioral/social learning perspective. Behavioral observations are frequently made in the child's natural environment,

although situations are sometimes created in clinic or laboratory settings to approximate naturally occurring interactions. Observations range from single, relatively simple, and discrete behaviors of the child, to observations of the child and peers, to complex systems of interactions of family members (Kolko, 1987; Israel, Pravder, & Knights, 1980; Reid, 1978). Clearly, ongoing interactions are more difficult to observe and code than are the behaviors of a single individual; however, they are likely to be theoretically and clinically relevant. An example of an observational method used by Dadds and his colleagues was described in Chapter 4 (p. 75).

The first step in any behavioral observation system involves explicitly pinpointing and defining behaviors. Observers are trained to use the system and note whether a particular behavior or sequence of behaviors occurs. Research indicates that a number of factors affect reliability as well as validity and clinical utility of observational systems (Hops, Davis, & Longoria, 1995). For example, the complexity of the observational system and changes over time in the observers' use of the system (observer drift) are two such factors. Reactivity (whether the knowledge that one is being observed changes one's behavior) is often cited as the greatest impediment to the utility of direct observation. Careful training, periodic monitoring of observers' use of the system, and use of observers already in the situation (e.g., teachers) are some recommended ways to reduce distortions in the information obtained from direct observation.

Behavioral observations are the most direct method of assessment and require the least inference. The difficulty and expense involved in training and maintaining reliable observers is probably the primary obstacle to their common use in nonresearch contexts. Since direct observation has long been considered the hallmark of assessment from a behavioral perspective, attempts have been made to create systems that are more amenable to widespread use. Direct observation is, however, just one aspect of a multimethod approach to behavioral assessment that can include self-monitoring of behavior, interviews, ratings and checklists, and self-report instruments.

Projective Tests

At one time the most common form of psychological test employed to assess children was the projective test. These tests are less commonly used today, in large part because of a continuing debate regarding lack of empirical norms, reliability, and validity (Anastasi & Urbina, 1997; Kleiger, 2001; Knoff, 1998).

Projective tests were derived from the psychoanalytic notion of projection as a defense mechanism: One of the ways in which the ego deals with unacceptable impulses is to project them onto some external object. It is assumed that the impulses cannot be expressed directly. Therefore, many projective tests present an ambiguous stimulus, allowing the youngster to project "unacceptable" thoughts and impulses, as well as other defenses against them, onto the stimulus. Projective tests are also used by some clinicians in a manner that involves less psychodynamic inference (Chandler, 2003). For example, the youngster may see an ambiguous stimulus in terms of past experiences and present desires and thus be prompted to report these. Also, analyses that examine formal aspects of a test response—for example, the distance between human figures that the child draws—may be used. Interpretations are then made on the basis of this response style rather than on the content of the response.

In the Rorschach test, the youngster is asked what he or she sees in each of ten ink blots (Figure 5–3). The most commonly used methods for scoring and interpretation are based on characteristics of the response, such as the portion of the blot responded to (location), factors such as color and shading (determinants), and the nature of what is seen in the blot (content) (Exner & Weiner, 1995).

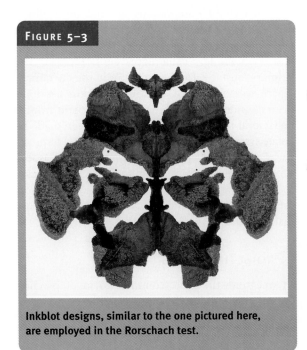

FIGURE 5–3

Inkblot designs, similar to the one pictured here, are employed in the Rorschach test.

The Human Figure Drawing, or Draw-a-Person test, (Koppitz, 1984; Machover, 1949) requires the youngster to draw a picture of a person and then a second person of the opposite sex. The House-Tree-Person technique (Buck, 1992) asks the child to draw a house, a tree, and a person. In the Kinetic Family Drawing technique (Burns & Kaufman, 1970), the child is asked to draw a picture of everyone in the family, including himself or herself, "doing something." Typically the clinician then asks questions about the drawings. Murray's (1943) Thematic Apperception Test (TAT), the Children's Apperception Test (CAT) (Bellak & Bellak, 1982; Bellak & Abrams, 1997), and the Roberts Apperception Test for Children (McArthur & Roberts, 1982) provide the youngster with pictures for which he or she is asked to make up a story. Figure 5–4 presents pictures similar to those used in the CAT.

INTELLECTUAL-EDUCATIONAL ASSESSMENT

The evaluation of intellectual-academic functioning is an important part of almost all clinical assessments. Intellectual functioning is a central defining feature for disorders such as mental retardation and learning disabilities, but it may also contribute to and be affected by a wide variety of behavioral problems. Compared with most other assessment instruments, tests of intellectual functioning tend to have better normative data, reliability, and validity. Although our present discussion of these instruments is brief, additional information will be presented in later chapters.

Intelligence Tests. By far the most commonly employed assessment devices for evaluating intellectual functioning are tests of general intelligence. In fact, they probably are the most frequently employed assessment device other than the interview. The Stanford-Binet (Roid, 2003); the Wechsler tests—the Wechsler Preschool and Primary Scale of Intelligence (Wechsler, 2002) and the Wechsler Intelligence Scale for Children (Wechsler, 2003); and the Kaufman Assessment Battery for Children (Kaufman & Kaufman, 2004) are some of the intelligence tests widely used in clinical settings. All are individually administered and yield an intelligence (IQ) score. The average score is 100, and an individual score reflects how far above or below the average person of his or her age an individual has scored.

Intelligence tests have long been the subject of heated controversy. Critics have argued that the use of IQ scores has resulted in intelligence being viewed

FIGURE 5-4

Drawings similar to those employed in the CAT.

as a real thing rather than as a concept. Furthermore, IQ scores have led to intelligence being viewed as a rigid and fixed attribute rather than as something complex and subtle. Critics also claim that intelligence tests are culturally biased and have led to social injustice (cf. Kamin, 1974; Kaplan, 1985). Although intelligence tests are popular and useful in predicting a variety of outcomes, criticism and continued concern with legal, ethical, and practical issues demand that they be used cautiously and that ongoing attention be paid to test improvement and monitoring of appropriate usage (Kamphaus, 1993; Perlman & Kaufman, 1990).

Developmental Scales. Assessment of intellectual functioning in very young children, and particularly in infants, requires a special kind of assessment instrument. A popular measure is the Bayley Scales of Infant Development (Bayley, 1993). The Bayley can be used to assess children from 2 to 42 months of age and includes a Motor Scale, a Mental Scale, and a Behavior Rating Scale that assesses behavioral style (e.g., attitude, interest). Performance on developmental tests yields a developmental index rather than an intelligence score. Unlike intelligence tests, which emphasize language and abstract reasoning abilities,

developmental scales emphasize sensorimotor skills and simple social skills. For example, the Bayley examines the ability to sit, walk, place objects, attend to visual and auditory stimuli, smile, and imitate adults. Perhaps because they tap different abilities, there is only a low correlation between developmental scales, particularly when administered early, and measures of intellectual functioning later in childhood. Early developmental test scores may, however, be predictive of later intellectual functioning for children with serious developmental disabilities (Sattler, 1992).

Ability and Achievement Tests. In addition to assessing general intellectual functioning, it is often necessary or helpful to assess functioning in a particular area. Ability and achievement tests have been developed for this purpose (Katz & Slomka, 1990; Stetson & Stetson, 2001). The Wide Range Achievement Test (Wilkinson, 1993) and the Woodcock Reading Mastery Tests (Woodcock, 1998), for example, are two measures of academic achievement that are administered to an individual youngster. Tests such as the Iowa Test of Basic Skills (Hoover, Dunbar, & Frisbie, 2001) and the Stanford Achievement Test (Harcourt Assessment, 2003) are group-administered achievement tests employed in many school settings. Specific ability and achievement tests are particularly important in working with children with learning and school-related problems.

ASSESSMENT OF PHYSICAL FUNCTIONING

General Physical Assessment. Assessment of physical functioning can provide several kinds of information valuable to understanding disordered behavior. Family and child histories and physical examinations may reveal genetic problems that are treatable by environmental manipulation. For example, phenylketonuria (PKU) is a recessive gene condition that is affected by dietary treatment. Avoidance of phenylalanine in the child's diet prevents most of the cognitive problems usually associated with the condition. In addition, diseases and defects may be diagnosed that affect important areas of functioning either directly (for example, a urinary tract infection causing problems in toilet training) or indirectly (for example, a sickly child being overprotected by parents). Also, signs of atypical or lagging physical development may be an early indication of developmental disorders that eventually influence many aspects of behavior.

Psychophysiological Assessment. Psychophysiological assessments are often conducted when one is considering anxiety disorders or other problems where arousal level is of concern. Because of the equipment that is necessary, such assessments are more common in research settings than in general clinical practice. Evaluation of heart rate, muscle tension, and respiration rate are examples of assessments conducted. Measures of electrical activity in the autonomic nervous system, such as skin conductance, or in the central nervous system, such as the electroencephalogram (EEG), are also often aspects of psychophysiological assessments.

Assessment of Nervous System Functioning. The assessment of the nervous system is considered important to understanding a variety of psychopathology. Disorders such as mental retardation, autism, learning disabilities, and attention-deficit disorders have received particular attention. The development of assessment techniques has benefited research regarding the relationship of brain disturbance to psychopathology and the mechanisms through which medications have their effects (Charney et al., 2002).

Current assessment of presumed neurological dysfunction often consists of a combination of direct neurological approaches and indirect neuropsychological assessment. Such assessment requires the coordinated efforts of neurologists, psychologists, and other professional workers.

NEUROLOGICAL ASSESSMENT. A number of procedures directly assess the integrity of the nervous system (Teodori, 1993). The computer has revolutionized neurological assessment, and new techniques have become the primary mode of evaluation. The electroencephalograph (EEG) is a procedure with a long history that has been improved by the availability of computers (Kuperman et al., 1990). The EEG and the event-related potential (ERP) require placing electrodes on the scalp that record activity of the brain cortex in general or during a time when the individual is engaged in information-processing tasks. Individual differences in EEG activation patterns have been found in studies of fearful and inhibited children and in infants of depressed mothers, and the ERP has been used to study learning and language disorders (Dawson et al., 1997; Nelson & Bloom, 1997).

Newer technologies such as brain imaging techniques have vastly improved our ability to assess brain structure and function, and have begun to be employed in research and clinical work with children and adolescents (Eliez & Reiss, 2000; Filipek, 1999; Tuma, 2001; Zametkin, Ernst, & Silver, 1998). For example, computerized tomography, or the CT scan (also referred to as computerized axial tomography—CAT scan), allows tens of thousands of readings of minute variations in the density of brain tissue, measured from an X-ray source, to be computer processed so that a photographic image of a portion of the brain can be obtained. The resulting image can reveal subtle structural abnormalities of the brain.

Positron emission tomography (PET) scans determine the rate of activity of different parts of the brain by assessing the use of oxygen and glucose, which fuel brain activity. The more active a particular part of the brain is, the more oxygen and glucose used. After a small amount of radioactive substance has been injected into the bloodstream, amounts of radiation appearing in different areas of the brain are measured while the person engages in some particular task. Many images are taken of the brain, and a computer-produced color-coded picture is created that indicates different levels of activity in different parts of the brain. Newer developments allow PET scans to estimate the production of brain neurotransmitters.

Magnetic resonance imaging (MRI) is a noninvasive procedure. A large magnet and radiowaves are used to create a magnetic field around the brain. The cells in the brain respond to the radiowaves and a 3D computer image of the brain is created. Functional magnetic resonance imaging (fMRI) uses the same technology and produces images by tracking subtle changes in oxygen in different parts of the brain. Particular parts of the brain are called on to perform some task, and these regions receive increased blood flow and thus increased oxygen. The MRI scanner detects these changes and produces pictures of the brain that indicate areas of activity. Related techniques, magnetic resonance spectography (MRS), permit the study of various brain chemicals. These relatively new assessment tools are likely to become increasingly important in research and individual assessment (Peterson, 2003).

NEUROPSYCHOLOGICAL EVALUATIONS. Neuropsychological evaluations employ tests that primarily assess general intellectual abilities, learning, sensorimotor and perceptual skills, verbal skills, and memory. From the individual's performance on these tasks, inferences are made about brain functioning.

Neuropsychological evaluations originally were employed in the hope that they could detect the presence or absence of brain damage. The failure to find evidence of brain damage in suspected populations and the development of direct methods of assessing the central nervous system have resulted in a shift of focus. One current emphasis is distinguishing groups of behavioral and learning disorders that are presumed to have a neurodevelopmental etiology. For example, any test that discriminates learning disabled from normal learners might be considered neuropsychological in this sense (Taylor, 1988b). Interest also exists in assessing changes arising out of alterations in the central nervous system, for example, evaluating recovery from head injury (Middleton, 2001).

The current interest in neuropsychological evaluation is attributable, at least in part, to increased sensitivity to the needs and legal requirements of providing services to children with handicapping conditions—some of whom exhibit problems presumed to have a neurological etiology. Also, advances in medicine have resulted in increasing numbers of children who survive known or suspected neurological trauma. The increase in survival rates of infants born prematurely is one example. Children with acute lymphocytic leukemia who receive treatment that includes substances injected directly into the spinal column and radiation to the head are yet another example.

Neuropsychological evaluation appreciates the need for broadly based assessment (Bengtson & Boll, 2001). Two of the most widely used collections of instruments are the Halstead-Reitan Neuropsychological Test Battery for Children (Reitan & Wolfson, 1993) and the Luria-Nebraska Neuropsychological Battery—Children's Revision (Golden, Purisch, & Hammeke, 1985). As the term *battery* implies, these instruments consist of several subtests or scales, each intended to assess one or more abilities. The use of a broad spectrum of tests is the usual strategy employed in neuropsychological approaches to assessment (Fletcher & Taylor, 1997; Luciana, 2003). The spectrum may be fixed batteries like the preceding, or flexible batteries based on combinations of existing tests. Figure 5–5 illustrates the Bender Visual-Motor Gestalt Test (Bender, 2003), which is used to assess visual-motor function. Table 5–3 lists some of the domains that are assessed by these various tests. The importance of these various domains of functioning will become apparent as we discuss specific disorders.

Neuropsychological evaluation of children (pediatric neuropsychology) is still a relatively young field. Part of this ongoing effort is the development of instruments that derive from evolving research on cognitive development, neurological development, and brain-behavior relationships. In addition, several traditional testing instruments used with adults continue to be employed in pediatric neuropsychological evaluations. To enhance the meaningfulness of these evaluations, efforts have been undertaken to compile pediatric normative data for these traditional neuropsychological instruments (Baron, 2004). Research is also being directed toward developing strategies that more clearly specify impairment and guide rehabilitation.

Treatment

Interventions designed to prevent and treat problems are an important concern of clinicians and researchers alike. In this discussion we provide a general sense of what may be involved in the treatment process and in clinical work with youngsters and their families. In the chapters that follow, we examine various multi-component interventions for specific disorders.

Clinicians are likely to be called on to help children and adolescents whose problems are multifaceted. A youngster, for example, may simultaneously have problems involving anxiety and depression,

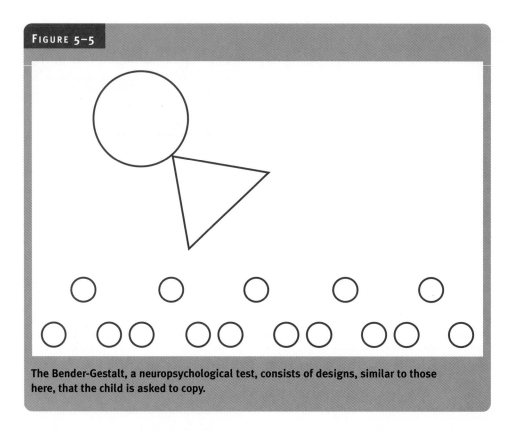

FIGURE 5-5

The Bender-Gestalt, a neuropsychological test, consists of designs, similar to those here, that the child is asked to copy.

social problems with peers, and academic difficulties. Indeed, it is likely that a youngster will have multiple presenting problems. Furthermore, problems may vary with situations and may be more broadly defined to include other individuals. Thus clinical attention often will be directed not only to the child but also to family members and perhaps school personnel and peers. Treatment is therefore likely to contain multiple elements that address different aspects of the clinical problem.

Multiple professionals from differing backgrounds may be involved in providing services to youngsters and their families. The clinician's theoretical conceptualization of the presenting problem and of the process by which change occurs will influence how treatment is provided. For example, a psychologist whose conceptualization of the disorder emphasizes environmental influences and contingencies is most likely to consider treatments that include both the youngster and significant others and that focus on modifying environmental stimuli and the consequences of behavior. Similarly, a psychologist whose conceptualization emphasizes cognitive processes is most likely to consider interventions aimed at modifying particular cognitions. Psychiatrists or other physicians whose conceptualization may emphasize biological contributions may be inclined to employ medications in their treatments. Nevertheless, many professionals conceptualize the development of behavioral problems as being subject to multiple influences and realize that treatment may involve multiple components.

TREATMENT MODES AND SETTINGS

Treatment may be delivered in a variety of modes (e.g., individual therapy, family therapy) and in different settings (e.g., office, school). Indeed, clinicians

TABLE 5-3	SOME OF THE DOMAINS EVALUATED IN NEUROPSYCHOLOGICAL ASSESSMENT

General intelligence
Memory/Learning
Language function
Attention
Motor function
Visual-motor function
Higher-order planning
Academic achievement

Adapted from Luciana, 2003.

may employ several different modes of treatment and youngsters may receive help in a variety of settings.

Individual and Group Psychotherapy. Therapists may see the young client in individual one-to-one sessions. A therapist working with a child with an anxiety disorder may, for example, help the child to understand the problem and teach the child active ways of confronting and coping with the anxiety. These sessions may resemble the verbal interchanges and activities of adult sessions or, particularly with young children, may employ play as the primary mode of interaction between the therapist and the child. In addition, various forms of individually focused treatment may be delivered in a group rather than in an individual format. The same assumptions and methods that guide individual therapies may be used. Although the group format may be selected in order to offer services to larger numbers of children and adolescents, there are other rationales for this choice (Johnson, Rasbury, & Siegel, 1997). Groups offer the opportunity for socialization experiences not present in the individual mode. Group treatment also may be more appealing to young people because it is less threatening, demonstrates that peers have difficulties, and often includes opportunities for activities not likely to occur in one-to-one relationships with an adult therapist.

Play Therapy. The need to alter treatment procedures to fit the young child's level of cognitive and emotional development is one factor that has produced nonverbal modes of working with children. The use of play as a therapeutic vehicle is a common mode of treatment with young children. This is consistent with the importance of play in the development of young children (Rubin, Fein, & Vandenberg, 1983; Smith, 1988). Rather than relying exclusively on abstract verbal interactions, the therapist uses play to facilitate communication. Play may also be a more familiar way for the child to interact with an adult and may help make the child feel at ease. A therapist may make use of puppets and dolls, have the child draw or paint, employ specially created board games, or use children's books that tell the story of children with similar difficulties. In this manner, most practitioners use play as a part of therapy. However, using play itself as a therapeutic vehicle and play therapy as a more structured and distinct approach to treatment also exists (Ablon, 1996; Russ, 1995). The two most well-known perspectives on play therapy are derived from the psychodynamic and the client-centered perspectives.

Early psychoanalytic therapists agreed that child patients required a different mode of treatment than the highly verbal, free association mode used in adult psychoanalysis. Melanie Klein (1932) was among the

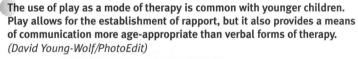

The use of play as a mode of therapy is common with younger children. Play allows for the establishment of rapport, but it also provides a means of communication more age-appropriate than verbal forms of therapy.
(David Young-Wolf/PhotoEdit)

first to emphasize play therapy. She gave the child's play a prominent role in the therapeutic process and used it as the basis for psychoanalytic interpretation. In contrast, Anna Freud viewed play as only one potential mode of expression and placed less emphasis on symbolic interpretation of play. For example, she disagreed with Klein that a child's opening a woman's handbag symbolically expresses curiosity regarding the contents of the mother's womb. Rather, the child may be responding to a previous experience in which someone brought a gift in a similar receptacle (A. Freud, 1946). The contemporary psychoanalytic position tends to favor Anna Freud's positions on play (Johnson et al., 1997). Indeed, the term *play therapy* as it is used today refers to child treatment in which play is the major mode of expression, regardless of the therapist's theoretical orientation.

Another major influence on the evolution of play therapy was the work of Virginia Axline, who developed her approach from the client-centered perspective associated with Carl Rogers. The basic principles outlined by Axline (1947) remain the guidelines for contemporary client-centered play therapy (Johnson et al., 1997). The principles of the client-centered approach are the same for adults and children of varying ages. The therapist makes adjustments in communication style to create the appropriate accepting, permissive, and nondirective therapeutic environment. The use of play with young children helps to create such an environment.

Family Therapy and Parent Training. Clinicians may also work with the youngster's parents or family. We will see that working with the family can take many forms. Here we highlight a few examples.

Including members of the family as part of the therapeutic process is consistent with defining a clinical problem as existing in a social context and of the family being a very important part of that context. Clinicians who treat adolescents with eating disorders, for example, frequently work with the entire family to change maladaptive family interaction patterns that may contribute to the development and maintenance of eating disorders (Robin, 2003; Steiner & Lock, 1998). Similarly, clinicians working with youngsters with significant conduct problems, such as juvenile offending and substance abuse, may seek to develop critical competencies and establish adaptive relationships by involving the family as well as other social systems in the treatment process (Henggeler & Lee, 2003).

Parent training is a common therapeutic tool employed by clinicians. Many professionals have taken the position that change in the child's behavior may best be achieved by producing changes in the way that the parents manage the child. This viewpoint is consistent with the observation that it may often be the parent's perception, along with the child's actual behavior, that results in the child being referred for treatment. Siblings of the referred youngster may also have similar problems (Fagan &

Treatment may involve the youngster, parent(s), or other family members.
(Michael Newman/PhotoEdit, Inc.)

Najman, 2003). This is another reason that it may be helpful to work with the entire family or provide parents with a general set of parenting skills.

Parent training procedures have been applied to a wide variety of childhood problems. A number of approaches have emerged, and a number of popular books appear on the shelves of bookstores everywhere. However, in terms of systematic applications and research, most work has come from the social learning/behavioral approach.

Behavioral parent training has received a great deal of clinical and research attention, and a number of reviews and discussions have appeared (Kazdin, 1997; McMahon & Wells, 1998; Webster-Stratton & Hancock, 1998). Original efforts focused on teaching parents to manage the consequences, or contingencies, that they applied to children's behavior. More recent approaches include a wider variety of skills, such as skills in verbal communication and expression of emotion. In addition, the impact of stressors such as socioeconomic disadvantage, single-parent status, social isolation, and maternal depression on the effectiveness of parent training may be considered (Forehand, Furey, & McMahon, 1984; Hartman, Stage, & Webster-Stratton, 2003; Israel, Silverman, & Solotar, 1986; Wahler & Dumas, 1984; Webster-Stratton & Hooven, 1998). Parent training is now frequently employed as part of a multifaceted approach to treatment. Other components may include additional therapeutic work with the parent, direct work with the child, or work with the teacher and the school (Kazdin, 2003; Webster-Stratton & Reid, 2003).

Pharmacological Treatment. Pharmacological treatments (medications) are part of the interventions employed for a variety of childhood and adolescent behavior disorders (McClellan & Werry, 2003; Riddle, Kastelic, & Frosch, 2001). These treatments are often used in combination with other modes of treatment. Medications that affect mood, thought processes, or overt behavior are known as psychotropic or psychoactive, and thus the term psychopharmacological treatment is often employed. Two examples of some of the pharmacological agents employed with children and adolescents include stimulants for attention-deficit hyperactivity disorder and selective serotonin reuptake inhibitors for obsessive-compulsive disorder, depression, and anxiety disorders. Table 5–4 provides examples of the generic and brand names of some of the medications in these and other classes of psychotropic agents.

The decision whether to use psychopharmacological treatment is, in part, determined by the nature of the presenting problem. However, other considerations such as possible side effects and a family's comfort with using medication need to be considered and discussed. Racial/ethnic and income differences seem to contribute to the rates of psychotropic medication use with young people. For example, Leslie and colleagues (2003) report that among a large sample of families receiving services through publicly funded services, caregivers of African American and Latino children were less likely to report past-year use of such medication than caretakers of white children. Higher income and private insurance also were associated with a greater likelihood of psychotropic medication use.

Psychotropic drugs produce therapeutic effects by their influence on the process of neurotransmission. Poling, Gadow, and Cleary (1991) describe some of the ways that these medications can affect neurotransmission:

- By altering the body's production of a neurotransmitter
- By interfering with the storage of a neurotransmitter
- By altering the release of a neurotransmitter
- By interfering with the inactivation of a neurotransmitter or the reuptake of a neurotransmitter
- By interacting with receptors for a neurotransmitter

For some psychoactive drugs, there is a specific and clearly hypothesized mechanism for action, whereas for others the specific reasons for effectiveness are unknown.

Children and adolescents have been increasingly treated with psychotropic medications. Indeed, an appreciable increase in children as young as 2 to 4 years of age receiving medications such as stimulants and antidepressants has caused particular concern (Greenhill et al., 2003a; Zito et al., 2000). Unfortunately, research regarding the efficacy and safety of many of these medications for children and adolescents lags behind their use (Gracious et al., 2004; Jensen et al., 1999; Riddle et al., 2001). Increased research holds promise for improved safety and effectiveness of psychotropic medications (Greenhill et al., 2003b).

Treatment Settings. Often when one thinks of treatment one thinks of therapy that takes place in the clinician's office. Treatment can also take place in other settings. For example, professionals may choose to conduct interventions in the schools. This may be done as a matter of convenience because this is a

TABLE 5-4	SOME OF THE PSYCHOTROPIC MEDICATIONS USED IN THE TREATMENT OF CHILDREN AND ADOLESCENTS	
CLASS	**GENERIC NAME**	**SELECTED TRADE (BRAND) NAMES**
Stimulants	Methylphenidate	Ritalin, Concerta
	Dextroamphetamine	Dexedrine
	Dextroamphetamine/ Amphetamine	Adderall
Selective Serotonin Reuptake Inhibitors (SSRIs)	Citalopram	Celexa
	Fluoxetine	Prozac, Serafem
	Fluvoxamine	Luvox
	Paroxetine	Paxil
	Sertraline	Zoloft
Tricyclic Antidepressants	Amitriptyline	Elavil, Endep
	Clomipramine	Anafranil
	Desipramine	Norpramin
	Imipramine	Tofranil, Norfranil
	Nortriptyline	Pamelor, Aventyl
Non-Tricylic Antidepressants	Bupropion	Wellbutrin
	Nefazodone	Serzone
	Venlafaxine	Effexor XR
Antianxiety (Anxiolytics)	Alprazolam	Xanax
	Buspirone	Buspar
	Chlordiazepoxide	Librium
	Clonazepam	Klonopin
	Diazepam	Valium
	Lorazepam	Ativan
Antipsychotics (Neuroleptics)	Clozapine	Clozaril
	Haloperidol	Haldol
	Olanzapine	Zyprexa
	Quetiapine	Seroquel
	Resperidone	Risperdal
	Trifluoperazine	Stelazine
	Ziprasidone	Zeldox
Mood Stabilizers	Carbamazepine	Tegretol
	Lithium	Eskalith, Lithobid
	Valproate	Depakote, Depakene

setting where youngsters spend an appreciable portion of their day. The school setting may also facilitate the ability to treat youngsters in groups. Also, working in the school may allow the clinician to intervene in the setting where many problems may occur.

RESIDENTIAL TREATMENT. It is sometimes necessary to remove children from their family home. Thus, alternative residences are another setting in which treatment may occur. Residential treatment is usually considered a mode of intervention for severe behavior problems (Johnson et al., 1997; Lyman & Wilson, 2001). The problems may be so difficult to treat that working with the youths on an outpatient basis while they continue to reside at home does not provide enough contact or control. Concern may also exist that children may harm themselves or others and, therefore, that closer supervision is necessary. The child may also be removed from the home because circumstances there are highly problematic, suggesting that successful interventions could not be achieved at home. Unfortunately, the lack of availability of alternative placements or appropriate funding can result in children being placed in institutional settings when interventions in the home with additional support provided to the family or in less restrictive environments, like foster homes, might be successful. Typically, professionals strive to use interventions that allow youngsters to remain at home and that permit families to stay intact. On the other hand, treatment in residential settings is often undertaken when other modes of intervention have not proven successful.

Inpatient child psychiatry units in general medical hospitals or psychiatric hospitals are one form of residential treatment. There has been increased use of hospitalization, but at the same time, the modal length of stay has dramatically decreased (Pottick et al., 2001). Thus rather than being used for long-term stays of many months or years, short-term stays of several weeks to a month are employed. Residential treatment may also occur in settings such as group homes, units in nonmedical settings, therapeutic camping programs, and juvenile facilities that are part of the legal/judicial system. Treatment in such settings usually involves a variety of services, including therapeutic, educational, and vocational interventions. Because programs differ so much in what the actual content is, they have been difficult to evaluate, and we know less than we would like about their effectiveness (Johnson et al., 1997; Lyman & Wilson, 2001).

EMPIRICALLY SUPPORTED TREATMENTS

In subsequent chapters in this text, as part of our discussion of various disorders of youth, we examine treatments for specific disorders. Interventions for which there is empirical support are emphasized— that is, treatments that have been deemed worthy through scientific evaluation. This approach follows from one of the themes of this text, an orientation toward empirical approaches and the methods of science.

This same emphasis, along with an increasing demand that professionals be accountable for the effectiveness of the services they offer, was among the considerations that led professional organizations to identify such interventions. As part of this evolving effort (Chorpita, 2003; Ollendick & Davis, 2004; Weisz & Kazdin, 2003) several different terms, including empirically supported treatments and evidence-based treatments have been used to describe treatments for which such evidence exists. Also, different criteria have been proposed to designate treatments as evidence-based or empirically supported.

For example, the Society of Clinical Psychology (a division of the American Psychological Association) formed the Task Force on Promotion and Dissemination of Psychological Procedures. The task force issued a report that indicated which treatments were empirically supported, specifying the level of research necessary to establish a treatment as empirically supported (Chambless, 1996; Chambless & Hollon, 1998; Chambless et al., 1996). Three categories were noted: well-established treatments, probably efficacious treatments, and experimental treatments. The primary distinction was between *well-established* and *probably efficacious* treatments. The principal differences between the two categories are as follows:

- Well-established treatments have been shown to be superior to placebo interventions or other treatments, whereas probably efficacious treatments have been shown to be superior only to a waiting-list or no-treatment control.
- Well-established treatments have been shown to be effective in studies by at least two different teams of investigators, whereas probably efficacious treatments need not be (e.g., two studies by the same investigators are adequate).

The research for both categories must be well-controlled group or single-subject designs, and characteristics of the treatment participants (e.g., age, sex, ethnicity, diagnosis) must be clearly specified. Furthermore, treatment must have been conducted with treatment manuals. Treatment manuals describe precisely the treatment procedures that are followed. This method allows for the evaluation of treatment integrity—that is, the degree to which therapists in the study have followed the treatment that is described and being evaluated.

Although the task force report and the movement behind it is supported by many professionals, there is considerable discussion and criticism. *One concern* is voiced by the question, "What treatment methods might clinicians use?" Perhaps types of therapies—from different orientations, for example—might be effective but have yet to be tested. And what course of action is appropriate for problems for which there are no empirically supported treatments? A *second concern* involves the reliance on manualized treatments. Does the use of manuals mean a "cookbook," inflexible approach to treatment that ignores clinical judgment? Or can manuals be viewed as a set of careful guidelines that may be used in a clinically responsible, flexible manner? A *third concern* revolves around the question of the applicability and transportability of treatments from the research setting to the real world and to real-world clients (see p. 80).

A full examination of these concerns and complexities of the effectiveness of treatment is beyond the scope of our present discussion (cf. Kazdin & Weisz, 2003; Ollendick & Davis, 2004; Ollendick & King, 2000). However, throughout the remaining chapters, our discussion of interventions is sensitive to the need for treatments for which the empirical evidence is strongest.

Clinical Work with Young Clients

It is in clinical interaction, such as assessment and intervention, that various professionals come into personal contact with children and adolescents—as well as with their families—who are experiencing difficulties. Young people not only have the needs that older clients have for competent, dependable, and respectful care, but also have special needs because of their developmental level and their minority status in the legal system (Schetky, 2000).

INTERDISCIPLINARY APPROACH

It is often the case that more than one professional is involved in assessing and treating a young person, among whom are psychologists, psychiatrists, social workers, and special education teachers. Most psychologists working with child and adolescent problems have specialized in clinical psychology; others may have specialized in school, developmental, or educational psychology. They usually hold the doctoral degree (Ph.D. or Psy.D.), which demands 5 to 6 years of university graduate study. Psychology has sturdy roots in the laboratory and an interest in both normal and abnormal behavior. Training in psychology thus includes psychological research, as well as direct contact in assessing and treating individuals who display behavioral problems.

Psychiatrists, on the other hand, hold the doctorate in medicine (M.D.); they are physicians who have specialized in the treatment of mental disturbance. Psychiatrists function in ways that are similar to those of psychologists, but they tend to view problem behavior more as a medical dysfunction. They thus have a greater tendency to conduct medical examinations and employ medical treatments, especially pharmacological treatments.

Social workers generally hold the master's degree (M.A.) in social work. Like psychologists and psychiatrists, they may counsel and conduct therapy, and historically their special focus has been working with the family and other social systems in which young people are enmeshed.

Special education teachers, who usually have obtained the master's degree, emphasize the importance of providing needy children and adolescents with optimal educational experiences. They are able to plan and implement individualized educational programs, thus contributing to the treatment of many disorders.

Youngsters with problems also come to the attention of nurses, general physicians, teachers in regular classrooms, and workers in the legal system. Indeed, these professionals may be the first to hear about a problem. Therefore, interdisciplinary consultation commonly occurs and often is ideal. A good amount of coordination is necessary if this approach is to be effective. Who functions as the coordinator may depend on the type of disorder, the developmental level of the client, the first point of professional contact, and the treatment setting.

WORKING WITH PARENTS

Dealing with disorders of youth almost always involves contact with at least one parent and frequently requires working closely with parents.

Parents vary greatly in their motivation to participate in psychological or mental health evaluation and treatment for their offspring. Consultation and help are sought for many reasons. Most parents, of course, are truly concerned about the welfare of their sons and daughters, and consequently seek help. Parents may also be motivated to alleviate conflicts with their child or to reduce their own worries. And they may be referred by schools or the courts, sometimes against their own wishes. All these reasons for seeking help can influence the success of treatment.

Parents also vary in the ability to understand, support, and carry out professional recommendations. The entire range of that ability exists, with some parents being superbly apt at forming a therapeutic alliance with the child and therapist. On the other hand, accommodation often must be made for parental concerns or issues. Some parents fear that they will be blamed for their offspring's problems (Kraemer, 1987), thus leading to defensiveness. Others may have inappropriate goals; for example, authoritarian parents may desire their child or adolescent to be excessively obedient. Parents can resent professional suggestions, be overly dependent, or expect therapists to "fix" the problem without the parents' involvement. Regardless of varying tendencies, however, parents frequently desire and can benefit from education and training relevant to the difficulties being experienced.

The importance of the parents' role is apparent in cases in which treatment is discontinued prior to successful completion. Family variables play a dominant role (Armbruster & Kazdin, 1994; Kazdin et al., 1997). The risk of dropping out of treatment is higher with socioeconomic disadvantage. This finding was confirmed in a study in Finland, where families of all social classes have equal access to mental health services (Pelkonen et al., 2000). Additional family factors implicated in discontinuance of treatment are young age of mother, single parenting, harsh child-rearing practices, parent psychopathology, and family stress. More immediate factors—such as parental belief that treatment is irrelevant or a less than satisfactory parent-therapist relationship—have been associated with discontinuance. In one study, dropping out of treatment was affected by both the referral source and parental dysfunction (Gould, Shaffer, & Kaplan, 1985). The dropout rate was especially high for families that had both disturbed parents and school referrals.

Whatever the situation, parents are vital in treatment, and they provide information and perceptions that no others can provide. Thus the competent and sensitive professional typically welcomes parental participation and works toward optimizing the quality of the child-parent relationship.

WORKING WITH AND FOR THE YOUNG CLIENT

Direct interaction with youngsters is both rewarding and demanding. Young children may be especially incapable of identifying problems and seeking treatment, and they most often enter treatment at the suggestion or coercion of adults. Adolescents sometimes have more input into the decision to seek clinical services, but special attention needs to be given to issues such as the heightened sensibility to autonomy that many adolescents experience (Cicchetti & Rogosch, 2002). Sensitivity to the young person's perspective and efforts to create and maintain motivation may be critical.

Mindfulness of the client's developmental level is imperative. Such knowledge is essential in evaluating problems and judging their significance. Understanding of developmental competencies and failures also provides guidelines for treatment. A clear example is training children to control their own behavior by giving themselves verbal directions in problem solving. Such a strategy can be therapeutic for particular kinds of problems. However, very young children would not be expected to do as well with this technique as would older children.

Finally, young people have basic rights that must be recognized and protected. They have a right to information about treatment procedures, to assent to treatment, and to participate in decisions about the goals of treatment. In addition, the basic rights to privacy and confidentiality apply to clients of all ages, although developmental level enters into determining the exact ways in which these considerations play out (Behnke & Warner, 2002). We would hardly expect to employ identical guidelines for a preschooler as for a ninth-grader. Nevertheless, immaturity of the child can demand, if anything, greater attention to ethical concerns and the child's welfare.

When they treat young people, mental health workers often face tough questions concerning clinical, ethical, and legal matters. Examples abound. Consider the following situation, which is adapted from descriptions provided by Schetky (2000).

| **Aaron** | **Clinical, Legal, and Ethical Considerations** |

Mrs. Schulz, recently divorced, is seeking therapy for her 6-year-old son, Aaron. The father has shared custody and is responsible for treatment costs. He insists that Aaron is fine and does not need therapy. Mr. Schulz suggests that the problem lies with his ex-wife. The therapist, believing that Aaron requires treatment, is in a bind. Legally, she needs the consent of only one parent to see a child, but she recognizes that proceeding without the father's consent might well lead to his undermining treatment. She must decide what is in the best interests of the child in the long run. She wishes that she had involved the father from the beginning. (p. 2944)

Several legal concerns can arise. For example, therapists frequently are called upon for legal testimony, raising issues of confidentiality and potential harm to the client (Schetky, 2000). Or to take yet another example, today's sensitivity to child abuse makes it of heightened concern with regard to legal rights (DeKraai, Sales, & Hall, 1998). Therapists are typically required by law to report abuse. In some cases, this mandate has the potential to complicate the professional's judgment about what is best for the child and the family in treatment. Nevertheless, professionals must understand and meet legal requirements, inform families of the kinds of things that must be reported, and work within the legal framework to fulfill their professional obligations to their clients. Ethical and legal dilemmas regarding behavioral disorders are not uncommon, but they are of special concern when they involve young people who are limited in speaking for themselves.

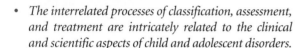

SUMMARY

- *The interrelated processes of classification, assessment, and treatment are intricately related to the clinical and scientific aspects of child and adolescent disorders.*

CLASSIFICATION AND DIAGNOSIS

- *Classification systems must have clearly defined categories or dimensions that can be clearly discriminated from each other. Any classification system must be reliable and valid. Diagnostic systems are also judged by their clinical utility.*

- *Clinically derived classification relies on consensus among clinicians regarding disorders and their definition. The DSM, the clinically derived system most likely to be employed in the United States, is a categorical approach to classification.*

- *The recent versions of the DSM include an increased number of categories of child and adolescent disorders, provide more highly structured rules for diagnosis, use a multiaxial system to assess various aspects of functioning, and draw on research data in a more consistent fashion.*

- *Although reliability of the DSM has been improved by more structured diagnostic rules, there is still considerable variation across categories, and reliability may be affected by the conditions under which information is obtained and diagnoses are made. The validity of some of the diagnostic categories has received considerable attention, but the validity of others is still questioned.*

- *The problem of comorbidity—youngsters' meeting the criteria for more than one disorder—presents particular challenges.*

- *Despite improvements, the DSM is still criticized by some regarding its relative inattention to issues of age, gender, and cultural context as well as other clinical, scientific, ethical, and social-political grounds.*

- *Empirical approaches to classification rely on behavior checklists and statistical analyses, and tend to be associated with dimensional rather than categorical approaches to classification.*

- *Achenbach's Child Behavior Checklist, Teacher Report Form, and Youth Self-Report are examples of checklists employed in the empirical approach. There is good support for two broad syndromes— externalizing and internalizing—and support for subcategories within each general syndrome.*

- *Information from multiple informants suggests sensitivity to the possible influence of situational differences on behavior and to differences due to the respondent's perspective.*

- *Critics of diagnostic systems remind us of the possible dangers of labeling children and adolescents.*

ASSESSMENT

- *Conducting a comprehensive assessment is necessary, not only for classification and diagnosis but also for planning and executing appropriate interventions. The complex process of assessment requires a multifaceted approach.*

- *The general clinical interview is the most common form of assessment. Structured interviews are often organized so as to provide information for a DSM diagnosis.*

- *Problem checklists can be employed to sample a wide range of behavior problems or those problems particular to a specific disorder. These checklists may enable the clinician to compare a child with appropriate norms and to examine issues such as situational aspects of a child's behavior and the perceptions of various informants.*

- *Self-report measures are available for both the youngster and the relevant adults in the youngster's life. These instruments can be used to assess constructs directly related to the presenting problem (e.g., anxiety, depression) or related constructs of potential interest (e.g., self-concept, self-control, parenting stress, family environment).*

- *Observation of behavior is central to a behavioral/social learning approach and is a direct method of assessment. The impracticality of implementing current observation systems in general clinical practice is an impediment to their widespread use.*

- *Projective tests are probably less widely used than was once the case as a result of questions concerning their reliability and validity.*

- *Intellectual-educational assessments are conducted for a wide variety of presenting problems. General intelligence and developmental levels are evaluated, as well as specific abilities and achievement. Although intelligence tests are popular, they are in many ways controversial. Given that they present a variety of concerns, they should be used cautiously.*

- *Assessment of physical functioning, especially of the nervous system, is important for many behavior problems. Methods include case histories, medical examinations, the EEG, and several newer techniques, such as the CT scan, PET scan, MRI, and MRS. Much attention has also been given to neuropsychological testing as a means of indirectly assessing known or suspected problems in central nervous system functioning.*

TREATMENT

- *It is likely that the treatment of children and adolescents will include several elements, because young people are likely to have multiple problems. Treatments are also likely to include family members and may need to incorporate school personnel and peers as well.*

- *Various modes and settings for treatment of youngsters and their families are available. Psychotherapy may be conducted with a single child or in groups. Play is an important aspect of therapy, especially with younger clients. Interventions also often include family members, focus on the family as a unit, or incorporate parent training in child management skills. Psychotropic medications have increasingly been employed in the treatment of child and adolescent disorders. Interventions may take place in a variety of settings including the clinician's office, schools, and various residential facilities.*

- *Demand for professionals to be accountable for the effectiveness of their services along with an increasing emphasis on empiricism has led professional organizations to develop treatments that are supported by research.*

CLINICAL WORK WITH YOUNG CLIENTS

- *Professional care of young clients is interdisciplinary and recognizes the important role that parents play in treatment. Treatment of youth requires special consideration of their motivation, developmental level, and rights to assent to treatment, to participate in decisions, and to have privacy. Social, legal, and ethical dilemmas can easily arise.*

KEY TERMS

classification *(p. 94)*

taxonomy *(p. 94)*

diagnosis *(p. 94)*

assessment *(p. 94)*

category *(p. 94)*

dimension *(p. 94)*

interrater reliability *(p. 95)*

test-retest reliability *(p. 95)*

validity *(p. 95)*

clinical utility *(p. 95)*

Diagnostic and Statistical Manual of Mental Disorders—DSM *(p. 95)*

International Classification of Diseases—ICD *(p. 95)*

clinically derived classification *(p. 95)*

categorical approach *(p. 95)*

multiaxial system *(p. 95)*

comorbidity *(p. 98)*

CHAPTER 6
Anxiety Disorders

With this chapter we begin our examination of specific problems and disorders. The children and adolescents discussed in this and the next chapter are variously described as anxious, fearful, withdrawn, timid, depressed, and the like. They seem to be very unhappy and to lack self-confidence. These youngsters are often said to have emotional difficulties that they take out on themselves; thus the term *internalizing disorders* is often employed to describe such problems.

An Introduction to Internalizing Disorders

Empirical efforts to classify child and adolescent behavior disorders have clearly found support for a broad syndrome composed of internalizing problems (see Chapter 5). Many of the problems included in clinically defined classifications would also be thought of as internalizing disorders. These problems were once broadly referred to as neuroses, a term that is now employed less frequently. Currently, more specific terms such as phobias,

obsessions and compulsions, anxiety disorders, and depression are more likely to be used.

The distinctness of these more specific clinical diagnostic categories, such as the various anxiety and depressive disorders described in the DSM system, is often questioned. Why is this the case? One reason is the difficulty encountered in achieving adequate interrater reliability for specific diagnostic categories. In addition, considerable evidence indicates that a given child or adolescent often meets the criteria for more than one of the different disorders (Angold, Costello, & Erkanli, 1999). The phenomenon of an individual's meeting the criteria for more than one disorder, which is often termed *comorbidity*, was discussed in Chapter 5. The dilemma is an appreciable one.

It has also been suggested that what are sometimes viewed as separate disorders may be different expressions of a general disposition toward the development of anxiety or internalizing difficulties. Particular environments or experiences shape this general disposition into a particular pattern of symptoms (disorder). Cultural differences may operate in this manner. Research findings suggest that there are no differences among cultural groups in the overall prevalence of anxiety disorders or in the temperamental qualities that may underlie the development of anxiety difficulties. However, differences in the prevalence of specific anxiety disorders and types of symptoms are reported (Austin & Chorpita, 2004; Pina & Silverman, 2004). For example, higher rates of separation anxiety disorder and of somatic/physiological symptoms in Hispanic than in European American children have been cited (Ginsburg & Silverman, 1996; Varela et al., 2004). The strong value Hispanic cultures place on familial interdependence (collectivism) and on empathizing with others and remaining agreeable (simpatia) has been suggested as contributing to this particular expression of anxiety by members of this cultural group.

With these considerations in mind, let us turn to an examination of internalizing disorders. In this chapter, we examine anxiety disorders, and in Chapter 7, we discuss mood disorders.

Defining and Classifying Anxiety Disorders

In general, anxiety and fear are viewed as a complex pattern of three types of reactions to a perceived threat (Barrios & O'Dell, 1998; Lang, 1984). This tripartite model describes overt behavioral responses (e.g., running away, trembling voice, eyes closing), physiological responses (e.g., changes in heart rate and respiration, muscle tension, stomach upset), and subjective responses (e.g., thoughts of being scared, self-deprecatory thoughts, images of bodily harm).

Fear and anxiety have much in common, and the terms are sometimes used interchangeably. However, a distinction is made between fear as a reaction to an *immediate/present* threat characterized by an alarm reaction and anxiety as a *future-oriented* emotion characterized by an elevated level of apprehension and lack of control. In contrast to the complex combination of three components that define fear and anxiety, worry—thoughts about possible negative outcomes that are intrusive and difficult to control—is viewed as a cognitive component of anxiety (Barlow, 2002; Vasey & Daleiden, 1994).

One of the challenges facing clinicians is to decide whether the anxiety exhibited by a child or adolescent is normal (Albano, Chorpita, & Barlow, 2003). Anxiety is a basic human emotion. It can serve an adaptive function by alerting the youngster to novel or threatening situations. Anxiety is thus part

of normal developmental processes by which the young person learns, for example, to identify and cope with arousal, develop competencies, and become more autonomous. Thus, young children learn to cope with the dark and separation and adolescents deal with the anxieties of beginning high school and dating. What then do we know about typical fear, worry, and anxiety?

NORMAL FEARS, WORRIES, AND ANXIETIES

General Prevalence. Several classic studies of general populations lead to the realization that children exhibit a surprisingly large number of fears, worries, and anxieties (Jersild & Holmes, 1935; MacFarlane, Allen, & Honzik, 1954). The prevalence of such concerns may sometimes be underestimated. For example, 43 percent of the 6- to 12-year-olds studied by Lapouse and Monk (1959) had seven or more fears. Mothers in this study reported 41 percent fewer fears than indicated by the children's own reports. This study and others suggest that parents may underestimate the prevalence of fears in their children. This tendency may be particularly true for older children who are increasingly able to mask their emotions (Gullone, 2000).

Although it appears that fears are quite common among children, the prevalence of intense fears is less clear. Early findings indicated lower levels of intense fears (Miller, Barrett, & Hampe, 1974; Rutter, Tizard, & Whitmore, 1970) than suggested by later

Fears and anxieties are quite common in children. It is only when these are persistent, are intense, interfere with functioning, or are developmentally inappropriate that they may require clinical attention.
(Geri Engberg/The Image Works)

findings (Bell-Dolan, Last, & Strauss, 1990; Ollendick, 1983; Rutter, 1989a).

Sex, Age, and Cultural Differences. Most research suggests that girls exhibit a greater number of fears than boys. This difference is most clear for older children and less clear for preschool and elementary school children. Studies generally suggest greater fear intensity in girls as well (Gullone, 2000). Findings of sex differences probably should be interpreted with caution because gender-role expectations may, in part, be responsible for differences between boys and girls in displaying and admitting to fears (Ginsburg & Silverman, 2000).

It is commonly reported that both the number and the intensity of fears experienced by children decline with age (Gullone, 2000). Figure 6–1 illustrates this general pattern. Worry becomes prominent in children at about 7 years of age and becomes more complex and varied as children develop.

Certain fears appear to be more common at particular ages: for example, fear of strangers at 6 to 9 months, fear of imaginary creatures during the second year, fear of the dark among 4-year-olds, and social fears and fear of failure in older children and adolescents (Gullone, 2000; Miller et al., 1974). Similarly, preschoolers may worry about imaginary threats, young children about their physical safety, and older children and adolescents about social situations and their competence. Thus, threats to youngsters' well-being are a prominent worry across age (Silverman, La Greca, & Wasserstein, 1995). However, changes in the content of fears and worries likely reflect ongoing cognitive, social, and emotional development.

Cross-cultural examinations of common fears suggest similarities across cultures. The Fear Survey Schedule for Children (FSSC-R; Ollendick, 1983) is an inventory of fear stimuli and situations. The FSSC-R has been translated into a number of different languages. The most common fears were similar across different countries and cultures and girls were found to score higher than boys (Fonesca, Yule, & Erol, 1994).

CLASSIFYING ANXIETY DISORDERS

Most authorities would not usually view age-appropriate anxieties as requiring clinical attention unless they were quite intense or continue longer than expected. Mild fear reactions and those specific to a developmental period might be expected to dissipate quickly. Indeed, in general, longitudinal studies suggest that normal fears are relatively transitory

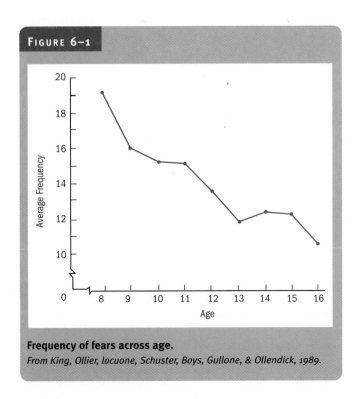

FIGURE 6–1

Frequency of fears across age.
From King, Ollier, Iacuone, Schuster, Bays, Gullone, & Ollendick, 1989.

(Gullone, 2000). However, if the fear or anxiety, even though short-lived, creates sufficient discomfort or interferes with functioning, intervention may be justified. Furthermore, anxiety disorders, if left untreated, may follow a chronic course and be associated with additional difficulties (Kendall et al., 2004).

How do we then define and classify disorders of childhood and adolescence in which anxiety is the principal feature? The answer is not a simple one, and there is considerable disagreement as to how anxiety disorders should be categorized (Barrios & Hartmann, 1997; Rabian & Silverman, 2000; Schniering, Hudson, & Rapee, 2000). Because the DSM approach is most commonly used, much of this chapter is organized using this system.

The DSM Approach. The DSM-IV-TR describes one type of anxiety disorder that is "usually first diagnosed in infancy, childhood, or adolescence," Separation Anxiety Disorder. In addition to this disorder, a child or an adolescent can be diagnosed with many of the other anxiety disorders included in the DSM: Specific Phobia, Social Phobia, Panic Disorder, Generalized Anxiety Disorder, Obsessive-Compulsive Disorder, Posttraumatic Stress Disorder, and Acute Stress Disorder. We will define and discuss each of these disorders when we turn to a discussion of specific anxiety disorders.

Studies of community samples have generally reported that between 12 and 20 percent of youngsters meet diagnostic criteria for one or more anxiety disorders (Albano et al., 2003). Two more recent studies using DSM-IV criteria suggest rates of about 3 to 7 percent in samples of Puerto Rican and British children and adolescents (Canino et al., 2004; Ford, Goodman, & Meltzer, 2003).

The Empirical Approach. Empirical systems that are based on statistical procedures have also yielded subcategories related to anxiety disorders. Within the broad category of internalizing disorders, for example, Achenbach (Achenbach & Rescorla, 2001) describes an anxious/depressed syndrome (see Table 6–1). There is not, however, a separate anxiety syndrome or other narrower syndromes that correspond to the specific anxiety disorders of the DSM, suggesting that in youngsters, the various anxiety and depression symptoms tend to occur together. Other internalizing syndromes, such as "somatic complaints" (e.g., feeling dizzy, having stomachaches) and "withdrawn/depressed" (e.g., refusing to talk, feeling withdrawn), also contain symptoms that are likely to be related to anxiety problems.

TABLE 6–1	BEHAVIOR PROBLEMS INCLUDED IN THE ANXIOUS/DEPRESSED SYNDROME
Cries a lot	Feels too guilty
Fears	Self-conscious
Fears school	Feels hurt when
Fears doing bad	criticized
Must be perfect	Talks or thinks
Feels unloved	of suicide
Feels worthless	Anxious to please
Nervous, tense	Fears mistakes
Fearful, anxious	Worries

From Achenbach & Rescorla, 2001.

Specific Phobias

Phobia is the term usually employed to describe fears that are exaggerated and disruptive to normal functioning. The essential feature of a specific phobia is a persistent fear of a specific object or situation that is unusual or excessive.

DIAGNOSTIC CRITERIA

The main features required for the DSM diagnosis of Specific Phobia are presented in Table 6–2. These criteria acknowledge developmental differences by noting that anxiety may be expressed differently by children and that children may not realize that their fears are unreasonable or excessive.

In addition to these main features, the fear must produce marked distress or must interfere significantly with the youngster's normal routine, academic functioning, or social relationships. Also, the fear must have a duration of at least 6 months.

The DSM suggests that specific phobias be further subcategorized into five types: animal, natural environment (e.g., heights, storms, water), blood-injection-injury, situational (e.g., airplanes, enclosed places), and other (e.g., in children, avoidance of loud sounds or costumed characters).

DESCRIPTION

Youngsters with specific phobias display symptoms representing the three domains of anxiety (behavioral, cognitive, physiological). Behaviorally, these youngsters try to avoid the situation or object that

TABLE 6–2	MAJOR FEATURES FOR THE DSM DIAGNOSIS OF SPECIFIC PHOBIA

1. Marked and persistent fear that is excessive or unreasonable, cued by the presence or anticipation of a specific object or situation (e.g., flying, heights, animals, receiving an injection, seeing blood).
2. Exposure to the phobic stimulus almost invariably provokes an immediate anxiety response. **Note:** In children, this anxiety may be expressed by crying, tantrums, freezing, or clinging.
3. The person must recognize that his or her fear is excessive or unreasonable. **Note:** In children this feature may be absent.
4. The person must avoid the phobic situation(s) or must endure exposure with intense anxiety and distress.

From American Psychiatric Association, 2000.

they fear. For example, children who have an extreme fear of dogs may refuse to go outside. When confronted with a large dog, they may "freeze" or run to their parent for protection. In crying out for help, the youngster may describe feelings of tension, panic, or even fear of death. The cognitive aspect of these reactions often includes thoughts of catastrophic events that may occur upon exposure to the phobic situation. Nausea, rapid heart rate, and difficulty in breathing are among the physiological reactions that may also occur. These reactions may occur even when contact with the feared situation is merely anticipated. Thus, not only is the youngster restricted in his or her activities, but fears of encountering the phobic object or situation are also likely to change the lifestyle and activities of the family as a whole.

EPIDEMIOLOGY

Specific phobias are among the most commonly diagnosed anxiety disorders in children and adolescents (King, Muris, & Ollendick, 2004). Although estimates vary somewhat, prevalence is generally reported as between 3 to 4 percent in community samples (Albano et al., 2003). A recent report based on a community sample of British youngsters ages 5 through 15 suggested a rate of about 1 percent (Ford et al., 2003), and in a community sample of German adolescents 12 to 17 years old, 3.5 percent met the criteria for specific phobia (Essau, Conradt, & Petermann, 2000). Specific phobias are often described as more prevalent in girls than in boys, but this gender difference is not consistently reported (Anderson, 1994; Costello & Angold, 1995b; Ford et al., 2003). Information regarding

ethnic differences are limited, but comparisons between European American and African American and Hispanic youngsters suggest more similarities than differences (Last & Perrin, 1993; Silverman & Ginsberg, 1998).

Youngsters with specific phobias are likely to meet the criteria for other disorders. Last, Strauss, and Francis (1987) found that among youngsters who were referred to a clinic with a primary diagnosis of specific phobia, the majority met criteria for one or more other disorders. Additional diagnoses included other anxiety disorders, depression and mood disorders, and externalizing disorders such as oppositional defiant disorder. Verduin and Kendall (2003) report that nearly half of clinically referred youngsters whose primary diagnosis was another anxiety disorder also met the criteria for a specific phobia. Similarly, in their community sample of adolescents, Essau and colleagues (2000) report that nearly half of the youngsters with a specific phobia met the criteria for another anxiety disorder, and depressive and somatoform disorders (physical symptoms in the absence of a known physical pathology) were also common.

DEVELOPMENTAL COURSE

Although there is relatively little research information on the natural course of specific phobias, there is often the impression that children's phobias are relatively benign and that improvement will occur over time with or without treatment. However, there is reason to question this perception and to think in terms of continuity over time (Albano et al., 2003).

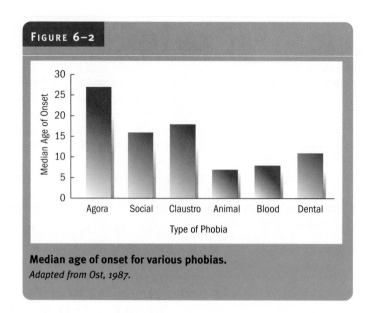

Median age of onset for various phobias.
Adapted from Ost, 1987.

Findings from Essau and colleagues' (2000) sample of German adolescents, for example, suggest that for a proportion of youngsters, phobic symptoms persist over time and are associated with impaired functioning. This finding is consistent with reports of phobic adults that suggest that specific phobias are likely to begin in childhood and may for some individuals persist into adulthood (Kendler et al., 1992b). Furthermore, the age of onset reported by adults with phobias (Öst, 1987), presented in Figure 6–2, illustrate that specific phobias appear to have an early age of onset. A reasonable suggestion, therefore, is that specific phobias are likely to begin during childhood and, that for at least some individuals, they may persist over time.

Social Phobia

DIAGNOSTIC CRITERIA

Another category of phobia specified by the DSM is Social Phobia (or Social Anxiety Disorder). The essential feature of social phobia is a marked and persistent fear of acting in an embarrassing or humiliating way in social or performance situations. The main features required for the diagnosis of social phobia are presented in Table 6–3.

As with specific phobias, these criteria acknowledge developmental differences by noting that anxiety may be expressed differently by children and that children may not realize that their fears are unreasonable

TABLE 6–3	MAJOR FEATURES FOR THE DSM DIAGNOSIS OF SOCIAL PHOBIA

1. A marked and persistent fear of one or more social or performance situations in which the person is exposed to unfamiliar people or to possible scrutiny by others. The individual fears that he or she will act in a way (or show anxiety symptoms) that will be humiliating or embarrassing. **Note:** In children there must be evidence of the capacity for age-appropriate social relationships with familiar people and the anxiety must occur in peer settings, not just in interaction with adults.
2. Exposure to the feared situation almost invariably provokes anxiety. **Note:** In children this anxiety may be expressed by crying, tantrums, freezing, or shrinking from social situations with unfamiliar people.
3. There must be recognition by the person that the fear is excessive or unreasonable. **Note:** This feature may be absent in children.
4. The feared situations are avoided or are endured with intense distress.

From American Psychiatric Association, 2000.

or excessive. Furthermore, to distinguish social phobia from other aspects of social development, children receiving the diagnosis would be expected to display appropriate social relationships with familiar people and to experience social anxiety with peers and not just with adults.

In addition to these main features, the phobia must interfere significantly with the youngster's normal routine, academic functioning, or social relationships or must produce marked distress. Also, the phobia must have a duration of at least 6 months.

DESCRIPTION

Youngsters with social phobia fear social activities and situations such as speaking, reading, writing or performing in public, initiating or maintaining conversations, speaking to authority figures, and interacting in informal social situations (Beidel, Turner, & Morris, 1999).

The behavioral component of this social anxiety is most frequently manifested by the avoidance of situations that involve social interactions or evaluation. Even everyday and seemingly mundane activities, such as eating in public, may be avoided. Albano, Chorpita, and Barlow (2003) describe a teenage girl who spent every lunch period in a bathroom stall so as to avoid the school cafeteria. In the cognitive realm, concerns about being embarrassed or negatively evaluated are common for these youngsters. They are likely to focus their thoughts on negative attributes that they perceive in themselves, to negatively evaluate their performance, and to interpret others' responses as critical or disapproving even when this is not the case. Examples of these concerns are illustrated in Table 6–4, which

presents examples of items from the Social Anxiety Scale for Children—Revised (LaGreca & Stone, 1993). Complaints of illness and stomachaches are common physiological symptoms, especially in younger children.

Because these youngsters try to avoid social situations, they may miss school and may be unlikely to participate in recreational activities. For example, younger children may not attend birthday parties or participate in Boy Scout or Girl Scout meetings, whereas adolescents are unlikely to attend school events, such as club meetings or dances, or to date. These young people may, therefore, have few friends. In school situations, teachers often describe them as "loners."

Youngsters with social phobia often report feelings of lesser self-worth as well as feeling sad and lonely. Over time they may also experience lesser educational achievement (Ginsburg, LaGreca, & Silverman, 1998; Velting & Albano, 2001). The potential consequences for a youngster are thus quite broad.

TABLE 6–4	EXAMPLES OF ITEMS FROM THE SOCIAL ANXIETY SCALE FOR CHILDREN—REVISED

I worry about what other kids think of me.
I'm afraid that other kids will not like me.
I feel that kids are making fun of me.
I feel shy around kids I don't know.
I feel nervous when I'm around certain kids.
I feel shy even with kids I know very well.
It's hard for me to ask other kids to play with me.

By permission of author Annette M. La Greca.

Louis | Social Phobia and Its Consequences

Louis, a 12-year-old white male, was referred by his school counselor because of periodic episodes of school refusal, social withdrawal, and excessive need for reassurance. On an almost daily basis Louis would claim he could not remain in the classroom. He would generally be sent to the nurse or counselor's office until his mother came and took him home early. Louis had few friends and rarely participated in social activities that involved other children. Louis found parties, eating in public, and using public restrooms particularly difficult. Spanish class was also particularly difficult because of regular assignments to read aloud or to carry on conversations with classmates. Louis's mother described him as always having been excessively fearful, timid, scared of everything, and needing constant reassurance. The mother herself had a history of anxiety problems, was fearful of meeting new people, and had little social contact, saying "it's basically just Louis and me." Louis received the diagnoses of Social Phobia and Generalized Anxiety Disorder.

Adapted from Silverman & Ginsburg, 1998, pp. 260–261.

EPIDEMIOLOGY

Social phobia is usually estimated to be present in approximately 1 percent of youngsters in the general community (e.g., Kashani & Orvaschel, 1990; Lewinsohn et al., 1993a; McGee et al., 1990). However, changes in diagnostic practices since the DSM-IV suggest somewhat higher rates (Beidel, Morris, & Turner, 2004; Canino et al., 2004). It is also a common diagnosis in clinic populations. Last and colleagues (1992) report that 14.9 percent of youngsters assessed at an anxiety disorders clinic were given a primary diagnosis of social phobia, and 32.4 percent had a lifetime history of the disorder. At present it is not clear whether there are gender differences in the prevalence of social phobias (Albano et al., 2003; Ford et al., 2003). On the basis of reports of children seen in clinics and retrospective reports, middle to late adolescence is the typical age of onset (Öst, 1987; Strauss & Last, 1993). This finding is consistent with the developmental considerations discussed below. Although social phobia is most frequently diagnosed in adolescents, it can occur earlier (Ford et al., 2003; Neal & Edelmann, 2003). Prevalence probably increases with age, and the disorder may be underrecognized, particularly in adolescents (Albano & Barlow, 1996; Clark et al., 1994). One reason that the problem may be underrecognized is

that youngsters with social phobia may minimize their problems in order to present themselves in a desirable way (DiBartolo et al., 1998). This tendency would be consistent with a concern about negative evaluation.

Most youngsters with social phobia also meet the criteria for one or more other disorders (Albano et al., 2003; Beidel et al., 1999). As with Louis, another anxiety disorder is the most common additional diagnosis (Verduin & Kendall, 2003). Adolescents, in particular, may also meet the criteria for a major depressive disorder.

DEVELOPMENTAL COURSE

The development of social phobia can be viewed within the context of normative developmental factors (Velting & Albano, 2001). In young children between the ages of 6 months and 3 years, stranger anxiety and separation anxiety are common. The self-consciousness that is an essential part of what we mean by social phobia, however, does not develop until later. The abilities to see oneself as a social object and to feel embarrassment may emerge at about 4 or 5 years of age. Taking the perspective of other people and then experiencing concern over their possible negative evaluation probably do not

---

ACCENT ●●●●

Selective Mutism and Social Phobia

A young kindergarten girl, Amy, does not speak in school or with her peers. She has been this way since beginning preschool. Children like Amy might be given a diagnosis of Selective Mutism.

Youngsters with selective mutism do not talk in specific social situations. These situations, such as the classroom or play activities, are ones in which their peers typically do talk or in which talking is important to development. Mutism occurs despite the fact that the children do speak in other situations. For example, they may speak easily with family members if no one else is present. The onset of the disorder is usually before age 5. These youngsters are typically described as shy, withdrawn, fearful, and clingy (American Psychiatric Association, 2000). Many of these children also display oppositional behavior (Ford et al., 1998). They may, for example, be stubborn, be disobedient, whine, or have temper tantrums.

Selective mutism is a separate DSM disorder, but some evidence suggests that it might be conceptualized as an extreme form of social phobia (Standart & Le Couteur, 2003). For example, 90 to 100 percent of children with selective mutism also meet diagnostic criteria for social phobia (Black & Uhde, 1995; Dummit et al., 1997). There is also some support for the idea that children with selective mutism are more socially anxious than children with social phobia who are not selectively mute. However, it remains unclear whether children with selective mutism simply have extreme levels of a social anxiety disorder (Yeganeh et al., 2003). Although this diagnostic distinction remains unclear, in working with children with selective mutism, clinicians may need to consider potentially severe levels of social anxiety and possible oppositional behavior in planning treatments.

Adolescence is a period during which involvement in a variety of social activities is expected. Some youngsters find these social demands particularly difficult.
(Richard Nawitz/Photo Researchers, Inc.)

emerge until about 8 years of age. By late childhood or early adolescence, these cognitive developmental prerequisites and the awareness that one's appearance and behavior can be the basis for others' evaluations are in place. So, for example, Westenberg and colleagues (2004) assessed fears among a sample of children and adolescents (8 to 18 years of age) from the Netherlands. Fears of social and achievement evaluation increased with age, and these age-related changes in fears were associated with level of social-cognitive maturity.

By late childhood or early adolescence, youngsters are regularly required to perform tasks that have a social-evaluative component. They are, for example, expected to speak in class, engage in group activities, and perform in athletic or musical events. Responsibility for initiating and arranging social activities is also shifting. Parents are no longer likely to be highly involved in arranging social interactions. Young adolescents also may be expected to engage in different social activities such as attending school dances and dating. The combination of these social demands and the development of self-awareness can set the stage for the emergence of social anxiety. Social phobia may be thought to evolve from anxiety that is typical in this developmental period but that is magnified for some youngsters by individual differences and social demands (Neal & Edelmann, 2003).

Because adolescence is a period during which social anxieties are quite common, making the distinction between normal and abnormal social anxiety may be particularly difficult. Interpretation of severity, defined in the DSM diagnostic criteria by phrases such as "almost invariably," "marked distress," "intense anxiety," and "interferes significantly," becomes particularly important in this age group (Clark et al., 1994). The view that some level of social anxiety is common during adolescence and that only some smaller proportion of youngsters go on to develop clinical level problems is supported by research data (Velting & Albano, 2001). For example, Essau, Conradt, and Peterman (1999) found that approximately 51 percent of a community sample of youngsters between the ages of 12 and 17 reported at least one specific social fear. And, in a longitudinal study of a cohort of young people from New Zealand, increased anxious/withdrawn behavior at age 8 was associated with increased risk for social phobia during adolescence and young adulthood (Goodwin, Fergusson, & Horwood, 2004).

Separation Anxiety and School Refusal

We have chosen to describe school refusal and separation anxiety together, because much of what has been written about the problem of school refusal and its etiology has derived from a separation anxiety perspective. In addition, given that compulsory education laws require all children to attend school, it seems likely that many children with separation anxiety would also have problems with school attendance.

DIAGNOSIS AND CLASSIFICATION

Separation Anxiety Disorder. The DSM category of Separation Anxiety Disorder (SAD) is intended to describe children with excessive anxiety regarding separation from a major attachment figure and/or home. Diagnostic criteria include eight symptoms involving worry or distress and related sleep and physical problems. These symptoms (Table 6–5) are associated with concerns of separation from or worry of harm befalling major attachment figures.

The DSM requires the presence of three or more symptoms for at least 4 weeks. The problems must be present prior to the age of 18 and cause significant distress or impairment in social, school, or other areas of functioning.

School Refusal. Some youngsters exhibit excessive anxiety regarding school attendance. These youngsters may not attend school and this is typically termed school refusal. Such reluctance or refusal to go to school is one of the eight symptoms listed for the DSM diagnosis of SAD, and some youngsters who exhibit school refusal do receive this diagnosis. However, since only three of the eight symptoms listed need to be present to receive the diagnosis of SAD, not all children with separation anxiety disorder exhibit school refusal. In addition, not all school refusers show separation anxiety (Kearney, Eisen, & Silverman, 1995; Last & Strauss, 1990). Some children, for example, may fear some aspect of the school experience. They might be diagnosed under the specific phobia or social phobia categories. For example, if children fear going to school because of anxiety regarding evaluation, speaking in public, or meeting new people, they may receive a diagnosis of Social Phobia.

Nevertheless, the most common conceptualization of school refusal attributes the problem to separation anxiety. Psychodynamic explanations describe the child's insistence on remaining at home as satisfying both the child's and the mother's needs and conflicts concerning separation. The basic notion is that strong attachment leads the child to fear that something may happen either to the self or to the mother during separation. In the latter instance, the child may have aggressive wishes toward the parent that the child fears will be fulfilled (Kessler, 1988). There is little information about the father's role in this process.

Behavioral explanations of school refusal as separation anxiety presume that the child has learned an avoidance response because of some association of school with an existing intense fear of losing the mother. Once avoidance behavior occurs, it may be reinforced by attention and other rewards,

TABLE 6–5	MAJOR FEATURES FOR THE DSM DIAGNOSIS OF SEPARATION ANXIETY DISORDER

Developmentally inappropriate and excessive anxiety concerning separation from home or from those to whom the individual is attached, as evidence by three (or more) of the following:

1. Recurrent excessive distress when separation from home or major attachment figures occurs or is anticipated
2. Persistent and excessive worry about losing, or about possible harm befalling, major attachment figures
3. Persistent and excessive worry that an untoward event will lead to separation from a major attachment figure (e.g., getting lost or being kidnapped)
4. Persistent reluctance or refusal to go to school or elsewhere because of fear of separation
5. Persistent and excessive fear or reluctance to be alone or without major attachment figures at home or to be without significant adults in other settings
6. Persistent reluctance or refusal to go to sleep without being near a major attachment figure or to sleep away from home
7. Repeated nightmares involving the theme of separation
8. Repeated complaints of physical symptoms (such as headaches, stomachaches, nausea, or vomiting) when separation from major attachment figures occurs or is anticipated

From American Psychiatric Association, 2000.

such as toys and special foods, which the child receives while at home.

However, it is best not to view all cases of school refusal as being similar or as having a unitary cause. Indeed, school refusal should probably be considered heterogeneous and multicausal. One suggestion is that it might be more useful to classify school refusal by the function that the behavior serves—by a functional analysis—rather than by symptoms (Kearney, 2001; Kearney & Silverman, 1996). Some youngsters may refuse school due to negative reinforcement. These youngsters may avoid negative affect such as anxiety and depression or may escape from aversive social (peer interactions) or evaluative situations (public speaking). Alternatively, youngsters may also refuse to go to school due to positive reinforcement. For them, school refusal behaviors (e.g., complaints of illness) may result in attention from their parents. Some children may receive positive tangible reinforcement (e.g., watching television or special treats). Using such an approach, treatment programs can be designed that address the functions that school refusal behavior serves for a particular youngster.

DESCRIPTION

Young children experiencing separation anxiety may be clingy, following their parents around. They may express general fear or apprehension, experience nightmares, or complain of somatic symptoms (e.g., dizziness, headaches, stomachaches, nausea). Older children may complain about not feeling well, may think about illness or tragedy that might befall them or their caregivers, become apathetic and depressed, and be reluctant to leave home or to participate in activities with their peers. Some youngsters may threaten to harm themselves. This threat is usually viewed as a means to escape or avoid separation, and serious suicidal behavior is rare.

Kenny   Separation Anxiety

Kenny, a 10-year-old boy, lived with his parents and his two half-siblings from his mother's previous marriage. He was brought to an anxiety disorders clinic by his parents because he was extremely fearful and had refused to go to school during the past several months. Kenny was also unable to be in other situations in which he was separated from his parents—such as when playing in the backyard, at Little League practice, staying with a sitter. When separated from his parents, Kenny cried, had tantrums, or threatened to hurt himself (e.g., jump from the school window). Kenny also exhibited high levels of anxiety, a number of specific fears, significant depressive symptomatology (e.g., sad mood, guilt about his problems, occasional wishes to be dead, and periodic early awakening). Kenny's separation problems appeared to have begun about a year earlier

Avoidance of school may be reinforced by attention and other rewards such as special foods or privileges the child receives while at home.
(Michael Newman/PhotoEdit, Inc.)

when his father was having drinking problems and was away from home for prolonged periods of time. Kenny's separation problems gradually worsened over the year.

Adapted from Last, 1988, pp. 12–13.

A certain degree of anxiety and fear about school is common for children, but some exhibit excessive anxiety regarding school attendance. The behaviors, thoughts, and somatic complaints characteristic of separation anxiety are often part of the picture of school refusal. Youngsters, particularly adolescents, may also show signs of depression. They are often absent from school on a regular basis, may fall behind in the academic work, and sometimes have to repeat a grade. In addition, because they miss opportunities for social experiences they are likely to experience peer difficulties as well. School refusal can be a serious problem that causes serious distress for both the child and caregivers and that may also interfere with the child's development. Clinical reports suggest that onset of these problems often follows some life stress such as a death, an illness, a change of school, or a move to a new neighborhood.

School refusal is often differentiated from truancy. Truants are usually described as unlikely to be excessively anxious or fearful about attending school. They typically are absent on an intermittent basis, often without parental knowledge. The school refuser, in contrast, is usually absent for continuous extended periods, during which time the parents are aware of the child's being at home. Also, truants are often described as poor students who exhibit other conduct problems such as stealing and lying. There is considerable disagreement as to whether truancy or school attendance problems associated with conduct problems and antisocial behaviors should be considered in the concept of school refusal (King & Bernstein, 2001).

EPIDEMIOLOGY

Separation Anxiety Disorder. Separation anxiety disorder is probably one of the most common anxiety disorders in children. Estimates of prevalence in community samples typically range from about 3 to 12 percent of children and among children referred to clinics, approximately 12 percent to as much as one-third receive a primary diagnosis of Separation Anxiety Disorder (Albano et al., 2003; Canino et al., 2004; Silverman & Dick-Niederhauser, 2004). Children with separation anxiety disorder often also

"But, sweetie, children are the backbone of our educational system."

Refusing to go to school and/or to be separated from parents is a common reason for referral for psychological services.
(Ed Lettau/Photo Researchers, Inc.)

meet diagnostic criteria for other disorders. At an outpatient clinic, about 80 percent of children with separation anxiety disorder were given one or more other diagnoses (Last, Strauss, & Francis, 1987). Generalized Anxiety Disorder seems to be the most common other diagnosis received (Last et al., 1987; Verduin & Kendall, 2003). Some studies report a greater prevalence of SAD among girls as compared with boys, but others report no gender differences (Albano et al., 2003; Ford et al., 2003). Prevalence declines after early childhood, and the disorder is probably uncommon in adolescence (American Psychiatric Association, 2000; Clark et al., 1994).

School Refusal. School refusal is usually estimated to occur in 1 to 2 percent of the general population and in about 5 percent of all clinic-referred cases; it is equally common in boys and girls (Elliott, 1999; King et al., 2000). It is interesting, however, that some reports suggest that as many as 69 percent of referrals for any kind of child phobia are for school refusal, and that the problem is seen in approximately 3 percent to 8 percent of clinic-referred children (Last & Strauss, 1990; Miller et al., 1972; Smith, 1970). Perhaps this outcome is because the problem creates considerable difficulty for parents and school personnel.

DEVELOPMENTAL COURSE

Anxiety concerning separation from a primary caregiver is part of the normal developmental process in infants. From the first year of life through the preschool years, children typically exhibit periodic distress and worry when they are separated from their parents or other individuals to whom they have an attachment. Indeed, the absence of any separation distress may indicate an insecure attachment. Even in older children, it is not uncommon for expectations, beliefs, and prior separation experiences to lead to feelings of homesickness when separated from parents (Thurber & Sigman, 1998). Such distress is viewed as problematic only when distress on separation persists beyond the expected age or is excessive.

For children with separation anxiety, symptoms often progress from milder to more severe. For example, children's histories reveal complaints of nightmares that may lead to allowing the child to sleep in the parents' bed on an intermittent basis. This often rapidly progresses to the child sleeping with one or both parents on a regular basis (Albano et al., 2003). Most children appear to recover from separation anxiety disorder (Kearney et al., 2003); however, for some, the symptoms may persist and they may develop a later disorder, with depression being particularly common (Last et al., 1996). In adolescents, separation anxiety, if present, may be the precursor of more serious problems (Blagg & Yule, 1994; Tonge, 1994). There is some suggestion, based on retrospective reports of adults, that youngsters with separation anxiety disorder may be at particular risk for developing panic disorder or agoraphobia (anxiety about being in a situation where escape may be difficult or embarrassing) as adults (Manicavasagar et al., 2000). However, even retrospective findings are mixed (Rabian & Silverman, 2000), and a follow-up study of youngsters diagnosed with separation anxiety disorder did not find support for this association (Aschenbrand et al., 2003). Young adults who had completed treatment for SAD when they were youngsters were reassessed approximately 7.5 years later using structured diagnostic interviews. Participants with a childhood diagnosis of SAD, compared to those with a childhood diagnosis of other anxiety disorders, were *not* more likely to meet diagnostic criteria for panic disorder or agoraphobia as young adults. They were, however, more likely to meet the criteria for other anxiety disorders as young adults.

School refusal, unlike separation anxiety disorder, can be found in children of all ages, but like separation anxiety disorder, it seems more likely to occur at major transition points. There is the suggestion that in younger children, the problem is likely to be related to separation anxiety, but children in middle-age groups and early adolescence are likely to have complex and mixed presentations of anxiety and depressive disorders. Prognosis seems best for children under the age of 10 years, and treatment seems to be particularly difficult with older children and those who are also depressed (Bernstein et al., 2001; Blagg & Yule, 1994). If problems are left untreated, serious long-term consequences seem possible (Elliott, 1999).

In working with school refusers, the majority of clinicians of all orientations stress the importance of getting the youngster back to school (Blagg & Yule, 1994; King, Ollendick, & Gullone, 1990). Successful strategies take an active approach to the problem—finding a way of getting the youngster back to school even if this is difficult or requires the threat of legal intervention. Cognitive-behavioral interventions that include exposure to fearful situations and teaching the youngster coping skills, as well as child-management training and advice for parents and teachers, have shown promise in achieving regular school attendance as well as overall improvement in functioning (King et al., 2000).

Generalized Anxiety Disorder

Phobias, school refusal, and separation anxiety represent relatively focused anxiety disorders. However, anxiety is sometimes experienced in a less focused manner.

DIAGNOSTIC CRITERIA

Prior versions of the DSM employed the diagnosis of Overanxious Disorder of Childhood and Adolescence (OAD) to recognize this clinical entity. Beginning with the DSM-IV, however, this diagnosis was eliminated. Instead, children and adolescents are now considered, along with adults, under the category of Generalized Anxiety Disorder (GAD). We will use both terms here, since much of the literature has employed the term *overanxious disorder*.

Generalized anxiety disorder is characterized by excessive anxiety and worry that the youngster finds difficult to control. The major diagnostic features of GAD as described by the DSM are presented in Table 6–6. Some of these symptoms must be present most days for the past 6 months, and the symptoms must cause significant distress or impairment in important areas of the youngster's functioning. The DSM acknowledges some developmental difference in that a child need only display one or more of the six symptoms listed in part C of Table 6–6. An adult must display at least three of these symptoms to receive the diagnosis of GAD.

DESCRIPTION

Clinicians frequently describe children and adolescents who worry excessively and exhibit extensive fearful behavior. These intense worries are not focused on any particular object or situation but rather occur in regard to a number of general life circumstances and are not due to a specific recent stress. Youngsters seem excessively concerned with their competence and performance in a number of areas (e.g., academics, peer relations, sports) to the point of being perfectionistic and setting unreasonably high standards for themselves. They may also worry about things like family finances and natural disasters. They are often described as "little worriers." These youngsters repeatedly seek approval and reassurance, and exhibit nervous habits (e.g., nail biting) and sleep disturbances. Physical complaints such as headaches and stomachaches are also common (Albano et al., 2003; American Psychiatric Association, 2000). The following description of John captures the clinical picture of generalized anxiety disorder.

> **TABLE 6–6   MAJOR FEATURES FOR THE DSM DIAGNOSIS OF GENERALIZED ANXIETY DISORDER**
>
> A. Excessive anxiety and worry occurring about a number of events or activities (e.g., school performance).
> B. The youngster finds it difficult to control the worry.
> C. The anxiety and worry are associated with one or more of the following symptoms:
>   1. Restlessness or feeling on edge
>   2. Being easily fatigued
>   3. Difficulty concentrating
>   4. Irritability
>   5. Muscle tension
>   6. Disturbed sleep
>
> *From American Psychiatric Association, 2000.*

John   Generalized Anxiety Disorder

Like his mother, John had a very low opinion of himself and his abilities . . . and found it difficult to cope with the "scary things" inside himself. His main problem had to do with the numerous fears that he had and the panic attacks that overtook him from time to time. He was afraid of the dark, of ghosts, of monsters, of being abandoned, of being alone, of strangers, of war, of guns, of knives, of loud noises, and of snakes. . . . Like his mother again, he had many psychosomatic complaints involving his bladder, his bowels, his kidneys, his intestines, and his blood. . . . He also suffered from insomnia and would not or could not go to sleep until his mother did. . . . He was also afraid to sleep alone or to sleep without a light, and regularly wet and soiled himself. He was often afraid but could not say why and was also fearful of contact with others.

Anthony, 1981, pp. 163–164.

EPIDEMIOLOGY

Epidemiological studies of nonclinic samples suggest that generalized anxiety disorder is a relatively common problem. Estimates, among youth of all ages, vary from about 2 to 14 percent (Anderson et al., 1987; Canino et al., 2004; Cohen et al., 1993b; Costello, 1989). The disorder is usually reported to be more common in girls, and the median age of onset is estimated to be about 10 years of age (Ford et al., 2003; Keller et al., 1992).

Generalized anxiety disorder is probably the most common anxiety disorder among adolescents (Clark et al., 1994). Estimates of rates in the general population of adolescents range from 3.7 to 7.3 percent (Kashani & Orvaschel, 1990; McGee et al., 1990; Whitaker et al., 1990). The findings of Cohen et al. (1993b) indicate a rate of about 14 percent for girls in both the 14–16 and the 17–20 age ranges, and a prevalence of about 5 percent for boys in both of these age groups.

The disorder is common among youngsters seen in clinical settings. Keller and colleagues (1992), for example, report that 85 percent of the youngsters with an anxiety disorder were diagnosed with overanxious disorder. Although other estimates are not quite this high, the disorder is commonly diagnosed.

Youngsters who meet the diagnostic criteria for GAD are likely to meet the diagnostic criteria for additional disorders (Masi et al., 2004), and rates of such co-occurrence seem higher for youngsters with GAD than for those with other diagnoses (Silverman & Ginsburg, 1998). Depression, separation anxiety, and phobias are common co-occurring disorders (Masi et al., 2004; Verduin & Kendall, 2003). However, GAD may be overdiagnosed (American Psychiatric Association, 2000), and some have questioned whether it is a distinct disorder. What is now considered a separate disorder (GAD) might instead be viewed as an indication of a general constitutional vulnerability toward anxiety or emotional reactivity (Flannery-Schroeder, 2004). It may be that help is sought when youngsters with this general vulnerability exhibit other anxiety or internalizing disorders (Beidel, Silverman, & Hammond-Laurence, 1996).

DEVELOPMENTAL COURSE

GAD does not seem transitory (Keller et al., 1992). Symptoms may persist for several years (Cohen, Cohen, & Brook, 1993a). Persistence may be particularly likely for those with more severe symptoms. A greater number of severe overanxious symptoms and increased impairment have been reported among adolescents with this disorder (Clark et al., 1994; Strauss, 1994).

An examination of developmental differences in co-occurring disorders provides some interesting information (Masi et al., 2004; Strauss et al., 1988). For example, although rates of co-occurrence are high for youngsters of all ages, young children seem more likely to receive a concurrent diagnosis of separation anxiety disorder, and adolescents a concurrent diagnosis of depression or social phobia. These findings may suggest a developmental difference in how generalized anxiety is experienced. Alternatively, since, in general, separation anxiety is more common in young children and depression and social anxiety more common in adolescents, these findings may also be viewed as consistent with questions, raised above, about whether GAD is a distinct disorder or an indication of a heightened general vulnerability.

Panic Attacks and Panic Disorder

Frank   Panic Attacks

While falling asleep, Frank often experienced discrete episodes of his heart beating quickly, shortness of breath, tingling in his hands, and extreme fearfulness. These episodes lasted only 15 to 20 minutes, but Frank could not fall asleep in his bedroom and began sleeping on the living room couch. His father brought him back to his bed once he was asleep, but Frank was tired during the day, and his schoolwork began to deteriorate.

Adapted from Rapoport & Ismond, 1996, pp. 240–241.

Intense, discrete experiences of extreme fear, like Frank's, that seem to arise quickly and often, and that occur without any clear cause, are known as panic attacks, and are another way that adolescents and children experience anxiety.

DIAGNOSTIC CRITERIA

A distinction is made between panic attacks and panic disorder.

Panic Attacks. A panic attack is a discrete period of intense fear or terror that has a sudden onset and reaches a peak quickly—10 minutes or less. The DSM describes 13 somatic or cognitive symptoms, 4 or more of which must be present during an episode (see Table 6–7). There are three different categories of panic attacks, defined by the presence or absence of triggers. *Unexpected (uncued) panic attacks* occur spontaneously or "out of the blue" with no apparent situational trigger. In contrast, *situationally bound (cued) panic attacks* occur on almost all occasions when the person is exposed to or anticipates a feared object or situation (e.g., a dog). *Situationally predisposed*

TABLE 6–7	SYMPTOMS OF A PANIC ATTACK ACCORDING TO THE DSM

1. Palpitations, pounding heart, or accelerated heart rate
2. Sweating
3. Trembling or shaking
4. Sensations of shortness of breath or smothering
5. Feeling of choking
6. Chest pain or discomfort
7. Nausea or abdominal distress
8. Feeling dizzy, unsteady, lightheaded, or faint
9. Derealization (feelings of unreality) or depersonalization (feeling detached from oneself)
10. Fear of losing control or going crazy
11. Fear of dying
12. Paresthesias (numbness or tingling sensations)
13. Chills or hot flushes

From American Psychiatric Association, 2000.

TABLE 6–8	MAJOR CRITERIA FOR THE DSM DIAGNOSIS OF PANIC DISORDER

1. Recurrent unexpected Panic Attacks (see Table 6–7)
2. At least one of the attacks has been followed by 1 month (or more) of one (or more) of the following:
   a. Persistent concern about having additional attacks
   b. Worry about the implications of the attack (e.g., losing control, having a heart attack, "going crazy")
   c. A significant change in behavior related to the attacks

From American Psychiatric Association, 2000.

panic attacks occur on exposure to a situational cue, but not all the time; that is, they do not occur invariably, and they may occur following exposure rather than immediately.

Panic attacks are not themselves a disorder within the DSM system, but rather they may occur in the context of several different anxiety disorders.

Panic Disorder. One of these disorders is Panic Disorder, which involves *unexpected* panic attacks that the person is concerned will reoccur without warning. The DSM criteria for a panic disorder are presented in Table 6–8. Panic disorder may occur with or without agoraphobia. In severe cases of panic a youngster may remain at home or become terrified of leaving home. This agoraphobia is an attempt to avoid certain circumstances in which an uncontrollable or embarrassing attack may occur or during which help may not be available.

Although there is an established literature regarding adults, it is only relatively recently that the occurrence of panic in children and adolescents has received attention (Kearney et al., 1997; Ollendick, Mattis, & King, 1994). This discrepancy was, in part, due to controversy regarding the existence of panic attacks and panic disorder in youngsters (Kearney & Silverman, 1992; Klein et al., 1992). Much of the controversy revolved around two issues.

One issue is whether youngsters experience both the physiological and cognitive symptoms of panic. Adults who experience panic attacks report fear of losing control, going "crazy," or dying during the attack. They also worry about future attacks. It has been reported that such cognitive symptoms do not occur in children or young adolescents, and it is

suggested that this absence is due to their limited cognitive development (Chorpita, Albano, & Barlow, 1996).

The second issue concerns whether panic is experienced by youngsters as spontaneous (uncued) or cued. Youngsters may report attacks as "out of the blue" because they may not be sufficiently aware of, or as likely to monitor, cues in their environment. Careful and detailed questioning may be needed to reveal precipitating cues. This problem is particularly true in relation to younger children.

EPIDEMIOLOGY

Although the diagnosis of panic may be difficult, literature is accumulating to suggest the presence of panic attacks and panic disorder in adolescents and, to a lesser degree, in prepubertal children (Ollendick, Birmaher, & Mattis, 2004). For example, many adults who experience panic attacks or panic disorder report that onset had occurred during adolescence or earlier.

Also, both community samples and clinic-based studies suggest that panic attacks and panic disorder may not be uncommon in adolescents. For example, 16 percent of youngsters between the ages of 12 and 17 in a community sample of Australian youth reported at least one full-blown panic attack in their lifetime (King et al., 1997) and similar rates have been reported in a sample of German adolescents (Essau, Conradt, & Petermann, 1999). Regarding panic disorder, the condition seems rarely to be diagnosed prior to mid or late adolescence. For example, Ford and colleagues (2003) found that while panic disorder was rarely diagnosed in younger British children, about 0.5 percent of youngsters between the ages of 13 and 15 met the criteria for panic disorder. Similar rates have been reported in a community sample of Puerto Rican, German, and U.S. youngsters (Canino et al., 2004; Essau et al., 1999; Whitaker et al., 1990). In clinical samples of adolescents, reported prevalence is higher—about 10 to 15 percent (e.g., Alessi, Robbins, & Dilsaver, 1987; Last & Strauss, 1989). Both panic attacks and panic disorder are typically reported as occurring more frequently in girls than in boys.

DESCRIPTION AND DEVELOPMENTAL PATTERN

Adolescents who experience panic attacks do experience considerable distress and impairment. Few, however, seem to seek treatment (Ollendick et al., 2004). With regard to how panic is experienced, studies of adolescents seen in clinics indicate that these youths evidence both the physiological and cognitive symptoms of panic. For example, Bradley and Hood (1993) found that seven of the physiological symptoms of panic attacks were reported by more than 50 percent of their sample. Cognitive symptoms were reported less frequently: "going crazy" was reported by 32 percent, and fear of dying by 25 percent.

Whether panic attacks are cued or spontaneous is less clear. Psychosocial stressors (e.g., family conflict, peer problems) were reported as possible precipitants by 26 of the 28 adolescents in this study. Some studies, however, report that for some youngsters, the panic attacks are judged to be spontaneous. As we have mentioned, though, there is a problem in judging the spontaneous nature of panic attacks in youngsters.

Less is known regarding panic in younger children. Although both panic attacks and panic disorder are reported in clinical samples of children, their expression may differ somewhat from the presentation in adolescents and adults. Young children may report a general fear of becoming sick rather than describing specific physiological symptoms (e.g., palpitations, breathlessness) or verbalizing fears of dying, going crazy, or losing control (Albano et al., 2003).

Youngsters with panic attacks or panic disorder who do present at clinics are likely to have a family history of panic attacks or other severe anxiety symptoms. They are also likely to present with a variety of other symptoms, and many meet the criteria for additional diagnoses, particularly other anxiety disorders and depression (Kearney et al., 1997; Masi et al., 2000). Many of the youngsters with panic disorder seen in clinical settings also exhibit agoraphobia. The high proportion of youngsters who report a history of separation anxiety led to the suggestion that separation anxiety disorder is a precursor to panic disorder. Findings of neurophysiological signs of greater arousal among infants of mothers with panic disorder as compared to controls is consistent with the idea of an early vulnerability (Warren et al., 2003). However, it seems likely that separation anxiety disorder would be only one of many possible paths to the development of panic disorder (Hayward et al., 2004; Ollendick et al., 2004).

Reactions to Traumatic Events

How do youngsters react to experiencing natural disasters such as hurricanes, other disasters such as fires or ship sinkings, the violence of a terrorist attack or kidnapping? Until relatively recently there had been little systematic study of children's reactions to such traumatic events.

Trauma is usually defined as an event outside everyday experience that would be distressing to almost anyone. Early descriptions of children's exposure to trauma suggested that reactions would be relatively mild and transient, and thus these experiences were not given a great deal of attention. However, reports began to emerge of more severe and long-lasting reactions.

The investigation of 26 children kidnapped from their Chowchilla, California, school bus in 1976 is one study that influenced how children's posttraumatic responses were understood. The children and their bus driver were held for 27 hours. At first they were driven around in darkened vans and then were moved to a buried tractor trailer, where they remained until some of the victims dug themselves out. The child victims and at least one parent of each child were interviewed within 5 to 13 months of the kidnapping. All of the children were found to be symptomatic, with 73 percent showing moderately severe or severe reactions. Assessments 2 to 5 years after the kidnapping revealed that many symptoms had persisted (Terr, 1979; 1983).

DIAGNOSTIC CRITERIA FOR ACUTE AND POSTTRAUMATIC STRESS DISORDERS

Systematic study of children's reactions to trauma was also stimulated by the introduction, in the third version of the DSM, of a specific diagnosis—Posttraumatic Stress Disorder (PTSD). The current DSM criteria for PTSD (Table 6–9) require exposure to a serious traumatic event to which the child or adolescent shows an intense fearful reaction. The youngster must also experience the PTSD triad of symptoms—reexperiencing, avoidance, and arousal—for more than one month. In addition, the disturbance must cause significant interference in important areas of the youngster's functioning.

There may need to be greater attention paid to developmental considerations in defining posttraumatic stress disorder in children (Salmon & Bryant, 2002). Indeed, some have suggested that existing criteria are not appropriate for infants or children under age 4, and alternative criteria have been proposed (Scheeringa et al., 2003). It has also been suggested that very young children can be given the diagnosis of PTSD following exposure to a traumatic event even if they do not exhibit intense fear at the time. Furthermore, there may be differences in the number and kind of symptoms of reexperiencing, avoidance, and arousal that young children exhibit.

The diagnostic criteria for Acute Stress Disorder (ASD) are essentially the same as those for PTSD, with two key exceptions. Perhaps the principal distinction is that ASD symptoms last for at least 2 days, but less than 4 weeks, whereas PTSD lasts for at least one month following the trauma or has a delayed onset. A youngster with a significant immediate reaction to a trauma may be given the diagnosis of ASD. This diagnosis may predict future PTSD, or help alert adults to the need for intervention to prevent such an outcome. The diagnosis of ASD also explicitly requires the presence of dissociative symptoms—that is, alterations in self awareness to escape an upsetting experience. Symptoms of dissociation can

---

TABLE 6–9	MAJOR CRITERIA FOR THE DSM DIAGNOSIS OF POSTTRAUMATIC STRESS DISORDER

A. The person has been exposed to a traumatic event that
  1. includes a threat of death, serious injury, or physical integrity to the self or others; and
  2. the person's response involves fear, helplessness, or horror (in children, this reaction may be expressed instead as disorganized or agitated behavior).

B. Reexperiencing the Traumatic Event (1 or more)[a]
  1. Recurrent distressing recollections (in young children may be trauma-related play)
  2. Recurrent distressing dreams
  3. Acting or feeling as if event were recurring
  4. Intense distress to cues that symbolize the event
  5. Physiological reactivity to cues that symbolize the event

C. Persistent Avoidance of Trauma-Related Stimuli and General Numbing (3 or more)[a]
  1. Avoidance of trauma-related thoughts, feelings, or conversations
  2. Avoidance of activities, places, or people associated with the trauma
  3. Inability to recall important aspects of the trauma
  4. Diminished interest in significant activities
  5. Feelings of detachment from others
  6. Restricted range of affect
  7. Sense of foreshortened future

D. Persistent Symptoms of Increased Arousal (2 or more)[a]
  1. Sleep difficulties
  2. Irritability, anger outbursts
  3. Difficulty concentrating
  4. Hypervigilance
  5. Exaggerated startle response

[a]Numbers in parentheses indicate the number of symptoms required in each category.

From American Psychiatric Association, 2000.

be displayed as a general numbing, detachment, or "appearing in a daze," or by *derealization* (a marked sense of unreality), *depersonalization* (feeling cut off from one's feelings or environment), or *dissociative amnesia* (inability to recall an important aspect of the trauma). Dissociation may be present with PTSD, but is not required for the diagnosis.

DESCRIPTION

The reactions of youngsters to traumatic events may vary considerably. Many exhibit symptoms without meeting the criteria for a diagnosis of PTSD, but still experience considerable distress and interference with functioning.

Most youngsters become upset at reminders of the trauma, and they experience repetitive, intrusive thoughts about the event. Even children who experience mild levels of exposure to life-threatening disasters may have such thoughts. Among preschool and school-age children, reenactment of aspects of the disaster is frequently observed in drawings, stories, and play. Initially such behavior may be part of reexperiencing symptoms, but it may become a useful part of the recovery process as well. Saylor, Powell, and Swenson (1992), for example, report that after Hurricane Hugo occurred in South Carolina, children's play progressed from blowing houses down to acting out the role of roofers during rebuilding.

Youngsters may also exhibit increased frequency and intensity of specific fears directly related to or associated with the traumatic experience. Thus adolescent British girls on a school trip who experienced the sinking of their cruise ship Jupiter developed fears of swimming, of the dark, or of boats and other forms of transportation. These girls, however, did not show elevated levels of unrelated fears when compared with schoolmates who did not go on the trip or with girls from a comparable school (Yule, Udwin, & Murdoch, 1990).

Separation difficulties and clingy, dependent behaviors are also common. These behaviors may be exhibited in reluctance to go to school or in a desire to sleep with parents. Other sleep problems, such as difficulty in getting to sleep, nightmares, and repeated dreams related to the traumatic event, are also common. A sense of vulnerability and loss of faith in the future have also been reported. In adolescents, this loss may interfere with planning for future education and careers; moreover, school performance is reported to suffer. Other commonly noted symptoms include depressed mood, loss of interest in previously enjoyed activities, irritability, and angry or aggressive outbursts. Guilt about surviving when others have died can also occur. It is also common for youngsters to meet the criteria for additional and multiple diagnoses (Pfefferbaum, 1997).

PTSD AND CHILD ABUSE

Child maltreatment is one form of trauma that has been viewed within the framework of PTSD. Indeed, many youngsters who experience abuse meet the diagnostic criteria for PTSD. In Chapter 3 (p. 57) we saw that a developmental traumatology model of child maltreatment suggests that trauma-induced changes in neurobiology underlie the development of psychopathology in maltreated children (De Bellis, 2001). In this model, PTSD symptoms are considered to be the key mediator linking maltreatment and subsequent psychopathology. Accordingly, as depicted in Figure 6–3, PTSD symptoms are the initial problems that then contribute to the potential development of a wide range of behavioral and emotional problems at different times of life.

EPIDEMIOLOGY

Natural disasters, terrorism, and accidents are catastrophic events that are unpredictable in nature, making it difficult to determine the number of children and adolescents who will be exposed to traumatic events each year (Fletcher, 2003). However, we do know that youngsters are frequently exposed to maltreatment and are frequent victims of violent crime. Some may be at particular risk. For example, infants and younger children are at greater risk for maltreatment (Wekerle & Wolfe, 2003) and homeless adolescents are at increased risk for victimization (Stewart et al., 2004). It seems likely that a good number of youngsters experience a traumatic event. Indeed, a survey of children and adolescents indicated that about one quarter had experienced a serious traumatic event by the age of 16 (Costello et al., 2002).

Fletcher (2003) indicates that about one third of youngsters exposed to traumatic events are diagnosed with PTSD—a rate that is slightly higher than traumatized adults. Most studies find a higher incidence of PTSD among girls. As indicated earlier, developmental differences may exist in how PTSD is expressed, particularly in very young children. Research also suggests that children, adolescents, and adults may differ with regard to some

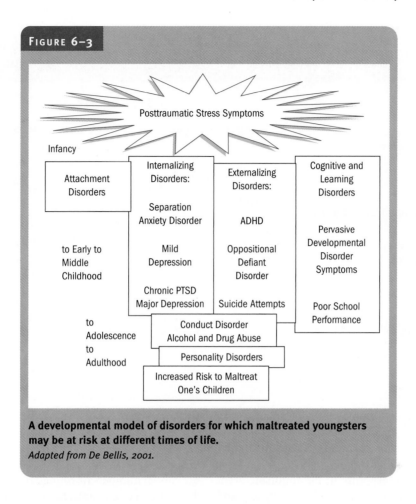

FIGURE 6-3

A developmental model of disorders for which maltreated youngsters may be at risk at different times of life.
Adapted from De Bellis, 2001.

basic neurobiological responses to trauma (De Bellis, 2001; Lipschitz et al., 2003). For example, there may be differences in the response of the hypothalamic-pituitary-adrenal (HPA) axis, a critical neurohormonal regulatory system that, under conditions of extreme stress, leads to the release of neurohormones, including cortisol. The response of this system is one of the mechanisms that is thought to underlie the development of PTSD and other difficulties.

On average, the incidence of particular PTSD symptoms appears to be above 20 percent. The PTSD cluster of symptoms (reexperiencing, avoidance, and arousal) has been reported in youngsters from a variety of different cultures (Perrin, Smith, & Yule, 2000). The most frequently occurring category of symptom is probably reexperiencing the event (Fletcher, 2003).

Not all children and adolescents experience the same pattern or intensity of symptoms, and not all children who experience traumas meet the criteria for PTSD. Reactions may also vary in how long symptoms persist and problems may fluctuate over

time. A number of factors seem to influence youngsters' initial reactions and the duration and severity of symptoms (La Greca, Silverman, & Wasserstein, 1998; Udwin et al., 2000).

The nature of the traumatic event may influence reactions. One can, for example, group stressors into two categories: (1) acute, nonabusive stressors—nonabusive traumatic events that occur only once (e.g., floods, accidents); and (2) chronic or abusive stressors—ongoing stressors (e.g., war) or physical or sexual abuse (Fletcher, 2003). Some symptoms of PTSD appear to be likely to occur regardless of the type of traumatic event (e.g., trauma-related fears, difficulty sleeping). However, other symptoms may vary depending on the type of trauma experienced. Also, while youngsters experiencing either kind of trauma appear equally likely to receive the diagnosis of PTSD, they may vary as to other diagnoses that they are likely to receive. These differences are illustrated in Table 6–10. It may seem surprising that some symptoms or problems are more likely to be observed among youngsters exposed to acute,

TABLE 6-10	RATES OF PTSD SYMPTOMS AND ASSOCIATED SYMPTOMS/DIAGNOSES IN RESPONSE TO ACUTE, NONABUSIVE STRESSORS AND CHRONIC OR ABUSIVE STRESSORS	
	TYPE OF STRESSOR	
	ACUTE-NONABUSIVE	**CHRONIC OR ABUSIVE**
DSM Symptom Cluster		
Reexperiencing	92%	86%
Avoidance/numbness	30%	54%
Overarousal	55%	71%
Associated Symptoms/Diagnoses		
PTSD	36%	36%
Generalized Anxiety	55%	26%
Separation Anxiety	45%	35%
Panic	35%	6%
Depression	10%	28%
ADHD	22%	11%

Adapted from Fletcher, 2003.

nonabusive trauma. One possible explanation may be that youngsters exposed to chronic stressors come to some kind of accommodation over time with their traumas (Fletcher, 2003).

The degree of exposure to the traumatic event also appears to be an important influence. Pynoos and his colleagues (1987), for example, studied 159 California schoolchildren who were exposed to a sniper attack on their school in which one child and a passerby were killed and 13 other children were injured. Children who were trapped on the playground showed much greater effects than those who had left the immediate vicinity of the shooting or were not in school that day. At a 14-month follow-up among the most severely exposed children, 74 percent still reported moderate to severe PTSD symptoms, whereas 81 percent of the nonexposed children reported no PTSD (Nader et al., 1991). Although level of exposure to this life-threatening trauma was an important factor, reactions did occur among children who did not experience a high degree of exposure. The child's subjective experience of threat and greater knowledge of the schoolmate who was killed were associated with increased reactions among less-exposed children.

Individual differences that existed prior to a traumatic event (e.g., anxiety level, ethnicity) are also likely to influence the youngster's reaction (La Greca et al., 1998). So, for example, a child's prior level of general anxiety may, in part, determine her or his reaction to the traumatic event.

DEVELOPMENTAL COURSE AND PROGNOSIS

In general, symptoms of PTSD decline over time, but substantial numbers of youngsters continue to report difficulties. For example, La Greca and her colleagues (1996) examined third- through fifth-grade children during the school year after Hurricane Andrew occurred in Florida. Symptoms of avoidance and general numbing decreased over time, being present in about 49 percent of the children at 3 months and about 24 percent of the children at 10 months. Similarly, the number of children with symptoms of arousal decreased from 67 to about 49 percent in the same time period. However, substantial numbers of children continued to report reexperiencing symptoms—approximately 90 percent at 3 months and 78 percent at 10 months.

Children's initial attempts at coping may also affect the course of their reactions. Children who tend to use negative coping strategies (e.g., blaming others, screaming) may be more likely to experience persistent symptoms (La Greca et al., 1996). The reactions of children and adolescents to traumatic events are also related to the reactions of their parents and others in their environment. If the parents themselves suffer severe posttraumatic stress or for some other reason are unable to provide an atmosphere of support and communication, their children's reactions are likely to be more severe.

ACCENT ● ● ● ● ●

Terrorism and Posttraumatic Stress

On September 11, 2001, terrorists struck the United States with attacks on New York City and Washington, DC. Many people suffered the loss of a loved one in the attack or in rescue efforts. Nearly 3,000 persons were known or presumed dead. Survivors, relatives, and many more were left with vivid images of planes crashing into buildings, buildings burning and falling, loss of human life, and terror and sadness on the faces of those involved. What is the impact of such events on children and adolescents?

In reaction to an earlier event, the Oklahoma City bombing, children who lost loved ones, friends, or acquaintances, or who simply lived nearby, experienced both immediate and continuing symptoms of posttraumatic stress (Allen et al., 1999; Pfefferbaum et al., 1999a; Whittlesey et al., 1999). Symptoms included trembling, nervousness, fear, shock, and fear that a family member or friend might be hurt. Nearly 2 months following the attack, the majority of youngsters in the Oklahoma City area still reported safety worries and many experienced difficulty handling demands and posttraumatic stress symptoms. The symptoms were greatest for those who had lost an immediate family member, but many of those who had lost a more distant relative, friend, or acquaintance remained affected as well (Pfefferbaum et al., 1999b).

Similar reactions occurred among youngsters in New York City and Washington, D.C. following the September 11 attacks. The impact on families was appreciable. Telephone interviews of Manhattan residents 1 to 2 months later indicated that many had a relative or friend killed or knew a teacher or coach who lost someone (Stuber et al., 2002). Over half reported that more

than 4 hours passed before the parent and child were reunited. Counseling was received by a youngster in 22 percent of these families. In the Washington, D.C., area, service use showed an increase over the same period for the previous year. There was an increase of 46 percent in child outpatient visits for anxiety disorders and a 50 percent increase in such visits for acute and posttraumatic stress reactions (Hoge & Pavlin, 2002).

Widespread and frequent media coverage also brought the trauma into many homes around the country. Surveys conducted days or months after the attacks suggested that many youngsters may have experienced stress-related symptoms and worry about safety (Saylor et al., 2003; Schuster et al., 2001; Whalen et al., 2004). Parents experiencing stress reactions were more likely to report stress symptoms in their child and, in families where children's television viewing had not been restricted, time watching TV significantly correlated with the number of reported stress symptoms (Schuster et al., 2001). Interestingly, viewing positive images (e.g., heroics and rescues) did not help—again greater viewing was associated with more child PTSD symptoms (Saylor et al., 2003).

Reactions to terrorism seem similar in many ways to reactions to other traumatic events, but there may be unique aspects (Fremont, 2004). Terrorism presents an unpredictable threat and there is extensive media coverage. There is also a profound effect on the adults and communities that typically provide support for young people. In the wake of the events of September 11, attention continues to be focused on developing successful interventions and on investigating the effects of such trauma.

These findings naturally lead to the question of how best to intervene when children and adolescents are exposed to traumatic events. Clear recommendations are difficult to make; however, clinical consensus suggests certain key components (AACAP, 1998b; Pfefferbaum, 1997; Vernberg & Vogel, 1993; Yule, 1994). Within a short time of the disaster, debriefing groups are usually employed to encourage youngsters and their families to share their feelings and open channels of communication, to prepare them for possible reactions in the future, and to help them realize that their initial reactions are normal reactions to abnormal events. Additional group work or

individual cognitive-behavioral interventions may be necessary for some youngsters (Cohen et al., 2004). These interventions should include parents and should involve exploration of the trauma and education about posttraumatic stress reactions. Treatments should also include some form of exposure to thoughts, emotions, and trauma-related situations; train youngsters in the use of specific stress management techniques; address thoughts and attributions; and include strategies to prevent relapse (Perrin et al., 2000). These components may facilitate coping or alleviate symptoms and may help to enhance a sense of control and mastery.

Obsessive-Compulsive Disorder

DIAGNOSTIC CRITERIA

Obsessions are unwanted, repetitive, intrusive thoughts, whereas compulsions involve repetitive, stereotyped behaviors that the child or adolescent feels compelled to perform. Obsessive-Compulsive Disorder (OCD) involves either obsessions or compulsions, or in a majority of youngsters, both (March & Mulle, 1998). The definitions employed in the DSM to characterize obsessions and compulsions are presented in Table 6–11. Beyond defining the nature of obsessions and compulsions, the DSM criteria for OCD indicate that the person realizes that the thoughts and behaviors are unreasonable. This particular feature is not required for the diagnosis of OCD in children but may become part of the clinical picture in older children and adolescents. Even among very young children, odd repetitive acts may be seen as strange. However, children, as we see in the case of Stanley, may initially have their own explanations. The child may come to recognize that the ideas or behaviors involved are unreasonable but still feel the need to repeat them.

Stanley   The Martian Rituals

Seven-year-old Stanley indicated that he had seen a show in which Martians contacted humans by putting strange thoughts in their heads. Stanley explained his compulsion to do everything in sequences of four as a sign that he had been picked as the Martians' contact on earth. After 2 years of no contact, Stanley gave up this explanation but not his ritual.

Rapoport, 1989, p. 84.

Another criteria for the diagnosis of OCD is that the obsessions or compulsions are highly time consuming and that they result in considerable interference with normal routines, academic functioning, and social relationships (Piacentini et al., 2003). The impact on Sergei's life illustrates the nature and consequences of the disorder.

Sergei   Impairment in Functioning

Sergei is a 17-year-old former high school student. Only a year or so ago Sergei seemed to be a normal adolescent with many talents and interests. Then, almost overnight he was transformed into a lonely outsider, excluded from social life by his psychological disabilities. Specifically, he was unable to stop washing. Haunted by the notion that he was dirty—in spite of the contrary evidence of his senses—he began to spend more and more of his time cleansing himself of imaginary dirt. At first his ritual ablutions were confined to weekends and evenings and he was able to stay in school while keeping them up, but soon they began to consume all his time, forcing him to drop out of school, a victim of his inability to feel clean enough.

Rapoport, 1989, p. 83.

TABLE 6–11	THE DSM DEFINITIONS OF OBSESSIONS AND COMPULSIONS

Obsessions: Intrusive, persistent thoughts, impulses, or images that
1. cause anxiety or distress;
2. are not simply excessive real-life worries;
3. the person attempts to ignore, suppress, or neutralize; and
4. are recognized as products of one's own mind.

Compulsions: Repetitive behaviors or mental acts that
1. the person feels driven to perform; and
2. are unrealistic attempts to prevent or reduce distress or some dreaded situation.

From American Psychiatric Association, 2000.

DESCRIPTION

Judith Rapoport and her colleagues at the National Institute for Mental Health (NIMH) conducted a series of studies that increased the attention given to obsessive-compulsive behavior in youngsters. Table 6–12 indicates the most common obsessions and compulsions among these children and adolescents seen by the NIMH group.

Subsequent reports have corroborated these findings (Henin & Kendall, 1997). Compulsive rituals are reported more frequently than obsessions; this finding is different from reports concerning adults, in which obsessions and compulsions are reported at fairly equivalent rates. There appear to be two broad themes: the first theme is a preoccupation with cleanliness, grooming, and averting danger; and the second theme is a pervasive doubting—not knowing when one is "right." Washing, repeating, and checking rituals are the most common. Obsessions involving dirt, germs, contamination, or fear of something terrible happening are the most frequently reported.

Childhood obsessive-compulsive disorder is often recognized only when symptoms are very severe. If a youngster reaches out for help, it is frequently only after years of suffering. Youngsters often admit having kept their problems a secret. Among those who do seek help, many indicate that their parents were unaware of their problem. For example, diagnostic interviews conducted with a community-based sample of youngsters ages 9 through 17 and their mothers found that of the 35 cases of OCD

TABLE 6–12	OBSESSIONS AND COMPULSIONS AMONG CHILDREN AND ADOLESCENTS RECEIVING THE DIAGNOSIS OF OBSESSIVE-COMPULSIVE DISORDER	PERCENT REPORTING SYMPTOM
Obsessions		
Concern with dirt, germs, or environmental toxins		40
Something terrible happening (fire, death, or illness of self or loved one)		24
Symmetry, order, or exactness		17
Scrupulosity (religious obsessions)		13
Concern or disgust with bodily wastes or secretions (urine, stool, saliva)		8
Lucky or unlucky numbers		8
Forbidden, aggressive, or perverse sexual thoughts, images, or impulses		4
Fear of harming others or oneself		4
Concern with household items		3
Intrusive nonsense sounds, words, or music		1
Compulsions		
Excessive or ritualized handwashing, showering, bathing, toothbrushing, or grooming		85
Repeating rituals (going in or out of a door, up or down from a chair)		51
Checking (doors, locks, appliances, emergency brake on car, paper route, homework)		46
Rituals to remove contact with contaminants		23
Touching		20
Measures to prevent harm to self or others		16
Ordering or arranging		17
Counting		18
Hoarding or collecting rituals		11
Rituals of cleaning household or inanimate objects		6
Miscellaneous rituals (such as writing, moving, speaking)		26

Note: Percentages total more than 100 percent because many youths had more than one symptom.

Adapted from Rapoport, 1989.

identified, 4 youngsters were diagnosed as having OCD on the basis of the parent's report, and 32 as the result of the child's report, but in only one case did the child and parent concur (Rapoport et al., 2000).

EPIDEMIOLOGY

Obsessive-compulsive disorder is probably not as rare as was once believed (March et al., 2004; Rapoport et al., 2000). Epidemiological studies of nonreferred adolescents suggest a prevalence rate of about 1 percent and a lifetime prevalence rate of about 1.9 percent in the general adolescent population (Flament et al., 1988; Rapoport et al., 2000). Most estimates also suggest that at younger ages, boys outnumber girls, but that by adolescence, the genders are equally represented (March et al., 2004; Rapoport et al., 2000). Among a sample of 70 consecutive child and adolescent cases seen at NIMH, 7 had an onset prior to the age of 7 years, and the mean age of onset was 10 years of age. The onset of obsessive-compulsive symptoms in boys tended to be prepubertal (mean age 9), whereas in girls, the average onset (mean of 11 years) was around puberty (Swedo et al., 1989c). Similar age differences in onset of OCD symptoms have also been reported among community samples (Rapoport et al., 2000).

Most youngsters diagnosed with obsessive-compulsive disorder meet the criteria for at least one other disorder (Geller et al., 2003a; Rapoport & Inhoff-Germain, 2000). Multiple anxiety disorders, attention-deficit hyperactivity disorder, developmental disabilities, conduct and oppositional disorders, substance abuse, and depression are commonly reported (Rapoport & Inhoff-Germain, 2000). Obsessive-compulsive disorder also often occurs with Tourette's syndrome (a chronic disorder with a genetic and neuroanatomical basis characterized by motor and vocal tics and related urges) or other tic disorders (Leckman et al., 1997). Tics are sudden, rapid, recurrent, stereotyped motor movements or vocalizations. Youngsters with tics may represent a distinct subtype of OCD with regard to symptomatology and response to treatment (Geller et al., 2003b; Scahill et al., 2003).

DEVELOPMENTAL COURSE AND PROGNOSIS

Behavior with obsessive-compulsive qualities occurs in various stages of normal development (Leonard et al., 1990). For example, very young children may have bedtime and eating rituals or may require things to be "just so." Disruption of these routines often leads to distress. Also, young children are often observed to engage in repetitive play and to show a distinct preference for sameness. Benjamin Spock (Spock & Rothenberg, 1992), in his widely read book for parents, noted that mild compulsions—such as stepping over cracks in the sidewalk or touching every third picket in a fence—are quite common in 8-, 9-, and 10-year-olds. Many readers of this text likely recall engaging in such behaviors. Behaviors that are common to the child's peer group are probably best viewed as games. Only when they dominate the child's life and interfere with normal functioning is there cause for concern. In addition, though, the specific content of OCD rituals generally does not resemble common developmental rituals, and OCD rituals have a later stage of onset. It is not clear whether developmental rituals represent early manifestations of obsessive-compulsive disorder in some children (Leonard et al., 1990).

Obsessive-compulsive disorder is described as following a course in which symptoms emerge and fade over time. Multiple obsessions and compulsions are usually present at any one time, and usually the symptoms change over time, although no clear progression is identified (Rettew et al., 1992).

Research also suggests that the disorder is likely to be chronic (Leonard et al., 1994). Although about three quarters of youngsters receiving treatment may show substantial improvement, problems persist (Wagner et al., 2003). For example, Leonard and her colleagues (1993) followed youngsters who had received pharmacological treatment and were

Keeping things in certain specific locations and order is common among children. It is only when these kinds of behaviors interfere with normal functioning that they should cause concern for clinicians and other adults.
Courtesy of A. C. Israel

reevaluated 2 to 7 years later. Seventy percent were still taking medication, 43 percent still met the diagnostic criteria for OCD, and only 11 percent exhibited no obsessive-compulsive symptoms.

Etiology of Anxiety Disorders

We have so far described several anxiety disorders. It is likely that such disturbances are influenced by multiple risk factors that interact with each other in complex ways (Barlow, 2002; Donovan & Spence, 2000). But risk factors and causal mechanisms are by no means clear. Much of the information that is available represents a downward extension from the adult literature.

One question we can ask is, How specific are the influences? Risk factors could be specific; that is, different combinations of influences could lead to different disorders. Alternatively, influences may be nonspecific—a particular risk factor or combination of risk factors may contribute to the development of anxiety disorders in general rather than to a specific anxiety disorder. As it turns out, risk factors may be quite nonspecific and may contribute to the development of several problems including, but not limited to, anxiety disorders. Finally, there may be multiple paths and different combinations of risk factors for the same outcome. Youngsters may experience different combinations of influences yet meet the criteria for the same disorder.

Genetics

Multiple sources indicate that anxiety disorders occur in families (Klein et al., 2001; Silverman & Ginsburg, 1998). The degree to which such familial aggregation results from genetic or environmental influences remains unclear, and there may be gender differences in the relative contributions of these influences (Lichtenstein & Annas, 2000; Thapar & McGuffin, 1995). However, findings from family and twin studies are consistent with a genetic contribution to anxiety disorders.

One type of family study indicates that children whose parents have an anxiety disorder are at risk for developing an anxiety disorder (e.g., Beidel & Turner, 1997). Family aggregation of anxiety disorders is also indicated by research that shows that parents whose children have anxiety disorders are themselves likely to have anxiety disorders (e.g., Last et al., 1991). In addition, more specific examinations of the influence of inheritance indicate genetic influences (Kendler et al., 1992b; Lichtenstein & Annas,

2000). Twin studies do indicate higher rates of concordance for monozygotic as compared with dizygotic twins. In the Virginia Twin Study of Adolescent Behavioral Development (Eaves et al., 1997), heritability estimates for anxiety tended to be lower than for other disorders. The findings are, however, consistent with other reports (King & Ollendick, 1997; Thapar & McGuffin, 1995) that suggest that genetic factors may play a role in the development of anxiety disorders. These influences may be expressed through differences in the biochemical functioning of the brain with regard to neurotransmitters such as serotonin (Neumeister et al., 2004).

What may be inherited, however, is a general tendency, such as emotional and behavioral reactivity to stimuli, rather than heritability of a specific anxiety disorder. Furthermore, this general tendency may be a risk factor for depression as well as anxiety (Eley & Stevenson, 1999; Thapar & McGuffin, 1997). The Virginia Twin Study and other findings also suggest that the genetic contribution to anxiety disorders may be greater for girls than for boys. Finally, we should remember that these findings indicate a substantial contribution of environment to anxiety disorders (Eaves et al., 1997; Lichtenstein & Annas, 2000). Thus, there may be a general genetic risk factor for anxiety disorders and depression and unique experiences may contribute to specific expressions of this vulnerability.

Biological Influences for OCD. Many workers have come to believe in a biological basis for obsessive-compulsive disorder (Grados & Riddle, 2001; March & Mulle, 1998). It may be particularly important to note evidence of genetic influence for obsessive-compulsive disorder (Leonard et al., 1994). The disorder has been found to be more prevalent among youngsters with a first-degree relative with obsessive-compulsive behavior than among the general population, and many parents of youngsters with the disorder meet diagnostic criteria for OCD or exhibit obsessive-compulsive symptoms (Lenane et al., 1990; Riddle et al., 1992; Swedo et al., 1989c). In addition, a number of studies have reported that both OCD and Tourette's syndrome (or less severe tic disorders) occur in the same persons at higher than expected rates and have found a familial association between the two disorders (Leonard et al., 1994). These findings are viewed as suggesting a possible genetic cause for obsessive-compulsive disorder.

Findings of an association between obsessive-compulsive symptoms and certain known neurological disorders provide further support for a biological basis for obsessive-compulsive disorder. Also, brain imaging studies have suggested that obsessive-compulsive disorder is linked to neurobiological abnormalities of the basal ganglia, a group of brain structures lying under the cerebral cortex (Luxenberg et al., 1988; Swedo et al., 1989a; Swedo et al., 1989b) and areas of the prefrontal cortex (Russell et al., 2003). A subset of cases of obsessive-compulsive disorder, known as PANDAS (pediatric autoimmune neuropsychiatric disorders associated with streptococcal infections), has been noted. These cases have a sudden onset or exacerbation of symptoms and include tics (Allen, Leonard, & Swedo, 1995; Snider & Swedo, 2003). They are believed to result from an autoimmune reaction produced when antibodies formed by the body against the streptococcal cells react with and cause inflammation in cells of the basal ganglia.

TEMPERAMENT

The general vulnerability to anxiety discussed earlier may be associated with the child's temperament—biologically based, possibly inherited, individual differences in emotionality, behavioral style, and the like.

An important model of the relationship of temperament and anxiety disorders has been described by Jerome Kagan and his colleagues (Kagan, 1997). Their findings are based on longitudinal research of behaviorally inhibited children, who are identified as extreme with respect to the probability of withdrawal or approach to unfamiliar people or events (see p. 33). Of particular interest is the development of internalizing problems in these inhibited children. At 5.5 years of age, children who were originally classified as inhibited had developed more fears than had uninhibited children. Furthermore, whereas fears in uninhibited children could usually be related to a prior trauma, this was not true for the inhibited children (Kagan, Resnick, & Snidman, 1990). Other research also suggests that inhibited children are at risk for the development of anxiety disorders. For example, in a study of two samples, Kagan's original sample and a sample of high-risk offspring of parents with panic disorder/agoraphobia and other disorders, significant differences between inhibited and not inhibited children were observed (Biederman et al., 1993). Inhibited children were more likely to meet the criteria for four or more disorders, for two or more anxiety disorders, and for specific anxiety disorders (avoidant disorder, separation anxiety disorder, and agoraphobia). Furthermore, the rates of anxiety

disorders for inhibited children increased over the 3-year period that they were followed. This and other evidence suggests that early anxious and withdrawn behaviors are associated with increased risk for the development of internalizing difficulties during later childhood, adolescence, and young adulthood (Goodwin, Fergusson, & Horwood, 2004; Hirshfeld-Becker, Biederman, & Rosenbaum, 2004).

Gray (1987) has described a functional brain system (described further in Chapter 8), part of which is a behavioral inhibition system (BIS) involving multiple areas of the brain. The BIS system is related to the emotions of fear and anxiety, and tends to inhibit action in novel or fearful situations or under conditions of punishment or nonreward. Gray's model of inhibition has also informed thinking about the contribution of temperament to the development of anxiety disorders (Chorpita, 2001; Lonigan et al., 2004).

Another approach to the contribution of temperament to anxiety disorders derives from Clark and Watson's (1991) model of emotion and the concept of negative affectivity (NA). NA is a temperamental dimension characterized by a general/persistent negative (e.g., nervous, sad, angry) mood and style of engagement with the environment. Research supports the hypothesis that the development of both anxiety and depression may be characterized by high levels of NA and that this may, in part, be responsible for high rates of co-occurrence of these disorders. Depression, but not anxiety, is thought to be characterized by low levels of the separate temperamental dimension of positive affectivity—pleasurable mood and engagement with the environment (Chorpita, 2002; Lonigan et al., 2004).

PSYCHOSOCIAL INFLUENCES

Psychosocial influences are clearly a part of the complex interplay of risk factors that can lead to the development of anxiety disorders. Children with a general vulnerability to anxiety may be exposed to a variety of experiences that increase their risk for anxiety disorders. For example, children may develop anxiety problems as a result of exposure to some traumatic event such as being attacked by a dog. As we saw earlier, exposure to traumatic events can result in posttraumatic stress reactions that may then set the stage for the development of other disorders. The reactions of parents to the trauma or to children's experience is one factor that can influence outcome. Not all children with anxiety difficulties, however, are exposed to traumatic events. How do we understand the development of anxiety in these youngsters?

It has been suggested that the various psychosocial influences on the development of anxiety can be organized around the concept of a child's experiences with and perceptions of control (cf. Chorpita & Barlow, 1998; Chorpita, 2001). The role of parents is, again, a principal focus of attention.

Parents may influence the development of anxiety in several ways (Wood et al., 2003). Children may learn to be anxious from their parents who prompt, model, and reinforce anxious behavior. Parents, who are themselves anxious, may model fearful behavior or transmit such information by telling stories of anxiety-provoking experiences. That children can learn from observing their parents' reactions is illustrated in a study of toddlers who were presented with a rubber snake or rubber spider (Gerull & Rapee, 2002). The toddlers' approach to or avoidance of these toys was measured. Toddlers whose mothers' expressions were negative toward a toy in an earlier trial were less likely to approach and more likely to show negative emotional reactions to the toy. Also, Ollendick, King, and Hamilton (1991) asked a large sample of Australian and American youngsters (9 to 14 years of age) to report retrospectively on the sources of their fears. They found that the development of highly prevalent fears was most frequently attributed to the transmission of information and modeling. A parent may also reinforce avoidant behavior once it is displayed by the child by attending to that behavior or by being oversolicitous to the child in situations that initially evoke anxious behavior.

In addition to modeling anxious behavior or relating stories of fearful and traumatic experiences, parents may influence the development of anxiety through other practices. For example, Dadds and his colleagues (1996) demonstrated that anxious children and their parents are more likely to perceive threat and therefore choose avoidant solutions to ambiguous social problems. Videotaped discussions between children (7 to 14 years old) and their families revealed that parents of anxious children listened less to their children, pointed out fewer positive consequences of adaptive behavior, and were more likely to respond to a child's solutions that were avoidant. In contrast, parents of nonclinic children were more likely to listen to and agree with their children's plans that were neither aggressive nor avoidant. Following the family discussion, children from both groups were asked for their plan for the situation. Anxious children offered more avoidant solutions. Parenting

practices may thus contribute to the development of certain cognitive styles, for example, to the perception of situations as hostile or threatening.

Parents of anxious children have also been described as intrusive. Intrusive parenting is defined as excessive regulation of children's activities, overprotection, autocratic parental decision making, or instruction of children in how to think or feel (Wood et al., 2003). Such parenting behavior may affect children's sense of control/effectiveness, and their development of adaptive problem-solving and coping styles. For example, mothers and clinic-referred children with anxiety disorders were observed while completing tasks together. Mothers of these anxious children were more intrusive and more critical while working with their children than were mothers of nonclinic children (Hudson & Rapee, 2001; 2002). These influences are likely bidirectional. A child's anxious temperament may also evoke an overprotective and intrusive parental response.

An additional indication of the contribution of parenting to the development of anxiety disorders comes from the literature concerning the impact of attachment (Main, 1996). Insecure mother-child attachments have been shown to be a risk factor for the development of anxiety disorders (Bernstein, Borchardt, & Perwien, 1996). For example, Warren and colleagues (1997) reported on the adolescent outcome of a group of youngsters who, as infants, had been assessed using Ainsworth's Strange Situation procedure. At 12 months of age, these youngsters had been classified as either securely attached, avoidantly attached, or anxiously/resistantly attached. When they were 17.5 years old, they were assessed by raters who did not know the child's past attachment status. Fifteen percent of the adolescents had at least one past or current anxiety disorder. Fifty-one percent of the adolescents had a disorder other than an anxiety disorder. More youngsters with anxiety disorders were, as infants, classified as having anxious/resistant attachments, and more children with other (nonanxiety) disorders were classified as having avoidant attachments. Also, 28 percent of children who were anxiously/resistantly attached as infants developed anxiety disorders, whereas 13 percent who were not anxiously/resistantly attached developed anxiety disorders. Furthermore, anxious/resistant attachment was found to contribute to the development of anxiety disorders even after maternal anxiety and measures of infant temperament were accounted for. Thus a specific kind of insecure attachment may contribute to the development of anxiety disorders.

We have been discussing how families may contribute to the development of anxiety problems in children. But we should also remember that families protect children from developing these problems. Family support, for example, has been found to protect children who are exposed to traumatic circumstances (Donovan & Spence, 2000). And families may foster children's abilities to cope with potentially anxiety-provoking circumstances.

Assessment of Anxiety Disorders

A comprehensive assessment of a youngster presenting with anxiety will likely involve a variety of assessment needs. Assessment strategies that are sensitive to developmental issues are required because they must address ongoing developmental changes and appreciate differences in children's comprehension and expressive abilities. The assessment process must also allow problems of clinical concern to be differentiated from the normal fears and worries that may be common in this age group (Kendall et al., 2000; March & Albano, 1998). Thus initial and ongoing assessment presents a considerable challenge.

Because it is likely that aspects of the environment may contribute to anxiety difficulties, the youngster's environment will need to be assessed as well. For example, it may be desirable to assess the specific environmental events that are associated with heightened anxiety, to evaluate patterns of family interactions and communication, to assess the reactions of adults or peers to the youngster's behavior, and to assess the existence of problems in other family members. The assessment of multiple aspects of the problem and the use of multiple informants, including the child or adolescent, are likely to yield valuable information.

Assessment of anxiety disorders is often guided by the tripartite model of anxiety. Thus assessment methods address one or more of the three response systems (behavioral, physiological, subjective). Various methods exist (Barrios & Hartmann, 1997; Greco & Morris, 2004).

INTERVIEWS AND SELF-REPORT INVENTORIES

As is usually the case, a general clinical interview is likely to yield information that is valuable to the clinician in formulating an understanding of the case and in planning an intervention. The youngster and at least one parent will typically be interviewed.

Structured diagnostic interviews are available and may be employed to derive a clinical diagnosis (Schniering et al., 2000). For example, the Anxiety Disorders Interview Schedule for Children (ADIS-C/P) is a semistructured interview for the child and parent (Silverman & Albano, 1997; Silverman, Saavedra, & Pina, 2001) designed to determine the DSM anxiety diagnoses.

The most widely used method for assessing childhood anxiety is self-report inventories. These are particularly important in assessing the subjective component of anxiety. It is clearly important to assess subjective symptoms from the child's or adolescent's viewpoint because it may be difficult for adults reliably to identify the existence of such discomfort in children. However, children may have difficulty in labeling and communicating their subjective feelings, thus creating a considerable assessment challenge.

Global self-ratings of degree of anxiety or of fear are often obtained. Youngsters may report how anxious they are in a specific situation. There are also self-report instruments that assess overall subjective anxiety, such as the State-Trait Anxiety Inventory for Children (Spielberger, 1973) and the Revised Children's Manifest Anxiety Scale (Reynolds & Richmond, 1978), which contains items such as "I have trouble making up my mind" and "I am afraid of a lot of things." The Multidimensional Anxiety Scale for Children (MASC) was developed by March and his colleagues (1997) to address the multidimensional nature of anxiety.

Assessment of the cognitive component of children's anxiety has probably received less attention then it should, given that various aspects of cognitions have been implicated in the maintenance and etiology of anxiety (Kendall et al., 2000; Schniering et al., 2000). The Negative Affect Self-Statement Questionnaire (Ronan, Kendall, & Rowe, 1994) is used to assess the cognitive content associated with negative affect. A subscale for assessing anxious self-talk (e.g., "I am going to make a fool of myself") has been found to discriminate between anxious and nonanxious children. The Coping Questionnaire—Child Version (Kendall et al., 1997a) assesses the child's ability to cope with anxiety in challenging situations.

Some instruments also exist to assess specific anxiety disorders; for example, the Revised Fear Survey Schedule for Children (Ollendick, 1983) to assess specific fears, the Social Anxiety Scale for Children—Revised (La Greca & Stone, 1993), and the Social Phobia and Anxiety Inventory for Children (Beidel, Turner, & Morris, 1995).

Given that youngsters with anxiety disorders often present with a variety of other problems as well, the assessment process should include a broader exploration of problem areas. Instruments, such as the Achenbach behavior checklists, can be employed to help in describing a range of behavior problems. These instruments also allow for an examination of various perspectives (the youngster, parents, teacher) on problems.

BEHAVIORAL OBSERVATIONS

Methods for assessing the overt behavioral aspects of fears and anxieties make use of direct observation (Dadds, Rapee, & Barrett, 1994). Behavioral avoidance tests require the youngster to perform a series of tasks involving the feared object or situation. Thus the youngster might be asked to move closer and closer to a feared dog and then increasingly to interact with the dog.

Observations can also be made by observers in the natural environment where the fear or anxiety occurs. Alternatively, self-monitoring procedures require the youngster to observe and to systematically record his or her own behavior. A daily diary of such observations may be part of an initial assessment and is also often part of treatment efforts.

Observation of the child's behavior in the natural environment can be made as the child encounters a feared situation.
(Tony Freeman/PhotoEdit)

PHYSIOLOGICAL RECORDINGS

The physiological component of anxiety is assessed by measuring parameters such as heart rate, skin conductance, and palmar sweat. Although practical difficulties often inhibit obtaining these measures, the development of portable and inexpensive recording devices has greatly facilitated such recording. However, the physiological aspects of anxiety are assessed less frequently than the other two response systems (Barrios & Hartmann, 1997; King, 1994).

Treatment of Anxiety Disorders

The treatment of anxiety in children and adolescents has a long history. However, research regarding effective treatments is less extensive than for adults. The systematic investigation of treatments for clinical-level anxiety problems and of interventions to prevent anxiety disorders has only recently received attention (D'Eramo & Francis, 2004; Feldner, Zvolensky, & Schmidt, 2004).

PSYCHOLOGICAL TREATMENTS

Much of the research on treatments for children and adolescents with anxiety disorders has supported the use of behavioral or cognitive-behavioral interventions (Ollendick & King, 1998). Several behavioral techniques for treating phobias, and cognitive-behavioral procedures for treating anxiety disorders (separation anxiety, social phobia, generalized anxiety disorders) are considered either "well-established" or "probably efficacious."

It is worth noting that exposure to feared stimuli is an essential element of successful fear-reduction programs (Öst et al., 2001). Thus many of the behavioral treatments for phobias can be conceptualized as various ways of facilitating exposure to the feared object or situation.

Relaxation and Desensitization. Relaxation training teaches youngsters to be aware of their physiological and muscular reactions to anxiety and provides them with skills to control these reactions. By tensing and relaxing various muscle groups, the youngster comes to sense early signs of bodily tension and to use these sensations as signals to relax. With practice the child is able to relax muscle groups in real-life situations when initial signs of tension are detected. Cue-controlled relaxation can also be taught. During muscle relaxation training, the child is taught to subvocalize a cue word such as "calm."

The cue word can be used in actual situations when anxiety is anticipated or experienced to help induce a relaxed state.

When relaxation training is combined with exposure to feared situations, the procedure is known as desensitization or systematic desensitization. In imaginal desensitization, a hierarchy of fear-provoking situations is constructed, and the youngster is asked to visualize scenes, starting with the least and progressing to the most fear-producing. These visualizations are presented as the youngster is engaged in relaxation. This process is repeated until the most anxiety-provoking scene can be comfortably visualized. In in vivo desensitization, the actual feared object or situation is employed rather than using visualizations.

Modeling. A commonly employed behavioral procedure is modeling. The early work of Bandura and his colleagues (e.g., Bandura & Menlove, 1968) was the impetus for subsequent research. In all modeling therapies, the child observes another person interacting adaptively with the feared situation. The model can be live or symbolic (e.g., on film). Participant modeling, in which observation is followed by the fearful child joining the model in making gradual approaches to the feared object, is one of the most potent treatments (Ollendick & King, 1998).

Lewis's (1974) early and often cited treatment of fear of the water illustrates the use of modeling, and participant modeling in particular. Boys in a modeling-plus-participation treatment observed a film of boys performing tasks such as those in a swimming test. These coping models initially exhibited fear but gradually increased their competency in dealing with the tasks. Immediately following the film, the children were taken to the pool for a 10-minute participation phase. They were encouraged to engage in the activities involved in the swimming test and were given social reinforcements for attempting these activities. When the behavioral swimming test was repeated the next day, a control group showed no change. Boys in modeling-only and participation-only conditions exhibited significant improvement, but the most effective treatment was the combination of modeling and participation. A follow-up evaluation 5 days later suggested that the gains had been maintained and had generalized to a different pool and different instructor. Once again the modeling-plus-participation boys seem to have fared the best.

Contingency Management. Modeling and systematic desensitization and its variants are treatments that were developed as ways of reducing a child's fear or anxiety. Contingency management procedures are based on operant principles and, instead, address the child's avoidant/anxious behavior directly by altering the contingencies for such behavior—ensuring that positive consequences follow exposure to but not avoidance of the feared stimulus and that the child is rewarded for improvement. These procedures are also sometimes described as reinforced practice. Contingency management or reinforced practice has been shown to be effective in treating children's fears and phobias (Ollendick & King, 1998). As we saw in the Lewis (1974) study, contingency management is often combined with modeling, relaxation, or desensitization procedures.

Cognitive-Behavioral Treatments. There is considerable support for the efficacy of cognitive-behavioral treatment programs for anxiety disorders in children and adolescents (Christophersen & Mortweet, 2001; D'Eramo & Francis, 2004; Silverman & Berman, 2001). These treatment programs integrate a number of behavioral and cognitive-behavioral strategies. The overall goals of these interventions are to teach

- recognition of the signs of anxious arousal,
- identification of the cognitive processes associated with anxious arousal, and
- strategies and skills for managing anxiety.

Cognitive-behavioral treatment programs employ a variety of therapeutic strategies to achieve these goals, as shown in Table 6–13 (Kendall et al., 2000).

Cognitive-behavioral treatment for children with anxiety disorders is illustrated by the work of Kendall and his colleagues (Kendall, Aschenbrand, & Hudson, 2003). A 16-week program, which makes use of a variety of behavioral and cognitive behavioral procedures (see Table 6–13), is divided into two segments. The first eight sessions are devoted to a progressive building of skills. During the second eight sessions, these skills are practiced in situations that expose the child to increasing levels of anxiety. The behavioral strategies include modeling, in vivo exposure, role play, relaxation training, and contingency management. Cognitive strategies address recognizing the physiological symptoms of anxiety, challenging and modifying anxious talk, developing a plan to cope with the situation, evaluating the success of coping efforts, and utilizing self-reinforcement. Throughout treatment the therapist serves as a coping model, demonstrating each of the new skills in each new situation. The preparation of a youngster

TABLE 6–13	TREATMENT STRATEGIES INCLUDED IN COGNITIVE-BEHAVIORAL TREATMENTS FOR ANXIETY DISORDERS IN CHILDREN AND ADOLESCENTS

Coping modeling
Identification and modification of anxious self-talk
Exposure to anxiety-provoking situations
Role playing and contingent reward procedures
Homework assignments
Education about emotions
Teaching awareness of bodily reactions and cognitive activities when anxious
Relaxation procedures
Practice in using newly acquired skills in increasingly anxiety-provoking situations

Adapted from Kendall, Chu, Pimentel, & Choudhury, 2000.

for an in vivo exposure—a visit to a mall—illustrates an exchange that might occur between a therapist and a child during Kendall's cognitive-behavioral treatment program.

Therapist: So are you feeling nervous now?

Child: I don't know. Not really.

Therapist: How would you know you were starting to get nervous?

Child: My heart would start beating faster.

Therapist: (recalling a common somatic complaint for this child) What about your breathing?

Child: I might start breathing faster.

Therapist: And what would you be thinking to yourself?

Child: I might get lost or I don't know where I am.

Therapist: And what are some things you could do if you start getting nervous?

Child: I could take deep breaths and say everything is going to be okay.

Therapist: That's good, but what if you were unsure where you were or got lost?

Child: I could ask somebody.

Therapist: Yes, you could ask somebody. Would it be a good idea to ask one of the guards or policemen? How are you feeling? Do you think you are ready to give it a try?

(Kendall et al., 2000, p. 269)

The program makes use of the Coping Cat Workbook (Kendall, 1992) and the acronym "FEAR" to highlight the four skills that the child learns in the program (Kendall et al., 2003).

F—Feeling frightened? (recognizing physical symptoms of anxiety)

E—Expecting bad things to happen? (recognizing anxious self-talk—See Figure 6–4)

A—Actions and attitudes that will help (behaviors and coping statements the child can use when anxious)

R—Results and rewards (self-evaluation and self-rewards)

Research supports the efficacy of this approach (Kendall et al., 2003). Youngsters diagnosed with anxiety disorders randomly assigned to a treatment condition fared better by the end of treatment than control youngsters on a number of anxiety measures. Treated children returned, on average, to the normal range on these measures. In addition, 64 percent of the treated youngsters no longer met diagnostic criteria for an anxiety disorder as compared with 5 percent (one case) in the control condition. Follow-up assessments at 1 year and 3 years following treatment indicated that these treatment gains were maintained (Kendall & Southam-Gerow, 1996). A second study found similar outcomes (Kendall et al., 1997a; 2003). Other research suggests the efficacy of delivering cognitive-behavior therapy in a group rather than an individual format (Flannery-Schroeder & Kendall, 2000; Silverman et al., 1999). Kendall's program is a child-focused program, but the

FIGURE 6-4

A therapist can make use of illustrations such as this to help elicit a child's anxiety-related cognitions or self-talk.

contextual influences on anxiety are appreciated. Thus, parents are involved as consultants and collaborators. They attend two sessions and actively participate in a supportive role.

An Australian adaptation has extended the role of family involvement (Barrett, Dadds, & Rapee, 1996; Barrett & Shortt, 2003). The program has a child-focused component using the Coping Koala Group Workbook, an adaptation of Kendall's Coping Cat Workbook and program. In addition, in the family component, the child and parents are treated in small family groups. Thus, in addition to the cognitive-behavioral procedures for the child's anxiety, parents are trained in and practice child management, anxiety management, and communication and problem-solving skills to build a supportive family environment.

Research evaluations of the program indicate that the vast majority of youngsters, in both child-only or child-plus-family treatments, no longer meet criteria for an anxiety disorder by the end of treatment and at follow-up several years later. Greater involvement of parents may be the treatment of choice for some youngsters. Findings from this research suggest that this may be the case for younger children and cases where the parents themselves are highly anxious (Cobham, Dadds, & Spence, 1998; Barrett & Shortt, 2003).

PHARMACOLOGICAL TREATMENTS

Selective serotonin reuptake inhibitors (SSRIs), tricyclic antidepressants, and antianxiety medications have been the most frequently suggested pharmacological agents for treating youngsters with anxiety disorders. However, there are limited studies of the effectiveness of medication in treating anxiety disorders in children and adolescents, and many of these have methodological shortcomings (Stein & Seedat, 2004; Stock, Werry, & McClellan, 2001). Suggestions of the efficacy of fluvoxamine, an SSRI, in treating social phobia, separation anxiety disorder, or generalized anxiety disorder (McClellan & Werry, 2003; Walkup et al., 2001) are limited and comparison with psychological treatment has not been addressed (Coyle, 2001). Systematic study is needed to establish safety and efficacy. Thus, in practice, the use of pharmacological treatment for anxiety in youth is probably not the treatment of first choice. If medication is employed, it is likely to be recommended as an adjunct to psychological interventions (AACAP, 1997; Stein & Seedat, 2004; Velosa & Riddle, 2000).

The treatment of obsessive-compulsive disorder is an area in which there does seem to be support for pharmacological approaches. The serotonin reuptake inhibitor (SRI) clomipramine and various SSRIs, such as fluoxetine (Prozac), sertraline (Zoloft), paroxetine

(Paxil), and fluvoxamine (Luvox), have been shown to be effective in treating OCD in children and adolescents (Geller et al., 2003b; Riddle, Kastelic, & Frosch, 2001).

TREATING OBSESSIVE-COMPULSIVE DISORDER

Obsessive-compulsive disorder differs in a number of ways from the other anxiety disorders we have reviewed (e.g., known and suspected etiological factors, patterns of co-occurrence, support for pharmacological treatment). We will therefore provide a brief separate discussion of treatment for this disorder.

Two kinds of intervention, alone or in combination, seem to be the current treatments of choice for obsessive-compulsive disorder (Franklin, Foa, & March, 2003; Pediatric OCD Treatment Study [POTS] Team, 2004; van Balkom et al., 1994). As previously indicated, clomipramine and SSRIs have been demonstrated as effective pharmacological treatments (Geller et al., 2003b; Grados & Riddle, 2001). Cognitive-behavioral interventions are the other treatment recommended. The treatment typically involves education about OCD, training in modifying cognitions to resist obsessions and compulsions and to enhance change, and contingency management and self-reinforcement. The central aspect of cognitive-behavioral approaches, however, is exposure with response prevention (Albano & DiBartolo, 1997; March & Mulle, 1998). The youngster is exposed to the situation that causes anxiety, and the compulsive ritual is prevented by helping the youngster resist the urge to perform it.

In imaginal exposure, the child is presented with a detailed and an embellished description of the feared situation for several minutes so as to create anxiety. At the same time, the child is not permitted to engage in any thoughts or behaviors to avoid the anxiety. The several-minute exposure is repeated until the anxiety is reduced to a predetermined level. The following is an example of imaginal exposure to anxiety-provoking germs.

You walk up to the school door and have to open the door with your hands. You forgot your gloves, so there is nothing to protect you from the germs. As you touch the handle, you feel some sticky and slimy wet stuff on your hand and your skin begins to tingle. Oh no! You've touched germs that were left there by someone and they're oozing into your skin and contaminating you with some sickness. You start to feel weak, and can feel the germs moving under your skin. You try to wipe your hands on your clothes, but it's too late. Already the germs are into your blood and moving all through your body. You feel weak and dizzy, and you can't even hold the door open. You start to feel like you're going to vomit, and you can taste some vomit coming up to your throat . . . (Albano & DiBartolo, 1997)

In addition to, or as an alternative to, imaginal exposure, the child may be exposed to the actual anxiety-provoking situations. The involvement of the family, especially with younger children, may be an important component (Freeman et al., 2003). The treatment of Amanda and her family illustrates the use of exposure in the actual anxiety-provoking situation.

Amanda   Rituals and Checking

Amanda, 8 years old, was referred because of her rituals and excessive checking behavior, which took more and more of her time (e.g., she was taking at least 20 minutes to dress in the morning instead of the 5 minutes which had been more than ample previously).

1. Every night she closed the curtains, turned down the bed and fluffed up her pillow three times before beginning to undress. Any disruption of this routine caused great distress.

2. The top bedcover had to be placed with the fringes only just touching the floor all around.

3. At night Amanda removed her slippers slowly and carefully, she then banged them on the floor upside-down, then the right-way-up, three times and nudged them gently and in parallel under the bed.

4. Before going to sleep Amanda had to go to the toilet three times. She often woke up in the middle of the night and carried out the same performance.

5. Before carrying out a ritual Amanda sang:

   "One, two, three, Come dance with me, Tra la la, Tra la la."

6. All dressing and undressing had to be done three times. This included pulling up her pants three times after every visit to the toilet.

7. All Amanda's toys had special places, which had to be checked and rechecked before leaving the bedroom.

8. The ornaments on top of the piano had special places. These positions were so precise that Amanda's mother found dusting and polishing almost impossible.

Adapted from Stanley, 1980, pp. 86–87.

Amanda's family was instructed not to give Amanda special attention and to treat her as a girl who did not have compulsive urges. The parents were also trained to initiate response prevention procedures. Starting with the least upsetting situation, the parents prevented Amanda from engaging in her rituals. Once she had coped with a situation, the next step up the hierarchy was taken. After the first 2 days, in which Amanda experienced considerable anxiety, she gradually began to relax. After 2 weeks, all her symptoms had disappeared. No new or additional problems arose, and Amanda was still symptom free at the 1-year follow-up.

SUMMARY

AN INTRODUCTION TO INTERNALIZING DISORDERS

- *There is appreciable evidence of a broad category of child and adolescent internalizing problems. The existence and definition of more specific disorders are, however, less certain. One issue of particular concern is the high rate of co-occurrence of multiple internalizing disorders.*

DEFINING AND CLASSIFYING ANXIETY DISORDERS

- *Anxiety or fear is generally viewed as a complex pattern of three response systems: overt behavioral, physiological, and subjective responses. Anxiety is part of normal developmental processes.*

- *Fears are quite common in children. There also seem to be age- and gender-related variations in numbers and content of fears. The most common fears seem to be similar across cultures.*

- *The DSM-IV-TR describes one anxiety disorder within the "usually first evident in infancy, childhood, or adolescence" grouping: Separation Anxiety Disorder. A youngster can also receive other anxiety disorder diagnoses.*

- *The empirical approach to classification describes subcategories of internalizing disorders. These subcategories do not, however, suggest separate anxiety disorders and suggest that anxiety and depression tend to co-occur.*

SPECIFIC PHOBIAS

- *Phobias, as distinguished from normal fears, are judged to be excessive, persistent, or nonadaptive. Specific phobias are among the most commonly diagnosed anxiety disorders in children and adolescents. They are likely to begin in childhood and may persist over time. Youngsters with this diagnosis, as with other anxiety disorders, frequently have co-occurring disorders.*

SOCIAL PHOBIA

- *Children and adolescents with social phobias are likely to be concerned about being embarrassed or negatively evaluated. Prevalence probably increases with age. Social anxieties are quite common during adolescence, making the interpretations of prevalence and degree of disturbance difficult.*

- *Youngsters with selective mutism do not talk in selected social situations. This disorder may be a type of social phobia.*

SEPARATION ANXIETY AND SCHOOL REFUSAL

- *Separation anxiety is a common problem among children but becomes less common by adolescence.*

- *School refusal describes children whose anxieties keep them from school. This term accommodates cases of both separation anxiety and phobias related to aspects of the school situation. School refusal in adolescence is likely to be complex.*

- *Treatment of school refusal is most successful if begun early, and it probably needs to be tailored to the specific kinds of school refusal exhibited.*

GENERALIZED ANXIETY DISORDER

- *Youngsters diagnosed with generalized anxiety disorder (GAD) exhibit excessive worry and anxiety that is not focused on any particular object or situation. GAD is probably the most common anxiety* disorder among adolescents. GAD is common among youngsters seen in clinical settings, and the disorder may persist. The question of overlap with other diagnoses is of concern.

PANIC ATTACKS AND PANIC DISORDER

- Panic attacks may be cued or uncued, and they may occur in the context of several anxiety disorders. Panic disorder is associated with recurrent uncued panic attacks. The presence of panic in adolescents seems likely, but the existence, particularly of uncued panic, in younger children is less clear. Family histories of panic and severe anxiety are commonly reported.

REACTIONS TO TRAUMATIC EVENTS

- The diagnosis of posttraumatic stress disorder requires reexperiencing of a traumatic event, avoidance of stimuli associated with the trauma, and symptoms of increased arousal.
- There may be age-related differences in reactions to trauma and reactions may differ based on the nature of the traumatic event.
- The diagnosis of acute distress disorder may be given during the first month following the trauma. In general, symptoms decline over time, but substantial numbers of youngsters continue to report symptoms.
- Degree of exposure to the trauma, preexisting child characteristics and coping abilities, and reactions of parents are among the influences that may determine a youngster's reaction to a trauma.

OBSESSIVE-COMPULSIVE DISORDER

- Obsessive-compulsive disorder (OCD) is characterized by repetitive and intrusive thoughts and/or behaviors. OCD is more common than once thought and often appears to follow a chronic course.

ETIOLOGY OF ANXIETY DISORDERS

- The development and maintenance of anxiety disorders are influenced by multiple factors that interact in complex ways.
- There is a familial aggregation for anxiety disorders. Genetic factors may play a role, but for many disorders, what may be inherited is a general tendency toward emotional reactivity. Evidence for a genetic

and biological basis seems strongest for obsessive-compulsive disorder.

- A general vulnerability to anxiety may be associated with the child's temperament. The temperamental characteristic of behavioral inhibition appears to be a risk factor for the development of anxiety disorders.
- Psychosocial influences play a considerable role in the development of anxiety disorders. Direct exposure, imitation, information transmission, and parenting practices are some of the mechanisms of influence.

ASSESSMENT OF ANXIETY DISORDERS

- In conducting assessments of anxiety, developmental issues need to be considered, and various perspectives on the youngster's problem, information about a full range of problems, and information about the youngster's environment should be obtained.
- Assessment of anxiety is typically guided by the three response systems: overt behavior, subjective responses, and physiological responses.
- The subjective aspects of anxiety are assessed through a variety of self-report measures. Direct observation and behavioral approach tests are employed to assess overt behavioral aspects. Physiological aspects of anxiety are less frequently assessed than the other two response systems.

TREATMENT OF ANXIETY DISORDERS

- Appreciable support exists for the effectiveness of psychological treatments for anxiety problems in youngsters. Many treatments are, at least in part, based on exposure to the feared stimulus.
- Procedures such as modeling, desensitization, and contingency management have proven to contribute to successful treatment. Cognitive-behavioral treatments that include a number of therapeutic strategies have proven effective in treating anxiety disorders. Pharmacotherapy, if employed, is usually an adjunct to psychological treatments.
- Cognitive-behavioral treatments involving exposure and response prevention and pharmacological treatment employing selective serotonin reuptake inhibitors have been shown to be effective in treating obsessive-compulsive disorder.

KEY TERMS

internalizing disorders (p. 123)

anxiety (p. 124)

fear (p. 124)

worry (p. 124)

phobia (p. 126)

specific phobia (p. 126)

Mood Disorders

In this chapter we examine what are known as problems of mood or affect. Youngsters can experience moods that are, on the one hand, unusually elated, or on the other hand, unusually sad. When these moods are particularly extreme or persistent or when they interfere with the youngster's functioning, they may be labeled as mania and depression, respectively, and they are another aspect of internalizing disorders.

Until relatively recently, mood disorders in children and adolescents had not received a great deal of attention. The increase in interest in affective problems can be traced to a number of influences. Promising developments in the identification and treatment of mood disorders in adults played a role. Also, the emergence of a number of assessment measures, particularly of depression, allowed researchers to examine the phenomenon in clinic and normal populations of youngsters. In addition, improvements in diagnostic practices have facilitated the study of mood disorders in children and adolescents. However, finding that we can apply adult diagnostic criteria to youngsters should not lead us to prematurely conclude that these phenomena are the same in children and adults.

In isolating mood disorders as separate categories, we confront many of the same problems that we found in examining anxiety disorders. For example, children and adolescents who meet the criteria for a diagnosis of depression are often also given other diagnoses. Thus the designation of these problems as distinct entities is not without controversy. Nonetheless, examining depression and mania makes sense in terms of how the research and treatment literature is organized. Particularly in children, but also in adolescents, the focus of clinicians and researchers interested in mood disorders has been primarily on the problem of depression.

A Historical Perspective

A brief look at recent history can aid our understanding of current views of childhood depression. The dominant view in child clinical work for many years was the orthodox psychoanalytic perspective. From this perspective, depression was viewed as a phenomenon of superego and mature ego functioning (Kessler, 1988). It was argued, for example, that in depression, the superego acts as a punisher of the ego. Because the child's superego is not sufficiently developed to play this role, it is impossible, within this perspective, for a depressive disorder to occur in children. It is not surprising, therefore, that depression in children received little attention.

A second major perspective added to the controversy regarding the existence of a distinct disorder of childhood depression. The concept of masked depression represented an interesting view. This view held that there is a disorder of childhood depression. However, it was proposed that the sad mood and other features usually considered essential to the diagnosis of depression frequently are not present. It was held that an underlying depressive disorder does exist but that the youngster's depression is "masked" by other problems (depressive equivalents), such as hyperactivity or delinquency. The "underlying" depression itself is not directly displayed but is inferred by the clinician. Some workers, indeed, suggested that masked depressions were quite common and may have resulted in underdiagnosis of childhood depression (Cytryn & McKnew, 1974; Malmquist, 1977).

The notion of masked depression was clearly problematic. There was no operational way to decide whether a particular symptom was or was not a sign of depression. Indeed, the symptoms that were suggested as masking depression included virtually the full gamut of problem behaviors evident in youngsters. The concept of masked depression was, therefore, quite controversial.

This concept was important, however. It clearly recognized depression as an important and a prevalent childhood problem. And the central notions of masked depression—that depression in children does exist and may be displayed in a variety of age-related forms different from adult depression—are still widely held. The concept that depression is manifested differently in children and adults contributed, in part, to the evolution of a developmental perspective.

Early in the evolution of a developmental perspective, some workers suggested that behaviors (e.g., insufficient appetite, excessive reserve) that led to the diagnosis of depression might be only transitory developmental phenomena—common among children in certain age groups (Lefkowitz & Burton, 1978). It was thus suggested that perhaps one of the reasons why clinicians gave the diagnosis of depression was the mistaken belief that such behaviors (symptoms) are rare and, therefore, important when manifested. A developmental perspective on depression has continued to evolve and will be described throughout this chapter. This early position, however, drew attention to the need to differentiate transient episodes of sadness and negative affect, which may be common reactions among children, from more long-lasting expressions of such emotions. Also, the distinction between depression as a *symptom* and depression as a *syndrome* is important to consider here. One or two depressive behaviors of a child may be viewed as typical of that developmental stage. However, it is different to suggest that a cluster of such behaviors accompanied by other problems and impaired functioning is likely to occur in a large number of children (Kovacs, 1997). The developmental perspective has become an important approach to the study of depression (Cicchetti & Toth, 1998; Schwartz, Gladstone, & Kaslow, 1998).

Definition and Classification of Mood Disorders

DEFINING DEPRESSION

Understanding depression in children and adolescents is a complex task. The phenomenon itself involves a complex interplay of influences and a complex clinical presentation. In addition, there have been a variety of perspectives on depression in young people and a variety of ways in which depression has been defined.

A study by Carlson and Cantwell (1980) illustrates this point. Three different criteria were employed to define depression in a randomly selected sample of clinic-referred youngsters. The presence of depressive symptoms at intake served as one criterion. The youngsters were also administered a version of the Children's Depression Inventory (a paper-and-pencil measure), a second criterion. Finally, as a third criterion, separate interviews with the youngsters and their parents were conducted to assess for the presence of a DSM mood disorder. The use of depressive symptoms at intake as the criterion led to the largest number of children being designated as depressed, the depression inventory led to fewer, and the DSM diagnosis led to the least. It is clear that the results were not simply a matter of using more or less stringent criteria. Rather, there appear to be some differences in definition. For example, not all children designated as depressed by the depression inventory were designated as depressed using the depressive symptom criterion, as would be expected if the former were just a more stringent definition. Similarly, not all DSM mood disorder children were designated as depressed using the criterion of depression inventory score. These and other findings indicate that different groups of youngsters may or may not be designated as depressed, depending on how depression is defined and assessed (Hammen & Rudolph, 2003; Kaslow & Racusin, 1990). Such variations can lead to different conclusions regarding the causes and correlates of depression.

A study by Kazdin (1989b) illustrates differences related to informants' views. DSM diagnoses of 231 consecutive child admissions to an inpatient psychiatric facility were made on the basis of direct interviews with the children and their parents. This method of diagnosing depression was compared with diagnosis based on exceeding a cutoff score on the Children's Depression Inventory (CDI). Both the children and their parents completed the CDI. In addition, children and/or their parents completed other measures to assess attributes reported to be associated with depression. Consistent with the findings of Carlson and Cantwell described previously, different groups of children appeared to be designated as depressed depending on the method employed. In addition, characteristics associated with depression varied depending on the method used. Some of these results are illustrated in Table 7–1. Defining depression as a high self-report score on the CDI indicated that depressed children were more hopeless; had lower self-esteem; made more internal (as opposed to external) attributions regarding negative events; and on the basis of a locus of control scale, were more likely to believe that control was due to external factors rather than to themselves.

Depressed and nondepressed children defined by the other two criteria (parent CDI and DSM) did not differ from each other on these characteristics. Employing the parent CDI criterion, children with high depression scores exhibited more problems across a wide range of symptoms (as measured by the Child Behavior Checklist—CBCL) than those with very low depression scores. Depression as designated by the other two criteria did not appear to be associated with this wide range of problems. Thus conclusions regarding correlates of depression may be affected by the method and informant employed to designate youngsters as depressed.

It is not possible at this point to make definitive statements about the "correct" definition of depression. It is probably fair, however, to state that the dominant view is that childhood depression is a syndrome, or disorder, and that the most often employed definitions are those offered by the DSM.

THE DSM APPROACH

In the DSM, depression and mania are described in the category of Mood Disorders. There are no separate diagnostic categories for mood disorders in children or adolescents. The diagnostic categories are the same for children, adolescents, and adults. Mood disorders are sometimes described as unipolar (one mood is experienced, typically depression) versus bipolar (both moods are experienced, depression and mania).

The DSM describes mood episodes that are not themselves diagnoses but that serve as the building

TABLE 7–1	MEAN CHARACTERISTIC SCORES OF DEPRESSED AND NONDEPRESSED CHILDREN AS DESIGNATED BY DIFFERENT CRITERIA FOR DEPRESSION					
			CRITERIA			
	CHILDREN'S DEPRESSION INVENTORY (BY CHILD)		CHILDREN'S DEPRESSION INVENTORY (BY PARENT)		DSM DIAGNOSIS	
MEASURES	HIGH	LOW	HIGH	LOW	DEPRESSED	NONDEPRESSED
Hopelessness	7.3	3.3	5.3	5.0	5.4	4.8
Self-esteem	22.7	38.9	28.2	30.8	29.2	30.9
Attributions	5.4	6.5	5.8	5.8	6.0	6.0
Locus of control	9.8	6.8	8.2	8.7	7.9	8.4
Total behavior problems (CBCL)	75.8	75.3	81.6	69.0	76.5	75.0

Adapted from Kazdin, 1989b.

blocks for the diagnosis of mood disorders. Four types of mood episodes are described. The essential characteristic of a *Major Depressive Episode* is a period of either depressed mood or loss of interest or pleasure in nearly all activities. The essential feature of a *Manic Episode* is a period of abnormally and persistently elevated, expansive, or irritable mood. A *Mixed Episode* includes symptoms of both Manic and Major Depressive Episodes. A *Hypomanic Episode* is characterized by the same symptoms as a Manic Episode, but symptoms are not as severe and do not cause impairment in functioning.

DEPRESSIVE DISORDERS: THE DSM APPROACH

Major Depressive Disorder (MDD) is the primary DSM category for defining depression. This disorder is described by the presence of one or more major depressive episodes. The symptoms required for the presence of a major depressive episode are the same for children, adolescents, and adults (with one exception), and these symptoms are listed in Table 7–2. The one exception is that in children or adolescents, irritable mood can be substituted for depressed mood. Indeed, some reports suggest that a majority of depressed youths (over 80 percent) exhibit irritable mood (Goodyer & Cooper, 1993; Ryan et al., 1987). To diagnose a Major Depressive Episode, the DSM requires the following:

- That five or more symptoms are present
- That one of these symptoms must be either depressed (or irritable) mood or loss of pleasure

- That the symptoms must be present for at least 2 weeks
- That symptoms must cause clinically significant distress or impairment in important areas of the youngster's functioning (e.g., social, school)

Dysthymic Disorder is the other principal depressive disorder included in the DSM. It is essentially a disorder in which many of the symptoms of a major depressive episode are present in less severe form but are more chronic—that is, they persist for a longer period of time. Depressed mood (or in children and adolescents, irritable mood) is present for at least one year along with two or more of the other symptoms indicated in Table 7–3. Again, the symptoms must cause clinically significant distress or impairment. The term double depression is sometimes employed to describe instances in which both dysthymia and a major depressive episode are present. Dysthymia is typically described as developing prior to the occurrence of a major depressive episode. The validity of separate diagnoses of dysthymia and major depressive disorders has been questioned. There is little evidence of differences in the features or correlates of these disorders other than an earlier age of onset for dysthymia (Goodman et al., 2000).

Youngsters who are depressed can also be given the diagnosis of Adjustment Disorder with Depressed Mood. This disorder is viewed as a response to a stressor in which depressive symptoms do not meet the criteria for other depressive disorders.

As was indicated before, the view inherent in the DSM approach is that depressive disorders found in youngsters are the same as those found in adults. There is some research consistent with this perspective. However, differences have also been found and certain findings require explanation. Differences

TABLE 7–2	SYMPTOMS USED BY THE DSM TO DIAGNOSE A MAJOR DEPRESSIVE EPISODE

1. Depressed or irritable mood
2. Loss of interest or pleasure
3. Change in weight or appetite
4. Sleep problems
5. Motor agitation or retardation
6. Fatigue or loss of energy
7. Feelings of worthlessness or guilt
8. Difficulty thinking, concentrating, or making decisions
9. Thoughts of death or suicidal thoughts/behavior

From American Psychiatric Association, 2000.

TABLE 7–3	SYMPTOMS USED BY THE DSM TO DIAGNOSE DYSTHYMIC DISORDER

1. Depressed or irritable mood
2. Poor appetite or overeating
3. Sleep disturbance
4. Low energy or fatigue
5. Low self-esteem
6. Concentration or decision-making problems
7. Feelings of hopelessness

From American Psychiatric Association, 2000.

such as the gender ratio in prevalence (Compas, Hinden, & Gerhardt, 1995; Nolen-Hoeksema & Girgus, 1994), biological correlates (Kazdin & Marciano, 1998), and the effectiveness of antidepressant medications (Ambrosini, 2000) are described in this chapter. Such differences are one reason why it may be premature to accept the use of the same criteria for depressive disorders across all age groups.

DEPRESSION: EMPIRICAL APPROACHES

Syndromes that involve depressive symptoms have also been identified by empirical approaches to taxonomy. This finding is illustrated by the syndromes of the Achenbach instruments (p. 101). The syndromes that include depressive symptoms that regularly occur together also include symptoms characteristic of anxiety and withdrawn behavior. Thus this research does not find a syndrome that includes symptoms of depression alone. A mixed presentation of depression and anxiety features has emerged consistently in research with children and adolescents. This finding again highlights the question of whether depression in youngsters manifests itself the same way as it does in adults.

How best to define and classify depression in children and adolescents remains a focus of ongoing research. One issue is that depression in young people may best be conceptualized as dimensional rather than categorical (Hankin et al., 2005). A second issue is determining developmentally sensitive criteria. Many workers have chosen to concern themselves with youngsters who exhibit constellations of depressive symptoms whether or not they meet the DSM criteria for a mood disorder. This approach makes sense in that it is not clear that the cutoff set by the diagnostic criteria is the critical one. Many youngsters who fall short of meeting diagnostic criteria may still exhibit impairment in everyday functioning (Kazdin & Marciano, 1998).

DESCRIPTION OF DEPRESSION

In everyday usage, the term *depression* refers to the experience of a pervasive unhappy mood. This subjective experience of sadness, or dysphoria, is also a central feature of the clinical definition of depression. Descriptions of youngsters viewed as depressed suggest that they experience a number of other problems as well. Concern may be expressed about the youngster's irritability and temper tantrums—sudden outbursts, tears, yelling, throwing things.

Sad affect, or dysphoria, is the central characteristic of most definitions of depression.
(David Young-Wolffe/PhotoEdit)

Adults may describe loss of the experience of pleasure, social withdrawal, lowered self-esteem, inability to concentrate, and poor schoolwork as changes they note in the youngster. Alterations of biological functions (sleeping, eating, elimination) and somatic complaints are often noted as well. The youngster may also express thoughts of wishing to die.

These youngsters frequently experience other psychological disorders. Anxiety disorders, such as separation anxiety disorder, are probably the most commonly noted. Conduct disorder and oppositional defiant disorder also occur among depressed youth. Among depressed adolescents, alcohol and substance abuse are also common additional problems.

The case of a 15-year-old boy, Nick, illustrates many of these features as well as some of the factors that contribute to the development and course of depression.

Nick The Problems of Depression

Nick lives with his mother. His father left before Nick was born. Nick was born with a curvature of the spine as a result of which he walks awkwardly and is limited in his physical abilities. The incident that resulted in Nick being brought to the clinic was his arrest for shoplifting.... (His mother) reports that Nick is irritable and sullen much of the time, that they are constantly fighting and arguing.... Nick's outbursts have escalated recently, including occasions when he has thrown things and punched holes in walls and doors....

Nick reveals that he is very unhappy, has few things in his life that give him pleasure, and feels hopeless about things improving for him. He is self-conscious about his appearance, his peers tease him and he feels that he is disliked, and he hates himself.

... Nick's typical day is described as: "He wakes up early in the morning after having stayed up late the night before watching television, but he lies in bed until 9:00 or 10:00 a.m. He then spends much of the day at home alone playing video games or watching television." Nick has gained considerable weight and he reports that he is having trouble controlling his appetite.... Nick's mother returns home from work late in the afternoon. They often argue about his having missed another day of school. They eat dinner together silently while watching television. The rest of the evening is filled with arguments....

Adapted from Compas, 1997, pp. 197–198.

BIPOLAR DISORDER: THE DSM APPROACH

The other major mood disorders included in the DSM fall into the category of Bipolar Disorders. They involve the presence of mania as well as depressive symptoms. Mania is typically described as a period of abnormally elevated (or irritable) mood characterized by features such as inflated self-esteem; high rates of activity, speech, and thinking; distractibility; and exaggerated feelings of physical and mental well-being. To meet the criteria for a Manic Episode, mania and at least three or more other symptoms must be present. These symptoms are described in Table 7–4. *Bipolar I disorder* involves a history of major depression and mania, whereas *Bipolar II disorder* includes a history of major depression and hypomania (less severe mania). *Cyclothymic disorder* involves chronic, but mild, fluctuations of mood that do not meet the diagnostic criteria for major depressive or manic episodes.

Less is known about these disorders in children and adolescents than in adults (Youngstrom, Findling, & Feeny, 2004). The same DSM criteria

TABLE 7–4	SYMPTOMS USED BY THE DSM TO DIAGNOSE A MANIC EPISODE

1. Persistent elevated, expansive, or irritable mood
2. Inflated self-esteem
3. Decreased need for sleep
4. Being more talkative than usual
5. Feeling of thoughts racing
6. Distractibility
7. Increased goal-directed activity or psychomotor agitation
8. Excessive pleasurable activity that can lead to negative consequences (e.g., buying sprees, sexual indiscretions)

From American Psychiatric Association, 2000.

used for adults are applied to children and adolescents. Important developmental differences in presentation, however, challenge clinicians to apply these criteria while being sensitive to developmental differences in expression (Hammen & Rudolph, 2003; Youngstrom et al., 2004). For example, there is the question of irritability. As we have seen, irritability is a common aspect of depressed mood in youngsters. Thus, is irritability a sign of depression, mania, or a mixed episode? Also, youngsters are likely to exhibit a chronic presentation of mixed moods with very rapid mood shifts. This is in contrast to the clinical picture in adults of acute onset of distinct episodes with periods of relatively good functioning between episodes (James & Javaloyes, 2001). Some have suggested that the chronic mixed mood pattern in youngsters may be similar to that seen in severe forms of adult bipolar disorder, raising the question of whether these youngsters' problems represent an early-onset severe form of the disorder (Geller et al., 2003).

Youngsters may also present with patterns of co-occurring problems and disorders (e.g., attention-deficit hyperactivity disorder) that are different than those seen in adults (Tillman et al., 2003). For example, manic episodes and bipolar disorders in adolescents, and particularly in older adolescents, may be similar to adult presentations. However, manic episodes in adolescents are more likely to be associated with antisocial behaviors, school truancy, academic failure, or substance use. Manic episodes in adolescents are also likely to include psychotic features and early-onset bipolar disorder may often be misdiagnosed as schizophrenia (James & Javaloyes, 2001). Bipolar disorder may initially present as depression with alterations of mood occurring only after some period of time. Thus, diagnosis of bipolar disorder even in adolescents may be difficult because of confusion regarding symptoms/co-occurring disorders (Hammen & Rudolph, 2003).

The description and diagnosis of mania in young children also has been criticized as overinclusive. Mania may be confused with concepts such as difficult temperament. And mistaking children's imaginative play, overactivity, exuberance, and such qualities for manic symptoms is a concern. Another potential difficulty is discriminating between bipolar disorders and severe forms of other disorders. Manic-like behaviors are very common among children with severe forms of a variety of other disorders, including attention-deficit hyperactivity disorder, oppositional defiant disorder, and depression (Carlson & Kelly, 1998). Thus the question arises, Should we diagnose a bipolar disorder in such youngsters, or is manic behavior a nonspecific symptom of severe child psychopathology?

Finally, another difficulty in diagnosing bipolar disorder in children is that many of the symptoms typical of mania in adults are unlikely to occur in children. Unlike adults, children, for example, do not have several credit cards that they "max out," undertake risky business ventures, or engage in excessive sexual behavior. Geller and her colleagues (2003), as part of an ongoing study of bipolar disorders in youngsters, have attempted to describe how various mania criteria may present in children. Table 7–5 provides examples of what may be viewed as symptoms of mania in children and contrasting examples of typical child behavior. Clinicians must make judgments of the child's behavior based on considerations such as age-appropriateness, appropriateness to context, and degree of impairment or interference.

Thus, if one accepts the existence of bipolar disorder in prepubertal children, the diagnosis may require considerable care so as to discriminate the

TABLE 7–5	EXAMPLES OF MANIFESTATIONS OF MANIA SYMPTOMS IN CHILDREN AND TYPICAL CHILD BEHAVIOR	
SYMPTOM	**CHILD MANIA**	**NORMAL CHILD**
Elated mood	A 9-year-old girl continually danced around the house saying "I'm high, over the mountain high." A 7-year-old boy was repeatedly taken to the principal for clowning and giggling in class (when no one else was).	Child was very excited when family went to Disneyland on Christmas morning.
Grandiose behaviors	An 8-year-old girl set up a paper flower store in her classroom and was annoyed and refused to do class work when asked to by the teacher. A 7-year-old boy stole a go-cart. He knew it was wrong to steal, but did not believe it was wrong for him. He thought that the police were arriving to play with him.	A 7-year-old boy pretended he was a fireman, directing others and rescuing victims. In his play, he did not call the firehouse. His play was age-appropriate and not impairing.
Hypersexual behavior	An 8-year-old boy imitated a rock star—gyrating his hips and rubbing his crotch during an interview. A 9-year-old boy drew pictures of naked ladies in public and said that they were his future wife.	A 7-year-old played doctor with a same-age friend.

Adapted from Geller et al., 2003.

disorder from other disorders and from nonclinical behavioral presentations (NIMH Developmental Psychopathology and Prevention Research Branch, 2001).

Epidemiology

EPIDEMIOLOGY OF DEPRESSION

Estimates of the prevalence of depression vary considerably, reflecting, in part, differences in how depression is defined and diagnosed (Hammen & Rudolph, 2003; Kessler, Avenevoli, & Merikangas, 2001). In addition, developmental considerations complicate getting accurate estimates. The difficulty of administering similar assessments to youngsters of different ages is one consideration. Also, widely employed assessment tools, such as interviews, require that the youngster think in terms of psychological constructs—such as hopelessness—and effectively communicate what is remembered. Such processes clearly depend on developmental level. Finally, it may be that there are real differences in prevalence that are related to developmental level.

Major depressive disorder (MDD) is by far the most prevalent form of affective disorder among children and adolescents (Lewinsohn, Rohde, & Seeley, 1998). Among youngsters with unipolar disorders, about 80 percent experience MDD, 10 percent dysthymia without MDD, and 10 percent "double depression." In community surveys, reported prevalence rates for major depressive disorder in children range between 0.4 and 2.5 percent, and in adolescents between 0.4 and 8.3 percent. The epidemiology of dysthymic disorder is less well studied. Reported prevalence rates among children range between 0.6 and 1.7 percent, and among adolescents between 1.6 and 8.0 percent (Birmaher et al., 1996a). Several reports suggest increasing rates of major depression in recent decades (Birmaher et al., 1996a; Kessler et al., 2001). This trend has been reported for youngsters as well as for adults (Kovacs & Gatsonis, 1994; Lewinsohn et al., 1993b).

Reported prevalence rates probably underestimate the scope of the problem. For example, lifetime prevalence rates, rather than prevalence rates at any one point in time, indicate that episodes of clinical depressions may be quite common, particularly among adolescents. In the Oregon Adolescent Depression Project (OADP), a large prospective epidemiological study of a representative community sample of adolescents ages 14 to 18, Lewinsohn and his colleagues (1998) estimate that by age 19, approximately 28 percent of adolescents will have experienced an episode of major depressive disorder (35 percent of the females and 19 percent of the males). Other information suggests lifetime prevalence rates of diagnosable depressive disorders among the general population as high as 20 to 30 percent (Compas, Ey, & Grant, 1993; Lewinsohn et al., 1993a). This finding means that about one out of four youngsters in the general population experiences a depressive disorder sometime during childhood or adolescence. Even higher estimates emerge when other definitions of clinical levels of depression are employed. For example, 40 to 50 percent of the OADP youngsters scored above the criteria for depression "caseness" on a standard self-report depression questionnaire. As a comparison, 16 to 20 percent of adults meet "caseness" criteria.

Finally, the extent of the problem is even clearer when one includes youngsters who exhibit depressive symptoms but who do not meet diagnostic criteria. These youngsters are not included in the prevalence estimates just cited. However, such youngsters often exhibit impairments in their academic, social, and cognitive functioning and also are at greater risk for future disorders than are youngsters not exhibiting depressive symptoms (Kazdin & Marciano, 1998; Lewinsohn et al., 1998).

Age and Gender. Age and gender are clearly relevant to estimates of the prevalence of depression in young people (Cyranowski et al., 2000; Harrington, 2001). Depression is less prevalent in younger children than in adolescents (Ford, Goodman, & Meltzer, 2003). Usually no gender differences are reported for children ages 6 to 12 (Angold & Rutter, 1992; Fleming, Offord, & Boyle, 1989). When differences are reported, depression is more prevalent in boys than in girls during this age period (Anderson et al., 1987). Yet among adolescents, depression is more common among girls and begins to approach the 2:1 female-to-male ratio usually reported for adults (Lewinsohn et al., 1994). This age-gender pattern is illustrated in Figure 7–1. It is worth noting that for adolescents of *both* sexes, there is a greater prevalence of depression than exists for younger children (Angold & Rutter, 1992; Cohen, Cohen, Kasen et al., 1993b; Lewinsohn et al., 1993a; Whitaker et al., 1990).

The OADP findings and other information (Nolen-Hoeksema & Girgus, 1994; Wade, Cairney, & Pevalin, 2002) suggest that the gender difference in major depressive disorder prevalence probably emerges between the ages of 12 and 14. Consistent with this picture are findings from the Dunedin

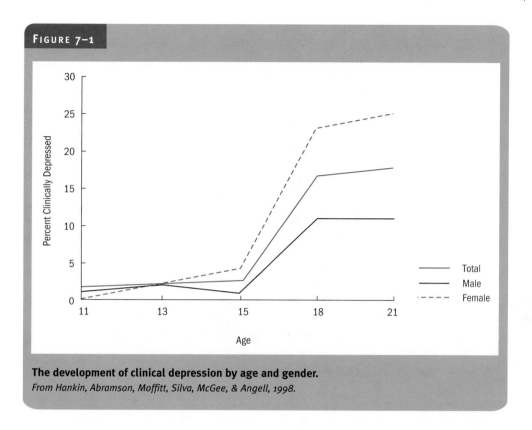

The development of clinical depression by age and gender.
From Hankin, Abramson, Moffitt, Silva, McGee, & Angell, 1998.

Multidisciplinary Health and Development Study, a large epidemiological study conducted in New Zealand (Hankin et al., 1998). Rates of clinical depression (major depressive episode or dysthymic disorder) in these youngsters were assessed at a number of points between the ages of 11 and 21. At age 11, males showed a tendency to have higher rates of depression than females; at 13, there were no gender differences; and females had higher rates of depression at ages 15, 18, and 21. Gender differences were greatest between 15 and 18, and rates of depression began to level off after age 18. Findings of other investigators suggest that gender differences in depression may be more pronounced among youngsters referred for mental health services than in nonreferred samples (Compas et al., 1997).

Socioeconomic, Ethnic, and Cultural Considerations. Lower socioeconomic status (SES) is reported to be associated with higher rates of depression. The link is probably through influences such as income, limited parental education, chronic stress, family disruption, environmental adversities, and racial/ethnic discrimination (Hammen & Rudolph, 2003; Wight, Sepúlveda, & Aneshensel, 2004). Although such SES differences may have a disproportionate impact on certain ethnic groups, there is not a great deal of information regarding racial and ethnic differences in the prevalence of depression. Comparable rates are typically reported in various ethnic groups (Canino et al., 2004; Gibbs, 2003; Hammen & Rudolph, 2003), except for higher rates among Mexican American children and adolescents (Organista, 2003). Although comparable rates are typically reported for African American (AA) and European American (EA) youngsters, a comparison of youngsters in grades 3 to 5 suggests an interesting ethnicity by sex interaction (Kistner, David, & White, 2003). These findings are illustrated in Figure 7–2. AA boys reported more depressive symptoms than EA boys, whereas there was no such ethnic difference for the girls. Also, AA boys were more depressed than AA girls, whereas EA girls were more depressed than EA boys. The results of this study also suggest that both perceived and actual differences in academic achievement were, at least in part, responsible for the elevated rates of depression among AA boys.

Co-occurring Difficulties. Finally, youngsters who are depressed typically experience other problems as well. For example, 40 to 70 percent of youngsters diagnosed with MDD also meet the criteria for another disorder, and 20 to 50 percent have two

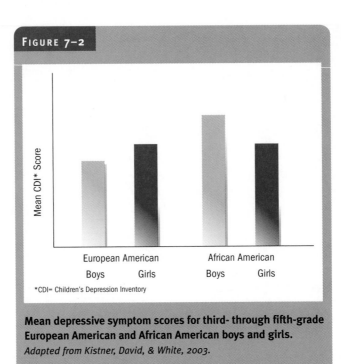

FIGURE 7–2

Mean depressive symptom scores for third- through fifth-grade European American and African American boys and girls.
Adapted from Kistner, David, & White, 2003.

or more additional disorders (Birmaher et al., 1996a). The most common additional nonmood disorders are anxiety disorders, disruptive behavior disorders, and substance abuse disorders (Hammen & Rudolph, 2003; Lewinsohn et al., 1998; TADS Team, 2005).

EPIDEMIOLOGY OF BIPOLAR DISORDER

Definitional issues make accurate estimates of prevalence difficult. Bipolar disorder is thought to be relatively rare in childhood and adolescence, but prevalence may be underestimated (James & Javaloyes, 2001; Youngstrom et al., 2004). In a community sample of adolescents aged 14 to 18 years, the lifetime prevalence was about 1 percent (Lewinsohn, Klein, & Seeley, 1995). The peak onset appears to be in the 15- to 19-year-old group with females and males equally represented. The prevalence of bipolar disorder in prepubertal youngsters is unclear, although it is generally believed that the rates are much lower than after puberty.

Similar to what we noted in our discussion of depression, in community samples of adolescents, manic-like symptoms of elevated, expansive, or irritable mood are present in youngsters who do not meet the criteria for a bipolar disorder. Again, the youngsters with these subsyndromal symptoms do

experience substantial impairment in functioning (Kessler et al., 2001). Indeed, evidence suggests a bipolar spectrum, that is, a continuum extending from hypomanic personality traits to subsyndromal symptoms to mild and severe forms of the disorder rather than a categorical distinction (Lewinsohn, Seeley, & Klein, 2003; Papolos, 2003).

A number of other conditions co-occur in youngsters diagnosed with bipolar disorder. Attention-deficit hyperactivity disorder, conduct disorder, oppositional defiant disorder, and substance abuse or dependence are among the problems commonly reported (Papolos, 2003; Spencer et al., 2001). These youngsters also experience significant impairment in school, social, and family functioning (Lewinsohn et al., 1995a; 2003). Their families face a considerable challenge and likely require assistance and support that is sensitive to the child's difficulties and the family's needs (Fristad & Goldberg-Arnold, 2003). The feelings of a mother who received support through an online support group illustrates this need.

| **Bipolar Disorder** | **The Need for Family Support** |

One of the biggest stressors is the total isolation and lack of support. I *never* have a moment to myself. I have no friends, I have no life. I spend almost every day with a feeling of mortal terror that we will return to the horror before diagnosis and stabilization. No parent or child should ever have to experience what we and the many other parents I've met at CABF (Child and Adolescent Bipolar Foundation) have had to go through. I am tired of this life. I grieve for the loss of what I thought motherhood would be. . . . If I did not have the lifeline, I don't know what I would do some nights. I can log on after a bad day and get the support and strength to start the new day with a smile so that I can be there for my boys.

Adapted from Hellander, Sisson, & Fristad, 2003, p. 314.

Developmental Course and Prognosis

DEPRESSION AND DEVELOPMENT

It is interesting to ask, How is depression manifested, and what is the prevalence of depression at different developmental periods? Although the diagnostic criteria in the DSM are largely the same for children, adolescents, and adults, depression may be manifested differently in these groups and, as we saw earlier in our discussion of epidemiology, there may be gender differences in developmental patterns (Compton et al., 2003; Harrington, 2001; Weiss & Garber, 2003).

Schwartz, Gladstone, and Kaslow (1998) describe the phenomenology of depression at different developmental stages. Infants and toddlers lack the cognitive and verbal abilities necessary to self-reflect and report depressive thoughts and problems. It is difficult, therefore, to know what the equivalent to adult depressive symptoms may be in this age group. Given cognitive, language, and other developmental differences, it is likely that depressive behavior in this age group may be quite different than in adults. Interestingly, the description of infants separated from their primary caregivers in many ways seems similar to that of depression (Bowlby, 1960; Spitz, 1946). These and other distressed infants, as well as infants of depressed mothers, have been observed to exhibit behaviors such as lethargy, feeding and sleep problems, irritability, sad facial expression, excessive crying, and decreased responsiveness—behaviors often associated with depression.

Depression in preschoolers is also difficult to assess. Many of the symptoms associated with later depression have been noted in youngsters in this age group (e.g., irritability, sad facial expression, changes of mood, feeding and sleep problems, lethargy, excessive crying). Differences in cognition and language, as well as limited information, make it difficult to know how these behaviors are related to the experience of depression and depressive syndromes in older individuals and whether or not these represent stable patterns.

For the period of middle childhood (6 to 12 years), there is more evidence that a prolonged pattern of depressive symptoms may emerge. Younger children in this age group typically do not verbalize the hopelessness and self-deprecation associated with depression. However, 9- to 12-year-olds who exhibit other symptoms of depression may verbalize feelings of hopelessness and low self-esteem. Still, in youngsters in this age group, depressive symptoms may not be a distinctive syndrome but may occur with a variety of symptoms usually associated with other disorders. So, for example, as mentioned before, mixed depressed/anxious syndromes rather than separate depressed syndromes emerge in empirical taxonomies (Achenbach & Rescorla, 2001).

During the early adolescent period, the manifestation of depression is in many ways similar to that of the childhood period. Over time, however, probably in relation to shifts in biological, social, and cognitive development, depression in older adolescents starts to resemble more closely the symptoms of adult depression (Cyranowski et al., 2000). In their community sample of adolescents, Lewinsohn and his colleagues (1998) report a median age of onset for major depressive disorder at 15.5 years.

As part of their longitudinal research and their effort to examine the relationship of age of onset and familial contributions to depression, Harrington and his colleagues (1997) compared a group of prepubertal-onset depressed youngsters to a group whose onset of depression was postpubertal. Rates of depression in relatives of youngsters in the two groups did not differ. There were, however, other differences in the families of the two groups. Manic disorders tended to be higher among relatives of the postpubertal-onset group, whereas relatives of the prepubertal depressed youngsters had higher rates of criminality and family discord. This evidence is consistent with viewing prepubertal-onset depressive disorders as distinct from postpubertal-onset depression. In addition, continuity to major depression in adulthood was lower among prepubertal-onset youngsters than among those with postpubertal onset of depression. This finding is also consistent with viewing adolescent-onset depression as more similar to adult forms of the disorder and different from earlier onset depression.

Adolescence thus appears to be a period when depressive syndromes similar to adult depression have their onset. As noted before, there is a significant increase in the prevalence of depression in adolescence, and prevalence may reach adult levels in late adolescence (Wight et al., 2004). What, then, is the clinical course of depression during adolescence and into adulthood? How long does an episode of major depression last? Are there future episodes?

Episodes of depression in adolescents may last for an appreciable period of time and for some youngsters may present a recurring problem. In the OADP community sample (Klein et al., 2001; Lewinsohn et al., 1998), the median duration of an episode of major depressive disorder was 8 weeks, the range was from 2 to 520 weeks, the mean duration of the longest episode was 6 months, and earlier onset of depression (at or before the age of 15) was associated with longer episodes. The recurrent nature of depression is illustrated by the finding that among these adolescents, 26 percent had a history of recurrent major depressive episodes. Kovacs (1996), in her review of studies of clinically referred youngsters, found a median duration of major depressive disorder episodes of 7 to 9 months. It was found that about 70 percent of these clinically referred youngsters had recurrences of major depressive disorder episodes when followed for 5 or more years. Thus the duration of episodes in clinical samples may be more than three times the duration in community samples, and the likelihood of recurrence of a major depressive episode more than twice as great.

A sample of participants in the OADP project was interviewed after their 24th birthday. Those who prior to age 19 had met criteria for major depressive disorder or adjustment disorder with depressed mood were more likely to meet criteria for major depressive disorder during young adulthood than their peers with a nonaffective disorder or no disorder prior to age 19 (Lewinsohn et al., 1999). In addition, follow-up studies suggest that some adolescents with major depressive disorder develop bipolar disorder within 5 years after the onset of depression, but the percentage of such outcomes is not clear (Birmaher et al., 1996a; Kovacs, 1996; Lewinsohn et al., 1999).

DEVELOPMENTAL COURSE OF BIPOLAR DISORDER

Lewinsohn, Klein, and Seeley (1995) examined the course of bipolar disorder in a large community sample of adolescents (ages 14 to 18). The median duration of the most recent manic episode for these youngsters was 10.8 months. Also, for youngsters with a diagnosis of bipolar disorder their first affective episode was earlier (mean age = 11.75 years old) than for adolescents with a history of major depression with no periods of mania (mean age = 14.95 years old). The total amount of time with an affective disorder was longer for these youngsters as well. The estimated mean duration of affective disorder for these youngsters with bipolar disorder was 80.2 months compared with a mean duration of 15.7 months for youngsters in the OADP sample with major depressive disorder. This finding suggests that in some youngsters, major depressive disorder may be an early stage of bipolar disorder. This course may be more likely to occur in youngsters with an earlier onset of depression.

| Joseph | **Early Bipolar Symptoms** |

Based on information gathered at his first hospital admission, Joseph suffered from childhood illnesses more than his eight siblings. By the time he started school at age 6 his parents described him as already having periods of being tired. Although Joseph was usually considered a "jolly boy who enjoyed himself," there were episodes of crying, irritability, and depressed moods. At school he was sometimes "extra good" and at others he "lost all interest."

By the time he was 13, the family said, "they could see it coming." Joseph began having alternating periods of "quietness and irritability." He would be at the playground ordering others around and being overly bossy at one moment and at the next he would be withdrawn, sitting quietly reading the Bible. For periods of a week or so, Joseph would sit around, tired, not talking and sometimes crying. During these times he seemed "scared."

There were rapid and extreme changes when Joseph would destroy whatever his siblings were playing with. During these times Joseph was overactive, restless, overtalkative, bold, loud, demanding, and exhibited hostile behavior and angry outbursts. The brief spells of being "quiet versus irritable" persisted through ages 13 and 14. Joseph's symptoms and the cycling worsened dramatically at age 15 when he was first admitted to the hospital meeting the criteria for a bipolar disorder.

Adapted from Egeland, Hostetter, Pauls, & Sussex, 2000, p. 1249.

Some of the adolescents in the OADP sample who met the criteria for bipolar disorder experienced a chronic/recurrent course. Twelve percent had not remitted by age 24 (that is, they continued to meet diagnostic criteria) and of those in remission at age 18, about one quarter had another episode between the ages of 19 and 24 (Lewinsohn et al., 2003). Individuals with bipolar disorder during adolescence were far more likely to meet criteria for bipolar disorder during young adulthood than adolescents with subsyndromal bipolar disorder. Adolescents with subsyndromal bipolar disorder, however, did experience high rates of major depressive disorder during young adulthood.

Geller and colleagues (2003) studied a group of prepubertal and early adolescent youngsters with bipolar disorder. These youngsters were assessed in a research setting, but received care from their own community practitioners. During a 2-year period about two thirds of these youngsters experienced recovery (defined as at least 8 consecutive weeks not meeting DSM criteria for mania or hypomania). A little over half of these youngsters relapsed after recovery and many continued to meet the criteria for another disorder during their recovery.

Longitudinal data are limited. However, the information that is available would seem to suggest that youngsters with bipolar disorders or symptoms might continue to display symptoms of affective and other disorders, at least into the early adult period.

Etiology of Mood Disorders

Most contemporary views of mood disorders suggest a model that integrates multiple determinants, including biological, social-psychological, family, and peer influences.

⬤ BIOLOGICAL INFLUENCES

Biological views of mood disorders in children and adolescents focus on genetic and biochemical influences. These views derive largely from adult literature. There are fewer data available on children and adolescents, but information has become increasingly available (Emslie et al., 1994; Rutter et al., 1999).

Genetic Influences. Adult studies are consistent in showing a strong genetic component for bipolar disorders. Heritability estimates of about 80 percent are reported and research employing linkage analysis and other methods is underway to identify specific genes that may be involved (DePaulo, 2004; Faraone et al., 2004; Rutter et al., 1999). Research has tended to focus on issues such as describing and differentiating the disorder and on the genetic contribution to the disorder. Environmental factors may influence the probability of an at-risk youngster developing bipolar symptoms, the degree of symptomatology, and whether other problems are evident. Attention to such influences should be part of ongoing research on bipolar disorder in children and adolescents.

Genetic influences are generally thought to play a role in depression in children and adolescents as well, although findings are less clear (Rice, Harold, & Thapar, 2002) and the genetic component is weaker than is the case for bipolar disorders. Support for the role of genetics in depression derives from a number of findings. For example, the data based on twin, family, and adoption studies of mood disorders in adults suggest a heritability component (Kendler et al., 1992a; Weissman, Kidd, & Prusoff, 1982; Wender et al., 1986). Also, onset of depression before 20 years of age has been associated with greater rates of depression among family members (Klein et al., 1995; Puig-Antich et al., 1989; Weissman et al., 1988). In addition, first-degree adult relatives of depressed children and adolescents have greater than expected rates of depressive disorders (Birmaher et al., 1996a; Kovacs et al., 1997). Findings from twin and blended family designs also suggest a genetic component for depressive symptomatology (O'Connor et al., 1998; Silberg et al., 1999). Research indicating that children of parents with major depressive disorder are at increased risk for major depression (discussed later) can also be seen as consistent with a genetic influence.

Although a genetic contribution seems possible, even research that suggests heritability in depression also indicates the importance of environmental influences. For example, O'Connor and his colleagues (1998) examined a sample of same-sex adolescent siblings between the ages of 10 and 18. The sample included monozygotic (MZ) and dizygotic (DZ) twins, full siblings, half siblings, and unrelated siblings. Results indicated an appreciable genetic component to depressive symptoms, but there were significant influences of shared and nonshared environment as well.

The complexity of these issues is illustrated in a study by Rende and his colleagues (1993). These investigators examined depressive symptomatology in a general (unselected) sample of 707 pairs of adolescent siblings. By comparing MZ twins, DZ same-sex twins, and same-sex full siblings from nondivorced families, as well as full, half, and unrelated same-sex siblings from stepfamilies, the authors were able to make use of twin and adoption study methodologies to examine genetic and environmental influences on depression. A significant genetic influence was found when the depressive symptomatology of the full sample was examined. However, surprisingly, a significant genetic influence on depression was not found if only youngsters with high levels of depression were considered. Instead, there was a significant influence of shared environment, that is, nongenetic influences shared by both siblings in a family. The authors suggest that one possible explanation for these findings is that genetic influence operates on personality and temperamental factors, such as emotionality and sociability, which affect the full range of depressive symptomatology. And, indeed, there is evidence for the contribution of temperamental characteristics to the development of depressive symptoms in children and adolescents (Compas, Connor-Smith, & Jaser, 2004). It might be reasoned that extreme depressive symptomatology may result, against this background of moderate genetic influence, from stressful experiences that are shared by siblings in a family. Furthermore, the same genetic liability to temperamental characteristics, such as emotionality, may contribute to the development of depression in another way. This genetic liability may also create a risk for styles of interpersonal interaction that predispose individuals to be exposed to stressful situations and affect their reactions to such experiences (Rutter et al., 1999; Silberg et al., 2001).

Brain Functioning and Neurochemistry. It is often presumed that nervous system functioning and biochemistry play an etiological role in depression and, indeed, this may be the case. However, the study of these processes in depression is complex and difficult. Research on several fronts with adults, children, and adolescents is ongoing (Hammen & Rudolph, 2003).

The role of neurotransmitters, such as norepinephrine, serotonin, and acetylcholine, has been a central aspect of the study of the biochemistry of depression. The impetus to study these neurotransmitters came largely from findings that the effectiveness of certain antidepressant medications with adults was related to levels of these chemicals or receptivity to them. For example, an early suggestion, the catecholamine hypothesis, proposed that low levels of norepinephrine were created by too much reabsorption by the neuron releasing it or by too efficient a breakdown by enzymes. This process was thought to result in too low a level of norepinephrine at the synapse to fire the next neuron. Current research continues to explore the role of neurotransmitters; however, the mechanisms of action are likely to be quite complicated, involving complex interactions among neurotransmitter systems and receptors rather than simply the amount of neurotransmitters available. Also, possible developmental differences in these neurotransmitter mechanisms require further exploration (Kaufman et al., 2001).

Studies of the neuroendocrine systems (connections between the brain, hormones, and various organs) add complexity to this picture. Dysregulation of the neuroendocrine systems involving the hypothalamus, pituitary gland, and the adrenal and thyroid glands is thought of as a hallmark of adult depression (Emslie et al., 1994). These systems are also regulated by neurotransmitters. Thus the picture regarding depression is likely to be a complex one. The rapid biological changes during childhood and adolescence (e.g., hormonal activity during puberty) offer a particular challenge (Sokolov & Kutcher, 2001).

Research on the biological aspects of depression suggests that during the earlier developmental periods of childhood and adolescence, the neuroregulatory system is not equivalent to that in adulthood (Kaufman et al., 2001; Sokolov & Kutcher, 2001). Biological indicators later in development (for example, in older adolescents who are more severely depressed) may be more similar to those for depressed adults. Thus although many workers still find evidence for a biological dysfunction in childhood depression, a simple translation of the adult findings is not sufficient (Ivanova, 1998; Puig-Antich, 1986).

For example, disturbances of sleep are associated with clinical levels of depression (Emslie et al., 2001). Research has indicated that EEG patterns during sleep are strong biological markers of major depressive disorders in adults (Gillin et al., 1979; Kupfer & Reynolds, 1992). Many of the sleep findings reported in adults are not characteristic of children diagnosed with major depressive disorders, but some of these patterns are reported in adolescents (Birmaher et al., 1996a; Brooks-Gunn et al., 2001; Kaufman et al., 2001). For example, some abnormalities related to the rapid eye movement (REM) stage of sleep may be present in depressed adolescents.

Also, adults with major depression produce excessive levels of cortisol, a stress hormone produced in the adrenal glands. Similar patterns have not been observed consistently in investigations of cortisol functioning in youngsters (Brooks-Gunn et al., 2001; Kaufman et al., 2001). Indeed, underproduction of cortisol sometimes has been found in depressed youngsters (Goenjian et al., 1996). However, increased cortisol levels, similar to those for depressed adults, may occur among older and more severely depressed adolescents (Rao et al., 1996). Also, the ratio of cortisol to dehydroepiandrosterone (DHEA), another hormone, rather than the level of cortisol levels alone, may be related to depression in children and adolescents (Brooks-Gunn et al., 2001). Thus, again, sensitivity to developmental differences is clearly suggested.

How can we understand these various findings? In general, differences in biological markers of depression might suggest that the child, adolescent, and adult disorders are different. Alternatively, such differences in biological markers may represent age-related differences in the same disorder.

SOCIAL-PSYCHOLOGICAL INFLUENCES

There has been greater attention to social-psychological influences on depression than on mania/bipolar disorder. Despite increased interest in recent years, much of the thinking regarding such influences on child and adolescent depression is still based on theories derived from work with depressed adults. We will examine several of the social-psychological influences and provide illustrations of work based on youth.

Separation and Loss. A common psychological explanation of depression is that it results from separation or loss. Psychoanalytic explanations of depression, following from Freud, emphasize the notion of object loss. The loss may be real (parental death, divorce) or symbolic. Identification with and ambivalent feelings toward the lost love object are thought to result in the person's directing hostile feelings concerning the love object toward the self. Some psychodynamic writers emphasize loss of self-esteem and feelings of helplessness that result from object loss, and they minimize the importance of aggression turned inward toward the self (Kessler, 1988).

Some behaviorally oriented explanations also involve separation and loss. Both Ferster (1974) and Lewinsohn (1974) emphasized the role of inadequate positive reinforcement in the development of depression. Loss of or separation from a loved one is likely to result in a decrease in the child's sources of positive reinforcement. However, inadequate reinforcement may also result from factors such as not having adequate skills to obtain desired rewards.

The theme of separation-loss is a central concept in many theories of depression. The loss may be real or imagined.
(Courtesy of A. C. Israel)

Past support for the theory that separation played a role in the genesis of depression came from several different sources. For example, a fairly typical sequence of reactions of young children to prolonged separation from their parents was described by investigators (e.g., Bowlby, 1960; Spitz, 1946). In this so-called anaclitic depression, the child initially goes through a period of "protest" characterized by crying, asking for the parents, and restlessness. This is followed shortly by a period of depression and withdrawal. Most children begin to recover after several weeks.

The connection between loss and depression has been examined in regard to adult depression. For a long time, the widely held view was that such early loss puts one at high risk for later depression—especially women. More recent examinations of this issue question this view, in part because most studies were plagued with methodological problems (Finkelstein, 1988; Tennant, 1988). The current view is that early loss is not in and of itself pathogenic. The link between such loss and later depression is not direct. Rather, it is hypothesized that loss, as well as other circumstances, can set in motion a chain of adverse circumstances such as lack of care, changes in family structure, and socioeconomic difficulties that put the individual at risk for later disorder (Bifulco, Harris, & Brown, 1992; Saler & Skolnick, 1992).

Much of the research on the association between loss and depression has relied on the retrospective reports of adults. However, investigation of the impact of loss on children has received some attention (Dowdney, 2000; Tremblay & Israel, 1998). For example, Sandler and his colleagues found support for a model consistent with the indirect effects of loss (West et al., 1991). Among a sample of 92 families who had lost a parent within the previous 2 years, depression in youngsters (ages 8 to 15) was not directly linked to the loss. Rather, the level of parental demoralization, family warmth, and stable positive events following the loss mediated the effects of parental death on depression in these youngsters. Thus, children who experience the positive aspects of these family variables are likely to be resilient following the loss of a parent (Lin et al., 2004).

Cognitive-Behavioral/Interpersonal Perspectives. Behavioral, cognitive, and cognitive-behavioral perspectives encompass many related and overlapping concepts (Hammen, 1992; Kaslow, Adamson, & Collins, 2000). Influences such as interpersonal skills, cognitive distortions, views of self, control beliefs, self-regulation, and stress are the focus of these perspectives on child and adolescent depression. The ways in which depressed youngsters relate to others and are viewed by others, and the ways that these youngsters view themselves and think, are believed to contribute to how depression develops and is maintained.

As indicated earlier, writers such as Ferster (1974) and Lewinsohn (1974) suggested that a combination of lowered activity level and inadequate interpersonal skills plays a role in the development and maintenance of depression. Interpersonal theories of depression emphasize a transactional relationship. Depressed youngsters both contribute and react to problematic relationships. It is suggested that depressed individuals do not elicit positive interpersonal responses from others. Indeed, there is evidence that depressed youths display deficits in social functioning, have negative interpersonal expectations and perceptions, and are viewed as less likable by others (Hammen & Rudolph, 2003; Kaslow, Brown, & Mee, 1994; Schwartz, Gladstone, & Kaslow, 1998). For example, Bell-Dolan, Reaven, and Peterson (1993) obtained self, peer, and teacher reports of both depression and social functioning for 112 fourth- to sixth-graders. Negative social behavior (aggression and negative support seeking), social withdrawal, and low social competence were all related to higher ratings of depression.

A learned helplessness explanation of depression (Seligman & Peterson, 1986) suggests that some individuals, as a result of their learning histories, come to perceive themselves as having little control of their environment. This learned helplessness is in turn associated with the mood and behaviors characteristic of depression. Separation may be a special case of learned helplessness: The child's attempts to bring the parent back may result in the child's thinking that personal action and positive outcome are independent of each other.

Helplessness conceptualizations emphasize how the person thinks about activity and outcome—a person's attributional or explanatory style. An explanatory style in which one blames oneself (internal) for negative events and views the causes of events as being stable over time (stable) and applicable across situations (global) is thought to be characteristic of depressed individuals. The opposite style, external-unstable-specific attributions for positive events, may also be viewed as part of this depressed style. In revisions of this perspective, the interaction of stressful life events with cognitive style is given greater emphasis (Abramson, Metalsky, & Alloy, 1989). This revision is

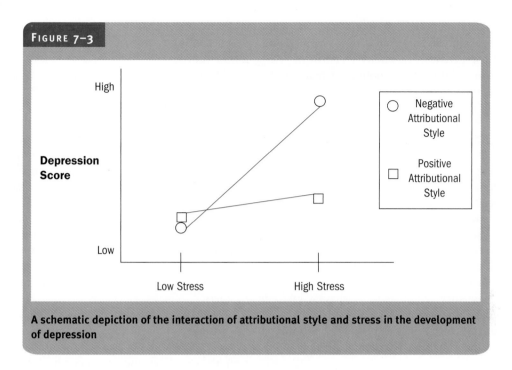

FIGURE 7–3

A schematic depiction of the interaction of attributional style and stress in the development of depression

referred to as the hopelessness theory of depression. Attributional style (a vulnerability or diathesis) acts as a moderator between negative life events that the person sees as important (a stress) and hopelessness. Hopelessness, in turn, leads to depression. Figure 7–3 illustrates how the hopelessness theory of depression views the development of depression. The theory predicts that a youngster with a diathesis of a negative attributional style who is also exposed to the stress of high levels of negative life events is more likely to develop depression. A number of studies have reported maladaptive attributional styles and hopelessness in depressed youngsters (Kaslow et al., 2000; Schwartz et al., 2000), and the vulnerability-stress notions of hopelessness theory have received some support (Conley et al., 2001; Joiner, 2000). However, additional attention needs to be given to inconsistencies in findings, investigation of developmental patterns, exploration of potential gender differences, and a clearer articulation of the relationship of attributional style and life events (Abela, 2001; Kaslow et al., 2000).

The role of cognitive factors in depression is also the major emphasis of other theorists. Beck (1967; 1976), for example, assumes that depression results from negative views of the self, others, and the future. Depressed individuals, Beck hypothesizes, have developed certain errors in thinking that result in their distorting even mildly annoying events into opportunities for self-blame and failure. Although findings are mixed, some research studies have found evidence in depressed youngsters of cognitive distortions such as those suggested by Beck's theory (Gencöz et al., 2001; Stark, Schmidt, & Joiner, 1996). Depressed youngsters exhibit a tendency to catastrophize, overgeneralize, personalize, and selectively attend to negative events.

The nature of the link between cognitive influences such as attributional style, hopelessness, or cognitive distortion and depression requires further clarification (Hammen & Rudolph, 2003; Kaslow et al., 2000). For example, cognitive processes may be specific to depression or may be more generally associated with a variety of disorders. Perhaps cognitive distortions that are associated with depression may not be general, but instead may be limited to certain kinds of situations, such as those that are interpersonal and emotional. It is also not clear whether these cognitions play a causal role in depression as an underlying vulnerability or whether they are associated with depression in some other way—perhaps co-occurring with depression, being a consequence of depression, or being part of an ongoing reciprocal interplay with depression. Research, including cross-cultural comparisons, supports a reciprocal view of the relationship between cognitions and depression (Stewart et al., 2004).

The dimension of control, part of a helplessness perspective discussed before, has also been the focus of additional consideration. Weisz and colleagues, for example, have found that low levels of perceived competence (the ability to perform relevant behavior) and perceived noncontingency (outcomes are not contingent on behavior) are both related to levels of depression in children (Weisz et al., 1993b). Similarly, researchers have examined style of coping with stress as a component of the development of depression. For example, lower levels of active coping (e.g., problem solving) and greater levels of disengagement coping (e.g., avoidance) have been associated with youngsters' depression. Evolving models of stress and coping are likely to contribute to a greater understanding of the development of depression (Compas et al., 2004). Given the suggestion of these difficulties in depressed youngsters, it may be worthwhile to examine the type of coping and self-regulatory (competence) behavior evoked or encouraged by parents of depressed youngsters (Kaslow et al., 2000). With this observation in mind, we turn to the influences of parental depression on youngsters.

IMPACT OF PARENTAL DEPRESSION

A major area of research on childhood depression has been an examination of children of depressed parents. There are several reasons for the proliferation of such research. Because family aggregation of mood disorders in adults was known to exist, it was presumed that examining children of parents with mood disorders would reveal a population likely to experience childhood depression. Such a high-risk research strategy has the potential to be a more efficient means of investigating a problem than a random sampling of the population would be. In addition, such research might provide information on the continuity among child, adolescent, and adult mood disorders.

Numerous studies have found that youngsters from homes with a depressed parent are at increased risk for developing a psychological disorder (Beardslee, Versage, & Gladstone, 1998). A number of longitudinal studies have been particularly informative. Hammen and her colleagues (1990) compared the long-term effects of maternal depression and maternal chronic medical illness. Over the course of a 3-year period, with evaluations at 6-month intervals, children of both depressed mothers and medically ill mothers exhibited elevated rates of psychological disorder as compared with children of non-ill mothers. Rates of disorder were higher for children of depressed mothers than for those with medically ill mothers.

Weissman and her colleagues (1997) followed the offspring of two groups of parents over a 10-year period. At the time of the follow-up, the offspring were in late adolescence or were adults. Parents and offspring were assessed with a structured diagnostic interview. Offspring for whom neither parent had a psychological disorder (low risk) were compared with offspring for whom one or both parents had a diagnosis of major depressive disorder (high risk). The offspring of the depressed parents had increased rates of MDD, particularly before puberty. The high-risk group also had increased rates of other disorders, including phobias and alcohol dependence. These results are illustrated in Table 7–6. In addition, more serious depression was experienced by offspring of depressed parents as compared with depression experienced by offspring of nondepressed parents. However, the depressed offspring

TABLE 7–6	PERCENTAGE OF YOUNGSTERS WITH DISORDERS AMONG OFFSPRING OF PARENTS WITH MDD AND WITH NO DIAGNOSIS	
	PARENTAL DIAGNOSIS	
DIAGNOSIS IN OFFSPRING	**MDD**	**NONE**
Any mood disorder	85	38
MDD	56	25
Any anxiety disorder	42	15
Phobias	21	8
Panic disorder	13	0
Alcohol dependence	22	7

Adapted from Weissman, Warner, Wickramaratne, Moreau, & Olfsen, 1997.

of depressed parents were less likely to receive treatment; in fact more than 30 percent never received any treatment.

Beardslee and his colleagues have examined the question of the impact of parental depression in a non–clinically referred population (Beardslee et al., 1996; 1998). Families were recruited from a large health maintenance organization. Assessments, including a structured diagnostic interview, were conducted initially and 4 years later. Families were divided into three categories: parents with no diagnosis, parents with a nonaffective disorder, and one or both parents with an affective disorder. Parental nonaffective disorder, parental MDD, and the number of diagnosed disorders that the child experienced prior to the first assessment predicted whether the youngster experienced a serious affective disorder in the time between assessments.

The findings presented here suggest that the risk associated with parental depressions may not be specific. Children with a depressed parent appear to be at risk for a variety of problems, not just depression. And children of parents with other diagnoses or with chronic medical conditions may also be at risk for depression. Perhaps various disorders that youngsters experience share common risk factors, whereas some risk factors are specific to depression. It is also possible that some disruptions to effective parenting are common to parents with various disorders, whereas other disruptions are more likely to occur among parents with a particular disorder.

There may be a variety of mechanisms whereby depressive mood states in parents are associated with dysfunction in their children (Cummings, Davies, & Campbell, 2000). As suggested before, shared heredity may play a role in the link between parental and child depression. However, parental depression may have an impact through a variety of nonbiological pathways. For example, parents can influence their child through parent-child interactions, through coaching and teaching practices, and by arranging their child's social environment. Before we turn to a discussion of these mechanisms, it is important to remember that influences between parent and child are likely to be bidirectional (Elgar et al., 2004). A depressed youngster may, for example, generate additional stress that lessens the adult's ability to parent effectively.

Mechanisms of Parental Influence. As we indicated before, both depression in adults and depression in young people are associated with certain characteristic ways of thinking and cognitive styles.

Depressed parents may transmit these styles to their children. Garber and Flynn (2001), for example, assessed mothers and their youngsters annually over 3 years starting in sixth grade. They found that a maternal history of depression was associated with lower perceived self-worth, a negative attributional style, and hopelessness in offspring. Maladaptive ways of thinking may be modeled by parents and may also affect the general manner in which depressed adults parent their offspring (Nolen-Hoeksema et al., 1995).

Parental depression may result in disruption of effective parenting (Lovejoy et al., 2000). For example, the behavior of depressed parents may be accompanied by negative affect such as anger or hostility. Also, the depressed parents' absorption in their own difficulties may lead them to be withdrawn or make them less attentive and aware of their children's behavior. Monitoring of a child's behavior is a key element in effective parenting. Depressed parents may also perceive behaviors to be problematic that other parents do not. This difference in perception is important, because being able to ignore or tolerate low levels of problematic behavior is likely to lead to less family disruption. In addition, studies involving direct observation of families with a depressed parent or child indicate that interactional patterns in these families may serve to maintain the depression in the parent or child (Dadds et al., 1992; Ge et al., 1995; Hops et al., 1987). Depressed behavior by one family member may be maintained because it serves to avoid aggressive and conflictual behavior with and among other family members. Indeed, an association between marital conflict and parental depression is frequently reported (Beach, Fincham, & Katz, 1998; Whisman, 2000). These two variables are in turn related to problematic outcomes in children and adolescents (Du Rocher Schudlich & Cummings, 2003).

Mary | Family Interactions and Depression

Mary is an adolescent with considerable problems with anxiety and depression. Mary's mother was diagnosed with major depression. Her parents fought often and frequently the topic was money or problems and stresses related to her father's job. Mary's mother dealt with these difficulties by self-medicating with alcohol and developed a serious drinking problem. The conflicts, alcohol abuse, and other stresses seemed to have contributed to the development of symptoms of depression in Mary's mother. For the good of all the family members and because of her concern for her mother, Mary felt that she had to serve as a mediator for her parents' disputes and that she was responsible for alleviating her mother's sadness. Over time these family conflicts and problems contributed to Mary developing psychological difficulties of her own.

Adapted from Cummings, Davies, & Campbell, 2000, pp. 305–306.

In addition to marital discord, families with a depressed parent may exist in adverse contexts (e.g., social disadvantage/standard of living) and experience high levels of stressful life events (e.g., health and financial difficulties). These circumstances in turn are likely to exacerbate a parent's depressive episodes and contribute to disruptions in parenting. For example, high levels of stress may restrict the parent's ability to involve the child in activities outside the home and may limit the family's social networks. Thus the child may have limited opportunity to interact with other adults outside the family or to have access to other sources of social support. This deficiency may be particularly problematic in that one of the mechanisms by which depressed parents may affect the functioning of their offspring is the parents' own problems in interpersonal functioning and their perceptions of others (Hammen & Brennan, 2001).

Finally, the link between parent and child depression has been viewed in the context of attachment (Cicchetti & Toth, 1998; Elgar et al., 2004). The emotional unavailability and insensitivity that may be associated with parental depression have been shown to be strong and reliable predictors of insecure parent-child attachments. Attachment theory holds that children's internal working models or representations of the self and the social world are importantly influenced by early attachments. It is in these early relationships that the child first experiences and learns to regulate intense emotions and arousal, experiences the social world, and develops a concept of the self. In other words, working models that guide future experiences are thought to be first developed in these early attachment relationships. In children with insecure parent-child attachments, the cognitive and emotional contents of these working models have been described as remarkably similar to the cognitive and emotional patterns characteristic of depression (Cummings et al., 2000). Insecure attachments may interfere with the child's developing capacity to regulate affect and arousal and may be associated with poorer self-concept and less trust in the availability and responsiveness of the social world.

From very early on, infants are affected by their mothers' or caregivers' behavior. Infants of depressed mothers may develop a depressed mood style that generalizes to their reactions to others and that may persist (Field, 1992). A study by Murray (1992) illustrates the relationship between maternal depression and attachment. Women were screened for depression after childbirth. These women and their infants were followed and at 18 months mother-child attachment was assessed. Maternal postnatal depression increased the risk of insecure attachment. The results are illustrated in Figure 7–4. The relationship

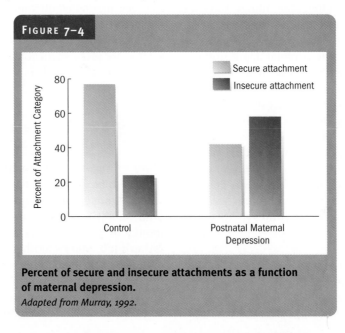

FIGURE 7–4

Percent of secure and insecure attachments as a function of maternal depression.
Adapted from Murray, 1992.

of maternal depression to other variables was also illustrated. For example, the adverse effect of lower social class on infant cognitive development was found primarily when mothers had experienced their first onset of depression following childbirth. At a 5-year follow-up, attachment security at 18 months of age mediated a negative relation between maternal postnatal depression (at 2 months of age) and the child's prosocial behavior at age 6 (Murray et al., 1999).

Age and gender differences are likely regarding the effects of parental depression on offspring (Hops, 1995; Lovejoy et al., 2000). Furthermore, although children of depressed parents are at increased risk for a number of difficulties, not all these children experience adverse outcomes (see the descriptions of Joe and Frank). Many form secure attachments, experience good parenting, and do not develop disorders (Beardslee et al., 1998; Brennan, Le Brocque, & Hammen, 2003). For example, the National Institute of Child Health and Human Development (NICHD) Early Child Care Research Network study (1999) provides a longitudinal examination of the effects of mother-child interaction. Among depressed women, mothers who were observed to be more sensitive and responsive to their infants had children with better language development and fewer behavioral problems at 36 months.

Joe and Frank   Different Outcomes

Joe's father was diagnosed with major depression and his paternal grandfather also experienced episodes of depression . . . but both his parents were attentive and responsive to him. Even when Joe's father's depressive symptoms were severe, he remained attentive and emotionally warm. Joe's mother was very supportive of his father and they had a secure marriage. . . . Joe also had a close and supportive relationship with his two sisters. Joe did well in school and was popular, although he tended to be shy in large groups. He attended an excellent university, studied medicine, and became a pediatrician. Joe married and he and his wife were happy and were attentive and responsive parents. Joe experienced periods of anxiety and occasional mild to moderate symptoms of depression. The symptoms were rarely more than subclinical and Joe never felt the need to seek therapy.

Frank's mother was diagnosed with major depressive disorder and her mother has also been depressed. His mother and father were divorced when Frank was 10. This followed many years of intense marital conflict. . . . Both parents had also been generally emotionally unresponsive toward the children, . . . and they involved Frank and his sister in their marital conflicts. . . . Frank and his sister fought with each other and were never close to each other. In preschool Frank was highly aggressive and difficult. . . . By adolescence, Frank was habitually delinquent, and he dropped out of high school. As an adult, Frank was diagnosed with a depressive disorder and his interpersonal relationships were tumultuous and typically short-lived.

Adapted from Cummings, Davies, & Campbell, 2000, pp. 299–300.

Peer Relations and Depression

Although problems with peers are common in the general population, these problems do discriminate youngsters referred to psychological services from nonreferred youngsters (Achenbach & Rescorla, 2001). Consistent with views that emphasize interpersonal aspects of depression, peer relation difficulties would appear to contribute to the development and maintenance of depression (Goodyer, 2001; McCauley, Pavlidis, & Kendall, 2001). Peer status, for example, has been found to be associated with adjustment difficulties, including depression.

A study by Kupersmidt and Patterson (1991) illustrates the relationship between peer status and adjustment. The sociometric status of a sample of second-, third-, and fourth-graders was assessed through nominations for being liked most and liked least. A peer status grouping was determined for each child. Two years later when the children were in the fourth through the sixth grade, several assessment instruments were completed, including a modified version of the Achenbach Youth Self-Report (YSR). As an index of a negative outcome, the authors examined whether a child had scores in the clinical range in one or more specific problem areas (the narrowband syndromes of the YSR). Rejected boys and girls exhibited higher than expected rates of clinical-range difficulties. In addition, girls with neglected peer status had even higher levels of clinical-range difficulties.

The authors also examined the relationship between peer status and each of the more specific problem areas defined by the various narrowband behavior problem scores. There was no relationship between peer status and any specific behavior problem for boys. However, a finding of particular interest emerged for girls. Rejected girls were more than twice as likely to report high levels of depression than average, popular, and controversial girls. Furthermore, neglected girls were more than twice as likely as rejected girls and more than five times as likely as the other groups of girls to report depression problems.

A study by Nangle and colleagues (2003) suggests that peer status/popularity may influence dyadic friendship quantity and quality that, in turn, influences loneliness and thus depression. Indeed, depression in young people has been found to be associated with a number of interpersonal characteristics important to peer relations and friendships. For example, depressed youngsters may perceive themselves as less interpersonally competent, have negative views of peers, have problematic social problem-solving styles, and exhibit distortions in processing of social information (Rudolph & Asher, 2000). Many of the problems in social relationships that accompany depression in young people may arise, in part, from the depressed youth's perceptions, including that others are rejecting and critical. This perception may then lead to behaviors by the depressed youngster that annoy peers, limit friendships, and result in isolation.

Suicide

Suicide is often mentioned in discussions of depression. This association probably occurs because depression is an important risk factor for suicide, and the two problems share etiological and epidemiological patterns. However, although the two problems overlap, they are also distinct. The majority of depressed youngsters do not attempt or commit suicide, and not every suicidal youth is depressed. Interest in suicide includes not only concern with completed suicides, but also with attempted suicides and suicidal thought. There is reason to attend to the full range of suicidal behavior.

PREVALENCE OF COMPLETED SUICIDES

The rate of completed suicide is relatively low among youngsters as compared with adults and lower for prepubertal children than for adolescents. Completed suicide by young people is nevertheless of concern and efforts to prevent suicide among young people have been developed (see Chapter 15). Each year approximately 1,900 youngsters in the United States between the ages of 10 and 19 die by suicide, making it the third leading cause of death in this age group (Anderson & Smith, 2003).

Suicides among younger children are occurring at a higher rate than two decades ago. In 1980, the suicide rate among youngsters between the ages of 10 and 14 was 0.4 per 100,000. Although suicides

A withdrawn or socially isolated child may need assistance in developing appropriate social skills and in increasing peer interactions.
(Ellen B. Senisi/The Image Works)

TABLE 7-7	SUICIDE RATES PER 100,000 BY AGE, GENDER, AND RACE FOR YEARS 1980, 1995, AND 2001								
	ALL RACES			**WHITE**			**BLACK**		
	1980	**1995**	**2001**	**1980**	**1995**	**2001**	**1980**	**1995**	**2001**
AGES 10–14									
Males	1.21	2.61	1.90	1.37	2.82	2.00	.52*	1.64	1.70
Females	.29	.83	.60	.33	.90	.60	.15*	.42*	—*
AGES 15–19									
Males	13.79	17.41	12.90	15.00	18.38	14.00	5.61	13.70	7.30
Females	3.02	3.11	2.70	3.26	3.26	2.90	1.60	2.30	1.30

*Rare occurrence—rate may be unreliable

From Anderson & Smith, 2003.

remained a relatively rare event in this age group, the 2001 rate was 1.3 youngsters per 100,000—an increase of over 200 percent. In contrast, although suicide rates are higher among youngsters 15 to 19 years of age, the trend over time is quite different. The 1980 rate among 15- to 19-year-olds was 12.3 per 100,000, and the 2001 rate was 7.9 per 100,000—a decrease of over 35 percent. Table 7–7 presents suicide data for 1980, 1995, and 2001 by age, gender, and two racial groups. We see that the rate of completed suicides is highest for white males. An overall leveling off or decrease in rates since 1995 can be seen except in black males ages 10–14, where in 2001 the rate increased slightly. In addition, the 2001 rates for Hispanic youth were comparable to those reported for black youngsters. The high rates of suicide among American Indian youth, particularly males in the 15- to 19-age range (an alarming 27.7 per 100,000), are worth noting (Anderson & Smith, 2003).

An increased availability of guns appears to be one of the factors contributing to suicide among young people. Based on the national Youth Risk Behavior Survey (Grunbaum et al., 2002) the percentage of youngsters in grades 9 to 12 in the United States who seriously considered suicide or made a suicide plan significantly decreased between 1991 and 2001. However, during this same period, there was a significant increase in the number of youngsters who made an injurious suicide attempt. Moreover, a survey of suicides among 15- to 24-year-olds in 34 of the wealthiest nations indicated that 34 percent of suicides were firearm-related (Johnson, Krug, & Potter, 2000). The percentage in the United States was 68 percent, and the United States accounted for 62 percent of all firearm-related suicides.

SUICIDAL IDEATION AND ATTEMPTS

Patty   A Suicide Attempt

Patty, a pretty 8-year-old, took an overdose of two of her mother's imipramine tablets just before going to sleep. Nobody knew about this until the next morning when Patty's mother had to wake her when she did not get up in time for school. Patty complained of a headache, dizziness, and tiredness. She was tearful and irritable and argued that her mother should "Leave me alone. I want to die." Alarmed, Patty's mother brought her to the pediatrician, who recommended that Patty be hospitalized for evaluation of suicidal behavior. . . . He believed that Patty would not be safe at home. Patty insisted that the "best thing would be for me to die."

Patty's mother told the pediatrician that the last 2 months had been very stressful for the family. She and her husband had separated and were planning to divorce. The mother described feeling very depressed and anxious over the last year. Her husband often came home drunk and would be very hostile to her and threaten her. . . .

Patty is a fine student and has many friends. . . . Patty's teacher had spoken to her mother about Patty's behavior over the previous 2 months. Patty was fidgety in class and unable to concentrate; she often day-dreamed. Her homework assignments were often not completed and her grades had dropped. Unlike her earlier behavior, Patty, in the last month, had preferred to be alone and had not joined her peers in after-school activities. She also had several arguments with her best friend.

Adapted from Pfeffer, 2000, p. 238.

If one considers the entire range of suicidal behavior, prevalence appears quite high, particularly among adolescents and, to a lesser extent, among children. Clearly it is difficult to assess the prevalence of suicidal behavior. Many attempts may go undetected and unreported, because not all cases seek medical or some therapeutic care. Also, methodological and definitional issues may limit interpretation of self-reports of suicidal ideation and attempts. Even some completed suicides may be mistakenly viewed as accidents.

A prospective longitudinal study of approximately 1,500 adolescents between 14 and 18 years of age by Lewinsohn and his colleagues (1996) gives us a picture of the prevalence of adolescent suicidal behavior. A total of 19.4 percent of these adolescents had a history of suicidal ideation. Such ideation was more prevalent in females (23.7 percent) than in males (14.8 percent). And although more frequent suicidal ideation predicted future suicide attempts, even mild and relatively infrequent suicidal thoughts increased the risk for an attempt.

Suicide attempts had occurred in 7.1 percent of this community sample. Females (10.1 percent) were more likely than males (3.8 percent) to attempt suicide. Suicide attempts before puberty were uncommon. The majority of attempts made by females consisted of either ingestion of harmful substances (55 percent) or cutting themselves (31 percent). Males employed a wider variety of methods—ingestion (20 percent), cutting (25 percent), gun use (15 percent), hanging (11 percent), and other methods, such as shooting air into one's veins or running into traffic (22 percent). Some adolescents attempted suicide more than once. The first 3 months after an attempt were a period of particularly high risk for a repeated attempt. Reattempts were made by approximately 27 percent of the boys and 21 percent of the girls. The likelihood of a suicidal attempt by these youngsters remained above the rates expected in the general population for at least 2 years. At 24 months, 39 percent of the boys and 33 percent of the girls had reattempted.

Suicide attempts by adolescents and children are often conceptualized as a "cry of pain"—as expressing "I want to stop feeling pain" (De Wilde, Kienhorst, & Diekstra, 2001). Young people are often thought to be vulnerable to suicide because their problem-solving and self-regulatory skills and their abilities to cope with stressful circumstances may be limited. Some youngsters may be faced with circumstances that cause considerable stress that they view as beyond their control. These youngsters may also have limited understanding that undesirable situations can and often do change.

SUICIDE AND PSYCHOPATHOLOGY

Suicide is often thought of as a symptom of disorders such as depression. Indeed, depression is related to suicide among children and adolescents (Flisher, 1999; Lewinsohn, Rohde, & Seeley, 1996), and constructs such as hopelessness that are associated with depression have been found to predict suicidal behavior (Levy, Jurkovic, & Spiro, 1995). For example, in a longitudinal study, Kovacs, Goldston, and Gatsonis (1993) found that a significantly greater proportion of youngsters with depressive disorders attempted suicide than did youngsters with other disorders. However, suicidal behavior can be associated with a variety of disorders, and the presence of two or more disorders appreciably increases the risk of suicidal attempts (Fergusson & Lynskey, 1995; Lewinsohn, Rohde, & Seeley, 1995). Conduct disorder and substance abuse diagnoses are common among completed suicides. Indeed, some research suggests considerable diagnostic heterogeneity among young suicide completers. Therefore, although depression is an important risk factor, the presence of a depressive disorder is neither necessary nor sufficient for the occurrence of suicidal behavior. It is probably important to be aware that some workers indicate that the presence of problems (e.g., aggression and impulsivity in combination with or independent of depression) at levels below criteria for any diagnosis of disorder also increase the risk of suicidal behavior (King et al., 1992).

RISK FACTORS

There is no typical suicidal youngster, and multiple factors likely contribute to risk for suicide (De Wilde et al., 2001; Gould et al., 2003; King et al., 2001). A history of prior suicide attempts is a strong predictor of completed suicide. However, multiple characteristics of youngsters themselves appear to be risk factors of suicidal behavior. Figure 7–5 illustrates the clusters of variables found to be significant risk factors in the adolescents studied by Lewinsohn and his colleagues (1996). Risk factors may have both direct and indirect effects. Indirect effects on suicidal behavior in this group of youngsters were mediated by the adolescents' cognitive/coping styles, which in turn had an impact on suicidal behavior.

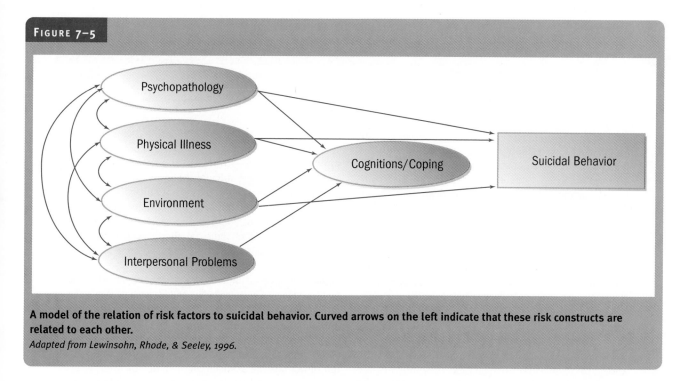

FIGURE 7–5

A model of the relation of risk factors to suicidal behavior. Curved arrows on the left indicate that these risk constructs are related to each other.

Adapted from Lewinsohn, Rhode, & Seeley, 1996.

Individual risk factors include poor interpersonal problem-solving ability, physical illness, and psychological disorders that are characterized by attributes such as depression, hopelessness, impulsivity, and aggression. Sexual orientation may be a risk factor among adolescent youth. (See Accent: "Sexual Orientation and Suicide Risk.")

A family history of suicidal behavior increases risk. Family factors (such as abuse, low parental monitoring, and poor communication) and family disruption are also frequently cited as risk factors. Although improved research is needed, it would appear that youngsters who attempt suicide are likely to grow up in families characterized by high levels of turmoil (De Wilde et al., 2001; Wagner, 1997). However, high levels of involvement and support may serve a protective function (Gould et al., 2003).

Other factors such as high levels of stress in school, social relations, and sociocultural influences—including the ready availability of firearms—are also thought to contribute to increased risk. Considerable concern also exists regarding contagion ("imitation" or increased suicidal behavior) following media reports or presentations of stories of youth suicide (Gould et al., 2003).

Research, conducted primarily with adults, suggests possible biological factors such as abnormalities in serotonin function and possible genetic influences. At present biological findings have little impact on clinical practice (Gould et al., 2003).

Assessment of Mood Disorders

The assessment of mood disorders is likely to involve a number of strategies and to sample a broad spectrum of attributes (Stark et al., 2000; Youngstrom et al., 2004). Structured interviews may be employed to yield a DSM mood disorder diagnosis, although they are more likely to be employed in research than in typical clinical settings. As we have seen, mood disorders may manifest themselves in a number of ways throughout development, and youngsters who experience a mood disorder are likely to exhibit other difficulties. A general clinical interview and the use of a general dimensional instrument like the Child Behavior Checklist are common. Because a variety of influences may contribute to the development of these disorders, assessing the parents, family, and social environments as well as individual characteristics of the youngster is likely to prove informative.

With regard to depression, a variety of measures that focus more specifically on depression and related constructs have been developed (Compas, 1997; Hodges, 1994; Reynolds, 1994). Of these, self-report instruments are among the most commonly employed. They are particularly important, given

ACCENT

Sexual Orientation and Suicide Risk

It is frequently suggested that suicide is more common among gay and lesbian youth as compared with the general adolescent population. At present there does not appear to be evidence for a higher rate of completed suicide in these groups (American Academy of Child and Adolescent Psychiatry [AACAP], 2001; Catalan, 2000). However, the view that these young people are at increased risk for suicidal ideation and suicidal attempts is widely held. Several studies of sizeable community samples suggest a two- to seven-fold increase in risk, and these youngsters also may be more likely to make suicide attempts that require medical attention (AACAP, 2001). Why might this be the case?

Research suggests that gay, lesbian, and bisexual youth are likely to report experiences that are known to be important risk factors. They may engage in early and more frequent drug and alcohol use and are more likely to be bullied and victimized at school. Many clinicians believe that the difficulties of dealing with the stigma of homosexuality and the interpersonal difficulties that this may bring might lead to depression, and there are reports of high levels of depression in such youth.

Data from the National Study of Adolescent Health (Add Health Study), a nationally representative study of U.S. adolescents, support the view that sexual orientation is a risk factor for suicidal ideation and suicide attempts, and suggest that this risk is, in part, due to known adolescent risk factors (Russell & Joyner, 2001). About 12,000 adolescents completed the survey in their homes, and information regarding the issues of sexuality and suicide was collected in a

manner to minimize issues of privacy and confidentiality. Youths with a same-sex orientation (having a same-sex romantic attraction or relationship) were more likely to report suicidal thoughts and were more than two times as likely to attempt suicide than their same-sex peers. It is important to note, however, that the vast majority of youth with a same-sex sexual orientation reported no suicidal thoughts or attempts (about 85 percent of boys and 72 percent of girls). Youngsters with a same-sex orientation also scored higher on several important adolescent suicide risk factors: more alcohol abuse and depression, higher rates of suicide attempts by family members and friends, and victimization experiences.

These and other findings suggest that sexual orientation, per se, is not a risk factor for suicide attempts, but rather it is the association of same-sex orientation with known risk factors common to all adolescents. Indeed, the same risk factors (e.g., low self-esteem, early sexual debut, unsafe sex, substance use) are reported to be equally elevated in sexual minority and heterosexual suicide attempters (Savin-Williams & Ream, 2003). Again, it is important to remember that most youth with a same-sex orientation do not attempt suicide and are resilient in the face of considerable risk (Savin-Williams, 2001). Sexual minority youth who attempt suicide may exist in a context that amplifies the experience of other risk factors (Savin-Williams & Ream, 2003). Appreciation of this context can inform our understanding of the difficulties faced by these youngsters. It should also encourage us to continue to create environments in which risk will be decreased.

that many of the key problems that characterize depression, such as sadness and feelings of worthlessness, are subjective. The Children's Depression Inventory (CDI) (Kovacs, 1992) is probably the most frequently used measure of this type. It is an offspring of the Beck Depression Inventory, commonly used for adults. The CDI asks youngsters to choose which of three alternatives best characterizes them during the past 2 weeks. Twenty-seven items sample affective, behavioral, and cognitive aspects of depression. Research on gender and age differences, reliability, validity, and clinically meaningful cutoff scores

has been conducted for the CDI (Reynolds, 1994). The Reynolds Child Depression Scale (Reynolds, 1989) and Reynolds Adolescent Depression Scale (Reynolds, 1987) also have been reported to have good psychometric properties (Reynolds, 1994). Despite their wide use, some research suggests caution in assuming equivalent measurement of depression by measures such as the CDI with minority populations such as African Americans and Spanish-language Mexican Americans (Prelow et al., 2002).

Many self-report measures are also rephrased so that they can be completed by significant others such as the child's parents (Clarizio, 1994). Measures completed by both the child and the parent often show only low levels of correlation, and agreement may vary with the age of the youngster (Kazdin, 1994; Renouf & Kovacs, 1994). These results suggest that information provided by different sources may tap different aspects of the child's behavior. Assessment measures can also be completed by teachers, clinicians, or other adults (Clarizio, 1994). Ratings by peers can likewise provide a unique perspective. The Peer Nomination Inventory of Depression (Lefkowitz & Tesiny, 1980) asks children to nominate peers who fit certain descriptions. Table 7–8 presents questions regarding depression, happiness, and popularity to which the peers are asked to respond.

Measures of constructs related to depression have also been developed, and many characteristics might be assessed. For example, attributes such as self-esteem (e.g., Harter, 1985) and perceived control over events (e.g., Connell, 1985) are likely candidates for evaluation. In addition, assessing various cognitive processes such as hopelessness (Kazdin, Rodgers, &

Colbus, 1986), attributional style (Seligman & Peterson, 1986), and cognitive distortions (e.g., Leitenberg, Yost, & Carroll-Wilson, 1986) have been and are likely to be helpful for both clinical and research purposes.

A number of observational and performance-based measures exist to assist in the assessment of depression in children and adolescents (Garber & Kaminski, 2000). Systematic observations of depressed youngsters interacting with others in controlled laboratory settings can potentially provide an opportunity to observe the social behavior of these youngsters with significant others. Table 7–9 lists some of the categories of behaviors that can be observed using existing systems for coding social interactions relevant to depression. Observational measures may not be used as frequently as other assessment measures because they require considerable training and coding itself is very labor intensive. There is also concern regarding the ecological validity of these observations, that is, the extent to which a brief laboratory interaction reflects real-world social interactions.

As one might expect, the assessment of bipolar disorders in children and adolescents is less well developed. A broad spectrum of information is, again, the assessment goal (Youngstrom et al., 2004). Structured diagnostic interviews such as versions of

TABLE 7–8	PEER NOMINATION INVENTORY OF DEPRESSION ITEMS

Who often plays alone? (D)
Who thinks they are bad? (D)
Who doesn't try again when they lose? (D)
Who often sleeps in class? (D)
Who often looks lonely? (D)
Who often says they don't feel well? (D)
Who says they can't do things? (D)
Who often cries? (D)
Who often looks happy? (H)
Who likes to do a lot of things? (H)
Who worries a lot? (D)
Who doesn't play? (D)
Who often smiles? (H)
Who doesn't take part in things? (D)
Who doesn't have much fun? (D)
Who is often cheerful? (H)
Who thinks others don't like them? (D)
Who often looks sad? (D)
Who would you like to sit next to in class? (P)
Who are the children you would like to have for your best friends? (P)

Note: D = items that are included in depressed score
H = items in happiness score
P = items in popularity score

Adapted from Lefkowitz & Tesiny, 1980.

TABLE 7–9	CATEGORIES AND EXAMPLES OF DEPRESSION-RELATED BEHAVIORS THAT CAN BE OBSERVED IN SOCIAL INTERACTION TASKS

Emotions: smiling, frowning, crying, happiness, sadness, anger, fear
Affect Regulation: control or expression of affect
Problem Solving: identifying problems, proposing solutions
Nonverbal Behaviors: eye contact, posture
Conflict: noncompliance, ignoring, demanding, negotiating
Cognitive Content: criticism, praise, self-derogation
Speech: rate, volume, tone of voice, initiation
Engaged or Disengaged: enthusiasm, involvement, persistence
On or Off Task Behavior
Physical Contact: threatening, striking, affection
Symptoms: depression, irritability, psychomotor agitation, retardation, fatigue concentration

Adapted from Garber & Kaminski, 2000.

the K-SADS have been employed to make diagnostic decisions and to obtain additional information. There are no established mania rating scales developed specifically for children and adolescents. The Young Mania Rating Scale (Young et al., 1978) has been adapted for use with children and adolescents (Youngstrom et al., 2004). The General Behavior Inventory (Depue et al., 1989) designed to assess symptoms of depression, hypomania, mania, and mixed mood states has been adapted for use with children and adolescents and as a parent-report measure (Danielson et al., 2003; Youngstrom et al., 2001).

Treatment of Mood Disorders

The treatment of depression in young people, particularly adolescents, has received increasing attention (Asarnow, Jaycox, & Tompson, 2001; Wolraich, 2003). There is far less information available regarding the treatment of bipolar disorder, but, here too, interest has increased (Carlson et al., 2003; Goldberg-Arnold & Fristad, 2003; James & Javaloyes, 2001). However, even in regard to depression, less is known about the treatment of youth compared with that for adults, and treatments often are adaptations of those that seem to be successful for adults. Our discussion of treatment emphasizes pharmacological and cognitive-behavioral treatments, because these interventions, alone and in combination, have received the most research attention (Treatment for Adolescents with Depression Study [TADS], 2005).

PHARMACOLOGICAL TREATMENTS FOR DEPRESSION

The practice of prescribing antidepressant medication for children and adolescents is still controversial, because the effectiveness and safety of pharmacotherapy with depressed youngsters remains unclear (Vitiello & Swedo, 2004; Wagner & Ambrosini, 2001). Tricyclic antidepressants (TCAs) such as imipramine, amitriptyline, nortriptyline, and desipramine have been widely used to treat depression in young people. Selective serotonin reuptake inhibitors (SSRIs) such as fluoxetine and paroxetine and other second-generation antidepressants such as bupropion and venlafaxine have more recently been employed with depressed youth. TCAs have not been demonstrated to be effective in treating depressed youth, and they have more side effects than SSRIs. Thus, despite mixed research results, SSRIs are viewed as more

promising and are more likely to be recommended when medication is prescribed.

However, the use of such medications is for the most part based on clinical trials or on a small number of controlled studies (McClellan & Werry, 2003). This research does not clearly support the superiority of these antidepressant medications in either prepubertal children or adolescents. At present it is difficult to know whether or why these medications, many of which are reported effective in treating adult depression, are ineffective for youth (Wagner & Ambrosini, 2001). It may be that adequately designed research is lacking. Additionally, differences in response to these medications may lead us to question the assumption that depression is the same across age groups. As we have discussed, there may be neurodevelopmental, biological, psychological, and interpersonal differences in depression in children, adolescents, and adults.

These medications are widely employed, however, and these or other pharmacological agents may ultimately prove to be effective, alone or in combination with other treatments (TADS Team, 2004). However, because antidepressant medications are principally developed and marketed for adults, there are less well-established guidelines for their administration and little systematic data on their safety. Issues of safety and side effects are of particular concern, because little is known regarding the long-term impact of these medications on development, particularly in young children. Particular concern has been expressed about the possible association between SSRIs and increases in suicidal behavior (Vitiello & Swedo, 2004).

PSYCHOSOCIAL TREATMENTS FOR DEPRESSION

Much of the literature on psychosocial interventions for depressed youngsters has suggested treatments based on downward extensions of interventions employed with adults. Although this was a reasonable way to begin to explore effective treatment, there are limitations to such an approach (Hammen et al., 1999; Stark, Rouse, & Kurowski, 1994). For example, the lives of depressed youngsters differ from those of adults. Children and adolescents have ongoing daily contact with parents that may contribute to the problem of depression. Also, youngsters are exposed on a daily basis to the potential negative consequences of social skill difficulties and the impact of peer relation difficulties. Adults, on the other hand, may arrange their lives to avoid familial and social contacts. As we develop a better understanding of the social-psychological factors that contribute to depression in children and adolescents, treatments that differ from those employed with adults and that address relevant developmental experiences of depressed children and adolescents are likely to be the most effective.

Most psychological interventions for depression in children and adolescents derive from a cognitive-behavioral perspective. Cognitive aspects of these treatments confront and modify the youngster's maladaptive cognitions (e.g., problematic attributions, excessively high standards, negative self-monitoring). The behavioral aspects focus on goals such as increasing pleasurable experiences; increasing social skills; and improving communication, conflict resolution, and social problem-solving skills.

In general, findings are positive and promising (Michael & Crowley, 2002). However, support for the effectiveness of treatment is still somewhat limited, particularly in cases involving clinical levels of depression and preadolescents. Also, which specific components of these multielement treatments are most effective remains unclear (Asarnow et al., 2001; Bachanas & Kaslow, 2001). Several studies are described here to illustrate interventions derived from a cognitive-behavioral perspective.

Weisz and his colleagues (2003) have developed a manualized cognitive-behavioral intervention, PASCET (Primary and Secondary Control Enhanced Training), that is based on the relationship between perceived control and depression. In an initial test of this program, children, in grades 3 to 6, who exhibited mild to moderate depressive symptoms were treated in small groups during school hours. The eight-session program emphasized control skills that helped identify and develop activities that the child found mood enhancing and that the child valued; that identified and modified maladaptive thoughts; that fostered cognitive techniques for mood enhancement; and that aided relaxation and positive imagery. At the end of treatment and at a 9-month follow-up, the treatment group showed significantly greater change (decrease) in depressive symptoms than did the no-treatment control group. These results are illustrated in Figure 7–6. Weisz and colleagues have adapted this program to a primary care setting with a more distressed and disturbed sample of clinic-referred youth. Evaluation of this program is underway (Weisz et al., 2003).

A cognitive-behavioral intervention, known as the Adolescent Coping with Depression program, a skills-training, multicomponent intervention, has been developed by Lewinsohn, Clarke, and colleagues (Clarke, DeBar, & Lewinsohn, 2003). In an initial study (Lewinsohn et al., 1990) adolescents

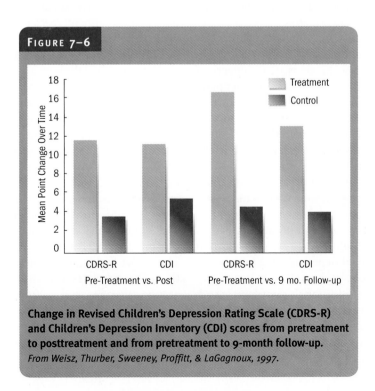

FIGURE 7–6

Change in Revised Children's Depression Rating Scale (CDRS-R) and Children's Depression Inventory (CDI) scores from pretreatment to posttreatment and from pretreatment to 9-month follow-up.
From Weisz, Thurber, Sweeney, Proffitt, & LaGagnoux, 1997.

aged 14 to 18 who met diagnostic criteria for depression were randomly assigned to one of three conditions: adolescent-only, adolescent-and-parent, and wait-list control. Adolescents attended sixteen 2-hour sessions, twice a week, in a group or classlike setting, that focused on teaching methods of relaxation, increasing pleasant events, controlling irrational and negative thoughts, increasing social skills, and teaching conflict resolution (communication and problem-solving) skills. In the parent-involvement condition, parents met for nine weekly sessions. They were provided with information on the skills being taught to their teenagers and were taught problem-solving and conflict resolution skills.

As compared with the control group, treatment groups improved on depression measures. For example, at the end of treatment, the recovery rate for treated adolescents was 46 percent whereas only 5 percent of the control group no longer met diagnostic criteria. The teenagers in the treatment conditions were followed for 2 years after the end of treatment, and their treatment gains were maintained. Control participants were not available for follow-up, because they were offered treatment at the end of the treatment period. A second similar study (Clarke et al., 1999) yielded comparable findings. In both studies there were few or no significant advantages for parent involvement.

Brent and colleagues (1997) compared the relative efficacy of two treatments—cognitive-behavioral therapy (CBT) and behavioral family systems therapy—with a supportive therapy condition included to control for the nonspecific effects of receiving treatment. All of the adolescents met diagnostic criteria for major depressive disorder. Participants received 12 to 16 sessions of therapy over a 3- to 4-month period. Youngsters in the CBT condition showed greater improvement than those in the other two conditions. However, also clear was the necessity to improve short-term efficacy of treatment for at least some youth, as well as long-term efficacy, perhaps by longer treatment or continuing care. For example, more than half of the participants in the study required additional treatment beyond that provided. Severity of depression, the presence of co-occurring disorders, and family problems predicted the need for additional treatment. And, despite the superiority of the CBT condition, it was not as successful for all participants. Forty percent of adolescents treated with CBT remained symptomatic at posttreatment. In addition, at 2-year follow-up there were no differences in depression between adolescents who received CBT and those in other conditions (Weersing & Brent, 2003).

The effectiveness of interpersonal psychotherapy (IPT) for adolescents, modified from interpersonal psychotherapy for depressed adults, has also been examined. IPT is based on the premise that whatever the causes, depression is intertwined with the individual's interpersonal relationships. The treatment addresses current interpersonal issues of adolescents such as grief, interpersonal disputes, role transitions, interpersonal deficits, and single-parent family status through a variety of active strategies (Mufson & Dorta, 2003). Mufson and colleagues (1999) found that adolescents diagnosed with major depressive disorder who received ITP showed improvement in depressive symptoms, social functioning, and problem-solving skills compared with control youngsters whose clinical condition was monitored. Rosselló and Bernal (1999) compared IPT with cognitive-behavioral therapy and a wait-list control in a sample of clinically depressed adolescents in Puerto Rico. Both treatment groups showed significant improvements in depressive symptoms (see Figure 7–7) and self-esteem as compared with the control condition.

It is interesting to note that the study by Mufson and colleagues included a large proportion of Latino youths and that Rosselló and Bernal made efforts to incorporate interpersonal aspects of Latino culture into their treatment: *personalismo*—the preference for interpersonal contacts, and *familismo*—a strong identification with and attachment to family. This was accomplished through a variety of adaptations to the treatment, such as selection of examples, sayings, and images from the youngsters' culture and context; emphasis on the interpersonal nature of the therapeutic approach; and discussion of family dependence and independence (Rosselló & Bernal, 1996; 1999). Although youngsters in both treatment groups in the Rosselló and Bernal study had comparable improvements in depression, improvement for some other outcome measures was better in the IPT group. The authors suggest that this may be because of the consonance of IPT with Puerto Rican cultural values. This effort highlights the importance of evaluating the efficacy of treatments for different cultural groups (Asarnow et al., 2001).

Treatments that are derived from a cognitive-behavioral perspective and treatments that address interpersonal and family aspects of depression in children and adolescents are promising. However, additional large-scale controlled treatment studies

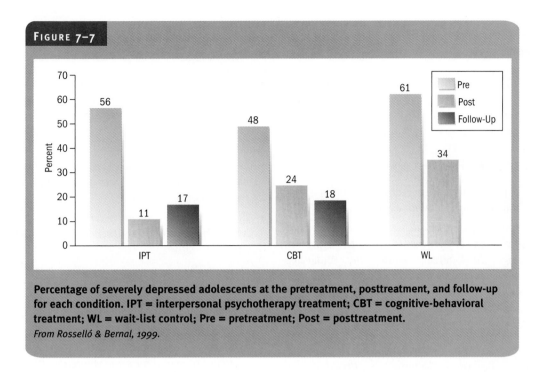

FIGURE 7-7

Percentage of severely depressed adolescents at the pretreatment, posttreatment, and follow-up for each condition. IPT = interpersonal psychotherapy treatment; CBT = cognitive-behavioral treatment; WL = wait-list control; Pre = pretreatment; Post = posttreatment.
From Rosselló & Bernal, 1999.

are needed. Successful treatment strategies will need to address the multiple aspects of depression and of the social and family environments of depressed youngsters. While such treatments seem promising, several aspects of depression in children and adolescents suggest the potential value of preventive interventions (Birmaher et al., 1996b; Kazdin & Marciano, 1998). (See Chapter 15.)

TREATMENT OF BIPOLAR DISORDER

The treatment of bipolar disorder requires a multimodal approach to the disorder itself as well as attention to likely co-occurring difficulties and the considerable impact on family life (James & Javaloyes, 2001). The young patient with mania may need to be admitted to a child or adolescent hospital unit so as to insure the youngster's safety and to provide an adequately controlled environment. The choice of an inpatient setting would be guided by the level of disturbance displayed by the youngster, the risk of harm or suicide, the level of support that the family is able to provide, and the need for medical supervision of medication.

The most common treatment for bipolar disorder is pharmacotherapy (Kowatch et al., 2005). Because bipolar disorder in childhood and adolescence is a relatively rare disorder, information

regarding treatment is sparse (McClellan & Werry, 2003; Ryan, 2003). That treatments rely heavily on the adult literature is problematic, and information regarding possible side effects is needed (Carlson et al., 2003; Gracious et al., 2004). Mood stabilizers such as lithium, valproate, carbamazepine, or combinations of these and other medications are the pharmacological agents likely to be employed (Ryan, 2003). Treatment of the depressive aspects of the disorder may include the use of medications such as the selective serotonin reuptake inhibitors.

Although the primary treatment for bipolar disorder is pharmacological, education of the patient and family about the disorder is important. In addition, individual and family therapy is often recommended. Programs designed for youngsters and their families that provide educational and psychotherapeutic components have been developed and are undergoing evaluation (Fristad & Goldberg-Arnold, 2003; Goldberg-Arnold & Fristad, 2003; Pavuluri et al., 2004). These treatment programs include many of the cognitive-behavioral elements described in the psychosocial treatment of depression. Support groups and other forms of assistance for families are likely to be needed as well (Hellander et al., 2003). Research regarding all aspects of treatment for bipolar disorder in adolescents and children is needed.

SUMMARY

●●●●●●○○○

- *Interest in mood disorders in young people is relatively recent. Particularly in children, but also in adolescents, interest has been mainly on depression.*

A HISTORICAL PERSPECTIVE

- *The psychoanalytic theory of depression suggested that the problem would not exist in children.*

- *The concept of masked depression, although problematic, resulted in greater attention to the problem and highlighted developmental issues. A developmental perspective to understanding depression has continued to evolve.*

DEFINITION AND CLASSIFICATION OF MOOD DISORDERS

- *What is defined as depression is affected by how depression is measured and who provides information.*

- *The dominant view of mood disorders is that offered by the DSM.*

- *Major Depressive Disorder, Dysthymic Disorder, and Adjustment Disorder with Depressed Mood are the DSM diagnoses typically given to depressed youngsters.*

- *Empirical approaches to classification suggest syndromes that include a mixed presentation of depression and anxiety features in children and adolescents.*

- *Youngsters who are depressed are likely to experience a number of other difficulties and to meet the diagnostic criteria for a variety of other disorders.*

- *Bipolar disorders involve the presence of mania as well as depression. Less is known about these disorders in children and adolescents.*

- *Developmental differences in presentation of mood disorders challenge the use of the same diagnostic criteria in all age groups.*

EPIDEMIOLOGY

- *Major depressive disorder is the most prevalent form of affective disorders among children and adolescents.*

- *Episodes of clinical depression are quite common among adolescents. Depression is more prevalent among adolescents than children and among girls during adolescence.*

- *Higher rates of depression are reported among low SES groups. Although comparable rates of depression are typically reported for different ethnic groups, research suggests attention to possible differences.*

- *Definitional issues make estimates difficult, but bipolar disorder is rare, particularly in prepubertal youngsters.*

- *Evidence suggests thinking in terms of a continuum—a bipolar spectrum—rather than in categorical terms.*

DEVELOPMENTAL COURSE AND PROGNOSIS

- *How mood disorders are manifested varies by developmental period.*

- *Episodes of depression may last for an appreciable period of time and for some youngsters may present a recurring problem.*

- *Youngsters who meet the criteria for bipolar disorder may experience a chronic and recurrent course of difficulties.*

ETIOLOGY OF MOOD DISORDERS

- *Most contemporary views of depression in children and adolescents suggest a model that integrates multiple determinants.*

- *A strong genetic contribution to the development of bipolar disorder is suggested. Research suggests a genetic component to depression as well but also considerable influence of shared and nonshared environment.*

- *Research on the biochemistry of depression emphasizes the role of neurotransmitters and the neuroendocrine system. Findings suggest that during childhood and early adolescence, the biological aspects of depression differ from adult cases.*

- *Separation/loss has been a major theme in many theories of depression. Cognitive and behavioral theories also suggest other contributions to the development of depression, including interpersonal and cognitive aspects of functioning.*

- *A learned helplessness perspective suggests that a learned perception of lack of control leads to a cognitive style and behaviors characteristic of depression. Hopelessness theory emphasizes the interaction of stressful life events and cognitive style.*

- *Cognitive theories, such as Beck's, and self-control models of depression have also received attention.*

- *Maternal depression appears to be related to childhood dysfunctions, but this relationship does not seem to be either specific to childhood depression or inevitable. Various mechanisms may link maternal depression and child dysfunction.*

- *Interpersonal relationships with peers contribute to the development of depression, and a youngster's depression contributes to peers' relationships with the depressed youngster.*

SUICIDE

- *Completed suicide represents a considerable concern. The range of suicidal behavior that includes suicidal thoughts and suicide attempts is more prevalent.*

- *Suicidal behavior is related to depression but to other problems as well.*

- *The factors that contribute to suicidal behavior are often multiple and complex.*

ASSESSMENT OF MOOD DISORDERS

- *Assessment of depression is likely to sample a broad spectrum of attributes and to involve a number of strategies. Obtaining information from a variety of informants and with a variety of measures seems important.*

- *Assessment has been facilitated by the development of structured diagnostic interviews. In addition, self-report measures are frequently employed.*

- *Instruments available to assess attributes associated with depression (e.g., hopelessness) and observational and performance-based measures add to our ability to conduct a thorough assessment.*

- *Assessment of bipolar disorders in children and adolescents is less well developed.*

TREATMENT OF MOOD DISORDERS

- *The prescription of antidepressant medications to treat children and adolescents with depression is widespread and may be an important component of treatment for some youngsters. However, the use of medications continues to be controversial, because effectiveness and safety remain unclear. Selective serotonin reuptake inhibitors are most commonly employed.*

- *Treatments derived from behavioral and cognitive-behavioral perspectives and treatments that address interpersonal and family aspects of depression in youngsters seem promising. However, continued development of treatments that are sensitive to multiple aspects of psychological, social, and family influences and to cultural differences are needed.*

- *Treatment of bipolar disorder requires a multimodal approach. The primary treatment involves the use of pharmacological agents, particularly mood stabilizers. Research regarding all aspects of treatment for bipolar disorder in youth is needed.*

KEY TERMS

masked depression *(p. 162)*

unipolar mood disorder *(p. 163)*

bipolar mood disorder *(p. 163)*

major depressive disorder *(p. 164)*

dysthymic disorder *(p. 164)*

double depression *(p. 164)*

adjustment disorder with depressed mood *(p. 164)*

bipolar disorder *(p. 166)*

mania *(p. 166)*

subsyndromal *(p. 170)*

remission *(p. 173)*

learned helplessness *(p. 176)*

attributional (explanatory) style *(p. 176)*

hopelessness *(p. 177)*

cognitive distortions *(p. 177)*

contagion *(p. 185)*

selective serotonin reuptake inhibitors *(p. 188)*

CHAPTER 8

Conduct Problems

In this chapter and the next we discuss problems often described as externalizing. This term reflects problems that seem to place the youngster in conflict with others and is in contrast to the seemingly more inner-directed problems discussed in the two previous chapters. Various other terms also are employed to describe these types of problems—acting out, disruptive, impulsive, undercontrolled, oppositional, antisocial, conduct-disordered, and delinquent. Although there is a general understanding of this broad category, attempting to understand, define, and subcategorize such behavior is a continuing goal.

Among disruptive behavior problems, a distinction has often been made between inattention, hyperactivity, and impulsivity on the one hand, and aggression, oppositional behaviors, and more serious conduct problems on the other (Waldman, Lillienfeld, & Lahey, 1995). The behaviors in the first grouping are discussed in greater detail in the next chapter, which is on attention-deficit hyperactivity disorder (ADHD). The oppositional and conduct-disordered behaviors of the second grouping are considered in this chapter. Labels such as conduct disorder, oppositional defiant disorder, and

juvenile delinquency are often applied to young people who exhibit such behavior. These youngsters have high rates of referral for mental health and other social and legal services and some portion of these youngsters have contributed to broad societal concern with levels of violence and crime. Conduct problems are thus the focus of considerable societal and scientific concern.

Classification and Description

Disruptive behaviors are common at various stages of development. Clinicians commonly hear complaints of a youngster's noncompliant, aggressive, and antisocial behavior. Parents and teachers often describe young children and adolescents who do not follow directions, do not comply with requests or seem irritable or angry. Also various forms of aggression and bullying may be common from early school years through middle school. Many adolescents may engage in dangerous behaviors and use illegal substances. The fact that these problems are common and disruptive makes them a topic of concern for parents and for those who work with children. They may cause considerable distress for parents and teachers, create discord among family members, or interfere with classroom functioning. Extreme and persistent forms of these behaviors cause a degree of disturbance and destruction well beyond the common experience. Thus they are of particular concern not only for the family but also for institutions such as the school and for society at large. The seeming persistence of these behaviors over time for some individuals—perhaps from early childhood through adult life—also contributes to their importance.

EMPIRICALLY DERIVED SYNDROMES

An empirically derived syndrome involving aggressive, oppositional, destructive, and antisocial behavior has been identified in a wide variety of studies. This syndrome has been given a variety of names, including externalizing, undercontrolled, or conduct disorder. It is robust in that it emerges employing a variety of measures, reporting agents, and settings. There have also been efforts to distinguish narrower groupings within this broad externalizing/conduct disorder syndrome.

Achenbach and Rescorla (2001), for example, have described two syndromes, aggressive behavior (e.g., argues a lot, destroys things, is disobedient, fights) and rule-breaking behavior (e.g., breaks rules, lies, steals, is truant), within the broader externalizing syndrome. The behaviors that are characteristic of these two narrow syndromes are listed in Table 8–1. Children may exhibit only one or both types of problems. The validity of this distinction is supported by a variety of research findings (Achenbach & Rescorla, 2001). For example, research suggests a higher degree of heritability for the aggressive than the rule-breaking syndrome (Edelbrock et al., 1995). Developmental differences also exist between the two syndromes. In a longitudinal analysis, Stanger, Achenbach, and Verhulst (1997) found that the average scores of the two syndromes declined between ages 4 and 10. After age 10, however, the scores on the aggressive syndrome continued to decline, whereas scores on the delinquent syndrome (now called rule-breaking) increased. These findings are illustrated in Figure 8–1. These same authors also found that the stability (the similarity of a particular individual's behavior at two points in time) was higher for the aggressive than for the delinquent (rule-breaking) syndrome. These and other findings suggest that it is important to distinguish

TABLE 8–1	BEHAVIORS FROM THE AGGRESSIVE AND RULE-BREAKING SYNDROMES
AGGRESSIVE BEHAVIOR	**RULE BREAKING BEHAVIOR**
Argues a lot	Drinks alcohol
Defiant	Lacks guilt
Mean to others	Breaks rules
Demands attention	Bad friends
Destroys own things	Lies, cheats
Destroys other's things	Prefers older kids
Disobedient at home	Runs away
Disobedient at school	Sets fires
Gets in fights	Sex problems
Attacks people	Steals at home
Screams a lot	Swearing
Explosive	Thinks of sex too much
Easily frustrated	Tardy
Stubborn, sullen	Uses tobacco
Mood changes	Truant
Sulks	Uses drugs
Suspicious	Vandalism
Teases a lot	
Temper	
Threatens others	
Loud	

Items listed are summaries of the actual content (wording) of items on the instruments. Most items are included in the Child Behavior Checklist (CBCL), Teacher Report Form (TRF), and Youth Self Report (YSR) versions of these syndromes, whereas others are specific to one or two of these instruments. Adapted from Achenbach & Rescorla, 2001.

between types of externalizing/conduct disorder problems.

Empirical approaches to classifying conduct disorders also suggest other ways of grouping problem behaviors within this broad category. These approaches are not mutually exclusive and indeed do overlap with the aggressive/rule-breaking distinction and with each other. Some approaches suggest a distinction based on *age of onset* (Hinshaw, Lahey, & Hart, 1993): a later- or an adolescent-onset category consisting principally of nonaggressive and rule-breaking behaviors, and an early-onset category that includes these behaviors as well as aggressive behaviors. The *salient symptom* approach is based on the primary behavior problem being displayed. Distinguishing antisocial children whose primary problem is aggression from those whose primary problem is

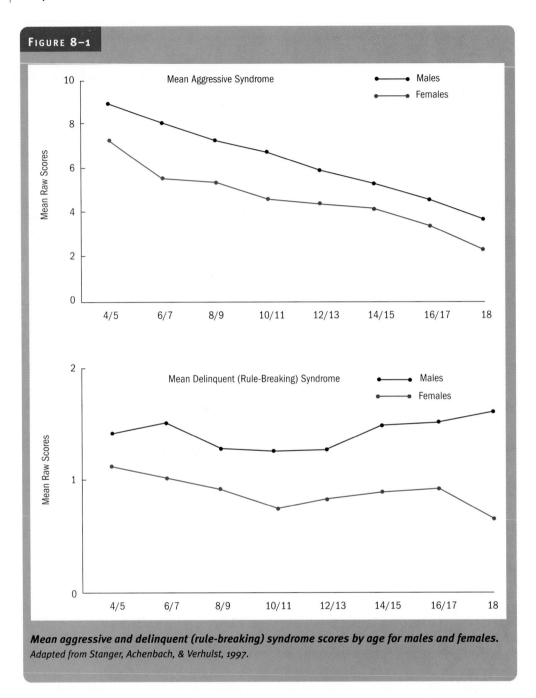

FIGURE 8-1

Mean aggressive and delinquent (rule-breaking) syndrome scores by age for males and females.
Adapted from Stanger, Achenbach, & Verhulst, 1997.

stealing is an example. Aggressive behavior may be particularly important to single out in this way. There is support for distinguishing aggression from other conduct-disordered behavior in terms of its social impact, correlates, gender differences, and developmental course (Loeber & Stouthamer-Loeber, 1998).

Expansion of the salient symptom distinction suggests a broader distinction (Loeber & Schmaling, 1985; Willoughby, Kupersmidt, & Bryant, 2001)

between overt, confrontational antisocial behaviors (e.g., arguing, fighting, temper tantrums), and covert, or concealed, antisocial behaviors (e.g., fire setting, lying, stealing, truancy). A further expansion suggests the grouping of conduct problems by employing two dimensions: the overt-covert distinction and a destructive-nondestructive dimension of behavior (Frick, 1998b). This approach and the clusters of behaviors based on it are illustrated in Figure 8–2. These kinds of distinctions continue to be

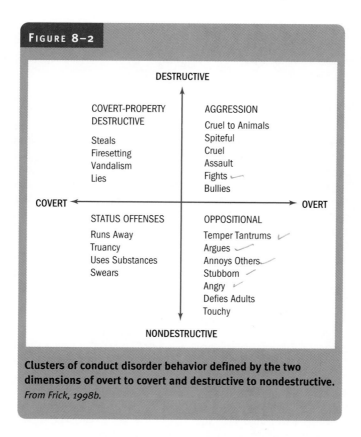

FIGURE 8-2

DESTRUCTIVE

COVERT-PROPERTY DESTRUCTIVE

Steals
Firesetting
Vandalism
Lies

AGGRESSION

Cruel to Animals
Spiteful
Cruel
Assault
Fights
Bullies

COVERT ← → OVERT

STATUS OFFENSES

Runs Away
Truancy
Uses Substances
Swears

OPPOSITIONAL

Temper Tantrums
Argues
Annoys Others
Stubborn
Angry
Defies Adults
Touchy

NONDESTRUCTIVE

Clusters of conduct disorder behavior defined by the two dimensions of overt to covert and destructive to nondestructive.
From Frick, 1998b.

explored in the context of an empirical and a developmental approach to understanding conduct-disordered behavior.

DSM APPROACH: OVERVIEW

Within the section on Disorders Usually First Diagnosed in Infancy, Childhood and Adolescence, the DSM has a category of Attention-Deficit and Disruptive Behavior Disorders. This larger category includes the diagnostic categories of Attention-Deficit Hyperactivity Disorder (discussed in Chapter 9) and the diagnoses of Oppositional Defiant Disorder and Conduct Disorder, which are discussed in the present chapter.

Although our focus is children and adolescents, it is important to note that among Personality Disorders, the DSM includes a diagnosis of Antisocial Personality Disorder (APD). This diagnosis may be applied to some individuals who displayed a persistent pattern of aggressive and antisocial behavior once they reached the age of 18. APD is characterized by "a pervasive pattern of disregard for and violation of the rights of others" and by multiple illegal and aggressive behaviors (American Psychiatric Association, 2000). Adults with APD may also display

psychopathy—an interpersonal trait defined by characteristics such as deceitfulness, callousness, lack of remorse, and impulsivity. The diagnosis of APD requires that the pattern be present since the age of 15 with evidence that the individual did meet, or would have met, the criteria for Conduct Disorder with an onset before 15 years of age.

Later we will discuss a subgroup of youngsters who display a developmental pattern of persistent aggressive and antisocial behavior. Some of these youngsters may continue this developmental trajectory and receive the diagnosis of APD as adults. There is evidence suggesting that some of these youngsters may display the callous/unemotional traits characteristic of psychopathy (Frick, 1998a; Silverthorn, Frick, & Reynolds, 2001). Youngsters high on such traits are described as displaying shallow emotions, a lack of anxiety, a lack of empathy, and little or no guilt.

DSM APPROACH: OPPOSITIONAL DEFIANT DISORDER

Young children are often stubborn, do not comply with requests or directions from adults, and in a variety of ways exhibit oppositional behavior. Not all

ACCENT ●●●●●

Fire Setting

Much of the information that we describe in this chapter addresses what can be termed overt conduct-disordered behavior (e.g., oppositional defiant behavior, aggression). Fire setting represents a behavior that would be described as covert.

Juvenile fire setting accounts for the majority of arrests for arson in the United States (U.S. Bureau of the Census, 2001). It produces serious damage in terms of loss of life, injury, posttraumatic symptoms, and property damage. It is associated with serious difficulties for the child, family, and community (Barnett & Spitzer, 1994; Kolko, 2001). Fire setters are at increased risk for later juvenile court referral and arrest for a violent crime beyond what would be predicted by the presence of conduct disorder (Becker et al., 2004).

Playing with fire is probably a part of normal development for many children as well as for those who become fire setters (Kolko, 1985). One can then ask, What other factors may be associated with the onset and persistence of a fire-setting problem? According to Kolko (2001) there are two categories of influence. The first category is unusual involvement with, interest in, and/or awareness of fire. It includes playing with matches, being attracted to fire, and having limited competence regarding fire. The second domain addresses factors that may contribute to the development of conduct-disordered behavior in general. These factors include aspects of the youngster (e.g., aggression), parents (e.g., poor monitoring of the child), and family (e.g., conflict). In this way, fire setting may be seen as part of a cluster of covert antisocial behaviors that include destruction of property, stealing, lying, and truancy. In fact, among both community and clinically referred youngsters, level of covert antisocial behavior predicted later fire setting (Kolko et al., 2001).

Family difficulties related to fire setting may be an extreme form of those that have been described for conduct disorders in general (Barnett & Spitzer, 1994; Kolko, 1989). For example, child fire setters were more likely to come from homes with marital violence and to have fathers who drank and abused pets (Becker et al., 2004). Also, Kazdin and Kolko (1986) found poorer marital adjustment and higher levels of psychological difficulties, depression in particular, among mothers of fire setters compared with mothers of non–fire setters.

such behavior is indicative or predictive of clinical problems (see the case of Henry). Indeed, appropriate and skilled assertions of autonomy may be desirable and may facilitate development (Johnston & Ohan, 1999). It is the less skilled and excessive oppositional and defiant behavior that may indicate present or future problems.

Henry | Preschool Oppositional Behavior

Mrs. Sweet reported that her 3.5-year-old son, Henry, was causing problems. She viewed Henry as a normal, active, bright boy. However, she felt the need to talk with a professional because her friends and family had made some comments about Henry's escalating disruptive behavior.

Henry was the older of two children and had a 9-month-old sister. Mrs. Sweet's responses to initial questionnaires indicated that she perceived Henry as engaging in a significant amount of disruptive behavior but the behavior was not problematic to her. The mother's log of the past week contained descriptions of inappropriate behaviors such as: "Henry hit his grandfather on the shin with a baseball bat" and "Henry scraped a knife across the kitchen wall."

Mr. Sweet did not attend the initial interview because he saw the difficulty as primarily "my wife's problem." Mrs. Sweet indicated that Henry's developmental milestones were within normal limits but that from birth Henry was a "difficult" child. Henry spent three mornings a week at a preschool and these were problem-free. The teachers initially reported, however, that they had to be rather "firm" in their expectations. When Henry was invited to spend time with friends in their homes things went well. Difficulties were reported when friends visited him—his behavior was described as very active, getting into things that were forbidden, and in general creating chaos. Henry's father often took Henry on full-day outings and thoroughly enjoyed this time. Mr. Sweet felt that his wife should be firmer with Henry. Mrs. Sweet described the major problems as "not listening," "refusing to do as requested," and "talking back." All of these occurred primarily with her, but were beginning to occur with other people in the family.

According to Mrs. Sweet, on a typical day Henry managed routine events such as eating and bathing easily. However, when any demands were placed on him, he would refuse to comply. To avoid confrontations, Mrs. Sweet spent much of her time rearranging her schedule, but this was becoming increasingly difficult as her 9-month-old demanded more of her attention.

Henry came to a clinic-observation session wearing an army camouflage outfit, cowboy hat, and boots, and carrying two six-shooters and a toy machine gun. He greeted the clinician with "I'm going to shoot your eyes out." The clinician responded with a firm "We don't talk like that in my office." Henry quickly responded in a contrite voice, "Oh, I'm sorry." Observation of parent-child interaction indicated that Mrs. Sweet gave Henry a high rate of noncontingent positive reinforcement, placed many demands on him, and tried to get compliance through reasoning. Henry placed many demands on his mother and rarely complied with her requests. Henry and his mother seemed to enjoy playing together. Henry refused to comply with his mother's requests to pick up the toys; however, he readily complied with the clinician's requests to clean up the toys.

A recommendation was made that both parents attend classes on child development and management. Both parents and Henry were also involved in treatment sessions to increase positive parent-child interactions, to set age-appropriate limits, to increase Henry's compliance, and to determine a consistent method of discipline. This parent training program was carried out over a 6-week period with (two) follow-up appointments. After treatment, Henry was still described as "headstrong"; however, both parents felt that his behavior was acceptable and for the most part easily managed.

Adapted from Schroeder & Gordon, 2002, pp. 374–376.

TABLE 8–2	BEHAVIORS USED BY THE DSM TO DEFINE OPPOSITIONAL DEFIANT DISORDER

- Loses temper
- Argues with adults
- Actively defies or refuses to comply with adult requests or rules
- Deliberately annoys others
- Blames others for own mistakes or misbehavior
- Is touchy or easily annoyed
- Is angry and resentful
- Is spiteful or vindictive

From American Psychiatric Association, 2000.

Oppositional Defiant Disorder (ODD) is described as a pattern of negativistic, hostile, and defiant behavior that is developmentally extreme. The major criteria used to define the disorder are listed in Table 8–2. To receive the diagnosis of Oppositional Defiant Disorder, at least four of these behaviors must be present for a period of at least 6 months. To distinguish the behaviors from expected levels of opposition and assertiveness, any behavior must be judged to occur more frequently than is typical for a child of comparable age. Furthermore, the oppositional defiant behavior must cause clinically meaningful impairment in the youngster's social or academic functioning. The case of Jeremy illustrates the behaviors displayed by children who might receive the diagnosis of Oppositional Defiant Disorder.

Jeremy Oppositional Defiant Disorder

Jeremy, age 9, was increasingly disobedient and difficult to manage at school. Recently he swore at a teacher and was suspended from school for several days. He also rode his bike into a store window and shattered it (once before he had broken a window when riding his bike with a friend). These and other experiences convinced his mother that she had to do something about his behavior.

Jeremy's problems have slowly escalated; however, he has been difficult to manage since nursery school. He is most likely to get into trouble when he is without close supervision. In school, Jeremy has been reprimanded for teasing, tripping, and kicking other children and calling them names. It often appears that he is deliberately trying to annoy other children, but Jeremy always claims that others have started the problem. Jeremy is described as bad-tempered and irritable. He does not become involved in serious fights, but there are occasionally minor physical exchanges with another child. Jeremy sometimes refuses to do what his teachers tell him to do, arguing and giving reasons why he should not have to do his work. Despite this, his grades have been good.

At home Jeremy's behavior is quite variable. On some days he is defiant and rude. Although he eventually complies, he needs to be told several times before he will do anything. On other days he is charming and volunteers to help but unhelpful days predominate. Jeremy's mother reports that "The least thing upsets him, and then he shouts and screams." She describes Jeremy as spiteful and mean with his younger brother.

Jeremy completes his work and his concentration is generally good. His mother describes him as "on the go all the time," but not restless. His teachers are not concerned that he is restless but are concerned about his attitude. His mother indicates that Jeremy tells minor lies, but that he is truthful about important things, if pressed.

Adapted from Spitzer et al., 2000, pp. 342–343.

Oppositional and noncompliant behavior is clearly a common problem, particularly during preschool age and again during adolescence (Coie & Dodge, 1998; Loeber et al., 2000). Diagnosis should therefore require high levels of such problems. Although such behavior is prevalent among nonclinic children, it is also one of the most frequently reported problems of children referred to clinics and is more common among clinic-referred children than nonreferred children (Achenbach & Rescorla, 2001; Rey, 1993). Noncompliance represents a practical problem for parents, teachers, and clinicians. Also, noncompliant, stubborn, and oppositional behavior may represent for some youngsters the earliest steps on a developmental path of persistent antisocial behavior (Hinshaw et al., 1993; Loeber et al., 1993). The appropriateness of the ODD diagnosis thus rests, in part, on a balance between "overdiagnosing" common problems of children and adolescents versus ignoring potential early precursors of more serious antisocial behaviors.

DSM Approach: Conduct Disorder

The diagnosis of Conduct Disorder represents more seriously aggressive and antisocial behaviors. Indeed, the violence and property destruction characteristic of many of these behaviors may considerably impact individuals, families, and communities. Nonaggressive conduct-disordered behaviors (e.g., truancy, theft) also can result in considerable harm.

The essential feature of the diagnosis is a repetitive and persistent pattern of behavior that violates the basic rights of others as well as major age-appropriate societal norms. The criteria used to define the disorder are presented in Table 8–3. The diagnosis of Conduct Disorder requires that three or more of these behaviors be present during the past 12 months, with at least one of them present in the past 6 months. Also the behavior must cause clinically meaningful impairment in social or academic

TABLE 8–3	BEHAVIORS USED BY THE DSM IN DIAGNOSING CONDUCT DISORDER

Aggression toward People and Animals

Bullies, threatens, or intimidates ✓
Initiates physical fights ✓ hit
Has used a weapon
Is physically cruel to people
Is physically cruel to animals
Has stolen while confronting a victim
Has forced someone into sexual activity

Destruction of Property

Has deliberately engaged in fire setting with the intention of causing serious damage
Has deliberately destroyed others' property (other than by fire setting)

Deceitfulness or Theft

Has broken into house, building, or car
Often lies to obtain goods or favors or to avoid obligations
Has stolen items of nontrivial value without confronting a victim

Serious Violations of Rules

Stays out at night despite parental prohibitions, beginning before age 13
Has run away from home overnight at least twice (or once without returning for a lengthy period)
Is often truant from school, beginning before age 13

From American Psychiatric Association, 2000.

functioning. Two subtypes, Childhood-Onset and Adolescent-Onset, are specified on the basis of whether one or more of the criterion behaviors had an onset prior to age 10 years.

The symptoms listed in the DSM criteria for Conduct Disorder include diverse behaviors. They represent problems from different categories of externalizing/disruptive behaviors described earlier (pp. 195–197). For example, both overt and covert behaviors are listed. Because only three symptoms are required for a diagnosis, the diagnosis of Conduct Disorder may represent a heterogeneous group of youngsters with different subtypes of conduct disorder. Such heterogeneity may be of particular concern for research investigations.

The following description of Doug describes many of the features that characterize children who exhibit persistent aggressive and antisocial behavior and illustrates the behavior and background of children who may receive a conduct disorder diagnosis.

Doug	**Early Aggressive and Antisocial Behavior**

Doug, 8 years old, was brought for treatment because of his unmanageable behavior at home. The specific concern was with Doug's aggressive behavior. When Doug is angry, he chokes and hits his 18-month-old brother and constantly makes verbal threats of physical aggression. Recently, Doug's behavior became more out of control, and his mother felt she was unable to cope. Apart from his aggression, Doug has played with matches and set fires over the last 3 years. These episodes have included igniting fireworks in the kitchen, setting fires in trash dumpsters, and starting a fire in his bedroom, which the local fire department had to extinguish. At school his behavior has been disruptive over the last few years. His intellectual performance is within the normal range (IQ = 96) and his academic performance is barely passing. His aggressive behavior against peers and disruption of class activities have led to his placement in a special class for emotionally disturbed children. Even so, his behavior is not well controlled. The school has threatened expulsion if treatment is not initiated.

Doug is the second born of three brothers. Doug's father frequently abused alcohol. When drunk, he would beat his wife and children. The parents separated on a number of occasions and eventually were divorced when Doug was 5 years old. After the divorce, the mother and children moved in with the maternal grandfather who also drank excessively, and physically abused the children. Less than 2 years ago, the mother had another child by her former husband. With the stress of the new child, the death of her father, and Doug's continuing problems, the mother became depressed and began to drink. Although she is not employed, she spends much of her time away from the home. She leaves the children unsupervised for extended periods with a phone number of a neighbor for the children to call if any problems arise with the baby.

Adapted from Kazdin, 1985, pp. 3–4.

GENDER DIFFERENCES: RELATIONAL AGGRESSION

Throughout this chapter we will see gender differences in conduct problems. Gender differences exist in prevalence, developmental course, and in factors and processes that contribute to the development of conduct problems (Crick & Zahn-Waxler, 2003; Kerr et al., 2004). Perhaps the most basic aspect of gender differences is the way that conduct problems are expressed in boys and girls.

Much of the research on conduct disorders has been based on male samples. We saw earlier how focusing on one gender can influence estimates of prevalence of a disorder and how a disorder is defined. In addition, we will see that aggression is a central aspect of the definition of conduct disorders and that physical aggression has received much of the attention in studies of conduct problems.

It is frequently reported that boys exhibit significantly higher levels of aggression than do girls. Is this because girls are less aggressive? Crick and colleagues (Crick & Grotpeter, 1995; Crick & Zahn-Waxler, 2003) started with a general definition of aggression as intent to hurt or harm others. They noted that during early and middle childhood peer interactions tended to be gender segregated. This suggested that children's aggression would focus on social issues most salient in same-gender peer groups. In studying externalizing behaviors, aggression has generally been defined in terms of overt physical or verbal behaviors intended to hurt or harm others (e.g., hitting or pushing, threatening to beat up others). It was reasoned that this is consistent with the characteristics of instrumentality and physical dominance typical of boys during childhood. Girls, in contrast, are focused on developing close, dyadic relationships. It was thus hypothesized that

ACCENT ● ● ● ●

Are Conduct Problems a Mental Disorder?

The diagnosis of Conduct Disorder is frequently part of the controversy over what constitutes psychopathology or mental disorder (Hinshaw & Lee, 2003; Richters & Cicchetti, 1993). Richters and Cicchetti addressed this question, in part, by asking if Mark Twain's characters of Tom Sawyer and Huckleberry Finn suffered from a mental disorder. As these authors point out, the two boys engaged in a sustained pattern of antisocial behavior that would warrant a diagnosis of conduct disorder—lying, stealing, aggression, truancy, running away, cruelty to animals. The boys were judged by the townspeople in social-moral terms and opinions were mixed as to whether, at heart, they were good or bad boys.

The issues of what constitutes a conduct disorder are complex. However, one concern is placing the locus of the deviant behavior entirely within the individual and ignoring the social context. As can be seen from the following quotation, the DSM acknowledges this issue.

Concerns have been raised that the Conduct Disorder diagnosis may at times be misapplied to individuals in settings where patterns of undesirable behavior are sometimes viewed as protective (e.g., in threatening, impoverished, high-crime settings). Consistent with the DSM-IV definition of mental disorder, the Conduct Disorder diagnosis should be applied only when the behavior in question is symptomatic of an underlying dysfunction within the individual and not simply a reaction to the immediate social context. (American Psychiatric Association, 2000, p. 96)

How does one determine whether a youngster's behavior is a reaction to a problematic environment or an indication of individual psychopathology? Clinicians and researchers must be sensitive and aware of both typical development and the real impact of poverty, stress, and violent communities on the development of antisocial behavior.

girls' attempts to harm others may focus on relational issues—behaviors intended to damage another child's feelings or friendships. Examples of such relational aggression include the following:

- Purposefully leaving a child out of some play or other activity
- Getting mad at someone and excluding the person from a peer group
- Telling lies about someone so that the other kids won't like the person
- Telling someone you will not like him or her unless the person does what you say
- Saying mean things about someone so that others will not like the person (Crick & Grotpeter, 1996)

Indeed, girls are more relationally aggressive than boys. Relational aggression is found from preschool age through adolescence (Crick, Casas, & Ku, 1999; Prinstein, Boergers, & Vernberg, 2001). Moreover, relational aggression is associated with peer rejection, depression, anxiety, and feelings of loneliness and isolation (Crick & Grotpeter, 1995; Crick, Casas, & Mosher, 1997; Crick & Nelson, 2002). Interestingly, youngsters who engage in gender nonnormative forms of aggression (i.e., overtly

aggressive girls and relationally aggressive boys) exhibit a greater number of behavior problems than those who engage in gender normative aggression or are nonaggressive (Crick, 1997).

Thus, it appears important to broadly define aggression. For one thing, a sole focus on physical aggression might fail to identify aggressive girls. For example, Crick and Grotpeter (1995) found that over 80 percent of aggressive girls (those who were relationally, but not physically, aggressive) would not have been identified by a definition limited to physical aggression. The concept of relational aggression challenges the view that girls are nonaggressive and suggests caution in making non-gender-specific interpretations of findings.

DELINQUENCY

In addition to empirical and DSM approaches to classifying antisocial and conduct-disordered behavior, it is important to consider the notion of delinquency. The term *delinquency* is primarily a legal rather than a psychological one. As a legal term, it refers to a juvenile (usually under 18) who has committed an index crime or a status offense. An index crime is an act that would be illegal for adults as well as for juveniles (e.g., theft, aggravated assault, rape, or murder). A status offense is an act that is illegal only for juveniles (e.g., truancy, association with "immoral" persons, violation of curfews, or incorrigibility). It is important also to make a distinction between delinquent behavior and what might be called official delinquency.

This distinction is important because some behaviors described as delinquent are quite common. Surveys based on adolescent self-reports show that as many as 80 to 90 percent of youths report involvement in delinquent activity before reaching the age of 18. In contrast, if one examines official records (e.g., police, courts), a much lower rate of delinquency is suggested—15 to 35 percent for males and 2 to 14 percent for females. The estimate of rate varies with the stringency of the definition of "official record" (Moore & Arthur, 1989).

Whether an act by a juvenile gets classified as official delinquency may depend as much on the actions of others as it does on the youth's behavior. The norm violation must, of course, be noticed by someone and must be reported to a law-enforcement official. A police officer then can either arrest the youth or merely issue a warning. If the youth is arrested, he or she may or may not be brought to court. Once in juvenile court, only some individuals receive the legal designation of delinquent; others may be warned or released in the custody of their parents. Various definitions of delinquency can be used anywhere in this process.

A Trio of Conduct-Related Behaviors: Violence, Bullying, Substance Use

As discussion so far makes clear, conduct problems encompass diverse behaviors that are viewed as disruptive and harmful to individuals engaging in them as well as to society more generally. Oppositional and conduct disorders slide into, or overlap with, several areas that are currently of particular societal concern. The purpose of this section is to emphasize three of these areas—violence, bullying, and substance use.

VIOLENCE

Violence is typically defined as an extreme form of physical aggression. For example, violence might be defined as aggressive acts that cause serious harm to others, such as aggravated assault, rape, robbery, and homicide, whereas aggression might be defined as acts that inflict less serious harm (Loeber & Stouthamer-Loeber, 1998). Thus much of what we discuss throughout this chapter regarding topics such as the etiology and developmental course of aggressive and conduct-disordered behavior applies to violence as well. However, additional factors may influence the development of violence, and different needs may exist for the prevention and treatment of violent behavior.

When one speaks about youth violence, there are at least two concerns. First, there is the concern regarding youth as perpetrators of violent acts. Second is the concern that youngsters are the most frequent victims of violence by their peers. (See Accent: "Some Facts on Violence and Youth.")

As illustrated in Table 8–4, there have been a large number of violent crimes committed by youth. Between 1985 and 1998, there was an increase of about 54 percent in the number of cases of violent offenses handled by juvenile courts. High arrest rates of youths between 10 and 17 years of age have been reported, and some surveys indicate that as many as 1 in 20 students carries a weapon regularly (Tolan, 2001).

Young people exposed to violence also are at significant risk. Part of this exposure is contact with

TABLE 8–4	**NUMBER OF CASES DISPOSED BY JUVENILE COURTS, BY REASON FOR REFERRAL, OF YOUTHS AGES 10 TO 17**			
	YEAR			
REASONS FOR REFERRAL	**1985**	**1990**	**1995**	**2000**
Violent offenses	67,000	94,000	137,000	81,000
Property offenses	489,000	773,000	888,000	661,000
Delinquency offenses (e.g., vandalism, drug law violations)	555,000	660,000	1,001,000	1,079,000

From U.S. Bureau of the Census, 1998; 2003.

ACCENT ●●●●●

Some Facts on Violence and Youth

One way to get a picture of the magnitude of the problem of violence is to look at statistics concerning the matter. The following facts address youth and violence during 2001/2002 (Anderson & Smith, 2003; Egley & Major, 2004; Grunbaum et al., 2002):

- Assault (homicide) was the fifth leading cause of death among young people 10 to 14 years of age, and the second leading cause of death for those 15 to 19 years of age.

- Slightly over 17 percent of youth in grades 9 through 12 reported carrying a weapon (e.g., gun, knife, club) during the previous 30 days, whereas 6.4 percent reported having carried a weapon to school.

- Over 30 percent of students, grades 9 through 12, reported being part of a physical fight during the previous year, with 4 percent requiring medical assistance.

- During the previous year, 9.5 percent of youth in grades 9 through 12 were intentionally hit, slapped, or physically hurt by a boyfriend or girlfriend.

- Nearly 8 percent of students had at some time been forced to have sexual intercourse when they did not want to.

- Close to 9 percent of high school students were threatened or injured with a weapon on school grounds during the previous year.

- More than 21,500 gangs were reported to be active in the United States, with more than 731,500 members.

violent peers, but youth are exposed to violence in a number of other ways, including watching television, seeing movies, and playing video games. If one also includes youngsters who are physically abused, who witness domestic violence, and who reside in neighborhoods with high rates of violence, the picture is even more troubling. Youngsters exposed to violence, either as victims or as witnesses, are at increased risk for developing aggressive, antisocial, and other externalizing problems. But they are also at risk for developing internalizing difficulties such as anxiety, depression, and somatic symptoms (Schwab-Stone et al., 1999). Youngsters chronically exposed to violence may suffer abnormal neurological development and dysregulation in the biological systems that are involved in arousal and managing stress. These changes can have far-reaching psychological and physical consequences (Margolin & Gordis, 2000).

The problem of youth and violence has become a major national concern (Margolin & Gordis, 2000; Reppucci, Woolard, & Fried, 1999). A variety of governmental and professional efforts have been directed at this problem (Weist & Cooley-Quille, 2001). For example, the American Psychological Association formed a special Task Force on Violence and Youth, and several organizations have taken initiatives to promote professional training in this area, to develop and disseminate position statements, and to advocate for relevant legislation. In addition, there has been an increase in research related to violence and youth (Acosta et al., 2001; Weist & Cooley-Quille, 2001).

Schools are one arena given considerable governmental and public attention. Concern exists about youngsters' bringing dangerous weapons to school and with the high rate of violence in schools. In the wake of several highly publicized incidents, such as those in Littleton, Colorado, and Pearl, Mississippi, schools and communities felt pressure to do something to reduce the risk of violence in the community and to protect their schoolchildren. Changes in school procedures were implemented to increase security, educational efforts were initiated to increase student awareness and to emphasize nonviolent social problem-solving strategies, and pressure was exerted to provide additional services to students at risk for committing violent acts.

Although the intense media attention to dramatic school incidents increased community awareness and efforts, it probably also contributed to other actions that may be somewhat more controversial regarding the ultimate benefit to young people. Metal detectors were installed in schools, some school administrators requested youngsters to report any strange behavior by their peers, and a variety of similar policies were widely initiated. Although there is reason for concern about school violence, a number of questions have been raised. For example, the view that there has been a drastic increase in rates of violence in schools has been questioned, and concern has been raised regarding the effects on youngsters of some of the actions that have been taken. It also has been noted that only a small percentage of youth violence takes place on school grounds and that the rate of violent crimes committed by youth remains low during the school day but spikes at the close of the school day (Mulvey & Cauffman, 2001). School violence should therefore probably be considered and addressed with an appreciation of violence in the larger community and society. Also, programs to reduce violence in schools should do so in a manner that creates a school atmosphere that facilitates the overall development of young people while ensuring their safety.

BULLYING

Bullying is another form of aggression that has received increased attention, in part because of a concern that some of the youngsters who committed dramatic violent acts were themselves victims of bullying.

Many people are familiar with the problem of bullying either through personal experience or through literature, television, or movies. Recent interest in this topic was generated by the work of Olweus (1993; 1994) in Scandinavia and by media attention following incidents of school violence in which bullying was implicated.

Estimates of the incidence of bullying depend on definitions employed, which probably need to consider developmental and cultural variations (Smith et al., 2002). Bully–victim relationships begin to emerge in the preschool years and are common among elementary school children (Hay, Payne, & Chadwick, 2004; Schwartz et al., 1997). Data from a sample of over 15,000 youngsters from throughout the United States suggest the scope of the problem during middle school and beyond (Nansel et al., 2001). Youngsters in grades 6 through 10 reported involvement in bullying. About 30 percent reported moderate or frequent involvement (about 13 percent as a bully, 11 percent as a victim, and 6 percent as both). Males were more likely than females to be involved as both perpetrators and victims, and the frequency of bullying was higher for sixth-grade through eighth-grade youngsters than among students in the ninth and tenth grades. Similar percentages are reported in various countries and, in general, the percentage of youngsters who report being bullied decreases with age (Kumpulainen, Räsänen, & Henttonen, 1999; Wolke et al., 2000). Bullying itself is more stable.

Boys are exposed to more direct open attacks than are girls. Indirect bullying can occur in the form of spreading of rumors, manipulation of friendship relationships, and social isolation. This form of bullying may be harder to detect. Girls are exposed to a greater extent to this more subtle form of bullying than to open attacks. Boys, however, may be exposed to this indirect bullying at rates comparable to that of girls.

The typical bully is described by Olweus (1994) as being highly aggressive to both peers and adults; having a more positive attitude toward violence than students in general; being impulsive; having a strong need to dominate others; having little empathy toward victims; and, if a boy, being physically stronger than boys in general. Not all highly aggressive youngsters are bullies. Differences between bullies and other aggressive youngsters and the processes that underlie bullying remain to be clarified (Hay et al., 2004).

The typical victim is more anxious and insecure than other students—is cautious, sensitive, quiet, nonaggressive, and suffering from low self-esteem. If victims are boys, they are likely to be physically weaker. This so-called submissive, nonassertive style often seems to precede being selected as a victim (Schwartz, Dodge, & Coie, 1993). Also, victims generally do not have a single good friend in their class. One student's awareness of the protective importance of having a friend, especially a popular one, was revealed in an interview with Eric Crouch, the 2001 Heisman Trophy winner as the outstanding college football player:

It was a source of pride to his mother . . . that as a popular grade school kid, Eric often befriended students whom others teased. "I talk to them, become friends with them," he would tell his mother, "and they didn't get teased anymore." (Murphy, 2001, p. 64)

In addition to warding off victimization, support from a close friend may buffer the effects of victimization (Prinstein et al., 2001).

It is clearly important to address the bully–victim problem. Bullying may be part of a more general antisocial, conduct-disordered developmental pattern, and thus bullies are at risk. Indeed, Olweus (1994) reports that 60 percent of boys classified as bullies in grades 6 through 9 were convicted of at least one officially registered crime by age 24 and that 35 to 40 percent of former bullies had three or more convictions by this age as compared with only 10 percent of control boys.

The consequences for the victims of bullying also suggest the importance of intervening early. Victims experience a variety of negative outcomes, particularly depression and loneliness (Hawker & Boulton, 2000). The victims of bullying form a large group of youngsters whom, to a great extent, many schools may ignore, and whose parents may be relatively unaware of the problem. One can imagine the effects of going through years of school in a state of fear, anxiety, and insecurity. Some portion of these youngsters' self-esteem is so poor and their hope for change so low that they view suicide as the only possible option (Olweus, 1994). A case described by Olweus illustrates the pain that youngsters may suffer.

| **Henry**   **A Victim of Bullying** |

Henry was a quiet and sensitive 13-year-old. For several years he had been harassed and attacked occasionally by some of his classmates. . . . During the past couple of months, the attacks had become more frequent and severe.

Henry's daily life was filled with unpleasant and humiliating events. His books were pushed from his desk, his tormentors broke his pencils and threw things at him, they laughed loudly and scornfully when he occasionally responded to the teacher's questions. Even in class, he was often called by his nickname, the "Worm."

As a rule, Henry did not respond; he just sat there expressionless at his desk, passively waiting for the next attack. The teacher usually looked in another direction when the harassment went on. Several of Henry's classmates felt sorry for him but none of them made a serious attempt to defend him.

A month earlier, Henry had been coerced, with his clothes on, into a shower. His two tormentors had also threatened him several times to give them money and steal cigarettes for them.

One afternoon, after having been forced to lie down in the drain of the school urinal, Henry quietly went home, found a box of sleeping pills and swallowed a handful. Henry's parents found him unconscious but alive on the sofa in the living room. A note on his desk told them that he couldn't stand the bullying any more, he felt completely worthless, and believed the world would be a better place without him.

Adapted from Olweus, 1993, pp. 49–50.

SUBSTANCE USE

Adolescent substance use is an important clinical and public health problem. The use of alcohol and other drugs can be part of the constellation of antisocial and rule-breaking behaviors exhibited by conduct-disordered youngsters. However, the fact that the use of such substances is common among adolescents and preadolescents suggests that the problem warrants some separate discussion (Johnston, O'Malley, & Bachman, 2003; U.S. Bureau of the Census, 2003). There is widespread concern regarding illegal (illicit) drugs such as marijuana, cocaine/"crack," ecstasy, hallucinogens (e.g., LSD), and heroin. There also is concern regarding use of licit drugs (drugs that are legal for adults or by prescription) and other substances. Alcohol, nicotine, psychoactive medications (e.g., stimulants, sedatives), over-the-counter medications (e.g., sleep aids and weight reduction aids), steroids, and inhalants (e.g., glue, paint thinner) are accessible and potentially harmful. They may also play a role in starting some young people on a course of long-term and increased substance use (Bailey, 1989; Cambor & Millman, 1996).

Classification and Description. Many adolescents experiment with substance use. Those working with youngsters are faced with the challenge of discriminating between patterns of experimentation or lesser use that are developmentally normative and patterns that may have serious short- and long-term consequences (Monti, Colby, & O'Leary, 2001).

The DSM substance use disorders are often employed to diagnose maladaptive use of alcohol or other drugs by adolescents. Substance dependence (Table 8–5) refers to a maladaptive pattern of substance use that continues for at least 12 months and that includes symptoms of *tolerance* (needing increased amounts of the substance), *withdrawal* (changes upon discontinuation), and *psychological dependence* (compulsive use). Symptoms of tolerance

TABLE 8–5	MAJOR FEATURES FOR THE DSM DIAGNOSIS OF SUBSTANCE DEPENDENCE

A maladaptive pattern of substance use, leading to clinically significant impairment or distress, as manifested by three (or more) of the following occurring at any time in the same 12-month period:

1. Tolerance
2. Withdrawal
3. The substance is often taken in larger amounts or over a longer period of time than was intended
4. Persistent desire or unsuccessful efforts to control substance use
5. A great deal of time is spent in activities necessary to obtain the substance
6. Important activities are given up or reduced because of substance use
7. The substance use is continued despite knowledge of having a persistent or recurrent physical or psychological problem that is likely caused or exacerbated by the substance

From American Psychiatric Association, 2000.

TABLE 8–6	MAJOR FEATURES FOR THE DSM DIAGNOSIS OF SUBSTANCE ABUSE

A. A maladaptive pattern of substance use leading to clinically significant impairment or distress, manifested by one (or more) of the following, occurring within a 12-month period:
   1. Recurrent substance use resulting in failure to fulfill major role obligations at work, school, or home
   2. Recurrent substance use in situations in which it is physically hazardous
   3. Recurrent substance-related legal problems
   4. Continued substance use despite having persistent or recurrent social or interpersonal problems caused or exacerbated by the effects of the substance
B. The symptoms have never met the criteria for Substance Dependence for this class of substance.

From American Psychiatric Association, 2000.

and withdrawal indicate a physiological dependence. However, the diagnosis may be given in the absence of physiological dependence. Substance abuse (Table 8–6) indicates maladaptive use, which recurs over a 12-month period and leads to one or more repeated harmful consequences. The diagnosis of substance abuse is not given if the individual meets the criteria for dependence for that substance. For both diagnoses, the criteria for adolescents are the same as those for adults. The adequacy of these criteria and their ability to capture the nature of adolescent substance use has been questioned (Chassin et al., 2003).

One alternative definition views any use of alcohol or other substance by a minor as abuse, since such use is illegal. Less extreme and more prevalent are definitions that address patterns of use and related negative consequences whether or not they meet diagnostic criteria.

Rodney   Alcohol and Nicotine Use

"It was so hard to start, I had no idea it would be harder to stop." Rodney, age 17, didn't recall much about the motorcycle accident that had put him in the hospital. It involved quite a few brandy Alexanders and too little about hanging onto the passenger bar of the motorcycle. He

was clear-headed enough to realize that he badly needed a cigarette.

By the time Rodney was 12, he was already attending high school classes, had won several statewide scholastic contests, and had appeared twice on a popular TV quiz show. When he was 14, his parents reluctantly let him accept a scholarship to a small but prestigious liberal arts college. "Of course I was the smallest one there . . . I'm sure I started smoking and drinking to compensate for my size."

Six months into college, Rodney was smoking a pack and a half a day. When studying for exams (he often felt he wasn't "measuring up"), he found himself lighting one cigarette from another, going through several packs in a day this way—far more than he meant to. The following year, he read the Surgeon General's report on smoking and saw a video about lung cancer ("in living—no dying—color"). He swore he would never smoke again, but he noticed that he became restless, depressed, and "so irritable my roommate begged me to light up again." Over the next year he had tried twice more to quit.

Rodney's parents were hardworking churchgoers who had never touched a drop of alcohol.

Both had been appalled at what alcohol had done to their own fathers. Several times in the last few months, when he was so badly hung over he couldn't attend classes, Rodney had vaguely wondered whether he was about to follow in his grandfathers' unsteady footsteps.

When Rodney first awakened after the accident he had pins through his femur and a terrific hangover. Now, 2 days later, his vital signs were stable and normal except for a pulse of only 56. "I don't suppose you could smuggle in some nicotine gum?" Rodney asked.

Adapted from Morrison & Anders, 1999, pp. 286–287.

Epidemiology. The reason for widespread concern about substance use is clear when one examines prevalence data. According to the Monitoring the Future (MTF) study—a long-term study of American adolescents that annually surveys large samples of eighth-, tenth-, and twelfth-graders—over half (53 percent) of young people have tried an illicit drug by the time they finish high school (Johnston et al., 2003). If one includes inhalant use in the definition of illicit drugs, approximately one third have done so by the eighth grade. Marijuana is the most widely used illicit drug; however, over 29 percent of youngsters have tried some illicit drug other than marijuana by

the end of twelfth grade, and 21 percent of twelfth-graders have used some illicit drug other than marijuana in the prior year.

Information regarding the use of licit drugs is also reason for concern. Alcohol, which is the most widely used substance among all age groups, including young people (U.S. Bureau of the Census, 2003), remains in widespread use, according to the MTF study. Of particular concern is the finding that 62 percent of twelfth-graders and 21 percent of eighth-graders report having been drunk at least once in their life. Rates of cigarette smoking remain a concern as well. Among twelfth-graders, 27 percent are current smokers, and 11 percent of eighth-graders report that they are current smokers.

The MTF data suggest that overall there has been a stabilization or decline in substance use among young people in recent years. However, levels remain above those of a decade ago, and there is an increase in the use of some substances (tranquilizers, barbiturates). The authors of this study suggest that increases and decreases in the use of particular drugs are due to shifts in the perceived benefits and perceived risks that youngsters come to associate with each drug. Their concern is that rumor of the supposed benefits spreads faster than information about adverse consequences. Figure 8–3 illustrates the reported use of various

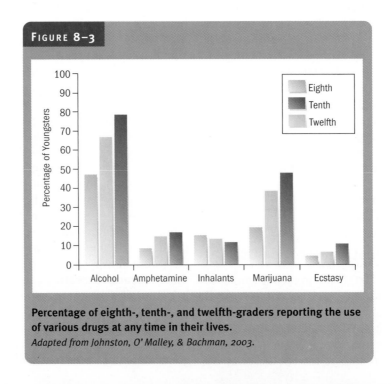

FIGURE 8-3

Percentage of eighth-, tenth-, and twelfth-graders reporting the use of various drugs at any time in their lives.
Adapted from Johnston, O'Malley, & Bachman, 2003.

substances by eighth-, tenth-, and twelfth-graders, on the basis of the MTF data.

Findings regarding gender and SES differences in substance use are not consistent. Issues of how substance use is defined, how epidemiological information is obtained, and which substances are studied probably contribute to different conclusions. It is often assumed that substance use problems are more prevalent among certain ethnic groups such as African Americans, American Indians, and various groups of Latino Hispanic youngsters, than they are among European American youngsters. Here, too, findings are inconsistent (Gibbs, 2003; LaFromboise & Dizon, 2003; Organista, 2003). One limitation of available information may be that many findings are derived from school-based studies. The differential school drop-out rates among ethnic groups may make it difficult to obtain an accurate picture regarding prevalence.

Adolescents with abuse or dependence problems typically display a number of other difficulties (Armstrong & Costello, 2002). Many use multiple drugs. Alcohol and marijuana, and alcohol and hallucinogens, are common combinations. Academic and family difficulties are common, as are delinquent behaviors. As indicated earlier, substance use is often conceptualized as a later-occurring part of a constellation of conduct problem behaviors. It is not surprising, therefore, that youngsters often meet the criteria for externalizing/ disruptive behavior disorders (ODD, CD). Mood and anxiety disorders also are frequently associated with substance use problems.

Etiology and Developmental Course. Researchers and clinicians agree that multiple etiological pathways exist by which young people begin and maintain substance use. Cavell, Ennett, and Meehan (2001) have suggested a model of the various risk and protective factors thought to be involved in these developmental pathways. These factors overlap considerably with the factors that influence the development of conduct problems in general, and they are discussed more fully later in this chapter. Here we draw on Cavell and Colleagues' (2001) conceptualization to provide examples of risk and protective factors.

Individual differences, in temperament and self-regulation, for example, are implicated in the onset and escalation of substance use (Wills & Dishion, 2004). Cognitive-affective components— attitudes, expectations, intentions, and beliefs about control—are prominent in conceptualizations of adolescent substance use. For instance, the anticipation of positive or negative consequences for drinking is an important proximal influence on alcohol use. The importance of expectancy regarding the effects of alcohol is illustrated in a study of the development of drinking behavior (Smith & Goldman, 1994; Smith et al., 1995). Over a 2-year period during which many of the youngsters first began to drink,

Association with a peer group that supports the use of alcohol and other drugs may be a contributing influence to the development of substance use and abuse.
(Bill Aron/PhotoEdit, Inc.)

expectations that drinking would facilitate social interactions predicted initiation into drinking. Those who expected social facilitation also drank more over the 2-year period, and future expectations regarding the effects of drinking became more positive.

Youngsters who have been physically or sexually assaulted or who have witnessed violence also appear to be at increased risk for substance abuse (Kilpatrick et al., 2000). Other individual characteristics, including the presence of early conduct problems and aggression and genetic endowment, may also influence initiation into and the course of substance use.

Families are an important influence on adolescent substance use patterns. Aspects of parent-child relationships such as the quality of attachment, level of family conflict, and effectiveness of parenting skills have been linked to adolescent substance use. Also, social learning theory explanations have drawn attention to the role of modeling of behavior and attitudes. Because parents and older siblings are potential models for such behavior, the child of a parent who is an alcoholic or a substance abuser may be at particular risk (Chassin et al., 1996). Research by Hops and his colleagues (Hops et al., 2000), for example, indicates that when parents or older siblings use tobacco, alcohol, or marijuana, adolescents are more likely to initiate use of these substances. More than the specific behavior observed is affected by modeling. The youngster may also initiate the use of other substances that serve a similar function (e.g., escape, perceived facilitation of social interactions). Furthermore, the attitude displayed by the parent can affect the youngster's behavior. Adolescents are more likely to use substances when they perceive less parental disapproval for use (Chassin et al., 1998).

Peer factors are considered among the strongest influences on adolescent substance use. Perceived peer substance use and perceived peer approval have been shown to be important factors. Social learning theory explanations suggest that adolescents who interact with substance-using peer models and who expect positive consequences from substance use will initiate and continue substance use. However, it is difficult to establish direct peer influence. To begin with, adolescent substance users tend to choose friends who use drugs. Also, research findings are based on adolescents' perceptions of their peers' behavior, and such perceptions may be affected by the bias to see one's own choices as common (Cavell et al., 2001).

School, neighborhood, and community influences are likely to contribute to adolescent substance use. Poor academic performance and low involvement in school activities, for example, have been linked to substance use. In contrast, schools that foster a sense of commitment and community have lower rates of use. Although some information suggests that low-income and high-risk neighborhoods are associated with greater adolescent substance use, findings are mixed. Some studies suggest higher rates of initial experimentation in more affluent and suburban neighborhoods (Cavell et al., 2001; Luthar & D'Avanzo, 1999). Apart from the issue of rate differences, the risks associated with substance experimentation may be greater for youngsters who reside in poorer neighborhoods, particularly if other members of their families also use or abuse substances (Luthar & Cushing, 1999). Clearly, more research on these influences is needed.

A variety of theories and conceptualizations have been suggested as ways of explaining how risk and protective factors contribute to the development of substance use. Social learning theory, as we have seen, emphasizes processes such as imitation, expectancy, and consequences. We will briefly examine a selection of other theoretical and conceptual models.

One particular model views adolescence as a period of transition that is marked by certain behaviors deemed appropriate for adults but not for adolescents (e.g., Jessor & Jessor, 1977). Use of alcohol is an example of such a behavior. This transitional notion is consistent with findings that not all adolescents who are problem drinkers abuse alcohol as adults. Individual differences and environmental variables are assumed to affect the rate at which an individual makes the transition to adulthood and thereby the age of onset of these behaviors. There may be developmental changes in neurocircuitry during adolescence that make this a period of greater vulnerability for experimentation with substances and substance use disorders (Chambers, Taylor, & Potenza, 2003).

Adolescent substance use has also been viewed within the context of a stress and coping model (Wills & Filer, 1996). Youngsters facing greater negative life events and perceived stress, and/or those with elevated physiological responses to stress, may be more likely to use alcohol and other substances (Chassin et al., 2003). Substance use serves a coping function for the adolescent, or at least it is perceived to do so. Whereas some young people employ a variety of adaptive-active coping mechanisms (e.g., seeking information, considering alternatives, taking direct action), others rely more heavily on the use of avoidant coping mechanisms (e.g., distraction, social withdrawal, wishful thinking) and use alcohol and other substances to deal with stress.

As we noted, youngsters frequently use more than one substance. One way of explaining this trend, as we have seen, is imitation of substance-using models. Another explanation posits a developmental sequence (Kandel, 1982). The use of legal drugs such as alcohol and tobacco precedes the use of illicit drugs. It is virtually never the case that a nonuser goes directly to the use of illegal drugs. Participation in one stage does not necessarily mean that the young person will progress to the next stage; rather, only a subgroup at each stage progresses to the next level. The earlier the youngster begins one stage, the greater is the likelihood of other drug use (Windle, 1990). Thus the earlier that legal drugs are used, the greater the likelihood of illicit drug use (Kandel & Yamaguchi, 1993). Also, heavier use at any stage seems to be associated with "progress" to the next stage. Findings that alcohol and drug use are beginning early, even before the teenage years (e.g., Huizinga, Loeber, & Thornberry, 1993), are particularly disturbing in the context of a developmental stage model.

Following from reports that the use of other drugs occurs together with the use of alcohol, Lynskey, Fergusson, and Horwood (1998) suggest that a common or shared vulnerability to substance use may help explain the correlation between use of different drugs. They examined the correlation between the use of alcohol, tobacco, and cannabis among a group of 16-year-old New Zealand youngsters. Their results suggested a model in which affiliation with delinquent or substance-using peers, novelty seeking, and parental illicit drug use contributed to a common vulnerability to substance use. This model, which is illustrated in Figure 8–4, suggests that the correlation between use of different substances in adolescents is due to the fact that there are shared risk factors that create a common or shared vulnerability. This vulnerability then leads to increased likelihood of using various substances.

Clearly, no single factor or theory can easily explain which youths start or persist in problematic substance use (Huizinga, Loeber, & Thornberry, 1993; White et al., 1999). Explanations must include an array of variables—biological, psychological, and social—that interactively affect development over time (Cicchetti & Luthar, 1999; Glantz & Leshner, 2000). It seems clear, however, that early conduct

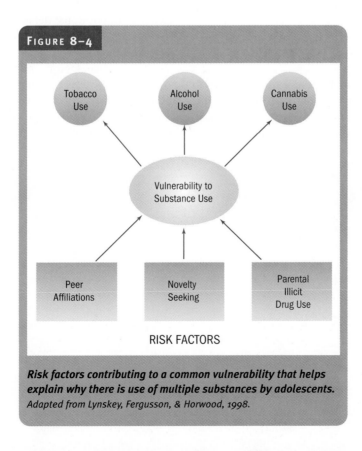

FIGURE 8–4

Risk factors contributing to a common vulnerability that helps explain why there is use of multiple substances by adolescents.
Adapted from Lynskey, Fergusson, & Horwood, 1998.

problems are associated with later substance use (Lynskey & Fergusson, 1995). Bearing in mind this association—as well as what we know about youth violence and bullying—let us proceed to examine the epidemiology, developmental course, etiology, assessment, and treatment of conduct problems.

Epidemiology

Conduct problems are one of the most frequent reasons for referral to child and adolescent treatment services (Kazdin, 1995). The exact prevalence is difficult to establish, and a number of methodological and definitional factors contribute to this difficulty (Hinshaw & Lee, 2003; Loeber et al., 2000). One important consideration is that diagnostic criteria for ODD and CD have changed considerably, and rates vary according to which criteria are employed. Studies of prevalence in community samples report rates of between 1 and 16 percent for both ODD and CD (Breton et al., 1999; Loeber et al., 2000). Many estimates are based on earlier definitions. More recent investigations employing DSM-IV criteria report rates for ODD of between about 2.3 and 5.5 percent, and rates for CD of between about 1.5 and 2.2 percent in Puerto Rico, Brazil, and Great Britain (Canino et al., 2004; Fleitlich-Bilyk & Goodman, 2004; Ford et al., 2003).

Gender, Age, and Context

Conduct disorders are more commonly diagnosed in boys than in girls; a ratio of about 3:1 or 4:1 is typically cited. Higher rates of ODD are also reported in boys. However, the degree of gender difference for ODD remains less clear (Loeber et al., 2000; Maughan et al., 2004). Gender and age differences in the prevalence of ODD and CD, based on a nationally representative sample in Great Britain (Maughan et al., 2004), are illustrated in Figure 8–5. The greater prevalence in boys does not mean CD and ODD are unimportant problems among girls. Both are relatively common diagnoses for girls in clinical settings and are associated with a variety of negative outcomes, such as early pregnancy and criminal records. It also is important to remember that the DSM definition of conduct disorder may emphasize "male" expressions of aggression. Thus conduct disorder may be underestimated in girls.

With regard to age, conduct problems or delinquent behaviors that are not as serious and that do not persist over time are common among adolescents (White, Moffitt, & Silva, 1989). Professionals may likely think of them as within the normal range of adolescent experimentation. It is persistent or chronic conduct problems that are of greater concern. An increasing prevalence of conduct disorder with age is often reported for both boys and girls and there is some suggestion that, due to particular risk for girls in the period around puberty, the gender ratio narrows temporarily in the mid-teens (Maughan et al., 2004; Moffitt et al., 2001). Some reports suggest a decline in oppositional defiant disorder with age, but findings are much less consistent (Maughan et al., 2004).

Contextual factors such as poverty and the stress of high-crime neighborhoods are thought to increase the risk for conduct-disordered behavior. Greater prevalence is reported in urban as compared to rural environments (Canino et al., 2004;

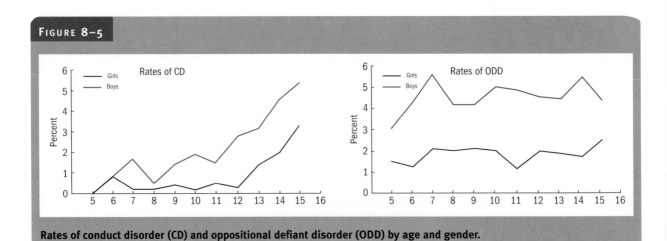

Figure 8–5

Rates of conduct disorder (CD) and oppositional defiant disorder (ODD) by age and gender.
Adapted from Maughan et al., 2004.

Fleitlich-Bilyk & Goodman, 2004). Also, official records often indicate greater delinquency among lower class and minority youths and in neighborhoods characterized by high crime rates. One might question whether such differences are due to selection of certain groups for prosecution and consider definitions other than official records. However, estimates based on alternative methods, such as self-report, present other methodological difficulties. Although further documentation is needed, real associations between conduct-disordered behavior/delinquency and social class and neighborhoods probably do exist; however, they are probably more moderate than was once contended. The influence of these variables on child and adolescent antisocial behavior is probably mediated by their impact on factors such as the ability of adults to parent effectively (Capaldi et al., 2002).

PATTERNS OF CO-OCCURRENCE

Youngsters who receive one of the disruptive disorder diagnoses also frequently experience other difficulties and receive other diagnoses. In considering the issue of the overlap between the ODD and CD diagnoses, the DSM-IV acknowledges that oppositional defiant behavior is a common precursor of the childhood-onset type of Conduct Disorder and stipulates that a youngster cannot receive both diagnoses (American Psychiatric Association, 2000). If a youngster meets the criteria for both Conduct Disorder and Oppositional Defiant Disorder, he or she is given only the Conduct Disorder diagnosis. However, the question remains of how these two disorders relate. Are they, for example, separate disorders, or is oppositional defiant disorder a developmental precursor to conduct disorder?

Most youngsters who receive the diagnosis of CD also meet the criteria for ODD. In the Developmental Trends Study of clinic-referred boys 7 to 12 years old, 96 percent of those who met criteria for CD also met criteria for ODD. The reported average age of onset was about 6 years for ODD and about 9 years for CD, suggesting that among boys with conduct disorder, this disorder is preceded by behaviors characteristic of oppositional defiant disorder and that these behaviors are "retained" as additional antisocial behaviors emerge. On the other hand, ODD does not always result in CD. Of the boys with ODD (but no CD) at the initial assessment, 75 percent had not progressed to CD 2 years later. About half of the boys with ODD at Year 1 continued to meet the criteria for ODD at Year 3, and about one quarter no

longer met the criteria for ODD. Thus, although most cases of conduct disorder meet the criteria for oppositional defiant disorder, most youngsters with oppositional defiant behaviors do not progress to a conduct disorder (American Psychiatric Association, 2000; Hinshaw, Lahey, & Hart, 1993).

There is also considerable co-occurrence of oppositional defiant disorder and conduct disorder with attention-deficit hyperactivity disorder (Waschbusch, 2002). Among children diagnosed with ADHD, it is estimated that between 35 and 70 percent develop ODD, and between 30 and 50 percent develop CD (Johnston & Ohan, 1999). When these disorders co-occur, ADHD seems to precede the development of the other disorders. It might be speculated that the impulsivity, inattention, and overactivity of ADHD present a particular parenting challenge. In instances where limitations in parenting skills exist, a pattern of noncompliant and aversive parent-child interactions may be set in motion (Patterson, DeGarmo, & Knutson, 2000). The challenges of parenting an ADHD child may thus play a role in the early onset of ODD behaviors and may continue over the course of development to maintain and exacerbate ODD/CD behaviors. Parent-child relationships are only one of the potential mechanisms whereby the presence of ADHD may increase the risk for ODD/CD. However, findings from a twin study suggest that although ADHD, ODD, and CD are each influenced by genetic and environmental factors, the covariation of the three disorders seems to be primarily influenced by a shared environmental factor (Burt et al., 2001). Such a finding is consistent with the potential contribution of parenting. Whatever factors contribute to the co-occurrence of these disorders, it would appear that ADHD is one possible path toward more persistent and more severe conduct disorders (Fergusson & Horwood, 1998; Hinshaw & Lee, 2003; Loeber et al., 2000).

In addition, youngsters with disruptive behavior disorders commonly experience a variety of other difficulties. Young aggressive children are frequently rejected by their peers (Newcomb, Bukowsi, & Pattee, 1993). Youngsters with persistent conduct problems are also frequently described as having certain neurocognitive impairments and lower school achievement (Caspi & Moffitt, 1995; Maguin & Loeber, 1996; Moffitt et al., 2001). Verbal/language deficits, in particular, have been reported among community and clinical samples, as well as deficits in executive functions (higher order cognitive functions that permit one to process information and to problem solve) (Gilmour et al., 2004; Moffitt et al.,

2001). How such difficulties and conduct disorders relate to each other is a complex issue. In what ways do cognitive and language difficulties contribute to the development of conduct disorders? What is the relationship among these deficits, conduct disorder, and poor academic performance? To what extent are some of these deficiencies related to ADHD—are they characteristic of only the subset of youngsters with conduct disorder who also have ADHD? These and other questions remain to be resolved.

Internalizing disorders also occur at higher than expected rates among youngsters with disruptive disorders, particularly conduct disorder (Loeber & Keenan, 1994; Loeber et al., 2000). Estimates of the rate of co-occurrence of conduct problems and anxiety disorders vary widely from 19 to 53 percent (Nottelmann & Jensen, 1995). Also, the literature on the nature of the association between anxiety and conduct problems is unclear and often contradictory (Hinshaw & Lee, 2003; Rutter, Giller, & Hagell, 1998). At question is whether anxiety increases or decreases the risk for conduct disordered behavior. Gender and age differences may be a consideration (Hinshaw, Lahey, & Hart, 1993). A distinction between kinds of co-occurring anxiety-related symptoms may also be important. Kerr and colleagues (1997) differentiated between the concepts of behavioral inhibition and social withdrawal (p. 33). They found that in aggressive boys, behavioral inhibition was a protective factor against delinquency, whereas social withdrawal was not. In any event, the co-occurrence of anxiety and conduct problems is likely to be due to multiple influences, with the same family environmental factors influencing both problems (Gregory, Eley, & Plomin, 2004).

The co-occurrence of depression and conduct disorder is also clearly appreciable and in community samples has been estimated as between 12 and 25 percent (Angold, Costello, & Erkanli, 1999; Loeber & Keenan, 1994; Nottelmann & Jensen, 1995). Among a community sample of older adolescents, Lewinsohn, Rohde, and Seeley (1995) found that a major depressive disorder co-occurred in 38 percent of youngsters with a disruptive behavior disorder (CD, ODD, or ADHD). In clinical samples, approximately 33 percent of children and adolescents have a co-occurrence of conduct and depressive disorders (Dishion, French, & Patterson, 1995). In both community and clinic populations, boys show greater co-occurrence than girls (Dishion et al., 1995; Lewinsohn et al., 1995). Numerous factors may help account for the frequent co-occurrence of conduct problems and depression, and the developmental sequence of the two disorders remains unclear (Loeber et al., 2000). It may be that one disorder creates a risk for the other. For example, frequent failures and conflict experiences may contribute to depression in youngsters with conduct problems, or depression may be expressed as irritable, angry, antisocial behavior. Alternatively, the disorders may co-occur because of shared etiology such as shared genetic influences. One behavior genetic study found that approximately 45 percent of the covariation between depressive and antisocial symptoms could be attributed to a common genetic liability, the remainder being explained by shared and nonshared environmental influences (O'Connor et al., 1998).

Developmental Course

STABILITY OF CONDUCT PROBLEMS

An important aspect of conduct problems is their reported stability over time (Fergusson, Lynskey, & Horwood, 1997; Loeber et al., 2000; Stanger et al., 1996; Tolan & Thomas, 1995). Considerable evidence exists that the presence of early conduct-disordered behavior is related to the development of later aggressive and antisocial behavior and to a range of adverse psychological and social-emotional outcomes (Brame, Nagin, & Tremblay, 2001; Caspi, Elder, & Bem, 1987; Hafner, Quast, & Shea, 1975; Loeber & Farrington, 2000; Robins et al., 1971).

However, like most other issues related to behavior disorders in children and adolescents, the question of the stability or continuity of antisocial/conduct-disordered behavior is a complex one (Loeber & Stouthamer-Loeber, 1998; Maughan & Rutter, 1998). Measurements of conduct problems taken several years apart do result in relatively high correlations (Stanger et al., 1996). But it is also important to recognize what these correlations suggest—that the relative positions of individuals regarding these behaviors remain somewhat stable between Time 1 and Time 2. This stability of relative position does not mean that the *level* of disordered behavior remains the same for all individuals. If the levels of aggression in most of the children decreased about the same amount over time, a high correlation could still be produced.

It nevertheless appears that some but not all youngsters continue to exhibit aggressive and antisocial behavior (NICHD Early Child Care Research Network, 2004). Although change can occur at any time, decreases may particularly occur during preschool age and adolescence. Campbell and her colleagues (Campbell, 1997) found that whereas there was some stability of externalizing behaviors from the ages of 4 to 6, only 30 to 50 percent of preschoolers identified as hard to manage met the criteria for externalizing problems at school entry. Loeber and Stouthamer-Loeber (1998) reported that among a community sample of inner-city boys, the prevalence of physical fighting started to decrease by age 15.

A study by Brame and colleagues (2001) illustrates the variety of possible developmental trajectories that may exist. The authors found that in a community sample of boys, followed from kindergarten to late adolescence, overall there was a considerable reduction in aggression no matter what the original childhood level. However, a variety of patterns was evident. For example, among boys with high levels of childhood aggression, a small group showed continued high levels during adolescence. However, a second group of youngsters, which was three times larger, reported virtually no aggression during adolescence. Different patterns of aggression over time were also seen in the groups of youngsters with low and moderate levels of childhood aggres-

sion. The challenges are to describe patterns of both continuity and discontinuity, characterize shifts in the form that antisocial behaviors may take, and identify variables that influence the course of antisocial behavior over time.

AGE OF ONSET

Many studies have found that early age of onset is related to more serious and persistent antisocial behavior (Babinski, Hartsough, & Lambert, 1999; Fergusson & Woodward, 2000; Loeber & Farrington, 2000; Tolan & Thomas, 1995). A number of authors have proposed two distinct developmental patterns leading toward antisocial behavior, one with a childhood onset and the other with a late or an adolescent onset (Hinshaw et al., 1993; Moffitt, 1993a; Raine et al., 2005).

Childhood Onset. The childhood-onset developmental pattern fits with the notion of the stability of conduct-disordered behavior. Indeed, Moffitt (1993a) terms this pattern "life-course persistent antisocial behavior." Retrospective studies of antisocial adults are consistent with this picture of stable

"I'm afraid my youthful transgressions may already have eliminated any chance for me to be President."

conduct-disordered behavior. It must be remembered, however, that a substantial number of children with an early onset of antisocial behavior do not persist on this pathway. The early-onset pathway is less common than the adolescent-onset pattern, with estimates of about 3 to 5 percent in the general population (Hinshaw et al., 1993; Moffitt, 1993a). Youngsters following this pattern are also more likely from early on to exhibit other problems, such as attention-deficit hyperactivity disorder, neurocognitive deficits, and academic difficulties (Raine et al., 2005). Indeed, it is hypothesized that these early difficulties are associated with early oppositional-defiant and disruptive behavior. In this way, they may be the starting point for one developmental pathway characterized by early onset and persistent disruptive and antisocial behavior during childhood and adolescence. For some this pathway may lead to Antisocial Personality Disorder and other negative outcomes in adulthood (Lahey et al., 1999; Loeber et al., 2000; Maughan & Rutter, 1998; Patterson et al., 2000).

Even though there is stability of problematic behavior for some youngsters with an early onset, antisocial behaviors exhibit qualitative change in the course of development. Hinshaw and colleagues (1993) describe the features of this heterotypic continuity of antisocial behavior:

> *The preschooler who throws temper tantrums and stubbornly refuses to follow adult instructions becomes the child who also initiates fights with other children and lies to the teacher. Later, the same youth begins to vandalize the school, torture animals, break into homes, steal costly items, and abuse alcohol. As a young adult, he or she forces sex on acquaintances, writes bad checks, and has a chaotic employment and marital history. (p. 36)*

There is also the suggestion that this pattern may have an even earlier start for some individuals with a difficult temperament during infancy (Frick & Morris, 2004).

Adolescent Onset. An adolescent-onset developmental pattern is illustrated in the Dunedin Multidisciplinary Health and Development Study (McGee et al., 1992). Prospective examination of a birth cohort of New Zealand youngsters revealed a large increase in the prevalence of nonaggressive conduct disorder but no increase in aggressive conduct disorder at age 15 compared with age 11. These youngsters were clearly exhibiting problem behavior; for example, they were as likely to be arrested for their delinquent offenses as were childhood-onset delinquents. However, their offenses were less aggressive, and the adolescent-onset cases included slightly more females than males, in contrast to the predominance of males among conduct disorder cases at age 11. This rather common emergence during adolescence of nonaggressive antisocial behavior is contrasted to early-onset antisocial behavior.

The adolescent-onset pattern is the more common developmental pathway. There is little oppositional or antisocial behavior exhibited during childhood. During adolescence, many youngsters begin to engage in illegal activities, and although most exhibit only isolated antisocial acts, some engage in enough antisocial behavior to qualify for a diagnosis of conduct disorder. However, the antisocial behaviors are less likely to persist beyond adolescence and thus are sometimes termed *adolescent-limited* (Moffitt, 1993a). Some of the youngsters do continue to have difficulties later in life though these difficulties may not be as severe as the outcomes for the life-course-persistent individuals (Moffitt et al., 2002). It remains important to determine which of these individuals do discontinue and which of them persist in or escalate their antisocial behavior as they enter adulthood, and to identify the variables that affect the developmental process at different points in time (White, Bates, & Buyske, 2001).

DEVELOPMENTAL PATHS

In addition to groupings of individuals by age of onset, much attention also has been given to the conceptualization of developmental progressions of conduct problems (e.g., Dodge, 2000; Farrington, 1986; Loeber et al., 1993; Patterson, DeBaryshe, & Ramsey, 1989). Loeber (1988) proposed a model that illustrates some of the attributes that might characterize the developmental course of conduct disorders within individuals. The model suggests that at each level, less serious behaviors precede more serious ones but that only some individuals progress to the next step. Progression on a developmental path is characterized by increasing diversification of antisocial behaviors. Youngsters who progress show new antisocial behaviors, and previous behaviors may also be retained rather than replaced. Individuals may differ in their rate of progression.

Loeber's Three-Pathway Model. Loeber and colleagues (1993) suggest that it is best to conceptualize antisocial behavior as occurring along multiple

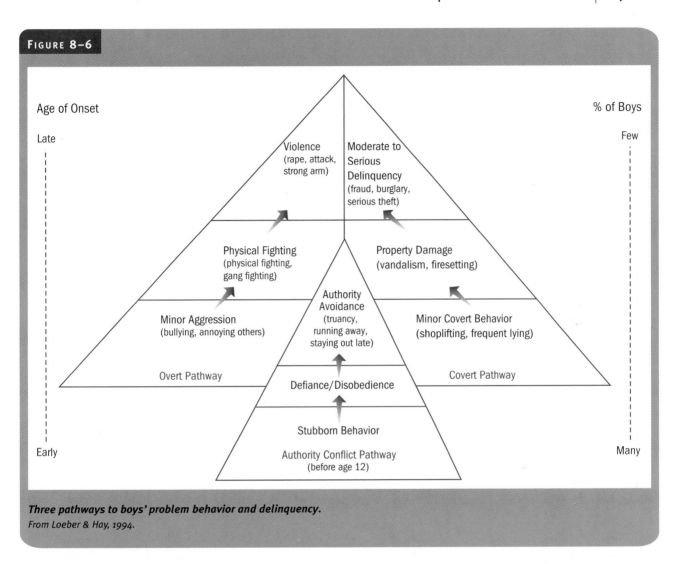

FIGURE 8-6

Three pathways to boys' problem behavior and delinquency.
From Loeber & Hay, 1994.

pathways. On the basis of a longitudinal study of inner-city youth and following from distinctions between conduct problem behaviors described earlier, Loeber proposed a triple-pathway model (see Figure 8–6):

- an overt pathway starting with minor aggression, followed by physical fighting, followed by violence;
- a covert pathway starting with minor covert behaviors, followed by property damage, and then moderate to serious delinquency; and
- an authority conflict pathway prior to age 12, consisting of a sequence of stubborn behavior, defiance, and authority avoidance.

Individuals may progress along one or more of these pathways. As illustrated in Figure 8–6, entry into the authority conflict pathway typically begins earlier than entry into the other two pathways, and not all individuals who exhibit early behaviors on a pathway

progress through the subsequent stages. The percentage of youngsters exhibiting behaviors characteristic of later stages is less than those exhibiting earlier behaviors on a pathway.

Investigators continue their efforts to describe the developmental pathways of antisocial, conduct-disordered behavior. At the same time, they also seek to identify the influences that first put youngsters on those pathways and that determine whether the antisocial behavior will continue or desist.

Etiology

The development of conduct problems is likely to involve the complex interplay of a variety of influences (Hill, 2002; Rutter, 2003). Table 8–7, reproduced from Loeber and Farrington (2000), provides a list of empirically validated risk factors for

| TABLE 8–7 | RISK FACTORS FOR CHILD AGGRESSION AND LATER SERIOUS AND VIOLENT JUVENILE OFFENDING |

Child Factors

Difficult temperament
Impulsive behavior
Hyperactivity (but only when co-occurring with
  disruptive behavior)
Impulsivity
Substance use
Aggression
Early-onset disruptive behavior
Withdrawn behavior
Low intelligence
Lead toxicity

Family Factors

Parental antisocial or delinquent behavior
Parental substance abuse
Parents' poor child-rearing practices
  Poor supervision
  Physical punishment
  Poor communication
Poor parent-child relations
Parental physical and sexual abuse
Parental neglect
Maternal depression
Mother's smoking during pregnancy
Teenage motherhood
Parents disagree on child discipline

Single parenthood
Large family
High turnover of caretakers
Low socioeconomic status of the family
Unemployed parent
Poorly educated mother
Family members' carelessness in allowing chil-
  dren access to weapons, especially guns

School Factors

Poor academic performance
Old for grade
Weak bonding to school
Low educational aspirations
Low school motivation
Poorly organized and functioning schools

Peer Factors

Association with deviant or delinquent siblings
  and peers
Rejection by peers

Neighborhood Factors

Neighborhood disadvantage and poverty
Disorganized neighborhoods
Availability of weapons
Media portrayal of violence

Adapted from Loeber & Farrington, 2000.

childhood aggression and later delinquency. Although this listing is informative, how the various influences came together in the development of conduct problems is quite complex. In our description we present influences in separate sections, but, again, it is important to remember that causal explanations typically involve multiple transactional influences and variations of how influences are associated. Each set of influences may directly and/or indirectly affect the development of antisocial behavior. Here we will give primary attention to intrapersonal and relationship influences, but the larger contexts in which these occur is not to be ignored (Barrera, Prelow et al., 2002).

THE SOCIOECONOMIC CONTEXT

Multiple findings suggest the importance of considering the larger social context. For example, the impact of poverty on oppositional and conduct problems in an American Indian sample has been described (p. 81;

Costello et al., 2003) and demonstrated among other ethnic groups as well (e.g., Macmillan, McMorris, & Kruttschnitt, 2004). Influences associated with poverty also have received attention. For example, Prelow, Danoff-Burg, and colleagues (2004) found that ecological risks (i.e., neighborhood disadvantage and urban-related stress events) were associated with frequency of delinquent/rule-breaking behavior for both African American and European American youngsters. Moreover, perceived discrimination amplified the effect of ecological risks for African American youth. Socioeconomic and other disadvantages likely reflect a process in which adverse individual, family, school, and peer factors combine to increase a youngster's likelihood of developing conduct problems (Fergusson, Swain-Campbell, & Horwood, 2004).

AGGRESSION AS A LEARNED BEHAVIOR

Aggression is a central part of the definition of conduct-disordered behavior and a common difficulty among nonreferred children. Children clearly may learn to be aggressive by being rewarded for such behavior (Patterson, 1976). Also, as we saw earlier (p. 48), children may learn through imitation of aggressive models. Bandura's (1965) classic work with nursery school children demonstrated that children imitated an aggressive filmed model. Furthermore, the consequences experienced by the model affected the performance, but not the learning of aggression. Thus in one set of circumstances, a young boy may not perform aggressive behavior that he has learned. However, at another time, when the boy anticipates positive consequences for aggression, the behavior will be performed. It has also been demonstrated not only that children may learn new and novel aggressive responses following observation of an aggressive model but also that aggressive responses already in the child's repertoire are more likely to occur—that is, disinhibition of aggression may occur.

Children certainly have ample opportunity to observe aggressive models. Parents who engage in physical aggression toward their spouse or who physically punish their children serve as models for aggressive behavior. In fact, children exhibiting excessive aggressive or antisocial behaviors are likely to have siblings, parents, and even grandparents with histories of conduct problems and records of aggressive and criminal behavior (Farrington, 1995; Huesmann et al., 1984; Waschbusch, 2002) and to have observed especially high rates of aggressive behavior in their homes (Kashani et al., 1992; Margolin, 1998; Patterson, DeBaryshe, & Ramsey, 1989). Aggression is also ubiquitous in television programs and in other media (Anderson et al., 2003; Bushman & Anderson, 2001).

FAMILY INFLUENCES

The family environment can play an important role in the genesis of various conduct-disordered behaviors. As indicated before, a high incidence of deviant or criminal behavior has been reported in families of youngsters with conduct problems. Longitudinal studies, in fact, suggest that such behavior is stable across generations (Glueck & Glueck, 1968; Huesmann et al., 1984). It seems, then, that conduct-disordered children may be part of a deviant family system. Numerous family variables have been implicated, including family socioeconomic status, family size, marital disruption, poor-quality parenting, parental abuse and neglect, and parental psychopathology (Frick, 1994; Patterson, Reid, & Dishion, 1992; Waschbusch, 2002). We highlight a few of these influences.

Parent-Child Interactions and Noncompliance. The manner in which parents interact with their children contributes to the genesis of conduct-disordered behavior. Defiant, stubborn, and noncompliant behaviors are often among the first problems to develop in children. Given that these occur in both clinic and nonclinic families, what factors might account for the greater rates in some families? One possible factor is suggested by evidence that parents differ in both the number and the types of commands that they give. Parents of clinic-referred children issue more commands, questions, and criticisms. Also, the use of prohibitions and commands that are presented in an unclear, an angry, a humiliating, or a nagging manner are less likely to result in child compliance (Dumas & Lechowicz, 1989; Forehand et al., 1975; Kuczynski & Kochanska, 1995). Consequences that parents deliver also affect the child's noncompliant behavior (Brinkmeyer & Eyberg, 2003; Forehand & McMahon, 1981). A combination of negative consequences (time-out) for noncompliant behavior and rewards and attention for appropriate behavior seems to be related to increased levels of compliance.

The Work of Patterson and His Colleagues. Gerald Patterson and his colleagues have created the Oregon Model—a developmental intervention

A child may engage in aversive behaviors in order to get something that he or she wants. If the parent repeatedly gives in, this capitulation may contribute to coercive patterns of interaction in the family.
(Dennis MacDonald/PhotoEdit, Inc.)

model for families with aggressive antisocial children—based on a social learning perspective (Patterson et al., 1975; Patterson et al., 1992; Reid, Patterson, & Snyder, 2002). Although this approach recognizes that characteristics of the child may play a role, the emphasis is on the social context.

> *If we are to change aggressive childhood behavior, we must change the environment in which the child lives. If we are to understand and predict future aggression, our primary measures will be of the social environment that is teaching and maintaining these deviant behaviors. The problem lies in the social environment. If you wish to change the child, you must systematically alter the environment in which he or she lives. (Patterson, Reid, & Eddy, 2002, p. 21)*

Patterson developed what he refers to as coercion theory to explain how a problematic pattern of behavior develops. Observations of referred families suggested that acts of physical aggression were not isolated behaviors. On the contrary, such acts tended to occur along with a wide range of noxious behaviors that were used to control family members in a process labeled as coercion. How and why does this process of coercion develop?

One factor is parents who lack adequate family management skills. According to Patterson (1976; Patterson et al., 1992), parental deficits in child management lead to an increasingly coercive interaction within the family. Central to this process are the notions of negative reinforcement and the reinforcement trap. Here is an example:

- A mother gives in to her child's tantrums in the supermarket and buys him a candy bar.
- The short-term consequence is that things are more pleasant for both parties:
  - The child has used an aversive event (tantrum) to achieve the desired goal (candy bar).
  - The mother's giving in has terminated an aversive event (tantrum and embarrassment) for her.
- Short-term gains, however, are paid for in long-term consequences:
  - The mother, although receiving some immediate relief, has increased the probability that her child will employ tantrums in the future.
  - The mother has also been provided with negative reinforcement that increases the likelihood that she will give in to future tantrums.

In addition to this negative reinforcement trap, coercive behavior may also be increased by direct positive reinforcement. Aggressive behavior, especially in boys, may meet with social approval.

The concept of reciprocity adds to our understanding of how aggression and coercion may be learned and sustained. Children as young as nursery school age can learn in a short time that attacking another person in response to some intrusion can terminate that intrusion. In addition, the victim of the attack may learn from the experience and is more likely to initiate attacks in the future. The eventual victim of escalating coercion also provides a negative reinforcer by giving in, thereby increasing the likelihood that the "winner" will start future coercions at higher levels of intensity and thus will get the victim to give in more quickly.

This process is exacerbated by the ineffectiveness of punishment. In problem families punishment does not suppress coercive behavior but may serve to increase it. The ineffectiveness of punishment may be due to the strong reinforcement history for coercive behavior and to inconsistent use of punishment in these families (Patterson, 1982).

The description of a coercive process and ineffective parenting has served as the basis for Patterson's intervention project and for his evolving developmental model (Patterson et al., 1992; Patterson et al., 2002). In addition to describing the "training" of antisocial behavior in the home, the Oregon Model describes a relationship between antisocial behavior in boys and poor peer relationships and other adverse outcomes (Snyder, 2002). It is suggested that ineffective parenting produces the coercive, noncompliant core of antisocial behavior, which in turn leads to these other disruptions. Furthermore, it is hypothesized that each of these outcomes serves as a precursor to subsequent drift into deviant peer groups.

The perspective of Patterson and his coworkers has expanded to include a wide array of variables that affect the family process and many problems known to be associated with antisocial behavior. However, at the core of this complex theoretical model is the parent training model (Figure 8–7) that has proven to be so robust that Patterson and his colleagues call it basic black; "it is simple, elegant and seems appropriate for more than one setting" (Patterson et al., 1992, p. 62).

Parental discipline and parental monitoring are described as contributing to and being influenced by the child's antisocial behavior. Parental discipline is defined by an interrelated set of skills: accurately

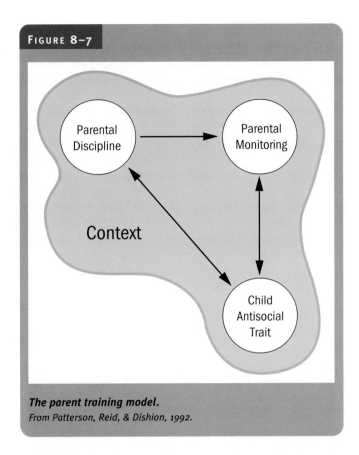

The parent training model.
From Patterson, Reid, & Dishion, 1992.

tracking and classifying problem behaviors, ignoring trivial coercive events, and using effective consequences when necessary to back up demands and requests. Parents of problem children as compared with other parents have been found to be overinclusive in the behaviors that they classify as deviant. Thus these parents differ in how they track and classify problem behavior. These parents also "natter" (nag, scold irritably) in response to low levels of coercive behavior or to behavior that other parents see as neutral and are able to ignore. Parents of antisocial children fail to back up their commands when the child fails to comply, and they also fail to reward compliance when it does occur.

Parental monitoring of child behavior is also important to the development and persistence over time of antisocial behavior. The amount of time a child spends unsupervised by parents increases with age. The amount of unsupervised time also is positively correlated with antisocial behavior. Patterson describes his treatment families as having little information as to where their children are, whom they are with, what they are doing, or when they will be home. This situation probably arises from a variety of considerations, including the repeated failures

that these parents have experienced in controlling their children even when difficulties occurred right in front of them. Also, requesting information would likely lead to a series of confrontations that the parents prefer to avoid. These parents have low expectations regarding the likelihood of positive responses to their involvement either from their own children or from social agencies such as schools (Patterson et al., 1992).

Extrafamilial Influences and Parental Psychopathology. The question of why some families and not others exhibit inept management practices has received some attention. Patterson (Patterson et al., 1992) posits that any number of variables may account for changes over time in family management skills. Patterson's own findings and those of other investigators support the relationship between extrafamilial stressors (e.g., daily hassles, negative life events, financial problems, family health problems) and parenting practices (Capaldi et al., 2002; Wahler & Dumas, 1989). In addition, the handing down of faulty parenting practices from one generation to the next seems to help explain the problematic parenting characteristics of antisocial families. Social disadvantage and living in neighborhoods that require a very high degree of parenting skills also place some families at risk. Finally, various forms of parental psychopathology are associated with poor parenting practices. Parents who themselves have antisocial difficulties may be particularly likely to have parenting practices (e.g., inconsistent discipline, low parental involvement) associated with the development of conduct-disordered behavior (Capaldi et al., 2002). Also, heavy drinking by parents may lower their threshold for reacting adversely to their child's behavior and also may be associated with inept monitoring of the child and less parental involvement (Lahey et al., 1999; West & Prinz, 1987). Figure 8–8 illustrates a model of how a variety of influences may lead to disruption of effective parenting and to child antisocial behavior.

Marital Discord. Parental conflict and divorce have frequently been cited in homes of children and adolescents with conduct problems (Cummings, Davies, & Campbell, 2000; O'Leary & Emery, 1985). The conflict leading to and surrounding the divorce are principal influences in this relationship, and less conflict and greater cooperation are associated with fewer problems in children (Amato & Keith, 1991; Hetherington, Bridges, & Insabella, 1998). If aggression between the parents is also present, childhood disorder seems even more likely than would be expected on the basis of marital discord alone (Cummings, Goeke-Morey, & Papp, 2004; Jaffee, Poisson, & Cunningham, 2001; Jouriles, Murphy, & O'Leary, 1989). The relationship between marital conflict and conduct disorders can be explained in a number of ways. Parents who engage in a great deal of marital conflict or aggression may serve as models for their children. The stress of marital discord may also interfere with parenting practices and the ability to monitor the child's behavior. The relationship between discord and conduct problems may also operate in the opposite causal direction; that is, the child's disruptive behavior may contribute to marital discord.

Also, both conduct problems and marital discord may be related to a "third variable," such as the presence of parental antisocial disorder (Lahey et al., 1988). Indeed, there are high rates of antisocial personality disorder (APD) among parents of conduct-disordered youngsters, and APD is associated with high rates of marital instability (Frick, 1994).

The relationship between marital conflict and child adjustment is likely to be complex and change over time, and it is important to remember that these problems exist in a larger context (Cummings &

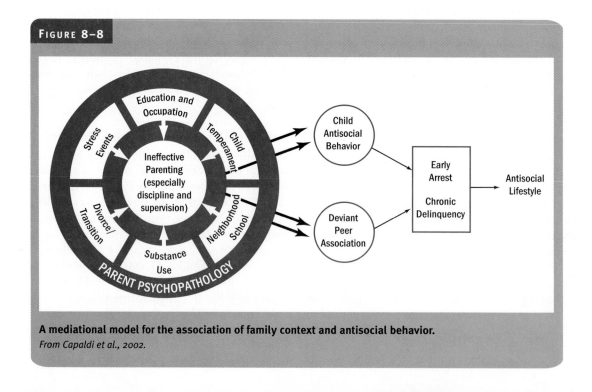

FIGURE 8–8

A mediational model for the association of family context and antisocial behavior.
From Capaldi et al., 2002.

Marital discord and aggression between parents can contribute to the development of conduct-disordered behavior in children.
(B. Daemmrich/The Image Works)

Davies, 2002). It may be that a high level of environmental risk (related to family and community/neighborhood factors) directly affects the youngster and is also experienced by the parents, contributing to marital and parenting difficulties (Herrenkohl et al., 2001; Luthar, 1999; Paschall & Hubbard, 1998; Wahler & Dumas, 1989). Socioeconomic difficulties and the challenge of living in high-crime neighborhoods, for example, may make it difficult to execute essential parenting skills such as monitoring a youngster's behavior (Richards et al., 2004).

ACCENT ● ● ● ● ●

Maltreatment and Conduct Problems

Early maltreatment, particularly physical abuse, is a risk factor for serious conduct problems (Lansford et al., 2002; Wekerle & Wolfe, 2003). Physically maltreated youngsters often display high levels of hostility and aggression and have frequent angry outbursts. These youngsters have higher than expected rates of conduct and oppositional defiant disorders.

A variety of mechanisms probably account for the association between maltreatment and conduct problems. As might be expected, persistent maltreatment may be particularly detrimental. For example, Bolger and Patterson (2001) found that chronically maltreated children were more likely to be aggressive and rejected by peers. A suggested mechanism for this maltreatment-aggression-peer rejection pattern is the coercive interactional style the child has learned in the family of origin.

Physical maltreatment may also contribute to learning of problematic cognitive/social information-processing patterns. Indeed, the relationship between early maltreatment and later aggressive behavior is, in part, mediated by these biased social information-processing patterns (Dodge, 2003). Thus, physical maltreatment may contribute to conduct problems through the development of problematic peer relationship and cognitive processes.

Peer Relations

Peer relations are part of the complex interplay of influences that contribute to the development of conduct problems (Hay et al., 2004). Parents are often concerned that their children are being influenced by peers whose behavior they view as "bad" or "dangerous." Such concern may be reasonable. Early exposure to aggressive peers may be one factor in initiating early aggressive and antisocial behavior, and later association with deviant peers can contribute to the maintenance and escalation of such behavior (Fergusson & Horwood, 1998; Laird et al., 2001; Snyder, 2002).

Difficulties in interpersonal relations have repeatedly been found among youngsters with conduct problems (Lochman, Whidby, & FitzGerald, 2000). Peers often reject children who display disruptive and aggressive behavior (Bierman, 2004; Coie, Belding, & Underwood, 1988). Rejected aggressive children suffer immediate social consequences and are at risk for negative long-term outcomes such as delinquency, adult criminality, educational failure, and adult psychological maladjustment (Laird et al., 2001; Parker & Asher, 1987; Rudolph & Asher, 2000).

Not all aggressive youngsters are rejected, however, and those who are may not be without friends. In late childhood and into adolescence, conduct-disordered and delinquent youngsters may have friends who also engage in aggressive and antisocial behaviors. The case of Delano, described in an earlier chapter (p. 62), is a dramatic example of this. Research shows that these deviant peer associations play a role in the initiation and maintenance of antisocial behavior (Fergusson & Horwood, 1996; Keenan et al., 1995). Fergusson and Horwood (1998) reported on the linkages between early conduct problems and outcomes at age 18 in a group of New Zealand children studied longitudinally since birth. They found that conduct problems at age 8 were associated with poorer outcomes, such as leaving school by age 18 without appropriate educational qualifications and a period of 3 months or more of unemployment. One of the factors that mediated the relationship between early aggression and later poor outcomes was peer affiliations. Adolescents who between the ages of 14 and 16 had reported having friends who were delinquent or who used illegal substances were at greater risk for negative outcomes.

Peer influences are not independent of other contextual factors. So, for example, in their longitudinal study of New Zealand youngsters, Fergusson and Horwood (1999) found that family variables such as parental conflict, parental history of drug abuse and criminal behavior, and early mother-child interactions were predictive of affiliation with deviant peers at age 15. Cultural and community influences come into play as well. Brody and colleagues (2001), for example, found in a sample of African American children that difficulty with deviant peers was less likely if parents were nurturing and involved, but more likely if parenting was harsh and inconsistent. Furthermore, affiliation with deviant peers was less likely in neighborhoods with collective socialization practices (e.g., willingness of adults to monitor and supervise youth from both their own and other families). Community economic disadvantage also was associated with greater likelihood of deviant peer affiliation, and the benefits of nurturant/involved parenting and collective socialization were most pronounced for youngsters from the most disadvantaged neighborhoods.

Cognitive-Emotional Influences

Consider the adolescent boy who is walking down the street and is approached by a group of peers who begin to call him names, laugh, and tease him. Some boys respond to this situation by getting angry, escalating the conflict, and perhaps reacting violently, whereas other boys are able to deflect attention to another topic, ignore it, laugh, make light of the teasing, or firmly ask that the teasing stop. The cognitive and emotional processes that occur during this situation constitute proximal mechanisms for aggressive behavior. (Dodge, 2000, p. 448)

Examining how youngsters think and feel about social situations is part of understanding conduct disorders. For example, they may attribute hostility to another child's actions or may fail to take another person's perspective, fail to use social problem-solving skills, fail to think before they act, or fail to use self-verbalizations to control their emotions and behavior. These social-cognitive-emotional processes are part of the development and persistence of aggressive and antisocial behavior (Dodge, 2000; Lochman et al., 2000). Specific social information-processing patterns such as a focus on the positive aspects of aggression and a lack of responsiveness to emotional stimuli may, for example, be characteristic of youngsters with the callous/unemotional traits described earlier (Pardini, Lochman, & Frick, 2003; Loney et al., 2003).

The model articulated by Dodge and his colleagues that was described in Chapter 2 (p. 35) illustrates how one might address social-emotional cognitions (Crick & Dodge, 1994; Dodge, 2003). The model suggests that cognitive processing begins with encoding (looking for and attending to) and then interpreting social and emotional cues. The next steps include searching for possible alternative responses, selecting a specific response, and finally enacting the selected response. Investigations reveal that youngsters with conduct problems have poorer social problem-solving skills and display cognitive deficits and distortions in various parts of this process (Fontaine, Burks, & Dodge, 2002). For example, aggressive youngsters make use of fewer social cues and misattribute hostile intent to their peers' neutral actions. They also generate fewer responses and ones that are less likely to be effectively assertive and more likely to be aggressive solutions. They may also expect that aggressive responses will lead to positive outcomes. Furthermore, aggressive youngsters may be more likely to perceive and label the arousal they experience in conflict situations as anger rather than other emotions. These reactions to internal arousal may contribute to further distortion and restricted problem solving (Lochman et al., 2000).

Problematic social-cognitive-emotional processes may start quite early in life and be part of the stability of early-onset conduct-disordered behavior. Coy and colleagues (2001), for example, presented two groups of preschool boys with hypothetical peer-related social dilemmas to resolve. The tasks were presented when the boys were about 4 or 5 years old, and again 1 and 2 years later. At the first assessment, clinic-referred boys with a primary diagnosis of ODD were more likely to give hostile or aggressive solutions to stories than were comparison community boys who were viewed as typical and had no clinical diagnosis. This group difference in aggressive solutions continued at the following two assessments.

Dodge and his colleagues (Dodge, 1991; Schwartz et al., 1998) have made a distinction between two types of aggressive behavior: reactive aggression and proactive aggression. Reactive aggression is an angry ("hot-blooded") retaliatory response to a perceived provocation or frustration. Proactive aggression, in contrast, is generally not associated with anger and is characterized by deliberate aversive behaviors (starting fights, bullying, teasing) that are oriented to specific goals or supported by positive environmental outcomes. These different types of aggression are associated with different social-cognitive deficiencies (Schippell et al., 2003). Reactively aggressive youngsters display deficiencies in early stages of the social-cognitive process; for example, they underutilize social cues and attribute hostile intent to others. Proactively aggressive youngsters display deficiencies in later stages of the process; they are likely to positively evaluate aggressive solutions and to expect that they will lead to positive outcomes. The two types of aggression also seem to be related to different outcomes. Reactively aggressive boys were found to display higher rates of other problems and to have an earlier onset of such difficulties than were proactively aggressive boys (Dodge et al., 1997). Reactively aggressive boys also seem more likely to be the targets of negative peer attitudes and behaviors (Schwartz et al., 1998).

A study by Brendgen and colleagues (2001) further illustrates the value of the reactive-proactive distinction. This study also reminds us, once again, of the interrelatedness of influences. A sample of Caucasian, French-speaking boys from low socioeconomic neighborhoods in Montreal, Canada, were categorized at 13 years of age as either nonaggressive, proactive-aggressive, reactive-aggressive, or both proactive- and reactive-aggressive. At ages 16 through 17 the boys were asked to report on their delinquency-related physical violence (e.g., beat up other boys, used a weapon in a fight) and on their physical violence against a dating partner. As can be seen in Table 8–8, proactive aggression was associated with greater delinquency-related violence, and reactive aggression with greater dating violence. It is interesting that the relationship between proactive aggression and delinquency-related violence was moderated by level of parental supervision. The relationship was strong for boys who had experienced low levels of parental supervision during their early adolescent years, but the relationship was weak for boys who had experienced higher levels of parental supervision during this period. Similarly, the relationship between reactive aggression and dating violence was mediated by level of maternal warmth and caregiving. The relationship was strong for boys who had experienced low levels of maternal warmth and caregiving during their development, but this relationship was weak among boys who had experienced higher levels of maternal warmth and caregiving. Thus, although development of proactive and reactive aggression may be influenced by social-cognitive style, the developmental course of such behavior seems to be affected by styles of parenting.

TABLE 8–8	MEAN SCORES OF DELINQUENCY-RELATED VIOLENCE AND DATING VIOLENCE BY AGGRESSIVE GROUP			
		AGGRESSIVE GROUP		
	NONAGRESSIVE	**PROACTIVE-ONLY**	**REACTIVE-ONLY**	**REACTIVE-PROACTIVE**
Delinquency-related violence	.19	.42	.25	.42
Dating violence	.10	.05	.19	.21

Adapted from Brendgen, Vitaro, Tremblay, & Lavoie, 2001.

BIOLOGICAL INFLUENCES

The idea that antisocial and criminal behavior has strong biological roots has a long history. As early as the late nineteenth century, the Italian physician Lombroso wrote of the "stigmata of degeneration." Law violators were described as a distinct physical type at birth, with distinct physical features such as long earlobes, fleshy and protruding lips, and abundant wrinkles. Females were said to commit fewer crimes because their lesser intelligence and sexual coldness overcame their naturally jealous and vengeful nature (cited in Empey, 1978). This conceptualization had an extensive impact on criminology and social policy for over a third of a century, but current-day scientists have accumulated sufficient evidence to reject it. Contemporary understanding of the role of biological influences emphasize transactions among multiple biological and nonbiological influences (Lahey & Waldamn, 2003; Susman, 1993).

Genetics. Until recently there was little or no evidence regarding genetic contributions to childhood conduct problems, and there was limited evidence regarding the role of genetics in adolescent delinquency. The findings that existed suggested a lesser genetic component for adolescent delinquency than for adult criminal behavior. How might this difference be explained? The childhood-onset versus adolescent-limited distinction discussed earlier may be germane. Conduct-disordered behavior and delinquent behavior are quite common during adolescence, and in many cases, they do not persist into adulthood. It might, therefore, be reasonable to hypothesize an increased genetic component in antisocial behavior that is more aggressive and persists from childhood into adult life (Eley, Lichtenstein, & Moffitt, 2003; Rutter et al., 1999; Taylor, Iacono, & McGue, 2000).

Early findings from a number of longitudinal behavior genetic studies of children and adolescents do suggest a genetic component to conduct-disordered/externalizing behavior. The Virginia Twin Study of Adolescent Behavioral Development (Eaves et al., 1997; Hewitt, et al., 1997), for example, examined genetic and environmental influences in a large sample of Caucasian twin pairs ages 8 to 16. There was evidence for a considerable genetic influence; however, there was considerable variability in the findings, depending on the informant (e.g., mother or father) and the source of information (interview versus questionnaires). There was also support for the effects of shared environment. The Nonshared Environment and Adolescent Development Project examined a sample of same-sex adolescent siblings (monozygotic and dizygotic twins, full siblings, half-siblings, and unrelated siblings) between the ages of 10 and 18. Again, there was evidence for moderate genetic influence on externalizing behavior scores and also evidence for the impact of shared environment (Deater-Deckard et al., 1997).

Conclusions regarding the nature of genetic contributions to antisocial/conduct-disordered behavior must be made with caution. Findings are preliminary and far from unequivocal. Also, Rosenthal (1975) hypothesized that what is inherited is certain characteristics; for example, body build, sensitivity to alcohol, or temperamental qualities such as irritability, impulsivity, and sensation seeking. The hypothesis that such qualities make an individual prone to antisocial behavior in response to environmental pressures seems reasonable (Frick & Morris, 2004). Although genetic influences may play some role, they are likely to be indirect and interact in complex ways with environmental influences, such as social conditions, family variables, and certain social learning experiences that are major factors in determining etiology (Rhee & Waldman, 2003; Rutter et al., 1999).

Neurophysiological Influences. Psychophysiological variables have been frequently hypothesized to be related to antisocial behavior. Support for this notion comes from studies that find differences between delinquent or conduct-disordered youth and control youngsters on psychophysiological measures such as electrodermal responding (skin conductance) and heart rate (Beauchaine et al., 2001).

Quay (1993) hypothesized a biological foundation for aggressive, life-course persistent conduct disorders. This hypothesis is based on Gray's (1987) theory of brain systems: a behavioral inhibition system (BIS) and a behavioral activation (or approach) system (BAS) that have distinct neuroanatomical and neurotransmitter systems. The BIS is related to the emotions of fear and anxiety, and tends to inhibit action in novel or fearful situations or under conditions of punishment or nonreward. The BAS tends to activate behavior in the presence of reinforcement; it is associated with reward seeking and pleasurable emotions. An imbalance between the two systems is hypothesized to create a predisposition that in combination with adverse environmental circumstances produces behavior problems. Figure 8–9 (p. 228) depicts how an imbalance might contribute to either externalizing (antisocial) or internalizing (anxious/depressed) behavior. Quay (1993) suggested that an underactive behavioral inhibition system (BIS; e.g., reflected in skin conductance) combined with an overactive reward system (BAS; e.g., reflected in heart rate) may be implicated in the genesis of persistent aggressive conduct disorders.

An alternative model of how the two systems may operate has also been suggested. In this view, conduct-disordered, aggressive behavior results from an underactive BAS system in combination with an underactive BIS system (Beauchaine et al., 2001). Conduct-disordered and aggressive behavior represent a form of sensation seeking in response to chronic underarousal created by an underactive BAS system. Youngsters characterized as conduct-disordered also have low levels of inhibition and engage in aggressive and other antisocial behaviors to achieve satisfactory reward states and positive arousal.

A third system described by Gray (1987) might also be involved in conduct disorders. The fight/flight system (F/F) also involves distinct brain and autonomic nervous system functioning. It is proposed to mediate defensive reactions under conditions of frustration, punishment, or pain. Thus, stimuli that are viewed as threatening would activate the F/F system. Certain youth, such as those with conduct-disordered behavior, may have a reduced threshold for F/F responding, whereas higher thresholds may be associated with characteristics such as social competence and empathy toward others in distress. In general, the BIS and BAS are viewed as motivational, whereas the F/F system is viewed as an emotion regulation system (Beauchaine et al., 2001).

Neuropsychological Deficits. The idea that brain dysfunction is among the causes of antisocial behavior is not new, but the scientific investigation of such influence is relatively recent. The role of the frontal lobes, in particular, and of deficits in verbal and executive functions (e.g., sustaining attention, abstract reasoning, goal formation, planning, self-awareness) has been suggested (Ishikawa & Raine, 2003; Moffitt, 1993b; Nigg & Huang-Pollock, 2003).

Neuropsychological measures have been found to be related to indications of poor outcomes, such as early onset and stability of conduct disorder, aggressiveness, and attention-deficit hyperactivity disorder symptoms. Moffitt (1993b) proposed a developmental model that hypothesizes early insults to the infant nervous system due to factors such as prenatal or postnatal exposure to toxic agents. Compromised neurological functioning affects a variety of areas, including temperament. This effect, in turn, may set in motion a chain of problematic parent-child interactions, particularly under conditions of family adversity. Conduct disorder is thus viewed as evolving from early individual differences in neuropsychological functioning that may be perpetuated and exacerbated by transactions with the social environment. Neuropsychological conceptualizations of conduct disorder development may apply to only some conduct-disordered youngsters, and additional research and refinements of theoretical concepts are needed (Ishikawa & Raine, 2003).

Assessment

As is the case for most child and adolescent problems, assessment of conduct problems is likely to be a complex and multifaceted process. The various manifestations of conduct-disordered behavior and other problem domains such as attentional deficits, hyperactivity, impulsivity, and depression need to be evaluated. Furthermore, given the appreciable involvement of family, peers, and school, these environments and individuals may also need to be included in the

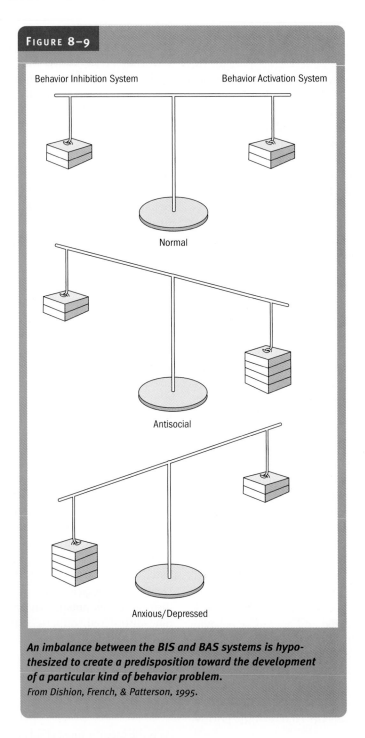

FIGURE 8–9

Behavior Inhibition System   Behavior Activation System

Normal

Antisocial

Anxious/Depressed

An imbalance between the BIS and BAS systems is hypo-thesized to create a predisposition toward the development of a particular kind of behavior problem.
From Dishion, French, & Patterson, 1995.

assessment process. In the following sections we describe the primary procedures likely to be used by clinicians working to assess these youngsters. However, it should be recognized that the assessment process may also include evaluation of other aspects of the presenting problems, others' problems, attitudes, and skills (e.g., parenting), and ongoing life stresses (Frick & Loney, 2000; Lochman et al., 2000).

INTERVIEWS

A general clinical interview with the parents is typically conducted, and older children and adolescents themselves can be interviewed. An interview with younger children may not be as easily conducted or may not be a reliable source of information; however, the opportunity to interact with the young child may be helpful to the clinician in formulating hypotheses and in establishing rapport. An interview with the entire family may also provide valuable information. In addition, an interview with the teacher or school personnel is frequently part of the assessment process and can provide important information about certain spheres of functioning. Structured interviews with the youngster and parent are often conducted, and can help provide a comprehensive understanding of problems and their context, as well as the perspectives of multiple individuals. Structured interviews can also be used for determining a diagnosis.

BEHAVIORAL RATING SCALES

Among general rating scales useful for assessing conduct problems are the Achenbach instruments (Achenbach & Rescorla, 2001) and the Behavioral Assessment System for Children (BASC; Reynolds & Kamphaus, 1992). They allow evaluation of a broad array of problems through the reports of multiple informants.

Available, too, are behavioral rating scales that focus specifically on conduct problems and disruptive behavior. The Conners parent and teacher rating scales—revised (Conners et al., 1998a,b), the Eyberg Child Behavior Inventory (ECBI), and the Sutter-Eyberg Student Behavior Inventory (SESBI) are examples (Eyberg, 1992). The ECBI is completed by parents, and the SESBI is completed by teachers. Described as measures of conduct problems, these instruments do contain items sampling the range of "disruptive behavior" problems that correspond to the DSM diagnoses of Oppositional Defiant Disorder and Attention-Deficit Hyperactivity Disorder, as well as Conduct Disorder. Although the majority of items represent conduct problems rather than ADHD, children who exceed the cutoff may represent a heterogeneous group of children with disruptive behavior problems (McMahon & Estes, 1997).

The Self-Report Delinquency Scale (SRD; Elliott, Huizinga, & Ageton, 1985) is a widely used youth self-report measure of conduct problems. Consisting of items derived from the Uniform Crime Reports and including index offenses (e.g., theft, aggravated assault), other delinquent behaviors, and drug use, it is intended for use with youngsters 11 to 19 years old. Self-report measures are less commonly used with younger children because of concern with their ability to accurately report conduct problems.

BEHAVIORAL OBSERVATIONS

Behavioral observation systems have long been a part of the assessment of conduct problems. There are a large number of systems designed for use in clinic, home, and school settings (McMahon & Estes, 1997). Behavioral observations are viewed as a desirable part of the assessment process because of the potential bias of reports based on interviews and questionnaires.

The Behavioral Coding System (Forehand & McMahon, 1981) and the Dyadic Parent-Child Interaction Coding System II (Eyberg et al., 1994) are two similar observational systems for assessing parent-child interactions in the clinic. Both place the parent and the child in situations that vary from free-play/child-directed to adult-directed activities. Various child and parent behaviors are observed and scored. Many of these focus on parental commands (antecedents) and consequences for child compliance or noncompliance. The Interpersonal Process Code (Rusby, Estes, & Dishion, 1991) is another observational system that is an outgrowth of observational systems developed by Patterson and his colleagues.

The three observational systems just described have also been used in home settings, and these and other systems have been employed in the schools (e.g., The Fast Track School Observation Program; Conduct Problems Prevention Research Group, 1992). Observation in these locales is desirable, because these are the settings where many of the conduct problem behaviors and interactions occur. Such use, however, for practicing clinicians is rare. The systems are complex and require extensive periods of training and the use of trained observers. The observations themselves are lengthy, and coordination with times when relevant behaviors are occurring in homes or schools is challenging.

An alternative to using trained observers in the home or other natural environments is to train adults in the child's environment to record and observe certain behaviors. An advantage of this approach is the opportunity to observe and record behaviors that occur at low rates (e.g., stealing or fire setting) and that would likely be missed by trained observers making occasional visits. The Parent Daily Report (PDR; Chamberlain & Reid, 1987) is one measure of this kind. During brief telephone interviews, the parent is asked whether any of the targeted behaviors occurred during the past 24 hours. The Daily Telephone Discipline Interview (Webster-Stratton & Spitzer, 1991) was developed as an extension to the

PDR to provide more information about parental interventions surrounding child behaviors reported on the PDR.

Most of the observational systems described here are targeted for children and their parents, teachers, and peers. Observational systems also are available for coding parent-adolescent conflict, problem solving, and communication (Foster & Robin, 1997).

Treatment

Because of the challenges posed by youngsters with conduct problems and the impact they have on others, many different treatments have been attempted. Only a portion of these has received careful empirical evaluation regarding effectiveness. Here we will briefly describe some of the treatments that research suggests are supported or promising (Brestan & Eyberg, 1998; Christophersen & Mortweet, 2001; Kazdin, 1997; Ollendick & King, 2000).

PHARMACOLOGICAL INTERVENTION

There is a paucity of well-controlled research regarding the use of medication in treating oppositional defiant disorder or conduct disorder. It is important to remember that many youngsters with these disorders show symptoms of or meet the diagnostic criteria for attention-deficit hyperactivity disorder. There is considerable support for pharmacological interventions for ADHD (McClellan & Werry, 2003). Thus youngsters who also present with this co-occurrence may benefit from the use of medications such as stimulants. However, from a research perspective, evaluations of pharmacological treatments for ODD or CD would need to ensure that the medication's effectiveness was not due to the presence of ADHD symptoms in the population studied. Much of the available research can be critiqued for failing to control adequately for such considerations.

In the literature on pharmacological treatments, a distinction is made between impulsive aggression and predatory (or planned) aggression (Botteron & Geller, 1999). This distinction appears to be similar to the reactive versus proactive distinction. To the extent that research supports the use of medication, it is for the treatment of impulsive aggression and not predatory aggression (Botteron & Geller, 1999; McLeer & Wills, 2000).

Mood stabilizers are the category of medication most likely to be considered for use in treating extreme aggressive and conduct-disordered behaviors (McLeer & Wills, 2000; Riddle, Kastelic, & Frosch, 2001). Research support is limited, however. Given a broad uneasiness regarding increased use of psychoactive medications with children, especially in the context of limited or no proof of their effectiveness in youngsters, there is concern regarding the use of such medications (Coyle, 2000; Zito et al., 2000). If psychoactive medication were employed in the treatment of aggressive conduct-disordered youngsters, it should be part of a multimodal treatment approach that includes parent training and other psychological interventions.

PARENT TRAINING

Parent training is among the most successful approaches to reducing aggressive, noncompliant, and antisocial behaviors in youth (Brestan & Eyberg, 1998; Kazdin, 1997; Nock, 2003). A variety of parent training programs have been implemented, and they have a number of features in common (see Table 8–9).

Some parent training programs have focused on oppositional and defiant behavior. There are ethical issues involved in reducing such noncompliance in children. Compliance is not always a positive behavior, and the child's ability to say "no" to certain requests may be desirable either to train or to retain. In this regard, it is important to assure that parents do not expect perfect compliance, which is neither the norm nor highly desirable in our society. A quiet, docile child should not be the treatment goal.

The program developed by Forehand and his colleagues illustrates parent training that focuses on noncompliant behavior (Forehand & Long, 1996). A treatment program for noncompliant children (4 to 7 years old) and their families was developed in which parents were taught to give direct, concise commands, allow the child sufficient time to comply, reward compliance with contingent attention, and apply negative contingencies to noncompliance (Forehand & McMahon, 1981). Research studies indicate that this program was effective (McMahon & Wells, 1998; Powers & Roberts, 1995). Successful treatment of noncompliance also seems to reduce other problem behaviors, such as tantrums, aggression, and crying (Wells, Forehand, & Griest, 1980). Furthermore, at follow-up, treated children were

TABLE 8–9	COMMON FEATURES OF PARENT TRAINING PROGRAMS

- Treatments are conducted primarily with the parents.
  - The therapist teaches the parents to alter interactions with their child so as to increase prosocial behavior and to decrease deviant behavior.
  - Young children may be brought into sessions to train both the parents and the child in how to interact. Older youths may participate in negotiating and developing behavior change programs.
- New ways of identifying, defining, and observing behavior problems are taught.
- Social learning principles and procedures that follow from them are taught (e.g., social reinforcement, points for prosocial behavior, time out from reinforcement, loss of privileges).
- Treatment sessions are an opportunity to see how techniques are implemented and to practice using techniques. Behavior change programs implemented in the home are reviewed.
- The child's functioning in school is usually incorporated into treatment.
  - Parent-managed reinforcement programs for school and school-related behavior are often part of the behavior-change program.
  - If possible, the teacher plays a role in monitoring behavior and providing consequences.

Adapted from Kazdin, 1997.

not different from nonclinic community children across multiple areas such as academic performance, relationships with parents, and adjustment (Long et al., 1994). An additional benefit appeared to be that untreated siblings increased their compliance, and it seems likely that this outcome was due, at least in part, to the mother's use of her improved skills with the untreated child (Humphreys et al., 1978).

Attention to the effective use of parent commands to increase compliance and decrease inappropriate behavior is also part of the parent-child interaction therapy (PCIT) program developed by Eyberg and her colleagues (Brinkmeyer & Eyberg, 2003). This program seeks to enhance parent-child attachment and to improve the poor behavior management skills of the parent. Several studies have provided support for the effectiveness of PCIT. Here we highlight the portion of the program that teaches parents to use effective commands (Querido, Bearss, & Eyberg, 2002). The rules for effective use of commands that parents are taught (along with examples) are presented in Table 8–10.

As we have seen, Patterson's conceptualization of the development of antisocial behavior evolved in the context of treating these children and their families. The importance of parenting skills in Patterson's formulation led to the development of a treatment program that focused on improving these skills (Patterson et al., 1975; Patterson et al., 1992; Reid et al., 2002). The program teaches parents to pinpoint problems, to observe and record behavior, to more effectively use social and nonsocial reinforcers for appropriate or prosocial behavior, and to more effectively withdraw reinforcers for undesirable behavior. Each family attends clinic and home sessions and has regular phone contact with a therapist, who helps develop interventions for particular targeted behaviors and who models desired parenting skills. Problematic behaviors in the school setting are also targeted, and interventions involve both the parents and school personnel. Active treatment is terminated when both the therapist and the family believe that a sufficient number of problematic behaviors have ceased, appropriate behavior has stabilized, overall family functioning has become more positive, and the parents have become able to handle additional problems with little, if any, assistance (Patterson, Chamberlain, & Reid, 1982).

Webster-Stratton and her colleagues (1984; 1994; Webster-Stratton & Hammond, 1997; Webster-Stratton, Hollinsworth, & Kolpacoff, 1989; Webster-Stratton & Reid, 2003) have developed a multifaceted treatment program for young children (2 to 8 years old) with conduct problems, including oppositional defiant and conduct disorder, known as the Incredible Years Training Series. One component of the program is a standard package of videotaped programs of modeled parenting skills. These videos, which contain a large number of vignettes of about 2 minutes each, include examples of parents interacting with their children in both appropriate and inappropriate ways. The videos are shown to groups of parents, and following each vignette, there is a therapist-led discussion of the relevant interactions. Parents are also given homework assignments that allow them to practice parenting skills at home with their children.

The treatment program has been evaluated in a number of studies in which it has been compared with various control conditions (Reid, Webster-Stratton, & Baydar, 2004; Webster-Stratton & Reid, 2003). Parents

TABLE 8–10	RULES FOR EFFECTIVE COMMANDS FROM THE **PCIT** PROGRAM.
RULE	**EXAMPLE**
Be *direct* rather than indirect.	Please hand me the block. *Instead of* Will you hand me the block?
State command *positively*.	Come sit beside me. *Instead of* Don't run around the room!
Give commands *one at a time*.	Put your shirt in the hamper. *Instead of* Clean your room.
Be *specific* rather than vague.	Get down off the chair. *Instead of* Be careful.
Be *age appropriate*.	Draw a square. *Instead of* Draw a hexagon.
Be *polite and respectful*.	Please hand me the block. *Instead of* Hand me that block this instant!
Explain commands *before* they are given or *after* they are obeyed.	Go wash your hands. *After the child obeys* It is good to be all clean when you go to school.
Use commands only when necessary or appropriate.	(*As child is running around*) Please sit in this chair. (Good time) *But not* Please hand me glass from the counter. (Not good time)

Adapted from Querido, Bearss, & Eyberg, 2002.

completing the program have rated their children as having fewer problems than have control parents and rated themselves as having better attitudes and more confidence regarding their parenting role. Observations in the home have also shown these parents to have better parenting skills and their children to have greater reductions in problem behavior. These improvements were maintained at 1- and 3-year follow-up evaluations. Webster-Stratton (Webster-Stratton & Reid, 2003; Webster-Stratton, Reid, & Hammond, 2004) has also expanded the program to include components that enhance parents' interpersonal skills and the social support that the family receives, improve the child's social problem-solving skills, promote parental involvement in school and academic activities, and train teachers in effective classroom management strategies.

COGNITIVE PROBLEM-SOLVING SKILLS TRAINING

Parent training approaches focus on family aspects of conduct-disordered behavior. Other treatments focus more specifically on aspects of the child's functioning. Among these are ones that derive from the interpersonal and social-cognitive aspects of conduct-disordered behavior. These interventions address social-cognitive deficiencies and distortions (Kendall & Panichelli-Mindel, 1995; Lochman, Barry, & Pardini, 2003). Such problem-solving skills training programs share a number of features (see Table 8–11).

Webster-Stratton and colleagues' cognitive-behavioral, social skills, problem-solving, and anger management training program (part of the Incredible Years series) is an example of interventions that address such deficits and skills (Webster-Stratton,

TABLE 8–11	COMMON FEATURES OF PROBLEM-SOLVING SKILLS TRAINING PROGRAMS

- The emphasis is on the thought processes involved in the child's approach to interpersonal situations.
  - In step-by-step approaches, the child is taught to solve interpersonal problems.
  - The child makes statements to himself or herself that direct attention to the aspects of problems that lead to effective solutions.
- Solutions (behaviors) that are selected are important as well.
  - Prosocial behaviors are fostered (e.g., through modeling, direct reinforcement).
- Through games, academic activities, and stories, use is made of structured tasks to teach cognitive problem-solving skills.
  - As treatment progresses, these skills are increasingly applied to real-life situations.
- Therapists usually play an active role. They
  - model cognitive processes by making verbal self-statements,
  - apply a sequence of statements to problems,
  - provide cues to prompt appropriate skills, and
  - apply feedback and praise for correct skills.
- Treatment usually combines several different procedures, including modeling and practice, role playing, and consequences for the skills displayed.

Adapted from Kazdin, 1997.

Reid, & Hammond, 2004). Youngsters, ages 4 to 8, with early-onset conduct problems receive the treatment in small groups. The program addresses interpersonal difficulties typically encountered by young children who have conduct problems. With therapist guidance, the children are taught to cope with such situations through a variety of techniques. Videotaped vignettes of children in stressful situations are viewed and discussed, and acceptable solutions and coping skills are practiced. The intervention is made developmentally appropriate and includes the use of materials such as child-size puppets, coloring books, cartoons, stickers, and prizes to enhance learning. Strategies to insure generalization to other settings are included in the children's sessions. Also, parents and teachers, who are involved through receiving regular letters, are asked to reinforce the targeted skills whenever they notice the child using them at home or at school and to complete weekly good-behavior charts. As compared with a waiting-list group of children, at posttreatment those in the treatment program exhibited significantly less aggressive, noncompliant, and other externalizing problems at home and school, more prosocial behavior with peers, and more positive conflict management strategies. Most of the posttreatment changes were maintained at a 1-year follow-up.

Combined Treatments. Kazdin and his colleagues (Kazdin, 2003; Kazdin, Siegel, & Bass, 1992; Kazdin & Wassel, 2000) have demonstrated the potential benefit of combining parent training and cognitive problem-solving skills training in treating children with conduct problems. A combination of cognitive problem-solving skills training (PSST) and parent management training (PMT), similar to the procedures described before, proved superior to either treatment alone for youngsters 7 years of age and older. (PMT alone is offered to children aged 6 and younger, and PSST alone is offered when the parent cannot or will not participate.) Treatment led to significant improvements in the youngsters' functioning at home, at school, and in the community both immediately after treatment and at a 1-year follow-up, as well as to improvements in parental stress and functioning. In addition, the combined treatments resulted in a greater proportion of the youngsters' falling within normative levels of functioning. These findings along with those of Webster-Stratton, described earlier, suggest the value of interventions that address the multiple influences operating in conduct-disordered youth and their families.

FUNCTIONAL FAMILY THERAPY

The kinds of interventions described as successful with younger conduct-disordered children, such as parent training, may be less successful with adolescents and chronic juvenile delinquents (Kazdin, 1993; McMahon & Wells, 1998). Functional family therapy (FFT) is a treatment program developed by Alexander and his colleagues that integrates behavioral-social learning, cognitive-behavioral, and family systems perspectives (Alexander et al., 1998; Alexander, Holtzworth-Munroe, & Jameson, 1994). The problem behavior of the youngster is assumed to serve a purpose—it is the only way that some of the interpersonal functions of the family can be met. Specific interventions drawn from parent management training are included. Treatment, however, also focuses on the interpersonal processes of the family system. The goals of therapy are to improve the communication skills of families; modify cognitive sets, expectations, attitudes, and affective reactions; and establish new interpretations and meanings of behavior.

Treatment sessions focus on directly altering communication patterns in the family. Therapists employ a variety of techniques: modeling, prompting, shaping and rehearsing effective communication skills, and feedback and reinforcement for positive changes. In addition, contracts are created to establish reciprocal patterns of positive reinforcement. For example, a contract regarding a privilege for a certain family member also specifies that person's responsibilities for securing those privileges and provides bonuses for all parties for compliance with the contract.

The treatment program has been demonstrated to improve the interactions of families, to lower rates of recidivism, and to lower rates of court referrals for siblings of initially referred delinquents (Alexander & Parsons, 1973; Barton et al., 1985; Klein, Alexander, & Parsons, 1977).

COMMUNITY-BASED PROGRAMS

Placing severely conduct-disordered or delinquent youth in institutions that are a part of the criminal justice system is a frequently considered alternative.

Concerns exist regarding the effectiveness of such interventions and the impact of placement in such institutions that exposes youngsters to a subculture in which deviant behaviors may be learned and reinforced. These concerns and the success of some community-based programs (Davidson & Basta, 1989) have led to the search for effective alternatives to institutionalization.

The Teaching Family Model (TFM) developed at Achievement Place is an oft-cited example of a community-based program for delinquent youth and an example of behaviorally based (largely operant) interventions. It is a home-style residential treatment program begun in 1967 by the faculty and students of the Department of Human Development at the University of Kansas (Fixsen, Wolf, & Phillips, 1973; Phillips, 1968). Adolescents who were declared delinquent or dependent neglect cases lived in a house with two trained teaching parents. The youths attended school during the day and also had regular work responsibilities. The academic problems, aggression, and other norm-violating behaviors exhibited by these adolescents were viewed as an expression of failures of past environments to teach appropriate behaviors. Accordingly, these deficits were corrected through modeling, practice, instruction, and feedback. The program centered on a token economy in which points and praise are gained for appropriate behaviors and are lost for inappropriate behaviors. Points could be used to purchase a variety of privileges that were otherwise unavailable. If a resident met a certain level of performance, the right to go on a merit system and thus avoid the point system could be purchased. This process was seen as providing a transition to usual sources of natural reinforcement and feedback, such as praise, status, and satisfaction. The goal was gradually to transfer a youngster who is able to perform adequately on merit to his or her natural home. Teaching parents helped the natural parents or guardians to structure a program to maintain gains made at Achievement Place.

One of the outstanding features of the TFM approach is the extensive research that the program produced (Willner et al., 1978). Numerous single-subject design experiments evaluated the components of the program, thereby suggesting cause-and-effect relationships. Both the program's developers and independent investigators evaluated the effectiveness of TFM (Kirigin et al., 1982; Weinrott, Jones, & Howard, 1982). These evaluations suggested that the TFM approach was more effective than comparison programs while the adolescents were involved in the group home setting. However, once they left this setting, differences disappeared.

Difficulties in transitions back to the youths' own families and long-term effectiveness are common in all interventions with delinquent populations. Given this consideration, the developers of TFM suggested a "long-term supportive family model" in which specially trained foster parents would provide care for a single adolescent into early adulthood (Wolf, Braukmann, & Ramp, 1987). Multidimensional treatment foster care (MTFC) interventions have been developed (Chamberlain & Smith, 2003). Like the TFM approach, many of these programs are based on behavioral-social learning theory, place youth in family-like settings, and intervene with problem behaviors in a natural setting. However, one or perhaps two youngsters, rather than a group of youngsters, are placed in a specialized foster care home. This decision was based on literature suggesting the value of not permitting these youngsters to associate with peers with similar antisocial histories. Foster parents are trained in behavior management skills and are provided with supervision and support by program staff. Explicit behavioral goals are set, and a systematic program including a point system is employed. The youngster's school is also involved. Individual weekly sessions with a therapist that emphasize building skills are also provided for the youngster. During the MTFC stay, staff also work with the youngster's parents or other aftercare personnel to prepare them (and the youngster) for reunification. Research indicates that youngsters in the MTFC program as compared with those in out-of-home *group* programs were less likely to engage in delinquent activities and at 1 year postdischarge had fewer arrests (Chamberlain & Reid, 1998; Chamberlain & Smith, 2003).

Ⓜultisystemic Therapy

Interventions with antisocial youth are likely to require the cooperation of multiple human service agencies. Often the coordination of services is difficult to achieve, and individualizing such efforts to fit the needs of youngsters and their families is even more challenging. Approaches, which are known as individualized care or wraparound services, employ interdisciplinary teams to develop a plan that is both individualized and comprehensive (Borduin, 1994; Burchard & Clark, 1990).

| **Maggie** | **The Need for Multiple Services** |

Maggie is a 13-year-old white seventh-grader who lives with her unemployed, crack-addicted mother, mother's live-in boyfriend, two sisters (ages 10 and 8), and a daughter of one of her mother's crack-addicted friends. Maggie was referred because she was physically violent at home (e.g., she was arrested several times for assaulting family members), at school (e.g., she beat a classmate with a stick and threatened to kill a teacher), and in the neighborhood (e.g., she was arrested twice for assaulting residents of her housing development). Many of Maggie's aggressive actions followed all-night binges by her mother. Maggie, who primarily associates with delinquent peers, was placed in a special class, and was recommended for expulsion from school. The family resides in a high-crime neighborhood, and the only source of income is welfare benefits.

Adapted from Henggeler et al., 1998, p. 23.

Multisystemic therapy (MST; Henggeler & Lee, 2003; Henggeler et al., 1998) is a family- and community-based approach. The youngster is considered to exist in a number of systems, including family, peers, school, neighborhood, and community—a social ecology (Bronfenbrenner, 1989). MST uses treatment strategies derived from family systems therapy and from behavior therapy to treat adolescents with serious difficulties and their families. The approach seeks to preserve the family and to maintain the youths in their homes. MST addresses not only the family system but also skills of the youngster and extrafamilial influences, such as peers, school, and neighborhood. Figure 8–10 is a sample of the results of an initial assessment regarding Maggie, which describes both strengths and needs in the various systems considered by MST. Family sessions, which are conducted in the home and community settings, are flexible and individualized for each family.

A report on a comparison of MST to the usual services offered to serious juvenile offenders and their families illustrates this approach (Henggeler, Melton, & Smith, 1992). These youths were viewed as at imminent risk for out-of-home placement. They averaged 3.5 previous arrests, 54 percent had at least one arrest for a violent crime, and 71 percent had

FIGURE 8–10

FAMILY NAME: Maggie   **DATE OF ADMISSION:**

STRENGTHS	NEEDS

Individual

Athletic, enjoys sports. Attractive and likeable. Average intelligence. Takes care of siblings. Antisocial behavior limited to aggression. Cares deeply for her mother and wants things to be better at home and school. She responds well to praise.	History of school and community aggression. Physically fights mother. Victim of child sexual abuse.

Family

Extended family lives close by and are concerned about M's behavior and home life. Grandmother and aunts willing to do "whatever it takes." Mother is seriously concerned about her drug use and M's school and home behavior. Children's basic needs are met by the mother—she is a survivor. Strong family bond.	Maternal crack cocaine dependence. Poor monitoring. High conflict, crowded living conditions. Low financial resources. Mother feels hopeless about changing her and M's behavior. Mother has minimal parenting skills. Family is socially isolated. Grandmother has cancer.

Peers

Prosocial peers in grandmother's neighborhood.	Aggressive and antisocial peers. Peers have little commitment to school.

School

Athletic programs. A counselor has a close relationship with Maggie and wants her to do well.	Limited resources. Policy of zero tolerance for threatening teachers. View behavior problems as moral flaw. Quick to expel students. Poor relationship to surrounding community. History of conflict with the family.

Neighborhood/Community

Several churches located in the neighborhood.	Drug infested. Criminal subculture. Minimal prosocial outlets.

A sample of results from an initial assessment that describes strengths and needs in the various systems considered by MST.

From Henggeler, Schoenwald, Borduin, Rowland, & Cunningham, 1998.

been incarcerated previously for at least 3 weeks. The findings of this study (illustrated in Figure 8–11) indicate that MST was significantly more effective than the usual services. In addition, families receiving the MST intervention reported increased family cohesion, whereas reported cohesion decreased in the other families. Also, aggression with peers decreased for MST youths but remained the same for the youths receiving usual services. Several other reports by Henggeler and his colleagues indicate the usefulness of MST with a variety of populations, including youth presenting for psychiatric emergencies, and suggest the long-term effectiveness of this approach

(Henggeler & Lee, 2003; Henggeler et al., 1998; Henggeler et al., 2003).

The difficulties in treating adolescents with serious and persistent conduct disorders has led some to suggest a change in the way in which conduct disorders are conceptualized. The suggestion is that the disorder be viewed as "social disability" (Wolf et al., 1987) or as analogous to a chronic physical disease such as diabetes (Kazdin, 1987; Mulvey, Arthur, & Reppucci, 1993). This kind of model suggests not single and short-term treatments, but rather multiple interventions beginning early (Brody et al., 2004; Reid & Eddy, 2002; Reid et al., 2004) and continuing

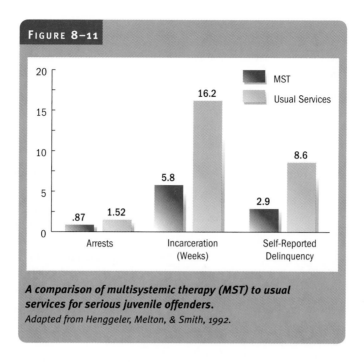

FIGURE 8–11

A comparison of multisystemic therapy (MST) to usual services for serious juvenile offenders.
Adapted from Henggeler, Melton, & Smith, 1992.

throughout the youngster's life—perhaps into early adulthood. The multidetermined nature of antisocial behavior and the potential stability of conduct-disordered behavior certainly suggest early, multifaceted, flexible, and ongoing interventions for some youngsters.

SUMMARY

CLASSIFICATION AND DESCRIPTION

• *Aggression, oppositional behavior, and other antisocial behaviors are among the most common problems of referred youngsters as well as in the general population.*

• *Empirical approaches have consistently identified a syndrome of aggressive, oppositional, antisocial behaviors. This syndrome has been labeled externalizing, undercontrolled, or conduct disorder. Two narrow syndromes within this broad syndrome have been designated as aggressive behavior and rule-breaking behavior.*

• *Other ways of distinguishing among groupings of conduct-disordered behavior, such as age of onset, an overt versus covert distinction, and a further destructive-nondestructive distinction, have also been suggested.*

• *The DSM contains a grouping of disorders that includes Oppositional Defiant Disorder (ODD) and Conduct Disorder (CD), along with Attention-Deficit Hyperactivity Disorder (ADHD).*

• *ODD is described as a pattern of negativistic, hostile, and defiant behavior. CD is described as a repetitive and persistent pattern of behavior that violates both the basic rights of others and societal norms. Two subtypes, childhood-onset and adolescent-onset, are indicated.*

• *There are gender differences in prevalence, developmental course, and etiological influences of conduct problems. In part, such differences may be related to how aggression is expressed. The concept of relational aggression has contributed to understanding gender differences.*

• *Delinquency is primarily a legal term rather than a psychological term. Some behaviors described as delinquent are quite common.*

A TRIO OF CONDUCT-RELATED BEHAVIORS: VIOLENCE, BULLYING, SUBSTANCE USE

• *There is concern regarding high rates of violent behavior. This has led to action on multiple fronts, particularly in schools.*

- It is important to address bullying since bullying may be part of a more general antisocial developmental pattern. The victims of bullying can also be considered to be at considerable risk.

- The use of alcohol and drugs may be a part of a pattern of antisocial and rule-breaking behavior. Substance dependence and substance abuse are the DSM diagnoses related to substance use problems. The high rate of substance use by young people is a widespread concern. A variety of theories, models, and risk factors have been suggested to explain substance use.

EPIDEMIOLOGY

- Conduct problems are one of the most frequent reasons for referral to child and adolescent treatment services.

- Conduct disorder and oppositional defiant disorder are more commonly diagnosed in boys, but are also a common diagnosis for girls in clinical settings.

- Conduct-disordered behavior that is less serious and does not persist is common in adolescence.

- Contextual factors such as poverty and the stress of high-crime neighborhoods are thought to increase the risk for conduct problems.

- An important question is whether oppositional defiant disorder is a precursor of conduct disorder.

- Youngsters who receive the diagnoses ODD or CD are likely to experience other difficulties. There is a high rate of co-occurrence of ODD/CD with ADHD. ADHD appears to be a risk factor for the other two disorders.

DEVELOPMENTAL COURSE

- An important aspect of conduct problems is their reported stability over time. However, the issue of stability is a complex one.

- Age of onset is an important aspect of the development of conduct problems. A childhood-onset or life-course persistent pathway is of great concern. An adolescent-onset path is the more common, and antisocial behavior among such youngsters may be less likely to persist beyond adolescence.

- Conduct-disordered behavior has been conceptualized in terms of developmental progressions or paths. Pathways characterized by overt, covert, and authority conflict behaviors have been described.

ETIOLOGY

- Conduct problems likely develop through a complex interaction of influences.

- Influences from the socioeconomic context, such as poverty, neighborhood disadvantage, and related stress, affect the development of conduct-disordered behavior.

- Aggression and other conduct-disordered behavior can be learned through imitation and the consequences that such behavior receives.

- Family variables also are an important influence on the development of conduct-disordered behavior. Important mechanisms through which family influence occurs are parental involvement and parenting practices. The work of Patterson and his colleagues has contributed to our knowledge in this area.

- The impact of the parents' own psychological difficulties, marital discord, and child maltreatment are also noted.

- Peer relations both contribute to and are affected by conduct problems. Aggressive youngsters are often rejected by their peers with both immediate and long-term consequences. However, these youngsters may not be without friends and the influence of bad companions is a concern.

- Cognitive-emotional characteristics of the youngster, such as social information-processing skills and interpersonal problem-solving skills, are also thought to contribute to the development and persistence of conduct-disordered behavior.

- Biological influences, such as genetic, neurophysiological, and neuropsychological influences, may also play a role.

ASSESSMENT

- Assessment of conduct problems is likely to be complex and multifaceted. Interviews, behavioral rating scales, and behavioral observations are among the methods employed.

TREATMENT

- Support for the use of pharmacological interventions is best for the use of stimulants with those ODD/CD youngsters who also exhibit symptoms of ADHD.

- Parent training is among the most successful approaches. Interventions employing cognitive problem-solving skills training focus more specifically on aspects of the youngster's functioning.

Treatment programs that combine these approaches and address multiple influences have been developed.

- *Functional Family Therapy integrates cognitive-behavioral and family systems approaches to work with youth and their families.*

- *Community-based programs such as the Teaching Family Model and Multidimensional Treatment Foster Care are among the approaches to working with youthful offenders. Multisystemic Therapy is a systems-based intervention that attempts to keep the youngsters in their homes. It addresses the child and various systems such as family, peers, school, neighborhood, and community.*

KEY TERMS

aggressive behavior syndrome *(p. 195)*

rule-breaking behavior syndrome *(p. 195)*

overt conduct problems *(p. 196)*

covert conduct problems *(p. 196)*

destructive-nondistructive conduct problems *(p. 196)*

antisocial personality disorder *(p. 197)*

psychopathy *(p. 197)*

callous/unemotional traits *(p. 197)*

oppositional defiant disorder *(p. 199)*

conduct disorder *(p. 200)*

relational aggression *(p. 202)*

delinquency *(p. 202)*

violence *(p. 202)*

bullying *(p. 205)*

illicit drugs *(p. 206)*

licit drugs *(p. 206)*

substance dependence *(p. 206)*

substance abuse *(p. 207)*

childhood-onset developmental pattern *(p. 215)*

adolescent-onset developmental pattern *(p. 216)*

coercion *(p. 220)*

negative reinforcement *(p. 220)*

reinforcement trap *(p. 220)*

discipline *(p. 220)*

monitoring *(p. 221)*

reactive aggression *(p. 225)*

proactive aggression *(p. 225)*

behavioral inhibition system *(p. 227)*

behavioral activation system *(p. 227)*

fight/flight system *(p. 227)*

parent training *(p. 230)*

token economy *(p. 234)*

CHAPTER 9

Attention-Deficit Hyperactivity Disorder

[Cory's] mother, Mrs. Conner, called the therapist's office in tears. . . . [Cory's] teacher, Ms. Hall, had recommended that [he] be immediately placed on Ritalin, as his hyperactivity was disturbing the class. . . . Mrs. Conner reported that [Cory] was an active child who was always running around the house and crashing into the furniture. She stated that he had walked early, at ten months, and had been keeping her running ever since. . . .

Mr. Conner . . . believed that [Cory] was being allowed to disrupt class and the teachers just didn't punish him. . . . He went on to report that if he had acted the way [Cory] was acting in school he would have "gotten a beating." . . .

[Cory] reported that he knew his parents and his teacher were mad at him for being "so bad." (Morgan, 1999, pp. 6–8)

The presenting problems for children who receive the diagnosis of attention-deficit hyperactivity disorder (ADHD) are recognized in both dimensional and categorical classifications of behavioral disorders. Only a few disturbances of

youth have garnered as much public interest and have been so surrounded by controversy as ADHD. Most of the general public has at least passing knowledge of the disorder, which is widely referred to as "hyperactivity" or "attention deficit disorder," terms that reflect the changing conceptualizations of the disorder. Controversy about ADHD especially has focused on both its nature and the pharmacological treatment that was widely introduced in the late 1960s.

Evolving Ideas about ADHD

What we now refer to as ADHD has traveled a winding path of definitions (Barkley, 2003; Milich, Balentine, & Lynam, 2001). One early account of the disorder was given by the English physician George Still, who described a group of boys with a "defect in moral control" as inattentive, impulsive, overactive, lawless, and aggressive, among other things. In the United States, epidemics of encephalitis in 1917–1918 aroused interest in patients who suffered this brain infection and who were left with similar attributes. A comparable clinical picture also was noted in children who had suffered head injury, birth trauma, and exposure to infections and toxins.

By the late 1950s, emphasis was given to overactivity or motor restlessness in these children, and the terms *hyperkinesis*, *hyperkinetic syndrome*, and *hyperactive child syndrome* were variously applied. In time, hyperactivity was downgraded in importance, and attention deficits took center stage. The shift was reflected in the DSM-III (1980), which recognized attention deficit disorder (ADD) either *with* hyperactivity or *without* hyperactivity.

More change was yet to come. In the DSM-III-R (1987), the disorder was relabeled Attention Deficit Hyperactivity Disorder. Children were identified on the basis of displaying 8 of 14 behaviors, which could be different mixes of inattention, hyperactivity, and impulsivity. That is, the disorder was viewed as unidimensional, so that any mix of symptoms met the criteria. Nevertheless, the relationship of these three primary features of ADHD was unsettled. Were they best viewed as part of a single dimension? Or as co-occurring but independent of each other? Might two of them be alike but different from the third? In fact, the unidimensional view fell by the wayside in the DSM when factor analytic research designed to better understand the nature of ADHD suggested that it consists of two factors: inattention and hyperactivity-impulsivity.

DSM Classification and Diagnosis

This finding became the basis of the present conceptualization, first presented in the DSM-IV (1994) and labeled Attention-Deficit/Hyperactivity Disorder. The two factors of inattention and hyperactivity-impulsivity compose three subtypes: Predominantly Inattentive Type (ADHD-I), Predominantly Hyperactive-Impulsive Type (ADHD-HI), and a Combined Type (ADHD-C). The major symptoms and criteria for the subtypes of ADHD appear in Table 9–1. Diagnosis of ADHD demands the presence of some symptoms before age 7, and display of symptoms for at least 6 months. Because all the criterion behaviors are observed to some degree in normal children and may vary with developmental level, diagnosis is given only when symptoms are at odds with developmental level. There also must be clear evidence of impaired social, academic, or occupational functioning. In addition, symptoms must be pervasive; that is, they must occur in at least two settings (e.g., home and school).

TABLE 9–1	THE DSM SYMPTOMS OF ATTENTION-DEFICIT/ HYPERACTIVITY DISORDER

A. Symptoms of Inattention

Fails to attend to details or makes careless mistakes in schoolwork or other activities.
Has difficulty in sustaining attention.
Does not seem to listen when spoken to.
✓Does not follow through on instructions or duties.
✓Has difficulty organizing tasks and activities.
Avoids, dislikes tasks requiring sustained mental effort.
✓Often loses things necessary for tasks or activities.
Is distracted by extraneous stimuli.
✓Is forgetful in daily activities.

B. Symptoms of Hyperactivity-Impulsivity

Hyperactivity

Fidgets with hands or feet or squirms.
✓Leaves seat inappropriately.
Runs about or climbs inappropriately (in adolescents or adults, may only be feelings of restlessness).
Has difficulty playing quietly or in quiet activities.
Is often "on the go" as if "driven by a motor."
Talks incessantly.

Impulsivity

Blurts out answers before questions are completed.
✓Has difficulty awaiting turn.
✓Interrupts or intrudes on others.

Requirements for Diagnosis

ADHD Predominantly Inattentive Type: Six or more symptoms of A
ADHD Predominantly Hyperactive-Impulsive Type: Six or more symptoms of B
ADHD Combined Type: Six or more symptoms of both A and B

From American Psychiatric Association, 2000.

Some concern has been expressed about this conceptualization of attention-deficit hyperactivity disorder. The criterion of pervasiveness raises the question of whether cases with relatively mild symptoms go unidentified (August & Garfinkel, 1993). Then, too, although the age criterion appears appropriate for most cases of ADHD, it may apply less well to the inattentive subtype (Willoughby et al., 2000). As we will see, other issues about the inattentive subtype have also been raised. First, though, we discuss the core features of ADHD and the difficulties that are secondarily associated with the disorder. We use the general label attention-deficit hyperactivity disorder (ADHD) to refer to youth diagnosed with the disorder.

Description: Core Features

INATTENTION

Adults who come into contact with children with ADHD report various signs of inattention. These children do not stick to a task but skip rapidly from one activity to another, do not attend to what is said to them, are easily distracted, daydream, or lose things. One baffling aspect of adult reports is that the children appear as sometimes unable to focus and concentrate but at other times as able to sit for hours drawing or building with blocks. Attention is situational, appearing normal when the child is interested or otherwise motivated but problematic when the task is boring, routine, or repetitious.

Although the reports of adults provide reasonably good global descriptions of ADHD, formal observation and controlled research have been conducted to validate and elucidate attention deficits. Children and adolescents with ADHD do pay less attention to their work than children with learning disabilities or normal controls (Barkley, 1998). In the laboratory, children with ADHD do less well than control children on many tasks that demand attention.

However, attention is a complex ability that has been conceptualized in different ways and linked to various psychopathologies and brain structures or systems (Anderson et al., 2001). Numerous attention abilities are recognized, such as the ability to focus on select stimuli, maintain focus, deal simultaneously with more than one stimulus, and efficiently shift from one stimulus to another. Such abilities are viewed as developing over different time frames prior to adulthood and as playing vital roles in information processing. A distinction is often made between more automatic, early-developing attention and that which develops later and is more voluntary and immersed in higher order cognition.

One of the areas examined regarding ADHD is selective attention. This refers to the ability to focus on relevant environmental stimuli, to not be distracted by irrelevant stimuli. Some studies indicate that irrelevant stimuli do distract children with ADHD (Brodeur & Pond, 2001; Leung & Connolly, 1996; Lorch et al., 2000). Nevertheless, research findings are mixed. It appears that distraction is more likely when the tasks are boring or difficult, or when the irrelevant stimuli are novel, salient, or embedded in the task (Douglas, 1983).

Sustained attention (vigilance)—paying attention to a task over a period of time—also has been examined. One of the ways in which it has been evaluated is through continuous performance tests (CPTs). Although several versions exist, the fundamental task is for the person to push a button to identify a target stimulus over trials, such as a letter when it appears in a series of letters projected onto a screen (e.g., *t* must be identified when it follows *m*). Errors can be made by not reacting to the target (which shows inattention or lack of vigilance) and by reacting to nontarget stimuli (which may show impulsivity or failed inhibition). Children with ADHD often make more of both errors and are slower in responding than normal children and children with other diagnoses (Epstein et al., 2003; Losier, McGrath, & Klein, 1996; Taylor, 1995). However, such sustained attention deficits do not specifically define ADHD, because they often occur in other behavioral disorders (Swaab-Barneveld et al., 2000). Also, a true deficit in sustained attention would lead to a worsening of performance as the length of the task increases, a condition that only sometimes holds for ADHD.

What can be made of these findings? Although deficits in selective attention are recognized, they are generally considered less central than in sustained attention. Moreover, the rather complex findings, combined with other research, have led many investigators to conclude that although inattention is problematic something else is central in ADHD (Huang-Pollock & Nigg, 2003; Slusarek et al., 2001; Taylor, 1995). A fundamental problem may be one of more general control and self-regulation, which includes the control and allotment of attention.

HYPERACTIVITY AND IMPULSIVITY

Hyperactivity. Children with ADHD are described as always on the run, restless, fidgety, and unable to sit still. These children squirm, wiggle, and tap their fingers (Greenhill, 1991; Whalen, 1989). All too often they have minor mishaps, such as spilling drinks and knocking over objects, as well as more serious accidents that result in bodily harm. The quality of motion may appear excessively energetic, haphazard, disorganized, and lacking in goals. Youth with hyperactivity seem to have difficulty in regulating their actions to suit the demands of the particular situation.

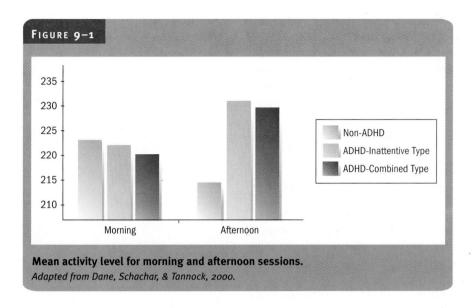

FIGURE 9-1

Mean activity level for morning and afternoon sessions.
Adapted from Dane, Schachar, & Tannock, 2000.

Much of the information about activity problems comes from parent and teacher reports. More objective assessment can be made with direct observations and with small devices worn by the child that measure movement. Both kinds of measures indicate the excessive movement of children with ADHD, as well as variation across youngsters and situations. In one study, a device was used to monitor motor activity during morning and afternoon sessions (Dane, Schachar, & Tannock, 2000). Differences existed between non-ADHD and ADHD youngsters only in the afternoon, when non-ADHD youngsters became less active and ADHD youngsters became more active (Figure 9–1). Another study that recorded movement continuously for one week showed that boys with hyperactivity were more active than controls during school reading and mathematics but not physical education and lunch/recess (Porrino et al., 1983). In general, motor excess and restlessness are more likely to occur in highly structured situations that demand children to sit still and regulate their behavior in the face of little reinforcement (Dane et al., 2000; Greenhill, 1991).

Impulsivity. The essence of impulsivity is a deficiency in inhibiting behavior, holding back, or controlling behavior, which appears as "acting without thinking." The child may interrupt others, cut in line in front of others, or heedlessly engage in dangerous behaviors. Activities that require patience or restraint are not well accomplished. Impulsivity often leads others to judge the child as careless, irresponsible, immature, lazy, or rude (Barkley, 1998).

In the laboratory, impulsivity has been assessed in different ways. Variations of the stop-signal task

are widely used (Nigg, 2001). For example, stimuli—say the letter X and the letter O—are presented on a screen, and the child is told to press one of two keys depending on which stimulus is presented. Key presses are to be withheld on a minority of trials when a special signal (a tone) comes on, so that the child must sometimes rapidly inhibit (stop) the response. Deficits on the stop-signal task have been shown in several studies with ADHD children (Oosterlaan, Logan, & Sergeant, 1998). This finding, in conjunction with other research, makes clear that inhibition of motor responses is an important aspect of attention-deficit hyperactivity disorder.

Description: Secondary Features

In addition to the core problems of ADHD, youth with the disorder experience more than their share of difficulties in diverse areas of functioning that are important both clinically and theoretically. These findings may largely apply to children displaying what is now considered the combined subtype of ADHD, and the degree to which they apply to those exhibiting only inattention requires further investigation.

MOTOR PROBLEMS

Motor incoordination may affect as many as 60 percent of children with ADHD, a figure that exceeds that for normal children (Barkley, 2003). Various tests indicate deficits in fine motor coordination, motor timing, and the execution of sequences of complex motor behavior. Children with ADHD appear especially affected when the tasks involve complex movement and sequencing, which implicates higher order control processes such as organization and regulation of behavior (Kalff et al., 2003).

INTELLIGENCE, LEARNING DISABILITIES, ACADEMIC DEFICITS

As a group, children with ADHD perform somewhat lower on intelligence tests than normal control groups, but they display a range of general intelligence, including above average. An association with learning disabilities is established. Impairments occur in reading, mathematics, and other academic areas that at least in some cases are not due to lowered intelligence.

Academic failure is striking among youth with ADHD. Preacademic skill deficits have been shown in preschoolers with ADHD (DuPaul et al., 2001), and academic problems may be obvious in the first few years of school (Lahey et al., 1998). Failure is evidenced by achievement test scores, school grades, being held back in grade, and placement in special education classes. As many as 30 percent of children may repeat a grade, and 30 to 40 percent may experience at least one special education placement (Barkley, 1998). Moreover, from 10 to 35 percent may fail to graduate high school. Failure to meet the requirements of the classroom has been shown in several countries.

COGNITION: EXECUTIVE DYSFUNCTION

Children with attention-deficit hyperactivity disorder exhibit deficits on numerous experimental and neuropsychological tasks that are interpreted as difficulties with executive functions (Hinshaw et al., 2002; Nigg et al., 2002; Pennington & Ozonoff, 1996). Executive functions refer to several cognitive processes necessary for goal-directed behavior (Clark, Prior, & Kinsella, 2002). Executive functions are involved in planning and organizing actions and in self-regulation. Among other processes, they include working memory, verbal self-regulation, self-monitoring, inhibition of behavior, regulation of emotion, and motor control. These higher order processes are frequently associated with the brain's frontal lobe and its connections.

ADAPTIVE FUNCTIONING

Relative to their level of general intelligence, children with ADHD have been shown to have deficiencies in many domains of everyday adaptive behavior, including communication and social skills. Deficits in self-care and independence are sometimes at the level that would be expected with much greater cognitive impairment (Hinshaw, 1998). Many of the children engage in behavior more immature than what their abilities seem to warrant, and greater monitoring by adults is required than what might otherwise be anticipated.

A failure to acquire various kinds of skills may underlie adaptive disability, but a failure to *perform* learned skills might well be crucial (Barkley et al., 2002). Indeed, because ADHD involves deficits in executive functions that aid in the performance of goal-directed behavior, ADHD might best be seen as a disorder of "doing" rather than of "knowing" (Clark, Prior, & Kinsella, 2002).

SOCIAL BEHAVIOR AND RELATIONSHIPS

Social difficulties, which are reported in high percentages of cases of ADHD, may be an important reason for adults to seek professional help for the child. How do many children with ADHD actually behave that so upsets others? To begin with, they have high social impact (Whalen & Henker, 1985; 1998). They are talkative and tend to be louder, faster, and more forceful than peers. Their vigor, intensity, and emotionality are out of keeping with the social situation and the needs of others. Their behavior is often bothersome, intractable, disruptive, noncompliant, and disagreeable. In some instances, annoying actions may seem unintentional or even reflective of a desire to be helpful. Nonetheless, some of the children are highly aggressive.

Various explanations have been offered for these social behaviors. The youngsters may only inadequately process social-emotional cues (Cadesky, Mota, & Schachar, 2000). Or they may know what is appropriate but are unable to enact the proper behavior, especially when excited or irritated. They sometimes may have social goals that could be expected to create problems; for example, they may prefer fun and risk trouble at the expense of breaking rules (Melnick & Hinshaw, 1996). Relevant too is that children with ADHD-C have a positive bias regarding their social competence, behavioral conduct, and academic competence (Gerdes, Hoza, & Pelham, 2003; Hoza et al., 2004). In general, they

Although roughhouse play is a part of typical childhood activities, the youngster with ADHD often displays excessively energetic and undercontrolled behavior.
(Jennie Woodcock/Corbis)

appear to lack awareness of their negative impact on others, rate their relationships as overly positive, and overestimate the degree to which they are liked and accepted.

Peer and Teacher Relations. Given their profile of social behaviors, it is not surprising that children with ADHD have trouble making and keeping friends; they frequently are disliked and rejected by peers. Whereas these negative reactions apply more strongly to children who are impulsive and hyperactive, those with only attention problems tend to be ignored or neglected (Hinshaw, 1998). Teacher reaction to ADHD is also problematic. For example, in one study, teachers of young children associated all types of ADHD with less cooperation and other positive behaviors, and hyperactivity-impulsivity with disruptive and less self-controlled behaviors (Lahey et al., 1998). Perhaps it is unsurprising that teacher behavior tends to be directive and controlling.

Family Relations. ADHD also takes a toll on family interaction and well-being. Parents are excessively negative, directive, and intrusive (Barkley, 2003). This appears especially true for mothers, and negative exchanges may occur as early as the child's preschool years. Much of this interaction appears to stem from the child's behavior, with conflicts strongly associated with the child's being oppositional. In time, negative interactions become reciprocal. Father-child exchanges are less problematic but

still affected, and sibling-child interactions are characterized by high conflict.

Broader family malfunctioning associated with ADHD undoubtedly plays a role in child-parent relationships. Family difficulties include parenting stress; lowered sense of parenting competence; decreased contact with extended family; increased alcohol use; and increased marital conflict, separation, and divorce (Barkley, 2003). This profile is especially associated with the child's being oppositional or displaying conduct problems. The parents themselves are at genetic risk for a variety of problems, including the symptoms of ADHD. In addition, of course, family members influence each other in complex ways.

SLEEP AND ACCIDENT RISK

It is not unusual for parents to report sleep problems in children with ADHD. It appears that prevalence of these difficulties in ADHD is higher than in non-clinic children but not higher than in some clinic populations (Corkum et al., 1999). The problems include falling asleep, difficulties with arising, and involuntary movements during sleep (e.g., teeth grinding). Several reasons are suggested for the difficulties. For example, when ADHD children are treated with stimulant medication too close to bedtime, sleep onset may be hindered. In addition, behavioral difficulties and the anxiety that is sometimes associated with ADHD may interfere with sleep.

Relatively well documented is that children with ADHD suffer more accidental injury. For example, Szatmari and colleagues (1989) found that 7 percent suffered an accidental poisoning and that 23 percent had bone fractures, compared with 3 percent and 15 percent in controls. Several studies show that accidental poisoning is two to three times more likely in children with ADHD (Barkley, 2003).

Older youth with ADHD are at greater risk for automobile accidents, driving offenses such as speeding, and drinking and driving. Such outcomes were found for young adults who had scored high on ADHD symptoms during adolescence (Woodward, Fergusson, & Horwood, 2000). The findings were largely accounted for by the participants' being male, having conduct problems, and spending much time driving but with relatively little driving experience. However, after these influences were accounted for, inattention was still linked to serious motor accidents and possibly to risky driving behavior. In general, inattention and hyperactivity-impulsivity may play a direct or an indirect role in putting youth at risk for injury and accidents.

DSM Subtypes

We have seen that the DSM recognizes three subtypes of ADHD: Predominantly Inattentive (ADHD-I), Predominantly Hyperactive-Impulsive (ADHD-HI), and the combination of these symptoms (ADHD-C). Many investigations, including studies in different countries, generally validate and support the usefulness of these subtypes (Gadow et al., 2000; Gomez et al., 1999; Graetz et al., 2001; Hudziak et al., 1998; Lahey et al., 1994). Symptoms tend to cluster according to these types, and other characteristics also differentiate the three subgroups. Nonetheless, the subtypes have not been equally studied and important questions are raised about them.

Interest in the inattentive subtype (ADHD-I) has existed for many years. Recall, if you will, that the DSM had once recognized a category of attention deficit disorder without hyperactivity. In contrast, research on ADHD-HI is relatively scant. It is the combined subtype (ADHD-C) that most often has been clinically described and investigated. The following case description illustrates ADHD-C, exhibited in a child of almost 7 years of age. The presence of inattention, hyperactivity, and impulsivity are obvious.

Jimmy | **Combined Subtype of ADHD**

Jimmy was not seen as a "bad" child by his parents; he was not ill tempered, oppositional, or aggressive. But he was in constant motion, and often wandered off, sometimes getting into dangerous situations such as running into the road without looking and putting keys in an electric socket. Jimmy frequently did not follow through on his parents' requests, although this did not appear to be deliberate. Rather it seemed that Jimmy got sidetracked by things he found more interesting. He had constantly to be reminded to stay on task. His parents adopted an active style of dealing with him—monitoring him, reminding him, using immediate reinforcement and punishment.

When Jimmy was enrolled in preschool, his inattentive, overactive, and impulsive behaviors led his parents to withdraw him from one program and his being asked to leave a second program. Among the difficulties were talking out of turn, dropping out of group activities, distracting others, and engaging in too much imaginative play. Similar kinds of behaviors were reported in kindergarten, where he had problems focusing attention, being too active, and being unable to work independently. An evaluation at that time showed Jimmy to have high average intelligence but achieving at somewhat lower levels.

By first grade, Jimmy's impulsivity began to interfere with his social relationships. He was described as immature and silly. His peers complained of his bothering them, grabbing them, and pulling them, and although Jimmy was friendly he was unable to maintain friendships. His behavior, more acceptable at early ages, was no longer accepted by peers. Teachers too had complaints. The coach noted an inability to participate in organized sports and that Jimmy was off-task and silly. In the classroom he failed to follow instructions, often did not complete work in time, and disrupted others by constant activity and noise making.

From Hathaway, Dooling-Litfin, & Edwards, 1998, pp. 313–316.

The description of Jimmy's behavior can be compared to depictions of the inattentive subtype of ADHD. It is important to note that research with inattentive children has sometimes found a factor referred to as sluggish cognitive tempo. Children displaying a sluggish cognitive tempo tend to be lethargic, daydreamy, confused, and more socially withdrawn (Hartman et al., 2004; Milich et al., 2001). Some researchers suggest that sluggish cognitive tempo may best differentiate the combined and the inattention subgroups, even though the DSM does not include it on its symptoms list. Sluggish cognitive tempo presents a very different clinical picture than that of the restless, on-the-go, and disruptive behaviors of the child with hyperactive and impulsive behaviors. The contrast between the inattentive subtype and ADHD-C is captured in the following portrayal of Tim.

Tim	**Predominantly Inattentive Subtype of ADHD**

Tim was a quiet, somewhat introverted child who easily faded into the crowd. His early development was unremarkable, and he was not a behavior problem.

In elementary school, Tim's behavior and academic performance were adequate. But he did not volunteer information, often appeared in a daze, and often did not catch what teachers said when they called upon him. He could read but had difficulty staying with a train of thought, which created comprehension problems. Approaching third grade, Tim began to have increased difficulties in school, including completing his work on time, but he was not found eligible for special services. Teachers commented on his daydreaming, attention lapses, poor focusing, and being "spacey." His grades became less consistent, ranging from Bs to Ds. Tim's attention problems and poor study habits took a larger toll in high school, and academic failures resulted in a transfer to vocational education.

Despite academic problems, Tim made and kept friends, although he was reserved and indifferent to organized recreational activities. His academic performance was a source of strain and conflict with his mother, who reported that Tim was often irritable, talked back, and blamed others for his mistakes. He was, however, compliant in other ways. Based on assessment when he was almost eighteen years of age, Tim was described as presumably of average intelligence, with a chronic history of inattentiveness, distractibility, and underachievement.

From Hathaway, Dooling-Litfin, & Edwards, 1998, pp. 329–330.

For subtypes of a disorder to be valid, they must be different not only in symptoms but also in other important ways. Children with ADHD-I are thought to be distinct from ADHD-C in several ways (Faraone et al., 1998; Milich et al., 2001). Age of onset appears to be later, and girls with ADHD are more likely to be diagnosed with the inattentive subtype than other subtypes (Zalecki & Hinshaw, 2004). Social problems are differentially exhibited. ADHD-I children appear more passive and shy; they engage in less fighting and aggression. ADHD-I also is less associated with externalizing disorders and perhaps more strongly linked with internalizing symptoms. Unsurprising then, inattentive children are less rejected by their peers. In addition, some differences may exist in academic achievement, although the findings are inconsistent. Limited evidence also exists for differences in brain functioning (evoked potentials) between the inattentive and combined groups (Smith, Johnstone, & Barry, 2003).

Although these differences are viewed as demonstrating that ADHD-I is a valid subtype of ADHD, the matter is not completely settled. Some investigators point out that findings are mixed at best for several domains of functioning. With some exceptions, few differences between the groups have been found on neuropsychological testing and most laboratory studies of inattention and impulsivity (Hinshaw, 2001; Lahey, 2001; Nigg et al., 2002; Pelham, 2001). Moreover, some suggest that inattention as characterized by sluggish, dreamy behavior might represent a unique disorder, not a subtype of ADHD at all (Milich et al., 2001). Barkley (2003) has adopted this position, proposing that central to the disorder are deficits in selective attention and slow cognitive processing, in contrast to the inability to inhibit behavior that characterizes hyperactivity-impulsivity. Clearly, there is a need for continuing research on the nature of attention-deficit hyperactivity disorder and its subtypes.

ADHD and Co-Occurring Disorders

A remarkable fact about ADHD, especially ADHD-C, is the degree to which it coexists with other disorders. As is usually the case, rates of co-occurrence vary considerably depending on the samples, measures, the specific disorders, and the like. Rates are higher in clinic than in community samples, with more of the referred youngsters likely than not to have another disorder (Costin et al., 2002) and a sizable number exhibiting two or more disorders. Comorbidity generally is related to greater impairment and developmental risk.

LEARNING DISORDERS

The range of 15 to 40 percent co-occurrence has been suggested for ADHD and specific learning disabilities, including reading disorders (Rucklidge & Tannock, 2002; Schachar & Tannock, 2002).

Although the developmental paths between ADHD and learning disorders—and poor academic performance—are not definitively determined, some evidence bears on this issue. ADHD, and especially inattention, adversely affects later reading ability (McGee et al., 2002). However, it also appears that early reading problems can lead to attentional difficulties. It has been observed that after children make reading errors they experience moments of inattention—which might function as distractions that interfere with the further acquisition of reading.

ADHD, learning problems, and academic outcomes probably are linked in more than one way. For instance, in a study of 7- to 16-year-olds, support was found for a dual pathway from ADHD to academic achievement (Rapport, Scanlon, & Denney, 1999). On the one hand, ADHD led to cognitive deficits (inattention and memory problems) and thence to poor scholastic achievement. On the other hand, ADHD and associated conduct problems led to poor classroom performance and thence to poor scholastic achievement. Thus, both cognitive deficits and behavioral misconduct appeared to mediate the association of ADHD and academic achievement.

EXTERNALIZING DISORDERS

Children with ADHD are frequently reported as noncompliant, oppositional, annoying, and argumentative—behaviors that fall into the DSM category of Oppositional Defiant Disorder (ODD). Furthermore, ODD may lead to Conduct Disorder (CD), which involves aggression, deceit, and violations of rules. It is estimated that between 35 and 70 percent of children with ADHD develop ODD and that between 30 and 50 percent develop CD (Johnston & Ohan, 1999). Given the diagnosis of either ADHD or CD, children are over ten times more likely to get the second diagnosis than if they did not have the first diagnosis (Barkley, 2003).

The similarity of ADHD, ODD, and CD is reflected in their being considered together in the DSM as Attention-Deficit and Disruptive Behavior Disorders. Given this similarity and their high co-occurrence, it is reasonable to ask: Are these disorders actually only one common disorder? Researchers have considered this issue and answered "no" (Hinshaw & Lee, 2003; Nadder et al., 2001). ADHD and conduct disorders share genetic and family risk factors (Barkley, 2003). However, epidemiologic and clinic studies in different countries indicate that the disorders have distinct symptom clusters and other distinct features (e.g., Leung et al., 1996; Pillow et al., 1998; Waschbusch, 2002). ADHD generally is more strongly associated with cognitive impairment and neurodevelopmental abnormalities. Conduct problems are more strongly related to adverse family factors and psychosocial disadvantage (Waschbusch, 2002).

Much research has been devoted to studying the co-occurrence of ADHD symptoms and conduct/oppositional symptoms in clinic and nonreferred groups. Important differences exist in children having only ADHD, only oppositional/conduct problems, or the combination of these. Children displaying the combination appear more disturbed and impaired, both in ADHD symptoms and conduct problems (Barkley, 1998; Jensen, Martin, & Cantwell, 1997; Waschbusch, 2002). This general finding holds for preschoolers as well (Gadow & Nolan, 2002). Importantly, behavioral difficulties appear earlier in these children's lives and problems are likely to persist. Other differences are noteworthy. Comorbid ADHD is generally more strongly related to coercive child-parent interactions, parental symptomatology and substance abuse, and disadvantaged social class (e.g., Hinshaw & Lee, 2003; Waschbusch, 2002).

The several differences between ADHD and comorbid ADHD have led to the suggestion that the comorbid condition may be a valid subcategory of ADHD (Jensen, et al., 1997). At the same time, the effects of the double set of problems appear simply to add—rather than to act in more complex ways—a finding that argues for a simple view of co-occurrence (Waschbusch, 2002). What is clear is that knowing whether a child with ADHD also has conduct problems tells us much about the child.

INTERNALIZING DISORDERS

The overlap of ADHD and obsessive-compulsive disorder—although estimated as high as 30 percent—has hardly been studied relative to anxiety and mood disorders (Geller et al., 2002).

It is estimated that perhaps 25 to 30 percent of youth with ADHD, either in clinic or in community samples, have anxiety disorders (Barkley, 2003; Jensen et al., 1997; Manassis, Tannock, & Barbosa, 2000). These children reportedly are less hyperactive and impulsive than ordinarily found in ADHD, and they may display fewer conduct problems. Limited data suggest that ADHD plus anxiety, compared to either disorder alone, is associated with some differences in performance on cognitive tasks and differential response to interventions (Manassis et al., 2000). The comorbid condition also shows greater persistence of ADHD symptoms, but little risk for anxiety in adolescence and early adulthood.

The co-occurrence of ADHD and depressive disorders or symptoms is found at varying rates in children and adolescents and in clinic and community samples (Barkley, 2003; Biederman, Faraone, Mick et al., 1996). Mild depressive symptoms, major depression, and bipolar disorder are all observed. Perhaps 25 to 30 percent of ADHD cases have major depression, and the link has been found in adolescents. It is interesting that the overly positive perception that some children with ADHD have of their own competence appears to be absent in the presence of co-occurring depression (Hoza et al., 2004).

The overlap between ADHD and bipolar disorder may range from 10 to 20 percent (Barkley, 2003). Reportedly, the diagnosis of childhood bipolar disorder substantially increases the risk for ADHD rather than the other way around. Moreover, in the presence of the two conditions bipolar disorder has an earlier onset than when it appears alone.

The reasons for the association of ADHD with internalizing symptoms are unclear (Barkley, 1998, 2003). Personal stress as well as family stress and adversity seem to have some influence. Family risk studies provide possible support for genetic influence on comorbidity. To take an example, family risk for ADHD or depression increases risk among family members for the other disorder. However, much more investigation is needed in this area. It is quite possible that the factors underlying co-occurrence vary somewhat, depending on the internalizing symptoms or disorders involved.

Epidemiology

The prevalence of ADHD varies a good deal, depending on the criteria employed, age, gender, informants, country, and other variables. Overall prevalence estimates in U.S. school-age children vary from 3 to 7 percent (American Psychiatric Association, 2000). When parents or teachers provide data in community studies, prevalence of symptoms can reach over 20 percent (Nolan, Gadow, & Sprafkin, 2001). Community studies are typically based solely on parents' or teachers' ratings of symptoms, whereas additional criteria, such as age of onset and pervasiveness of symptoms, are employed for clinical diagnosis.

In general, less is known about prevalence in the preschool and adolescent years than in childhood. Age is related to diagnosed ADHD, however: there is a decline from childhood to adolescence. The disorder may indeed be less common in adolescence, but it is also possible that diagnostic items are a poor fit with adolescent behavior (e.g., "fidgets," "squirms"), which could result in fewer cases being diagnosed (Barkley, 2003).

The prevalence of the DSM subtypes appears to vary depending on whether community or clinic populations are sampled. Several community studies indicate that ADHD-I is least prevalent (Gomez et al., 1999; Nolan, Gadow, & Sprafkin, 2001). In clinic studies, ADHD-C is most common, suggesting that youth with the combination of symptoms are viewed as having greater impairment or intolerably disruptive behavior. It has been suggested that ADHD-HI, which seems relatively uncommon, may appear earlier than ADHD-C and at least in some cases develops into ADHD-C (Gomez et al., 1999).

GENDER

More boys than girls consistently receive the diagnosis of ADHD, with two to nine boys for every girl, depending on the type of ADHD and the setting (American Psychiatric Association, 2000). The sex ratio is higher in clinic samples than in community samples, which report on average a ratio of roughly three boys to one girl (Barkley, 2003). The gender difference in prevalence may be affected by the diagnostic criteria being biased toward the manifestation of the disorder in males. Running, climbing, and leaving one's seat in the classroom, for example, more readily occur in boys than in girls. Perhaps relevant, too, is the finding that when boys, but not girls, exhibit oppositional defiant behaviors teachers may overidentify ADHD symptoms—which could inflate prevalence in boys (Jackson & King, 2004). No matter what the true cause, the gender disparity in prevalence probably helped produce the neglect of girls with ADHD, which only more recently is being addressed. (See Accent: "Girls and ADHD.")

ACCENT ● ● ● ● ●

Girls and ADHD

The view that ADHD is a disorder of school-age boys is shifting. Nonetheless, a clear picture of ADHD in girls has not yet emerged. Among the numerous findings is that relative to boys with the disorder girls have lower IQs, poorer language skills, perhaps fewer executive function abilities, different patterns of EEG abnormalities, and more frequent diagnosis of ADHD-I (Rucklidge & Tannock, 2002; Sowell et al., 2003).

One of the more comprehensive studies of girls with ADHD was conducted by Hinshaw and colleagues (Hinshaw, 2002b; Hinshaw et al., 2002). The 6- to 12-year-olds, recruited from a variety of community sources, comprised an ethnically and socioeconomically diverse sample. Multiple measures were taken prior to and during their attendance at summer camp. These included neuropsychological, intelligence, and achievement tests; parent and staff reports; peer evaluations; and direct observation. Girls were identified with ADHD according to cut-off scores on well-established behavioral scales; they were compared with an age- and ethnically-matched group of girls who did not meet the ADHD criteria.

Among the findings are that girls with ADHD

- exhibited more deficits in executive functions, with more deficits in girls with the combined subtype of ADHD than those with the inattentive subtype;

- had histories of grade retention, special education, and speech and language problems;

- exhibited higher rates of anxiety, mood disorder, and conduct problems, the latter especially high in the combined ADHD subtype;

- displayed higher rates of both overt and relational aggression, with girls in the combined subtype higher than girls in the inattentive subgroup (Zalecki & Hinshaw, 2004);

- were regarded more negatively by peers—this was especially true for the combined subtype but girls in the inattentive subtype were more isolated;

- experienced higher parental hostility and emotional overinvolvement (Peris & Hinshaw, 2003); parents of the girls with the combined subtype also reported being more authoritarian and more overwhelmed; and

- had a history of adoption, and also a history of abuse in the girls with the combined subtype.

Many of the findings of this study are similar to those reported in other investigations with girls. The researchers caution, however, that different results are possible depending on the samples and measures employed. Indeed, there is a need for continuing examination of ADHD in girls and adolescent females and for studies that directly compare females and males.

SOCIAL CLASS AND CULTURE

The relationship of prevalence and social class is unclear. We know that ADHD appears in all social classes and also that higher rates are sometimes associated with lower social class (Barkley, 2003). The latter finding perhaps can be explained by other factors, such as the source of information or social class differences in the conduct disturbance that often co-occurs with ADHD. Similarly, it remains to be seen whether the reported higher rates of disorder among African American than European American children are attributable to methodological or social class factors.

The symptoms of ADHD are observed in many countries, which report similar gender ratios and an association of ADHD with learning and conduct problems (Whalen & Henker, 1998). Quite striking, however, is the cross-cultural variation in overall prevalence. This may be due, of course, to differences in sampling, in how ADHD is defined, who does the observing, and cultural values. The possible role of cultural influence was suggested, for example, in a study in which clinicians from China, Indonesia, Japan, and the United States were asked to rate the behaviors of boys presented in video vignettes. Ratings of hyperactivity and disruptive behaviors were higher for the Chinese and Indonesian than for the Japanese and U.S. mental health workers (Tao, 1992). Thus it appeared that cultural expectations and values affected the interpretation of the boys' behaviors.

Developmental Course and Prognosis

The importance of studying attention-deficit hyperactivity disorder across developmental levels has become increasingly clear. Because ADHD is believed to emerge by age 7, examination of the earlier years of life can be critical to understanding the origin of the disorder. At the same time, children do not necessarily "outgrow" ADHD, as was once believed, so that the development course of ADHD can be understood only by determining the persistence of symptoms into adolescence and adulthood. In addition, of course, we want to know how children with ADHD fare more generally in later life.

INFANCY AND THE PRESCHOOL YEARS

It is believed that at least some cases of ADHD begin in infancy, but this possibility is not easily established. How would ADHD manifest itself so early in life? It is reasonable that temperamental differences in activity level, distractibility, and the like might forecast ADHD, at least in part. Sanson and colleagues (1993) reported that a group of children who were hyperactive and aggressive at age 8 had displayed early difficult temperament, and by age 3 to 4 had been more active and less cooperative and manageable. The hypothesis has been put forth that temperamental tendencies for emotional reactivity and poor self-regulation may be precursors of later forms of ADHD (Nigg, Goldsmith, & Sachek, 2004).

Behaviors that are symptomatic of attention-deficit hyperactivity disorder are commonly reported in preschoolers but often lessen with time (Campbell, 1990; 1995). For some children the symptoms persist and can meet the criteria for diagnosis. These young children may exhibit social skill and preacademic skill deficits, and their parents report particularly high levels of stress (DuPaul et al., 2001). Continuance of the disorder seems more likely when the child displays a high level of defiant behavior and there is considerable parent-child conflict (Barkley, 2003).

CHILDHOOD

The advent of school is likely to increase demands for paying attention, following rules, getting along with others, and otherwise regulating one's own behavior (Campbell, 2000). Most cases of ADHD are diagnosed during the elementary school years, with ADHD-I perhaps being identified somewhat later than the other subtypes. Once the behavioral symptoms of ADHD are exhibited, they often remain stable or may increase throughout childhood.

These are the years that have been well documented. Self-regulation and self-organization are problematic, social relationships can be far from satisfactory, peer rejection becomes obvious, and poor academic achievement is observed. Clinical-level oppositional behaviors, conduct problems, and internalizing symptoms also can become more apparent in some children.

"You're so organized!"

ADOLESCENCE AND ADULTHOOD

In adolescence, the core symptoms of ADHD—especially hyperactive-impulsive behaviors—may decrease in a substantial number of cases, and the diagnosis of ADHD may no longer apply. Still, the disorder frequently persists, with estimates ranging widely from perhaps 40 to 80 percent of affected youth (Barkley, 2003; Hansen, Weiss, & Last, 1999; Willoughby, 2003). Two aspects of symptom manifestation are noteworthy. Even when diagnostic criteria are not met, some adolescents may experience the core manifestations of ADHD to some degree. Moreover, heterotypic continuity of symptoms is likely. That is, the core symptoms may carry over in somewhat different forms; for example, overactive running about in childhood may later be manifest as inability to relax (Willoughby, 2003).

Several longitudinal studies of the outcome of childhood ADHD leave no doubt that the disorder puts these children at risk for a variety of other problems in adolescence. These include poor school achievement, reading problems, conduct disorder, antisocial behavior, drug use or abuse, social problems, low self-esteem, and emotional problems (Fischer et al., 1993; McGee et al., 2002; Slomkowski, Klein, & Mannuzza, 1995).

Studies that followed cases of child ADHD into young adulthood indicate that substantial but varying percentages still display some core deficits and/or impaired social relationships, depression, low self-concept, antisocial behavior, drug use, and educational and occupational disadvantage (Barkley et al. 2004; Mannuzza et al., 1993; 1998; Weiss & Hechtman, 1986). Most of these young adults are employed, although their work history is somewhat unstable, and job status is on the low end.

More recently, interest has grown in adults who for the first time are identified with the symptoms of ADHD and retrospectively report a history of childhood ADHD symptoms (Barkley, 1998: Ernst et al., 2003). Of course, the question of reliability must be raised regarding such retrospective report and caution must be taken in generalizing from adult ADHD to child ADHD. Nonetheless, these cases of adult ADHD do suggest that the disorder can be a chronic, lifelong condition.

VARIATION AND PREDICTION OF OUTCOME

In examining developmental data for ADHD, it is important to consider the overall picture. *First*, the sizable percentage of children continuing to have difficulties varies a good deal over studies, which may reflect true sample differences or methodological factors. *Second*, the core symptoms of ADHD, especially hyperactivity-impulsivity, appear to lessen with development. *Third*, many associated problems can exist into later years, although the trend is for difficulties to weaken over time. *Fourth*, ADHD comorbid with conduct disorder is especially associated with poorer outcomes in core and secondary problems. *Fifth*, heterogeneity exists in developmental course and outcome; some children overcome earlier problems and are reasonably adjusted in adulthood, whereas others show various kinds and degrees of problems. This latter fact poses the question, What variables predict outcome?

Many predictors of adolescent or adult problems have been identified (Table 9–2). However, the picture is a complex one. Risk factors may be related to outcome for some subtypes of ADHD and not others. For example, early age of onset may predict worse outcome for ADHD-C than for ADHD-I (Willoughby et al., 2000). Risks also appear different for different areas of functioning (Campbell, 1995; Fergusson, Lynskey, & Horwood, 1997; Lambert, 1988; McGee et al., 2002). Educational outcome appears especially associated with earlier deficits in attention, intelligence, and academic skill, as well as with some child-rearing practices. In contrast, the continuance of antisocial behavior is associated with early-occurring conditions such as family disturbance and the child's aggression and conduct problems. In this latter case, it appears that early ADHD symptoms combined with adverse child-parent interactions and/or other family adversities put the child on an early path to oppositional behavior and subsequent conduct disorder—which leads to

TABLE 9–2   SOME VARIABLES THAT MAY PREDICT ADOLESCENT AND ADULT OUTCOMES OF CHILDHOOD ADHD

Age of onset
Severity of symptoms
Aggression; conduct problems
Academic performance
General intelligence
Family adversities
Parents' ADHD and psychiatric disorder
Parents' child-rearing practice; parent-child interaction
Peer relationships

persistent antisocial behavior (Loeber et al., 1995; Patterson, DeGarmo, & Knutson, 2000). Genetic or other biological influences may also play a role here (Silberg et al., 1996). Overall then, the outcomes of childhood ADHD appear to vary with a host of risk and protective factors.

Psychological Explanations of ADHD

Many cognitive, perceptional, and motivational deficits have been associated with ADHD, and various explanatory accounts of the disorder have been offered. They have emphasized, for example, attention, arousal, response to reward, time perception, working memory, inhibition, executive functions, or self-regulation (Nigg, 2001; Rapport et al., 2001). These accounts, which vary in how comprehensive they are, frequently reference brain functioning. Our discussion highlights a few of the approaches from the voluminous research literature and then examines one model in greater detail.

SENSITIVITY TO REWARD

Unusual sensitivity to reinforcement has been inconsistently noted in children with ADHD. For example, they have been shown to do especially poorly under partial schedules of reinforcement and otherwise low incentives (e.g., Slusarek et al., 2001). They also have been shown to have an atypically high preference for immediate reward over delayed reward (Tripp & Alsop, 2001). Interestingly, limited brain scan data from typically functioning adults and adults with childhood-onset ADHD suggest differences in the activation of brain circuits during a task in which participants made decisions for high reward/risk for high loss or low reward/risk for low loss (Ernst et al., 2003). All these findings suggest that an abnormality in the reward system leads to differences in responding to the usual contingencies involved in paying attention, staying on task, following rules, and the like.

AVERSION TO DELAY

Sonuga-Barke and colleagues have proposed that one path to ADHD involves an aversion to delay. This idea is similar to the emphasis on reduced sensitivity to reward in that both suggest a deficit, or deviation, in motivation. In general, delay aversion would be manifested by attempts to avoid or escape delay

(Sonuga-Barke et al, 2004). Thus, the preference that children with ADHD show for immediate over delayed reward may have more to do with avoiding delay than with the reward itself (Sonuga-Barke, 1994). It is argued that in situations where delay cannot be escaped or avoided, children will attend to aspects of the environment that help "speed up" the perception of time. Antrop and colleagues (2000) evaluated this idea by observing children with and without ADHD when they had to wait in a room with little available stimulation. On some measures, the children with ADHD engaged in more activity, presumably to lessen a subjective sense of delay. In another study, Sonuga-Barke and colleagues (2004) predicted that children with ADHD would be more sensitive to environmental cues for delay due to the emotional or motivational significance that delay has for them. The findings, which the researchers consider preliminary, supported the prediction.

WORKING MEMORY

Deficits in working memory are described in ADHD. Denny and Rapport put these deficits at the center of one account of the disorder (Rapport et al., 2001). Working memory is involved in constructing a cognitive representation of incoming stimuli, maintaining it for short periods of time, and manipulating it. As part of the process, working memory searches and activates stored, older memories relevant to the incoming stimuli, including memories of relevant actions. When things go well, appropriate behaviors can then be enacted. When working memory fails, cognitive representations rapidly fade and behavior is disorganized—a feature that characterizes ADHD. According to this formulation, other mechanisms may also be at work. For example, failed working memory may motivate the child to direct attention to other environmental stimuli—to increase the rate of incoming stimuli to replace the representations that fade so easily. Such stimulus seeking behavior is reflected in the rapid shifts of attention and activity that are observed in ADHD.

INHIBITION AND EXECUTIVE FUNCTIONS

As already noted, children with ADHD exhibit deficits in executive functions, the higher order skills required for planning, organizing, and implementing goal-directed behavior. One component of executive functions is the ability to inhibit responses. Deficits in inhibition, which are well

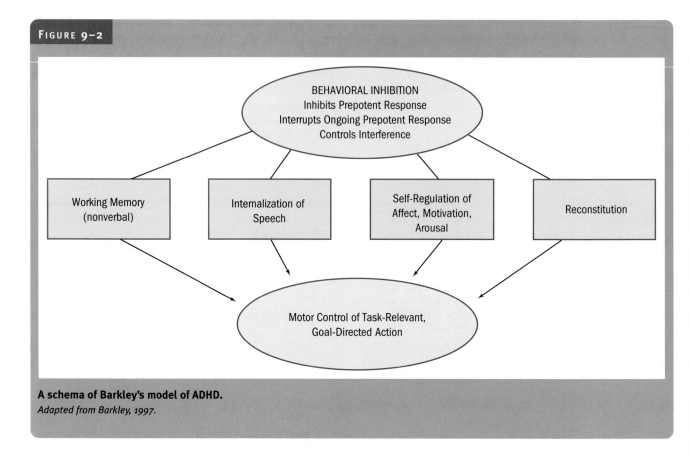

FIGURE 9–2

A schema of Barkley's model of ADHD.
Adapted from Barkley, 1997.

documented in ADHD, have moved to the forefront in explaining the disorder.

Barkley's Model. Barkley's (1998; 2003) multi-faceted model, which applies only to cases in which hyperactivity-impulsivity are observed, gives response inhibition a central role in ADHD. As Figure 9–2 indicates, behavioral inhibition is viewed as critical to the performance of four other executive functions—which influence the motor control of behavior.

Behavioral inhibition is seen as consisting of three abilities. *First* is the ability to inhibit prepotent responses, that is, responses that are likely to be reinforced or have a history of reinforcement. *Second* is the ability to inhibit, or interrupt, prepotent responses that are already underway. These two inhibitory functions allow a span of time during which the executive functions can be employed for self-regulation. The *third* inhibitory ability then comes into play, which is the ability to inhibit competing events—to protect the operation of the executive functions from interference. In these ways, behavioral inhibition facilitates the workings of the subordinate executive functions.

The model incorporates four subordinate executive functions, briefly noted below, each of which has several elements:

- Working memory allows the person to hold information in mind so that it may be considered.
- Internalization of speech facilitates the person's mental reflection on rules and instructions to guide behavior.
- Self-regulation of affect and motivation involves processes that allow the person to modulate emotion and motivation.
- Reconstitution involves processes that allow the person to analyze and synthesize experiences and to think creatively.

These four executive functions provide the means for the individual to self-regulate his or her behavior. Accordingly, the child is able to engage in task relevant, goal-directed, flexible behavior; is sensitive to feedback; and displays complex motor sequences. In contrast, when inhibition is disordered, these executive functions—and thus self-regulation and adaptability—are adversely affected.

Barkley's model is obviously complex and some of its components are better supported than others (Nigg, 2001). Relatively strong support exists for the involvement of inhibition and the executive functions in ADHD. Nonetheless, some suggest that ADHD is heterogeneous and, for example, that inhibitory deficits and delay of aversion may be two independent paths to ADHD (Hughes & Graham, 2002; Solanto et al., 2001; Sonuga-Barke, Dalen, & Remington, 2003). The roles that various psychological components play in ADHD and their relationship to underlying biological and environmental etiologies await further investigation.

Etiology

Brain damage or injury was once considered the primary cause of ADHD. When it became evident that brain damage could not be identified in most children who showed such difficulty, it was assumed that some undetectable "minimal brain dysfunction" existed. By the late 1950s and early 1960s, the need for better empirical evidence was recognized. Theories of brain dysfunction subsequently became more closely tied to empirical evidence.

Of course, even if one assumes abnormalities of the brain, the reason for brain dysfunction remains. In a small percentage of cases, brain damage from vehicle and bicycle accidents and other traumatic events is related to symptoms of ADHD in children and adolescents (Max et al., 1998). But what explains the majority of cases? Is the cause genetic, or is it due to disease, poor diet, environmental teratogens? What role might the psychosocial environment play? All these, and other questions as well, have been posed about etiology.

Brain Structure and Activity

Numerous brain systems or structures are implicated in ADHD, including the frontal lobe and underlying regions, parietal lobe, temporal lobe, corpus callosum, and the cerebellum. For example, subtle reductions in volume have been found in the temporal lobe, corpus callosum (which connects the hemispheres), and cerebellum (involved in motor coordination and executive functions) (Sowell et al., 2003). Increased gray and decreased white tissue have been observed in several regions.

Interest has focused particularly on the frontal lobes and connections to the striatal region (Figure 9–3). Frontal lobe functioning and damage has been associated with the core symptoms of ADHD; inhibition, working memory, and other executive functions; and higher order motor control (Casey et al., 1997; Semrud-Clikeman et al., 2000). Various measures (e.g., MRI, fMRI, SPECT, EEG) point to brain abnormalities of the frontal lobe and connected underlying regions. A relatively consistent and telling abnormality is the smaller than average size of the right frontal area, the caudate nucleus, and the globus pallidus (Barkley, 1998; Tannock, 1998; Yeo et al., 2003). Brain scans also show that children with ADHD have decreased blood flow and decreased glucose utilization—signs of underactivity—in the frontal areas and pathways connected to the striatal areas and the cerebellum (Rapport & Chung, 2000). This finding extends to the parents of ADHD children who themselves displayed symptoms of hyperactivity: they too showed lowered metabolism in the frontal area (Hechtman, 1991; Taylor, 1994; Zametkin & Rapoport, 1986).

Another focus of neurobiological research is the biochemistry of the brain. Several neurotransmitters may be involved in ADHD but the best evidence implicates deficiencies in dopamine and norepinephrine, which are important in the functioning of the frontal and related areas of the brain (Biederman & Spencer, 2000). Consistent with this finding, stimulant medications used to treat ADHD block the reuptake of dopamine and norepinephrine into the presynaptic membrane of neurons, making them more available in synapses.

Several conclusions can be drawn from investigations of the brain. *First*, although abnormalities in the frontal and striatal regions appear central, other areas are involved. *Second*, underarousal of the brain is implicated. *Third*, dopamine and norepinephrine deficiency are implicated. *Fourth*, ADHD is undoubtedly a heterogeneous disorder with various disturbances in brain regions or networks involved in the regulation of attention and behavior.

Genetic Factors

Numerous studies indicate that the families of children with ADHD have higher rates of psychopathology, including ADHD, than would be expected (Barkley, 2003; Tannock, 1998). Between 10 to 35 percent of first-degree family members are likely to have ADHD. Moreover, children of parents with ADHD are at high risk for the disorder. Family aggregation studies also suggest some genetic influence on the co-occurrence of ADHD with

FIGURE 9-3

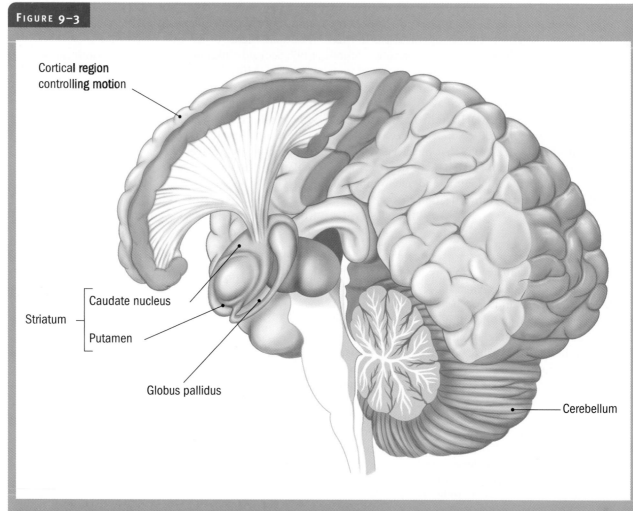

Cortical **region controlling motion**

Striatum
— Caudate nucleus
— Putamen

Globus pallidus

Cerebellum

Drawing of the brain indicating some of the structures implicated in ADHD. Part of the hemisphere is cut away to allow a view of the striatal area.

Adapted from Youdin & Riederer, 1997.

other disorders. Limited research shows, too, that some brain abnormalities found in ADHD occur in the unaffected siblings of children with ADHD, raising the possibility of family risk (Durston et al., 2004).

Twin studies provide clearer evidence of inheritance. Estimates of heritability fall roughly into the .50 to .85 range (Rietveld et al., 2004; Rutter et al., 1999). Heritability has been documented across a variety of definitions, measures, informants, and populations. Further support for genetic influence comes from a limited number of adoption studies (Sprich et al., 2000).

An interesting finding from genetic studies is that the symptoms of attention-deficit hyperactivity disorder are inherited in degree rather than in categorical fashion, suggesting that the disorder is better conceptualized as dimensional instead of an all-or-nothing category (Denney, 2001).

Although the mode of inheritance for ADHD is not established, the influence of multiple genes might well be suspected. Molecular genetic studies have linked specific genes to symptoms of the disorder (Rutter et al., 1999; Sunohara et al., 2000). Evidence for an association with the gene DRD4 is significant (Plomin & McGuffin, 2003). DRD4 is a gene on chromosome 11 that codes for a dopamine receptor site that inhibits activity in receiving neurons (Barr, 2001). There is also some evidence for associations with DAT1, DRD5, and 5HT1B.

PRENATAL INFLUENCES AND BIRTH COMPLICATIONS

Prenatal conditions and birth complications are only inconsistently associated with symptoms of ADHD or diagnosed ADHD. Some studies indicate that very low birthweight (Sykes et al., 1997) and length of labor and hemorrhage can put children at risk (Chandola et al., 1992). Prenatal maternal tobacco smoking and alcohol consumption also can be hazardous (Linnet et al., 2003). A large population study conducted in Finland showed an association of maternal smoking with hyperactivity after adjustment for sex, family structure, SES, maternal age, and maternal alcohol use (Kotimaa et al., 2003). In an extensive U.S. study that followed women from pregnancy to the time their offspring were 14 years old, prenatal alcohol use was linked to activity level, attention deficits, and difficulties in organizing tasks (Streissguth et al., 1984; 1989; 1995). Animal studies showing adverse effects on the brain due to alcohol and nicotine exposure are consistent with reported size reduction of the neuronal networks involved in ADHD (Mick et al., 2002).

DIET AND LEAD

For many years interest has been expressed in the possible etiological role of diet and exposure to lead. One controversial idea was that foods containing artificial dyes and flavors, certain preservatives, and naturally occurring salicylates (for example, in tomatoes and cucumbers) were related to hyperactivity. Subsequent research did not support the claim, nor was behavior improved when children were put on the recommended Feingold diet (Harley & Matthews, 1980; Spring, Chiodo, & Bowen, 1987). Similarly, meta-analysis of research showed that neither behavior nor cognitive functioning of children with ADHD was affected by sugar intake (Wolraich, Wilson, & White, 1995). The overall evidence suggests that diet does not play a strong role and currently there is little interest in this area.

That lead should be suspected of causing ADHD is not unreasonable, as high levels of lead have been associated with serious deficits in biological functioning, cognition, and behavior (Tesman & Hills, 1994). Low levels of exposure over long periods of time also can adversely affect children. Several studies have examined the correlation of lead levels with attention and activity level. Lead levels of blood typically have been examined and also occasionally the amount of lead in the dentine of children's deciduous ("baby") teeth. Major studies sensitive to methodological issues have found significant but small links (Fergusson, Horwood, & Lynskey, 1993; Silva et al., 1988; Thomson et al., 1989). However, even when children have high lead levels, perhaps no more than 4 percent of the variance in ADHD symptoms can be attributed this factor (Barkley, 2003). It is worth noting, however, that blood lead levels lower than what is considered safe by the Centers for Disease Control and Prevention have recently been associated with decreased IQ (Canfield et al., 2003). Although this finding may have little implication for ADHD, caution should not be thrown to the wind regarding the protection of children from lead-based paints, automobile emissions, leaded crystal and ceramic dishes, and solder on old copper pipes.

PSYCHOSOCIAL FACTORS

Few researchers and clinicians believe that psychosocial factors are a primary cause of ADHD, but the symptoms of the disorder are malleable to environmental influences and psychosocial factors are likely to affect the severity, continuity, and nature of the symptoms, as well as associated and co-occurring disturbances. Some investigators note that the possible interaction of environmental factors, including psychosocial variables, with genetic influence has not been given adequate consideration (Christakis et al., 2004; Schachar & Tannock, 2002). Some express concern that early psychosocial influences may adversely affect brain development in ways that are relevant to ADHD. (See Accent: "TV Viewing and Attention Problems in Young Children.")

Unsurprisingly, family factors are among the psychosocial variables thought to be especially influential. Numerous family correlates of children's ADHD have been described. The link with family adversity—such as economic disadvantage, family conflict and separation, and poorer mental health and coping—is reported in several studies (Goodman & Stevenson, 1989; McGee et al., 2002). Nigg and Hinshaw (1998) observed that boys with ADHD with or without antisocial behavior were more likely to have mothers with a history of depression and/or anxiety and fathers with a childhood history of ADHD. The parent-child relationship has been shown to be important. For example, Tully and colleagues (2004) examined ADHD symptoms displayed by 5-year-old twins who had been born with low birthweight; they found that maternal warmth had a moderating effect

ACCENT ●●●●●

TV Viewing and Attention Problems in Young Children

Christakis and colleagues (2004) note that there is too little appreciation of the possible influence of early experience on the development of attention in children. They point to the considerable evidence that environmental exposure can be crucial to synaptic development in the brain and its functions. They suggest that television, with its rapidly changing images, could play a role in shaping the brain and could lead to attention problems. With this in mind, the hypothesis was tested that early exposure to television is associated with later attention problems.

The investigators drew data from the National Longitudinal Survey of Youth, a study of a large national sample of youth. The children in the investigation were 50 percent male and 57 percent white, the latter due to the deliberate effort to oversample nonwhites. The mothers of these children had reported on the amount of television their children viewed at age 1 (mean = 1.8 years) and age 3 (mean = 3.8 years). The mothers also had reported inattention at age 7 by rating their children on five items derived from known rating scales, items that inquired about the child's difficulty with concentration, confusion, impulsivity, obsessions, and restlessness. Based on a specific cut-off score, 10 percent of the children were considered to have attention problems. The question then was, For these children, did a link exist between television exposure at ages 1 and 3 and inattention at age 7? Indeed, it did.

The researchers appropriately note that although adjustments were made for several confounding factors—among them home environment, cognitive stimulation, maternal depression—causal conclusions cannot be drawn from this correlational study. Nor is there a claim that the data apply to diagnosed ADHD. However, the investigators argue that the findings suggest the advisability of limiting TV exposure during the formative years of children's brain development, a position also taken by the American Academy of Pediatrics.

on ratings of symptoms. And as we have already seen, the parents of children with ADHD are more restrictive, impatient, and authoritarian (Campbell, 1995; Woodward, Taylor, & Dowdney, 1998; Stormont-Spurgin & Zentall, 1995). Overall, there is evidence that ADHD in children can affect parent behavior and that parent behavior can influence the nature and perhaps development of ADHD (Johnston & Mash, 2001). Still, family influence needs to be regarded cautiously as findings have been inconsistent and relatively little is known about how the family psychosocial environment interacts with genetic influences and child characteristics to shape ADHD or protect children from developing the disorder.

It is also possible that teacher behaviors play a role in shaping a child's attentiveness and reflectivity. How a classroom is organized and how activities are structured can influence academic achievement, perhaps especially for children predisposed to ADHD behaviors (Whalen, 1989). As with parents, teacher perception and tolerance of student behavior may influence daily social interactions.

Overall, after much research, the etiology of ADHD remains uncertain. Etiology, and certainly developmental paths, likely vary with different subgroups of ADHD and perhaps with gender. Progress is being made in establishing genetic contributions to etiology, in understanding how brain functioning is related to the symptoms of the disorder, and in recognizing how psychosocial influences may shape and maintain the problem behaviors.

Assessment

Whether the purpose of assessment is identification of ADHD, planning for treatment, or both, several aspects of the disorder serve as useful guidelines (Barkley, 1990; 1997; Hinshaw & Erhardt, 1993).

- Because ADHD is best conceptualized as a biopsychosocial disorder, assessment must be broad-based.

TABLE 9-3	INTERVIEW FORMAT SUGGESTED BY BARKLEY
QUESTIONS	**SITUATIONS**
1. Is this a problem area?	Overall interactions
2. What does the child do in this situation?	Play alone
3. What is your response?	Play with others
4. What will the child do next?	Mealtimes
5. If the problem continues, what will you do next?	Dressing in morning
6. What is usually the outcome of this interaction?	Washing and bathing
7. How often do these problems occur in this situation?	Parent on telephone
8. How do you feel about these problems?	During television
9. On a scale of 0 to 10 (0 = no problem, 10 = severe problem), how severe is this problem to you?	Visitors at home
	Visiting others' homes
	In public places
	While mother is occupied
	Father at home
	Chores
	Bedtime
	Other situations

From Barkley, 1981.

- Because ADHD is developmental, a developmental history is important and assessment will vary somewhat with developmental level.

- Because ADHD is pervasive and may manifest itself differently in different settings, individuals familiar with the child and the settings should be consulted.

- Because ADHD has high rates of co-occurrence with other behavioral disorders, assessment requires careful distinctions of other disorders.

The following discussion emphasizes the psychological and social factors most pertinent to assessment, and draws most heavily on the approach of Barkley (1990; 1997; 1998) and his colleagues.

INTERVIEWS

Because ADHD is most often assessed early in life, parents are critical in the interview process. Information needs to be obtained about the child's problems, strengths, history, family stress, and the school. Direct and systematic questions about family dysfunction are recommended so that family adversity is not underestimated (Overmeyer et al., 1999). Questions about peer relationships can also be useful.

It is important to assess specific parent-child interactions, not only for diagnosis but also for treatment planning. Parents may tend to emphasize the past and general aspects—such as how the child might have been affected by a divorce—but information about current interaction is critical (Barkley, 1998). It is helpful to pose specific questions and to direct attention to specific situations (Table 9–3). For example, questions are asked about what the child does, how the parents respond, and how often problems occur in the situation.

The youth being assessed should also be interviewed. With younger children, the interview may simply be a time for getting acquainted, establishing rapport, and observing the child's appearance and behavior. Such observations must be interpreted cautiously, however, because children with ADHD may act more appropriately during office visits than they do in other settings. Older children and adolescents are more able to report reliably on their problems, school performance, peer relationships, the way that they see family functioning, what they think would make life better, and the like.

Teacher interviews can address difficulties in the school setting that may not be validly assessed by parents (Mitsis et al., 2000). A direct interview is valuable, with a focus on learning and academic problems and on peer interaction. In addition, information can be obtained about parent-school interaction and cooperation, as well as school services. Some youth with ADHD have rights to special evaluation and educational services. (Indeed, many of these children receive special education services under the Individuals with Disabilities Education Act, often under the categories of learning disabilities or behavior/emotional disturbance. See page 297 for relevant discussion.)

RATING SCALES

Parent and teacher rating scales and checklists, which are popular tools for assessing ADHD, can provide much information with relatively little time and effort. Many of the scales are reliable and valid, are consistent with the DSM conceptualization of ADHD, and can contribute to clinic and research efforts (Collett, Ohan, & Myers, 2003). Some of these tools are broad in scope and identify not only ADHD but also its co-occurrence with other disorders. Scales with a narrower focus are useful in assessing specific aspects of ADHD.

An example of widely employed scales is the Conners Rating Scales–Revised. Both parent and teacher scales exist in long and abbreviated forms. Table 9–4 shows the seven major factors of the long version of the Conners Parent Rating Scale–Revised

TABLE 9–4	SEVEN FACTORS OF THE REVISED CONNERS PARENT RATING SCALE, WITH EXAMPLES

1. Cognitive Problems
   Careless mistakes
   Arithmetic problems
2. Oppositional
   Loses temper
   Defies adults
3. Hyperactivity-Impulsivity
   Always on the go
   Excitable
4. Anxious-Shy
   Many fears
   Clings to parents
5. Perfectionism
   Everything just so
   Sets high goals
6. Social Problems
   Does not make friends
   Feels inferior
7. Psychosomatic
   Aches and pains
   Seems tired

Adapted from Conners, Sitarenios, Parker, & Epstein, 1998b.

and examples of items as they are distributed across the factors (Conners et al., 1998b). The comparable version of the teacher scales has six similar factors (Conners et al., 1998a). In addition to the parent and teachers scales, there is a self-report adolescent instrument, the Conners-Wells Adolescent Self-Report Scales.

DIRECT OBSERVATION

Direct observation can be extremely useful because the behavioral manifestations of attention-deficit hyperactivity disorder are relatively situational. Home and school observations for initial observation can be well worth the time they require, and observations to target behaviors for intervention can be critical to successful treatment (Jacob & Pelham, 2000). Signs of the core features of ADHD are of utmost importance, of course, but so also are indications of noncompliance, aggression, attention-seeking, and other characteristics of social interactions and relationships. Several observational coding systems for ADHD are available.

OTHER PROCEDURES

Additional assessment methods are often necessary and/or useful. Procedures to specifically evaluate inattention and impulsivity have been developed. For example, the Conners' Continuous Performance Test II requires the client to press a computer key at the sight of any letter except X in the middle of the screen (Epstein et al., 2003; CPT II, 2004). Designed for youngsters 6 years and over, this 14-minute test differentiates ADHD and normative samples.

Standardized tests of intelligence, academic achievement, and adaptive behavior may be essential. Medical evaluation does not usually identify ADHD but when biological factors are highly suspect it can provide information potentially useful in treatment or in understanding the disorder. Such assessment reasonably includes a medical/developmental history and a medical examination that contains a neurological evaluation.

Treatment

Among the treatments for attention-deficit hyperactivity disorder are pharmacotherapy, parent training, behavioral programs, cognitive-behavioral training, social skills training, academic remediation, and individual counseling (Anastopoulos & Farley, 2003;

Antshel & Remer, 2003; Whalen & Henker, 1998). Most widely employed, and considered the most efficacious, are pharmacological and behaviorally oriented parent training and school-based approaches.

PHARMACOLOGICAL TREATMENT

A report by Bradley in 1937 is usually cited as the first instance of the treatment of childhood behavioral disorders with stimulant medication (Greenhill et al., 2002). Many pharmacological agents have been used for ADHD since then, but stimulant medications are by far the treatment of choice (Table 9–5). They are the psychotropic medication most frequently studied and prescribed to youth in the United States, primarily for attention-deficit hyperactivity disorder (Wolraich, 2003). These stimulants affect dopamine and norepinephrine, likely in the midbrain or frontal cortex (Biederman & Spencer, 2000; DuPaul, Barkley, & Connor, 1998).

Most often used are methylphenidate, dextroamphetamine, and the combination of dextroamphetamine and amphetamine. The effects of most stimulants are rapid but wear off within a few hours, and so they are often given two or three times a day. However, slow release forms (Concerta, Adderall XR) are proving to be effective (McCracken et al., 2003; Swanson et al., 2003). Because these are necessary only once daily, they are obviously more convenient

TABLE 9–5	MEDICATIONS MOST COMMONLY USED TO TREAT ADHD

Medications of First Choice

Stimulants
   Methylphenidate (Ritalin; Concerta)
   Dextroamphetamine (Dexedrine)
   Combined Amphetamine and Dextroamphetamine (Adderall; Adderall XR)

Medications of First Alternative Choice

Antidepressants
   Tricyclics (e.g., desipramine; imipramine)
   Other antidepressants
Antihypertensives
   Clonidine

Less Used Medications

Anticonvulsants
Antipsychotics

and can avoid the lack of privacy likely in receiving medication at school.

Although much controversy surrounds the use of stimulants, it is not, in the view of most professionals, due to their failure to rapidly alleviate the primary deficits of ADHD. An estimated 75 percent of medicated children show increased attention and reduced impulsivity and activity level, both in the laboratory and in natural environments (Whalen & Henker, 1998). In addition to alleviating the core symptoms of ADHD, stimulant medications can reduce co-occurring aggressive, noncompliant, oppositional behaviors (Hinshaw et al., 1989). The strongest effects have been documented for measures of attention, distractibility, and impulsivity and for social and classroom behavior (Wolraich, 2003). Perhaps not surprising, then, parents and teachers interact more positively with their children who are benefiting from medication (Chronis et al., 2003; Murphy, Greenstein, & Pelham, 1993). Pharmacological treatment thus appears to alleviate ADHD not only directly but also through improving social relationships. Whatever the route, an impressive amount of data supports the claim for effectiveness across settings, measures, and age (Riddle, Kastelic, & Frosch, 2001; Swanson et al., 1995; Whalen & Henker, 1998). Despite this, parents hold various views on the acceptability of medication for ADHD and more generally. (See Accent: "Parental Attitudes about Medication Use.")

Concerns about Medication. One concern about medication for ADHD is its limitations. Symptoms are alleviated, but medication normalizes behavior in only about 50 percent of children, has only small to modest effect on academic achievement, and does not at all benefit a minority of youth (Schachar & Tannock, 2002; Wolraich, 2003). In addition, long-term effects have not been well documented (Klein et al., 2004).

A second concern about stimulant treatment is possible adverse biological side effects. Moderate side effects occur in 4 to 10 percent of cases (Greenhill et al., 2002), and preschoolers may experience more difficulties than older children. Sleep problems, decreased appetite, stomach pain, headaches, irritability, and jitteriness have all been reported. The effects are often mild to moderate and may diminish in 2 or 3 weeks or after a reduction in dosage. Suppression of growth is also reported, but height does not seem to be affected in the long run (NIH Consensus Development Panel, 2000). Only inconsistently reported is a worsening or an initiation of

ACCENT ● ● ● ● ●

Parental Attitudes about Medication Use

The beliefs and attitudes held by parents about their offspring's using medications for psychological problems is a crucial factor in whether medication will be accepted or rejected. For young children, the attitudes of parents may be *the* decisive factor, whereas the feelings of older children and adolescents are more likely to be given greater consideration in decisions about intervention. A minority of parents may be content to take what they see as an easy road to helping their children—the taking of a few pills every day. For most parents, however, the issues are more complex. Rappaport and Chubinsky (2000), commenting on the dearth of research about this matter, offer some "food for thought."

These investigators point out that parents may be quite comfortable with their child's using cold remedies and antibiotics while being opposed to medications that will affect mood or behavior. We can speculate about parental feelings regarding medications that affect brain functioning. Then, too, the need for medication might carry multiple meanings for parents. As Rappaport and Chubinsky note, prescription of medication may indicate that parents are not overreacting or exaggerating their child's problems. Parents might also be relieved that a solution may be at hand for difficulties that they were unable to rectify. On the other hand, recommendation for medications can raise the possibility that the child has a serious and chronic mental illness, which in turn may bring grief and a sense of loss. Parents may also question whether they genetically transmitted problems to the child or behaved in ways that produced symptoms in the child.

These sensitive issues require careful evaluation by mental health workers. Parental attitudes and beliefs need to be included in discussion about treatments so that, for example, alternative interventions are considered. Parental satisfaction may affect the success of treatment and translate into more general attitudes about mental health matters.

---

motor and vocal tics in a small minority of children (Varley et al., 2001; Wolraich, 2003).

In general, when stimulants are prescribed and used appropriately, they are considered relatively safe drugs for most youth. This does not mean, of course, that the need for monitoring should be taken lightly. Individuals vary in their responses to different dosages and different stimulants. In fact, warnings have been given of an association of the stimulant pemoline with liver failure and death (Wolraich, 2003). Medications must always be viewed as potentially adverse or dangerous for some persons, no matter how small the number.

A third concern about childhood stimulant use is whether it increases the risk for later alcohol and substance use or abuse. The weight of the evidence is that treatment with medication does not readily explain any later drug dependency and may actually decrease risk (Barkley et al., 2003; Wilens et al., 2003). Nevertheless, concern about the illicit use of the stimulants themselves by youth with or without ADHD may warrant a watchful eye.

At one time, concern was expressed that pharmacological treatment might result in children's experiencing undue worries and detrimental cognitions, for example, worries that they would become "hyper" without medications or beliefs that their behavior is controlled by external forces rather than by their own efforts. There is little evidence for this outcome, and children can actually gain feelings of competence and self-control (Schachar & Tannock, 2002; Whalen & Henker, 1998). Still, sensitive assessment is necessary because individual children and adolescents report a variety of attitudes about taking medications (Rappaport & Chubinsky, 2000).

In addition to the concerns already discussed, critics have argued that medication is too readily prescribed. Some believe that it is overused because it is a "quick fix" for the schools and for some parents. In fact, prescription of stimulant medications has risen (Greenhill et al., 2002). The use of methylphenidate (Ritalin) has increased in the United States every year, except for three, since it was first monitored in 1971 (Wolraich, 2003). Relatively recent increases for preschoolers have been striking (Zito et al., 2000) and, along with concern about other medications, have led to a call for research on the safety and efficacy of medications in very young children (Greenhill et al., 2003). The overall rise in medication use may be due to an actual increase in ADHD or to the diagnosis being more readily applied. Or it may be related to the use of medication for a longer treatment time or to increased use with preschoolers, adolescents, adults, girls, children with ADHD-I, and youngsters with learning disabilities. In any event, it appears that uneven practices warrant scrutiny. For example, a survey of four communities reported that only one-eighth of children meeting the criteria for ADHD received adequate intervention with stimulants, whereas another survey found that 72 percent of the children receiving stimulants failed to meet the ADHD criteria (Greenhill et al., 2002). Several government agencies and professional groups are involved in studying the treatment of ADHD and in promulgating guidelines and regulations for pharmacotherapy.

Concern about the use and misuse of medication for ADHD has at times led to heated controversy that was fed by media coverage in major magazines and on television. Media attention that serves to educate is beneficial, of course. Unfortunately, concerns about medications have sometimes been expressed in emotionally charged, exaggerated— and perhaps harmful—ways by parents, professionals, and organized groups (Barkley, 1998; Swanson et al., 1995). Although extreme emotional reaction and exaggeration are rarely helpful, professionals who recognize the benefits of stimulants also point to their limitations and warn against their misuse or overuse.

BEHAVIORALLY ORIENTED INTERVENTION

Behavioral interventions are the most developed and the most documented alternative treatments; they are often combined with other treatments. Emphasis is placed on the consequences of behavior in controlling attention, impulsivity, rule adherence, academic effort, and social interaction. Reinforcers typically include not only tokens or points that can be exchanged for a variety of rewards but also social consequences such as praise. Negative consequences are often required as well, in which the child loses opportunity for reinforcers (time out) or must give up privileges or earned reinforcers (response cost). Most behavioral interventions are conducted in the home or school, with parents or teachers working directly with the child.

Parent Training. Parent training is a commonly employed psychological treatment for ADHD (Schachar & Tannock, 2002). Managing a child with ADHD can be stressful for families, and parents tend to become exhausted and overly directive. They may also begin to view themselves as lacking the normal skills of parenting (Anastopoulos, Smith, & Wien, 1998). These facts coupled with the obvious influence that parents have on their children's behavior make families a natural focus of intervention.

Although parent training programs vary somewhat, they share the goal of teaching child management techniques (Anastopoulos & Farley, 2003). As an example, we briefly describe an intervention that emphasizes the management of the core symptoms of ADHD and noncompliance and defiance in children between 4 and 12 years of age. This focus is consistent with the view that ADHD involves a deficit in behavioral inhibition and risk for conduct disturbances. Appropriate parental management of child behavior is viewed as bringing the child's behavior under increased parental control, facilitating the child's awareness of behavioral consequences, preventing the development of comorbid conditions, and alleviating parental stress. The program is considered suitable when ADHD is contributing to family difficulties.

The treatment program consists of ten components that are covered in 8 to 12 sessions with an individual family or groups of families. As Table 9–6 indicates, in addition to training in behavioral management, the components include information to increase understanding of ADHD, discussion of special and future problems, consideration of the child's school situation and parental involvement in the school, and booster sessions as needed for review and troubleshooting.

Although, in general, parent interventions can result in improved child and family functioning (Anastopoulos et al., 1998), relatively few studies have examined effectiveness specifically for children with ADHD. Limited data show that significant improvement can occur in approximately half of preschoolers exhibiting ADHD symptoms whose parents have had parenting training (Sonuga-Barke et al., 2001). Other data suggest that parent training can favorably influence family functioning and parental satisfaction with treatment (Anastopoulos & Farley, 2003). There is a need, however, to better understand the components of parent training programs that are effective, as well as the conditions that limit or interfere with successful outcome. Excessive family stress or marital conflict may work against a

TABLE 9–6	COMPONENTS OF THE PARENT TRAINING PROGRAM DESCRIBED BY ANASTOPOULOS AND FARLEY (2003)

1. Overview of ADHD (e.g., symptoms, etiology)
2. Discussion of child-parent relationships, principles of behavioral management
3. Facilitating skills in providing positive attention to the child ("catching the child being good") and ignoring "bad" behavior
4. Promoting appropriate independent play and compliance with simple requests; issuing commands more effectively
5. Setting up a reward-oriented home token or point system
6. Using response cost for noncompliance and minor rule violation
7. Using time out for serious rule violations
8. Handling disruptive child behavior in public places, such as grocery stores and churches
9. Preparing for termination of parent training; handling potential future problems; fading out home reward program; discussing school issues
10. As needed, booster session to review training and troubleshoot problems

Adapted from Anastopoulos & Farley, 2003.

TABLE 9–7	HYPOTHETICAL CHILD-TEACHER CONTINGENCY CONTRACT

I agree to do the following:
1. Take my seat by 8:10 every morning.
2. Remain in my seat unless Ms. Duffin gives permission to me or the class to leave seats.
3. Not interrupt other students when they are speaking.
4. Complete morning written work as assigned before lunch break.
5. Complete afternoon written work as assigned before gym or recess in the afternoon.

I agree that when I do the above, I will:
. . . earn extra time in the computer corner
. . . earn extra time to do artwork
. . . earn extra checkmarks that I can trade for art supplies.

I agree that if I do not do 1–5 above each day, I will:
. . . not be able to participate in recess activities.

Based on DuPaul, Guevremont, & Barkley, 1991.

positive outcome. Another factor that appears to hinder success is the presence of ADHD symptoms in the parents themselves, which is probably not uncommon given the familial nature of the disorder (Sonuga-Barke, Daley, & Thompson, 2002).

Classroom Management. School-based behavioral intervention is effective in addressing inattention, disruptive behavior, and academic failure. Most commonly the teacher administers contingency management intervention, and typically receives training and consultation from a mental health specialist (Jacob & Pelham, 2000). Procedures usually include token reinforcement, time out, and response cost. Contingency contracting, in which the child and the teacher sign a written agreement specifying how the child will behave and the contingencies that will accrue, can be helpful (Table 9–7). Often essential is the daily report card sent to parents, which reflects the child's performance regarding targeted behaviors. The report card serves as feedback to the child, informs the parents so that they can reward the child for progress, and promotes communication between the teacher and the parents.

Research suggests that classroom structure and organization may also be important to enhancing learning in children with ADHD (Pfiffner & Barkley, 1998). Increasing stimulation within the task—for example, by the use of color, shape, or tape recordings—might facilitate attention to the task. Keeping the length of the task within the child's attention span and using timers to pace performance might be of benefit. Rules that are written and clearly displayed also may help guide the child. Placing the child's desk away from other children and near the teacher can reduce peer reinforcement of inappropriate behavior and also facilitate teacher monitoring and feedback.

Teachers are crucial, of course, in influencing the learning environment of the classroom and in implementing behavioral programs. Limited data show that elementary school teachers are knowledgeable about ADHD and recognize it as a legitimate problem (Pisecco, Huzinec, & Curtis, 2001). They appear to favor the daily report card relative to response cost and medication, although several factors play a role in their acceptance of treatments. In general, teacher beliefs and attitudes, flexibility, tolerance for the disruptions common in ADHD, and interactional style might well be important variables regarding the success of classroom-based programs (Greene, 1995).

The well-being of children with ADHD is undoubtedly influenced by teachers' attitudes and abilities to manage and organize classroom activities.
(Will Hart/PhotoEdit, Inc.)

MULTIMODAL TREATMENT

There seems little doubt that behaviorally oriented methods can frequently help alleviate ADHD in the short run. Empirical investigations show that on-task, attentive, appropriate behaviors can be shaped and academic performance improved. However, behavioral programs often require much effort and time, and benefits, although notable, can be smaller than those from medication. At the same time, the limitation and criticism of medication have continued to raise questions about its use for ADHD. This situation has resulted in comparisons of the effects of medication alone, psychosocial treatments alone, and multimodal interventions that combined medication and psychosocial approaches.

A major effort was initiated in 1990 at two large medical centers in Montreal and New York (Klein et al., 2004). Seven- to 9-year-olds were randomly assigned to receive methylphenidate, methylphenidate plus psychosocial intervention (including parent training, academic assistance, social skills training, psychotherapy), and a control treatment consisting of medication plus professional attention that avoided the components of the psychosocial intervention. The children had been diagnosed according to DSM-III-R, which allowed diagnosis based on a mix of symptoms of inattention, hyperactivity, and impulsivity. They did not have diagnoses of specific learning disorders or conduct disorder, and prior to the study they were shown to respond to medication. The investigators were particularly interested in enhancing the effects of medication with a relatively intense psychosocial treatment aimed at specific areas of functioning. Overall, evaluation after the 2-year project indicated improvements in several areas of behavior in all conditions but did not indicate additional benefits when psychosocial components were combined with medication (Abikoff et al., 2004a; 2004b; Hechtman et al., 2004).

MTA Study. The Multimodal Treatment Assessment study (MTA) is the largest long-term evaluation of treatment options. This six-center investigation was initiated by the National Institutes of Mental Health. Close to 600 children, age 7 to 9 years, were randomly assigned to one of four treatment conditions lasting for 14 months (MTA Cooperative Group, 1999a). The children were diagnosed with ADHD-C. The treatments were as follows:

- **Medication Treatment.** Children received medication, mostly methylphenidate, with dosage carefully assigned, monitored, and adjusted at monthly sessions with the child and parents. Teacher input was also available for these sessions. Medication was given for the entire time period.

- **Behavioral Treatment.** The intensive program consisted of parent training sessions; school-based intervention including teacher consultation and a trained aid who worked with the child part time for 60 days; and a child-focused, behaviorally oriented summer camp experience. Training gradually leveled off, with parents being seen once monthly or not at all by the end of the investigation.

- **Combined Treatment.** Medication and behavioral treatments were integrated.
- **Community Care Treatment.** Children in this comparison group received various routine treatments in their communities. As it turned out, 67 percent were on medication, with dosage levels lower than for the medication treatment group. The child was seen only one or two times by a physician and there was no teacher contact for feedback.

Initial evaluations of the MTA study were conducted before, during, and at the end of the 14 months. Numerous measures were taken of core ADHD symptoms, associated problems, and family factors. A follow-up assessment was conducted 10 months after the termination of treatment.

Core ADHD symptoms were reduced for children in all groups over the 14-month treatment, but the amount of improvement varied with the type of treatment (MTA Cooperative Group, 1999a; 1999b). The medication and combined treatments were generally superior to behavioral and community care treatments. Overall direct comparison showed that the medication and combined groups did not differ. However, interesting differences emerged with further analyses. The findings are numerous and complex, as briefly demonstrated by specific examples:

- For several measures, the combined treatment had the greatest effect (MTA Cooperative Group, 1999a). This was true for parent ratings of their children's externalizing and internalizing symptoms, and for reading achievement.
- For children with comorbid ADHD and anxiety, behavioral treatment was as effective as the medication or the combination treatments (Rieppi et al., 2002).
- Social class moderated some of the outcomes. Families with more education benefited the most from the combined treatment, but this was not so for families with less education (Rieppi et al., 2002). Also, in poorer but not other families the use of medication was associated with decreased closeness between families and their children (MTA Cooperative Group, 1999b).

Additional findings regarding medication are interesting. The MTA study supports previous finding that lower dosage medication is used when behavioral components are part of the treatment package. In addition, the difficulties that some families have in accepting medication treatment are apparent in the MTA study. Prior to intervention, 6 percent of families refused medication, whereas virtually none refused behavioral treatment (Vitiello et al., 2001). Moreover, MTA families expressed less satisfaction with the medication treatment than with the behavioral and the combined interventions.

TEN-MONTH FOLLOW-UP. A 10-month posttreatment assessment examined the persistence of effects of the four treatments on select measures (MTA Cooperative Group, 2004a; 2004b). Of immediate interest here is that the general superiority of the medication and combined treatments was again demonstrated for reducing ADHD and oppositional defiant symptoms (but not some other problems). However, the effects were about 50 percent weaker than at the end of treatment. Figure 9–4 depicts this outcome for parent and teacher ratings of ADHD symptoms at the beginning of treatment, the end of treatment, and the posttreatment follow-up.

In an exploration of why benefits weakened in the medication and combined groups, the researchers analyzed parents' reports of actual medication use at the end of treatment (not assignment to treatment group) and at the time of the follow-up (MTA Cooperative Group, 2004a). Four patterns of medication use emerged: some children used medication across treatment and posttreatment time; some used none; some used medication only during treatment; some only during post-treatment time. From the data the researchers concluded that the reduction of benefits in the medication and combined treatment groups may be due to these groups' having a larger number of children who stopped medication and a smaller number who started medication during the posttreatment phase. The investigators commented that it is surprising that an unexpected number of children helped by medication during treatment quit taking it. This finding is perhaps related to the fact that parents had not viewed any one treatment as more effective than the others and had expressed greater satisfaction with the behavioral approach.

It is also interesting that at follow-up, children who had received behavioral treatment maintained treatment gains, which the researchers speculated

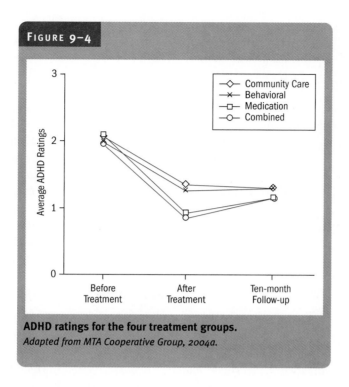

ADHD ratings for the four treatment groups.
Adapted from MTA Cooperative Group, 2004a.

was due to the carryover of what had been learned during treatment. Once again, we see the complexities of treatment for ADHD. Planned assessments of the MTA children into adolescence and adulthood promise to shed more light on several issues.

The MTA study has been widely discussed and analyzed. Some researchers point to lessons that can be gleaned from the findings. Whalen (2001), for instance, suggested the need for exploring new psychosocial treatments, such as teaching adolescents with ADHD to recognize their strengths and weaknesses and to match them to occupations. Investigators also point to the importance of matching youth and their families to treatments (Harwood & Beutler, 2001). Taken together, the MTA findings support previous findings of the effects of well-managed medication treatment and argue against a "one size fits all" approach to treating ADHD.

Comment On Care

It is probably fair to say that at the present time, practitioners take various stances with regard to treatments. Medication is widely employed but is not preferred by every family or clinician. Many believe that a combination of medical and psychosocial treatments is the best approach for many children,

because different treatments might address different deficits (Schachar & Tannock, 2003). Parent training in child management is judged important, as is educational support and the treatment of disorders that co-occur with ADHD. The requirement for treatment to be tailored to individual needs is apparent, even as these needs change as the child develops.

A broader issue concerns the availability and quality of treatments. The rate of outpatient care for 3- to18-year-olds with ADHD showed a threefold increase from 1987 to 1997, across all social class groups and especially for poorer families (Olfson et al., 2003). Even so, it is estimated that perhaps two-thirds of these needy children receive no treatment and that the availability of service varies across communities, social class, and ethnic groups (Jensen, 2000; Schachar & Tannock, 2002). Moreover, when youth receive medical services, services may be determined less by established standards of care than by the type of professional involved (Hoagwood et al., 2000). For example, family physicians are more likely to prescribe stimulant medications—which may not be optimally monitored—and less likely to use or provide other services, such as mental health counseling and follow-up services. An apparent gap exists between the guidelines for care published by the medical community and actual community practice (Schachar & Tannock, 2002).

SUMMARY

EVOLVING IDEAS ABOUT ADHD

- *Accounts of ADHD have shifted over time regarding symptoms and their conceptualization. Two factors are now widely recognized: inattention and hyperactivity-impulsivity.*

DSM CLASSIFICATION AND DIAGNOSIS

- *The DSM recognizes three subtypes of ADHD: Predominately Inattentive, Predominately Hyperactive-Impulsive, and the Combined Type.*

- *Diagnosis demands the presence of symptoms for at least 6 months by age 7 and impairment in at least two settings.*

DESCRIPTION: CORE FEATURES

- *The core problems of inattention, hyperactivity, and impulsivity, which occur more in certain situations than others, are widely observed by parents and teachers and measured by instruments such as continuous performance and stop-signal tests.*

DESCRIPTION: SECONDARY FEATURES

- *As a group, youth with ADHD display several secondary difficulties, among which are motor problems, somewhat lowered intelligence, academic failure, executive dysfunction, and social and conduct problems.*

DSM SUBTYPES

- *Many differences exist between ADHD-I and ADHD-C, but questions remain about all the subtypes. ADHD-HI may be a precursor of ADHD-C.*
- *Some children with ADHD-I exhibit a dreamy, sluggish cognitive tempo, which some investigators suggest is a unique disorder rather than a subtype of ADHD.*

ADHD AND CO-OCCURRING DISORDERS

- *ADHD co-occurs at high rates with learning disabilities, externalizing, disorders, and internalizing disorders. These comorbid conditions are associated with not only different symptoms pictures but also different risks and complex developmental paths. Both genetic and psychosocial factors are implicated.*

EPIDEMIOLOGY

- *About 3 to 7 percent of school-age children are estimated to have ADHD, and rates decline in adolescence. Boys are diagnosed more frequently than girls, prevalence appears somewhat higher in lower social classes, and notable cross-cultural differences in prevalence are reported.*

- *Girls with ADHD are being studied more than in past times, although much is yet to be learned about how and the degree to which the disorder manifests itself relative to ADHD in boys.*

DEVELOPMENTAL COURSE AND PROGNOSIS

- *Temperamental precursors of ADHD may appear very early in life, and hyperactivity and impulsivity can be observed at preschool age. The school environment increases demands on the child and academic, social, and conduct problems become obvious.*

- *The core features of childhood ADHD substantially continue into adolescence and to a lesser degree into adulthood. Hyperactivity and impulsivity appear to weaken over time and heterotypic continuity occurs. In addition, other difficulties, such as poor school achievement and antisocial behavior, are observed. Continuity of problems is linked complexly to several variables.*

PSYCHOLOGICAL EXPLANATIONS OF ADHD

- *Psychological theories of ADHD emphasize various deficits, including unusual sensitivity to reinforcement, aversion to delay, working memory deficits, and problems of inhibition and executive functions.*
- *Barkley's model, which applies to ADHD-C, proposes that inhibitory deficits interfere with other executive functions to produce impairment in the regulation of behavior.*

ETIOLOGY

- *Evidence exists for structural and functional abnormalities of the brain. Several regions are implicated but especially the right frontal-striatal and connecting regions. There is evidence for underactivity and dopamine and norepinephrine are implicated.*

- *Substantial genetic transmission of ADHD is indicated by family and twin studies, and a handful of genes has been identified as relevant to ADHD. Pregnancy/birth complications are inconsistently linked to ADHD, but maternal alcohol and cigarette use, low birthweight, and adverse birth conditions may underlie some cases. Diet is thought to have small influence; exposure to lead is linked to ADHD but likely is causal in only a small number of cases.*

- *The psychosocial environment plays a role in shaping and maintaining ADHD behaviors. Family factors are viewed as particularly important, and consideration is given to teacher behavior. Greater appreciation of early experiences that may shape brain development, such as excessive TV viewing, is suggested.*

ASSESSMENT

- *The identification of ADHD requires broad-based assessment that takes into account developmental level, various settings, and co-occurrence with other disorders.*

- *A comprehensive model includes interviews with the children/adolescents, parents, and teachers; standardized rating scales; direct observation; intelligence and achievement testing; and appropriate medical evaluations.*

TREATMENT

- *Stimulant medication, which is widely employed, can relieve both the core and associated symptoms of ADHD in most cases. However, limitations exist and numerous concerns are expressed about such pharmacotherapy.*

- *Some efficacy has been shown for behaviorally oriented parent training, as well as school-based interventions.*

- *Findings from the MTA study reveal the overall superiority of treatment with stimulant medication or medication combined with behavioral treatment, with some persistence of effects. However, this study points to the complexities of treatment effects and argues for matching treatments to children and their families.*

- *The availability and quality of treatment of ADHD appear to fall short of guidelines provided by the medical community.*

KEY TERMS

Predominately Inattentive Type (ADHD-I) *(p. 241)*

Predominately Hyperactive-Impulsive Type (ADHD-HI) *(p. 241)*

Combined Type (ADHD-C) *(p. 241)*

selective attention *(p. 242)*

sustained attention *(p. 242)*

continuous performance tests *(p. 242)*

stop-signal tasks *(p. 243)*

executive functions *(p. 244)*

sluggish cognitive tempo *(p. 247)*

delay aversion *(p. 253)*

behavioral inhibition (Barkley's model) *(p. 254)*

CHAPTER 10

Language and Learning Disorders

Specific problems that arise in the development of language and learning are discussed in this chapter. These disabilities can vary from subtle to severe, interfere with innumerable daily activities and social relationships, cast a shadow of failure and frustration over the school years, and adversely affect adult occupational life. Indeed, it can be argued that language and learning disorders have had increasing impact on individual lives because of escalating demands for certain kinds of skills and learning in our industrial and technologically sophisticated world.

Child or adolescent difficulties in communication and learning are associated with many known medical, genetic, and behavioral syndromes. Such conditions are not, however, the focus of this chapter. Rather, our primary interest is in youth who historically have been viewed as displaying specific impairments that are out of keeping with other aspects of their development. It is assumed that disturbance occurs relatively early and is not readily explained by social factors.

Professionals from diverse disciplines have been interested in language and learning problems—notably educators, psychologists, physicians, and language specialists. Approaching their work from different perspectives, they have generated diverse albeit often overlapping terminology, definitions, emphases, causal theories, and treatments. This rich history is reflected throughout the present chapter.

A Bit of History: Unexpected Disabilities, Unmet Needs

Specific language and learning problems have been recognized for a long time. Two major themes have been associated with the field as we know it today (Lyon, Fletcher, & Barnes, 2003). One is scientific and clinical interest in understanding individuals who display specific deficits that appear discrepant with their intelligence or other abilities. The other, more applied, theme is an emphasis on the need to improve services to young people exhibiting such deficits.

Curiosity about discrepant, or uneven, abilities within individuals can be traced to work in Europe in the 1800s. Consider as an example the following early description of a 10-year-old boy.

| Thomas | So Many Abilities |

He was apparently a bright and in every respect an intelligent boy. He had been learning music for a year and had made good progress in it. . . . In all departments of his studies where the instruction was oral he had made good progress, showing that his auditory memory was good. . . . He performs simple sums quite correctly, and his progress in arithmetic has been regarded as quite satisfactory. He has no difficulty in learning to write. His visual acuity is good.

Hinshelwood, 1917, pp. 46–47.

Yet, despite the boy's successes, it was reported that he was unable to learn to read. Many similarly puzzling cases were presented by physicians, and the field developed an early medical orientation that linked specific impairments with brain abnormalities. For example, in the latter 1880s, Broca described the inability of his adult patients to express themselves verbally while maintaining the capacity to comprehend what others said. Soon after, Wernicke documented brain lesions in patients who had problems in understanding language but otherwise did not exhibit language and cognitive

impairment. Each of these men traced the specific disability to an area in the brain that now carries his name. Over many years, brain damage in adults was linked to behavioral symptoms such as specific speech problems, learning difficulties, and inattention (Hammill, 1993). Similar problems in children were hypothesized to be caused by brain injury or dysfunction of some sort, perhaps too subtle to be identified.

As Table 10–1 indicates, behavioral scientists in the United States, building on the European work, began to contribute a psychological orientation to the study of learning problems (Hallahan & Mock, 2003). Although brain dysfunction was often assumed, etiology was downplayed in favor of understanding the characteristics of learners and the educational remediation of learning deficits (Lyon et al., 2003). By the mid-1900s, several kinds of interventions were recommended. Nevertheless, concern was growing that a group of children had educational needs that were not being met by the schools.

In 1963, representatives from several organizations met at a symposium sponsored by the Fund for Perceptually Handicapped Children. In addressing the participants, Samuel Kirk, a well-respected psychologist, noted that the children of their concern exhibited a variety of deficiencies that were

TABLE 10–1 HISTORICAL OVERVIEW OF THE FIELD OF LEARNING DISABILITIES

European Foundation Period (c. 1800–1920)	European physicians and researchers explore links between brain injury and disabilities (e.g., in language and reading)
U.S. Foundation Period (c. 1920–1960)	Building on European work, psychologists, educators, and others focus on identification of disabilities and remediation in educational settings via language, perceptual, and motor approaches
Emergent Period (c. 1960–1975)	Emergence of the concept of learning disabilities (LD) Various groups offer definitions of LD Advocacy by parents and professionals for effective educational services
Solidification Period (c. 1975–1985)	Solidification of federal definition and regulations for LD A focus on empirically validated research (e.g., on memory)
Turbulent Period (c. 1895–2000)	Efforts to reach consensus on definition Dramatic growth in number of LD students Continued research; progress on etiology, intervention Continued vexing questions (e.g., about definition, special education)

Based on Hallahan & Mock, 2003.

presumed to be related to neurological dysfunction—especially learning difficulties, perceptual problems, and hyperactivity. Kirk suggested and defined "learning disabilities" as a suitable term that he believed could encourage and guide the assessment and educational intervention so needed by these children. That evening the conferees organized into what is today called the Learning Disabilities Association of America (Hammill, 1993).

Kirk's presentation was a milestone in the emergence of the concept of learning disabilities, and parents and educators henceforth played an important role in an area previously dominated by physicians and psychologists (Hallahan & Kauffman, 1978; Taylor, 1988a). Parents were given hope that the problem was limited and treatable; teachers were relieved of the suspicion that they were to blame for student failure; concerned professionals were provided a term that could make children eligible for special services. It was recognized that youth labeled as "learning disabled" constituted a heterogeneous group.

By the late 20th century, efforts were made to reach consensus on the definition of learning disabilities, provide special education services, and conduct research into many areas. The last few decades have seen progress, and the number of youth categorized as learning disabled has dramatically increased. Nonetheless, challenges remain regarding the definition and conceptualization of specific language and learning disabilities, as well as related issues.

Definitional Concerns

To understand the problems of definition we turn to the **Education for All Handicapped Children Act** of 1975 (Public Law 94-142), which has had enormous influence on the field of learning disorders or disabilities. A sweeping educational mandate, it has been amended over the years and retitled the **Individuals with Disabilities Education Act** (IDEA). Its definition of learning disabilities has had an impact on the educational system, children and families, clinicians and researchers.

Specific learning disability means a disorder in one or more of the basic psychological processes involved in understanding or in using language, spoken or written, in which the disorder may manifest itself in an imperfect ability to listen, think, speak, read, write, spell, or to do mathematical calculations. The term includes such conditions as perceptual handicaps, brain injury, minimal brain dysfunction, dyslexia, and developmental aphasia. The term does not include children who have learning problems which are primarily the result of visual, hearing, or motor handicaps, or mental retardation, or emotional disturbance, or of environmental, cultural, or economic disadvantage. (U.S. Office of Education, 1977, p. 65083)

This is a general definition that refers to disorder in basic psychological processes, but does not identify them. Reference is made to several conditions, including neurological anomalies, in only a general way. The definition also lacks specific criteria for identifying disabilities. In addition, it explicitly excludes children whose disabilities are due to several factors that could be expected to cause learning problems. The exclusionary criteria have been questioned, partly because it may be difficult to distinguish underachievement due to emotional disturbance, lack of motivation, or cultural or economic disadvantage. The presence of exclusionary criteria, in combination with the lack of specific criteria to define learning disabilities, has led to the statement that learning disabilities are defined more by what they are *not* than by what they are.

Definitional concerns have resulted in different, albeit overlapping, definitions and ways to identify disabilities (Dean & Burns, 2002; Hammill, 1993; Lyon et al., 2003). Definitional problems have led to different prevalence rates, incomparability of groups chosen for research purposes, and varying standards to determine whether children will receive special education services. Here, we provide a snapshot of the definitional problem by considering how learning disabilities have often been identified.

IDENTIFYING SPECIFIC DISABILITIES

A lack of agreed-upon criteria to identify learning disabilities has been a continuing problem. What criteria and methods are to be used to decide that language or academic skills are below expectations for the child? In fact, different guidelines have been offered and several methods generated. Most often they do not target underlying psychological processes, and they raise questions.

One approach to identifying specific disabilities has been to determine that the child is performing below expected grade level in at least one academic area. Variations occur in the specific criterion, however.

Thus, a sixth-grader, for example, might be labeled with a learning disability when achievement is at the fourth or the fifth grade. A general problem in this method of identification is that a large discrepancy would seem more serious for a younger than an older child: being 2 years behind is more serious for a third-grader than for a six-grader. The problem can be reduced by setting the criterion, for instance, at 1-year deficiency for younger children and 2 years for older children, but judgment still must be made as to the criterion for each grade level.

A second approach to identification has been to compare the child's performance with age-mates on standardized tests of language, reading, writing, and arithmetic. The degree to which performance must fall below expected performance varies with school districts and researchers. The criterion is usually set in the range of one to two standard deviations below the mean on these tests.

A particularly prevalent way to identify disabilities has been by a discrepancy between the individual's intellectual ability and specific achievement level. It is assumed that if a specific disability exists, performance on measures of *general* ability (typically IQ tests) will exceed performance on achievement tests of the hypothesized *specific* impairment. Guidelines often call for the discrepancy to be severe or significant, but this has been defined somewhat differently. A discrepancy of two or more standard deviations between intelligence and achievement is often set, although smaller difference has been acceptable. As popular as this IQ-achievement discrepancy approach has been, it is criticized on several grounds (Dyck et al., 2004). For example, it is argued that intelligence tests rely strongly on language abilities so that intelligence may be underestimated in children with language or learning disabilities—making a discrepancy less probable. Serious question also is raised about a related issue, the exclusion of children considered to be "slow learners," that is, for whom a discrepancy is not found (Siegel, 1989; Stanovich, 1989; Vellutino et al., 2004). There is growing recognition that in several ways specific disabilities do not differ much from general learning problems that show no such discrepancy (Scruggs & Mastropieri, 2002).

Overall, the arguments against the IQ-achievement discrepancy approach have somewhat weakened it (Dean & Burns, 2002). Nonetheless, intelligence is frequently considered by requiring that the child with low achievement also exhibit average intelligence, or that IQ not fall below the level that typically defines mental retardation (about 70).

The incorporation of children with both low achievement and relatively low intelligence into the concept of learning disabilities is a contentious issue (e.g., Kavale & Forness, 2003).

To be sure, despite the problems of definitional confusion, substantial progress has been made. In this chapter, we examine specific developmental disabilities in language and reading, and briefly in writing and mathematics. We begin with language disorders because they are likely to be identified earlier than learning disorders and because language problems often are involved in other disabilities.

Language Disorders

The study and treatment of language disorders has been both independent of and integrated with those of learning disorders, which typically refer to reading, writing, and arithmetic. Language disabilities have historically been referred to as *aphasia*, a term that means loss of language due to brain damage or dysfunction. When the matter at hand is developmental disorder in youth—as it is in our discussion—aphasia is not an accurate fit, and the terms *developmental aphasia* and *developmental dysphasia* were once employed. These terms have largely given way to *specific language disorder* and *specific language impairment*. We use these terms interchangeably. Discussion begins with an overview of normal language development to provide a framework for understanding disordered language.

NORMAL LANGUAGE DEVELOPMENT

Language, as we usually know it, is a system of communication based on sounds that are combined into words and sentences to represent experience and carry meaning. Table 10–2 defines the basic components of language that must be mastered by all users of oral and written language.

Phonology has to do with the basic sounds of a language. English has 42 basic sounds, or phonemes. As a written language, it has 26 alphabet letters, which singly or in combinations are called graphemes. There is a correspondence between phonemes and graphemes. Of course, letters are combined to form words, which carry meaning. Morphology has to do with the formation of words, and syntax refers to the organization of words into phrases and sentences. Morphology and syntax are parts of grammar, the system of rules that organize a language. Thus, English speakers who follow the rules say "He dances

TABLE 10–2	BASIC COMPONENTS OF LANGUAGE
Phonology	Sounds of a language and rules for combining them
Morphology	Formation of words, including the use of prefixes and suffixes (e.g., un, ed, s) to give meaning
Syntax	Organization of words into phrases and sentences
Semantics	Meanings in language
Pragmatics	Use of language in specific contexts

the social customs of language such as taking turns when speaking with another person or judging when to initiate conversation.

Superimposed on the basic components of language are reception and expression. Reception has to do with the comprehension of messages sent by others. Expression concerns the production of language, that is, sending messages. Reception is developmentally acquired earlier than expression—as anyone who tries to learn a second language quickly discovers.

Infants typically come into the world geared for language; their amazing capacity progresses rapidly and in sequential milestones during the first few years of life (Table 10–3). During the first year, infants can distinguish and produce sounds that are not part of their language, and then this ability contracts to the sounds of their language. Thus, infants come into the world with a general ability to process language sounds, and this is refined with experience.

well," not "He well dance." The rules of language help facilitate meaningful communication, which is referred to as semantics. Finally, pragmatics is the use of language in context; in social situations it includes

TABLE 10–3	EARLY ACQUISITION OF LANGUAGE AND COMMUNICATION	
	RECEPTION	**EXPRESSION**
Birth to 6 months	Reacts to sudden noise. Is quieted by a voice. Locates sound. Recognizes name and words like "bye-bye."	Cries. Babbles, laughs. Initiates vocal play. Vocalizes to self. Experiments with voice.
6 to 12 months	Stops activity to "no." Raises arms to "come up." Obeys simple instructions. Understands simple statements.	Makes sounds of the culture's language. Combines vowel sounds. Imitates adult sounds. Says first words.
12 to 18 months	Carries out two consecutive commands. Understands new words. Listens to nursery rhymes.	Uses ten words. Requests by naming objects. Connects sounds so that they flow like a sentence.
18 to 24 months	Recognizes many sounds. Understands action words like "show me."	Uses short sentences. Uses pronouns. Echoes last words of a rhyme.
24 to 36 months	Follows commands using "in," "on," "under." Follows three verbal commands given in one utterance.	Uses possessive, noun-verb combinations. Mother understands 90 percent of communications.
36 to 48 months	Increases understanding of others' messages and social context of communication.	Uses increasingly complex language forms, such as conjunctions and auxiliary verbs.

Based on Bryant, 1977; Whitehurst, 1982.

TABLE 10–4	THE DSM CRITERIA FOR THREE COMMUNICATION DISORDERS	
PHONOLOGICAL	**EXPRESSIVE**	**RECEPTIVE-EXPRESSIVE**
A. There is failure to use developmentally appropriate and dialect-appropriate speech sounds (e.g., use of substitutions and omissions).	A. Scores from standardized measures of expressive language are substantially below scores for nonverbal intelligence and receptive language.	A. Scores from standardized measures of both receptive and expressive language are substantially below those for nonverbal intellectual capacity.

B. The difficulties interfere with academic or occupational achievement or with social communication.

C. If mental retardation, a speech-motor or sensory deficit, or environmental deprivation is present, the language difficulties are in excess of those usually associated with these problems.

From American Psychiatric Association, 2000.

By their first birthdays, most infants are saying a few words. Some speech sounds are more difficult than others, and individual differences in pronunciation, or articulation, become obvious. Even before this time, infants have begun to understand the communications of others.

By 2 years of age, most children have gone from saying single words, to two-word utterances, to longer strings of words set in meaningful phrases or sentences. Vocabulary increases dramatically, different parts of speech are acquired, and the ability to arrange words improves. Comprehension also grows, and parents of 3-year-olds perceive that they are talking with someone who is no longer a "baby." Indeed, infancy—a term derived from a Latin word that means "incapable of speech"—is usually said to be over at age 2. Progress continues at a rapid rate and includes pragmatics. By age 7, many of the basics of language are acquired, although language development continues into adolescence and even into adulthood.

DSM CLASSIFICATION AND DIAGNOSIS

From even a brief review of language development, it is obvious that a variety of impairments might occur; problems can exist in phonology, syntax, semantics, and so forth. It is possible, then, to classify disabilities in several ways. Although attempts to subgroup language disabilities have not been very successful, a basic distinction is often made between children who have difficulty in expression, or performance, and those who have problems in reception, or comprehension (Leonard, 1998).

Under the category of Communication Disorders, the DSM considers three disorders of interest to our discussion. Table 10–4 provides a summary of the diagnostic criteria for these. For Phonological Disorder to be diagnosed, a child must fail to display developmentally appropriate and dialect-appropriate speech sounds. Diagnosis of Expressive Disorder or Mixed Receptive-Expressive Disorder requires assessment with standardized, individually given language and intelligence tests. Expressive Disorder exists when language expression is inferior to the person's nonverbal intelligence and reception (comprehension) of language. The category of Mixed Receptive-Expressive Disorder reflects the fact that receptive problems do not typically occur alone. Diagnosis requires that both reception and expression of language are below the child's nonverbal intelligence. In all cases of language disorders, impairments must be severe enough to interfere with daily functioning. Furthermore, the impairments cannot be due to mental retardation or sensorimotor deficits, nor to insufficient environmental stimulation.

DESCRIPTION

Phonological Disorder. Children with this disorder have difficulty in articulating speech sounds. They make incorrect speech sounds, substitute easy-made sounds for more difficult ones, or omit sounds. Most children display some misarticulation as they acquire speech, and developmental norms are thus crucial in diagnosis of disorder.

Problems in articulation are sometimes differentiated from language disorders and are referred to as speech disorder. (In fact, children with simple misarticulations but no other difficulties are not considered to have specific language disorder according to some definitions, although they may profit from remedial work [Leonard, 1998].) However, problems in phonology can go beyond a simple inability to accurately produce speech sounds to a broader problem in the child's understanding of the sound structure of the language (Snowling, Bishop, & Stothard, 2000; Whitehurst & Fischel, 1994). Thus, for example, the child may have difficulty in knowing which word rhymes with another or whether "soup" or "coat" starts with the same sound as "Sam" (Bishop, 2002). Such problems have more serious implications for the development of language.

Expressive Language Disorder. This disorder involves the production of language with regard to vocabulary, grammar, and other aspects of language output. Youngsters with expressive problems may have a limited amount of speech and may speak in extremely short, simple sentences. Vocabulary may be small; critical parts of sentences may be missing; unusual word order may be displayed. Especially problematic, children may exhibit undue errors in marking word forms such as plurals or verb tense. In addition, phonological problems may be observed. However, children with expressive problems understand speech and age-level concepts, and thus they can appropriately respond to others' communications.

These characteristics are seen in the following description of Jennifer, a sociable, active 5-year-old with expressive language disorder (Johnson & Beitchman, 2000a). One day while Jennifer was playing with her friend Sarah, each girl told the story of Little Red Riding Hood to her doll.

Jennifer | Problems in Language Expression

Sarah's story began: "Little Red Riding Hood was taking a basket of food to her grandmother who was sick. A bad wolf stopped Riding Hood in the forest. He tried to get the basket from her but she wouldn't give it to him."

By contrast, Jennifer's story illustrated her marked difficulties in verbal expression: "Riding Hood going to grandma house. Her taking food. Bad wolf in a bed. Riding Hood say, what big ears, grandma? Hear you, dear. What big eyes, grandma? See you, dear. What big mouth, grandma? Eat you all up!"

Many features of Jennifer's story were characteristic of children with expressive language disorder, including the short, incomplete sentences; the simple sentence structure; the omission of grammatical function words (e.g., is, the) and endings (e.g., possessive -'s, present tense verb -s); the problem in question formation; and the incorrect use of pronouns (e.g., "her" for she). Nonetheless, when tested by methods that did not require verbal responding, it was clear that Jennifer understood the details and plot of the Riding Hood tale as well as Sarah did. Jennifer also demonstrated adequate comprehensive skills in her kindergarten classroom, where she readily followed the teacher's multistep verbal instructions.

Adapted from Johnson & Beitchman, 2000a, pp. 2636–2637.

Receptive-Expressive Language Disorder. This disorder involves difficulties comprehending the communication of others. Single words, phrases, sentences, the multiple meanings of a word, or the past tense may all be problematic. The child may fail to respond to speech, seem deaf, respond inappropriately to others' speech, or be uninterested in television. In addition, there are difficulties in expressing language. Problems may occur in phonology as well—although these are not central to the disorder. Perhaps not surprising, receptive-expressive language disorders are generally the most severe language impairments.

The description of a 5-year-old boy, Trang, illustrates receptive-expressive impairments (Johnson & Beitchman, 2000b). This child lived with his parents and siblings, who were proficient in both English and Vietnamese. His development in both languages was much slower than that of his siblings, and kindergarten assessment revealed impairments in both reception and expression.

Trang | Problems in Language Reception and Expression

Trang understood a limited number of words for objects, actions, and relations. He often failed to follow classroom instruction, particularly those that involved words for time (e.g., yesterday, after, week) and space (e.g., beneath, in front of, around). . . . His conversation with other children often broke down because he did not understand fully what they were saying, nor could he express his own ideas clearly. As a result he was not a favored playmate, and most of the children in his class ignored him. His limited interactions further reduced Trang's opportunities for improving and practicing his already weak language skills. Additional assessment, conducted with the assistance of a Vietnamese interpreter, revealed that Trang showed similar receptive and expressive language deficits in Vietnamese. His nonverbal skills, however, were generally appropriate for his age. He readily constructed intricate buildings and vehicles with small, plastic building blocks; he easily completed complex jigsaw puzzles; and he successfully solved numerical, conceptual, or analogical problems, as long as they were presented nonverbally.

Adapted from Johnson & Beitchman, 2000b, p. 2642.

When considering any type of language disorder, it is helpful to keep in mind the considerable variation across children in the kinds and severity of problems experienced. Imagine, if you will, the difference between a child with only articulation deficits and a child who is unable to comprehend much of what is being communicated by others. Life is different too for the child who has minor articulation deficits and one whose speech can hardly be understood by others.

EPIDEMIOLOGY AND DEVELOPMENTAL COURSE

The prevalence of specific language impairments has not been easy to establish because of differences in definitions, assessment instruments, and other factors. Children referred for psychiatric services have very high rates, for example, 40 to 50 percent (Toppelberg et al., 2002). Limited epidemiologic studies suggest rates of about 7 percent for 5-year-olds (Bishop, 2002). Even so, prevalence depends on age and type of disorder.

Boys are widely reported as having higher rates than girls (American Psychiatric Association, 2000; Leonard, 1998). Although higher prevalence in clinic samples may reflect referral bias, this does not seem to completely account for the gender difference (Viding et al., 2004). Higher rates also have been noted in children from low socioeconomic groups (Toppelberg & Shapiro, 2000). This finding raises questions, however, about the identification of disorders when children use dialects different from the standard English employed in standardized assessment instruments. Moreover, the SES difference does not appear to be strong (Bishop, 2002).

Language disorders usually appear by age 3 or 4, but mild difficulties may not be identified until later (American Psychiatric Association, 2000). Some impairments may become apparent with the demands of schoolwork and greater complexity of language. It may be more difficult to ascertain what a child understands than to observe impairments in the expression of speech.

Retrospective and prospective studies of children and adults of various ages, followed for various periods of time, indicate that improvement can occur over time and that language abilities can reach the normal range (Leonard, 1998). However, a hierarchy of risk based on the type of disorder has been noted. Children who display only articulation problems are at lowest risk, those with expressive problems are at middle risk, and those with receptive-expressive problems are at highest risk for later language impairments (Baker & Cantwell, 1989; Rutter, Mawhood, & Howlin, 1992; Whitehurst & Fischel, 1994).

Phonological problems, especially when mild, are quite common during the preschool years, but about 75 percent of mild to moderate cases remit by age 6 (American Psychiatric Association, 2000). Such difficulties have low rates in adolescence. A substantial group of children with early expressive difficulties continues to exhibit impairment whereas others reach the typical range of language development but still fall somewhat short of most of their peers (Bishop, 2002; Rescorla, 2002; Tomblin et al., 2003). In contrast, receptive-expressive difficulties, which probably are less common than expressive disabilities, often increase over time and many children may never develop completely normal language. For example, boys with receptive-expressive impairments were evaluated in early adulthood; 20 percent had a level of comprehension below that of 10-year-old children and about 25 percent had equally poor expressive skills (Mawhood, Howlin, & Rutter, 2000). In general then, although children diagnosed with specific language impairments are often said to be "delayed" in language development, many get a late start and develop more slowly, with abilities leveling off or falling behind and never catching up (Leonard, 1998; Miller & Tallal, 1995; Tallal & Benasich, 2002). Further study is needed of the factors that influence outcome (Botting et al., 2001).

The burden of language disorder is seen in its association with adverse psychosocial and behavioral outcomes. School achievement is affected: more students are retained at grade level and fewer students attend high school (Tomblin et al., 2000). At least in

TABLE 10–5	RISK OF HAVING A LEARNING DISABILITY* AT AGE 19 IN A GROUP IDENTIFIED WITH LANGUAGE IMPAIRMENTS AT AGE 5

LEARNING DISABILITY	RISK
Reading	4.6
Spelling	4.1
Math	3.7
Reading + spelling	4.7
Reading + math	9.4
Spelling + math	4.4
Reading + spelling + math	7.8

*A learning disability was defined by performance below the 25th percentile on tests of reading, spelling, or math and an IQ (verbal or performance) of at least 80.

Adapted from Young et al., 2002.

part, this finding undoubtedly is due to the association of language disorders with learning disabilities (Tomblin et al., 2000; Young et al., 2002). For instance, one longitudinal study found that language-impaired children were 4.6 times as likely to have later reading disability compared to typically developing children (Table 10–5). In another study, 51 percent of children with language disorder had reading disability and 55 percent of children with reading disability had language impairment. (McArthur et al., 2000). The role that language plays in reading problems is suggested by the finding that preschoolers who have weaknesses in oral language (e.g., vocabulary, grammar) and in knowing the names and sounds of letters are at risk for later reading problems (Lonigan, Burgess, & Anthony, 2000; Raitano et al., 2004).

UNDERLYING COGNITIVE DEFICITS

Children with language impairments commonly exhibit subtle, nonlinguistic cognitive deficits and proposals have been put forth as to how these deficits might contribute to language disorder (Bishop, 1992b; Leonard, 1998). Given the complexity of this work, our discussion only aims to give the flavor of the research.

An important hypothesis is that a general limitation in information-processing capacity is involved in language disorder (Leonard, 1998). The information-processing model focuses on the mental manipulation of information. It assumes, among other things, that rapid handling of information facilitates processing. Limitation in speed of processing is notable in children with specific language impairments. They appear to more slowly respond across a variety of tasks, such as mentally rotating stimuli and moving pegs. In other words, the limitation potentially affects learning or performance across domains. Regarding language itself, detrimental effects reasonably would be expected when the specific language operation requires especially rapid processing.

A second, more specific, hypothesis relates language impairments to the slow processing and production of brief, rapidly successive events, notably auditory events. The perception of many of the details of language depends on sound cues of brief duration (Leonard, 1998), and so a child who cannot catch rapidly flowing cues might well have language difficulties. Through a series of studies in which sound of various duration and sequences were presented, Tallal and colleagues have argued for deficits in such processing. Children with language impairments have been shown to have difficulty in identifying very fast sounds embedded in speech (Tallal & Benasich, 2002). Moreover, infants at family risk for language/learning impairments exhibited longer processing times for auditory stimuli. Further support for the hypothesis comes from studies indicating that when sound cues in speech syllables are experimentally extended, speech discrimination improves.

Still a third proposal implicates working, or short-term, memory involved in the processing of sound (Gathercole, 1998). Working memory is hypothesized to include a system, the phonological loop, to deal specifically with processing language-related information (Baddeley, 1992; 2001). The operation of this component of working memory can be evaluated by saying aloud a string of words, or nonwords, and then asking the person to repeat them back immediately. The number of stimuli repeated is a measure of phonological short-term memory. In typically developing children, phonological memory is related to the acquisition of vocabulary, comprehension, syntactic processing, and speech production (Marton & Schwartz, 2003). Moreover, poor phonological short-term memory has been shown in children with language disorder, even when matched on language ability with other children (e.g., Bishop, 2002; Conti-Ramsden, 2003).

Although progress is being made in understanding subtle cognitive deficits exhibited by children with language impairments, much is yet to be done. Given the heterogeneity of problems, several deficits could be involved.

Learning Disorders: Reading, Writing, Arithmetic

The terms *learning disabilities* (LD) and *learning disorders* refer to specific developmental problems in reading, writing, and arithmetic—the "three Rs" essential to classroom learning and everyday functioning. These disorders respectively have been called *dyslexia, dysgraphia*, and *dyscalculia*—terms that are used less today. Although learning disabilities are often described as if they are "pure," deficits frequently occur in combinations. Most children with learning disorder have reading problems, and many have additional learning difficulties. Specific learning disabilities are recognized by the educational system and by the DSM and ICD.

DSM CLASSIFICATION AND DIAGNOSIS

Table 10–6 provides a summary of the DSM criteria for diagnosis of Reading Disorder, Disorder of Written Expression, and Mathematics Disorder. Diagnosis is based on a substantial discrepancy between how well a person performs on individually given, standardized achievement tests relative to the person's age, intelligence, or age-appropriate education. The disturbance must interfere significantly with academic achievement or daily living. It cannot be accounted for by a sensory deficit.

We discuss select topics for each of these disorders before examining more general issues. Emphasis is placed by far on reading disabilities because of their high prevalence and because they have been most investigated.

READING DISORDER

Description. Reading can be defined as "the process of extracting and constructing meaning from written text for some purpose" (Vellutino et al., 2004, p. 5). It requires the ability to readily identify words in running text so that the meaning of the text can be computed. Among the many skills involved in this "on-line" process are language abilities, cognitive skills, understanding of the conventions of written text (e.g., reading from left to right on a page), and a store of knowledge about the world.

An enormously complex process, reading virtually always entails instruction. When it is not mastered, children may struggle to recognize single written words or to pronounce them correctly when reading aloud, read excessively slowly or haltingly, have limited vocabulary, be able to read but not to understand what they have read, or not remember what they have read. Given the complexities of reading, it is unsurprising that extensive efforts have been made to discover whether reading problems fall into subtypes based on underlying cognitive deficits. These efforts have not resulted in well-delineated subtypes (Culbertson, 1998; Siegel, 2003). However, a distinction often is made between problems in word-level reading and problems in the comprehension of written text.

Epidemiology and Developmental Course. The reported prevalence of reading disorder (RD) has varied considerably. Lyon and colleagues (2003) note that estimates historically have fallen between at least 10 and 15 percent of the U.S. school-age population. Discrepancies in reported rates are due perhaps to definitional inconsistency, sampling differences, and the lumping together of different types of learning disorders.

Boys have been more often identified than girls, but there is reason to suspect a selection bias. Willcutt and Pennington (2000) suggest that the male to female ratio is about 3 to 1 in clinic samples but only about 1.5 to 1 in the general child population.

Reading disorders have been identified at varying rates across many countries (Grigorenko, 2001).

TABLE 10–6	THE DSM CRITERIA FOR DISORDERS OF READING, WRITTEN EXPRESSION, AND MATHEMATICS

A. Achievement or ability, as measured by standardized tests, is substantially below that expected given the person's age, measured intelligence, and age-appropriate education.
B. The disturbance significantly interferes with academic achievement or activities of daily living that require the ability.
C. If a sensory deficit is present, the difficulties are in excess of those usually associated with the sensory deficit.

From American Psychiatric Association, 2000.

Further research would be useful in clarifying the degree to which this might be explained by the differing structures of different languages, societal attitudes toward reading disabilities, or methodological factors.

Reading problems tend to persist during the school years into adolescence and adulthood (McGee et al., 2002). Still, variation is seen in outcome, including improvement (Shaywitz et al., 2003; Williams & McGee, 1996). Some children with poor reading skills in early childhood have been reported as catching up with their peers by preadolescence or adolescence, and improvement can occur from adolescence into early adulthood. General intelligence, mother's reading ability, and initial severity of reading problems may predict outcome. Youngsters with initially severe problems are further disadvantaged by not being able to practice reading, because experience and practice with print material is considered important in improving literacy skills.

Underlying Processes. Many perceptual and cognitive processes have been implicated in RD, including auditory and visual processes. Theories of visual system abnormalities were the most influential throughout the 20th century until the 1970s and 1980s (Vellutino, et al., 2004). For example, Samuel Orton, a central figure in early research on reading, noted that among other difficulties visual-perceptual deficits caused dyslexic children to reverse letters (*d* for *b; saw* for *was*) and even to write in mirror images (Vellutino, 1979). Other theorists have suggested that dyslexia is caused by eye defects that lead to impairments in scanning, tracking, or processing visual stimuli.

Despite the early popularity of visual-perceptual hypotheses, it is presently believed that perceptual processing deficits may be involved in reading problems for some children (e.g., Solan et al., 2001), but that reading disorder fundamentally is related to language impairment. In a simple demonstration of this view, Vellutino (1987) asked poor readers in the second through sixth grades to copy words and other stimuli after a brief visual presentation. They then were requested to name the words. Poor readers correctly copied words—vision did not appear problematic—but they had difficulties in naming the words. For instance, they copied *was* correctly, even correctly named the letters, but named the word *saw*. The incorrect naming suggested a language rather than a visual problem.

Considerable research now gives a central role to phonological processing, that is, using the sound structure of language to process written material.

Before they can learn to read, children must realize that spoken words can be segmented into sounds, an ability referred to as phonological awareness. For instance, they must recognize that the word *sad* contains three sounds, even though *sad* is said as one unit of sound. Also necessary is phonological decoding, that is, understanding that letters (graphemes) correspond to sounds (phonemes) and being able to map letters to sounds. Young children who are aware of the sounds of their native language and who can decode letters, syllables, and words develop better reading. In contrast, core phonological processing deficits are associated with difficulty in naming single words, reading, and spelling. It is thought that phonological processing deficits are involved in most cases of reading disorder. Moreover, interventions that target phonological processing deficits improve single word identification and reading. Of further interest are cross-cultural studies pointing to the importance of phonological processes in the reading of alphabet-based languages other than English (Grigorenko, 2001; Paulesu et al., 2001). (For more on these studies see Accent: "Vulnerability and Reading in Different Languages.")

For all these reasons, much emphasis has been given to phonological awareness and decoding as the core deficit in reading. Nevertheless, other reading problems exist. Of notable interest is that some children—perhaps 5 to 10 percent—who are not deficient in phonological processing have difficulties in understanding what they read (Lyon et al., 2003). These children can decode and recognize single words, but they variously exhibit small vocabulary, poor understanding of syntax, and deficits in working memory and drawing inferences from text. They may often go unidentified by teachers (Nation et al., 2004).

In the view of some researchers, an overemphasis on phonological deficits is too narrow a perspective of reading. Snowling (2000) has pointed out that decoding skills certainly aid the child in reading words that follow the usual grapheme-phoneme rules, but they do not help much for words such as *yacht* and *biscuit*. The same is true for knowing how to read the word *bow* in "The magician took a bow," and understanding *she* in "Susan gave Jane an apple and she was happy" (p. 246). Snowling, and others, emphasize that reading involves phonological, syntactic, and semantic components, and that the demands placed on these components change over time. Phonology is likely to be especially important in early learning to read.

In an interesting study, Snowling, Gallagher, and Frith (2003) conducted three assessments (at age

ACCENT ● ● ● ● ●

Vulnerability and Reading in Different Languages

The value of cross-cultural investigation is demonstrated in studies of reading in different languages. Even some basic findings give us food for thought.

To begin with, alphabet-based languages vary in the consistency in which letters map to sounds—German and Italian are more consistent than English and French. Reading skills are more readily acquired in the more consistent languages, and there are fewer cases of reading disorder as shown in the accurate recognition of single words (Paulesu et al., 2001). However, even in cultures using the more consistent languages, some individuals will read less well than others, but this is not very evident in phonological awareness and decoding. Reading problems are manifested more in short-term memory and rapid naming of words (Vellutino et al., 2004). It has also been shown that German-speaking children with reading problems are able to read long unfamiliar words and nonwords as well as their nonimpaired peers—presumably because of the relatively consistent matching of letters and sounds. They do, however, show problems in fluency.

Perhaps even more striking is the comparison of reading disabilities in alphabet-based languages and logographic languages, such as Chinese, which requires knowledge and recognition of hundreds of complex visual symbols with different meanings. Preliminary research suggests that learning to read in Chinese is associated with several deficits rather than with difficulties in phonological awareness and decoding. Visual skills are a stronger predictor of reading ability in Chinese than in alphabet languages. Moreover, brain scans indicate that functioning of a right frontal area is disrupted in impaired reading of Chinese rather than a left posterior area typically seen in impaired reading of English (Siok et al., 2004).

What can be made of these fascinating findings? For Vellutino and his colleagues (2004), the findings underscore the fact that reading disorder depends on certain innate susceptibilities interacting with environmental factors, including the language specific to the culture in which children learn to read. Some alphabet languages, such as German, may be less demanding on the vulnerable child whereas others, such as English, may present heightened challenges. Moreover, different languages may make different demands on specific abilities. Thus, the child with a particular vulnerability may be likely to develop a reading disorder in one culture but not in another.

---

3 years, 9 months; 6 years; 8 years) of children at family risk for reading problems and children not at risk. Many more at-risk youngsters exhibited reading problems at age 8; they had experienced continuous language impairments as well. Other at-risk children did not meet the criteria for reading problems at age 8, but they did show poorer performance than the control group in language and reading skills (e.g., spelling, nonword reading, reading comprehension, and mild impairments in phonological awareness and verbal short-term memory). This pattern, shown in other but not all research, suggests that reading disability is not an all-or-none condition but rather is multidimensional and continuous. That is, children exhibit different language and reading deficits, with only some meeting the threshold defined as reading disorder.

Also suggested in the Snowling and colleagues (2003) study are two pathways to reading abilities. One path originates with language skills and the other with early letter knowledge (phonological path)—and both paths lead to word-level and comprehension reading skills (Figure 10–1). Based on the data, the investigators propose that at-risk children only slowly developed the phonological path but that some were protected from reading problems at age 8 because (1) they had sufficient language skills to rely more on the language-related path and (2) as learning to read proceeds, reading depends more on language-related skills (e.g., using the context of a sentence to read). The investigators recognize that language skills are not the only factor that might protect high-risk children; others include instruction, children's ability to attend, and models who foster the practice of reading. Moreover, the analysis does not rule out the possibility of the protected children's developing later reading problems. In fact, some evidence suggests that reading problems—both word-level and/or comprehension—can first emerge around the fourth or fifth grade (Leach, Scarborough, &

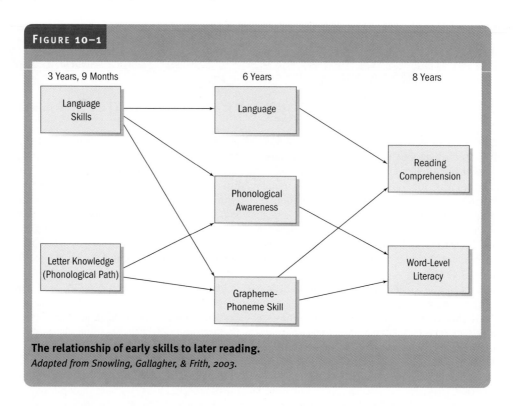

FIGURE 10–1

The relationship of early skills to later reading.
Adapted from Snowling, Gallagher, & Frith, 2003.

Rescorla, 2003). As is obvious, much is yet to be known about reading. At the same time, the importance of phonological processing in learning to read is clear.

DISORDER OF WRITTEN EXPRESSION

Children with writing disabilities may be the last to hand in classwork and may sit for hours over homework. Their writings may be rife with errors, be difficult to decipher, and contain disorganized content lacking in length and richness. Despite definitional variation, there is consensus that writing is multidimensional, and it has been helpful to make a distinction between transcription and text generation.

Transcription involves putting ideas into written form; it is fundamental in the early development of writing (Berninger & Amtmann, 2003). Many deficiencies are observed in poor transcription—in punctuation, capitalization, word placement—but problems in handwriting and spelling are central. Disabilities can occur in one or both or these (Figure 10–2). In typical development, smooth, rapid, and clear handwriting develops gradually and entails effort. In the presence of specific disabilities, producing letters and words on paper goes especially slowly, is laborious, and not always successful. Good handwriting requires not only motor skill, but also that letters be stored in working and long-term memory, planned for, and retrieved from memory. Good spelling depends, among other abilities, on understanding the connections between sounds and conventional spelling, on word recognition, and on knowledge and retrieval of learned letters/words from memory (Berninger & Amtmann, 2003; Lyon et al., 2003).

Text generation can be viewed as the creation of meaning in written form. Among other requirements it demands that the child be able to retrieve from memory words, sentence structure, and stored information about the topic of interest. Also critical are higher order executive functions and metacognitive skills, the latter involving the understanding of the cognitive processing system (Graham & Harris, 2003; Schumaker & Deshler, 2003; Wong et al., 1997). Disabled writers lack skills in understanding the goal of their writing, developing a plan, organizing the points to be made, linking ideas, monitoring and revising their work, and the like. Many of these components apply to language and thinking more generally and are thus less specific to writing disorders than is transcription (Lyon et al., 2003). This does not mean, of course, that these skills are less important in understanding and ameliorating children's difficulties in writing. Figure 10–3 provides an example of the work of an adolescent assigned to

FIGURE 10-2

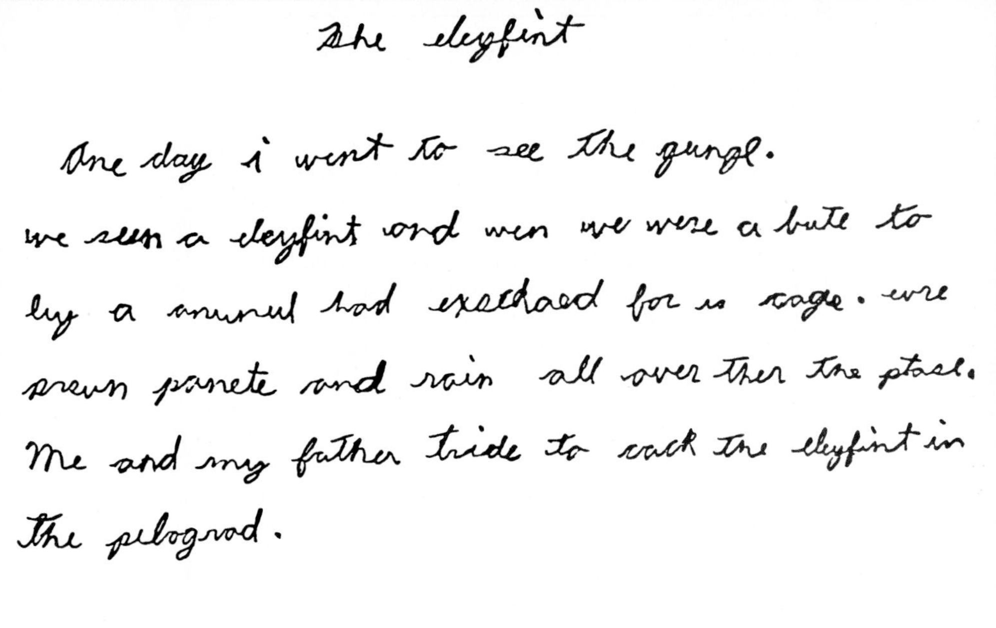

The Elephant

One day I went to see the jungle. We seen a elephant and when we were about to leave an animal escaped from his cage. Every person panicked and ran all over the place. Me and my father tried to catch the elephant in the playground.

The writing of an 11-year-old boy and the probable translation. The writing shows imagination, a rich vocabulary, and a basic grasp of storytelling. There also are misspellings of common and uncommon words, poorly formed letters, and retracing of letters that suggest difficulty in mechanics of writing. *Adapted from Taylor, 1988a.*

write a compare-and-contrast essay. The essay is comprehensible but demonstrates weak sentence construction, awkward phrasing, lack of paragraphing, and deficits in organization. This student's writing greatly improved through an intervention program aimed at teaching cognitive and metacognitive skills.

Epidemiology and Developmental Course. The prevalence of writing disorders is not definitively known and further epidemiological study is needed. It is estimated that 10 percent of school-age children have some form of writing disability (Lyon et al., 2003). Standardized tests for writing skill are not well developed and assessment may require analyses of samples of a child's written work. Developmental norms are important, of course, in judging the quality of writing; for example, before age 8 or so motor skills may not be well developed, and only simple narrative can be expected (e.g., Spagna, Cantwell, & Baker, 2000a). By second grade, though, the disorder is usually apparent (American Psychiatric Association, 2000), and referral for problems sharply increases around the fourth grade (Berninger & Amtmann, 2003). It is assumed that writing disorder lessens over time but persists for some youth.

MATHEMATICS DISORDER

Mathematics disabilities can affect many domains—for example, arithmetic or geometry—and also any single domain (Geary, 2003). Descriptions of mathematics disorder in children indicate an array of

FIGURE 10–3

Hokey and basketball are two sports they both have comparesions they both sports, they contrast in many ways like in hokey you use a stick and a puck, but in basketball you use one ball and your hands. They also compare in that when you play them the goal is to get the puck or basketball into a goal or net. Another contrast is that hokey is played on ice and basketball is played on courts. When you play hokey or basketball you noticed that the puck and ball both touch the ground that is another way to compare. In hokey the goal.net is placed on the ground and in basketball the net is on a backboard in the air that is another contrast. If you have ever been to a hokey or basketball game there is always quaters or periods in a game so that the players can take a break, in that way they compare. Basketball has four quarters and Hockey has three periods to a game and they are different in that way. But the best comparisions in hokey and basketball is the fans, many people love hockey and basketball that's why they are one of most played and favored sports in the world.

A compare-and-contrast essay written by an adolescent with learning disabilities.
From Wong, Butler, Ficzere, & Kuperis, 1997.

difficulties including problems in accurately reading numbers, performing simple addition and subtraction, understanding arithmetic terms and symbols, memorizing mathematical facts, and understanding spatial organization. (See Figure 10–4.)

Early Procedural and Strategy Impairments. Research has emphasized basic understanding of children's early counting and arithmetic abilities (Geary, 2003; 2004; Torbeyns, Verschaffel, & Ghesquière, 2004). Even the relatively simple calculations accomplished by very young children require some conceptual and procedural understanding of number and counting. By age 5, many typically developing children understand basic principles of counting (e.g., an object in an array of objects can be counted only once), although they may yet have difficulties with other principles (e.g., objects in an array can be counted in any order). As they take on simple calculations, there is a gradual transition to more advanced procedures. For example, *counting all* (e.g., 2 + 3 is added by counting 1-2-3-4-5) gradually gives way to *counting on* (e.g., the child starts with 2 and then adds on 3-4-5). Counting procedures are soon represented in memory and arithmetic facts can then be called up automatically. The addition of 2 + 3 no longer requires counting: 5 is quite effortlessly and rapidly retrieved. Children with arithmetic disabilities more slowly acquire many of these procedures and strategies and employ them less frequently and with less speed and accuracy. In addition, deficits or delays exist in memory-based retrieval processes, which persist through the elementary school years.

In examining these select findings, the following are worth noting. *First*, longitudinal investigations are necessary for a more complete understanding of developmental course. *Second*, some investigators have fail to distinguish children with only mathematics disability from children who also have reading disabilities. In fact, the co-occurring condition is linked to more pronounced difficulties and is being further differentiated (Geary, 2004; Fuchs, Fuchs, & Prentice, 2004; Jordan, Hanich, & Kaplan, 2003). *Third*, research is needed on more

FIGURE 10–4

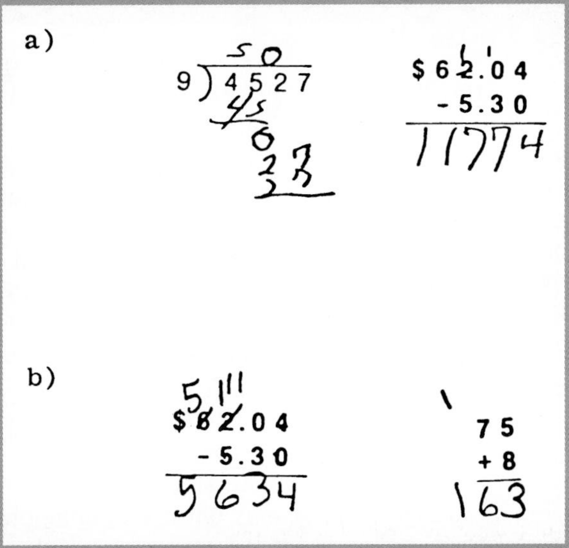

a)

b)

Arithmetic computation errors made by (a) a 12-year-old boy and (b) a 10-year-old girl with learning disabilities.
From Taylor, 1988a.

complex mathematics and on understanding possible underlying cognitive deficits, such as working memory, executive functions, and visual-spatial skills (e.g., Wilson & Swanson, 2001). *Fourth*, although there is evidence that specific regions of the brain subserve different arithmetic operations, brain studies of children with mathematics disorder are lacking (Lyon et al., 2003).

Epidemiology and Developmental Course. There are relatively few studies of the prevalence of mathematics disabilities and they vary in how they define and measure deficits. Given this, it appears that 5 to 8 percent of school-age children display some form of mathematics disabilities (Geary, 2004; Lyon et al., 2003). This figure may drop to 1 percent when cases with co-occurring reading disabilities and ADHD are excluded (American Psychiatric Association, 2000). Gender differences have not been found in most studies.

There is indication of some persistence of disabilities; for example, Prior and colleagues (1999) found that 57 percent of children with arithmetic disorder at age 7 to 8 had arithmetic problems 4 years later. Although further study is required, mathematics disabilities can be identified during the early

school years and can persist into adolescence (Lyon et al., 2003).

Co-Occurring Behavior Problems

Youngsters with language and learning problems—in both clinic and community samples—have a higher than average risk for a variety of behavioral disturbances (Beitchman et al., 1996; Conti-Ramsden & Botting, 2004; Rutter, Mawhood, & Howlin, 1992).

Language impairment has been associated with externalizing and internalizing problems. Such difficulties exist as early as preschool age and are demonstrated during childhood and into early adulthood. Stevenson (1996) found that overactivity and behavioral immaturity (such as dependency, tantrums, and poor bowel control) were more common in young children, whereas internalizing problems were more common in older children. The continuity of behavioral disturbance is suggested by a longitudinal study of a community sample identified with language deficits at age 5 (Beitchman et al., 1996; 2001). A follow-up conducted at about age 19

ACCENT

Nonverbal Learning Disabilities (NVLD)

As a matter of general interest, we mention that not all learning disabilities relate strongly to language difficulties. One group of children described as displaying a unique profile of learning impairments, in which language skills are relatively intact, are said to exhibit Nonverbal Learning Disabilities (NVLD). The disorder has been given other names, including "right hemisphere deficit syndrome" and "social–emotional learning disabilities." The conceptualization of NVLD is uncertain, and it has been likened to a few different pervasive developmental and mental retardation syndromes.

Abnormal brain development or damage, involving the white matter and right hemisphere, is thought to underlie NVLD (Anderson et al., 2001; Rourke & Fuerst, 1995). Relative strengths exist in verbal abilities and relative deficits in mathematics, visual-spatial skills, and social competence. Visual-spatial deficits are thought to be responsible for problems in interpreting other people's facial expressions, gestures, and other nonverbal signals. NVLD also is associated with the development of internalizing behavioral symptoms. Youngsters with NVLD may be identified later than children with obvious language impairments, and on the basis of social-emotional rather than cognitive problems (Anderson et al., 2001). The following is a brief description of a girl diagnosed with NVLD whose neuropsychological functioning was evaluated at ages 5 and 14.

Jenny   A Profile of NVLD

Jenny was evaluated due to learning and social problems. She reportedly had experienced some neonatal problems, relatively early development of expressive language, and somewhat slow development of motor skills. Formal evaluation showed intact intellectual and linguistic abilities with less well-developed nonverbal abilities, especially visual and visual-motor skills. She appeared disorganized and displayed difficulties on memory tasks requiring her to encode and retain material. Educational and social strategies were recommended to minimize Jenny's difficulties.

Jenny's childhood years were characterized by continual problems and intervention. Psychotherapy was discontinued when Jennie's parents felt it was unhelpful. A diagnosis of ADHD led to treatment with medication. Later occurring symptoms of obsessive-compulsive behaviors and the sensation that she was being watched led to hospitalization to determine whether Jennie suffered from a psychotic illness.

At age 14, a second neuropsychological evaluation was precipitated by depressive symptoms as well as ongoing behavioral and learning difficulties. During assessment Jenny was quiet, passive, reflective, cooperative, and anxious. Her language and literacy skills were intact, as were sustained attention and verbal learning. But many abilities were now well below average, with particular difficulties in social comprehension, visual perception and memory, visuomotor coordination, and mathematics. A similar ongoing pattern of difficulty and decline in cognitive, academic, and social behavior has been observed in other children with NVLD.

From Anderson et al., 2001, pp. 425–432.

indicated rates of anxiety disorder higher than for a control group and males were at risk for antisocial personality.

Of interest is evidence that behavioral disturbance associated with language impairments can be mediated by the reading problems that often develop (Tomblin et al., 2000). Reading disorder obviously cannot account for behavioral disorder of preschoolers, but older children with language impairment may be at risk for behavioral disturbance because they are unable to meet expectations for the acquisition of reading.

The association of learning disabilities with ADHD is well established, as we saw in Chapter 9.

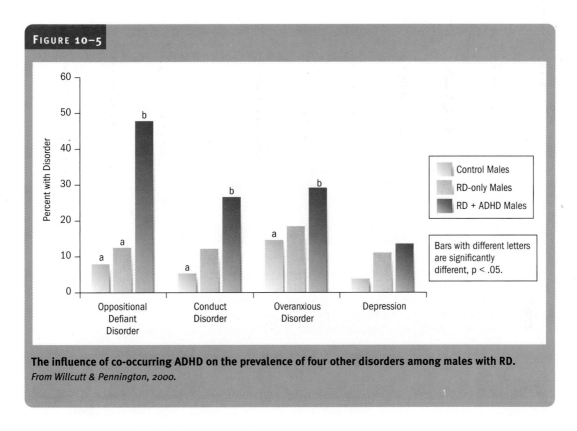

FIGURE 10–5

The influence of co-occurring ADHD on the prevalence of four other disorders among males with RD.
From Willcutt & Pennington, 2000.

In an interesting study, Willcutt and colleagues (2001) compared the cognitive deficits of nonreferred twins who displayed reading disorder, ADHD, or both disorders. Reading disability was associated with deficits regarding the sounds and memory of words, ADHD with deficits in inhibition. Children who exhibited both disorders had deficits in both areas that added to make them the most disabled. Similar results, which also show increased impairment for the co-occurring group, have come from other samples (Purvis & Tannock, 2000; Rucklidge & Tannock, 2002). Moreover, the presence of ADHD with RD has been associated with heightened risk for still other disorders. Figure 10–5 demonstrates this finding in males; a somewhat different and weaker effect was found for females.

Reading disorder has frequently been associated with conduct disturbance. Although several causal connections are theoretically possible, longitudinal research suggests that the path from reading disorder to later conduct problems is indirect. Early behavior problems and family factors are thought to play a role (Fergusson & Lynskey, 1997; Prior et al., 1999; Williams & McGee, 1996). Thus only some youth with reading problems develop later conduct difficulties, and boys appear more at risk than girls.

Social and Motivational Problems

Although many children and adolescents with language and learning disabilities do quite well socially, develop a positive sense of self, and maintain interest in learning, these areas are problematic for others.

SOCIAL RELATIONS AND COMPETENCE

The social relations of at least some children with disabilities are less than satisfactory. Teachers associate learning disabilities with a variety of problematic behaviors—anxiety, immaturity, disruptiveness, lack of cooperation, lack of self-control, hyperactivity, among others (Heavey et al., 1989; Mishna, 2003). In addition, children with learning disorders are often rated by peers as less popular and more rejected and neglected than nondisabled youngsters. Figure 10–6 represents the general findings, which have been shown in meta-analyses (Nowicki, 2003; Ochoa & Palmer, 1995). Risk for social rejection can begin in the early school years and continue into young adulthood (Bryan, 1997). This finding does not mean, of

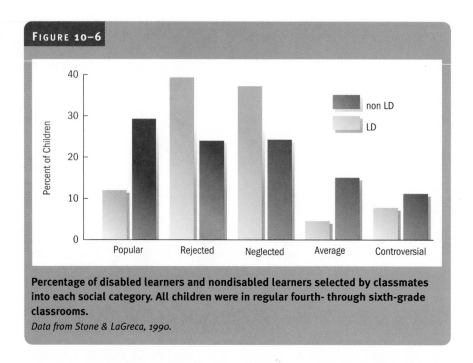

FIGURE 10–6

Percentage of disabled learners and nondisabled learners selected by classmates into each social category. All children were in regular fourth- through sixth-grade classrooms.
Data from Stone & LaGreca, 1990.

course, that all children with learning disabilities are rejected or otherwise have poor relationships; research suggests that risk varies from approximately 35 to 60 percent.

What underlies such social difficulties? There is no definitive answer to this question. Behavioral problems associated with learning disabilities, such as ADHD, may adversely affect peers (Vaughn, LaGreca & Kuttler, 1999). In addition, children with learning disorders appear to have lower social competence than their nondisabled peers, which might well affect social relationships (Nowicki, 2003; Rourke & Fuerst, 1995; Toro et al., 1990). Difficulties exist in identifying the emotional expression of others, understanding social situations, guessing how other youngsters feel in particular situations, and solving social problems.

Whatever the underlying causes, poor social relationships and poor social skills increase risk for school alienation and dropout, loneliness, and

Social interaction and motivational factors play an important role in the development of learning and learning difficulties.
(Courtesy of A. C. Israel)

withdrawal (Deater-Deckard, 2001; Vaughn et al., 1999). Risk for victimization or bullying by peers may also be increased (Nowicki, 2003). For example, in one study three times as many 11-year-olds with language impairments than typically developing age-mates reported experiencing victimization more than once a week (Conti-Ramsden & Botting, 2004).

ACADEMIC SELF-CONCEPT AND MOTIVATION

Meta-analyses indicate that learning disorders are associated with a lowered sense of worth (Elbaum & Vaughn, 2003; Nowicki 2003). These children are aware of their poor academic abilities and also tend to rate their global sense of self as relatively low.

School experiences contribute to children's self worth, and by age 4 or 5, some children already are sensitive to teacher criticism and respond to it, for example, by downgrading the quality of their work (Cutting & Dunn, 2002). Research generally suggests that some youngsters respond to criticism with a *mastery orientation*; they are more likely to attribute failure to lack of effort or to task difficulty, expect future improvement, and maintain problem solving and positive affect. Other children respond with a *helplessness orientation*; they do not expect future success, give up easily, and experience negative self-cognitions and affect. Helplessness is hypothesized to be related to self-concept (Burhans & Dweck, 1995).

Given these related considerations, it is easy to see that children with disabilities can enter a vicious cycle of academic failure and low motivation that works against them (Licht & Kistner, 1986). As a result of academic failure, they come to doubt their intellectual abilities and believe that their efforts to achieve are futile. Such learned helplessness exacerbates the situation as the youngsters are more likely to give up in the face of difficulty. In turn, further failure is experienced, which reinforces their belief in lack of ability and control (Figure 10–7).

To put this discussion into perspective, not all children with learning disabilities have serious motivational problems—and such difficulties can occur in youngsters without specific disabilities. It is reasonable to assume, however, that youth with disabilities are at particular risk for academic motivational difficulties.

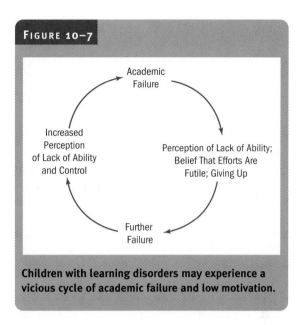

FIGURE 10–7

Children with learning disorders may experience a vicious cycle of academic failure and low motivation.

Etiology of Language and Learning Disorders

BRAIN ABNORMALITIES

Language/learning disabilities are associated with cerebral palsy, epilepsy, nervous system infections, head injury, prenatal alcohol use, and neurological delays and soft signs (e.g., Snowling, 1991; Taylor, 1989; Vellutino et al., 2004). Direct study of the brain indicates how it might be implicated in specific disabilities. Many regions of the brain are likely to be involved in some way; for example, the cerebellum and certain visual and auditory pathways could play a role in perceptual processing in reading disorder (Fawcett, Nicolson, & Maclagan, 2001). A major focus of investigation, however, is the left hemisphere, long considered crucial to language functions.

Brain Structure. Structures of the brain have been investigated with postmortem examination and brain scans. Especially implicated is the planum temporale and the surrounding region (Hynd, Marshall, & Gonzalez, 1991; Hynd & Semrud-Clikeman, 1989a; 1989b; Peterson, 1995). This area, which roughly corresponds with Wernicke's area and is implicated in language, involves the upper surface of the temporal lobe extending to the lower surface of the parietal lobe. In most—but not all—adults in the general population the area is larger in the left hemisphere than the right. In persons with specific language and reading disorders, asymmetry often is absent. The right side has been found as large or even larger than the left, and decreased size of the left temporal lobe has been found (Eliez et al., 2000). In addition, cell abnormalities in the brain have been observed to be more common in reading disabilities.

As informative and interesting as these and other structural findings are, caution is needed in drawing conclusions. Differences in the brain of adults with reading disabilities may or may not be the same as in the still developing brain of children. And the research findings are not completely consistent. For example, hemisphere symmetry, as well as group differences in the size of the corpus callosum, are sometimes found and other times not found (Vellutino et al., 2004). In addition, research samples are often small and brain measurement is not easily accomplished.

Brain Functioning. Much attention recently has been given to evaluating brain functioning with a variety of scanning methods as children and adults engage in language and reading tasks. Differences have been shown between impaired and nonimpaired readers in brain regions involved in language and reading (Shaywitz, 2003). (See Figure 10–8.) An area in the front of the brain (corresponding to Broca's area) aids in word analysis. The second area, the parietal-temporal area (including Wernicke's area) plays a central role in phonological processing, that is, in integrating the visual and sound aspects of language. The third area at the junction of the occipital and temporal lobes is especially involved in rapid word recognition; it becomes increasing important as readers come to rely more on automatic, almost instantaneous word recognition rather than on basic phonological processes. In general, strong readers rely more on the back areas of the brain in reading, and most processing occurs on the left side.

It has been proposed that reading disorder involves faulty wiring of the system necessary for good language and reading. Several studies show that patterns of brain activation is different in children and adults with or without reading problems when they engage in various phonological and reading tasks. In reading disabilities, the posterior left side appears underactive and the corresponding posterior right side may be overactive (Breier et al., 2003; Shaywitz et al., 1998). There is also some evidence that the front left area of the brain may be relatively overactive, and that as children with reading disabilities get older they may increasingly employ the frontal area of the brain (Shaywitz & Shaywitz, 2003).

In examining these findings, it is helpful to be mindful that the brain is a dynamic network:

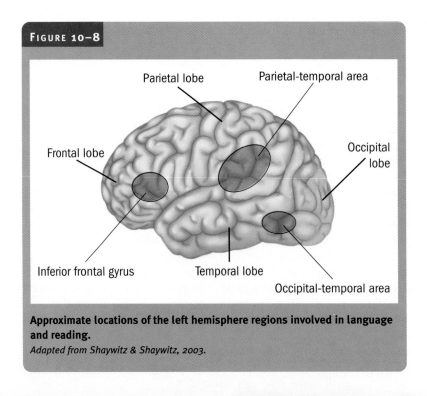

FIGURE 10–8

Parietal lobe

Parietal-temporal area

Frontal lobe

Occipital lobe

Inferior frontal gyrus

Temporal lobe

Occipital-temporal area

Approximate locations of the left hemisphere regions involved in language and reading.
Adapted from Shaywitz & Shaywitz, 2003.

abnormalities in one area might affect another, perhaps as an effort to compensate for what is not working properly. Shaywitz and colleagues suggest that the use of alternative routes—greater reliance on the front brain area and the right hemisphere—allows some readers to achieve accurate, although not rapid and fluent, reading (Shaywitz, 2003; Shaywitz et al., 2003).

These investigators, based largely on the study of early reading problems that do or do not persist, also speculate that there may be two groups of poor readers. Children in one group may be born with an abnormality affecting the posterior reading area and reading skills, but they develop relatively good general cognitive skills (and the potential to compensate). In the second group, the posterior brain system may initially be adequate but experiences—such as poor reading instruction or a disadvantaged family language environment—result in both reading problems and relatively lower cognitive skills.

Further research is required to better understand brain functioning in reading disorders. Meanwhile, important results are coming from research that shows brain changes associated with interventions for reading and language deficits. We will return to these fascinating findings later in the chapter.

GENETIC INFLUENCE

Genetic effects on language and learning disabilities have been investigated with the gamut of genetic methods, including linkage studies.

Language. Specific language disorders aggregate in families, although 30 to 60 percent of index cases appear to be the only member of their family with a language disorder (Tallal & Benasich, 2002). Concordance is about 85 percent for identical twins, about 50 percent for fraternal pairs (Spinath et al., 2004). These findings indicate a substantial environmental contribution as well as genetic influence.

Molecular genetics studies, although still limited in number, are beginning to reap benefits (Plomin & McGuffin, 2003). In one investigation, 252 children from 98 families, in which at least one sibling exhibited language problems, were examined for possible gene linkages. The children's DNA was genotyped for 400 genetic markers. The investigators identified linkages on chromosomes 16 and 19, each associated with a different language deficit (nonword repetition, expressive language).

Reading. Parents of youth with RD have high rates of reading problems and, conversely, youth whose parents have reading difficulties are at higher risk for these problems (Carroll & Snowling, 2004; Grigorenko, 2001). Twin comparisons give evidence of genetic influence. For example, data from the Colorado Reading Project show 68 percent concordance for identical twins and 40 percent for fraternal twins (DeFries & Light, 1996). Influence on several components of reading also has been shown, including on phonological processing and single-word reading. This is a particularly interesting finding given the importance of these processes in language and reading disorders.

Some progress is being made in identifying specific chromosomes that might contribute to RD. Chromosomes 6 and 15 were the first to be identified and subsequent linkage studies implicated chromosome 18 and 2 (DeFries & Light, 1996; Grigorenko, 2001; Plomin & McGuffin, 2003).

The genetic studies can be interpreted as supporting both single-gene and multiple-gene effects (Schulte-Körne, 2001). The involvement of multiple genes is supported by evidence that reading skills in children at family risk appear to be continuously distributed (Pennington & Lefly, 2001; Snowling et al., 2003). In other words, there is no "disease" gene for dyslexia but rather a number of genes—which ones and how many may vary—that may work together with other risk factors to produce susceptibility for reading disorders (Pennington, 1999).

The overlap of language and reading difficulties raises the question of whether they share a genetic predisposition. There is some evidence for this proposition. The co-occurrence of language and reading problems appears in the families of children with disabilities (Flax et al., 2003), and a study of phonological processing, language, and reading suggested a shared genetic basis in a sample of 6- and 7-year-olds (Hohnen & Stevenson, 1999).

Writing and Mathematics. Less is known about genetic effects on other learning disabilities. Family aggregation has been revealed in a few studies of spelling disabilities (e.g., Schulte-Körne, 2001). And Shalev and colleagues (2001) found that parents and siblings of probands with mathematics disabilities exhibited rates of impairment about ten times higher than what would be expected in the general population. In addition, limited twin data indicate higher concordance for mathematics disability in identical than fraternal pairs (Lyon et al., 2003). It also appears that mathematics and reading disabilities may have a shared genetic vulnerability.

PSYCHOSOCIAL INFLUENCES

Although biological variables are of etiological importance in language and learning disabilities, genetic behavior studies indicate a role for environmental influence on normal and impaired development (Chapman, 2000; Grigorenko, 2001).

From other types of research, we know of the importance of several psychosocial variables in the development of language (Chapman, 2000; Weizman & Snow, 2001). Early vocabulary growth is predicted by the number or sophistication of words the child hears from its mother. And more rapid language development is predicted by, for example, the mother's elaborating on the child's speech and commenting on what the child is paying attention to. Family variables may not be the root of language problems but can play a role in maintaining deficits (Whitehurst & Fischel, 1994).

Stevenson and Fredman (1990) found that large family size and certain aspects of mother-child interaction were linked to reading problems, and they noted that family involvement in the child's learning may be especially influential on early reading acquisition. The child's motivation to read can also make a difference as amount of reading is related to reading skills (Snowling, 2000; 2002). Lowered expectation of teachers and children themselves—as well as learned helplessness—may be especially hazardous for those whose learning requires extraordinary effort. It is also generally believed that factors such as overcrowded classrooms, math anxiety, and quality of instruction can affect the acquisition of mathematics skills (Shalev et al., 2001). Of course, care must be taken not to thoughtlessly generalize influences on normal development to poor reading in low achieving children or to those who exhibit specific disabilities.

However, educational instruction is viewed by some researchers as an important environmental influence (Snowling, 2000). Particularly for reading but in other areas as well instructional differences can matter. Thus, it can be argued that special instruction is appropriate for most children who appear at risk for reading or other learning disabilities. Although some children may be at particularly high neurobiological risk for reading problems, greater or lesser risk can be identified by children's performance on reading-related tasks such as letter naming and on response to early intervention (Vellutino et al., 2004).

Assessing Language and Learning Disorders

When language disorders are suspected in preschoolers, parents seek assessment from a variety of professionals. Family and child history; speech and language evaluation; assessment of verbal and nonverbal intelligence; and screening for hearing, neurological, and medical problems are generally appropriate (Bishop, 2002). Speech and language specialists can make a critical contribution in early assessment and/or later ongoing assessment necessary for intervention. A multidisciplinary team may be formed to plan intervention; it may include language specialists, preschool teachers, psychologists, and physicians, among others (Kirk, Gallagher, & Anastasiow, 2000).

Later occurring or more subtle language problems and learning handicaps may be assessed in mental health settings, but are often evaluated in the educational system, following procedures recommended by government regulations for the assessment and education of handicapped youth.

Crucial in identifying language and learning disabilities—and understanding a child's particular deficits—are psychological tests that evaluate academic achievement; general intelligence; and specific language, cognitive, perceptual, or motor skills. The focus of academic assessment is usually on reading, spelling, and arithmetic skills, although tests are available for other academic areas. It is important to evaluate components of academic domains (Beitchman & Young, 1997). Evaluations for reading, for example, might include measures of sounding out words, matching letters and sounds, and comprehending written material. Strengths also need to be assessed. A large number of standardized tests are available for these purposes.

When it is relevant, the evaluator should also discuss the child's study habits, motivations, self-esteem, and concerns (e.g., Bryan, 1997). Because language and learning disabilities are essentially defined in terms of achievement and cognition, there is probably a tendency to assess inadequately the behavioral, social, and motivational contexts in which the child is operating. Taylor (1989) has provided a model for comprehensive assessment of disabilities that includes the child's psychological adjustment and motivation (Figure 10–9). It also

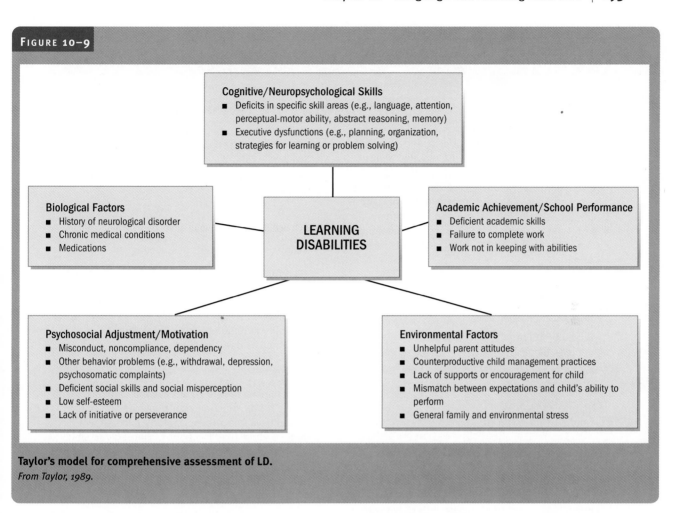

FIGURE 10-9

Taylor's model for comprehensive assessment of LD.
From Taylor, 1989.

takes into account environmental factors that can promote or have adverse influence on the child's functioning, such as parental attitudes and the match between the child's abilities and others' expectations.

Finally, especially as the benefits of early intervention have become better documented, early assessment is highly desirable. Excepting severe cases, it can be challenging to identify meaningful language impairments in toddlers. Children 2 to 3 years old who are late talkers or exhibit other expressive problems can fall into the normal range of language development by early school age or they can continue to have difficulties (e.g., Rescorla, 2002). Thus, early language problems require monitoring. Reading problems can be predicted in kindergarten or first grade (Lyon & Cutting, 1998). Yet most reading disabilities go undetected until second or third grade, partly because parents and teachers believe that the difficulties are short-lived (Shaywitz, 2003). (See Accent: "Some Clues for Identifying Reading Disorder.") Unfortunately, later intervention is less

successful than earlier treatment. Many children are not referred for learning problems until after they have experienced several years of academic failure, a delay that can take its toll on the child's development and psychosocial well-being.

Intervention for Language and Learning Disorders

Interventions targeting specific language, learning, and academic problems are creating excitement these days. However, some children and adolescents might also profit from individual and family counseling, including a focus on social and behavioral problems. On the other hand, some treatments are viewed with skepticism by researchers and clinicians. Interventions involving eye exercises, tinted lenses, antihistamines and diet, among others, have not been shown effective and should be avoided (e.g., American Academy of Pediatrics, 1998).

ACCENT

Some Clues for Identifying Reading Disorder

Sally Shaywitz (2003), a neuroscientist and physician who has been in the forefront of reading disorder research, notes that parents can play an important role in the identifying reading disorder. This requires careful observation, knowing what to look for, and a willingness to spend time listening to the child speak and read. With this in mind, Shaywitz has presented clues for recognizing that a child may need further assessment.

Clues during the Preschool Years

Delayed language

Difficulty in learning and appreciating common nursery rhymes

Mispronounced words: persistent baby talk

Difficulty in learning (and remembering) names of letters

Failure to know the letters in child's own name

Clues during Kindergarten and First Grade

Failure to understand that words can be segmented and sounded out

Inability to learn to associate letters with their appropriate sounds

Reading errors not connected to the sounds of the letters, for example, *big* is read as *goat*

Inability to read common one-syllable words or to sound out even simple words

Complaints about the difficulty of reading or avoiding reading

History of reading difficulties in parents or siblings

Clues from Second Grade and Beyond

Among the many clues in speaking:

mispronunciation of long, unfamiliar, or complicated words; influent speech (hesitations, pauses, use of "ums"), inability to find the exact word; inability to reply rapidly when questioned; difficulty in remembering bits of verbal information such as dates and lists.

Among the many clues in reading:

slow reading progress; difficulty in reading unfamiliar words, function words such as *that* and *in*, or multisyllable words; omitting parts of words; oral reading that is choppy, labored, or slow; avoidance of reading; reading that improves in accuracy but not in fluency; family history of reading and spelling difficulties.

In keeping with the notion that specific reading disorder is discrepant with a child's general abilities, Shaywitz recommends looking for indications of strengths such as the ability to figure things out; an understanding of new concepts; comprehension of stories read or told by others; and good reasoning and abstraction skills.

APPROACHES TO INTERVENTION

Intervention for learning disorders historically has reflected the multidisciplinary nature of the field. Psychologists, physicians, educators, optometrists, and communication therapists have all had a hand in treatment. In the late 1960s and 1970s, many different approaches were employed (Hammill, 1993; Lyon & Cutting, 1998). Particularly prevalent was the early psychoeducational model (also known as the diagnostic-remedial approach), which targeted various perceptual and cognitive processes assumed

to underlie disabilities (Hammill, 1993). Training programs that involved practice in eye-hand coordination, spatial relationships, or language were offered by educational specialists. Many of these fell by the wayside due to lack of success (Dean & Burns, 2002; Hammill, 1993). On the other hand, the behavioral model made no assumptions about underlying deficits. It aimed at identifying and improving academic or social skills through learning principles, such as contingency management, feedback, and modeling (Lyon & Cutting, 1998). Behavioral techniques continue to play a role in the interventions that are favored today. They are often combined with direct instruction and cognitive approaches.

Direct instruction pinpoints the acquisition of needed skills and teaches to them. That is, if the child has a disability in writing, exercises and practice are provided in writing sentences and paragraphs. Among other things, direct instruction entails selecting and stating goals, presenting new material in small steps and with clear and detailed explanations, incorporating student practice and student feedback, guiding students, and monitoring student progress (Gettinger & Koscik, 2001; Lyon & Cutting, 1998). Some direct instruction programs are highly organized and scripted regarding curriculum and teacher behavior, for example, programs developed by Engelmann and colleagues, which have proven effective for high risk students (Adams & Carnine, 2003).

The *cognitive approach* emphasizes executive functions and/or metacognition. Instruction emphasizes the child's increased awareness of task demands, use of appropriate strategies, monitoring success of the strategies, and switching to another strategy when necessary. The approach has been applied to reading comprehension, mathematics, written expression, memory skills, and study skills (Maccini & Hughes, 1997; Wong et al., 2003). When special emphasis on students' monitoring and directing their own learning is added, the approach may be referred to as cognitive-behavioral. In this case, students assess, record, and self-reinforce their own behavior.

EFFECTIVENESS OF INTERVENTION

The voluminous reports on intervention can only be briefly discussed here. Reviews indicate that intervention can be ameliorative and also fall short of ideal effectiveness.

Intervention for Language Impairments.
Reviews and meta-analyses of interventions indicate that language development can be enhanced, although effects depend in part on type of disability and measures employed (Law & Garrett, 2004; Leonard, 1998). Phonological and expressive skills (e.g., syntax, vocabulary) are more easily remediated than receptive abilities. There is some evidence that both clinician- and parent-directed therapy can be effective, and a few studies found indirect benefits for child behavior and parent outcomes.

In his discussion of treatments, most of which focused on expressive disorders, Leonard (1998) noted that in many ways, interventions appear similar to how parents and other adults teach language to typically developing children. Operant procedures and modeling are widely used, and it is not unusual for toys and pictures to be a part of the training procedures. For example, the trainer presents language forms (e.g., plural nouns) and the child is encouraged to imitate them, and/or reinforcers are given for the child's communication in natural settings.

Leonard reported that some children on some tasks closed the gap between themselves and their typically developing peers. Some evidence exists for the generalization of training; for instance, an acquired language form may be used in different sentences in spontaneous speech. In addition, follow-up evaluations showed that the effects of training may endure over time. Despite these findings, though, the picture is not all positive. Language often improved but did not reach adequate levels, so that many youngsters remained socially and academically disadvantaged. Thus, both success and the need to improve treatments are evident.

Intervention for LD.
Direct instruction and cognitive approaches have generally been shown to be more effective than other approaches to learning disabilities (Lyon et al., 2003; Hatcher, Hulme, & Snowling, 2004; Torgesen et al., 2001). For example, explicit training in phonological skills with the application of these skills to text appears more effective in early reading intervention than approaches that focus on context and meaning. One of the more comprehensive examinations of intervention outcomes was undertaken by Swanson and Hoskyn (1998). The meta-analysis contrasted 180 interventions "over and above" typical classroom programs with control comparisons. A variety of learning disabilities, including language deficits, were targeted with reading disabilities the most frequently treated. The interventions were reported between 1972 and 1997. Four models were compared: Direct Instruction; Strategy Instruction (emphasizing prompts, explanations, and modeling of strategies and cognitive approaches); Combined Treatment of both Direct and Strategy Instruction; and interventions that appeared to have no components of Direct Instruction or Strategy Instruction. The analysis showed positive effects of moderate size for Direct Instruction alone and for Strategy Instruction alone, and a larger effect for Combined Treatment. What these

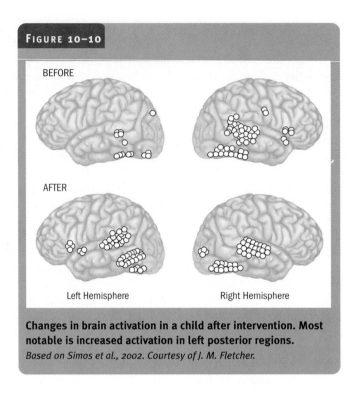

FIGURE 10–10

BEFORE

AFTER

Left Hemisphere

Right Hemisphere

Changes in brain activation in a child after intervention. Most notable is increased activation in left posterior regions.

Based on Simos et al., 2002. Courtesy of J. M. Fletcher.

findings suggested to Swanson and Hoskyn is that optimal training includes both lower order (instruction at the skill level) and higher order instruction (emphasis on the knowledge base and explicit strategies). They speculate that both instructional approaches are valuable because reading, mathematics, and other areas of functioning involve several component processes. The analysis also showed that all areas of academic disabilities responded to intervention—although effects were stronger in some areas than others and varied from high to low-moderate. Overall, the possibility of substantial remediation of learning disabilities through thoughtfully designed and implemented interventions is indicated.

Intervention and Brain Change. An especially interesting endeavor is the attempt to demonstrate the association of treatment effects with changes in brain functioning.

Simos and colleagues (2002) worked with a small group of 7- to 17-year-olds with average intelligence but severe disabilities in word recognition and phonological skills. Preintervention brain scans indicated an abnormal activation pattern for phonological tasks: little or no activation of the left parietal-temporal region and increased activation of the corresponding region of the right brain. The children received about 80 hours of phonological training over 8 weeks. Not only did measures of word accuracy show improvement into the normal range, but brain scans also indicated increased activation in the left posterior hemisphere relative to the corresponding right side. No changes over time were shown in activation patterns for the normal control group. Figure 10–10 exemplifies the findings in one of the children who received intervention.

A more extensive investigation of 6- to 9-year-olds with reading disabilities and comparison groups examined the outcome of a phonologically based intervention delivered at school over 8 months (Shaywitz et al., 2004). Daily 50-minute sessions focused on letter-sound associations, phoneme analysis of words, timed reading of words, oral story reading, and word dictation. As progress was made in basic skills, more emphasis was given to narrative texts. After intervention, the treated participants significantly improved on reading measures, and brain activation measured by fMRI was more in keeping with activation found for the non-impaired control group. Notably, there was increased activation in parts of the left posterior and frontal systems and decreased activation in two right-side areas. Follow-up of some of the children one year after intervention indicated continued improvement in the occipital-temporal region, known for its involvement with automatic word processing.

A different intervention approach has been evaluated with the Fast ForWord reading program. Fast ForWord is based on extensive research that grew from the hypothesis that reduced capacity to process rapid, successive perceptual stimuli underlies language impairment (Tallal, 2000; Tallal & Benasich, 2002). Intervention exercises aim at increasing the rate of neural processing. The child is presented with acoustically modified speech stimuli (e.g., slowed speech), and depending on the child's progress the exercises gradually incorporate rapid natural speech. The commercially available program consists of a hierarchy of seven computer-based training exercises to improve speech perception, phonological processing, and language comprehension. Research on the effectiveness of the approach moved from the laboratory to the clinic and classroom, and the program currently is employed by numerous school districts. A recent evaluation compared 20 treated children, ages 8 to 12, with reading disability to matched typical readers on both reading measures and fMRI scans (Temple et al., 2003). Treatment consisted of 100 minutes of daily exercises, 5 days a week, for an average of about 28 days. The children with learning disabilities improved on several reading measures; brain changes in the posterior language areas were similar to those of other intervention studies and they correlated with improvement in oral language.

The research that documents both improvement in select language/reading skills and correlated neurobiological change is impressive because it suggests that psychosocial treatment can affect brain development. Questions remain, however. Relatively small numbers of children have been evaluated over short periods of time. Virtually nothing is known about why some children benefit from intervention and others do not. Nor is it determined exactly what components of some of the treatments were responsible for improvement in specific skills. In addition, of course, these studies do not definitely establish the original cause of the reading disabilities.

Overall, recent progress is nonetheless quite remarkable. It holds promise for remediation of reading problems for both specific reading disorder and general reading problems. Moreover, it suggests the kinds of early reading instruction that would likely benefit most children who are learning to read—thereby either nipping problems in the bud or preventing them from occurring at all (Coyne et al., 2004; Hatcher et al., 2004).

Educational Services

In the United States, educational services for persons with various kinds of disabilities have evolved dramatically over the last decades. Criticisms, legal decisions, and a growing social commitment to the rights of children with disabilities to appropriate education resulted in the Education for All Handicapped Children Act of 1975. Subsequent federal regulations extended opportunities and rights. Public Law 99-457 amended the Education for All Handicapped Children Act, extending provisions to developmentally delayed 3- to 5-year-olds and creating voluntary intervention for infants. The Education for All Handicapped Children Act was expanded under the title the Individuals with Disabilities Education Act (IDEA) in 1990, and IDEA was reauthorized and amended in 1997 and in 2004. IDEA encompasses several categories for serving youth with disabilities, including speech or language disability; learning disability; mental retardation; emotional disturbance; developmental delay; and sensory and medical impairments such as blindness, deafness, and orthopedic problems.

The four purposes of IDEA have remained essentially unchanged over the years (U.S. Department of Education, 2000):

- To ensure that all students with disabilities obtain an appropriate free public education that emphasizes special education and related services to meet their particular needs

- To ensure that the rights of these students and their parents are protected

- To assist states and localities in providing education to children with disabilities

- To assess and ensure the effectiveness of these educational efforts

Appropriate education fundamentally means educational experiences tailored to each child's needs. An individualized education plan (IEP) is constructed for each student receiving special education. IEPs must consider the child's present functioning, short-term and long-term educational goals, educational services to be provided, expected duration of services, procedures for evaluations, and for older students the transition from school to work (Mercer & Mercer, 2001). The plans must be reviewed annually by a committee and the child's parents.

Under IDEA students with disabilities must be educated in the least restrictive environment, that is,

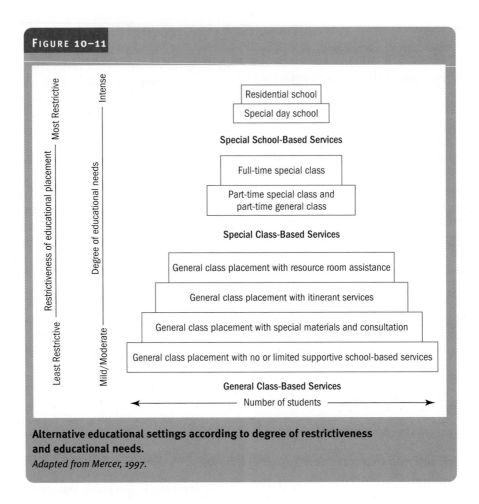

FIGURE 10–11

Alternative educational settings according to degree of restrictiveness and educational needs.
Adapted from Mercer, 1997.

with their nonhandicapped peers to the maximum extent appropriate. Because many handicapped students had once been viewed as a poor fit for public community schools, mainstreaming—the attendance of students with disabilities in neighborhood schools—became a central feature of educational placement. The late 1980s saw an initiative that further affected the education of students with special needs. Through the Regular Education Initiative, a call went out for inclusion of students beyond mainstreaming. The inclusion position holds that most children with disabilities can best be educated in general education classrooms. Its underlying premise is that schools should be restructured to be supportive, nurturing communities that meet the needs of all students (Mercer & Mercer, 2001).

Consistent with the concept of appropriate education in the least restrictive environment, several options are available for students in need of special education services. The options range from the general education classroom, with or without supplemental services, to the special residential school (Figure 10–11). These settings provide increasing levels of support, and appropriate education means matching the child with the appropriate setting.

Increasing numbers of infants, children, and adolescents are served under IDEA. From 1991–92 to 2000–01 there was a 28 percent increase of students age 6 through 21 (U.S. Department of Education, 2003). Quite striking is that of all youth in this age range served in 2000–01, about 50 percent were diagnosed with specific learning disabilities and almost 19 percent with speech or language impairments.

Equally compelling is the dramatic shift over the years in the LD and mental retardation categories. Figure 10–12 shows this change from the late 1970s to 1995, when the number of students diagnosed with LD about doubled and the number with mental retardation substantially declined. The reasons for this shift are likely to be multiple, involving diagnostic issues, sensitivity to student needs,

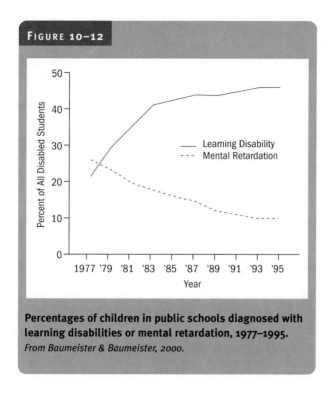

Percentages of children in public schools diagnosed with learning disabilities or mental retardation, 1977–1995.
From Baumeister & Baumeister, 2000.

motivation for learning experiences perceived as optimal, or the desire to avoid the stigma of mental retardation (e.g., Grigorenko & Lockery, 2002; Reschley, 1996).

Currently, the overwhelming number of students with LD attend neighborhood schools, where they are in general education classrooms with varying degrees of supplemental services, such as special instruction in the classroom or in resource rooms.

BENEFITS AND CONCERNS

The effectiveness of special education services, particularly those provided in special contained classrooms, has been questioned over the years. This is not an easy matter to settle, because research must address a variety of kinds and severity of disabilities, as well as many alternative programs. Even within a type of school setting, the activities, quality of teaching, and support services vary a good deal. Given these complexities, a considerable amount of past research did not clearly support the once-anticipated academic and social benefits of special education classrooms (Howlin, 1994; Detterman & Thompson, 1997). Nevertheless, some research indicated slightly better academic outcomes for students in these classrooms (Hocutt, 1996). It is likely that it is not the

setting per se as much as the quality of instruction that influences outcome.

With the policy of full inclusion came questions about its benefits or disadvantages. By the late 1990s, 75 percent of students with disabilities were educated in general education classrooms and the trend seems to be a hearty one (U.S. Department of Education, 2000). Inclusion nevertheless can elicit strong approval or opposition. Advocates point to research showing benefits to academic achievement and social outcomes for the included students (Hobbs & Westling, 1998; Rea, McLaughlin, & Walther-Thomas, 2002; Waldron & McLeskey, 1998). Students have been found to do better on standardized achievement tests and in relating to others, with no greater behavioral difficulties. Outcomes for nonhandicapped students in these classrooms have also been reported as favorable (Cole, Waldron, & Majd, 2004; Staub & Peck, 1994/1995). Advocates of full inclusion believe that concern is best directed not toward whether inclusive education should be provided but toward *how* it should be implemented to maximize its effectiveness.

In contrast, critics of full inclusion point to data that do not support it, including little academic advantage and lower levels of self-esteem among students with disability (Cole et al., 2004). It is also argued that although the full inclusion policy has helped reduce discrimination and segregation of students with disabilities, it has strengthened a false belief that no student requires special consideration and that placement in special education settings is a harmful discriminatory approach (Kauffman, McGee, & Brigham, 2004). Moreover, those opposed to full inclusion view it as violating both children's rights and federal mandates for appropriate educational placement. They argue that a continuum of educational settings best serves varying student needs—and is consistent with the desires of many parents and educators (Mercer & Mercer, 2001).

A central issue is whether teachers have the knowledge, support, and motivation to maintain optimal teaching strategies while also accommodating students with special needs. Teachers sometimes lack the specialized training to adapt curricula for learning disabilities and to deal with behavior problems. In a study of elementary school teachers, negative attitudes toward students with disabilities in their inclusive classrooms were related to attributes of the children that made class management and instruction difficult (Cook et al., 2000). Teachers also have reported problems with peer rejection that lead to the included child's being isolated, teased, and the like (Hobbs & Westling, 1998).

Inclusion can be challenging in other ways. Many special education teachers, who formerly taught in relatively autonomous special classrooms, now work in collaboration with regular teachers in general classrooms (Klingner & Vaughn, 2002). The attitudes of school principals are important in implementing inclusion—and yet one study showed that most were uncertain of its benefits (Praisner, 2003). Parents of children with disabilities tend to have mixed views of inclusion; they desire quality educational experiences but have concerns about the welfare of their children in integrated settings. This may be especially true in families with children with severe disabilities (Palmer et al., 2001).

The policy of inclusion clearly has brought benefits and has also made demands on the educational system. Presently, both "good" and "poor" programs are being implemented (Cole et al., 2004), and increased understanding of what constitutes successful programs is necessary (Wallace et al., 2002).

SUMMARY

A BIT OF HISTORY: UNEXPECTED DISABILITIES, UNMET NEEDS

- *Today's field of language and learning disorders can be traced to interest in individuals who exhibited discrepant abilities and to advocacy to improve services to them.*

- *Kirk's 1963 definition of learning disability was a milestone for the interdisciplinary field as we know it today.*

DEFINITIONAL CONCERNS

- *The influential definition of specific learning disability offered by the federal government has been criticized on several counts and has led to variation in how specific disabilities are defined and identified.*

- *Specific disorders are identified by a discrepancy between a person's performance and what is expected in terms of grade level, age, or the individual's intelligence. Criticism of the achievement-intelligence discrepancy approach has weakened it somewhat but IQ is still often considered.*

LANGUAGE DISORDERS

- *Language development is well under way by 2 to 3 years of age, and basic abilities are acquired by about age 7.*

- *As conceptualized by the DSM, specific language disorders include phonological, expressive, and receptive-expressive disorders.*

- *Limited epidemiologic studies suggest a rate of about 7 percent for 5-year olds, but rates vary with age and with type and severity of disorder. Boys have higher rates than girls.*

- *Simple articulation problems often remit; outcome is more variable for early expressive problems and poorest for receptive-expressive disorder. Risks include continuing language disabilities, learning disabilities, and academic difficulties—as well as social and behavioral problems.*

- *Among the cognitive deficits proposed to explain language disorders are slow general information processing, impairment in processing brief auditory signals, and deficits in phonological working memory.*

LEARNING DISORDERS: READING, WRITING, ARITHMETIC

- *Specific reading disorder, the most common LD, may occur in at least 10 to 15 percent of school-age children. Rates are probably higher in boys, but selection bias may exaggerate the gender difference. Reading problems tend to persist but can diminish.*

- *Reading disorders (RD) can be viewed in terms of word-level and/or comprehension problems. Perceptual deficits may be involved, but emphasis is currently given to language deficits. Phonological processing deficits play a critical role in RD, especially in learning to read, but problems in other language components are implicated.*

- *Specific writing disorder is multidimensional, involving deficits that affect transcription and text generation. Prevalence is estimated at about 10 percent of school-age children, and many children also display reading problems. The disorder is usually apparent by second grade, referral may increase at grade four, and improvement and persistence of difficulties are noted.*

- *Specific mathematics disorder has been most studied with regard to arithmetic competency, and further research is needed in many areas. Although 5 to 8 percent of school-age children may be affected, this figure includes children who also exhibit reading difficulties. Mathematics disabilities can be identified during the early school years and can persist.*

CO-OCCURRING BEHAVIOR PROBLEMS

- *Children and adolescents with specific disabilities are at risk for a variety of maturational, internalizing, and externalizing behavioral difficulties, including co-occurring ADHD. The developmental paths are likely to vary.*

SOCIAL AND MOTIVATIONAL PROBLEMS

- *A disproportionate number of students with language and learning disorders are at risk for poor social relations. Behavioral problems and low social competence may be underlying factors.*

- *These students are also at high risk for low academic self-concept and motivation, which can lead to a detrimental motivational cycle.*

ETIOLOGY OF LANGUAGE AND LEARNING DISORDERS

- *Abnormalities of brain structure and activation are associated with language and reading disabilities. Most centrally involved are the temporal-parietal, temporal-occipital, and frontal lobes. Poor readers*

show different activation patterns, some of which may be compensatory.

- *Genetic transmission of disabilities is documented, particularly for language and reading. Progress is slowly being made in identifying specific genes. There is evidence for multiple gene effects on normal and problem reading.*

- *Family and school factors are likely to play some role in disabilities. The effects of instruction are of considerable interest and some workers argue that well-crafted special programs are appropriate for all at-risk children.*

ASSESSING LANGUAGE AND LEARNING DISORDERS

- *Parents may call on a variety of professionals to assess early language disorders. Evaluation of later occurring language and learning problems is commonly conducted in the educational setting.*

- *Tests of academic achievement, intelligence, and cognitive processes are central in identifying and understanding disabilities. Broad assessment is ideal, however, and early identification can be crucial.*

INTERVENTION FOR LANGUAGE AND LEARNING DISORDERS

- *Current interventions emphasize direct instruction and practice in the deficient area, the use of behavioral methods, and the training of strategies and metacognition.*

- *Well-implemented interventions can be effective, for both language and learning disorders, although there is continuing need to improve treatments.*

- *Recent research has shown that intervention can lead to improved reading-related performance and correlated brain change.*

EDUCATIONAL SERVICES

- *Under IDEA, individuals up to age 21 with language and learning disabilities are entitled to educational services.*

- *Of the increasing numbers of children served by the schools, about half are categorized under learning disability and another almost one-fifth under language impairment. Most attend general education classrooms with varying degrees of supplemental supports.*

- *Disagreement and controversy continue over the drawbacks and benefits of special education and inclusion.*

KEY TERMS

Education for All Handicapped Children Act
  (p. 272)

Individuals with Disabilities Education Act *(p. 272)*

phonology *(p. 273)*

phonemes *(p. 273)*

graphemes *(p. 273)*

morphology *(p. 273)*

syntax *(p. 273)*

grammar *(p. 273)*

semantics *(p. 274)*

pragmatics *(p. 274)*

receptive language *(p. 274)*

expressive language *(p. 274)*

articulation (of language) *(p. 275)*

phonological disorder *(p. 275)*

expressive disorder *(p. 275)*

mixed receptive-expressive disorder *(p. 275)*

phonological loop (working memory) *(p. 278)*

phonological processing *(p. 280)*

phonological awareness *(p. 280)*

phonological decoding *(p. 280)*

individualized education plan *(p. 297)*

least restrictive environment *(p. 297)*

mainstreaming *(p. 298)*

inclusion *(p. 298)*

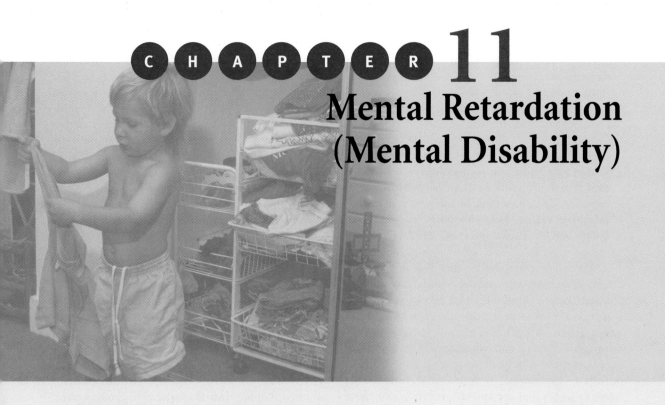

CHAPTER 11

Mental Retardation (Mental Disability)

Mental retardation is not something you have, like blue eyes or a bad heart. Nor is it something you are, like being short or thin. It is not a medical disorder.... Nor is it a mental disorder.... Mental retardation refers to a particular state of functioning. (Luckasson et al., 1992, p. 9)

Mental retardation (MR) has long been recognized, but until about 1700 it was little understood and scarcely viewed as different from other disorders (Reschly, 1992). In the early 1800s, the concept of mental retardation more firmly took root as involving deficient mental functioning and handicaps in the daily tasks of living. These two features remain central, although ideas about mental disability have evolved and are evolving even today.

Perhaps more strongly than many other disorders, mental retardation has been seen as a trait of the individual. This perspective is largely being replaced by the view that functioning is best described as a fit between the abilities of the individual and his or her personal and social environment. Biological causation is recognized, but the numerous ways in which the environment plays a role are being given more than passing attention.

The labels applied to mental retardation have also changed over time. The terms *idiot*, from the

Greek meaning "ignorant person," *imbecile*, from the Latin meaning "weakness," and *moron*, meaning "foolish or having deficient judgment," were all once employed in the professional literature (Potter, 1972; Scheerenberger, 1983). Although these terms were used by professionals as clinical descriptions, they took on increasingly negative connotations, and changes in terminology were partly an attempt to substitute more positive labels. Currently, we are witnessing another transition. The influential American Association on Mental Retardation has decided to drop the term *mental retardation*, although its replacement is not yet selected (Luckasson et al., 2002). Terms such as *intellectual disability* and *learning disabilities* are used in Europe. In this chapter, we employ *mental retardation* because it still appears in the major classification systems and the literature, but we simultaneously use *mental* or *intellectual disability*.

Definition and Classification

AAMR Approach

We begin discussion with the definition offered by the American Association on Mental Retardation (AAMR), which has led efforts to understand and ameliorate mental disability. Founded in 1876, this organization has long provided conceptualizations of mental retardation.

In its latest manual, published in 2002, *Mental Retardation: Definition, Classification, and Systems of Support*, AAMR offered the following definition:

> ***Mental retardation is a disability characterized by significant limitations both in intellectual functioning and in adaptive behavior as expressed in conceptual, social, and practical adaptive skills. This disability originates before age 18. (Luckasson et al., 2002, p. 8)***

Three criteria must be met before a person can be diagnosed with mental retardation. The age criterion, before 18, signifies that mental retardation is seen as a developmental disorder. Age 18 approximates when individuals in our society usually assume adult roles and when crucial psychosocial development and brain development have typically occurred. Limitation in intellectual functioning refers to scores that are approximately two or more standard deviations below the mean on standardized general tests of intelligence, such as the Stanford-Binet and the Wechsler scales. In practice, given the standard error of measurement, scores of about 70 to 75 or below usually meet this criterion. Limitation in adaptive skills is defined as performance on standardized tests of adaptive skills that is at least two standard deviations below the mean. The requirement of *both* intellectual and adaptive behavior deficits means that individuals who fall into the retarded range on intelligence tests but otherwise get along adequately at home, school, or work do not meet the criteria for mental retardation. Nor do those with deficits in adaptive behavior without poor performance on intelligence tests warrant the diagnosis. In addition, valid assessment and judgments of functional limitation must consider contexts of the individual's life—the community, cultural diversity, and the like.

AAMR has presented a theoretical model of mental retardation that incorporates influences, supports, and individual functioning. As indicated in Figure 11–1, five influences are mediated by supports provided to the individual. Mental retardation is not viewed as an absolute trait of the individual, and it is assumed that appropriate sustained supports generally result in improved functioning. Moreover, children or adolescents with mental disability are viewed as complex individuals who have strengths as well as limitations.

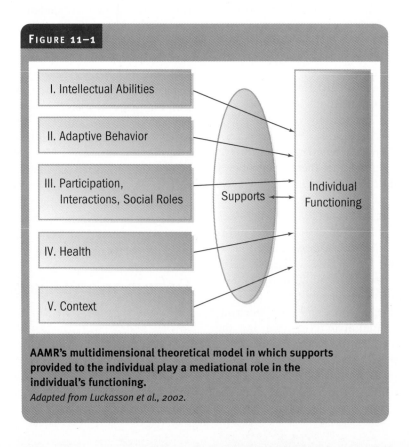

FIGURE 11–1

I. Intellectual Abilities

II. Adaptive Behavior

III. Participation, Interactions, Social Roles

IV. Health

V. Context

Supports

Individual Functioning

AAMR's multidimensional theoretical model in which supports provided to the individual play a mediational role in the individual's functioning.
Adapted from Luckasson et al., 2002.

TABLE 11–1	AREAS IN WHICH THE AAMR RECOMMENDS ASSESSMENT FOR NEEDED SUPPORTS

- Human development
- Teaching and education
- Home living
- Community living
- Employment
- Health and safety
- Behavioral
- Social
- Protection and advocacy

Luckasson et al., 2002.

| TABLE 11–2 | LEVELS OF MENTAL RETARDATION RECOGNIZED BY THE DSM |

LEVEL	IQ RANGE	PERCENTAGE OF MR POPULATION
Mild	50–55 to about 70	85
Moderate	35–40 to 50–55	10
Severe	20–25 to 35–40	3–4
Profound	below 20–25	1–2

Levels of Needed Supports. Because great variability exists in the abilities of people with mental retardation, it seems reasonable that subgrouping based on severity of retardation might be helpful in intervention and research. Following this line of reasoning, AAMR once employed four levels of retardation: mild, moderate, severe, and profound. Individuals were assigned to a subgroup according to their intelligence test scores. This approach has been widely employed by other classification systems. Nonetheless, AAMR eliminated the approach in 1992 and recommended that each individual with MR be assessed for levels of needed environmental supports, that is, resources and strategies that will promote development and well-being. The identification and amount of supports needed are judged for nine areas, as shown in Table 11–1. This approach recognizes that needs for supports might be different in one area of functioning than another and might change over time. It also indicates AAMR's concept of mental retardation as dynamically linked to the environment rather than being viewed as a static quality of the individual.

DSM AND PAST APPROACHES

The DSM approach to diagnosis and classification is both similar and dissimilar to the AAMR approach (American Psychiatric Association, 2000). Concurrent intellectual and adaptive limitations are required for diagnosis, as is onset of the disorder before age 18. The DSM requires an IQ of approximately 70 or below on standardized tests of intelligence and recognizes that measurement error for intelligence tests is approximately 5 points. The criteria call for deficits in at least two areas of adaptive behavior, and the DSM notes the usefulness of several adaptive behavior scales.

The area in which the DSM departs significantly from the AAMR is in its continued classification of individuals according to level of intelligence. (The ICD-10 does the same.) It is argued that the elimination of classification by IQ would leave clinicians and researchers with an inadequately reliable and meaningful way to group individuals (Baumeister & Baumeister, 2000). Table 11–2 shows the four levels employed by the DSM. About 85 percent of all cases are of mild retardation, with percentages dropping sharply for the remaining levels. Persons with mild retardation are viewed as quite different in functioning and in other important ways from persons classified at the other three levels. Thus a distinction is commonly made between mild retardation and more severe retardation, with the IQ of about 50 marking the boundary.

It is worth noting that mild and moderate retardation were respectively labeled educable and trainable by educators in the United States based on expectations for learning. Although recent changes in educational policy and practices regarding exceptional students have made this classification less relevant, it guided the management of intellectually handicapped students for many years and is still sometimes referenced.

Also noteworthy is change in the diagnostic criteria for mental retardation over time. For instance, many professionals criticized AAMR in 1992 when it appeared to raise the upper limit of the IQ criterion from 70 to 75, a change that would double the number of persons who would potentially meet the criterion (King, Hodapp, & Dykens, 2000). Such a change also could especially affect the labeling of persons from certain socially disadvantaged groups. To put this matter in broader perspective, it is not the first time that controversy has existed with regard to the IQ criterion. In 1959, AAMR employed a definition that allowed individuals to be diagnosed

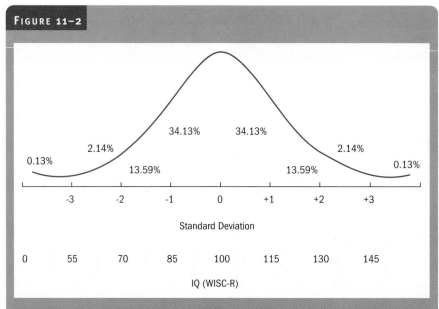

FIGURE 11–2

The distribution of scores on the WISC-R test of general intelligence fitted to the normal distribution. Standard deviation units indicate how far above or below a score is from the mean of 100. The standard deviation for the WISC-R is 15 points. When MR is defined by one or more standard deviations below the mean, approximately 16 percent of the population is mentally retarded. When MR is defined by two or more standard deviations below the mean, 2 to 3 percent of the population is mentally retarded.

with MR when they scored one or more standard deviations below the mean on intelligence tests (Figure 11–2). Those who scored in the approximate range of 69 to 85 were labeled as retarded at the borderline level. By this definition, about 16 percent of the population could be diagnosed as mentally deficient. Arguments ensued about the unreasonableness of the criterion, particularly because certain disadvantaged groups were disproportionately labeled retarded. In 1973, AAMR shifted the IQ criterion to approximately 70 or below. Changes in and controversy about the definition of mental retardation demonstrate the degree to which MR is a socially constructed category that has sometimes provoked heated debate.

Nature of Intelligence and Adaptive Behavior

Because measures of intelligence and adaptive behavior are central to defining mental disability, it is important to look more closely at their development and the concepts that underlie them.

MEASURED INTELLIGENCE

Tested intelligence is the most prominent criterion for mental retardation, and it is inextricably woven with retardation (Baumeister & Baumeister, 2000). As simple as the concept of intelligence seems on the surface, its meaning has raised many questions. We might agree, as have theorists, that it involves the knowledge possessed by a person, the ability to learn or think, or the capacity to adapt to new situations. Beyond these general definitions, however, we might run into disagreements. Theorists themselves argue, at times passionately, about the precise nature of intelligence, and they hold various perspectives on it (Anderson, 2001). We can hardly do justice to this topic, and our goal is to address issues that are most relevant to understanding mental retardation.

Modern intelligence testing goes back to the work of Alfred Binet and his colleagues at the beginning of the 20th century. Their approach—the traditional psychometric approach—focused on individual differences and on the idea that underlying abilities explained differences in intellectual functioning (Beirne-Smith, Ittenbach, & Patton, 1998). Intelligence is often viewed as consisting of a general ability, called *g*, and numerous specific abilities, for example, motor and verbal abilities (Johnson et al., 2004). Intelligence is measured by the presentation of tasks that tap both general and specific abilities. This psychometric approach is sometimes described as examining the products of intellectual, or cognitive, abilities rather than the processes involved in the abilities.

In recent years, information-processing theories have come to the fore, focusing on the processes by which individuals perceive sensory stimuli, store information, manipulate information, and perhaps act on it. Different theorists have somewhat different ways of conceptualizing these processes, but in any case, intelligence is measured according to how well a person performs on processing tasks. For example, the abilities to attend to and simultaneously deal with several bits of information might be measured (Anastasi & Urbina, 1997). Information-processing approaches contribute much to the understanding of mental retardation and are increasingly integrated into the measurement of intelligence. However, it was the psychometric approach that largely shaped views of intelligence throughout most of the 20th century.

Early Test Construction and Assumptions.

When Binet and his colleague Simon were asked by school officials in Paris to find a way to identify children who needed special educational experiences, they tested children of different ages on brief tasks relevant to classroom learning. In 1905, the first intelligence scale was published, consisting of tasks that average children of various ages passed. Age ordering of tasks reflected the belief that mental development increases with age throughout childhood. On the basis of their performance, children were assigned a mental age (MA), which is the age corresponding to the chronological age (CA) of children whose performance they equaled. Thus a 7-year-old who passed the tests that average 7-year-olds passed was assigned a MA of 7; a 7-year-old who passed the tests that the average 5-year-old passed obtained a MA of 5.

Binet made several assumptions about intelligence (Siegler, 1992). He believed that intelligence encompassed many complex processes, was malleable within limits, and was influenced by the social environment. Binet argued that carefully constructed standardized tests were necessary to minimize children's being inaccurately evaluated. Moreover, he and his colleagues devised methods to improve intellectual functioning, and they recommended that educational programs be fitted to each child's special needs.

TABLE 11–3	MEASURES RELEVANT TO TESTS OF INTELLIGENCE
CA	Chronological age.
MA	Mental age. The age score corresponding to the chronological age of children whose performance the examinee equals. For the average child, MA = CA.
IQ (ratio)	The ratio of mental age to chronological age multiplied by 100. IQ = MA/CA x 100.
IQ (deviation)	A standard score derived from statistical procedures that reflects the direction and degree to which an individual's performance deviates from the average score of the age group.

Intelligence testing was brought to the United States when Henry Goddard translated and used the Binet scales with residents of the Vineland Training School in New Jersey. Then in 1916, about 5 years after Binet's death, Lewis Terman—working at Stanford University—revised the early scales into the Stanford-Binet test. Terman adopted the idea of the intelligence quotient (IQ) as the ratio of an individual's mental age to chronological age, multiplied by 100 to avoid decimals. The ratio IQ enabled direct comparison between children of different ages. Today the major intelligence tests employ statistical comparison, so that what is often referred to as IQ is no longer a quotient but a score that nevertheless denotes age comparison (Table 11–3).

Goddard and Terman made some markedly different assumptions from those of Binet about the nature of intelligence. They assumed that the tests measured inherited intelligence that would remain stable over the life of the individual (e.g., Cravens, 1992). They also saw the need for *eugenics*, the improvement of the human species by control of inheritance. These beliefs had broad social implications that were to generate heated debate about the assumptions and uses of intelligence tests, as well as the more general treatment of persons with retardation. (See Accent: "Mental Disability: A History of Abusive Ideas.")

Stability and Validity of Tested Intelligence.

Intrinsic to the debates about intelligence is the issue of whether measured intelligence is stable over time. The issue can be examined by studying a

ACCENT

Mental Disability: A History of Abusive Ideas

It is unfortunate that mental retardation and its identification have been associated with some regrettable, even abusive, ideas and practices.

Not very long after their introduction, intelligence tests began to play a role in shaping U.S. public policy, even though the tests used and their administration were of questionable quality. IQ tests played a role in establishing quotas for people of southern European background who wished to immigrate to the United States and in introducing laws for the sterilization of people considered mentally deficient (Strickland, 2000). In fact, "unsexing" the "unfit" had begun prior to 1900 in the United States due to a complex of social and economic events, and the procedure increased during the early 1900s (Wehmeyer, 2003). Indiana was the first of many states to pass a sterilization law, and such law was upheld in 1927 by the Supreme Court in a Virginia case, *Buck v. Bell*. California law called for the sterilization of state hospital inmates and feeble-minded children residing in state-run homes. Forced sterilization affected over 50,000 before scientists and others overtly criticized it.

Although perhaps not as dramatic, the use of intelligence tests in the schools also has been criticized. With the passage of compulsory education laws, the public schools soon employed intelligence tests to assess children's capacity for school learning (MacMillan & Reschly, 1997). Children of poor families and of some minority families generally perform relatively poorly on the tests. In more recent times, this group has included children of African American, Hispanic, and Native American background, although it should be recognized that social class is often confounded with racial/ethnic background. This finding has raised considerable concern about test results being used to disproportionately identify minority and poor children as intellectually deficient—resulting in placements in special education classrooms, lowered self-esteem, and the like. Confrontations with the educational system, some of which have reached the courts, have ensued over a variety of testing practices and test fairness issues (MacMillan, Keogh, & Jones, 1986). Questions were raised about bilingual students' being assessed with standard English tests, about the content of tests not relating well to the subcultures in which students were being reared, and about the quality of the tests being used. Legal outcomes often, but not always, favored plaintiffs for minority groups. The influential *Larry P. v. Riles* case, a class action suit in which the plaintiffs were black people, resulted in severe restrictions on the use of intelligence tests for identifying and placing black children into special education programs in California. Overall, the educational system has been forced to stringently monitor the use and administration of intelligence tests.

Inherent in the uses and abuses of tests was the assumption that measured intelligence is a stable, biologically programmed characteristic of individuals. The more accepted view today is that intelligence tests assess important, circumscribed behaviors that result from the interaction of heredity and environment and that at least to some degree can be modified throughout life by environmental factors (Fagan & Holland, 2002).

group of people longitudinally and correlating earlier IQ scores with later IQ scores. When such test-retest measurements are made after preschool age, IQ scores are quite stable for groups of typically functioning individuals. It is important to note that such analyses examine groups of people, but individual scores can also be examined over time. When this is done we see that conditions such as the family situation and educational opportunity can be associated with change in individual IQs. At the same time, the IQs of persons with mental disability are more stable than IQs of persons with average or above scores, and the lower the score, the greater the stability.

Another central issue about intelligence is what an IQ score tells us about a person. This is, of course, a question about the validity of intelligence tests. If intelligence is defined as ability that relates to school performance, evidence exists for validity. After age 5, the correlations of IQ with school grades and reading, spelling, and mathematics achievement scores are moderately high, generally in the range of .40 to .75 (Berger & Yule, 1985; Matarazzo, 1992). On the other hand, intelligence test scores are correlated with out-of-school achievements (e.g., adaptive behavior, job success) relatively weakly (Baumeister, 1987). However, IQ scores that fall below the average range are generally better predictors of academic and nonacademic performance than those in the normal range.

Caution is necessary in interpreting measured intelligence and in using scores to categorize youngsters as mentally retarded. IQ scores are relatively stable, but they are not cast in stone. They provide important information about individual functioning but cannot tell us everything. Serious questions have been raised about the cultural bias of intelligence tests as well as their limitations. Factors that might contribute to intelligence—such as motivation and social responsiveness—are not well discriminated by the tests (Scarr, 1982; Siegler, 1992), and IQ tests may not well reflect problem solving in the real world (Sternberg et al., 1995). Thus, intelligence tests are an important tool, but they need to be interpreted within the context of the individual's life, including how the person functions in different cultural and situational environments and with supports.

ADAPTIVE FUNCTIONING

Working at the Vineland Training School several decades ago, Edgar Doll emphasized the importance of social adequacy and the ability of persons with retardation to manage their lives. He published a scale to measure what he called social competence, a forerunner of the present concept of adaptive behavior and the Vineland Adaptive Behavior Scales (Myers, Nihira, & Zetlin, 1979). In 1959, AAMR first included deficits in adaptive functioning as a criterion for mental retardation. Adaptive behavior was viewed as overlapping with but not identical to intelligence, and research shows a moderate relationship between the two measures (DeStefano & Thompson, 1990). That is, as measured intelligence decreases, individuals are more likely to have greater difficulty in everyday functioning (King et al., 2000).

Adaptive behavior has generally been thought of as "what people do to take care of themselves and to relate to others in daily living . . ." (Grossman, 1983, p. 42). The ideas of personal self-help skills, social competence and social responsibility, and community living skills appear central in major tests of adaptive behavior (Luckasson et al., 1992; 2002). Behaviors associated with sensorimotor, communication, self-help, and primary socialization skills are emphasized in early life, whereas during later childhood and adolescence, reasoning and judgments

The ability to perform everyday behaviors is of critical importance to the adjustment and well-being of youth with mental retardation.
(Michelle D. Bridwell/PhotoEdit, Inc.)

about the environment and social relationships increase in importance.

In a broader sense, consideration needs to be given to culture: what is judged as adaptive may vary across cultures that hold different expectations for behavior. The demands of the immediate situation—and how the individual matches them—may also enter into what is considered adaptive (Scott, 1994). For example, children sometimes appear disabled with regard to academic demands at school but adequately meet the requirements of home and neighborhood—a phenomenon referred to as six-hour retardation.

Not all professionals are in favor of weighing adaptive behavior as heavily as intelligence in the definition of retardation (Baumeister & Baumeister, 2000; King et al., 2000.) They tend to view adaptive behavior as the result or correlate of mental disability. And they have expressed concerns about measurement problems, reflecting the fact that the development of adaptive behavior tests lagged behind that of intelligence tests. Nevertheless, it is widely agreed that daily living competences are critical to the adjustment and satisfaction of persons with mental retardation.

Description

Mental retardation encompasses a heterogeneous set of syndromes and conditions. In some cases, the effects are confined to mild deficits in intellectual and adaptive behavior but in others there are severe impairments in cognitive, sensory, motor, language, socioemotional, or behavioral systems. The enormous differences in functioning can be illustrated in several ways.

One way is to examine functioning that generally describes individuals according to levels of intelligence. Table 11–4 provides a brief description for mild, moderate, severe, and profound disability with a focus on expectations for communication skills, academic learning, and eventual living arrangements.

It is also informative to compare the developmental profiles of individual cases of children with mental disability. As an example, Figure 11–3 presents profiles for Bob and Carol, 10-year-olds whose functioning has been judged respectively as mildly and severely retarded (Kirk, Gallagher, & Anastasiow, 2000). Bob's physical characteristics (height, weight, motor coordination) do not vary much from those of his typically developing peers, but his functioning in language, academic, and social areas lags behind approximately 3 years (or grade-levels). In contrast, Carol is somewhat more behind in physical attributes and otherwise functioning at the 4-year-old level. With appropriate support, Bob might benefit from typical academic experiences but specialized training would be required to help Carol develop her potential.

A third way in which the clinical picture can be filled out is by further description of the physical/medical, learning/cognitive, and social functioning of children with mental disability. Most youth with mental retardation, particularly those with mild disability, show no unusual physical characteristics and blend into the general population. But a sizable number do show atypical appearance that ranges from minor abnormalities to distorted body size or shape. Disturbances in physical functions also occur. Up to 20 percent of persons with MR have a seizure disorder; other problems include motor difficulties, impaired eyesight or blindness, and deafness (Singh et al., 1998). Abnormalities of physical appearance and function are especially associated with the more severe levels of mental retardation, as are many medical conditions, such as cerebral palsy, epilepsy, cardiac problems, and kidney disease. The life span of

those with MR has increased in recent decades but it is still lower than average, specifically at the lower levels of mental retardation (Patja et al., 2000).

Investigators have described learning and cognition in MR. Children with mental retardation can learn, but there is immense variability with level of disability and etiology. Early investigations of classical and operant conditioning showed that basic learning is possible at all levels of mental retardation.

TABLE 11–4   BRIEF DESCRIPTION OF FUNCTIONING ACCORDING TO LEVELS OF MENTAL RETARDATION

MILD RETARDATION
Usually develops social and communication skills in preschool years
Has minimal sensorimotor deficits
Can acquire about sixth-grade academic skills by late teens
Usually achieves adult vocational and social skills for self-support
May need guidance, assistance, supervised living, but often lives successfully in the community

MODERATE RETARDATION
Usually develops communication skills in early childhood
Can attend to personal care, with support
Is unlikely to progress beyond second-grade academic skills
Can benefit from social and occupational skills training and perform unskilled or semiskilled work
Can adapt to supervised community living

SEVERE RETARDATION
May learn to talk and minimally care for self at school age
Has limited ability to profit from preacademic training
In adulthood, may perform simple tasks with supervision
In most cases, can adapt to community living with family or in group homes

PROFOUND RETARDATION
In most cases, has a neurological condition
Has sensorimotor impairments in childhood
With training, may show improvement in motor, self-care, and communication skills
May do simple supervised tasks
Requires structure and constant supervision with individual caregiver for optimal development

Based on American Psychiatric Association, 2000; Singh, Oswald, & Ellis, 1998.

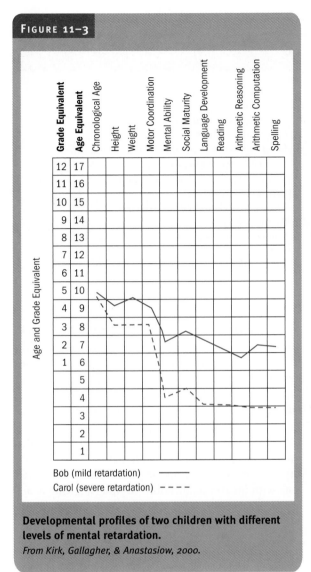

FIGURE 11-3

Developmental profiles of two children with different levels of mental retardation.

From Kirk, Gallagher, & Anastasiow, 2000.

on many tasks, and rehearsal of information as a memory strategy (Bray, Fletcher, & Turner, 1997). The study of different syndromes of retardation is instructive in demonstrating differential cognitive strengths and weaknesses, a topic to which we later return. All of these research approaches are valuable, of course, in informing us about the kinds and extent of training that might improve the intellectual and adaptive functioning of people with various abilities.

Finally, substantial heterogeneity is observed in communication and social abilities. These skills are especially important if youngsters with mental disability are to have more normal life experiences than they did in past times. Research has emphasized the social competencies of those with mild and moderate retardation (Greenspan & Love, 1997). In addition to language difficulties, some young people with mental retardation communicate in ways that can be detrimental to personal relationships (Davies & Rogers, 1985). Impairment is indicated, for example, in inappropriate facial expression and body contact, lack of verbal greetings and small talk, inappropriate comments, excessive friendliness, and lack of empathy in responding to others. Social cognition is also impaired, such as the understanding of others' perspectives, social situations, and social cues. It appears that social cognitive skills can gradually improve and that skills develop in the same order as they do for typically developing children (Greenspan & Love, 1997). There seems little doubt that some of the social and communication problems of youngsters with MR are attributable to intellectual disability and physical/medical impairments. It would be mistaken, however, not to recognize the influence of certain experiences on social development. Children with MR tend to experience greater social isolation despite today's heightened commitment to include them in typical social and educational activities. Then too, it is likely that other people, because of discomfort or other reasons, behave somewhat differently during social interactions. This behavior may result in lack of appropriate social models or unusual social relations that adversely affect those with mental disability.

Behavioral Problems and Co-Occurring Psychopathology

The well-being and social adaptation of individuals with mental retardation are hindered by various emotional and behavioral problems, some of which are sufficiently severe to meet criteria for clinical

Over the years, operant learning has been of special interest. New behaviors can be shaped by successive approximations; desirable behaviors can be maintained and undesirable behaviors weakened by consistent application of appropriate contingencies. Research based on information-processing approaches, primarily with individuals with mild or moderate disability, has been fruitful in documenting numerous problems. Deficits in attention, working memory, the use of effective strategies to mentally organize information, monitoring one's own thinking, and generalizing learning to new situations have been described (e.g., Tomporowski & Tinsley, 1997). Disability is not all-or-none, of course. For instance, competence has been displayed in visual recognition memory, long-term memory diagnoses. Reports of prevalence are highly inconsistent. Perhaps 30 to 40 percent of nonreferred individuals with MR have significant problems as rated by others (Dekker & Koot, 2003a; Volkmar & Dykens, 2002). According to the American Psychiatric Association (2000), the rate may be three to four times the rate in the general population. This finding applies to children and adolescents as well as adults. There is some indication that the frequency of problems in young people increases with age (Handen, 1998). In addition, behavior problems increase as retardation becomes more severe.

Although exact prevalence rates are arguable, the kinds of disturbances exhibited are similar to those shown in the general population. Anxiety, depression, attention problems, hyperactivity, aggression, obsessive-compulsive behavior, schizophrenia, autism, stereotypes, and self-injury have all been reported (Bregman, 1991; Lee et al., 2003; Szymanski, King et al., 1999). The rates for particular disturbances may differ, though, from rates in the general population. For example, there may be less substance abuse and more psychoses and autism in the MR population (Moss et al., 1997). Also observed is that depressive feelings, anxiety, and antisocial problems may be more common in mild disability whereas psychosis and autism may be more prevalent with lower intellectual ability (Dekker & Koot, 2003b).

It can be difficult to accurately identify or diagnose psychopathology. One reason is that the salience of intellectual disability may interfere with the recognition of other difficulties (Jopp & Keys, 2001). Such overshadowing, as it is called, has been documented among different professionals working in different settings. A second reason is that the cognitive and communication impairments of MR can make it difficult to identify problems, especially in severe retardation. This might be particularly so for symptoms requiring descriptions of internal feelings and experiences—a task that may be difficult even for youth with mild retardation. We would expect, for example, that depressive symptoms might be challenging to assess because the individual must be able to identify and label sadness, hopelessness, and the like. Still another factor can hinder diagnosis of psychopathology. Although standard diagnostic criteria apply quite well when IQ is about 50 or higher, they do not apply well at lower levels of retardation (Handen, 1998).

What accounts for high rates of problems or disorders in MR? Neurological factors (e.g., seizures) no doubt explain some disturbed behavior and probably play a stronger role in more severe retarda-

TABLE 11–5	FACTORS THAT MAY CONTRIBUTE TO BEHAVIORAL DISTURBANCES IN MR

Neurobiological processes responsible for mental retardation
Side effects of medication
Communication deficits
Inadequate problem-solving and coping skills
Reduced opportunity for development of social skills
Reduced opportunity for development of supportive social relationships
Stigma leading to low self-concept
Family stress
Vulnerability to exploitation and abuse

Based in part on King, Hodapp, & Dykens, 2000.

tion. Biological causation is suggested by the association of specific genetic syndromes with specific problem behaviors (Moldavsky, Lev, & Lerman-Sagie, 2001). The stigma of MR, lack of developmental opportunities, and qualities of living arrangements are among other factors that might be influential (Table 11–5).

Co-occurring problems undoubtedly lower the quality of life for young people with mental disability, interfere with community adjustment, and correlate with institutionalization (Szymanski, King et al., 1999; Scott, 1994). Currently there is greater recognition that disordered behavior warrants attention, whether or not it is inherent in mental retardation; however, it is likely that mental health care is inadequate (Dekker & Koot, 2003a).

Epidemiology

The prevalence of mental retardation is estimated as between 1 and 3 percent of the general population, but it varies with the criterion used and other factors (Singh, Oswald, & Ellis, 1998). If intelligence tests scores in the population with mental disability follow the normal distribution and an IQ of about 70 is taken as the criterion, a rate of over 2 percent would be expected from the theoretical distribution of IQ scores (see Figure 11–2). In fact, an even larger percentage could be expected because a greater number of cases than predicted by the normal distribution actually cluster at the low end of performance. Nonetheless, when MR is defined by *both* IQ and adaptive behavior deficits, a prevalence around

1 percent is suggested (American Psychiatric Association, 2000; Hodapp & Dykens, 2003). It is assumed that some individuals with mild retardation as defined by IQ scores are not identified with MR because their behavior is sufficiently adaptive in their environments.

Prevalence data are especially interesting when age and severity of mental retardation are inspected. Rates are lower prior to school age, and the young children identified tend to have moderate to lower IQ scores. It appears that the more severe cases attract more immediate attention, although not all of such cases are identified this early. A dramatic shift then occurs when children enter school. Prevalence increases as more mild cases are diagnosed, undoubtedly because the children are unable to meet the new demands in this situation. Rates appear to level off in adolescence and a decline occurs in adulthood. Decline may in part be due to the capacity of some adults to successfully work in unskilled jobs and otherwise function adequately, or perhaps be less available for evaluation. At the lower levels of MR, rates may drop because of the shorter lifespan of those with more severe mental retardation compared with the general population.

Other variables are important when prevalence is examined (Hodapp & Dykens, 2003; King et al., 2000). MR appears more in males than females—perhaps due to reporting bias, other environmental factors, and male vulnerability to biological influences. In fact, males are at higher risk for particular genetic syndromes associated with mental disability.

Low socioeconomic groups account for a disproportionate number of cases of MR, specifically mild cases—an important finding revisited later in the chapter. Overall, the epidemiology of mental retardation is a reminder that prevalence often varies with many factors, including the demands of different environments and the likelihood of cases being identified and labeled as MR. As was noted in Chapter 10, it appears that many children once identified in the schools with mental retardation may now be identified in the schools with learning disabilities.

Developmental Course and Considerations

Very different life trajectories can be anticipated for youngsters with mental disability. Stability of diagnosis is not inevitable and individuals with mild disability can, with appropriate training and opportunity, develop adequate intellectual or adaptive skills so that criteria for the disorder are no longer met (American Psychiatric Association, 2000). For most children, though, mental disability is lifelong. As might be expected, severity and cause of the disorder make a difference in course and outcome, as do factors such as associated medical problems and psychopathology and family variables (Volkmar & Dykens, 2002).

DEVELOPMENTAL ISSUES

Theorists and practitioners have been interested in several issues pertaining to the development of intelligence in mental retardation compared to what is known or hypothesized about typical cognitive development. Earlier research tended to focus on milder retardation for which there was no identified cause; later efforts included more severe retardation with known organic etiologies.

The *rate* of intellectual developmental has been of interest. Typical development is generally seen as occurring gradually over time throughout childhood and adolescence, with some spurts and regressions. What happens in retardation? Does cognition grow too slowly, become permanently arrested at a specific time, change through a series of spurts and lags? In fact, such questions are far from answered, although different patterns in the rates of development have been observed for some specific syndromes.

A second developmental consideration has to do with the *sequence* of intellectual growth. Intelligence normally develops in some orderly way. Does this course hold for retardation? Early research focused on whether youngsters with retardation followed the four stages of cognitive growth that, according to Jean Piaget, all typically developing youngsters display as they come to think in more complex ways. Research confirmed that children with mental disability generally do progress through the same Piagetian stages—and other cognitive sequences—as do nonretarded children, but do so more slowly and ultimately do not progress as far (Hodapp & Dykens, 2003; Hodapp & Zigler, 1997). The participants in this early research were children with retardation for which there was no clear organic cause but subsequently included children with Down syndrome.

Another issue addressed was whether children with retardation with no known organic cause exhibit similar intelligence as nonretarded children *matched on mental age*. Although this issue is theoretically complex, it was intertwined with the belief that typically developing youngsters more or less function at the same level across various domains of cognition. It was hypothesized that intelligence would not be different in those with mental retardation with no known organic cause. Put in another way, it was proposed that these children had no outstanding "defect" that caused the retardation. The hypothesis was supported for Piagetian tasks that required reasoning about classification, length, number, and the like (Hodapp, 1998). However, the children with retardation did not do as well on certain aspects of information-processing tasks. What was even clearer is that children with organically based mental retardation did not perform as well as MA-matched peers on either Piagetian or information-processing tasks. Thus, they appeared to have one or more specific areas of deficits (Hodapp & Dykens, 2003). Currently, this line of investigation is murky because questions have been raised about cross-domain performance in typically developing children. Nevertheless, strengths and weaknesses in areas of both cognition and language are observed in syndromes of mental disability, and differences between strong and weak areas may become more pronounced over time (Hodapp & Dykens, 2003).

What then can generally be concluded from research about the development of intelligence in mental retardation? It appears that some youngsters, especially those with milder levels of disability, will follow the typical order of growth and show few specific deficits, but will be delayed in development and fail to reach higher levels of abilities. Youngsters with more severe levels of retardation (and organic etiology) may exhibit specific deficits that can result in their performing relatively less well in some areas than others compared with children matched on mental age. These findings have practical implications for working with children with retardation. For example, the fact that the sequence of development in mental retardation is often similar to that for typical development provides a guideline for constructing curricular materials for teaching children.

Etiology

Although mental retardation is associated with hundreds of specific medical and genetic conditions, as well as with physical and psychosocial environmental circumstances, causation is not clearly identified in an estimated 30 to 40 percent of individuals seen in clinical settings (American Psychiatric Association, 2000). Etiology is more likely to be puzzling in milder cases of disability.

Johnny   Unknown Cause of MR

Johnny is a 10-year-old boy with mild mental retardation. Although from birth his parents considered him somewhat "slow," Johnny was not diagnosed . . . until his early grade-school years. To this day, no clear [cause] has been provided for Johnny's mild mental retardation. As measured by the Stanford-Binet IV, his I.Q. is 67, with no significant difference between his verbal and perceptual processing scores. Johnny does, however, show impulsivity and problems in attending. . . . Johnny's mental retardation first became apparent at the end of the first grade. At that time, a student study team at his school worked with Johnny's classroom teacher and the resource room teacher to help Johnny improve his basic work organizational skills and increase his attention span. At his parents' request, Johnny was also evaluated for attention-deficit hyperactivity disorder by the local psychiatrist, who subsequently prescribed stimulant medication that seemed to help.

Adapted from King et al., 2000, p. 2599.

Historically the two-group approach to mental disability has been a central organizing perspective in both theory and research (Volkmar & Dykens, 2002). Accordingly, individuals with MR are viewed as falling into two categories that differ from each other in several ways, including causation or suspected causation. The groups, as indicated in Table 11–6, are referred to as the organic group and the cultural-familial group. Biological etiology is clear for the organic group, and in the 1960s and 1970s causation for the cultural-familial group was primarily attributed to environmental deprivation, as reflected in the term *cultural-familial*. Current knowledge and theory indicates the wisdom of viewing causation as more complex and interactive. A multicausal model underlies our discussion, although we distinguish organic, multigenic, and psychosocial etiology or risks.

ORGANIC INFLUENCES

Attributing mental retardation to pathological organic factors implies that biological conditions are crucial in accounting for disordered brain function and thus intellectual disability. The idea that mental disability is caused by inherited biological "defect" has a strong place in the history of MR. In past times the argument was often based on flimsy or flawed

TABLE 11–6	THE TWO-GROUP APPROACH TO MENTAL RETARDATION

ORGANIC	CULTURAL-FAMILIAL
Individual shows a clear organic cause of mental retardation	Individual shows no obvious cause of retardation; sometimes another family member is also retarded
More prevalent at moderate, severe, and profound levels of retardation	More prevalent in mild mental retardation
Equal or near-equal rates across all ethnic and SES levels	Higher rates within minority groups and low-SES groups
More often associated with other physical disabilities	Few associated physical or medical disabilities

Adapted from Hodapp & Dykens, 2003.

"proof." For example, in his influential study of the Kallikak family, Goddard (1912) traced the quite distinct genealogical lines of Martin Kallikak. One line originated from Kallikak's liaison with a barmaid, the second from later marriage to a woman of "better stock." From information on several hundred of Kallikak's descendants, Goddard found a pronounced difference in the two families, namely, that the first liaison had resulted in more mental deficiency, criminality, alcoholism, and immorality. Obvious weaknesses existed in this study, most notably the questionable accuracy of the data. But the results were taken as evidence that mental disability was an inherited trait—although family environment could just as well have played a role.

Today there is much greater understanding of biological risk and causation. Zigler and his colleagues pointed out that although IQ scores are said to be normally distributed in the general population, they actually fall into a distribution that resembles the normal curve except for a "bump" at the low end (Burack, 1990; Zigler, Balla, & Hodapp, 1984). This excess of low scores, they suggested, is accounted for by individuals who have suffered major biological impairment (Simonoff, Bolton, & Rutter, 1996). In fact, evidence exists for a group of individuals with more severe mental retardation, coming about equally from all social classes, that shows an excess of specific genetic abnormalities, multiple congenital anomalies, clear evidence of brain dysfunction such as cerebral palsy, and reduced life expectancy.

It is currently estimated that 50 percent of cases of MR have some known organic cause (Volkmar & Dykens, 2002). Although associated with all levels of

MR, the presence of organic factors is more strongly related to greater disability. Biological risk, regardless of the level of retardation involved, may be due to abnormal genetic mechanisms, prenatal or birth variables, or postnatal circumstances (Table 11–7).

TABLE 11–7	ORGANIC-RELATED CAUSES OR RISKS FOR MENTAL RETARDATION

Prenatal

Genetic disorders
    Chromosome abnormalities
    Single-gene and other mutations
    Multigenes
Congenital malformations
Exposure
    Maternal infections
    Teratogens
    Toxemia; placental insufficiency
    Malnutrition

Perinatal

Low birth weight; prematurity
Delivery complications (trauma, anoxia)
Infections

Postnatal

Infections
Toxins
Accidents; trauma
Diseases
Malnutrition

Adapted from King, Hodapp, & Dykens, 2000.

TABLE 11–8	SOME PHYSICAL ATTRIBUTES AND BEHAVIORAL PROBLEMS ASSOCIATED WITH THREE SYNDROMES OF MENTAL RETARDATION	
	PHYSICAL	**BEHAVIORAL**
Down	Upward slant and folds at corner of eyes, flat facial features, fissured tongue, broad hands and feet, poor muscle tone	Relatively good social skills and mild manner but also noncompliance, stubbornness, augumentativeness, inattention, overactivity. Dementia in adulthood
Fragile X	Boys tend to have velvetlike skin, double-jointed thumbs, and by adolescence long faces, large ears, oversized testicles	Inattention, hyperactivity, stereotyped movements, anxiety, social avoidance, poor peer interaction (Girls: shyness, anxiety, social avoidance). Co-occurring autism that is associated with greater developmental delay
Williams	"Elfinlike" face (e.g., small lower jaw, prominent cheeks), growth deficiency, often an aged appearance in late adolescence or early adulthood	Anxiety, fears and phobias, inattention, hyperactivity, indiscriminate and overly friendly social interaction, poor social judgment

Based on Aman, Hammer, & Rojahn, 1993; Bailey et al., 2000; Capone, 2001; Karmiloff-Smith & Thomas, 2003; Moldavsky et al., 2001; State, King, & Dykens, 1997; Volkmar & Dykens, 2002; Whitman, O'Callaghan, & Sommer, 1997.

Genetic Syndromes. The exact ways in which genetic syndromes, both inherited and noninherited, affect intelligence and other attributes is being vigorously pursued. In some disorders, chromosome aberrations in which whole or parts of chromosomes are duplicated or deleted are quite obvious, and newer technologies are uncovering more subtle chromosome abnormalities (Knight et al., 1999). Many genetic syndromes involve single-gene mutations that often affect metabolism; recessive inheritance is common although dominant and sex-linked patterns are observed. Examples are the recessively inherited PKU and Lesch-Nyhan syndrome.

A few syndromes account for a high percentage of cases of mental retardation. We will highlight two of these—Down and fragile X—and also the less frequently found Williams syndrome. The study of these syndromes is important not only because of the disorders themselves but also because they provide opportunity to investigate and compare groups of individuals affected by known organic etiology. The syndromes are notably different in their genetic basis, physical features, intellectual strengths and weaknesses, behavioral manifestations, and probably developmental course. The association between specific syndromes and specific behaviors has led to

the notion of behavioral phenotypes. Some of the physical/medical characteristics and problem behaviors associated with the three syndromes are summarized in Table 11–8 and further description follows.

DOWN SYNDROME. Down syndrome, the most common single disorder of mental retardation, accounts for an estimated 5 percent of mild retardation and 30 percent of more severe cases (Gillberg, 1997). It occurs in 1 in 800 to 1,000 live births (Capone, 2001). The condition was described in 1866 by John Langdon Down, a British physician, who attributed it to maternal tuberculosis. In 1959, only 3 years after human chromosomes were described, trisomy 21 was discovered in persons with Down syndrome. As shown in Figure 11–4, chromosome 21 appears in a triplet instead of a pair. Ninety-five percent of all cases are attributed to this abnormality, which is caused by failure of the chromosome pair to divide in meiosis, the process in which ova and sperm are formed. Trisomy 21 seems to occur almost randomly and is not inherited. It is related to advancing maternal age, though, and risk is notably higher after age 40. Younger women who have a child with trisomy 21 have a small risk for having another child with Down syndrome (Simonoff et al., 1996). In a minority of

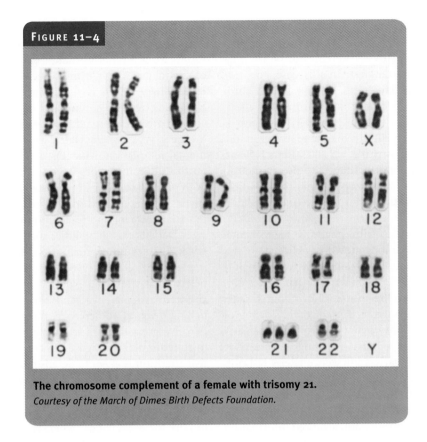

FIGURE 11-4

The chromosome complement of a female with trisomy 21.
Courtesy of the March of Dimes Birth Defects Foundation.

cases, the extra chromosome has been traced to fathers (Evans & Hammerton, 1985; Holmes, 1978).

Although the mechanism through which the extra set of genes influences development is unknown, several parts of the brain are affected, with abnormalities that include reduced brain size, reduced number and density of neurons, and abnormal dendrites (Capone, 2001). Brain pathology virtually identical to the abnormal plaques and tangles found in Alzheimer's disease is observed by age 35 to 40, and the symptoms of this disease are seen in three-quarters of persons with MR by the time they reach 70. In addition, there is risk of serious health problems, such as heart defects and hearing impairment. Although life expectancy is below normal, it has climbed substantially in recent years (Patja et al., 2000).

Mental disability usually is evident during the first few years of life, and amidst many spurts and regressions, the rate of development slows throughout childhood and adolescence (Capone, 2001). Retardation typically ranges from moderate to severe (Moldavsky et al., 2001). Unusually large declines in cognitive and adaptive functioning have inconsistently been reported in adults; these are perhaps related to the development of dementia (Hawkins et al., 2003).

The relative cognitive impairments and strengths associated with Down syndrome are becoming better understood. Most children acquire speech but it is delayed, and expressive language is more affected than comprehension. Evidence exists for deficits in verbal short-term memory and auditory processing (Laws & Gunn, 2004). Visual-spatial abilities are relatively good.

FRAGILE X SYNDROME. This syndrome is second to Down syndrome as a cause of mental retardation and is the most common inherited form of mental retardation. It occurs in 1 of 4,000 male births and 1 of 8,000 female births (Reiss & Dant, 2003). Although genetic transmission was apparent early-on, much investigative work was necessary to track down the underlying X-linked process (Simonoff et al., 1996; Thapar et al., 1994). The disorder involves repeats of a mutation of a triplet of DNA nucleotides (cytosine, guanine, guanine). Persons in the general population have between 6 and 50 of these repeats. Male and female carriers of fragile X syndrome have 50 to 200 repeats; this condition is known as the premutation. Males can pass on the premutation to their daughters, who become carriers. But it is when females transmit the premutation that the number of repeats can expand to over 200, in which case the FMR-1 gene is not expressed and the full-blown fragile X syndrome is manifest. In this case, sons are more affected than daughters, whose second X chromosome is likely to be normal. Through its influences on protein synthesis, the FMR-1 gene is thought to adversely affect synaptic maturation and brain circuitry (Grossman et al., 2003; Reiss & Dant, 2003). Structural abnormalities have been found in several brain areas, and it appears that there is difficulty in brain activation in response to increased task difficulty.

Nearly all males with fragile X have mental retardation, usually moderate. Most children are not identified until about age 3, although parents report earlier concerns (Bailey, Skinner, & Sparkman, 2003). Language skills develop to a level of about 4 years and then plateau. There is a predictable slowing of cognition and adaptive behavior beginning as early as age 5, with development reaching a plateau by later childhood or early adolescence (Reiss & Dant, 2003). Weaknesses are notable in visual-spatial cognition, sequential information processing, motor coordination, arithmetic, and executive functions. Verbal long-term memory and acquired information appear to be relative strengths (Volkmar & Dykens, 2002). Nowhere near as many females with fragile X syndrome display mental retardation, and when they do, it tends to be mild although similar to the male profile. Learning disabilities, behavior problems, and social impairments are common in females with one affected X chromosome.

WILLIAMS SYNDROME. This syndrome is a rare disorder, occurring in an estimated 1 case in 20,000, which results from a random mutation involving deletions of several genes on chromosome 7 (Karmiloff-Smith & Thomas, 2003). Cardiac and kidney problems, hypersensitivity to sound, and deficient depth perception are among the difficulties reported. The syndrome is typically associated with mild to moderate mental retardation, with IQs mostly in the range of 50 to 70. Brain studies have linked the disorder to both scarcity of tissue in the visual system for making spatial judgments and in the frontal lobe implicated in social behavior and fear responses (Bower, 2004).

Deficits exist in abilities such as general knowledge, abstract conceptualization, and problem solving (Rossen et al., 1996). Visual-spatial skills are below what would be expected in keeping with the children's mental age, and the deficits are compelling. Even at adolescence, there is an inability to perceive gross differences in spatial orientation and to copy simple stick figures. In copying figures, selective attention is given to details rather than to whole configurations, an example of which is provided in Figure 11–5. Here we see that adolescents with Williams syndrome focused on the local feature (Y) in their drawings, whereas those with Down syndrome focused on the global feature (D). Despite such visual-spatial deficits, individuals with Williams syndrome are interested in human faces and can infer "wanting" and "thinking" from facial cues (Elgar & Campbell, 2001).

Particularly striking in Williams syndrome is the level of language ability relative to visual-spatial

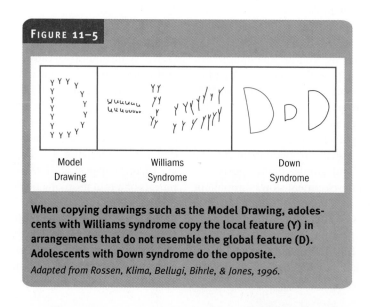

FIGURE 11–5

| | | |
| Model Drawing | Williams Syndrome | Down Syndrome |

When copying drawings such as the Model Drawing, adolescents with Williams syndrome copy the local feature (Y) in arrangements that do not resemble the global feature (D). Adolescents with Down syndrome do the opposite.

Adapted from Rossen, Klima, Bellugi, Bihrle, & Jones, 1996.

deficits, and often relative to children with other genetic disorders. Verbal IQ is usually significantly higher than performance IQ. Whereas weaknesses exist in aspects of language such as syntax and reading, children and adults with Williams syndrome are described as having a sophisticated vocabulary and ability to employ it (Laing et al., 2001; Karmiloff-Smith & Thomas, 2003). Their communication style has been described as fluent and "pseudo-mature" (Hodapp & Zigler, 1997; State et al., 1997). In fact, although language may be weak in meaning, the use of unusual, socially engaging vocabulary and expression can be captivating, as depicted in the following account of Crystal. Continued study of Williams and other genetic syndromes holds promise in advancing our understanding of gene-brain-behavior relationships in development.

Crystal	An "Elegant" Friend and a "Sweet Petunia"

In describing her future aspirations, Crystal, a 16-year-old adolescent, states: "You're looking at a professional book writer. My books will be filled with drama, action, and excitement. And everyone will want to read them. I'm going to write books, page after page, stack after stack. . . . I'll start on Monday." Crystal describes a meal as "a scrumptious buffet," an older friend as "quite elegant," and her boyfriend as "my sweet petunia"; when asked if someone could borrow her watch, she replies "My watch is always available for service." Crystal can spontaneously create stories—she weaves a tale of a chocolate princess who changes the sun color to save the chocolate world from melting; she recounts with detail a dream in which an alien from a different planet emerges from a television. Her creativity extends to music; she has composed the lyrics to a love song. . . . In view of her facility with language, proclivity for flowery, descriptive terms, and professed focus on drama and action, her aspiration may seem plausible; but in fact, Crystal has an IQ of 49, with an IQ equivalent age of 8 years.

Rossen et al., 1996, p. 367.

MULTIGENIC INFLUENCES

The genetic risks and syndromes just discussed are assumed to cause mental retardation through abnormal brain development or brain damage. In contrast, multigenic, or polygenic, influences derive from multiple genes whose effects combine to produce variation in intelligence in normal populations. Mental retardation is viewed as representing the lower scores in this nonpathological variation.

Current understanding of hereditary influence on intelligence in populations has a basis in behavior genetic research (Plomin, DeFries, & McClearn, 1990). Intelligence test performance of identical twins is more similar than that of fraternal twins; when identical twins are reared apart, similarity decreases but is still high. Studies of families and adopted children lend support to the twin findings. In general, it is estimated that about 50 percent of the variation in tested intelligence in populations is due to genetic transmission of multiple genes. By far, most of this research has been conducted with non-retarded persons, but the few studies conducted with individuals with mental retardation similarly implicate multigenic inheritance (Thompson, 1997).

Research studies also suggest that the influence of multiple genes may vary with the level of MR. Whereas pathological organic factors are more strongly associated with the more severe levels of disability, the opposite appears to hold for multigenic influences. One family study, for example, revealed that the IQs of siblings of children with severe retardation averaged 103, hinting that severe retardation did not "run in families" and that some specific organic factor had caused retardation in the affected child. In contrast, the IQs of siblings of children with mild retardation averaged 85, suggesting general family influence, perhaps multigenic inheritance, psychosocial effects, or a combination of these (Broman et al., 1987; Scott, 1994).

This is not to say, of course, that pathological organic factors never cause mild mental retardation. Indeed, we might anticipate that biological advances will reveal now-undetected organic abnormalities that contribute to mild impairments. Nevertheless, multiple factors are likely involved in the etiology of mild cases and these include multiple genes as well as psychosocial influences (Hodapp & Dykens, 2003).

PSYCHOSOCIAL INFLUENCES

Interest in psychosocial causation of mental disability was tied to the conceptualization of cultural-familial retardation (Table 11–6). The terms *garden variety* and *undifferentiated* also were used, reflecting the large number of cases that were not readily distinguished from one another (Crnic, 1988). These children appeared quite normal, possessed relatively good adaptive skills, were often first identified on entering school, and as adults often blended into the general population. Their family members were frequently described in similar ways.

It has been observed for many years that mild retardation in families occurs disproportionately in the lower socioeconomic classes and in some minority groups, and could be caused by psychosocial/cultural disadvantage. Of course, many psychosocial variables correlated with social class put children at risk—such as parental education, parental attitudes, social support, and stressful life events (Sameroff, 1990). The adverse effects of psychosocial variables may operate through more than one pathway. Inadequate intellectual stimulation might hinder early brain development, especially the growth of synaptic networks. Behaviors conducive to success in the classroom and other learning environments may not be acquired or supported. Attitudes and motivation favorable to achievement may be inadequately established.

Specific associations have been demonstrated between home environment variables, social class, and children's intellectual development. One study found, for instance, that ability at age 3 was related to lower social class and parental practices, that is, interacting with the child, talking to the child, and being actively interested in what the child did (Hart & Risley, 1992). As a group, educationally and economically deprived parents may lack skills, or otherwise be unable to stimulate children's language and cognitive development. The investigators of this study and their colleagues have for many years been engaged in the Juniper Gardens Children's Project, an intervention and research program for disadvantaged preschool children (Greenwood et al., 1992; 1994). They have proposed a model for the development of retardation that reaches across generations. Accordingly, young children, because of limited parental interactions, begin to fall behind intellectually. On reaching school, this situation combines with school practices that lead to low educational motivation, exposure, and achievement—resulting in a high rate of school dropout. In turn, when these children become parents, they are unable to contribute optimally to the cognitive growth of their offspring.

It is, nevertheless, difficult to pinpoint any one cause of MR in disadvantaged children. This population is also at risk for major inherited abnormalities, prenatal and birth adversities, postnatal malnutrition and disease, and other adversities that can affect the developing brain. Variation due to multiple-gene inheritance is not ruled out. Given what is known about the intricacies of development, multifactor explanations might frequently apply.

MULTIFACTOR CAUSATION

Although it is still too easy to fall back on the historical tendency to view the cause of MR as falling into *either* biological *or* psychosocial factors, more complex explanations are now clearly recognized. As AAMR points out, multifactor explanations of the causes and risk underlying mental disability are not inconsistent with the two-group approach. In some instances, biomedical factors may predominate whereas in others social, behavioral, or educational factors may predominate. Even when a known medical disorder is strongly associated with mental retardation, the level of disability may be determined, within limits, by some mix of other biological factors and attributes of the psychosocial environment. For example, intelligence, adaptive behavior, and behavioral problems are influenced by the home and school environment in children with fragile X syndrome (Reiss & Dant, 2003). AAMR views the development of mental disability within a multiple risk model that encompasses biomedical, social, behavioral, and educational factors that can operate at different times in life (Table 11–9).

Family Coping and Accommodation

The birth of a child with a disability is likely to be a traumatic and sad event for a family. Parents feel the loss of expectations that will never be fulfilled and face demands for special care for their child. An unusual amount of attention must be given to the intellectual, emotional, and behavioral needs of the child, and often to physical needs as well.

How should we think about families who have a child with retardation or other developmental disorders? Early investigations focused on determining adverse effects on family members, but families are currently viewed in a more normative way—as similar to other families coping with stress. They are seen as accommodating their lifestyles to their child's needs even as these needs and other circumstances vary over time (Seltzer et al., 2001; von Gonard et al., 2002). This is a different perspective from earlier, more negative and static views of family adjustment. For example, earlier stage perspectives proposed that family adjustment moved from shock and denial *to*

TABLE 11–9	THE FOUR AAMR CATEGORIES OF RISK AND ETIOLOGY PERTAINING TO MENTAL DISABILITY			
TIMING	**BIOMEDICAL**	**SOCIAL**	**BEHAVIORAL**	**EDUCATIONAL**
Prenatal	1. Chromosomal disorders 2. Single-gene disorders 3. Syndromes 4. Metabolic disorders 5. Cerebral dysgenesis 6. Maternal illnesses 7. Parental age	1. Poverty 2. Maternal malnutrition 3. Domestic violence 4. Lack of access to prenatal care	1. Parental drug use 2. Parental alcohol use 3. Parental smoking 4. Parental immaturity	1. Parental cognitive disability without supports 2. Lack of preparation for parenthood
Perinatal	1. Prematurity 2. Birth injury 3. Neonatal disorders	1. Lack of access to birth care	1. Parental rejection of caretaking 2. Parental abandonment of child	1. Lack of medical referral for intervention services at discharge
Postnatal	1. Traumatic brain injury 2. Malnutrition 3. Meningoencephalitis 4. Seizure disorders 5. Degenerative disorders	1. Impaired child-adult relationship 2. Lack of adequate stimulation 3. Family poverty 4. Chronic illness in the family 5. Institutionalization	1. Child abuse and neglect 2. Domestic violence 3. Inadequate safety measures 4. Social deprivation 5. Difficult Child behaviors	1. Impaired parenting 2. Delayed diagnosis 3. Inadequate early intervention services 4. Inadequate special-educational services 5. Inadequate family support

From Luckasson et al., 2002.

chronic sadness, hopelessness, and anger *to* emotional reorganization and adjustment (Blacher, 1984). Even though families report the experiences just described, any stage model is probably too simple because families appear continually to adjust and readjust in various ways. Moreover, joy and satisfaction are part and parcel of the experiences of parenthood.

One variable that can affect how families function is the severity of their child's mental retardation. Moderate and severe levels demand much immediate care but also planning for lifetime care and supervision; mild retardation can mean a long period of uncertainty about the existence of deficits. The diagnostic process can be stressful and frustrating for parents (Bailey et al., 2003). Looking back on first being informed about their child's disability, parents suggested that it is beneficial to be told the truth as early as possible, to receive information about the disorder, and to be treated sympathetically (Quine & Rutter, 1994). Other influences on family coping include parental beliefs and coping skills, marital interaction, parental intellectual functioning, siblings' perceptions, social class variables, professional services, and social support (e.g., Atkinson et al., 1995; Flynt, Wood, & Scott, 1992; Sloper et al., 1991; Wolf et al., 1998). These numerous factors—child characteristics, family characteristics, and social variables—create a complex picture.

Family members likely are affected in different ways and to varying degrees. Mothers may elect not to work outside the home or to work part time (Seltzer et al., 2001). When they are employed, they face greater than usual work-related stress, for example, in finding child care for a youngster with unique

Youngsters with mental retardation or other developmental disabilities require and benefit from extraordinary care and nurturing from their families. The extent to which these families experience stress, adjust to high demands, and are fulfilled depends on many factors.
(Frank Siteman/Stock Boston)

needs (Warfield, 2001). Mothers may be more affected overall than fathers, but we should not oversimplify how family members are challenged. One study showed, for instance, that mothers are more affected by the child's behavior and fathers by variables external to the child, such as unemployment and financial strain (Sloper et al., 1991). Siblings undoubtedly are influenced by family stress and needs to accommodate the child with diasabilities. For example, siblings may have difficulties in knowing how to talk to others about their sister or brother with disabilities, and they are often socialized to anticipate caring for the child with disabilities in the future (Orsmond & Seltzer, 2000; Turnbull, 2004).

It is worth noting that the effects of having a child with disabilities may vary with family ethnic/racial background (Neely-Barnes & Marchenko, 2004). Differences have been reported across ethnic/racial groups in perceptions about disability, how disability affects family caregivers, and participation in the systems that provide services.

LIVING ARRANGEMENTS

At one time, families were encouraged to place their children in out-of-home care (Llewellyn et al., 1999). This attitude has dramatically shifted, and today most youngsters with intellectual disability live at home. Nevertheless, many families consider other

options and some decide, for a variety of reasons, in favor of group homes, foster care, or institutions (Table 11–10). In a study of children who had severe disabilities, families that were committed to at-home care expressed more satisfaction with the routines of everyday life and viewed their child as part of family

TABLE 11–10	FACTORS REPORTED BY AT LEAST 40 PERCENT OF PARENTS AS STRONGLY OR VERY STRONGLY INFLUENCING THE DECISION FOR OUT-OF-HOME PLACEMENT

FACTOR	PERCENT
Day-to-day stress	81
My child's level of functioning and potential for future learning	75
My child's behavior	60
Feelings of my nonhandicapped children	55
My spouse's attitude toward placement	48
Medical or physical problems of my handicapped child	48
Availability of respite care	46
Availability of babysitters	43
Advice from professionals	41

Adapted from Bromley & Blacher, 1991.

life and the community (Llewellyn et al., 1999). In contrast, families that were searching for alternative placements or had already placed their child believed that the child needed better care than they could provide and expressed concern about other family members. Although decisions about the child's living arrangement often weigh heavily on parents, Eisenberg, Baker, and Blacher (1998) found that families come to terms with their choice. They appear to choose what they believe will benefit everyone and cite positive consequences of their decision. It is also the case that families may recognize that as youngsters with mental retardation approach adulthood, leaving home may be a natural transition with risks and opportunity for growth, much as it is for other young people (Blacher, 2001).

REWARDS AND SATISFACTIONS

Research on families rearing a child with developmental disabilities has a history of emphasizing stress, loss, grief, frustration, guilt, and other negative reactions (Helff & Glidden, 1998). And yet, siblings can be well adjusted (Kaminsky & Dewey, 2000), and they report that they acquire increased empathy, maturity, patience, acceptance of differences, ability to help others, and appreciation for health and family (Eisenberg, Baker, & Blatcher, 1998). Scorgie and Sobsey (2000) investigated the transformations in the lives of parents of children with disabilities. Transformational outcomes were defined as substantial and lasting psychological change for the better that are set into motion by a traumatic or challenging event that provides opportunity for change. Several transformational outcomes were reported by parents (Table 11–11). These parents recognized negative aspects of rearing a child with special needs—for example, career limitations and reduced social participation—and they emphasized the importance of balancing negative and positive aspects.

Fortunately, considerable recognition is being given to more complete portraits of family interaction and functioning. (See Accent: "Family Context and Development.") Family systems perspectives focus on understanding numerous family needs and facilitating family quality of life (Turnbull, 2004). Efforts are being made to provide economic assistance, medical care, child and family therapy, training in child management, and training of parents as teachers for their handicapped children. Research indicates that helping families obtain services from

TABLE 11–11	PARENTAL REPORTS OF POSITIVE TRANSFORMATIONS IN THEIR LIVES

ITEMS MOST PARENTS AGREED OR STRONGLY AGREED WITH

Learned to speak out
Can achieve
Became stronger
Met other people/friends
See life from another perspective
Make a difference for another
Have a more authentic view of success
Learned what is important in life
Am more compassionate

Adapted from Scorgie & Sobsey, 2000.

community resources rather than solely from professional agencies can be especially advantageous (Handen, 1998).

Assessment

Our discussion of the assessment of mental retardation draws heavily on Handen's (1997) review. Assessment may serve several purposes. Diagnosis may be required for school placement or for obtaining special services. Parents also may seek a second opinion about their child's functioning, or they may seek help in facilitating the diagnosed child's development or managing behavior. Thus, employing a standard battery of assessment instruments or methods will not appropriately serve every child. Rather, the purpose of the evaluation can best determine the comprehensiveness of the assessment and the procedures and instruments used. Assessment of intelligence, adaptive behavior, behavior adjustment and problems, academic progress, family functioning, and medical concerns are all appropriate, depending on the case.

TESTS OF GENERAL INTELLIGENCE

Standardized, individually given intelligence tests are the single most important instruments to diagnose mental retardation. For infants, toddlers, or children with severe deficiency, developmental tests substitute for intelligence tests.

ACCENT

Family Context and Development

Any view of mental disability that assumes a relationship between functioning and environmental support would argue that the home environment is at least as important for the development of children with MR as it is for typical youngsters. How families function day by day and how family members interact with the child with disabilities can be critical to the well-being of both children and the family. The following example points to the importance of understanding the interface of mothers and their children with disabilities.

In some ways, there is little difference in the manner in which mothers of children with retardation interact compared with mothers of typical children of the same mental age (King et al., 2000). Both groups of mothers speak in short sentences with simple vocabulary, repeat key words, and use high pitch—in short, employ the "motherese" that is universally observed in mother-child "talk." What appears to be different is that some mothers with a child with intellectual disability are more directive and controlling.

They dominate turn-taking time, speak more when the child is speaking, teach rather than play, and so forth (Hodapp, 1998). These mothers may be especially worried about their child's not meeting developmental norms and may be especially motivated to instruct their child. The child's behavior may play an important role as well, as some of the infants tend to be less socially responsive and to give less predictable and appropriate social signals (Roach et al., 1998). Limited data suggest that an overly directive and controlling maternal style is detrimental to the development of the children (King et al., 2000). However, it appears that maternal sensitivity and support can moderate adverse effects. Roach and colleagues (1998) note that mothers can simultaneously direct their child's behavior and show support, for example, by making it easier for the child to succeed and by appropriately praising the child. In fact, the combination of parental directiveness and sensitive support has been linked to positive child outcome.

Developmental Tests. Several standardized, individually given developmental scales exist. Among the most popular is the Bayley Scales of Infant Development-II, which covers age 1 month to 42 months (Bayley, 1969/1993). Performance on this test is termed developmental quotient (DQ), because it evaluates different abilities than do tests for older children. Infant scales give greater emphasis to sensorimotor functioning and less emphasis to language and abstraction. This feature may partly account for the fact that performance on infant tests is not highly correlated with later IQ in the normal population. However, developmental tests may be better predictors of mental disability, especially of severe retardation, than of average or superior intelligence. They may also be especially helpful when used in conjunction with histories and neurodevelopmental assessments (Bregman & Hodapp, 1991).

Stanford-Binet. The Stanford-Binet Intelligence Scale is now in its fifth edition (Roid, 2003). The previous edition was substantially reorganized by grouping subtests into four cognitive areas. The fifth edition retains many of these subtests, and five areas

are now assessed: Fluid Reasoning, Knowledge, Quantitative Reasoning, Visual-Spatial Processing, and Working Memory. The S-B includes toys and objects helpful in assessing young children, and nonverbal evaluation is possible in each cognitive area. Scores can be obtained for each cognitive area and a Nonverbal, Verbal, and Full-Scale IQ can be obtained. The standardization group for the S-B fifth edition is a representative U.S. sample, ages 2 to 85 years.

Wechsler Tests. Immensely popular for assessing MR are the Wechsler Preschool and Primary Scale of Intelligence (WPPSI-R) (Wechsler, 2002) and the Wechsler Intelligence Scale for Children–Fourth Edition (WISC-IV) (Wechsler, 2003). Designed for ages 4 to 6.5, the WPPSI-R contains subscales that are designated as either verbal or performance tasks. Three IQ scores are calculated: Verbal IQ, Performance IQ, and Full-Scale IQ that combines that verbal and performance scores.

The WISC-IV is based more on cognitive models than earlier versions of this test. Examples of subtests are vocabulary, block design, digit span, and coding. Instead of earning a verbal and performance

IQ, the child obtains four index scores. These are Verbal Comprehension, Perceptual Reasoning, Working Memory, and Processing Speed. A Full-Scale IQ is derived from ten core subtests included in these four indices. The WISC-IV was standardized on a sample of U.S. children ages 6 to 16.

Kaufman Tests. The Kaufman Assessment Battery for Children–Revised (KABC-II), designed for individuals ages 3 to 18, emphasizes cognitive processing (Kaufman & Kaufman, 2004). Five scales are offered. For example, the sequential processing/short-term memory scale requires step-by-step processing of content, whereas the simultaneous processing scale requires integrating several pieces of visual-spatial information at the same time. The KABC-II permits the evaluator to employ either 4 or 5 scales based on two different models relevant to the reason for referral or the child's background. One of the models is more applicable to the child from a mainstream language and cultural background, whereas the other may be more suitable for a child of different background. Both models result in a global intelligence score. The Kaufman tests also include the Adolescent and Adult Intelligence Test (KAIT) that is designed for ages 11 and up. Based on several theories of intelligence, it appears psychometrically sound (Anastasi & Urbina, 1997).

ASSESSING ADAPTIVE BEHAVIOR

Adaptive behavior can be assessed through interviews with families or caretakers, direct observation, and self-report in some cases. Several standardized scales have been constructed, and attention has been given to reliability and validity.

Vineland Adaptive Behavior Scales. These scales were originated by Doll at the Vineland Training School. A major revision was constructed by Sparrow, Balla, and Cicchetti in 1984, and the fifth revision (Vineland-II) nears completion (American Guidance Service, 2005). Information can be collected for individuals from birth to age 89 through semistructured interviews or rating scales with parents or caregivers. Also available is a questionnaire for teachers to assess individuals ages 3 through 21 years. The scales cover four major behavioral domains: communication, daily living skills, socialization, and motor skills. In addition, an optional domain of maladaptive behavior can be used. Scores from the separate domains and an overall score can be compared with scores from a normal standard group and special groups with disabilities. Research has suggested that the Vineland

TABLE 11–12	SOME DOMAINS ASSESSED BY THE ADAPTIVE BEHAVIOR SCALES

Independent functioning
Physical development
Language development
Self-direction
Responsibility
Socialization
Numbers and time
Prevocational/vocational activity
Violent and antisocial behavior
Rebellious behavior
Withdrawal
Eccentric and self-abusive behavior

scales differentiated among different disorders and measured what they were intended to measure (Balboni et al., 2001).

AAMR'S Adaptive Behavior Scales. For several years, AAMR has published adaptive behavior scales to be employed in the schools and community (Luckasson et al., 2002). The ABS–School Edition (ABS-S:2) examines a wide range of behaviors that tap personal self-sufficiency, community self-sufficiency, personal–social responsibility, social adjustment, and personal adjustment (Table 11–12). The comparison norm groups consist of public school children, ages 3 through 16, with or without disabilities. The ABS–Residential and Community (ABC-RC:2), which largely taps the same factors as the school-based scale, is based on performance of persons, ages 18 and over, with developmental disabilities.

OTHER APPROACHES TO ASSESSMENT

Additional assessment approaches may be employed when the goal is to provide intervention or support to children and adolescents with mental disabilities. For example, curriculum-based assessment goes hand in hand with programmatic intervention. Typically it is geared to a specific curriculum and measures a child's individual progress, which in turn guides teaching or treatment. The curriculum-based approach is especially useful for severe and profound retardation, partly because norm-referenced intelligence tests are not sufficiently sensitive to developmental change in children within this range of intelligence (Handen, 1997). In comparison, the functional assessment approach is particularly appropriate in understanding the factors maintaining maladaptive behaviors, and thus in efforts to change these behaviors. (We more fully describe the approach later in the chapter.)

AAMR, in addition to recommending the usual standardized tests of intelligence and adaptive behavior, has developed guidelines for assessing each person's needs for supports (Luckasson et al., 2002). Consistent with AAMR's philosophy, the aim of this assessment is to provide services to improve the functional capabilities of those with mental handicaps (p. 305). The process involves identifying the areas in which support is needed, appropriate support activities, and the level of support needed in each activity. For example, an adolescent may require aid in interacting with community members or in personal hygiene. Such support could be provided through simple monitoring, teaching activities, or physical supports. The level of support judged necessary could range from minimal to substantial.

Treatment

BROADENING OF OPPORTUNITY

The long history of treatment for mental deficiency has been characterized by different approaches and fluctuations in quality, which reflected the attitudes held about mental disability. (See Accent: "Changing Views of Mental Retardation.") Viewing treatment from a broad perspective, the last several decades have been marked by favorable attitudes and service models. The 1960s brought widespread interest in the rights of poor, handicapped, and minority populations. The concept of normalization, first popularized in Scandinavia, served as a framework for how people with mental deficiency would be treated. Accordingly, each person is seen as having the right to experiences that are as normal and as least restrictive as possible. When applied to treatment, the central idea of normalization is that intervention should aim at producing behaviors that are as normal as

ACCENT ● ● ● ●

Changing Views of Mental Retardation

Attitudes about mental deficiency have reflected the general beliefs of the times and have influenced how those with retardation would be treated by the societies in which they lived (Cytryn & Lourie, 1980). Roman laws permitted extermination of those with mental retardation; medieval Europe looked upon them as jesters or creatures of the devil.

We can trace modern attitudes to the late 1700s and the case of the "Wild Boy of Aveyron," otherwise known as Victor. The boy was first seen running naked through the woods, searching for roots and acorns to eat. He was captured and assigned to a medical officer, Jean M. Itard, at the National Institute for the Deaf and Dumb in Paris. Victor's senses were underdeveloped; his memory, attention, and reasoning were deficient; and his ability to communicate was almost nil (Itard, as cited in Harrison & McDermott, 1972). Itard attributed the boy's deficits to lack of contact with civilized people, but the treatment designed for Victor failed, and he remained in custodial care until his death.

Despite the unfortunate outcome, Itard's effort did much to stimulate interest in the "feebleminded" or "retarded" (Rie, 1971). The middle to late 1800s saw a favorable climate, with special education. Itard's student Sequin was a leader during this optimistic era, and promising ideas spread rapidly across the United States. Residential schools opened to educate children with retardation and then to return them to the community (Szymanski & Crocker, 1985). This enlightened view was marked in 1876 by the formation of AAMR.

Optimism then was gradually overcome by several developments. Increased interest in biology as a cause of MR, the rise of psychoanalysis, and the misuse or misunderstanding of IQ tests strengthened the belief that persons with mental retardation could not be helped and were a detriment, if not a danger, to society. This attitude led to widespread institutionalization and custodial care rather than treatment, with institutions growing in number and size throughout the first half of the 20th century. Subsequent developments, framed by recognition of the rights of persons with mental disability, brought renewed optimism and efforts to improve conditions—which characterize present-day approaches to mental retardation.

possible and should accomplish this goal by methods as culturally normal as possible (Mesibov, 1992; Thompson & McEvoy, 1992; Wolfensberger, 1980).

The philosophy of normalization has been widely applied to the lives of people with MR and developmental disabilities, and has influenced many aspects of life, including living arrangements, work life, and educational services. For example, residence in state institutions in the United States dramatically decreased from the late 1970s, whereas residence in small group homes in the community increased (Lakin et al., 2003). Similarly, opportunity for supported employment in the community has risen over several years (Braddock, Rizzolo, & Hemp, 2004; Figure 11–6). Under the Americans with Disabilities Act, states are required to provide programs, activities, and services in the least restrictive environments. Thus, progress has been made, although continued effort is needed to maintain and strengthen these efforts (e.g., Kormann & Petronko, 2004). Because mental disability usually persists at some level, concern for children and adolescents with MR includes attention to social and work opportunities for their future years.

Turning more specifically to educational services and behavioral treatment for young people, interventions must consider not only intellectual and adaptive functioning but also associated behavioral difficulties and physical impairments. In a substantial number of cases, particularly involving severe retardation, medical conditions must be attended. Thus professionals from various disciplines are involved. Treatment can be as varied as special diet to prevent or check retardation due to PKU, training programs to teach self-help or social skills, medication to control seizures, academic classes in reading or arithmetic, and the like. Although the overall goal of treatment is to help youngsters attain the best possible functioning and life circumstance, the aim of any single intervention depends on the specific needs being addressed. We will examine, to varying degrees, educational services, behavioral intervention, pharmacological treatment, and psychotherapy.

EDUCATIONAL SERVICES

Educational services are the most extensive and common interventions for mental retardation (Handen, 1998). Adoption of the Individuals with Disabilities Education Act (IDEA) has dramatically, if gradually, changed access to public education for persons with mental disability. It has strengthened individualized programming for children with retardation, increased parents' participation in the education of their youngsters, and provided greater opportunity for alternative educational settings. Despite the variation that exists across school districts and regions,

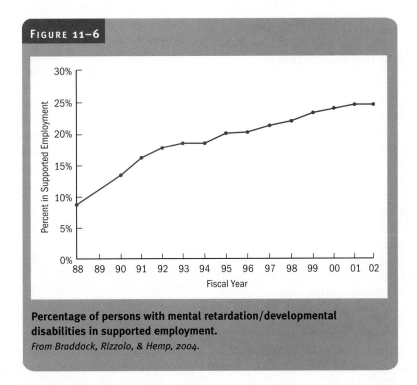

FIGURE 11–6

Percentage of persons with mental retardation/developmental disabilities in supported employment.
From Braddock, Rizzolo, & Hemp, 2004.

Increased numbers of children with mental handicaps now are attending community schools in which they are fully or partially integrated into general education classrooms.
(Richard Hutchings/Photo Researchers, Inc.)

more children with mental disabilities are attending local schools and joining their peers in general classrooms. The following description provides a glance into one child's school experiences.

Harold   Life in the Mainstream

Harold is a 16-year-old boy with moderate mental retardation. Diagnosed at birth with Down syndrome, Harold has been mainstreamed with same-age peers throughout his schooling. Harold, whose IQ is 53, has some difficulties with articulation, and his language consists mainly of two- to four-word sentences. Recently, Harold was introduced to reading; he now can read 50 sight words. Although he can occasionally be stubborn and argumentative, Harold is well liked by his teachers and classmates, and his parents boast that Harold has been a charming, pleasant child from infancy on. In addition to attending his classes at the local high school, Harold serves as the assistant manager for his high school's cross-country team and actively participates in Special Olympics.

King et al., 2000, p. 2599.

The benefits of special educational settings, mainstreaming, and inclusion have been challenged, just as they have been for other kinds of disabilities (p. 299). However, students with mental retardation can be successfully integrated into community schools, where they experience increased social interaction, and nonhandicapped students can profit by increased awareness of the needs of others. Hocutt (1996) has emphasized that outcome is influenced more by instructional and other classroom features than by placement itself; and that effective interventions require considerable investment of resources, time, effort, and teacher support.

Despite some positive evaluations and arguments for integrated school classrooms, students with severe retardation—many of whom also have physical disabilities and special health needs—have largely remained on the periphery of the inclusion movement. The vast majority of these children continue to be served in traditional special education settings (Palmer et al., 2001). Among the reasons for this circumstance may be lack of support from parents of these students. In a study that asked parents whether full inclusion would be a "good idea," 45 percent answered in the negative regarding their child. The most cited reason was belief that the child's impairments precluded any benefit:

> *[My child's] mentality is around two years olds or less and he is 8 years old. He would not benefit from a regular classroom environment, other than socially, because he does not have the mentality at this time to comprehend subjects.*
>
> *My daughter is like an infant physically and a toddler emotionally, socially, intellectually . . . advancing a child like my daughter along with her peer group would be isolating and inappropriate. (Palmer et al., 2001, p. 475)*

The second most commonly cited reason was the belief that full inclusion would place undue burden on teachers and be detrimental to typically developing students. These parents also were concerned that their child's needs for a curriculum that emphasizes basic living skills or functional skills would not be met and that their child might be neglected, harmed, or ridiculed.

Concern about what happens to children with retardation when they reach adulthood is shared by most educators. IDEA mandates transition plans for handicapped students, which must be given consideration by age 14. These plans must be drawn to fit the individual student. Mercer and Mercer (2001) note that all successful plans must include academic programs that prepare the student for independent work or further schooling; vocational education; self-advocacy training; and collaboration among professionals, family, and potential employers. Analysis indicates that present efforts and implementation fall short of insuring adequate postschool transition (Johnson et al., 2002). More optimistically, though, it is promising that mental retardation is increasingly viewed in terms of supports required for optimal development and community integration across the lifespan.

BEHAVIORAL INTERVENTION

In the 1960s, advocates of behavior modification began to work in institutions that previously provided custodial care but little training or education (Whitman, Hantula, & Spence, 1990). Behavior modification gradually became dominant, and an enormous amount of research was conducted. A wide range of behaviors at all levels of handicap was targeted. Operant procedures were used to enhance adaptive skills and reduce maladaptive behavior.

In recent years, behavioral techniques have progressed notably. Guidelines have been established for various methods, and precision in teaching and generalization of learned skills have been advanced (Handen, 1998). An important distinction has been made between discrete trial learning and naturalistic, or incidental, learning. In discrete trial learning, the clinician selects the task to be learned and provides clear directives, prompts, and consequences for appropriate behavior. Teaching is usually conducted in a quiet place, away from distractions. In naturalistic learning the teaching situation is informal, less structured, and more natural. It is more likely to be initiated by the child, amidst everyday contexts; for example, the child's asking for a toy is used as an opportunity for teaching. Both discrete trial learning and naturalistic learning have been shown to be effective, and naturalistic learning is believed to be especially effective for generalization of learning.

Efforts have also been made to train those who work with youngsters with mental retardation—in the home, school, community programs, or residential placements (e.g., Whitman et al., 1990). Training can focus on general principles or on management of a specific child, and it may be delivered to groups or to individual families. Training courses and curricula have been developed to disseminate information to caretakers. Evaluation of outcomes has been conducted, with attempts to establish the value of programs to the everyday activities of the child (Kiernan, 1985). Parent training has been shown to be effective, and parents can profit from ongoing contact with professionals (Handen, 1998).

Overall, behavior modification has had considerable success in serving young people with MR. This is not to say that the application of behavioral techniques is simple; in fact, it requires skill, effort, and perseverance. But enormous gains have been made.

Enhancing Adaptive Behaviors. Operant techniques have been employed to enhance a variety of adaptive behaviors. These include self-help skills, imitation, language, social behavior, academic skills, and work behaviors. Here, we comment on two of these areas.

The acquisition of daily living skills has been recognized as crucial (Danforth & Drabman, 1990; Taras & Matese, 1990). Children and adolescents who cannot dress and feed themselves or otherwise cannot take care of their basic needs are often limited from participating in educational and social activities. Those who are unable to shop, order food in restaurants, swim, or bowl can hardly enjoy independence in community living. Thus self-help programs target a gamut of self-help behaviors.

Considerable attention also has been given to assess and facilitate social skills, mostly but not exclusively for mild and moderate retardation (e.g., Matson, LeBlanc, Weinheimer, 1999). Training has been provided in various settings and has included instruction, self-instruction, modeling, role playing, and reinforcement (Hughes, 1999; Marchetti & Campbell, 1990). Normally developing peers have been shown to facilitate social interaction, as have environmental features such as type of activity and teacher prompts (Handen, 1998). Curricula for the teaching of social skills are available. In addition to these treatments, it is recognized that everyday activities can enhance social development. For example, participation in the Special Olympics by persons with mental retardation has been linked with social competence (Dykens & Cohen, 1996).

Reducing Maladaptive Behaviors. Self-stimulation, bizarre speech, tantrums, aggression, and self-injury are among the behaviors that

Special Olympics is an example of community programs that attempt to normalize the lives of youth with retardation and to provide opportunities to develop social skills as well as a sense of accomplishment and self-worth.
(AP/Wide World Photos)

interfere with social relationships, learning, and community living—and sometimes even directly harm individuals with mental retardation. A variety of techniques have been employed to reduce these behaviors, and success has been documented with single-subject research designs.

In this discussion, we emphasize self-injury because intervention for this behavior has been especially problematic. Repetitious self-injurious behavior (SIB), which usually disappears in typically developing children by school age, is observed in an estimated 35 to 40 percent of persons with MR (Baumeister & Baumeister, 2000). Self-injurious behaviors vary in form—head banging, biting, hitting the self, and such—and intensity ranges from minor to life-threatening damage. Biological or environmental factors, or their combination, may underlie the behavior (Mace et al., 1998). The association of SIB with Lesch-Nyhan and other genetic syndromes, as well as with middle ear infection, suggests an abnormal organic need for sensory stimulation that self-injurious behavior might provide. Even so, SIB is clearly influenced by environmental factors.

The history of treating SIB shows that it can be relatively difficult to change (Bregman & Gerdtz, 1997). Medications are only somewhat successful, and early behavioral interventions often failed. When self-injury threatened the child and interventions were ineffective, punishment was sometimes employed. Punishments included lemon juice squirted into the mouth and contingent electric shock. Although such aversive consequences can be effective, they raised serious ethical questions (Public Interest, 1989; Schopler, 1994). It is now recommended that aversive treatment be employed only in brief interventions for severe cases, and only after review and consent (Bregman & Gerdtz, 1997). Effective and more acceptable procedures have evolved and they often emphasize improved assessment of the factors influencing behavior.

COMPREHENSIVE ANALYSIS. Newsom (1998) has offered a general approach to comprehensive analysis of the variables that can influence maladaptive, or challenging, behaviors. Figure 11–7 presents the schema for organizing such influences. Setting events are background variables that can change the probability that a behavior will occur. For example, fatigue can make it more likely that the child will respond with SIB. Antecedent stimuli occur just prior to self-injury and precipitate the behavior. Positive consequences for SIB are also viewed as critical. Self-injury can be positively reinforced with tangibles such as food and activities, or attention from caretakers as they try to comfort or verbally deter a child from engaging in self-injury. Self-injury also can be negatively reinforced. For example, when unwanted demands are made, the child may engage in self-injury, with the result that caregivers may cease to make the demands—thereby negatively reinforcing SIB.

The purpose of a comprehensive analysis is to serve as a guideline for intervention. Modification of setting events and antecedent stimuli can prevent SIB from occurring at all. Modification of reinforcement contingencies can reduce already-occurring behavior.

FUNCTIONAL COMMUNICATION TRAINING. This is an approach to reducing challenging behavior by encouraging the child to substitute in its place an adaptive behavior. It is assumed that maladaptive behaviors are often used intentionally as a way to communicate needs or desires (Durand & Carr, 1991). The behaviors are "adaptive" in the sense that the child often obtains a desired end, but in the long run, the behaviors work against the child's well-being. The first step in Functional Communication

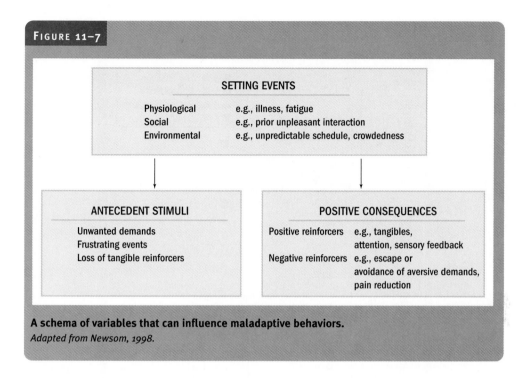

FIGURE 11–7

SETTING EVENTS

Physiological	e.g., illness, fatigue
Social	e.g., prior unpleasant interaction
Environmental	e.g., unpredictable schedule, crowdedness

ANTECEDENT STIMULI

Unwanted demands
Frustrating events
Loss of tangible reinforcers

POSITIVE CONSEQUENCES

Positive reinforcers	e.g., tangibles, attention, sensory feedback
Negative reinforcers	e.g., escape or avoidance of aversive demands, pain reduction

A schema of variables that can influence maladaptive behaviors.
Adapted from Newsom, 1998.

Training is functional analysis; the second is to select and train a more positive way to communicate.

The functional analysis determines the factors influencing the challenging behavior in the specific situation in which it occurs (Durand, 1993). Naturalistic observations of the child, interviews with caregivers, and rating scales are helpful. The Motivation Assessment Scale is a convenient rating scale used to determine the influence of attention, tangible reinforcement, escape from an unwanted situation, and sensory feedback on SIB (Durand & Crimmins, 1988). In addition, functional analysis can be conducted by exposing the youngster to different conditions while the rate of the maladaptive behavior is observed, in order to determine the variables that are influencing the behavior. Functional analyses have been shown to be effective (Hanley, Iwata, & McCord, 2003).

Functional Communication Training is exemplified in the case of Matt, a 5-year-old boy who was diagnosed with moderate mental retardation and cerebral palsy (Durand, 1999). Matt lived with his parents and attended a school for students with developmental disabilities. He lacked verbal language, but he was able to point to express his desires. Matt frequently bit his hand and screamed—behaviors that had not succumbed to prior interventions. The treatment strategy had several components:

- Matt's teacher was trained to conduct the intervention in the classroom.

- The teacher determined the circumstances in which Matt most frequently engaged in self biting and screaming. She gave the Motivation Assessment Scale, and she systematically observed Matt's behavior under four conditions: low teacher attention during a task, low access to a preferred tangible object during a task, a more difficult task, and a control condition. This analysis showed that Matt's maladaptive behavior occurred when he was faced with a difficult task.

- Matt was trained to ask for help on difficult tasks. Help could be obtained by his pressing a pad on a device, which activated a voice saying "I need help."

- The effectiveness of the training was evaluated.

The entire intervention required several weeks. The results of the functional analysis (A) and the final evaluation of Matt's behavior (B) are shown in Figure 11–8. The positive outcome is consistent with similar studies showing the effectiveness of Functional Communication Training in which youngsters are taught to communicate their desires through adaptive spoken language or with mechanical devices when needed. This particular study is interesting in that it also included trips to a

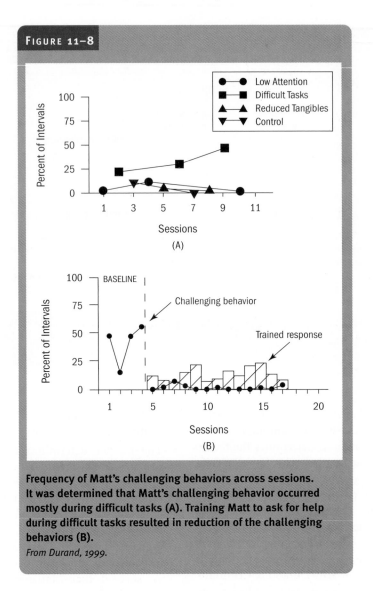

FIGURE 11–8

Frequency of Matt's challenging behaviors across sessions. It was determined that Matt's challenging behavior occurred mostly during difficult tasks (A). Training Matt to ask for help during difficult tasks resulted in reduction of the challenging behaviors (B).
From Durand, 1999.

community store in which Matt had experienced difficulty and frustration handling money as he purchased candy. After intervention, Matt used the mechanical device to ask the shopkeeper for help in managing his money.

PHARMACOLOGICAL TREATMENT

Medications are not known to strengthen intellectual functioning in cases of retardation but are employed for medical and behavioral symptoms. One study reported that 2 to 7 percent of children living in the community received psychotropic drugs, and this number rose to 19 to 33 percent when antiseizure medications were considered (Singh et al., 1998). As might be expected, drug treatment generally increases with the number and severity of behavioral problem. And it is generally higher for those living in institutions, particularly in larger institutions or institutions with restrictive environments. Features of these institutions certainly may be partly responsible for high medication use, but individuals who are institutionalized also are more likely to have behavioral problems to begin with.

The management of medication for MR requires special consideration. It may be difficult to ascertain the efficacy and possible side effects of drugs because the youngsters may be unable to describe clearly what they are experiencing. In addition, the difficulty of diagnosing behavioral problems increases the need to monitor the effects of medications. Possible drug interactions require a watchful eye, too, particularly in cases involving medical conditions (King et al., 2000).

There is some evidence for the efficacy of psychopharmacology. For example, stimulant medication results in some reduction of symptoms of ADHD when this disorder co-occurs with mental retardation in school age children (Pearson et al., 2004). However, there is concern about questionable practices. Antipsychotic medications appear to be overused and perhaps inappropriately employed with adults in response to challenging behavior (Robertson et al., 2000.) Baumeister and Baumeister (2000) believe that the extent to which antipsychotic medications are used to control behavior in institutions has bordered on abuse. Indeed, inappropriate use of drugs and overdosing have been documented, resulting in close government monitoring. The lack of controlled research with individuals with MR is also striking, a problem not unique to MR but perhaps particularly worrisome given the difficulty of evaluating medication effects.

PSYCHOTHERAPY

Research into the use and effectiveness of psychotherapy with individuals with MR appears to be scant (Beail, 2003). Although not as widely employed as other approaches, "talking" therapies are not precluded in the presence of mild and moderate intellectual deficits, although modifications may be required (Bregman, 1991; King et al., 2000). Certainly, psychotherapeutic techniques must be adapted to the developmental level of the child or adolescent. It is probably best that therapists be directive and set specific goals. Language must be concrete and clear, and nonverbal techniques need to be used in the presence of communication difficulties (e.g., play or other activities). Short, frequent sessions may be necessary.

SUMMARY

IDENTIFICATION AND CLASSIFICATION

- *Mental retardation is defined by subaverage intellectual functioning with concurrent deficits in adaptive skills manifested before age 18.*

- *The AAMR model of MR views retardation as multidimensional, with environmental supports mediating outcome. AAMR classifies MR by levels of needed supports; the DSM-IV classifies MR by four IQ levels. About 85 percent of cases are of mild retardation.*

NATURE OF INTELLIGENCE AND ADAPTIVE BEHAVIOR

- *Binet and colleagues assumed that intelligence is somewhat malleable and influenced by the social environment. Subsequent assumptions of fixed inheritance and misuse of intelligence tests resulted in controversies and legal battles.*

- *Measured intelligence is relatively stable for most people and correlates reasonably well with academic performance; IQ scores must be interpreted with care.*

- *Adaptive behavior refers to domains of everyday behavior, such as self-help and social competence. Judgments of adaptive skills must consider cultural expectations and specific situations.*

DESCRIPTION

- *The abilities of young people with retardation show immense variation, as exemplified by IQ levels and individual profiles of characteristics. Various levels of difficulties are manifest in physical and medical attributes, learning ability, and social functioning.*

BEHAVIORAL PROBLEMS AND CO-OCCURRING PSYCHOPATHOLOGY

- *Rates of behavior problems and psychopathology are high in MR, and the kinds of difficulties are overall similar to those in the general population. It can be difficult to identify and diagnose behavioral disturbance.*

EPIDEMIOLOGY

- *The prevalence of mental retardation in the general population is 1 to 3 percent, depending on the criterion used and on sampling. Rates are disproportionately high in persons of school age, male gender, and lower social class.*

DEVELOPMENTAL COURSE AND CONSIDERATIONS

- *The developmental course and outcome of mental retardation varies widely but most children will require a degree of support throughout life.*

- *Depending on level of retardation and/or etiology, it appears that intelligence develops at different rates, often in the same sequences as it typically does, or is characterized by specific deficits.*

ETIOLOGY

- *The two-group approach to etiology conceptualized MR as falling into an organic or a cultural-familial group.*

- *Organic influences, which are more closely associated with more severe retardation, include many genetic, pre-, peri-, and postnatal adversities. Much is being learned from the study of specific syndromes, such as Down, fragile X, and Williams syndromes.*

- *Multiple-gene effects are considered especially important in mild MR, which is viewed as representing the lower end of the distribution of intelligence in the population.*

- *Psychosocial influences, which may operate across generations of socially disadvantaged families, is also viewed as particularly relevant to milder levels of retardation.*

- *AAMR's multiple risk model reflects the current perspective of etiology as complex and interactive.*

FAMILY COPING AND ACCOMMODATION

- *Family accommodation to having a child with retardation is influenced by child characteristics, family characteristics, and social variables. Most children with disabilities live at home and caretakers recognize rewards and satisfactions. Families appear to come to terms with their varied decisions.*

ASSESSMENT

- *Assessment of MR is best guided by its goals. In addition to evaluation of intelligence and adaptive behavior with standardized scales, it can include curriculum-based performance, functional assessment, and needed supports, as well as medical status and family functioning.*

TREATMENT

- *Historically, treatment for mental retardation has varied in approach and quality, reflecting attitudes toward MR. During recent decades, concern for the rights of youngsters with handicaps and the philosophy of normalization have been primary considerations.*

- *IDEA and related policies have brought increased educational integration, although questions remain about mainstreaming and inclusion, particularly regarding students with severe retardation.*

- *The wide range of behavioral techniques used to strengthen appropriate skills and to weaken maladaptive behaviors are generally effective for mental retardation. Comprehensive and functional analysis is helpful in treating challenging behaviors.*

- *Pharmacological treatment and psychotherapy are both in need of controlled outcome studies. The former is relatively common; it can be effective for some medical and behavioral disturbances but requires especially careful monitoring. Psychotherapy, with adaptations, may have limited usefulness in mild or moderate MR.*

KEY TERMS

mental age *(p. 307)*

intelligence quotient *(p. 307)*

six-hour retardation *(p. 309)*

overshadowing *(p. 312)*

two-group approach *(p. 314)*

organic group *(p. 314)*

cultural-familial group *(p. 314)*

behavioral phenotypes *(p. 316)*

normalization *(p. 326)*

discrete trial learning *(p. 329)*

naturalistic (incidental) learning *(p. 329)*

self-injurious behavior *(p. 330)*

Functional Communication Training *(p. 330)*

CHAPTER 12
Autism and Schizophrenia

Autism and schizophrenia are now considered independent from each other, but they have a history of being intricately connected. Moreover, both involve pervasive and often continuing problems in social, emotional, and cognitive functioning, which have a basis in neurobiological abnormality. Development may be qualitatively different from normal development in ways that have compelled an enormous amount of interest and investigation.

A Bit of History: Autism and Schizophrenia

Despite the longtime recognition of the disorders that we are about to discuss, confusion and debate have surrounded them. Historically, these disorders were associated with adult psychoses—that is, severely disruptive disturbances implying abnormal perceptions of reality. Psychotic disturbances were noted in early 20th-century classifications of mental disorders based on Kraepelin's work. Bleuler applied the term *schizophrenias* to these disorders, which involve disturbances in reality, such as hearing voices and seeing images that did not exist. Investigators

noted a small percentage of cases that had begun in childhood (Marenco & Weinberger, 2000).

Ideas about psychoses and other severe disturbances developed gradually over many years. Investigators described groups of children as having early onset of schizophrenia, and still others pointed to syndromes that appeared similar, but not identical, to schizophrenia. Various diagnostic terms were applied, including *disintegrative psychoses* and *childhood psychoses*. Beginning around 1930 and for several years afterward, *childhood schizophrenia* served as a general label, while numerous subcategories were employed (Volkmar, 1987; Rutter & Schopler, 1987).

In 1943, Leo Kanner described what he called "early infantile autism," arguing that it was different from other cases of severe disturbance, which generally had later onset. One year later, Hans Asperger described a group of children whose symptoms overlapped with Kanner's cases. Although these men did not know each other—and apparently believed that they were writing about different types of disturbance—today autism and Asperger syndrome are viewed as similar disorders (Frith, 2004).

By the early 1970s, data from several countries showed that severe disturbances were age related, with a relatively large number of cases before age 3, remarkably low prevalence in childhood, and increased prevalence in adolescence (Kolvin, 1971). This pattern suggested that different syndromes might underlie the earlier-occurring and later-occurring disturbances. Several investigators argued that children whose problems appeared early were different from those whose problems came later, not only in behavior but also in social class, family history, and other factors (Dawson & Castelloe, 1992).

Only gradually did the view evolve that autism and schizophrenia are distinct disorders. They now appear in separate categories in the major diagnostic systems. Autism is considered a pervasive developmental disorder that, along with similar disorders, is observed early in life and does not include symptoms of psychosis. Schizophrenia is a psychotic disturbance that affects a small number of children, rises in frequency in adolescence, and increases still more in early adulthood.

Autistic Disorder

Kanner concluded that of particular importance in autism were communication deficits, good but atypical cognitive potential, and behavioral problems such as obsessiveness, repetitive actions, and unimaginative play. He emphasized, however, that the fundamental disturbance was an inability to relate to people and situations from the beginning of life. He quoted parents as referring to their disturbed children as "self-sufficient," "like in a shell," "happiest when left alone," and "acting as if people weren't there" (1973, p. 33). To this extreme disturbance in emotional contact with others, Kanner applied the term *autistic*. The following is an abbreviated description of a case presented by Kanner.

| Paul | Autistic Aloneness |

Paul was a slender, well built, attractive child, whose face looked intelligent and animated. . . . He rarely responded to any form of address, even to the calling of his name. . . . He was obviously so remote that the remarks did not reach him. He was always vivaciously occupied with something and seemed to be highly satisfied. . . . There was, on his side, no affective tie to people. He behaved as if people as such did not matter or even exist. It made no difference if one spoke to him in a friendly or harsh way. He never looked up at people's faces. When he had any dealings with persons at all, he treated them, or rather parts of them, as if they were objects.

Adapted from Kanner, 1943, reprinted, 1973, pp. 14–15.

DSM Classification and Diagnosis

Most of the characteristics originally described by Kanner were subsequently observed by others and are central in defining the disorder. Since 1980, the DSM has recognized autism as a subcategory of Pervasive Developmental Disorders (PDDs), which are characterized by early occurring, severe impairments that are qualitatively deviant relative to the person's developmental level (American Psychiatric Association, 2000). Both the DSM and the ICD recognize several such disorders, which have symptoms similar to autism and have historically been difficult to distinguish from autism and from each other. Autism has been the most studied but greater attention is being given to the other disorders, especially Asperger's disorder, and to the idea of a spectrum of autistic disorders. Our discussion focuses on autism, given its dominant role in the research literature, but we also address the related disorders.

Table 12–1 indicates the DSM diagnostic features for what is called Autistic Disorder. The primary symptoms are impaired social interaction, disturbed communication, and the presence of restrictive repetitive behaviors and interests—which are sometimes referred to as the triad of impairments. Diagnosis requires a total of at least six items, with all three features present. Onset must occur prior to age 3.

Description: Autism's Triad of Impairments

Descriptions of autism focus more heavily on preschool and school-age children. These youngsters can appear quite different from each other, both in specific symptoms and in severity of problems.

Social Interaction. Parental accounts and home video recordings of infants prior to their family's suspicion of problems indicate that subtle differences in social interaction can begin very early. Even before one year, some of the infants are less likely than control infants to be visually responsive, less likely to respond to their names, and more likely to show aversion to being touched by another person

TABLE 12–1   THE DSM FEATURES OF AUTISTIC DISORDER

A Total of Six or More from 1, 2, and 3

1. Qualitative impairment in social interaction manifested by at least two of the following:
   Impaired nonverbal behaviors
   — Failure to develop age-appropriate peer-relationships
   Lack of spontaneous sharing of enjoyment or interests
   — Lack of social or emotional reciprocity

2. Qualitative impairment in communication manifested by at least one of the following:
   Delay or lack of spoken language
   — When speech is adequate, impairment in initiating or sustaining conversation
   Stereotyped, repetitive, or idiosyncratic language
   — Lack of varied, age-appropriate, spontaneous make-believe or social imitative play

3. Restricted, repetitive, stereotyped patterns of behavior, interests, or activities manifested by at least one of the following:
   — Abnormal preoccupation with stereotyped and restrictive interests
   Inflexible adherence to nonfunctional routines or rituals
   Stereotyped and repetitive motor mannerisms
   Persistent preoccupation with parts of objects

From American Psychiatric Association, 2000.

(Baranek, 1999; Werner et al., 2000). Older infants fail to track people visually, avoid eye contact, exhibit an "empty" gaze, fail to respond to others with emotional expression and positive affect, and show little interest in being held (e.g., Adrien et al., 1993; Stone, 1997). Figure 12–1 demonstrates this behavior with data from a laboratory study showing that 4-year-olds with autism gazed at their mothers less than children with Down syndrome and those with typical development.

Quite striking in autism are deficits in joint attention interactions, which in typical youngsters begin to develop after 6 months. These interactions involve gestures, such as pointing, and eye contact—that is, joint visual attention—that center the child's and caregiver's attention on an object, in order to share an experience. In addition, young children with autism imitate the actions of others less than typically developing youngsters (Rogers et al., 2004). They appear to miss out on the mutual connection between two people and the potential it holds for learning about themselves and others.

Because such behaviors interfere with social interaction, we might expect a lack of attachment to parents. This is largely not the case (Sigman et al., 1997). These children can exhibit secure, insecure, or disorganized attachment (Willemsen-Swinkels et al., 2000). A recent meta-analysis indicates that slightly over half of the children with autism showed secure attachment in the Strange Situation (Rutgers et al., 2004). Despite attachment bonds, however, parents come to suspect that something is wrong—that their child's social behavior is unusual or deficient or delayed.

Abnormal processing of social stimuli, specifically the face, appears to be another of the elements of deviant social interaction. Typically developing infants recognize the faces of their mothers, and the processing of faces, including emotional expression, is considered crucial to development. Children with autism often, although not always, show impaired recognition of human faces, remember faces less than objects, and have problems recognizing facial expressions of happiness and sadness (e.g., Boucher, Lewis, & Collis, 1998; Celani, Battacchi, & Arcidiacono, 1999). Laboratory studies indicate unusual processing styles (Klinger, Dawson, & Renner, 2003; McPartland et al., 2004). For example, typically developing youngsters have relative difficulty in processing photographs of faces that appear upside down, but this is not so in autism.

During childhood, a variety of social deficits, such as lack of understanding of social cues and inappropriate social actions, also are evident. There is a certain aloofness, disinterest, and lack of social reciprocity. The child may ignore others, fail to engage in cooperative play, or seem overly content to be alone (Volkmar et al., 1997). Even higher functioning adolescents and adults may seem "odd," have difficulty with the subtleties of social interaction, and have problems in forming friendships as they move through life.

Communication. Disturbed communication—both nonverbal and verbal—is the second aspect of the triad of difficulties in autism. As we have already seen, nonverbal communication involving the face and eyes is atypical or deficient, and some of these problems may be specific to autism. In addition, even when children with autism use simple instrumental gestures, complex gestures that express feelings may be lacking, even into adolescence (Attwood et al., 1988). Thus, pointing to something or communicating "come here" or "be quiet" may occur, but putting the

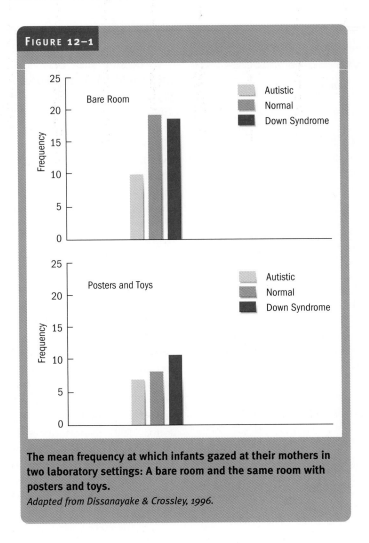

FIGURE 12-1

The mean frequency at which infants gazed at their mothers in two laboratory settings: A bare room and the same room with posters and toys.

Adapted from Dissanayake & Crossley, 1996.

arms around someone to express feelings or friendship may still be absent.

Speech and language expression are problematic. About 50 percent of children with autism remain mute or rarely say more than words or simple phrases—although this figure may be declining with more effective early intervention (Klinger et al., 2003). Babbling and verbalizations may be abnormal in tone, pitch, and rhythm (Sheinkopf et al., 2000; Tager-Flüsberg, 1993). In those who acquire language, development is delayed and often abnormal (Lord & Bailey, 2002). Echolalia and pronoun reversal are commonly observed. In echolalia the person echoes back what another has said. This behavior can be a passing feature of normal development, and it is also seen in dysfunctions such as language disorders, schizophrenia, and blindness. Pronoun reversal is more common in autism than in

other disorders or normal development. The child may refer to others as *I* or *me*, and to the self as *he, she, them,* or *you.*

Difficulties with the syntax of language and delay in comprehension have been reported, but most notable is impairment in pragmatics, the social use of language (Klinger et al., 2003). Conversation is characterized by irrelevant details, inappropriate shifts in topic, disregard of the normal give-and-take of conversation—or there may be an overall failure to develop conversation. Nevertheless, some children do function at a higher level. They may be able to tell stories, communicate better when given prompts (Loveland & Tunali-Kotoski, 1997), and read. And some exhibit hyperlexia, a little-understood feature in which single-word reading is extraordinary but comprehension of what is read is problematic (Grigorenko, Klin, & Volkmar, 2003).

Restricted, Repetitive, Stereotyped Behavior and Interests. The third major impairment of autism is atypical and often odd behaviors that are described as restricted, repetitive, stereotyped, obsessive, or rigid behaviors and interests. These behaviors often are not observed before age 3 (Lord & Bailey, 2002).

Repetitive, stereotyped motor behaviors commonly reported by parents include rocking; walking on the toes; whirling; and arm, hand, or finger flapping (Klinger et al., 2003). Although many of these oddities are seen in normally developing young children and select behavioral disorders, they occur in autism more frequently and with greater severity (Bodfish et al., 2000; Turner, 1999). They appear to be especially common in younger children with autism and those with lower intelligence.

Also particularly characteristic of autism are higher order repetitive, obsessive activities and interests (Turner, 1999). These include unusual preoccupations with aspects of the environment. Children may seem obsessed with numbers or some object; they may compulsively collect articles or be overly absorbed in hobbies. They may adopt motor routines, such as rearranging objects, and insist on following rituals for eating and going to bed. Minor changes in the environment, such as rearrangement of furniture or schedules, can cause much upset, a reaction seldom reported in nonautistic groups. In addition, play behavior may lack spontaneity, imagination, imitation, and themes (Baron-Cohen, 1993).

DESCRIPTION: AUTISM'S ASSOCIATED IMPAIRMENTS

Although not necessary for the diagnosis of autism, several features are associated with it and are meaningful in understanding the disorder.

Sensory/Perceptual Impairments. The sensory organs are intact but abnormal responses to stimuli make sensation and perception suspect. Indeed, parents note sensory anomalies in their children and many investigators believe that these abnormalities are fundamental (Rogers, Hepburn, & Wehner, 2003; Newsom, 1998).

Both oversensitivity and undersensitivity to stimulation are reported (Klinger & Dawson, 1996). In oversensitivity the child is disturbed by moderate stimulation, for example, the noise of a kitchen appliance or a light touch on the skin. Thus there may be dislike, fear, or avoidance of sensory input. Undersensitivity, perhaps more common, is demonstrated in many ways. Children may fail to respond to sounds, verbal communications, or the sight of others. The clinical picture may be puzzling; for example, a child may seem unaware of a loud noise but fascinated by the quiet ticking of a watch (Volkmar & Klin, 2000). In some cases, the failure to respond to sound leads parents to think that their child is deaf.

Children with autism also seem to have difficulty with complex perceptual stimuli. They may seem "stuck" on a particular stimulus while

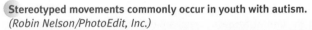
Stereotyped movements commonly occur in youth with autism.
(Robin Nelson/PhotoEdit, Inc.)

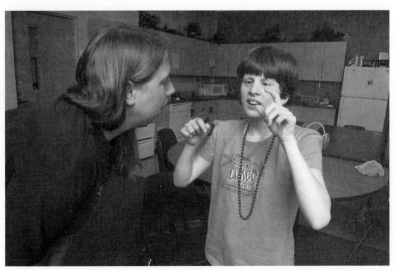

ignoring competing stimuli, which may implicate attentional processes (Landry & Bryson, 2004). Such overselectivity may be manifested in the obsessive attention paid to a toy or a piece of paper. And failure to respond to the complexity of stimuli in the environment can interfere with the child's learning. (Other anomalies involving perception and attention are documented, and we will later examine these.)

Intellectual Performance. Although there is a wide range of intelligence in autism, including above average, about 75 percent of all cases show mental retardation, with many exhibiting severe or profound deficiency (Joseph, Tager-Flüsberg, & Lord, 2002; Volkmar & Klin, 2000). The distinction is made between individuals functioning at a higher or lower level, with an IQ of about 70 being the defining score. This is an important way in which persons with autism differ. Intelligence levels are quite stable over time, and higher functioning is associated with less severe symptoms, different educational needs, and greater chance of normal functioning in later life (Howlin et al., 2004; Stevens et al., 2000; Wing, 1997).

The test profiles of persons with autism generally indicate uneven cognitive development. Deficits exist in abstract and conceptual thinking, language, and social understanding. Relative strengths appear in rote learning, rote memory, and visual-spatial skills (Happé, 1994; Volkmar & Klin, 2000). Performance scores are usually higher than verbal scores across the IQ range. This discrepancy can lessen from preschool age to adolescence in higher functioning autism, perhaps due to developing language skills (Joseph et al., 2002).

That autistic symptoms occur amidst such wide variability in general intelligence is puzzling. To make matters more perplexing, a small minority of youth exhibit so-called splinter skills—abilities much higher than expected on the basis of their general intelligence—and savant abilities that are strikingly better than among normally developing youth (Miller, 1999). (See Accent: "Savant Abilities and Autism.")

Adaptive Behavior. Autism is characterized by difficulties in dealing with the comings and goings of everyday life. Performance on the Vineland Adaptive Behavior Scales shows a unique profile for persons

ACCENT ● ● ● ● ●

Savant Abilities and Autism

The prevalence of savant abilities is unknown; they are particularly associated with autism, although they appear more generally, including in mental retardation. Spectacular abilities—usually in memory, mathematics, calendar calculations, word recognition, drawing, and music—are displayed (Miller, 1999; Heaton & Wallace, 2004). Some of these abilities are indeed amazing (Treffert, 1988). One individual needed only 1.5 minutes to calculate the number of seconds in 70 years, 17 days, and 12 hours, even considering the effects of leap years. And one 5-year-old, despite limited language and retarded daily living skills, had perfect music pitch, a classical piano repertoire, and the ability to improvise music. Savant abilities are often associated with higher IQ levels but have been reported with IQs as low as 55 and in children whose deficits preclude testing (Miller, 1999).

There is no known explanation for these abilities, and numerous proposals have been put forth. It is unlikely that savant abilities can be simply explained by rote memory or practice, as had sometimes been suggested. Heaton and Wallace (2004) note that savant talents in art and music defy such simple explanations and that, moreover, savant abilities often entail the use of rule-based knowledge and domain-relevant strategies. For example, savant skills in calendar calculation involve abstraction of the regularities that inhere in calendars. Heaton and Wallace are inclined to believe that many of the information-processing skills found in typical functioning are present in those with autism and savant abilities. In addition, some individuals with autism tend to overfocus on detail, which may give them an advantage in acquiring basic knowledge in some domains. Savant skills tend to be related to repetitive and obsessive behaviors, suggesting that the individual is highly interested in them and motivated to practice them (Pring, Hermelin, & Heavey, 1995). Any ultimate explanation of savant abilities is likely to involve several influences, including genetic influences (Nurmi et al., 2003).

with autism compared with peers matched on intelligence (Carter et al., 1998; Kraijer, 2000). Self-help and daily living skills are roughly what is expected on the basis of mental ability; communication skills fall somewhat short of this; and social skills are far below the expected level.

Other Features. Although young children with autism are frequently described as physically attractive, some show minor physical anomalies. A certain gracefulness and bodily agility have been noted, but so also have poor balance, uncoordinated gait, and motor awkwardness in adolescence (Molloy, Dietrich, & Bhattacharya, 2003; Volkmar & Klin, 2000). These children also can exhibit tantrums, aggression, hyperactivity, and self-injurious behavior, perhaps partly out of frustration and inability to communicate through language. Shifts in mood, fear and anxiety, and depression in adolescence are also reported. So also are unusual eating preferences and sleep problems, although these require further investigation (Klinger et al., 2003). None of these problems are specific to autism, of course, but they can interfere with the child's everyday functioning and require good management.

EPIDEMIOLOGY

Over 30 epidemiological studies of autism, involving close to 5 million persons ranging in age from birth to early adulthood, have been conducted in several countries since the mid-1960s (Fombonne, 2003; Volkmar et al., 2004). The increase in prevalence over this time period is quite striking. Research published between 1966 and 1991 reported a median rate of 4.4 cases per 10,000; from 1992 to 2001 the rate was 12.7. Although great variation exists among the studies, the data have stirred considerable discussion.

Is it likely that the rates of autism have risen so substantially? Although an increase is possible, better detection of cases through improved assessment and increased public awareness of the disorder likely play a role. So also may the use of broader diagnostic criteria or a broader conceptualization of autism. Given numerous considerations, a prevalence of 10 persons in 10,000 has been proposed as a reasonable estimate for autistic disorder (Fombonne, 2003; Tanguay, 2000; Volkmar & Klin, 2000). This rate rises to an estimated 27.5 per 10,000 when Asperger's disorder and unspecified pervasive developmental disorders are included (Fombonne, 2003).

In both epidemiologic and clinic studies, boys display autism more than girls, with the ratio of 3.5–4 boys to 1 girl (Volkmar et al., 2004). An interesting sex difference exists. When intelligence is in the normal range, the ratio of boys to girls is highest; when intelligence falls into the range of profound mental retardation, the ratio of boys to girls is lowest. It is possible that autism is more readily expressed in boys and that more severe underlying pathology is required before the disorder is expressed in girls.

Social class is unrelated to autism. Early reports of high rates in upper social classes probably resulted from unrepresentative samples (Fombonne, 2003).

DEVELOPMENTAL COURSE AND PROGNOSIS

Although social and communication symptoms of autism are documented for the first 2 years of life, diagnosis typically occurs somewhat later (Charmon & Baird, 2002). Looking back, parents report variation in the onset of symptoms. Some children always seemed different to their parents, whereas others appeared to develop normally for a while and then failed to maintain developmental milestones, and still others regressed and displayed qualitatively different development (Davidovitch et al., 2000). A substantial percentage of parents report regression, which often emerged during the second half of the second year of life. Among other behaviors, the children stopped gazing at others, orienting to their names, spontaneously imitating others, and using meaningful words (Goldberg et al., 2003; Lord, Shulman, & DiLavore, 2004). An obvious weakness of this research is reliance on retrospective reports, and although regression may occur, further investigation is warranted (Volkmar et al., 2004).

Childhood often brings improvement in social, communication, and self-help skills (Piven et al., 1996; Sigman, 1998). Repetitive movements tend to lessen and obsessive interests tend to increase (Klinger et al., 2003). Adolescence can be relatively uneventful, show improvement that may persist into adulthood, or be marked by deterioration and a variety of behavior problems, such as aggression and anxiety (American Psychiatric Association, 2000; Mesibov & Handlan, 1997). This is a time of high risk for the occurrence of epilepsy.

In young adulthood, progress is possible but perhaps two-thirds or more individuals do not achieve independent living. Numerous studies conducted in different countries have shown that outcome is poor when early IQ is below 50 or communicative language is lacking by age 5 or 6

(Howlin et al., 2004; Volkmar & Klin, 2000). A recent follow-up of children with IQs of at least 50 found that those with childhood IQs of 70 or above did notably better, suggesting that this IQ level is the better predictor of adulthood independent living. In general, improvement occurs in childhood into adulthood, although not universally, and symptoms endure for many persons (Seltzer et al., 2003). Perhaps 10 percent achieve successful work placement and some social life (Volkmar & Klin, 2000). For these individuals, life may include typical achievements and rewards, although some behavioral difficulties may persist. (See Accent: "A Personal Account of Autism.")

UNDERLYING PSYCHOLOGICAL DEFICITS

We have so far focused on defining the core and associated features of autism, but controlled research gives a more complete and subtle picture of the psychological deficits that might underlie autism.

Investigators have asked whether particular impairments might account for the various symptoms of autism and have emphasized theory of mind, central coherence, and executive functions (Volkmar et al., 2004).

Theory of Mind. Attention has been given to the idea that autism and autism-like disorders entail a disturbance in the ability to mentally represent the social world (Dorris et al., 2004). Extensively studied is theory of mind—the ability to infer mental states in others and in one's self (Perner et al., 1989). Having a theory of mind (ToM) means that we understand that mental states exist—that humans have desires, intentions, beliefs, feelings, and so forth—and that these mental states are connected to action. Theory of mind can be thought of as the ability to read others' minds, which guides our interaction with others. Theory of mind typically develops gradually. Children of 3 to 4 years usually have first-order abilities, that is, some understanding of people's

ACCENT ● ● ● ● ●

A Personal Account of Autism

Temple Grandin (1997), a university professor of animal science, has written a firsthand account of autism. She attributes a good part of her success to educational opportunity and mentors. She was provided early structured nursery school and language training; she was mainstreamed from kindergarten through sixth grade; she then attended boarding school before enrolling in a small liberal arts college. She had wise mentors: her mother and aunt, teachers, and people in industry who hired her and helped her develop her abilities.

Ms. Grandin's descriptions of autism are instructive. She experienced "horrible oversensitivity" to sound and touch; as a child, someone's touch brought "an overwhelming, drowning wave of stimulation." Ms. Grandin experiences difficulties in memory and in learning verbally. She relies heavily on images that she has stored in her mind, and she thinks in pictures. Concepts are visualizations of many examples. For instance, she has no general or abstract concept of a boat, just images of several boats she has seen. Any one image is linked to other memories; her father's boat is linked to fishing and to picnics. To think about boats, she must search her visual memory for specific

boats and then find associated images. Thinking in pictures is slower than verbal thinking, but it lends itself to Ms. Grandin's occupational task of designing equipment.

Ms. Grandin reports that she has become better at handling social situations. She uses prerehearsed responses for common interactions. For example, she has stored images of previous encounters with jealous engineers and of effective responses. Depending on logic rather than emotion, these responses are employed. In fact, Ms. Grandin characterizes her functioning by intellectual more than emotional intensity. And she speaks of the motivations and balances in her life this way:

Many people with autism become disillusioned and upset because they do not fit in socially and they do not have a girlfriend or boyfriend. I have just accepted that such a relationship will not be part of my life. . . . I want to be appreciated for the work I do. I am happiest when I am doing something for fun, like designing an engineering project, or making something that makes a contribution to society. (Grandin, 1997, p. 1039)

FIGURE 12–2

(A)   The Sally-Anne task. The child is asked where Sally will look for the
marble when she returns to the room.

Sally puts the marble in the basket,
then exits the room

Anne enters and transfers the
marble to a box

(B)   Examples of faux pas stories. The child is asked, In the story, did someone say something
that he or she should not have said?

Kim helped her Mum make an apple pie
for her uncle when he came to visit. She
carried it out of the kitchen. "I made it
just for you," said Kim. "Mmm,"
replied Uncle Tom. "That looks lovely.
I love pies, except for apple, of course!"

James bought Richard a toy airplane
for his birthday. A few months later,
they were playing with it, and James
accidentally dropped it. "Don't worry,"
said Richard. "I never liked it anyway.
Someone gave it to me for my birthday."

Two theory of mind tasks.
From Baron-Cohen et al., 1999.

private mental states (Wellman, 1993). At about age 6, children acquire second-order abilities: They can think about another person's thinking about a third person's thoughts.

Aspects of ToM have been evaluated with different tasks. Widely used is the Sally-Anne test that evaluates the understanding that another person can hold a false belief (Baron-Cohen, 1989). Here, the child is told that Sally places a marble in a basket and exits the room; Anne then transfers the marble to a box, and Sally returns to the room (Figure 12–2). The child is asked where Sally will look for the marble. To be correct, the child must understand that Sally falsely believes the marble is in the basket where she had placed it and that this belief will guide her action. This first-order task can be modified to evaluate second-order ability. Here, when Sally leaves the room, she peeks back and sees Anne transfer the marble. The child being tested is asked, "Where does Anne think Sally will look for the marble?" The child must "read" what Anne is thinking about Sally's

thoughts. There is compelling evidence that the majority of children with autism fails such first-order tests and that a greater number fails second-order tests (Baron-Cohen & Swettenham, 1997).

Because some children with autism are able to pass second-order tasks, more challenging tasks have been constructed. In one of these, for example, children hear brief stories in which character A commits a faux pas—that is, unintentionally says something without considering its negative impact on character B. The child being evaluated is asked to identify the faux pas. Recognizing the faux pas requires "mind reading" because it requires the understanding that (1) the two characters have different knowledge and that (2) the statement of character A emotionally affects character B. On this test, children with autism (or a related disorder) who were able to pass second-order ToM tests did less well than typically developing children (Baron-Cohen et al., 1999). The findings suggest that the faux pas test is an advanced test of ToM and that it can be difficult even for children with higher functioning autism.

ToM impairments are not shown in all studies (e.g., Russell & Hill, 2001), but there is little doubt that deficits exist across age and can be present in higher functioning autism. Baron-Cohen and others believe that such "mind blindness" underlies many of the social and communication deficits of autism—for example, failure to understand facial expression, relate to others, acquire the pragmatics of language, and engage in pretend play (Tager-Flüsberg, 1997; Baron-Cohen & Swettenham, 1997; Waterhouse & Fein, 1997). An important challenge to this proposition is that particular social abnormalities of autism are present before ToM skills would be expected to develop (Lord & Bailey, 2002).

Weak Central Coherence. In normal cognition, individuals have a tendency to use context to weave together bits of information to make a whole, to give global meaning. This penchant, which is referred to as central coherence, is viewed as varying from strong to weak in the general population (Happé, Briskman, & Frith, 2001). On the basis of performance on specific visual-perceptual tasks, Frith and Happé proposed that individuals with autism are weak in central coherence; that is, they tend to focus on parts of stimuli rather than on integrating information into wholes. Simply put, they see the trees rather than the forest.

Performance on some perceptual tasks can be interpreted in this way. For example, children with autism generally perform better than controls on embedded figure tasks, which call for recognizing a stimulus figure that is embedded within a larger picture. In an important study, Shah and Frith (1993) investigated the quite striking superior performance that persons with autism show on the block design task of the Wechsler intelligence test. They not only perform well compared with their achievement on other IQ tasks, but also outperform typically developing children and matched children with mental retardation. Superior ability to break the block design into segments helps on this task (Figure 12–3).

The hypothesis of weak central coherence has also been applied to reading tasks in which it is important to consider the whole context. For example, the correct pronunciation of "tear" is greatly aided by sentence context, as in "There is a tear in her eye" versus "There is a tear in her dress" (Baron-Cohen & Swettenham, 1997). Deficits in pronunciation suggests that individuals with autism have

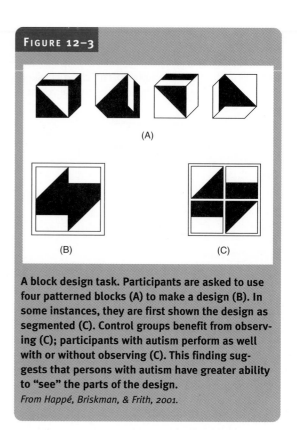

FIGURE 12–3

A block design task. Participants are asked to use four patterned blocks (A) to make a design (B). In some instances, they are first shown the design as segmented (C). Control groups benefit from observing (C); participants with autism perform as well with or without observing (C). This finding suggests that persons with autism have greater ability to "see" the parts of the design.
From Happé, Briskman, & Frith, 2001.

difficulty in extracting global meaning from the sentences (Happé, 1996).

All these findings suggest that youth with autism process information in a more analytic, less global and integrative way than normally—which can lead to exceptional performance on some tasks and poor performance on others. In fact, an interesting aspect of this research is that it offers an explanation of particular cognitive strengths of autism. Further understanding of deficits in central coherence is being sought in research offering refined or alternative explanations for the findings (Mann & Walker, 2003; Lopez & Leekam, 2003; Mottron et al., 2003).

Executive Dysfunction. In several investigations, children and adults with autism performed more poorly than control groups on tests of executive functions (McEvoy, Rogers, & Pennington, 1993; Ozonoff, 1997). This result led to the proposal that such impairment may underlie autism's symptoms. However, poor performance can be hard to interpret because executive functions involve several components (Liss et al., 2001). Moreover, depending on the specific task, executive deficits may or may not be present in autism—thus raising the question of the exact nature of the impairments. In addition, because executive dysfunction exists in other disorders, it is unlikely to uniquely explain autism.

Ozonoff and Jensen (1999) addressed these issues by comparing typically developing children and children with autism, ADHD, or Tourette syndrome on three measures of executive function. The profiles of deficits for the disorders differed. Children with autism did significantly worse on tasks requiring the child to be flexible—to shift strategies and plan ahead. In fact, it is commonly found that people with autism do less well on such tasks. Autism apparently entails deficits in disengaging from a stimulus, switching to a new rule or set, and planning ahead (Bailey, Phillips, & Rutter, 1996; Liss et al., 2001). The data suggest that impairments on a subset of executive functions may be central to autism, although the relationship of executive deficits to degree of social impairment in autism is not established (Volkmar et al., 2004).

Multiple Psychological Deficits. Inherent in the research we examined above is the question of whether any single psychological deficit can explain the symptoms of autism. In fact, each of the deficits appears to account better for some but not all of the symptoms (Bailey et al., 1996; Baron-Cohen & Swettenham, 1997). It is also doubtful that these cognitive deficits appear in all persons with autism and the deficits do not seem specific to autism (Plaisted, Swettenham, & Rees, 1999; Peterson, 2004). This suggests that although they are important in the disorder, they are not fundamental (Liss et al., 2001; Yirmiya et al., 1998). Moreover, the tasks used to evaluate a specific cognitive impairment may also tap other deficits (Heavey et al., 2000; Russell, Saltmarsh, & Hill, 1999). Finally, it is important to note that much of the research has been conducted with individuals displaying higher levels of functioning.

Due in part to these issues, but also to increased opportunity to study very young children with autism, researchers are turning to early-occurring behaviors such as following another person's gaze, joint visual attention, face perception, and imitation (Kylliäinen & Hietanen, 2004; Volkmar et al., 2004). Many of these are thought to be involved in the development of affective-social development that appears so deviant in autism. To some extent this interest harks back to a perspective that has persisted since Kanner's time—that is, to intersubjectivity, a special awareness that persons have of each other that motivates them, from the moment of birth, to communicate with the emotions and interests of others (Trevarthen & Aitken, 2001).

It is, in any event, unlikely that any single psychological impairment underlies all of the varied features of autism. More probably, specific impairments might be responsible for different features of autism. The clinical picture would depend on which particular deficit—or combination of deficits—is present. It is also possible that psychological impairments may interact to produce features of autism or that other deficits are yet to be identified. In looking at the immediate research agenda, Volkmar and colleagues (2004) comment on the need to relate underlying basic psychological deficits both to the disabilities actually displayed in the daily lives of those with autism and also to neurobiological and genetic processes.

NEUROBIOLOGICAL ABNORMALITIES

Diverse evidence exists for neurobiological anomalies in autism. Neurological examination may indicate soft signs of brain dysfunction, and the association of autism with epilepsy and mental retardation suggests brain anomalies (e.g., Minshew, Sweeney, & Bauman, 1997; Volkmar & Klin, 2000). Various brain structures and regions have been considered with postmortem examination, brain imaging, and animal models. Most consistently studied and implicated are the temporal lobe–limbic system, the frontal lobes, and the cerebellum (Minshew et al., 1997; Pennington & Welsh, 1997; Schultz & Klin, 2002). These connected regions are part of what is sometimes referred to as the "social brain" (Frith, 2004).

An interesting finding is unusually large brain size—perhaps by 5 to 10 percent—in toddlers (Fombonne et al., 1999; Volkmar et al., 2004). Large brain size is apparently not evident at birth and only inconsistently evident in adolescence and adulthood. This suggests an atypical growth spurt soon after birth and during childhood that then levels off. It is unclear whether some lobes of the brain are affected more than others.

Whatever developmental process underlies size abnormality, some evidence exists for disproportionately large cerebral white matter in toddlers and young children, but small size in adolescence. Other studies have shown the corpus callosum connecting the hemispheres to be small in older persons with autism. This pattern suggests disturbances in brain connectivity.

Microscopic studies of the temporal-limbic system, frontal lobes, and cerebellum show abnormalities (Filipek, 1999; Tanguay, 2000). These include decreased number and size of cells, high cell density, less dendritic branching, and abnormal cell migration. Also shown are abnormalities in the mini-columns (a functional cell unit) of the cortex of the temporal and frontal lobes (Casanova et al., 2002). This finding points to decreased inhibition of activity, which could cause widespread cognitive and behavioral problems (Volkmar et al., 2004). Some of the microscopic studies suggest that brain anomalies may develop prenatally.

Reduced activity has been shown in several regions of the brain (Volkmar et al., 2004). Under-activity in the amygdala has been demonstrated while individuals engage in face perception and ToM tasks. Similarly, reduced activity occurs in areas of the frontal lobe and other brain regions considered important in social and emotional functioning (Mundy, 2003). In addition, activity of the cerebellum has been implicated in attention problems in autism.

Although interest exists in the biochemical systems, consistent findings are lacking (Volkmar et al., 2004). Limited data indicate abnormalities of brain serotonin during childhood (Filipek, 1999) and of dopamine in the frontal lobes in adolescence (Ernst, 2000). Unclear is the significance of the most dependable biochemical finding—high blood levels of dopamine in 25 to 50 percent of cases (Bailey et al., 1996; Mulder et al., 2004).

Understanding of the neurobiology of autism is progressing, although a definitive portrait has not yet emerged. Given the research findings and the mix of symptoms of the disorder, abnormalities of multiple brain structures, regions, or networks are likely.

ETIOLOGY

Dominant among early etiological proposals was that parenting played a critical causative role in autism. Kanner described the parents as highly intelligent, professionally accomplished people who were preoccupied with scientific, literary, and artistic concerns, and who treated their offspring in a coldly mechanical way (1943; Kanner & Eisenberg, 1956). Inadequate, "refrigerator" parenting became implicated in causing autism, even though Kanner also hypothesized an innate social deficit. Bettelheim's (1967a,b) psychoanalytic theory was an especially influential psychosocial explanation (Mesibov & Van Bourgondien, 1992). Accordingly, autism was caused by parental rejection or pathology that resulted in the young child's retreating into an autistic "empty fortress." This approach eventually suffered from

doubts about psychoanalytic theories and treatment, and perhaps most important from the lack of support for parental deviancy (Klinger & Dawson, 1996; Mesibov & Van Bourgondien, 1992). Fortunately, blame is no longer placed on parents, who are now playing stronger roles in advocacy and treatment for their children. Moreover, current interest is in organic-based causal factors.

Prenatal and Early-Life Risk. Seasonal birth pattern has been suspect as a prenatal or early-life risk, because time of year is associated with potentially dangerous viral infections, testosterone levels, and so forth. However, recent research does not support the idea that children with autism are born during any particular season of the year (Tanguay, 2000; Yeates-Frederikx et al., 2000).

Many pregnancy and birth variables have been associated with autism, but the complications are relatively minor and autism is not always associated with such factors (Piven et al., 1993). Then too, pregnancy and birth complications could result from, rather than cause, an abnormal fetus (Bailey et al., 1996; Bolton et al., 1997). It is nevertheless possible that these adversities underlie or play some role in some cases of autism.

Medical Conditions and Vaccines. Numerous medical conditions are associated with autism—epilepsy, cerebral palsy, infections such as meningitis, hearing impairment, and some genetic disorders (Bailey et al., 2000; Rutter et al., 1999; Volkmar & Klin, 2000). The strength of the association with these conditions is debatable, but is stronger when mental disability is present. About 25 percent of those with autism have seizure disorders (Schultz & Klin, 2002). Two other conditions associated with autism beyond what would be expected are the genetic disorders fragile X syndrome (p. 317) and tuberose sclerosis (Volkmar et al., 2004). The latter, caused by inherited or new gene mutations, involves the growth of tumors in the brain and other organs that cause varied effects, including developmental delays, behavioral problems, and mental disabilities. Whether this condition or fragile X syndrome plays a causal role in autism or simply coexists with autism is unknown.

Related to medical issues is the question of a relationship between autism and vaccines given to prevent diseases that are otherwise unassociated with autism. The issue was raised by parents who associated their children's onset of pervasive developmental disorders with the vaccine that the youngsters had received to prevent measles, mumps, and rubella

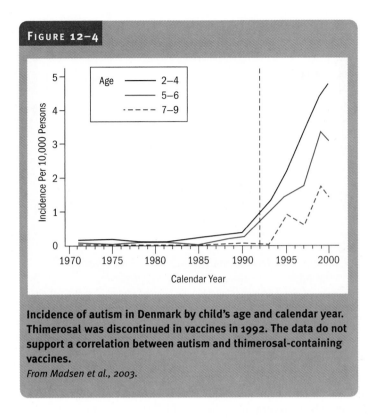

FIGURE 12-4

Incidence of autism in Denmark by child's age and calendar year. Thimerosal was discontinued in vaccines in 1992. The data do not support a correlation between autism and thimerosal-containing vaccines.

From Madsen et al., 2003.

(Wakefield et al., 1998). Concern was expressed elsewhere that vaccines with thimerosal, a mercury-containing preservative, put children at risk for the disorder (Madsen et al., 2003). Research examining the incidence of autism over several years does not appear currently to support either proposition (Institute of Medicine, 2004; Taylor et al., 1999, see Figure 12–4). However, doubts are not completely laid to rest and the Autism Society of America has called for further investigation. Meanwhile, some experts fear that parents may endanger their children by refusing vaccines.

Genetic Influence. Major twin studies document much higher concordance in monozygotic twins than in dizygotic twins (Bailey et al., 1995; Steffenburg et al., 1989). Monozygotic twins of probands have about a 60 percent chance of having autism, and an even greater probability of an autism-like disorder (Veenstra-vanderweele & Cook, 2003). The comparative figure for dizygotic cotwins is only 4.5 percent.

Family studies of autism are generally consistent with twin study findings. The rate of autism in siblings of autistic children varies from 2 to 7 percent, and about 8 percent of extended families have an additional autistic member (Bailey et al., 1996; Newsom, 1998; Rutter et al., 1999). This rate is higher than what would be expected in the general population. Yet other interesting findings have emerged. *First*, a higher than expected rate of other pervasive developmental disorders is found in families. *Second*, family members exhibit impairments in social, communicative, and repetitive behaviors that are similar to autism but not severe enough for any diagnosis (Piven & Palmer, 1997; Szatmari et al., 2000). For example, social reticence, pragmatic language deficits, and rigid, obsessive traits occur in undiagnosed family members (Folstein et al., 1999). These problems decrease as the genetic relationship becomes more distant (Pickles et al., 2000). There is also some suggestion that theory of mind deficits, executive planning skills, and weak central coherence "run" in families (Happé et al., 2001; Rutter et al., 1999).

Inheritance rather than social transmission is likely to be responsible for the family aggregation of impairments. For example, Szatmari and his colleagues (2000) found that impairments occurred more significantly in biological than adoptive families in three major areas of function (Figure 12–5). Despite some weaknesses in the overall research, these findings together indicate that a broad genetic predisposition may run in families, leading to autism, autism-like disorders, or milder related problems—that is, to a spectrum of disorder.

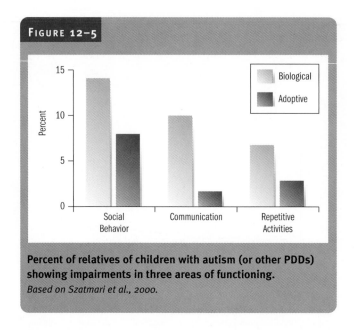

FIGURE 12-5

Percent of relatives of children with autism (or other PDDs) showing impairments in three areas of functioning.
Based on Szatmari et al., 2000.

The modes and mechanisms of genetic transmission are not established, but genetic heterogeneity is highly likely, and investigators favor the idea that various interacting genes best explain most cases (Rutter et al., 1999; Veenstra-vanderweele & Cook, 2003). This possibility is suggested by the spectrum of disorder and the varied clinical picture. Chromosomes 7 and 2 are the most commonly implicated in linkage studies and a few other genes related to serotonin are implicated (Plomin & McGuffin, 2003; Veenstra-vanderweele & Cook, 2003). In addition, a duplication of a sequence of genes on chromosome 15 has been observed in an estimated 1 to 3 percent of cases of autism, apparently transmitted maternally (Sutcliffe & Nurmi, 2003).

ASPERGER'S DISORDER AND OTHER PDDS

As noted earlier much current interest exists in disorders that appear similar to autism and each other. In addition to Autistic Disorder, the DSM includes four disorders under the category of Pervasive Developmental Disorders (for three of these, see Table 12–2). Of these, Asperger's disorder is receiving the most attention. Consistent with the DSM approach, these disorders are viewed as discrete and quite distinct from each other, but questions have been raised about this conceptualization.

Rett's Disorder. Upon noticing that two young girls in his waiting room were exhibiting similar hand-wringing movements, Andreas Rett, an Austrian physician, discovered among patient records six more cases with similar symptoms and developmental history (Van Acker, 1997). This discovery led to the first publication, in 1966, describing Rett's disorder, or Rett syndrome.

Children with Rett's disorder display apparently normal development during the first months of life and then regress and deteriorate in distinctive ways. There is severe or profound retardation. Brain neurons are smaller and more densely packed than normal, and there are fewer dendritic connections, especially in the motor, temporal, and hippocampal areas (Kerr, 2002). The brain stem is also implicated. Several biochemical abnormalities have been noted. In 1999, causation was linked to a gene on the X chromosome that regulates other genes; over one hundred mutations have now been described. Although the mutation likely occurs in either parent, it is more probable in the father, who passes it to his daughter. Indeed, Rett's disorder primarily is known in females, but can occur in boys when the mutation is transmitted by the mother.

The prevalence of the syndrome is not well established, although 1 in 10,000 or less has been suggested for females—with lower rates for males (Kerr, 2002). The condition is categorized as a PDD because of the presence of autistic-like behaviors, particularly during the preschool years (Volkmar & Klin, 2000). However, this lifelong disorder has a more negative outcome than autism (Van Acker, 1997). The child may become somewhat more interested in social interaction during childhood and

TABLE 12–2	THE DSM FEATURES OF THREE NONAUTISTIC PERVASIVE DEVELOPMENTAL DISORDERS

RETT'S DISORDER

All of the Following after a Period of Normal Development:

Deceleration of head growth, 5 to 48 months
Loss of hand skills, 5 to 30 months; subsequent stereotyped hand movements
Loss of social engagement early (although interaction may develop later)
Poorly coordinated gait or trunk movement
Severely impaired language development with severe psychomotor retardation

CHILDHOOD DISINTEGRATIVE DISORDER

After Normal Development for at Least 2 Years, Significant Loss (Before Age 10) in at Least Two of the Following:

Expressive or receptive language
Social skills or adaptive behavior
Bowel or bladder control
Play
Motor skills

Abnormal Functioning in at Least Two of the Following:

Qualitative impairment in social interaction
Qualitative impairment in communication
Restricted, repetitive, stereotyped patterns of behavior, interests, and activities, including motor stereotypies and mannerisms

ASPERGER'S DISORDER

Qualitative Impairment in Social Interaction, Manifested by at Least Two of the Following:

Deficits in use of nonverbal behaviors to regulate social interaction
Failure to develop age-appropriate peer relationships
Lack of spontaneous sharing of enjoyment or interests with others
Lack of social or emotional reciprocity

Restricted, Repetitive, Stereotyped Behavior, Interests, and Activities, Manifested by at Least One of the Following:

Preoccupation with restricted pattern of interest, abnormal in intensity or focus
Inflexible adherence to nonfunctional routines or rituals
Stereotyped and repetitive motor mannerisms
Persistent preoccupation with parts of objects

No Significant General Delay in Language

No Significant Delay in Cognitive Development or in Self-help Skills, Adaptive Behavior (Except in Social Interaction), and Curiosity about the Environment in Childhood

From American Psychiatric Association, 2000.

adolescence, but communicative and behavioral problems remain relatively stable while there is a progressive loss of skills.

Childhood Disintegrative Disorder (CDD).

Theodore Heller first described childhood disintegrative disorder in 1908. He termed the condition dementia infantilis, and it also has been called Heller's syndrome and disintegrative psychosis (Volkmar & Klin, 2000). The onset of CDD is time-bound in that development must be normal for at least 2 years and symptoms must be present before age 10. By this time, many acquired skills are lost. The manifestations of CDD are very similar to autism's triad of disturbance, but diagnosis requires impairment in only two areas. The disorder is usually associated with severe mental retardation.

Bob   Childhood Disintegrative Disorder

Bob's early history was within normal limits. By age 2, he was speaking in sentences and his development appeared to be proceeding appropriately. At 40 months he was noted to exhibit, abruptly, a period of marked behavioral regression shortly after the birth of a sibling. He lost previously acquired skills in communication and was no longer toilet trained. He became uninterested in social interaction, and various unusual self-stimulatory behaviors became evident. . . . Behaviorally, he exhibited features of autism. At follow-up at age 12 he still was not speaking, apart from an occasional single word, and was severely retarded.

Adapted from Volkmar, 1996a, pp. 496–497.

The evidence for neurological disturbance in CDD includes abnormal EEGs and seizures (Volkmar & Klin, 2000). CDD occurs in perhaps only 1 child in 50,000 and prevalence is greater in males than females (American Psychiatric Association, 2000; Volkmar et al., 2004). Onset is usually between 3 and 4 years of age and may be gradual or abrupt. Impairments seem to remain fairly constant over time, although improvement may occur in a small number of cases.

Because the symptom picture is similar to autism, time of onset could be important in differentiating the disorders; however, regression and symptom onset after age 2 are reported by some parents of children with autism (Davidovitch et al., 2000; Lord et al., 2004). This has raised the question of whether the disorders are actually different from each other (Hendry, 2000). Nevertheless, evidence exists that more children with CDD than with autism are mute, display loss of self-help skills, and have IQ scores less than 40 (Volkmar & Klin, 2000). These youngsters are among the lowest functioning of children with PDDs; outcome is less favorable than in autism, with high rates of institutionalization. The regression and marked loss of skills found in CDD suggest an underlying genetic disorder (Volkmar et al., 2004).

Asperger's Disorder (AD). Although Asperger first wrote of this syndrome in 1944, many years passed before English-speaking professionals took notice and the diagnosis was not recognized by the DSM and ICD until the early 1990s (Klin & Volkmar, 1997). Asperger's disorder, or Asperger syndrome, is marked by qualitative deficits in social interaction and by restrictive, repetitive, stereotyped interests and behaviors. In these ways, it resembles autism. However, according to the DSM criteria, children with AD display no significant delay in language, cognitive development, adaptive behavior (except in the social domain), or curiosity about the environment. Language skills may actually appear precocious and verbalization excessive.

Individuals with the syndrome have difficulties in establishing friendships and other positive social bonds. Deficits appear in the use of nonverbal social gestures, emotional expression, and early sharing behaviors. Social awkwardness, inappropriateness, lack of empathy, and insensitivity are apparent. There seems to be some interest in other people, but life is often marked by loneliness. Although research indicates impairment in ToM skills and the perception of complex emotions, the exact nature of the social deficits are not fully understood (Frith, 2004).

Particularly striking are obsessive and restricted interests, the focus of which seems to know few bounds; astronomy, kitchen appliances, historical events, and geographical locales are a few examples. The child may collect an inordinate number of facts and recite them in a pedantic, egocentric, long-winded style. Indeed, Asperger referred to his patients as "little professors." Adults with AD are known for their meticulous work—whether in art or science (Frith, 2004). At the same time, children and adults often exhibit imagination as displayed, for example, in art.

Other problems not required for diagnosis also have been observed. A variety of motor difficulties may exist, as well as behavioral problems such as noncompliance, negativism, and aggression (Miller & Ozonoff, 2000; Volkmar & Klin, 2000). Some of the difficulties of Asperger's disorder can be seen in the following description.

Robert   Asperger's Disorder

Robert's parents had no concerns about his early development. Peer interaction problems became noticeable in preschool, where he was seen as somewhat eccentric, partly due to an intense interest in astronomy. By age 10, numerous problems and concerns (e.g., visual-motor difficulties, social isolation) had led to therapy and educational accommodation.

Evaluated in his twelfth year, Robert had a verbal IQ of 150 and a performance IQ of 116. His visual-motor coordination and executive skills were far below average—indicating poor manual dexterity, slow motor function, poor visual-spatial skills, and a tendency toward getting "stuck" on a stimulus or behavior. His receptive and expressive vocabulary were excellent, but he communicated in a rather formal and pedantic style. When asked, for example, to provide another word for "thin" he offered, "dimensionally challenged."

In social interaction, Robert often failed to respond to the facial expressions and gestures of others; he avoided eye contact and appeared to look through people. After an initial reserve, he appeared to become more comfortable with the evaluator, and he discussed his interest in astronomy. He engaged in a long, intense, vigorous monologue—and was insensitive to the evaluator's efforts to change the subject. He also described two children he considered friends; their relationship seemed based on their interest in computers. Robert saw himself as isolated and withdrawn in a novel group situation, but said he was an excellent public speaker in informal presentations for which he memorized and rehearsed.

Adapted From Volkmar et al., 2000.

The prevalence of Asperger's disorder is estimated as 2.5 in 10,000 persons (Fombonne, 2003). Boys are diagnosed more than girls. Systematic study is lacking with regard to the course and outcome of the disorder, but outcome appears variable (Frith, 2004). Asperger himself thought that many of his patients could do reasonably well, and current clinical impressions agree that outcome can be favorable in terms of living independently, finding employment, and having a family. Social impairments, however, may persist over time.

Of notable interest regarding Asperger's disorder is its relationship to higher functioning autism. Although the lack of language problems is supposed to differentiate these syndromes, the distinction is often difficult to make. For Asperger's disorder, there are reports of later onset, more complex speech, higher verbal IQ, less severe social and communication problems, fewer motor mannerisms, and more noticeable restricted interests (Ghaziuddin et al., 2000; Miller & Ozonoff, 2000; Volkmar & Klin, 2000). Nonetheless, a recent review concluded that Asperger's disorder has not so far been shown to be *qualitatively* different than higher functioning autism

in symptoms, associated features, and biological factors (Macintosh & Dissanayake, 2004). It can thus be argued that Asperger's disorder may be best seen as higher functioning autism. The research is not without flaws, and one problem is that Asperger's disorder is defined somewhat differently by various clinicians and investigators. A cautious stance, therefore, appears appropriate at this time.

Pervasive Developmental Disorder Not Otherwise Specified (PDDNOS). Children whose symptoms appear related to the PDD category but fail to meet specific criteria can be diagnosed with PDDNOS. They must display impaired reciprocal social interaction and either impaired communication or stereotyped behavior and interests (American Psychiatric Association, 2000). Cases of so-called atypical autism fall into the PDDNOS category, that is, cases in which criteria for autistic disorder are not met because of late onset, atypical symptoms, lesser symptoms, or all of these.

Children who receive the diagnosis may have social interaction problems in common but otherwise show a varied mix of difficulties (Sicotte & Stemberger, 1999). A complex history of definition has hindered reliable diagnosis and investigation, and studies of PDDNOS are quite scarce and with confusing findings (Serra et al., 2002; Volkmar et al., 2004). Although controversy exists as to how PDDNOS is related to other PDDs, it is often considered similar to but less severe than autism.

Conceptualizing PDDs. Based on the clinic and research data, how should autism and other PDDs be conceptualized? Evidence appears to support Rett syndrome as a discrete disorder, whereas some question exists regarding childhood disintegrative disorder. However, it is the distinction among autism, Asperger's disorder, and PDDNOS that appears most at issue (Mayes, Calhour, & Crites, 2001; Volkmar et al., 2004). A shift has occurred toward viewing the latter two disorders as "lesser variants" of autism. In other words, the three disorders—and especially autism and Asperger's disorder—are seen as falling along a continuum of severity of symptoms rather than into separate categories (Frith, 2004; Szatmari, 2000; Werry, 2001). This conceptualization, which requires further investigation, has theoretical and practical implications concerning, for example, etiology and intervention (Macintosh & Dissanayake, 2004). One recommendation is for clinicians to use the broader conceptualization of "autism spectrum disorder" while also specifying the "discrete" subcategory that best fits the clinical findings.

ASSESSMENT OF AUTISM

Because autism encompasses many areas of functioning and implicates neurobiological deficits, broad-based assessment is appropriate (American Academy of Child and Adolescent Psychiatry, 1999; Charman & Baird, 2002). Parental involvement is needed to provide a unique picture of the child's functioning and also to lay the groundwork for collaboration should treatment be needed. A history is needed of prenatal, birth, developmental, familial, and medical factors—as well as past intervention. Medical examination may be valuable in helping to identify autism, investigate its causes, and treat associated conditions such as seizures.

Psychological and behavioral evaluations typically include interviews, direct observation of the child, and psychological tests. Tests of intelligence, adaptive behavior, and language are among the useful instruments, depending on the individual case. Several instruments exist to specifically assess autistic behaviors. We briefly describe three of these that serve somewhat different purposes or employ somewhat different approaches. Ratings are based on actual observation of the child and/or reports of past or present behavior.

Evaluating Autistic Behaviors. The early identification of autism has high priority because of the value placed on early intervention (Charmon & Baird, 2002). Increased knowledge of early social and communication behaviors has led to efforts to identify children who may be exhibiting few blatant problems. The Checklist for Autism in Toddlers (CHAT) is an example; it is designed to help detect autism as early as 18 months (Baird et al., 2000; Scambler, Rogers, & Wehner, 2001). CHAT consists of a brief set of questions asked of parents or professionals concerning, for example, joint attention and imaginative play.

The Childhood Autism Rating Scale (CARS) is an example of a widely employed screening tool for children and older persons (Newsom & Hovanitz, 1997; Western Psychological Services, 2004). It consists of 15 items on which the child is rated after observation, usually by professionals. The items cover many areas of functioning, including emotional response, imitation, social relations, communication, perception, and intelligence (Schopler

et al., 1980; Schopler, Reichler, & Renner, 1988). Each item is rated in terms of severity, and points are summed to diagnose mild to moderate or severe autism. Identification of autism highly corresponds to DSM diagnosis of the disorder (Rellini et al., 2004).

The Autism Diagnostic Observation Schedule (ADOS) consists of four modules of activities, one of which is selected as relevant to the age and language abilities of the person being evaluated (e.g., Lord et al., 2000). It is useful for a wide range of individuals. Each module creates opportunity for the client to display behaviors relevant to autism, for example, by engaging the person in play or in story telling. ADOS provides cutoff scores for the diagnosis of autism and also the broader diagnosis of PDD but, as with most instruments, additional information from parents is necessary for a more complete profile of functioning (Klinger et al., 2003).

TREATMENT AND EDUCATION

Extensive efforts to alleviate autism have been motivated by the compelling needs of youth with PDDs and by family and societal advocacy for treatment. Today, an array of treatments is available, as well as the call for rigorous scientific evaluation.

Concern is expressed about possible harm from unconventional and untested treatments, some of which make excessive therapeutic claims (Klin & Cohen, 1997). Among these are megavitamins, hugging therapy, auditory training, visual training, psychomotor skills patterning, and facilitated communication. In facilitated communication (FC), for example, the client types messages on a keyboard while the client's hand or arm is guided by a facilitator-therapist. It was claimed that children with autism and other severe disabilities who previously had little ability to communicate were able to send complex and poetic messages. Some intelligence test scores were said to have dramatically risen. Questions about treatment effects eventually led to systematic research, which showed that FC messages largely originate with the facilitator-therapists, who seem unaware that their help goes beyond guidance (e.g., Perry, Bryson, & Bebko, 1998; Saloviita & Sariola, 2003; Simon, Toll, & Whitehair, 1994). With regard to treatment effects, Goldstein (2000) has warned: Remember that "If it is too good to be true, it is too good to be true."

Despite some unfortunate occurrences regarding treatment, real progress has been achieved.

Behavioral and educational approaches are the mainstay treatments. Also employed is pharmacotherapy and, for convenience, we turn first to this approach.

Pharmacological Treatment. The typical antipsychotic medications that are antagonistic to dopamine can help some youth in reducing problematic behaviors, but adverse side effects occur over time in a minority of cases (Campbell et al., 1997). Of particular concern are motor problems, including tardive dyskinesia (involuntary repetitive movements of the tongue, mouth, and jaw). These medications have thus been largely replaced by atypical antipsychotic medications that are antagonistic to dopamine and serotonin and generally have fewer side effects. The targeted behaviors include agitation, self-injury, and stereotypes. Risperidone has been most investigated and has been shown to bring behavioral improvement across all ages (Arnold et al., 2003; Malone et al., 2002; Nicolson, Awad, & Sloman, 1998).

Medications that are antagonistic to opiate peptides (endorphins) are of interest because heightened opiate levels may be related to self-injury and social and cognitive deficits (Klinger et al., 2003). Naltrexone sometimes reduces hyperactivity and irritability (Kolmen et al., 1998; Volkmar & Klin, 2000). The use of stimulants to reduce hyperactivity is questionable due to reported worsening of stereotypies (Lord & Bailey, 2002).

Overall, some medications may alleviate some of the primary and secondary symptoms of autism but much is yet to be known about drug effects. Medications are best used as an adjunct to behavioral and educational interventions (Lord & Bailey, 2002).

Behavioral Intervention. Early behavioral intervention consisted of simple demonstrations of behavior change in youth with the disorder (Koegel, Koegel, & McNerney, 2001; Schreibman, 2000). Subsequent efforts were made to teach a variety of adaptive behaviors and to discourage undesirable behaviors. An outstanding example of this early work was the approach taken by Lovaas and his colleagues at the University of California at Los Angeles, who were among the first to teach verbal communication to autistic children (Lovaas, Young, & Newsom, 1978; Newsom, 1998). In highly structured sessions, the usual tools of operant intervention were employed—such as contingent reinforcement, prompts, shaping, modeling, and procedures to facilitate the generalization of learning.

Early behavioral efforts enjoyed success but were also challenged by failure. For instance, youngsters receiving language training too often failed to initiate speech or use speech in everyday activities (Koegel, 2000). With regard to other kinds of behaviors, acquired responses often did not generalize, punishment appeared necessary to modify some maladaptive behaviors, and some behaviors were hardly modifiable (Schreibman, 1997).

Improved behavioral procedures have brought increased success. Functional analysis of maladaptive behavior and Functional Communication Training (p. 330) have been successfully used with children with autism. Adaptive behaviors can be acquired through both discrete trial and naturalistic learning that is more likely to generalize to other settings. In addition, the teaching of some skills can facilitate other positive behaviors; for example, teaching children to initiate social and academic interactions may promote the learning of language and social skills. These various behavioral approaches have been incorporated into strategies known as Incidental Teaching, Milieu Teaching, Pivotal Response Training, and the like (Schreibman, 2000). The approach taken in pivotal response training, for example, is to target core pivotal behaviors that, when improved, may effect improvement in other behaviors as well (Koegel et al., 2001; Koegel, Koegel, & Brookman, 2003). Because impairments in autism tend to be extensive—and targeting each problem is extremely time consuming and expensive—pivotal response training holds promise for time-efficient and cost-effective intervention (Table 12–3).

COMPREHENSIVE BEHAVIORAL INTERVENTION: THE YOUNG AUTISM PROJECT. Although the targeting of specific behaviors can be helpful, early, intensive, comprehensive programs are necessary to bring about substantial improvement in the lives of children with autism. In 1970, a groundbreaking intervention was developed by Lovaas and his colleagues that aimed at multiple positive outcomes, a treatment effort known as the Young Autism Project (Lovaas, 1987; Lovaas & Smith, 1988). Children under age 4 are selected—because early age maximizes new learning—and they must be free of major medical problems (Lovaas & Smith, 2003). Most receive 40 hours per week of one-to-one intervention with experienced behavioral therapists, with sessions tapering off near the end of the approximately 3-year program.

Discrete trial learning is employed throughout training, incidental learning begins after the first few

TABLE 12–3	PROCEDURES USED IN PIVOTAL RESPONSE TRAINING TO STRENGTHEN THE CHILD'S MOTIVATION TO INITIATE AND RESPOND TO ENVIRONMENTAL STIMULI

To Increase Motivation to Respond
   Child is permitted to select activities and objects.
   Tasks are varied.
   Reinforcement is given liberally to the child's
      attempts to respond.
   Natural reinforcers are employed.
   Opportunity is given to the child to use acquired
      responses as new ones are learned.
Child Is Taught to Respond to Multiple Cues in the
   Environment
Child Is Taught Self-Regulation
Child Is Taught to Initiate Behavior

Based on Koegel, Koegel, & McNerney, 2001.

months, and small group teaching in preschool occurs during the final years (see Table 12–4). Initially, it is usually necessary to reduce maladaptive behaviors that interfere with learning, such as tantrums, to teach imitation and compliance with verbal commands, and to train basic behaviors such as dressing and playing with toys. Considerable effort is then given to language and communication skills, as well as to peer interaction and interactive play. During the last year or so, emphasis is placed on advanced communication and school adjustment. Parents are an integral part of intervention. They attend all meetings regarding their child, work with therapists for the first 3 to 4 months implementing discrete trial learning, and subsequently use incidental learning to encourage communication, self-help, and other behaviors in everyday settings.

The Early Autism Project and related programs have been among the most extensively evaluated. A 1987 report compared outcome for three groups:

TABLE 12–4	TREATMENT STAGES IN THE YOUNG AUTISM PROJECT		
STAGE	**LENGTH**	**TEACHING METHOD(S)**	**GOALS (EXAMPLES)**
1. Establishing a teaching relationship	~2–4 weeks	Primarily discrete trial training (DTT)	Following directions such as "sit" or "come here," reducing interfering behaviors such as tantrums
2. Teaching foundational skills	~1–4 months	Primarily DTT	Imitating gross motor actions, identifying objects, dressing, beginning play with toys
3. Beginning communication	~6+ months	DTT, incidental teaching	Imitating speech sounds, expressively labeling objects, receptively identifying actions and pictures, expanding self-help and play skills
4. Expanding communication, beginning peer interaction	~12 months	DTT, incidental teaching, dyads with typical peers	Labeling colors and shapes, beginning language concepts such as big/little and yes/no, beginning sentences such as "I see _____," beginning pretend play and peer interaction
5. Advanced communication, adjusting to school	~12 months	DTT, incidental teaching, small group, regular education preschool	Conversing with others, describing objects and events, comprehending stories, understanding perspective of others, working independently, helping with chores

Adapted from Lovaas & Smith, 2003.

TABLE 12–5	EDUCATIONAL PLACEMENT AND MEAN IQ SCORE AT INITIAL FOLLOW-UP IN THE YOUNG AUTISM PROJECT		
	PERCENT OF CHILDREN COMPLETING REGULAR FIRST GRADE	PERCENT OF CHILDREN IN LANGUAGE HANDICAPPED AND LD CLASS	PERCENT OF CHILDREN IN FIRST GRADE FOR AUTISTIC-RETARDED
Group I	47 IQ: 107	42 IQ: 70	11 IQ: 30
Group II	0	42 IQ: 74	58 IQ: 36
Group III	5 IQ: 99	48 IQ: 67	48 IQ: 44

Adapted from Lovaas, 1987.

Group I received behavioral treatment for more than 40 hours each week; Group II received almost the same treatment but for less than 10 hours each week; Group III, an outside group of children with autism, received no training in the project. The groups were similar in characteristics and intervention lasted for 2 or more years. At initial follow-up, Group I children averaged 7 years of age. They had significantly higher educational placement and IQ than the other two groups, which did not differ from each other (see Table 12–5). A second follow-up when Group I children averaged 13 years of age showed that they had maintained improvements over Group II youngsters (McEachin, Smith, & Lovaas, 1993). Eight of the nine Group I children who had done well at the first follow-up were holding their own in regular classrooms and approached normal functioning.

Although this study had a stronger scientific design than most treatment studies at that time (Rogers, 1998), criticisms were expressed (Mundy, 1993; Rogers, 1998; Schopler, Short, & Mesibov, 1989). Since then, outcome studies of improved design, involving interventions with fewer hours of treatment, have shown positive but weaker findings (Lovaas & Smith, 2003; Smith, Groen, & Wynn, 2000). A multisite study is further examining outcome. Evidence so far indicates that both intellectually impaired children and older children with relatively higher functioning may benefit from treatment. At the same time, interventions initiated and based in the community, rather than in clinic-directed settings, probably have less favorable outcome—due perhaps to excessive demands on parents, relatively unexperienced therapists, and the like.

The overall findings from extensive behavioral intervention have made the behavioral approach a leading treatment option. Drawing on evaluations of behavioral approaches—and also of psychoeducational interventions such as TEACCH, which is discussed in the next section—Schreibman (2000) has noted that the following are now well documented with regard to intensive treatments:

- Intensive treatments—that is, treatments given for many hours a day and/or in many of the child's daily environments—can be extremely effective.

- Intervention when children are very young has the potential for widespread gains.

- Effective treatments are associated with carefully controlled learning situations.

- Effective interventions must use techniques to promote generalization and maintenance of acquired learning (e.g., parent training, naturalistic teaching).

- When parents are trained to be major treatment providers, generalization and maintenance of learning are more likely.

- There is a great deal of variation in outcome; different children may benefit from different approaches.

TEACCH: Comprehensive Psychoeducational Treatment. TEACCH, which stands for <u>T</u>reatment and <u>E</u>ducation of <u>A</u>utistic and related <u>C</u>ommunication handicapped <u>Ch</u>ildren, is a university-based statewide program mandated by law to provide services, research, and training for autism and related disorders (Schopler, 1997). The approach has evolved over 30 years as an alternative to a psychoanalytic-based approach used in the 1960s at the University of North Carolina. From the beginning, families played

TABLE 12–6	SHARED VALUES OF THE TEACCH TREATMENT PROGRAM

Characteristics of autism are understood from observation rather than through professional theory.

Parent-professional collaboration is vital.

The child's adaptation is improved through teaching new skills and making environmental accommodations to deficits.

Assessment for individualized treatment occurs through formal instruments or informal observation.

Priority is given to cognitive and behavior theory.

Enhancement of skills and acceptance of deficits go hand in hand.

A holistic orientation deals with the whole situation.

Lifelong community-based services are crucial.

Based on Schopler, 1997

The successful teaching of children with autism usually requires special strategies. This photograph of a seven-year-old boy with autism interacting with a classmate captures the social communication difficulties that sometimes must be overcome.
(Ellen B. Senisi/Photo Researchers, Inc.)

a critical role in developing TEACCH, and priority was given to three areas: home adjustment, education, and community adaptation. A clear philosophy and set of values emerged over the years, as shown in Table 12–6.

TEACCH operates regional centers, a Developmental Evaluation Center, and an Area Health Education Center. The regional centers provide individual assessment, training for parents to serve as cotherapists for their children, family support, consultation, professional training, and collaboration with other relevant agencies. TEACCH affiliates with hundreds of North Carolina classrooms and is involved in selecting and training the teachers. Students are enrolled in the classrooms after they are assessed by TEACCH and receive an individualized educational plan. Parents and professionals also collaborate on educating the wider community about autism and on developing additional community services.

TEACCH has been evaluated in various ways (Schopler, 1994; 1997; Ozonoff & Cathcart, 1998). It has been recognized for excellence and implemented across the United States and in Europe. At the same time, weaknesses in the outcome studies, including lack of control groups, have been noted (Smith, 1999).

Educational Opportunities. Autism is among the disabilities included in the Individuals with Disabilities Education Act (IDEA) (p. 297). Thus school districts are obliged to identify children with autism, provide services from birth, include families in evaluation and intervention, and deliver appropriate educational programs. The commitment to the least restrictive alternatives and school inclusion has diminished institutionalization and has increased educational opportunities.

Although data are limited, it appears that some children with autism can benefit academically and socially from classroom interaction with typical peers. Factors such as adaptation of curricula, social skills training, teacher attitude, and encouragement of peer interaction make a difference (Durand, 2001). Perhaps unsurprising, opinions about full school inclusion run the gamut from advocacy to arguments for varied educational settings (Burack, Root, & Zigler, 1997). Numerous workers and professional organizations, including those associated with TEACCH, favor the philosophy of least restrictive placement and argue that the marked differences in abilities in persons with autism require alternative educational settings (Division TEACCH, 2004).

In the broader schemes of things, educational efforts need to focus on preparation for appropriate independent functioning and quality of life. However, progress is being made in improving the lives of youth with the disorder and their families. In part, this is the result of both rigorous research and the commitment and advocacy of families and professionals alike.

Schizophrenia

As we noted at the beginning of this chapter, for many years the term childhood schizophrenia was applied to heterogeneous groups of children with certain severe impairments. Even after diagnostic confusion was reduced—for example, by the conceptualizing of autism as distinct—a fundamental question remained: Does schizophrenia appearing in children and adolescents differ from adult schizophrenia or, alternatively, is there a basic disorder manifesting itself at different times of life? By 1980, some consensus was reached that the essential features of schizophrenia hold across age, and the same basic diagnostic criteria were applied to individuals of all ages. This approach is not without problems, but the diagnosis of youth with schizophrenia is reasonably reliable (Hollis, 2000; 2002).

Although research problems—such as small samples, retrospective designs, and lack of control groups—have hindered the understanding of childhood-onset schizophrenia, there is considerable impetus to study the disorder (Asarnow & Asarnow, 2003; Nicolson & Rapoport, 2000). Of course, early-occurring disturbance is of interest in itself, both for scientific and humanitarian reasons. It is also important to study schizophrenia across childhood and adolescence to better understand its developmental course and the relationship to adult-onset disorder. Our primary interest in this chapter is schizophrenia of young people, but adult-onset schizophrenia is considered as well. In keeping with the clinical and research literature, our discussion often distinguishes childhood schizophrenia (with onset usually defined as prior to age 13) and schizophrenia that first occurs during adolescence or during adulthood.

DSM CLASSIFICATION AND DIAGNOSIS

Table 12–7 indicates the DSM major diagnostic features for schizophrenia. At least two features usually are required, and signs of disorder must be continuous for at least 6 months. Schizophrenia disrupts normal adaptation and relationships. Thus young people so diagnosed must have failed to reach normal levels of interpersonal, academic, or occupational achievement.

The first four features listed in Table 12–7 are considered reflections of psychosis (American Psychiatric Association, 2000). Referred to as positive symptoms, they indicate an excess or distortion of

| TABLE 12–7 | MAJOR DSM FEATURES FOR SCHIZOPHRENIA |

1. Delusions
2. Hallucinations
3. Disorganized speech
4. Disorganized or catatonic behavior
5. Negative symptoms: diminished affect, speech content, and goal-directed activities

From American Psychiatric Association, 2000.

normal functioning. Hallucinations, or erroneous perceptions, and delusions, or erroneous beliefs, often are viewed as the hallmarks of schizophrenia. But disorganized speech, which reflects thought disorder, is a critical feature. Disorganized behavior is manifested in many ways: inappropriate silliness, unexpected agitation and aggression, lack of self-care, and the like. Catatonic behaviors are motor disturbances, such as decreased or excessive motor reactivity, and rigid and strange bodily postures.

Individuals with schizophrenia also may display negative symptoms, that is, a diminution or lack of normally occurring behaviors. Thus they may exhibit little emotion (flat affect), their speech may consist of brief replies that do not seem to convey much information (alogia), or they may neither initiate nor maintain goal-directed actions (avolition).

Although youth can be successfully diagnosed, the strong reliance on positive symptoms, such as hallucinations and delusions, for diagnosis has implication for very young children. Early developmental level may not lend itself to these psychotic manifestations, nor to such symptoms being reported by the child or being reliably assessed. In fact, it is difficult to diagnose schizophrenia until age 7 or 8 (Gooding & Iacono, 1995). This means, of course, that if schizophrenia manifests itself very early, it is unlikely to be identified and its very early developmental course unlikely to be studied.

The DSM criteria for schizophrenia are similar to that of the ICD. Both systems also include subcategories for schizophrenia, such as paranoid and disorganized schizophrenia. However, subgroups have not been extensively applied to children. A study of child cases that identified subtypes found changes in the subtypes over time (Eggers et al., 2000).

TABLE 12–8   SOME CHARACTERISTICS OF CHILDHOOD SCHIZOPHRENIA IN FOUR STUDIES

	MEAN AGE	MALE: FEMALE	MEAN IQ	AUDITORY HALLUCINATIONS	VISUAL HALLUCINATIONS	DELUSIONS	THOUGHT DISORDER
				PERCENT OF CASES SHOWING SYMPTOMS			
Kolvin et al., 1971							
N = 33	≈11.1	2.66:1	86	82	30	58	60
Green et al., 1992							
N = 38	9.58	2.17:1	86	84	47	55	100
Russell et al., 1989							
N = 35	9.54	2.2:1	94	80	37	63	40
Volkmar et al., 1988							
N = 14	≈7.86	2.5:1	82	79	28	86	93

Adapted from Green et al., 1992: Russell et al., 1989; and Volkmar, 1991.

DESCRIPTION

The core psychotic features of schizophrenia are striking; however, associated characteristics are important considerations. We first focus on the core features and then on the associated characteristics.

TABLE 12–9   PERCENTAGE OF CHILDREN WITH HALLUCINATIONS AND DELUSIONS

TYPES OF HALLUCINATIONS	PERCENT
Nonaffective auditory	80
Command	69
Visual	37
Conversing voices	34
Religious	34
Persecutory	26
Commenting voices	23
Tactile	17
Olfactory	6
Somatic	6

TYPES OF DELUSIONS	PERCENT
Persecutory	20
Somatic	20
Bizarre	17
Reference	14
Grandiose	11
Thought insertion	11
Control/influence	9
Mind reading	9
Thought broadcasting	6
Thought control	3
Religious	3

From Russell, Bott, & Sammons, 1989.

Hallucinations. Hallucinations are false perceptions that occur in the absence of identifiable stimuli. Individuals experiencing hallucinations report hearing, seeing, or smelling things that others do not hear, see, or smell. Such perceptual abnormalities can vary in content and in complexity. For example, simple hallucinations are indistinct shapes or sounds, whereas complex hallucinations are more organized, such as identifiable figures or voices (Volkmar et al., 1995).

Table 12–8 shows some of the characteristics of four samples of children diagnosed with schizophrenia, including the hallucinations they reported. Hallucinations occurred at high rates and with notable consistency across the samples. Auditory hallucinations were by far the most common. Visual hallucinations were reported fairly often, whereas those involving touch and smell were quite rare. These findings are consistent with other studies of children, adolescents, and adults with schizophrenia.

Table 12–9 details the variety of hallucinations reported by children in one study, as well as the percentage of children who experienced each type (Russell, Bott, & Sammons, 1989). It was not uncommon for a single child to report several types. The following are examples of the children's accounts of their experiences:

Auditory: The kitchen light said to do things and "shut up."

Command: A man's voice said "murder your stepfather" and "go play outside."

Visual: A ghost with a red, burned, and scarred face was seen several times in different places.

Religious: God said, "Sorry D., but I can't help you now, I'm helping someone else."

Persecutory: Monsters said that the child is "stupid" and that they will hurt him.

Delusions. Delusions are false beliefs that are maintained even in the face of realistic contradiction. They vary in content. For example, delusions of persecution involve beliefs of impending harm from someone, whereas delusions of reference involve inaccurate beliefs that certain events or objects have particular significance. Delusions can also be simple or complex, and fragmented or organized. As shown in Table 12–8, delusions occurred relatively frequently and with consistency across the samples of children. Table 12–9 indicates the many types of delusions reported by the children, and some youngsters reported several types. The following are examples:

Persecutory: A child believed his father had escaped jail and was coming to kill him.

Somatic: A child believed that a boy and a girl spirit lived inside his head.

Bizarre: A boy was convinced he was a dog and growing fur. One time he refused to leave a veterinarian's office unless he got a shot.

Grandiose: A boy had the firm belief that he was different and able to kill people. He believed that when God zoomed through him, he became strong.

Thought Disorder. Delusions are a disturbance in the content of thought, but the form of thinking is also distorted in schizophrenia. Thought disorder involves difficulties in organizing thoughts and is reflected in disorganized speech. Several indications of thought disorder are recognized. The person may display loose associations, that is, jump from topic to topic with no obvious connection between topics and without awareness of the problem. Speech may be illogical, incoherent, and incomprehensible to others. It may also have impoverished content, conveying little information because it is vague, too abstract or concrete, or repetitive. It may include neologisms, made-up words that are meaningless to others. Thought disorder is suggested in this excerpt from an interview with a 7-year-old boy:

I used to have a Mexican dream. I was watching TV in the family room. I disappeared outside of this world and then I was in a closet. Sounds like a vacuum dream. It's a Mexican dream. When I was close to that dream earth I was turning upside down. I don't like to turn upside down. Sometimes I have Mexican dreams and vacuum dreams. It's real hard to scream in dreams. (Russell et al., 1989, p. 404)

Table 12–8 shows high percentages of thought disorder in the four samples of children studied, but it also reveals a large variation across the samples. These differences may be real, but they may also be due to difficulty in identifying thought disorder in children (McClellan, 2000).

Associated Characteristics. Among the features associated with childhood schizophrenia are motor abnormalities that include awkwardness, delayed milestones, poor coordination, and peculiar posture (Eggers, 1978; Nicolson & Rapoport, 2000; Watkins, Asarnow, & Tanguay, 1988).

Basic language skills are not as deficient as in autism, but impaired communication is common (McClellan, Werry et al., 2001). For example, when asked a question, children with schizophrenia may be less likely to give any reply, and when they do reply, they may be less likely to give information to supplement their simple answers (Abu-Akel et al., 2000). The youngsters also use fewer conjunctions and other speech devices to connect ideas (Caplan et al., 2000). Atypical features such as echolalia and neologisms occur.

Many children with schizophrenia score at borderline to average levels on intelligence tests; perhaps 10 to 20 percent of cases show low IQ scores (McClellan, 2000). There is some evidence for a decline in intelligence during at least the first few years after psychotic symptoms appear (Jacobsen & Rapoport, 1998).

Emotional and social disturbances also are evident. Some of these difficulties indicate the flat affect and lack of social interest—the negative symptoms—that reportedly are more common in early-onset than adult schizophrenia (Hollis, 2002). Social problems include shyness, withdrawal, isolation, and ineptness (Bettes & Walker, 1987; Eggers et al., 2000; Watkins et al., 1988). In addition, inappropriate emotion, moodiness, anxiety, and depression have been reported (e.g., Green et al., 1992; Prior & Werry, 1986).

TABLE 12–10	CHILDREN'S AGES AT ONSET OF SYMPTOMS AND DIAGNOSIS OF SCHIZOPHRENIA		
AGE (APPROXIMATE YEARS)	**PERCENT SHOWING ONSET OF NONPSYCHOTIC SYMPTOMS**	**PERCENT SHOWING ONSET OF PSYCHOTIC SYMPTOMS**	**PERCENT DIAGNOSED**
0–3	8	0	0
3–5	18	0	0
5–7	45	18	5
7–9	13	42	29
9–11	13	29	37
11–12	3	11	29

Adapted from Green, Padron-Gayol, Hardesty, & Bassiri, 1992.

EPIDEMIOLOGY

The prevalence of schizophrenia in children is not established, but the disorder is considered quite rare, with rates much smaller than the adult rate of about 1 percent (Eggers, Bunk, & Krause, 2000). Prevalence climbs during adolescence into early adulthood. Schizophrenia often, but not always, is reported as more common in boys than in girls, with the sex ratio perhaps flattening out in adolescence (Asarnow & Asarnow, 2003). This compares with later-onset schizophrenia, in which males are diagnosed at earlier age and also appear to be at somewhat greater risk for the disorder (e.g., Aleman, Kahn, & Selten, 2003).

Childhood-onset schizophrenia may occur at higher rates in less educated and less professionally successful families; however, the data are mixed and may be biased by reliance on hospital samples (McClellan, Werry et al., 2001). In adulthood, schizophrenia is more prevalent in the lower social classes. It also is observed in cultures all over the world, with similar rates and symptom profiles.

DEVELOPMENTAL COURSE AND PROGNOSIS

The onset of schizophrenia in childhood is likely to be gradual, or insidious (McClellan, Werry et al., 2001). Nonpsychotic symptoms occur prior to psychotic symptoms and diagnosis. These early occurring characteristics include delays and aberrations in language and in motor, sensory, and cognitive functions—as well as social withdrawal, peer difficulties, school problems, and "odd" personality

(Asarnow, Tompson, & McGrath, 2004; McClellan et al., 2003; Nicolson & Rapoport, 2000). The question has been raised as to whether early symptoms should be viewed as precursors or as early manifestations of the disorder (Asarnow & Asarnow, 2003). As it is, psychotic symptoms—and thus diagnosis—become more likely at school age. Table 12–10 reflects this developmental course for 38 children hospitalized with schizophrenia.

As we might expect, developmental level makes its way into children's psychotic experiences (Eggers, 1978; Russell et al., 1989). Early hallucinations are likely to include animals, toys, and monsters, and to be simple. Similarly, when delusions first appear, they are quite simple (e.g., a monster wants to kill me), and then they gradually become more elaborate, complex, abstract, and systematized. These changes are in keeping with cognitive and socioemotional development (Volkmar, 1996b).

Adolescent onset of schizophrenia is perhaps not as insidious as child onset. Many diagnosed adolescents nonetheless have histories of attention, motor-perceptual, and other neurodevelopmental problems as well as worry, shyness, moodiness, and aggression. This picture seems more similar to adult-onset schizophrenia, in which there is considerable variation in the timing, severity, and nature of early features (Rossi et al., 2000). The psychotic symptoms exhibited by adolescents also are more similar to those of adults'. For instance, persecutory and grandiose delusions are more common than in childhood cases, and delusions are more complex and systematized (Volkmar et al., 1995).

Further research is needed on the course and outcome of schizophrenia in youth. Much variation has been reported in the course of the disorder (Eggers et al., 2000). It does appear that, as in adult cases, some youth have a chronic condition, others experience episodes of difficulties that come and go, and still others partly or fully recover (e.g., Hollis, 2000). Nevertheless, full recovery is not common. A 42-year follow-up of cases with onset by age 14 found that roughly 25 percent had recovered, 25 percent had partial recovery, and 50 percent had a continuing severe course (Eggers & Bunk, 1997). From other investigations we can surmise that from roughly half to three-quarters of cases may not do well (Asarnow et al., 2004; Gillberg, Hellgren, & Gillberg, 1993; Jarbin, Ott, & von Knorring, 2003; Krausz & Muller-Thomsen, 1993).

Research suggests that poor adjustment before onset, insidious onset, an extended initial psychotic episode, negative symptoms, and a longer time lapse before treatment may predict poor outcome (Hollis, 2002). In any event, though, early age of onset is associated with poor outcome, suggesting that child and adolescent schizophrenia are more ominous than adult-onset schizophrenia (Hollis, 2000; McClellan, Werry et al., 2001).

Unfortunately, child and adolescent schizophrenia, as shown in a limited number of studies, carries a higher than usual risk for premature death, as does later-onset schizophrenia (Hollis, 2002; Meltzer et al., 2003). There appears to be a mix of causes, such as undetected medical conditions and suicide and other violent events. The following case description illustrates several of the developmental features of childhood-onset schizophrenia that terminated in tragedy.

Mary	**Developmental Course of Childhood Schizophrenia**

Mary had always been a very shy child. She would become mute at times, had severe difficulties making friends, was frequently oppositional, and had occasional enuresis. By the time she reached roughly 10 years of age, Mary showed academic difficulties in addition to continuing social isolation. She became depressed, felt that the devil was trying to make her do bad things, believed that her teacher was trying to hurt her, and became preoccupied with germs. Her behavior became increasingly disorganized; she talked of killing herself, appeared disheveled, and ran in front of a moving car in an apparent suicide attempt.

This episode precipitated an inpatient psychiatric evaluation, during which Mary continued to show bizarre behavior. . . . Although Mary's functioning improved during hospitalization and she returned to her family, throughout her childhood and adolescent years she was tormented by fears, hallucinations, the belief that others were out to get her, and occasional bouts of depression often accompanied by suicide attempts. She continued to be socially isolated and withdrawn, and to perform poorly in school. At age 17 (after several brief inpatient hospitalizations), Mary was admitted to a state hospital, where she remained until the age of 19. During this period her affect was increasingly flat, and her psychotic symptoms persisted. One week after discharge from the hospital, Mary went into her room, locked the door, and overdosed on her medications. She was found dead the next morning.

Adapted from Asarnow & Asarnow, 2003, p. 455.

NEUROBIOLOGICAL ABNORMALITIES

Nervous system anomalies have been revealed for schizophrenia. Although many of the findings come from adult cases and from children at high risk who were later diagnosed in adolescence or adulthood, findings have begun to accumulate for childhood schizophrenia. The findings are notably similar across age groups.

Neurological dysfunction is suggested by general symptoms of children with schizophrenia, such as motor delay, coordination problems, and other soft neurological signs (Jacobsen & Rapoport, 1998). In addition, minor physical abnormalities—including irregularities of the face, head, hands, and feet—occur at elevated rates in schizophrenia (Brennan & Walker, 2001; Marenco & Weinberger, 2000). These suggest genetic influence or prenatal insult during the first and second trimesters, when the nervous system is rapidly developing.

Postmortem and especially imaging studies show structural abnormalities of the brain across age, although not universally (Asarnow & Asarnow, 2003; Jacobsen & Rapoport, 1998). Among the most common findings are reduced volume of the brain, most consistently in the frontal, temporal-limbic (e.g., hippocampus, amygdala), and thalamus areas. Reduction also has been found in the cerebellum. For the most part, reduced volume involves gray matter, but white matter reduction is reported

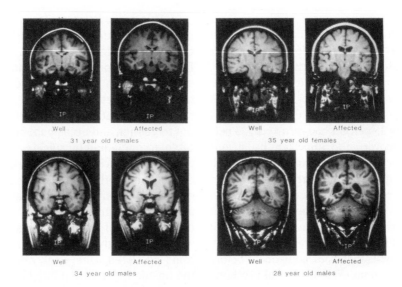

Well   Affected

31 year old females

Well   Affected

35 year old females

Well   Affected

34 year old males

Well   Affected

28 year old males

Increased size of the brain ventricles has been found across age groups with schizophrenia. The above images are from MRI scans for four sets of identical twins discordant for the disorder. In each set, the twin affected by schizophrenia shows increased ventricle size relative to the unaffected twin.
(Dr. E. Fuller Torrey and Dr. Weinberger/National Institute of Mental Health)

(Davis et al., 2003). Also found across age groups is enlargement of the fluid-filled ventricles. Reduced brain volume and enlarged ventricles have been associated with negative symptoms, poor adjustment before diagnosis, and neuropsychological deficits (Buchanan & Carpenter, 2000; Davis et al., 2003; Gur et al., 1998). Structural abnormalities of brain cells also have been noted. Neurons sometimes have been reported as abnormal and in atypical locations. They appear densely packed, with fewer synaptic processes and connections, and altered synaptic chemistry.

Brain disturbance is demonstrated in other ways. Symptoms have been associated with increased or decreased activity in the frontal and temporal lobes, most consistently negative symptoms with reduced frontal lobe activity (Hollis, 2002). Indirect evidence of brain involvement comes from neuropsychological and experimental testing that indicates deficits in attention and information processing, such as in verbal and spatial memory, abstraction, language, and executive functions (Asarnow & Asarnow, 2003; Cannon et al., 1994; Kumra et al., 2000). These deficits are similar to those of adult schizophrenia (McClellan, Werry et al., 2001). In addition, low reactivity of the autonomic nervous system, which might involve the hippocampus, has been widely reported for a subgroup of adults with schizophrenia, and a study of children suggested similar abnormality

(Jacobsen & Rapoport, 1998; Ohman & Hultman, 1998).

For many years, dopamine has been implicated in schizophrenia. Dopamine is important in several cerebral pathways, including the frontal and temporal-limbic areas. Also, typical antipsychotic medications block dopamine, whereas symptoms are made worse by substances that increase dopamine. Still, typical antipsychotic medications help only some patients—primarily improving positive but not negative symptoms—and dopamine's role in schizophrenia is not understood. Numerous subtle transmitter dysfunctions might exist, including an imbalance between the dopamine and other neurotransmission systems (Asarnow & Asarnow, 2003). The involvement of other neurotransmitters, such as GABA and glutamate, is being pursued.

What is to be made of the various, and sometimes inconsistent, findings about the brain? Taken together, the evidence suggests that several brain areas and neurotransmitters, functioning in complex ways, are likely to be involved. Current proposals suggest that schizophrenia involves abnormalities in the connections among parts of a widely distributed network, predominately of frontal and temporal-limbic circuits but perhaps also of more posterior and subcortical areas (Buchanan & Carpenter, 2000; Davis et al., 2003; White et al., 2003).

ETIOLOGY

Given the evidence of brain anomalies, it is not surprising that etiological hypotheses and investigations have sought to explain the origins of these abnormalities and how they might account for schizophrenia.

Genetic Factors. The extensive research conducted in several countries on adult-onset schizophrenia indicates that risk for the disorder increases as genetic relationship to an adult proband increases (Gottesman, 1993; Mortensen et al., 1999). For example, risk is about 13 percent for children of a schizophrenic parent but only 2 percent for first cousins. Twin data show greater concordance in identical than fraternal twins—45 versus 17 percent (Plomin & Crabbe, 2000). Moreover, genetic vulnerability may express itself in disorders similar to but less severe than schizophrenia (e.g., schizoaffective and schizotypal disorders) and in cognitive processing deficits associated with schizophrenia (Hollis, 2002; MacDonald et al., 2003). The findings suggest the inheritance of not a distinct disorder but rather of a more general vulnerability.

A limited number of studies in which schizophrenia arose in childhood provides interesting findings. The family members of the probands are at greater risk for schizophrenia or schizophrenia-like disorders than what would be expected in the general population—and risk appears even higher than for relatives of adult-onset probands (Hollis, 2002; Nicolson & Rapoport, 2000; Ross et al., 1999). Thus, genetic vulnerability may play an especially important role in producing schizophrenia early in life.

Researchers are working to determine the mode(s) of transmission and gene(s) involved in schizophrenia. Single-gene effects have been associated with schizophrenia. For example, velocardiofacial syndrome has been found in over 6 percent of a sample of children with schizophrenia, which is higher than in the general population (Usiskin et al., 1999). This syndrome involves deletions on chromosome 22 and physical/medical problems (Gothelf & Lombroso, 2001). It is nonetheless generally believed that multiple genes are involved in most cases of schizophrenia. Attempts to identify genes have met with limited success. Linkage studies implicate several chromosomes (e.g., 6, 8, 22), but the findings are inconsistent (Plomin & McGuffin, 2003; Kendler, 2000; Rutter et al., 1999). Genetic association analyses provide some evidence that specific genes related to dopamine and serotonin receptor sites increase risk for schizophrenia.

If many genes having small influence are involved in schizophrenia—especially in various combinations—it will be difficult to obtain a complete picture of genetic effects. It is also clear that the genetic data do not seem to tell the entire story. How can we explain the fact that so many identical cotwins of adults with schizophrenia are unlikely to have schizophrenia? Nongenetic influence apparently plays a role in producing schizophrenia. A recent meta-analysis of later-onset twin studies found evidence for a modest influence of shared environmental influences, which could include early exposure to toxins, infections, and prenatal effects (Sullivan, Kendler, & Neale, 2003).

Pregnancy and Birth Complications. Prenatal and birth adversities are only minimally linked to childhood schizophrenia, and their association with adult-onset is sometimes but not always found (Matsumoto et al., 1999; Asarnow & Asarnow, 2003). Many variables have been examined, and structural brain deficits have sometimes been associated with these complications, as has a more severe course of schizophrenia.

The association of schizophrenia with prenatal influenza has been examined in several studies. Particularly interesting findings came from a study of Finnish people who had been exposed prenatally to influenza virus during an epidemic (Mednick et al., 1988). Those exposed during the second trimester of pregnancy had a greater risk for eventually developing schizophrenia. Nevertheless, not all influenza epidemics are linked to schizophrenia (Marenco & Weinberger, 2000).

Cannon and Rosso (2002) note that birth complications, most particularly those in which the infant is deprived of oxygen, show a strong association with schizophrenia relative to other environmental factors. Further, hypoxia may be related to specific brain abnormalities. While not ruling out a small direct effect of birth complications, these investigators tend toward the view that birth complications might operate through interaction with family vulnerability for schizophrenia.

Overall, it appears that pregnancy and birth complications may play a role in some cases of schizophrenia, although we must consider that genetically abnormal fetuses might cause prenatal and perinatal complications.

Psychosocial Influences. Among the psychosocial factors that have been explored as contributing to the development of schizophrenia are life events and family variables. For adult-onset schizophrenia, adverse life events increase in the weeks prior to symptoms, and stress may interact with other factors to contribute to etiology (Fowles, 1992). The degree to which life events play a role in childhood schizophrenia has yet to be determined.

Family characteristics have a long history of being suspected as causing adult-onset schizophrenia. Indeed, the phrase "schizophrenogenic mothering" was once used to capture the idea that pathological parenting was the basic cause of the condition. There has been vacillating interest in the role of family interaction and climate, with much of the research conducted in families of an adult diagnosed with schizophrenia.

The possible influence of family climate is shown in the Finnish Adoption Study, which followed adopted children of mothers with schizophrenia (Tienari et al., 1990). The adoptees who were later diagnosed with schizophrenia had been reared in families rated as having disturbed relationships. Adoptees with rates of schizophrenia at about the general population rates had experienced healthy family relationships. This finding suggests that family climate played a role in etiology.

Research has examined the possible role of communication deviance (CD), that is, distorted and vague communication that indicates dysfunctional thinking and attention. Among the findings is that CD was higher in parents of children with schizophrenia or a related condition than it was in parents of comparison children (Asarnow, Goldstein, & Ben-Meir, 1988). Moreover, in families that had children with schizophrenia, high CD was related to greater impairment in the children. It is unclear how these findings should be interpreted (Asarnow & Asarnow, 2003). Are they a reflection of family stress, parental psychopathology, or additional variables? Other investigations have considered the possible influence of parental expression of criticism and hostility. Although high expressed emotion (EE) was linked to the eventual diagnosis of schizophrenia (or related disorders) in high-risk adolescents (Valone, Goldstein, & Norton, 1984), doubt remains that parents of children with schizophrenia are more critical than other parents (Hollis, 2002). It is worth noting, however, that in adult-onset schizophrenia, high EE is correlated with the return of symptoms after remission (Butzlaff & Hooley, 1998).

Results from family research can be interpreted as suggesting that genetically vulnerable children who experience certain kinds of family interactions or disturbances are at heightened risk for schizophrenia. Although this interactional interpretation is not unreasonable, perhaps adverse family interactions are shaped by the characteristics of dysfunctional members rather than the other way around. We must consider too that genetic influences shared by parents and offspring might underlie parent-child interactions and family climate.

Multifactor and Developmental Models. Present knowledge about schizophrenia (mostly later-onset) has led to the proposal that etiology involves multiple factors. A vulnerability-stress model is often invoked as a general framework. It assumes that an organismic vulnerability, probably genetic but possibly and/or prenatal insult, interacts with environmental stress to produce somewhat different developmental paths and outcomes. Some individuals thus reach a threshold to exhibit diagnosable schizophrenic symptoms or similar but less severe symptoms whereas others do not.

The neurodevelopmental hypothesis is common today in explaining schizophrenia (Weinberger & McClure, 2002). Accordingly, early development of the brain goes awry, affecting critical brain circuits. Although some difficulties may be present early in life, the full-blown consequences are not usually manifested until the brain further matures in adolescence or early adulthood, "enabling" clinical expression of the disorder (Marenco & Weinberger, 2000). Various investigators hypothesize how adolescent brain development may be related to schizophrenia. The shaping of the brain through selective pruning of synapses in the frontal lobes and association areas peaks around late adolescence (Cannon & Rosso, 2002). Schizophrenia could involve excessive pruning at this time.

The exact way or extent to which the neurodevelopmental model of schizophrenia applies to childhood schizophrenia is unclear. As we have seen, substantial evidence exists that childhood and later-onset schizophrenia are similar clinically and biologically (Nicholson & Rapoport, 2000). Such similarities argue that they are not different disorders. However, childhood schizophrenia may have more severe nonpsychotic symptoms prior to diagnosis and less favorable course and outcome. Perhaps then, childhood schizophrenia is a severe form of later-onset schizophrenia (Jacobsen & Rapoport, 1998). Greater genetic vulnerability may play an important role and/or greater environmental adversities combined with biological vulnerability may produce the disorder so early in life (e.g., Nicholson & Rapoport,

2000; Ross et al., 1999). This issue awaits further research.

ASSESSMENT

The following categories can serve as a guide for comprehensive assessment for suspected child or adolescent schizophrenia (McClellan, Werry et al., 2001; Volkmar, 1996b).

- Historical information, including data on pregnancy complications, early development, age of onset, course of symptoms, medical and family history.
- Assessment for the positive and negative symptoms of schizophrenia and associated features.
- Psychological assessment that includes intelligence, communication, and adaptive skills testing.
- Physical examination; EEG, brain scans, laboratory tests may be needed in some cases.
- Consultation with the school and social services as necessary.

Although early identification can facilitate appropriate treatment, it presents particular challenges. The early-occurring nonpsychotic behavioral maladjustments of schizophrenia are observed in other disorders. Indeed, children with schizophrenia may initially receive diagnoses of PDD, ADHD, mood disorders, and anxiety disorders, among others (Schaeffer & Ross, 2002). Even after the onset of psychotic symptoms, some professionals may lack adequate training or hesitate to diagnose schizophrenia, perhaps to avoid stigmatizing the young child.

In addition, as previously noted, it may be difficult to identify the psychotic symptoms of childhood schizophrenia. Standardized rating scales (e.g., the Kiddie Positive and Negative Syndrome Scale) and semistructured interviews (e.g., the Kiddie-SADS, the Schedule for Affective Disorders and Schizophrenia for School-aged Children) can be helpful. Still, it may be difficult to identify true hallucinations in young children (McKenna et al., 1994). Children may report distorted perceptions that simply reflect vivid imaginations. Also, youngsters in nonclinic and clinic populations report seeing ghosts or shapes, hearing voices, and the like—but such hallucinations often do not indicate psychosis (McGee, Williams, & Poulton, 2000; Mertin & Hartwig, 2004; Vickers & Garralda, 2000). Similarly, it can be difficult to tell whether bizarre ideas, obsessions, and

preoccupations reported by the young should be considered psychotic delusions. This is especially true in children younger than 5 or 6, who are still limited in thinking logically and in distinguishing reality from fantasy (Volkmar et al., 1995). In addition, assessment of thought disorder has been especially difficult. It can be affected by a child's language skills, which are crucial in evaluating thinking processes. Moreover, what is considered abnormal thinking varies with developmental level (Caplan, 1994; Caplan et al., 2000).

Assessment of adolescents, especially older adolescents, seems less problematic than that of children. Psychotic symptoms appear more similar to those of adult-onset schizophrenia, although they do not always indicate full-blown schizophrenia (Altman, Collins, & Mundy, 1997; Mertin & Hartwig, 2004). Moreover, psychotic symptoms can be associated with several disorders, including substance abuse, epilepsy, and mood disorders (Calderoni et al., 2001; McClellan et al., 2003; Ulloa et al., 2000). Thus, manifestations of psychosis must be interpreted within the broader clinic presentation. The need for generally improved assessment is evident in data showing misdiagnosis of schizophrenia in youth.

TREATMENT

As with other aspects of early-onset schizophrenia, there is a lack of systematic research on treatment, and we must generalize from what is known about treatment of adults. Treatment can vary substantially, depending on the severity of the case, whether the case is in an acute or a chronic phase, opportunity for intervention, community/family support, and the perspective of the therapist. With severe disturbance, some youth remain at home and may attend special schools; others are placed in hospitals and other residential settings for periods of time. Hospitalization is more likely to occur during the first episode of disturbance (Clark & Lewis, 1998). Early intervention is desirable, because it is associated with fewer symptoms in the future (Hollis, 2002). The best treatment strategy employs multiple methods to alleviate the multiple problems frequently encountered. Pharmacological and psychosocial interventions are the treatments of choice.

Pharmacological Intervention. Although electroconvulsive shock (ECS) therapy was once a widely used medical treatment of adult schizophrenia, today, for patients of all ages, the medical treatment of choice is pharmacotherapy. In adults, hallucinations, delusions, thought disturbance, and other symptoms can be alleviated by antipsychotic medications that block dopamine. Limited research—for example, with haloperidol—shows modest improvement for children and adolescents (Campbell, Rapoport, & Simpson, 1999; McClellan, 2000). The motor side effects of these medications have been of concern and, in addition, they are less effective for negative than positive symptoms.

Atypical antipsychotic medications—such as risperidone, olanzapine, and clozapine—increasingly are used and evaluated for youth (Findling et al., 2003; Kumra et al., 1997; McClellan, Werry et al., 2001). These medications, most of which affect dopamine and serotonin, do not have the side effects of the typical antipsychotics, and they may act on both positive and negative symptoms. But they, too, have some adverse side effects, such as weight gain and sedation (Hollis, 2002). Clozapine, which appears especially effective for children and adolescents, carries risks for seizures and serious blood abnormalities, and thus is recommended only in cases that do not respond to other medications (Asarnow et al., 2004). Systematic studies with children and adolescents are still crucially needed.

Psychosocial Intervention. Medications largely aim at reducing psychotic symptoms, whereas psychosocial treatment encompasses broader objectives. These interventions for youth rely heavily on what is know about adult treatments, some of which have been shown to be ameliorative or promising. Presumably some are more relevant to children and adolescents than others.

The family psychoeducational approach is a popular strategy for adults that is likely to be critical for youth. Today's interventions are fueled by a collaborative philosophy in which blame is not placed on families, as it sometimes had been in the past (Asarnow et al., 2004). Table 12–11 indicates some of the major components of family interventions. Individual and group approaches also may be effective for later-onset disorder, but the extent to which they generalize to children and young adolescents requires investigation. The use of psychodynamic therapy is not indicated; more promising are individual interventions providing support, education, and training of skills such as emotional awareness, self-monitoring, and coping during social interaction. Behavioral approaches are important components of many interventions that target skills training, with operant

TABLE 12–11	MAJOR COMPONENTS OF FAMILY INTERVENTIONS FOR SCHIZOPHRENIA

Education about schizophrenia (e.g., causal hypotheses, course, treatments)

Enhancing strategies for coping with schizophrenia

Training in family communication emphasizing clarity and feedback tactics

Training in problem solving; managing everyday situations and stress

Crisis intervention during severe stress and/or signs of relapse of the disorder

Adapted from Asarnow, Tompson, & McGrath, 2004.

and cognitive-behavioral methods being dominant. Operant intervention was early introduced into hospitals and other institutions, with the underlying aim to help maintain clients as active agents in their own lives and to facilitate their leaving hospitals for less restrictive environments. Now that most individuals with schizophrenia are living in the community for long periods of time, the behavioral approach is applied in many different settings.

A comprehensive approach and a supportive environment are needed in treating later-onset schizophrenia. Meta-analysis indicates that the combination of pharmacological and psychosocial treatments is more effective than only medications (Mojtabai, Nicholson, & Carpenter, 1998). Although outcome data are limited for children and adolescents, we know that the hardship of schizophrenia for the young person stems from both the disturbing symptoms and the disruption of normal development (McClellan, Werry et al., 2001). Treatment thus must consider the reduction of specific symptoms and also the facilitation of psychological, educational, and social development. Medication, family therapy, individual therapy, the teaching of specific academic or developmental skills, and occupational considerations—and combinations of these—are important. Treatment components may vary over time, but support is crucial across all phases of the disorder, not just during the acute phase. Because an array of services are usually required, intensive care management and coordination is likely to be beneficial (Asarnow et al., 2004). And as with other aspects of early-onset schizophrenia, the importance of research in advancing knowledge about the effectiveness of intervention can hardly be overstated.

SUMMARY

A BIT OF HISTORY: AUTISM AND SCHIZOPHRENIA

- *Autism, schizophrenia, and similar disorders were historically associated with each other but are now often viewed as independent of each other.*

AUTISTIC DISORDER

- *The primary manifestations of autistic disorder are early-occurring impaired social interaction, impaired communication, and restricted preoccupations and stereotyped behaviors. Associated problems include deficits in perception, intelligence, adaptive behavior, and motor skills.*

- *The prevalence of autism is about 10 persons in 10,000, and rates are much higher when autism-like disorders are included. Prevalence is higher in boys and unrelated to social class.*

- *Parents report variable onset of autistic symptoms, including regression. Symptoms can lessen throughout childhood; adolescence is marked by variable course. Perhaps two-thirds or more individuals with autism do not achieve independent living.*

- *Research on psychological deficits underlying autistic symptoms has emphasized deficits in theory of mind, central coherence, and executive functions. Multiple impairments likely account for autistic symptoms.*

- *Neurobiological research suggests that autism involves impairment in multiple brain areas or networks.*

- *The evidence for an inherited predisposition for autism—and a spectrum of autistic symptoms—is substantial. Associated medical conditions and prenatal/birth complications may play some causal role.*

- *The pervasive developmental disorders and their relationship to each other are receiving substantial study. Autism, Asperger's disorder, and to a lesser extent PDDNOS are often conceptualized as a spectrum of autism.*

- *Comprehensive assessment for autism includes evaluation of intelligence and adaptive behavior. Numerous psychological tools exist for assessing autistic symptoms.*

- *Behavioral and educational interventions are the mainstay of treatment, with medication as an adjunct. Autism falls under the mandates of the Individuals with Disabilities Education Act.*

SCHIZOPHRENIA

- *The hallmarks of schizophrenia are hallucinations, delusions, thought disorder, disorganized behavior, and negative symptoms.*

- *The prevalence of schizophrenia is small in childhood and escalates in adolescence. It may be higher in males during childhood but not later.*

- *The onset of schizophrenia in youth often is insidious, with nonpsychotic symptoms appearing prior to psychotic symptoms. The course of schizophrenia varies, but full recovery is unlikely in most cases.*

- *Neurological abnormalities in schizophrenia are evidenced in several ways. Frontal and temporal-limbic circuits and dopamine are especially implicated, and the disorder likely involves brain connectivity.*

- *Genetic influence, pregnancy/birth variables, and psychosocial factors are causally implicated in schizophrenia. Multifactor vulnerability-stress and neurodevelopmental models are hypothesized. Childhood schizophrenia is hypothesized to be a severe form of adult-onset schizophrenia.*

- *Comprehensive assessment is required for schizophrenia. Identifying psychotic symptoms in childhood can be problematic.*

- *Guidelines for treating schizophrenia in youth are largely based on treatment of later-onset cases. A multimethod approach is recommended, which includes medications and psychosocial treatments.*

KEY TERMS

pervasive developmental disorders (*p. 336*)

autistic disorder (*p. 336*)

joint attention (*p. 337*)

echolalia (*p. 338*)

pronoun reversal (*p. 338*)

splinter skills/savant abilities (*p. 340*)

theory of mind *(p. 342)*

central coherence *(p. 344)*

intersubjectivity *(p. 345)*

Rett's disorder *(p. 348)*

childhood disintegrative disorder *(p. 349)*

Asperger's disorder *(p. 350)*

PDDNOS *(p. 351)*

childhood schizophrenia *(p. 357)*

positive symptoms *(p. 357)*

hallucinations *(p. 357)*

delusions *(p. 357)*

disorganized speech *(p. 357)*

disorganized behavior *(p. 357)*

catatonic behavior *(p. 357)*

negative symptoms *(p. 357)*

loose associations *(p. 359)*

neologisms *(p. 359)*

insidious onset *(p. 360)*

CHAPTER 13

Disorders of Basic Physical Functions

In this chapter and the next we discuss problems of physical functioning and health. Because, in many ways, these problems represent the interface between psychology and pediatrics, the term *pediatric psychology* is often applied to this field of research and practice. For many of the problems discussed, parents first turn to their pediatrician for help (Roberts & Lyman, 1990). For example, difficulties in getting children to sleep, in starting and managing toilet training, and in the feeding of infants and toddlers are among the problems brought to pediatricians (Gross & Drabman, 1990). Many problems discussed here involve issues of physical functioning that require collaboration between psychologists and physicians. The life-threatening starvation of anorexic adolescents and the problem of enlarged colons in encopretic children are two examples.

It is common for children to exhibit some difficulty in acquiring appropriate habits of elimination, sleep, and eating. Both the child's ability to master these relevant tasks and the parents' ability to train the child are important to the immediate well-being of both. Parents may be judged by themselves and others by how they manage these early child-rearing tasks. Also, how these tasks are handled can set the foundation for later difficulties. Problems may occur in the same area (for example, the later eating disorder of anorexia nervosa) or in more general ways (for example, problems with authority figures). Although parents solve many early difficulties themselves, professional assistance is also frequently sought (Schroeder & Gordon, 2002). In this chapter, attention is given to some commonly encountered difficulties that are part of normal development. The principal focus, however, is on problems that are serious enough to make them of clinical concern.

Problems of Elimination

TYPICAL ELIMINATION TRAINING

Toilet training is an important concern for parents of young children (Mesibov, Schroeder, & Wesson, 1977; Schroeder & Gordon, 2002). Parents may view control of elimination as a developmental milestone for the child. Furthermore, entry into day care or another program may depend on achievement of appropriate toileting. For the child, pleasing the parent, a sense of mastery, and the feeling of no longer being a "baby" may all contribute to the importance of achieving toileting control.

The usual sequence of acquisition of control over elimination is nighttime bowel control, daytime bowel control, daytime bladder control, and finally, nighttime bladder control. Although there is considerable variation as to when children are developmentally ready to achieve control over elimination, bowel and daytime bladder training usually are completed between the ages of 18 and 36 months.

Parents differ as to when they feel it is appropriate to begin daytime training. Much of this decision is related to cultural values, attitudes, and real-life pressures on the parent (e.g., day-care requirements, other siblings). An example of how day-to-day considerations probably affect this decision is illustrated by the advent of the disposable diaper. Ready availability of disposable diapers reduced many parents' inclinations toward the desirability of starting training early.

There are probably several factors that contribute to successful training. Being able to determine that the child is developmentally ready to begin training is certainly of importance. Also, correctly judging when the child has to go to the toilet can lead to important early success experiences. Adequate preparation, such as using training pants rather than a diaper, having the child in clothes that are easy to remove, and having a child-size potty seat available are also helpful. Finally, the common practice of providing praise and concrete positive reinforcers (e.g., stickers, raisins) for appropriate toileting behavior, and doing so in a relaxed manner, has been demonstrated to be effective (O'Leary & Wilson, 1987; Schroeder & Gordon, 2002).

ENURESIS

Jay   Enuresis and Its Consequences

Jay, a seven-year-old, had never achieved nighttime continence but had been continent during daytime for several years. He wets his bed an average of four days per week. No other significant behavior problems are present except for mild academic difficulties, and Jay's developmental history is unremarkable except for mild oxygen deprivation at birth and a delay in acquiring speech. Jay's biological father wet the bed until age nine.

Jay's mother and stepfather disagree on how they view his bedwetting. His mother feels he will grow out of it. His stepfather views Jay's bedwetting as laziness and removes privileges following episodes of enuresis. Both parents change the sheets when they are wet and attempt to restrict Jay's fluids prior to bedtime. They see the enuresis as a significant source of distress for the family and the conflict over how to handle it as exacerbating the problem.

Adapted from Ondersma & Walker, 1998, pp. 364–365.

Description and Classification. The term enuresis comes from the Greek word meaning "I make water." It refers to the repeated voiding of urine during the day or night into the bed or clothes when such voiding is not due to a physical disorder (e.g., diabetes, urinary tract infection). A lack of urinary control is not usually diagnosed as enuresis prior to the age of 5 when continence might be expected. Also, a certain frequency of lack of control is required before one would make a diagnosis of enuresis, and this frequency varies with the age of the child. The DSM definition requires either a frequency of twice weekly for at least three consecutive months or wetting that is associated with clinically significant distress or impairment in important areas of functioning (American Psychiatric Association, 2000).

A distinction is often made between the more common nocturnal enuresis (nighttime bedwetting) and diurnal enuresis (daytime wetting). Enuresis is also referred to as primary if the child has never demonstrated bladder control and as secondary when the problem is preceded by a period of urinary continence. About 85 percent of all cases of enuresis are of the primary type (Walker, 2003).

Epidemiology. Estimates of prevalence indicate that among 5-year-olds 7 percent of boys and 3 percent of girls exhibit enuresis and that by 10 years of age the percentages are 3 and 2 percent, respectively. By age 18 prevalence decreases to 1 percent for males and less than 1 percent for females (Walker, 2003).

Etiology. A number of factors have been proposed as causes of enuresis, but no definitive cause has been established. At one time, the view that enuresis was the result of emotional disturbance was widely held (Gerard, 1939). However, evidence does not support the view that enuresis is primarily a psychopathological disorder (Christophersen & Mortweet, 2001). When emotional difficulties are present in a child with enuresis, they most commonly are a consequence of enuresis rather than a cause. Enuretic children, especially as they become older, are very likely to experience difficulties with peers and other family members. It would not be surprising if the child's self-image suffered (Wagner, Smith, & Norris, 1988). Also, enuresis and emotional problems may occur together because similar factors contribute to the development of both. For example, a chaotic home environment may contribute to both inadequate toilet training and behavior problems.

It is frequently suggested that sleep abnormalities contribute to the development of enuresis. Many adults, for example, assume that nocturnal enuresis occurs because the child is an unusually deep sleeper. Indeed, parents often spontaneously report difficulty in arousing their enuretic children during the night. However, research regarding the role of sleep and arousal is inconsistent (Mikkelsen, 2001). Wetting can occur in any of the stages of sleep, not just in deep sleep. This and other evidence raises doubts about viewing all or most cases of enuresis as a disorder of sleep arousal (King & Noshpitz, 1991; Walker 2003). However, in some subgroups of youngsters, enuresis may, at least in part, be due to sleep arousal patterns.

Another biological pathway that has been suggested is a lack of normal nocturnal increases in antidiuretic hormone (ADH), which might lead to a higher production of urine. Among evidence for this hypothesis is the fact that some enuretic children respond well when an antidiuretic medication (desmopressin acetate, a hormone analog) is administered. However, evidence is not consistent and does not support viewing low levels of ADH as the only or the primary cause of enuresis, although it may be a factor in some cases (Mikkelsen, 2001).

Family histories of youngsters with enuresis frequently reveal a number of relatives with the same problem. Higher rates of concordance for enuresis also have been reported among monozygotic than dizygotic twins, and multigenerational studies further support the notion of a significant genetic contribution to the disorder. Several different chromosomes have been implicated, and there may be a number of different modes of genetic transmission (Mikkelsen, 2001).

Overall, information regarding biological influences strongly suggests that at least some portion of enuretic children may have an organic predisposition toward enuresis. This as yet unspecified risk factor(s) may or may not result in the development of enuresis, depending on various experiential factors, such as parental attitude and training procedures.

The central tenet of behavioral theories of enuresis is that wetting results from a failure to learn control over reflexive wetting. Failure can result from either faulty training or other environmental influences that interfere with learning (e.g., a chaotic or stressful home environment). Many behavioral theories incorporate some maturational/physical difficulty, such as bladder capacity or arousal deficit, into their explanation.

Treatment. Prior to beginning any treatment, the child should be evaluated by a physician to rule out any medical cause for the urinary difficulties. If a parent seeks treatment for a very young child, a discussion of developmental norms may be helpful. Finally, if treatment for enuresis is to be initiated, careful preparation and ensuring of parental cooperation are necessary.

A variety of pharmacological agents have been used in the treatment of enuresis. Imipramine hydrochloride (Tofranil), a tricyclic antidepressant, was at one time the most commonly employed. The effectiveness of imipramine seems to rely on the child's continuing to take the medication. Moreover, there is reason for concern regarding possible side effects (Houts, 2003; Walker, 2003). Desmopressin acetate (DDAVP) has become the primary pharmacological treatment for enuresis, in part because it may have less risk of side effects than imipramine. Desmopressin was suggested as a treatment on the basis of its ability to control high urine output during sleep. Research findings suggest that DDAVP may reduce bedwetting even in cases that are difficult to treat. However, as with imipramine, relapse occurs; that is, wetting resumes if the drug is discontinued (Mikkelsen, 2001; Walker, 2003).

Behavioral treatments for nocturnal enuresis have received considerable research attention (Christophersen & Mortweet, 2001; Mellon & McGrath, 2000). The most well-known method is the urine-alarm system. This procedure was originally introduced by the German pediatrician Pflaunder in 1904 and was adapted and systematically applied by Mowrer and Mowrer (1938). Since then, the device and the procedures have been refined by a number of investigators. The basic device consists of an absorbent sheet between two foil pads. When urine is absorbed by the sheet, an electric circuit is completed that activates an alarm that sounds until manually turned off (see Figure 13–1). The parents are instructed to awaken the child when the alarm sounds. The child is taught to turn off the alarm and to go to the bathroom to finish voiding. The bedding

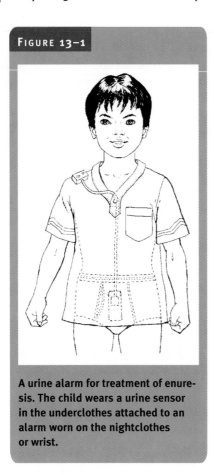

FIGURE 13–1

A urine alarm for treatment of enuresis. The child wears a urine sensor in the underclothes attached to an alarm worn on the nightclothes or wrist.

is then changed, and the child returns to sleep. Usually records of dry and wet nights are kept, and after 14 consecutive nights of dryness, the device is removed.

Research conducted on the urine-alarm system indicates that it is successful in a clear majority of cases and that it is the treatment of choice for enuresis. It is also more cost-effective than medications such as DDAVP (Houts, 2003; Mikkelsen, 2001). Treatment durations range between 5 and 12 weeks. Relapse has been reported in about 40 percent of cases, but reinstituting training often results in a complete cure (Christophersen & Mortweet, 2001).

Modifications of the standard urine-alarm procedures have been introduced to reduce relapses. Full Spectrum Home Training was designed to build on initial treatment success, to reduce relapse, and to decrease the rate at which families dropped out of treatment (Houts, 2003; Houts, Liebert, & Padawar, 1983). The procedure, which is cost-effective, is a treatment manual-guided package that includes urine-alarm; cleanliness training (having the child change his or her bed and night clothes); a procedure to increase bladder capacity, which is known as retention control training; and overlearning, a

process of training children to a higher criterion of successive dry nights than is usually thought to be necessary. The training program is delivered in a single one-hour group session, and the parents and children then contract to complete the training at home with regular calls from the treatment staff as the only additional contact.

A study by Houts, Peterson, and Whelan (1986) illustrated the program's success and examined the contribution of the components to reducing relapse. Participating families received one of three treatment combinations: Group 1 received bell-and-pad plus cleanliness training (BP), Group 2 received these two components plus retention control training (BP-RCT), and Group 3 received these three components plus overlearning (BP-RCT-OL)—the full package. A control group of children was followed over an 8-week period. No spontaneous remission of wetting occurred in control children, and they were then randomly assigned to one of the three treatment conditions. The findings of this study indicate that the three conditions were equally effective in treating enuresis. However, at 3-month follow-up, relapse was significantly less in the BP-RCT-OL group than in the other two groups. These results suggest the importance of overlearning in preventing relapse.

ENCOPRESIS

Susan | Encopresis and Its Consequences

Susan, a six-year-old, has been soiling at least once per day since birth. The frequency of soiling had not decreased despite nearly constant attempts to convince her to use the toilet. Following careful medical examination, Susan's physician was certain that all medical causes for her condition had been ruled out. Tests, however, did reveal a considerable amount of fecal matter in her colon. During the course of the assessment, Susan's mother indicated that both she and her daughter were becoming very frustrated. It was also revealed that Susan was experiencing significant anxiety and pain with toileting. It appeared that Susan had learned to retain feces and to fear toileting following early experiences with large and painful bowel movements. The toileting problems had begun to affect Susan's social functioning and self-esteem.

Adapted from Ondersma & Walker, 1998, pp. 371–372.

Description and Classification. Functional encopresis refers to the passage of feces into the clothing or other unacceptable area when this is not due to physical disorder. The diagnosis is given when this event occurs at least once a month, for at least 3 months, in a child of at least 4 years of age (American Psychiatric Association, 2000). Two subtypes of encopresis are recognized on the basis of the presence or absence of constipation. The vast majority of encopretic children are chronically constipated and are classified as having constipation with overflow incontinence (or retentive encopresis).

Epidemiology. Less writing and research have been done concerning encopresis than concerning enuresis (Christophersen & Mortweet, 2001; Mikkelsen, 2001). Estimates of prevalence range between 1.5 and 7.5 percent of children. Percentages appear to decrease with age, and the condition is very rare by adolescence. The problem occurs more frequently in males (Walker, 2003).

Pediatricians, who are likely to see a broad population of children, argue that the majority of children with encopresis have no associated psychopathology, a position supported by other workers (Christophersen & Mortweet, 2001; King & Noshpitz, 1991). However, because encopresis occurs during the day more often than at night, it is more socially evident than enuresis and also is more likely to carry a social stigma. Consequently, encopresis is likely to be a source of considerable distress to both parents and children, and may therefore be associated with more behavior problems, particularly among referred samples. For example, in the Worcester Encopresis Study (Young et al., 1996), children with encopresis who had been referred to a pediatric gastroenterology clinic were reported to have higher total behavior problem and lower social competence scores than children without toileting problems. Following treatment, these children had fewer behavior problems and improved social skills. To the extent that associated psychological difficulties do exist, they may be a consequence, rather than an antecedent, of encopresis, or both may be related to common environmental factors (e.g., stressful family circumstances).

Etiology. Most theories acknowledge that encopresis may result from a variety of causative mechanisms (McGrath, Mellon, & Murphy, 2000). Initial constipation/soiling may be influenced by factors such as diet, fluid intake, medications, environmental stresses, or inappropriate toilet training. The rectum and colon may become distended by the hard feces. The bowel then becomes incapable of responding with a normal defecation reflex to normal amounts of fecal matter.

Medical perspectives on the problem tend to stress a neurodevelopmental approach (Christophersen & Mortweet, 2001; Mikkelsen, 2001). Encopresis is viewed as more likely to occur in the presence of developmental inadequacies in the structure and functioning of the physiological and anatomical mechanisms required for bowel control. These organic inadequacies are viewed as temporary.

A behavioral perspective on encopresis stresses faulty toilet training procedures. Encopresis may be explained by poor dietary choices and a failure to apply appropriate training methods consistently. Some cases of encopresis may also be accounted for by avoidance conditioning principles. Avoidance of pain or fear reinforces retention. Positive consequences may also maintain soiling, and inadequate reinforcement may be given for appropriate toileting (Doleys, 1989). These various learning explanations are not incompatible with physiological explanations. For example, poor child training may compound insufficient physiological-neurological mechanisms.

Treatment. Most treatments for encopresis combine medical and behavioral management (McGrath et al., 2000; Mikkelsen, 2001). After the parent and the child have been educated about encopresis, the first step usually consists of an initial cleanout phase using enemas or high fiber intake to eliminate fecal impactions. Next, parents are asked to schedule regular toilet times and to use suppositories if defecation does not occur. Modifications in diet, laxatives, and stool softeners are employed to facilitate defecation. Positive consequences, such as a shared activity chosen by the child, are used to reward unassisted (no suppository) bowel movements in the toilet, as well as clean pants. If soiling occurs, children may be instructed to clean themselves and their clothes. Use of laxatives and suppositories is withdrawn. Research suggests that such treatment is highly effective and that relapse rates are low (Christophersen & Mortweet, 2001; Mikkelsen, 2001). In relatively infrequent cases where soiling is being used to manipulate the environment (e.g., being allowed to leave school, getting the mother's time and attention) additional family therapy may be indicated (Walker, 2003).

Sleep Problems

Parents commonly complain of difficulties in getting their young children to go to sleep and to sleep through the night. Nightmares are another concern that parents often report. To understand these problems, as well as more serious sleep disorders, it is necessary to understand the variations in what is normal sleep for children.

SLEEP DEVELOPMENT

At all ages, there is considerable individual variability in what would be considered a normal sleep pattern. Furthermore, patterns of sleep change with development (Horne, 1992; Mindell & Owens, 2003). For example, the average newborn infant sleeps between 16 and 20 hours per day. By the time that children are 1 year old, the average amount of sleep has fallen to 12 hours. The typical 6- to 12-year-old sleeps 10 to 11 hours each day. In addition to the number of hours of sleep, other aspects change as well. For example, newborns distribute their sleeping equally between day and night. Fortunately for parents, by about 3 months of age, the day-night pattern typical in adults is present in infants; and by 18 months, sleep patterns are usually quite stable.

Within sleep periods there are two broad phases: rapid eye movement, or REM, sleep; and nonrapid eye movement, or NREM, sleep. NREM sleep is divided into four stages. Stages 3 to 4, the deepest part of sleep, are characterized by very slow waves in the EEG and are thus sometimes referred to as slow wave sleep (SWS). Throughout the night, the brain cycles through these stages of sleep. The time spent in different stages of sleep varies and changes with development. In the first year of life, for example, active REM sleep changes from about 8 hours to about half this amount, thus also reducing the proportion of time spent in REM relative to other phases of sleep. The sequencing, or patterns in which the various stages of sleep occur, also changes. The phases of sleep are intermixed in irregular patterns in infants. However, as the child develops, regular patterns of light NREM, deep NREM, and REM sleep are gradually established.

COMMON SLEEP PROBLEMS

What, then, are the common complaints regarding children's sleep, and how are disorders of sleep defined? During the first year of life, the parents'

most frequent complaint is that the child does not sleep through the night. A reluctance to go to sleep and nightmares often occur during the second year, and the 3- to 5-year-old presents a variety of problems, including difficulty in going to sleep, nighttime awakenings, and nightmares. Surveys suggest that approximately one-quarter to one-third of infants and younger children experience some form of sleep problem that is disturbing to the family (Goodlin-Jones, Burnham, & Anders, 2000; Mindell, 1993). Some infants' and young children's sleep difficulties may be associated with conditions such as colic, with feeding practices, or with dietary problems such as milk intolerance.

School-age children also experience a variety of sleep problems, including bedtime resistance, delayed sleep onset, and night waking (Blader et al., 1997; Sadeh, Raviv, & Gruber, 2000). Indeed, sleep problems in older children may be underestimated, because older children are less likely to alert their parents to their difficulties (Owens et al., 2000). Even in adolescence, complaints regarding sleep are common, particularly the need for more sleep and difficulty in falling asleep. In fact, whereas many might think of sleep problems as being associated with young children, they are common in adolescents as well. Decreasing amounts of sleep due to later bedtimes combined with earlier school start times are of concern. Insufficient sleep may lead to problems such as poor academic performance and symptoms of depression (Fredriksen et al., 2004; Mindell & Owens, 2003; Morrison, McGee, & Stanton, 1992).

Whether early sleep difficulties continue and/or develop into more serious sleep disorders is probably a function of a complex interplay of individual (e.g., difficult temperament) and environmental (e.g., parental depression) influences (Goodlin-Jones et al., 2000). Indeed, clear discrimination between common sleep difficulties and some sleep disorders is difficult. However, sleep problems that are frequent, persistent, and associated with other problems for the child are considered sleep disorders. Sleep problems that do not cause the child significant distress or do not result in impairment in important areas of functioning would not be considered a diagnosable disorder (American Psychiatric Association, 2000).

SLEEP DISORDERS

There are many types of sleep disorders that are of concern to clinicians working with infants, children, and adolescents (Anders & Eiben, 1997; Streisand & Efron,

2003). The sleep disorders of primary concern are usually classified into two major categories: dyssomnias, or difficulties in initiating and maintaining sleep or of excessive sleepiness; and parasomnias, or disorders of arousal, partial arousal, or sleep-stage transitions (American Sleep Disorders Association, 1997).

Dyssomnias. Problems of getting to sleep and sleeping through the night, if severe and chronic enough, fall into the category of dyssomnias. These sleep and waking problems are indeed common. They frequently are viewed as manifestations of the child's neurophysiological development and therefore are expected eventually to clear up. However, child, parental, and environmental factors do seem to play a role in a substantial number of cases. For example, parent-child interactions may be of importance. Rocking and soothing a young child to assist falling asleep at night may not allow the child to learn to soothe herself or himself and to return to sleep during a normal night waking. A comparison of poor sleepers and good sleepers, between 12 and 36 months of age, revealed some surprising findings (Minde et al., 1993). Mothers' sleep diaries indicated more night wakings for the poor sleepers. However, filmed recordings indicated no differences in the actual number of wakings for the two groups. The poor sleepers were unable or unwilling to go back to sleep and woke their parent. In contrast, good sleepers were able to return to sleep on their own either by looking around and falling asleep or by quieting themselves, for example, by hugging a toy animal or sucking their thumbs. Whatever the cause, these problems may persist over many years, and they can result in considerable distress to the families involved (Stores, 1996).

The presence of dyssomnias may be underestimated. Young children's reports of difficulty in getting to sleep or staying asleep may be mistaken for attention seeking. The child's level of cognitive development is also a factor in identifying sleep difficulties. For children to recognize a sleep problem, they must be able to conceptualize difficulties in initiating and maintaining sleep as such (Wilson & Haynes, 1985). Sleep problems that are not identified by either the child or the parent are sometimes detected when objective recording of sleep is conducted (Sadeh et al., 2000). Dyssomnias may result in impairment in social, educational, or other areas of functioning. Yet there may not be awareness that sleep difficulties are contributing to these problems.

The relationship between sleep disorders and other childhood problems is probably complex. Children's fear or worries may contribute to the development of problems in falling and staying asleep. In older children, sleep problems may be associated with worrisome cognitions—concerns about school or peers, ruminations about past or anticipated experiences, or fears. In addition, adolescents may have difficulty in establishing good sleep habits in the context of changing lifestyles. Another reason that sleep difficulties and other childhood problems may occur together is that they may be manifestations of a common set of etiological mechanisms such as difficult temperament, family discord, or parenting practices.

Parasomnias. Several of the childhood sleep disorders that cause concern for parents fall into the category of parasomnias. These include sleepwalking, sleep terrors, and nightmares.

SLEEPWALKING. An episode of sleepwalking (somnambulism) begins with the child's sitting upright in bed. The eyes are open but appear "unseeing." Usually the child leaves the bed and walks around, but the episode may end before the walking stage is reached. An episode may last for a few seconds or 30 minutes or longer. There is usually no later memory of the episode. It was once believed that the sleepwalking child was exceptionally well coordinated and safe. This belief has proven to be a myth, and physical injury is a danger of the disorder.

Danielle Sleepwalking

Danielle, 11 years old, told her mother that she thought that she was "going crazy." During the past two months there were several occasions when she awoke confused about where she was. Although she had gone to sleep in her own room, she awoke in other locations around the house. When she awoke in her older brother's room she felt concerned and guilty. Her younger sister reported that several times she had seen Danielle walking around the house at night like a "zombie" and not responding when she called her name. Danielle feared that she might have "amnesia" because she had no memory of anything happening during these nights. A medical history and examination revealed no history of seizures or current physical problems. Other than anxiety about her sleep problem and usual age-appropriate concerns, Danielle seemed well adjusted and she was functioning very well in school and with her family.

Adapted from Spitzer et al., 2000, pp. 337–338.

ACCENT

Sleep Apnea

Children may experience disrupted or inadequate sleep for a number of reasons. One of these is obstructive sleep apnea (OSA), a respiratory sleep disorder characterized by repeated brief episodes of upper airway obstruction and resulting multiple transient arousals from sleep. These events result in fragmented and insufficient sleep and daytime fatigue and inattention. Mindell and Owens (2003) provide some basic information about the disorder.

Common nighttime symptoms of sleep apnea include loud snoring, pauses and difficulty in breathing, restless sleep, sweating during sleep, and bedwetting. Episodes may occur primarily during REM sleep in the later part of the night. In addition to fatigue, daytime symptoms may include mouth breathing, chronic nasal congestion or infection, and morning headaches.

Parents may be unaware of the symptoms that occur during sleep or otherwise fail to report them to their pediatricians. Instead, parents often initially complain of difficulties such as behavior problems, hyperactivity, inattentiveness and academic problems. OSA symptoms may only become evident after direct questioning about sleep. Information from interview and physical examination is important, but the only way to reliably diagnose OSA is by a sleep study. The youngster sleeps overnight in a laboratory. EEG and other physiological measurements are taken and the youngster's sleep is observed.

OSA is a common sleep disorder with peaks of prevalence between the ages of 2 and 6 years and in adolescence. In young children enlarged tonsils and adenoids are the most common risk factors. In adults the disorder is most commonly associated with obesity. Increasing prevalence of obesity suggests that this may become more of a relative risk for children and adolescents.

Removal of the tonsils and adenoids is the most common treatment in children, and symptom relief typically follows. Not all youngsters are candidates for such surgery, however. The use of a CPAP (continuous positive airway pressure) device can relieve apnea symptoms, but does not cure the problem. The youngster wears a nasal/face mask during sleep and the device delivers pressure to keep the airways open. For youngsters who are obese, weight loss is recommended.

Approximately 15 percent of children between the ages of 5 and 12 have isolated experiences of walking in their sleep. Sleepwalking disorder, that is, persistent sleepwalking, is estimated to occur in 1 to 6 percent of the population. The problem usually continues for a number of years but then disappears by adolescence (American Psychiatric Association, 2000).

The vast majority of sleepwalking episodes occur in the first 1 to 3 hours following sleep onset. The fact that sleepwalking occurs during the later stages of NREM sleep (deep sleep) appears to invalidate the idea that sleepwalking is the acting out of a dream, because dreams occur in REM sleep. A characteristic EEG pattern has been found to precede each episode of sleepwalking. This EEG pattern exists in 85 percent of all children during the first year of life but is present in only 3 percent of 7- to 9-year-olds. Thus it has been suggested that central nervous system immaturity is of significance in sleepwalking disorder, and knowledge that the disorder is usually outgrown is consistent with that conceptualization.

This view does not, however, rule out psychological or environmental factors. Frequency of sleepwalking has been reported to be influenced by the specific setting, stress, fatigue, and physical illness (American Psychiatric Association, 2000; Mindell & Owens, 2003). Greater concordance rates for sleepwalking among monozygotic twins than among dizygotic twins and family patterns of sleepwalking have also been reported, leading some to propose a genetic component to the disorder. Unlike the case for adults, the presence of sleepwalking in children has not been found to be associated with psychological disturbance (Dollinger, 1986; Stores, 1996).

SLEEP TERRORS AND NIGHTMARES. Both sleep terrors and nightmares are fright reactions that occur during sleep. Sleep terrors, also known as night terrors or pavor nocturnus, are experienced by approximately 3 percent of children. Sleep terrors typically occur between the ages of 4 and 12 and most individuals outgrow the problem by adolescence (Mindell & Owens, 2003). Nightmares and sleep terrors are often

TABLE 13–1	CHARACTERISTICS DIFFERENTIATING NIGHTMARES AND SLEEP TERRORS
NIGHTMARES	**SLEEP TERRORS**
Occur during REM sleep	Occur during NREM sleep
During middle and latter portions of the night	During first third of night
Verbalizations, if any, are subdued	Child wakes with cry or scream, and verbalizations usually present
Only moderate physiological arousal	Intense physiological arousal (increased heart rate, profuse sweating, pupils dilated)
Slight or no movements	Motor activity, agitation
Easy to arouse and responsive to environment	Difficult to arouse and unresponsive to environment
Episodes frequently remembered	Very limited or no memory of the episode
Quite common	Somewhat rare (1 to 6 percent)

Adapted from Wilson & Haynes, 1985.

confused, but they differ in a number of ways (see Table 13–1).

Sleep terrors occur during deep, slow wave sleep and at a fairly constant time, usually about 2 hours into sleep. The event is quite striking in that the still-sleeping child suddenly sits upright in bed and screams. The face shows obvious distress, and there are signs of autonomic arousal, such as rapid breathing and dilated pupils. In addition, repetitive motor movements may occur, and the child appears disoriented and confused. Attempts to comfort the child are largely unsuccessful. The child most often returns to sleep without full awakening and has little or no memory of this event the next morning. The conceptualization of the causes of sleep terrors is similar to that previously described for sleepwalking, and, indeed, they occur in the same part of the sleep cycle.

Nightmares are the other fright reaction that occurs during sleep and are common in children between the ages of 3 and 6 years (Mindell & Owens, 2003; American Sleep Disorders Association, 1997). These dreams occur during REM sleep. Parents may underestimate their children's nighttime fears. The findings illustrated in Figure 13–2 suggest that this may be particularly true for older children (Muris et al., 2001). It is frequently thought that the dreams are a direct manifestation of anxieties that the child faces. It has been suggested that children typically extinguish their fears by gradually exposing themselves during daytime hours to the feared stimulus (Kellerman, 1980). Factors such as parental protectiveness or lack of awareness of their children's fears, however, might limit the child's ability to engage in such daytime exposure or coping. In the absence

of exposure and coping, anxieties and associated nightmares may continue or be exacerbated.

Matthew   Recurrent Nightmares

The recurrent nightmares that 11-year-old Matthew experienced led his parents to seek help. Matthew was doing well in school, was involved in many activities, and had friends. His parents described him as sensitive and serious, but quite happy. A sleep diary indicated that nightmares had occurred on 11 of 14 nights. Matthew went to sleep in his own bed, but after the nightmare slept in his parents' or older brother's bedroom. Although his parents and brother did not mind, Matthew felt it was immature to have to sleep in their rooms. Recently, Matthew was taking longer to fall asleep at night. Matthew complained of being tired during the day and upset about having another nightmare.

The parents indicated that Matthew had experienced occasional night terrors between the ages of 4 and 6. These had begun at the time of his maternal grandfather's death and after a difficult bout with the flu and high fever. During his preschool years Matthew had at least one nightmare a week, but since then only occasional nightmares until the past month. There were no health or other problems in the family except that the paternal grandfather had experienced a heart attack 2 months earlier, but he was home and recovering.

Matthew described his life as enjoyable and stimulating, but reported a number of situations that made him very sad or angry. Several bullies

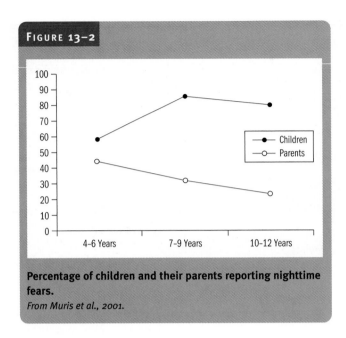

FIGURE 13–2

Percentage of children and their parents reporting nighttime fears.
From Muris et al., 2001.

on the school bus repeatedly teased and pushed younger children including his younger brother. Matthew was also having difficulty completing a particular Scout badge and he described his older brother as being particularly irritating to the entire family.

The parents and Matthew were reassured and told that he was a child with many strengths and also sensitivity to injustices and others being hurt. It was suggested that his nightmares were related to these stresses at home and at school. A brief intervention was recommended. The treatment consisted of Matthew discussing the content of his nightmares with his parents and keeping a diary of the content. Matthew was also taught relaxation techniques. The clinician and Matthew reviewed the content of the nightmares and role played responses that resulted in a victory over the scary events. There was also a focus on the events that were creating stress. Matthew and the clinician took a problem-solving approach to the bullies on the bus and the parents had the school principal investigate and intervene in the bullying incidents. The family discussed sibling squabbles and the older brother was encouraged to spend more time with his own friends.

Matthew's nightmares decreased over the next month. This coincided with Matthew's having greater control over daily events and the resolution of the bullying problem. Matthew realized that he might have occasional nightmares and that if they became recurrent he would identify and cope with stressors in his environment.

Adapted from Schroeder & Gordon, 2002, pp. 214–216.

No single theoretical framework has proven successful in explaining the development of nightmares, and explanations allowing for multiple causes (e.g., developmental, physiological, and environmental factors) are most likely to have the greatest utility.

TREATING SLEEP PROBLEMS

Initiating and Maintaining Sleep. A number of different interventions have been demonstrated to be effective in dealing with the problems of bedtime refusal, difficulty in falling asleep, and nighttime wakings (Christophersen & Mortweet, 2001; Mindell, 1999).

Extinction (ignoring) procedures are based on the assumption that attention to nighttime fussing maintains children's sleep problems. Thus parents are taught to put the child to bed at a designated time and then to ignore the child until a set time the next morning. Some parents find it very stressful to ignore long periods of bedtime crying. A variant of the extinction procedure, graduated extinction, has been found to be successful. First, parents ignore bedtime crying for an agreed-upon time for which they feel comfortable, and then over several nights,

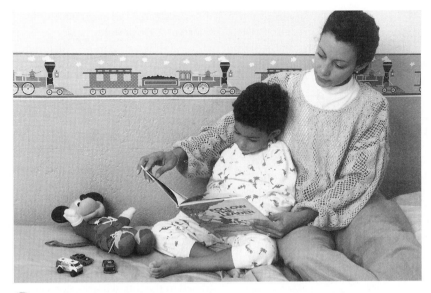

Establishing a predictable bedtime routine is helpful in reducing children's sleep problems.
(Laura Dwight/Laura Dwight Photography)

the period is increased before they check on the child.

Establishing positive bedtime routines also appears to be a promising intervention. Parents are taught to develop a consistent bedtime routine at a regularly scheduled bedtime. The routine involves calm activities that the child enjoys. Another successful procedure, scheduled awakenings, involves having the parent awake and console the child approximately 15 minutes before typical spontaneous awakening. These scheduled awakenings are gradually faded out.

Finally, there is research to support the value of parent education in preventing the development of these kinds of sleep problems. Parents of infants are provided information about infant sleep, the importance of routine, and the importance of putting the infant into the crib while partially awake so that the child can learn to go to sleep without an adult's being present.

Pharmacological agents have been among the most widely used treatments. However, good support for their effectiveness is lacking, and there is concern regarding negative side effects and recurrences of sleep disturbances with discontinuation of treatment. Given such concerns, behavioral interventions are usually recommended for most problems prior to the use of pharmacological treatments (e.g., Anders & Eiben, 1997; Mindell & Owens, 2003).

Parasomnias. In many cases of sleep terrors and sleepwalking, intensive treatment may not be indicated, because the episodes usually disappear spontaneously. Education and support may be sufficient. However, a number of treatments have been suggested. These include scheduled awakenings, contingency management, instructional procedures, and anxiety-reduction procedures (Christophersen & Mortweet, 2001). Durand and Mindell (1999) used a multiple baseline design to evaluate the effectiveness of scheduled awakenings for three boys, each with a several-year history of sleep terrors. During the baseline period, data on the occurrence of sleep terrors were recorded. During the intervention phase, parents were provided with an explanation of the procedures. They were instructed to awaken their son approximately 30 minutes prior to the typical sleep-terror time by lightly touching him until the child opened his eyes, and then to allow him to fall back to sleep. The scheduled awakening intervention quickly reduced the frequency of sleep terrors, and success was maintained at a 12-month follow-up.

Pharmacological treatments of sleep terror and sleepwalking have also been reported; however, the medications may actually produce effects that set the stage for recurrences of these disorders, and side effects are a concern (Shaffer & Waslick, 1996).

Consistent with anxiety's being viewed as the basis for nightmares, the majority of treatments for nightmares have involved anxiety-reduction techniques. However, no treatment strategy can be stated as most effective, nor are the active components of the various treatments known.

Problems of Feeding, Eating, and Nutrition

Establishing eating habits and food preferences is one of the primary aspects of early socialization. Mealtimes are often an occasion for family interactions and rituals, and other social interactions frequently revolve around food and eating. These and other considerations suggest the importance of food and eating-related behaviors.

COMMON EATING AND FEEDING PROBLEMS

A wide range of problems having to do with eating and feeding are commonly reported in young children (Budd & Chugh, 1998). These include undereating, finicky eating, overeating, problems in chewing and swallowing, bizarre eating habits, annoying mealtime behaviors, and delays in self-feeding. Many of these problems can cause considerable concern for parents and appreciable disruption of family life. For example, Crist and Nappier-Phillips (2001) indicate that over 50 percent of parents report one problem feeding behavior and more than 20 percent report multiple problems. Also, O'Brien (1996) found that approximately 30 percent of a sample of parents of infants and toddlers reported that their children refuse to eat the foods presented to them. Adequate nutrition and growth are clearly a concern, but restricted eating is also often accompanied by behavioral problems such as tantrums, spitting, and gagging. Severe cases of food refusal may be associated with even more difficult social and psychological problems, and may result in medical complaints and malnourishment. Indeed, some cases of failure to thrive (life-threatening weight loss or failure to gain weight) can be conceptualized as a special case of such refusal (Kelly & Heffer, 1990; Kerwin & Berkowitz, 1996). Thus some feeding and eating problems may actually endanger the physical health of the child. The disorders discussed in the following sections are some that appear in the DSM and have attracted attention from researchers and clinicians.

EARLY FEEDING AND EATING DISORDERS

Rumination Disorder. First described in 1687, rumination (or mercyism) is a syndrome with a long history (Kanner, 1972). It is characterized by the voluntary and repeated regurgitation of food or liquid in the absence of an organic cause. When infants ruminate, they appear deliberately to initiate

Young children often exhibit feeding and eating problems. This difficulty may result in disruption and cause their parents considerable distress. *(SuperStock. Inc.)*

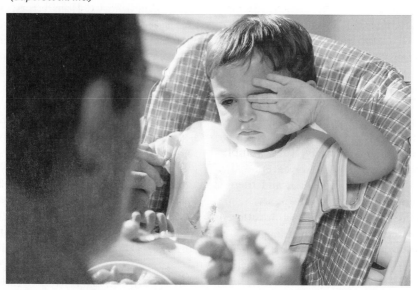

regurgitation. The child's head is thrown back, and chewing and swallowing movements are made until food is brought up. In many instances, the child initiates rumination by placing his or her fingers down the throat or by chewing on objects. The child exhibits little distress; rather, pleasure appears to result from the activity. If rumination continues, serious medical complications can result, with death being the outcome in extreme cases (American Psychiatric Association, 2000).

Rumination is most often observed in two groups, in infants and in persons with developmental disabilities. Among children who are developmentally normal, rumination usually appears during the first year of life. In individuals with mental retardation, later onset is often observed, and the incidence of the disorder seems to increase with greater degrees of mental retardation. In both groups, rumination appears to be more prevalent in males (Kerwin & Berkowitz, 1996; Mayes, 1992).

ETIOLOGY AND TREATMENT. Rumination in infants is often attributed to a disturbance in the mother-infant relationship (Mayes, 1992). The mother is described either as having psychological difficulties that prevent her from providing the infant with a nurturant relationship or as experiencing significant life stress that interferes with her ability to attend to the infant. Rumination is sometimes seen as the infant's attempt to provide this missing stimulation. Alternatively, others view the act as habitual in nature. The pattern may start, for example, with the normal occurrence of spitting up by the infant. The behaviors may then be reinforced by a combination of pleasurable self-stimulation and the increased attention from adults that follows (e.g., Kanner, 1972; Linscheid & Rasnake, 2001). It is possible to integrate these explanations by hypothesizing that the learning of rumination may be more likely in circumstances in which the mother does not provide adequate stimulation and attention. Rumination among individuals diagnosed with mental retardation is commonly viewed as a learned habit.

Management of the problem will probably involve a multidisciplinary team. Treatments emphasizing use of social attention contingent on appropriate behavior have been successful, and there is some suggestion that with infant ruminators, improving mothers' ability to provide a nurturing and responsive environment is effective (Mayes, 1992; Nicholls, 2004). These procedures have the advantage of being easily implemented by the parents in the home and of being acceptable to them.

However, controlled evaluations of interventions are needed.

Pica. *Pica* is the Latin term for magpie, a bird known for the diversity of objects that it eats. Pica is characterized by the habitual eating of substances usually considered inedible, such as paint, dirt, paper, fabric, hair, and bugs.

During the first year of life, most infants put a variety of objects into their mouths, partly as a way of exploring the environment. Within the next year, they typically learn to explore in other ways and come to discriminate between edible and inedible materials. The diagnosis of pica is therefore usually made when there is a persistent eating of inedibles beyond this age, and pica is most common in 2- and 3-year-olds.

Information regarding prevalence is limited, but pica is reported to be particularly high among individuals with developmental disabilities (American Psychiatric Association, 2000; McAlpine & Singh, 1986; Nicholls, 2004). Pica can lead to a variety of damage, including parasitic infection and intestinal obstruction due to the accumulation of hair and other materials. The disorder also appears to be related to accidental poisoning (American Psychiatric Association, 2000; Halmi, 1985).

ETIOLOGY AND TREATMENT. A number of causes for pica have been postulated (Kerwin & Berkowitz, 1996). Because youngsters have been observed eating strange substances when food is unavailable, it has been proposed that pica is an attempt to satisfy nutritional deficits. Parental inattention, lack of supervision, and lack of adequate stimulation have also been proposed. Cultural influences such as superstitions regarding eating certain substances should also be considered (Millican & Lourie, 1970; Paniagua, 2000).

Educational approaches aimed at informing parents of the dangers of pica and at encouraging them to deter the behavior may be somewhat successful. However, there is the need to supplement such interventions with more intensive therapeutic endeavors in some cases. Behavioral interventions that address antecedents and consequences of pica behavior have been suggested (Bell & Stein, 1992; Linscheid & Rasnake, 2001). Interventions vary from less intrusive procedures, such as reinforcement of behaviors incompatible with pica, to more intrusive aversive procedures, such as contingent squirts of water to the child's face and restraining the child. These procedures are often combined with reinforcement for appropriate behavior and increased attention to the child. In general, less intrusive procedures should be attempted prior to employing more aversive interventions.

Feeding Disorder of Infancy or Early Childhood.

The essential feature of this disorder is a persistent failure to eat adequately that results in the child's failing to gain weight or experiencing a significant weight loss. The DSM criteria for Feeding Disorder of Infancy or Early Childhood requires that this problem must be present for at least one month and not be due to a gastrointestinal or other medical condition, to other disorders (e.g., rumination disorder), or to the lack of available food (American Psychiatric Association, 2000). The problem is often discussed as one aspect of "failure to thrive," and conceptualization of these feeding problems and their treatment often are discussed as part of this larger construct.

Approximately 1 to 5 percent of pediatric hospital admissions are due to failure to thrive, and about one-half of these may be due to feeding disturbances. The prevalence of failure to thrive based on community samples is estimated at about 3 percent. Feeding disorder of infancy and early childhood appears to be equally common in males and females (American Psychiatric Association, 2000).

That an infant or a young child would cease to eat adequately is puzzling and clearly troublesome. This problem and associated malnutrition can result in disruption in multiple areas of physical, cognitive, and social-emotional development at this critical time. The young child may be irritable and difficult to console or may appear apathetic and withdrawn—characteristics that may further contribute to feeding difficulties.

Multiple causes most likely contribute to the development of feeding disorders (Benoit, 2000). The particular influences that contribute are difficult to determine, in part because it is difficult to observe the child and family prior to the development of the problem. Drotar and Robinson's (2000) review and discussion of failure to thrive suggests that one might conceptualize the development of a feeding disorder in terms of the parent's competence—defined as sensitivity to the child's developing repertoire and as communication and involvement with the child. In this conceptualization, the parent's competence is viewed as being influenced by three sets of factors.

The first set is the parent's personal resources. Identification with the parental role, learning of effective parenting skills, and attachment and relationships with their children may be disrupted in these parents. This problem may, in part, be due to traumatic experiences in their own childhood that resulted in disruptions in the development of these parenting processes. Parental psychopathology, particularly depression, may also contribute to diminished parental resources.

The second set of factors is characteristics of the infant or child that may contribute to the problem by increasing the complexity of child-rearing for parents with limited personal resources. Thus factors such as low birthweight, acute physical illnesses, various disabilities, and temperamental characteristics may contribute to the development of a problem.

Finally, the family's social context is likely to interact with personal parental resources and child characteristics to affect parenting competence. Poverty or economic stress, serious parental or family conflict, the family's social networks and resources, and availability of community resources are among the contextual factors that may be implicated.

The focus of intervention has been on treating the physical/nutritional symptoms so as to improve growth and developmental outcome. Multidisciplinary treatments that include medical, nutritional, educational, and psychological components are typical, but controlled studies indicate mixed and often disappointing outcomes (Benoit, 2000).

OBESITY

Obesity is typically defined in terms of body mass index (BMI, weight in kilograms divided by square of height in meters). While there are various criteria, a BMI at or above a certain percentile (85th or 95th) for age and gender is often employed to define overweight and obesity, respectively.

Obesity is an important health problem and is among the most prevalent nutritional diseases in children and adolescents. Prevalence increases with age (Aristimuno et al., 1984; Garn & Clark, 1976; Huse et al., 1982), and with age there is also an increase in the percentage of obese children who will become obese adults (Garn et al., 1986; Rolland-Cachera et al., 1987). What is perhaps most striking are reports that indicate increasing rates of childhood obesity. Data from the National Health and Nutrition Examination Survey (NHANES) illustrate this problem (Figure 13–3). Findings such as these have lead the U.S. Surgeon General and the American Academy of Pediatrics to call for a plan to reduce obesity (American Academy of Pediatrics, 2003).

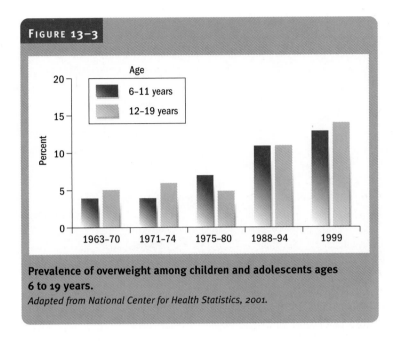

FIGURE 13–3

Prevalence of overweight among children and adolescents ages 6 to 19 years.

Adapted from National Center for Health Statistics, 2001.

Obesity in childhood is associated with numerous physical health problems, including those related to the risk of diabetes and heart disease (Aristimuno et al., 1984; Cooperberg & Faith, 2004). In addition, there are associations with social and psychological difficulties (Gortmaker et al., 1993; Pierce & Wardle, 1993; Zametkin et al., 2004). For example, in a study by Israel and Shapiro (1985), the behavior problem scores of children who were enrolled in a weight-loss program were significantly higher than the norms for the general population, but significantly lower than the norms for children referred to clinics for psychological services. These findings are illustrated in Figure 13–4. Clearly, it cannot be determined from

ACCENT

Obesity Epidemic? Certain Ethnic Groups at Particular Risk

Increases in the prevalence of childhood obesity have been noted for some time. Dietz (1988), comparing national health survey data over a 15-year period beginning in the mid-1960s, found that rates of obesity increased 54 percent among 6- to 11-year-old children and 39 percent among 12- to 17-year-old adolescents during this period. Several reports suggest that this trend has continued (Robinson & Killen, 2001). In 1999, approximately 13 percent of children ages 6 to 11 years and 14 percent of adolescents ages 12 to 19 were overweight (National Center for Health Statistics, 2001). Strauss and Pollack (2001), based on a nationally representative sample of children 4 to 12 years of age, found that between 1986 and 1998 the percentage of overweight youngsters increased steadily.

Although the prevalence of obesity is high for all children and adolescents, it is particularly high among certain ethnic groups including African American, American Indian, and Latino youth (Ruiz, Pepper, & Wilfley, 2004). For example, Strauss and Pollack (2001) report that in 1998 overweight prevalence was 21.5 percent for African American children, 21.8 percent for Hispanic youngsters, and 12.3 percent for non-Hispanic whites. This finding represents increases of more than 120 percent for African American and Hispanic children, and more than 50 percent for non-Hispanic white children. These racial and ethnic disparities remained statistically significant after controlling for income and other possible confounding variables.

There is widespread concern regarding the rates of obesity among children and adolescents. Prevalence is particularly high among certain ethnic groups.
(David Young-Wolff/PhotoEdit, Inc.)

this study whether these problems contribute to or result from being overweight.

The obese child's social interactions may be adversely affected by negative evaluations (Bell & Morgan, 2000; Tiggermann & Anesbury, 2000). Because children hold negative views of obesity, children who are perceived as overweight are ranked as less liked. Children as young as 6 described obese children as "lazy," "stupid," "cheats." Furthermore, the reduction of activity and dexterity that often accompanies obesity makes social isolation and rejection even more likely. These effects appear to continue

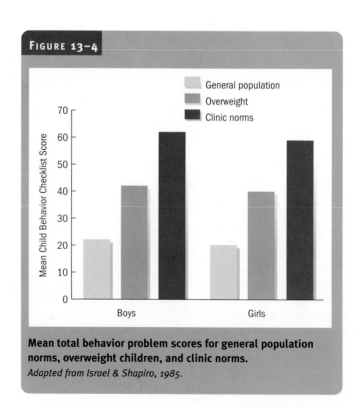

FIGURE 13-4

Mean total behavior problem scores for general population norms, overweight children, and clinic norms.
Adapted from Israel & Shapiro, 1985.

throughout development. College acceptance rates are lower for obese adolescent girls than for nonobese girls with comparable academic credentials (Dietz, 1995; Stunkard & Sobal, 1995). The obese youngster's self-esteem may be adversely affected by such experiences. However, many obese youngsters do not have adjustment difficulties and they may maintain their general self-esteem despite reactions to their physical appearance (Israel & Ivanova, 2002).

Etiology. The causes of obesity are certainly multiple and complex. Any explanation must include biological, psychological, and social/cultural influences (Cope, Fernández, & Allison, 2004; Henderson & Brownell, 2004; Jelalian & Mehlenbeck, 2003).

Biological influences include genetic factors and the metabolic effects of dieting and exercise (Price, 1995; Saris, 1995). Leptin deficiency in severely obese children is an example of a potential mechanism (Cope et al., 2004; Montague et al., 1997). Leptin is a protein that is believed to be involved in signaling the brain to end eating; a gene identified in mice appears to control the production of leptin. Genetic contributions are likely to be complex rather than simple. Of course, biological influences are not independent of environmental influences; rather, these influences interact. So for example, leptin levels can be affected by eating styles associated with obesity (Laessle, Wurmser, & Pirke, 2000).

Psychosocial factors are also important in the development of obesity. Both logic and research suggest that the food intake and activity level of obese children are in need of change (Klesges & Hanson, 1988; Schlicker, Borra, & Regan, 1994). Problematic food intake and inactivity are presumed to be affected by environmental influences and to be learned in the same manner as any other behavior (Laessle, Uhl, & Lindel, 2001). Children, for example, observe and imitate the eating behavior of their parents and others around them, and are reinforced for engaging in that style of eating (Klesges & Hanson, 1988). Eating and inactivity may also become strongly associated with physical and social stimuli, so that they become almost automatic in some circumstances. Moreover, people may learn to use food to overcome stress and negative mood states, such as boredom and anxiety. The treatment of obesity that has been developed from a social learning perspective seeks to break these learned patterns and to develop more adaptive ones.

Larger cultural influences are also germane. Television provides a striking example of how the larger society might contribute to the development of weight problems in children. American children have easy access to high-caloric foods, watch a great deal of television, frequently play video games, and in general lead a sedentary lifestyle (Jelalian & Mehlenbeck, 2004; Robinson & Killen, 2001). In addition to the negative effects of inactivity associated with television watching, children's diets are probably adversely influenced by the contents of advertising. Indeed, the probability of being overweight is associated with the amount of television viewing, and reduction in viewing may lead to decreases in degree of obesity (Gordon-Larsen, Adair, & Popkin, 2002; Robinson, 1999).

Sean   **Obesity and Family Environment**

Sean, a ten-year-old who was 50 percent overweight for his height and age, enrolled in a treatment program for obese children and their families. Sean's pediatrician described a history of steady, greater than expected weight gains with extreme increases in the last three years. Sean's father was normal weight, but his mother was about 40 percent overweight and had made numerous unsuccessful weight-loss attempts. Neither of Sean's two siblings was overweight. Sean snacked frequently on large amounts of high-calorie food, with most of his calories consumed after school while his parents were at work. His mother often found candy wrappers in Sean's room and clothes' pockets. Sean's parents reported that as Sean gained weight, his physical activity had decreased and most of his leisure time was spent watching television. They were concerned with his frequent shortness of breath. Sean had no close friends and was something of a loner. He was teased about his weight at school and by his siblings. Although the parents indicated that they were committed to Sean's losing weight, there were indications of some family "sabotage." Much of the family's activities revolved around food, and food was used as a reward. Sean's father described himself as a gourmet cook, and his high-calorie, high-fat meals were "family times." Sean spent considerable time at his grandmother's, who took pleasure in providing him with food and snacks.

Adapted from Israel & Solotar, 1988.

Behavioral Treatment. Multifaceted programs that emphasize behavioral interventions and education are the most effective treatments for childhood obesity (Cooperberg & Faith, 2004; Jelalian & Saelens, 1999). The work of Israel and his colleagues (Israel et al., 1994; Israel & Solotar, 1988) illustrates the general approach. Children and parents attend meetings during which the following four areas are regularly addressed: *intake*, which includes nutritional information, caloric restriction, and changes in actual eating and food preparation behaviors; *activity*, which includes both specific exercise programs and increasing the energy expended in daily activities, for example, walking to a friend's house rather than being driven; *cues*, which identify the external and internal stimuli associated with excessive eating or inactivity; and *rewards*, which provide positive consequences for progress by both the child and the parent. Homework assignments are employed to encourage the families to change their environments and to practice more appropriate behavior.

Research supports the effectiveness of the behavioral approach to children's weight reduction (Cooperberg & Faith, 2004; Epstein et al., 1995; Israel, 1990; Israel & Zimand, 1989). However, there is still a need for improved interventions that produce greater, more consistent, and more long-lasting weight loss and for attention to issues of setting appropriate treatment goals (Faith et al., 2001; Israel, 1999). In developing improved interventions, the importance of certain treatment components, including parental involvement, has been emphasized. Israel, Stolmaker, and Andrian (1985), for example, provided parents with a brief course in the general principles of child management. The parents then participated with their children in a behavioral weight-reduction program during which the application of the general parenting skills to weight reduction was emphasized. Another group of parents and children received only the behavioral weight-reduction program. At the end of treatment, both groups achieved a significantly greater weight loss than the control children who were not receiving treatment. One year following treatment, children whose parents had received separate child-management training had maintained their weight losses better than other treated children.

These results and others suggest the importance of changing family lifestyles and of providing parents with the skills necessary to maintain appropriate behavior once the treatment program has ended (Israel, 1988). This is a particularly important issue in light of repeated evidence that individuals frequently regain the weight they have lost. In addition to parental involvement, the importance of increased activity, particularly when it is part of the family's lifestyle, and various other family factors have been shown to be related to treatment outcome (Foreyt & Goodrick, 1993; Israel, Silverman, & Solotar, 1986).

"Tracy could be a good little poet someday if she'd lose some weight."

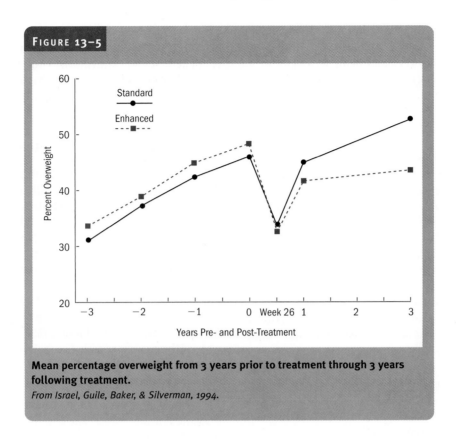

FIGURE 13–5

Mean percentage overweight from 3 years prior to treatment through 3 years following treatment.

From Israel, Guile, Baker, & Silverman, 1994.

Parallel to the need to improve parental involvement, the value of enhancing the child's self-regulatory skills has also been suggested (Israel et al., 1994). Children receiving a multidimensional treatment program, comparable to the four-area program described before, were compared with children receiving a similar intervention plus enhanced training in comprehensive self-management skills. The results of this study are presented in Figure 13–5. In the 3 years prior to treatment, children in the two conditions had shown similar patterns of increasing percentage of overweight. Both treatment conditions resulted in comparable reductions in the percentage of overweight during treatment. However, whereas children in the standard condition appeared to return to pretreatment trends in the 3 years following intervention, children in the enhanced self-regulation condition did not.

Although treatment findings are encouraging, broader interventions and prevention efforts are also needed (Campbell et al., 2004). Programs targeting the general population, or high-risk groups in particular, need to be part of the effort to deal with this common problem. These programs seek, through the media and schools, to educate youngsters and their families and to actively change nutritional and activity lifestyles.

Eating Disorders: Anorexia and Bulimia Nervosa

Anorexia nervosa and bulimia nervosa are eating disorders that involve maladaptive attempts to control body weight, significant disturbances in eating behavior, and abnormal attitudes about body shape and weight. Not very long ago these disorders were considered quite rare. The number of cases reported, as well as "subclinical" levels of these problems, has increased (Lucas & Holub, 1995; Phelps et al., 1993; Thompson & Smolak, 2001). This increase may be due to actual increases in eating disorders and/or to greater awareness and reporting of these problems. Revelations of anorexic and bulimic behavior among celebrities also has increased popular interest.

DEFINITION AND CLASSIFICATION: AN OVERVIEW

There has been considerable debate regarding the best way to define eating disorders and the degree to which disorders overlap. When distinctions between eating disorders are considered or when attempts to subcategorize a particular disorder are made, several dimensions are usually considered. An individual's weight status is one such consideration. A person with an eating disorder may be underweight, within the normal weight range, or overweight.

A second consideration is whether the individual engages in binge eating. A binge is defined by the DSM as (1) eating a larger amount of food during a discrete period of time (e.g., one hour) than most people would be expected to eat during that time and (2) feeling a lack of control of eating during this episode. However, there is some question as to whether the individual must consume a large amount of food in order for an episode to be considered a binge (Anderson & Paulosky, 2004). Some suggest that it is the feeling of loss of control and violation of dietary standards that is the central characteristic of a binge.

A third consideration is the method that the person uses to control her or his weight. A distinction is often made between restricting and purging strategies. The first strategy refers to a person's severely restricting food intake and/or engaging in highly vigorous exercise. The second strategy involves purging oneself of unwanted calories through methods such as vomiting or the misuse of laxatives, diuretics, or enemas.

Weight status, the presence or absence of binge eating, and the method employed to control one's weight therefore are important considerations in thinking about eating disorders. We turn now to how these dimensions are involved in describing eating disorders.

CLASSIFICATION AND DESCRIPTION: DSM APPROACH

The DSM describes two primary eating disorder diagnoses: Anorexia Nervosa and Bulimia Nervosa. The DSM also includes a category of Eating Disorder Not Otherwise Specified (EDNOS). This diagnosis may be applied to eating disorders that would not meet the criteria for either anorexia nervosa or bulimia nervosa. One such disorder is Binge-Eating Disorder (BED). BED is characterized by recurrent binge eating; however, the individual does not engage in the inappropriate weight-control behaviors that are part of bulimia nervosa (described below). The DSM considers BED as requiring further study prior to making it a separate diagnosis.

Anorexia Nervosa. Individuals with eating disorders whose body weight is well below expected levels (15 percent below or more) are likely to be given the diagnosis of anorexia nervosa (AN). A drive for extreme thinness and a fear of gaining weight are characteristics of individuals with this diagnosis. The seriousness of extreme weight loss is illustrated by Bruch's (1979) classic description of one of her clients.

Alma	**Like a Walking Skeleton**

. . . she (Alma) looked like a walking skeleton, with her legs sticking out like broomsticks, every rib showing, and her shoulder blades standing up like little wings. Her mother mentioned, "When I put my arms around her I feel nothing but bones, like a frightened little bird." Alma's arms and legs were covered with soft hair, her complexion had a yellowish tint, and her dry hair hung down in strings. Most striking was the face—hollow like that of a shriveled-up old woman with a wasting disease, . . . Alma insisted that she looked fine and that there was nothing wrong with her being so skinny. "I enjoy having this disease and I want it." (pp. 2–3)

The DSM criteria employed to diagnose AN are presented in Table 13–2. The criterion of less than 85 percent of expected weight can be the result of the youngster's refusal to gain weight or if the youngster is still growing, the failure to gain enough weight to meet the 85 percent criterion. Some definitions have stressed that psychological variables, such as a sense of personal inadequacy, are also central to defining the disorder (Bruch, 1973; 1986; Yates, 1989).

The DSM distinguishes between two subtypes of AN. This distinction is based on whether or not the person binges:

- *Binge-eating/purging anorexics* exhibit a persistent pattern of binge eating and purging.

TABLE 13–2	CRITERIA USED BY THE DSM TO DIAGNOSE ANOREXIA NERVOSA

1. Body weight less than 85 percent of expected weight
2. Intense fear of gaining weight
3. Disturbance in perception of body weight and shape or denial of seriousness of low body weight
4. Absence of three consecutive menstrual cycles in postmenarcheal females

From American Psychiatric Association, 2000.

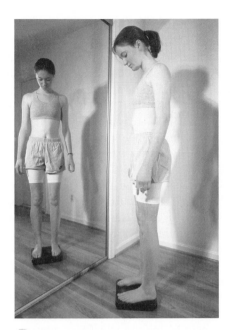

Extreme concern with weight and body shape has become common among girls and young women.
(Richard T. Nowitz/Photo Researchers, Inc.)

TABLE 13–3	CRITERIA USED BY THE DSM TO DIAGNOSE BULIMIA NERVOSA

1. Recurrent episodes of binge-eating
2. Recurrent inappropriate compensatory behavior to prevent weight gain
3. Occurrence of items 1 and 2 at least twice a week for 3 months
4. Self-evaluation unduly influenced by body shape and weight

From American Psychiatric Association, 2000.

- *Restricting anorexics*, on the other hand, achieve their weight loss by fasting and/or excessive exercise and do not binge eat.

Bulimia nervosa. In contrast to anorexia nervosa, individuals with eating disorders whose body weight is not below expected levels are likely to be given the diagnosis of bulimia nervosa (BN). In general, BN is characterized by recurrent binge eating. A persistent overconcern with body shape and weight is also exhibited. Such overconcern means, of course, that the bulimic individual needs to employ some method of compensating for binge eating. The most frequently cited method is purging by vomiting or the use of laxatives.

The DSM criteria used to diagnose BN are presented in Table 13–3. To receive this diagnosis, the symptoms must not occur exclusively during episodes of anorexia nervosa—that is, a person who displays the symptoms as part of anorexia nervosa would not receive both diagnoses.

The issue of subtyping has also arisen in diagnosing BN. The principal consideration is whether purging is employed to compensate for binge eating. Thus there are two subtypes of BN in the DSM:

- The *purging type* is one in which the person regularly induces vomiting or misuses laxatives, diuretics, or enemas.

- The *nonpurging type* is one in which the person fasts and/or exercises excessively but does not regularly purge.

EPIDEMIOLOGY

Prevalence estimates for eating disorders are largely based on samples that combine adolescents and young adults. These disorders occur predominantly in young women. The rate of occurrence in males is about one-tenth of that in females (American Psychiatric Association, 2000; Thompson & Smolak, 2001). Thus, females represent over 90 percent of all cases. AN is reported to occur in about 0.5 percent of females. BN is more commonly diagnosed, occurring in 1 to 3 percent of females (American Psychiatric Association, 2000). Lewinsohn and colleagues (1993a) reported a lifetime prevalence rate for bulimia of approximately 1 to 1.5 percent in a random sample of high school females, and this finding seems consistent with other estimates of prevalence in the general population of adolescent females (Wilson, Becker, & Heffernan, 2003).

These numbers may actually underestimate the prevalence of eating disorders, because individuals with these disorders may be overrepresented among those who do not cooperate with prevalence studies (Wilson et al., 2003). Perhaps of more importance, the stated prevalence rates are based on individuals' meeting full diagnostic criteria for AN or BN. But many other individuals exhibit various aspects of disordered eating and disturbances of body image. Of these individuals, many may meet the criteria for an Eating Disorder Not Otherwise Specified, and this diagnosis may be more common than AN or BN in youngsters (Steiner & Lock, 1998). These cases are also sometimes described as a "partial syndrome" or as "subclinical." They may be of concern, given the widely held view that eating disorders are the extreme of a continuum that begins with more "normative" weight concern, body dissatisfaction, and dieting (Shisslak, Crago, & Estes, 1995). In fact, youngsters with a partial syndrome may experience substantial social and educational impairment. And adolescents who do not fully meet diagnostic criteria may in many ways resemble those who do and appear to be at considerable risk for the development of other disorders, especially depression (le Grange et al., 2004; Lewinsohn, Striegel-Moore, & Seeley, 2000; Patton et al., 1997).

Of particular interest is the finding that subclinical concerns with weight and shape and unusual eating behaviors are increasingly common among younger adolescents and even preadolescent girls. Thus although eating disorders that meet full diagnostic criteria typically occur in late adolescence, disordered eating behaviors and attitudes are appearing in younger children (Thompson & Smolak, 2001). These problems may be precursors of more serious eating disorders.

There is some suggestion that by the fourth and fifth grade, girls are worried about being or becoming overweight and desire to become thinner. For example, in a sample of girls aged 9 to 18, 58 percent perceived themselves to be overweight, whereas only 15 percent were overweight by objective standards (Mellin, Irwin, & Scully, 1992). Also, among 10-year-olds, approximately 55 percent reported fear of fatness, and 81 percent reported restrained eating/dieting.

Among middle school children, concerns about weight remain prevalent, and more extreme weight control behaviors seem to be employed (Childress et al., 1993). Evidence suggests that extreme weight concern in these young girls is predictive of the emergence of later eating disorder symptoms and of depression, lowered self-esteem, and feelings of inadequacy and personal worthlessness (Killen et al., 1994a,b; Lewinsohn et al., 1993a; Stice & Bearman, 2001). Such feelings may, in turn, lead to increased concern with weight and shape among girls who already place great personal value on these physical attributes (Cohen-Tovee, 1993).

Even at this young age concerns with weight and shape have been reported to be more prevalent among girls than boys (Shapiro, Newcomb, & Loeb, 1997; Thelen et al., 1992). However, there is also increasing concern regarding disordered eating and body dissatisfaction among young males (McCabe & Ricciardelli, 2004). (See Accent: "Being Buff: Weight and Shape Concerns in Young Men.")

Gender, Ethnic, and Cultural Differences. Eating disorders occur predominantly in young women, and young white women from middle to upper class backgrounds appear to be at greatest risk (Connors, 1996). Ethnic and cultural differences deserve further consideration (Smolak & Striegel-Moore, 2001; Wilson et al., 2003). There is probably not sufficient evidence regarding ethnic minorities. Research does suggest, however, that African American and Hispanic females report less body dissatisfaction than European American females even though rates of obesity are higher in the former ethnic groups. Eating disorders appear to be culturally related phenomena, particularly bulimia nervosa (Keel & Klump, 2003). Evidence suggests that the more "Westernized" young women from other cultures become, the more likely they are to develop eating disorders.

Within Western culture certain groups are thought to be at particular risk (Wilson et al., 2003). These include individuals (particularly women) involved in activities such as gymnastics, wrestling, ballet, and cheerleading in which weight-control behaviors and abnormal eating are engaged in to enhance performance or appearance. Rigorous large-scale research is lacking; however, analysis of existing literature does suggest small, but significant, differences (Smolak, Murnen, & Ruble, 2000). Elite female athletes involved in some of the activities listed above appear to be at highest risk. Interestingly, gymnasts do not appear to be at greater risk than nonathletes, and nonelite high school female athletes may be less likely than nonathletes to have an eating disorder or to report body dissatisfaction.

Co-occurring Disorders. Eating disorders commonly co-occur with a number of other disorders (O'Brien & Vincent, 2003). Lewinsohn, Striegel-Moore, and Seeley (2000) report that in a community sample of adolescent girls, among those with full syndrome eating disorders, 90 percent experienced one or more co-occurring disorders. Depression, anxiety disorders, substance use disorders, and personality disorders are commonly reported as co-occurring with both anorexia and bulimia nervosa (Wilson et al., 2003).

DEVELOPMENTAL COURSE AND PROGNOSIS

Anorexia Nervosa. The age of onset of AN is during adolescence, with peaks at ages 14 and 18 (Thompson & Smolak, 2001). Cases of earlier onset are rare but do exist (Gowers et al., 1991; Lask & Bryant-Waugh,

ACCENT ●●●●●

Being Buff: Weight and Shape Concerns in Young Men

Prevalence statistics and much of the literature has focused on eating disordered behavior and weight and body image concerns in young women. This is, at least in part, due to the high rates of such difficulties among females. More recently, attention has begun to turn to young men, and whether eating, weight, and body shape concerns are underestimated in the male population. Part of what we should recognize here is a possible gender bias in how a disorder is defined. So, for example, drawing from the literature on young women, interest has largely focused on issues such as the desire for a smaller and thinner body and losing weight. Although losing weight may be a concern for some young men who are overweight, they may not desire a small thin body. The ideal for many young men may be a larger or at least more muscular body. Perhaps defining body dissatisfaction and weight concerns in a different way might paint a different picture regarding body image concerns and disordered eating in young men.

Indeed, it has become accepted among researchers and others that weight and shape concerns and body dissatisfaction have become more common among males. McCabe and Ricciardelli (2004) highlighted some of the reasons for this trend. Male bodies are more often featured in popular magazines and models have become more muscular. Popular athletes, film stars, and many other male icons also have become increasingly more muscular. Action figures, such as GI Joe, have followed the same trend and are likely to have physiques equal to or exceeding those of advanced body builders. Also, weight training has become more prevalent among young men and may have come to be viewed as normative. Thus, similar to what young women have experienced, cultural pressures may be increasingly likely to affect young men.

What may be the consequences of these trends? Appearance and weight have, for a long time, been considered overly important influences on young women's self-esteem. Similar concerns may be emerging as central to men's feelings of self-worth (Pope et al., 2000). Problematic eating styles may be increasing. In addition, excessive exercise and muscle-building strategies may be escalating among young males, including the use of steroids to achieve results.

The literature is not extensive regarding disordered eating and body dissatisfaction in young men. Nonetheless, there is information available that suggests that both disordered eating and the pursuit of muscularity in adolescent males are influenced by similar factors. Furthermore, several factors consistently associated with disordered eating in young women (e.g., body mass index, negative affect, self-esteem, perfectionism, and pressure from others to lose weight) also appear to be associated with problematic eating behaviors in young men (Ricciardelli & McCabe, 2004).

Increased attention to disordered eating and the pursuit of muscularity in young males is likely to clarify the nature and extent of this problem and its associated psychological and health consequences. Such information can inform the development of necessary prevention and treatment strategies.

1992). Some individuals may experience a single episode; others fluctuate between periods of restoration of normal weight and relapse (perhaps to dangerously low levels that require hospitalization). Still others may gain weight but continue eating disordered behaviors that meet the criteria for BN or EDNOS (American Psychiatric Association, 2000; Wilson et al., 2003).

Anorexia nervosa is a serious disorder, and a substantial proportion of young women with the disorder have poor outcomes (Grinspoon et al., 2000; Steinhausen, 1997; Wentz et al., 2001). Extreme weight loss can lead to significant medical complications (e.g., anemia, hormonal changes, cardiovascular problems, dental problems, loss of bone density), and the disorder may be life-threatening. It has been reported that over 10 percent of cases end in death, half of which may result from suicide (American Psychiatric Association, 2000; Pike, 1998; Steiner & Lock, 1998).

Bulimia Nervosa. The onset of BN extends from adolescence into early adulthood. Binge eating often begins during or after a period of restrictive dieting driven by extreme dissatisfaction with body shape and weight. The DSM describes the course of the disorder as either chronic or intermittent, with periods of remission alternating with recurrences of binge eating. However, over the long term, symptoms of BN diminish in many individuals (American Psychiatric Association, 2000). Although some individuals may no longer meet the diagnostic criteria for BN, problems may persist—some individuals may meet the criteria for EDNOS, and many meet the criteria for major depressive disorder (Fairburn et al., 2000; Lewinsohn et al., 2000).

The recurrent vomiting associated with BN may result in dental problems due to the loss of tooth enamel. Other medical problems such as fluid and electrolyte disturbances may also occur, particularly among those who purge (American Psychiatric Association, 2000). As we will see later, promising treatments for BN are available that can help individuals recover from what otherwise might be chronic difficulties.

ETIOLOGY

A variety of causal mechanisms have been proposed to explain the development of eating disorders. Indeed, it is likely that AN and BN are multiply determined and result from a variety of different patterns of causal factors (Bryant-Waugh & Lask, 1995; Garner & Desai, 2001; Wilson et al., 2003). Most current explanations incorporate multiple influences into conceptualizations of how eating disorders may develop. What are some of the influences that have been considered?

Cultural Influences. Any discussion of the development of eating disorders must address cultural influences and gender roles for women (Paniagua, 2000; Smolak & Murnen, 2004). Our society's emphasis on and valuing of slim and young bodies, particularly for women, likely contributes to the development and prevalence of eating disorders (Garner & Desai, 2001; Mirkin, 1990; Wilfley & Rodin, 1995). Families, peers, and the media transmit these cultural messages (Wertheim, Paxton, & Blaney, 2004). Guillen and Barr (1994), for example, examined the messages contained in articles, advertisements, and other materials in *Seventeen* over two decades. In this magazine for female adolescents, the primary reasons presented for following nutrition or fitness plans were to lose weight and become more attractive. Body shapes of models were less curvaceous than those in adult women's magazines; in fact, the hip:waist ratio of models decreased over the years studied. Additional research points to the influence of the media (Levine & Harrison, 2004) and suggests that young people may unfavorably compare themselves to persons depicted in music videos and other media (Tiggerman & Slater, 2004).

Thus one perspective on the development of eating disorders emphasizes contemporary social influences, particularly on young women, that place too great an emphasis on physical appearance, create a "culture of thinness," and may transmit a message that social and economic opportunity are associated with a thin body (Anderson-Fye & Becker, 2004; Gilbert & Thompson, 1996).

Some authors remind us that unusual eating styles are not recent phenomena, and that historical accounts can assist us in examining our conceptualization of eating disorders (Attie & Brooks-Gunn, 1995). There were, for example, a group of women living in the High Middle Ages (13th through 16th centuries) who exhibited extreme restrictions of eating and what might be viewed as bizarre and pervasive behaviors and images regarding eating and food (Bell, 1985; Brumberg, 1986). Descriptions of the behavior of these women bear a remarkable similarity to contemporary eating disorders. The most interesting twist to this tale, however, is that these women were later canonized as saints. Bell (1985) chose the term "holy anorexia" to describe the condition of these women and to call attention to the cultural dimension that may be lost in current diagnostic efforts. Questions such as why a set of behaviors at one time is viewed as pious and at another as a disease force us to address important issues. To say that AN merely went undiagnosed in the past fails to appreciate that behaviors that appear similar may have very different origins, meanings, and functions. For example, Habermas (1992) has suggested that if fear of becoming overweight is considered as essential in defining eating disorders, then both AN and BN should be considered historically new syndromes (late 19th and early 20th centuries) and Western. Indeed, even contemporary investigations suggest that such extreme fear of being overweight may not exist among individuals with eating disorders in all cultures (Anderson-Fye & Becker, 2004). This is just one of the many complexities presented when one includes a cultural perspective in thinking about eating or other kinds of disorders.

Early Feeding Difficulties. Continuities from early childhood feeding difficulties to later eating problems and disorders have been hypothesized. Clinical reports mention early feeding difficulties in individuals with eating disorders, and there is some research support for this position. For example, Marchi and Cohen (1990) longitudinally traced maladaptive eating patterns in a group of children. Their findings suggested that early childhood pica was a risk factor and that picky eating was a protective factor for bulimic symptoms in adolescence. On the other hand, picky eating and digestive problems in early childhood were risk factors for elevated symptoms of AN in adolescence. Kotler and colleagues (2001) found that maternal reports during early childhood of eating conflicts, struggles with food, and unpleasant meals were predictive of later AN in adolescence or young adulthood, whereas eating too little during childhood was somewhat protective regarding a future diagnosis of BN. Certainly, more research is needed to clarify the relationship between early eating/feeding difficulties and later eating disorders. However, it does seem that experiences that begin early in childhood regarding food acceptance pattern, the balance between external and self-control of eating, and other experiences in which parents play a crucial role are important factors in shaping later eating problems (Fisher & Birch, 2001).

Weight History and Concerns. Family weight history and the individual's previous weight history are frequently considered as possible etiological factors. There is much debate about the idea that the self-starvation that is characteristic of AN begins as an attempt to control genuine obesity. It has been suggested that comments that the young girl is "getting plump" may stimulate normal dieting, which evolves into anorexic refusal to eat. However, the role of a personal and family history of being overweight in the development of AN remains unclear, and the frequency of dieting among adolescent girls raises the question of why some girls who begin this common social ritual persist well beyond the point of socially desired slimness.

Similar considerations have been discussed regarding BN, and there does seem to be evidence that supports personal and family history of overweight as a risk factor (Wilson et al., 2003). Some young women with such a history may become bulimic, and the problematic behaviors may have begun as more typical attempts to reduce weight that could not meet the thin cultural ideal.

Research by Fairburn and his colleagues (1997) supports the role of weight history. Three groups of participants were recruited from a community sample: a group with BN, a group with other disorders (depression and anxiety), and a group of healthy controls. The groups were compared on a number of putative risk factors for BN. Whereas participants with BN experienced a significantly greater exposure to most risk factors as compared with healthy controls, there were very few differences in risk exposure for the bulimia group as compared with the participants with other disorders. A history of childhood obesity and negative self-evaluation were two of the risk factors to which the BN group experienced greater exposure. These factors thus appear to increase the risk for developing the specific disorder of BN.

Research by Killen and his colleagues (1996) supports the notion that extreme weight concerns contribute to the development of eating disorders. A community sample of high-school-age girls was followed over a 4-year period. Four percent (36 girls) developed a "partial syndrome eating disorder." These girls, even though they might not have met diagnostic criteria for AN or BN, exhibited binge-eating episodes, compensatory behavior to prevent weight gain, and overconcern with body weight and shape or lack of control of eating during a binge. A baseline measure of weight concerns was significantly associated with the onset of the partial syndrome eating disorder. Whereas girls in the top quartile on the measure of weight concerns had the highest incidence of the syndrome, none of the girls in the lowest quartile developed eating disorder symptoms.

Independent of the question of weight history, dissatisfaction with weight and body shape has come to be viewed as part of the defining characteristics of eating disorders and as one of the early aspects of the development of such problems. Pictorial instruments that graphically assess body dissatisfaction in young children have been developed as part of a comprehensive assessment of eating disorders (Collins, 1991; Gardner, 2001; Stewart & Williamson, 2004). Use of such instruments (see Figure 13–6) has contributed to the view that body dissatisfaction and other problematic beliefs and behaviors are common and are present even in very young children.

Developmental Stress. Another notion regarding the etiology of eating disorders is that they evolve out of a response to the stress of certain developmental changes. Because eating disorders generally begin

FIGURE 13–6

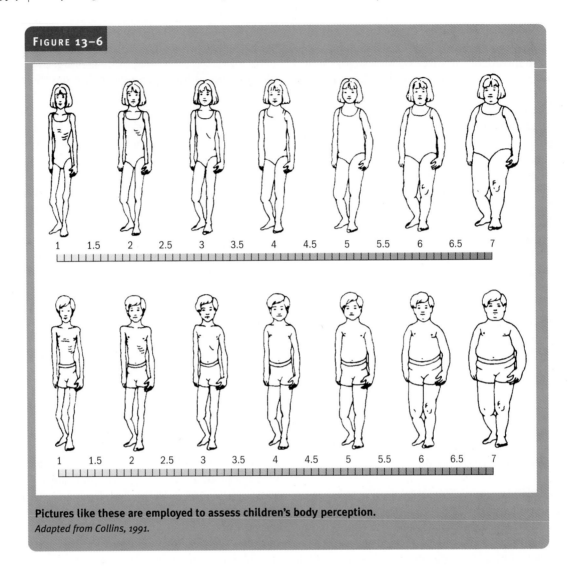

Pictures like these are employed to assess children's body perception.
Adapted from Collins, 1991.

during the adolescent years, stresses associated with this period—such as the onset of puberty and associated bodily changes, expectations of greater autonomy and responsibility, and increased social demands—are implicated (Levine et al., 1994). The coping skills of some young girls may not be adequate for such challenges. For example, AN has been viewed as an avoidant coping response: Stringent dieting prevents the appearance of a mature body and also results in menstruation's being avoided or reversed. Some view the individual's fear of weight gain as related to concerns about psychosexual maturity (Crisp, 1984); however, this association has not been established empirically (Wilson et al., 2003). The feasibility of stress contributing to the development of BN is supported by findings of early menarche as a risk factor for development of the disorder (Fairburn et al., 1997).

Sexual Abuse. Reports based on clinical cases have suggested early sexual abuse as a cause of eating disorders, particularly BN. Studies involving children are limited (Connors, 2001) but reviews suggest a small but significant association between childhood sexual abuse and eating disordered behavior (Smolak & Murnen, 2002). The nature of this relationship remains unclear. However, sexual abuse would appear to be a risk factor for psychopathology in general, rather than a specific risk for the development of eating disorders (Fairburn et al., 1997; Levine, Smolak, & Striegel-Moore, 1996; Romans et al., 2001). This, of course, does not mean that clinicians working with young people should not consider the occurrence of sexual abuse, which may be part of a pathway to eating disturbance for some individuals (Wonderlich et al., 2001).

Family Influences. Many explanations regarding the development of eating disorders have emphasized family variables. Bruch's (1979) description of an anorexic girl, Ida, is a classic example of family influences. The girl is described as the object of much family attention and control and as trapped by a need to please. AN, according to Bruch, is a desperate attempt by the child to express an individual identity.

| Ida | **A Sparrow in a Golden Cage** |

She enjoyed being home but missed the fuss they had made about her in the past, when everybody was acutely concerned about her. . . . Even as a child, Ida had considered herself not worthy of all the privileges and benefits that her family offered her, because she felt she was not brilliant enough. An image came to her, that she was like a sparrow in a golden cage, too plain and simple for the luxuries of her home, but also deprived of the freedom of doing what she truly wanted to do.

Adapted from Bruch, 1979, pp. 23–24.

It is difficult, however, to determine whether any pattern observed in a family subsequent to the onset of a disturbance is a cause or an effect. This is especially the case in AN, in which family observations have frequently followed the offspring's life-threatening refusal to eat. Reviews of research do suggest that family patterns are associated with eating disorders; however, there is no single pathway of influence (Steinberg & Phares, 2001). Such families are described as having a high incidence of weight problems, affective disorder, and alcoholism or drug abuse. Also, aspects of the family environment, such as periods of low parental contact and high parental expectations, are implicated as risk factors (Fairburn et al., 1997). Families of young women with eating disorders have also been described as exhibiting controlling, interdependent family relationships, together with parental discord (Kog & Vandereycken, 1985; Strober & Humphrey, 1987).

Parental attitudes and beliefs concerning eating, weight, and body shape may be particularly important. Pike and Rodin (1991), for example, found that compared with mothers of daughters with low levels of eating disturbances, mothers of daughters with disordered eating viewed their daughters as less attractive and were more likely to think that their daughters should lose more weight. These mothers were also more dissatisfied with the functioning of their family system. In addition, they themselves had more eating problems and different dieting histories than other mothers. How and when family variables come into play is complex and difficult to determine.

Biological Influences. Because eating and the biological mechanisms behind it are complex, numerous biological mechanisms have been studied. Eating behavior can both be influenced by and effect changes in neurobiological and neuroendocrine systems, so determining causal relationships is not easy. It has been difficult to determine whether a particular biological difference found in young women with eating disorders placed them at initial risk for the disorder or resulted from change in the biological system due to disordered eating.

For example, faulty hormonal regulation is suggested by the nature of some of the symptoms associated with AN (e.g., amenorrhea) and the fact that onset is frequently around puberty. However, many of the physical abnormalities that have been found seem to result from starvation rather than to cause it (Fairburn, 1995; Pirke & Platte, 1995). These abnormalities are also found in nonanorexic individuals who have reached starvation weight and in whom hormonal indicators typically return to normal when adequate weight is gained. Another possible influence is suggested by reports of abnormalities in brain neurotransmitters (e.g., norepinephrine, serotonin) among individuals with AN and BN (Ferguson & Pigott, 2000; Kaye, Gendall, & Strober, 1998). For example, serotonin plays a major role in the inhibition of feeding, and decreased serotonin activity in bulimic individuals has been observed. It remains unclear whether initial dieting is due to decreased serotonin activity or whether problematic eating leads to changes in serotonin levels that then help sustain bulimic behavior.

A genetic contribution to eating disorders has also been suggested (Bulik, 2004; Grice et al., 2002; Strober et al., 2000). There are higher than expected rates of eating disorders among family members of individuals with AN and BN. Family studies also suggest that AN and BN may have some shared etiology (Strober et al., 2000). Twin studies also suggest a genetic component to eating disorders (Bulik, 2004). However, such research is difficult to conduct for AN because of the relatively low prevalence of the disorder. Despite limitations, it seems likely that additive genetic influences (cumulative impact of multiple genes) contribute to the development of AN and BN and interact with environmental influences (Bulik,

2004). The manner in which genes contribute to eating disorders remains unclear, but the mechanisms may involve complex contributions to personal styles, such as rigidity/obsessionality or general anxiety level, or to biological processes involved in the regulation of eating behavior (Bulik, Wade, & Kendler, 2001; Klump, McGue, & Iacono, 2000).

TREATMENT

In general there is research support regarding treatment of BN, but this is far less the case for AN. Furthermore, treatments specific to the needs of children and younger adolescents have received limited attention and, thus, recommendations are largely based on downward extensions of controlled studies with older adolescents and adults (Gore, Vander Wal, & Thelan, 2001; Gowers & Bryant-Waugh, 2004; Robin, Gilroy, & Dennis, 1998). Because eating disorders likely derive from and are maintained by a variety of influences, and because of considerable heterogeneity among individuals, treatments that address multiple influences need to be developed. Here we briefly highlight some treatment approaches.

Family Approaches. Family therapy for eating disorders derives from the observation by clinicians of varying persuasions that families are intimately involved in the maintenance of this behavior. There are a variety of approaches to therapy with families of eating disordered young women (Lock, 2004). Family therapy is widespread in clinical practice, but research support is more limited. There is some support for the effectiveness of family interventions for adolescents with AN (Lock, 2004; Robin, 2003). The work of Minuchin and his colleagues (1978) is one of the early family systems approaches to AN.

The families of young women with AN, according to Minuchin, can be described as enmeshed. The members of the family do not have distinct identities. In this kind of family, the youngster learns to subordinate the self (individuality) to family loyalty. The young girl's overinvolvement with the family prevents the individualization that is necessary at this time of life. The families of the young girls have also always had a special concern with eating, diet, and rituals pertaining to food. The anorexic adolescent begins to challenge the family system, and rebellion is exhibited through refusal to eat. The family maintains its stability by making the child a sick, incompetent person who requires care. It follows from this conceptualization that the entire family system must be treated. Indeed, in many family approaches, the family system

rather than the eating disorder symptoms or the adolescent is the primary focus of treatment. Although controlled research is lacking, Minuchin and his colleagues (1978) reported that 86 percent of the 53 cases they treated recovered from both the AN and its psychosocial components.

It is not clear that there is empirical support for the hypothesized differences in families that serve as the basis for many approaches to family therapy (Dare & Eisler, 1997; Vandereycken, 1995). However, the logic for incorporating family issues into treatment, particularly for children and adolescents, seems compelling, and indeed has become part of many approaches to intervention (Lock, 2004; Robin et al., 1998).

Research is ongoing and suggests promise for some family-based therapies such as the Maudsley approach (Dare & Eisler, 1997; LeGrange, Binford, & Loeb, 2005; Lock et al., 2001). This approach, developed by Dare, Eisler, and their colleagues at the Maudsley Hospital in London, avoids viewing families as pathological and blaming them for the development of AN. The position taken is that the causes of the disorder are unknown and the family is considered the most important resource for the adolescent's recovery. Treatment incorporates elements of other family therapy approaches and is designed to take place over one year, with initial intense support of the family gradually faded over time. Treatment is broadly divided into three phases. The first phase is highly focused on the eating disorder, refeeding, and weight gain. Families are encouraged to work out for themselves the best way to refeed their anorexic child. Once the adolescent is gaining weight and eating takes place with minimal struggle, the second phase begins. Eating disorder symptoms are the main subject of sessions, but the goal is to assist the family in finding ways to return control back to the adolescent. As this occurs other family issues can begin to be reviewed. Once the adolescent achieves a healthy weight the final phase is undertaken. General issues of adolescent development and the ways they have been affected by AN are addressed (Lock, 2004).

Cognitive-Behavioral Treatments. Cognitive-behavioral treatment of BN has appreciable research support and is viewed by many as a treatment of choice for this disorder (Anderson & Maloney, 2001; Robin et al., 1998; Pike, Devlin, & Loeb, 2004). Treatment involves a multifaceted program that is based on the rationale that cognitive distortions and a loss of control over eating are at the core of the disorder (Fairburn, 1997). According to this view, cognitions regarding shape and weight are the primary features of the disorder, and other features—such as dieting and self-induced vomiting—are secondary expressions of these concerns. In the initial stage of treatment, the patient is educated regarding BN, and the cognitive view of the disorder is made clear. During this early stage, behavioral techniques are also employed to reduce bingeing and compensatory behaviors (e.g., vomiting) and to establish control over eating patterns. These techniques are supplemented with cognitive restructuring techniques, and as treatment progresses, there is an increasingly cognitive focus on targeting inappropriate weight-gain concerns and on training self-control strategies for resisting binge eating. Next, additional cognitively oriented interventions address inappropriate beliefs concerning food, eating, weight, and body image. Finally, a maintenance strategy to sustain improvements and to prevent relapses is also included.

Controlled research has shown the cognitive behavioral approach to the treatment of BN to be superior to no treatment and to alternative treatments, including pharmacotherapy and a variety of other psychotherapies (Pike et al., 2004; Wilson & Fairburn, 2002).

Treatment of AN from a cognitive-behavioral perspective has often been conceptualized as consisting of two phases: intervention to restore body weight and to save the patient's life; and subsequent extended interventions to ameliorate long-standing adjustment and family difficulties and to maintain normal weight. Behavioral interventions focus on the first phase and rely heavily on operant learning principles to promote weight gain (Touyz & Beumont, 1997). These interventions have successfully employed positive and negative consequences contingent on weight change to produce weight gain in a relatively brief period of time. Most interventions treat hospitalized patients at a fairly critical point in the disorder, and their effectiveness at this life-threatening point is an obvious contribution. However, there has been less success regarding both the long-term maintenance of weight gain and the social-emotional adjustment of patients after they have left the hospital. Cognitive-behavioral treatments, similar to those for BN, have been developed to address the second phase. However, there is only limited research regarding the effectiveness of this approach (Pike et al., 2004). The development of a behavioral family systems therapy for adolescents with AN has shown some initial promise (Robin, 2003). This approach combines behavioral, cognitive, and family systems perspectives and interventions in working with adolescents and their parents.

Interpersonal Psychotherapy. Interpersonal psychotherapy (IPT) focuses on interpersonal problems involved in the development and maintenance of a disorder. This therapeutic approach does not directly target eating symptoms, but seeks to enhance interpersonal functioning and communication skills. The rationale for such an approach is based, in part, on research indicating the role of interpersonal influences (e.g., actions of peers, friends, family; comparison with others) on the development of body image and self-esteem (Tantleff-Dunn, Gokee-LaRose, & Peterson, 2004). An assessment of the individual's interpersonal history is obtained. One or more of four interpersonal problem areas are the focus of the intervention: grief, role transitions, role disputes, and interpersonal deficits. To illustrate one of these, the case of Gayle describes the contribution of role transitions to the development of an eating disorder.

IPT has proven to be effective in the treatment of BN. There is not empirical support for the effectiveness of IPT in treating AN (Fairburn et al., 1995; Tantleff-Dunn et al., 2004).

| **Gayle** | **Interpersonal Role Transitions** |

Gayle, an 18-year-old with bulimia, graduated from a small high school and began attending a large university far from home. Gayle was an only child, was very close to her parents, and had been part of a small circle of childhood friends. She was both excited and frightened about going away to college. Quickly she felt pressured by the need to impress others and make new friends. Gayle described herself as having been "sheltered" and "catapulted into adulthood." The therapy began by focusing on facilitating Gayle's transition to college, independence, and adulthood. As she developed a network of social support and gained confidence in her abilities to care for herself, Gayle's purging and preoccupation with her physical appearance decreased.

Adapted from Tantleff-Dunn, Gokee-LaRose, & Peterson, 2004, p. 170.

Pharmacological Treatment. Although case reports suggest that different pharmacological treatments can be successful with eating disordered patients, controlled research, particularly regarding children and adolescents, is either lacking or presents a somewhat more cautious picture (de Zwaan, Roerig, & Mitchell, 2004; Gowers & Bryant-Waugh, 2004).

There seems to be little support for the effectiveness of any pharmacological approach to the treatment of AN. However, research is ongoing regarding some antidepressant medications, particularly for maintaining weight once it is gained and as adjuncts to psychological intervention (de Zwaan et al., 2004; Gowers & Bryant-Waugh, 2004).

In controlled studies with adults, antidepressant medication has been reported effective for treating BN (de Zwaan et al., 2004; Werry & Aman, 1999). Effectiveness may be limited to only some patients, and at present, medication would not appear to be the primary treatment of choice. The role of antidepressants in treating BN in adolescents remains unclear (Gowers & Bryant-Waugh, 2004). Moreover, caution regarding side effects with individuals who are already psychologically and physiologically at risk is indicated.

SUMMARY

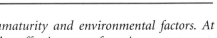

- *It is common for children to exhibit some difficulty in acquiring habits of elimination, sleep, and eating. For some youngsters these problems are serious enough to make them of clinical concern.*

PROBLEMS OF ELIMINATION

- *Toilet training is an important concern for parents of young children. Knowledge of the typical sequence of control over elimination and of appropriate parenting practices can contribute to successful training.*

- *Enuresis and encopresis are disorders of elimination that seem best explained by a combination of biological predisposition and failure to train and/or learn bodily control.*

- *Desmopressin is the best-supported medically oriented procedure for treating enuresis. Behavioral interventions that include a urine-alarm procedure have high success rates and low rates of remission, and they seem to be the treatments of choice at present.*

- *Encopresis is probably best dealt with through a combination of medical and behavioral procedures.*

SLEEP PROBLEMS

- *Parents often report that their children have problems involving sleep. Knowledge of normal sleep development helps in understanding sleep difficulties and disorders. Sleep problems are common in infants, children, and adolescents. Sleep disorders are persistent sleep difficulties that cause the child distress or interfere with other functioning.*

- *Difficulties in initiating and maintaining sleep (dyssomnias) are most effectively dealt with by establishing bedtime routines and the appropriate cues for sleep. Sleep disorders such as sleepwalking and sleep terrors (parasomnias) are probably best conceptualized as resulting from a combination of nervous system immaturity and environmental factors. At present the effectiveness of various treatments remains unclear.*

PROBLEMS OF FEEDING, EATING, AND NUTRITION

- *A wide range of problems having to do with eating and feeding are commonly reported in young children. Many of these problems cause considerable concern for parents and appreciable disruption of family life.*

- *Some eating and feeding problems are more serious and persistent, and may actually endanger the physical health of the young person.*

- *The early feeding and eating disorders in the DSM are Rumination Disorder, Pica, and Feeding Disorder of Infancy or Early Childhood, which is also often discussed as failure to thrive.*

- *Childhood obesity is an important health problem and, unfortunately, is quite prevalent. The development of obesity is influenced by a complex interaction of biological, psychosocial, and cultural influences.*

- *The learning of adaptive eating and activity patterns is the basis of behavioral treatment programs for obesity. This approach to treatment is probably the most successful. However, greater weight loss and better maintenance still need to be achieved and priority given to prevention and early intervention.*

EATING DISORDERS: ANOREXIA AND BULIMIA NERVOSA

- *The DSM describes two primary eating disorder diagnoses: Anorexia Nervosa and Bulimia Nervosa. A category of Eating Disorders Not Otherwise*

Specified is also included. A potential category of Binge-Eating Disorder is being studied.

- *Anorexia nervosa (AN) is a serious disorder characterized by extreme weight loss, an intense fear of becoming fat, and disturbance in the perception of body weight and shape. A number of other physical and psychological problems are present as well. A distinction is made between restricting and binge-eating/purging anorexia.*

- *Bulimia nervosa (BN) refers to a repeated pattern of binge eating followed by some inappropriate compensatory mechanism. A distinction is made between purging and nonpurging types.*

- *Females represent about 90 percent of all cases of eating disorders (AN and BN). Increasing prevalence of eating disordered behavior and attitudes among young girls has been noted. There is also increased concern regarding disordered eating and body dissatisfaction in young males.*

- *Ethnic and cultural differences deserve further consideration and certain groups, such as some athletes and dancers, may be at particular risk.*

- *Age of onset for AN is typically during adolescence. For many individuals the disorder, or other eating problems, persists over a considerable period of time. For some, the disorder may be life threatening.*

- *The onset of BN extends from adolescence into early adulthood. Although symptoms diminish for many individuals, there is concern regarding persistent eating difficulties and depression if treatment is not undertaken.*

- *Explanations that incorporate multiple influences are most likely needed to understand the development of eating disorders. Cultural influences, early feeding difficulties, weight history, stress and coping, family influences, and genetic and other biological influences should be considered.*

- *Treatments for AN and BN specific to children and younger adolescents have received less attention, and current treatment recommendations are therefore based on downward extensions of studies with older adolescents and adults.*

- *The use of family therapy or family involvement in treatment is widespread in clinical practice, although further empirical support is required. Cognitive-behavioral treatment is the intervention for BN for which there is the best-controlled research support. Interpersonal psychotherapy has also proven to be effective.*

- *Although AN has proven difficult to treat, some treatments involving family members show promise. The effectiveness of pharmacological treatments with children and adolescents is unclear.*

KEY TERMS

● ● ● ● ● ● ○ ○

enuresis *(p. 370)*

nocturnal enuresis *(p. 370)*

diurnal enuresis *(p. 370)*

primary enuresis *(p. 370)*

secondary enuresis *(p. 370)*

urine-alarm system *(p. 371)*

encopresis *(p. 373)*

rapid eye movement (REM) sleep *(p. 374)*

nonrapid eye movement (NREM) sleep *(p. 374)*

dyssomnias *(p. 375)*

parasomnias *(p. 375)*

sleepwalking *(p. 375)*

obstructive sleep apnea *(p. 376)*

sleep terrors *(p. 376)*

nightmares *(p. 377)*

failure to thrive *(p. 380)*

rumination *(p. 380)*

pica *(p. 381)*

feeding disorder of infancy or early childhood *(p. 382)*

obesity *(p. 382)*

body mass index *(p. 382)*

binge *(p. 388)*

restricting *(p. 388)*

purging *(p. 388)*

eating disorder not otherwise specified *(p. 388)*

binge-eating disorder *(p. 388)*

anorexia nervosa *(p. 388)*

bulimia nervosa *(p. 389)*

CHAPTER 14

Psychological Factors Affecting Medical Condition

This chapter continues the discussion of the problems of physical conditions and health. We turn to an examination of how psychological factors contribute to our understanding of youngsters with chronic medical conditions. The prevalence of such conditions and the associated medical and psychological challenges make this a topic of high interest. We also examine how psychological influences contribute to the delivery of effective medical treatment. In addressing these topics, we touch on issues such as the role of the family, chronic conditions and youngsters' adaptation and adjustment, and the adherence of youngsters and families to regimens recommended by health care practitioners. In order to illustrate the interfaces between psychology and medicine, we describe their application to various medical conditions such as asthma, cancer, diabetes, and HIV/AIDS. To understand the evolution of current thinking and practice, it is helpful to have some appreciation of the history of such endeavors.

Historical Context

The topics discussed in this chapter would in the past have come under the heading of psychosomatic disorders. The main focus of interest was on actual physical conditions, such as asthma, headaches, ulcers, and nausea. These disorders were known or presumed to be affected by psychological factors. The terminology for describing these disorders has undergone a number of changes in the last few decades. The term *Psychosomatic Disorders* was replaced in the DSM-II by *Psychophysiological Disorders*, and in the DSM-III and III-R with the term *Psychological Factors Affecting Physical Condition*. The term has been modified in the DSM-IV and DSM-IV-TR to Psychological Factors Affecting Medical Condition.

The uncertainty over terminology reflects a long-standing controversy over the nature of the relationship between mind and body, the psyche and the soma. During the 20th century, interest in the effects of psychological processes on the body resulted in the development of the field of psychosomatic medicine. Early workers began to accumulate evidence and to develop theories of how psychological factors played a causative role in specific physical disorders (Alexander, 1950; Grace & Graham, 1952; Selye, 1956). As this field developed, several trends emerged. An increasing number of physical disorders were seen to be related to psychological factors. Even the common cold was thought to be affected by emotional factors. The question therefore arose as to whether it was fruitful to identify a specific group of psychosomatic disorders or whether psychological factors were operating in all physical conditions. In addition, the focus began to shift from psychogenesis, that is, psychological cause, to multicausality, the idea that social and psychological (as well as biological) factors all contribute to both health and illness at multiple points. The latter view is holistic, assuming a continuous transaction among influences. This broad scope and interactive perspective has continued to develop (Brown, 2002; Eiser, 1994; Wood, 1994).

With this shift in thinking, the field began to expand considerably. The ongoing role of social and psychological factors in the development of medical conditions, their consequences, and treatment, and in prevention and health maintenance all began to receive increased attention (Drotar, 1981; Routh, Schroeder, & Koocher, 1983; Winett, 1995). This chapter is in keeping with these changes. However, it is clearly not possible to survey completely this rapidly expanding field. Whole volumes have been dedicated to the topic or segments of it (Drotar, 2000; La Greca et al., 1992; Roberts, 2003), and several scientific journals have emerged to deal exclusively with research in this area (e.g., *Journal of Pediatric Psychology, Behavioral Medicine, Health Psychology*). In this chapter, we will examine some of the specific medical problems of children that have received the attention of psychologists and other selected topics of interest. This examination will allow us to illustrate the changes that have occurred and the current status and diversity of this field.

Psychological and Family Influences on Medical Conditions

In this section, we will look at information on asthma to illustrate how psychological and family variables may influence the symptoms of pediatric medical problems. This examination of asthma will begin to allow us to see how thinking about the role of psychological variables in physical illness has changed and expanded.

THE EXAMPLE OF ASTHMA

Loren　Managing Asthma

Loren is a twelve-year-old boy with moderate to severe asthma. For the fourth time in a year, he was hospitalized because of asthma. At hospital rounds, Loren's physician pointed out that his asthma could be controlled if he avoided triggers of his asthma, including exercise-induced attacks, and if he complied with his medication regimen. It was also pointed out that Loren did not use his nebulizer properly. Instead of alleviating his respiratory distress, most of the medication was wasted because of inappropriate inhaler use. Lack of quick relief frustrated Loren. As a result he tended to become angry, a behavior that only exacerbated his asthma. It was decided to (1) teach Loren to identify and avoid triggers of his asthma, (2) review his medication and adjust the regimen if possible, (3) improve his compliance to his medical treatment regimen, (4) teach him how to use his nebulizer correctly, and (5) teach him skills to control his frustration.

Adapted from Creer, 1998, p. 411.

Description and Prevalence. Defining and describing asthma is complex and remains an ongoing process (McQuaid & Walders, 2003; National Institutes of Health, 1997). Asthma is a disorder of the respiratory system that is characterized by hyperresponsiveness of the airways to a variety of stimuli. Hyperresponsiveness results in inflammation and narrowing of air passages, and air exchange is impaired, particularly during expiration. Intermittent episodes of wheezing and shortness of breath (dyspnea) result. Within the same individual, as well as across individuals, attacks may vary in severity. Thus asthma is an illness that is quite unpredictable, a problem for both research and management of the disorder. Severe attacks, known as status asthmaticus, which are life threatening and require emergency medical treatment, are another challenge in treating asthmatic children. The fear of not being able to breathe and the danger of severe attacks are likely to create appreciable anxiety in the young person and in family members.

Asthma is a common chronic illness in young people. Approximately 10 percent of youngsters are asthmatic, and minority and poor children are overrepresented (Brown & Macias, 2001; Creer, 1998; Miller, 2000). Asthma is a potentially reversible disorder, but the impact of the disease on the youngster is considerable. In addition to hospitalization and emergency room use, many school days are lost because of asthma (Weiss, Gergen, & Hodgson, 1992; Yeatts & Shy, 2001).

Clearly, the greatest threat is loss of life, and all measures used to treat the physical symptoms of asthma—daily medication to prevent wheezing, environmental control of potential irritants, desensitization to allergens, avoidance of infection, and emergency treatment to stop wheezing—are geared to prevent death. Although much has been done to improve treatment, the prevalence of asthma, as well as increases in medical costs, hospitalization, and mortality rates, are reasons for continuing concern (Creer, 1998; McQuaid & Walders, 2003).

Etiology. The causes of asthma are complex, and there is a considerable history of controversy concerning etiology. Indeed, the exact cause remains unknown (Creer, 1998; McQuaid & Walders, 2003). However, it is broadly acknowledged that genetic or other factors place some youngsters at risk for developing asthma (National Institutes of Health, 1997). Some cause or a variety of causes produce a hypersensitivity of the air passages. Once established, this hypersensitivity results in the youngster's responding to various irritants more easily than would a nonasthmatic individual.

Whatever its etiology, individuals with highly sensitive and labile respiratory tracts are potentially exposed to a second set of factors that influence whether asthmatic attacks occur. This second set of influences has come to be thought of as *trigger* mechanisms or *irritants*, rather than as causes of asthma. Every child or adolescent has different triggers and triggers can differ over time for the same youngster (Creer, 1998).

Repeated respiratory infection may play a role in the development of asthma, and respiratory viral infections can set off or worsen the severity of an attack. Allergies may also be related to the development and occurrence of asthmatic attacks. Allergies may exist to inhaled substances (such as dust, the dander of a pet, pollen) or to ingested substances (such as milk, wheat, or chocolate). Physical factors such as cold temperatures, tobacco smoke, pungent odors, and exercise and rapid breathing may also contribute to wheezing. Furthermore, psychological stimuli and emotional upset are often considered important triggers of asthma attacks (Creer, 1998; Miller & Wood, 1994). Indeed, it is virtually impossible to assess and analyze asthma without recognizing the multiple psychological factors involved.

Changing Views. Although we have come to view the causes of asthma differently, in much of the early literature asthma was viewed primarily as a disease with psychological causes. Possibly the earliest and most widely known psychosomatic explanation of asthma was the psychoanalytic explanation originally offered by French and Alexander (1941). Asthma was hypothesized to arise from an excessive, unresolved dependence on the mother and a resultant fear of separation. The symptoms of wheezing and shortness of breath were viewed as "a suppressed cry for the mother," brought on because crying, and the desire for the mother that it represents, become intolerable to the parent. It is probably important to examine the specifics of this hypothesis and its validity, because as Creer (1982) has pointed out, French and Alexander's ideas about psychological and family factors in asthma had as much impact as anything previously written. Moreover, these ideas were applied to other disorders.

Renne and Creer (1985) summarized the basic aspects of the explanation and the information concerning its validity. The four major conclusions offered by French and Alexander were that (1) in asthmatic patients, a universal conflict exists between an infantile dependent attachment to their mothers and other emotions (particularly sexual wishes) that are incompatible with this dependent attitude; (2) asthma attacks are related to an inhibited suppressed cry for the mother; (3) there is a unique personality pattern characteristic of asthmatic patients; and (4) psychoanalysis will alleviate the asthmatic symptoms. French and Alexander were clearly influenced by their psychoanalytic training, and much of the support for this theory came from other psychoanalysts and from individual case studies. Reviews of research conducted since the publication of the original monograph by French and Alexander suggest that there is little, if any, support for their conclusions (Renne & Creer, 1985). No unique relationship appears to exist between asthmatic children and their mothers. To the extent that asthmatic children cry less, this behavior is more likely due to the realization that crying may trigger an attack. Furthermore, there is no evidence for a personality pattern unique to asthma, and asthmatic patients would seem to be as psychologically healthy as other people. Finally, psychotherapy has not been effective in alleviating the disorder.

All in all, there is little, if any, convincing evidence that psychological or family factors play a significant role as an original cause of the reduced respiratory capacity characteristic of asthma. However, there is evidence that these factors may play an important role in precipitating or triggering asthmatic attacks in at-risk youngsters.

Like many other investigators, Purcell and his colleagues (1969)—working at the Children's Asthma Research Institute and Hospital (CARIH) in

Parental concern over precipitating a symptomatic attack may often lead children with chronic illnesses, such as asthma, to spend appreciable time isolated from their peers.
By permission of U.S. Department of Health and Human Services— Public Health Service (ADM, 77–497).

Denver—observed that some children became free of symptoms fairly soon after being sent away from their parents for treatment. Indeed, in the 1950s, "parentectomy" was suggested as the treatment of choice for some children (Peshkin, 1959). Were these effects due to changes in the emotional environment or in the physical environment? What other variables accounted for this reaction?

An interesting study on separation suggested some answers to these questions (Purcell et al., 1969). Prior to the beginning of the study, parents of asthmatic children were interviewed and asked about the degree to which emotions precipitated asthmatic attacks. Children for whom emotions were important precipitants were expected to respond positively to separation from their parents (predicted positive), whereas children for whom emotions played less of a role were not expected to show improvement.

For the predicted positive group, all measures of asthma improved during the separation period. The children who were not predicted to respond to separation exhibited no differences across phases on any measure.

The findings of this research study, and of others like it, led investigators to view changes in the psychological atmosphere as the basis for improvement in asthmatic symptoms. However, over time both the investigators at CARIH and other investigators came to view such findings somewhat differently. Although the magnitude of changes reported might be statistically significant, they were not clinically significant. And changes might have been due to increased compliance with prescribed medical regimens when the substitute parents moved in and the children's parents lived in a hotel. Indeed, current treatments to improve asthmatic functioning do focus on improving adherence (Lemanek, Kamps, & Chung, 2001).

This does not mean that psychological factors and family functioning play no role in asthma. There seems little doubt that these factors, in general, do play a role (Klinnert, Mrazek, & Mrazek, 1994; McQuaid & Walders, 2003). For example, home environment (e.g., dust, animal dander), activities of family members (e.g., smoking, outdoor activities), and stress (e.g., family fights, divorce) may act as triggers for asthmatic attacks. Beyond the anxiety that parents experience, the youngster's asthma may have consequences for the parents (e.g., days lost at work because of their child's illness, medical costs) and siblings (e.g., loss of attention, restrictions in choice of family activities). Also, family members likely have to assist in the management of the disease, especially for younger children. It is therefore not surprising that psychological interventions have focused on educating families about the triggers of asthma attacks, on the consequences of asthma, and on helping youngsters and their families manage the disease (Creer, 2000; McQuaid & Walders, 2003).

We have seen, then, how the focus on psychological and family factors has shifted from the cause of a chronic illness such as asthma to an interest in how youngsters, parents, and family may influence the frequency and severity of the symptoms and can manage the disorder (Bleil et al., 2000; Kaugars, Klinnert, & Bender, 2004; Markson & Fiese, 2000). This is one example of how those who study and work with children with chronic conditions have shifted and broadened their focus of interest. An interest in the consequences of chronic conditions is another example.

Consequences of Chronic Conditions

The effects of any chronic illness are likely to be pervasive, particularly if the illness is life threatening. The youngster is likely to experience substantial stress and anxiety. In addition, limitations due to illness often place obstacles in the way of normal development. For example, contact with peers may be limited or school attendance may be disrupted.

Of course, the family, too, needs to cope with the illness, its treatment, and its effects over long periods of time. Such long-term demands are bound to be difficult to handle, and the consistency required by treatment regimens is stressful in its own right. Thus the entire family may experience considerable anxiety and have appreciable stress placed on its daily routines.

ADJUSTMENT AND CHRONIC ILLNESS

Research on chronic illness has become a priority for pediatric psychologists (Kazak, 2002). One frequent question is, Does chronic illness lead to poor adjustment? The answer would appear to be not necessarily, but these illnesses and related life experiences probably place the child at increased risk for adjustment problems, particularly those of an internalizing nature (LeBovidge et al., 2003; McQuaid, Kopel, & Nassau, 2001; Soliday, Kool, & Lande, 2000; Vila et al., 2000). Research findings suggest that there is considerable variation in adjustment among chronically ill youngsters. Although the majority of young people with a chronic illness do not experience adjustment problems, subsets of more vulnerable patients do exist (Patenaude & Kupst, 2005; Wallander, Thompson, & Alriksson-Schmidt, 2003).

However, measuring adjustment at any one time is unlikely to provide a complete picture. Adjustment for the youngster and family members is likely to be an ongoing process, beginning at diagnosis and continuing through treatment, treatment completion, perhaps relapse, and the long-term course that is inherent in a chronic illness (Friedman, Latham, & Dahlquist, 1998; Kazak, 2005).

How might we best understand variation in reactions among young people and their families? Increasingly, pediatric psychology has recognized that research must be guided by theories that suggest variables that might influence psychological outcomes (Dantzer et al., 2003; Fritz & McQuaid, 2000; Thompson et al., 1992; Wallander & Varni, 1998). Several models are available to guide research, many of which view chronic illness as an ongoing chronic stressor to which the youngster and family must continue to adapt and continue to develop appropriate coping mechanisms (Miceli, Rowland, & Whitman, 1999; Wallander & Varni, 1998).

Adjustment to chronic illness is best thought of as a complex function of a number of variables, each of which requires continued investigation. Characteristics of the young person would seem likely to contribute to the adjustment of both the youngster and the family; for example, the child's existing competencies and the types and variety of coping skills that the youngster possesses are likely to be important in this process. A second category of variables is disease factors, such as severity, degree of impairment, and the functional independence of the

FIGURE 14–1

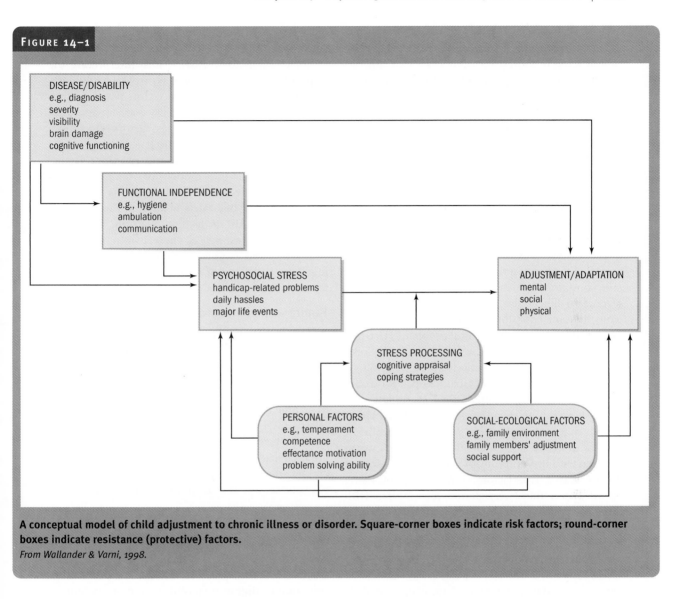

A conceptual model of child adjustment to chronic illness or disorder. Square-corner boxes indicate risk factors; round-corner boxes indicate resistance (protective) factors.

From Wallander & Varni, 1998.

youngster. In addition, the youngster's environment (e.g., family, school, health care) is likely to be a factor in variations in adjustment. An appreciation of the complexity of the problem is illustrated in the model offered by Wallander, Varni, and their colleagues (Wallander & Varni, 1998; see Figure 14–1).

In the following sections, we examine two of the categories of influences on adjustment to chronic illness: illness parameters and family functioning.

Illness Parameters and Adjustment. In searching to understand the adjustment among youngsters with chronic illnesses, it is reasonable to ask, Do aspects of the illness itself contribute to differences in adjustment? In attempting to answer this question, the type of disease, the severity of the illness, and the

degree of impairment of functioning produced by the illness are among the variables that have been examined. Of course, analyzing these dimensions separately is not always possible. For example, certain illnesses are more severe than others, and severity is likely related to greater restrictions in normal functioning. However, each of these variables seems important.

Some research findings suggest that certain types of chronic conditions put youngsters at greater risk than others (Bennett, 1994; Miceli et al., 1999). For example, Vila and colleagues (1999) compared youngsters with asthma and diabetes. Parents of youngsters with asthma reported more problems than did parents of youngsters with diabetes. These youngsters with asthma also had higher self-reports of anxiety. However, the two groups of youngsters did not differ in their reports of symptoms of depression or levels of self-esteem. Other research suggests no differences in adjustment between youngsters with different chronic conditions (Garstein et al., 1999). For example, Meijer and her colleagues (2000) studied the social functioning of youngsters diagnosed with one of a variety of chronic conditions, including cystic fibrosis, diabetes, arthritis, and asthma. There were no differences between children with different chronic conditions with regard to social activities, social aggressive or submissive behavior, or social self-esteem.

The inconsistency of findings regarding the impact of type of chronic condition may be due, in part, to differences in the severity of the illness. Certain conditions are more severe than others, but severity of illness also can vary among youngsters with the same condition. What, then, might be the impact of severity of the medical problem? Here too, findings are conflicting (Miceli et al., 1999). Some research does suggest a relationship between illness severity and adjustment (McQuaid, Kopel, & Nassau, 2001). For example, a longitudinal examination of youngsters with juvenile rheumatoid arthritis (JRA) found that although there were no significant overall differences in social functioning between children with JRA and control youngsters, severity of disease was a risk factor. Peers ratings of liking declined over the 2-year period for children with more severe disease as compared to those with mild disease. Also, children with active disease were chosen fewer times as a best friend than children in remission (Reiter-Purtill et al., 2003). However, more severe forms of a disorder are not always associated with poorer adjustment, and relationships are likely to be complex (Klinnert et al., 2000; Wallander & Varni, 1998).

Adjustment also may be associated with the degree of functional limitation (how restricted the youngster is) due to the chronic condition (Bleil et al., 2000; Meijer et al., 2000). For example, functional limitations may affect the number of absences from school or relationships with friends. The degree to which the illness is controlled also appears to be important. Although these results suggest that anxiety, depression, and the like are outcomes of illness-related parameters, investigators acknowledge that the direction of causation is not clearly established. Anxiety, depression, and the like may contribute to illness parameters such as poor illness control, more severe illness symptoms, and greater functional limitations (Wiebe et al., 1994).

Ethically, we cannot manipulate emotional conditions or illness severity, nor can we randomly assign children to diseases. Thus, interpreting the impact of aspects of illness is inevitably difficult. Furthermore, although illness factors may help predict adjustment, predictive ability does not appear to be that strong. Integrating illness factors into a more normative approach—one that combines these factors with the stress, risk, and resilience factors included in etiological models for youngsters without chronic medical disorder—seems suggested (Soliday et al., 2000). Such an approach would allow for identification of factors relatively unique to chronic illness, as well as those common to other youngsters and families. Among the variables that might be the focus of such a normative approach, family functioning has received some attention.

Family Functioning and Adjustment. It is not surprising that family functioning is related to the psychological adjustment of chronically ill youngsters (Kaugars et al., 2004; Kell et al., 1998). Without denying the particular risks and stressors associated with chronic conditions, it is reasonable as a starting point to assume that some of the family influences that are related to adjustment of other children and adolescents, such as parental depression and marital conflict, are also related to the adjustment of young people with chronic illness. Indeed, this seems to be the case (Lavigne & Faier-Routman, 1993; Soliday et al., 2000).

| **Lisa** | **Diabetes Management and Family Context** |

Lisa is a fourteen-year-old with a history of insulin-dependent diabetes mellitus and a variety of behavior and health status problems. Her mother reports difficulties with Lisa's diabetes management, which have gotten worse recently, resulting in ten hospitalizations in the past twelve months.

Lisa is the only adopted child in a family of four youngsters. She has three brothers, ages twenty years, two years, and one month. The two-year-old was born seriously ill and required several operations, although he is now in good health. During the assessment process, Mrs. L openly expressed her hostility toward Lisa. In contrast, the oldest son is seen as perfect. Mrs. L is also exceptionally nurturing towards her two younger sons.

The births of the two younger brothers have clearly changed Lisa's role in the family from youngest child and the focus of Mrs. L's nurturance, to sibling caretaker. Mrs. L is feeling increasingly stressed and recently left work to care for the two boys. She is angry at her husband for his passive stance, but this remains largely unexpressed. The oldest son's decision to leave home for college leaves her without any male support. Mrs. L directs much of her anger towards Lisa. Lisa is angry also, and this is directed primarily toward her father. It is possible that she may be receiving subtle encouragement from her mother for this. At the same time, Lisa's difficulties draw her parents together. Lisa's behavior and hospitalizations also shift the family focus of attention away from her brothers and toward her.

Adapted from Johnson, 1998, pp. 428–429.

A variety of family influences known to be related to youngsters' adjustment in general have also been investigated in populations of youngsters with chronic conditions (Wallander et al., 2003). Timko and her colleagues (1993), working with youngsters with JRA, examined how parental risk and resilience factors predicted disease-related functional disabilities (e.g., gripping things, doing routine household chores), pain, and psychosocial adjustment. After the age of the youngsters and initial levels of their functioning were controlled for, parents' personal strain and depressed mood and fathers' drinking were associated with poorer adjustment in the youngsters 4 years after initial contact. Better parental social functioning, the mothers' involvement in social activities, and the fathers' number of close relationships, on the other hand, seemed to facilitate the children's adjustment. Given that attention has often concentrated on the contribution of maternal factors, it is interesting that the fathers' risk and resilience factors contributed to the children's functioning and adjustment beyond what was already accounted for by maternal factors and other influences.

Illness-related and family factors may moderate or mediate each other's relationship to adjustment. Findings by Wagner and her colleagues (2003), for example, suggest that parental distress may interact with illness-related factors to affect child adjustment. Among youngsters with JRA, the impact of parental distress was evident for those youngsters who perceived their illness to be more intrusive—that is, interfering with their ability to engage in activities. These youngsters were more depressed. In contrast, parental distress was unrelated to the depression of youngsters with low levels of perceived illness intrusiveness.

Bleil and her colleagues (2000) also studied the contribution of illness-related functional status and family factors. The degree to which a youngster was restricted by asthma was related to symptoms of depression. This relationship, however, was mediated by the security of the relationship between the mother and youngster (Figure 14–2). That is, functional status appeared to affect security of mother-child relatedness, which in turn affected the youngster's level of depression.

Differences in family variables such as conflict, control, and organization also appear to be associated with adjustment. In their comparison of diabetic youngsters and matched controls with acute illness, Wertlieb, Hauser, and Jacobson (1986) found that overt expression of family conflict was related to greater problem behavior in both groups. However, other factors differentiated the groups. One particularly interesting finding involved differences in attempts to control and maintain the family system. Among the acutely ill youngsters, a greater control orientation in the family was strongly related to a greater probability of behavior problems. In contrast, low levels of family organization were associated with high levels of behavior problems among

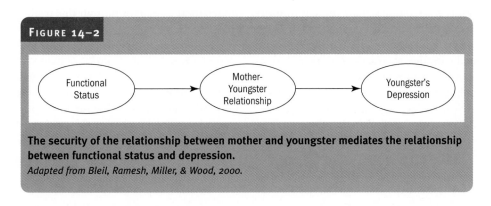

FIGURE 14–2

Functional Status → Mother-Youngster Relationship → Youngster's Depression

The security of the relationship between mother and youngster mediates the relationship between functional status and depression.
Adapted from Bleil, Ramesh, Miller, & Wood, 2000.

the diabetic youth. Families with a diabetic child have appreciable demands placed on them to organize daily routines involved in the management of the illness. Successful management of the diabetes probably requires appreciable organization and structure, as well as overtly dealing with issues of control. Structured and controlling family environments may be associated with better metabolic control of the diabetic condition. The relationship of family environment to adjustment relationships, however, is likely to be complex (Seiffge-Krenke, 1998; Wallander et al., 2003; Weist et al., 1993).

Cohesion is another family variable that seems to be important. It is often suggested that a life-threatening illness draws family members closer together. Increased cohesion, although not a universal reaction to illness, has been observed in families coping with a variety of illnesses (Ross et al., 1993; Wood et al., 1989). Level of cohesion also is frequently associated with the adjustment of the youngster and other family members (Helgeson et al., 2003; Lavigne & Faier-Routman, 1993; Sloper, 2000).

A study of adolescent cancer survivors illustrates the importance of cohesion; however, it too suggests that relationships are likely to be complex (Rait et al., 1992). Adolescents who had previously been treated for leukemia, Hodgkin's disease, or non-Hodgkin's lymphoma and who were currently in remission participated in the study. The participants were 12 to 19 years old at the time of the assessment. Given the literature on chronic illness and family functioning, the authors hypothesized that the experience of cancer would result in greater family cohesion and that cohesion would be associated with the psychosocial adjustment of these cancer survivors.

The adolescents completed a standard measure of family adaptability and cohesion. The cancer survivors' scores did differ from a normative community group, but not in the predicted direction. The adolescents who had survived cancer described their families as less cohesive than the community sample. There was, though, the expected relationship between cohesion and adjustment. Greater cohesion was associated with better posttreatment psychological adjustment. However, an interesting complexity was suggested. Among "recent" survivors (treatment completed a year or less ago) and "long-term" survivors (treatment completed more than 5 years ago), there was the described strong relationship between family cohesiveness and adjustment. For "intermediate" survivors (treatment completed between 1 and 5 years ago), however, the association between family cohesiveness and adjustment was dramatically decreased.

In a related finding, Varni and his colleagues (1996) studied children with newly diagnosed cancer with respect to the predictive effects of family functioning on adjustment over the first 9 months after diagnosis. Higher levels of family cohesion and expressiveness were predictive of better adjustment. However, family functioning was more predictive of concurrent adjustment than of later adjustment. That is, family cohesion at one time was more closely related to adjustment at that same time than it was to adjustment 6 months later.

These findings illustrate the importance of studying adjustment as a process over time. The child's condition may change, and the effect of the illness on the family may not be static. Furthermore, changes in the youngster and in the illness may require changing styles of family involvement. Because youngsters with chronic illnesses have a greater chance of survival than ever before, these findings suggest the need for continued exploration of how time since treatment, current age, age at diagnosis, and other variables may be related to the association of family environment and the youngsters' psychological adjustment.

As more youngsters survive chronic illnesses, the complexities of studying long-term adjustment become clear. Are perceived deficiencies (e.g., lower achievement), when found, due to poorer adjustment or to reasonable life choices about what is important? Rather than asking about better disease adjustment, it may be more reasonable to ask, how does the experience of chronic illness affect individual development (Eiser, 1998)?

CANCER: ADAPTING TO CHRONIC ILLNESS

Cancer has long been viewed as a fatal and little understood disease. Although this frightening image still remains, it is not as accurate as was once the case. With increasing survival rates, the emphasis has shifted from "dying from" to "living with" cancer (Eiser, 1998). It may now, for many youngsters, be more appropriate to view cancer as a chronic condition rather than a fatal disease. For example, in 1960 acute lymphocytic leukemia, the most common form of childhood cancer, had a survival rate of 1 percent 5 years after diagnosis. By the mid-1970s, the survival rate had increased to about 49 percent, and by the end of the 20th century, to about

83 percent (Ries et al., 2001). Advances in treatment have improved the overall 5-year survival rate for childhood cancer to over 75 percent (National Cancer Institute, 2004).

However, treatments are often lengthy, highly invasive, stressful, and accompanied by considerable pain. Working with this population thus presents multiple and complex challenges. In addition to the initial task of helping the youngster and family understand and come to accept the illness, it is important to assist them in coping with a long and stressful treatment regimen and the additional stressors that the illness and its treatment place on them. For example, advice regarding the youngster's school, teacher, and peer group is likely to be important during treatment and afterward. Also, the youngster's and family's concerns regarding the longer-term impact of the disease are considerable (Vannatta & Gerhardt, 2003). Potential effects are probably related to developmental period. For adolescents the disease may interfere with the development of autonomy as a result of increased dependence on family and medical staff, and it may impose restrictions on social life and the development of close interpersonal relationships. Adolescence also is a developmental period during which some high-risk behaviors (substance use) may be somewhat normative. Even brief involvement in such behaviors can have significant consequences for young people with cancer. Problematic outcomes, however, are not inevitable. The provision of ongoing psychosocial services to families throughout this process may buffer the impact of the cancer experience and allow the youngsters to develop and function much like their peers. Such services may also assist siblings and other family members who are also impacted (Kazak, 2005; Vannatta & Gerhardt, 2003; Woznick & Goodheart, 2002).

One must also be aware that the very treatments that have resulted in longer survival may contribute to the long-term challenges. Advances in treatments such as chemotherapy and radiation have contributed to increased life expectancy. However, youngsters who have completed these treatments are at increased risk for growth and reproductive difficulties as well as cardiac, pulmonary, renal/urological, gastrointestinal, ocular, and dental problems. Cosmetic impairments and functional limitations (e.g., diminished stamina) have also been frequently noted. Some of these effects may not be apparent immediately after treatment, but may occur later among survivors, and their impact may evolve over time (Moore, 2005; Vannatta & Gerhardt, 2003).

The immediate and long-term impact on cognitive and neurobehavioral functioning—of treatments such as irradiation and chemotherapy to prevent central nervous system occurrence of leukemia—are not entirely clear. However, it appears that impairment does occur in areas such as attention, memory, and academic achievement (Brown et al., 1998; Espy et al., 2001; Lockwood, Bell, & Colegrove, 1999; Moore, 2005; Raymond-Speden et al., 2000).

Families may require continuing assistance to help them in supporting their child with cancer.
(Sean Cayton/The Image Works)

ACCENT ● ● ● ● ●

The Impact of HIV/AIDS in Children and Adolescents

An appreciable number of those infected with HIV and AIDS are women of childbearing age. The HIV-positive children born to these women are one of the sadder images of the AIDS story. Indeed, about 90 percent of youngsters infected with the virus acquire it through their mothers (Armstrong, Willen, & Sorgen, 2003). These babies are often very sick and frequently were given away or taken from their mothers. Many of them were taken in by foster parents who were willing to take on the challenge of caring for such a child. Fortunately, with medical advances, the number of HIV babies born to HIV-positive women has dropped dramatically. However, this problem remains a considerable international concern.

Although the majority of youngsters become infected through vertical transmission from their mothers, some youngsters, such as those with hemophilia, become infected through the blood supply. For older children and adolescents, there is also concern regarding transmission by drug use or sexual contact.

With medical advances producing greater survival rates, attention has shifted from terminal care for affected youngsters to management of the condition and improving quality of life (Armstrong et al., 2003).

We have known for some time that children born infected with HIV are likely to have developmental and cognitive problems. HIV progresses faster in children than in adults and is more likely to result in neurological abnormalities because of the effects of the virus on immature nervous and immune systems (Wachsler-Felder & Golden, 2002). By school age these neurological problems result in significant learning, language, and attention difficulties, and emotional and social difficulties are also evident. The impact may be greater for youngsters with greater compromise of their immune system (Bordeaux et al., 2003). Young people with HIV/AIDS are thus likely to have to continue to adapt to extraordinary circumstances and are also likely to present their caregivers with exceptional challenges.

It is important to remember that not all HIV-infected youngsters have clinically significant emotional and behavioral problems (Bachanas et al., 2001). However, among those who do, particularly those born to HIV-positive mothers, it is difficult to fully know what is contributing to the difficulties. Clearly, some of the problems are direct outcomes of their disease (Wachsler-Felder & Golden, 2002). The medical treatments and the stress of adhering to a long-term medical regimen and a chronic illness are probably factors as well. However, these young people were born to mothers whose prenatal care may not have been optimal, who may have abused drugs when they were pregnant, and who may have had serious psychopathology themselves. All of these powerful influences, as well as family and environmental risks that the young people may have faced after their births, make current problematic outcomes understandable. The adaptation challenges are considerable and call for a coordinated and intensive program of assistance for these young people and their families.

The shift to coping, adjusting, and adapting to cancer is clearly a more optimistic approach. However, while we continue to attempt to understand this process and assist young people and families, we must also monitor youngsters for long-term outcomes of their conditions and side effects of treatment. In addition, relapse remains possible, and there is an increased risk for secondary cancers. Maintaining such vigilance without creating additional and undue anxiety, and at the same time promoting an optimistic and adaptive attitude, presents a considerable challenge.

A similar perspective on adaptation applies to other chronic illnesses such as sickle cell disease and HIV/AIDS (see Accent: "The Impact of HIV/AIDS in Children and Adolescents") and to conditions such as head injury (Lewis, 2001; Noll et al., 2001; Thompson et al., 2002; Yeates et al., 2001). The consequences of the illness or condition itself as well as the impact of intensive, demanding, and long-term treatments need to be addressed in understanding adaptation to these chronic conditions over time.

Facilitating Medical Treatment

Attempts to provide psychological treatment that would improve a patient's medical condition have long been one of the aspects of the interface between psychology/psychiatry and medicine. The vast majority of early attempts sought to provide the patient with psychotherapy as a means of reducing physical symptoms or curing illness. Such direct assaults on illness through psychotherapy proved to be largely ineffective (Werry, 1986). More recent efforts have taken a somewhat different approach to integrating a psychological perspective into the clinically relevant, empirically supported treatment of medical problems (Drotar & Lemanek, 2001). Although a comprehensive review of these multiple efforts and strategies is beyond the scope of the present chapter, a few important illustrations follow.

ADHERENCE TO MEDICAL REGIMENS

The terms adherence and compliance are most commonly used to describe how well a youngster or family follows recommended medical treatments such as taking medications, following diets, or implementing lifestyle changes. Diabetes provides an excellent illustration of the way psychologists have increasingly attempted to understand the complex tasks encountered by families managing chronic childhood disorders (Delamater, 2000; Drotar, et al., 2000; La Greca & Bearman, 2003).

A Description of Diabetes. Diabetes is one of the most common chronic diseases in youngsters, affecting approximately 1.8 youth per 1,000. Type 1 (DM1), also known as insulin-dependent diabetes mellitus, is a lifelong disorder that results from the pancreas's producing insufficient insulin. Daily replacement of insulin by injection is required. Because the onset of DM1 typically occurs in childhood, this form of diabetes is often referred to as a childhood or juvenile diabetes. In Type 2 diabetes (DM2), rather than insulin deficiency, insulin resistance occurs, impairing cellular uptake of insulin. DM2 was previously viewed as an adult-onset disorder; however, 10 to 20 percent of new cases of diabetes in youth are of this type. DM2 is disproportionately high among African American, American Indian, and Hispanic populations. DM2 may be managed by weight reduction, exercise, and careful diet. However, insulin injections may also be required for many youngsters with this form of diabetes (Brown & Macias, 2001; Gortmaker & Sappenfield, 1984; Wysocki, Greco, & Buckloh, 2003).

Onset of DM1 occurs most often around puberty. However, the onset of the disease can occur at any time from infancy to early adulthood. Although the exact etiology of DM1 is unclear,

genetic factors appear to be involved. Diabetes is thought to be an autoimmune disease in which the body attacks its own pancreatic cells (Johnson, 1998).

Both forms of diabetes increase the long-term risk for damage to the heart, kidneys, eyes, and nervous system. If the disorder is not controlled, a condition known as ketosis, or ketoacidosis, may occur. This is a very serious condition that can lead to coma and death (Johnson, 1998; Wysocki et al., 2003).

The youngster and family face a treatment regimen that includes dietary restrictions, daily injections of insulin, monitoring of urine, and testing of blood glucose levels (see Table 14–1). On the basis of the daily tests for level of sugar—and factors such as timing of meals, diet, exercise, physical health, and emotional state—the daily dosages of insulin must be adjusted. Even under the best of circumstances, "insulin reactions" occur often. Thus the youngster must be sensitive to the signs and symptoms of both hyperglycemia (excessively high levels of blood glucose) and hypoglycemia (excessively low blood glucose). Adverse reactions involve irritability, headache, shaking, and—if not detected early enough—unconsciousness and seizures. The fact

TABLE 14–1	SOME ACTIVITIES REQUIRED OF DIABETIC CHILDREN AND FAMILIES

Inject insulin regularly
Test blood regularly
Exercise regularly
Avoid sugar
Check for symptoms—low
Check for symptoms—high
Be careful when sick
Shower regularly
Wear diabetes ID
Watch weight
Eat meals regularly
Adjust diet to exercise
Carry sugar
Test blood as directed
Change injection site
Inject insulin as directed
Watch dietary fat
Take care of injuries
Eat regular snacks
Control emotions
Inspect feet

Adapted from Karoly & Bay, 1990.

that symptoms are different for different youngsters and are subjectively experienced makes the task of identifying them complicated. Parents and youngsters are therefore faced with a difficult, often unpredictable, and emotion-laden therapeutic program that requires careful integration into daily life (Delamater, 2000; Johnson, 1998).

Management of the Diabetic Condition. The first task in treatment is for the team of professionals to gain and maintain control of the diabetic condition. As this task is achieved, insulin requirements often decrease, and the initial fears and concerns of the youngster and family are often reduced. This has come to be known as the "honeymoon period." This period of partial remission may terminate gradually and often ends about 1 to 2 years after initial diagnosis. Beginning a diabetes self-management program with families during the first few months after diagnosis may avoid this initial deterioration in metabolic function, and early intervention with young children may help to reduce adherence problems and problems in diabetic control during later periods (Davis et al., 2001; Delamater et al., 1990). Transferring control for management of the disease from the professional to the family and child or adolescent, as well as requiring maintenance of such control over long periods of time, is one of the challenges of working with chronic illness (Meltzer et al., 2003; Palmer et al., 2004).

Adherence to the Diabetic Regimen. The concept of adherence is multifaceted (La Greca & Bearman, 2003; Riekert & Drotar, 2000). Appreciation of this complexity has led to the development of intervention programs that combine strategies such as education, training in self-management skills, and parent/family involvement. Such programs appear to be promising (Christophersen & Mortweet, 2001; La Greca & Bearman, 2003; Lemanek et al., 2001). The initial step addressed in most programs is to educate the youngster and family about the disease. Although such efforts are regularly made, adequate knowledge cannot be assumed. Therefore, efforts have been made toward developing methods to assess knowledge. Behavioral observation methods have been employed to assess whether the youngster knows how to execute necessary skills such as urine and blood glucose testing. Questionnaires are frequently used to measure knowledge of the disease and the application of that knowledge to different situations (e.g., the role of insulin, and adjusting diet based on blood sugar readings). However, adherence is not just a matter of accurate information and knowledge; it requires that the prescribed tasks be accurately and consistently carried out.

In this chapter, it is not possible to examine all aspects of adherence. However, several important variables can be highlighted. Developmental level is an important variable affecting adherence (Iannotti & Bush, 1993; Johnson, 1993; Palmer et al., 2004). For example, children under 9 years may have difficulty accurately measuring and injecting insulin. In general, knowledge and skills seem to increase with age (Rovet & Fernandes, 1999). However, it may be unwise, even with adolescents, for parents to withdraw from participation (Johnson, 1998; McQuaid et al., 2003; Meltzer et al., 2003).

Adolescence is a period during which management of diabetes often deteriorates (Anderson et al., 2000; Johnson, 1995). During this period control is often gradually transferred to the youngster, and parental participation often ceases, but total withdrawal of adult involvement may not be advisable (Wiebe et al., 2005). The adolescent's knowledge of the disease and its management may be overestimated. Adolescents may, for instance, make errors in estimating their blood glucose levels, particularly when blood glucose levels are quite variable (Meltzer et al., 2003). Despite better problem-solving abilities, adolescents with diabetes also may show decreased adherence (Thomas, Peterson, & Goldstein, 1997). Whereas increasing cognitive development potentially allows the adolescent to better understand the illness and to manage a complex routine, there are other aspects of cognition that may interfere with adherence. Murphy, Thompson, and Morris (1997) examined the cognitive appraisal processes of 12- to 18-year-olds with diabetes. They found that adolescents who (1) have a negative perception of their bodies, (2) perceive little control over health when ill, and (3) have an external attributional style (see p. 176) for negative events were at greatest risk for poor adherence.

Palmer and colleagues (2004) studied youngsters between the ages of 10 and 15 who had a diagnosis of DM1 for at least 1 year. Mothers' and children's perceptions of who was responsible for various aspects of diabetes management were assessed. Measures of the youngsters' developmental maturity were also obtained. The youngsters also completed a measure of their level of self-reliance/autonomy, and their pubertal status was assessed through mothers' reports of the extent to which their child displayed specific signs of puberty. Metabolic control of the diabetes was assessed through medical records of Hba_{1c} (glycosylated hemoglobin test—reflecting average blood glucose levels). With low levels of child self-reliance/autonomy and when pubertal status was low,

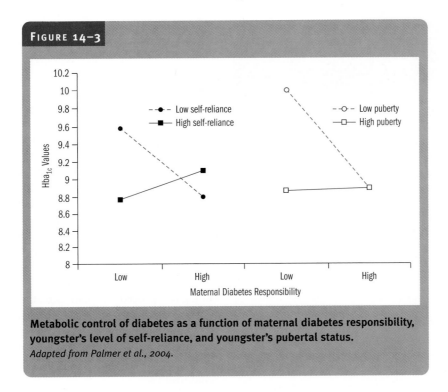

FIGURE 14–3

Metabolic control of diabetes as a function of maternal diabetes responsibility, youngster's level of self-reliance, and youngster's pubertal status.
Adapted from Palmer et al., 2004.

transfer of diabetes responsibility from mother to child was associated with higher Hba_{1c} values (poorer control). The effects on metabolic control of self-reliance, pubertal status, and maternal responsibility for diabetes are illustrated in Figure 14–3.

Social and emotional concerns, such as peer acceptance and greater participation in activities, also are associated with decreased adherence (Thomas et al., 1997). Youngsters with diabetes may wish to avoid appearing different. The unusual behaviors required (e.g., injections, glucose testing) and the dietary demands of eating frequently (when others are not) and avoiding high-fat foods and sweets (when others are eating junk food) make conformity difficult. Some of these social challenges are illustrated in Table 14–2. These vignettes are used to assess social problem solving among diabetic youth. Conflicts with parents over issues of independence are also likely to be present. Such social and interpersonal issues most likely combine with actual physical changes, like those associated with delayed puberty, to increase management and compliance difficulties for adolescents (Brooks-Gunn, 1993; Johnson, 1998). Interventions that maintain parental involvement yet minimize parent-adolescent conflict and improve communication and problem-solving skills are needed (Anderson et al., 2000; Wysocki et al., 2003).

Many other problems regarding adherence are worthy of continued attention. For example, anticipating environmental obstacles to compliance is important. Creating interventions that help adolescents deal with peers concerning their diabetes and that facilitate appropriate peer support, for instance, may greatly facilitate compliance with recommendations (Greco et al., 2001). The realization that the immediate consequences of diabetes management are often negative, and therefore more consistent with nonadherence than with adherence, may also help to anticipate difficulties. For example, the immediate consequence of injections is discomfort, whereas the adverse effect of skipping injections is not immediate. Thus interventions that reduce the immediate negative effects of compliance may be of value.

Attention to the role of the health care system and primary care providers (pediatrician, nurse) is another important aspect of the adherence process (Dunbar-Jacob, 1993; La Greca & Bearman, 2003). Changes in the health care system have resulted in shortened medical visits and a less personal relationship with providers. These conditions may contribute to poorer communication and poorer adherence.

The behavior of health care providers also is important. For example, there may be a considerable

---

TABLE 14–2 | **EXAMPLES OF VIGNETTES TO EVALUATE SOCIAL PROBLEM-SOLVING IN DIABETIC YOUTH**

Glucose Testing

Your friends ask you to go to a video arcade, and it's almost time for you to test your glucose. You don't have your test materials with you, and your friends are impatient to leave. If you stop and test, they will leave without you.

Diet—Sweets

You are invited to your best friend's birthday party, where they are going to serve cake and ice cream at a time when you are supposed to have a snack. But cake and ice cream would not fit into your diet plan at all, since you are supposed to have a snack that is low in sugar and fat.

Diet—Time of Eating

Your friends invite you out for dinner at your favorite restaurant, but they want to go really late, a lot later than you would normally eat.

Alcohol

Your friends invite you to a big party. You go there, and you find out that almost everyone is drinking beer. Your friends offer you some beer and seem to expect that you will drink it just as everyone else did.

Adapted from Thomas, Peterson, & Goldstein, 1997.

---

discrepancy between what primary providers believe they have recommended and what patients and families recall. Also, information provided may not be sufficient to permit the family to carry out complex regimens (DiMatteo, 2000; Ievers et al., 1999). It seems, too, that health care providers may not be sufficiently aware of the child's level of cognitive development and so treat youngsters of varying ages as essentially the same. Thus younger children's understanding may be overestimated, whereas the cognitive abilities of older children may be underestimated. Doctors and patients also may not share the same goals for treatment (La Greca & Bearman, 2001; Marteau et al., 1987). And family nonadherence to the health care provider's recommendation may be the family's way of adapting the regimen so as to incorporate considerations of the child's quality of life. These issues suggest the importance of training health care providers to be sensitive to the needs of individual families and children and to

improve professional-patient communication (DiMatteo, 2000; Korsch & Marcy, 2000).

PSYCHOLOGICAL MODIFICATION OF CONDITION-RELATED PAIN

The Eastern mystic who walks on hot coals, voluntarily slows the heart, and by the power of the mind closes a wound has always fascinated inhabitants of the Western world. Fascinating, too, are the shaman's cures by removal of evil spirits, the miracles of faith healers, and cures of medical ailments by inert placebos (Ullmann & Krasner, 1975). These phenomena highlight in a dramatic fashion the possible role of psychological interventions in the treatment of medical disorders. Each phenomenon suggests that psychological procedures can directly affect physical functioning. The systematic and scientific study of how psychology can be used to directly treat physical symptoms such as pain has become part of the shifting emphasis in understanding mind-body relationships.

The use of relaxation and biofeedback to treat children's headaches is one example of attempts to directly modify physical functioning through psychological interventions. Headaches are usually classified as tension, migraine, or a combination of the two. The pain and suffering that can accompany intense headaches, and the desire to avoid potential negative aspects of drug treatment led to the exploration of nonpharmacological approaches (Andrasik, Blake, & McCarran, 1986; Lofland, Sturges, & Payne, 1999).

Biofeedback refers to a procedure in which some device gives immediate feedback to the person about a particular biological function. Feedback is usually provided by a signal such as a light or tone or by some graphic display. Such feedback, some form of relaxation training or a combination of the two, seem effective in producing clinically meaningful levels of improvement in children's headaches (Holden, Deichmann, & Levy, 1999; Labbé, 1998; Scharff, Marcus, & Masek, 2002).

Osterhaus and her colleagues (1993), for example, treated a group of school-aged youngsters (12 to 19) with migraine headaches by using a combination of relaxation training, biofeedback, and cognitive training (to challenge irrational thoughts and to replace them with more rational thoughts that might produce pleasant feelings and less stress). The treatment was a school-based, after-school program. Regular home practice was also required. Youngsters in the treatment group improved more than the waiting list control group. Forty-five percent of the treatment group, as compared with 11 percent of the control group, achieved clinically meaningful reductions in a headache index. At a 7-month follow-up evaluation, the treatment group experienced significant further posttreatment improvement. The youngsters in the control group were no longer available for comparison since, because of ethical considerations, they now were receiving treatment for their headaches.

REDUCING PROCEDURE-RELATED PAIN AND DISTRESS

Developing psychologically based procedures for enhancing the effectiveness of medical treatment is another important and growing area of interest. Procedures for dealing with pain and discomfort associated with medical treatment illustrate this potentially important contribution.

Pain and Distress. Despite its seeming simplicity, pain is a complex phenomenon that is difficult to assess. It is difficult, for example, to separate the pain or discomfort that the person is suffering from the anxiety that the person is experiencing while undergoing a painful medical procedure. This difficulty has led some to use the term *distress* to encompass pain, anxiety, and other negative affect (Jay, 1988; Varni, Katz, & Waldron, 1993). Whatever term is employed, three different response systems might be assessed: cognitive-affective, behavioral, and physiological (Blount, Piira, & Cohen, 2003; Johnson & Rodrigue, 1997).

Self-report measures of the cognitive-affective component of pain are the measures most frequently employed. This is probably an intentional choice. Because pain is a subjective experience, assessing the youth's experience of pain is important (Dahlquist & Switkin, 2003). In addition, the greater accessibility of this component and the relative ease of measurement are certainly factors. However, measurement is not without its difficulties. For example, the youngster's developmental level plays a large role in selecting a self-report measure. Because older children may be able to describe pain in semantic terms, interviews and questionnaires may be employed. Younger children need to rely on concrete and visual methods. The use of a pain thermometer that visually represents degrees of pain in numerical terms is one procedure that has been employed (see Figure 14–4). In very young children who may not have the number concepts and discriminations

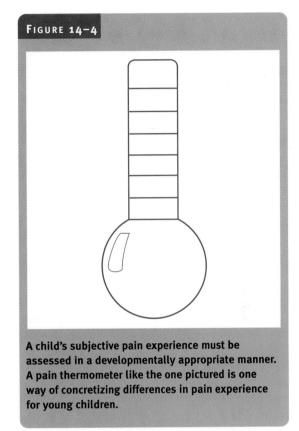

FIGURE 14–4

A child's subjective pain experience must be assessed in a developmentally appropriate manner. A pain thermometer like the one pictured is one way of concretizing differences in pain experience for young children.

required by this method, different measures can be employed. In that instance, faces with expressions from broad smiles to severe frowns, along with colors to indicate intensity of pain, may be useful. If photographs are employed, use of ethnically appropriate images may be important (Beyer & Knott, 1998; Hicks et al., 2001).

The behavioral component of children's distress (for example, behaviors that require the child to be physically restrained) can often interfere with effective medical treatment. Observational methods are often used to assess children's distress behaviors. Structured behavioral observations employing a system of defined behaviors and trained observers have been employed in a variety of contexts (Blount et al., 2003; Elliot, Jay, & Woody, 1987). Because such procedures can be expensive and time consuming, global ratings of youngsters' distress behaviors by parents or nurses are often used.

Assessment of the physiological aspect of pain is far less common (Christophersen & Mortweet, 2001). Melamed and Siegel's (1975) measurement of palmar sweat before and after youngsters underwent elective surgery and Jay and colleagues' (1987) monitoring of pulse rate prior to bone marrow aspiration are examples of use of physiological measures. However, the sophisticated equipment necessary and the difficulty involved in reliably obtaining measures such as heart rate, blood pressure, and skin conductance make such measures less likely to be employed.

Helping the Child Cope. Procedures have been developed to assist youngsters in coping with the pain associated with their disease or disorder, or with the treatments they receive (Blount et al., 2003; Powers, 1999; Walco et al., 1999). Many of the medical procedures used to assess and treat children with chronic disorders are aversive. Well-timed preparation of the youngster that contains appropriate information is the first step in reducing distress and in helping the youngster cope (Peterson & Mori, 1988; Spafford, von Baeyer, & Hicks, 2002). The basic rationale for preparation is that unexpected stress is worse than predictable stress. From the simple statement that preparation is good follows the complex question of how this is best achieved for each young person. Research provides some guidelines and suggests certain procedures (Kazak, 2005; Powers, 1999).

Children's distress and experiences of pain during medical procedures are related to the behavior of their parents (Friedman et al., 1998). When parents use strategies to distract the child or to direct the child to use coping techniques, the child exhibits less distress. In contrast, when parents attempt to comfort the child by reassuring statements or apologies, distress is greater (Harbeck-Weber & Peterson, 1996; Manimala et al., 2000; Salmon & Pereira, 2002).

The behavior of the medical practitioner is also likely to affect the youngster. An interesting finding is that information presented in a reassuring manner may reduce child distress (Dahlquist, Power, & Carlson, 1995). It may be that youngsters respond differently to parents and to staff and that a combination of distraction/direction and reassurance, respectively, from these two sources may be most beneficial to the youngster (Friedman et al., 1998).

Youngsters themselves have made some recommendations regarding coping strategies (Ross, 1988). Many of these suggestions cluster around the perception of being in control (Carpenter, 1992), and many involve the youngster's controlling the environment during the aversive treatment procedure. The following comment by a 10-year-old boy undergoing emergency room burn treatment illustrates this phenomenon:

> I said, "How about a hurting break?" and he (intern) said, "Hey, man, are you serious?" And I said, "Sure. Even when ladies are having babies they get a little rest between the bad pains." And they (the pediatric emergency room personnel) all laughed and he said, "OK,

It is common for children to exhibit distress during medical procedures. Particularly for children who must undergo frequent treatment, techniques that reduce distress can facilitate good medical care.
(Chuck Pefley/Stock Boston)

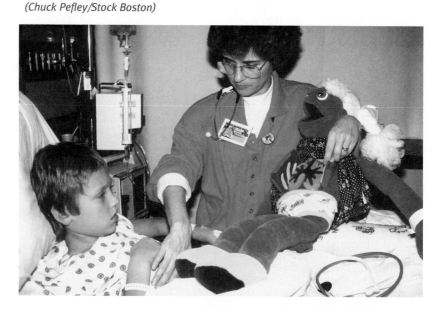

you get a 60-second break whenever you need it," and then it was much, much better, like you wouldn't believe it. (Ross, 1988, p. 5)

Although children may be capable of generating their own strategies for coping with pain and distress, procedures for teaching effective stress management/coping skills are also needed. Most interventions consist of a variety of coping strategies derived from behavioral and cognitive-behavioral perspectives. Table 14–3 lists some of the skills included in such programs.

The work of Jay and her colleagues on reducing the stress of youngsters undergoing bone marrow aspirations is a good example of such efforts (Jay et al., 1987; 1991; 1995). Bone marrow aspirations (BMAs) are often conducted for youngsters with leukemia in order to examine the marrow for evidence of cancer cells. The procedure, in which a large needle is inserted into the hip bone and the marrow is suctioned out, is very painful. The use of general anesthesia and intramuscular injections of sedatives are avoided because there is concern regarding substantial medical risks and side effects.

The intervention package developed by Jay and her colleagues consists of five major components: filmed modeling, breathing exercises, emotive imagery/distraction, positive incentive, and behavioral rehearsal. The intervention package is administered on the day of the scheduled BMA, about 30 to 45 minutes prior to the procedure.

TABLE 14–3	SOME SKILLS TAUGHT TO ASSIST CHILDREN IN COPING WITH MEDICAL PROCEDURES

Deep breathing exercises (deep inhalation and slow exhalation)
Distraction (e.g., counting ceiling tiles, music)
Emotive imagery (reconceptualizing the setting or pain)
Relaxing imagery
Progressive muscle relaxation (relaxing muscle groups)
Modeling or active coaching of coping skills
Behavioral or imaginal rehearsal (of the medical procedures)
Rewards for using coping strategies

Adapted from Dahlquist, 1992.

In the first step, youngsters are shown an 11-minute film of a same-age model undergoing BMA. The model, on a voice overlay, narrates the steps involved in the procedure, as well as his or her thoughts and feelings at crucial points. The model also exhibits positive coping behaviors and self-statements. The child in the film exhibits a realistic amount of anxiety but copes with it rather than exhibiting no anxiety and distress at all. After observing the film, the youngsters are taught simple breathing exercises, which are intended as active attention distracters but may also promote some relaxation.

The youngsters are then taught imagery/distraction techniques. Emotive imagery (Lazarus & Abramavitz, 1962) is a technique in which images are used to inhibit anxiety. A child's hero images are ascertained in a discussion with the child. They are then woven into a story that elicits positive affect that is presumed to be incompatible with anxiety, that transforms the meaning of the pain, and that encourages mastery rather than avoidance of pain. One girl's emotive imagery resembled the following story:

She pretended that Wonderwoman had come to her house and asked her to be the newest member of her Superpower Team. Wonderwoman had given her special powers. These special powers made her very strong and tough so that she could stand almost anything. Wonderwoman asked her to take some tests to try out these superpowers. The tests were called bone marrow aspirations and spinal taps. These tests hurt, but with her new superpowers, she could take deep breaths and lie very still. Wonderwoman was very proud when she found out that her superpowers worked, and she made the Superpower team. (Jay et al., 1985, p. 516)

Another imagery distraction technique involves teaching the youngster to form a pleasant image that is incompatible with the experience of pain (e.g., a day at the beach). The youngster chooses either the emotive or the incompatible strategy and is given guidance during the bone marrow procedure to help in forming the images.

A positive incentive component of the intervention includes a trophy presented as a symbol of mastery and courage. The youngster is told she can win the trophy if she does "the best that she can possibly do." The situation is structured so that every youngster can be successful in getting the trophy.

During a behavioral rehearsal phase, younger children "play doctor" with a doll, whereas older children are guided in conducting a "demonstration." The youngsters are instructed step-by-step in the administration of the BMA. As the youngster goes through the procedure, the doll is instructed to lie still and do the breathing exercises and imagery.

Jay and her colleagues (1987) compared this cognitive-behavioral package with a low-risk pharmacological intervention (oral Valium) and a minimal treatment-attention control condition. Each youngster experienced each of these interventions during three different BMAs. Which of the six possible orders of these interventions a youngster received was randomly determined. When in the cognitive-behavioral intervention condition, youngsters had significantly lower behavioral distress, lower pain ratings, and lower pulse rates than when they were in the control condition. When youngsters were in the Valium condition, they showed no significant differences from the control condition except that they had lower blood pressure scores.

The findings of this study represent one example of interventions that can help youngsters and families cope with the distress associated with certain medical procedures. The incorporation of parents or other family members into such programs can improve the maintenance of child coping, reduce parent/family distress, and improve the cost effectiveness of interventions that otherwise might require a great deal of professional time (Powers et al., 1993; Schiff et al., 2001). Such interventions hold the promise of making delivery of effective medical treatment more likely (Blount et al., 2003).

PREPARATION FOR HOSPITALIZATION

Youngsters suffering from chronic illness often require periodic hospitalization to stabilize their functioning. Other youngsters, too, often need to enter the hospital for scheduled surgery, some other procedure, or in an emergency. Indeed, about one-third of all youngsters are hospitalized at least once. Siegel and Conte (2001), writing on the history and status of hospitalization for medical care, indicated that in the mid-1950s the importance of the child's psychological reaction to early hospitalization and surgery began to be recognized. Two films by James Robertson at the Tavistock Clinic are suggested to have been instrumental in changing attitudes and practices. One film portrayed a young child's intense distress at being separated from his parents for a week while undergoing minor surgery. The other

film demonstrated the positive adjustment of a youngster whose mother remained with him while he was hospitalized for surgery. Also, a substantial research literature developed that documented the stressful effects of hospitalization (Siegel & Conte, 2001). Improvements have occurred since the 1950s and 1960s, when much of this research was conducted. For example, in 1954 most New York hospitals allowed parental contact only during two visiting hours per week. In contrast, Roberts and Wallander (1992), describing a 1988 survey of 286 hospitals in the United States and Canada, found that 98 percent of the hospitals had unrestricted visiting for parents and that 94 percent allowed parent rooming-in.

Most hospitals now also offer prehospital preparation for both the child and the parents when admissions are planned (O'Byrne, Peterson, & Saldana, 1997; Roberts & Wallander, 1992). One well-supported method involves models who, although apprehensive, cope with the hospitalization stresses. Melamed and Siegel's (1975) film, *Ethan Has an Operation*, showed a 7-year-old boy prior to, during, and after surgery. The child narrates the story and shows realistic but adaptive reactions to the procedures. The film has been shown to be an effective means of preparation for hospitalization and surgery (Melamed & Siegel, 1980; Peterson et al., 1984). This is but one example of the use of modeling. Other films and the use of puppets have been shown to be effective as well (Peterson et al., 1984), and interventions often combine modeling with explicit training of coping techniques. Current efforts are directed at preparation procedures that are well-timed; matched to individual characteristics of the child, parent, and family; and are cost effective and therefore likely to be used (Peterson et al., 1990; Siegel & Conte, 2001; Vernon & Thompson, 1993).

Despite the improvements in hospitalization procedures, children are still faced with stressors. Spirito, Stark, and Tyc (1994), for example, found that 50 percent of the chronically ill youngsters whom they asked to name a stressor since they had been in the hospital, described a specific aspect of hospitalization (e.g., noises preventing sleep, rude staff, slow service). By way of comparison, only 33 percent and 17 percent, respectively, indicated pain-related concerns or an illness-related problem (e.g., side effects of treatment, problems or limitations caused by their illness). In contrast, the percentages of youngsters hospitalized for acute illness or injuries who indicated hospital-, pain-, or illness-related stressors were 39 percent, 51 percent, and

ACCENT ● ● ● ● ●

Preventing Childhood Injury

Prevention and health maintenance is another aspect of current pediatric psychology. The prevention of injury to children is an example of this aspect of ongoing efforts at the interface of psychology and physical health.

Each year millions of children are injured. Indeed, injuries are the leading cause of death and hospitalization for youths over the age of one in the United States. Clearly the loss of life and function is tragic, and the medical costs considerable (Deal et al., 2000; Peterson, Reach, & Grabe, 2003).

Tremblay and Peterson (1999) describe some clinical and policy challenges to injury prevention. One obstacle is that serious injuries are often mistakenly assumed to occur infrequently and to be chance events and, thus, unavoidable. Such assumptions do not encourage an active prevention effort. Professionals have therefore come to suggest abandoning the common term *accident* in favor of *unintentional injury,* a term that acknowledges that the event, though not deliberate, might have been avoided.

Another challenge to injury prevention described by Tremblay and Peterson (1999) is the variety of modes of injury and thus potential interventions: "A toddler mastering the operation of the gate blocking access to the swimming pool, a 7-year-old riding a bicycle without a helmet, and a 16-year-old driving with peers who ridicule him when he stays within the speed limit are all candidates for a variety of potential interventions. . . ."

A basic contribution of psychology is the perspective that there are important behavioral antecedents to injury prevention and that behavioral responses play a critical role in maintaining those conditions. Both child (e.g., risk taking) and parent (e.g., protectiveness) behaviors can contribute to child injury (Morrongiello, Ondejko, & Littlejohn, 2004a). The risk, for example, of a child's ingesting household poisons is increased when the child is old enough to explore his or her environment but still young enough impulsively to ingest a substance, and by a setting in which poisons are accessible and constant supervision is lacking.

Prevention efforts can involve tactics directed at the entire population (multimedia campaigns), particular subsets of the population (bicycle safety programs for families with young children), or at certain milestones (yearly visits to the pediatrician). Education about the seriousness and extent of childhood injuries is part of the effort. However, more specific multiple-component prevention programs aimed at modifying risk behaviors and that include contingencies and incentives for appropriate injury-prevention behavior are also likely to be needed (Peterson et al., 2003).

It is important for parents not to rely on child-based strategies (e.g., teaching rules) prematurely (Morrongiello, Ondejko, & Littlejohn, 2004b). They should also not be lulled into a false sense of security. Parents whose children use safety equipment such as bicycle helmets may allow their child to take greater risks. This practice may offset some of the benefits of safety equipment (DeLillo & Tremblay, 2001).

---

10 percent, respectively. This finding highlights the potential differing needs of children with prior hospitalization experiences. Hospital stressors require attention, because improvements in these areas are likely to enhance the mood state and adjustment of youngsters, particularly those who are chronically ill and may require frequent hospitalizations.

The Dying Child

Clearly, one of the most distressing aspects of working with severely ill youngsters is the prospect of death. Even though much progress has been made at increasing survival rates, the numbers still fall appreciably short of 100 percent (National Cancer Institute, 2004). Increased survival rates may make the death of a child even harder to bear when it does occur (Eiser, 1994). Several important questions are raised:

- What is the child's understanding of death?
- How can we best prepare the youngster and the family?
- How do we prepare people for death while sustaining their motivation for treatment?
- Can we help the family begin to accept the child's impending death but prevent the family from premature distancing from the child?

- What do we do after the youngster dies?
- How is the helper affected by working with the dying child?

These are difficult questions.

Children's ideas about death change during development and are influenced by experiences, family attitude, and cultural factors (Candy-Gibbs, Sharp, & Petrun, 1985; McIntosh, 1999). Cognitive development plays a role in the evolving conceptualization of death (Ferrari, 1990: Oltjenbruns, 2001). Young children may think of death as being less alive and assume it to be reversible. At about 5 years of age, an appreciation of the finality of death may be present, but death still does not seem inevitable. An understanding of death as final and inevitable and of personal mortality emerges at about age 9 or 10. Nevertheless, children may be aware of death and be worried about their fatal illness even if they do not have a fully developed concept of death. And fatally ill youngsters' concepts of death do not appear to be more advanced than those of physically well youth (Jay et al., 1987). Although adolescents' understanding of death may be similar to that of adults, attention to the particular aspects of this stage of development is needed (Balk & Corr, 2001).

What of family members? They must certainly be made aware of the seriousness of the youngster's illness (Wolfe et al., 2000b). However, an appropriate balance between acceptance of death and hope for life is probably adaptive. It is a genuine challenge to prepare parents for the death of their child, while also enabling them to help the child emotionally and to assist with the treatment regimen. This undertaking requires knowledgeable and sensitive mental health staff. As our ability to lengthen survival—and perhaps to raise hopes of some future cure—increases, the problem becomes even more difficult. Integration of support services into the total treatment program and immediate availability and access are important in delivering needed help. Once a point is reached where the child's death is likely, the focus of intervention must shift. Information and support are still needed, but the focus must change to helping the child and family to be most comfortable and to make the best use of the remaining time. Moreover, the family should not be abandoned after the young person's death. Continued assistance is needed and such support should be a part of the total treatment (Friedman et al., 1998; Wolfe et al., 2000a).

Caregivers, too, are not immune to the effects of observing a youngster's dying. Efforts must be made to educate caregivers and to reduce the high cost of helping: the inevitable stress, the feelings of helplessness, and the likelihood of burnout (Koocher, 1980; Sahler et al., 2000). These are not trivial matters. The helpers' adjustment and efficiency are not the only concern, so also is the potential impact of their behavior on the family and youngster (Hilden et al., 2001). In *Who's Afraid of Death on a Leukemia Ward?* Vernick and Karon (1965) offered poignant anecdotes to this effect. One anecdote describes the impact of helpers' behavior on a 9-year-old patient who, after taking a turn for the worse, received some medical treatment and began to show improvement:

> *One day while she was having breakfast I commented that she seemed to have gotten her old appetite back. She smiled and agreed. . . . I mentioned that it looked as if she had been through the worst of this particular siege. She nodded in agreement. I went on to say that it must have been very discouraging to feel so sick that all she could do was worry—worry about dying. She nodded affirmatively. I recognized that the whole episode must have been very frightening and that I knew it was a load off her mind to be feeling better. She let out a loud, "Whew," and went on to say that except for me, nobody really talked with her. "It was like they were getting ready for me to die." (p. 395)*

Certainly, one of the most difficult decisions is what to tell the dying youngster. A protective approach or "benign lying" was once advocated. The youngster was not to be burdened, and a sense of normalcy and optimism was to be maintained. Most professionals now feel that this approach is not helpful and probably is doomed to failure anyway. The stress on the family of maintaining this deception is great, and the likelihood that the youngster will believe the deception is questionable. In this decision, and in other aspects of working with the child and family, some balance must be struck that takes into consideration the child's developmental level, past experiences, timing, and an understanding of the family's culture and belief system (Dolgin & Jay, 1989; Oltjenbruns, 2001). An example of such a balance is illustrated in the following excerpt:

> *A child with a life-threatening illness should be told the name of the condition, given an accurate explanation of the nature of the*

illness (up to the limit of his ability to compre-hend), and told that it is a serious illness of which people sometimes die. At the same time, however, the child and family can be told about treatment options and enlisted as allies to fight the disease. An atmosphere must be established in which all concerned have the opportunity to ask questions, relate fantasies, and express concerns, no matter how scary or far fetched they may seem. When the patient is

feeling sick, weak, and dying, there is no need to [be reminded] of the prognosis. If a family and patient know a prognosis is poor but per-sist in clinging to hope, one has no right to wrest that from them. The truth, humanely tempered, is important, but we must be mind-ful of the patient and how [the patient's] needs are served. To tell the "whole truth" or a "white lie" for the benefit of the teller serves no one in the end. (Koocher & Sallan, 1978, p. 300)

SUMMARY

HISTORICAL CONTEXT

- *The current view that psychological factors are rele-vant to physical disorders in a number of different ways represents a shift from the earlier, more limited view of psychosomatic diseases caused by emotional factors.*

PSYCHOLOGICAL AND FAMILY INFLUENCES ON MEDICAL CONDITIONS

- *Current conceptualizations of the role of psycholog-ical and family factors in chronic illness are illustrated through the example of asthma. Psycho-logical and family influences are among a variety of possible trigger mechanisms that can bring on an asthmatic episode, the child's asthma may impact other family members, and family assistance is needed in managing the medical condition.*

CONSEQUENCES OF CHRONIC CONDITIONS

- *There is likely to be considerable individual vari-ability in how youngsters and families cope with chronic conditions. Adjustment is likely to be an ongoing process and is best understood as being influenced by a number of variables.*

- *Researchers have sought to determine the impact of parameters of the illness, such as severity, and of aspects of family functioning, such as control and organization, on the chronically ill youngster's adjustment.*

- *With increasing survival rates for youngsters with chronic conditions, the adaptation over time of the youngster and family to the illness and its treatment*

are of great interest. Adaptation to cancer and HIV/AIDS are two examples.

FACILITATING MEDICAL TREATMENT

- *Psychology can contribute to effective treatment of medical conditions in a number of ways.*

- *Medical treatment may be rendered ineffective because of difficulties that the patient and family experience in trying to adhere to prescribed treat-ment regimens. Attempts to improve adherence require attention to multiple dimensions such as the youngster's developmental level, peer and social influences, family patterns of interaction, and the role of the health care professional.*

- *Psychological treatments (for example, relaxation and biofeedback) may modify physical functioning and the pain associated with chronic conditions. Treatment of migraine headaches is an example of this kind of application.*

- *Psychologically based procedures may also facilitate the delivery of medical interventions. Treatment pro-grams to reduce the pain and distress felt by youngsters who are undergoing medical procedures and prepara-tion for hospitalization are examples of psychological influences enhancing medical interventions.*

THE DYING CHILD

- *Despite increasingly high survival rates, the prospect of death is one of the most distressing aspects of working with some chronically ill youth. Psycholog-ical contributions to helping these children, their families, and the professionals who work with them can be an aid in effective and caring treatment.*

KEY TERMS

●●●●●●○○○

psychosomatic disorders *(p. 400)*

psychological factors affecting medical condition *(p. 400)*

psychosomatic medicine *(p. 400)*

functional limitation *(p. 406)*

functional disabilities *(p. 407)*

adherence to (compliance with) medical regimens *(p. 411)*

honeymoon period *(p. 412)*

biofeedback *(p. 414)*

emotive imagery *(p. 417)*

Prevention and Evolving Concerns for Youth

It is a truism that the future of every society depends on its youth, and that the welfare of children and adolescents is tied to many factors. The lives of youth are affected by what is happening in the personal lives of their parents and in their communities, the value assigned to the young, the priorities given to health care and education, and a host of other variables. The economic resources of nations make a difference, and it is not surprising that even basic care and opportunity are especially problematic in developing countries. Nevertheless, because the implementation of programs devoted to youth also depends on social attitudes, care can vary enormously even when resources are adequate. Sensitive and attentive adults are looking at such influences with an eye toward better care for youth.

Progress in understanding human development also is stimulating efforts toward optimizing the potential of the young. Although no one would deny that knowledge about development is incomplete, we have come far from viewing children and adolescents simply as incomplete adults. Their unique needs are better known; the general course of physical, intellectual, and social growth is well on the way to being mapped; and developmental influences, including risk and protective factors, are increasingly understood. Enthusiasm exists for using this knowledge to reduce behavioral disorder, enhance development, and enrich lives. Thus both societal and professional factors are shaping concerns for youth and the ways in which these concerns are manifested in programs and policies.

Our discussion in this chapter is necessarily selective. Emphasizing behavioral and psychological issues, we recognize many interacting influences, as is consistent with our general view of development. A major theme of the chapter is the progress being made in preventing behavioral and developmental disorders, and we begin there. In turn, we look at selected topics regarding the care of youth in different family circumstances, mental health services for young people, and the well-being of children and adolescents living in countries other than the United States.

Preventing Behavioral Disorder

In the United States, interest in prevention can be traced to the early 20th-century writings of Clifford Beers, the mental hygiene movement, and the creation of the child guidance clinics (Coie, Miller-Johnson, & Bagwell, 2000; Heller, 1996). However, progress did not come easily. Several reasons accounted for this situation. Mental health professionals are trained for treatment, and they are financially rewarded for treatment. And it has always been difficult to deflect funding from the obvious needs of those already displaying problems, a need that is never completely met. As a result, prevention usually has been poorly funded. In addition, doubts have been expressed about the basis for prevention. Disorders with known etiology are clearly preventable, at least in principle. If we know that an infection of the brain causes disturbed behavior, we can work toward finding ways to prevent the infection. But the etiology of behavioral disorder is often difficult to establish and is likely to be multifactorial. In addition, prevention efforts—such as sex education and drug programs—have sometimes been resisted by the general public as intruding on parental prerogatives or values (Enzer & Heard, 2000).

More recently, interest in prevention has increased. From a humanitarian viewpoint, prevention clearly is more desirable, because it averts discomfort and suffering. And even with treatment, some disorders are difficult to reverse. Practical considerations also argue for prevention. The number of professionals required to treat mental disorder might never exist (Coie et al., 2000), intervention is especially unlikely to be available to certain groups of people, and treatment is exceedingly costly. In addition, much more is now known about risk and protective factors in psychopathology, providing a firmer basis for prevention efforts. Finally, evidence for the effectiveness of prevention programs and for principles to guide programs has become clearer (DiLillo & Peterson, 2001; Durlak & Wells, 1997; Nation et al., 2003).

Conceptualizing Prevention

Caplan is usually credited with being a catalyst for the preventive approach in mental health (Lorion, 2000). He took the public health approach, with its underlying belief that major diseases have been controlled only by preventive efforts. Caplan's (1964) three-prong model has served as a general framework for thinking about prevention. In this model, prevention is viewed as primary, secondary, or tertiary. *Primary prevention*, which attempts to stave off disorders in the first place, involves both general health enhancement and prevention of specific dysfunction. *Secondary prevention* is usually defined as the effort to shorten the duration of existing cases through early referral, diagnosis, and treatment. It is a "nipping in the bud" strategy. *Tertiary prevention* aims to reduce problems that are residual to disorders; it might thus seek to minimize the negative impact of labeling a child as learning disabled or to rehabilitate a person who has suffered a severe mental disorder. Tertiary prevention is clearly worthwhile, but it is an after-the-fact strategy that reduces dysfunction.

Subsequent to Caplan's approach, prevention has been defined in several ways. More recent conceptualizations tend to view it in terms of prevention that occurs prior to the full onset of disorders or problems. Figure 15–1, loosely based on the Institute of Medicine's approach (a component of the National Academy of Science), shows one way to depict prevention. Prevention is set apart from treatment and from aftercare that might reduce additional dysfunction, and it has three components (Munoz, Mrazek, & Haggerty, 1996).

1. Universal prevention strategies are targeted to entire populations for which greater than average risk has not been identified in individuals. Ideally, cost of interventions is low, the interventions are acceptable to the populations, and risk of adverse outcome from the interventions is low. Hypothetical examples are encouraging parents to read to their children to maximize cognitive growth and promoting exercise and proper diet to avoid obesity.

2. The second component, high-risk prevention strategies (also called selective strategies), targets individuals who are at higher than average risk for disorder. Thus intervention might be directed toward individuals or subgroups with biological risk, high stress, family dysfunction, or poverty.

3. The third component, indicated strategies, is targeted to high-risk individuals who show minimal symptoms or signs forecasting a disorder, or who have biological markers for a disorder, but do not meet the criteria for the disorder.

The Wellness Goal. One of the more notable ways in which definitions of prevention vary has to do with acceptance or rejection of the goal of wellness. The Institute of Medicine defines prevention in terms of averting illness or disorder but deliberately does not include efforts designed for wellness, that is, the enhancement of optimal functioning or health (Munoz et al., 1996). The contrasting position

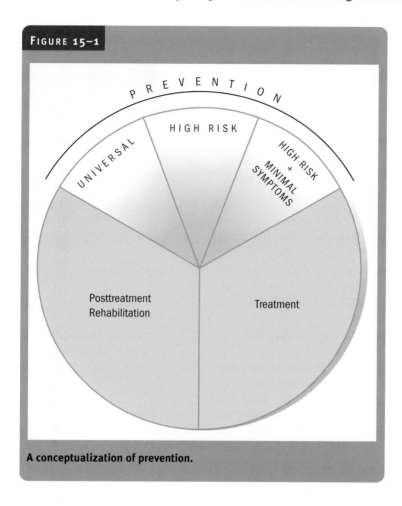

FIGURE 15–1

A conceptualization of prevention.

recommends the building of individual competence, connections to others, security, and optimism as protection from disorder and disease (Albee, 1986, 1996; Weissberg, Kumpfer, & Seligman, 2003). In this regard, Albee noted that many mental disorders are linked to poverty, sexism, and racism and that such social ills must be confronted. Cowen (1991; 1994) also argued for wellness, defining it as going beyond the absence of malfunction to such things as belongingness, purpose, control, and satisfaction with oneself and one's life.

The American Psychological Association's Task Force on Prevention: Promoting Strength, Resilience, and Health in Young People has endorsed the wellness approach (Weissberg et al., 2003). Programs to enhance wellness can take many forms, occur in different settings, and involve the promotion of specific social policies. Such programs require input from diverse fields, such as mental health, human development, community planning, social policy, and the like. Relevant to young people, a developmental psychopathology approach is valuable in pointing to

factors that facilitate optimal growth and resilience (Cicchetti & Rogosch, 2002).

DIVERSE PREVENTION PROGRAMS

Prevention programs vary tremendously in strategy, focus, and setting. Primary prevention programs for children have emphasized the modification of either the environment or children's learning or behavior and have involved mental health professionals, teachers, parents, and college students as change agents (Durlak & Wells, 1997). In practice, many prevention interventions target at-risk populations, for example, children with developmental delay or single-parent families.

A distinction can be made between programs that focus on preventing a potential array of negative outcomes and programs that focus more on specific symptoms or disorders. The former include, for example, interventions with economically disadvantaged children to enhance general development and prevent the varied cognitive, social, and emotional adversities associated with poverty (e.g., Peters, Petrunka, & Arnold, 2003). Programs focusing more on specific psychopathology include, for example, interventions for deterring the development of depression or conduct-disordered behaviors (Clarke et al., 2003; Hinshaw, 2002; Reid, Webster-Stratton, & Bayder, 2004).

PREVENTION PROGRAMS TARGETING MULTIPLE ADVERSE OUTCOMES

A considerable number of well-designed and evaluated programs that seek to prevent multiple adverse outcomes currently exist. To give the flavor of them, we detail two that are family or community based and two that are more school based. These examples also illustrate interventions at different points in development.

Intervention for Low Birthweight Infants. These programs target the development of low birthweight or premature infants. The association of low birthweight with a variety of adverse outcomes (e.g., medical complications, developmental delays, behavioral problems, poor academic performance) that may persist into adolescence is well established (Field, Hernandez-Reif, & Freedman, 2004). Extraordinary medical intervention is often critical to favorable outcome, but so too is the quality of care given to the infants. The hope of many prevention programs is that adverse effects can be reduced or overcome by high-quality programs that enhance parents' attitudes and skills, family resources, and social support (Greenberg & Crnic, 1988; Sameroff, 1990).

An example of such an effort is the Infant Health and Development Program, a comprehensive 3-year randomized clinical trial that consisted of home visits, family education and support, and educational day care for the children (Bradley et al., 1994). It was conducted at several sites. Evaluations when the children were age 3 showed positive effects on infant health and cognitive development compared to a group of follow-up control children. However, outcomes at age 8 indicated attenuation of effects; only treated children of relatively higher birthweight (2100–2500 grams versus 2100 grams or less) maintained some cognitive and academic gains (McCarton et al., 1997). These findings raised questions about expectations for such prevention programs (Baumeister & Bacharach, 2002). We do not know, of course, whether lengthier intervention would have brought more meaningful benefits (Blair & Wahlsten, 2002). It would not be unreasonable that sustained support and special educational input are

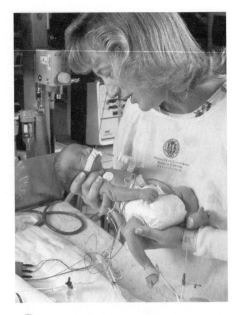

Medical advances have lowered the death rate of premature or low birthweight infants and investigations are under way in how best to optimize development and prevent problems.
(Jonathan Nourok/PhotoEdit, Inc.)

required by infants who come into the world at markedly low birthweight/prematurity.

In part due to the limited success of this type of prevention program, some workers have advocated for even earlier intervention. Stimulation programs for preterm and low birthweight infants that begin before hospital discharge are an example (Field et al., 2004). Infant massage is one type of stimulation program. Preterm newborns, once they are medically stabilized, receive massage therapy (e.g., Dieter et al., 2003). Three times per day, for 5 to 10 days, infants are stroked (with moderate pressure) during the first and third 5-minute phases and are moved passively during the middle 5-minute phase. Infants receiving massage therapy achieve significantly greater weight gain than control low birthweight infants and thus earlier hospital discharge. Research findings suggest that the effects of infant massage are related to physiological and biochemical changes associated with normal growth. No adverse effects have been reported and other developmental benefits have been noted as well. Some of these outcomes, such as reduced irritability, enhanced sleep, and better orientation, may improve parent-infant interactions, and this may be a key mechanism to enhance development. It has been recommended that parents, other family members, and hospital volunteers can be trained to perform these massage procedures, thus improving the cost-effectiveness of intervention and allowing for continuation of stimulation after hospital discharge (Field et al., 2004). Such family involvement may also enhance caregiver-infant interactions. Investigations of various types of infant stimulation programs, of which types of interventions are best for which infants, and of the long-term effects of such programs are needed (Lester, Bigsby, & Miller-Loncar, 2004).

Overall, the modest success of interventions for low birthweight and premature infants suggests efforts to improve at-risk preventive approaches and also to reduce the incidence of preterm birth and low birthweight (Field et al., 2004; McCarton, Wallace, & Bennett, 1996).

Preschool Intervention for Disadvantaged Children. Among the most important of interventions designed to reduce the risks of poverty and

disadvantage are early school programs. An initial underlying assumption was that brief interventions might allow poor children to be on equal footing with more economically fortunate youngsters. It was assumed that early experience is especially important for intellectual and social growth. Thus it was anticipated that preschool intervention might put children on a path to academic achievement that, in turn, could boost their chances of attaining self-worth, decent jobs, and healthy, fulfilling lives. The intent was well captured in the name Head Start, given to the federally funded program initiated in 1965 that included preschool programs (Ripple & Zigler, 2003.) (See Accent: "A Head Start for Children at Risk.")

Innumerable early intervention programs have been funded by private, local, and federal agencies. Over a 30-year period, the effectiveness of early

ACCENT ● ● ● ● ●

A Head Start for Children at Risk

Head Start was initiated as part of the federal government's War on Poverty. Although preschool education is an important element, from the beginning Head Start was conceptualized as a comprehensive developmental program to enhance cognitive, social, and emotional growth; health; and family and community relationships (Ripple & Zigler, 2003; Zigler, 1999). It now serves children from birth to age 5 and their low-income families. Head Start encompasses several major components.

- **Child Education.** The educational component places preschoolers into classes with a high teacher-student ratio. The ethnic and cultural characteristics of the community are considered; for example, by incorporating bilingual staff.

- **Health.** Physical and mental health is emphasized. Nutritious meals are served, and parents are offered education in nutrition. Hearing, vision, and dental checkups are obtained; follow-up medical treatment is provided when appropriate. Mental health consultation is available to evaluate special needs and to provide training in child development for staff and parents.

- **Parent Involvement.** Community involvement is fundamental to Head Start. Parents participate in decisions about the program, many serve as volunteers or employees, and many participate in workshops related to the welfare of their children or family.

- **Social Services.** When Head Start families have needs for other social services, they are aided in

obtaining services. The object is to strengthen the family unit so that it may do the best job possible in rearing children and supporting its adult members.

In general, home-based programs, research and evaluation activities, and relationships with communities and universities are part of the program (Ramey, 1999). The Early Head Start program provides services to infants, pregnant women, and their families.

In 2003, Head Start enrolled nearly 910,000 children, mostly 3- and 4-year-olds (Head Start Statistical Fact Sheet, 2004). About 13 percent of them had disabilities. Parents of current or past attendees comprised 28 percent of the staff, and 880,000 parents volunteered in local programs.

Despite criticism and some difficulties over the years, research indicates that Head Start can improve school readiness and several areas of child and parent functioning (Ripple & Zigler, 2003). The process has been likened to a relay race: A burst of cognitive and school readiness fades, but not before the baton has been given to other runners on the team—teacher expectations, self-confidence, school promotions, avoidance of special education, parental aspirations, and so forth (Woodhead, 1988). However, due to the lack of large-scale, well-controlled outcome data, a major longitudinal study is underway to compare Head Start and non–Head Start children through the first grade. Additional factors will also be examined, such as the quality of programs, parenting practices, and community support.

A critical component of Head Start is preschool experience that offers multiple activities and a high teacher-to-child ratio.
(Bob Daemmrich/The Image Works)

school interventions, including that of Head Start, has been studied. This large literature is in fundamental agreement on many points (Guralnick, 1998; Ramey, 1999; Ramey & Ramey, 1998; St. Pierre & Layzer, 1998). The following are among the conclusions that have been drawn.

- High-quality interventions show positive effects on cognitive and social development.
- The child's participation for 2 years is better than for 1 year.
- Greater benefits are associated with greater intensity of the program (that is, positive experiences tightly packed into time).
- The quality of teachers strongly influences program effectiveness.
- Parent involvement is critical for the young child's success.
- Programs that provide more comprehensive services have greater benefits.
- Some children benefit more than others, and benefits appear related to initial risk status.
- Initial benefits on standardized intellectual tests fade over time, especially when learning and motivation are not supported by the social environment.
- Longer-term benefits can be observed in the school environment. These include reduced grade retention and special education placement, and increased rates of high school graduation. Some

studies also show higher employment rates and reduction of antisocial behavior.

These findings indicate that quality programs can make a difference in the lives of many children disadvantaged by poverty and special disabilities. (See p. 79 for the Abecedarian Project.) Nevertheless, there is agreement that continuous educational and other support is important and that early prevention programs, even when of high quality, cannot be expected to alleviate all of the ills of persistent poverty.

The Primary Mental Health Project (PMHP). The PMHP is an important aspect of the contributions of Emory Cowen to our knowledge regarding the prevention of mental health problems and the promotion of wellness in children (Cicchetti et al., 2001). This project, initiated in 1957 at the University of Rochester, took the elementary school as its focus for preventive efforts (Cowen et al., 1975; Zax & Cowen, 1967). The school was selected not only because it is the setting for much socialization and learning, but also because children were experiencing school maladjustment. These students were not being well served, the rest of the class was being disrupted, and teacher morale was suffering.

Although the PMHP has evolved over the years, its continuing thrust has been systematic early identification and prompt preventive intervention for school maladjustment. What follows is a brief description of the principal aspects of the program. More extensive descriptions are available elsewhere (e.g., Cowen et al., 1996; Cowen & Hightower, 1989; 1990).

The PMHP model has four basic structural elements (Braden & Hightower, 1998; Hightower, 1997):

- A focus on young primary-grade children and provision of preventive services before problems become entrenched;

- An emphasis on an active screening process that makes use of multiple brief, reliable, and valid measures to identify children showing early signs of school adjustment difficulties;

- A use of carefully selected, trained, and supervised paraprofessionals to provide direct services to children; and

- A change from traditional direct-service roles for school-based mental health professionals to services such as consultation and training.

An innovative aspect of the PMHP was mass screening of youngsters soon after they began school. Screening methods have consisted of parental interviews, psychological testing, teacher reports, and direct observations. Children identified by the PMHP either as already manifesting maladjustment or as likely to do so in the future, become the recipients of special treatment by nonprofessional child aides. Many of the child aides are mothers with relatively modest formal education. They receive training and supervision at the project, and are selected for personal qualities such as warmth, empathy, flexibility, and a history of enjoying and working well with children and adults. Although the use of nonprofessional child aides was initially justified on the basis of professional shortages and financial austerity, the child aides are now seen as an asset of the program rather than a compromise (Braden & Hightower, 1998; Cowen et al., 1996).

Conversation, books, games, and media provide a framework for the child associate's interaction with the child. The child is encouraged to deal with problem areas and feelings, and enhancement of self-esteem is considered important. Specific activities depend on the needs of the individual child. The program has been flexibly applied so as to meet the demands of particular situations and communities, and research findings have been incorporated to guide such applications (Braden & Hightower, 1998; Spomer & Cowen, 2001).

Research has been an essential component of the PMHP; it was designed from the start to improve the program and to demonstrate possible benefit (Cowen et al., 1996). Evaluations over the years suggest that the program has been effective, and research findings have been fed back into the program to structure improvements (Braden & Hightower, 1998). Research has been conducted, for example, on assessment instruments to initially screen children and to evaluate their progress (Gesten, 1976; Hightower et al., 1987). And when some data indicated that those most helped were shy-anxious children, greater efforts were made to aid students with learning disabilities and acting-out problems (Cowen, Gesten, & Wilson, 1979; Lorion, Cowen, & Caldwell, 1974). These are examples of an appreciable body of research that has guided the development and dissemination of the program.

The PMHP began as a single demonstration project, but by 1983, twenty PMHP projects were operating in the Rochester, New York, area. Through active dissemination efforts, the program was also adopted elsewhere, and an estimated 1,500 schools in more than 700 school districts around the world are believed to have implemented the project (Cowen et al., 1996).

On the basis of their experiences in the PMHP, Cowen and his colleagues also developed several additional projects to expand the dissemination and provision of prevention services. The Rochester Child Resilience Project (RCRP) is an example (Cowen et al., 1996). This project is rooted in understanding the impact of chronic life stress on children and the resilience of some children experiencing monumental adverse circumstances. The project was designed to investigate the correlates and antecedents of resilient outcomes among highly stressed fourth- to sixth-grade urban children. Results from the RCRP identified variables that differentiate stress-affected and stress-resilient children and their parents (Cowen et al., 1990; 1996; Magnus et al., 1999a,b). Some of these were child variables, such as a realistic sense of control, problem-solving skills, coping strategies, empathy, and self-esteem. Other variables involved the parent-child relationship, such as a warm caregiving environment, more positive and age-appropriate discipline practices, and the caregiver's sense of being an effective parent. This research is an example of how investigations of resilience can be useful to those concerned with enhancing the wellness of children and families at risk because of highly stressful environments (Cowen, 1994; 2000).

The School Transitional Environment Project (STEP). STEP is designed to avert future difficulties for students who are functioning adaptively in their schools (Felner & Adan, 1988; Felner et al., 1993;

Braden & Hightower, 1998). The focus is on a normative life event—the transition into middle/junior high school, or high school. School transition can be a risky time for youngsters; it is associated with diminished academic performance, substance abuse, delinquency, and school dropout. Transition is considered riskier in schools that provide little social support and have a complex organization (e.g., students feeding in from many other schools, many new social demands). STEP targets such schools.

Central to STEP is the creation of units—groups of four or five homerooms. Students in a STEP unit are assigned to a homeroom and to the same academic classes as well. The STEP homerooms and classes are placed in physical proximity, so that cohesion is increased and complexity of the large school decreased. A second component of STEP has homeroom teachers take on new tasks in guidance and monitoring. For example, they assist students in selecting classes, provide brief counseling, and oversee attendance and truancy. Teachers receive training in these areas. A team approach to solving problems is structured through regular teacher meetings to discuss student functioning, needs for referral, and problems. In this way, STEP units simulate small schools by creating small units in which groups of people are in close contact and responsible to each other. The intervention largely focuses on modifying the environment.

Evaluations have shown STEP's effectiveness (Felner et al., 2001). Compared with control students, STEP students attended school at higher rates, had higher academic performance, and rated the school environment favorably. Three- to five-year follow-ups found that STEP students were significantly less likely to drop out of school and more likely to maintain their academic performance and achievement levels. They also had reduced levels of social, emotional, and behavioral problems and of substance abuse compared with control/comparison students who showed more of these problems following transitions. This favorable outcome generally held in subsequent STEP programs, which serviced students from working, semiskilled, and blue-collar families; minority students; and students in urban, suburban, and rural settings (Braden & Hightower, 1998; Felner et al., 2001).

The finding that STEP students no longer showed significant declines in academic performance and achievement was an important outcome. However, it was also the case that students did not show gains in these areas over time. It was, in part, from such considerations that the Project on High-Performing Learning Communities (Project HiPlaces)

emerged as an outgrowth of STEP. This project seeks to provide practitioners and policy makers with a knowledge base and model for "what works" in educational reform. Project HiPlaces focuses on all students in grades K–12 by seeking school change rather than more individually focused change. According to Felner and colleagues (2001), the question that summarizes the project's concerns is "How do we create educational contexts in which all students are nurtured and challenged in ways that lead them to be highly effective learners, to perform and achieve at high levels, and to be healthy, responsible, and successful citizens in our democracy" (p. 190). Thus, Project HiPlaces is broadly concerned with the well-being of youth.

PREVENTION PROGRAMS TARGETING SPECIFIC ADVERSE OUTCOMES

Those who undertake these prevention interventions are especially concerned about the prevalence or consequences of particular problems. Prevention programs targeting depression and suicide serve as examples of such efforts.

Prevention of Depression. Several aspects of depression in children and adolescents suggest the potential value of prevention interventions and of high-risk approaches (Birmaher et al., 1996b; Kazdin & Marciano, 1998). Information has accumulated regarding identifiable risk factors for depression. Risk factors such as familial risk (e.g., depressed parents), peak periods of incidence (adolescence), and early episodes of subclinical levels of depression can be used to identify at-risk youngsters. A preventive approach is also suggested by the nature of depression. Depression is often characterized by recurring episodes; thus, early intervention may affect the long-term course of the disorder. Although few studies of prevention of depression in youngsters have been reported, there is some suggestion that such efforts hold promise.

A prevention program—the Coping with Stress course—has been derived from the Adolescent Coping with Depression program discussed in Chapter 7 (p. 189). The Coping with Stress course focuses on a single module of the larger program—cognitive restructuring. Fifteen one-hour sessions, delivered over five weeks to groups of six to ten adolescents, target cognitions such as irrational or highly negative beliefs, guilt, hopelessness, and worthlessness. This prevention program has been evaluated, and significantly fewer prospective cases of major depression were found among high-risk participants (Clarke et al., 2003). For example, Clarke and colleagues (1995) screened 1,652 adolescents and identified youngsters who experienced depressive symptoms but did not meet the criteria for diagnosed depression. These adolescents were randomly assigned either to a 15-session cognitive-behavioral intervention or to an "usual care" control condition. Both groups were also allowed to pursue whatever outside sources of care they desired. There was a significant difference in the incidence of major depression or dysthymia at 12-month follow-up—14.5 percent in the treated group versus 25.7 percent in the control group. Similar findings were obtained for an intervention with at-risk offspring of depressed parents (Clarke et al., 2001).

Another prevention effort is illustrated by the work of Jaycox and colleagues (1994). Youngsters between 10 and 13 years of age who had elevated scores on the Children's Depression Inventory and had reported high levels of parental conflict in their families were identified. The children were assigned either to a group that received cognitive interventions and social problem-solving training or to a no-intervention control condition. Children receiving the intervention experienced significantly greater relief and prevention of depressive symptoms at the end of the intervention and at 6-month and 2-year follow-ups. Indeed, differences between the two conditions increased over time (Gillham et al., 1995).

Suicide Prevention. The Centers for Disease Control and Prevention has identified strategies to improve the prevention of suicide among young people. Table 15–1 summarizes these recommendations. A variety of preventive efforts can be derived from these recommendations, and indeed, efforts in multiple domains are likely to be needed.

Gould and colleagues (2003) reviewed a number of youth suicide prevention efforts. We briefly highlight a few of the preventive strategies. Many of these are school based. Suicide awareness curricula add information about suicide to the school curriculum. The hope is that student will be more likely to self-disclose difficulties and that youngsters will be more likely to refer or report peers for support. Evidence regarding effectiveness, however, is mixed. Some reports indicate desired changes in knowledge, attitude, and help-seeking behavior. However, other reports suggest detrimental effects, such as decreases in desired attitude and help-seeking behavior, or they express concern that suicidal behaviors might be inadvertently imitated.

TABLE 15–1	STRATEGIES TO IMPROVE THE PREVENTION OF SUICIDE AMONG YOUNG PERSONS RECOMMENDED BY THE CENTERS FOR DISEASE CONTROL AND PREVENTION

Build support for families, communities, and neighborhoods.
Ensure accessible and effective clinical care for mental, physical, and substance abuse disorders.
Expand suicide prevention efforts for youths, emphasizing nonviolent handling of disputes, conflict resolution, and skill building in problem solving.
Promote awareness of suicide intervention resources such as mental health centers, counseling centers, and hotlines.
Restrict inappropriate access to firearms.

From Centers for Disease Control and Prevention, 2001.

Peer helper programs educate and train selected youngsters in skills related to mental health problems. The role that peer helpers play can vary considerably by program. Youngsters may be more likely to confide in a peer than an adult, and trained peers can provide information, support, and encouragement to seek help. They can also report warning signs to a responsible adult. An additional strategy, gatekeeper training programs, helps school personnel develop the knowledge and skills needed to identify youngsters at risk and to make appropriate referrals. These strategies are frequently employed. However, so far there is insufficient evidence to support their effectiveness.

Skill training programs typically have multiple components that emphasize the development of problem-solving, coping, and cognitive skills. Suicidal youth are thought to have deficits in these areas. High-risk youngsters are often targeted. Evidence of the effectiveness of such programs exists, but additional research is needed to identify which components are responsible for risk reduction.

Screening is a prevention strategy aimed at finding cases of suicidal behavior by conducting multiple-stage schoolwide assessments focused on recent and frequent suicidal ideation, past suicide attempts, depression, and substance abuse. After initial screenings, those identified can receive a second stage of assessment to eliminate false positives (those identified as potentially a suicide risk who are actually not). The ultimate effectiveness of screening depends on the availability of services for these youth and the effectiveness of the referral process for seeking help.

Postvention/crisis intervention programs seek to make timely responses to a suicide. The goal is to reduce suicide contagion or the onset or exacerbation of problems (e.g., posttraumatic stress disorder, depression) among students following the suicide of a schoolmate. These interventions seek to provide assistance in the grief process, facilitate support, and identify and refer youngsters who may be at risk. Research on the effectiveness of such programs is limited.

Efforts at preventing suicide may also take place in the community. Crisis centers and telephone hotlines are available in many communities. Because suicidal behavior is often impulsive and time limited, efforts to restrict the availability of firearms are a part of prevention efforts. Limiting access to a lethal method during a high-risk time period may prevent suicide. Educating media professionals about how to report suicide also can be successful in reducing suicide contagion. Indeed, following the implementation of media guidelines on how to report suicidal behavior, subsequent suicide rates have declined. Educating primary health care workers, who often see youth during crucial periods, can also be a part of community-based efforts. As with other prevention programs, continued evaluation and strengthening are crucial.

Who Cares for Children: Family Issues

The centrality of family influences on child and adolescent development has been evident throughout this book. We are all aware that U.S. families have changed dramatically in the last several decades, most obviously through increased rates of divorced, single-parent, and step-parent households. (For a review of divorce, see p. 58.) Family roles also have shifted, largely because wives and mothers are employed outside the home. Many individuals voice concerns about the health of the family. Nevertheless, scholars who have studied the history of the family in the United States have challenged the idea that the family has decayed from some past idyllic form, and they point out that various family forms have always been sizable in number. Research, too,

has led us away from a focus on family *structure* with findings that it is family *processes* (e.g., warmth, communication, support) that are of critical importance for the well-being of family members.

It is, nonetheless, appropriate to ask questions about the impact of family changes on the family and, more specifically, on who is caring for children, under what circumstances, and with what consequences. Although the scope of this matter is beyond what we can do in the present discussion, it is our purpose to draw attention to the issue by examining maternal employment and day care for children. In addition, we look at two other areas—adoption and foster care—that directly implicate the daily care and experiences of a subset of children.

MATERNAL EMPLOYMENT AND CHILD CARE

The increase of women in the labor force has transformed family life (Cabrera et al., 2000; Steil, 2001). In 1950, 12 percent of married women with a preschool child worked outside the home. In 2003, that figure was 60 percent—and 77 percent for married women with a child age 6 to 17 (U.S. Bureau of the Census, 2004–2005).

Studies of the effects of mothers' employment on the women themselves, the marital relationship, and children show few overall differences between families in which mothers do or do not work (Harvey, 1999; Muller, 1995; Silverstein, 1991). The impact depends on a host of factors, including the child's age, the amount of time parents spend at work, the way remaining time is used by the family, the quality of child-care arrangements, parental attitudes, family structure, and the like (Gottfried & Gottfried, 1988; Hoffman, 1989; Scarr, Phillips, & McCartney, 1989). With regard to child effects, perhaps no factor has been of more concern than children's being cared for by adults other than their mothers or parents.

Is Nonparental Child Care Harmful to Young Children? Unsurprising is that nonparental care for children, birth through 6 years of age, is higher when mothers are employed for longer hours outside of the home. These children are cared for in many different arrangements. Care is provided by relatives or nonfamily, in or out of the child's home, or by nonfamily in center-based settings. The young child's age affects the type of care provided, with nonparental care—especially in center-based programs—increasing notably after age 2 (Federal Interagency Forum on

Child and Family Statistics, 2004). Family income and ethnic/racial background are also associated with type of care. For example, more children are cared for by relatives in families below the poverty line, and more white (non-Hispanic) and black children are cared for in child-care facilities than Hispanic children.

What is known about the impact of non-parental care on young children's well-being? Decades of research on this topic have been marked by debate—some rancorous—among professionals and in the public press (Belsky, 2001; Scarr, 1998). Investigators have examined cognitive and social outcomes for children and have especially considered the quality and amount of care, as well as some characteristics of the family. Interpretation of the findings are made difficult by the fact that quality of day care may be correlated with characteristics of the family and child. For example, if highly competent parents are likely to select high-quality day care, the cause of positive child outcomes of day-care may be unclear. For this reason, the more recent research has tended to control for the possible effects of family selection of care.

Many studies indicate that the effects of early child care depend in part on the quality of day care, which is defined by several indices—such as the ratio of caregivers to children, responsive staff-child interaction, staff training, developmentally appropriate curricula, and health and safety standards (Scarr, 1998). High-quality care is positively related to the development of cognition and language for youngsters who enter day care early in life (Belsky, 2001; NICHD Early Child Care Research Network, 2003b). In addition, smaller benefits have been found for psychosocial behavior across studies that observed children in different types of care (Phillips & Adams, 2001). Recent studies of psychosocial outcomes have focused the most on troublesome behavior such as aggression and noncompliance.

There is greater debate about the effects of the amount of day care that children receive—that is, the cumulative hours of care per week or the age at which children begin nonparental care (Phillips & Adams, 2001). Debate has centered on psychosocial outcomes, with some studies claiming that more time in care is associated with troublesome behavior but with other studies not showing this link (Loeb et al., 2004; NICHD Early Child Care Research Network, 2003a).

The somewhat mixed findings have led investigators to give more attention to differences in outcome that might exist for low-income families.

Interest in these families also increased after 1996 federal regulations put higher employment demands on women on welfare, resulting in greater employment of these women. In this regard, Borge and colleagues (2004) noted that when risks of day care are considered, there is a danger of overlooking risks associated with at-home care in socially disadvantaged families under stress. Their study indicated that at-home children in very high-risk families were more aggressive than those in day care, as rated primarily by the mothers. In this study, the mothers who provided home care for their preschool children differed from the mothers who selected day care: they were less educated, had lower occupational status, had a larger number of children, and showed less adaptive family functioning. Loeb and colleagues (2004) found positive cognitive outcomes for children of low-income families who attended day-care centers and whose mothers entered the workforce when the children were between 12 and 42 months of age. Quality and stability of care had some influence in the expected direction. The children cared for by family members showed no cognitive effects but more behavioral problems. Still another study of low-income families found that both high quality of care and more extensive time in care were linked to beneficial effects on cognitive and behavioral development (Votruba-Drzal, Coley, & Chase-Lansdale, 2004). This and other research suggest that high-quality nonparental child care may have particularly strong positive effects on children who are exposed to highly disadvantaged family circumstance.

The larger lesson to be learned from research is that the effects of different arrangements of child care may vary depending on the broad context of children's lives. More generally, the issue of non-parental care has implications for social policy. Although the size of the effects of child-care arrangements tend to be in the small to moderate range, even small effects can be important when they involve large numbers of children (Belsky, 2001; Youngblade, 2003).

Care of School-Age Children. Although professional debate over child care has focused on early care, concern exists for children of school age. Some older children have no formal provisions for after-school care. These are the so-called latchkey children, or children in self-care, who must use a key to let themselves into their empty homes after school. The term *self-care* is typically applied to children of elementary and middle school age, because it is usually agreed that preschool children should always have

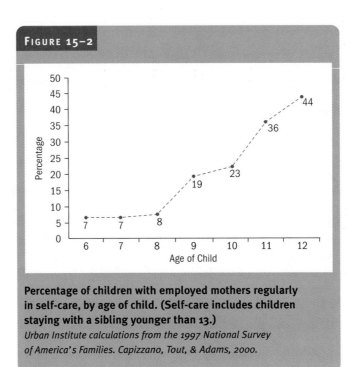

FIGURE 15–2

Percentage of children with employed mothers regularly in self-care, by age of child. (Self-care includes children staying with a sibling younger than 13.)
Urban Institute calculations from the 1997 National Survey of America's Families. Capizzano, Tout, & Adams, 2000.

supervision and that high school age youngsters do not need the level of supervision that would be considered child care. Accurate estimates of the prevalence of self-care are hard to come by, but national surveys indicate that self-care as a primary arrangement rises dramatically from age 8 to age 12 (Federal Interagency Forum on Child and Family Statistics, 2004; Figure 15–2).

The developmental implications of self-care likely are affected by the amount of time in self-care, the child's developmental level, family influences, neighborhood characteristics, and available social supports. Unsurprisingly, then, studies of the impact of self-care on children's development have yielded variable findings (Vandell & Shumow, 1999). Some studies suggest no differences in outcomes for children in self-care as compared with other after-school arrangements. Other studies suggest problematic outcomes. Factors such as younger age and time spent hanging out with peers rather than being at home seem to be associated with poorer outcomes for children in self-care. The negative effects of self-care may also be more evident for children from low-income families.

The choice of self-care is probably determined by multiple considerations, but one factor is the availability of after-school programming. Evidence supports the benefit of quality after-school programming, including extracurricular activities (NICHD

Many children return to empty homes after school. The impact of such self-care requires further study. *(Courtesy of A. C. Israel)*

Early Child Research Network, 2004). Posner and Vandell (1999), for example, found that low-income urban third- to fifth-grade children who attended after-school recreational and academically oriented programs rather than being in informal care with neighbors and relatives accrued some developmental benefits. Structured programming may help children avoid potentially harmful situations such as exposure to deviant peers, illegal activities, or violence. In general, evidence for positive effects of after-school programs is strongest for low-income children, children in high-crime urban neighborhoods, younger children, and boys (Vandell & Shumow, 1999). Nevertheless, even supervised out-of-home programs are not necessarily beneficial—characteristics of the programs (e.g., adult leadership, scheduled meetings) can be important in predicting positive behavioral outcomes (Coley, Morris, & Herdandez, 2004). Such considerations have led to recommendations for government and communities to address children's out-of-school time and to develop more and better-quality after-school programming (Larner, Zippiroli, & Behrman, 1999).

Self-care, even if not ideal, may still be an alternative arrangement for some children. When self-care is employed, it is necessary to ensure that the child is adequately prepared. Peterson (1989) suggested that three major areas need to be considered in preparation: injury risk, emotional difficulties, and selection of activities. Preparation has several components, including discussion with the child and arrangements for a contact person if the child feels that help is needed. Also essential is that the child has a safe and secure environment.

ADOPTIVE FAMILIES

Our discussion so far has focused on youth living with at least one biological parent, but millions of children live in other kinds of arrangements, including adoptive families. Adoption has traditionally been viewed in a positive way, as an alternative family structure that meets the needs of both the child and the parents. In the United States and similar countries, adoption has most often involved middle-class couples choosing to enlarge their families, and the children as frequently coming from less advantaged situations. It is nevertheless appropriate to keep in mind the various circumstances; adoptive children may or may not have contact with kin families, may be adopted by different race/ethnic families, or may have prior experiences in foster care or orphanages (Borchers et al., 2003).

Despite the view of adoption as a happy situation, the welfare of adoptive youth has been an issue. A substantial amount of research indicates that these young people are at risk for behavioral and learning problems. Adopted children show up in disproportionate numbers in mental health settings. Might reasons other than actual behavioral disturbance be responsible for overrepresentation? Debate exists about this possibility (Miller et al., 2000). Some argue that adoptive parents might be particularly sensitive to their children's behavior, come more readily into contact with mental health professionals, or use their greater resources to seek professional help. Research with nonclinic populations avoids the issue of referral bias, although it is not completely free of bias when parents are asked to report on their children's behavior. These investigations contribute to knowledge about the development of adoptees.

For example, Simmel and colleagues (2001) studied the prevalence of attention-deficit hyperactivity disorder and oppositional defiant disorder, using survey data from the California Long-Range Adoption Study, a prospective statewide research study into the characteristics of adoptive families. Overall, 29 percent of the 4- to 18-year-olds manifested some externalizing symptomatology and the rate of ADHD in adoptees was at least double the rate of that for comparable nonadoptees. Maughan, Collishaw, and Pickles (1998) examined school achievement in children from the National Child Development Study, a prospective study of all British children born in one week in March 1958. This study found positive outcome for adoptive children. The adoptees seemingly had benefited from the higher social class and material circumstances of their lives, and the greater interest in education and richer educational environment in their homes.

In general, it appears that most adopted youngsters function within the normal range but that there is some risk, mostly small to moderate, for behavioral and learning problems (Miller et al., 2000; Simmel et al., 2001). Late age of adoption and male gender are generally associated with greater risk. So also are a variety of preadoption factors, such as neglect/abuse, prenatal drug exposure, and foster care. Characteristics and functioning of the adoptive family as well as broader environmental factors can also make a difference as to how well the child does.

Intercountry and Transracial Adoption. In 2003, there were over 21,000 intercountry adoptions in the United States (Center for Adoption Research and Policy, 2004). Children have been brought "home" from countries as diverse as China, Peru, Korea, Russia, Poland, and the Philippines (Kaslow, 2001). A substantial number of these adoptions are transracial as well as transcultural. The sense of identity that these

International and interracial adoptions, illustrated by this Western-Japanese family, can bring unique enrichments and challenges.
(Margaret Ross/Stock Boston)

youngsters develop may be linked to successful adaptation, particularly during adolescence (Cederblad et al., 1999). International adoptees do report being teased and being aware of their "foreignness," but there also are reports of their being popular with peers. The potential for "foreignness" to be problematic undoubtedly is affected by the degree to which multiculturalism is accepted by the larger society and the local communities in which these children live. Given these considerations, how well do the children do in their adoptive homes and countries? The weight of the evidence appears to favor as positive an outcome as for other adopted groups. And similar to other groups, preadoption experiences, adoptive family functioning, age at adoption, and gender can moderate outcome.

We should also note that transracial adoptions occur within countries—as when children from Australia's indigenous people are adopted by mainstream white families and African American black children are adopted by European American white families in United States (Rushton & Minnis, 1997). Identity issues and a sense of dislocation are not identical to those in international adoptions, but they still exist and can be substantial. Moreover, the context can be fraught with sociopolitical controversy. In the United States, the adoption of black children into white families has variously been viewed as "cultural genocide," harm to the identity of the children, positive influence on racial integration, and

positive influence on children who are provided loving, advantaged homes. Despite the sometimes strong opinions, transracial adoptions and placements appear satisfactory in over 70 percent of cases, which is comparable to same-race outcomes (Rushton & Minnis, 1997).

We do not wish to oversimplify the many questions that require further research regarding adoption. Does the quality of the lives of the adopted children compensate for broken bonds with birth family and cultural roots? What can be done to encourage multicultural families (Kaslow, 2001)? What coping mechanisms are employed by adopted children over what issues (Smith & Brodzinsky, 2002)? In the final analysis, though, these issues and the risk for behavioral disorders do not detract from the positive aspects of this kind of family (Miller et al., 2000). Rather, they suggest the need for research and for specific policies (e.g., early adoption) and support for adoptive families.

FOSTER CARE

Although it is ordinarily preferable for children and adolescents to remain with their birth families, substitute care is not always avoidable. Substitute placement occurs involuntarily or voluntarily when families are unable to care for their offspring. In earlier times in the United States and other countries, these youth were placed in institutions and had little connections to their families. Concerns about harmful effects of institutionalization led to family foster care, with a major goal of returning the children to their biological families (Benoit, 2000). However, many youth remained in foster care for long periods of time, some until they reached the legal age to be independent. Although foster care certainly can have positive influences, it also can be inadequate; moreover, the rate of disruption is high, with children's being moved from placement to placement (Barber, Delfabbro, & Cooper, 2001; Minty, 1999).

In an effort to improve this situation, the federal government enacted the Adoption and Safe Family Act (ASFA) in 1997 (see Figure 15–3). Among other changes brought by ASFA, the provision of a permanent home now is given priority. Within a specified time each child must either be returned to the biological family or be adopted or permanently placed with a foster family, which can include relatives or legal guardians (Allen & Bissell, 2004). The ASFA provides the states financial incentive for the adoption of children in temporary foster care. In some circumstances, it may be difficult to attain this goal. The experiences of one professional involved in facilitating children's movement into permanent adoptive families are described in Accent: "Finding 'Forever' Parents."

The system can go awry at many points. Administrative agencies, including the courts, can be so overloaded that they are unable to operate in a competent and timely fashion. And the task has been made more difficult by an overall increase of children and adolescents—disproportionately of minority background—in foster care, and by the experiences of these youth. Many reasons exist for out-of-home care, among them poverty, homelessness, parental substance abuse, HIV/AIDS, domestic violence, and maternal incarceration (Bass, Shields, & Behrman, 2004; Rosenfeld et al., 1997). Children entering foster care often have lived in disorganized homes, been traumatized, have developmental and behavioral problems, and require special medical and educational care. Foster parents do not always receive the support and training that are needed to facilitate the development of these youth.

The foster care system is attempting to respond to these circumstances. For example, because youth in foster care are at risk for behavioral problems, treatment foster care programs have been created (Benoit, 2000; Rosenfeld et al., 1997). Here, foster parents understand, prior to the placement, that the child requires mental health services and that they will serve as change agents. Special training and help is given to foster care parents, and links are forged with community mental health services. In the Family to Family approach, communities where foster care is especially needed are targeted, and financial incentive is given to foster parents to

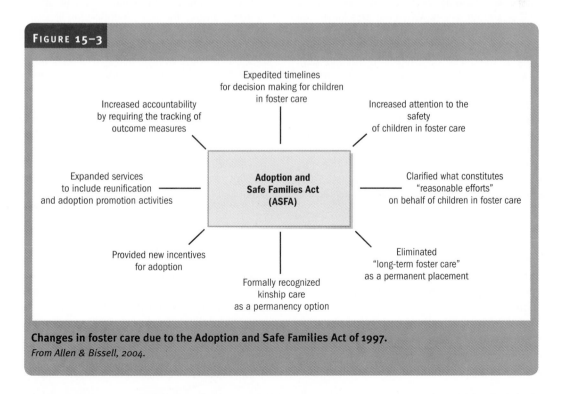

FIGURE 15–3

Expedited timelines for decision making for children in foster care

Increased accountability by requiring the tracking of outcome measures

Increased attention to the safety of children in foster care

Expanded services to include reunification and adoption promotion activities

Adoption and Safe Families Act (ASFA)

Clarified what constitutes "reasonable efforts" on behalf of children in foster care

Provided new incentives for adoption

Eliminated "long-term foster care" as a permanent placement

Formally recognized kinship care as a permanency option

Changes in foster care due to the Adoption and Safe Families Act of 1997.
From Allen & Bissell, 2004.

ACCENT

Finding "Forever" Parents

For the past 12 years, I have been a caseworker for an adoption agency. Our mission is to rescue children from inadequate or damaging foster care. Almost all of our "kids" are considered "hard to place." Most are between the ages of eight and fifteen; some have handicapping conditions; the majority exhibit behavioral problems such as ADHD, conduct problems, poor school performance, and inability to bond with the adoptive families who love and want them. Most of the kids have been neglected or maltreated by their birth parents and the foster care system for so long that they and their adoptive families face special life-long challenges. Given all the problems, it's a wonder that adoption works at all.

Our agency believes that the foundation for a good adoption develops while the child and family are getting to know each other. During the many months of visiting before the kids actually move into the homes, we work closely with the families. Part of our job is to assuage the nearly overwhelming terror felt by some perspective adoptive parents who are about to embark on an unknowable future with these children. We also work closely with the youngsters, so they feel empowered to determine their futures. In the end, I know that parental commitment to our kids is what makes adoption work. When our kids know that their "forever" parents aren't going to abandon them no matter what they are or do, then the youngsters, too, are able to commit themselves to the adoption. This is when they take control of their behavior and make the needed changes.

Thinking about why our kids need adoption, I realize the real culprit is social inequity. Birth parents can be criticized for not taking care of these kids, but until you see the role poverty plays in the parents' lives, you won't understand. Many of the birth parents are unemployed and unemployable, and some have no place to live. Many of their lives are defined by racism, limited education, family disorganization and multiple single-parenting, addiction and alcoholism, criminal behavior, and physical and mental illness. The hardest part of my job is dealing with those occasional birth parents still involved with their children. I figure, once they lose their kids, there isn't much else for them to lose, but I also know I can't let this circumstance affect me if I'm going to help the children.

As a caseworker, I bury the harsh reality of social inequity, and I focus on everyday practical issues, such as the courts and finding good families. Our state law demands that children in foster care for more than twelve months be freed for adoption, but this hardly ever happens. The courts appear insensitive to the harm done by children's languishing in temporary homes and to the benefits of permanent families. I find that judges take too long in deciding that a birth family isn't retrievable, and I am frustrated by how long it takes to finalize an adoption. Three-year-old children are transformed into preteenagers with lots of psychological "baggage."

Another chronic problem is to find families for our minority teenage boys who have been in foster care for years and have not one person they can depend on. Middle-class, stable families have a lot to offer, but they aren't always the most suitable families. In my experience, families that had to overcome their own difficulties understand better what our kids have been through, and know what it takes to overcome problems. Besides this, when a family takes a difficult child, especially one who looks different, I find that rather than chipping in to help, the community often looks down on the family. Our youngsters need unconditional acceptance from their new communities as well as their families if they are to trust again and abide by social norms. All of us need to examine our prejudices, and most of us need to change our attitudes towards these children and their adoptive families.

develop a mentoring relationship with birth parents (Chipungu & Bent-Goodley, 2004). Both sets of parents ideally work with professionals to reunite birth families.

Another change that has occurred in foster care over the last two decades is an increase in placement of children in the homes of relatives. Some disagreement exists as to the disadvantages and benefits of this arrangement. Kinship, compared to nonkin, foster parents tend to be older, in poorer health, and with less income; they often are grandparents (Green, 2004). The needs of these families may be greater, and they receive less service and supervision. There is also concern that birth parents will have inappropriate access to the children. At the same time, kin placements may be less disruptive and result in greater stability for the child. With decreases in the availability of nonfamily foster families, most states now view kinship foster care as a feasible and preferable option (Benoit, 2000).

Developments in the foster care system give some reason for optimism. It is important to acknowledge that most individuals working in the system are well intentioned and caring. Increased resources, innovative problem solving, increased services for foster children and families, and improved coordination of services are among the recommendations for improving substitute care (Bass et al., 2004).

Mental Health Services for Youth

We now turn to a brief discussion of mental health services for youth. Over the years, many studies of mental health services have been conducted. It is widely agreed that children and adolescents are underserved. Fewer than one-third of needy youth receive services (Weist, 1997), and that figure has been estimated to be as low as one-fourth (Kestenbaum, 2000). Particularly underserved are specific groups such as those of minority background and those with physical handicaps.

Analyses of mental health needs have recognized a lack of adequate funding. To various degrees, funding is provided by federal and state governments, third-party (health insurance) providers, and clients themselves. It has usually been more difficult to obtain financial coverage for mental health than other kinds of health needs. Escalating costs adversely affect both middle- and lower-class families, with the health care system in flux regarding the effort to control costs through managed care (Kiesler, 2000). Because some families have inadequate access to private care, greater efforts are being made to ensure that children's needs are being met through federal and state programs.

Early mental health services for youth emphasized a community approach (Pumariega & Glover, 1998). Child guidance clinics provided interdisciplinary and low-cost services to children and adolescents and their families. Services subsequently became more hospital-based, and guidance and mental health clinics experienced lack of funding and support. Hospital and residential care increased during the 1970s and 1980s, partly because of increased third-party payment. All the while there was a dramatic increase in the population of poor minority children who needed but could not obtain mental health services. Many of these children went into the child welfare system when their parents were unable to care for them, and many were placed into residential and detention facilities. This dire situation and growing medical costs resulted in a call for publicly funded community-based services. Today's services are delivered in various settings, including mental health clinics, psychiatric or full service hospitals, residential centers, private professional practices, child welfare and juvenile agencies, and schools. Community mental health clinics and schools are dominant settings (Hoagwood & Johnson, 2003; Weist, 1997).

Some professionals believe that the school can play an important role in the delivery of services to the millions of enrolled students and their families (Kestenbaum, 2000; Weist, 1997). Traditional mental health services in schools are largely limited to children enrolled in special education and a relatively small number involved in interventions with school psychologists. Yet the school setting has clear advantages in that it is accessible to all students, contact can be frequent, and the stigma of mental health consultation can be avoided. In making this point, Kestenbaum (2000) quotes a colleague as saying the following:

I decided to adopt what I have come to refer to as the Willie Sutton Theory of Children's Mental Health. When reporters asked Willie Sutton, the notorious bank robber of the 1930s, why he robbed banks, he answered "that's where the money is." If you wanted to provide mental health services to children, I reasoned, you had to go where the children were: in the schools. (p. 6)

The movement to expand school services includes the entire range from prevention to treatment to posttreatment monitoring. To varying degrees, increases in the kinds of programs offered and improved coordination are commonly recommended. For example, partnerships could be set up between schools and community mental health agencies, which could variously expand school services. Many schools now have general health centers, and mental health services could be readily embedded in these. A call has gone out for school psychology to incorporate a public health perspective with an emphasis on serving populations, prevention and strengthening of positive behaviors, and evaluation

(Strein, Hoagwood, & Cohn, 2003). The model of the school as the provider of comprehensive services has also been employed (Holtzman, 1997). "Full-service schools" are the primary neighborhood institution for promoting child and family development, which includes educational, health, and mental health goals within a framework of community-based participation.

FRAGMENTATION, UTILIZATION, EVALUATION

Concerns have generally been expressed about the fragmentation of mental health services, especially for more serious disturbances. In recognition of the need for better coordinated services, efforts have been made to develop community-based, interagency systems of care (Mental Health: A Report of the Surgeon General, 2001). For example, the federal government instituted the Child and Adolescent Service System Program (CASSP). By providing leadership and funding to the states, CASSP has encouraged a comprehensive model of care, interagency collaboration, parental involvement, and sensitivity to the needs of minority groups (Pumariega & Glover, 1998). Other aspects of the model include treatment in the least restrictive environment, early identification of problems and intervention, and smooth transition into adult care systems when necessary. A similar approach also was taken by the Comprehensive Community Mental Health Services for Children and Their Families Program; it provides financial support to the states, territories, and Indian tribal organizations to care for millions of children through a coordinated, comprehensive network of mental health and other services (Mental Health: A Report of the Surgeon General, 2001). Overall, evaluations of such systems of care indicate benefits such as reduced use of residential and out-of-state treatments, parental satisfaction with care, and improved functional behavior of the children. However, it is unclear whether child clinical outcomes are better than they are in other approaches to mental health.

Whereas fragmentation of mental health services can certainly be problematic, so too can low utilization of available services. Help-seeking behavior is likely to be complex and vary with personal and other variables (Sears, 2004; Yeh et al., 2004). Several demographic variables predict service use (Logan & King, 2001). Caucasian families, those of higher social class, and those living in urban areas are more likely to use professional services. Minority group families are more likely to seek help from family and community contacts rather than professionals, and premature termination of services is higher for Hispanic and African American youngsters and their families (Mental Health: A Report of the Surgeon General, 2001). If programs are to successfully serve ethnic/racial populations, they must incorporate cultural traditions, beliefs, and ways of interpersonal interactions.

Finally, with regard to youth services, there is a need both to continue to evaluate services and to disseminate information about effective services. It is clear that evidence-based treatment for young people can be ameliorative for a variety of disorders in a variety of settings (Kazdin & Weisz, 2003; Christophersen & Mortweet, 2001). However, families need specific information about the availability, effectiveness, and costs of care (e.g., Newman & Tejeda, 1996). Similarly, agencies and institutions providing services would profit from greater dissemination of information about efficacious prevention programs and treatment (e.g., Rotheram-Borus & Duan, 2004).

Youth in the Global Society

As we turn our attention to the international scene, one striking fact is that mass transportation and communication, including the Internet, are making the functional world smaller day by day. The lives of youth are already being strongly influenced by this phenomenon, and the impact will become even more pervasive throughout the 21st century.

THIRD WORLD POVERTY AND HEALTH

Although poverty in the United States is rightly of concern, the effects of being poor are dramatically worse in developing countries. The link between poverty and bodily and psychological well-being is observed in various measures—nutrition, disease, lack of opportunity, and death. For example, malnutrition and specific mineral deficiencies (e.g., iron) are associated with developmental, cognitive, and behavioral risk (Chang et al., 2002; Pollitt et al., 1996). In developing countries, 150 million children are malnourished (We the Children, 2001).

Youth in developing countries can benefit from public health programs that include prenatal care, immunization, screening for medical conditions, improved nutrition, child safety, family planning,

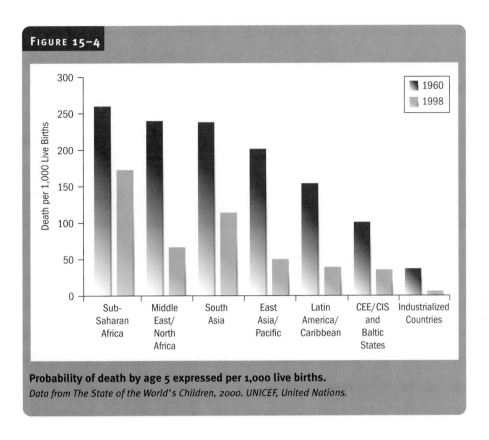

FIGURE 15-4

Legend: 1960, 1998

(Bar chart showing Death per 1,000 Live Births by region)

Probability of death by age 5 expressed per 1,000 live births.
Data from The State of the World's Children, 2000. UNICEF, United Nations.

and the like (Rahman et al., 2000). Progress has been made on several fronts. For instance, disease has been reduced, fewer children are underweight, and more families are consuming iodine in their diets. Figure 15–4 shows the reduction that occurred from 1960 to 1998 in the mortality of children under the age of 5 years, a measure viewed as an overall indication of how well children are doing. Nonetheless, enormous needs yet exist. Indeed, Figure 15–4 indicates the large differences in children's death rates across the world. Continuing efforts are required for further improvements and to maintain any gains accomplished. At the present time, huge resources and efforts are required to deal with the HIV/AIDS epidemic. Since the late 1970s, over 2.7 million children have died of AIDS-related disease (Wachsler-Felder & Golden, 2002). In sub-Saharan Africa, 12.3 million children have been orphaned because of the AIDS virus (Children On the Brink, 2004).

Only quite recently has international attention turned to the risk of behavioral problems in children and adolescents (Rahman et al., 2000). Epidemiologic reports attest to a substantial rate and range of disabilities (e.g., internalizing, externalizing, mental retardation, pervasive developmental disorders). If

interventions are to be successful, local community involvement as well as standards and values are important considerations. For example, conduct "disturbance" may be viewed in some communities as a disciplinary rather than a mental health concern, and certain interventions might well be more acceptable than others. Thus, as with other health programs, cultural sensitivity is critical.

EXPOSURE TO ARMED OR SOCIOPOLITICAL CONFLICT

Exposure to armed conflict or to threatening sociopolitical environments influences the development of a significant minority of young people throughout the world (Barenbaum, Ruchkin, & Schwab-Stone, 2004). Cambodian youth suffered extensive hardships and violence during the 1975–1979 Pol Pot regime and subsequently lived in refugee camps for extended periods of time (Mollica et al., 1997; Savin et al., 1996). Youth are currently living in areas in which the threat of war is chronic and may vary from low to high (e.g., some Middle East and African countries). In addition to direct traumatic experiences and bodily threats to the self and loved ones, these situations can be characterized by uncertainty, temporary or permanent separation from family and community, inadequate nutrition, lack of shelter, control by the "enemy," and the like.

It is worth noting that research on the effects of war itself is not easy to accomplish. It is difficult to collect data immediately or soon after armed conflict, and longer-term outcome is confounded by less-than-optimal experiences following war. Investigations often have been conducted with immigrant groups and especially refugee groups, which may be living in camps and still experiencing trauma, loss, and poor living conditions.

Given this circumstance, rates of psychopathology vary tremendously across studies, anywhere from 22 to 94 percent (Barenbaum et al., 2004). In some cases, symptoms may occur after a delay, and in general it appears that both persistence of symptoms and their relatively rapid alleviation are reported. A variety of problems occurs, including anxiety, depression, somatic complaints, grief reactions, and social withdrawal. Of these, posttraumatic stress disorder (PTSD) and depression have been most noted, perhaps with PTSD more associated with war experiences, and depression with subsequent life conditions (Thabet, Abed, & Vostanis, 2004).

Although psychological upset is widely associated with actual or threatening situations, many youngsters show remarkable adaptation (Lustig et al., 2004). Resilience can be attributed to personal coping tendencies as well as to factors such as supportive families and communities and religious beliefs. Coping strategies may seem quite ordinary. For example, Sudanese children living in refugee camps in Northern Uganda did what they could to cope. The large camps were crowded with no space to play games or sports, people were dependent on food rations, and the bureaucracy was ever-present. Little opportunity existed for problem solving, and the children coped by seeking the company of others, engaging in wishful thinking, and praying (Paardekooper, de Jong, & Hermanns, 1999).

Despite resilient outcomes, there is considerable need for intervention and prevention. Such efforts will vary, of course, depending on the situation—that is, whether young people and their families remain in war-threatened countries, live in refugee camps, or are adjusting to resettlement in communities and countries new to them. For example, when families have relocated, they usually are of disadvantaged minority status and often are isolated. The presence of community workers who can link them to psychological services can be crucial

(Howard & Hodes, 2000). In other situations, interventions at a broader level are appropriate. An example is an effort to alleviate distress caused by war in Bosnia (Yule, 2000). Teachers were trained to understand the needs of the children and how they might help, and counseling was set up at youth clubs for adolescents and at a child-parent outpatient clinic.

The more we understand about treating the victims of war and conflict—including the mediators and moderators of stress reactions and resilience—the better the chance of alleviating and preventing emotional adversity. Nevertheless, few would dispute the opinion that war "must be regarded with abhorrence in terms of its terrible human toll in human suffering, especially on its most innocent bystanders—children and adolescents" (Jensen & Shaw, 1993, p. 697).

DIVERSITY AND INTERNATIONAL COOPERATION

An obvious implication of the shrinking world is the increased need to deal well with others of different facial appearance, color, dress, custom, and belief. It is estimated that at least 5,000 ethnocultural groups exist around the world (Marsella, 1998). Furthermore, we are currently witnessing massive relocations of people into foreign countries and cultures. The challenge of adapting to ethnic and racial differences, although not new by any means, is substantial.

In the United States, the challenge of diversity has a long history. Prejudice and fears often have had adverse effects on peoples of various groups—Native Americans, African Americans, Irish, Poles, Asians, Arabs, Jews, and Catholics, to name a few. Being of minority status remains a risk factor for quality of life and opportunity (Hawkins, Cummins, & Marlatt, 2004; Nyborg & Curry, 2003). And the United States is becoming increasingly multicultural with cross-cultural and cross-religion marriages and bicultural adoptions (Kaslow, 2001).

As a discipline, psychology has participated in the study of issues related to diversity, although perhaps not always as timely as could be expected. A historic example is the work of Kenneth Clark and his colleagues that played a role in the 1957 Supreme Court decision, *Brown v. Board of Education*, which overthrew the "separate but equal" doctrine that had permitted segregation in the public schools (Clark, Chein, & Cook, 2004). Clark, an African American, became president of the American Psychological

Association in the late 1960s (Pickren & Tomes, 2002). At about that time, the American Psychological Association became more committed to addressing problems of race and related matters. Today, concerns exist about the conditions and progress of numerous cultural and racial groups living in the United States (Gibbs, Huang, & Associates, 2003; Pettigrew, 2004).

The need also exists for increased study across cultures and the processes of international cooperation. In fact, an important outgrowth of closer communication among the peoples of the world is greater international effort to solve problems and to optimize living conditions. Over several decades, world attention has been drawn to promoting the healthy development of youth. The United Nations declared 1979 as the International Year of the Child and subsequently drafted the U.N. Convention on the Rights of the Child. Among other rights, this document cites the rights of children to a family environment, an adequate standard of living, education, freedom of religion and self-expression, as well as rights to be free from specific harms such as abuse, torture, and exploitation (Murphy-Berman & Weisz, 1996). The United Nations also has sponsored world summits and conferences, innumerable programs to benefit children, and the collection of data on youth to monitor progress and make recommendations.

Many other concerned organizations, both public and private, are addressing global issues such as poverty, high birth rates, infant mortality, medical and mental health needs, violence, and environmental pollution. Because all of these problems can have dramatic influence on the development of children and adolescents, international cooperation holds promise of improving the lives of young people.

SUMMARY

- *The care received by children and adolescents reflects not only what is known about development but also the social, political, and economic conditions in which they live.*

PREVENTING BEHAVIORAL DISORDER

- *Prevention of behavioral disorders is receiving increased attention.*

- *Kaplan conceptualized prevention as primary, secondary, and tertiary. Today, it is most commonly viewed as intervention that occurs prior to the onset of full-blown disorder and is often labeled universal, high-risk (selective), or indicated.*

- *Promotion of wellness is arguably a part of prevention and is endorsed by a task force of the American Psychological Association.*

- *Prevention programs vary in goals, methods, and settings. Examples are programs for low birthweight infants, economically disadvantaged children, and youngsters at risk for depression.*

WHO CARES FOR CHILDREN: FAMILY ISSUES

- *The employment of women has led to increased nonparental child care of various forms. The effects of out-of-home care on young children depend on many factors. High-quality care can have beneficial effects on cognitive and behavioral development. The effects of amount of care are still debated. Children of highly disadvantaged families may particularly benefit from center-based care.*

- *The effects of self-care by older children are variable. However, supervised, high-quality out-of-school programs have been shown to be advantageous, perhaps especially for disadvantaged families.*

- *Adoption is associated with mild to moderate risk for behavioral and learning problems. Gender, age at adoption, preadoption experiences, and adoptive family functioning are associated with outcome. International and transracial adoptions appear as satisfactory as other adoptions.*

- *Current policy regarding foster care assumes that it is temporary and that the child will return to the birth family within a designated time or will join a permanent adoptive or foster care family. Many concerns are expressed about foster care and efforts are being made to address them.*

MENTAL HEALTH SERVICES FOR YOUTH

- *Consensus exists that mental health services for youth are underfunded, fragmented, and underutilized by certain groups. Services are offered in various settings, with mental health clinics and schools being dominant. Federally sponsored efforts encourage integrated, comprehensive services. There is continued need to provide and encourage quality services to ethnic/racial minority groups.*

Youth in the Global Society

- *Many challenges to the development of young people are evident worldwide, such as poverty, disease, and poor nutrition. International efforts have brought improvements but enormous needs persist.*

- *Millions of children and adolescents suffer loss and physical and psychological damage from armed and sociopolitical conflicts.*

- *A functionally smaller world has brought heightened need for people to adapt to and be enriched by diversity. International cooperation holds promise for improving the lives of needy children and adolescents.*

KEY TERMS

universal prevention strategies *(p. 424)*

high-risk (selective) prevention strategies *(p. 424)*

indicated prevention strategies *(p. 424)*

wellness *(p. 424)*

treatment foster care *(p. 437)*

Glossary

ABA (reversal) research design Single-subject experimental design in which the relevant behavior is measured during a baseline period (A), manipulation (B), and a period in which the manipulation is removed (A). The reintroduction of the manipulation (B) is added when treatment is the goal.

Acute onset The sudden (rather than gradual) onset of a disorder.

Adaptive behavior scales Psychological instruments that measure an individual's ability to perform in the everyday environment, for example, to wash one's hair, interact socially, and communicate.

Adoption studies In genetic research, the comparison of adopted children with their biological and their adoptive families to determine hereditary and environmental influences on characteristics.

Affect As a noun, affect is used to refer to emotion or mood. Thus the term affective disorder is often employed to refer to a mood disorder such as depression or mania.

Agoraphobia Excessive anxiety about being in a situation where escape might be difficult or embarrassing.

Anoxia Lack of oxygen.

Antisocial behavior A pattern of behavior that violates widely held social norms and brings harm to others (e.g., stealing, lying).

Aphasia A general term referring to language loss or disturbances caused by brain anomalies. Developmental aphasia refers to language disorders in childhood.

Attachment A strong socioemotional bond between individuals. Usually discussed in terms of the child–parent or child–caretaker relationship, attachment is generally viewed as having a strong influence on a child's development.

Attention The focusing or concentration of mental energy on an object or event. Selective attention refers to focusing on a stimulus and not being distracted by other stimuli. Sustained attention refers to maintaining concentration on a stimulus over time.

Attribution (attributional style) The way an individual thinks about or explains actions and outcomes, for example, a child's attributing his or her school failure to lack of innate intelligence.

Authoritative parenting Style of parenting in which parents set rules and expectations for their children, follow through with consequences, and simultaneously are warm, accepting, and considerate of their children's needs. This style is thought to be associated with positive development in children.

Autoimmune disorder A condition in which the body's immune system attacks its own healthy tissue.

Autonomic nervous system A part of the nervous system that regulates functions usually considered involuntary, such as the operation of smooth muscles and glands. The system controls physiological changes associated with emotion. (*See* central nervous system.)

Baseline The measured rate of a behavior before an intervention is introduced. Baseline rates of the behavior can then be compared to rates during and following the intervention.

Behavior modification An approach to the treatment of behavior disorders that is based primarily on learning principles. Sometimes also referred to as behavior therapy.

Behaviorally inhibited temperament The temperamental tendency to be highly reactive to and stressed by unfamiliar stimuli.

Binge A relatively brief episode of excessive consumption (e.g., of food) over which the individual feels no control.

Biofeedback Procedures by which an individual is provided immediate information (feedback) about his or her physiological functioning (e.g., muscle tension, skin temperature). It is assumed that the individual can come to control bodily functioning through such feedback.

Case study Method of research in which an individual case is described. The case study can be informative but cannot be generalized to other persons or situations with confidence.

Central coherence The tendency of individuals to weave bits of information together so as to create a whole, or global meaning. It is contrasted with the (analytic) tendency to focus on parts of stimuli, rather than the whole.

Central nervous system In humans, the brain and spinal cord. (*See* autonomic nervous system.)

Child guidance movement An early to mid-20th century effort in the United States to treat and prevent childhood mental disorders. Importance was given to influences of family and wider social systems on the child.

Chromosome A threadlike structure in the cell nucleus that contains the genetic code. Human cells possess 23 pairs, except the ova and sperm, which possess 23 single chromosomes.

Chromosome abnormalities Abnormalities in the number and/or structure of the chromosomes, which can lead to fetal death or anomalies in development.

Classical conditioning A form of learning, also referred to as Pavlovian conditioning. An individual comes to respond to a stimulus (conditioned stimulus or CS) that did not previously elicit a response. Classical conditioning occurs when a CS is paired with another stimulus (the unconditioned stimulus, or UCS) that does elicit the desired response (unconditioned response, or UCR). When this response is elicited by the conditioned stimulus alone it is called a conditioned response (CR).

Clinical significance   The degree to which research findings are meaningful regarding real-life applications.

Clinical utility   The adequacy of a classification system, diagnosis, or assessment instrument based on how fully the observed phenomena are described and on how useful the descriptions are.

Coercion   A process in which a noxious or aversive behavior of one person (e.g., aggression by a child) is rewarded by another person (e.g., a parent). Often applied to the development of conduct-disordered behavior.

Cognitive strategies   Information processing and memory strategies, for example, rehearsing and categorizing information to facilitate memory.

Cohort   A particular age group of individuals. A cohort may differ in life experiences and values from an age group born and raised during a different era.

Comorbidity   A term used when an individual meets the criteria for more than one disorder (e.g., Attention-Deficit Hyperactivity Disorder and Oppositional Defiance Disorder). (*See* co-occurrence.)

Compulsions   Behaviors the individual feels compelled to repeat over and over again, even though they appear to have no rational basis.

Computerized tomography (CT scan)   A procedure that assesses density of brain tissue and produces a photographic image of the brain. This allows investigators to directly assess abnormalities of brain structures. Also sometimes referred to as computerized axial tomography or CAT scan.

Concordant   In genetic research, refers to individuals who are similar in particular attributes, for example, concordant for hair color or activity level.

Conditioned stimulus (CS)   A neutral stimulus, which through repeated pairings with a stimulus (unconditioned stimulus) that already elicits a particular response, comes to elicit a similar response (conditioned response).

Contingency management   Use of procedures that seek to modify behavior by altering the causal relationship between stimulus and response events, for example, between a behavior and a reinforcer or punisher.

Continuous performance test (CPT)   A method to evaluate sustained attention and impulsivity. The individual must identify a target stimulus when it appears in a series of stimuli. Errors are made by not reacting to the target stimulus or by reacting to nontarget stimuli.

Control group   In an experiment, a group of participants treated differently than the participants who receive the experimental manipulation and are later compared with them. The purpose of control groups is to ensure that the results of the experiment can be attributed to the manipulation rather than to other variables.

Co-occurrence   A term used when individuals experience the problems (symptoms) associated with more than one disorder (e.g., anxiety and depression). (*See* comorbidity.)

Correlation coefficient   A number obtained through statistical analysis that reflects the presence or absence of a correlation, the strength of a correlation, and the direction (positive or negative) of a correlation. Pearson *r* is a commonly used coefficient. (*See* positive correlation; negative correlation.)

Correlational research   A research method aimed at establishing whether two or more variables covary, or are associated. (*See* positive correlation; negative correlation.) The establishment of a correlation permits prediction of one variable from the other, but does not automatically establish a causal relationship.

Covert behaviors   Behaviors that are not readily observable. When describing antisocial behaviors this term refers to behaviors that are concealed, such as lying, stealing, and truancy. (*See* overt behaviors.)

Critical period   A relatively limited period of development during which an organism may be particularly sensitive to specific influences.

Cross-sectional research   A research strategy that observes and compares different groups of subjects at one point in time. It is a highly practical way to gather certain kinds of information.

Cultural familial retardation   A term, less popular now, referring to the majority of cases of milder mental retardation that "runs in families" and for which biological causation is not established.

Defense mechanisms   In psychoanalytic theory, psychological processes that distort or deny reality so as to control anxiety. Examples are repression, projection, reaction formation.

Deinstitutionalization   The movement to place/treat people with disorders at home or in various community settings rather than in institutions.

Delinquency   A legal term that refers to an illegal act by a person under 18. Such behavior may be illegal for an adult as well, such as theft, or may only be illegal when committed by a juvenile, for example, truancy.

Delusion   An idea or belief that is contrary to reality and is not widely accepted in the culture (e.g., delusions of grandeur or persecution).

Dependent variable   In the experimental method of research, the measure of behavior that may be influenced by the manipulation (independent variable).

Development   Change in structure and function that occurs over time in living organisms. Typically viewed as change from the simple to the complex, development is the result of transactions among several variables.

Developmental level   The level at which an individual is functioning with regard to physical, intellectual, or socioemotional characteristics.

Developmental psychopathology   The study of behavioral disorders within the context of developmental influences.

Developmental quotient (DQ)   A measure of performance on infant tests of development, paralleling the intelligence quotient (IQ) derived from intelligence tests for older children.

Diathesis   Vulnerability for a disease or disorder.

Differential reinforcement of other behaviors (DRO)   In behavior modification, refers to applying relatively more reinforcement to desirable behaviors that are incompatible with specific undesirable behaviors.

Difficult temperament   Tendency of an individual to display negative mood, intense reactions to stimuli, irritability, and the like. It is a risk factor for behavior problems.

Discordant In genetic research, refers to individuals who are dissimilar in particular attributes, for example, discordant in hair color or activity level.

Discrete trial learning Method of modifying behavior or teaching in which the clinician or teacher presents specific tasks or material in small steps, provides clear directives or prompts, and applies consequences. The setting is structured for learning. (*See* incidental learning.)

Discrimination The process by which an individual comes to learn that a particular stimulus, but not others, signals that a certain response is likely to be followed by a particular consequence.

Dizygotic (fraternal) twins Twins resulting from two independent unions of ova and sperm that occur at approximately the same time. Dizygotic twins are genetically no more alike than are nontwin siblings.

DNA Deoxyribonucleic acid. The chemical carrier of the genetic code, found in the chromosomes, composed of sugar, phosphates, and nucleotides. The nucleotides carry the hereditary information.

Dyslexia General term referring to reading disorder not due to general intellectual deficiency.

Echolalia The repetition of the speech of others, either immediately or delayed in time. A pathological speech pattern commonly found in autism and psychoses.

Education for All Handicapped Children Act of 1975 Public Law 94–142 that set influential federal guidelines for the rights of handicapped children to an appropriate public education. Reauthorized and expanded, it now is titled the Individuals with Disabilities Education Act (IDEA).

Ego According to psychoanalytic theory, the structure of the mind that operates predominantly at the conscious level. It mediates between instinctual urges and reality and is responsible for decision making.

Electroencephalograph (EEG) A recording of the electrical activity of the brain.

Empirical The process of verification or proof by accumulating information or data through observation or experiment (in contrast to reliance on impression or theory).

Empirically supported treatments Interventions for which there is empirical support for effectiveness; treatments that have been deemed worthy through scientific evaluation.

Epidemiology The study of the occurrence and distribution of a disorder within a population. Seeks to understand risk and etiology.

Equifinality The concept that diverse factors or paths can result in the same or similar developmental outcomes. For example, somewhat different paths can lead to conduct disordered behavior.

Etiology The cause or origin of a disease or behavior disorder.

Eugenics Efforts to improve human characteristics through systematic control of reproduction and thus genetics.

Evidence-based assessment/treatment *See* empirically supported treatments.

Executive functions Higher-order mental abilities involved in goal-directed behavior. Included are planning and organizing behavior, working memory, inhibiting responses, and evaluating and switching strategies.

Experimental research A research strategy that can establish causal relationships between or among variables. Subjects are treated to the independent variable to determine possible effects on the dependent variable. Comparison groups are included and procedures carefully controlled to help rule out possible effects of extraneous factors.

External validity In research, refers to the degree to which findings of an investigation can be generalized to other populations and situations.

Externalizing disorders Behavioral disorders in which the problems exhibited seem directed at others, for example, aggression and lying.

Extinction A weakening of a learned response that is produced when reinforcement that followed the response no longer occurs.

Factor analysis A statistical procedure that correlates each item with every other item and then groups correlated items into factors.

Fraternal twins *See* dizygotic twins.

Functional analysis Behavior analysis, that is, assessment of variables that might be influencing the occurrence and maintenance of a behavior. Determining such antecedent variables and consequences for behavior can be crucial in modifying the behavior.

Functional magnetic resonance imaging (fMRI) A noninvasive magnetic radiowave technology, which by tracking subtle changes in oxygen in different parts of the brain, produces images that indicate areas of brain activity. (*See* magnetic resonance imaging.)

Gene The unit of the chromosome that transmits genetic information.

Generalization of learning The process by which a response is made to a new stimulus that is different but similar to the stimulus present during learning.

Generalized imitation The tendency to imitate across persons, situations, and time.

Genotype The complement of genes that a person carries; the genetic endowment.

Goodness-of-fit Degree to which an individual's attributes or behaviors match or fit the attributes or demands of the individual's environment.

Grapheme A unit of a writing system—a letter or combination of letters—that represent the sounds of a language (the phonemes).

Hallucination A false perception (e.g., hearing a noise, seeing an object) that occurs in the absence of any apparent environmental stimulation.

Heritability The degree to which genetic influences account for variations in an attribute among individuals in a population.

Heterotypic continuity The continuity of a disorder over time in which the form of the problem behaviors changes over time. Contrasts with homotypic continuity, in which the form does not change.

Hypothesis In science, a proposition or "educated guess" put forth for evaluation by some scientific method.

Id According to psychoanalytic theory, the structure of the mind present at birth. The source of all psychic energy, the id operates entirely at the unconscious level, seeking immediate gratification of all instinctual urges, such as sexual urges.

Identical twins   *See* monozygotic twins.

Impulsivity   Acting without thinking; a failure to inhibit behavior. Some children with attention-deficit hyperactvity disorder exhibit impulsivity.

Incidence   Number or proportion of persons in a population newly diagnosed with a disorder during a specific time period.

Incidental learning   Method of modifying behavior or teaching in informal, natural settings. Takes advantage of the everyday context, for example, by teaching tasks relevant to what the child is engaging in at the moment. Learning procedures, such as contingency management, are typically employed.

Inclusion   Refers to the idea that all children with disabilities can best be educated, and should be included, in regular classrooms. (*See* Regular Education Initiative.)

Independent variable   In the experimental method of research, the variable manipulated by the researcher.

Individual Education Plan (IEP)   Detailed educational plan legally mandated for each person being served by the Individuals with Disabilities Act.

Individuals with Disabilities Act (IDEA)   Current federal law to ensure the rights of handicapped persons (birth to age 21) to appropriate public education. It ensures education and services in the least restrictive settings possible, parent participation, and assistance to the states in carrying out mandates. (*See* Education for All Handicapped Children Act of 1975.)

Information processing   Complex mental processes by which the organism attends to, perceives, interprets, and stores information. (*See* attention; working memory; executive functions; metamemory; cognitive strategies.)

Informed consent   In research or treatment, the ethical and legal guideline that potential participants be reasonably informed about the research or treatment as a basis for their consent or willingness to participate.

Insidious onset   Gradual rather than sudden (acute) onset of a disorder.

Intelligence quotient (IQ), deviation   A standard score derived from statistical procedures that reflects the direction and degree to which an individual's performance on an intelligence test deviates from the average score of the individual's age group.

Intelligence quotient (IQ), ratio   The ratio of mental age (MA), derived from performance on tests of intelligence, to chronological age (CA), multiplied by 100. IQ = MA/CA × 100.

Interactional model of development   The view that development is the result of the interplay of organismic and environmental variables. (*See* transactional model of development.)

Internalizing disorders   The large category of disorders—many of which were traditionally referred to as neuroses—in which the problems exhibited seem directed more at the self than at others, for example, fears, depression, and withdrawal.

Internal validity   In research, refers to the degree to which findings can be attributed to certain factors. Frequently concerns the degree to which the result of an experiment can be attributed to the experimental manipulation (the independent variable) rather than to extraneous factors.

Interrater reliability   The extent to which different raters agree on a particular diagnosis or measurement.

In vivo   A term referring to the natural context in which behavior occurs. For example, in vivo treatment is delivered in the setting in which the behavior problem occurs (e.g., the home rather than the clinic).

Joint attention interactions   Behaviors, such as pointing and eye contact, that simultaneously focus the attention of two or more people on the same object or situation, presumably for sharing an experience.

Learned helplessness   Passivity and a sense of lack of control over one's environment that is learned through experiences in which one's behavior was ineffective in controlling events.

Least restrictive environment   Regarding education, refers to the idea that individuals with disabilities have the right to be educated with their typically developing peers to the extent that is maximally feasible.

Lifetime prevalence   Number or proportion of persons in a population diagnosed with a disorder at any time during life.

Longitudinal research   A research strategy that observes the same participants over a relatively long period of time, measuring behavior at certain points. It is particularly helpful in tracing developmental change.

Magnetic resonance imaging (MRI)   A noninvasive procedure that creates a magnetic field around the brain. Cells in the brain respond to the radiowaves, and a three-dimensional image of the structures of the brain is created. (*See* functional magnetic resonance imaging.)

Mainstreaming   The educational practice of placing individuals with disabilities into community schools and into the least restrictive settings appropriate to their needs. Most of the children spend most school time in classrooms with typically developing peers, with various degrees of special support.

Maturation   Changes that occur in individuals relatively independent of the environment, provided that basic conditions are satisfied. For example, most humans develop the ability to walk, given normal physical health and opportunity for movement.

Maturational lag   A slowness or falling behind in development; often implies a lag in brain or nervous system development.

Mediating influence   The effect that a variable has to bring about or cause an outcome.

Mental age (MA)   The score corresponding to the chronological age (CA) of children whose intellectual test performance the examinee equals. For the average child, MA = CA.

Mental hygiene movement   An effort organized in the United States early in the 20th century to bring effective, humane treatment to the mentally ill and to prevent mental disorders. Closely associated with the child guidance movement.

Metacognition   The understanding of one's own information processing system.

Metamemory   The understanding of the working of one's memory or the strategies used to facilitate memory.

Minimal brain dysfunction (MBD)   The assumption that the central nervous system or brain is functioning in a pathological way to a degree that is not clearly detectable.

Moderating influence   The effect that a variable has to temper (e.g., reduce or strengthen) an outcome.

Monozygotic (identical) twins   Twins resulting from one union of an ovum and sperm. The single zygote divides early into two, with the new zygotes having identical genes (and thus being of the same sex).

Morphology   Refers to the forms of words or the study of word formation.

Multifinality The concept that a factor may lead to different developmental outcomes. For example, child abuse may result in different kinds of behavior problems.

Multigenic influence The influence of multiple genes on an attribute or behavior, with the effects of the genes combining in some way. Also referred to as polygenic influence.

Multiple baseline research designs Single subject experimental designs in which a manipulation is made and multiple behaviors or multiple participants are measured over time.

Mutation Spontaneous change in the genes that can be transmitted to the next generation. One of the genetic mechanisms that accounts for variation in species and individuals.

Nature vs. nurture controversy The continuing debate about the relative influence of innate and experiential factors on the shaping of the individual. Also known as the maturation vs. learning and heredity vs. environment controversy.

Negative (inverse) corrrelation When two (or more) variables are negatively correlated they co-vary such that high scores on one variable are associated with low scores on the other, and vice versa.

Negative reinforcement The process whereby the probability of a response increases because the response was followed by the removal of an aversive stimulus.

Neuropsychological assessment The use of psychological tests and behavioral measures to indirectly evaluate the functioning of the nervous system. Performance on these measures is known or presumed to reflect specific aspects of the functioning of the brain.

Neurotransmitter A chemical that carries the nerve impulse from one neuron across the synaptic space to another neuron. Examples are serotonin, dopamine, and norepinephrine.

Nonnormative development influences The effects on development that stem from events that are not necessarily unusual in themselves but that occur to only some individuals, perhaps at unpredictable times. Examples are serious injury in childhood and premature death of a parent. These influences may be especially stressful. (*See* normative developmental influences.)

Nonshared environmental influence The portion of environmental influences on an attribute that is experienced by one family member but not other members. (*See* shared environmental influence.)

Normal distribution (curve) The bell-shaped theoretical distribution or probability curve that describes the way in which many attributes (e.g., height, intelligence) occur in the population or are assumed to occur.

Normalization Philosophy that persons with disabilities have the right to experiences that are as normal as possible for the individual. (*See* mainstreaming; least restrictive environment.)

Normative developmental influences The effects on development that stem from events that happen to most individuals in some more-or-less predictable way, for example, puberty. (*See* nonnormative developmental influences.)

Norms Data based on information gathered from a segment of the population that represents the entire population. Norms serve as standards to evaluate individual development or functioning.

Nuclear family A family unit consisting of the father, mother, and children.

Observational learning Learning that occurs through viewing the behavior of others. Modeled behavior can be presented in live or symbolic form.

Obsessions Recurring and intrusive irrational thoughts over which the individual feels no control.

Operant learning Learning in which responses are acquired, maintained, or eliminated as the result of consequences (e.g., reinforcement, punishment) and other learning processes.

Operational criteria (definition) A specified set of observable operations that are measurable and allow one to define some concept. For example, maternal deprivation might be defined by the amount of time the child is separated from its mother.

Overlearning The procedure whereby learning trials are continued beyond the point at which the child has completed the stated criteria. This is intended to increase the likelihood that the new behavior will be maintained.

Overt behaviors Behaviors that are readily observable. When describing antisocial behaviors this term refers to behaviors that are confrontational such as physical aggression, temper tantrums, and defiance. (*See* covert behaviors.)

Panic attack A discrete period of intense apprehension, fear, or terror that has a sudden onset and reaches a peak quickly.

Paradigm A shared perspective, set of assumptions, and conceptions held by a group of scientists that guide their work.

Partial correlation statistical procedure A statistical procedure that aids in the interpretation of a demonstrated correlation by removing the effects of one or more specific variables.

Perinatal The period at or around the time of birth.

Perspective *See* paradigm.

Phenotype The observable attributes of an individual that result from genetic endowment, developmental processes, and the transactions of these.

Phobia Anxiety about, and avoidance of, some object or situation. This reaction is judged to be excessive, overly persistent, unadaptive, or inappropriate.

Phonological awareness The understanding that spoken words can be segmented into sounds (for example, that "cat" has three sounds) and that sounds are represented by letters or combinations of letters of the alphabet.

Phonological decoding In alphabet-based languages, mapping letters to sounds.

Phonological processing Using the sound structure of a language to process written material. Deficits in such processing are central in reading disorders.

Phonology Refers to the sounds of a language or the study of speech sounds.

Pica The habitual eating of substances usually considered inedible such as dirt, paper, and hair.

Placebo A treatment—psychological or chemical—that alters a person's behavior because he or she expects that change will occur. Placebos are often employed as control conditions to evaluate whether a treatment being tested is effective for reasons other than the person's belief in it.

Positive (direct) correlation When two (or more) variables are positively correlated they co-vary with each other such that high scores on one variable are associated with high scores on the other variable, and low scores on the one variable are associated with low scores on the other.

Positive reinforcement The process whereby the probability or strength of a response increases because the response is followed by a positive stimulus.

Positron emission tomography (PET scan) A procedure to directly assess activity in different parts of the brain by assessing the use of oxygen and glucose that fuel brain activity.

Posttraumatic stress disorder A reaction to a trauma that is characterized by the reexperiencing of the trauma accompanied by symptoms of increased arousal and by avoidance of stimuli associated with the traumatic event.

Pragmatics (of language) The use of speech and gesture in a communicative way, considering the social context. Pragmatic skills include using appropriate gestures and language style.

Predictive validity The extent to which predictions about future behavior can be made (e.g., by knowing an individual's diagnosis or performance on some test).

Premorbid adjustment The psychological, social, or academic/vocational adjustment of a person prior to onset of the symptoms of a disorder or its diagnosis.

Prenatal The period of development that occurs during pregnancy or gestation.

Prevalence Number or proportion of persons in a population with a disorder at a given time.

Primary prevention The prevention of disorders in the population by methods implemented before their full occurrence.

Proband The designated individual whose relatives are assessed to determine if an attribute occurs in other members of that family. Also called an index case.

Projection A defense mechanism whereby the ego protects against unacceptable thoughts or impulses by attributing them to another person or some object.

Projective tests Psychological tests that present ambiguous stimuli to the person. The person's response is presumed to reflect unconscious thoughts and feelings that are unacceptable to the ego and therefore cannot be expressed directly.

Pronoun reversal Deviant speech pattern in which speakers refer to themselves as "you" or "she" or "he" and refer to others as "I" or "me." Often found in autism.

Prospective research designs Designs that identify participants and then follow them over time. (*See* retrospective research designs.)

Protective factors Variables that lessen the effects of risk.

Psychoactive (psychotropic) drugs Chemical substances that influence psychological processes (e.g., behavior, thinking, emotions) by their influence on nervous system functioning. Examples are stimulants and antidepressants.

Psychogenesis The view that development of a behavior or disorder is due to psychological influence.

Psychosis A general term for severe mental disorder that affects thinking, the emotions, and other psychological systems. The hallmark of a psychosis is disturbed contact with reality.

PTSD *See* posttraumatic stress disorder.

Punishment A process whereby a response is followed by either an unpleasant stimulus or the removal of a pleasant stimulus, thereby decreasing the frequency of that response.

Qualitative research A research approach that assumes that events are best understood when they are observed in context and from a personal frame of reference. The methods employed include in-depth interviews and intensive case studies. (*See* quantitative research.)

Quantitative research A research approach that places high value on objective quantitative measurement in highly controlled situations, as characterized by the experiment. (*See* qualitative research.)

Random assignment In research, the assignment of individuals to different groups so that each individual has an equal chance of being assigned to any group. Such chance assignment helps make the groups comparable on factors that might influence the findings.

Recidivism The return to a previous undesirable pattern. The juvenile delinquent who again commits a crime after completing a treatment program illustrates recidivism.

Regular Education Initiative (REI) Controversial proposal that all children with disabilities be educated in regular classrooms rather than special education settings.

Reinforcement A process whereby a stimulus that occurs contingent on a particular behavior results in an increase in the likelihood of that behavior. (*See* positive reinforcement; negative reinforcement.)

Relapse The reoccurrence of a problem after it has been successfully treated.

Reliability The degree to which an observation is consistently made. The term can be applied to a test or other measurement or to a system of classification. (*See* test-retest reliability; interrater reliability.)

Resilience The ability to overcome risk factors, to function adaptively despite negative circumstances.

Response prevention A behavioral treatment procedure in which the person is not allowed to engage in, or is discouraged from engaging in, a compulsive ritual or avoidant behavior.

Retrospective research designs Designs that utilize information about past events; follow-back designs. (*See* prospective research designs.)

Risk The degree to which variables (risk factors) operate to increase the chance of behavior problems. (*See* protective factors.)

Rumination The voluntary regurgitation of food—most likely to occur among infants and persons with mental retardation.

Savant abilities Specific and remarkable cognitive abilities (e.g., in memory or arithmetic) of individuals who otherwise exhibit intellectual disability.

Scientific method An empirical approach to understanding phenomena. The scientific approach involves systematic formulation, observation and measurement, and interpretation of findings.

Secondary prevention The prevention of disorders in the population by shortening the duration of existing cases through early diagnosis and treatment.

Self-injurious behavior Repetitious action that damages the self physically, such as head banging or pulling one's own hair. Observed especially in autism and mental retardation.

Self-monitoring A procedure in which the individual observes and records his or her own behaviors or thoughts and the circumstances under which they occur.

Self-stimulatory behavior Sensory-motor behavior that serves as stimulation for the person. Often refers to a pathological process, for example, as when an autistic child repetitiously flaps his or her hands.

Semantics   The study of meanings in language.

Separation anxiety   Childhood anxiety regarding separation from the mother or other major attachment figures.

Sequential research designs   Various designs that combine the longitudinal and cross-sectional research strategies to maximize the strengths of these methods.

Shared environmental influences   The portion of environmental influences on an attribute that is experienced by two or more family members. (*See* nonshared environmental influences.)

Single-subject experiments   Experimental research designs employed with a single (or a few) participant(s), in which a manipulation is made and measurements are taken across time periods. (*See* ABA; multiple baseline designs.)

Socioeconomic status (SES)   Social class. Indices of SES include income, amount of education, and occupational level.

Somatogenesis   The view that development of a behavior or disorder is due to biological—rather than psychosocial—causes.

Stage theories of development   Explanations of development that postulate that growth occurs in a recognizable order of noncontinuous stages or steps that are qualitatively different from each other. Examples are Piaget's cognitive theory and Freud's psychosexual theory.

Statistical significance   In research, refers to a low probability that the findings are merely chance occurrences. By tradition a finding is statistically significant when there is a 5 percent or less probability that it occurred by chance ($p \le .05$).

Stereotypy   A repetitive action or movement, such as hand flapping.

Stop-signal task   A method to evaluate behavioral inhibition. The individual must press a button when a target stimulus comes on a screen but must withhold this response when a special signal also comes on.

Stress   A situation or event that brings strain to the individual. Considered a risk factor for behavioral and physical health.

Superego   According to psychoanalytic theory, the structure of the mind that is the conscience or self-critical part of the individual. It reflects society's morals and standards as they have been learned from parents and others.

Sympathetic nervous system   A part of the autonomic nervous system that, among other things, accelerates heart rate, increases blood glucose, inhibits intestinal activity, and in general seems to prepare the organism for stress or activity.

Syndrome   A group of behaviors or symptoms likely to occur together.

Syntax   The aspect of grammar that deals with the way words are put together to form phrases, clauses, and sentences.

Systematic desensitization   A behavioral treatment for anxiety. The client visualizes a hierarchy of scenes, each of which elicits more anxiety than the previous scene. These visualizations are paired with relaxation until they no longer produce anxiety.

Systematic direct observation   Observation of specific behaviors of an individual or group of individuals in a particular setting, with the use of a specific observational code or instrument.

Temperament   Individual differences in emotionality, social responsiveness, activity level, and self-control. Biologically-based disposition that can be transformed by experience.

Teratogens   Conditions or agents that are potentially harmful to the prenatal organism.

Tertiary prevention   The prevention of disorders in the population by reducing problems residual to disorders. An example is support groups for persons who are returning to the community after hospitalization for mental disorders.

Test-retest reliability   The degree to which a test or diagnostic system yields the same result when applied to the same individuals at different times.

Theory   An integrated set of propositions that explains phenomena and guides research.

Theory of mind   The ability to infer mental states (e.g., beliefs, knowledge) in others or the self.

Time-out   Behavior modification technique in which an individual displaying an undesirable behavior is removed from the immediate environment, usually by placement in an isolated room. Time-out is viewed conceptually as elimination of positive reinforcement or as punishment.

Token economy   A behavioral treatment procedure developed from operant conditioning principles. A set of behaviors that earns or costs reward points, given in the form of some scrip, such as poker chips, is set up. These tokens can then be exchanged for prizes, activities, or privileges.

Transactional model of development   The view that development is the result of the continuous interplay of organismic and environmental variables. It is conceptually similar to the interactional model of development but emphasizes the ongoing, mutual influences of factors.

Trauma   An event outside of everyday experience that would be distressing to almost anyone.

Treatment foster care   An effort to alleviate behavioral problems of children in foster care by working with foster parents and linking the child to the community mental health system.

Twin study   A type of research investigation frequently employed to examine the effects of hereditary and environmental variables. Pairs of genetically-identical monozygotic twins and dizygotic twins, which share on average half their genes, are examined to determine whether the former are more alike than the latter.

Unconditioned stimulus (UCS)   A stimulus that elicits a particular response prior to any conditioning trials. The loud noise that causes an infant to startle is an example of an unconditioned stimulus.

Validity   A term used in several different ways, all of which address issues of correctness, meaningfulness, and relevancy. (*See* internal validity; external validity; predictive validity.)

Wait-list (waiting-list) control group   Participants in a research study who do not receive the treatment being investigated. This allows the investigators to compare changes in a group of individuals who received treatment to a group of similar individuals who did not receive treatment. The term *wait list* is derived from the fact that those in the control group are offered treatment once the comparison is completed.

Working memory   Part of the memory system that briefly holds and actively manipulates, or works on, information that it receives from the sensory systems and/or calls up from long-term memory. May be referred to as short-term memory.

Zygote   The cell mass formed by the joining of an ovum and sperm; the fertilized egg.

AACAP. (1997). Practice parameters for the assessment and treatment of children and adolescents with anxiety disorders. *Journal of the American Academy of Child and Adolescent Psychiatry, 36,* 69S–84S.

AACAP. (1998). Practice parameters for the assessment and treatment of children and adolescents with posttraumatic stress disorder. *Journal of the American Academy of Child and Adolescent Psychiatry, 37,* 4S–26S.

Abela, J. R. Z. (2001). The hopelessness theory of depression: A test of the diathesis-stress and causal mediation components in third and seventh grade children. *Journal of Abnormal Child Psychology, 29,* 241–254.

Abidin, R. R. (1995). *Parenting Stress Index: Professional manual* (3rd ed.). Odessa, FL: Psychological Assessment Resources.

Abikoff, H., Hechtman, L., Klein, R. G., Gallagher, R., Fleiss, K., Etcovitch, J. et al. (2004a). Social functioning in children with ADHD treated with long-term methylphenidate and multimodal treatment. *Journal of the American Academy of Child and Adolescent Psychiatry, 43,* 820–829.

Abikoff, H., Hechtman, L., Klein, R. G., Weiss, G., Fleiss, K., Etcovitch, J. et al. (2004b). Symptomatic improvement in children with ADHD treated with long-term methylphenidate and multimodal psychosocial treatment. *Journal of the American Academy of Child and Adolescent Psychiatry, 43,* 802–811.

Ablon, S. L. (1996). The therapeutic action of play. *Journal of the American Academy of Child and Adolescent Psychiatry, 35,* 545–547.

Abramson, L. Y., Metalsky, G. I., & Alloy, L. B. (1989). Hopelessness depression: A theory-based subtype of depression. *Psychological Bulletin, 96,* 358–372.

Abu-Akel, A., Caplan, R., Guthrie, D., & Komo, S. (2000). Childhood schizophrenia: Responsiveness to questions during conversation. *Journal of the American Academy of Child and Adolescent Psychiatry, 39,* 779–786.

Achenbach, T. M. (1982). *Developmental psychopathology.* New York: Wiley.

Achenbach, T. M. (1990). Conceptualizations of developmental psychopathology. In M. Lewis & S. M. Miller (Eds.), *Handbook of developmental psychopathology.* New York: Plenum.

Achenbach, T. M. (1998). Diagnosis, assessment, taxonomy and case formulations. In T. H. Ollendick & M. Hersen (Eds.), *Handbook of child psychopathology* (3rd ed.). New York: Plenum Press.

Achenbach, T. M. (2000). Assessment of psychopathology. In A. J. Sameroff, M. Lewis, & S. M. Miller (Eds.), *Handbook of developmental psychopathology* (2nd ed.). New York: Kluwer Academic/Plenum Publishers.

Achenbach, T. M., & Rescorla, L. A. (2001). *Manual for the ASEBA School-Age Forms & Profiles.* Burlington, VT: University of Vermont, Research Center for Children, Youth, & Families.

Achenbach, T. M., Dumenci, L., & Rescorla, L. A. (2003a). Are American children's problems getting worse? A 23-year comparison. *Journal of Abnormal Child Psychology, 31,* 1–11.

Achenbach, T. M., Dumenci, L., & Rescorla, L. A. (2003b). DSM-oriented and empirically based approaches to constructing scales from the same item pools. *Journal of Clinical Child and Adolescent Psychology, 32,* 328–340.

Achenbach, T. M., Howell, C. T., McConaughy, S. H., & Stanger, C. (1995). Six-year predictors of problems in a national sample of children and youth: II. Signs of disturbance. *Journal of the American Academy of Child and Adolescent Psychiatry, 34,* 488–498.

Achenbach, T. M., McConaughy, S. H., & Howell, C. T. (1987). Child/adolescent behavioral and emotional problems: Implications of cross-informant correlations for situational specificity. *Psychological Bulletin, 101,* 213–232.

Achenbach, T. M., Rescorla, L. A., & Ivanova, M. Y. (2005). Cross-cultural consistencies and variations in child and adolescent psychopathology. In K. F. Frisbay & C. Reynolds (Eds.), *Handbook of multicultural school psychology.* New York: John Wiley.

Acosta, O. M., Albus, K. E., Reynolds, M. W., Spriggs, D., & Weist, M. D. (2001). Assessing the status of research on violence-related problems among youth. *Journal of Clinical Child Psychology, 30,* 152–160.

Adams, G., & Carnine, D. (2003). Direct instruction. In H. L. Swanson, K. R. Harris, & S. Graham (Eds.), *Handbook of learning disabilities.* New York: Guilford Press.

Adelman, H. S. (1996). Appreciating the classification dilemma. In W. Stainback & S. Stainback (Eds.), *Controversial issues confronting special education: Divergent perspectives* (2nd ed.). Boston: Allyn and Bacon.

Adrien, J. L., Lenoir, P., Martineau, J., Perrot, A., Hameury, L., Larmande, C., & Sauvage, D. (1993). Blind ratings of early symptoms of autism based upon home movies. *Journal of the American Academy of Child and Adolescent Psychiatry, 32,* 617–626.

Ainbinder, J. G., Blanchard, L. W., Singer, G. H. S., Sullivan, M. E., Powers, L. K., Marquis, J. G., & Santelli, B. (1998). A qualitative study of Parent to Parent support for parents of children with special needs. *Journal of Pediatric Psychology, 23,* 99–109.

Alarcón, R. D., Bell, C. C., Kirmayer, L. J., Lin, K. M., Üstün, B., & Wisner, K. L. (2002). Beyond the funhouse mirrors. Research agenda on culture and psychiatric diagnosis. In D. J. Kupfer,

M. B. First, & D. A. Regier (Eds.), *A research agenda for DSM-V*. Washington, DC: American Psychiatric Association.

Albano, A. M., & Barlow, D. H. (1996). Cognitive behavioral group treatment for adolescent social phobia. In E. D. Hibbs & P. S. Jensen (Eds.), *Psychosocial treatment research of child and adolescent disorders*. Washington, DC: American Psychological Association Press.

Albano, A. M., Chorpita, B. F., & Barlow, D. H. (2003). Childhood anxiety disorders. In E. J. Mash & R. A. Barkley (Eds.), *Child psychopathology* (2nd ed.). New York: Guilford Press.

Albano, A. M., & DiBartolo, P. M. (1997). Cognitive-behavioral treatment of obsessive-compulsive disorder and social phobia in children and adolescents. In L. VandeCreek (Ed.), *Innovations in clinical practice* (Vol. 15). Sarasota, FL: Professional Resource Exchange.

Albee, G. W. (1986). Toward a just society. Lessons from observations on the primary prevention of psychopathology. *American Psychologist, 41*, 891–898.

Albee, G. W. (1996). Revolutions and counterrevolutions in prevention. *American Psychologist, 51*, 1130–1133.

Aleman, A., Kahn, R. S., & Selten, J-P. (2003). Sex differences in the risk of schizophrenia. *Archives of General Psychiatry, 60*, 565–591.

Alessi, N. E., Robbins, D. R., & Dilsaver, S. C. (1987). Panic and depressive disorders among psychiatrically hospitalized adolescents. *Psychiatry Research, 20*, 275–283.

Alexander, F. (1950). *Psychosomatic medicine*. New York: W. W. Norton and Co.

Alexander, J., Barton, C., Gordon, D., Grotpeter, J., Hansson, K., Harrison, R., Mears, S., Mihalic, S., Parsons, B., Pugh, C., Schulman, S., Waldron, H., & Sexton, T. (1998). *Blueprints for violence prevention: Functional family therapy*. Boulder, CO: Venture.

Alexander, J. F., Holtzworth-Munroe, A., & Jameson, P. B. (1994). The process and outcome of marital and family therapy research: Review and evaluation. In A. E. Bergin & S. L. Garfield (Eds.), *Handbook of psychotherapy and behavior change* (4th ed.). New York: John Wiley & Sons.

Alexander, J. F., & Parsons, B. V. (1973). Short-term behavioral intervention with delinquent families: Impact on family process and recidivism. *Journal of Abnormal Psychology, 81*, 219–225.

Algozzine, B. (1977). The emotionally disturbed child: Disturbed or disturbing? *Journal of Abnormal Child Psychology, 5*, 205–211.

Allen, A. J., Leonard, H. L., & Swedo, S. E. (1995). A new infection-triggered, autoimmune subtype of pediatric OCD and Tourette's syndrome. *Journal of the American Academy of Child and Adolescent Psychiatry, 34*, 307–311.

Allen, M., & Bissell, M. (2004, Winter). Safety and stability for foster children: The policy context. *The Future of Children, 14*, 49–73.

Allen, S. F., Dlugokinski, E. L., Cohen, L. A., & Walker, J. L. (1999). Assessing the impact of a traumatic community event on children and assisting with their healing. *Psychiatric Annals, 29*, 93–98.

Altman, H., & Collins, M., & Mundy, P. (1997). Subclinical hallucinations and delusions in nonpsychotic adolescents. *Journal of Child Psychology and Psychiatry, 38*, 413–420.

Amato, P. R. (2000). The consequences of divorce for adults and children. *Journal of Marriage and the Family, 62*, 1269–1287.

Amato, P. R., & Keith, B. (1991). Parental divorce and the well-being of children: A metaanalysis. *Psychological Bulletin, 110*, 26–46.

Ambrosini, P. J. (2000a). A review of pharmacotherapy of major depression in children and adolescents. *Psychiatric Services, 51*, 627–633.

Ambrosini, P. J. (2000b). Historical development and present status of the Schedule for Affective Disorders and Schizophrenia for School-Age Children (K-SADS). *Journal of the American Academy of Child and Adolescent Psychiatry, 39*, 49–58.

American Academy of Child and Adolescent Psychiatry. (1999). Practice parameters for the assessment and treatment of children, adolescents, and adults with autism and other pervasive developmental disorders. *Journal of the American Academy of Child and Adolescent Psychiatry 38* (suppl.): 32s–54s.

American Academy of Child and Adolescent Psychiatry. (2001). Practice parameters for the assessment and treatment of children and adolescents with suicidal behavior. *Journal of the American Academy of Child and Adolescent Psychiatry, 40*, 24S–51S.

American Academy of Pediatrics. (2003). Prevention of pediatric overweight and obesity. *Pediatrics, 112*, 424–430.

American Academy of Pediatrics, Committee on Children with Disabilities. (1998). Learning disabilities, dyslexia, and vision: A subject review. *Pediatrics, 102*, 1217–1219.

American Academy of Pediatrics. (2000). Fetal alcohol syndrome and alcohol-related neurodevelopmental disorders. *Pediatrics, 106*, 358–361.

American Guidance Service. (2005). *Vineland Adaptive Behavior Scales, Second Edition (Vineland-II)*. Circle Pines, MN: AGS Publishers.

American Psychiatric Association. (1952, 1968, 1980, 1987, 1994). *Diagnostic and statistical manual of mental disorders*. Washington, DC: American Psychiatric Association.

American Psychiatric Association. (2000). *Diagnostic and statistical manual of mental disorders (4th ed.). Text Revision*. Washington, DC: American Psychiatric Association.

American Psychological Association. (2002). *Ethical principles of psychologists and code of conduct*. Washington, DC: Author.

American Sleep Disorders Association. (1997). *The international classification of sleep disorders, revised: Diagnostic and coding manual*. Rochester, MN: American Sleep Disorders Association.

Anastasi, A., & Urbina, S. (1997). *Psychological testing*. Upper Saddle River, NJ: Prentice Hall.

Anastopoulos, A. D., & Farley, S. E. (2003). A cognitive-behavioral training program for parents of children with attention-deficit/hyperactivity disorder. In A. E. Kazdin & J. R. Weisz (Eds.), *Evidence-based psychotherapies for children and adolescents*. New York: Guilford Press.

Anastopoulos, A. D., Smith, J. M., & Wien, E. E. (1998). Counseling and training parents. In R. A. Barkley, *Attention-deficit hyperactivity disorder*. New York: Guilford Press.

Anders, T. F., & Eiben, L. A. (1997). Pediatric sleep disorders: A review of the past 10 years. *Journal of the American Academy of Child and Adolescent Psychiatry, 36*, 9–20.

Anderson, B. J., Brackett, J., Ho, J., & Laffel, L. M. B. (2000). An intervention to promote family teamwork in diabetes management tasks: Relationships among parental involvement, adherence to blood glucose monitoring, and glycemic control in young adolescents with Type 1 diabetes. In D. Drotar (Ed.), *Promoting adherence to medical treatment in chronic childhood illness: Concepts, methods, and interventions*. Mahwah, NJ: Lawrence Erlbaum Associates.

Anderson, C. A., Berkowitz, L., Donnerstein, E., Huesmann, R., Johnson, J. D., Linz, D. et al. (2003). The influence of media violence on youth. *Psychological Science in the Public Interest, 4*, 81–110.

Anderson, D. A., & Maloney, K. C. (2001). The efficacy of cognitive-behavioral therapy on the core symptoms of bulimia nervosa. *Clinical Psychology Review, 21*, 971–988.

Anderson, D. A., & Paulosky, C. A. (2004). Psychological assessment of eating disorders and related features. In J. K. Thompson (Ed.), *Handbook of eating disorders and obesity*. Hoboken, NJ: John Wiley.

Anderson-Fye, E. P., & Becker, A. E. (2004). Sociocultural aspects of eating disorders. In J. K. Thompson (Ed.), *Handbook of eating disorders and obesity*. Hoboken, NJ: John Wiley.

Anderson, J. C. (1994). Epidemiology. In T. H. Ollendick, N. J. King, & W. Yule (Eds.), *International handbook of phobic and anxiety disorders in children and adolescents*. New York: Plenum Press.

Anderson, J. C., Williams, S., McGee, R., & Silva, P. A. (1987). DSM-III disorders in preadolescent children: Prevalence in a large sample from the general population. *Archives of General Psychiatry, 44*, 69–76.

Anderson, M. (2001). Annotation: Conceptions of intelligence. *Journal of Child Psychology and Psychiatry, 42*, 287–298.

Anderson, R. N., & Smith, B. L. (2003). Deaths: Leading causes for 2001. *National Vital Statistics Reports (Vol. 52)*. Hyattsville, MD: National Center for Health Statistics.

Anderson, V., Northam, E., Hendy, J., & Wrennall, J. (2001). *Developmental neuropsychology. A clinical approach*. Philadelphia: Taylor & Francis.

Andrasik, F., Blake, D. D., & McCarran, M. S. (1986). A biobehavioral analysis of pediatric headache. In N. A. Krasnegor, J. D. Arasteh, & M. F. Cataldo (Eds.), *Child health behavior: A behavioral pediatrics perspective*. New York: Wiley.

Angold, A., Costello, E. J., & Erkanli, A. (1999). Comorbidity. *Journal of Child Psychology and Psychiatry, 40*, 57–87.

Angold, A., & Rutter, M. (1992). Effects of age and pubertal status on depression in a large clinical sample. *Development and Psychopathology, 4*, 5–28.

Anthony, E. J. (1970). Behavior disorders. In P. H. Mussen (Ed.), *Carmichael's manual of child psychology*, Vol. II. New York: John Wiley.

Anthony, E. J. (1981). The psychiatric evaluation of the anxious child: Case record summarized from the clinic records. In E. J. Anthony & D. C. Gilpin (Eds.), *Three further clinical faces of childhood*. New York: S P Medical & Scientific Books.

Antrop, I., Roeyers, H., Van Oost, P., & Buysse, A. (2000). Stimulation seeking and hyperactivity in children with ADHD. *Journal of Child Psychology and Psychiatry, 41*, 225–231.

Antschel, K. M., & Remer, R. (2003). Social skills training in children with attention deficit hyperactivity disorder: A randomized-controlled clinical trial. *Journal of Clinical Child and Adolescent Psychology, 32*, 153–165.

Ariès, P. (1962). *Centuries of childhood*. New York: Vintage Books.

Aristimuno, G. G., Foster, T. A., Voors, A. W., Srinivasan, S. R., & Berenson, G. S. (1984). Influence of persistent obesity in children on cardiovascular risk factors: The Bogalusa Heart Study. *Circulation, 69*, 895–904.

Armbruster, P., & Kazdin, A. E. (1994). Attrition in child psychotherapy. In T. H. Ollendick & R. J. Prinz (Eds.), *Advances in clinical child psychology*. New York: Plenum Press.

Armistead, L., Forehand, R., Steele, R., & Kotchick, B. (1998). Pediatric AIDS. In T. H. Ollendick & M. Hersen (Eds.), *Handbook of child psychopathology* (3rd ed.). New York: Plenum Press.

Armstrong, F. D., Willen, E. J., & Sorgen, K. (2003). HIV and AIDS in children and adolescents. In M. C. Roberts (Eds.), *Handbook of pediatric psychology* (3rd ed.). New York: Guilford Press.

Armstrong, T. D., & Costello, E. J. (2002). Community studies of adolescent substance use, abuse, or dependence and psychiatric comorbidity. *Journal of Consulting and Clinical Psychology, 70*, 1224–1239.

Arnold, L. E., Vitiello, B., McDougle, C., Scahill, L., Shah, B., Gonzalez, M. N. et al. (2003). Parent-defined target symptoms respond to risperidone in RUPP Autism Study: Customer approach to clinical trials. *Journal of the American Academy of Child and Adolescent Psychiatry, 42*, 1443–1450.

Arsenio, W. F., & Lemerise, E. A. (2004). Aggression and moral development: Integrating social information processing and moral domain models. *Child Development, 75*, 987–1002.

Asarnow, J. R., & Asarnow, R. F. (2003). Childhood-onset schizophrenia. In E. J. Mash & R. A. Barkley (Eds.), *Child psychopathology*. New York: Guilford Press.

Asarnow, J. R., Goldstein, M. J., & Ben-Meir, S. (1988). Parental communication deviance in childhood onset schizophrenia spectrum and depressive disorders. *Journal of Child Psychology and Psychiatry, 29*, 825–838.

Asarnow, J. R., Jaycox, L. H., & Tompson, M. C. (2001). Depression in youth: Psychosocial interventions. *Journal of Clinical Child Psychology, 30*, 33–47.

Asarnow, J. R., Tompsom, M. C., & McGrath, E. P. (2004). Annotation: Childhood-onset schizophrenia: Clinical and treatment issues. *Journal of Child Psychology and Psychiatry, 45*, 180–194.

Asbury, K., Dunn, J. F., Pike, A., & Plomin, R. (2003). Nonshared environmental influences on individual differences in early behavioral development: A monozygotic twin difference study. *Child Development, 74*, 933–943.

Aschenbrand, S. G., Kendall, P. C., Webb, A., Safford, S. M., & Flannery-Schroeder, E. (2003). Is childhood separation anxiety disorder a predictor of adult panic disorder and agoraphobia? A seven-year longitudinal study. *Journal of the American Academy of Child and Adolescent Psychiatry, 42*, 1478–1485.

Atkinson, L., Scott, B., Chrisholm, V., Blackwell, J., Dickens, S., Tam, F., & Goldberg, S. (1995). Cognitive coping, affective distress, and maternal sensitivity: Mothers of children with Down syndrome. *Developmental Psychology, 31*, 668–676.

Attie, I., & Brooks-Gunn, J. (1995). The development of eating regulation across the life span. In D. Cicchetti & D. J. Cohen (Eds.), *Developmental psychopathology* (Vol. 2: *Risk, disorder, and adaptation*). New York: John Wiley.

Attwood, A., Frith, U., & Hermelin, B. (1988). The understanding and use of interpersonal gestures by autistic and Down's Syndrome children. *Journal of Autism and Developmental Disorders, 18*, 241–257.

August, G. J., & Garfinkel, B. D. (1993). The nosology of attention-deficit hyperactivity disorder. *Journal of the American Academy of Child and Adolescent Psychiatry, 32*, 155–165.

Austin, A. A., & Chorpita, B. F. (2004). Temperament, anxiety, and depression: Comparisons across five ethnic groups of children. *Journal of Clinical Child and Adolescent Psychology, 33*, 216–226.

Axline, V. M. (1947). *Play therapy*. Boston: Houghton Mifflin.

Azar, S. T., & Bober, S. L. (1999). Children of abusive parents. In W. K. Silverman & T. H. Ollendick (Eds.), *Development issues in the clinical treatment of children*. Boston: Allyn & Bacon.

Azar, S. T., Ferraro, M. H., & Breton, S. J. (1998). Intra-familial child maltreatment. In T. H. Ollendick & M. Hersen (Eds.), *Handbook of child psychopathology* (3rd ed.). New York: Plenum Press.

Babinski, L. M., Hartsough, C. S., & Lambert, N. M. (1999). Childhood conduct problems, hyperactivity-impulsivity, and inattention as predictors of adult criminal activity. *Journal of Child Psychology and Psychiatry, 40*, 347–355.

Bachanas, P. J., & Kaslow, N. J. (2001). Depressive disorders. In J. N. Hughes, A. M. La Greca, & J. C. Conoley (Eds.), *Handbook of psychological services for children and adolescents*. New York: Oxford University Press.

Bachanas, P. J., Kullgren, K. A., Schwartz, K. S., Lanier, B., McDaniel, J. S., Smith, J., & Nesheim, S. (2001). Predictors of psychological adjustment in school-age children infected with HIV: Stress, coping, and family factors. *Journal of Pediatric Psychology, 26*, 343–352.

Baddeley, A. (1992). Working memory. *Science, 255*, 5556–5559.

Baddeley, A. D. (2001). Is working memory still working? *American Psychologist, 56*, 851–864.

Bailey, A., Le Couteur, A., Gottesman, I., Bolton, P., Simonoff, E., Yuzda, E., & Rutter, M. (1995). Autism as a strongly genetic disorder: Evidence from a British twin study. *Psychological Medicine, 25*, 63–78.

Bailey, A., Phillips, W., & Rutter, M. (1996). Autism: Towards an integration of clinical, genetic, neuropsychological, and neurobiological perspectives. *Journal of Child Psychology and Psychiatry, 37*, 89–126.

Bailey, D. B., Hatton, D. D., Mesibov, G., Ament, N., & Skinner, M. (2000). Early development, temperament, and functional impairment in autism and fragile X syndrome. *Journal of Autism and Developmental Disorders, 30*, 49–59.

Bailey, D. B., Skinner, D., & Sparkman, K. L. (2003). Discovering fragile X syndrome: Family experiences and perceptions. *Pediatrics, 111*, 407–416.

Bailey, G. W. (1989). Current perspectives on substance abuse in youth. *Journal of the American Academy of Child and Adolescent Psychiatry, 28*, 151–162.

Baird, G., Charman, T., Baron-Cohen, S., Cox, A., Swettenham, J., Wheelwright, S., & Drew, A. (2000). A screening instrument for autism at 18 months of age: A 16-year follow-up study. *Journal of the American Academy of Child and Adolescent Psychiatry, 39*, 694–702.

Baker, L., & Cantwell, D. P. (1989). Specific language and learning disorders. In T. H. Ollendick & M. Hersen (Eds.), *Handbook of child psychopathology*. New York: Plenum.

Balboni, G., Pedrabissi, L., Molteni, M., & Villa, S. (2001). Discriminant validity of the Vineland Scales: Score profiles of individuals with mental retardation and a specific disorder. *American Journal of Mental Retardation, 106*, 162–172.

Balk, D. E., & Corr, C. A. (2001). Bereavement during adolescence: A review of research. In M. S. Stroebe, R. O. Hansson, W. Stroebe, & H. Schut (Eds.), *Handbook of bereavement research: Consequences, coping, and care*. Washington, DC: American Psychological Association.

Bandura, A. (1965). Influence of models' reinforcement contingencies on the acquisition of imitative responses. *Journal of Personality and Social Psychology, 1*, 589–595.

Bandura, A. (1977). *Social learning theory*. Englewood Cliffs, NJ: Prentice Hall.

Bandura, A. (1997). *Self-efficacy: The exercise of control*. New York: Freeman.

Bandura, A., Barbaranelli, C., Caprara, G. V., Pastorelli, C. (2001). Self-efficacy beliefs as shapers to children's aspirations and career trajectories. *Child Development, 72*, 187–206.

Bandura, A., & Menlove, F. L. (1968). Factors determining vicarious extinction of avoidance behavior through symbolic modeling. *Journal of Personality and Social Psychology, 8*, 99–108.

Baranek, G. T. (1999). Autism during infancy: A retrospective video analysis of sensory-motor and social behaviors at 9–12 months of age. *Journal of Autism and Developmental Disorders, 29*, 213–224.

Barber, J. G., Delfabbro, P. H., & Cooper, L. L. (2001). The predictors of unsuccessful transition to foster care. *Journal of Child Psychology and Psychiatry, 42*, 785–790.

Barenbaum, J., Ruchkin, V., & Schwab-Stone, M. (2004). The psychosocial aspects of children exposed to war: Practice and policy initiatives. *Journal of Child Psychology and Psychiatry, 45*, 41–62.

Barkley, R. (1981). Hyperactivity. In E. J. Mash & L. G. Terdal (Eds.), *Behavioral assessment of childhood disorders*. New York: Guilford Press.

Barkley, R. A. (1990). *Attention-deficit hyperactivity disorder*. New York: Guilford.

Barkley, R. A. (1997). Attention-deficit/hyperactivity disorder. In E. J. Mash & L. G. Terdal (Eds.), *Assessment of childhood disorders*. New York: Guilford Press.

Barkley, R. A. (1998). *Attention-deficit/hyperactivity disorder*. New York: Guilford Press.

Barkley, R. A. (2003). Attention-deficit/hyperactivity disorder. In E. J. Mash & R. A. Barkley (Eds.), *Child psychopathology*. New York: Guilford Press.

Barkley, R. A., Fischer, M., Smallish, L., & Fletcher, K. (2003). Does the treatment of attention-deficit/hyperactivity disorder with stimulants contribute to drug use/abuse? A 13-year prospective study. *Pediatrics, 111*, 97–109.

Barkley, R. A., Fischer, M., Smallish, L., & Fletcher, K. (2004). Young adult follow-up of hyperactive children: antisocial activities and drug use. *Journal of Child Psychology and Psychiatry, 45*, 195–211.

Barkley, R. A., Shelton, T. L., Crosswait, C., Moorehouse, M., Fletcher, K., Barrett, S., Jenkins, L., & Metevia, L. (2002). Preschool children with disruptive behavior: Three-year outcome as a function of adaptive disability. *Development and Psychopathology, 14*, 45–67.

Barlow, D. H. (2002). *Anxiety and its disorders: The nature and treatment of anxiety and panic* (2nd ed.). New York: Guilford Press.

Barnett, W., & Spitzer, M. (1994). Pathological fire-setting 1951–1991: A review. *Medicine Science and the Law, 34*, 4–20.

Baron, I. S. (2004). *Neuropsychological evaluation of the child.* New York: Oxford University Press.

Baron-Cohen, S. (1989). The autistic child's theory of mind: A case of specific developmental delay. *Journal of Child Psychology and Psychiatry, 30*, 285–297.

Baron-Cohen, S. (1993). From attention-goal psychology to belief-desire psychology: the development of a theory of mind, and its dysfunction. In S. Baron-Cohen, H. Tager-Flusberg, & D. J. Cohen (Eds.), *Understanding other minds.* New York: Oxford Press.

Baron-Cohen, S., O'Riordan, M., Stone, V., Jones, R., & Plaisted, K. (1999). Recognition of faux pas by normally developing children and children with Asperger syndrome or high-functioning autism. *Journal of Autism and Developmental Disabilities, 29*, 407–418.

Baron-Cohen, S., & Swettenham, J. (1997). Theory of mind in autism: Its relationship to executive functions and central coherence. In D. J. Cohen & F. R. Volkmar (Eds.), *Handbook of autism and pervasive developmental disorders.* New York: John Wiley.

Barr, C. L. (2001). Genetics of childhood disorders: XXII. ADHD, Part 6: The dopamine D4 receptor gene. *Journal of the Academy of Child and Adolescent Psychiatry, 40*, 118–121.

Barrera, M. Jr., Prelow, H. M., Dumka, L. E., Gonzales, N. A., Knight, G. P., Michaels, M. L., Roosa, M. W., & Tein, J. Y. (2002). Pathways form family economic conditions to adolescents' distress: Supportive parenting, stressors outside the family, and deviant peers. *Journal of Community Psychology, 30*, 135–152.

Barrett, P. M., Dadds, M. R., & Rapee, R. M. (1996). Family treatment of childhood anxiety: A controlled trial. *Journal of Consulting and Clinical Psychology, 64*, 333–342.

Barrett, P. M., & Shortt, A. L. (2003). Parental involvement in the treatment of anxious children. In A. E. Kazdin & J. R. Weisz (Eds.), *Evidence-based psychotherapies for children and adolescents.* New York: Guilford Press.

Barrios, B. A., & Hartmann, D. P. (1997). Fears and anxieties. In E. J. Mash & L. G. Terdal (Eds.), *Assessment of childhood disorders* (3rd ed.). New York: Guilford Press.

Barrios, B. A., & O'Dell, S. L. (1998). Fears and anxieties. In E. J. Mash & R. A. Barkley (Eds.), *Treatment of childhood disorders* (2nd ed.). New York: Guilford Press.

Barton, C., Alexander, J. F., Waldron, H., Turner, C. W., & Warburton, J. (1985). Generalizing treatment effects of functional family therapy: Three replications. *The American Journal of Family Therapy, 13*, 16–26.

Bass, S., Shields, M. K., & Behrman, R. E. (2004, Winter). Children, families, and foster care: Analysis and recommendations. *The Future of Children, 14*, 5–29.

Baumeister, A. A. (1987). Mental retardation: Some conceptions and dilemmas. *American Psychologist, 42*, 796–800.

Baumeister, A. A., & Bacharach, V. R. (2002). Early generic intervention has no enduring effect on intelligence and does not prevent mental retardation: The Infant Health and Development Program. *Intelligence, 28*, 161–192.

Baumeister, A. A., & Baumeister, A. A. (2000). Mental retardation: Causes and effects. In M. Hersen & R. T. Ammerman (Eds.), *Advanced abnormal child psychology.* Mahwah, NJ: Lawrence Erlbaum.

Bayley, N. (1969, 1993). *Bayley Scales of Infant Development: Birth to two years.* San Antonio, TX: Psychological Corporation.

Beach, S. R. H., Fincham, F. D., & Katz, J. (1998). Marital therapy in the treatment of depression: Toward a third generation of therapy and research. *Clinical Psychology Review, 18*, 635–661.

Beail, N. (2003). What works for people with mental retardation? Critical commentary on cognitive-behavioral and psychodynamic psychotherapy research. *Mental Retardation, 41*, 468–472.

Beals, J., Piasecki, J. Nelson, S., Jones, M., Keane, E., Dauphinais, Red Shirt, R., Sack, W. H., & Manson, S. M. (1997). Psychiatric disorder among American Indian adolescents: Prevalence in Northern Plains youth. *Journal of the American Academy of Child and Adolescent Psychiatry, 36*, 1252–1259.

Beardslee, W. R., Keller, M. B., Seifer, R., Lavorie, P. W., Staley, J., Podorefsky, D., & Shera, D. (1996). Prediction of adolescent affective disorder: Effects of prior parenteral affective disorders and child psychopathology. *Journal of the American Academy of Child and Adolescent Psychiatry, 35*, 279–288.

Beardslee, W. R., Versage, E. M., & Gladstone, T. R. G. (1998). Children of affectively ill parents: A review of the past 10 years. *Journal of the American Academy of Child and Adolescent Psychiatry, 37*, 1134–1141.

Beauchaine, T. P. (2003). Taxometrics and developmental psychopathology. *Development and Psychopathology, 15*, 501–527.

Beauchaine, T. P., Katkin, E. S., Strassberg, Z., & Snarr, J. (2001). Disinhibitory psychopathology in male adolescents: Discriminating conduct disorder from attention-deficit/hyperactivity disorder through concurrent assessment of multiple autonomic states. *Journal of Abnormal Psychology, 110*, 610–624.

Beck, A. T. (1967). *Depression: Clinical, experimental, and theoretical aspects.* New York: Harper & Row.

Beck, A. T. (1976). *Cognitive theory and emotional disorders.* New York: International Universities Press.

Becker, K. D., Stuewig, J., Herrera, V. M., & McCloskey, L. A. (2004). A study of firesetting and animal cruelty in children: Family influences and adolescent outcomes. *Journal of the American Academy of Child and Adolescent Psychiatry, 43*, 905–912.

Behnke, S. H., & Warner, E. (2002). Confidentiality in the treatment of adolescents. *Monitor on Psychology, 33*, 44–45.

Beidel, D. C., Morris, T. L., & Turner, M. W. (2004). Social phobia. In T. L. Morris & J. S. March (Eds.), *Anxiety disorders in children and adolescents.* New York: Guilford Press.

Beidel, D. C., Silverman, W. K., & Hammond-Laurence, K. (1996). Overanxious disorder: Subsyndromal state or specific disorder? A comparison of clinic and community samples. *Journal of Clinical Child Psychology, 25*, 25–32.

Beidel, D. C., & Turner, S. M. (1997). At risk for anxiety: I. Psychopathology in the offspring of anxious parents. *Journal of the American Academy of Child and Adolescent Psychiatry, 36,* 918–924.

Beidel, D. C., Turner, S. M., & Morris, T. L. (1995). A new inventory to assess childhood social anxiety and phobia: The Social Phobia and Anxiety Inventory for Children. *Psychological Assessment, 7,* 73–79.

Beidel, D. C., Turner, S. M., & Morris, T. L. (1999). Psychopathology of childhood social phobia. *Journal of the American Academy of Child and Adolescent Psychiatry, 38,* 630–646.

Beirne-Smith, M., Ittenbach, R. F., & Patton, J. R. (1998). *Mental retardation.* Upper Saddle River, NJ: Prentice Hall.

Beitchman, J. H., Wilson, B., Brownlie, E. B., Walters, H., Inglis, A., & Lancee, W. (1996). Long-term consistency in speech/language profiles: II. behavioral, emotional, and social outcomes. *Journal of the American Academy of Child and Adolescent Psychiatry, 35,* 815–825.

Beitchman, J. H., Wilson, B., Johnson, C. J., Atkinson, L., Young, A., Adlaf, E. et al. (2001). Fourteen-year follow-up of speech/language-impaired and control children: Psychiatric outcome. *Journal of the American Academy of Child and Adolescent Psychiatry, 40,* 75–82.

Beitchman, J. H., & Young, A. R. (1997). Learning disorders with a special emphasis on reading disorders: A review of the past 10 years. *Journal of the American Academy of Child and Adolescent Psychiatry, 36,* 1020–1032.

Belar, C. D., Nelson, P. D., & Wasik, B. H. (2003). Rethinking education in psychology and psychology in education. *American Psychologist, 58,* 678–684.

Bell, K. E., & Stein, D. M. (1992). Behavioral treatments for pica: A review of empirical studies. *International Journal of Eating Disorders, 11,* 377–389.

Bell, R. (1985). *Holy anorexia.* Chicago: University of Chicago Press.

Bell, S. K., & Morgan, S. B. (2000). Children's attitudes and behavioral intentions toward a peer presented as obese: Does a medical explanation for the obesity make a difference? *Journal of Pediatric Psychology, 25,* 137–145.

Bellak, L., & Abrams, D. M. (1997). *The T.A.T., C.A.T., and S.A.T. in clinical use* (6th ed.). Needham Heights, MA: Allyn and Bacon.

Bellak, L., & Bellak, S. (1982). *The Children's Apperception Test and Manual.* New York: C.P.S., Inc.

Bell-Dolan, D. J., Last, C. G., & Strauss, C. C. (1990). Symptoms of anxiety disorders in normal children. *Journal of the American Academy of Child and Adolescent Psychiatry, 29,* 759–765.

Bell-Dolan, D. J., Reaven, N. M., & Peterson, L. (1993). Depression and social functioning: A multidimensional study of the linkages. *Journal of Clinical Child Psychology, 22,* 306–315.

Belsky, J. (1993). Etiology of child maltreatment: A developmental-ecological analysis. *Psychological Bulletin, 114,* 413–434.

Belsky, J. (2001). Developmental risks (still) associated with early child care. *Journal of Child Psychology and Psychiatry, 42,* 845–859.

Bender, L. (2003). *Bender Visual-Motor Gestalt Test, Second Edition.* San Antonio, TX: Psychological Corporation.

Bendersky, M., & Lewis, M. (1994). Environmental risk, biological risk, and developmental outcome. *Developmental Psychology, 30,* 484–494.

Benedict, R. (1934a). Anthropology and the abnormal. *Journal of General Psychology, 10,* 59–82.

Benedict, R. (1934b). *Patterns of culture.* Boston: Houghton-Mifflin.

Bengtson, M. L., & Boll, T. J. (2001). Neuropsychological assessment of the child. In C. E. Walker & M. C. Roberts (Eds.), *Handbook of clinical child psychology* (3rd ed.). New York: John Wiley & Sons.

Bennett, D. S. (1994). Depression among children with chronic medical problems: A meta-analysis. *Journal of Pediatric Psychology, 19,* 149–169.

Benoit, D. (2000). Feeding disorders, failure to thrive, and obesity. In C. H. Zeanah, Jr. (Ed.), *Handbook of infant mental health* (2nd ed.). New York: Guilford Press.

Benoit, M. B. (2000). Foster care. In B. J. Sadock and V. A. Sadock (Eds.), *Comprehensive textbook of psychiatry* (Vol. II). Philadelphia: Lippincott Williams & Wilkins.

Berger, M., & Yule, W. (1985). IQ tests and assessment. In A. M. Clarke, A. D. B. Clarke, & J. M. Berg (Eds.), *Mental deficiency: The changing outlook.* New York: The Free Press.

Berninger, V. W., & Amtmann, D. (2003). Preventing written expression disabilities through early and continuing assessment and intervention for handwriting and/or spelling problems: Research into practice. In H. L. Swanson, K. R. Harris, & S. Graham (Eds.), *Handbook of leaning disabilities.* New York: Guilford Press.

Bernstein, D. M. (1996). The discovery of the child: A historical perspective on child and adolescent psychiatry. In M. Lewis (Ed.), *Child and adolescent psychiatry: A comprehensive textbook.* Baltimore: Williams & Wilkins.

Bernstein, G. A., Borchardt, C. M., & Perwien, A. R. (1996). Anxiety disorders in children and adolescents: A review of the past 10 years. *Journal of the American Academy of Child and Adolescent Psychiatry, 35,* 1110–1119.

Bernstein, G. A., Hektner, J. M., Borchardt, C. M., & McMillan, M. H. (2001). Treatment of school refusal: One-year follow-up. *Journal of the American Academy of Child and Adolescent Psychiatry, 40,* 206–213.

Bettelheim, B. (1967a). *The empty fortress.* New York: Free Press.

Bettelheim, B. (1967b, Feb. 12). Where self begins. *New York Times.*

Bettes, B. A., & Walker, E. (1987). Positive and negative symptoms in psychotic and other psychiatrically disturbed children. *Journal of Child Psychology and Psychiatry, 28,* 555–568.

Beyer, J. E., & Knott, C. (1998). Construct validity estimation for the African-American and Hispanic Oucher Scale. *Journal of Pediatric Nursing, 13,* 20–31.

Biederman, J., Faraone, S., Mick, E., Moore, P., & Lelon, E. (1996). Child Behavior Checklist findings further support comorbidity between ADHD and major depression in a referred sample. *Journal of the American Academy of Child and Adolescent Psychiatry, 35,* 734–742.

Biederman, J., Rosenbaum, J. F., Bolduc-Murphy, E. A., Faraone, S. V., Chaloff, J., Hirshfeld, D. R., & Kagan, J. (1993). A 3-year follow-up of children with and without behavioral inhibition. *Journal of the American Academy of Child and Adolescent Psychiatry, 32,* 814–821.

Biederman, J., & Spencer, T. J. (2000). Genetics of childhood disorder: XIX. ADHD, Part 3: Is ADHD a noradrenergic disorder? *Journal of the American Academy of Child and Adolescent Psychiatry, 39,* 1330–1333.

Bierman, K. L. (2004). *Peer rejection: Developmental processes and intervention strategies.* New York: Guilford Press.

Bierman, K. L., & Schwartz, L. A. (1986). Clinical child interviews: Approaches and developmental considerations. *Journal of Child and Adolescent Psychotherapy, 3,* 267–278.

Bierman, K. L., & Welsh, J. A. (1997). Social relationship deficits. In E. J. Mash & L. G. Terdal (Eds.), *Assessment of childhood disorders* (3rd edition). New York: Guilford Press.

Bifulco, A., Harris, T., & Brown, G. (1992). Mourning or early inadequate care? Reexamining the relationship of maternal loss in childhood with adult depression and anxiety. *Development and Psychopathology, 4,* 433–449.

Bijou, S. W., Peterson, R. F., Harris, F. R., Allen, K. E., & Johnston, M. S. (1969). Methodology for experimental studies of young children in natural settings. *The Psychological Record, 19,* 177–210.

Binggeli, N. J., Hart, S. N., & Brassard, M. R. (2001). *Psychological maltreatment of children.* Thousand Oaks, CA: Sage Publications.

Birch, S. H., & Ladd, G. W. (1998). Children's interpersonal behavior and the teacher-child relationship. *Developmental Psychology, 34,* 934–946.

Bird, H. R. (1996). Epidemiology of childhood disorders in a cross-cultural context. *Journal of Child Psychology and Psychiatry, 37,* 35–50.

Birmaher, B., Ryan, N. D., Williamson, D. E., Brent, D. A., & Kaufman, J. (1996). Childhood and adolescent depression: A review of the past 10 years. Part II. *Journal of the American Academy of Child and Adolescent Psychiatry, 35,* 1575–1583.

Birmaher, B., Ryan, N. D., Williamson, D. E., Brent, D. A., Kaufman, J., Dahl, R. E., Perel, J., & Nelson, B. (1996). Childhood and adolescent depression: A review of the past 10 years. Part I. *Journal of the American Academy of Child and Adolescent Psychiatry, 35,* 1427–1439.

Bishop, D. V. M. (1992). The underlying nature of specific language impairment. *Journal of Child Psychology and Psychiatry, 33,* 3–66.

Bishop, D. V. M. (2002). Speech and language difficulties. In M. Rutter & E. Taylor (Eds.), *Child and adolescent psychiatry,* Oxford, UK: Blackwell Publishing.

Blacher, J. (1984). Sequential stages of parental adjustment to the birth of a child with handicaps: Fact or artifact? *Mental Retardation, 22,* 55–68.

Blacher, J. (2001). Transition to adulthood: Mental retardation, families, and culture. *American Journal on Mental Retardation, 106,* 173–188.

Black, B., & Uhde, T. W. (1995). Psychiatric characteristics of children with selective mutism: A pilot study. *Journal of the American Academy of Child and Adolescent Psychiatry, 34,* 847–856.

Blader, J. C., Koplewicz, H. C., Abikoff, H., & Foley, C. (1997). Sleep problems of elementary school children: A community survey. *Archives of Pediatrics and Adolescent Medicine, 151,* 473–480.

Blagg, N., & Yule, W. (1994). School refusal. In T. H. Ollendick, N. J. King, & W. Yule (Eds.), *International handbook of phobic and anxiety disorders in children and adolescents.* New York: Plenum Press.

Blair, C., & Wahlsten, D. (2002). Why early intervention works. A reply to Baumeister and Bacharach. *Intelligence, 30,* 129–140.

Bleil, M. E., Ramesh, S., Miller, B. D., & Wood, B. L. (2000). The influence of parent-child relatedness on depressive symptoms in children with asthma: Tests of moderator and mediator models. *Journal of Pediatric Psychology, 25,* 481–491.

Blount, R. L., Piira, T., & Cohen, L. L. (2003). Management of pediatric pain and distress due to medical procedures. In M. C. Roberts (Eds.), *Handbook of pediatric psychology* (3rd ed.). New York: Guilford Press.

Bodfish, J. W., Symons, F. J., Parker, D. E., & Lewis, M. H. (2000). Varieties of repetitive behavior in autism: Comparisons to mental retardation. *Journal of Autism and Developmental Disorders, 30,* 237–243.

Bolger, K. E., & Patterson, C. J. (2001). Developmental pathways from child maltreatment to peer rejection. *Child Development, 72,* 549–568.

Bolton, P. F. et al. (1997). Obstetric complications in autism: Consequences or causes of the condition? *Journal of the American Academy of Child and Adolescent Psychiatry, 36,* 272–281.

Bonner, B. L., Kaufman, K. L., Harbeck, C., & Brassard, M. R. (1992). Child maltreatment. In C. E. Walker & M. C. Roberts (Eds.), *Handbook of clinical child psychology.* New York: Wiley.

Borchers, D., & Committee on Early Childhood, Adoption, and Dependent Care. (2003). Families and adoption: The pediatrician's role in supporting communication. *Pediatrics, 112,* 1437–1441.

Bordeaux, J. D., Loveland, K. A., Lachar, D., Stehbens, J., Bell, T. S., Nichols, S. et al. (2003). Hemophilia growth and development study: Caregiver report of youth and family adjustment to HIV disease and immunologic compromise. *Journal of Pediatric Psychology, 28,* 175–183.

Borduin, C. M. (1994). Innovative models of treatment and service delivery in the juvenile justice system. *Journal of Clinical Child Psychology, 23 (Suppl.),* 19–25.

Borge, A. I. H., Rutter, M., Cote, S., & Tremblay, R. E. (2004). Early childcare and physical aggression: Differentiating social selection and social causation. *Journal of Child Psychology and Psychiatry, 45,* 367–376.

Botteron, K., & Geller, B. (1999). Disorders, symptoms, and their pharmacotherapy. In J. S. Werry & M. G. Aman (Eds.), *Practitioner's guide to psychoactive drugs for children and adolescents* (2nd ed.). New York: Plenum Medical Book Company.

Botting, N., Faragher, B., Simkin, Z., Knox, E., & Conti-Ramsden, G. (2001). Predicting pathways of specific language impairment: What differentiates good and poor outcome? *Journal of Child Psychology and Psychiatry, 42,* 1013–1020.

Boucher, J., Lewis, V., & Collis, G. (1998). Familiar face and voice matching and recognition in children with autism. *Journal of Child Psychology and Psychiatry, 39,* 171–182.

Bower, G. (2004, Sept. 11). A very spatial brain defect. *Science News, 166,* 165–166.

Bowlby, J. (1960). Grief and mourning in infancy and early childhood. *Psychoanalytic Study of the Child, 15,* 9–52.

Bowlby, J. (1969). *Attachment and loss* (Vol. 1). New York: Basic Books.

Braddock, D., Rizzolo, M. C., & Hemp, R. (2004). Most employment services growth in developmental disabilities during 1988–2002 was in segregated settings. *Mental Retardation, 42,* 317–320.

Braden, J. P., & Hightower, A. D. (1998). Prevention. In R. J. Morris & T. R. Kratochwill (Eds.), *The practice of child therapy* (3rd ed.). Boston: Allyn and Bacon.

Bradley, R. H., Whiteside, L., Mundfrom, D. J., Casey, P. H., Kelleher, K. J., & Pope, S. K. (1994). Contributions of early interventions and early caregiving experiences to resilience in low-birthweight, premature children living in poverty. *Journal of Clinical Child Psychology, 23,* 425–434.

Bradley, R. H., & Whiteside-Mansell, L. (1997). Children in poverty. In R. T. Ammerman & M. Hersen (Eds.), *Handbook of prevention and treatment with children and adolescents.* New York: John Wiley.

Bradley, S. J., & Hood, J. (1993). Psychiatrically referred adolescents with panic attacks: Presenting symptoms, stressors, and comorbidity. *Journal of the American Academy of Child and Adolescent Psychiatry, 32,* 826–829.

Brady, E., & Kendall, P. C. (1992). Comorbidity of anxiety and depression in children and adolescents. *Psychological Bulletin, 111,* 244–255.

Brame, B., Nagin, D. S., & Tremblay, R. E. (2001). Developmental trajectories of physical aggression from school entry to late adolescence. *Journal of Child Psychology and Psychiatry, 42,* 503–512.

Brassard, M. R., Hart, S. N., & Hardy, D. B. (2000). Psychological and emotional abuse of children. In R. T. Ammerman & M. Hersen, (Eds.), *Case studies in family violence* (2nd ed.). New York: Kluwer Academic/Plenum Publishers.

Braungart-Rieker, J., Rende, R. D., Plomin, R., DeFries, J. C., & Fulker, D. W. (1995). Genetic mediation of longitudinal associations between family environment and childhood behavior problems. *Development and Psychopathology, 7,* 233–245.

Braver, S. L., Ellman, I. M., & Fabricius, W. V. (2003). Relocation of children after divorce and children's best interests: New evidence and legal considerations. *Journal of Family Psychology, 17,* 206–219.

Bray, N. W., Fletcher, K. L., & Turner, L. A. (1997). Cognitive competencies and strategy use in individuals with mental retardation. In W. E. MacLean (Ed.), *Ellis' handbook of mental deficiency, psychological theory and research.* Mahwah, NJ: Lawrence Erlbaum.

Bregman, J. D. (1991). Current developments in the understanding of mental retardation: Part II. Psychopathology. *Journal of the American Academy of Child and Adolescent Psychiatry, 30,* 861–872.

Bregman, J. D., & Gerdtz, J. (1997). Behavioral interventions. In D. J. Cohen & F. R. Volkmar (Eds.), *Handbook of autism and pervasive developmental disorders.* New York: John Wiley.

Bregman, J. D., & Hodapp, R. M. (1991). Current developments in the understanding of mental retardation: Part I. Biological and phenomenological perspectives. *Journal of the American Academy of Child and Adolescent Psychiatry, 30,* 707–719.

Breier, J. I., Simos, P. G., Fletcher, J. M., Castillo, E. M., Zhang, W., & Papanicolaou, A. C. (2003). Abnormal activation of temporoparietal language areas during phonetic analysis in children with dyslexia. *Neuropsychology, 17,* 610–621.

Brendgen, M., Vitaro, F., Tremblay, R. E., & Lavoie, F. (2001). Reactive and proactive aggression: Predictions to physical violence in different contexts and moderating effects of parental monitoring and caregiving behavior. *Journal of Abnormal Child Psychology, 29,* 293–304.

Brennan, P. A., Le Brocque, R., & Hammen, C. (2003). Maternal depression, parent-child relationships, and resilient outcomes in adolescence. *Journal of the American Academy of Child and Adolescent Psychiatry, 42,* 1469–1477.

Brennan, P. A., & Walker, E. F. (2001). Vulnerability to schizophrenia: Risk factors in childhood and adolescence. In R. E. Ingram & J. M. Price (Eds.), *Vulnerability to psychopathology: Risk across the lifespan.* New York: The Guilford Press.

Brent, D., Holder, D., Kolko, D., Birmaher, B., Baugher, M., Roth, C., Iyenagar, S., Johnson, B. (1997). A clinical psychotherapy trial for adolescent depression comparing cognitive, family, and supportive therapy. *Archives of General Psychiatry, 54,* 877–885.

Brestan, E. V., & Eyberg, S. M. (1998). Effective psychosocial treatments of conduct-disordered children and adolescents: 29 years, 82 studies, and 5,272 kids. *Journal of Clinical Child Psychology, 27,* 180–189.

Breton, J.-J., Bergeron, L., Valla, J.-P., Berthiaume, C., & Gaudet, N. (1999). Quebec child mental health survey: Prevalence of DSM-III-R mental health disorders. *Journal of Child Psychology and Psychiatry, 40,* 375–384.

Briggs, K., Hubbs-Tait, L., Culp, R. E., & Morse, A. S. (1994). Sexual abuse label: Adults' expectations for children. *The American Journal of Family Therapy, 22,* 304–314.

Briggs-Gowan, M. J., Carter, A. S., Skuban, E. M., & Horwitz, S. M. (2001). Prevalence of social-emotional behavioral problems in a community sample of 1- and 2-year-old children. *Journal of the American Academy of Child and Adolescent Psychiatry, 40,* 811–819.

Brinkmeyer, M. Y., & Eyberg, S. M. (2003). Parent-child interaction therapy for oppositional children. In A. E. Kazdin & J. R. Weisz (Eds.), *Evidence-based psychotherapies for children and adolescents.* New York: Guilford Press.

Brodeur, D. A., & Pond, M. (2001). The development of selective attention in children with attention deficit hyperactivity disorder. *Journal of Abnormal Child Psychology, 29,* 229–239.

Brody, G. H., Ge, X., Conger, R., Gibbons, F. X., Murry, V. M., Gerrard, M., & Simons, R. L. (2001). The influence of neighborhood disadvantage, collective socialization, and parenting on African-American children's affiliation with deviant peers. *Child Development, 72,* 1231–1246.

Brody, G. H., Murry, V. M., Gerrard, M., Gibbons, F. X., Molgaard, V., McNair, L. et al. (2004). The Strong African American Families Program: Translating research into prevention programming. *Child Development, 75,* 900–917.

Broman, S., Nichols, P. L., Shaughnessy, P., & Kennedy, W. (1987). *Retardation in young children: A developmental study of cognitive deficit.* Hillsdale, NJ: Erlbaum.

Bronfenbrenner, U. (1989). Ecological systems theory. In R. Vasta (Ed.), *Annals of child development* (Vol. 6: *Six theories of child development: Revised formulations and current issues*). London: JAI Press.

Brooks-Gunn, J. (1993). Why do adolescents have difficulty adhering to health regimes? In N. A. Krasnegor, L. Epstein, S. B. Johnson,

& S. Yaffe (Eds.), *Developmental aspects of health compliance behavior*. Hillsdale, NJ: Lawrence Erlbaum Associates.

Brooks-Gunn, J., Auth, J. J., Peterson, A. C., & Compas, B. E. (2001). Physiological processes and the development of childhood and adolescent depression. In I. M. Goodyer (Ed.), *The depressed child and adolescent* (2nd ed.). Cambridge, UK: Cambridge University Press.

Brown, J. V., Bakeman, R., Coles, C. D., Platzman, K. A., & Lynch, M. E. (2004). Prenatal cocaine exposure: A comparison of 2-year-old children in parental and nonparental care. *Child Development, 75,* 1282–1295.

Brown, R. T. (2002). Toward a social ecology of pediatric psychology. *Journal of Pediatric Psychology, 27,* 191–201.

Brown, R. T., & Macias, M. (2001). Chronically ill children and adolescents. In J. N. Hughes, A. M. La Greca, & J. C. Conoley (Eds.), *Handbook of psychological services for children and adolescents*. New York: Oxford University Press.

Brown, R. T., Madan-Swain, A., Walco, G. A., Cherrick, I., Ievers, C. E., Conte, P. M., Vega, R., Bell, B., & Lauer, S. J. (1998). Cognitive and academic late effects among children previously treated for acute lymphocytic leukemia receiving chemotherapy as CNS prophylaxis. *Journal of Pediatric Psychology, 23,* 333–340.

Bruch, H. (1973). *Eating disorders: Obesity, anorexia nervosa, and the person within*. New York: Basic Books.

Bruch, H. (1979). *The golden cage: The enigma of anorexia nervosa*. New York: Vintage Books.

Brumberg, J. J. (1986). "Fasting girls": Reflections on writing the history of anorexia nervosa. In A. B. Smuts & J. W. Hagen (Eds.), History and research in child development. *Monographs of the Society for Research in Child Development, 50*(4–5, Serial No. 211).

Bryan, K. (1977). Speech and language development. In M. J. Krajicek & A. I. Tearney (Eds.), *Detection of developmental problems in children*. Baltimore: University Park Press.

Bryan, T. (1997). Assessing the personal and social status of students with learning disabilities. *Learning Disabilities Research & Practice, 12,* 63–76.

Bryant-Waugh, R., & Lask, B. (1995). Eating disorders in children. *Journal of Child Psychology and Psychiatry, 36,* 191–202.

Buchanan, R. W., & Carpenter, W. T. (2000). Schizophrenia: introduction and overview. In B. J. Sadock & V. A. Sadock (Eds.), *Comprehensive textbook of psychiatry* (Vol. II). Philadelphia: Lippincott Williams & Wilkins.

Buck, J. N. (1992). *House-Tree-Person projective drawing technique (H-T-P): Manual and interpretive guide* (Revised by W. L. Warren). Los Angeles: Western Psychological Services.

Buckner, J. C., Mezzacappa, E., & Beardslee, W. R. (2003). Characteristics of resilient youth living in poverty: The role of self-regulatory processes. *Development and Psychopathology, 15,* 139–162.

Budd, K. S., & Chugh, C. S. (1998). Common feeding problems in young children. In T. H. Ollendick & R. J. Prinz (Eds.), *Advances in clinical child psychology* (Vol. 20). New York: Plenum Press.

Buhs, E. S., & Ladd, G. W. (2001). Peer rejection as an antecedent of young children's school adjustment: An examination of mediating processes. *Developmental Psychology, 37,* 550–560.

Bukowski, W. M., & Adams, R. (2005). Peer relationships and psychopathology: Markers, moderators, mediators, mechanisms, and meanings. *Journal of Clinical Child and Adolescent Psychology, 34,* 3–10.

Bulik, C. M. (2004). Genetic and biological risk factors. In J. K. Thompson (Ed.), *Handbook of eating disorders and obesity*. Hoboken, NJ: John Wiley.

Bulik, C. M., Wade, T. D., & Kendler, K. S. (2001). Characteristics of monozygotic twins discordant for bulimia nervosa. *International Journal of Eating Disorders, 29,* 1–10.

Burack, J. A. (1990). Differentiating mental retardation: The two-group approach and beyond. In R. M. Hodapp, J. A. Burack, & E. Zigler (Eds.), *Issues in the developmental approach to mental retardation*. New York: Cambridge University Press.

Burack, J. A., Root, R., & Zigler, E. (1997). Inclusive education for students with autism: Reviewing ideological, empirical, and community considerations. In D. J. Cohen and F. R. Volkmar (Eds.), *Handbook of autism and pervasive developmental disorders*. New York: John Wiley.

Burchard, J., & Clark, R. (1990). The role of individualized care in a service delivery system for children and adolescents with severely maladjusted behavior. *Journal of Mental Health Administration, 17,* 48–60.

Burgess, K. B., Marshall, P. J., Robin, K. H., & Fox, N. A. (2003). Infant attachment and temperament as predictors of subsequent externalizing problems and cardiac physiology. *Journal of Child Psychology and Psychiatry, 44,* 819–831.

Burhans, K. K., & Dweck, C. S. (1995). Helplessness in early childhood. *Child Development, 66,* 1719–1738.

Burns, R. C., & Kaufman, S. H. (1970). *Kinetic Family Drawing (K-F-D) research and applications*. New York: Bruner/Mazel.

Burt, S. A., Krueger, R. F., McGue, M., & Iacono, W. G. (2001). Sources of covariation among attention-deficit/hyperactivity disorder, oppositional defiant disorder, and conduct disorder: The importance of shared environment. *Journal of Abnormal Psychology, 110,* 516–525.

Bushman, B. J., & Anderson, C. A. (2001). Media violence and the American public: Scientific facts versus media misinformation. *American Psychologist, 56,* 477–489.

Butzlaff, R. L., & Hooley, J. M. (1998). Expressed emotion and psychiatric relapse. *Archives of general psychiatry, 55,* 547–552.

Cabrera, N. J., Tamis-LeMonda, C. S., Bradley, R. H., Hofferth, S., & Lamb, M. E. (2000). Fatherhood in the twenty-first century. *Child Development, 71,* 127–136.

Cadesky, E. B., Mota, V. L., & Schachar, R. J. (2000). Beyond words: How do children with ADHD and/or conduct problems process nonverbal information about affect? *Journal of the American Academy of Child and Adolescent Psychiatry, 39,* 1160–1167.

Calderoni, D., Wudarsky, M., Bhangoo, R., Dell, M. L., Nicolson, R., Hamburger, S. D. et al. (2001). Differentiating childhood-onset schizophrenia from psychotic mood disorders. *Journal of the American Academy of Child and Adolescent Psychiatry, 40,* 1190–1196.

Calkins, S. D., & Fox, N. A. (2002). Self-regulatory processes in early personality development: A multilevel approach to the study of childhood social withdrawal and aggression. *Development and Psychopathology, 14,* 477–498.

Cambor, R. L., & Millman, R. B. (1996). Alcohol and drug abuse in adolescents. In M. Lewis (Ed.), *Child and adolescent psychiatry: A comprehensive textbook*. Baltimore: Williams & Wilkins.

Campbell, D. T., & Stanley, J. C. (1963). *Experimental and quasi-experimental designs for research*. Chicago: Rand McNally.

Campbell, F. A., Ramey, C. T., Pungello, E. P., Miller-Johnson, S., & Burchinal, M. (2001). The development of cognitive and academic abilities: Growth curves from an early childhood educational experiment. *Developmental Psychology, 37*, 231–242.

Campbell, K., Waters, E., O'Meara, S., Kelly, S., & Summerbell, C. (2004). Interventions for preventing obesity in children (Cochrane Review). *The Cochrane Library, Issue 3*. Chichester, UK: John Wiley.

Campbell, M., Armenteros, J. L., Maone, R. P., Adams, P. B., Eisenberg, Z. W., & Overall, J. E. (1997). Neuroleptic-related dyskinesias in autistic children: A prospective longitudinal study. *Journal of the American Academy of Child and Adolescent Psychiatry, 36*, 835–843.

Campbell, M., Rapoport, J. L., & Simpson, G. M. (1999). Antipsychotics in children and adolescents. *Journal of the American Academy of Child and Adolescent Psychiatry, 38*, 537–545.

Campbell, S. B. (1990). The socialization and social development of hyperactive children. In M. Lewis & S. M. Miller (Eds.), *Handbook of developmental psychopathology*. NY: Plenum.

Campbell, S. B. (1995). Behavior problems in preschool children: A review of recent research. *Journal of Child Psychology and Psychiatry, 36*, 113–149.

Campbell, S. B. (1997). Behavior problems in preschool children. Developmental and family issues. In T. H. Ollendick & R. J. Prinz (Eds.), *Advances in clinical child psychology* (Vol. 19). New York: Plenum Press.

Campbell, S. B. (2000). Attention-deficit/hyperactivity disorder. In A. J. Sameroff, M. Lewis, & S. M. Miller (Eds.), *Handbook of developmental psychopathology*. New York: Kluwer Academic/Plenum.

Candy-Gibbs, S. E., Sharp, K. C., & Petrun, C. J. (1985). The effects of age, object, and cultural/religious background on children's concepts of death. *Omega Journal of Death and Dying, 15*, 329–346.

Canfield, R. L., Henderson, C. R., Cory-Slechta, D. A., Cox, C., Jusko, T. A., & Lanphear, B. P. (2003). Intellectual impairment in children with blood lead concentrations below 10 μg per deciliter. *New England Journal of Medicine, 348*, 1517–1526.

Canino, G., Shrout, P. E., Rugio-Stipic, M., Bird, H. R., Bravo, M., Ramirez, R. et al. (2004). The DSM-IV rates of child and adolescent disorders in Puerto Rico. *Archives of General Psychiatry, 61*, 85–93.

Cannon, T. D., & Rosso, I. M. (2002). Levels of analysis in etiological research on schizophrenia. *Development and Psychopathology, 14*, 653–666.

Cannon, T. D., Zorilla, L. E., Shtasel, D., Gur, R. E., Gur, R. C., Marco, E. J., Moberg, P., & Price, A. (1994). Neuropsychological functioning in siblings discordant for schizophrenia and healthy volunteers. *Archives of General Psychiatry, 51*, 651–661.

Cantor, S., & Kestenbaum, C. (1986). Psychotherapy with schizophrenic children. *Journal of the American Academy of Child Psychiatry, 25*, 623–630.

Cantwell, D. P. (1980). The diagnostic process and diagnostic classification in child psychiatry: DSM-III. *Journal of the American Academy of Child Psychiatry, 19*, 345–355.

Cantwell, D. P. (1996). Classification of child and adolescent psychopathology. *Journal of Child Psychology and Psychiatry, 37*, 3–12.

Capaldi, D., DeGarmo, D., Patterson, G. R., & Forgatch, M. (2002). Contextual risk across the early life span and association with antisocial behavior. In J. B. Reid, G. R. Patterson, & J. Snyder (Eds.), *Antisocial behavior in children and adolescents: A developmental analysis and model for intervention*. Washington, DC: American Psychological Association.

Capizzano, J., Tout, K., & Adams, G. (2000). Child care patterns of school-age children with employed mothers. Washington, DC: Urban Institute.

Caplan, G. (1964). *The principles of preventive psychiatry*. New York: Basic Books.

Caplan, R. (1994). Thought disorder in childhood. *Journal of the American Academy of Child and Adolescent Psychiatry, 33*, 605–615.

Caplan, R., Guthrie, D., Tang, B., Komo, S., & Asarnow, R. F. (2000). Thought disorder in childhood schizophrenia: Replication and update of concept. *Journal of the American Academy of Child and Adolescent Psychiatry, 39*, 771–778.

Capone, G. T. (2001). Down syndrome: Advances in molecular biology and the neurosciences. *Developmental and behavioral pediatrics, 22*, 40–59.

Carlson, G. A., & Cantwell, D. P. (1980). Unmasking masked depression in children and adolescents. *American Journal of Psychiatry, 137*, 445–449.

Carlson, G. A., Jensen, P. S., Findling, R. L., Meyer, R. E., Calabrese, J., DelBello, M. P. et al. (2003). Methodological issues and controversies in clinical trials with child and adolescent patients with bipolar disorder: Report of a consensus conference. *Journal of Child and Adolescent Psychopharmacology, 13*, 1–15.

Carlson, G. A., & Kelly, K. (1998). Manic symptoms in psychiatrically hospitalized children—what do they mean? *Journal of Affective Disorders, 51*, 123–135.

Carpenter, P. J. (1992). Perceived control as a predictor of distress in children undergoing invasive medical procedures. *Journal of Pediatric Psychology, 17*, 757–773.

Carroll, J. M., & Snowling, M. J. (2004). Language and phonological skills in children at high risk of reading difficulties. *Journal of Child Psychology and Psychiatry, 45*, 631–640.

Carson, C., & Rutter, M. (1991). Comorbidity in child psychopathology: Concepts, issues and research strategies. *Journal of Child Psychology and Psychiatry, 32*, 1063–1080.

Carter, A. S., Volkmar, F. R., Sparrow, S. S., Wang, J-J., Lord, C., Dawson, G. et al. (1998). The Vineland Adaptive Behavior Scales: Supplementary norms for individuals with autism. *Journal of Autism and Developmental Disorders, 28*, 287–302.

Casanova, M. F., Buxhoeveden, D. P., Switala, A. E., & Roy, E. (2002). Minicolumnar pathology in autism. *Neurology, 58*, 428–432.

Casey, B. J., Castellanos, F. X., Giedd, J. N., Marsh, W. L., Hamburger, S. D., Schubert, A. B., Vauss, Y. C., Vaituzis, A. C., Dickstein, D. P., Sarfatti, S. E., & Rapoport, J. L. (1997). Implication of right frontostriatal circuitry in response inhibition and Attention-deficit/Hyperactivity Disorder. *Journal of the American Academy of Child and Adolescent Psychiatry, 36,* 374–383.

Caspi, A., Elder, G. H. Jr., & Bem, D. J. (1987). Moving against the world: Life-course patterns of explosive children. *Developmental Psychology, 23,* 308–313.

Caspi, A., & Moffitt, T. E. (1995). The continuity of maladaptive behavior: From description to understanding in the study of antisocial behavior. In D. Cicchetti & D. J. Cohen (Eds.), *Developmental psychopathology.* (Vol 2: *Risk, disorder, and adaptation*). New York: John Wiley & Sons.

Catalan, J. (2000). Sexuality, reproductive cycle and suicidal behaviour. In K. Hawton & K. van Heeringen (Eds.), *The international handbook of suicide and attempted suicide.* Chichester, UK: John Wiley & Sons, LTD.

Caughty, M. O., O'Campo, P. J., Randolph, S. M., & Nickerson, K. (2002). The influence of racial socialization practices on the cognitive and behavioral competence of African American preschoolers. *Child Development, 73,* 1611–1625.

Cavell, T. A., Ennett, S. T., & Meehan, B. T. (2001). Preventing alcohol and substance abuse. In J. N. Hughes, A. M. La Greca, & J. C. Conoley (Eds.), *Handbook of psychological services for children and adolescents.* New York: Oxford University Press.

Ceballo, R., & McLoyd, V. (2002). Social support and parenting in poor, dangerous neighborhoods. *Child Development, 73,* 1310–1321.

Ceballo, R., Ramirez, C., Heran, K. D., & Maltese, K. L. (2003). Community violence and children's psychological well-being: Does parental monitoring matter? *Journal of Child and Adolescent Psychology, 32,* 586–592.

Cederblad, M., Höök, B., Irhammar, K., & Mercke, A-M. (1999). Mental health in international adoptees as teenagers and young adults: An epidemiological study. *Journal of Child Psychology and Psychiatry, 40,* 1239–1248.

Celani, G., Battacchi, M. W., & Arcidiacono, L. (1999). The understanding of the emotional meaning of facial expressions in people with autism. *Journal of Autism and Developmental Disorders, 29,* 57–66.

Center for Adoption Research and Policy. Homepage: *Frequently asked questions.* Retrieved September, 2004 from www.centerforadoptionresearch.org.

Centers for Disease Control and Prevention (2001). *Safe USA: Preventing Suicide.* Retrieved November 10, 2001, from http://www.cdc.gov.

Chamberlain, P., & Reid, J. B. (1987). Parent observation and report of child symptoms. *Behavioral Assessment, 9,* 97–109.

Chamberlain, P., & Reid, J. B. (1998). Comparison of two community alternatives to incarceration for chronic juvenile offenders. *Journal of Consulting and Clinical Psychology, 66,* 624–633.

Chamberlain, P., & Smith, D. K. (2003). Antisocial behavior in children and adolescents: The Oregon multidimensional treatment foster care model. In A. E. Kazdin & J. R. Weisz (Eds.), *Evidence-based psychotherapies for children and adolescents.* New York: Guilford Press.

Chambers, R. A., Taylor, J. R., & Potenza, M. N. (2003). Developmental neurocircuitry of motivation in adolescence: A critical period of addiction vulnerability. *American Journal of Psychiatry, 160,* 1041–1052.

Chambless, D. L. (1996). In defense of dissemination of empirically supported psychological interventions. *Clinical Psychology: Science and Practice, 3,* 230–235.

Chambless, D. L., & Hollon, S. D. (1998). Defining empirically supported therapies. *Journal of Consulting and Clinical Psychology, 66,* 7–18.

Chambless, D. L., Sanderson, W. C., Shoham, V., Bennett Johnson, S., Pope, K. S., Crits-Cristoph, P., Baker, M., Johnson, B., Woody, S. R., Sue, S., Beutler, L., Williams, D. A., & McCurry, S. (1996). An update on empirically validated therapies. *The Clinical Psychologist, 49(2),* 5–18.

Chandler, L. A. (2003). The projective hypothesis and the development of projective techniques for children. In C. R. Reynolds & R. W. Kamphaus (Eds.), *Handbook of psychological & educational assessment of children: Personality, behavior, and context* (2nd ed.). New York: Guilford Press.

Chandola, C. A., Robling, M. R., Peters, T. J., Melville-Thomas, G., & McGuffin, P. (1992). Pre- and perinatal factors and the risk of subsequent referral for hyperactivity. *Journal of Child Psychology and Psychiatry, 33,* 1077–1090.

Chang, S. M., Walker, S. P., Grantham-McGregor, S., & Powell, C. A. (2002). Early childhood stunting and later behaviour and school achievement. *Journal of Child Psychology and Psychiatry, 43,* 775–783.

Chapman, R. S. (2000). Children's language learning: An interactionist perspective. *Journal of Child Psychology and Psychiatry, 4,* 33–54.

Charmon, T., & Baird, G. (2002). Practitioner review: Diagnosis of autism spectrum disorder in 2- and 3-year-old children. *Journal of Child Psychology and Psychiatry, 43,* 289–305.

Charney, D. S., Barlow, D. H., Botterman, K., Cohen, J. D., Goldman, D., Gur, R. et al. (2002). Neuroscience research agenda to guide development of a pathophysiologically based classification system. In D. J. Kupfer, M. B. First, & D. A. Regier (Eds.), *A research agenda for DSM-V.* Washington, DC: American Psychiatric Association.

Chassin, L., Curran, P. J., Hussong, A. M., & Colder, C. R. (1996). The relation of parental alcoholism to adolescent substance use: A longitudinal follow-up study. *Journal of Abnormal Psychology, 105,* 70–80.

Chassin, L., Presson, C. C., Todd, M., Rose, J., & Sherman, S. J. (1998). Maternal socialization of adolescent smoking: The intergenerational transmission of parenting and smoking. *Developmental Psychology, 34,* 1189–1201.

Chassin, L., Ritter, J., Trim, R. S., & King, K. M. (2003). Adolescent substance use disorders. In E. J. Mash & R. A. Barkley (Eds.), *Child psychopathology* (2nd ed.). New York: Guilford Press.

Chatoor, I., Conley, C., & Dickson, L. (1988). Food refusal after an incident of choking: A posttraumatic eating disorder. *Journal of the American Academy of Child and Adolescent Psychiatry, 27,* 105–110.

Chess, S., & Thomas, A. (1972). Differences in outcome with early intervention in children with behavior disorders. In M. Roff, L. Robins, & M. Pollack (Eds.), *Life history research in psychopathology,* Vol. 2. Minneapolis: University of Minnesota Press.

Chess, S., & Thomas, A. (1977). Temperamental individuality from childhood to adolescence. *Journal of American Academy of Child Psychiatry, 16,* 218–226.

Children on the Brink. 2004. *A joint report of new orphan estimates and a framework for action.* Retrieved September 30, 2004 from www.UNAIDS.org.

Childress, A. C., Brewerton, T. D., Hodges, E. L., & Jarrell, M. P. (1993). The Kids' Eating Disorders Survey (KEDS): A study of middle school students. *Journal of the American Academy of Child and Adolescent Psychiatry, 32,* 843–850.

Chipungu, S. S., & Bent-Goodley, T. B. (2004). Meeting the challenges of contemporary foster care. *The Future of Children, 14,* 75–93.

Chorpita, B. F. (2001). Control and the development of negative emotions. In M. W. Vasey & M. R. Dadds (Eds.), *The developmental psychopathology of anxiety.* New York: Oxford University Press.

Chorpita, B. F. (2002). The tripartite model and dimensions of anxiety and depression: An examination of structure in a large school sample. *Journal of Abnormal Child Psychology, 30,* 177–190.

Chorpita, B. F. (2003). The frontier of evidence-based practice. In A. E. Kazdin & J. R. Weisz (Eds.), *Evidence-based psychotherapies for children and adolescents.* New York: Guilford Press.

Chorpita, B. F., Albano, A. M., & Barlow, D. H. (1996). Cognitive processing in children: Relation to anxiety and family influences. *Journal of Clinical Child Psychology, 25,* 170–176.

Chorpita, B. F., & Barlow, D. H. (1998). The development of anxiety: The role of control in the early environment. *Psychological Bulletin, 124,* 3–21.

Christakis, D. A., Zimmerman, F. J., DiGiuseppe, D. L., & McCarty, C. A. (2004). Early television exposure and subsequent attentional problems in children. *Pediatrics, 113,* 708–713.

Christophersen, E. R., & Mortweet, S. L. (2001). *Treatments that work with children: Empirically supported strategies for managing childhood problems.* Washington, DC: American Psychological Association.

Chronis, A. M., Pelham, W. E., Gnagy, E. M., Roberts, J. E., & Aronoff, H. R. (2003). The impact of late-afternoon stimulant dosing for children with ADHD on parent and parent-child domains. *Journal of Clinical Child and Adolescent Psychology, 32,* 118–126.

Cicchetti, D. (1984). The emergence of developmental psychopathology. *Child Development, 55,* 1–7.

Cicchetti, D. (1989). Developmental psychology: Some thoughts on its evolution. *Development and Psychopathology, 1,* 1–3.

Cicchetti, D., & Cohen, D. J. (1995). Perspectives on developmental psychopathology. In D. Cichetti & D. J. Cohen (Eds.), *Developmental psychopathology.* New York: John Wiley.

Cicchetti, D., & Dawson, G. (2002). Editorial: Multiple levels of analysis. *Development and Psychopathology, 14,* 417–420.

Cicchetti, D., & Hinshaw, S. P. (2002). Editorial: Prevention and intervention science: Contributions to developmental theory. *Development and Psychopathology, 14,* 667–671.

Cicchetti, D., & Luthar, S. S. (1999). Developmental approaches to substance use and abuse. *Development and Psychopathology, 11,* 655–656.

Cicchetti, D., & Lynch, M. (1995). Failures in the expectable environment and their impact on individual development: The case of child maltreatment. In D. Cicchetti & D. J. Cohen (Eds.), *Developmental psychopathology: Risk, disorder, and adaptation* (Vol. 2). New York: John Wiley & Sons.

Cicchetti, D., & Manly, J. T. (2001). Operationalizing child maltreatment: Developmental processes and outcomes. *Development and Psychopathology, 13,* 755–757.

Cicchetti, D., & Olsen, K. (1990). The developmental psychopathology of child maltreatment. In M. Lewis & S. M. Miller (Eds.), *Handbook of developmental psychopathology.* New York: Plenum Press.

Cicchetti, D., & Rogosch, F. A. (2001). The impact of child maltreatment and psychopathology on neuroendocrine functioning. *Development and Psychopathology, 13,* 783–804.

Cicchetti, D., & Rogosch, F. A. (2002). A developmental psychopathology perspective on adolescence. *Journal of Consulting and Clinical Psychology, 70,* 6–20.

Cicchetti, D., & Schneider-Rosen, K. (1986). An organizational approach to childhood depression. In M. Rutter, C. Izard, & P. Read (Eds.), *Depression in young people: Clinical and developmental perspectives.* New York: Guilford.

Cicchetti, D., & Sroufe, L. A. (2000). Editorial: The past as prologue to the future: The times, they've been a-changin'. *Development and Psychopathology, 12,* 255–264.

Cicchetti, D., Rappaport, J., Sandler, I., & Weissberg, R. P. (2001). Emory L. Cowen (1926–2000). *American Psychologist, 56,* 514–515.

Cicchetti, D., & Toth, S. L. (1998). The development of depression in children and adolescents. *American Psychologist, 53,* 221–241.

Cicchetti, D., Toth, S., & Bush, M. (1988). Developmental psychopathology and incompetence in childhood: Suggestions for intervention. In B. B. Lahey & A. E. Kazdin (Eds.), *Advances in clinical child psychology,* Vol. 11. New York: Plenum.

Cicchetti, D., Toth, S. L., & Maughan, A. (2000). An ecological-transactional model of child maltreatment. In A. J. Sameroff, M. Lewis, & S. M. Miller (Eds.), *Handbook of developmental psychopathology* (2nd ed.). New York: Kluwer Academic/Plenum Publishers.

Clarizio, H. F. (1994). Assessment of depression in children and adolescents by parents, teachers, and peers. In W. M. Reynolds and H. F. Johnston (Eds.), *Handbook of depression in children and adolescents.* New York: Plenum Press.

Clark, A. F., & Lewis, S. W. (1998). Treatment of schizophrenia in childhood and adolescence. *Journal of Child Psychology and Psychiatry, 39,* 1071–1082.

Clark, C., Prior, M., & Kinsella, G. (2002). The relationship between executive function abilities, adaptive behavior, and academic achievement in children with externalizing behaviour problems. *Journal of Child Psychology and Psychiatry, 43,* 785–796.

Clark, D. B., Smith, M. G., Neighbors, B. D., Skerlec, L. M., & Randall, J. (1994). Anxiety disorders in adolescence: Characteristics, prevalence, and comorbidities. *Clinical Psychology Review, 14,* 113–137.

Clark, K. B., Chein, I., & Cook, S. W. (2004). The effects of segregation and the consequences of desegregation: A (September 1952) Social Science Statement in the *Brown v. Board of Education of Topeka* Supreme Court Case. *American Psychologist, 59,* 495–501.

Clark, L. A., & Watson, D. (1991). Tripartite model of anxiety and depression: Psychometric evidence and taxonomic implications. *Journal of Abnormal Psychology, 100,* 316–336.

Clark, R., Anderson, N. B., Clark, V. R., & Williams, D. R. (1999). Racism as a stressor for African Americans. *American Psychologist, 54,* 805–816.

Clarke, G. N., DeBar, L. L., & Lewinsohn, P. M. (2003). Cognitive-behavioral group treatment for adolescent depression. In A. E. Kazdin & J. R. Weisz (Eds.), *Evidence-based psychotherapies for children and adolescents.* New York: Guilford Press.

Clarke, G. N., Hawkins, W., Murphy, M., Sheeber, L. B., Lewinsohn, P. M., & Seeley, J. R. (1995). Targeted prevention of unipolar depressive disorder in an at-risk sample of high-school adolescents: A randomized trial of a group cognitive intervention. *Journal of the American Academy of Child and Adolescent Psychiatry, 34,* 312–321.

Clarke, G. N., Hornbrook, M. C., Lynch, F. L., Polen, M., Gale, J., O'Connor, E. A. et al. (2001). A randomized trial of a group cognitive intervention for preventing depression in adolescent offspring of depressed parents. *Archives of General Psychiatry, 58,* 1127–1134.

Clarke, G. N., Rhode, P., Lewinsohn, P. M., Hops, H., & Seeley, J. R. (1999). Cognitive-behavioral treatment for adolescent depression: Efficacy of acute group treatment and booster sessions. *Journal of the American Academy of Child and Adolescent Psychiatry, 38,* 272–279.

Cobham, V. E., Dadds, M. R., & Spence, S. H. (1998). The role of parental anxiety in the treatment of childhood anxiety. *Journal of Consulting and Clinical Psychology, 66,* 893–905.

Cohen, J. A., Deblinger, E., Mannarino, A. P., & Steer, R. A. (2004). A multisite, randomized controlled trial for children with sexual abuse-related PTSD symptoms. *Journal of the American Academy of Child and Adolescent Psychiatry, 43,* 393–402.

Cohen, P., Cohen, J., & Brook, J. (1993a). An epidemiological study of disorders in late childhood and adolescence-II. Persistence of disorders. *Journal of Child Psychology and Psychiatry, 34,* 869–877.

Cohen, P., Cohen, J., Kasen, S., Velez, C. N., Hartmark, C., Johnson, J., Rojas, M., Brook, J., & Streuning, E. L. (1993b). An epidemiological study of disorders in late childhood and adolescence-I. Age- and gender-specific prevalence. *Journal of Child Psychology and Psychiatry, 34,* 851–867.

Cohen-Tovee, E. M. (1993). Depressed mood and concern with weight and shape in normal young women. *International Journal of Eating Disorders, 14,* 223–227.

Coie, J. D., Belding, M., & Underwood, M. (1988). Aggression and peer rejection in childhood. In B. B. Lahey & A. E. Kazdin (Eds.), *Advances in clinical child psychology,* Vol. 11. *New York: Plenum.*

Coie, J. D., & Dodge, K. A. (1998). Aggression and antisocial behavior. In W. Damon (Series Ed.) & N. Eisenberg (Vol. Ed.), *Handbook of child psychology: Vol. 3. Social, emotional, and personality development* (5th ed.). New York: John Wiley.

Coie, J. D., Miller-Johnson, S., & Bagwell, C. (2000). Prevention science. In A. J. Sameroff, M. Lewis, & S. M. Miller (Eds.), *Handbook of developmental psychopathology.* New York: Kluwer Academic/Plenum.

Coie, J. D., Watt, N. F., West, S. G., Hawkins, J. D., Asarnow, J. R., Markman, H. J. et al. (1993). The science of prevention: A conceptual framework and some directions for a national research program. *American Psychologist, 48,* 1013–1022.

Colder, C. R., Mott, J. A., & Berman, A. S. (2002). The interactive effects of infant activity level and fear on growth trajectories of early childhood behavior problems. *Development and Psychopathology, 14,* 1–23.

Cole, C. M., Waldron, N., & Majd, M. (2004). Academic progress of students across inclusive and traditional settings. *Mental Retardation, 42,* 136–144.

Coley, R. L. (2001). (In)visible men: Emerging research on low-income, unmarried, and minority fathers. *American Psychologist, 56,* 743–753.

Coley, R. L., Morris, J. E., & Hernandez, D. (2004). Out-of-school care and problem behavior trajectories among low-income adolescents: Individual, family, and neighborhood characteristics as added risks. *Child Development, 75,* 948–965.

Collett, B. R., Ohan, J., & Myers, K. M. (2003). Ten-year review of rating scales. V: Scales assessing attention-deficit/hyperactivity disorder. *Journal of the American Academy of Child and Adolescent Psychiatry, 42,* 1015–1037.

Collins, E. (1991). Body figure perceptions and preferences among preadolescent children. *International Journal of Eating Disorders, 10,* 199–208.

Compas, B. E. (1997). Depression in children and adolescents. In E. J. Mash & L. G. Terdal (Eds.), *Assessment of childhood disorders* (3rd ed.). New York: Guilford Press.

Compas, B. E., Connor-Smith, J., & Jaser, S. S. (2004). Temperament, stress reactivity, and coping: Implications for depression in childhood and adolescence. *Journal of Clinical Child and Adolescent Psychology, 33,* 21–31.

Compas, B. E., Connor-Smith, J. K., Saltzman, H., Thomsen, A. H., & Wadsworth, M. E. (2001). Coping with stress during childhood and adolescence: Problems, progress, and potential in theory and research. *Psychological Bulletin, 127,* 87–127.

Compas, B. E., Ey, S., & Grant, K. E. (1993). Taxonomy, assessment, and diagnosis of depression during adolescence. *Psychological Bulletin, 14,* 323–344.

Compas, B. E., Hinden, B. R., & Gerhardt, C. (1995). Adolescent development: Pathways and processes of risk and resilience. *Annual Review of Psychology, 46,* 265–293.

Compas, B. E., Oppedisano, G., Connor, J. K., Gerhardt, C. A., Hinden, B. R., Achenbach, T. M., & Hammen, C. (1997). Gender differences in depressive symptoms in adolescence: Comparison of national samples of clinically referred and nonreferred youths. *Journal of Consulting and Clinical Psychology, 65,* 617–626.

Compton, K., Snyder, J., Schrepferman, L., Bank, L., & Shortt, J. W. (2003). The contribution of parents and siblings to antisocial and depressive behavior in adolescents: A double jeopardy coercion model. *Development and Psychopathology, 15,* 163–182.

Conduct Problems Prevention Research Group (1992). A developmental and clinical model for the prevention of conduct disorder: The FAST Track Program. *Development and Psychopathology, 4,* 509–527.

Conley, C. S., Haines, B. A., Hilt, L. M., & Metalsky, G. I. (2001). The Children's Attributional Style Interview: Developmental tests of cognitive diathesis-stress theories of depression. *Journal of Abnormal Child Psychology, 29,* 445–463.

Connell, J. P. (1985). A new multidimensional measure of children's perceptions of control. *Child Development, 56,* 1018–1041.

Connelly, C. D., & Straus, M. A. (1992). Mother's age and risk for physical abuse. *Child Abuse & Neglect, 16*, 709–718.

Conners, C. K., Sitarenios, G., Parker, J. D. A., & Epstein, J. N. (1998a). Revision and restandardization of the Conners Teacher Rating Scale (CTRS-R): Factor structure, reliability, and criterion validity. *Journal of Abnormal Child Psychology, 26*, 279–291.

Conners, C. K., Sitarenios, G., Parker, J. D. A., & Epstein, J. N. (1998b). The revised Conners Parent Rating Scale (CPRS-R): Factor structure, reliability, and criterion validity. *Journal of Abnormal Child Psychology, 26*, 257–268.

Connors, M. E. (1996). Developmental vulnerabilities for eating disorders. In L. Smolk, M. P. Levine, & R. Striegel-Moore (Eds.), *The developmental psychopathology of eating disorders: Implications for research, prevention, and treatment.* Mahwah, NJ: Lawrence Erlbaum.

Connors, M. E. (2001). Relationship of sexual abuse to body image and eating problems. In J. K. Thompson & L. Smolak (Eds.), *Body image, eating disorders, and obesity in youth: Assessment, prevention, and treatment.* Washington, DC: American Psychological Association.

Conti-Ramsden, G. (2003). Processing and linguistic markers in young children with specific language impairment (SLI). *Journal of Speech, Language, and Hearing Research, 46*, 1029–1037.

Conti-Ramsden, G., & Botting, N. (2004). Social difficulties and victimization in children with SLI at 11 years of age. *Journal of Speech, Language, and Hearing Research, 47*, 145–161.

Cook, B. G., Tankersley, M., Cook, L., & Landrum, T. J. (2000). Teachers' attitudes toward their included students with disabilities. *Exceptional Children, 67*, 115–135.

Cooperberg, J., & Faith, M. S. (2004). Treatment of obesity II: Childhood and adolescent obesity. In J. K. Thompson (Ed.), *Handbook of eating disorders and obesity.* Hoboken, NJ: John Wiley.

Cope, M. B., Fernández, J. R., & Allison, D. B. (2004). Genetic and biological risk factors. In J. K. Thompson (Ed.), *Handbook of eating disorders and obesity.* Hoboken, NJ: John Wiley.

Corkum, P., Moldofsky, H., Hogg-Johnson, S., Humphries, T., & Tannock, R. (1999). Sleep problems in children with attention-deficit/hyperactivity disorder: Impact of subtype, comorbidity, and stimulant medication. *Journal of the American Association of Child and Adolescent Psychiatry, 38*, 1285–1293.

Costello, E. J. (1989). Developments in child psychiatric epidemiology. *Journal of the American Academy of Child and Adolescent Psychiatry, 28*, 836–841.

Costello, E. J., & Angold, A. (1995a). Developmental epidemiology. In D. Cicchetti & D. J. Cohen (Eds.), *Developmental Psychopathology.* New York: John Wiley.

Costello, E. J., & Angold, A. (1995b). Epidemiology. In J. S. March (Ed.), *Anxiety disorders in children and adolescents.* New York: Guilford Press.

Costello, E. J., & Angold, A. C. (2000). Developmental epidemiology: A framework for developmental psychopathology. In A. J. Sameroff, M. Lewis, & S. M. Miller (Eds.), *Handbook of developmental psychopathology.* New York: Kluwer Academic/Plenum Publishers.

Costello, E. J., & Angold, A. (2001). Bad behaviour: An historic perspective on disorders of conduct. In J. Hill & B. Maughan (Eds.), *Conduct disorders in childhood and adolescence.* New York: Cambridge University Press.

Costello, E. J., Compton, S. N., Keeler, G., & Angold, A. (2003). Relationships between poverty and psychopathology. *Journal of the American Medical Association, 290*, 2023–2029.

Costello, E. J., Erkanli, A., Fairbank, J. A., & Angold, A. (2002). The prevalence of potentially traumatic events in childhood and adolescence. *Journal of Traumatic Stress, 15*, 99–112.

Costello, E. J., Mustillo, S., Erkanli, A., Keeler, G., & Angold, A. (2003). Prevalence and development of psychiatric disorders in childhood and adolescence. *Archives of Psychiatry, 60*, 837–844.

Costin, J., Vance, A., Barnett, R., O'Shea, M., & Luk, E. S. (2002). Attention deficit hyperactivity disorder and comorbid anxiety: Practitioner problems in treatment planning. *Child and Adolescent Mental Health, 7*, 16–24.

Cotler, S. (1986). Epidemiology and outcome. In J. M. Reisman (Ed.), *Behavior disorders in infants, children, and adolescents.* New York: Random House.

Cowen, E. L. (1991). In pursuit of wellness. *American Psychologist, 46*, 404–408.

Cowen, E. L. (1994). The enhancement of psychological wellness: Challenges and opportunities. *American Journal of Community Psychology, 22*, 149–179.

Cowen, E. L. (2000). Now that we all know that primary prevention in mental health is great, what is it? *Journal of Community Psychology, 28*, 5–16.

Cowen, E. L., Gesten, E. L., & Wilson, A. B. (1979). The Primary Mental Health Project (PMHP): Evaluation of current program effectiveness. *American Journal of Community Psychology, 3*, 293–303.

Cowen, E. L., & Hightower, A. D. (1989). The Primary Mental Health Project: Alternatives in school based preventive interventions. In T. B. Gutkin & C. R. Reynolds (Eds.), *Handbook of school psychology* (2nd ed.). New York: Wiley.

Cowen, E. L., & Hightower, A. D. (1990). The Primary Mental Health Project: Alternative approaches in school-based prevention interventions. In R. E. Hess (Ed.), *Prevention in human services.* New York: Haworth Press.

Cowen, E. L., Hightower, A. D., Pedro-Carroll, J. L., Work, W. C., Wyman, P. A., & Haffey, W. G. (1996). *School-based prevention for children at risk: The Primary Mental Health Project.* Washington, DC: American Psychological Association.

Cowen, E. L., Trost, M. A., Lorion, R. P., Dorr, D., Izzo, L. D., & Issacson, R. V. (1975). *New ways in school mental health: Early detection and prevention of school maladaptation.* New York: Human Sciences Press.

Cowen, E. L., Wyman, P. A., Work, W. C., & Parker, G. R. (1990). The Rochester Child Resilience Project: Overview and summary of first year findings. *Development and Psychopathology, 2*, 193–212.

Cowen, E. L., Zax, M., Izzo, L. D., & Trost, M. A. (1966). Prevention of emotional disorders in the school setting: A further investigation. *Journal of Consulting Psychology, 30*, 381–387.

Cox, A., & Rutter, M. (1985). Diagnostic appraisal and interviewing. In M. Rutter & L. Hersov (Eds.), *Child and adolescent psychiatry: Modern approaches.* Oxford: Blackwell Scientific Publications.

Coy, K., Speltz, M. L., DeKlyen, M., & Jones, K. (2001). Social-cognitive processes in preschool boys with and without oppositional defiant disorder. *Journal of Abnormal Child Psychology, 29,* 107–119.

Coyle, J. T. (2000). Psychotropic drug use in very young children. *Journal of the American Medical Association, 283,* 1059–1060.

Coyle, J. T. (2001). Drug treatment of anxiety disorders in children. *New England Journal of Medicine, 344,* 1326–1327.

Coyne, M. D., Kame'enui, E. J., Simmons, D. C., & Harn, B. A. (2004). Beginning reading intervention as inoculation or insulin: First-grade reading performance of strong responders to kindergarten intervention. *Journal of Learning Disabilities, 37,* 90–104.

CPT II. (2004). *MHS 2004 catalogue.* North Tonawanda, NY.

Cravens, H. (1992). A scientific project locked in time: The Terman genetic studies of genius, 1920s–1950s. *American Psychologist, 47,* 183–189.

Creer, T. L. (1982). Asthma. *Journal of Consulting and Clinical Psychology, 50,* 912–921.

Creer, T. L. (1998). Childhood asthma. In T. H. Ollendick & M. Hersen (Eds.), *Handbook of child psychopathology* (3rd ed.). New York: Plenum Press.

Creer, T. L. (2000). Self-management and the control of chronic illness. In D. Drotar (Ed.), *Promoting adherence to medical treatment in chronic illness: Concepts, methods, and interventions.* Mahwah, NJ: Erlbaum.

Crick, N. R. (1997). Engagement in gender normative versus nonnormative forms of aggression: Links to social-psychological adjustment. *Developmental Psychology, 33,* 610–617.

Crick, N. R., Casas, J. F., & Ku, H. C. (1999). Relational and physical forms of peer victimization in preschool. *Developmental Psychology, 35,* 376–385.

Crick, N. R., Casas, J. F., & Mosher, M. (1997). Relational and overt aggression in preschool. *Developmental Psychology, 33,* 579–588.

Crick, N. R., & Dodge, K. A. (1994). A review and reformulation of social information-processing mechanisms in children's social adjustment. *Psychological Bulletin, 115,* 74–101.

Crick, N. R., & Grotpeter, J. K. (1995). Relational aggression, gender, and social-psychological adjustment. *Child Development, 66,* 710–722.

Crick, N. R., & Grotpeter, J. K. (1996). Children's treatment by peers: Victims of relational and overt aggression. *Development and Psychopathology, 8,* 367–380.

Crick, N. R., & Nelson, D. A. (2002). Victimization within peer relationships and friendships: Nobody told me there'd be friends like these. *Journal of Abnormal Child Psychology, 30,* 599–607.

Crick, N. R., & Zahn-Waxler, C. (2003). The development of psychopathology in females and males: Current progress and future challenges. *Development and Psychopathology, 15,* 719–742.

Crijnen, A. A. M., Achenbach, T. M., & Verhulst, F. C. (1997). Comparisons of problems reported by parents of children in 12 cultures: Total problems, externalizing and internalizing. *American Academy of Child and Adolescent Psychiatry, 36,* 1269–1277.

Crisp, A. H. (1984). The psychopathology of anorexia nervosa: Getting the 'heat' out of the system. In A. J. Stunkard & E. Stellar (Eds.), *Eating and its disorders.* New York: Raven Press.

Criss, M. M., Petit, G. S., Bates, J. E., Dodge, K. A., & Lapp, A. L. (2002). Family adversity, positive peer relationships, and children's externalizing behavior: A longitudinal perspective on risk and resilience. *Child Development, 73,* 1220–1237.

Crist, W., & Napier-Phillips, A. (2001). Mealtime behaviors of young children: A comparison of normative and clinical data. *Journal of Developmental and Behavioral Pediatrics, 22,* 279–286.

Crnic, K. A. (1988). Mental retardation. In E. J. Mash & L. G. Terdal (Eds.), *Behavioral assessment of childhood disorders: Selected core problems.* New York: Guilford.

Culbertson, J. L. (1998). Learning disabilities. In T. H. Ollendick & M. Hersen (Eds.), *Handbook of child psychopathology.* New York: Plenum Press.

Cummings, E. M., & Davies, P. T. (2002). Effects of marital conflict on children: Recent advances and emerging themes in process-oriented research. *Journal of Child Psychology and Psychiatry, 43,* 31–63.

Cummings, E. M., Davies, P. T., & Campbell, S. B. (2000). *Developmental psychopathology and family process: Theory, research, and clinical implications.* New York: The Guilford Press.

Cummings, E. M., Goeke-Morey, M. C., Papp, L. M. (2004). Everyday marital conflict and child aggression. *Journal of Abnormal Child Psychology, 32,* 191–202.

Curtis, W. J., & Cicchetti, D. (2003). Moving research on resilience into the 21st century; Theoretical and methodological considerations in examining the biological contributions to resilience. *Development and Psychopathology, 15,* 773–810.

Cutting, A. L., & Dunn, J. (2002). The cost of understanding other people: Social cognition predicts young children's sensitivity to criticism. *Journal of Child Psychology and Psychiatry, 43,* 849–860.

Cyranowski, J. M., Frank, E., Young, E, & Shear, M. K. (2000). Adolescent onset of the gender difference in lifetime rates of major depression: A theoretical model. *Archives of General Psychiatry, 57,* 21–27.

Cytryn, L., & Lourie, R. S. (1980). Mental retardation. In H. I. Kaplan, A. M. Freedman, & B. J. Sadock (Eds.), *Comprehensive textbook of psychiatry/III,* Vol. 3. Baltimore: Williams & Wilkins.

Cytryn, L., & McKnew, D. (1974). Factors influencing the changing clinical expression of the depressive process in children. *American Journal of Psychiatry, 131,* 879–881.

Dadds, M. R., Barrett, P. M., Rapee, R. M., & Ryan, S. (1996). Family process and child anxiety and aggression: An observational analysis. *Journal of Abnormal Child Psychology, 24,* 715–734.

Dadds, M. R., Rapee, R. M., Barrett, P. M. (1994). Behavioral observation. In T. H. Ollendick, N. J. King, & W. Yule (Eds.), *International handbook of phobic and anxiety disorders in children and adolescents* (pp. 349–364). New York: Plenum Press.

Dadds, M. R., Sanders, M. R., Morrison, M., & Rebgetz, M. (1992). Childhood depression and conduct disorder: II. An analysis of family interaction patterns in the home. *Journal of Abnormal Psychology, 101,* 505–513.

Dahlquist, L., Power, T., & Carlson, L. (1995). Physician and parent behavior during invasive cancer procedures: A multidimensional assessment. *Journal of Pediatric Psychology, 20,* 477–490.

Dahlquist, L. M. (1992). Coping with aversive medical treatments. In A. M. La Greca, L. J. Siegel, L. J. Wallander, & C. E. Walker (Eds.), *Stress and coping in child health.* New York: Guilford.

Dahlquist, L. M., & Switkin, M. C. (2003). Chronic and recurrent pain. In M. C. Roberts (Ed.), *Handbook of pediatric psychology* (3rd ed.). New York: Guilford Press.

Dane, A. V., Schachar, R. J., & Tannock, R. (2000). Does actigraphy differentiate ADHD subtypes in a clinical research setting? *Journal of the American Academy of Child and Adolescent Psychiatry, 39,* 752–760.

Danforth, J. S., & Drabman, R. S. (1990). Community living skills. In J. L. Matson (Ed.), *Handbook of behavior modification with the mentally retarded.* New York: Plenum.

Danielson, C. K., Youngstrom, E. A., Findling, R. L., & Calabrese, J. R. (2003). Discriminative validity of the General Behavior Inventory using youth report. *Journal of Abnormal Child Psychology, 31,* 29–39.

Dantzer, C., Swendsen, J., Maurice-Tison, S., & Salamon, R. (2003). Anxiety and depression in juvenile diabetes: A critical review. *Clinical Psychology Review, 23,* 787–800.

Dare, C., & Eisler, I. (1997). Family therapy for anorexia nervosa. In D. M. Garner & P. E. Garfinkel (Eds.), *Handbook of treatment for eating disorders* (2nd ed.). New York: Guilford Press.

Davidovitch, M., Glick, L., Holtzmam, G., Tirosh, E., & Safir, M. P. (2000). Developmental regression in autism: Maternal perception. *Journal of Autism and Developmental Disorders, 30,* 113–119.

Davidson, W. S., & Basta, J. (1989). Diversion from the juvenile justice system: Research evidence and a discussion of issues. In B. B. Lahey & A. E. Kazdin (Eds.), *Advances in clinical child psychology,* Vol. 12, New York: Plenum.

Davies, R. R., & Rogers, E. S. (1985). Social skills training with persons who are mentally retarded. *Mental Retardation, 23,* 186–196.

Davis, C. L., Delamater, A. M., Shaw, K. H., La Greca, A. M., Edison, M. S., Perez-Rodriguez, J. E., & Nemery, R. (2001). Parenting styles, regimen adherence, and glycemic control in 4- to 10-year-old children with diabetes. *Journal of Pediatric Psychology, 26,* 123–129.

Davis, K. L., Stewart, D. G., Friedman, J. I., Buchsman, M., Harvey, P. D., Hof, P. R. et al. (2003). White matter changes in schizophrenia. *Archives of General Psychiatry, 60,* 443–456.

Dawson, G., & Castelloe, P. (1992). Autism. In C. E. Walker & M. C. Roberts (Eds.), *Handbook of clinical child psychology.* New York: Wiley.

Dawson, G., Frey, K., Panagiotides, H., Osterling, J., & Hessl, D. (1997). Infants of depressed mothers exhibit atypical frontal brain activity: A replication and extension of previous findings. *Journal of Child Psychology and Psychiatry, 38,* 179–186.

De Bellis, M. D. (2001). Developmental traumatology: The psychobiological development of maltreated children and its implications for research, treatment, and policy. *Development and Psychopathology, 13,* 539–564.

de Groot, A., Koot, H. M., & Verhulst, F. C. (1996). Cross-cultural generalizability of the Youth Self-Report and Teacher's Report Form cross-informant syndromes. *Journal of Abnormal Child Psychology, 24,* 651–664.

De Wilde, E. J., Kienhorst, C. W. M., & Diekstra, R. R. W. (2001). Suicidal behaviour in adolescents. In I. M. Goodyer (Ed.), *The depressed child and adolescent* (2nd ed.). Cambridge, UK: Cambridge University Press.

de Zwaan, M., Roerig, J. L., & Mitchell, J. E. (2004). Pharmacological treatment of anorexia nervosa, bulimia nervosa, and binge eating disorder. In J. K. Thompson (Ed.), *Handbook of eating disorders and obesity.* Hoboken, NJ: John Wiley.

Dean, V. J., & Burns, M. K. (2002). Inclusion of intrinsic processing difficulties in LD diagnostic models: A critical review. *Learning Disability Quarterly, 25,* 170–176.

Deal, L. W., Gomby, D. S., Zippiroli, L., & Behrman, R. E. (2000). Unintentional injuries in childhood: Analysis and recommendations. *The Future of Children, 10(1),* 4–22.

Deater-Deckard, K. (2001). Recent research examining the role of peer relationships in the development of psychopathology. *Journal of Child Psychology and Psychiatry, 42,* 565–579.

Deater-Deckard, K., Reiss, D., Hetherington, E. M., & Plomin, R. (1997). Dimensions and disorders of adolescent adjustment: A quantitative genetic analysis of unselected samples and selected extremes. *Journal of Child Psychology and Psychiatry, 38,* 515–525.

DeFries, J. C., & Light, J. G. (1996). Twin studies of reading disability. In J. H. Beitchman, N. J. Cohen, M. M. Konstantareas, & R. Tannock (Eds.), *Language, learning, and behavior disorders.* New York: Cambridge University Press.

Dekker, M. C., & Koot, H. M. (2003a). DSM-IV disorders in children with borderline to moderate intellectual disability. I: Child and family predictors. *Journal of the American Academy of Child and Adolescent Psychiatry, 42,* 923–931.

Dekker, M. C., & Koot, H. M. (2003b). DSM-IV disorders in children with borderline to moderate intellectual ability. II: Prevalence and impact. *Journal of the American Academy of Child and Adolescent Psychiatry, 42,* 915–922.

Dekovic, M., & Janssens, A. M. (1992). Parents' child-rearing style and child's sociometric status. *Developmental Psychology, 28,* 925–932.

DeKraai, M. D., Sales, B. D., & Hall, S. R. (1998). Informed consent, confidentiality, and duty to report laws in the conduct of child therapy. In R. J. Morris & T. R. Kratochwill (Eds.), *The practice of child therapy* (3rd ed.). Boston: Allyn and Bacon.

Delamater, A. M. (2000). Critical issues in the assessment of regimen adherence in children with diabetes. In D. Drotar (Ed.), *Promoting adherence to medical treatment in chronic childhood illness: Concepts, methods, and interventions.* Mahwah, NJ: Lawrence Erlbaum Associates.

Delamater, A. M., Bubb, J., Davis, S. G., Smith, J. A., Schmidt, L., White, N. H., & Santiago, J. V. (1990). Randomized prospective study of self-management training with newly diagnosed diabetic children. *Diabetes Care, 13,* 492–498.

Demos, J., & Demos, V. (1972). Adolescence in historical perspective. In D. Rogers (Ed.), *Issues in adolescent psychology.* Englewood Cliffs, NJ: Prentice-Hall.

Denham, S. A., Caverly, S., Schmidt, M., Blair, K., DeMulder, E., Caal, S. et al. (2002). Preschool understanding of emotions: Contributions to classroom anger and aggression. *Journal of Child Psychology and Psychiatry, 43,* 901–916.

Denney, C. B. (2001). Stimulant effects in attention deficit hyperactivity disorder: Theoretical and empirical issues. *Journal of Clinical Child Psychology, 30,* 98–109.

DePaulo, J. R. (2004). Genetics of bipolar disorder: Where do we stand? *American Journal of Psychiatry, 161,* 595–597.

Depue, R. A., Krauss, S., Spoont, M. R., & Arbisi, P. (1989). General Behavior Inventory identification of unipolar and bipolar affective conditions in a nonclinical university population. *Journal of Abnormal Psychology, 98,* 117–126.

D'Eramo, K. S., & Francis, G. (2004). Cognitive-behavioral psychotherapy. In T. L. Morris & J. S. March (Eds.), *Anxiety disorders in children and adolescents.* New York: Guilford Press.

DeStefano, L., & Thompson, D. S. (1990). Adaptive behavior: The construct and its measurement. In C. R. Reynolds & R. W. Kamphaus (Eds.), *Handbook of psychological & educational assessment of children: Personality, behavior, and context.* New York: Guilford.

Detterman, D. K., & Thompson, L. A. (1997). What is so special about special education? *American Psychologist, 52,* 1082–1090.

DiBartolo, P. M., Albano, A. M., Barlow, D. H., & Heimberg. R. G. (1998). Cross-informant agreement in the assessment of social phobia in youth. *Journal of Abnormal Child Psychology, 26,* 213–220.

Dieter, J. N. I., Field, T., Hernandez-Reif, M., Emory, E. K., & Redzepi, M. (2003). Stable preterm infants gain more weight and sleep less after five days of massage therapy. *Journal of Pediatric Psychology, 28,* 403–411.

DiLillo, D., & Peterson, L. (2001). Prevention of childhood disorders. In C. E. Walker & M. C. Roberts (Eds.), *Handbook of clinical child psychology.* New York: John Wiley.

DiLillo, D., & Tremblay, G. (2001). Maternal and child reports of behavioral compensation in response to equipment usage. *Journal of Pediatric Psychology, 26,* 175–184.

Dietz, W. H. (1988). Metabolic aspects of dieting. In N. A. Krasnegor, G. D. Grave, & N. Kretchmer (Eds.), *Childhood obesity: A biobehavioral perspective.* Caldwell, NJ: The Telford Press.

Dietz, W. H. (1995). Childhood obesity: Prevalence and effects. In K. D. Brownell & C. G. Fairburn (Eds.), *Eating disorders and obesity: A comprehensive handbook.* New York: Guilford Press.

DiMatteo, M. R. (2000). Practitioner-family-patient communication in pediatric adherence: Implications for research and clinical practice. In D. Drotar (Ed.), *Promoting adherence to medical treatment in chronic childhood illness: Concepts, methods, and interventions.* Mahwah, NJ: Lawrence Erlbaum Associates.

Dishion, T. J. (1990). The family ecology of boys' relations in middle childhood. *Child Development, 61,* 874–892.

Dishion, T. J., French, D. C., & Patterson, G. R. (1995). The development and ecology of antisocial behavior. In D. Cicchetti & D. J. Cohen (Eds.), *Developmental psychopathology* (Vol. 2: *Risk, disorder and adaptation*). New York: John Wiley & Sons.

Division TEACCH. (2004). *Inclusion for children with autism.* Retrieved August 23, 2004, from www.teacch.com.

Dodge, K. A. (1991). The structure and function of reactive and proactive aggression. In D. Pepler & K. Rubin (Eds.), *The development and treatment of childhood aggression.* Hillsdale, NJ: Erlbaum.

Dodge, K. A. (2000). Conduct disorder. In A. J. Sameroff, M. Lewis, & S. M. Miller (Eds.), *Handbook of developmental psychopathology* (2nd ed.). New York: Kluwer Academic/Plenum Publishers.

Dodge, K. A. (2003). Do social information-processing patterns mediate aggressive behavior? In B. B. Lahey, T. E. Moffitt, & A. Caspi (Eds.), *Causes of conduct disorder and juvenile delinquency.* New York: Guilford Press.

Dodge, K. A., Lochman, J. E., Harnish, J. D., Bates, J. E., & Pettit, G. S. (1997). Reactive and proactive aggression in school children and psychiatrically impaired chronically assaultive youth. *Journal of Abnormal Psychology, 106,* 37–51.

Dodge, K. A., & Rabiner, D. L. (2004). Returning to roots: On social information processing and moral development. *Child Development, 75,* 1003–1008.

D'Onofrio, B. M., Turkheimer, E. M., Eaves, L. J., Cory, L. A., Berg, K., Solaas, M. H., & Emery, R. E. (2003). The role of the Children of Twins design in elucidating causal relations between parent characteristics and child outcomes. *Journal of Child Psychology and Psychiatry, 44,* 1130–1144.

Doleys, D. M. (1989). Enuresis and encopresis. In T. H. Ollendick & M. Hersen (Eds.), *Handbook of child psychopathology* (2nd ed.). New York: Plenum.

Dolgin, M. J., & Jay, S. M. (1989). Childhood cancer. In T. H. Ollendick & M. Hersen (Eds.), *Handbook of child psychopathology* (2nd ed.). New York: Plenum.

Dollinger, S. J. (1986). Childhood sleep disturbances. In B. B. Lahey & A. E. Kazdin (Eds.), *Advances in clinical child psychology,* Vol. 9. New York: Plenum.

Donovan, C. L., & Spence, S. H. (2000). Prevention of childhood anxiety disorders. *Clinical Psychology Review, 20,* 509–531.

Dorris, L., Espie, C. A. E., Knott, F., & Salt, J. (2004). Mind-reading difficulties in the siblings of people with Asperger's syndrome: Evidence for a genetic influence in the abnormal development of a specific cognitive domain. *Journal of Child Psychology and Psychiatry, 45,* 412–418.

Douglas, V. I. (1983). Attentional and cognitive problems. In M. Rutter (Ed.), *Developmental neuropsychiatry.* New York: Guilford.

Dowdney, L. (2000). Childhood bereavement following parental death. *Journal of Child Psychology and Psychiatry, 41,* 819–830.

Doyle, K. W., Wolchik, S. A., Dawson-McClure, S. R., & Sandler, I. N. (2003). Positive events as a stress buffer for children and adolescents in families in transition. Journal of *Clinical Child and Adolescent Psychology, 32,* 536–545.

Drotar, D. (1981). Psychological perspectives in chronic childhood illness. *Journal of Pediatric Psychology, 6,* 211–228.

Drotar, D. (Ed.) (2000). *Promoting adherence to medical treatment in chronic childhood illness: Concepts, methods, and interventions.* Mahwah, NJ: Lawrence Erlbaum Associates.

Drotar, D., & Lemanek, K. (2001). Steps toward a clinically relevant science of interventions in pediatric settings: Introduction to the special issue. *Journal of Pediatric Psychology, 26,* 385–394.

Drotar, D., Riekert, K. A., Burgess, E., Levi, R., Nobile, C., Kaugars, A. S., & Walders, N. (2000). Treatment adherence in childhood chronic illness: Issues and recommendations to enhance practice, research, and training. In D. Drotar (Ed.), *Promoting adherence to medical treatment in chronic childhood illness: Concepts, methods, and interventions.* Mahwah, NJ: Lawrence Erlbaum Associates.

Drotar, D., & Robinson, J. (2000). Developmental psychopathology of failure to thrive. In A. J. Sameroff, M. Lewis, & S. M. Miller (Eds.), *Handbook of developmental psychopathology* (2nd ed.). New York: Kluwer Academic/Plenum Publishers.

DuBois, D. L., Burk-Braxton, C., Swenson, L. P., Tevendale, H. D., & Hardesty, J. L. (2002). Race and gender influences on adjustment in early adolescence: Investigation of an integrative model. *Child Development, 73*, 1573–1592.

Dumas, J. E., & Lechowicz, J. G. (1989). When do noncompliant children comply? Implications for family behavior therapy. *Child and Family Behavior Therapy, 11*, 21–38.

Dummit, E. S., Klein, R. G., Tancer, N. K., Asche, B., Martin, J., & Fairbanks, J. A. (1997). Systematic assessment of 50 children with selective mutism. *Journal of the American Academy of Child and Adolescent Psychiatry, 36*, 653–660.

Dunbar-Jacob, J. (1993). Contributions to patient adherence: Is it time to share the blame? *Health Psychology, 12*, 91–92.

Duncan, G. J., & Brooks-Gunn, J. (2000). Family poverty, welfare reform, and child development. *Child Development, 71*, 188–196.

Dunn, J. (1996). Children's relationships: Bridging the divide between cognitive and social development. *Journal of Child Psychology and Psychiatry, 37*, 507–518.

Dunn, J., Deater-Deckard, K., Pickering, K., O'Connor, T. G., Golden, J., & The ALSPAC Study Team. (1998). Children's adjustment and prosocial behaviour in step-, single-parent, and non-stepfamily settings: Findings from a community study. *Journal of Child Psychology and Psychiatry, 39*, 1083–1095.

Dunn, J., & McGuire, S. (1992). Sibling and peer relationships in childhood. *Journal of Child Psychology and Psychiatry, 33*, 67–105.

DuPaul, G. J., Barkley, R. A., & Connor, D. F. (1998). Stimulants. In R. A. Barkley (Ed.), *Attention-deficit hyperactivity disorder.* New York: Guilford Press.

DuPaul, G. J., Guevrement, D. C., & Barkley, R. A. (1991). Attention-deficit hyperactivity disorder. In R. A. Barkley (Ed.), *Attention-deficit hyperactivity disorder.* New York: Guilford Press.

DuPaul, G. J., McGoey, K. E., Eckert, T. L., & VanBrakle, J. (2001). Preschool children with attention-deficit/hyperactivity disorder: Impairments in behavioral, social, and school functioning. *Journal of the American Academy of Child and Adolescent Psychiatry, 40*, 508–509.

Durand, V. M. (1993). Functional communication training using assistive devices: Effects on challenging behavior and affect. *Augmentative Alternative Communication, 9*, 168–176.

Durand, V. M. (1999). Functional communication training using assistive devices: Recruiting natural communities of reinforcement. *Journal of Applied Behavior Analysis, 32*, 247–267.

Durand, V. M. (2001). Future directions for children and adolescents with mental retardation. *Behavior Therapy, 32*, 633–650.

Durand, V. M., & Carr, E. G. (1991). Functional communication training to reduce challenging behavior: Maintenance and application in new settings. *Journal of Applied Behavior Analysis, 24*, 251–264.

Durand, V. M., & Crimmins, D. B. (1988). Identifying the variables maintaining self-injurious behavior. *Journal of Autism and Developmental Disorders, 18*, 99–117.

Durand, V. M., & Mindell, J. A. (1999). Behavioral intervention for childhood sleep terrors. *Behavior Therapy, 30*, 705–715.

Durlak, J. A., & Wells, A. M. (1997). Primary prevention mental health programs for children and adolescents: A meta-analytic review. *American Journal of Community Psychology, 25*, 115–152.

Du Rocher Schudlich, T. D., & Cummings, E. M. (2003). Parental dysphoria and children's internalizing symptoms: Marital conflict styles as mediators of risk. *Child Development, 74*, 1663–1681.

Durston, S., Pol, H. E. H., Schnack, H. G., Buitelaar, J. K., Steenhuis, M. P., Minderaa, R. B. et al. (2004). Magnetic resonance imaging of boys with attention-deficit/hyperactivity disorder. *Journal of the American Academy of Child and Adolescent Psychiatry, 43*, 332–340.

Dyck, M. K., Hay, D., Anderson, M., Smith, L. M., Piek, J., & Hallmayer, J. (2004). Is the discrepancy criteria for defining developmental disorders valid? *Journal of Child Psychology and Psychiatry, 45*, 979–995.

Dykens, E. M., & Cohen, D. J. (1996). Effects of Special Olympics International on social competence in persons with mental retardation. *Journal of the American Academy of Child and Adolescent Psychiatry, 35*, 223–229.

Eaves, L. J., Silberg, J. L., Meyer, J. M., Maes, H. H., Simonoff, E., Pickles, A., Rutter, M., Neale, M. C., Reynolds, C. A., Erickson, M. T., Heath, A. C., Loeber, R., Truett K. R., & Hewitt, J. K. (1997). Genetics and developmental psychopathology: 2. The main effects of genes and environment on behavioral problems in the Virginia Twin Study of Adolescent Behavioral Development. *Journal of Child Psychology and Psychiatry, 38*, 965–980.

Eccles, J. S., & Wigfield, A. (2002). Motivational beliefs, values, and goals. *Annual Review of Psychology, 53*, 109–132.

Edelbrock, C., Rende, R., Plomin, R., & Thompson, L. A. (1995). A twin study of competence and problem behavior in childhood and early adolescence. *Journal of Child Psychology and Psychiatry, 36*, 775–785.

Egeland, J. A., Hostetter, A. M., Pauls, D. L., & Sussex, J. N. (2000). Prodromal symptoms before onset of manic-depressive disorder suggested by first hospital admission histories. *Journal of the American Academy of Child and Adolescent Psychiatry, 39*, 1245–1252.

Eggers, C. (1978). Course and prognosis of childhood schizophrenia. *Journal of Autism and Childhood Schizophrenia, 8*, 21–36.

Eggers, C. & Bunk, D. (1997). The longterm course of childhood-onset schizophrenia: A 42-year followup. *Schizophrenia Bulletin, 23*, 105–117.

Eggers, C., Bunk, D., & Krause, D. (2000). Schizophrenia with onset before the age of eleven: Clinical characteristics of onset and course. *Journal of Autism and Developmental Disorders, 30*, 29–38.

Egley, A., & Major, A. K. (2004). *Highlights of the 2003 National Youth Gang Survey.* Washington, DC: Office of Juvenile Justice and Delinquency Prevention.

Eisenberg, L. (2001). The past 50 years of child and adolescent psychiatry: A personal memoir. *Journal of the American Academy of Child and Adolescent Psychiatry, 40*, 743–748.

Eisenberg, L., Baker, B. L., & Blacher, J. (1998). Siblings with children with mental retardation living at home or in residential placement. *Journal of Child Psychology and Psychiatry, 39*, 355–363.

Eisenberg, N., Cumberland, A., Spinrad, T. L., Fabes, R. A., Shepard, S. A., Reiser, M., Murphy, B. C., Losoya, S. H., & Guthrie, I. K. (2001). The relations of regulation and emotionality to children's externalizing and internalizing problem behavior. *Child Development, 72*, 1112–1134.

Eisenberg, N. et al. (1997). Contemporaneous and longitudinal prediction of children's social functioning from regulation and emotionality. *Child Development, 68*, 642–664.

Eiser, C. (1994). The eleventh Jack Tizard Memorial Lecture. Making sense of chronic disease. *Journal of Child Psychology and Psychiatry, 35*, 1373–1389.

Eiser, C. (1998). Long-term consequences of childhood cancer. *Journal of Child Psychology and Psychiatry, 39*, 621–633.

Eisner, E. W. (2003). On the art and science of qualitative research in psychology. In P. M. Camic, J. E. Rhodes, & L. Yardley (Eds.), *Qualitative research in psychology*. Washington, DC: American Psychological Association.

Elbaum, B., & Vaughn, S. (2003). Self-concept and students with learning disabilities. In H. L. Swanson, K. R. Harris, & S. Graham (Eds.), *Handbook of learning disabilities*. New York: Guilford Press.

Eley, T. C. (1997). General genes: A new theme in developmental psychopathology. *Current Directions in Psychological Science, 6*, 90–95.

Eley, T. C., Lichtenstein, P., & Moffitt, T. E. (2003). A longitudinal behavioral genetic analysis of the etiology of aggressive and nonaggressive antisocial behavior. *Development and Psychopathology, 15*, 383–402.

Eley, T. C., & Stevenson, J. (1999). Using genetic analyses to clarify the distinction between depressive and anxious symptoms in children. *Journal of Abnormal Child Psychology, 27*, 105–114.

Elgar, F. J., McGrath, P. J., Waschbusch, D. A., Stewart, S. H., & Curtis, L. J. (2004). Mutual influences on maternal depression and child adjustment problems. *Clinical Psychology Review, 24*, 441–459.

Elgar, K., & Campbell, R. (2001). The cognitive neuroscience of face recognition: Implications for developmental disorders. *Journal of Child Psychology and Psychiatry, 42*, 705–717.

Eliez, S., & Reiss, A. L. (2000). MRI neuroimaging of childhood psychiatric disorders: A selective review. *Journal of Child Psychology and Psychiatry, 41*, 679–694.

Eliez, S., Rumsey, J. M., Giedd, J. N., Schmitt, E. J., Padwardhan, A. J., & Reiss, A. L. (2000). Morphological alteration of temporal lobe gray matter in dyslexia: An MRI study. *Journal of Child Psychology and Psychiatry, 41*, 637–644.

Elliot, C. H., Jay, S. M., & Woody, P. (1987). An observational scale for measuring children's distress during painful medical procedures. *Journal of Pediatric Psychology, 12*, 543–551.

Elliot, D. S., Huizinga, D., & Ageton, S. S. (1985). *Explaining delinquency and drug use*. Beverly Hills, CA: Sage.

Elliott, J. G. (1999). School refusal: Issues of conceptualization, assessment, and treatment. *Journal of Child Psychology and Psychiatry, 40*, 1001–1012.

Emery, R. E., & Kitzmann, K. M. (1995). The child in the family: Disruptions in family functions. In D. Cicchetti & D. J. Cohen (Eds.), *Developmental psychopathology: Risk, disorder, and adaptation* (Vol. 2). New York: John Wiley & Sons.

Empey, L. T. (1978). *American delinquency*. Homewood, IL: Dorsey.

Emslie, G. J., Armitage, R., Weinberg, W. A., Rush, A. J., Mayes, T. L., & Hoffmann, R. F. (2001). Sleep polysomnography as a predictor of recurrence in children and adolescents with major depressive disorder. *International Journal of Neuropsychopharmacology, 4*, 159–168.

Emslie, G. J., Weinberg, W. A., Kennard, B. D., & Kowatch, R. A. (1994). Neurobiological aspects of depression in children and adolescents. In W. M. Reynolds & H. F. Johnston (Eds.), *Handbook of depression in children and adolescents*. New York: Plenum.

English, D. J. (1998). The extent and consequences of child maltreatment. *The Future of Children, 8(1)*, 39–53.

Enzer, N. B., & Heard, S. L. (2000). Psychiatric prevention in children and adolescents. In B. J. Sadock & V. A. Sadock (Eds.), *Comprehensive textbook of psychiatry* (Vol. II). Philadelphia: Lippincott Williams & Wilkins.

Epstein, J. N., Erkanli, A., Conners, C. K., Klaric, J., Costello, J. E., & Angold, A. (2003). Relations between continuous performance test performance measures and ADHD behaviors. *Journal of Clinical Child Psychology, 31*, 543–554.

Epstein, L. H., Valoski, A. M., Vara, L. S., McCurley, J., Wisniewski, L., Kalarchian, M. A., Klein, K. R., & Schrager, L. R. (1995). Effects of decreasing sedentary behavior and increasing activity on weight change in obese children. *Health Psychology, 14*, 109–115.

Ernst, M. (2000). Commentary: Considerations on the characterization and treatment of self-injurious behavior. *Journal of Autism and Developmental Disorders, 30*, 447–450.

Ernst, M., Kimes, A. S., London, E. D. et al. (2003). Neural substrates of decision making in adults with attention deficit hyperactivity disorder. *American Journal of Psychiatry, 160*, 1061–1070.

Ernst, M., Moolchan, E. T., & Robinson, M. L. (2001). Behavioral and neural consequences of prenatal exposure to nicotine. *Journal of the American Academy of Child and Adolescent Psychiatry, 40*, 630–641.

Espy, K. A., Moore, I. M., Kaufmann, P. M., Kramer, J. H., Matthay, K., & Hutter, J. J. (2001). Chemotherapeutic CNS prophylaxis and neuropsychologic change in children with acute lymphoblastic leukemia: A prospective study. *Journal of Pediatric Psychology, 26*, 1–9.

Essau, C., Conradt, J., & Petermann, F. (1999). Frequency and comorbidity of social phobia and social fears in adolescents. *Behaviour Research and Therapy, 37*, 831–843.

Essau, C. A., Conradt, J., & Petermann, F. (1999). Frequency of panic attacks and panic disorder in adolescents. *Depression and Anxiety, 9*, 19–26.

Essau, C. A., Conradt, J., & Petermann, F. (2000). Frequency, comorbidity, and psychosocial impairment of specific phobia in adolescents. *Journal of Clinical Child Psychology, 29*, 221–231.

Evans, J. A., & Hammerton, J. L. (1985). Chromosomal anomalies. In A. M. Clarke, A. D. B. Clarke, & J. M. Berg (Eds.), *Mental deficiency. The changing outlook*. New York: The Free Press.

Evans, R. B., & Koelsch, W. A. (1985). Psychoanalysis arrives in America. *American Psychologist, 40*, 942–948.

Evans, G. W. (2004). The environment of childhood poverty. *American Psychologist, 59*, 77–92.

Exner, J. E., Jr., & Weiner, I. B. (1995). *The Rorschach: A comprehensive system* (Vol. 3: *Assessment of children and adolescents*) (2nd ed.). New York: Wiley.

Eyberg, S. M. (1992). Parent and teacher behavior inventories for the assessment of conduct problem behaviors in children. In L. VandeCreek, S. Knapp, & T. L. Jackson (Eds.), *Innovations in clinical practice: A source book* (Vol. 11). Sarasota, FL: Professional Resource Exchange.

Eyberg, S. M., Bessmer, J., Newcomb, K., Edwards, D., & Robinson, E. (1994). *Dyadic Parent-Child Interaction Coding System II: A manual.* Unpublished manuscript, University of Florida.

Fabes, R. A., Martin, C. L., Hanish, L. D., & Updegraff, K. A. (2000). Criteria for evaluating the significance of developmental research in the twenty-first century: Force and counterforce. *Child Development, 71*, 212–221.

Fagan, A. A., & Najman, J. M. (2003). Association between early childhood aggression and internalizing behavior for sibling pairs. *Journal of the American Academy of Child and Adolescent Psychiatry, 42*, 1093–1100.

Fagan, J. F., & Holland, C. R. (2002). Equal opportunity and racial differences in IQ. *Intelligence, 30*, 361–387.

Fairburn, C. G. (1995). Physiology of anorexia nervosa. In K. D. Brownell & C. G. Fairburn (Eds.), *Eating disorders and obesity: A comprehensive handbook.* New York: Guilford Press.

Fairburn, C. G. (1997). Eating disorders. In D. M. Clark & C. G. Fairburn (Eds.), *Science and practice of cognitive behaviour therapy.* Oxford: Oxford University Press.

Fairburn, C. G., Cooper, Z., Doll, H. A., Norman, P., & O'Connor, M. (2000). The natural course of bulimia nervosa and binge eating disorder in young women. *Archives of General Psychiatry, 57*, 659–665.

Fairburn, C. G., Norman, P. A., Welch, S. L., O'Connor, M. E., Doll, H. A., & Peveler, R. C. (1995). A prospective study of outcome in bulimia nervosa and the long-term effects of three psychological treatments. *Archives of General Psychiatry, 52*, 304–312.

Fairburn, C. G., Welch, S. L., Doll, H. A., Davies, B. A., & O'Connor, M. E. (1997). Risk factors for bulimia nervosa: A community-based case-control study. *Archives of General Psychiatry, 54*, 509–517.

Faith, M. S., Saelens, B. E., Wilfley, D. E., & Allison, D. B. (2001). Behavioral treatment of childhood and adolescent obesity: Current status, challenges, and future directions. In J. K. Thompson & L. Smolak (Eds.), *Body image, eating disorders, and obesity in youth: Assessment, prevention, and treatment.* Washington, DC: American Psychological Association.

Faraone, S., Biederman, J., Mennin, D., Russell, R., Tsuang, M. T. (1998). Familial subtypes of attention deficit hyperactivity disorder: A follow-up study of children from antisocial-ADHD families. *Journal of Child Psychology and Psychiatry, 39*, 1045–1053.

Faraone, S. V., Glatt, S. J., Su, J., & Tsuang, M. T. (2004). Three potential susceptibility loci shown by a genome-wide scan for regions influencing the age of onset of mania. *American Journal of Psychiatry, 161*, 625–630.

Farrington, D. P. (1986). Stepping stones to adult criminal careers. In D. Olweus, J. Block, & M. R. Yarrow (Eds.), *Development of antisocial behavior and prosocial behavior.* New York: Academic Press.

Farrington, D. P. (1991). Longitudinal research strategies: Advantages, problems, and prospects. *Journal of the American Academy of Child and Adolescent Psychiatry, 30*, 369–374.

Farrington, D. P. (1995). The development of offending and antisocial behaviour from childhood: Key findings from the Cambridge Study in Delinquent Development. *Journal of Child Psychology and Psychiatry, 36*, 929–964.

Fawcett, A. J., Nicolson, R. I., & Maclagan, F. (2001). Cerebellar tests differentiate between groups of poor readers with and without IQ discrepancy. *Journal of Learning Disabilities, 34*, 119–135.

Federal Interagency Forum on Child and Family Statistics. 2004. *America's children: Key national indicators of well-being.* Washington, DC: U.S. Government Printing Office.

Feldner, M. T., Zvolensky, M. J., & Schmidt, N. B. (2004). Prevention of anxiety psychopathology: A critical review of the empirical literature. *Clinical Psychology: Science and Practice, 11*, 405–424.

Felner, R., Brand, S., Adam, A. A., Mulhall, P. F., Flowers, N., Sartain, B., & DuBois, B. L. (1993). Restructuring the ecology of the school as an approach to prevention during school transitions: Longitudinal follow-up and extensions of the School Transition Environment Project (STEP). *Prevention and Human Services, 10*, 103–136.

Felner, R. D., & Adan, A. M. (1988). The School Transition Environment Project: An ecological intervention and evaluation. In R. H. Price, E. L. Cowen, R. P. Lorion, & J. Ramos-McKay (Eds.), *Fourteen ounces of prevention: A casebook for practioners.* Washington, DC: American Psychological Association.

Felner, R. D., Favazza, A., Shim, M., Brand, S., Gu, K., & Noonan, N. (2001). Whole school improvement and restructuring as prevention and promotion. Lessons from STEP and the Project on High Performance Learning Communities. *Journal of School Psychology, 39*, 177–202.

Ferguson, C. P., & Pigott, T. A. (2000). Anorexia and bulimia nervosa: Neurobiology and pharmacotherapy. *Behavior Therapy, 31*, 237–264.

Ferguson, L. R. (1978). The competence and freedom of children to make choices regarding participation in research: A statement. *Journal of Social Issues, 34*, 114–121.

Fergusson, D., Swain-Campbell, N., & Horwood, J. (2004). How does childhood economic disadvantage lead to crime? *Journal of Child Psychology and Psychiatry, 45*, 956–966.

Fergusson, D. M., & Horwood, L. J. (1996). The role of adolescent peer affiliations in the continuity between childhood behavioral adjustment and juvenile offending. *Journal of Abnormal Child Psychology, 24*, 205–221.

Fergusson, D. M., & Horwood, L. J. (1998). Early conduct problems and later life opportunities. *Journal of Child Psychology and Psychiatry, 39*, 1097–1108.

Fergusson, D. M., & Horwood, L. J. (1999). Prospective childhood predictors of deviant peer affiliations in adolescence. *Journal of Child Psychology and Psychiatry, 40*, 581–592.

Fergusson, D. M., & Horwood, L. J. (2002). Male and female offending trajectories. *Development and Psychopathology, 14*, 159–177.

Fergusson, D. M., Horwood, L. J., & Lynskey, M. T. (1993). Early dentine lead levels and subsequent cognitive and behavioural development. *Journal of Child Psychology and Psychiatry, 34,* 215–227.

Fergusson, D. M., & Lynskey, M. T. (1995). Childhood circumstances, adolescent adjustment, and suicide attempts in a New Zealand birth cohort. *Journal of the American Academy of Child and Adolescent Psychiatry, 34,* 612–622.

Fergusson, D. M., & Lynskey, M. T. (1997). Early reading difficulties and later conduct problems. *Journal of Child Psychology and Psychiatry, 38,* 899–907.

Fergusson, D. M., Lynskey, M. T., & Horwood, L. J. (1997). Attentional difficulties in middle childhood and psychosocial outcomes in young adulthood. *Journal of Child Psychology and Psychiatry, 38,* 633–644.

Fergusson, D. M., & Woodward, L. J. (2000). Educational, psychological, and sexual outcomes of girls with conduct problems in early adolescence. *Journal of Child Psychology and Psychiatry, 41,* 779–792.

Ferrari, M. (1990). Developmental issues in behavioral pediatrics. In A. M. Gross & R. S. Drabman (Eds.), *Handbook of clinical behavioral pediatrics.* New York: Plenum.

Ferster, C. B. (1974). Behavioral approaches to depression. In R. J. Friedman & M. M. Katz (Eds.), *The psychology of depression: Contemporary theory and research.* Washington, DC: Winston.

Fetal Alcohol Syndrome. (2003). Retrieved March 2004 from http://www.cdc.gov/ncbdd/fas/fasask.htm.

Field, T. (1992). Infants of depressed mothers. *Development and Psychopathology, 4,* 49–66.

Field, T., Hernandez-Reif, M., & Freedman, J. (2004). Stimulation programs for preterm infants. *Social Policy Report, 18(1),* 3–19.

Fiese, B. H., & Bickman, N. L. (1998). Qualitative inquiry: An overview for pediatric psychology. *Journal of Pediatric Psychology, 23,* 79–86.

Filipek, P. A. (1999). Neuroimaging in the developmental disorders: The state of the science. *Journal of Child Psychology and Psychiatry, 40,* 113–128.

Findling, R. L., McNamara, N. K., Youngstrom, E. A., Branicky, L. A., Demeter, C. A., & Schulz, S. C. (2003). A prospective, open-label trial of olanzapine in adolescents with schizophrenia. *Journal of the American Academy of Child and Adolescent Psychiatry, 42,* 170–175.

Fine, R. (1985). Anna Freud. *American Psychologist, 40,* 230–232.

Fine, S. E., Izard, C. E., Mostow, A. J., Trentacosta, C. J., & Ackerman, B. P. (2003). First grade emotion knowledge as a predictor of fifth grade self-reported internalizing behaviors in children from economically disadvantaged families. *Development and Psychopathology, 15,* 331–342.

Finkelhor, D. (1994). The international epidemiology of child sexual abuse. *Child Abuse & Neglect, 18,* 409–417.

Finkelstein, H. (1988). The long term effects of early parent death: A review. *Journal of Clinical Psychology, 44,* 3–9.

Fischer, M., Barkley, R. A., Fletcher, K. E., & Smallish, L. (1993). The adolescent outcome of hyperactive children: Predictors of psychiatric, academic, social, and emotional adjustment. *Journal of the American Academy of Child and Adolescent Psychiatry, 32,* 324–332.

Fisher, J. O., & Birch, L. L. (2001). Body image in children. In J. K. Thompson & L. Smolak (Eds.), *Body image, eating disorders, and obesity in youth: Assessment, prevention, and treatment.* Washington, DC: American Psychological Association.

Fixsen, D. L., Wolf, M. M., & Phillips, E. L. (1973). Achievement place: A teaching-family model of community-based group homes for youth in trouble. In L. Hammerlynck, L. Handy, and E. Mash (Eds.), *Behavior change: Methodology, concepts and practice.* Champaign, IL: Research Press.

Flament, M. F., Whitaker, A., Rapoport, J. L., Davies, M., Berg, C. Z., Kalikow, K., Sceery, W., & Shafer, D. (1988). Obsessive compulsive disorder in adolescence: An epidemiological study. *Journal of the American Academy of Child and Adolescent Psychiatry, 27,* 764–771.

Flannery-Schroeder, E. C. (2004). Generalized anxiety disorder. In T. L. Morris & J. S. March (Eds.), *Anxiety disorders in children and adolescents.* New York: Guilford Press.

Flannery-Schroeder, E. C., & Kendall, P. C. (2000). Group and individual cognitive-behavioral treatments for youth with anxiety disorders: A randomized clinical trial. *Cognitive Therapy and Research, 24,* 251–278.

Flax, J. F., Realpe-Bonilla, T., Hirsch, L. S., Brzustowicz, L. M., Bartlett, C. W., & Tallal, P. (2003). Specific language impairments in families: Evidence for co-occurrence with reading impairments. *Journal of Speech, Language, and Hearing Impairments, 46,* 530–543.

Fleitlich-Bilyk, B., & Goodman, R. (2004). Prevalence of child and adolescent psychiatric disorders in southeast Brazil. *Journal of the American Academy of Child and Adolescent Psychiatry, 43,* 727–734.

Fleming, J. E., Offord, D. R., & Boyle, M. H. (1989). Prevalence of childhood and adolescent depression in the community: Ontario Child Health Study. *British Journal of Psychiatry, 155,* 647–654.

Fletcher, J. M., & Taylor, H. G. (1997). Children with brain injury. In E. J. Mash & L. G. Terdal (Eds.), *Assessment of childhood disorders* (3rd ed.). New York: Guilford Press.

Fletcher, K. E. (2003). Childhood posttraumatic stress disorder. In E. J. Mash & R. A. Barkley (Eds.), *Child psychopathology* (2nd ed.). New York: Guilford Press.

Flisher, A. J. (1999). Mood disorder in suicidal children and adolescents: Recent developments. *Journal of Child Psychology and Psychiatry, 40,* 315–324.

Flynt, S. W., Wood, T. A., & Scott, R. L. (1992). Social support of mothers of children with mental retardation. *Mental Retardation, 30,* 233–236.

Follette, W. C., & Houts, A. C. (1996). Models of scientific progress and the role of theory in taxonomy development: A case study of DSM. *Journal of Consulting and Clinical Psychology, 64,* 1120–1132.

Folstein, S. E., Santangelo, S. L., Gilman, S. E., Piven, J., Landa, R., Lainhart, J. et al. (1999). Predictors of cognitive test patterns in autistic families. *Journal of Child Psychology and Psychiatry, 40,* 1117–1128.

Fombonne, E. (2002). Case identification in an epidemiological context. In M. Rutter & E. Taylor (Eds.), *Child and adolescent psychiatry.* Oxford, UK: Blackwell Publishing.

Fombonne, E. (2003). Epidemiological surveys of autism and pervasive developmental disorders: An update. *Journal of Autism and Developmental Disorders, 33*, 365–382.

Fombonne, E., Rogé, B., Claverie, J., Courty, S., & Frémolle, J. (1999). Microcephaly and macrocephaly in autism. *Journal of Autism and Developmental Disorders, 29*, 113–119.

Fonesca, A. C., Yule, W., & Erol, N. (1994). Cross-cultural issues. In T. H. Ollendick, N. J. King, & W. Yule (Eds.), *International handbook of phobic and anxiety disorders in children and adolescents.* New York: Plenum Press.

Fontaine, R. G., Burks, V. S., & Dodge, K. A. (2002). Response decision processes and externalizing behavior problems in adolescents. *Development and Psychopathology, 14*, 107–122.

Ford, M. A., Sladeczek, I. E., Carlson, J., & Kratochwill, T. R. (1998). Selective mutism: Phenomenological characteristics. *School Psychology Quarterly, 13*, 192–227.

Ford, T., Goodman, R., & Meltzer, H. (2003). The British child and adolescent mental health survey 1999: The prevalence of DSM-IV disorders. *Journal of the American Academy of Child and Adolescent Psychiatry, 42*, 1203–1211.

Forehand, R., Furey, W. M., & McMahon, R. J. (1984). The role of maternal distress in a parent training program to modify child non-compliance. *Behavioral Psychotherapy, 12*, 93–108.

Forehand, R., King, H. E., Peed, S., & Yoder, P. (1975). Mother-child interactions: Comparisons of a noncompliant clinic group and a non-clinic group. *Behaviour Research and Therapy, 13*, 79–84.

Forehand, R. L., & Long, N. (1996). *Parenting the strong-willed child.* Chicago: Contemporary Books.

Forehand, R., & McMahon, R. J. (1981). *Helping the noncompliant child: A clinician's guide to parent training.* New York: Guilford.

Foreyt, J. P., & Goodrick, G. K. (1993). Obesity in children. In R. T. Ammerman & M. Hersen (Eds.), *Handbook of behavior therapy with children and adults: A developmental and longitudinal perspective.* Boston: Allyn & Bacon.

Foster, G. G., & Salvia, J. (1977). Teacher response to the label of learning disabled as a function of demand characteristics. *Exceptional Children, 43*, 533–534.

Foster, S. L., & Robin, A. L. (1997). Family conflict and communication in adolescence. In E. J. Mash & L. G. Terdal (Eds.), *Assessment of childhood disorders* (3rd ed.). New York: Guilford Press.

Fowles, D. C. (1992). Schizophrenia: Diathesis-stress revisited. *Annual Review of Psychology, 43*, 303–336.

Frances, A., & Ross, R. (2001). *DSM-IV-TR case studies: A clinical guide to differential diagnosis.* Washington, DC: American Psychiatric Association.

Franklin, M., Foa, E., & March, J. S. (2003). The Pediatric Obsessive-Compulsive Disorder Treatment Study: Rationale, design, and methods. *Journal of Child and Adolescent Psychopharmacology, 13*, S39–S51.

Fredriksen, K., Rhodes, J., Reddy, R., & Way, N. (2004). Sleepless in Chicago: Tracking the effects of adolescent sleep loss during the middle school years. *Child Development, 75*, 84–95.

Freeman, J. B., Garcia, A. M., Fucci, C., Karitani, M., Miller, L., & Leonard, H. L. (2003). Family-based treatment of early-onset obsessive-compulsive disorder. *Journal of Child and Adolescent Psychopharmacology, 13*, S71–S80.

Fremont, W. P. (2004). Childhood reactions to terrorism-induced trauma: A review of the past 10 years. *Journal of the American Academy of Child and Adolescent Psychiatry, 43*, 381–392.

French, T. M., & Alexander, F. (1941). Psychogenic factors in bronchial asthma. *Psychosomatic Medicine Monograph, 4*, 2–94.

Freud, A. (1946). *The psycho-analytical treatment of children.* London: Imago.

Freud, S. (1953). Analysis of a phobia in a five-year-old boy (1909). *Standard Edition.* Vol. 10. Ed. and trans. James Strachey, London: The Hogarth Press.

Frick, P. J. (1994). Family dysfunction and the disruptive disorders: A review of recent empirical findings. In T. H. Ollendick & R. J. Prinz (Eds.), *Advances in clinical child psychology.* Vol. 16. New York: Plenum Press.

Frick, P. J. (1998a). Callous-unemotional traits and conduct problems: A two-factor model of psychopathy in children. In D. J. Cooke, A. Forth, & R. D. Hare (Eds.), *Psychopathy: Theory, research, and implications for society.* Dordrecht, The Netherlands: Kluwer.

Frick, P. J. (1998b). Conduct disorders. In T. H. Ollendick & M. Hersen (Eds.), *Handbook of child psychopathology* (3rd ed.). New York: Plenum Press.

Frick, P. J. (2004). Integrating research on temperament and childhood psychopathology: Its pitfalls and promise. *Journal of Clinical Child and Adolescent Psychology, 33*, 2–7.

Frick, P. J., & Kamphaus, R. W. (2001). Standardized rating scales in the assessment of children's behavioral and emotional problems. In C. E. Walker & M. C. Roberts (Eds.), *Handbook of clinical child psychology* (3rd ed.). New York: John Wiley & Sons.

Frick, P. J., & Loney, B. R. (2000). The use of laboratory and performance-based measures in the assessment of children and adolescents with conduct disorders. *Journal of Clinical Child Psychology, 29*, 540–554.

Frick, P. J., & Morris, A. S. (2004). Temperament and developmental pathways to conduct problems. *Journal of Clinical Child and Adolescent Psychology, 33*, 54–68.

Fried, P. A. (2002). Conceptual issues in behavioral teratology and their implication in determining long-term sequelae of prenatal marihuana exposure. *Journal of Child Psychology and Psychiatry, 43*, 81–102.

Friedman, A. G., Latham, S. A., & Dahlquist, L. M. (1998). Childhood cancer. In T. H. Ollendick & M. Hersen (Eds.), *Handbook of child psychopathology* (3rd ed.). New York: Plenum Press.

Fristad, M. A., & Goldberg-Arnold, J. S. (2003). Family interventions for early-onset bipolar disorder. In B. Geller & M. P. DelBello (Eds.), *Bipolar disorder in childhood and early adolescence.* New York: Guilford Press.

Frith, U. (2004). Emmanuel Miller lecture: Confusions and controversies about Asperger syndrome. *Journal of Child Psychology and Psychiatry, 45*, 672–686.

Fritz, G. K., & McQuaid, E. L. (2000). Chronic medical conditions: Impact on development. In A. J. Sameroff, M. Lewis, & S. M. Miller (Eds.), *Handbook of developmental psychopathology* (2nd ed.). New York: Kluwer Academic/Plenum.

Fuchs, L. S., Fuchs, D., & Prentice, K. (2004). Responsiveness to mathematical problem-solving instruction: Comparing students at risk of mathematics disability with and without risk of reading disability. *Journal of Learning Disabilities, 37*, 293–306.

Gabbard, G. O. (2000). Psychoanalysis and psychoanalytic psychotherapy. In B. J. Sadock & V. A. Sadock (Eds.), *Kaplan & Sadock's Comprehensive textbook of psychiatry* (Vol. II). Philadelphia: Lippincott Williams & Wilkins.

Gadow, K. D., & Nolan, E. E. (2002). Differences between preschool children with ODD, ADHD, and ODD+ADHD symptoms. *Journal of Child Psychology and Psychiatry, 43*, 191–201.

Gadow, K. D., Nolan, E. E., Litcher, L., Carlson, G. A., Panina, N., Golovakha, E. et al. (2000). Comparison of attention-deficit/hyperactivity disorder symptom subtypes in Ukrainian schoolchildren. *Journal of the American Academy of Child and Adolescent Psychiatry, 39*, 1520–1527.

Garber, J., & Flynn, C. (2001). Predictors of depressive cognitions in young adolescents. *Cognitive Therapy and Research, 25*, 353–376.

Garber, J., & Kaminski, K. M. (2000). Laboratory and performance-based measures of depression in children and adolescents. *Journal of Clinical Child Psychology, 29*, 509–525.

Garcia Coll, C., Crnic, K., Lamberty, G., Wasik, B. H., Jenkins, R., Garcia, H. V. et al. (1966). An integrative model for the study of developmental competencies in minority children. *Child Development, 67*, 1891–1914.

García Coll, C., & Garrido, M. (2000). Minorities in the United States: Sociocultural context for mental health and developmental psychopathology. In A. J. Sameroff, M. Lewis, & S. M. Miller (Eds.), *Handbook of developmental psychopathology*. New York: Kluwer/Plenum Publishers.

Gardner, R. M. (2001). Assessment of body image disturbance in children and adolescents. In J. K. Thompson & L. Smolak (Eds.), *Body image, eating disorders, and obesity in youth: Assessment, prevention, and treatment*. Washington, DC: American Psychological Association.

Garmezy, N., & Masten, A. S. (1994). Chronic adversities. In M. Rutter, E. Taylor, & L. Hersov (Eds.), *Child and adolescent psychiatry: Modern approaches*. Cambridge, MA: Blackwell Scientific.

Garn, S. M., & Clark, D. C. (1976). Trends in fatness and the origins of obesity: Ad hoc committee to review the ten-state nutrition survey. *Pediatrics, 57*, 443–456.

Garn, S. M., LaVelle, M., Rosenberg, K. R., & Hawthorne, V. M. (1986). Maturational timing as a factor in female fatness and obesity. *The American Journal of Clinical Nutrition, 43*, 879–883.

Garner, D. M., & Desai, J. J. (2001). Eating disorders in children and adolescents. In J. N. Hughes, A. M. LaGreca, & J. C. Conoley (Eds.), *Handbook of psychological services for children and adolescents*. New York: Oxford University Press.

Garstein, M. A., Short, A. D., Vannatta, K., & Noll, R. B. (1999). Psychosocial adjustment of children with chronic illness: An evaluation of three models. *Journal of Developmental and Behavioral Pediatrics, 20*, 157–163.

Gathercole, S. E. (1998). The development of memory. *Journal of Child Psychology and Psychiatry, 39*, 3–27.

Ge, X., Conger, R. D., Lorenz, F. O., Shanahan, M., & Elder, G. H. (1995). Mutual influences in parent and adolescent psychological distress. *Developmental Psychology, 31*, 406–419.

Geary, D. C. (2003). Learning disabilities in arithmetic: Problem-solving differences and cognitive deficits. In H. L. Swanson, K. R. Harris, & S. Graham (Eds.), *Handbook of learning disabilities*. New York: Guilford Press.

Geary, D. C. (2004). Mathematics and learning disabilities. *Journal of Learning Disabilities, 37*, 4–15.

Geller, B., Craney, J. L., Bolhofner, K., DelBello, M. P., Axelson, D., Luby, J., Williams, M., Zimerman, B., Nickelsburg, M. J., Frazier, J., & Beringer, L. (2003). Phenomenology and longitudinal course of children with prepubertal and early adolescent bipolar disorder phenotype. In B. Geller & M. P. DelBello (Eds.), *Bipolar disorder in childhood and early adolescence*. New York: Guilford Press.

Geller, D. A, Biederman, J., Faraone, S. V., Cradock, K., Hagermoser, L., Zaman, N. et al. (2002). Attention-deficit hyperactivity disorder in children and adolescents with obsessive-compulsive disorder: Fact or artifact? *Journal of the American Academy of Child and Adolescent Psychiatry, 41*, 52–58.

Geller, D. A., Biederman, J., Stewart, E., Mullin, B., Farrell, C., Wagner, K. D., Emslie, G., & Carpenter, D. (2003a). Impact of comorbidity on treatment response to paroxetine in pediatric obsessive-compulsive disorder: Is the use of exclusion criteria empirically supported in randomized clinical trials? *Journal of Child and Adolescent Psychopharmacology, 13*, S19–S29.

Geller, D. A., Biederman, J., Stewart, S. E., Mullin, B., Martin, A., Spencer, T., & Faraone, S. V. (2003b). Which SSRI? A meta-analysis of pharmacotherapy trials in pediatric obsessive-compulsive disorder. *American Journal of Psychiatry, 160*, 1919–1928.

Gencöz, T., Voelz, A. R., Gencöz, F., Pettit, J. W., & Joiner, T. E. (2001). Specificity of information processing styles to depressive symptoms in youth psychiatric inpatients. *Journal of Abnormal Child Psychology, 29*, 255–262.

Gerard, M. W. (1939). Enuresis: A study in etiology. *American Journal of Orthopsychiatry, 9*, 48–58.

Gerdes, A. C., Hoza, B., & Pelham, W. E. (2003). Attention-deficit hyperactivity disordered boys' relationships with their mothers and fathers: Child, mother, and father perceptions. *Development and Psychopathology, 15*, 363–382.

Gerull, F. C., & Rapee, R. M. (2002). Mother knows best: The effects of maternal modeling on the acquisition of fear and avoidance behaviour in toddlers. *Behaviour Research and Therapy, 40*, 279–287.

Gesten, E. L. (1976). A Health Resources Inventory: The development of a measure of the personal and social competence of primary grade children. *Journal of Consulting and Clinical Psychology, 44*, 775–786.

Gettinger, M., & Koscik, R. (2001). Psychological services for children with learning disabilities. In J. N. Huges, A. M. La Greca, & J. C. Conoley (Eds.), *Handbook of psychological services for children and adolescents*. New York: Oxford University Press.

Ghaziuddin, M., Thomas, P., Napier, E., Kearney, G., Tsai, L., Welch, K., & Fraser, W. (2000). Brief report: Brief syntactic analysis in Asperger's syndrome: A preliminary study. *Journal of Autism and Developmental Disorders, 30*, 67–70.

Giaconia, R. M., Reinherz, H. Z., Silverman, A. B., Pakiz, B., Frost, A. K., & Cohen, E. (1994). Ages of onset of psychiatric disorders in a community population of older adolescents. *Journal of the American Academy of Child and Adolescent Psychiatry, 33*, 706–717.

Gibbs, J. T. (2003). African American children and adolescents. In J. T. Gibbs, L. N. Huang, and Associates (Eds.), *Children of color: Psychological interventions with culturally diverse youth.* San Francisco: Jossey-Bass.

Gibbs, J. T., Huang, L. N., & Associates. (2003). *Children of color: Psychological interventions with culturally diverse youth.* San Francisco: Jossey-Bass.

Gil, A. G., Wagner, E. F., & Vega, W. A. (2000). Acculturation, familism, and alcohol use among Latino adolescent males: Longitudinal relations. *Journal of Community Psychology, 28,* 443–458.

Gilbert, S., & Thompson, J. K. (1996). Feminist explanations of the development of eating disorders: Common themes, research findings, and methodological issues. *Clinical Psychology: Science and Practice, 3,* 183–202.

Gillberg, C. (1997). Practitioner review: Physical investigations in mental retardation. *Journal of Child Psychology and Psychiatry, 38,* 889–897.

Gillberg, I. C., Hellgren, L., & Gillberg, C. (1993). Psychotic disorders diagnosed in adolescence. Outcome at age 30 years. *Journal of Child Psychology and Psychiatry, 34,* 1173–1185.

Gillham, J. E., Reivich, K. J., Jaycox, L. H., & Seligman, M. E. P. (1995). Prevention of depressive symptoms in school children: A two-year follow-up. *Psychological Science, 6,* 343–351.

Gillin, J. C., Duncan, W., Pettigrew, K. D., Frankel, B., & Synder, F. (1979). Successful separation of depressed, normal and insomniac subjects by EEG sleep data. *Archives of General Psychiatry, 36,* 85–90.

Gilmour, J., Hill, B., Place, M., Skuse, D. H. (2004). Social communication deficits in conduct disorder: a clinical and community survey. *Journal of Child Psychology and Psychiatry, 45,* 967–978.

Ginsburg, G. S., & Silverman, W. K. (1996). Phobic and anxiety disorders in Hispanic and Caucasian youth. *Journal of Anxiety Disorders, 10,* 517–528.

Ginsburg, G. S., & Silverman, W. K. (2000). Gender role orientation and fearfulness in children with anxiety disorders. *Journal of Anxiety Disorders, 14,* 57–67.

Ginsburg, G. S., LaGreca, A. M. & Silverman, W. K. (1998). Social anxiety in children with anxiety disorders: Relation with social and emotional functioning. *Journal of Abnormal Psychology, 26,* 175–185.

Gjone, H., & Stevenson, J. (1997). The association between internalizing and externalizing behavior in childhood and early adolescence: Genetic or environment common influences? *Journal of Abnormal Child Psychology, 25,* 277–286.

Glantz, L. H. (1996). Conducting research with children: Legal and ethical issues. *Journal of the American Academy of Child and Adolescent Psychiatry, 35,* 1283–1291.

Glantz, M. D., & Leshner, A. I. (2000). Drug abuse and developmental psychopathology. *Development and Psychopathology, 12,* 795–814.

Gliner, J. A., Morgan, G. A., & Harmon, R. J. (2000). Single-subject designs. *Journal of the American Academy of Child and Adolescent Psychiatry, 39,* 1327–1329.

Glueck, S., & Glueck, E. T. (1968). *Delinquents and nondelinquents in perspective.* Cambridge, MA: Harvard University Press.

Goddard, H. H. (1912). *The Kallikak family.* New York: Macmillan.

Goenjian, A. K., Yehuda, R., Pynoos, R. S., Steinberg, A. M., Tashjian, M., Yang, R. K., Najarian, L. M., Fairbanks, L. A. (1996). Basal cortisol, dexamethasone suppression of cortisol, and MHPG in adolescents after the 1988 earthquake in Armenia. *American Journal of Psychiatry, 153,* 929–934.

Goldberg, W. A., Osann, K., Filipek, P. A., Laulhere, T., Jarvis, K., Modahl, C. et al. (2003). Language and other regression: Assessment and timing. *Journal of Autism and Developmental Disorders, 33,* 607–616.

Goldberg-Arnold, J. S., & Fristad, M. A. (2003). Psychotherapy for children with bipolar disorder. In B. Geller & M. P. DelBello (Eds.), *Bipolar disorder in childhood and early adolescence.* New York: Guilford Press.

Golden, C. J., Purisch, A. D., & Hammeke, T. A. (1985). *Luria-Nebraska Neuropsychological Battery: Forms I and II manual.* Los Angeles: Western Psychological Services.

Goldstein, H. (2000). Commentary: Interventions to facilitate auditory, visual, and motor integration: "Show me the data." *Journal of Autism and Developmental Disorders, 30,* 423–425.

Gomez, R., Harvey, J., Quick, C., Scharer, I., & Harris, G. (1999). DSM-IV AD/HD: Confirmatory factor models, prevalence, and gender and age differences based on parent and teacher ratings of Australian primary school children. *Journal of Child Psychology and Psychiatry, 40,* 265–274.

Gooding, D. C., & Iacono, W. G. (1995). Schizophrenia through the lens of a developmental psychopathology perspective. In D. Cicchetti & D. J. Cohen (Eds.), *Developmental Psychology* (Vol. 2). New York: John Wiley Interscience.

Goodlin-Jones, B. L., Burnham, M. M., & Anders, T. F. (2000). Sleep and sleep disturbances: Regulatory processes in infancy. In A. J. Sameroff, M. Lewis, & S. M. Miller (Eds.), *Handbook of developmental psychopathology* (2nd ed.). New York: Kluwer Academic/Plenum Publishers.

Goodman, R., & Stevenson, J. (1989). A twin study of hyperactivity-II. The aetiological role of genes, family relationships and perinatal adversity. *Journal of Child Psychology and Psychiatry, 30,* 691–709.

Goodman, S. H., Schwab-Stone, M., Lahey, B., Shaffer, D., & Jensen, P. (2000). Major depression and dysthymia in children and adolescents: Discriminant validity and differentiated consequences in a community sample. *Journal of the American Academy of Child and Adolescent Psychiatry, 39,* 761–770.

Goodwin, R. D., Fergusson, D. M., & Horwood, L. J. (2004). Early anxious/withdrawn behaviours predict later internalising disorders. *Journal of Child Psychology and Psychiatry, 45,* 874–883.

Goodyer, I. M. (2001). Life events: Their nature and effects. In I. M. Goodyer (Ed.), *The depressed child and adolescent* (2nd ed.). Cambridge, UK: Cambridge University Press.

Goodyer, I. M., & Cooper, P. (1993). A community study of depression in adolescent girls: II. The clinical features of identified disorder. *British Journal of Psychiatry, 163,* 374–380.

Gordon-Larsen, P., Adair, L. S., & Popkin, B. M. (2002). Ethnic differences in physical activity and inactivity patterns and overweight status. *Obesity Research, 10,* 141–149.

Gore, S. A., Vander Wal, J. S., & Thelan, M. H. (2001). Treatment of eating disorders in children and adolescents. In J. K. Thompson & L. Smolak (Eds.), *Body image, eating disorders, and obesity in youth: Assessment, prevention, and treatment.* Washington, DC: American Psychological Association.

Gortmaker, S. L., Must, A., Perrin, J. M., Sobol, A. M., & Dietz, W. H. (1993). Social and economic consequences of overweight in adolescence and young adulthood. *New England Journal of Medicine, 329,* 1008–1012.

Gortmaker, S. L., & Sappenfield, W. (1984). Chronic childhood disorders: Prevalence and impact. *Pediatric Clinics of North America, 31,* 3–18.

Gothelf, D., & Lombroso, P. J. (2001). Genetics of childhood disorders: XXV. Velocardiofacial syndrome. *Journal of the American Academy of Child and Adolescent Psychiatry, 40,* 489–491.

Gottesman, I. I. (1993). Origins of schizophrenia: Past as prologue. In R. Plomin & G. E. McClearn (Eds.), *Nature and nurture & psychology.* Washington, DC: American Psychological Association.

Gottfried, A. E., & Gottfried, A. W. (1988). Maternal employment and children's development. An integration of longitudinal findings with implications for social policy. In A. E. Gottfried and A. W. Gottfried (Eds.), *Maternal employment and children's development.* New York: Plenum.

Gottlieb, G., & Halpern, C. T. (2002). A relational view of causality in normal and abnormal development. *Development and Psychopathology, 14,* 421–435.

Gould, M. S., Greenberg, T., Velting, D. M., & Shaffer, D. (2003). Youth suicide risk and preventive interventions: A review of the past 10 years. *Journal of the American Academy of Child and Adolescent Psychiatry, 42,* 386–405.

Gould, M. S., Shaffer, D., & Kaplan, D. (1985). The characteristics of dropouts from a child psychiatric clinic. *Journal of the American Academy of Child Psychiatry, 24,* 316–328.

Gowers, S., & Bryant-Waugh, R. (2004). Management of child and adolescent eating disorders: The current evidence base and future directions. *Journal of Child Psychology and Psychiatry, 45,* 63–83.

Gowers, S. G., Crisp, A. H., Joughin, N., & Bhat, A. (1991). Premenarcheal anorexia nervosa. *Journal of Child Psychology and Psychiatry, 32,* 515–524.

Graber, J. A., Seeley, J. R., Brooks-Gunn, J., & Lewinsohn, P. M. (2004). Is pubertal timing associated with psychopathology in young adulthood? *Journal of the American Academy of Child and Adolescent Psychiatry, 43,* 718–726.

Grace, W. J., & Graham, D. T. (1952). Relationship of specific attitudes and emotions to certain bodily diseases. *Psychosomatic Medicine, 14,* 243–251.

Gracious, B. L., Findling, R. L., Seman, C., Youngstrom, E. A., Demeter, C. A., & Calabrese, J. R. (2004). Elevated thyrotropin in bipolar youths prescribed both lithium and divalproex sodium. *Journal of the American Academy of Child and Adolescent Psychiatry, 43,* 215–220.

Grados, M. A., & Riddle, M. A. (2001). Pharmacological treatment of childhood obsessive-compulsive disorder: From theory to practice. *Journal of Clinical Child Psychology, 30,* 67–79.

Graetz, B. W., Sawyer, M. G., Hazell, P. L., Arney, F., & Baghurst, P. (2001). Validity of DSM-IV ADHD subtypes in a nationally representative sample of Australian children and adolescents. *Journal of the American Academy of Child and Adolescent Psychiatry, 40,* 410–417.

Graham, S., & Harris, K. R. (2003). Students with learning disabilities and the process of writing: A meta-analysis of SRSD studies. In H. L. Swanson, K. R. Harris, & S. Graham (Eds.), *Handbook of learning disabilities.* New York: Guilford Press.

Grandin, T. (1997). A personal perspective on autism. In D. J. Cohen & F. R. Volkmar (Eds.), *Handbook of autism and pervasive developmental disorders.* New York: John Wiley.

Grant, K. E., Compas, B. E., Stuhlmacher, A. F., Thurm, A. E., McMahon, S. D., & Halpert, J. A. (2003). Stressors and child and adolescent psychopathology: Moving from markers to mechanisms of risk. *Psychological Bulletin, 129,* 447–466.

Gray, J. A. (1987). *The psychology of fear and stress.* New York: Cambridge University Press.

Greco, L. A., & Morris, T. L. (2004). Assessment. In T. L. Morris & J. S. March (Eds.), *Anxiety disorders in children and adolescents.* New York: Guilford Press.

Greco, P., Pendley, J. S., McDonell, K., & Reeves, G. (2001). A peer group intervention for adolescents with type 1 diabetes and their best friends. *Journal of Pediatric Psychology, 26,* 485–490.

Green, J., & Goldwyn, R. (2002). Annotation: Attachment disorganization and psychopathology: New findings in attachment research and their potential implications for developmental psychopathology in childhood. *Journal of Child Psychology and Psychiatry, 43,* 835–846.

Green, R. (2004). The evolution of kinship care policy and practice. *The Future of Children, 14,* 131–149.

Green, W. H., Padron-Gayol, M., Hardesty, A. S., & Bassiri, M. (1992). Schizophrenia with childhood onset: A phenomenological study of 38 cases. *Journal of the American Academy of Child and Adolescent Psychiatry, 31,* 968–976.

Greenberg, M. T., & Crnic, K. A. (1988). Longitudinal predictors of developmental status and social interaction in premature and full-term infants at age two. *Child Development, 59,* 554–570.

Greene, R. W. (1995). Students with ADHD in school classrooms: Teacher factors related to compatibility, assessment, and intervention. *School Psychology Review, 24,* 81–93.

Greene, R. W., & Ablon, J. S. (2001). What does the MTA study tell us about effective psychosocial treatment for ADHD? *Journal of Clinical Child Psychology, 30,* 114–121.

Greenhill, L. L. (1991). Attention-deficit hyperactivity disorder. In J. M. Wiener (Ed.), *Textbook of child & adolescent psychiatry.* Washington, DC: American Psychiatric Press.

Greenhill, L. L., Jensen, P. S., Abikoff, H., Blumer, J. L., DeVeaugh-Geiss, J., Fisher, C. (2003a). Developing strategies for psychopharmacological studies in preschool children. *Journal of the American Academy of Child and Adolescent Psychiatry, 42,* 406–414.

Greenhill, L., Pliszka, S., Dulcan, M. K., & the Work Group on Quality Issues. (2002). Practice parameter for the use of stimulant medications in the treatment of children, adolescents, and adults. *Journal of the American Academy of Child and Adolescent Psychiatry, 41, Supplement,* 26S-49S.

Greenhill, L. L., Vitiello, B., Riddle, M. A., Fisher, P., Shockey, E., March, J. S. et al. (2003b). Review of safety assessment methods used in pediatric psychopharmacology. *Journal of the American Academy of Child and Adolescent Psychiatry, 42,* 627–633.

Greenspan, S., & Love, P. F. (1997). Social intelligence and developmental disorder: Mental retardation, learning disabilities, and autism. In W. E. MacLean (Ed.), *Ellis' handbook of mental deficiency, psychological theory and research.* Mahwah, NJ: Lawrence Erlbaum.

Greenwood, C. R., et al. (1992). Out of the laboratory and into the community: 26 years of applied behavior analysis at the Juniper Gardens Children's Project. *American Psychologist, 47,* 1464–1474.

Greenwood, C. R., Hart, B., Walker, D., & Risley, T. (1994). The opportunity to respond and academic performance revisited: A behavioral theory of developmental retardation and its prevention. In R. Gardner et al. (Eds.), *Behavior analysis in education: Focus on measurably superior instruction.* Pacific Grove, CA: Brooks/Cole.

Gregory, A. M., Eley, T. C., & Plomin, R. (2004). Exploring the association between anxiety and conduct problems in a large sample of twins aged 2–4. *Journal of Abnormal Child Psychology, 32,* 111–122.

Grice, D. E., Halmi, K. A., Fichter, M. M. et al. (2002). Evidence for a susceptibility gene for anorexia nervosa on chromosome 1. *American Journal of Human Genetics, 70,* 787–792.

Grigorenko, E. L. (2001). Developmental dyslexia: An update on genes, brains, and environments. *Journal of Child Psychology and Psychiatry, 42,* 91–125.

Grigorenko, E. L., Klin, A., & Volkmar, R. (2003). Annotation: Hyperlexia: Disability or superability? *Journal of Child Psychology and Psychiatry, 44,* 1079–1091.

Grigorenko, E. L., & Lockery, D. (2002). Smart is as stupid does: Exploring bases of erroneous reasoning of smart people regarding learning and other disabilities. In R. J. Sternberg (Ed.), *Why smart people can be so stupid.* New Haven, CT: Yale University Press.

Grinder, R. E. (1967). *A history of genetic psychology.* New York: John Wiley.

Grinspoon, S., Thomas, E., Pitts, S., Gross, E., Mickley, D., Miller, K., Herzog, D., & Klibanski, A. (2000). Prevalence and predictive factors for regional osteopenia in women with anorexia nervosa. *Annals of Internal Medicine, 133,* 790–794.

Gross, A. M., & Drabman, R. S. (1990). Clinical behavioral pediatrics: An introduction. In A. M. Gross & R. S. Drabman (Eds.), *Handbook of clinical behavioral pediatrics.* New York: Plenum.

Grossman, A. W., Churchill, J. D., McKinney, B. C., Kodish, I. M., Otte, S. L., & Greenough, W. T. (2003). Experience effects on brain development: Possible contributions to psychopathology. *Journal of Child Psychology and Psychiatry, 44,* 33–63.

Grossman, H. J. (1983). *Classification in mental retardation.* Washington, DC: American Association on Mental Deficiency.

Grunbaum, J. A., Kann, L., Kinchen, S. A., Williams, B., Ross, J. G., Lowry, R., & Kolbe, L. (2002). Youth risk behavior surveillance—United States, 2001. *Surveillance Summaries,* June 28, 2002. MMWR 2002; 51(no. SS-4): 1–66.

Grusec, J. E. (1992). Social learning theory and developmental psychology: The legacies of Robert Sears and Albert Bandura. *Developmental Psychology, 28,* 776–786.

Grych, J. H., & Fincham, F. D. (1999). Children of single parents and divorce. In W. K. Silverman & T. H. Ollendick (Eds.), *Developmental issues in the clinical treatment of children.* Boston: Allyn and Bacon.

Guidubaldi, J., & Perry, J. D. (1985). Divorce and mental health sequelae for children: A two-year follow-up of a nationwide sample. *Journal of the American Academy of Child Psychiatry, 24,* 531–537.

Guillen, E. O., & Barr, S. I. (1994). Nutrition, dieting, and fitness messages in a magazine for adolescent women, 1970–1990. *Journal of Adolescent Health, 15,* 464–472.

Gullone, E. (2000). The development of normal fear: A century of research. *Clinical Psychology Review, 20,* 429–451.

Gur, R. E., Cowell, P., Turetsky, B. I., Gallacher, F., Cannon, T., Bilker, W., & Gur, R. C. (1998). A follow-up magnetic resonance imaging study of schizophrenia. *Archives of General Psychiatry, 55,* 145–152.

Guralnick, M. J. (1998). Effectiveness of early intervention for vulnerable children: A developmental perspective. *American Journal on Mental Retardation, 102,* 319–345.

Habenstein, R., & Olson, R. A. (2001). Families and children in history. In C. E. Walker & M. C. Roberts (Eds.), *Handbook of clinical child psychology* (3rd ed.). New York: John Wiley & Sons.

Habermas, T. (1992). Further evidence on early case descriptions of anorexia nervosa and bulimia nervosa. *International Journal of Eating Disorders, 11,* 351–359.

Habermas, T., & Bluck, S. (2000). Getting a life: The emergence of the life story in adolescence. *Psychological Bulletin, 126,* 748–769.

Hafner, A. J., Quast, W., & Shea, M. J. (1975). The adult adjustment of one thousand psychiatric patients: Initial findings from a twenty-five year follow-up. In R. O. Wirt, G. Winokur, & M. Roff (Eds.), *Life history in psychopathology,* Vol. 4, Minneapolis: University of Minnesota Press.

Hallahan, D. P., & Kauffman, J. M. (1978). *Exceptional children: Introduction to special education.* Englewood Cliffs, NJ: Prentice Hall.

Hallahan, D. P., & Mock, D. R. (2003). A brief history of the field of learning disabilities. In H. L. Swanson, K. R. Harris, & S. Graham (Eds.), *Handbook of learning disabilities.* New York: Guilford Press.

Halmi, K. A. (1985). Eating disorders. In H. I. Kaplan & B. J. Sadock (Eds.), *Comprehensive textbook of psychiatry* (4th ed.). Baltimore: Williams & Wilkins.

Hammen, C. (1992). Cognitive, life stress, and interpersonal approaches to a developmental psychopathology model of depression. *Development and Psychopathology, 4,* 189–206.

Hammen, C., & Brennan, P. A. (2001). Depressed adolescents of depressed and nondepressed mothers: Tests of an interpersonal impairment hypothesis. *Journal of Consulting and Clinical Psychology, 69,* 284–294.

Hammen, C., Burge, D., Burney, E., & Adrian, C. (1990). Longitudinal study of diagnosis in children of women with unipolar and bipolar affective disorders. *Archives of General Psychiatry, 47,* 1112–1117.

Hammen, C., & Rudolph, K. D. (2003). Childhood mood disorders. In E. J. Mash & R. A. Barkley (Eds.), *Child psychopathology* (2nd ed.). New York: Guilford Press.

Hammen, C., Rudolph, K., Weisz, J., Rao, U., & Burge, D. (1999). The context of depression in clinic-referred youth: Neglected areas in treatment. *Journal of the American Academy of Child and Adolescent Psychiatry, 38,* 64–71.

Hammill, D. D. (1993). A brief look at the learning disabilities movement in the United States. *Journal of Learning Disabilities, 26*, 295–310.

Handen, B. L. (1997). Mental retardation. In E. J. Mash & L. G. Terdal (Eds.), *Assessment of childhood disorders.* New York: Guilford Press.

Handen, B. L. (1998). Mental retardation. In E. J. Mash & L. G. Terdal (Eds.), *Treatment of childhood disorders.* New York: Guilford Press.

Hanish, L. D., & Guerra, N. G. (2002). A longitudinal analysis of patterns of adjustment following peer victimization. *Development and Psychopathology, 14*, 69–89.

Hankin, B. L., Abramson, L. Y., Moffitt, T. E., Silva, P. A., McGee, R., & Angell, K. E. (1998). Development of depression from preadolescence to young adulthood: Emerging gender differences in a 10-year longitudinal study. *Journal of Abnormal Psychology, 107*, 128–140.

Hankin, B. L., Fraley, R. C., Lahey, B. B., & Waldman, I. D. (2005). Is depression best viewed as a continuum or discrete category? A taxometric analysis of childhood and adolescent depression in a population-based sample. *Journal of Abnormal Psychology, 114*, 96–110.

Hanley, G. P., Iwata, B. A., & McCord, B. E. (2003). Functional analysis of problem behavior: A review. *Journal of Applied Behavior Analysis, 36*, 147–185.

Hansen, C., Weiss, D., & Last, C. G. (1999). ADHD boys in young adulthood: Psychosocial adjustment. *Journal of the American Academy of Child and Adolescent Psychiatry, 38*, 165–171.

Happé, F. G. E. (1994). Wechsler IQ profile and theory of mind in autism: A research note. *Journal of Child Psychology and Psychiatry, 35*, 1461–1471.

Happé, F. G. E. (1996). Studying weak central coherence at low levels: Children with autism do not succumb to visual illusions. *Journal of Child Psychology and Psychiatry, 37*, 873–878.

Happé, F., Briskman, J., & Frith, U. (2001). Exploring the cognitive phenotype of autism: Weak "central coherence" in parents and siblings of children with autism: I. Experimental tests. *Journal of Child Psychology and Psychiatry, 42*, 299–307.

Harbeck-Weber, C., & Peterson, L. (1996). Health-related disorders. In E. J. Mash & R. A. Barkley (Eds.), *Child psychopathology.* New York: Guilford Press.

Harcourt Assessment. (2003). *The Stanford Achievement Test, Tenth Edition.* San Antonio, TX: Harcourt Assessment.

Harding, S. (1991). *Whose knowledge? Whose science? Thinking from women's lives.* Ithaca, NY: Cornell University Press.

Harkness, S., & Super, C. M. (2000). Culture and psychopathology. In A. J. Sameroff, M. Lewis, & S. M. Miller (Eds.), *Handbook of developmental psychopathology.* New York: Kluwer/Plenum Publishers.

Harley, J. P., & Matthews, C. G. (1980). Food additives and hyperactivity in children: Experimental investigations. In R. M. Knights and D. J. Bakker (Eds.), *Treatment of hyperactive and learning disordered children.* Baltimore: University Park Press.

Harrington, R. (2001). Adolescent depression: Same or different? *Archives of General Psychiatry, 58*, 21–22.

Harrington, R., Rutter, M., Weissman, M., Fudge, H., Groothues, C., Bredenkamp, D., Pickles, A., Rende, R., & Wickramaratne, P. (1997). Psychiatric disorders in the relatives of depressed probands: I. Comparison of prepubertal, adolescent and early adult onset cases. *Journal of Affective Disorders, 42*, 9–22.

Harris, P. L. (1994). The child's understanding of emotion: Developmental change and the family environment. *Journal of Child Psychology and Psychiatry, 35*, 3–28.

Harrison, S. I., & McDermott, J. K. (1972). *Childhood psychopathology.* New York: International University Press.

Hart, B., & Risley, T. R. (1992). American parenting of language-learning children: Persisting differences in family-child interactions observed in natural home environment. *Developmental Psychology, 28*, 1096–1105.

Hart, S. N., & Brassard, M. R. (1991). Psychological maltreatment: Progress achieved. *Development and Psychopathology, 3*, 61–70.

Harter, S. (1985). *Manual for the Self-Perception Profile for Children.* Denver, CO: University of Denver.

Hartman, C. A., Willcutt, E. G., Rhee, S. H., & Pennington, B. F. (2004). The relation between sluggish cognitive tempo and DSM-IV ADHD. *Journal of Abnormal Child Psychology, 32*, 491–503.

Hartman, R. R., Stage, S. A., & Webster-Stratton, C. (2003). A growth curve analysis of parent training outcomes: Examining the influence of child risk factors (inattention, impulsivity, and hyperactivity problems), parental and family risk factors. *Journal of Child Psychology and Psychiatry, 44*, 388–398.

Hartung, C. M., & Widiger, T. A. (1998). Gender differences in the diagnosis of mental disorders: Conclusions and controversies of the DSM-IV. *Psychological Bulletin, 123*, 260–278.

Hartup, W. W. (1970). Peer interaction and social organization. In P. H. Mussen (Ed.), *Carmicheal's manual of child psychology.* New York: Wiley.

Hartup, W. W. (1996). The company they keep: Friendships and their developmental significance. *Child Development, 67*, 1–13.

Harvey, E. (1999). Short-term and long-term effects of early parental employment on children of the National Longitudinal Survey of Youth. *Developmental Psychology, 35*, 445–459.

Harwood, T. M., & Beutler, L. E. (2001). Commentary on Greene and Ablon: What does the MTA study tell us about effective psychosocial treatment for ADHD? *Journal of Clinical Child Psychology, 30*, 141–143.

Hatcher, P. J., Hulme, C., & Snowling, M. J. (2004). Explicit phoneme training combined with phonic reading instruction helps young children at risk of reading failure. *Journal of Child Psychology and Psychiatry, 45*, 338–359.

Hathaway, W., Dooling-Litfin, J. D., & Edwards, G. (1998). Integrating the results of an evaluation: Eight clinical cases. In R. A. Barkley (Ed.), *Attention-deficit hyperactivity disorder.* New York: Guilford Press.

Hawker, D. S. J., & Boulton, M. J. (2000). Twenty years' research on peer victimization and psychosocial maladjustment: A meta-analytic review of cross-sectional studies. *Journal of Child Psychology and Psychiatry, 41*, 441–455.

Hawkins, B. A., Eklund, S. J., James, D. R., & Foose, A. K. (2003). Adaptive behavior and cognitive function of adults with Down syndrome: Modeling change with age. *Mental Retardation, 41*, 7–28.

Hawkins, E. H., Cummins, L. H., & Marlatt, G. A. (2004). Preventing substance abuse in American Indians and Alaska Native youths: Promising strategies for healthier communities. *Psychological Bulletin, 130*, 304–323.

Hay, D. F., Pawlby, S., Sharp, D., Schmucker, G., Mills, A., Allen, H., & Kumar, R. (1999). Parents' judgements about young children's problems: Why mothers and fathers might disagree yet still predict later outcomes. *Journal of Child Psychology and Psychiatry, 40*, 1249–1258.

Hay, D. F., Payne, A., & Chadwick, A. (2004). Peer relations in childhood. *Journal of Child Psychology and Psychiatry, 45*, 84–108.

Hays, S. C. (1998). Single case experimental design and empirical clinic practice. In A. E. Kazdin (Ed.), *Methodological issues & strategies in clinical research*. Washington, DC: American Psychological Association.

Hayward, C., Wilson, K. A., Lagle, K., Killen, J. D., & Taylor, C. B. (2004). Parent-reported predictors of adolescent panic attacks. *Journal of the American Academy of Child and Adolescent Psychiatry, 43*, 613–620.

Head Start. (2004). Head Start Statistical Fact Sheet, 2004. Head Start Bureau, U.S. Department of Human Services, Administration for Children and Families. Retrieved September 30, 2004, from www.2.acf.dhhs.gov/programs/hsb.

Heaton, P., & Wallace, G. L. (2004). Annotation: The savant syndrome. *Journal of Child Psychology and Psychiatry, 45*, 899–911.

Heavey, C. L., Adelman, H. S., Nelson, P., & Smith, D. C. (1989). Learning problems, anger, preceived control, and misbehavior. *Journal of Learning Disabilities, 22*, 47–50.

Heavey, L., Phillips, W., Baron-Cohen, S., & Rutter, M. (2000). The Awkward Moments Test: A naturalistic measure of social understanding in autism. *Journal of Autism and Developmental Disorders, 30*, 225–236.

Hechtman, L. (1991). Developmental, neurobiological, and psychosocial aspects of hyperactivity, impulsivity, and inattention. In M. Lewis (Ed.), *Child and adolescent psychiatry: A comprehensive textbook*. Baltimore: Williams & Wilkins.

Hechtman, L., Abikoff, H., Klein, R. G., Weiss, G., Respitz, C., Kouri, J. et al. (2004). Academic achievement and emotional status of children with ADHD treated with long-term methylphenidate and multimodal psychosocial treatment. *Journal of the American Academy of Child and Adolescent Psychiatry, 43*, 812–819.

Helff, C. M., & Glidden, L. M. (1998). More positive or less negative? Trends in research on adjustment of families rearing children with developmental disabilities. *Mental Retardation, 36*, 457–464.

Helgeson, V. S., Janicki, D., Lerner, J., & Barbarin, O. (2003). Adjustment to juvenile rheumatoid arthritis: A family systems perspective. *Journal of Pediatric Psychology, 28*, 347–353.

Hellander, M., Sisson, D. P., & Fristad, M. A. (2003). Internet support for parents of children with early-onset bipolar disorder. In B. Geller & M. P. DelBello (Eds.), *Bipolar disorder in childhood and early adolescence*. New York: Guilford Press.

Heller, K. (1996). Coming of age of prevention science: Comments on the 1994 National Institute of Mental Health–Institute of Medicine prevention reports. *American Psychologist, 51*, 1123–1127.

Henderson, K. E., & Brownell, K. D. (2004). The toxic environment and obesity: Contribution and cure. In J. K. Thompson (Ed.), *Handbook of eating disorders and obesity*. Hoboken, NJ: John Wiley.

Hendry, C. N. (2000). Childhood disintegrative disorder: Should it be considered a distinct disorder? *Clinical Psychology Review, 20*, 77–90.

Henggeler, S. W., & Lee, T. (2003). Multisystemic treatment of serious clinical problems. In A. E. Kazdin & J. R. Weisz (Eds.), *Evidence-based psychotherapies for children and adolescents*. New York: Guilford Press.

Henggeler, S. W., Melton, G. B., & Smith, L. A. (1992). Family preservation using multisystemic therapy: An effective alternative to incarcerating serious juvenile offenders. *Journal of Consulting and Clinical Psychology, 60*, 953–961.

Henggeler, S. W., Rowland, M., Halliday-Boykins, C., Sheidow, A., Ward, D. M., Randall, J. et al. (2003). One-year follow-up of multisystemic therapy as an alternative to the hospitalization of youths with psychiatric crisis. *Journal of the American Academy of Child and Adolescent Psychiatry, 42*, 543–551.

Henggeler, S. W., Schoenwald, S. K., Borduin, C. M., Rowland, M. D., & Cunningham, P. B. (1998). *Multisystemic treatment of antisocial behavior in children and adolescents*. New York: Guilford Press.

Henin, A., & Kendall, P. C. (1997). Obsessive-compulsive disorder in childhood and adolescence. In T. H. Ollendick & R. J. Prinz (Eds.), *Advances in clinical child psychology* (Vol. 19). New York: Plenum Press.

Hernandez, D. J. (1994). Children's changing access to resources: A historical perspective. *Social Policy Report: Society for Research in Child Development, 8(1)*, 1–23.

Herrenkohl, T. I., Hawkins, J. D., Chung, I. J., Hill, K. G., & Battin-Pearson, S. (2001). School and community risk factors and interventions. In R. Loeber & D. P. Farrington (Eds.), *Child delinquents: Development, interventions, and service needs*. Thousand Oaks, CA: Sage.

Hetherington, E. M., Bridges, M., Insabella, G. (1998). What matters? What does not? Five perspectives on the association between marital transitions and children's adjustment. *American Psychologist, 53*, 167–184.

Hetherington, E. M., & Kelly, J. (2002). *For better or worse: Divorce reconsidered*. New York: W. W. Norton & Company.

Hetherington, E. M., & Stanley-Hagan, M. (1999). The adjustment of children with divorced parents: A risk and resiliency perspective. *Journal of Child Psychology and Psychiatry, 40*, 129–140.

Hewitt, J. K., Silberg, J. L., Rutter, M., Simonoff, E., Meyer, J. M., Maes, H., Pickles, A., Neale, M. C., Loeber, R., Erickson, M. T., Kendler, K. S., Heath, A. C., Truett, K. R., Reynolds, C. A., & Eaves, L. J. (1997). Genetics and developmental psychopathology: 1. Phenotypic assessment in the Virginia Twin Study of Adolescent Behavioral Development. *Journal of Child Psychology and Psychiatry, 38*, 943–963.

Hicks, C. L., von Baeyer, C. L., Spafford, P. A., van Korlaar, I., & Goodenough, B. (2001). The Faces Pain Scale—Revised: Toward a common metric in pediatric pain measurement. *Pain, 93*, 173–183.

Higgins, E. L., Raskind, M. H., Goldberg, R. J., & Herman, K. L. (2002). Stages of acceptance of a learning disability: The impact of labeling. *Learning Disability Quarterly, 25*, 3–17.

Hightower, A. D. (1997). Primary Mental Health Project. In G. W. Albee & T. P. Gullotta (Eds.), *Primary prevention works*. Thousand Oaks, CA: Sage Publications.

Hightower, A. D., Cowen, E. L., Spinell, A. P., Lotyczewski, B. S., Guare, J. C., Rohrbeck, C. A., & Brown, L. P. (1987). The Child Rating Scale: The development and psychometric refinement of a socioemotional self-rating scale for young children. *School Psychology Review, 16*, 239–255.

Hilden, J. M., Emanuel, E. J., Fairclough, D. L., Link, M. P., Foley, K. M., Clarridge, B. C. et al. (2001). Attitudes and practices among pediatric oncologists regarding end-of-life care: Results of the 1998 American Society of Clinical Oncology survey. *Journal of Clinical Oncology, 19*, 205–212.

Hill, J. (2002). Biological, psychological, and social processes in the conduct disorders. *Journal of Child Psychology and Psychiatry, 43*, 133–164.

Hinshaw, S. P. (1998). Is ADHD an impairing condition in childhood and adolescence? Chapter prepared for NIH Consensus Development Conference on Attention-Deficit Hyperactivity Disorder (ADHD): Diagnosis and Treatment. Bethesda, MD.

Hinshaw, S. P. (2001, Winter). Is the inattentive type of ADHD a separate disorder? *Clinical Psychology: Science and Practice, 8*, 498–501.

Hinshaw, S. P. (2002). Prevention/intervention trials and developmental theory: Commentary on the Fast Track special section. *Journal of Abnormal Child Psychology, 30*, 53–60.

Hinshaw, S. P. (2002a). Intervention research, theoretical mechanisms, and causal processes related to externalizing behavior patterns. *Development and Psychopathology, 14*, 789–818.

Hinshaw, S. P. (2002b). Preadolescent girls with attention-deficit/hyperactivity disorder: I. Background characteristics, comorbidity, cognitive and social functioning, and parenting practices. *Journal of Consulting and Clinical Psychology, 70*, 1086–1098.

Hinshaw, S. P., Carte, E. T., Sami, N., Treuting, J. J., & Zupan, B. A. (2002). Preadolescent girls with attention-deficit/hyperactivity disorder: II. Neuropsychological performance in relation to subtypes and individual classification. *Journal of Consulting and Clinical Psychology, 70*, 1099–1111.

Hinshaw, S. P., & Erhardt, D. (1993). Behavioral treatment. In V. B. Van Hasselt & M. Hersen (Ed.), *Handbook of behavior therapy and pharmacotherapy for children: A comparative analysis.* Boston: Allyn and Bacon.

Hinshaw, S. P., Hanker, B., Whalen, C. K., Erhardt, D., & Dunnington, R. E. (1989). Aggressive, prosocial, and nonsocial behavior in hyperactive boys: Dose effects of methylphenidate in naturalistic settings. *Journal of Consulting and Clinical Psychology, 57*, 636–643.

Hinshaw, S. P., Lahey, B. B., & Hart, E. L. (1993). Issues of taxonomy and comorbidity in the development of conduct disorder. *Development and Psychopathology, 5*, 31–49.

Hinshaw, S. P., & Lee, S. S. (2003). Conduct and oppositional defiant disorders. In E. J. Mash & R. A. Barkley (Eds.), *Child psychopathology* (2nd ed.). New York: Guilford Press.

Hinshelwood, J. (1917). *Congenital word-blindness.* London: H. K. Lewis.

Hirshfeld-Becker, D. R., Biederman, J., & Rosenbaum, J. F. (2004). Behavioral inhibition. In T. L. Morris & J. S. March (Eds.), *Anxiety disorders in children and adolescents.* New York: Guilford Press.

Hoagwood, K. (2003). Ethical issues in child and adolescent psychosocial treatment research. In A. E. Kazdin & J. R. Weisz (Eds.), *Evidence-based psychotherapies for children and adolescents.* New York: Guilford Press.

Hoagwood, K., & Johnson, J. (2003). School psychology: A public health framework I. From evidence-based practices to evidence-based policies. *Journal of School Psychology, 41*, 3–21.

Hoagwood, K., Kelleher, K. J., Feil, M., & Comer, D. M. (2000). Treatment services for children with ADHD: A national perspective. *Journal of the American Academy of Child and Adolescent Psychiatry, 39*, 198–206.

Hobbs, N. (1975). *The futures of children.* San Francisco: Jossey-Bass.

Hobbs, T., & Westling, D. L. (1998). Promoting successful inclusion through collaborative problem-solving. *Teaching Exceptional Children, 31*, 12–19.

Hockfield, S., & Lombroso, P. J. (1998). Development of the cerebral cortex: IX. Cortical development and experience: I. *Journal of the American Academy of Child and Adolescent Psychiatry, 37*, 992–993.

Hocutt, A. M. (1996). Effectiveness of special education: Is placement the critical factor? *The Future of Children, 6*, 77–102.

Hodapp, R. M. (1998). *Development and disabilities.* Cambridge, UK: Cambridge University Press.

Hodapp, R. M., Burack, J. A., & Zigler, E. (1990). Summing up and going forward: New directions in the developmental approach to mental retardation. In R. M. Hodapp, J. A. Burack, & E. Zigler (Eds.), *Issues in the developmental approach to mental retardation.* New York: Cambridge University Press.

Hodapp, R. M., & Dykens, E. M. (2003). Mental retardation (Intellectual disabilities). In E. J. Mash & R. A. Barkley (Eds.), *Child psychopathology.* New York: Guilford Press.

Hodapp, R. M., & Zigler, E. (1997). New issues in the developmental approach to mental retardation. In W. E. MacLean (Ed.), *Ellis' handbook of mental deficiency, psychological theory and research.* Mahwah, NJ: Lawrence Erlbaum.

Hodges, K. (1994). Evaluation of depression in children and adolescents using diagnostic clinical interviews. In W. M. Reynolds and H. F. Johnston (Eds.), *Handbook of depression in children and adolescents.* New York: Plenum Press.

Hoffman, L. W. (1989). Effects of maternal employment in the two-parent family. *American Psychologist, 44*, 283–292.

Hogan, D. M. (1998). The psychological development and welfare of children of opiate and cocaine users: Review and research needs. *Journal of Child Psychology and Psychiatry, 39*, 609–620.

Hoge, C. W., & Pavlin, J. A. (2002). Psychological sequelae of September 11. *New England Journal of Medicine, 347*, 443.

Hohnen, B., & Stevenson, J. (1999). The structure of genetic influences on general cognitive, language, phonological, and reading abilities. *Developmental Psychology, 35*, 590–603.

Holden, E. W., Deichmann, M. M., & Levy, J. D. (1999). Empirically supported treatment in pediatric psychology: Recurrent pediatric headache. *Journal of Pediatric Psychology, 24*, 91–109.

Hollis, C. (2000). Adult outcomes of child- and adolescent-onset schizophrenia: Diagnostic stability and predictive validity. *American Journal of Psychiatry, 157*, 1652–1659.

Hollis, C. (2002). Schizophrenia and allied disorders. In M. Rutter & E. Taylor (Eds.), *Child and adolescent psychiatry.* Oxford, UK: Blackwell Publishing.

Hoover, H. D., Dunbar, S. B., & Frisbie, D. A. (2001). *The Iowa Tests of Basic Skills, Form A*. Itasca, IL: Riverside Publishing.

Holmes, L. B. (1978). Genetic counseling for the older pregnant woman: New data and questions. *New England Journal of Medicine, 298*, 1419–1421.

Holtzman, W. H. (1997). Community psychology in full-service schools in different cultures. *American Psychologist, 52*, 381–389.

Hops, H. (1995). Age- and gender-specific effects of parental depression: A commentary. *Developmental Psychology, 31*, 428–431.

Hops, H., Andrews, J. A., Duncan, S. C., Duncan, T. E., & Tildesley, E. (2000). Adolescent drug use development: A social interactional and contextual perspective. In A. J. Sameroff, M. Lewis, & S. M. Miller (Eds.), *Handbook of developmental psychopathology* (2nd ed.). New York: Kluwer Academic/Plenum Publishers.

Hops, H., Biglan, A., Sherman, L., Arthur, J., Friedman, L., & Osteen, V. (1987). Home observations of family interactions of depressed women. *Journal of Consulting and Clinical Psychology, 55*, 341–346.

Hops, H., Davis, B., & Longoria, N. (1995). Methodological issues in direct observation: Illustrations with the Living in Familial Environments (LIFE) coding system. *Journal of Clinical Child Psychology, 24*, 193–203.

Horne, J. (1992). Sleep and its disorders in children. *Journal of Child Psychology and Psychiatry, 33*, 473–487.

Horowitz, F. D. (1992). John B. Watson's legacy: Learning and environment. *Developmental Psychology, 28*, 360–367.

Horowitz, F. D. (2000). Child development and the PITS: Simple question, complex answers, and developmental theory. *Child Development, 71*, 1–10.

Houts, A. C. (2002). Discovery, invention, and the expansion of the modern Diagnostic and Statistical Manual of Mental Disorders. In L. E. Beutler & M. L. Malik (Eds.), *Rethinking the DSM*. Washington, DC: American Psychological Association.

Houts, A. C. (2003). Behavioral treatment of enuresis. In A. E. Kazdin & J. R. Weisz (Eds.), *Evidence-based psychotherapies for children and adolescents*. New York: Guilford Press.

Houts, A. C., Liebert, R. M., & Padawar, W. (1983). A delivery system for the treatment of primary enuresis. *Journal of Abnormal Child Psychology, 11*, 513–520.

Houts, A. C., Peterson, J. K., & Whelan, J. P. (1986). Prevention of relapse in full-spectrum home training for primary enuresis: A component analysis. *Behavior Therapy, 17*, 462–469.

Howard, M., & Hodes, M. (2000). Psychopathology, adversity, and service utilization of young refugees. *Journal of the American Academy of Child and Adolescent Psychiatry, 39*, 368–377.

Howlin, P. (1994). Special education treatment. In M. Rutter, E. Taylor, & L. Hersov (Eds.), *Child and adolescent psychiatry: Modern approaches*. Cambridge, MA: Blackwell Scientific.

Howlin, P., Goode, S., Hutton, J., & Rutter, M. (2004). Adult outcome for children with autism. *Journal of Child Psychology and Psychiatry, 45*, 212–229.

Hoza, B., Gerdes, A. C., Hinshaw, S. P., Arnold, L. E., Pelham, W. E., Molina, B. S. G. et al. (2004). Self-perceptions of confidence in children with ADHD and comparison children. *Journal of Consulting and Clinical Psychology, 72*, 382–391.

Huang-Pollock, C. L., & Nigg, J. T. (2003). Searching for the attention deficit in attention deficit hyperactivity disorder: The case of visuospatial orienting. *Clinical Psychology Review, 23*, 801–830.

Hudson, J. L., & Rapee, M. (2001). Parent-child interactions and anxiety disorders: An observational study. *Behaviour Research and Therapy, 39*, 1411–1427.

Hudson, J. L., & Rapee, M. (2002). Parent-child interactions in clinically anxious children and their siblings. *Journal of Clinical Child and Adolescent Psychology, 31*, 548–555.

Hudziak, J. J., Heath, A. C., Madden, P. F., Reich, W., Bucholz, K. K., Slutske, W., Bierut, L. J., Neuman, R. J., & Todd, R. D. (1998). Latent class and factor analysis of DSM-IV ADHD: A twin study of female adolescents. *Journal of the American Academy of Child and Adolescent Psychiatry, 37*, 848–857.

Huesmann, L. R., Eron, L. D., Lefkowitz, M. M., & Walder, L. O. (1984). Stability of aggression over time and generations. *Developmental Psychology, 20*, 1120–1134.

Hughes, C. (1999). Identifying critical social interaction behaviors among high school students with and without disabilities. *Behavior Modification, 23*, 41–60.

Hughes, C., & Graham, A. (2002). Measuring executive functions in childhood: Problems and solutions. *Child and Adolescent Mental Health, 7*, 131–142.

Huizinga, D., Loeber, R., & Thornberry, T. P. (1993). Longitudinal study of delinquency, drug abuse, sexual activity, and pregnancy among children and youth in three cities. *Public Health Reports, 108 (suppl. 1)*, 90–96.

Huizink, A. C., Mulder, E. J. H., & Buitelaar, J. K. (2004). Prenatal stress and risk for psychopathology: Special effects or induction of general susceptibility? *Psychological Bulletin, 130*, 115–142.

Huizink, A. C., Robles de Medina, P. G., Mulder, E. J. H., Visser, G. H. A., & Buitelaar, J. K. (2003). Stress during pregnancy is associated with developmental outcome in infancy. *Journal of Child Psychology and Psychiatry, 44*, 810–818.

Humphreys, L., Forehand, R., McMahon, R., & Roberts, M. (1978). Parent behavorial training to modify child noncompliance: Effects on untreated siblings. *Journal of Behavior Therapy and Experimental Psychiatry, 9*, 235–238.

Huntington's Disease Collaborative Research Group (1993). A novel gene containing a trinucleotide repeat that is expanded and unstable on Huntington's disease chromsomes. *Cell, 72*, 971–983.

Huse, D. M., Branes, L. A., Colligan, R. C., Nelson, R. A., & Palumbo, P. J. (1982). The challenge of obesity in childhood: I. Incidence, prevalence, and staging. *Mayo Clinic Proceedings, 57*, 279–284.

Hynd, G. W., Marshall, R., & Gonzalez, J. (1991). Learning disabilities and presumed central nervous system dysfunction. *Learning Disability Quarterly, 14*, 283–296.

Hynd, G. W., & Semrud-Clikeman, M. (1989a). Dyslexia and brain morphology. *Psychological Bulletin, 106*, 447–482.

Hynd, G. W., & Semrud-Clikeman, M. (1989b). Dyslexia and neurodevelopmental pathology: Relationships to cognition, intelligence, and reading skill acquisition. *Journal of Learning Disabilities, 22*, 205–218.

Iannotti, R. J., & Bush, P. J. (1993). Toward a developmental theory of compliance. In N. A. Krasnegor, L. Epstein, S. B. Johnson, &

S. Yaffe (Eds.), *Developmental aspects of health compliance behavior.* Hillsdale, NJ: Lawrence Erlbaum Associates.

Ievers, C. E., Brown, R. T., Drotar, D., Caplan, D., Pishevar, B. S., & Lambert, R. G. (1999). Knowledge of physician prescriptions and adherence to treatment among children with cystic fibrosis and their mothers. *Journal of Developmental and Behavioral Pediatrics, 20,* 335–343.

Institute of Medicine. 2004. *Immunization Safety Review: Vaccines and Autism (2004). A report of the Institute of Medicine.* Washington, DC: National Academies Press.

Ishikawa, S. S., & Raine, A. (2003). Prefrontal deficits and antisocial behavior: A causal model. In B. B. Lahey, T. E. Moffitt, A. Caspi (Eds.), *Causes of conduct disorder and juvenile delinquency.* New York: Guilford Press.

Israel, A. C. (1988). Parental and family influences in the etiology and treatment of childhood obesity. In N. A. Krasnegor, G. D. Grave, & N. Kretchmer (Eds.), *Childhood obesity: A biobehavioral perspective.* Caldwell, NJ: The Telford Press.

Israel, A. C. (1990). Childhood obesity. In A. S. Bellack, M. Hersen, & A. E. Kazdin (Eds.), *International handbook of behavoir modification and therapy.* New York: Plenum.

Israel, A. C. (1999). Commentary: Empirically supported treatments for pediatric obesity: Goals, outcome criteria, and the societal context. *Journal of Pediatric Psychology, 24,* 249–250.

Israel, A. C., Guile, C. A., Baker, J. E., & Silverman, W. K. (1994). An evaluation of enhanced self-regulation training in the treatment of childhood obesity. *Journal of Pediatric Psychology, 19,* 737–749.

Israel, A. C., & Ivanova, M. Y. (2002). Global and dimensional self-esteem in preadolescent and early adolescent children who are overweight: Age and gender differences. *International Journal of Eating Disorders, 31,* 424–429.

Israel, A. C., Pravder, M. D., & Knights, S. (1980). A peer-administered program for changing the classroom behavior of disruptive children. *Behavioural Analysis and Modification, 4,* 224–238.

Israel, A. C., & Shapiro, L. S. (1985). Behavior problems of obese children enrolling in a weight reduction program. *Journal of Pediatric Psychology, 10,* 449–460.

Israel, A. C., Silverman, W. K., & Solotar, L. C. (1986). An investigation of family influences on initial weight status, attrition, and treatment outcome in a childhood obesity program. *Behavior Therapy, 17,* 131–143.

Israel, A. C., & Solotar, L. C. (1988). Obesity. In M. Hersen & C. G. Last (Eds.), *Child behavior therapy casebook.* New York: Plenum.

Israel, A. C., Stolmaker, L., & Andrian, C. A. G. (1985). The effects of training parents in general child management skills in a behavioral weight loss program for children. *Behavior Therapy, 16,* 169–180.

Israel, A. C., & Zimand, E. (1989). Obestiy. In M. Hersen (Ed.), *Innovations in child behavior therapy.* New York: Springer.

Ivanova, M. Y. (1998). *Dysregulation of the hypothalamic-pituitary-adrenocortical system in childhood and adolescent major depression: Evidence for biological correlates?* Unpublished manuscript, University at Albany, State University of New York, Psychology Department.

Izard, C. E., Fine, S., Mostow, A., Trentacosta, C., & Campbell, J. (2002). Emotion processes in normal and abnormal development and prevention intervention. *Development and Psychopathology, 14,* 761–787.

Jacob, R. G., & Pelham, W. H. (2000). Behavior therapy. In B. J. Sadock & V. A. Sadock (Eds.), *Kaplan & Sadock's Comprehensive textbook of psychiatry* (Vol. II). Philadelphia: Lippincott Williams & Wilkins.

Jacobsen, L. K., & Rapoport, J. L. (1998). Research update: Childhood-onset schizophrenia: Implications of clinical and neurobiological research. *Journal of Child Psychology and Psychiatry, 39,* 101–113.

Jackson, D. A., & King, A. R. (2004). Gender differences in the effects of oppositional behavior on teacher ratings of ADHD symptoms. *Journal of Abnormal Child Psychology, 32,* 215–224.

Jaffee, P. G., Poisson, S. E., & Cunningham, A. (2001). Domestic violence and high-conflict divorce: Developing a new generation of research for children. In S. A. Graham-Bermann & J. L. Edleson (Eds.), *Domestic violence in the lives of children: The future of research, intervention, and social policy.* Washington, DC: American Psychological Association.

Jaffee, S. R., Caspi, A., Moffitt, T. E., & Taylor, A. (2004). Physical maltreatment victim to antisocial child: Evidence of an environmentally mediated process. *Journal of Abnormal Psychology, 113,* 44–55.

Jaffee, S. R., Moffitt, T. E., Caspi, A., & Taylor, A. (2003). Life with (or without) father: The benefits of living with two biological parents depend on the father's antisocial behavior. *Child Development, 74,* 109–126.

James, A. C. D., & Javaloyes, A. M. (2001). The treatment of bipolar disorder in children and adolescents. *Journal of Child Psychology and Psychiatry, 42,* 439–449.

Jarbin, H., Ott, Y., & von Knorring, A-L. (2003). Adult outcome of social function in adolescent-onset schizophrenia and affective psychosis. *Journal of the American Academy of Child and Adolescent Psychiatry, 42,* 176–183.

Jay, S. M. (1988). Invasive medical procedures: Psychological intervention and assessment. In D. K. Routh (Ed.), *Handbook of pediatric psychology.* New York: Guilford.

Jay, S. M., Elliott, C. H., Fitzgibbons, I., Woody, P., & Siegel, S. (1995). A comparative study of cognitive behavioral therapy versus general anesthesia for painful medical procedures in children. *Pain, 62,* 3–9.

Jay, S. M., Elliot, C. H., Katz, E., & Siegel, S. E. (1987). Cognitive behavioral and pharmacologic intervention for children's distress during painful medical procedures. *Journal of Consulting and Clinical Psychology, 55,* 860–865.

Jay, S. M., Elliot, C. H., Ozolins, M., Olson, R., & Pruitt, S. (1985). Behavioral management of children's distress during painful medical procedures. *Behavior Research and Therapy, 23,* 513–520.

Jay, S. M., Elliot, C. H., Woody, P. D., & Siegel, S. (1991). An investigation of cognitive-behavioral therapy combined with oral valium for children undergoing painful medical procedures. *Health Psychology, 10,* 317–322.

Jaycox, L. H., Reivich, K. J., Gillham, J. E., & Seligman, M. E. P. (1994). Prevention of depressive symptoms in school children. *Behaviour Research and Therapy, 32,* 801–816.

Jelalian, E., & Mehlenbeck, R. (2003). Pediatric obesity. In M. C. Roberts (Ed.), *Handbook of pediatric psychology* (3rd ed.). New York: Guilford Press.

Jelalian, E., & Saelens, B. E. (1999). Empirically supported treatments in pediatric psychology: Pediatric obesity. *Journal of Pediatric Psychology, 24*, 223–248.

Jenkins, J. M., Rasbash, J., & O'Connor, T. G. (2003). The role of the shared family context in differential parenting. *Developmental Psychology, 39*, 99–113.

Jensen, P. S. (2000). Commentary: The NIH ADHD consensus statement: Win, lose, or draw? *Journal of the American Academy of Child and Adolescent Psychiatry, 39*, 194–197.

Jensen, P. S., Bhatara, V. S., Vitiello, B., Hoagwood, K., Feil, M., & Burke, L. B. (1999). Psychoactive medication prescribing practices for U.S. children: Gaps between research and clinical practice. *Journal of the American Academy of Child and Adolescent Psychiatry, 38*, 557–565.

Jensen, P. S., Martin, B. A., & Cantwell, D. P. (1997). Co-morbidity in ADHD: Implications for research, practice, and DSM-IV. *Journal of the Academy of Child and Adolescent Psychiatry, 36*, 1065–1075.

Jensen, P. S., & Shaw, J. (1993). Children as victims of war: Current knowledge and future research needs. *Journal of the American Academy of Child and Adolescent Psychiatry, 32*, 697–708.

Jersild, A. T., & Holmes, F. B. (1935). Children's fears. *Child Development Monograph*, No. 20.

Jessor, R., & Jessor, S. L. (1977). *Problem behavior and psychosocial development*. New York: Academic Press.

Jockin, V., McGue, M., & Lykken, D. T. (1996). Personality and divorce: A genetic analysis. *Journal of Personality and Social Psychology, 71*, 288–299.

Johnson, C. J., & Beitchman, J. H. (2000a). Expressive language disorder. In B. J. Sadock & V. A. Sadock (Eds.), *Comprehensive textbook of psychiatry* (Vol. II). Philadelphia: Lippincott Williams & Wilkins.

Johnson, C. J., & Beitchman, J. H. (2000b). Mixed receptive-expressive language disorder. In B. J. Sadock & V. A. Sadock (Eds.), *Comprehensive textbook of psychiatry* (Vol. II). Philadelphia: Lippincott Williams & Wilkins.

Johnson, D. R., Stodden, R. A., Emanuel, E. J., & Mack, M. (2002). Current challenges facing secondary education and transition services: What research tells us. *Exceptional Children, 68*, 519–531.

Johnson, G. R., Krug, E. G., & Potter, L. B. (2000). Suicide among adolescents and young adults: A cross-national comparison of 34 countries. *Suicide and Life-Threatening Behavior, 30*, 74–82.

Johnson, J. H., Rasbury, W. C., & Siegel, L. J. (1997). *Approaches to child treatment: Introduction to theory, research, and practice* (2nd ed.). Boston: Allyn and Bacon.

Johnson, M. H. (2000). Functional brain development in infants: Elements of an interactive specialization framework. *Child Development, 71*, 75–81.

Johnson, S. B. (1993). Chronic diseases of childhood: Assessing compliance with complex medical regimens. In N. A. Krasnegor, L. Epstein, S. B. Johnson, & S. Yaffe (Eds.), *Developmental aspects of health compliance behavior*. Hillsdale, NJ: Lawrence Erlbaum Associates.

Johnson, S. B. (1995). Managing insulin-dependent diabetes mellitus in adolescence: A developmental perspective. In J. Wallander & L. Siegel (Eds.), *Adolescent health problems: Behavioral perspectives*. New York: Guilford Press.

Johnson, S. B. (1998). Juvenile diabetes. In T. H. Ollendick & M. Hersen (Eds.), *Handbook of child psychopathology* (3rd ed.). New York: Plenum Press.

Johnson, S. B., & Rodrigue, J. R. (1997). Health-related disorders. In E. J. Mash & L. G. Terdal (Eds.), *Assessment of childhood disorders* (3rd ed.). New York: Guilford Press.

Johnson, W., Bouchard, T. J., Krueger, R. F., McGue, M., & Gottesman, I. I. (2004). Just one *g*: Consistent results from three test batteries. *Intelligence, 32*, 95–107.

Johnston, C., & Mash, E. J. (2001). Families of children with attention deficit/hyperactivity disorder: Review and recommendations for future research. *Clinical Child and Family Psychology Review, 4*, 183–207.

Johnston, C., & Ohan, J. L. (1999). Externalizing disorders. In W. K. Silverman & T. H. Ollendick (Eds.), *Developmental issues in the clinical treatment of children*. Boston: Allyn and Bacon.

Johnston, L. D., O'Malley, P. M., & Bachman, J. G. (2003). *Monitoring the future national results on adolescent drug use: Overview of key findings, 2002*. (NIH Publication No. 03–5374). Bethesda, MD: National Institute on Drug Abuse.

Joiner, T. E. (2000). A test of hopelessness theory of depression in youth psychiatric inpatients. *Journal of Clinical Child Psychology, 29*, 167–176.

Jones, M. C. (1924). A laboratory study of fear: The case of Peter. *Pedagogical Seminary, 31*, 308–315.

Jopp, D. A., & Keys, C. B. (2001). Diagnostic overshadowing reviewed and reconsidered. *American Journal on Mental Retardation, 106*, 416–433.

Jordan, N. C., Hanich, L. B., & Kaplan, D. (2003). A longitudinal study of mathematical competencies in children with specific mathematical difficulties versus children with comorbid mathematics and reading difficulties. *Child Development, 74*, 834–850.

Joseph, R. M., Tager-Flüsberg, H., & Lord, C. (2002). Cognitive profiles and social-communicative functioning in children with autism spectrum disorder. *Journal of Child Psychology and Psychiatry, 43*, 807–821.

Jouriles, E. N., Murphy, C. M., & O'Leary, K. D. (1989). Interspousal aggression, marital discord, and child problems. *Journal of Consulting and Clinical Psychology, 57*, 453–455.

Kagan, J. (1997). Temperament and the reactions to unfamiliarity. *Child Development, 68*, 139–143.

Kagan, J. (2003). Biology, context, and developmental inquiry. *Annual Review of Psychology, 54*, 1–23.

Kagan, J., Reznick, J. S., & Snidman, N. (1990). The temperamental qualities of inhibition and lack of inhibition. In M. Lewis & S. M. Miller (Eds.), *Handbook of developmental psychopathology*. New York: Plenum Press.

Kagan, J., & Snidman, N. (1999). Early childhood predictors of adult anxiety disorders. *Journal of Biological Psychiatry, 46*, 1536–1541.

Kalff, A. C., de Sonneville, L. M. J., Hurks. P. P. M., Hendriksen, J. G. M., Kroes, M., Feron, F. J. M. et al. (2003). Low- and high-level controlled processing in executive motor control tasks in

5–6-year-old children at risk for ADHD. *Journal of Child Psychology and Psychiatry, 44,* 1049–1057.

Kamin, L. J. (1974). *The science and politics of IQ.* Potomac, MD: Erlbaum.

Kaminsky, L., & Dewey, D. (2002). Psychosocial adjustment in siblings of children with autism. *Journal of Child Psychology and Psychiatry, 43,* 225–232.

Kamphaus, R. W. (1993). *Clinical assessment of children's intelligence.* Boston: Allyn & Bacon.

Kamphaus, R. W., & Frick, P. J. (1996). *Clinical assessment of child and adolescent personality and behavior.* Boston: Allyn and Bacon.

Kandel, D. B. (1982). Epidemiological and psycho-social perspectives on adolescent drug use. *Journal of the American Academy of Child Psychiatry, 21,* 328–347.

Kandel, D., & Yamaguchi, K. (1993). From beer to crack: Developmental patterns of drug involvement. *American Journal of Public Health, 83,* 851–855.

Kanner, L. (1943). Autistic disturbances of affective contact, *Nervous Child, 2,* 217–250.

Kanner, L. (1972). *Child psychiatry* (4th ed.). Springfield, IL: Chas. C. Thomas.

Kanner, L. (1973). *Childhood psychoses: Initial studies and new insights.* Washington, DC: V. H. Winston & Sons.

Kanner, L., & Eisenberg, L. (1956). Early infantile autism, 1943–1955. *American Journal of Orthopsychiatry, 26,* 55–65.

Kaplan, R. M. (1985). The controversy related to the use of psychological tests. In B. Wolman (Ed.), *Handbook of intelligence.* New York: Wiley.

Karmiloff-Smith, A., & Thomas, M. (2003). What can developmental disorders tell us about the neurocomputational constraints that shape development? The case of Williams syndrome. *Development and Psychopathology, 15,* 969–990.

Karoly, P., & Bay, R. C. (1990). Diabetes self-care goals and their relation to children's metabolic control. *Journal of Pediatric Psychology, 15,* 83–95.

Kashani, J. H., Daniel, A. E., Dandoy, A. C., & Holcomb, W. R. (1992). Family violence: Impact on children. *Journal of the American Academy of Child and Adolescent Psychiatry, 31,* 181–189.

Kashani, J. H., & Orvaschel, H. (1990). A community study of anxiety in children and adolescents. *American Journal of Psychiatry, 147,* 313–318.

Kaslow, F. W. (2001). Families and family psychology at the millennium. *American Psychologist, 56,* 37–46.

Kaslow, N. J., Adamson, L. B., & Collins, M. H. (2000). A developmental psychopathology perspective on the cognitive components of child and adolescent depression. In A. J. Sameroff, M. Lewis, & S. M. Miller (Eds.), *Handbook of developmental psychopathology* (2nd ed.). New York: Kluwer Academic/Plenum Publishers.

Kaslow, N. J., Brown, R. T., & Mee, L. (1994). Cognitive and behavioral correlates of childhood depression: A developmental perspective. In W. M. Reynolds and H. F. Johnston (Eds.), *Handbook of depression in children and adolescents.* New York: Plenum Press.

Kaslow, N. J., & Racusin, G. R. (1990). Childhood depression: Current status and future directions. In A. S. Bellack,

M. Hersen, & A. E. Kazdin (Eds.), *International handbook of behavior modification and therapy* (2nd ed.). New York: Plenum.

Katz, L. J., & Slomka, G. T. (1990). Achievement Testing. In G. Goldstein & M. Hersen (Eds.), *Handbook of psychological assessment* (2nd ed.). New York: Pergamon.

Kaufman, A. S., & Kaufman, N. L. (2004). *Administration and scoring material for the Kaufman Assessment Battery for Children, Second Edition* (KABC-II). Circle Pines, MN: American Guidance Service.

Kaufman, J., & Charney, D. (2001). Effects of early stress on brain structure and function: Implications for understanding the relationship between child maltreatment and depression. *Development and Psychopathology, 13,* 451–471.

Kaufman, J., & Henrich, C. (2000). Exposure to violence and early childhood trauma. In C. H. Zenah Jr. (Ed.), *Handbook of infant mental health* (2nd ed.). New York: The Guilford Press.

Kaufman, J., Martin, A., King, R. A., & Charney, D. (2001). Are child-, adolescent-, and adult-onset depression one and the same disorder? *Biological Psychiatry, 49,* 980–1001.

Kaufman, J., & Zigler, E. (1987). Do abused children become abusive parents? *American Journal of Orthopsychiatry, 57,* 186–192.

Kauffman, J. M., McGee, K., & Brigham, M. (2004). Enabling or disabling? Observations on changes in special education. *Phi Delta Kappan, 85,* 613–620.

Kaugars, A. S., Klinnert, M. D., & Bender, B. G. (2004). Family influences on pediatric asthma. *Journal of Pediatric Psychology, 29,* 475–491.

Kavale, K. A., & Forness, S. R. (2003). Learning disability as a discipline. In H. L. Swanson, K. R. Harris, & S. Graham (Eds.), *Handbook of learning disabilities.* New York: Guilford Press.

Kaye, W. H., Gendall, K., & Strober, M. (1998). Serotonin neuronal function and selective serotonin reuptake inhibitor treatment in anorexia and bulimia nervosa. *Biological Psychiatry, 44,* 825–838.

Kazak, A. E. (2002). *Journal of Pediatric Psychology* (JPP), 1998–2002: Editor's vale dictum. *Journal of Pediatric Psychology, 27,* 653–663.

Kazak, A. E. (2005). Evidence-based interventions for survivors of childhood cancer and their families. *Journal of Pediatric Psychology, 30,* 29–39.

Kazdin, A. E. (1985). *Treatment of antisocial behavior in children and adolescents.* Homewood, IL: Dorsey.

Kazdin, A. E. (1987). Treatment of antisocial behavior in children: Current status and future directions. *Psychological Bulletin, 102,* 187–203.

Kazdin, A. E. (1989). Identifying depression in children: A comparison of alternative selection criteria. *Journal of Abnormal Child Psychology, 17,* 437–454.

Kazdin, A. E. (1993). Treatment of conduct disorder: Progress and directions in psychotherapy research. *Development and Psychopathology, 5,* 277–310.

Kazdin, A. E. (1994). Informant variability in the assessment of childhood depression. In W. M. Reynolds and H. F. Johnston (Eds.), *Handbook of depression in children and adolescents.* New York: Plenum Press.

Kazdin, A. E. (1995). *Conduct disorders in childhood and adolescence* (2nd ed.). Thousand Oaks, CA: Sage.

Kazdin, A. E. (1997). Practitioner review: Psychosocial treatments for conduct disorder in children. *Journal of Child Psychology and Psychiatry, 38*, 161–178.

Kazdin, A. E. (1998). Drawing valid inferences from case studies. In A. E. Kazdin (Ed.), *Methodological issues and strategies in clinical research*. Washington, DC: American Psychological Association.

Kazdin, A. E. (2003). Problem-solving skills training and parent management training for conduct disorder. In A. E. Kazdin & J. R. Weisz (Eds.), *Evidence-based psychotherapies for children and adolescents*. New York: Guilford Press.

Kazdin, A. E., Holland, L., Crowley, M. & Breton, S. (1997). Barriers to Treatment Participation Scale: Evaluation and validation in the context of child outpatient treatment. *Journal of Child Psychology and Psychiatry, 38*, 1051–1062.

Kazdin, A. E., & Kolko, D. J. (1986). Parent psychopathology and family functioning among childhood firesetters. *Journal of Abnormal Child Psychology, 14*, 315–329.

Kazdin, A. E., & Marciano, P. L. (1998). Childhood and adolescent depression. In E. J. Mash & R. A. Barkley (Eds.), *Treatment of childhood disorders* (2nd ed.). New York: Guilford Press.

Kazdin, A. E., Rodgers, A., & Colbus, D. (1986). The Hopelessness Scale for Children: Psychometric characteristics and concurrent validity. *Journal of Consulting and Clinical Psychology, 54*, 241–245.

Kazdin, A. E., Siegel, T. C., & Bass, D. (1992). Cognitive problem-solving skills training and parent management training in the treatment of antisocial behavior in children. *Journal of Consulting and Clinical Psychology, 60*, 733–747.

Kazdin, A. E., & Wassell, G. (2000). Therapeutic changes in children, parents, and families resulting from treatment of children with conduct problems. *Journal of the American Academy of Child and Adolescent Psychiatry, 39*, 414–420.

Kazdin, A. E., & Weisz, J. R. (2003). *Evidence-based psychotherapies for children and adolescents*. New York: Guilford Press.

Kearney, C. A. (2001). *School refusal behavior in youth: A functional approach to assessment and treatment*. Washington, DC: American Psychological Association.

Kearney, C. A., & Silverman, W. K. (1992). Let's not push the "panic button": A critical analysis of panic and panic disorder in adolescents. *Clinical Psychology Review, 12*, 293–305.

Kearney, C. A., & Silverman, W. K. (1996). The evolution and reconciliation of taxonomic strategies for school refusal behavior. *Clinical Psychology: Science and Practice, 3*, 339–354.

Kearney, C. A., Albano, A. M., Eisen, A. R., Allan, W. D., & Barlow, D. H. (1997). The phenomenology of panic disorder in youngsters: An empirical study of a clinical sample. *Journal of Anxiety Disorders, 11*, 49–62.

Kearney, C. A., Eisen, A., & Silverman, W. K. (1995). The legend and myth of school phobia. *School Psychology Quarterly, 10*, 65–85.

Kearney, C. A., Sims, K. E., Prusell, C. R., & Tillotson, C. A. (2003). Separation anxiety disorder in young children: A longitudinal and family analysis. *Journal of Clinical Child and Adolescent Psychology, 32*, 593–598.

Keel, P. K., & Klump, K. (2003). Are eating disorders culture-bound syndromes? Implications for conceptualizing their etiology. *Psychological Bulletin, 129*, 747–769.

Keenan, K., Loeber, R., Zhang, Q., Stouthamer-Loeber, M., & Van Kammen, W. (1995). The influence of deviant peers on the development of boys' disruptive and delinquent behavior: A temporal analysis. *Development and Psychopathology, 7*, 715–726.

Keiley, M. K., Howe, T. R., Dodge, K. A., Bates, J. E., & Pettit, G. S. (2001). The timing of child physical maltreatment: A cross-domain growth and analysis of impact on adolescent externalizing and internalizing problems. *Development and Psychopathology, 13*, 891–912.

Kell, R. S., Kliewer, W., Erickson, M. T., & Ohene-Frempong, K. (1998). Psychological adjustment of adolescents with sickle cell disease: Relations with demographic, medical, and family competence variables. *Journal of Pediatric Psychology, 23*, 301–312.

Keller, M. B., Lavori, P. W., Wunder, J., Beardslee, W. R., Schwartz, C. E., & Roth, J. (1992). Chronic course of anxiety disorders in children and adolescents. Journal of the *American Academy of Child and Adolescent Psychiatry, 31*, 595–599.

Kellerman, J. (1980). Rapid treatment of nocturnal anxiety in children. *Journal of Behavior Therapy and Experimental Psychiatry, 11*, 9–11.

Kelly, J. B. (2000). Children's adjustment in conflicted marriage and divorce: A decade review of research. *Journal of the American Academy of Child and Adolescent Psychiatry, 39*, 963–973.

Kelly, M. L., & Heffer, R. W. (1990). Eating disorders: Food refusal and failure to thrive. In A. M. Gross & R. S. Drabman (Eds.), *Handbook of clinical behavioral pediatrics*. New York: Plenum.

Kempe, C. H., Silverman, F. N., Steele, B. B., Droegemueller, W., & Silver, H. K. (1962). The battered child syndrome. *Journal of the American Medical Association, 181*, 17–24.

Kendall, P. C. (1991). Guiding theory for therapy with children and adolescents. In P. C. Kendall (Ed.), *Child and adolescent therapy: Cognitive-behavioral procedures*. New York: Guilford.

Kendall, P. C. (1992). *Coping cat workbook*. Ardmore, PA: Workbook Publishing.

Kendall, P. C., Aschenbrand, S. G., & Hudson, J. L. (2003). Child-focused treatment of anxiety. In A. E. Kazdin & J. R. Weisz (Eds.), *Evidence-based psychotherapies for children and adolescents*. New York: Guilford Press.

Kendall, P. C., Chu, B. C., Pimentel, S. S., & Choudhury, M. (2000). Treating anxiety disorders in youth. In P. C. Kendall (Ed.), *Child and adolescent therapy: Cognitive-behavioral procedures*. New York: Guilford.

Kendall, P. C., Flannery-Schroeder, E., Panichelli-Mindel, S., Southam-Gerow, M., Henin, A., & Warman, M. (1997a). Therapy for youth with anxiety disorders: A second randomized clinical trial. *Journal of Consulting and Clinical Psychology, 65*, 366–380.

Kendall, P. C., & Panichelli-Mindel, S. M. (1995). Cognitive-behavioral treatments. *Journal of Abnormal Child Psychology, 23*, 107–124.

Kendall, P. C., Panichelli-Mindel, S. M., Sugarman, A., & Callahan, S. A. (1997b). Exposure to child anxiety: Theory, research, and practice. *Clinical Psychology: Science and Practice, 4*, 29–39.

Kendall, P. C., & Southam-Gerow, M. A. (1996). Long-term follow-up of a cognitive-behavioral therapy for anxiety-disordered youth. *Journal of Consulting and Clinical Psychology, 64*, 724–730.

Kendall, P. C., Safford, S., Flannery-Schroeder, E., & Webb, A. (2004). Child anxiety treatment: Outcomes in adolescence and impact on substance use and depression at 7.4-year follow-up. *Journal of Consulting and Clinical Psychology, 72,* 276–287.

Kendler, K. S. (1996). Major depression and generalized anxiety disorder: Same genes, (partly) different environments—revisited. *British Journal of Psychiatry, 168 (suppl. 30),* 68–75.

Kendler, K. S. (2000). Schizophrenia: Genetics. In B. J. Sadock & V. A. Sadock (Eds.), *Comprehensive textbook of psychiatry* (Vol. I). Philadelphia: Lippincott Williams & Wilkins.

Kendler, K. S., Neale, M. C., Kessler, R. C., Heath, A. C., & Eaves, L. J. (1992a). A population-based twin study of major depression in women: The impact of varying definitions of illness. *Archives of General Psychiatry, 49,* 257–266.

Kendler, K. S., Neale, M. C., Kessler, R. C., Heath, A. C., & Eaves, L. J. (1992b). The genetic epidemiology of phobias in women: The interrelationship of agoraphobia, social phobia, situational phobia, and simple phobia. *Archives of General Psychiatry, 49,* 273–281.

Kerns, K. A. (1996). Individual differences in friendship quality: Links to child-mother attachment. In W. M. Bukowski, A. F. Newcomb, & W. W. Hartup (Eds.), *The company they keep: Friendship during childhood and adolescence.* New York: Cambridge University Press.

Kerns, K. A., Klepac, L., & Cole, A. K. (1996). Peer relationships and preadolescents' perceptions of security in the child-mother relationship. *Developmental Psychology, 32,* 457–466.

Kerr, A. (2002). Annotation: Rett syndrome: Recent progress and implications for research and clinical practice. *Journal of Child Psychology and Psychiatry, 43,* 277–287.

Kerr, D. C. R., Lopez, N. L., Olson, S. L., Sameroff, A. J. (2004). Parental discipline and externalizing behavior problems in early childhood: The roles of moral regulation and child gender. *Journal of Abnormal Child Psychology, 32,* 369–383.

Kerr, M., Tremblay, R. E., Pagani, L., & Vitaro, F. (1997). Boys' behavioral inhibition and the risk of later delinquency. *Archives of General Psychiatry, 54,* 809–816.

Kerwin, M. E., & Berkowitz, R. I. (1996). Feeding and eating disorders: Ingestive problems of infancy, childhood, and adolescence. *School Psychology Review, 25,* 316–328.

Kessler, J. W. (1966, 1988). *Psychopathology of childhood.* Englewood Cliffs, NJ: Prentice Hall.

Kessler, R. C., Avenevoli, S., & Merikangas, K. R. (2001). Mood disorders in children and adolescents: An epidemiologic perspective. *Biological Psychiatry, 49,* 1002–1014.

Kestenbaum, C. J. (2000). How shall we treat children in the 21st century? *Journal of the American Academy of Child and Adolescent Psychiatry, 39,* 1–10.

Kiernan, C. (1985). Behaviour modification. In A. M. Clarke, A. D. B. Clarke, & J. M. Berg (Eds.), *Mental deficiency. The changing outlook.* New York: The Free Press.

Kiesler, C. A. (2000). The next wave of change for psychology and mental health services in the health care revolution. *American Psychologist, 55,* 481–487.

Killen, J. D., Hayward, C., Wilson, D. M., Taylor, C. B., Hammer, L. D., Litt, I., Simmonds, B., & Haydel, F. (1994a). Factors associated with eating disorder symptoms in a community sample of 6th and 7th grade girls. *International Journal of Eating Disorders, 15,* 357–367.

Killen, J. D., Taylor, B., Hayward, C., Haydel, K. F., Wilson, D. M., Hammer, L., Kraemer, H., Blair-Greiner, A., & Strachowski, D. (1996). Weight concerns influence the development of eating disorders: A 4-year prospective study. *Journal of Consulting and Clinical Psychology, 64,* 936–940.

Killen, J. D., Taylor, C. B., Hayward, C., Wilson, D. M., Haydel, K. F., Hammer, L. D., Simmonds, B., Robinson, T. N., Litt, I., Varady, A., & Kraemer, H. (1994b). Pursuit of thinness and onset of eating disorder symptoms in a community sample of adolescent girls: A three-year prospective analysis. *International Journal of Eating Disorders, 16,* 227–238.

Kilpatrick, D. G., Acierno, R., Schnurr, P. P., Saunders, B., Resnick, H. S., & Best, C. L. (2000). Risk factors for adolescent substance abuse and dependence: Data from a national sample. *Journal of Consulting and Clinical Psychology, 68,* 19–30.

King, B. H., Hodapp, R. M., & Dykens, E. M. (2000). Mental retardation. In B. J. Sadock & V. A. Sadock (Eds.), *Comprehensive textbook of psychiatry* (Vol. II). Philadelphia: Lippincott Williams & Wilkins.

King, N. (1994). Physiological assessment. In T. H. Ollendick, N. J. King, & W. Yule (Eds.), *International handbook of phobic and anxiety disorders in children and adolescents* (pp. 365–396). New York: Plenum Press.

King, N. J., & Bernstein, G. A. (2001). School refusal in children and adolescents: A review of the past 10 years. *Journal of the American Academy of Child and Adolescent Psychiatry, 40,* 197–205.

King, N. J., & Ollendick, T. H. (1997). Treatment of childhood phobias. *Journal of Child Psychology and Psychiatry, 38,* 389–400.

King, N. J., Ollendick, T. H., & Gullone, E. (1990). School-related fears of children and adolescents. *Australian Journal of Education, 34,* 99–112.

King, N. J., Ollendick, T. H., Mattis, S. G., Yang, B., & Tonge, B. (1997). Nonclinical panic attacks in adolescents: Prevalence, symptomatology, and associated features. *Behaviour Change, 13,* 171–183.

King, N. J., Ollier, K., Iacuone, R., Schuster, S., Bays, K., Gullone, E., & Ollendick, T. H. (1989). Fears of children and adolescents: A cross-sectional Australian study using the Revised-Fear Survey Schedule for Children. *Journal of Child Psychology and Psychiatry, 30,* 775–784.

King, N. J., Muris, P., & Ollendick, T. H. (2004). Specific phobia. In T. L. Morris & J. S. March (Eds.), *Anxiety disorders in children and adolescents.* New York: Guilford Press.

King, N., Tonge, B. J., Heyne, D., & Ollendick, T. H. (2000). Research on the cognitive-behavioral treatment of school refusal: A review and recommendations. *Clinical Psychology Review, 20,* 495–507.

King, R. A., & Noshpitz, J. D. (1991). *Pathways of growth: Essentials of child psychiatry,* Vol. 2. New York: John Wiley & Sons.

King, R. A., Pfeffer, C., Gammon, G. D., & Cohen, D. J. (1992). Suicidality of childhood and adolescence: Review of the literature and proposal for establishment of a DSM-IV category. In B. B. Lahey & A. E. Kazdin (Eds.), *Advances in clinical child psychology,* Vol. 14, New York: Plenum.

King, R. A., Schwab-Stone, M., Flisher, A. J., Greenwald, S., Kramer, R. A., Goodman, S. H., Lahey, B. B., Shaffer, D., & Gould, M. S. (2001). Psychosocial and risk behavior correlates of suicide attempts and suicidal ideation. *Journal of the American Academy of Child and Adolescent Psychiatry, 40,* 837–846.

Kirigin, K. A., Braukmann, C. J., Atwater, J. D., & Wolf, M. M. (1982). An evaluation of Teaching-Family (Achievement Place) group homes for juvenile offenders. *Journal of Applied Behavior Analysis, 15,* 1–16.

Kirk, S. A., Gallagher, J. J., & Anastasiow, N. J. (2000). *Educating exceptional children.* Boston: Houghton Mifflin Company.

Kistner, J. A., David, C. F., & White, B. A. (2003). Ethnic and sex differences in children's depressive symptoms: Mediating effects of perceived and actual competence. *Journal of Clinical Child and Adolescent Psychology, 32,* 341–350.

Kleiger, J. H. (2001). Projective testing with children and adolescents. In C. E. Walker & M. C. Roberts (Eds.), *Handbook of clinical child psychology* (3rd ed.). New York: John Wiley & Sons.

Klein, D. F., Mannuzza, S., Chapman, T., & Fyer, A. (1992). Child panic revised. *Journal of the American Academy of Child and Adolescent Psychiatry, 31,* 112–113.

Klein, D. N., Lewinsohn, P. M., Seeley, J. R., & Rohde, P. (2001). A family study of major depressive disorder in a community sample of adolescents. *Archives of General Psychiatry, 58,* 13–20.

Klein, D. N., Riso, L. P., Donaldson, S. K., Shwartz, J. E., Anderson, R. L., Ouimette, P. C., Lizardi, H., & Aronson, T. A. (1995). Family study of early-onset dysthymia: Mood and personality disorders in relatives of outpatients with dysthymia and episodic major depression and normal controls. *Archives of General Psychiatry, 52,* 487–496.

Klein, M. (1932). *The psycho-analysis of children.* London: Hogarth Press.

Klein, N. C., Alexander, J. F., & Parsons, B. V. (1977). Impact of family systems intervention on recidivism and sibling delinquency: A model of primary prevention and program evaluation. *Journal of Consulting and Clinical Psychology, 45,* 469–474.

Klein, R. G., Abikoff, H., Hechtman, L., & Weiss, G. (2004). Design and rationale of controlled study of long-term methylphenidate and multimodal psychosocial treatment in children with ADHD. *Journal of the American Academy of Child and Adolescent Psychiatry, 43,* 792–801.

Klesges, R. C., & Hanson, C. L. (1988). Determining the environmental causes and correlates of childhood obesity: Methodological issues and future research directions. In N. A. Krasnegor, G. D. Grave, & N. Kretchmer (Eds.), *Childhood obesity: A biobehavioral perspective.* Caldwell, NJ: The Telford Press.

Kliewer, C., & Biklen, D. (1996). Labeling: Who wants to be called retarded? In W. Stainback & S. Stainback (Eds.), *Controversial issues confronting special education: Divergent perspectives* (2nd ed.). Boston: Allyn and Bacon.

Klin, A., & Cohen, D. J. (1997). Ethical issues in research and treatment. In D. J. Cohen & F. R. Volkmar (Eds.), *Handbook of autism and pervasive developmental disorders.* New York: John Wiley.

Klin, A., & Volkmar, F. R. (1997). Asperger's Syndrome. In D. J. Cohen & F. R. Volkmar (Eds.), *Handbook of autism and pervasive development disorders.* New York: John Wiley.

Klinger, L. G., & Dawson, G. (1996). Autistic disorder. In E. J. Mash & R. A. Barkley (Eds.), *Child psychopathology.* New York: Guilford Press.

Klinger, L. G., Dawson, G., & Renner, P. (2003). Autistic disorder. In E. J. Mash & R. A. Barkley (Eds.), *Child psychopathology.* New York: Guilford Press.

Klingner, J. K., & Vaughn, S. (2002). The changing roles and responsibilities of an LD specialist. *Learning Disabilities Quarterly, 25,* 19–31.

Klinnert, M. D., McQuaid, E. L., McCormich, D., Adinoff, A. D., & Bryant, N. E. (2000). A multimethod assessment of behavioral and emotional adjustment in children with asthma. *Journal of Pediatric Psychology, 25,* 35–46.

Klinnert, M. D., Mrazek, P. J., & Mrazek, D. A. (1994). Early asthma onset: The interaction between family stressors and adaptive parenting. *Psychiatry: Interpersonal and Biological Processes, 57,* 51–61.

Klump, K. L., McGue, M., & Iacono, W. G. (2000). Age differences in genetic and environmental influences on eating attitudes and behaviors in preadolescent and adolescent female twins. *Journal of Abnormal Psychology, 109,* 239–251.

Knight, S. J. L., Regan, R., Nicod, A., Horsley, S. W., Kearney, L., Homfray, T. et al. (1999). Subtle chromosomal rearrangements in children with unexplained mental retardation. *The Lancet, 354,* 1676–1681.

Knoff, H. M. (1998). Review of the Children's Apperception Test (1991 Revision). In J. C. Impara & B. S. Plake (Eds.), *The thirteenth mental measurement yearbook.* Lincoln: The University of Nebraska–Lincoln.

Koegel, L. K. (2000). Interventions to facilitate communication in autism. *Journal of Autism and Developmental Disorders, 30,* 383–391.

Koegel, R. L., Koegel, L. K., & Brookman, L. I. (2003). Empirically supported pivotal response interventions for children with autism. In A. E. Kazdin & J. R. Weisz (Eds.), *Evidence-based psychotherapies for children and adolescents.* New York: Guilford Press.

Koegel, R. L., Koegel, L. K., & McNerney, E. K. (2001). Pivotal areas in intervention for autism. *Journal of Clinical Child Psychology, 30,* 19–32.

Koegel, R. L., O'Dell, M. C., & Koegel, L. K. (1987). A natural language teaching paradigm for nonverbal autistic children. *Journal of Autism and Developmental Disorders, 17,* 187–200.

Kog, E., & Vandereycken, W. (1985). Family charcteristics of anorexia nervosa and bulimia: A review of the research literature. *Clinical Psychology Review, 5,* 159–180.

Koger, S. M., Schettler, T., & Weiss, B. (2005). Environmental toxicants and development disabilities. *American Psychologist, 60,* 243–255.

Kolko, D. J. (1985). Juvenile firesetting: A review and methodological critique. *Clinical Psychology Review, 5,* 345–376.

Kolko, D. (1987). Simplified inpatient treatment of nocturnal enuresis in psychiatrically disturbed children. *Behavior Therapy, 18,* 99–112.

Kolko, D. J. (1989). Fire setting and pyromania. In C. Last & M. Hersen (Eds.), *Handbook of child psychiatric diagnosis.* New York: Wiley.

Kolko, D. J. (2001). Efficacy of cognitive-behavioral treatment and fire safety education for children who set fires: Initial and follow-up outcomes. *Journal of Child Psychology and Psychiatry, 42,* 359–369.

Kolko, D. J., Day, B. T., Bridge, J. A., & Kazdin, A. E. (2001). Two-year prediction of children's firesetting in clinically referred and nonreferred samples. *Journal of Child Psychology and Psychiatry, 42*, 371–380.

Kolmen, B. K., Feldman, H. M., Handen, B. L., & Janosky, J. E. (1998). Letters to the editor: Naltrexone in children with autism. *Journal of the American Academy of Child and Adolescent Psychiatry, 37*, 801–802.

Kolvin, I. (1971). Psychoses in childhood—a comparative study. In M. Rutter (Ed.), *Infantile autism: Concepts, characteristics, and treatments*. London: Churchill-Livingstone.

Koocher, G. P. (1980). Pediatric cancer: Psychosocial problems and the high costs of helping. *Journal of Clinical Child Psychology, 9*, 2–5.

Koocher, G. P., & Sallan, S. E. (1978). Pediatric oncology. In P. R. Magrab (Ed.), *Psychological management of pediatric problems*, Vol. 1. Baltimore: University Park Press.

Kopp, C. B. (1994). Trends and directions in studies of developmental risk. In C. A. Nelson (Ed.), *Threats to optimal development: Integrating biological, psychological, and social risk factors: The Minnesota symposium on child psychology. Vol. 27*. Hillsdale, NJ: Erlbaum.

Koppitz, E. M. (1984). *Psychological evaluation of human figure drawings by middle school pupils*. Orlando, FL: Grune & Stratton.

Korbin, J. E., Coulton, C. J., Chard, S., Platt-Houston, C., & Su, M. (1998). Impoverishment and child maltreatment in African American and European American neighborhoods. *Development and Psychopathology, 10*, 215–233.

Kormann, R. J., & Petronko, M. R. (2004). Community inclusion of individuals with behavioral challenges: Who supports the caregivers? *Mental Retardation, 42*, 223–228.

Korsch, B. M., & Marcy, S. N. (2000). Pediatric compliance from a patient and family perspective. In D. Drotar (Ed.), *Promoting adherence to medical treatment in chronic childhood illness: Concepts, methods, and interventions*. Mahwah, NJ: Lawrence Erlbaum Associates.

Kotimaa, A. J., Moilanen, I., Taanila, A., Ebeling, H., Smalley, S. L., McGough, J. J. et al. (2003). Maternal smoking and hyperactivity in 8-year-old children. *Journal of the American Academy of Child and Adolescent Psychiatry, 42*, 826–833.

Kotler, L. A., Cohen, P., Daview, M., Pine, D. S., & Walsh, B. T. (2001). Longitudinal relationships between childhood, adolescent, and adult eating disorders. *Journal of the American Academy of Child and Adolescent Psychiatry, 40*, 1434–1440.

Kovacs, M. (1992). *Children's Depression Inventory*. North Tonawanda, NY: Multi-Health Systems.

Kovacs, M. (1996). Presentation and course of Major Depressive Disorder during childhood and later years of the life span. *Journal of the American Academy of Child and Adolescent Psychiatry, 35*, 705–715.

Kovacs, M. (1997). Depressive disorders in childhood: An impressionistic landscape. *Journal of Child Psychology and Psychiatry, 38*, 287–298.

Kovacs, M., Devlin, B., Pollack, M., Richards, C., & Mukerji, P. (1997). A controlled family history study of childhood-onset depressive disorder. *Archives of General Psychiatry, 54*, 613–623.

Kovacs, M., & Gatsonis, C. (1994). Secular trends in age of onset of major depressive disorder in a clinical sample of children. *Journal of Psychiatric Research, 28*, 319–329.

Kovacs, M., Goldston, D., & Gatsonis, C. (1993). Suicidal behaviors and childhood-onset depressive disorders: A longitudinal investigation. *Journal of the American Academy of Child and Adolescent Psychiatry, 32*, 8–20.

Kowatch, R. A., Fristad, M., Birmaher, B., Wagner, K. D., Findling, R. L., & Hellander, M. (2005). Treatment guidelines for children and adolescents with bipolar disorder. *Journal of the American Academy of Child and Adolescent Psychiatry, 44*, 213–235.

Kozol, J. (1991). *Savage inequalities: Children in America's schools*. New York: Crown Publishers.

Kraemer, S. (1987). Working with parents: Casework or psychotherapy? *Journal of Child Psychology and Psychiatry, 28*, 207–213.

Krahn, G. L., Hohn, M. F., & Kime, C. (1995). Incorporating qualitative approaches into clinical child psychology research. *Journal of Clinical Child Psychology, 24*, 204–213.

Kraijer, D. (2000). Review of adaptive behavior studies in mentally retarded persons with autism/pervasive developmental disorder. *Journal of Autism and Developmental Disorders, 30*, 39–47.

Kratochwill, T. R., & Levin, J. R. (1992). *Single-case research design and analysis*. Hillsdale, NJ: Lawrence Erlbaum.

Krausz, M., & Muller-Thomsen, T. (1993). Schizophrenia with onset in adolescence: An 11-year followup. *Schizophrenia Bulletin, 19*, 831–841.

Kuczynski, L., & Kochanska, G. (1995). Function and contexts of maternal demands: Developmental significance of early demands for competent action. *Child Development, 66*, 616–628.

Kuhn, T. S. (1962). *The structure of scientific revolutions*. Chicago: University of Chicago Press.

Kumpulainen, K., Räsänen, E., & Henttonen, I. (1999). Children involved in bullying: Psychological disturbance and the persistence of the involvement. *Child Abuse and Neglect, 23*, 1253–1262.

Kumra, S., Bedwell, J., Smith, A. K., Arling, E., Albus, K. et al. (2000). Neuropsychological deficits in pediatric patients with childhood-onset schizophrenia and psychotic disorder not otherwise specified. *Schizophrenia Research, 42*, 135–144.

Kumra, S., Giedd, J. N., Vaituzis, A. C., Jacobsen, L. K., McKenna, K., Bedwell, J. et al. (2000). Childhood-onset psychotic disorders: Magnetic resonance imaging of volumetric differences in brain structure. *American Journal of Psychiatry, 157*, 1467–1474.

Kumra, S., Herion, D., Jacobsen, L. K., Briguglia, S., & Grothe, D. (1997). Case study: Risperidone-induced hepatotoxicity in pediatric patients. *Journal of the American Academy of Child and Adolescent Psychiatry, 36*, 701–705.

Kuperman, S., Gaffney, G. R., Hamdan-Allen, G., Preston, D. F., & Venkatesh, L. (1990). Neuroimaging in child and adolescent psychiatry. *Journal of the American Academy of Child and Adolescent Psychiatry, 19*, 159–172.

Kupersmidt, J. B., & Patterson, C. J. (1991). Childhood peer rejection, aggression, withdrawal, and perceived competence as predictors of self-reported behavior problems in preadolescence. *Journal of Abnormal Child Psychology, 19*, 427–449.

Kupfer, D. J., First, M. B., & Regier, D. A. (2002). Introduction. In D. J. Kupfer, M. B. First, & D. A. Regier (Eds.), *A research agenda for DSM-V*. Washington, DC: American Psychiatric Association.

Kupfer, D. J., & Reynolds, C. F. (1992). Sleep and affective disorders. In E. S. Paykel (Ed.), *Handbook of affective disorders* (2nd ed.). New York: Guilford Press.

Kvernmo, S., & Heyerdahl, S. (1998). Influence of ethnic factors on behavior problems in indigenous Sami and majority Norwegian adolescents. *Journal of the American Academy of Child and Adolescent Psychiatry, 37,* 743–751.

Kvernmo, S., & Heyerdahl, S. (2003). Acculturation strategies and ethnic identity as predictors of behavior problems in arctic minority adolescents. *Journal of the American Academy of Child and Adolescent Psychiatry, 42,* 57–65.

Kylliäinen, A., & Hietanen, J. K. (2004). Attention orienting by another's gaze direction in children with autism. *Journal of Child Psychology and Psychiatry, 45,* 435–444.

Ladd, G. W., & Troop-Gordon, W. (2003). The role of chronic peer difficulties in the development of children's psychological adjustment problems. *Child Development, 74,* 1344–1367.

LaFromboise, T., & Dizon, M. R. (2003). American Indian children and adolescents. In J. T. Gibbs, L. N. Huang and Associates (Eds.), *Children of color: Psychological interventions with culturally diverse youth.* San Francisco: Jossey-Bass.

Laessle, R. G., Uhl, H., & Lindel, B. (2001). Parental influences on eating behavior in obese and nonobese preadolescents. *International Journal of Eating Disorders, 30,* 447–453.

Laessle, R. G., Wurmser, H., & Pirke, K. M. (2000). Restrained eating and leptin levels in overweight preadolescent girls. *Physiology and Behavior, 70,* 45–47.

La Greca, A. M. (1993). Social skills training with children: Where do we go from here. *Journal of Clinical Child Psychology, 22,* 288–298.

La Greca, A. M., & Bearman, K. J. (2001). If "an apple a day keeps the doctor away," why is adherence so darn hard? *Journal of Pediatric Psychology, 26,* 279–282.

La Greca, A. M., & Bearman, K. J. (2003). Adherence to pediatric treatment regimens. In M. C. Roberts (Ed.), *Handbook of pediatric psychology* (3rd ed.). New York: Guilford Press.

La Greca, A. M., Siegel, L. J., Wallander, J. L., & Walker, C. E. (Eds.). (1992). *Stress and coping in child health.* New York: Guilford.

La Greca, A. M., Silverman, W. K., & Wasserstein, S. B. (1998). Children's predisaster functioning as a predictor of posttraumatic stress following Hurricane Andrew. *Journal of Consulting and Clinical Psychology, 66,* 883–892.

La Greca, A. M., Silverman, W. K., Vernberg, E. M., & Prinstein, M. J. (1996). Symptoms of posttraumatic stress in children after Hurricane Andrew: A prospective study. *Journal of Consulting and Clinical Psychology, 64,* 712–723.

La Greca, A. M., & Stone, W. L. (1993). Social anxiety scale for children-revised: Factor structure and concurrent validity. *Journal of Clinical Child Psychology, 22,* 17–27.

Lahey, B. B. (2001, Winter). Should the combined and predominantly inattentive types of ADHD be considered distinct and unrelated disorders? *Clinical Psychology: Science and Practice, 8,* 494–497.

Lahey, B. B., Applegate, B., McBurnett, K., Biederman, J., Greenhill, L., Hynd, G. W., Barkley, R. A., Newcorn, J., Jensen, P., Richters, J., Garfinkel, B., Kerdyk, L., Frick, P. J., Ollendick, T., Perez, D., Hart, E. L., Waldman, I., & Shaffer, D. (1994). DSM-IV field trials for attention deficit hyperactivity disorder in children and adolescents. *American Journal of Psychiatry, 151,* 1673–1685.

Lahey, B. B., Hartdagen, S. E., Frick, P. J., McBurnett, K., Conner, R., & Hynd, G. W. (1988). Psychopathology and antisocial behavior in the parents of children with conduct disorder and hyperactivity. *Journal of the American Academy of Child and Adolescent Psychiatry, 29,* 620–626.

Lahey, B. B., Pelham, W. E., Stein, M. A., Loney, J., Trapani, C., Nugent, K., Kipp, H., Schmidt, E., Lee, S., Cale, M., Gold, E., Hartung, C. M., Willcutt, E., & Baumann, B. (1998). Validity of DSM-IV Attention-deficit/Hyperactivity Disorder for younger children. *Journal of the American Academy of Child and Adolescent Psychiatry, 37,* 695–702.

Lahey, B. B., & Waldman, I. D. (2003). A developmental propensity model of the origins of conduct problems during childhood and adolescence. In B. B. Lahey, T. E. Moffitt, A. Caspi (Eds.), *Causes of conduct disorder and juvenile delinquency.* New York: Guilford Press.

Lahey, B. B., Waldman, I. D., & McBurnett, K. (1999). The development of antisocial behavior: An integrative causal model. *Journal of Child Psychology and Psychiatry, 40,* 669–682.

Laing, E., Hulme, C., Grant, J., & Karmiloff-Smith, A. (2001). Learning to read in Williams syndrome: Looking beneath the surface of atypical reading development. *Journal of Child Psychology and Psychiatry, 42,* 729–739.

Laird, R. D., Jordan, K. Y., Dodge, K. A., Petit, G. S., & Bates, J. E. (2001). Peer rejection in childhood, involvement with antisocial peers in early adolescence and the development of externalizing behavior problems. *Development and Psychopathology, 13,* 337–354.

Lakin, K. C., Prouty, R., Polister, B., & Coucouvanis, K. (2003). Selected changes in residential service systems over a quarter century, 1977–2002. *Mental Retardation, 41,* 303–306.

Lambert, N., Leland, H., & Nihira, K. (1993). *AAMR Adaptive Behavior Scales–School.* Austin, TX: PRO-ED.

Lambert, N. M. (1988). Adolescent outcomes for hyperactive children: Perspectives on general and specific patterns of childhood risk for adolescent educational, social, and mental health problems. *American Psychologist, 43,* 786–799.

Landry, R., & Bryson, S. E. (2004). Impaired disengagement of attention in young children with autism. *Journal of Child Psychology and Psychiatry, 45,* 1115–1122.

Lang, P. J. (1984). Cognition in emotion: Concept and action. In C. E. Izard, J. Kagan, R. B. Zajonc (Eds.), *Emotions, cognition, and behavior.* New York. Cambridge University Press.

Langer, D. H. (1985). Children's legal rights as research subjects. *Journal of the American Academy of Child Psychiatry, 24,* 653–662.

Lansford, J. E., Dodge, K. A., Pettit, G. S., Bates, J. E., Crozier, J., & Kaplow, J. (2002). A 12-year prospective study of the long-term effects of early childhood physical maltreatment on psychological, behavioral, and academic problems in adolescence. *Archives of Pediatrics and Adolescent Medicine, 156,* 824–830.

Lapouse, R., & Monk, M. (1958). An epidemiologic study of behavior characteristics in children. *American Journal of Public Health, 48,* 1134–1144.

Lapouse, R., & Monk, M. A. (1959). Fears and worries in a representative sample of children. *American Journal of Orthopsychiatry, 29,* 803–818.

Larner, M. B., Zippiroli, L., & Behrman, R. E. (1999). When school is out: Analysis and recommendations. *The Future of Children, 9(2),* 4–20.

Lask, B. & Bryant-Waugh, R. (1992). Early-onset anorexia nervosa and related eating disorders. *Journal of Child Psychology and Psychiatry, 33,* 281–300.

Last, C. G. (1988). Separation anxiety. In M. Hersen & C. G. Last (Eds.), *Child behavior therapy casebook.* New York: Plenum Press.

Last, C. G., Hersen, M., Kazdin, A. E., Orvaschel, H., & Perrin, S. (1991). Anxiety disorders in children and their families. *Archives of General Psychiatry, 48,* 928–934.

Last, C. G., & Perrin, S. (1993). Anxiety disorders in African-American and white children. *Journal of Abnormal Child Psychology, 21,* 153–164.

Last, C. G., Perrin, S., Hersen, M., & Kazdin, A. E. (1992). DSM-III-R anxiety disorders in children: Sociodemographic and clinical characteristics. *Journal of the American Academy of Child and Adolescent Psychiatry, 31,* 1070–1076.

Last, C. G., Perrin, S., Hersen, M., & Kazdin, A. E. (1996). A prospective study of childhood anxiety disorders. *Journal of the American Academy of Child and Adolescent Psychiatry, 35,* 1502–1510.

Last, C. G., & Strauss, C. C. (1989). Panic disorder in children and adolescents. *Journal of Anxiety Disorders, 3,* 87–95.

Last, C. G., & Strauss, C. C. (1990). School refusal in anxiety-disordered children and adolescents. *Journal of the American Academy of Child and Adolescent Psychiatry, 29,* 31–35.

Last, C. G., Strauss, C. C., & Francis, G. (1987). Comorbidity among childhood anxiety disorders. *Journal of Nervous and Mental Disease, 175,* 726–730.

Lavigne, J. V., & Faier-Routman, J. (1993). Correlates of psychological adjustment to pediatric physical disorders: A meta-analytic review and comparison with existing models. *Developmental and Behavioral Pediatrics, 14,* 117–123.

Lau, A. S., & Weisz, J. R. (2003). Reported maltreatment among clinic-referred children: Implications for presenting problems, treatment attrition, and long-term outcomes. *Journal of the American Academy of Child and Adolescent Psychiatry, 42,* 1327–1334.

Law, J., & Garrett, Z. (2004). Speech and language therapy: Its potential role in CAMHS. *Child and Adolescent Mental Health, 9,* 50–55.

Laws, G., & Gunn, D. (2004). Phonological memory as a predictor of language comprehension in Down syndrome: A five-year follow-up study. *Journal of Child Psychology and Psychiatry, 45,* 326–327.

Lazarus, A., & Abramavitz, A. (1962). The use of emotive imagery in the treatment of children's phobia. *Journal of Mental Science, 108,* 191–192.

Leach, J. M., Scarborough, H. S., & Rescorla, L. (2003). Late-emerging reading disabilities. *Journal of Educational Psychology, 95,* 211–224.

LeBovidge, J. S., Lavigne, J. V., Donenberg, G. R., & Miller, M. L. (2003). Psychological adjustment of children and adolescents with chronic arthritis: A meta-analytic review. *Journal of Pediatric Psychology, 28,* 29–39.

Leckman, J. F., Peterson, B. S., Anderson, G. M., Arnsten, F. T., Pauls, D. L., & Cohen, D. J. (1997). Pathogenesis of Tourette's Syndrome. *Journal of Child Psychology and Psychiatry, 38,* 119–142.

Lee, P., Moss, S., Friedlander, R., Donnelly, T., & Honer, W. (2003). Early-onset schizophrenia in children with mental retardation: Diagnostic reliability and stability of clinical features. *Journal of the American Academy of Child and Adolescent Psychiatry, 42,* 162–169.

Lefkowitz, M., & Burton, N. (1978). Childhood depression: A critique of the concept. *Psychological Bulletin, 85* (4), 716–726.

Lefkowitz, M., & Tesiny, E. (1980). Assessment of childhood depression. *Journal of Consulting and Clinical Psychology, 48,* 43–50.

le Grange, D., Binford, R., & Loeb, K. L. (2005). Manualized family-based treatment for anorexia nervosa: A case series. *Journal of the American Academy of Child and Adolescent Psychiatry, 44,* 41–46.

le Grange, D., Loeb, K. L., Van Orman, S., & Jellar, C. C. (2004). Bulimia nervosa in adolescents: A disorder in evolution? *Archives of Pediatric & Adolescent Medicine, 158,* 478–482.

Leinonen, J. A., Solantaus, T. S., & Punamäki, R-L. (2003). Parental mental health and children's adjustment: The quality of marital interaction and parenting as mediating factors. *Journal of Child Psychology and Psychiatry, 44,* 227–241.

Leitenberg, H., Yost, L. W., & Carroll-Wilson, M. (1986). Negative cognitive errors in children: Questionnaire development, normative data, and comparisons between children with and without self-reported symptoms of depression, low self-esteem, and evaluation anxiety. *Journal of Consulting and Clinical Psychology, 54,* 528–536.

Lemanek, K. L., Kamps, J., & Chung, N. B. (2001). Empirically supported treatments in pediatric psychology: Regimen adherence. *Journal of Pediatric Psychology, 26,* 279–282.

Lemerise, E. A., & Arsenio, W. F. (2000). An integrated model of emotion processes and cognition in social information processing. *Child Development, 71,* 107–118.

Lenane, M. C., Swedo, S. E., Leonard, H. L., Pauls, D. L., Sceery, W., & Rapoport, J. L. (1990). Psychiatric disorders in first degree relatives of children and adolescents with obsessive compulsive disorder. *Journal of the American Academy of Child and Adolescent Psychiatry, 29,* 407–412.

Leonard, H. L., Goldberger, E. L., Rapoport, J. L., Cheslow, D. L., & Swedo, S. E. (1990). Childhood rituals: Normal development or obsessive-compulsive symptoms? *Journal of the American Academy of Child and Adolescent Psychiatry, 29,* 17–23.

Leonard, H. L., Swedo, S. E., Allen, A. J., & Rapoport, J. L. (1994). Obsessive-compulsive disorder. In T. H. Ollendick, N. J. King, & Yule, W. (Eds.), *International handbook of anxiety disorders in children and adolescents.* New York: Plenum.

Leonard, H. L., Swedo, S. E., Lenane, M. C., Rettew, D. C., Hamburger, S. D., Bartko, J. J., & Rapoport, J. L. (1993). A two to seven year follow-up study of 54 obsessive compulsive children and adolescents. *Archives of General Psychiatry, 50,* 429–439.

Leonard, L. B. (1998). *Children with specific language impairment.* Cambridge, MA: The MIT Press.

Lerner, R. M., Fisher, C. B., & Weinberg, R. A. (2000). Toward a science for and of the people: Promoting civil society through the application of developmental studies. *Child Development, 71,* 11–20.

Leslie, L. K., Weckerly, J., Landsverk, J., Hough, R. L., Hurlbut, M. S., & Wood, P. A. (2003). Racial/ethnic differences in the use of psychotropic medication in high-risk children and adolescents. *Journal of the American Academy of Child and Adolescent Psychiatry, 42,* 1433–1442.

Lester, B. M., Bigsby, R., & Miller-Loncar, C. (2004). Infant massage: So where's the rub? *Social Policy Report, 18(1),* 8.

Leung, P. W. L., & Connolly, K. J. (1996). Distractibility in hyperactive and conduct-disordered children. *Journal of Child Psychology and Psychiatry, 37,* 305–312.

Leung, P. W. L., Ho, T. P., Luk, S. L., Taylor, E., Bacon-Shone, J., & Lieh Mak, F. (1996). Separation and comorbidity of hyperactivity and conduct disturbance in Chinese schoolboys. *Journal of Child Psychology and Psychiatry, 37,* 841–853.

Leventhal, T., & Brooks-Gunn, J. (2000). The neighborhoods they live in: The effects of neighborhood residence on child and adolescent outcomes. *Psychological Bulletin, 126,* 309–337.

Levine, M. P., & Harrison, K. (2004). Media's role in the perpetuation and prevention of negative body image and disordered eating. In J. K. Thompson (Ed.), *Handbook of eating disorders and obesity.* Hoboken, NJ: John Wiley.

Levine, M. P., Smolak, L., Moodey, A. F., Shuman, M. D., & Hessen L. D. (1994). Normative developmental challenges and dieting and eating disturbances in middle school girls. *International Journal of Eating Disorders, 15,* 11–20.

Levine, M., Smolak, L., & Streigel-Moore, R. (1996). Conclusions, implications, and future directions. In L. Smolak, M. P. Levine, & R. Streigel-Moore (Eds.), *The developmental psychopathology of eating disorders: Implications for research, prevention, and treatment.* Mahwah, NJ: Lawrence Erlbaum.

Levine, R. J. (1991). Respect for children as research subjects. In M. Lewis (Ed.), *Child and adolescent psychiatry. A comprehensive textbook.* Baltimore: Williams & Wilkins.

Levy, S. R., Jurkovic, G. L., & Spiro, A. (1995). A multisystems analysis of adolescent suicide attempters. *Journal of Abnormal Child Psychology, 23,* 221–234.

Lewinsohn, P. (1974). A behavioral approach to depression. In R. J. Friedman & M. M. Katz (Eds.), *The psychology of depression: Contemporary theory and research.* Washington, DC: Winston.

Lewinsohn, P. M., Clarke, G. N., Hops, H., & Andrews, J. (1990). Cognitive behavioral treatment for depressed adolescents. *Behavior Therapy, 21,* 385–402.

Lewinsohn, P. M., Clarke, G. N., Seeley, J. R., & Rohde, P. (1994). Major depression in community adolescents: Age at onset, episode duration, and time to recurrence. *Journal of the American Academy of Child and Adolescent Psychiatry, 33,* 809–818.

Lewinsohn, P. M., Hops, H., Roberts, R. E., Seeley, J. R., & Andrews, J. A. (1993a). Adolescent psychopathology: I. Prevalence and incidence of depression and other DSM-III-R disorders in high school students. *Journal of Abnormal Psychology, 102,* 133–144.

Lewinsohn, P. M., Klein, D. N., & Seeley, J. R. (1995a). Bipolar disorders in a community sample of older adolescents: Prevalence, phenomenology, comorbidity, and course. *Journal of the American Academy of Child and Adolescent Psychiatry, 34,* 454–463.

Lewinsohn, P. M., Rohde, P., & Seeley, J. R. (1995b). Adolescent psychopathology: III. The clinical consequences of comorbidity. *Journal of the American Academy of Child and Adolescent Psychiatry, 34,* 510–519.

Lewinsohn, P. M., Rohde, P., & Seeley, J. R. (1996). Adolescent suicidal ideation and attempts: Prevalence, risk factors, and clinical implications. *Clinical Psychology: Science and Practice, 3,* 25–46.

Lewinsohn, P. M., Rohde, P., & Seeley, J. R. (1998). Major Depressive Disorder in older adolescents: Prevalence, risk factors, and clinical implications. *Clinical Psychology Review, 18,* 765–794.

Lewinsohn, P. M., Rohde, P., Klein, D. N., & Seeley, J. R. (1999). Natural course of adolescent Major Depressive Disorder: I. Continuity into young adulthood. *Journal of the American Academy of Child and Adolescent Psychiatry, 38,* 56–63.

Lewinsohn, P. M., Rohde, P., Seeley, J. R., & Fischer, S. A. (1993b). Age-cohort changes in the lifetime occurrence of depression and other mental disorders. *Journal of Abnormal Psychology, 102,* 110–120.

Lewinsohn, P. M., Seeley, J. R., & Klein, D. N. (2003). Bipolar disorder in adolescents: Epidemiology and suicidal behavior. In B. Geller & M. P. DelBello (Eds.), *Bipolar disorder in childhood and early adolescence.* New York: Guilford Press.

Lewinsohn, P. M., Striegel-Moore, R. H., & Seeley, J. R. (2000). Epidemiology and natural course of eating disorders in young women from adolescence to young adulthood. *Journal of the American Academy of Child and Adolescent Psychiatry, 39,* 1284–1292.

Lewis, S. (1974). A comparison of behavior therapy techniques in the reduction of fearful avoidance behavior. *Behavior Therapy, 5,* 648–655.

Lewis, S. Y. (2001). Coping over the long haul: Understanding and supporting children and families affected by HIV disease. *Journal of Pediatric Psychology, 26,* 359–361.

Liaw, F., & Brooks-Gunn, J. (1994). Cumulative familial risk and low-birthweight children's cognitive and behavioral development. *Journal of Clinical Child Psychology, 23,* 360–372.

Licht, B. G., & Kistner, J. A. (1986). Motivational problems of learning-disabled children: Individual differences and their implications for treatment. In J. K. Torgesen & B. Y. L. Wong (Eds.), *Psychological and educational perspectives on learning disabilities.* New York: Academic Press.

Lichtenstein, P., & Annas, P. (2000). Heritability and prevalence of specific fears and phobias in childhood. *Journal of Child Psychology and Psychiatry, 41,* 927–937.

Lilienfeld, S. O. (2003). Comorbidity between and within childhood externalizing and internalizing disorders: Reflections and directions. *Journal of Abnormal Child Psychology, 31,* 285–291.

Lilienfeld, S. O., Lynn, S. J., & Lohr, J. M. (2003). *Science and pseudoscience in clinical psychology.* New York: Guilford Press.

Lilienfeld, S. O., Waldman, I. D., & Israel, A. C. (1994). A critical examination of the use of the term and concept of comorbidity in psychopathology research. *Clinical Psychology: Science and Practice, 1,* 71–83.

Lilly, M. S. (1979). Special education. Emerging issues. In M. S. Lilly (Ed.), *Children with exceptional needs*. New York: Holt, Rinehart and Winston.

Lin, K. K., Sandler, I. N., Ayers, T. S., Wolchik, S. A., & Luecken, L. J. (2004). Resilience in parentally bereaved children and adolescents seeking preventive services. *Journal of Clinical Child and Adolescent Psychology, 33*, 673–683.

Linnet, K. M., Dalsgaard, S., Obel, C. et al. (2003). Maternal lifestyle factors in pregnancy risk of attention deficit hyperactivity disorder and associated behaviors: Review of the current literature. *American Journal of Psychiatry, 160*, 1028–1040.

Linscheid, T. R., & Rasnake, L. K. (2001). Eating problems in children. In C. E. Walker & M. C. Roberts (Eds.), *Handbook of clinical child psychology* (3rd ed.). New York: John Wiley & Sons.

Lipschitz, D. S., Rasmusson, A. M., Yehuda, R., Wang, S., Anyan, W., Gueoguieva, R. et al. (2003). Salivary cortisol responses to dexamethasone in adolescents with posttraumatic stress disorder. *Journal of the American Academy of Child and Adolescent Psychiatry, 42*, 1310–1317.

Liss, M., Fein, D., Allen, D., Dunn, M., Feinstein, C., Morris, R. et al. (2001). Executive functioning in high-functioning children with autism. *Journal of Child Psychology and Psychiatry, 42*, 261–270.

Little, M., & Kobak, R. (2003). Emotional security with teachers and children's stress reactivity: A comparison of special-education and regular-education classrooms. *Journal of Clinical Child and Adolescent Psychology, 32*, 127–138.

Llewellyn, G., Dunn, P., Fante, M., Turnbull, L., & Grace, R. (1999). Family factors influencing out-of-home placement decisions. *Journal of Intellectual Disability Research, 43*, 219–233.

Lochman, J. E., Barry, T. D., & Pardini, D. A. (2003). Anger control training for aggressive youth. In A. E. Kazdin & J. R. Weisz (Eds.), *Evidence-based psychotherapies for children and adolescents*. New York: Guilford Press.

Lochman, J. E., Whidby, J. M., & FitzGerald, D. P. (2000). Cognitive-behavioral assessment and treatment with aggressive children. In P. C. Kendall (Ed.), *Child and adolescent therapy: Cognitive-behavioral procedures* (2nd ed.). New York: Guilford.

Lock, J. (2004). Family approaches for anorexia nervosa and bulimia nervosa. In J. K. Thompson (Ed.), *Handbook of eating disorders and obesity*. Hoboken, NJ: John Wiley.

Lock, J., Le Grange, D., Agras, W. S., & Dare, C. (2001). *Treatment manual for anorexia nervosa: A family-based approach*. New York: Guilford Press.

Lockwood, K. A., Bell, T. S., & Colegrove, R. W., Jr. (1999). Long-term effects of cranial radiation therapy on attention functioning in survivors of childhood leukemia. *Journal of Pediatric Psychology, 24*, 55–66.

Loeb, S., Fuller, B., Kagan, S. L., & Carrol, B. (2004). Child care in poor communities: Early learning effects of type, quality, and stability. *Child Development, 75*, 47–65.

Loeber, R. (1988). Natural histories of conduct problems, delinquency, and associated substance use: Evidence for developmental progressions. In B. B. Lahey & A. E. Kazdin (Eds.), *Advances in clinical child psychology*, Vol. 11. New York: Plenum.

Loeber, R., Burke, J. D., Lahey, B. B., Winters, A., & Zera, M. (2000). Oppositional defiant and conduct disorder: A review of the past 10 years, Part I. *Journal of the American Academy of Child and Adolescent Psychiatry, 39*, 1468–1484.

Loeber, R., & Farrington, D. P. (2000). Young children who commit crime: Epidemiology, developmental origins, risk factors, early interventions, and policy implications. *Development and Psychopathology, 12*, 737–762.

Loeber, R., Green, S. M., Keenan, K., & Lahey, B. (1995). Which boys will fare worse? Early predictors of the onset of conduct disorder in a six-year longitudinal study. *Journal of the American Academy of Child and Adolescent Psychiatry, 34*, 499–509.

Loeber, R., & Hay, D. F. (1994). Developmental approaches to aggression and conduct problems. In M. Rutter & D. F. Hay (Eds.), *Development through life: A handbook for clinicians*. Malden, MA: Blackwell Scientific.

Loeber, R., & Keenan, K. (1994). Interaction between conduct disorder and its comorbid conditions: Effects of age and gender. *Clinical Psychology Review, 14*, 497–523.

Loeber, R., & Schmaling, K. B. (1985) Empirical evidence for overt and covert patterns of antisocial conduct problems: A meta-analysis. *Journal of Abnormal Child Psychology, 13*, 337–354.

Loeber, R., & Stouthamer-Loeber, M. (1998). Development of juvenile aggression and violence: Some common misconceptions and controversies. *American Psychologist, 53*, 242–259.

Loeber, R., Wung, P., Keenan, K., Giroux, B., Stouthamer-Loeber, M., Van Kammen, W. B., & Maughan, B. (1993). Developmental pathways in disruptive child behavior. *Development and Psychopathology, 5*, 103–133.

Lofland, K. R., Sturges, J. M., & Payne, T. J. (1999). Headache. In A. J. Goreczny & M. Hersen (Eds.), *Handbook of pediatric and adolescent health psychology*. Boston: Allyn and Bacon.

Logan, D. E., & King, C. A. (2001). Parental facilitation of adolescent mental health service utilization: A conceptual and empirical review. *Clinical Psychology: Science and Practice, 8*, 319–333.

Loney, B. R., Firck, P. J., Clements, C. B., Ellis, M. L., & Kerlin, K. (2003). Callous-unemotional traits, impulsivity, and emotional processing in adolescents with antisocial behavior problems. *Journal of Clinical Child and Adolescent Psychology, 32*, 66–80.

Long, P., Forehand, R., Wierson, M., & Morgan, A. (1994). Does parent training with young noncompliant children have long term effects? *Behaviour Research and Therapy, 32*, 101–107.

Lonigan, C. J., Burgess, S. R., & Anthony, J. L. (2000). Development of emergent literacy and early reading skills in preschool children: Evidence from a latent-variable longitudinal study. *Developmental Psychology, 36*, 596–613.

Lonigan, C. J., Vasey, M. W., Phillips, B. M., & Hazen, R. A. (2004). Temperament, anxiety, and the processing of threat-relevant stimuli. *Journal of Clinical Child and Adolescent Psychology, 33*, 8–20.

López, B., & Leekam, S. R. (2003). Do children with autism fail to process information in context? *Journal of Child Psychology and Psychiatry, 44*, 285–300.

Lorch, E. P., Milich, R., Sanchez, R. P., van den Broek, P., Baer, S., Hooks, K. et al. (2000). Comprehension of televised stories in boys with attention deficit/hyperactivity disorder and nonreferred boys. *Journal of Abnormal Psychology, 109*, 321–330.

Lord, C., & Bailey, A. (2002). Autism spectrum disorders. In M. Rutter & E. Taylor (Eds.), *Child and adolescent psychiatry*. Oxford, UK: Blackwell Publishing.

Lord, C., Risi, S., Lambrecht, L., Cook, E. H., Levanthal, B. L., DiLavore, P. C. et al. (2000). The Autism Diagnostic Observation Schedule-Generic: A standard measure of social and communicative deficits associated with the spectrum of autism. *Journal of Autism and Pervasive Developmental Disorders, 30,* 205–223.

Lord, C., Shulman, C., & DiLavore, P. (2004). Regression and word loss in autistic spectrum disorders. *Journal of Child Psychology and Psychiatry, 45,* 936–955.

Lorian, R. P. (2000). Community, prevention, and wellness. In M. Hersen & R. T. Ammerman (Eds.), *Advanced abnormal child psychology*. Mahwah, NJ: Lawrence Erlbaum Associates.

Lorion, R. P., Cowen, E. L., & Caldwell, R. A. (1974). Problem types of children referred to a school based mental health program: Identification and outcome. *Journal of Consulting and Clinical Psychology, 42,* 491–496.

Losier, B. J., McGrath, P. J., & Klein, R. M. (1996). Error patterns on the continuous performance test in non-medicated and medicated samples of children with and without ADHD: A meta-analytic review. *Journal of Child Psychology and Psychiatry, 37,* 971–987.

Lott, B. (2002). Cognitive and behavioral distancing from the poor. *American Psychologist, 57,* 100–110.

Lovaas, O. I. (1987). Behavioral treatment and normal educational and intellectual functioning in young autistic children. *Journal of Consulting and Clinical Psychology, 55,* 3–9.

Lovaas, O. I., & Smith, T. (1988). Intensive behavioral treatment for young autistic children. In B. B. Lahey & A. E. Kazdin (Eds.), *Advances in clinical child psychology*, Vol. 2. New York: Plenum.

Lovaas, O. I., & Smith, T. (2003). Early and intensive behavioral intervention in autism. In A. E. Kazdin & J. R. Weisz (Eds.), *Evidence-based psychotherapies for children and adolescents*. New York: Guilford Press.

Lovaas, O. I., Young, D. B., & Newsom, C. D. (1978). Childhood psychosis: Behavioral treatment. In B. B. Wolman (Ed.), *Handbook of treatment of mental disorders in childhood and adolescence*. Englewood Cliffs, NJ: Prentice Hall.

Lovejoy, M. C., Graczyk, P. A., O'Hare, E., & Newman, G. (2000). Maternal depression and parenting behavior: A meta-analytic review. *Clinical Psychology Review, 20,* 561–592.

Loveland, K. A., & Tunali-Kotoski, B. (1997). The school-age child with autism. In D. J. Cohen, & F. R. Volkmar (Eds.). *Handbook of pervasive and developmental disorders*. New York: John Wiley.

Lucas, A. R., & Holub, M. I. (1995). The incidence of anorexia nervosa in adolescent residents of Rochester, Minnesota, during a 50-year period. In H. C. Steinhausen (Ed.), *Eating disorders in adolescence: Anorexia and bulimia nervosa*. Berlin: Walter de Gruyter.

Luciana, M. (2003). Computerized assessment of neuropsychological function in children: Clinical and research applications of the Cambridge Neuropsychological Testing Automated Battery (CANTAB). *Journal of Child Psychology and Psychiatry, 44,* 649–663.

Luckasson, R. et al. (1992). *Mental retardation: Definition, classification, and systems of supports*. Washington, DC: American Association on Mental Retardation.

Luckasson, R. et al. (2002). *Mental retardation: Definition, classification, and systems of support*. Washington, DC: American Association on Mental Retardation.

Lustig, S. L., Kia-Keating, M., Knight, W. G., Geltman, P., Ellis, H., Kinzie, J. D. et al. (2004). Review of child and adolescent mental health. *Journal of the American Academy of Child and Adolescent Psychiatry, 43,* 24–36.

Luthar, S. S. (1993). Methodological and conceptual issues in research on childhood resilience. *Journal of Child Psychology and Psychiatry, 34,* 441–453.

Luthar, S. S. (1999). *Poverty and children's adjustment*. Thousand Oaks, CA: Sage.

Luthar, S. S., & Becker, B. E. (2002). Privileged but pressured? A study of affluent youth. *Child Development, 73,* 1593–1610.

Luthar, S. S., & Cicchetti, D. (2000). The construct of resilience: Implications for intervention and social policies. *Development and Psychopathology, 12,* 857–885.

Luthar, S. S., & Cushing, G. (1999). Neighborhood influences and child development: A prospective study of substance abusers' offspring. *Development and Psychopathology, 11,* 763–784.

Luthar, S. S., & D'Avanzo, K. (1999). Contextual factors in substance use: A study of suburban and inner-city adolescents. *Development and Psychopathology, 11,* 845–867.

Luthar, S. S., & Goldstein, A. (2004). Children's exposure to community violence: Implications for understanding risk and resilience. *Journal of Clinical Child and Adolescent Psychology, 33,* 499–505.

Luxenberg, J. S., Swedo, S. E., Flament, M. F., Friedland, R., Rapoport, J. L., & Rapoport, S. I. (1988). Neuroanatomical abnormalities in obsessive-compulsive disorder detected with quantitative x-ray computed tomography. *American Journal of Psychiatry, 145,* 1089–1093.

Lyman, R. D., & Wilson, D. R. (2001). Residential and inpatient treatment of emotionally disturbed children and adolescents. In C. E. Walker & M. C. Roberts (Eds.), *Handbook of clinical child psychology* (3rd ed.). New York: John Wiley & Sons.

Lynskey, M. T., & Fergusson, D. M. (1995). Childhood conduct problems, attention deficit behaviors, and adolescent alcohol, tobacco, and illicit drug use. *Journal of Abnormal Child Psychology, 23,* 281–302.

Lynskey, M. T., Fergusson, D. M., & Horwood, L. J. (1998). The origins of the correlations between tobacco, alcohol, and cannabis use during adolescence. *Journal of Child Psychology and Psychiatry, 39,* 995–1005.

Lyon, G. R., & Cutting, L. E. (1998). Learning disabilities. In E. J. Mash & R. A. Barkley (Eds.), *Treatment of childhood disorders*. New York: Guilford Press.

Lyon, G. R., Fletcher, J. M., & Barnes, M. C. (2003). Learning disabilities. In E. J. Mash & R. A. Barkley (Eds.), *Child psychopathology*. New York: Guilford Press.

Lyons-Ruth, K., Zeanah, C. H., & Benoit, D. (2003). Disorder and risk for disorder during infancy and toddlerhood. In E. J. Mash, & R. A. Barkley (Eds.), *Child psychopathology*. New York: Guilford Press.

Maccini, P., & Hughes, C. A. (1997). Mathematics interventions for adolescents with learning disabilities. *Learning Disabilities Research and Practice, 12,* 168–176.

Maccoby, E. E. (1992). The role of parents in the socialization of children: An historic overview. *Developmental Psychology, 28*, 1006–1017.

Maccoby, E. E., & Martin, J. A. (1983). Socialization in the context of the family: Parent-child interaction. In P. H. Mussen (Ed.), *Handbook of child psychology,* Vol. IV. New York: John Wiley.

MacDonald, A. W., Pogue-Geile, M. F., Johnson, M. K., & Carter, C. S. (2003). A specific deficit in context processing in the unaffected siblings of patients with schizophrenia. *Archives of General Psychiatry, 60*, 57–63.

Mace, F. C., Vollmer, T. R., Progar, P. R., & Mace, A. B. (1998). Assessment and treatment of self-injury. In T. S. Watson & F. M. Gresham (Eds.), *Handbook of child behavior therapy.* New York: Plenum Press.

MacFarlane, J. W., Allen, L., & Honzik, M. P. (1954). *A developmental study of the behavior problems of normal children between 21 months and 14 years.* Berkeley: University of California Press.

Macfie, J., Cicchetti, D., & Toth, S. L. (2001). The development of dissociation in maltreated preschool-aged children. *Development and Psychopathology, 13*, 233–254.

Machover, K. (1949). *Personality projection in the drawing of the human figure.* Springfield, IL: Chas. C. Thomas.

Macintosh, K. E., & Dissanayake, C. (2004). Annotation: The similarities and differences between autistic disorder and Asperger's disorder: A review of the empirical evidence. *Journal of Child Psychology and Psychiatry, 45*, 421–434.

MacLean, K. (2003). The impact of institutionalization on child development. *Development and Psychopathology, 15*, 853–884.

MacMillan, D. L., Keogh, B. K., & Jones, R. L. (1986). Special educational research on mildly handicapped learners. In M. C. Wittrock (Ed.), *Handbook of research on teaching.* New York: Macmillan.

MacMillan, D. L., & Reschly, D. J. (1997). Issues of definition and classification. In W. E. MacLean, Jr. (Ed.), *Ellis' handbook of mental deficiency, psychological theory and research.* Mahwah, NJ: Lawrence Erlbaum.

MacMillan, R., McMorris, B. J., Kruttschnitt, C. (2004). Linked lives: Stability and change in maternal circumstances and trajectories of antisocial behavior in children. *Child Development, 75*, 205–220.

Madsen, K. M., Lauritsen, M. B., Pedersen, C. B., Thorsen, P., Plesner, A-M., Andersen, P. H., & Mortensen, P. B. (2003). Thimerosal and the occurrence of autism: Negative ecological evidence from Danish population-based data. *Pediatrics, 112*, 604–606.

Magnus, K. B., Cowen, E. L., Wyman, P. A., Fagen, D. B., & Work, W. C. (1999a). Correlates of resilient outcomes among highly stressed African-American and white urban children. *Journal of Community Psychology, 27*, 473–488.

Magnus, K. B., Cowen, E. L., Wyman, P. A., Fagen, D. B., & Work, W. C. (1999b). Parent-child relationship qualities and child adjustment in highly stressed urban black and white families. *Journal of Community Psychology, 27*, 55–71.

Maguin, E., & Loeber, R. (1996). Academic performance and delinquency. In M. Tonry (Ed.), *Crime and justice* (Vol. 20). Chicago: University of Chicago Press.

Main, M. (1996). Introduction to the special section on attachment and psychopathology: 2. Overview of the field of attachment. *Journal of Consulting and Clinical Psychology, 64*, 237–243.

Malmquist, C. P. (1977). Childhood depression: A clinical and behavioral prespective. In J. G. Schulterbrandt & A. Raskin (Eds.), *Depression in childhood: Diagnosis, treatment, and conceptual models.* New York: Raven Press.

Malone, R. P., Maislin, G., Choudhury, M. S., Gifford, C., & Delaney, M. A. (2002). Risperidone treatment in children and adolescents with autism: Short- and long-term safety and effectiveness. *Journal of the American Academy of Child and Adolescent Psychiatry, 41*, 140–147.

Manassis, K., Tannock, R., & Barbosa, J. (2000). Dichotic listening and response inhibition in children with comorbid anxiety disorders and ADHD. *Journal of the American Academy of Child and Adolescent Psychiatry, 39*, 1152–1159.

Manicavasagar, V., Silove, D., Curtis, J., & Wagner, R. (2000). Continuities of separation anxiety from early life into adulthood. *Journal of Anxiety Disorders, 14*, 1–18.

Manimala, R., Blount, R. L., & Cohen, L. L. (2000). The effects of parental reassurance versus distraction on child distress and coping during immunizations. *Child Health Care, 29*, 161–177.

Manly, J. T., Kim, J. E., Rogosch, F. A., & Cicchetti, D. (2001). Dimensions of child maltreatment and children's adjustment: Contributions of developmental timing and subtype. *Development and Psychopathology, 13*, 759–782.

Mann, T. A., & Walker, P. (2003). Autism and a deficit in broadening the spread of visual attention. *Journal of Child Psychology and Psychiatry, 44*, 274–284.

Mannuzza, S., Klein, R. G., Bessler, A., Malloy, P., & LaPadula, M. (1993). Adult outcome of hyperactive boys. *Archives of General Psychiatry, 50*, 565–576.

Mannuzza, S., Klein, R. G., Bessler, A., Malloy, P., & LaPadula, M. (1998). Adult psychiatric status of hyperactive boys grown up. *American Journal of Psychiatry, 155*, 493–498.

March, J. S., & Albano, A. M. (1998). New developments in assessing pediatric anxiety disorders. In T. H. Ollendick & R. J. Prinz (Eds.), *Advances in clinical child psychology* (Vol. 20). New York: Plenum Press.

March, J. S., Franklin, M. E., Leonard, H. L., & Foa, E. B. (2004). Obsessive-compulsive disorder. In T. L. Morris & J. S. March (Eds.), *Anxiety disorders in children and adolescents.* New York: Guilford Press.

March, J. S., & Mulle, K. (1998). *OCD in children and adolescents: A cognitive-behavioral treatment manual.* New York: Guilford Press.

March, J. S., Parker, J. D. A., Sullivan, K., Stallings, P., & Conners, C. K. (1997). The multidimensional anxiety scale for children (MASC): Factor structure, reliability and validity. *Journal of the American Academy of Child and Adolescent Psychiatry 36*, 554–565.

Marchetti, A. G., & Campbell, V. A. (1990). Social skills. In J. L. Matson (Ed.), *Handbook of behavior modification with the mentally retarded.* New York: Plenum.

Marchi, M., & Cohen, P. (1990). Early childhood eating behaviors and adolescent eating disorders. *Journal of the American Academy of Child and Adolescent Psychiatry, 29*, 112–117.

Marenco, S., & Weinberger, D. R. (2000). The neurodevelopmental hypothesis of schizophrenia: Following a trail of evidence from cradle to grave. *Development and Psychopathology, 12*, 501–527.

Margolin, G. (1998). Effects of domestic violence on children. In P. K. Trickett & C. J. Schellenbach (Eds.), *Violence against children in the family and the community.* Washington, DC: American Psychological Association.

Margolin, G., & Gordis, E. B. (2000). The effects of family and community violence on children. *Annual Review of Psychology, 51*, 445–479.

Markson, S., & Fiese, B. H. (2000). Family rituals as a protective factor for children with asthma. *Journal of Pediatric Psychology, 25*, 471–479.

Marsella, A. J. (1998). Toward a "global-community psychology": Meeting the needs of a changing world. *American Psychologist, 53*, 1282–1291.

Marteau, T., Johnston, M., Baum, J. D., & Bloch, S. (1987). Goals of treatment in diabetes: A comparison of doctors and parents of children with diabetes. *Journal of Behavioral Medicine, 10*, 33–48.

Martin, A., Scahill, L., Klin, A., & Volkmar, F. R. (1999). Higher-functioning pervasive developmental disorders: Rates and patterns of psychotropic drug use. *Journal of the American Academy of Child and Adolescent Psychiatry, 38*, 923–931.

Marton, K., & Schwartz, R. G. (2003). Working memory capacity and language processes in children with specific language impairment. *Journal of Speech, Language, and Hearing Research, 46*, 1138–1153.

Masi, G., Favilla, L., Mucci, M., & Millepiedi, S. (2000). Panic disorder in clinically referred children and adolescents. *Child Psychiatry and Human Development, 31*, 139–151.

Masi, G., Millepiedi, S., Mucci, M., Poli, P., Bertini, N., & Milantoni, L. (2004). Generalized anxiety disorder in referred children and adolescents. *Journal of the American Academy of Child and Adolescent Psychiatry, 43*, 752–760.

Masten, A. S. (2001). Ordinary magic: Resilience processes in development. *American Psychologist, 56*, 227–238.

Masten, A. S., & Coatsworth, J. D. (1998). The development of competence in favorable and unfavorable environments: Lessons from research on successful children. *American Psychologist, 53*, 205–220.

Matarazzo, J. D. (1992). Psychological testing and assessment in the 21st century. *American Psychologist, 47*, 1007–1018.

Matson, J. L., LeBlanc, L. A., & Weinheimer, B. (1999). Reliability of the Matson Evaluation of Social Skills with Severe Retardation (MESSIER). *Behavior Modification, 23*, 647–661.

Matsumoto, H., Takei, N., Saito, H., Kachi, K., & Mori, N. (1999). Childhood-onset schizophrenia and obstetric complications: A case-control study. *Schizophrenia Research, 38*, 93–99.

Mattison, R. E. (2000). School consultation: A review of research on issues unique to the school environment. *Journal of the American Academy of Child and Adolescent Psychiatry, 39*, 402–413.

Maughan, B., & Rutter, M. (1998). Continuities and discontinuities in antisocial behavior from childhood to adult life. In T. H. Ollendick & R. J. Prinz (Eds.), *Advances in clinical child psychology* (Vol. 20). New York: Plenum Press.

Maughan, B., Collishaw, S., & Pickles, A. (1998). School achievement and adult qualifications among adoptees: A longitudinal study. *Journal of Child Psychology and Psychiatry, 39*, 669–685.

Maughan, B., Rowe, R., Messer, J., Goodman, R., & Meltzer, H. (2004). Conduct disorder and oppositional defiant disorder in a national sample: Developmental epidemiology. *Journal of Child Psychology and Psychiatry, 45*, 609–621.

Mawhood, L., Howlin, P., & Rutter, M. (2000). Autism and developmental receptive language disorder—a comparative follow-up in early adult life. I: Cognitive and language outcomes. *Journal of Child Psychology and Psychiatry, 41*, 547–559.

Max, J. E., Arndt, S., Castillo, C. S., Bukura, H., Robin, D. A., Lindgren, S. D., Smith, W. L., Sato, Y., & Mattheis, P. J. (1998). Attention-deficit hyperactivity symptomatology after traumatic brain injury: A prospective study. *Journal of the American Academy of Child and Adolescent Psychiatry, 37*, 841–847.

Mayes, S. D. (1992). Rumination disorder: Diagnosis, complications, mediating variables, and treatment. In B. B. Lahey & A. E. Kazdin (Eds.), *Advances in clinical child psychology*, Vol. 14. New York: Plenum.

Mayes, S. D., Calhoun, S. L., & Crites, D. L. (2001). Does DSM-IV Asperger's disorder exist? *Journal of Abnormal Child Psychology, 29*, 263–271.

McAlpine, C., & Singh, N. N. (1986). Pica in institutionalized mentally retarded persons. *Journal of Mental Deficiency Research, 30*, 171–178.

McArthur, D. S., & Roberts, G. E. (1982). *Roberts Apperception Test for Children: Manual.* Los Angeles: Western Psychological Services.

McArthur, G. M., Hogben, J. H., Edwards, V. T., Heath, S. M., & Mengler, E. D. (2000). On the "specifics" of specific reading disability and specific language impairment. *Journal of Child Psychology and Psychiatry, 41*, 869–874.

McCabe, M. P., & Ricciardelli, L. A. (2004). Weight and shape concerns of boys and men. In J. K. Thompson (Ed.), *Handbook of eating disorders and obesity.* Hoboken, NJ: John Wiley.

McCarton, C. M., Brooks-Gunn, J., Wallace, I. F., & Bauer, C. R. (1997). Results at age 8 years of early intervention for low-birth-weight premature infants: The infant health and development program. *Journal of the American Medical Association, 277*, 126–132.

McCarton, C. M., Wallace, I. F., & Bennett, F. C. (1996). Early intervention for low-birth-weight premature infants: What can we achieve? *Annals of Medicine, 28*, 221–225.

McCauley, E., Pavlidis, K., & Kendall, K. (2001). Developmental precursors of depression: The child and the social environment. In I. M. Goodyer (Ed.), *The depressed child and adolescent* (2nd ed.). Cambridge, UK: Cambridge University Press.

McClellan, J. M. (2000). Early-onset schizophrenia. In B. J. Sadock & V. A. Sadock (Eds.), *Comprehensive textbook of psychiatry* (Vol. II). Philadelphia: Lippincott Williams & Wilkins.

McClellan, J. M., & Werry, J. S. (2000). Research psychiatric diagnostic interviews for children and adolescents. Introduction. *Journal of the American Academy of Child and Adolescent Psychiatry, 39*, 19–27.

McClellan, J. M., & Werry, J. S. (2003). Evidence-based treatments in child and adolescent psychiatry: An inventory. *Journal of the*

American Academy of Child and Adolescent Psychiatry, 42, 1388–1400.

McClellan, J. M., Werry, J. et al. (2001). Practice parameter for the assessment and treatment of children and adolescents with schizophrenia. *Journal of the American Academy of Child and Adolescent Psychiatry, 40:7 Supplement,* 4S–23S.

McClellan, J., Breiger, D., McCurry, C., & Hlastala, S. A. (2003). Premorbid functioning in early-onset psychotic disorders. *Journal of the American Academy of Child and Adolescent Psychiatry, 42,* 666–672.

McClure, E. B., Kubiszyn, T., & Kaslow, N. J. (2002). Advances in the diagnosis and treatment of childhood disorders. *Professional Psychology: Research and Practice, 33,* 125–134.

McCracken, J. T., Biederman, J., Greenhill, L. L., Swanson, J. M., McGough, J. J., Spencer, T. J. et al. (2003). Analog classroom assessment of a once-daily amphetamine formulation, SLI381 (ADDERALL XR), in children with ADHD. *Journal of the American Academy of Child and Adolescent Psychiatry, 42,* 673–683.

McEachin, J. J., Smith, T., & Lovaas, O. I. (1993). Long-term outcome for children with autism who received early intensive behavioral treatment. *American Journal on Mental Retardation, 97,* 359–372.

McEvoy, R. E., Rogers, S. J., & Pennington, B. F. (1993). Executive functions and social communication deficits in young autistic children. *Journal of Child Psychology and Psychiatry, 34,* 563–578.

McGee, R., Prior, M., Williams, S., Smart, D., & Sanson, A. (2002). The long-term significance of teacher-rated hyperactivity and reading ability in childhood: Finding from two longitudinal studies. *Journal of Child Psychology and Psychiatry, 43,* 1004–1017.

McGee, R. A., & Wolfe, D. A. (1991). Psychological maltreatment: Toward an operational definition. *Development and Psychopathology, 3,* 3–18.

McGee, R., Feehan, M., Williams, S., & Anderson, J. (1992). DSM-III disorders from age 11 to age 15 years. *Journal of the American Academy of Child and Adolescent Psychiatry, 31,* 50–59.

McGee, R., Feehan, M., Williams, S., Partridge, F., Silva, P. A., & Kelly, J. (1990). DSM-III disorders in a large sample of adolescents. *Journal of the American Academy of Child and Adolescent Psychiatry, 29,* 611–619.

McGee, R., Williams, S., & Poulton, R. (2000). Hallucinations in nonpsychotic children. *Journal of the American Academy of Child and Adolescent Psychiatry, 39,* 12–13.

McGloin, J. M., & Widom, C. S. (2001). Resilience among abused and neglected children grown up. *Development and Psychopathology, 13,* 1021–1038.

McGrath, J. E., & Johnson, B. A. (2003). Methodology makes meaning: How both qualitative and quantitative paradigms shape evidence and its interpretation. In P. M. Camic, J. E. Rhodes, & L. Yardley (Eds.), *Qualitative research in psychology.* Washington, DC: American Psychological Association.

McGrath, M. L., Mellon, M. M., & Murphy, L. (2000). Empirically supported treatments in pediatric psychology: Constipation and encopresis. *Journal of Pediatric Psychology, 25,* 225–254.

McGue, M., & Lykken, D. T. (1992). Genetic influence on risk of divorce. *Psychological Science, 6,* 368–373.

McIntosh, J. L. (1999). Death and dying across the life span. In T. L. Whitman, T. V. Merluzzi, & R. D. White (Eds.), *Life-span perspectives on health and illness.* Mahwah, NJ: Lawrence Erlbaum Associates.

McKenna, K., Gordon, C. T., Lenane, M., Kaysen, D., Fahey, K., & Rapoport, J. L. (1994). Looking for childhood-onset schizophrenia: The first 71 cases screened. *Journal of the American Academy of Child and Adolescent Psychiatry, 33,* 636–644.

McLanahan, S., & Sandefur, G. (1994). *Growing up with a single parent: What hurts, what helps?* Cambridge, MA: Harvard University Press.

McLeer, S. V., & Wills, C. (2000). Psychopharmacological treatment. In M. Hersen & R. T. Ammerman (Eds.), *Advanced abnormal child psychology* (2nd ed.). Mahwah, NJ: Lawrence Erlbaum Associates.

McLoyd, V. C. (1998). Socioeconomic disadvantage and child development. *American Psychologist, 53,* 185–204.

McMahon, R. J., & Estes, A. M. (1997). Conduct problems. In E. J. Mash & L. G. Terdal (Eds.), *Assessment of childhood disorders* (3rd ed.). New York: Guilford Press.

McMahon, R. J., & Wells, K. C. (1998). Conduct disorders. In E. J. Mash & R. A. Barkley (Eds.), *Treatment of childhood disorders.* New York: Guilford.

McNulty, M. A. (2003). Dyslexia and the life course. *Journal of Learning Disabilities, 36,* 363–381.

McPartland, J., Dawson, G., Webb, S. J., Panagiotides, H., & Carver, L. J. (2004). Event-related brain potentials reveal anomalies in processing of faces in autism spectrum disorder. *Journal of Child Psychology and Psychiatry, 45,* 1235–1245.

McQuaid, E. L., Kopel, S. J., Klein, R. B., & Fritz, G. K. (2003). Medication adherence in pediatric asthma: Reasoning, responsibility, and behavior. *Journal of Pediatric Psychology, 28,* 323–333.

McQuaid, E. L., Kopel, S. J., & Nassau, J. H. (2001). Behavioral adjustment in children with asthma: A meta-analysis. *Journal of Developmental and Behavioral Pediatrics, 22,* 430–439.

McQuaid, E. L., & Walders, N. (2003). Pediatric asthma. In M. C. Roberts (Eds.), *Handbook of pediatric psychology* (3rd ed.) New York: Guilford Press.

McReynolds, P. (1987). Lightner Witmer: Little-known founder of clinical psychology. *American Psychologist, 42,* 849–858.

Mednick, S. A., Machon, R. A., Huttunen, M. O., & Bonnett, D. (1988). Fetal viral infection and adult schizophrenia. *Archives of General Psychiatry, 45,* 189–192.

Meijer, S. A., Sinnema, G., Bijstra, J. O., Mellenbergh, G. J., & Wolters, W. H. G. (2000). Social functioning in children with a chronic illness. *Journal of Child Psychology and Psychiatry, 41,* 309–317.

Meins, E., Fernyhough, C., Fradley, E., Tuckey, M. (2001). Rethinking maternal sensitivity: Mothers' comments on infants' mental processes predict security of attachment at 12 months. *Journal of Child Psychology and Psychiatry, 42,* 637–648.

Melamed, B. G., & Siegel, L. J. (1975). Reduction of anxiety in children facing hospitalization and surgery by use of filmed modeling. *Journal of Consulting and Clinical Psychology, 43,* 511–521.

Melamed, B. G., & Siegel, L. J. (1980). *Behavioral medicine: Practical applications in health care.* New York: Springer.

Mellin, L. M., Irwin, C. E., & Scully, S. (1992), Prevalence of disordered eating in girls: A survey of middle-class children. *Journal of the American Dietetic Association, 92*, 851–853.

Mellon, M. W., & McGrath, M. L. (2000). Empirically supported treatments in pediatric psychology: Nocturnal enuresis. *Journal of Pediatric Psychology, 25*, 193–214.

Melnick, S. M., & Hinshaw, S. P. (1996). What they want and what they get: The social goals of boys with ADHD and comparison boys. *Journal of Abnormal Child Psychology, 24*, 169–185.

Meltzer, H. Y., Alphs, L., Green, A. I., Altamura, C., Anand, R., Bertoldi, A. et al. (2003). Clozapine treatment for suicidality in schizophrenia. *Archives of General Psychiatry, 60*, 82–91.

Meltzer, L. J., Johnson, S. B., Pappachan, S., Silverstein, J. (2003). Blood glucose estimation in adolescence with type 1 diabetes: Predictors of accuracy and error. *Journal of Pediatric Psychology, 28*, 203–211.

Mental Health: A Report of the Surgeon General. (2001). Surgeongeneral.gov/library/mentalhealth/index.html. Washington, DC: Office of the Surgeon General, Department of Health and Human Services.

Menning, C. L. (2002). Absent parents are more than money: The joint effect of activities and financial support on youth's educational attainment. *Journal of Family Issues, 23*, 648–671.

Mercer, C. D. (1997). *Students with learning disabilities.* Upper Saddle River, NJ: Prentice Hall.

Mercer, C. D., & Mercer, A. R. (2001). *Teaching students with learning problems.* Upper Saddle River, NJ: Merrill/Prentice Hall.

Mertin, P., & Hartwig, S. (2004). Auditory hallucinations in nonpsychotic children: Diagnostic considerations. *Child and Adolescent Mental Health, 9*, 9–14.

Mesibov, G. B. (1992). Letters to the editors. Response to Thompson and McEvoy. *Journal of Autism and Developmental Disorders, 22*, 672–673.

Mesibov, G. B., & Handlan, S. (1997). Adolescents and adults with autism. In D. J. Cohen & F. R. Volkmar (Eds.), *Handbook of autism and pervasive developmental disorders.* New York: John Wiley.

Mesibov, G. B., Schroeder, C. S., & Wesson, L. (1977). Parental concerns about their children. *Journal of Pediatric Psychology, 2*, 13–17.

Mesibov, G., B., & Van Bourgondien, M. E. (1992). Autism. In S. R. Hooper, G. W. Hynd, & R. E. Mattison (Eds.), *Developmental disorders. Diagnostic criteria and clinical assessment.* Hillsdale, NJ: Erlbaum.

Miceli, P. J., Rowland, J. F., & Whitman, T. L. (1999). Chronic illnesses in childhood. In T. L. Whitman, T. V. Merluzzi, & R. D. White (Eds.), *Life-span perspectives on health and illness.* Mahwah, NJ: Lawrence Erlbaum Associates.

Michael, K. D., & Crowley, S. L. (2002). How effective are treatments for child and adolescent depression? A meta-analytic review. *Clinical Psychology Review, 22*, 247–269.

Mick, E., Biederman, J., Faraone, S. V., Sayer, J., & Kleinman, S. (2002). Case-control study of attention-deficit hyperactivity disorder and maternal smoking, alcohol use, and drug use during pregnancy. *Journal of the American Academy of Child and Adolescent Psychiatry, 41*, 378–385.

Middleton, J. A. (2001). Psychological sequelae of head injury in children and adolescents. *Journal of Child Psychology and Psychiatry, 42*, 165–180.

Mikkelsen, E. J. (2001). Enuresis and encopresis: Ten years of progress. *Journal of the American Academy of Child and Adolescent Psychiatry, 40*, 1146–1158.

Milich, R., Balentine, A. C., & Lynam, D. R. (2001, Winter). ADHD combined type and ADHD predominantly inattentive type are distinct and unrelated disorders. *Clinical Psychology: Science and Practice, 8*, 463–488.

Milich, R., McAninch, C. B., & Harris, M. J. (1992). Effects of stigmatizing information on children's peer relations: Believing is seeing. *School Psychology Review, 21*, 400–409.

Miller, B. C., Fan, X., Christensen, M., Grotevant, H. D., & van Dulmen, M. (2000). Comparisons of adopted and non-adopted adolescents in a large, nationally representative sample. *Child Development, 71*, 1458–1473.

Miller, B. D., & Wood, B. L. (1994). Psychophysiologic reactivity in asthmatic children: A cholinergically mediated confluence of pathways. *Journal of the American Academy of Child and Adolescent Psychiatry, 33*, 1236–1245.

Miller, J. E. (2000). The effects of race/ethnicity and income on early childhood asthma prevalence and health care use. *American Journal of Public Health, 90*, 428–430.

Miller, J. N., & Ozonoff, S. (2000). The external validity of Asperger's Disorder: Lack of evidence from the domain of neuropsychology. *Journal of Abnormal Psychology, 109*, 227–238.

Miller, L. C., Barrett, C. L., & Hampe, E. (1974). Phobias of childhood in a prescientific era. In A. Davids (Ed.), *Child personality and psychopathology: Current topics*, Vol. 1. New York: John Wiley.

Miller, L. C., Barrett, C. L., Hampe, E., & Noble, H. (1972). Comparison of reciprocal inhibition psychotherapy and waiting list control for phobic children. *Journal of Abnormal Psychology, 79*, 269–279.

Miller, L. K. (1999). The savant syndrome: Intellectual impairment and exceptional skill. *Psychological Bulletin, 125*, 31–46.

Miller, S. A. (1998). *Developmental research methods.* Upper Saddle River, NJ: Prentice-Hall.

Miller, S. L., & Tallal, P. (1995). A behavioral neuroscience approach to developmental language disorders: Evidence for a rapid temporal processing deficit. In D. Cicchetti & D. J. Cohen (Eds.), *Developmental psychopathology.* Vol. 2. New York: John Wiley.

Millican, F. K., & Lourie, R. S. (1970). The child with pica and his family. In E. J. Anthony and C. Koupernik (Eds.), *The child in his family*, Vol. 1. New York: Wiley-Interscience.

Minde, K., Popiel, K., Leos, N., Falkner, S., Parker, K., & Handley-Derry, M. (1993). The evaluation and treatment of sleep disturbances in young children. *Journal of Child Psychology and Psychiatry, 34*, 521–533.

Mindell, J. A. (1993). Sleep disorders in children. *Health Psychology, 12*, 151–162.

Mindell, J. A. (1999). Empirically supported treatments in pediatric psychology: Bedtime refusal and night wakings in young children. *Journal of Pediatric Psychology, 24*, 465–481.

Mindell, J. A., & Owens, J. A. (2003). *A clinical guide to pediatric sleep: Diagnosis and management of sleep problems.* Philadelphia: Lippincott Williams & Wilkins.

Minnes, P. (1988). Family stress associated with a developmentally handicapped child. *International Review of Research on Mental Retardation, 15*, 195–226.

Minshew, N. J., Sweeney, J. A., & Bauman, M. L. (1997). Neurological aspects of autism. In D. J. Cohen & F. R. Volkmar (Eds.), *Handbook of autism and pervasive developmental disorders.* New York: John Wiley.

Minty, B. (1999). Annotation: Outcomes in long-term foster family care. *Journal of Child Psychology and Psychiatry, 40,* 991–999.

Minuchin, S., Rosman, B. L., & Baker, L. (1978). *Psychosomatic families: Anorexia nervosa in context.* Cambridge, MA: Harvard University Press.

Mirkin, M. P. (1990). Eating disorders: A feminist family therapy perspective. In M. P. Mirkin (Ed.), *The social and political contexts of family therapy.* Boston: Allyn & Bacon.

Mishna, F. (2003). Learning disabilities and bullying: Double jeopardy. *Journal of Learning Disabilities, 36,* 336–347.

Mitsis, E. M., McKay, K. E., Schulz, K. P., Newcorn, J. H., & Halperin, J. M. (2000). Parent-teacher concordance for DSM-IV Attention-Deficit/Hyperactivity Disorder in a clinic-referred sample. *Journal of the American Academy of Child and Adolescent Psychiatry, 39,* 308–313.

Moffitt, T. E. (1993a). Adolescence-limited and life-course-persistent antisocial behavior: A developmental taxonomy. *Psychological Review, 100,* 674–701.

Moffitt, T. E. (1993b). The neuropsychology of conduct disorder. *Development and Psychopathology, 5,* 135–152.

Moffitt, T. E., Caspi, A., Harrington, H., & Milne, B. J. (2002). Males on the life-course-persistent and adolescence-limited antisocial pathways: Follow-up at age 26 years. *Development and Psychopathology, 14,* 179–207.

Moffitt, T. E., Caspi, A., Rutter, M., & Silva, P. (2001). *Sex differences in antisocial behaviour: Conduct disorder, delinquency, and violence in the Dunedin longitudinal study.* Cambridge, UK: Cambridge University Press.

Mojtabai, R., Nicholson, R. A., & Carpenter, B. N. (1998). Role of psychosocial treatments in management of schizophrenia: A meta-analytic review of controlled outcome studies. *Schizophrenia Bulletin, 24,* 569–587.

Moldavsky, M., Lev, D., & Lerman-Sagie, T. (2001). Behavioral phenotypes of genetic syndromes: A reference guide for psychiatrists. *Journal of the American Academy of Child and Adolescence Psychiatry, 40,* 749–760.

Mollica, R. F., Poole, C., Son, L., Murray, C. C., & Tor, S. (1997). Effects of war trauma on Cambodia refugee adolescents' functional health and mental health status. *Journal of the American Academy of Child and Adolescent Psychiatry, 36,* 1098–1106.

Molloy, C. A., Dietrich, K. N., & Bhattacharya, A. (2003). Postural stability in autism spectrum disorder. *Journal of Autism and Developmental Disorders, 33,* 643–652.

Montague, C. T., Farooqui, I. S., Whitehead, J. P. et al. (1997). Congenital leptin deficiency is associated with severe early-onset obesity in humans. *Nature, 387,* 903–907.

Monti, P. M., Colby, S. M., & O'Leary, T. A. (Eds.) (2001). *Adolescents, alcohol, and substance abuse: Reaching teens through brief interventions.* New York: Guilford.

Moore, B. D. (2005). Neurocognitive outcomes in survivors of childhood cancer. *Journal of Pediatric Psychology, 30,* 51–63.

Moore, D. R., & Arthur, J. L. (1989). Juvenile delinquency. In T. H. Ollendick & M. Hersen (Eds.), *Handbook of child psychopathology,* 2nd ed. New York: Plenum.

Moos, R. H., & Moos, B. S. (1994). *Family Environment Scale Manual* (3rd ed.). Palo Alto, CA: Consulting Psychologists Press.

Morgan, D. L., & Morgan, R. K. (2001). Single-participant research design. *American Psychologist, 56,* 119–127.

Morgan, G. A., Harmon, R. J., & Gliner, J. A. (2001). Ethical problems and principles in human research. *Journal of the American Academy of Child and Adolescent Psychiatry, 40,* 1231–1233.

Morgan, R. K. (1999). *Case studies in child and adolescent psychopathology.* Upper Saddle River, NJ: Prentice-Hall.

Morrison, D. N., McGee, R., & Stanton, W. R. (1992). Sleep problems in adolescence. *Journal of the American Academy of Child and Adolescent Psychiatry, 31,* 94–99.

Morrison, J., & Anders, T. F. (1999). *Interviewing children and adolescents: Skills and strategies for effective DSM-diagnosis.* New York: The Guilford Press.

Morrongiello, B. A., Ondejko, L., & Littlejohn, A. (2004a). Understanding toddlers' in-home injuries: I. Context, correlates, and determinants. *Journal of Pediatric Psychology, 29,* 415–431.

Morrongiello, B. A., Ondejko, L., & Littlejohn, A. (2004b). Understanding toddlers' in-home injuries: II. Examining parental strategies, and their efficacy, for managing child injury risk. *Journal of Pediatric Psychology, 29,* 433–446.

Morrow-Bradley, C., & Elliot, R. (1986). Utilization of psychotherapy research by practicing psychotherapists. *American Psychologist, 41,* 188–197.

Mortensen, P. B. et al. (1999). Effects of family history and place and season of birth on the risk of schizophrenia. *New England Journal of Medicine, 340,* 603–608.

Moss, S., Emerson, E., Bouras, N., & Holland, A. (1997). Mental disorders and problematic behaviours in people with intellectual disability: Future directions for research. *Journal of Intellectual Research, 41,* 440–447.

Mottron, L., Burack, J. A., Iarocci, G., Belleville, S., & Enns, J. T. (2003). Locally oriented perception with intact global processing among adolescents with high-functioning autism: Evidence from multiple paradigms. *Journal of Child Psychology and Psychiatry, 44,* 904–913.

Mowrer, O. H., & Mowrer, W. M. (1938). Enuresis: A method for its study and treatment. *American Journal of Orthopsychiatry, 8,* 436–459.

MTA Cooperative Group. (1999a). A 14-month randomized clinical trial of treatment strategies for attention-deficit/hyperactivity disorder. *Archives of General Psychiatry, 56,* 1073–1086.

MTA Cooperative Group. (1999b). Moderators and mediators of treatment response for children with attention-deficit/hyperactivity disorder. *Archives of Psychiatry, 56,* 1088–1096.

MTA Cooperative Group. (2004a). National Institute of Mental Health Multimodal Treatment Study of ADHD follow-up: Changes in effectiveness and growth after the end treatment. *Pediatrics, 113,* 762–769.

MTA Cooperative Group. (2004b). National Institute of Mental Health Multimodal Treatment Study of ADHD follow-up:

24-month outcomes of treatment strategies for attention-deficit/hyperactivity disorder. *Pediatrics, 113*, 754–761.

Mufson, L., & Dorta, K. P. (2003). Interpersonal psychotherapy for depressed adolescents. In A. E. Kazdin & J. R. Weisz (Eds.), *Evidence-based psychotherapies for children and adolescents.* New York: Guilford Press.

Mufson, L., Weissman, M. M., Moreau, D., & Garfindel, R. (1999). Efficacy of interpersonal therapy for depressed adolescents. *Archives of General Psychiatry, 56*, 573–579.

Mulder, E. J., Anderson, G. M., Kema, I. P., De Bildt, A., van Lange, N. D. J., Den Boer, J. A., & Minderaa, R. B. (2004). Platelet serotonin levels in pervasive developmental disorders and mental retardation: Diagnostic group differences, within-group distribution, and behavioral correlates. *Journal of the American Academy of Child and Adolescent Psychiatry, 43*, 491–499.

Muller, C. (1995). Maternal employment, parent involvement, and mathematics achievement among adolescents. *Journal of Marriage and the Family, 57*, 85–100.

Mulvey, E. P., & Cauffman, E. (2001). The inherent limits of predicting school violence. *American Psychologist, 56*, 797–802.

Mulvey, E. P., Arthur, M. W., & Reppucci, N. D. (1993). The prevention and treatment of juvenile delinquency: A review of the research. *Clinical Psychology Review, 13*, 133–167.

Mundy, P. (1993). Normal versus high functioning status in children with autism. *American Journal on Mental Retardation, 97*, 381–384.

Mundy, P. (2003). Annotation: The neural basis of social impairments in autism: The role of the dorsal medial-frontal cortex and anterior cingulated system. *Journal of Child Psychology and Psychiatry, 44*, 793–809.

Munoz, R. F., Mrazek, P. J., & Haggerty, R. J. (1996). Institute of Medicine report on prevention of mental disorders: Summary and commentary. *American Psychologist 51*, 1116–1122.

Muris, P., Merckelbach, H., Ollendick, T. H., King, N. J., & Bogie, N. (2001). Children's nighttime fears: Parent-child ratings of frequency, content, origins, coping behaviors and severity. *Behaviour Research and Therapy, 39*, 13–28.

Murphy, A. (2001). Front-Runner. *Sports Illustrated*, 95(21), 62–66.

Murphy, D. A., Greenstein, J. J., & Pelham, W. E. (1993). Pharmacological treatment. In V. B. VanHasselt & M. Hersen (Eds.), *Handbook of behavior therapy and pharmacotherapy for children: a comparative analysis.* Boston: Allyn and Bacon.

Murphy, L. M. B., Thompson, R. J., Jr., & Morris, M. A. (1997). Adherence behavior among adolescents with type I insulin-dependent diabetes mellitus: The role of cognitive appraisal processes. *Journal of Pediatric Psychology, 22*, 811–825.

Murphy-Berman, V., & Weisz, V. (1996). U. N. Convention of the Rights of the Child: Current challenges. *American Psychologist, 51*, 1231–1233.

Murray, H. A. (1943). *Thematic Apperception Test.* Cambridge, MA: Harvard University Press.

Murray, L. (1992). The impact of postnatal depression on infant development. *Journal of Child Psychology and Psychiatry, 33*, 543–561.

Murray, L., Sinclair, D. Cooper, P., Ducournau, P., Turner, P., & Stein, P. (1999). The socioemotional development of 5-year-old children of postnatally depressed mothers. *Journal of Child Psychology and Psychiatry, 33*, 543–561.

Myers, C. E., Nihira, K., & Zetlin, A. (1979). The measurement of adaptive behavior. In N. R. Ellis (Ed.), *Handbook of mental deficiency.* Hillsdale, NJ: Erlbaum.

Nadder, T. S., Silberg, J. L., Rutter, M., Maes, H. H., & Eaves, L. J. (2001). Comparison of multiple measures of ADHD symptomatology: A multivariate genetic analysis. *Journal of Child Psychology and Psychiatry, 42*, 475–486.

Nader, K., Pynoos, R. S., Fairbanks, L. & Frederick, C. (1991). Childhood PTSD reactions one year after a sniper attack. *American Journal of Psychiatry, 147*, 1526–1530.

Nangle, D. W., Erdley, C. A., Newman, J. E., Mason, C. A., & Carpenter, E. M. (2003). Popularity, friendship quantity, and friendship quality: Interacting influences on children's loneliness and depression. *Journal of Clinical Child and Adolescent Psychology, 32*, 546–555.

Nansel, T. R., Overpeck, M., Pilla, R. S., Ruan, W. J., Simons-Morton, B., & Scheidt, P. (2001). Bullying behaviors among US youth: Prevalence and association with psychosocial adjustment. *Journal of the American Medical Association, 285*, 2094–2100.

Nathan, P. E., & Langenbucher, J. W. (1999). Psychopathology: Description and classification. *Annual Review of Psychology, 50*, 79–107.

Nation, K., Clarke, P., Marshall, K. M., & Durand, M. (2004). Hidden language impairments in children: Parallels between poor reading comprehension and specific language impairment? *Journal of Speech, Language, and Hearing Research*, 47, 199–211.

Nation, M., Crusto, C., Wandersman, A., Kumpfer, C. L., Seybolt, D., & Morrissey-Kane, et al. (2003). What works in prevention. *American Psychologist, 58*, 449–456.

National Cancer Institute. (2004, June). Annual report to the nation. Retrieved September 2004, from http://nci.nih.gov.

National Center for Health Statistics. (2001). *National Vital Statistics Report, Volume 49*, Hyattsville, MD: Author.

National Center for Health Statistics. (2001). *Prevalence of overweight among children and adolescents: United States, 1999.* [On-line]. Available: http://www.cdc.gov/nchs/products/pubs/pubd/hestats/overwght99.htm.

National Commission for the Protection of Human Subjects of Biomedical and Behavioral Research. (1979). *The Belmont Report: Ethical principles and guidelines for the protection of human subjects of research.* Washington, DC: U.S. Government Printing Office.

National Institute of Child Health and Human Development (NICHD) Early Child Care Research Network. (1999). Chronicity of maternal depressive symptoms, maternal sensitivity, and child functioning at 36 months. *Developmental Psychology, 35*, 1297–1310.

National Insitute of Mental Health. (1977). *Child abuse and neglect programs: Practice and theory.* Washington, DC: U.S. Government Printing Office.

National Institutes of Health. (1997). *Highlights of the expert panel Report 2: Guidelines for the diagnosis and management of asthma* (NIH publication No. 97-4051 A). Washington, DC: U.S. Department of Health and Human Services.

Neal, J. A., & Edelmann, R. J. (2003). The etiology of social phobia: Toward a developmental profile. *Clinical Psychology Review, 23,* 761–786.

Neely-Barnes, S., & Marchenko, M. (2004). Predicting impact of childhood disability on families: Results from the 1995 National Health Interview Survey Disability Supplement. *Mental Retardation, 42,* 284–293.

Nelson, C. A., & Bloom, F. E. (1997). Child development and neuroscience. *Child Development, 68,* 970–987.

Nelson, C. A., Bloom, F. E., Cameron, J. L., Amaral, D., Dahl, R. E., & Pine, D. (2002). An integrative, multidisciplinary approach to the study of brain-behavior relations in the context of typical and atypical development. *Development and Psychopathology, 14,* 499–520.

Neumeister, A., Bain, E., Nugent, A. C., Carson, R. E., Bonne, O., Luckenbaugh, D. A., Eckelman, W., Herscovitch, P., Charney, D. S., & Drevets, W. C. (2004). Reduced serotonin Type 1$_A$ receptor binding in panic disorder. *The Journal of Neuroscience, 24,* 589–591.

Newcomb, A. F., & Bagwell, C. L. (1995). Children's friendship relations: A meta-analytic review. *Psychological Bulletin, 117,* 306–347.

Newcomb, A. F., Bukowski, W. M., Pattee, L. (1993). Children's peer relations: A meta-analytic review of popular, rejected, neglected, controversial, and average sociometric status. *Psychological Bulletin, 113,* 99–128.

Newman, F. L., & Tejeda, M. J. (1996). The need for research that is designed to support decisions in the delivery of mental health services. *American Psychologist, 51,* 1040–1049.

Newsom, C. (1998). Autistic disorder. In E. J. Mash & R. A. Barkley (Eds.), *Treatment of childhood disorders.* New York: Guilford Press.

Newsom, C., & Hovanitz, C. A. (1997). Autistic disorder. In E. J. Mash & L. G. Terdal (Eds.), *Assessment of childhood disorders.* New York: Guilford Press.

NICHD Early Child Care Research Network. (2003a). Does amount of time spent in child care predict socioeconomic adjustment during the transition to kindergarten? *Child Development, 74,* 976–1005.

NICHD Early Child Care Research Network. (2003b). Modeling the impacts of child care quality on children's preschool cognitive development. *Child Development, 74,* 1454–1475.

NICHD Early Child Care Research Network. (2004a). Are child developmental outcomes related to before- and after-school care arrangements? Results from the NICHD study of early child care. *Child Development, 75,* 280–295.

NICHD Early Child Care Research Network (2004b). Trajectories of physical aggression from toddlerhood to middle childhood: Predictors, correlates, and outcomes. *Monographs of the Society for Research in Child Development, 69 (4, serial no. 278).*

Nicholls, D. (2004). Eating problems in childhood. In J. K. Thompson (Ed.), *Handbook of eating disorders and obesity.* Hoboken, NJ: John Wiley.

Nicolson, R., Awad, G., & Sloman, L. (1998). An open trial of risperidone in young autistic children. *Journal of the American Academy of Child and Adolescent Psychiatry, 37,* 372–376.

Nicolson, R., & Rapoport, J. L. (2000). Childhood-onset schizophrenia: What can it teach us? In J. L. Rapoport (Ed.). *Childhood onset of "adult" psychopathology.* Washington, DC: American Psychiatric Press.

Nietzel, M. T., Bernstein, D. A., & Milich, R. (1994). *Introduction to clinical psychology* (4th ed.). Englewood Cliffs, NJ: Prentice Hall.

Nigg, J. T. (2001). Is ADHD a disinhibitory disorder? *Psychological Bulletin, 127,* 571–598.

Nigg, J. T., Blaskey, L. G., Huang-Pollock, C. L., & Rappley, M. D. (2002). Neuropsychological executive functions and DSM-IV ADHD subtypes. *Journal of the American Academy of Child and Adolescent Psychiatry, 41,* 59–66.

Nigg, J. T., Goldsmith, H. H., & Sachek, J. (2004). Temperament and attention deficit hyperactivity disorder: The development of a multiple pathway model. *Journal of Clinical and Adolescent Psychology, 33,* 42–53.

Nigg, J. T., & Hinshaw, S. P. (1998). Parent personality traits and psychopathology associated with antisocial behaviors in childhood attention-deficit hyperactive disorder. *Journal of Child Psychology and Psychiatry, 39,* 145–159.

Nigg, J. T., & Huang-Pollock, C. L. (2003). An early-onset model of the role of executive functions and intelligence in conduct disorder/delinquency. In B. B. Lahey, T. E. Moffitt, A. Caspi (Eds.), *Causes of conduct disorder and juvenile delinquency.* New York: Guilford Press.

NIH Consensus Development Panel. (2000). National Institutes of Health consensus development conference statement: Diagnosis and treatment of attention-deficit/hyperactivity disorder (ADHD). *Journal of the American Academy of Child and Adolescent Psychiatry, 39,* 182–193.

NIMH Developmental Psychopathology and Prevention Research Branch. (2001). National Institute of Mental Health research roundtable on prepubertal bipolar disorder. *Journal of the American Academy of Child and Adolescent Psychiatry, 40,* 871–878.

Nock, M. K. (2003). Progress review of the psychosocial treatment of child conduct problems. *Clinical Psychology: Science and Practice, 10,* 1–28.

Nolan, E. E., Gadow, K. D., & Sprafkin, J. (2001). Teacher reports of DSM-IV ADHD, ODD, and CD symptoms in schoolchildren. *Journal of the American Academy of Child and Adolescent Psychiatry, 40,* 241–248.

Nolen-Hoeksema, S. N., & Girgus, J. S. (1994). The emergence of gender differences in depression during adolescence. *Psychological Bulletin, 115,* 424–443.

Nolen-Hoeksema, S. N., Mumme, D., Wolfson, A., & Guskin, K. (1995). Helplessness in children of depressed and nondepressed mothers. *Developmental Psychology, 31,* 377–387.

Noll, R. B., Stith, L., Garstein, M. A., Ris, M. D., Grueneich, R., Vannatta, K., & Kalinyak, K. (2001). Neuropsychological functioning of youths with sickle cell disease: Comparison with non-chronically ill peers. *Journal of Pediatric Psychology, 26,* 69–78.

Nottelmann, E. D., & Jensen, P. S. (1995). Comorbidity of disorders in children and adolescents: Developmental perspectives.

In T. H. Ollendick & R. J. Prinz (Eds.), *Advances in clinical child psychology* (Vol. 17). New York: Plenum Press.

Novins, D. K., Beals, J., & Mitchell, C. M. (2001). Sequences of substance abuse among American Indian adolescents. *Journal of the American Academy of Child and Adolescent Psychiatry, 40,* 1168–1174.

Novins, D. K., Duclos, C. W., Martin, C., Jewett, C. S., Manson, S. M. (1999). Utilization of alcohol, drug, and mental health treatment services among American Indian adolescent detainees. *Journal of the American Academy of Child and Adolescent Psychiatry, 38,* 1102–1108.

Nowicki, E. A. (2003). A meta-analysis of the social competence of children with learning disabilities compared to classmates of low and average to high achievement. *Learning Disability Quarterly, 26,* 171–188.

Nurmi, E. L., Dowd, M., Tadevosyan-Leyfer, O., Haines, J. L., Folstein, S. E., & Sutcliffe, J. S. (2003). Exploratory subsetting of autism families based on savant skills improves evidence of genetic linkage to 15q11-q13. *Journal of the American Academy of Child and Adolescent Psychiatry, 42,* 856–863.

Nyborg, V. M., & Curry, J. F. (2003). The impact of perceived racism: Psychological symptoms among African American boys. *Journal of Clinical Child and Adolescent Psychology, 32,* 258–266.

O'Brien, K. M., & Vincent, N. K. (2003). Psychiatric comorbidity in anorexia and bulimia nervosa: Nature, prevalence, and causal relationships. *Clinical Psychology Review, 23,* 57–74.

O'Brien, M. (1996). Child-rearing difficulties reported by parents of infants and toddlers. *Journal of Pediatric Psychology, 21,* 433–446.

O'Byrne, K. K., Peterson, L., & Saldana, L. (1997). Survey of pediatric hospitals' preparation programs: Evidence of the impact of health psychology research. *Health Psychology, 16,* 147–154.

Ochoa, S. H., & Palmer, D. J. (1995). A meta-analysis of peer rating of sociometric studies with learning disabled students. *Journal of Special Education, 29,* 1–19.

O'Connor, T. G. (2003). Natural experiments to study the effects of early experience: Progress and limitations. *Development and Psychopathology, 15,* 837–852.

O'Connor, T. G., McGuire, S., Reiss, D., Hetherington, E. M., & Plomin, R. (1998). Co-occurrence of depressive symptoms and antisocial behavior in adolescence: A common genetic liability. *Journal of Abnormal Psychology, 107,* 27–37.

O'Leary, K. D., & Emery, R. E. (1985). Marital discord and child behavior problems. In M. D. Levine & P. Satz (Eds.), *Developmental variation and dysfunction.* New York: Academic Press.

O'Leary, K. D., & Wilson, G. T. (1987). *Behavior therapy: Application and outcome* (2nd ed.). Englewood Cliffs, NJ: Prentice Hall.

Olfson, M., Gameroff, M. J., Marcus, S. C., & Jensen, P. S. (2003). National trends in the treatment of attention deficit hyperactivity disorder. *American Journal of Psychiatry, 160,* 1071–1077.

Ohman, A., & Hultman, C. M. (1998). Electrodermal activity and obstetric complications in schizophrenia. *Journal of Abnormal Psychology, 107,* 228–237.

Okun, A., Parker, G., & Levendosky, A. A. (1994). Distinct and interactive contributions of physical abuse, socioeconomic disadvantage, and negative life events to children's social, cognitive and affective adjustment. *Development and Psychopathology, 6,* 77–98.

Ollendick, T. H. (1983). Reliability and validity of the Revised Fear Survey Schedule for Children (FSSC-R). *Behaviour Research and Therapy, 21,* 685–692.

Ollendick, T. H., Birmaher, B., & Mattis, S. G. (2004). Panic disorder. In T. L. Morris & J. S. March (Eds.), *Anxiety disorders in children and adolescents.* New York: Guilford Press.

Ollendick, T. H., & Davis, T. E. (2004). Empirically supported treatments for children and adolescents: Where to from here? *Clinical Psychology: Science and Practice, 11,* 289–294.

Ollendick, T. H., & King, N. J. (1998). Empirically supported treatments for children with phobic and anxiety disorders: Current status. *Journal of Clinical Child Psychology, 27,* 156–167.

Ollendick, T. H., & King, N. J. (2000). Empirically supported treatment for children and adolescents. In P. C. Kendall (Ed.), *Child and adolescent therapy: Cognitive-behavioral procedures* (2nd ed.). New York: Guilford Press.

Ollendick, T. H., King, N. L., & Hamilton, D. I. (1991). Origins of childhood fears: An evaluation of Rachman's theory of fear acquisition. *Behaviour Research and Therapy, 29,* 117–123.

Ollendick, T. H., Mattis, S. G., & King, N. J. (1994). Panic in children and adolescents: A review. *Journal of Child Psychology and Psychiatry, 35,* 113–134.

Oltjenbruns, K. A. (2001). Developmental context of childhood grief and regrief phenomena. In M. S. Stroebe, R. O. Hansson, W. Stroebe, & H. Schut (Eds.), *Handbook of bereavement research: Consequences, coping, and care.* Washington, DC: American Psychological Association.

Olweus, D. (1993). *Bullying at school: What we know and what we can do.* Cambridge, MA: Blackwell.

Olweus, D. (1994). Bullying at school: Basic facts and effects of a school based intervention program. *Journal of Child Psychology and Psychiatry, 35,* 1171–1190.

Ondersma, S. J., & Walker, E. (1998). Elimination disorders. In T. H. Ollendick & M. Hersen (Eds.), *Handbook of child psychopathology* (3rd ed.). New York: Plenum Press.

Oosterlaan, J., Logan, G. D., & Sergeant, J. A. (1998). Response inhibition in AD/HD, CD, comorbid AD/HD+CD, anxious, and control children: A meta-analysis of studies with the Stop task. *Journal of Child Psychology and Psychiatry, 39,* 411–425.

Organista, K. C. (2003). Mexican American children and adolescents. In J. T. Gibbs, L. N. Huang and Associates (Eds.), *Children of color: Psychological interventions with culturally diverse youth.* San Francisco: Jossey-Bass.

Orobio de Castro, B., Slot, N. W., Bosch, J. D., Koops, W., & Weerman, J. W. (2003). Negative feelings exacerbate hostile attributions of intent in highly aggressive boys. *Journal of Clinical Child and Adolescent Psychology, 32,* 56–65.

Orsmond, G. I., & Seltzer, M. M. (2000). Brothers and sisters of adults with mental retardation: Gendered nature of the sibling relationship. *American Journal on Mental Retardation, 105,* 486–508.

Öst, L. (1987). Age of onset in different phobias. *Journal of Abnormal Psychology, 96,* 123–145.

Öst, L. G., Svensson, L., Hellström, K., & Lindwall, R. (2001). One-session treatment of specific phobias in youths: A randomized clinical trial. *Journal of Consulting and Clinical Psychology, 69,* 814–824.

Osterhaus, S. O. L., Passchier, J., vander Helm-Hylkema, H., de Jong, K. T., Orlebeke, J. F., de Grauw, A. J. C., & Dekker, P. H. (1993). Effects of behavioral psychophysiological treatment on school children with migraine in a nonclinical setting: Predictors and process variables. *Journal of Pediatric Psychology, 18,* 697–715.

Overmeyer, S., Taylor, E., Blanz, B., & Schmidt, M. H. (1999). Psychosocial adversities underestimated in hyperkinetic children. *Journal of Child Psychology and Psychiatry, 40,* 259–263.

Owens, J. A., Spirito, A., McGuinn, M., Nobile, C. (2000). Sleep habits and sleep disturbance in elementary school-aged children. *Developmental and Behavioral Pediatrics, 21,* 27–36.

Ozonoff, S. (1997). Casual mechanisms of autism: Unifying perspectives from an information-processing framework. In D. J. Cohen & F. R. Volkmar (Eds.), *Handbook of autism and pervasive developmental disorders.* New York: John Wiley.

Ozonoff, S., & Cathcart, K. (1998). Effectiveness of a home program intervention for young children with autism. *Journal of Autism and Developmental Disorder, 28,* 25–32.

Ozonoff, S., & Jensen, J. (1999). Brief report: Specific executive function profiles in three neurodevelopmental disorders. *Journal of Autism and Developmental Disorders, 29,* 171–177.

Paardekooper, B., de Jong, J. T. V. M., Hermanns, J. M. A. (1999). The psychological impact of war and the refugee situation on South Sudanese children in refugee camps in Northern Uganda: An exploratory study. *Journal of Psychology and Psychiatry, 40,* 529–536.

Palmer, D. L., Berg, C. A., Wiebe, D. J., Beveridge, R. M., Korbel, C.D., Upchurch, R., et al. (2004). The role of autonomy and pubertal status in understanding age differences in maternal involvement in diabetes responsibility across adolescence. *Journal of Pediatric Psychology, 29,* 35–46.

Palmer, D. S., Fuller, K., Arora, T., & Nelson, M. (2001). Taking sides: Parent views on inclusion for their children with severe disabilities. *Exceptional Children, 67,* 467–484.

Papolos, D. F. (2003). Bipolar disorder and comorbid disorders: The case for a dimensional nosology. In B. Geller & M. P. DelBello (Eds.), *Bipolar disorder in childhood and early adolescence.* New York: Guilford Press.

Paniagua, F. A. (2000). Culture-bound syndromes, cultural variations, and psychopathology. In I. Cuéllar & F. A. Paniagua (Eds.), *Handbook of multicultural mental health.* San Diego: Academic Press.

Pardini, D. A., Lochman, J., & Frick, P. J. (2003). Callous/unemotional traits and social-cognitive processes in adjudicated youths. *Journal of the American Academy of Child and Adolescent Psychiatry, 42,* 364–371.

Parker, J. G., & Asher, S. R. (1987). Peer relations and later personal adjustment: Are low-accepted children at risk? *Psychological Bulletin, 102,* 357–389.

Parker, J. G., Rubin, K. H., Price, J. M., & DeRosier, M. E. (1995). Peer relationships, child development, and adjustment: A developmental psychopathology perspective. In D. Cicchetti & D. Cohen (Eds.), *Developmental psychopathology* (Vol. 2: *Risk, disorder and adaptation*). New York: Wiley.

Paschall, M. J., & Hubbard, M. L. (1998). Effects of neighborhood and family stressors on African American male adolescents' self-worth and propensity for violent behavior. *Journal of Consulting and Clinical Psychology, 66,* 825–831.

Patenaude, A. F., & Kupst, M. J. (2005). Psychosocial functioning in pediatric cancer. *Journal of Pediatric Psychology, 30,* 9–27.

Patja, K., Iivanainen, M., Vesala, H., Oksanen, H., & Ruoppila, I. (2000). Life expectancy of people with intellectual disability: A 35-year follow-up study. *Journal of Intellectual Disability Research, 44,* 591–599.

Patterson, G. R. (1976). The aggressive child: Victim and architect of a coercive system. In L. A. Hamerlynck, L. C. Handy, & E. J. Mash (Eds.), *Behavior modification and families.* New York: Brunner/Mazel.

Patterson, G. R. (1982). *Coercive family process: A social learning approach,* Vol. 3. Eugene, OR: Castalia.

Patterson, G. R., Chamberlain, P., & Reid, J. B. (1982). A comparative evaluation of a parent-training program. *Behavior Therapy, 13,* 638–650.

Patterson, G. R., DeBaryshe, B. D., & Ramsey, E. (1989). A developmental perspective on antisocial behavior. *American Psychologist, 44,* 329–335.

Patterson, G. R., DeGarmo, D. S., & Knutson, N. (2000). Hyperactive and antisocial behaviors: Comorbid or two points in the same process? *Development and Psychopathology, 12,* 91–106.

Patterson, G. R., Reid, J. B., & Dishion, T. J. (1992). *Antisocial boys.* Eugene, OR: Castalia Publishing Company.

Patterson, G. R., Reid, J. B., & Eddy, J. M. (2002). A brief history of the Oregon Model. In J. B. Reid, G. R. Patterson, & J. Snyder (Eds.), *Antisocial behavior in children and adolescents: A developmental analysis and model for intervention.* Washington, DC: American Psychological Association.

Patterson, G. R., Reid, J. B., Jones, R. R., & Conger, R. E. (1975). *A social learning approach to family intervention,* Vol. 1. Eugene, OR: Castalia.

Patton, G. C., Carlin, J. B., Shao, Q., Hibbert, M. E., Rosier, M., Selzer, R., & Bowes, G. (1997). Adolescent dieting: Healthy weight control or borderline eating disorder. *Journal of Child Psychology and Psychiatry, 38,* 299–306.

Paulesu, E., Démonet, J.-F., Fazio, F., McCrory, E., Chanoine, V., Brunswick, N. et al. (2001). Dyslexia: Cultural diversity and biological unity. *Science, 291,* 2165–2167.

Pavuluri, M. N., Graczyk, P. A., Henry, D. B., Carbray, J. A., Heidenreich, J., & Miklowitz, D. J. (2004). Child- and family-focused cognitive-behavioral therapy for pediatric bipolar disorder: Development and preliminary results. *Journal of the American Academy of Child and Adolescent Psychiatry, 43,* 528–537.

Pearson, D. A., Lane, D. M., Santos, C. W., Casat, C. D., Jerger, S. W., Loveland, K. A. et al. (2004). Effects of methylphenidate treatment in children with mental retardation and ADHD: Individual variation in medication response. *Journal of the American Academy of Child and Adolescent Psychiatry, 43,* 686–698.

Pediatric OCD Treatment Study (POTS) Team (2004). Cognitive-behavior therapy, sertraline, and their combination for children and adolescents with obsessive-compulsive disorder: The Pediatric OCD Treatment Study (POTS) randomized controlled trial. *Journal of the American Medical Association, 292,* 1969–1976.

Pelham, W. E. (2001, Winter). Are ADHD/I and ADHD/C the same or different? Does it matter? *Clinical Psychology: Science and Practice, 8,* 502–506.

Pelham, W. E., Wheeler, T., & Chronis, A. (1998). Empirically supported psychosocial treatments for attention deficit hyperactivity disorder. *Journal of Clinical Child Psychology, 27,* 190–205.

Pelkonen, M., Marttunen, M., Laippala, P., & Lönnqvist, J. (2000). Factors associated with early dropout from adolescent psychiatry outpatient treatment. *Journal of the American Academy of Child and Adolescent Psychiatry, 39,* 329–336.

Pennington, B. F. (1999). Toward an integrated understanding of dyslexia: Genetic, neurological, and cognitive mechanisms. *Development and Psychopathology, 11,* 629–654.

Pennington, B. F., & Lefly, D. L. (2001). Early reading development in children at family risk for dyslexia. *Child Development, 74,* 816–833.

Pennington, B. F., & Ozonoff, S. (1996). Executive functions and developmental psychopathology. *Journal of Child Psychology and Psychiatry, 37,* 51–87.

Pennington, B. F., & Welsh, M. (1997). Neuropsychology and developmental psychopathology. In D. Cicchetti & D. J. Cohen (Eds.), *Developmental Psychopathology.* New York: John Wiley.

Peris, T. S., & Hinshaw, S. P. (2003). Family dynamics and preadolescent girls with ADHD: The relationship between expressed emotion, ADHD symptomology, and comorbid disruptive behavior. *Journal of Child Psychology and Psychiatry, 44,* 1177–1190.

Perlman, M. D., & Kaufman, A. S. (1990). Assessment of Child Intelligence. In G. Goldstein & M. Hersen (Eds.), *Handbook of psychological assessment* (2nd ed.). New York: Pergamon.

Perner, J., Frith, U., Leslie, A. M., & Leekam, S. R. (1989). Exploration of the autistic child's theory of mind: Knowledge, belief, and communication. *Child Development, 60,* 689–700.

Perrin, S., Smith, P., & Yule, W. (2000). The assessment and treatment of post-traumatic stress disorder in children and adolescents. *Journal of Child Psychology and Psychiatry, 41,* 277–289.

Perry, A., Bryson, S., & Bebko, J. (1998). Brief report: Degree of facilitator influence in Facilitated Communication as a function of facilitator characteristics, attitudes, belief. *Journal of Autism and Developmental Disorders, 28,* 87–90.

Peshkin, M. M. (1959). Intractable asthma of childhood: Rehabilitation at the institutional level with a follow-up of 150 cases. *International Archives of Allergy, 15,* 91–101.

Peters, R., Petrunka, K., & Arnold, R. (2003). The Better Beginnings, Better Futures Project: A universal, comprehensive, community-based prevention approach for primary school children and their families. *Journal of Child and Adolescent Psychology, 32,* 215–227.

Peterson, B. S. (1995). Neuroimaging in child and adolescent neuropsychiatric disorders. *Journal of the American Academy of Child and Adolescent Psychiatry, 34,* 1560–1576.

Peterson, B. S. (2003). Conceptual, methodological, and statistical challenges in brain imaging studies of developmentally based psychopathologies. *Development and Psychopathology, 15,* 811–832.

Peterson, C. C. (2004). Theory-of-mind development in oral deaf children with cochlear implants or conventional hearing aids. *Journal of Child Psychology and Psychiatry, 45,* 1096–1106.

Peterson, L. (1989). Latchkey children's preparation for self-care: Overestimated, underrehearsed, and unsafe. *Journal of Clinical Child Psychology, 18,* 36–43.

Peterson, L., Farmer, J., Harbeck, C., & Chaney, J. (1990). Preparing children for hospitalization and threatening medical procedures. In A. M. Gross & R. S. Drabman (Eds.), *Handbook of clinical behavioral pediatrics.* New York: Plenum.

Peterson, L., Reach, K., & Grabe, S. (2003). Health-related disorders. In M. C. Roberts (Ed.), *Handbook of pediatric psychology* (3rd ed.). New York: Guilford Press.

Peterson, L., Schultheis, K., Ridley-Johnson, R., Miller, D. J., & Tracy, K. (1984). Comparison of three modeling procedures on the presurgical and postsurgical reactions of children. *Behavior Therapy, 15,* 197–203.

Peterson, L. J., & Mori, L. (1988). Preparation for hospitalization. In D. K. Routh (Ed.), *Handbook of pediatric psychology.* New York: Guilford.

Pettigrew, T. F. (2004). Justice deferred: A half century after *Brown v. Board of Education. American Psychologist, 59,* 521–529.

Pfeffer, C. R. (2000). Suicidal behaviour in children: An emphasis on developmental influences. In K. Hawton & K. van Heeringen (Eds.), *The international handbook of suicide and attempted suicide.* Chichester, UK: John Wiley & Sons, Ltd.

Pfefferbaum, B. (1997). Posttraumatic stress disorder in children: A review of the past 10 years. *Journal of the American Academy of Child and Adolescent Psychiatry, 36,* 1503–1511.

Pfefferbaum, B., Nixon, S. J., Krug, R. S., Tivis, R. D., Moore, V. L., Brown, J. M., Pynoos, R. S., Foy, D., & Gurwitch, R. H. (1999a). Clinical needs assessment of middle and high school students following the 1995 Oklahoma City bombing. *American Journal of Psychiatry, 156,* 1069–1074.

Pfefferbaum, B., Nixon, S. J., Tuckerm, P. M., Tivis, R. D., Moore, V. L., Gurwitch, R. H., Pynoos, R. S., & Geis, H. K. (1999b). Posttraumatic stress responses in bereaved children after the Oklahoma City bombing. *Journal of the American Academy of Child and Adolescent Psychiatry, 38,* 1372–1379.

Pfiffner, L. J., & Barkley, R. A. (1998). Treatment of ADHD in school settings. In R. A. Barkley (Ed.), *Attention-deficit hyperactivity disorder.* New York: Guilford Press.

Phelps, L., Andrea, R., Rizzo, F. G., Johnston, L., & Main, C. M. (1993). Prevalence of self-induced vomiting and laxative-medication abuse among female adolescents: A longitudinal study. *International Journal of Eating Disorders, 14,* 375–378.

Phillips, D., & Adams, G. (2001, Spring/Summer). Child care and our youngest children. *The Future of Children, 11,* 35–51.

Phillips, E. L. (1968). Achievement Place: Token reinforcement procedures in a home-style rehabilitation setting for 'predelinquent' boys. *Journal of Applied Behavior Analysis, 1,* 213–223.

Piacentini, J., Bergman, L., Keller, M., & McCracken, J. (2003). Functional impairment in children and adolescents with obsessive-compulsive disorder. *Journal of Child and Adolescent Psychopharmacology, 13*, S61–S69.

Pickles, A., & Angold, A. (2003). Natural categories or fundamental dimensions: On carving nature at the joints and the rearticulation of psychopathology. *Development andPsychopathology, 15*, 529–551.

Pickles, A., Starr, E., Kazak, S., Bolton, P., Papanikolaou, K., Bailey, A. et al. (2000). Variable expression of the autism broader phenotype: Findings from extended pedigrees. *Journal of Child Psychology and Psychiatry, 41*, 491–502.

Pickren, W. E., & Tomes, H. (2002). The legacy of Kenneth B. Clark to APA. *American Psychologist, 57*, 51–59.

Pierce, J. W., & Wardle, J. (1993). Self-esteem, parental appraisal and body size in children. *Journal of Child Psychology and Psychiatry, 34*, 1125–1136.

Pike, K. M. (1998). Long-term course of anorexia nervosa: Response, relapse, remission, and recovery. *Clinical Psychology Review, 18*, 447–475.

Pike, K. M., Devlin, M. J., & Loeb, K. L. (2004). Cognitive-behavioral therapy in the treatment of anorexia nervosa, bulimia nervosa, and binge eating disorder. In J. K. Thompson (Ed.), *Handbook of eating disorders and obesity*. Hoboken, NJ: John Wiley.

Pike, K. M., & Rodin, J. (1991). Mothers, daughters, and disordered eating. *Journal of Abnormal Psychology, 100*, 198–204.

Pillow, D. R., Pelham, W. E., Hoza, B., Molina, B. S. G., & Stultz, C. H. (1998). Confirmatory factor analyses examining attention deficit hyperactivity disorder symptoms and other childhood disruptive behaviors. *Journal of Abnormal Child Pyschology, 26*, 293–309.

Pina, A. A., & Silverman, W. K. (2004). Clinical phenomenology, somatic symptoms, and distress in Hispanic/ Latino and European American youths with anxiety disorders. *Journal of Clinical Child and Adolescent Psychology, 33*, 227–236.

Pine, D. S., Alegria, M., Cook, E. H. Jr., Costello, E. J., Dahl, R. E., Koretz. D., et al. (2002). Advances in developmental science and DSM-V. In D. J. Kupfer, M. B. First, & D. A. Regier (Eds.), *A research agenda for DSM-V*. Washington, DC: American Psychiatric Association.

Pirke, K. M., & Platte, P. (1995). Neurobiology of eating disorders in adolescence. In H. C. Steinhausen (Ed.), *Eating disorders in adolescence: Anorexia and bulimia nervosa*. Berlin: Walter de Gruyter.

Pisecco, S., Huzinec, C., & Curtis, D. (2001). The effect of child characteristics on teachers' acceptability of classroom-based behavioral strategies and psychostimulant medication for the treatment of ADHD. *Journal of Clinical Child Psychology, 30*, 413–421.

Piven, J., Harper, J. Palmer, P., & Arndt, S. (1996). Course of behavioral change in autism: a retrospective study of high-IQ adolescents and adults. *Journal of the American Academy of Child and Adolescent Psychiatry, 35*, 523–529.

Piven, J., & Palmer, P. (1997). Cognitive deficits in parents from multiple-incidence autism families. *Journal of Child Psychology and Psychiatry, 38*, 1011–1022.

Piven, J., Simon, J., Chase, G., Wzorek, M., Landa, R., Gayle, J., & Folstein, S. (1993). The etiology of autism: Pre-, peri-, and neonatal factors. *Journal of the American Academy of Child and Adolescent Psychiatry, 32*, 1256–1263.

Plaisted, K., Swettenham, J., & Rees, L. (1999). Children with autism show local precedence in a divided attention task and global precedence in a selective attention task. *Journal of Child Psychology and Psychiatry, 40*, 733–742.

Plomin, R. (1994). Genetic research and identification of environmental influences. *Journal of Child Psychology and Psychiatry, 35*, 817–834.

Plomin, R. (1995). Genetics and children's experiences in the family. *Journal of Child Psychology and Psychiatry, 36*, 33–68.

Plomin, R., & Crabbe, J. (2000). DNA. *Psychological Bulletin, 126*, 806–828.

Plomin, R., DeFries, J. C., & McClearn, G. E. (1990). *Behavioral genetics: A primer* (2nd ed.). New York: W. H. Freeman and Company.

Plomin, R., & McGuffin, P. (2003). Psychopathology in the postgenomic era. *Annual Review of Psychology, 54*, 205–225.

Plomin, R., & Rutter, M. (1998). Child development, molecular genetics, and what to do with genes once they are found. *Child Development, 69*, 1223–1242.

Poling, A., Gadow, K. D., & Cleary, J. (1991). *Drug therapy for behavior disorders: An introduction*. New York: Pergamon.

Pollitt, E., Golub, M., Gorman, K., Grantham-McGregor, S., Levitsky, D., & Schürch, B. et al. (1996). A reconceptualization of the effects of undernutrition on children's biological, psychosocial, and behavioral development. *Social Policy Report, Society for Research in Child Development, X*, 1–22.

Pollock, L. A. (2001). Parent-child relations. In D. I. Kertzer & M. Barbagoli (Eds.), *The history of the European family. Vol. One. Family life in early modern times, 1500–1789*. New Haven, CT: Yale University Press.

Pope, H. G., Gruber, A. J., Mangweth, B., Bureau, B., deCol, C., Jouvent, R. et al. (2000). Body image perception among men in three countries. *American Journal of Psychiatry, 157*, 1297–1301.

Porrino, L., Rapoport, J. L., Behar, D., Sceery, W., Ismond, D. R., & Bunney, W. E. (1983). A naturalistic assessment of the motor activity of hyperactive boys: I. Comparison with normal controls. *Archives of General Psychiatry, 40*, 681–687.

Posner, J. K., & Vandell, D. L. (1999). After-school activities and the development of low-income urban children: A longitudinal study. *Developmental Psychology, 35*, 868–879.

Posner, M. I., & Rothbart, M. K. (2000). Developing mechanisms of self-regulation. *Development and Psychopathology, 12*, 427–441.

Potter, H. W. (1972). Mental retardation in historical perspective. In S. I. Harrison & J. F. McDermott (Eds.), *Childhood psychopathology*. New York: International Universities Press.

Pottick, K. J., Barber, C. C., Hansell, S., & Coyne, L. (2001). Changing patterns of inpatient care for children and adolescents at the Menninger Clinic, 1988–1994. *Journal of Consulting and Clinical Psychology, 69*, 573–577.

Powers, S. W. (1999). Empirically supported treatments in pediatric psychology: Procedure-related pain. *Journal of Pediatric Psychology, 24*, 131–145.

Powers, S. W., Blount, R. L., Bachanas, P. J., Cotter, M. W., & Swan, S. C. (1993). Helping preschoolleukemia patients and their parents cope during injections. *Journal of Pediatric Psychology, 18,* 681–695.

Powers, S. W., & Roberts, M. W. (1995). Simulation training with parents of oppositional children: Preliminary findings. *Journal of Clinical Child Psychology, 24,* 89–97.

Praisner, C. L. (2003). Attitudes of elementary school principals toward the inclusion of students with disabilities. *Exceptional Children, 69,* 135–145.

Prelow, H. M., Danoff-Burg, S., Swenson, R. R., & Pulgiano, D. (2004). The impact of ecological risk and perceived discrimination on the psychological adjustment of African American and European American Youth. *Journal of Community Psychology, 32,* 375–389.

Prelow, H. M., Michaels, M. L., Reyes, L., Knight, G. P., & Barrera, M. (2002). Measuring coping in low-income European American, African American, and Mexican American adolescents: An examination of measurement equivalence. *Anxiety, Stress, and Coping, 15,* 135–147.

Price, R. A. (1995). The search for obesity genes. In D. B. Allison & F. X. Pi-Sunyer (Eds.), *Obesity treatment: Establishing goals, improving outcomes, and reviewing the research agenda.* New York: Plenum Press.

Pring, L., Hermelin, B., & Heavey, L. (1995). Savants, segments, art, and autism. *Journal of Child Psychology and Psychiatry, 36,* 1065–1076.

Prinstein, M. J., Boergers, J., & Vernberg, E. M. (2001). Overt and relational aggression in adolescents: Social-psychological adjustment of aggressors and victims. *Journal of Clinical Child Psychology, 30,* 479–491.

Prior, M., Smart, D., Sanson, A., & Oberklaid, F. (1999). Relationship between learning difficulties and psychological problems in preadolescent children from a longitudinal sample. *Journal of the American Academy of Child and Adolescent Psychiatry, 38,* 429–436.

Prior, M., & Werry, J. S. (1986). Autism, schizophrenia, and allied disorders. In H. C. Quay and J. S. Werry (Eds.), *Psychopathological disorders of childhood.* New York: Wiley.

Public Interest. Self-injury "consensus" stirs strife, not accord. (1989, June). *APA Monitor.*

Puig-Antich, J. (1986). Psychobiological markers: Effects of age and puberty. In M. Rutter, C. E. Izard, & P. B. Read (Eds.), *Depression in young people: Developmental and clinical perspectives.* New York: Guilford.

Puig-Antich, J., Goetz, D., Davies, M., Kaplan, T., Davies, S., Ostrow, L., Asnis, L., Toomey, J., Iyengar, S., & Ryan, N. (1989). A controlled family history study of prepubertal major depressive disorder. *Archives of General Psychiatry, 46,* 406–418.

Pumariega, A. J., & Glover, S. (1998). New developments in service delivery research for children, adolescents, and their families. In T. H. Ollendick & R. J. Prinz (Eds.), *Advances in clinical child psychology* (Vol. 20). New York: Plenum Press.

Purcell, K., Brady, K., Chai, H., Muser, J., Molk, L., Gordon, N., & Means, J. (1969). The effect on asthma in children of experimental separation from the family. *Psychosomatic Medicine, 31,* 144–164.

Purvis, K. L., & Tannock, R. (2000). Phonological processing not inhibitory control differentiates ADHD and reading disability. *Journal of the American Academy of Child and Adolescent Psychiatry, 39,* 485–494.

Putnam, F. W. (2003). Ten-year research update review: Child sexual abuse. *Journal of the American Academy of Child and Adolescent Psychiatry, 42,* 269–278.

Pynoos, R. S., Frederick, C., Nader, K., Arroyo, W., Steinberg, A., Eth, S., Nunez, F., & Fairbanks, L. (1987). Life threat and posttraumatic stress in school-age children. *Archives of General Psychiatry, 44,* 1057–1063.

Quay, H. C. (1993). The psychobiology of undersocialized aggressive conduct disorder: A theoretical perspective. *Development and Psychopathology, 5,* 165–180.

Querido, J. G., Bearss, K., & Eyberg, S. M. (2002). Theory, research, and practice of parent-child interaction therapy. In F. W. Kaslow & T. Patterson (Eds.), *Comprehensive handbook of psychotherapy: Vol. 2. Cognitive/behavioral/ functional approaches.* New York: John Wiley.

Quine, L., & Rutter, D. R. (1994). First diagnosis of severe mental and physical disability: A study of doctor-parent communication. *Journal of Child Psychology and Psychiatry, 35,* 1273–1287.

Rabian, B., & Silverman, W. K. (2000). Anxiety disorders. In M. Hersen & R. T. Ammerman (Eds.), *Advanced abnormal child psychology* (2nd ed.). Mahwah, NJ: Lawrence Erlbaum Associates.

Rahman, A., Mubbashar, M., Harrington, R., & Gater, R. (2000). Annotation: Developing child mental health services in developing countries. *Journal of Child Psychology and Psychiatry, 41,* 539–546.

Raine, A., Moffitt, T. E., Caspi, A., Loeber, R., Stouthamer-Loeber, M., & Lynam, D. (2005). Neurocognitive impairments in boys on the life-course persistent antisocial path. *Journal of Abnormal Psychology, 114,* 38–49.

Rait, D. S., Ostroff, J. S., Smith, K., Cella, D. F., Tan, C., & Lesko, L. M. (1992). Lives in a balance—perceived family functioning and the psychosocial adjustment of adolescent cancer survivors. *Family Process, 31,* 383–397.

Raitano, N. A., Pennington, B. F., Tunick, R. A., Boada, R., & Shriberg, L. D. (2004). Pre-literacy skills of subgroups of children with speech sound disorders. *Journal of Child Psychology and Psychiatry, 45,* 821–835.

Ramey, C. T., & Campbell, F. A. (1984). Preventive education for high-risk children: Cognitive consequences of the Carolina Abecedarian Project. *American Journal of Mental Deficiency, 88,* 515–523.

Ramey, C. T., & Ramey, S. L. (1998). Early intervention and early experience. *American Psychologist, 53,* 109–120.

Ramey, S. L. (1999). Head Start and preschool education: Toward continued improvement. *American Psychologist, 54,* 344–346.

Rao, U., Dahl, D., Ryan, N. D., Birmaher, B., Williamson, D. E., Giles, D. E., Rao, R., Kaufman, J., & Nelson, B. (1996). The relationship between longitudinal clinical course and sleep and cortisol changes in adolescent depression. *Biological Psychiatry, 40,* 474–483.

Rapee, R. M., Barrett, P. M., Dadds, M. R., & Evans, L. (1994). Reliability of the DSM-III-R childhood anxiety disorders using structured interview: Interrater and parent-child agreement.

Journal of the American Academy of Child and Adolescent Psychiatry, 33, 984–992.

Rapoport, J. L. (1989). The biology of obsessions and compulsions. *Scientific American, 260,* 83–89.

Rapoport, J. L., & Inhoff-Germain, G. (2000). Treatment of obsessive-compulsive disorder in children and adolescents. *Journal of Child Psychology and Psychiatry, 41,* 419–431.

Rapoport, J. L., Inhoff-Germain, G., Weissman, M. M., Greenwald, S., Narrow, W. E., Jensen, P. S., Lahey, B. B., & Canino, G. (2000). Childhood obsessive-compulsive disorder in the NIMH MECA study: Parent versus child identification of cases. *Journal of Anxiety Disorders, 14,* 535–548.

Rapoport, J. L, & Ismond, D. R. (1996). *DSM-IV training guide for diagnosis of childhood disorders.* New York: Brunner/Mazel.

Rappaport, N., & Chubinsky, P. (2000). The meaning of psychotropic medications for children, adolescent, and their families. *Journal of the American Academy of Child and Adolescent Psychiatry, 39,* 1198–1200.

Rapport, M. D. (1993). Attention deficit hyperactivity disorder. In T. H. Ollendick & M. Hersen (Eds.), *Handbook of child and adolescent assessment.* Boston: Allyn and Bacon.

Rapport, M. D., & Chung, K-M. (2000). Attention deficit hyperactivity disorder. In M. Hersen & R. T. Ammerman (Eds.), *Advanced abnormal child psychology.* Mahwah, NJ: Lawrence Erlbaum.

Rapport, M. D., Chung, K-M., Shore, G., & Isaacs, P. (2001). A conceptual model of child psychopathology: Implications for understanding attention deficit hyperactivity disorder and treatment efficacy. *Journal of Clinical Child Psychology, 30,* 48–58.

Rapport, M. D., Scanlon, S. W., & Denney, C. B. (1999). Attention-deficit/hyperactivity disorder and scholastic achievement: A model of dual developmental pathways. *Journal of Child Psychology and Psychiatry, 40,* 1169–1183.

Raymond-Speden, E., Tripp, G., Lawrence, B., & Holdaway, D. (2000). Intellectual, neuropsychological, and academic functioning in long-term survivors of leukemia. *Journal of Pediatric Psychology, 25,* 59–68.

Rea, P. J., McLaughlin, V. L., & Walther-Thomas, C. (2002). Outcome for students with learning disabilities in inclusive and pullout programs. *Exceptional Children, 68,* 203–222.

Realmuto, G. M., August, G. J., & Hektner, J. M. (2000). Predictive power of peer behavioral assessment for subsequent maladjustment in community samples of disruptive and nondisruptive children. *Journal of Child Psychology and Psychiatry, 41,* 181–190.

Reddy, R., Rhodes, J. E., & Mulhall, P. (2003). The influence of teacher support on student adjustment in the middle school years: A latent growth curve. *Development and Psychopathology, 15,* 119–138.

Regier, D. A., & Burke, J. D. (2000). Epidemiology. In B. J. Sadock & V. A. Sadock (Eds.), *Kaplan & Sadock's comprehensive textbook of psychiatry* (Vol. I). Philadelphia: Lippincott Williams & Wilkins.

Reich, W. (2000). Diagnostic Interview for Children and Adolescents (DICA). *Journal of the American Academy of Child and Adolescent Psychiatry, 39,* 59–66.

Reid, J. B. (Ed.) (1978). *A social learning approach to family intervention* (Vol. 2: *Observations in home settings*). Eugene, OR: Castalia.

Reid, J. B., & Eddy, M. (2002). Prevention efforts during the elementary school years: The linking the interests of families and teachers (LIFT) project. In J. B. Reid, G. R. Patterson, & J. Snyder (Eds.), *Antisocial behavior in children and adolescents: A developmental analysis and model for intervention.* Washington, DC: American Psychological Association.

Reid, J. B., Patterson, G. R., & Snyder, J. (Eds.) (2002). *Antisocial behavior in children and adolescents: A developmental analysis and model for intervention.* Washington, DC: American Psychological Association.

Reid, M. J., Webster-Stratton, C., & Baydar, N. (2004). Halting the development of conduct problems in Head Start children: The effects of parent training. *Journal of Clinical Child and Adolescent Psychology, 33,* 279–291.

Reifman, A., Villa, L. C., Amans, J. A., Rethinam, V., & Telesca, T. Y. (2001). Children of divorce in the 1990s: A meta-analysis. *Journal of Divorce and Remarriage, 36,* 27–36.

Reiss, A. L., & Dant, C. C. (2003). The behavioral neurogenetics of fragile X syndrome: Analyzing gene-brain-behavior relationships in child developmental psychopathologies. *Development and Psychopathology, 15,* 927–968.

Reitan, R. M., & Wolfson, D. (1993). *The Halstead-Reitan Neuropsychological Test Battery: Theory and clinical interpretation* (2nd ed.). Tucson: Neuropsychology Press.

Reiter-Purtill, J., Gerhardt, C. A., Vannatta, K., Passo, M. H., & Noll, R. B. (2003). A controlled longitudinal study of the social functioning of children with juvenile rheumatoid arthritis. *Journal of Pediatric Psychology, 28,* 17–28.

Rellini, E., Tortolani, D., Trillo, S., Carbone, S., & Montecchi, F. (2004). Childhood Autism Rating Scale (CARS) and Autism Behavior Checklist (ABC) correspondence and conflicts with DSM-IV criteria in diagnosis of autism. *Journal of Autism and Developmental Disorders, 34,* 703–708.

Rende, R. D., Plomin, R., Reiss, D., & Hetherington, E. M. (1993). Genetic and environmental influences on depressive symptomatology in adolescence: Individual differences and extreme scores. *Journal of Child Psychology and Psychiatry, 34,* 1387–1398.

Renne, C. M., & Creer, T. L. (1985). Asthmatic children and their families. In M. Wolraich & D. Routh (Eds.), *Advances in developmental and behavioral pediatrics,* Vol. 6. Greenwich, CT: JAI.

Renouf, A. G., & Kovacs, M. (1994). Concordance between mothers' reports and children's self-reports of depressive symptoms: A longitudinal study. *Journal of the American Academy of Child & Adolescent Psychiatry, 33,* 208–216.

Reppucci, N. D., Woolard, J. L., & Fried, C. S. (1999). Social, community, and preventive interventions. *Annual Review of Psychology, 50,* 387–418.

Reschly, D. J. (1992). Mental retardation: Conceptual foundations, definitional criteria, and diagnostic operations. In S. R. Hooper, G. W. Hynd, & R. W. Mattison (Eds.), *Assessment and diagnosis of child and adolescent psychiatric disorders, Vol. II. Developmental disorders.* Hillsdale, NJ: Erlbaum.

Reschley, D. J. (1996). Identification and assessment of students with disabilities. *The Future of Children, 6,* 40–53.

Rescorla, L. (2002). Language and reading outcomes to age 9 in late-talking toddlers. *Journal of Speech, Language, and Hearing Research, 45*, 360–371.

Rettew, D. C., Swedo, S. E., Leonard, H. L., Lenane, M. C., & Rapoport, J. L. (1992). Obsessions and compulsions across time in 79 children and adolescents with obsessive compulsive disorder. *Journal of the American Academy of Child and Adolescent Psychology, 31*, 1050–1056.

Rey, J. M. (1993). Oppositional defiant disorder. *American Journal of Psychiatry, 150*, 1769–1778.

Reynolds, C. R., & Kamphaus, R. W. (1992). *The Behavior Assessment System for Children*. Circle Pines, MN: American Guidance Service.

Reynolds, C. R., & Kamphaus, R. W. (2002). *The clinician's guide to the Behavior Assessment System for Children*. New York: Guilford Press.

Reynolds, C. R., & Richmond, B. O. (1978). What I think and feel: A revised measure of children's manifest anxiety. *Journal of Abnormal Child Psychology, 6*, 271–280.

Reynolds, C. R., & Richmond, B. O. (1985). *Revised Children's Manifest Anxiety Scale*. Los Angeles: Western Psychological Service.

Reynolds, W. M. (1987). *Reynolds Adolescent Depression Scale: Professional Manual*. Odessa, FL: Psychological Assessment Resources.

Reynolds, W. M. (1989). *Reynolds Child Depression Scale*. Odessa, FL: Psychological Assessment Resources.

Reynolds, W. M. (1993). Self-report methodology. In T. H. Ollendick & M. Hersen (Eds.), *Handbook of child and adolescent assessment*. Boston: Allyn & Bacon.

Reynolds, W. M. (1994). Assessment of depression in children and adolescents by self-report questionnaires. In W. M. Reynolds and H. F. Johnston (Eds.), *Handbook of depression in children and adolescents*. New York: Plenum Press.

Rhee, S. H., & Waldman, I. D. (2003). Testing alternative hypotheses regarding the role of development on genetic and environmental influences underlying antisocial behavior. In B. B. Lahey, T. E. Moffitt, A. Caspi (Eds.), *Causes of conduct disorder and juvenile delinquency*. New York: Guilford Press.

Ricciardelli, L. A., & McCabe, M. P. (2004). A biopsychosocial model of disordered eating and the pursuit of muscularity in adolescent boys. *Psychological Bulletin, 130*, 179–205.

Rice, F., Harold, G., & Thapar, A. (2002). The genetic aetiology of childhood depression: A review. *Journal of Child Psychology and Psychiatry, 43*, 65–79.

Richards, M. H., Larson, R., Miller, B. V., Luo, Z., Sims, B., Parrella, D. P., & McCauley, C. (2004). Risky and protective contexts and exposure to violence in urban African American young adolescents. *Journal of Clinical Child and Adolescent Psychology, 33*, 138–148.

Richters, J. E., & Cicchetti, D. (1993). Mark Twain meets DSM-IIIR: Conduct disorder, development, and the concept of harmful dysfunction. *Development and Psychopathology, 5*, 5–29.

Riddle, M. A., Kastelic, E. A., & Frosch, E. (2001). Pediatric psychopharmacology. *Journal of Child Psychology and Psychiatry, 42*, 73–90.

Riddle, M. A., Scahill, L., King, R., Hardin, M. T., Towbin, K. E., Ort, S. I., Leckman, J. F., & Cohen, D. J. (1992). Obsessive compulsive disorder in children and adolescents: Phenomenology and family history. *Journal of the American Academy of Child and Adolescent Psychology, 29*, 766–772.

Rie, H. E. (1971). Historical perspectives of concepts of child psychopathology. In H. E. Rie (Ed.), *Perspectives in child psychopathology*. New York: Aldine-Atherton.

Riekert, K. A., & Drotar, D. (2000). Adherence to medical treatment in pediatric chronic illness: Critical issues and answered questions. In D. Drotar (Ed.), *Promoting adherence to medical treatment in chronic childhood illness: Concepts, methods, and interventions*. Mahwah, NJ: Lawrence Erlbaum Associates.

Rieppi, R. et al. (2002). Socioeconomic status as a moderator of ADHD treatment outcomes. *Journal of the American Academy of Child and Adolescent Psychiatry, 41*, 269–277.

Ries, L. A. G., Eisner, M. P., Kosary, C. L., Hankey, B. F., Miller, B. A., Clegg, L., & Edwards, B. K. (Eds.) (2001). SEER Cancer Statistics Review, 1973–1998, National Cancer Institute. Bethesda, MD, http://seer.Cancer.gov/Publications/CSR1973 1998/2001.

Rietveld, M. J. H., Hudziak, J. J., Bartels, M., van Beijstervelt, C. E. M., & Boomsma, D. I. (2004). Heritability of attention problems in children: Longitudinal results from a study of twins, age 3 to 12. *Journal of Child Psychology and Psychiatry, 45*, 577–588.

Ripple, C. H., & Zigler, E. (2003). Research, policy, and the federal role in prevention initiatives for children. *American Psychologist, 58*, 482–490.

Roach, M. A., Barratt, M. S., Miller, J. F., & Leavitt, L. A. (1998). The structure of mother-child play: Young children with Down syndrome and typically developing children. *Developmental Psychology, 34*, 77–87.

Roberts, M. C. (Ed.) (2003). *Handbook of pediatric psychology* (3rd ed.). New York: Guilford Press.

Roberts, M. C., & Lyman, R. D. (1990). The psychologist as a pediatric consultant: Inpatient and outpatient. In A. M. Gross & R. S. Drabman (Eds.), *Handbook of clinical behavioral pediatrics*. New York: Plenum.

Roberts, M. C., & Wallander, J. L. (1992). Family issues in pediatric psychology: An overview. In M. C. Roberts & J. L. Wallander (Eds.), *Family issues in pediatric psychology*. Hillsdale, NJ: Erlbaum.

Robertson, J., Emerson, E., Gregory, N., Hatton, C., Kessissoglou, S., & Hallam, A. (2000). Receipt of psychotropic medication by people with intellectual disability in residential settings. *Journal of Intellectual Disability Research, 44*, 666–676.

Robin, A. L. (2003). Behavioral family systems therapy for adolescents with anorexia nervosa. In A. E. Kazdin & J. R. Weisz (Eds.), *Evidence-based psychotherapies for children and adolescents*. New York: Guilford Press.

Robin, A. L., Gilroy, M., & Dennis, A. B. (1998). Treatment of eating disorders in children and adolescents. *Clinical Psychology Review, 18*, 421–446.

Robin, A. L., Koepke, T., & Moye, A. (1990). Multidimensional assessment of parent-adolescent relations. *Psychological Assessment, 2*, 451–459.

Robins, L. N., Murphy, G. E., Woodruff, R. A., Jr., & King, L. J. (1971). The adult psychiatric status of black school boys. *Archives of General Psychiatry, 24,* 338–345.

Robinson, T. N. (1999). Reducing children's television viewing to prevent obesity: A randomized controlled trial. *Journal of the American Medical Association, 282,* 1561–1567.

Robinson, T. N., & Killen, J. D. (2001). Obesity prevention for children and adolescents. In J. K. Thompson & L. Smolak (Eds.), *Body image, eating disorders, and obesity in youth: Assessment, prevention, and treatment.* Washington, DC: American Psychological Association.

Roeser, R. W., & Eccles, J. S. (2000). Schooling and mental health. In A. J. Sameroff, M. Lewis, & S. M. Miller (Eds.), *Handbook of developmental psychopathology.* New York: Kluwer Academic/ Plenum Publishers.

Rogers, A. G. (2000). When methods matter: Qualitative research issues in psychology. *Harvard Educational Review, 70,* 75–85.

Rogers, S. (1998). Empirically supported comprehensive treatments for young children with autism. *Journal of Clinical Child Psychology, 27,* 168–179.

Rogers, S. J., Hepburn, S. L., Stackhouse, T., & Wehner, E. (2004). Imitation performance in toddlers with autism and those with other developmental disorders. *Journal of Child Psychology and Psychiatry, 44,* 763–781.

Rogers, S. J., Hepburn, S., & Wehner, E. (2003). Parent reports of sensory symptoms in toddlers with autism and those with other developmental disorders. *Journal of Autism and Developmental Disorders, 33,* 631–642.

Roid, G. H. (2003). *Stanford-Binet Intelligence Scale* (5th ed.). Chicago: Riverside.

Rolland-Cachera, M. F., Deheeger, M., Guilloud-Bataille, M., Avons, P., Patois, E., & Sempe, M. (1987). Tracking the development of adiposity from one month of age to adulthood. *Annals of Human Biology, 14,* 219–229.

Romans, S. E., Gendall, K. A., Martine, J. L., & Mullen, P. E. (2001). Child sexual abuse and later disordered eating: A New Zealand epidemiological study. *International Journal of Eating Disorders, 29,* 380–392.

Ronan, K., Kendall, P. C., & Rowe, M. (1994). Negative affectivity in children: Development and validation of a self-statement questionnaire. *Cognitive Therapy and Research, 18,* 509–528.

Rosenfeld, A. A., Pilowsky, D. J., Fine, P., Thorpe, M., Fein, E., Simms, M. D., Halfon, N., Irwin, M., Alfaro, J., Saletsky, R., & Nickman, S. (1997). Foster care: An update. *Journal of the American Academy of Child and Adolescent Psychiatry, 36,* 448–458.

Rosenthal, D. (1975). Heredity in criminality. *Criminal Justice and Behavior, 2,* 3–21.

Ross, A. O. (1972). The clinical child psychologist. In B. J. Wolman (Ed.), *Manual of child psychopathology.* New York: McGraw-Hill.

Ross, C. K., Lavigne, J. V., Hayford, J. R., Berry, S. L., Sinacore, J. M., & Pachman, L. M. (1993). Psychological factors affecting reported pain in juvenile rheumatoid arthritis. *Journal of Pediatric Psychology, 18,* 561–573.

Ross, D. M. (1988). Aversive treatment procedures: The school-age child's view. *Newsletter of the Society of Pediatric Psychology, 12,* 3–6.

Ross, R. G. et al. (1999). Evidence for bilineal inheritance of physiological indicators of risk in childhood-onset schizophrenia. *American Journal of Medical Genetics, 88,* 188–199.

Rosselló, J., & Bernal, G. (1996). Adapting cognitive-behavioral and interpersonal treatments for depressed Puerto Rican adolescents. In E. D. Hibbs & P. S. Jensen (Eds.), *Psychosocial treatments for child and adolescent disorders: Empirically based strategies for clinical practice.* Washington, DC: American Psychological Association.

Rosselló, J., & Bernal, G. (1999). The efficacy of cognitive-behavioral and interpersonal treatments for depression in Puerto Rican adolescents. *Journal of Consulting and Clinical Psychology, 67,* 734–745.

Rossen, M., Klima, E. S., Bellugi, U., Bihrle, A., & Jones, W. (1996). Interaction between language and cognition: Evidence from Williams syndrome. In J. H. Beitchman, N. J. Cohen, M. M. Konstantareas, & R. Tannock (Eds.), *Language, learning, and behavior disorders.* New York: Cambridge University Press.

Rossi, A., Pollice, R., Daneluzzo, E., Marinangeli, M. G., & Stratta, P. (2000). Behavioral neurodevelopment abnormalities and schizophrenic disorder: A retrospective evaluation with the Childhood Behavior Checklist (CBCL). *Schizophrenia Research, 44,* 121–128.

Rothbart, M. K. (2004). Commentary: Differentiated measures of temperament and multiple pathways to childhood disorders. *Journal of Clinical Child and Adolescent Psychology, 33,* 82–87.

Rotheram-Borus, M. J., & Duan, N. (2004). Next generation of preventive interventions. *Journal of the American Academy of Child and Adolescent Psychiatry, 42,* 518–526.

Rourke, B. P., & Fuerst, D. R. (1995). Cognitive processing, academic achievement, and psychological functioning: A neurodevelopmental perspective. In D. Cicchetti & D. J. Cohen (Eds.), *Developmental psychopathology.* New York: John Wiley.

Routh, D. K., Schroeder, C. S., & Koocher, G. P. (1983). Psychology and primary health care for children. *American Psychologist, 38,* 95–98.

Rovet, J., & Fernandes, C. (1999). Insulin-dependent diabetes mellitus. In R. T. Brown (Ed.), *Cognitive aspects of chronic illness in children.* New York: The Guilford Press.

Rubin, K. H., Burgess, K. B., Kennedy, A. E., & Stewart, S. L. (2003). Social withdrawal in childhood. In E. J. Mash & R. A. Barkley (Eds.), *Child psychopathology* (2nd ed.). New York: Guilford Press.

Rubin, K. H., Fein, G. G., & Vandenberg, B. (1983). Play. In P. H. Mussen (Ed.), *Handbook of child psychology: Vol. 4, Socialization, personality, and social behavior.* New York: Wiley.

Rucklidge, J. J., & Tannock, R. (2002). Neuropsychological profiles of adolescents with ADHD: Effects of reading difficulties and gender. *Journal of Child Psychology and Psychiatry, 43,* 988–1003.

Rudolph, K. D., & Asher, S. R. (2000). Adaptation and maladaptation in the peer system: Developmental processes and outcomes. In A. J. Sameroff, M. Lewis, & S. M. Miller (Eds.), *Handbook of developmental psychopathology* (2nd ed.). New York: Kluwer Academic/ Plenum Publishers.

Ruiz, S. Y., Pepper, A., & Wilfley, D. E. (2004). Obesity and body image among ethnically diverse children and adolescents. In J. K. Thompson (Ed.), *Handbook of eating disorders and obesity.* Hoboken, NJ: John Wiley.

Rusby, J. C., Estes, A., & Dishion, T. (1991). *The Interpersonal Process Code (IPC).* Unpublished manuscript. Oregon Social Learning Center, Eugene.

Rushton, A., & Minnis, H. (1997). Transracial family placements. *Journal of Child Psychology and Psychiatry, 38,* 147–159.

Russ, S. W. (1995). Play psychotherapy research: State of the science. In T. H. Ollendick & R. J. Prinz (Eds.), *Advances in clinical child psychology.* Vol. 17. New York: Plenum.

Russell, A. T., Bott, L., & Sammons, C. (1989). The phenomenology of schizophrenia occurring in childhood. *Journal of the American Academy of Child and Adolescent Psychiatry, 28,* 399–407.

Russell, A., Cortese, B., Lorch, E., Ivey, J., Banerjee, P., Moore, G. J., & Rosenberg, D. R. (2003). Localized functional neurochemical marker abnormalities in dorsolateral prefrontal cortex in pediatric obsessive-compulsive disorder. *Journal of Child and Adolescent Psychopharmacology, 13,* S31-S38.

Russell, J., & Hill, E. L. (2001). Action-monitoring and intention reporting in children with autism. *Journal of Child Psychology and Psychiatry, 42,* 317–328.

Russell, J., Saltmarsh, R., & Hill, E. (1999). What do executive factors contribute to the failure on false belief tasks by children with autism? *Journal of Child Psychology and Psychiatry, 40,* 859–868.

Russell, S. T., & Joyner, K. (2001). Adolescent sexual orientation and suicide risk: Evidence from a national study. *American Journal of Public Health, 91,* 1276–1281.

Rutgers, A. H., Bakersman-Kranenburg, M. J., van Ijzendoorn, M. H., & van Berckelaer-Onnes, I. A. (2004). Autism and attachment: A meta-analytic review. *Journal of Child Psychology and Psychiatry, 45,* 1123–1134.

Rutter, M. (1983). School effects on pupils progress: Research findings and policy implications. *Child Development, 54,* 1–29.

Rutter, M. (1987). Psychosocial resilience and protective mechanisms. *American Journal of Orthopsychiatry, 57,* 316–331.

Rutter, M. (1989a). Isle of Wight revisited: Twenty-five years of child psychiatric epidemiology. *Journal of the American Academy of Child and Adolescent Psychiatry, 28,* 633–653.

Rutter, M. (1989b). Pathways from childhood to adult life. *Journal of Child Psychology and Psychiatry, 30,* 23–51.

Rutter, M. (2000). Psychosocial influences: Critiques, findings, and research needs. *Development and Psychopathology, 12,* 375–405.

Rutter, M. (2002). Nature, nurture, and development: From evangelism through science toward policy and practice. *Child Development, 73,* 1–21.

Rutter, M. (2003). Critical paths from risk indicator to causal mechanisms. In B. B. Lahey, T. E. Moffitt, A. Caspi (Eds.), *Causes of conduct disorder and juvenile delinquency.* New York: Guilford Press.

Rutter, M., Caspi, A., & Moffitt, T. E. (2003). Using sex differences in psychopathology to study causal mechanisms: Unifying issues and research strategies. *Journal of Child Psychology and Psychiatry, 44,* 1092–1115.

Rutter, M., Giller, H., & Hagell, A. (1998). *Antisocial behavior by young people.* Cambridge, England: Cambridge University Press.

Rutter, M., & Maughan, B. (2002). School effectiveness findings 1979–2002. *Journal of School Psychology, 40,* 451–475.

Rutter, M., Mawhood, L., & Howlin, P. (1992). Language delay and social development. In P. Fletcher & D. Hall (Eds.), *Specific speech and language disorders in children.* San Diego, CA: Singular Publishing Group.

Rutter, M., & Schopler, E. (1987). Autism and pervasive developmental disorders: Concepts and diagnostic issues. *Journal of Autism and Developmental Disorders, 17,* 159–186.

Rutter, M., & Silberg, J. (2002). Gene-environment interplay in relation to emotional and behavioral disturbance. *Annual Review of Psychology, 54,* 463–490.

Rutter, M., Silberg, J., O'Connor, T., & Simonoff, E. (1999). Genetics and child psychiatry: II Empirical research findings. *Journal of Child Psychology and Psychiatry, 40,* 19–55.

Rutter, M., & Smith, D. J. (1995). *Psychosocial disorders in young people: Time trends and their causes.* New York: Wiley.

Rutter, M., & Sroufe, L. A. (2000). Developmental psychopathology: Concepts and challenges. *Development and Psychopathology, 12,* 265–296.

Rutter, M., Tizard, J., & Whitmore, K. (Eds.) (1970). *Education, health, and behavior.* London: Longmans.

Ryan, N. D. (2003). The pharmacological treatment of child and adolescent bipolar disorder. In B. Geller & M. P. DelBello (Eds.), *Bipolar disorder in childhood and early adolescence.* New York: Guilford Press.

Ryan, N. D., Puig-Antich, J., Ambrosini, P., Ravinovich, H., Robinson, D., Neilson, B., Iyenhar, S., & Toomey, J. (1987). The clinical picture of major depression in children and adolescents. *Archives of General Psychiatry, 44,* 854–861.

Sadeh, A., Raviv, A., & Gruber, R. (2000). Sleep patterns and sleep disruptions in school-age children. *Developmental Psychology, 36,* 291–301.

Sahler, O. J., Frager, G., Levetown, M., Cohn, F. G., & Lipson, M. A. (2000). Medical education about end-of-life care in the pediatric setting: Principles, challenges, and opportunities. *Pediatrics, 105,* 575–584.

Saler, L., & Skolnick, N. (1992). Childhood parental death and depression in adulthood: Roles of surviving parent and family environment. *American Journal of Orthopsychiatry, 62,* 504–516.

Salmon, K., & Bryant, R. A. (2002). Posttraumatic stress disorder in children: The influence of developmental factors. *Clinical Psychology Review, 22,* 163–188.

Salmon, K., & Pereira, J. K. (2002). Predicting children's response to an invasive medical investigation: The influence of effortful control and parent behavior. *Journal of Pediatric Psychology, 27,* 227–233.

Saloviita, T., & Sariola, H. (2003). Authorship in facilitated communication: A re-analysis of a case of assumed representative authentic writing. *Mental Retardation, 41,* 374–379.

Salzinger, S., Feldman, R. S., Ng-Mak, D. S., Mojica, E., & Stockhammer, T. F. (2001). The effect of physical abuse on children's social and affective status: A model of cognitive and behavioral processes explaining the association. *Development and Psychopathology, 13,* 805–825.

Sameroff, A. J. (1990). Neo-environmental perspectives on developmental theory. In R. M. Hodapp, J. A. Burack, & E. Zigler (Eds.), *Issues in the developmental approach to mental retardation.* New York: Cambridge University Press.

Sandberg, S., Rutter, M., Pickles, A., McGuinness, D., & Angold, A. (2001). Do high-threat life events really provoke the onset of psychiatric disorder in children? *Journal of Child Psychology and Psychiatry, 42,* 523–532.

Sanson, A., Smart, D., Prior, M., & Oberklaid, F. (1993). Precursors of hyperactivity and aggression. *Journal of the American Academy of Child and Adolescent Psychiatry, 32,* 1207–1216.

Santostefano, S. (1978). A biodevelopmental approach to clinical child psychology. New York: Wiley-Interscience.

Saris, W. J. M. (1995). Metabolic effects of exercise in overweight individuals. In K. D. Brownell & C. G. Fairburn (Eds.), *Eating disorders and obesity: A comprehensive handbook.* New York: Guilford Press.

Sattler, J. M. (1992). *Assessment of children.* (Revised and updated 3rd ed.). San Diego: Jerome M. Sattler, Publisher.

Savin, D., Sack, W. H., Clarke, G. N., Meas, N., & Richart, I. (1996). The Khmer Adolescent Project: III. A study of trauma from Thailand's Site II refugee camp. *Journal of the American Academy of Child and Adolescent Psychiatry, 35,* 384–391.

Savin-Williams, R. C. (2001). Suicide attempts among sexual-minority youths: Population and measurement issues. *Journal of Consulting and Clinical Psychology, 69,* 983–991.

Savin-Williams, R. C., & Ream, G. L. (2003). Suicide attempts among sexual-minority male youth. *Journal of Clinical Child and Adolescent Psychology, 32,* 509–522.

Sawyer, M. G., Whaites, L., Rey, J. M., Hazell, P. L., Graetz, B. W., & Baghurst, P. (2002). Health-related quality of life of children and adolescents with mental disorders. *Journal of the American Academy of Child and Adolescent Psychiatry, 41,* 530–537.

Saylor, C. F., Boyce, G. C., & Price, C. (2003). Early predictors of school-age behavior problems and social skills in children with intraventricular hemorrhage (IVH) and/or extremely low birthweight (ELBW). *Child Psychiatry and Human Development, 33,* 175–192.

Saylor, C. F., Cowart, B. L., Lipovsky, J. A., Jackson, C., & Finch, A.J., Jr. (2003). Media exposure to September 11: Elementary school students' experiences and posttraumatic symptoms. *American Behavioral Scientist, 46,* 1622–1642.

Saylor, C. F., Powell, P., & Swenson, C. (1992). Hurricane Hugo blows down the broccoli: Preschoolers' post-disaster play and adjustment. *Child Psychiatry and Human Development, 22,* 139–149.

Scahill, L., Kano, Y., King, R. A., Carlson, A., Peller, A., LeBrun, U. et al. (2003). Influence of age and tic disorders on obsessive-compulsive disorder in a pediatric sample. *Journal of Child and Adolescent Psychopharmacology, 13,* S7–S17.

Scambler, D., Rogers, S. J., & Wehner, E. A. (2001). Can the Checklist for Autism in Toddlers differentiate young children with autism from those with developmental delay? *Journal of the American Academy of Child and Adolescent Psychiatry, 40,* 1457–1463.

Scarr, S. (1982). Testing for children: Assessment and the many determinants of intellectual competence. In S. Chess & A. Thomas (Eds.), *Annual progress in child psychiatry and child development 1982.* New York: Brunner/Mazel.

Scarr, S. (1998). American child care today. *American Psychologist, 53,* 95–108.

Scarr, S., Phillips, D., & McCartney, K. (1989). Working mothers and their families. *American Psychologist, 44,* 1402–1409.

Schachar, R., & Tannock, R. (2002). Syndromes of hyperactivity and attention deficit. In M. Rutter & E. Taylor (Eds.), *Child and adolescent psychiatry.* Oxford, UK: Blackwell Publishing.

Schaeffer, J. L., & Ross, R. G. (2002). Childhood-onset schizophrenia: Premorbid and prodromal diagnostic and treatment histories. *Journal of the American Academy of Child and Adolescent Psychiatry, 41,* 538–545.

Scharff, L., Marcus, D., & Masek, B. J. (2002). A controlled study of minimal-contact thermal biofeedback treatment in children with migraine. *Journal of Pediatric Psychology, 27,* 109–119.

Scheerenberger, R. C. (1983, 1987). *A history of mental retardation.* Baltimore: Brookes Publishing Co.

Scheeringa, M. S., Zeanah, C. H., Myers, L., & Putnam, F. W. (2003). New findings on alternative criteria for PTSD in preschool children. *Journal of the American Academy of Child and Adolescent Psychiatry, 42,* 561–570.

Schetky, D. H. (2000). Ethical issues in child and adolescent psychiatry. In B. J. Sadock & V. A. Sadock (Eds.), *Comprehensive textbook of psychiatry* (Vol. II). Philadelphia: Lippincott Williams & Wilkins.

Schiff, W. B., Holtz, K. D., Peterson, N., & Rakusan, T. (2001). Effect of an intervention to reduce procedural pain and distress for children with HIV infection. *Journal of Pediatric Psychology, 26,* 417–427.

Schippell, P. L., Vasey, M. W., Cravens-Brown, L. M., & Bretveld, R. A. (2003). Suppressed attention to rejection, ridicule, and failure cues: A unique correlate of reactive but not proactive aggression. *Journal of Clinical Child and Adolescent Psychology, 32,* 40–55.

Schlicker, S. A., Borra, S. T., & Regan, C. (1994). The weight and fitness status of United States children. *Nutrition Reviews, 52,* 11–17.

Schniering, C. A., Hudson, J. L., & Rapee, R. M. (2000). Issues in the diagnosis and assessment of anxiety disorders in children and adolescents. *Clinical Psychology Review, 20,* 453–478.

Schopler, E. (1994). Behavioral priorities for autism and related developmental disorders. In E. Schopler & G. B. Mesibov (Eds.), *Behavioral issues in autism.* New York: Plenum.

Schopler, E. (1997). Implementation of TEACCH philosophy. In D. J. Cohen & F. R. Volkmar (Eds.), *Handbook of autism and pervasive developmental disorders.* New York: John Wiley.

Schopler, E., Reichler, R. J., DeVellis, R. F., & Daly, K. (1980). Toward objective classification of childhood autism: Childhood Autism Rating Scale (CARS). *Journal of Autism and Developmental Disorders, 10,* 91–103.

Schopler, E., Reichler, R. J., & Renner, B. R. (1988). *The Childhood Autism Rating Scale (CARS).* Los Angeles: Western Psychological Services.

Schopler, E., Short, A., & Mesibov, G. (1989). Relation of behavioral treatment to "normal functioning": Comment on Lovaas. *Journal of Consulting and Clinical Psychology, 57*, 162–164.

Schreibman, L. (1997). Theoretical perspectives on behavioral intervention for individuals with autism. In D. J. Cohen & F. R. Volkmar (Eds.), *Handbook of autism and pervasive developmental disorders.* New York: John Wiley.

Schreibman, L. (2000). Intensive behavioral/psychoeducational treatments for autism: Research needs and future directions. *Journal of Autism and Developmental Disorders, 30*, 373–378.

Schroeder, C. S., & Gordon, B. N. (2002). *Assessment and treatment of childhood problems: A clinician's guide* (2nd ed.). New York: Guilford Press.

Schulte-Körne, G. (2001). Annotation: Genetics of reading and spelling disorder. *Journal of Child Psychology and Psychiatry, 42*, 985–997.

Schultz, D., Izard, C. E., Ackerman, B. P., & Youngstrom, E. A. (2001). Emotion knowledge in economically disadvantaged children: Self-regulatory antecedents and relations to social difficulties and withdrawal. *Development and Psychopathology, 13*, 53–67.

Schultz, R. T., & Klin, A. (2002). Genetics of childhood disorders: XLIII. Autism, Part 2: Neural foundations. *Journal of the American Academy of Child and Adolescent Psychiatry, 41*, 1259–1262.

Schumaker, J. B., & Deshler, D. D. (2003). Can students with LD become competent writers? *Learning Disability Quarterly, 26*, 129–141.

Schuster, M. A., Stein, B. D., Jaycox, L. H., Collins, R. L., Marshall, G. N., Elliott, M. N. et al. (2001). A national survey of stress reactions after the September 11, 2001 terrorist attacks. *New England Journal of Medicine, 345*, 1507–1512.

Schwab-Stone, M., Chen, C., Greenberger, E., Silver, D., Lichtman, J., & Voyce, C. (1999). No safe haven II: The effects of violence exposure on urban youth. *Journal of the American Academy of Child and Adolescent Psychiatry, 38*, 359–367.

Schwartz, D., Dodge, K. A., & Coie, J. D. (1993). The emergence of chronic peer victimization in boys' play groups. *Child Development, 64*, 1755–1772.

Schwartz, D., Dodge, K. A., Coie, J. D., Hubbard, J. A., Cillessen, A. H. N., Lemerise, E. A., & Bateman, H. (1998). Social-cognitive and behavioral correlates of aggression and victimization in boys' play groups. *Journal of Abnormal Child Psychology, 26*, 431–440.

Schwartz, D., Dodge, K. A., Pettit, G. S., & Bates, J. E. (1997). The early socialization of aggressive victims of bullying. *Child Development, 68*, 665–675.

Schwartz, J. A. J., Gladstone, T. R. G., & Kaslow, N. J. (1998). Depressive disorders. In T. H. Ollendick & M. Hersen (Eds.), *Handbook of child psychopathology* (3rd ed.). New York: Plenum Press.

Schwartz, J. A. J., Kaslow, N. J., Seeley, J., & Lewinsohn, P. (2000). Psychological, cognitive, and interpersonal correlates of attributional changes in adolescents. *Journal of Clinical Child Psychology, 29*, 188–198.

Scorgie, K., & Sobsey, D. (2000). Transformational outcomes associated with parenting children who have disabilities. *Mental Retardation, 38*, 195–206.

Scott, K. L., & Crooks, C. V. (2004). Effecting change in maltreating fathers: Critical principles for intervention planning. *Clinical Psychology: Science and Practice, 11*, 95–111.

Scott, S. (1994). Mental retardation. In M. Rutter, E. Taylor, & L. Hersov (Eds.), *Child and adolescent psychiatry. Modern approaches.* Cambridge, MA: Blackwell.

Scotti, J. R., Morris, T. L., McNeil, C. B., & Hawkins, R. P. (1996). DSM-IV and disorders of childhood and adolescence: Can structural criteria be functional? *Journal of Consulting and Clinical Psychology, 64*, 1177–1191.

Scruggs, T. E., & Mastropieri, M. A. (2002). On babies and bathwater: Addressing the problems of identification of learning disabilities. *Learning Disability Quarterly, 25*, 155–168.

Sears, H. A. (2004). Adolescents in rural communities seeking help: Who reports problems and who sees professionals? *Journal of Child Psychology and Psychiatry, 45*, 396–404.

Sears, R. R. (1975). *Your ancients revisited: A history of child development.* Chicago: University of Chicago Press.

Seifer, R. (2000). Temperament and goodness of fit: Implications for developmental psychopathology. In A. J. Sameroff, M. Lewis, & S. M. Miller (Eds.), *Handbook of developmental psychopathology.* New York: Kluwer Academic/Plenum Publishers.

Seiffge-Krenke, I. (1998). The highly structured climate in families of adolescents with diabetes: Functional or dysfunctional for metabolic control? *Journal of Pediatric Psychology, 23*, 313–322.

Seligman, M. P., & Peterson, C. (1986). A learned helplessness perspective on childhood depression: Theory and research. In M. Rutter, C. E. Izard, & P. B. Read (Eds.), *Depression in young people: Developmental and clinical perspectives.* New York: Guilford.

Seltzer, M. M., Greenberg, J. S., Floyd, S. J., Pettee, Y., & Hong, J. (2001). Life course impacts on parenting a child with a disability. *American Journal on Retardation, 106*, 265–286.

Seltzer, M. M., Krauss, M. W., Shattuck, P. T., Orsmond, G., Swe, A., & Lord, C. (2003). The symptoms of autism spectrum disorders in adolescence and adulthood. *Journal of Autism and Developmental Disorders, 33*, 565–581.

Selye, H. (1956). *The stress of life.* New York: McGraw-Hill.

Semrud-Clikeman, M., Steingard, R. J., Filipek, P., Biederman, J., Bekken, K., & Renshaw, P. F. (2000). Using MRI to examine brain-behavior relationships in males with attention deficit disorder with hyperactivity. *Journal of the American Academy of Child and Adolescent Psychiatry, 39*, 477–484.

Senf, G. M. (1986). LD research in sociological and scientific perspective. In J. K. Torgesen & B. Y. L. Wong (Eds.), *Psychological and educational perspectives on learning disabilities.* New York: Academic Press.

Serra, M., Loth, F. L., van Geert, P. L. C., Hurkens, E., & Minderaa, R. B. (2002). Theory of mind in children with "lesser variants" of autism: A longitudinal study. *Journal of Child Psychology and Psychiatry, 43*, 885–900.

Shadish, W. R., Cook, T. D., & Campbell, D. T. (2002). *Experimental and quasi-experimental designs for generalized causal inference.* Boston: Houghton Mifflin.

Shaffer, D., & Waslick, B. D. (1996). Elimination and sleep disorders. In J. M. Wiener (Ed.), *Diagnosis and psychopharmacology of childhood and adolescent disorders.* New York: John Wiley.

Shah, A., & Frith, U. (1993). Why do autistic individuals show superior performance on the block design task? *Journal of Child Psychology and Psychiatry, 34*, 1351–1364.

Shalev, R. S., Manor, O., Kerem, B., Ayali, M., Badichi, N., Friedlander, Y. et al. (2001). Developmental dyscalculia is a familial learning disability. *Journal of Learning Disabilities, 34*, 59–65.

Shapiro, S., Newcomb, M., & Loeb, T. B. (1997). Fear of fat, disregulated-restrained eating, and body-esteem: Prevalence and gender differences among eight- to ten-year-old children. *Journal of Clinical Psychology, 26*, 358–365.

Shapiro, T., & Esman, A. (1992). Psychoanalysis and child and adolescent psychiatry. *Journal of the American Academy of Child and Adolescent Psychiatry, 31*, 6–13.

Shaywitz, B. A., Shaywitz, S. E., Blachman, B. A., Pugh, K. R., Fulbright, R. K., Skudlarski, P. et al. (2004). Development of left occipitotemporal systems for skilled reading in children after a phonologically-based intervention. *Biological Psychiatry, 55*, 926–933.

Shaywitz, S. (2003). *Overcoming dyslexia.* New York: Knopf.

Shaywitz, S. E., Fletcher, J. M., & Shaywitz, B. A. (1996). A conceptual model and definition of dyslexia: Findings emerging from the Connecticut Longitudinal Study. In J. H. Beitchman, N. J. Cohen, M. M. Konstantareas, & R. Tannock (Eds.), *Language, learning, and behavior disorders.* New York: Cambridge University Press.

Shaywitz, S. E., & Shaywitz, B. A. (2003). Neurobiological indices of dyslexia. In H. L. Swanson, K. R. Harris, & S. Graham (Eds.), *Handbook of learning disabilities.* New York: Guilford Press.

Shaywitz, S. E., Shaywitz, B. A., Fulbright, R. K., Skudlarski, P., Mencl, W. E., Constable, R. T. et al. (2003). Neural systems for compensation and persistence: Young adult outcome of childhood reading disability. *Biological Psychiatry, 54*, 25–33.

Shaywitz, S. E., Shaywitz, B. A., Pugh, K. R., Fulbright, R. K., Constable, R. T., Mencl, W. E., Shankweiler, D. P., Liberman, A. M., Skudlarski, P., Fletcher, J. M., Katz, L., Marchione, K. E., Lacadie, C., Gatenby, C., & Gore, J. C. (1998). Functional disruption in the organization of the brain for reading in dyslexia. *Proceedings of the National Academy of Sciences, 95*, 2636–2641.

Sheinkopf, S. J., Munday, P., Oller, D. K., & Steffens, M. (2000). Vocal atypicalities of preverbal autistic children. *Journal of Autism & Developmental Disorders, 30*, 345–354.

Shields, A. M., Cicchetti, D., & Ryan, R. M. (1994). The development of emotional and behavioral self-regulation and social competence among maltreated school-age children. *Development and Psychopathology, 6*, 57–76.

Shisslak, C. M., Crago, M., & Estes, L. S. (1995). The spectrum of eating disturbances. *International Journal of Eating Disorders, 18*, 209–219.

Sicotte, C., & Stemberger, R. M. T. (1999). Do children with PDDNOS have a theory of mind? *Journal of Autism and Developmental Disorders, 29*, 225–233.

Siegel, L. J., & Conte, P. (2001). Hospitalization and medical care of children. In C. E. Walker & M. C. Roberts (Eds.), *Handbook of clinical child psychology* (3rd ed.). New York: John Wiley & Sons, Inc.

Siegel, L. S. (1989). IQ is irrelevant to the definition of learning disabilities. *Journal of Learning Disabilities, 22*, 469–478, 486.

Siegel, L. S. (2003). Basic cognitive processes and reading disabilities. In H. L. Swanson, K. R. Harris, & S. Graham (Eds.), *Handbook of learning disabilities.* New York: Guilford Press.

Siegler, R. S. (1992). The other Alfred Binet. *Developmental Psychology, 28*, 179–190.

Sigman, M. (1998). Change and continuity in the development of children with autism. *Journal of Child Psychology and Psychiatry, 39*, 817–828.

Sigman, M., Dissanayake, C., Arbelle, S., & Ruskin, E. (1997). Cognition and emotion in adolescents with autism. In D. J. Cohen & F. R. Volkmar (Eds.), *Handbook of autism and pervasive developmental disorders.* New York: John Wiley.

Silberg, J., Pickles, A., Rutter, M. et al. (1999). The influence of genetic factors and life stress on depression among adolescent girls. *Archives of General Psychiatry, 56*, 225–232.

Silberg, J., Rutter, M., Meyer, J., Maes, H., Hewitt, J., Simonoff, E., Pickles, A., Loeber, R., & Eaves, L. (1996). Genetic and environmental influences on the covariation between hyperactivity and conduct disturbance in juvenile twins. *Journal of Child Psychology and Psychiatry, 37*, 803–816.

Silberg, J., Rutter, M., Neale, M., & Eaves, L. (2001). Genetic moderation of environmental risk for depression and anxiety in adolescent girls. *British Journal of Psychiatry, 179*, 116–121.

Silk, J. S., Nath, S. R., Siegel, L. R., & Kendall, P. (2000). Conceptualizing mental disorders in children: Where have we been going and where are we going? *Development and Psychopathology, 12*, 713–735.

Silva, P. A., Hughes, P., Williams, S., & Faed, J. M. (1988). Blood lead, intelligence, reading attainment, and behaviour in eleven year old children in Dunedin, New Zealand. *Journal of Child Psychology and Psychiatry, 29*, 43–52.

Silverman, W. K., & Albano, A. M. (1997). *The Anxiety Disorders Interview Schedule for Children (DSM-IV).* San Antonio, TX: Psychological Corporation.

Silverman, W. K., & Berman, S. L. (2001). Psychosocial interventions for anxiety disorders in children: Status and future directions. In W. K. Silverman & P. D. A. Treffers (Eds.), *Anxiety disorders in children and adolescents: Research, assessment and intervention.* Cambridge, UK: Cambridge University Press.

Silverman, W. K., & Dick-Niederhauser, A. (2004). Separation anxiety disorder. In T. L. Morris & J. S. March (Eds.), *Anxiety disorders in children and adolescents.* New York: Guilford Press.

Silverman, W. K., & Ginsburg, G. S. (1998). Anxiety disorders. In T. H. Ollendick & M. Hersen (Eds.), *Handbook of child psychopathology* (3rd ed.). New York: Plenum.

Silverman, W. K., Kurtines, W. M., Ginsburg, G. S., Weems, C. F., Lumpkin, P. W., & Carmichael, D. H. (1999). Treating anxiety disorders in children with group cognitive-behavior therapy: A randomized clinical trial. *Journal of Consulting and Clinical Psychology, 67*, 995–1003.

Silverman, W. K., La Greca, A. M., & Wasserstein, S. (1995). What do children worry about? Worries and their relation to anxiety. *Child Development, 66*, 671–686.

Silverman, W. K., Saavedra, L. M., & Pina, A. A. (2001). Test-retest reliability of anxiety symptoms and diagnoses with the Anxiety Disorders Interview Schedule for DSM-IV: Child and Parent

Versions. *Journal of the American Academy of Child and Adolescent Psychiatry, 40*, 937–944.

Silverstein, L. B. (1991). Transforming the debate about child care and maternal employment. *American Psychologist, 46*, 1025–1032.

Silverthorn, P., Frick, P. J., & Reynolds, R. (2001). Timing of onset and correlates of severe conduct problems in adjudicated girls and boys. *Journal of Psychopathology and Behavioral Assessment, 23*, 171–181.

Simmel, C., Brooks, D., Barth, R. P., & Hinshaw, S. (2001). Externalizing symptomatology among adoptive youth: Prevalence and preadoptive risk factors. *Journal of Abnormal Child Psychology, 29*, 57–69.

Simon, E. W., Toll, D. M., & Whitehair, P. M. (1994). A naturalistic approach to the validation of facilitated communication. *Journal of Autism and Developmental Disorders, 24*, 647–657.

Simonoff, E., Bolton, P., & Rutter, M. (1996). Mental retardation: Genetic findings, clinical implications and research agenda. *Journal of Child Psychology and Psychiatry, 37*, 259–280.

Simonton, D. K. (2003). Qualitative and quantitative analysis of historical data. *Annual Review of Psychology, 54*, 617–640.

Simos, P. G., Fletcher, J. M., Bergman, E., Breier, J. I., Foorman, B. R., & Castillo, E. M. et al. (2002). Dyslexia-specific brain activation profile becomes normal following successful remedial training. *Neurology, 58*, 1203–1213.

Singer, L., Arendt, R., Farkas, K., Minnes, S., Huang, J., & Yamashita, T. (1997). Relationship of prenatal cocaine exposure and maternal postpartum psychological distress to child development outcome. *Development and Psychopathology, 9*, 473–489.

Singh, N. N., Oswald, D. P., & Ellis, C. R. (1998). Mental retardation. In T. H. Ollendick & M. Hersen (Eds.), *Handbook of child psychopathology*. New York: Plenum Press.

Siok, W. T., Perfetti, C. A., Jin, Z., & Tan, L. H. (2004). Biological abnormality of impaired reading is constrained by culture. *Nature, 431*, 71–76.

Skinner, B. F. (1948). *Walden two*. London: Macmillan.

Skinner, B. F. (1953). *Science and human behavior*. New York: Macmillan.

Skinner, B. F. (1968). *The technology of teaching*. New York: Appleton-Century-Crofts.

Slomkowski, C., Klein, R., & Mannuzza, S. (1995). Is self-esteem an important outcome in hyperactive children? *Journal of Abnormal Child Psychology, 23*, 303–315.

Sloper, P. (2000). Predictors of distress in parents of children with cancer: A prospective study. *Journal of Pediatric Psychology, 25*, 79–91.

Sloper, P., Knussen, C., Turner, S., & Cunningham, C. (1991). Factors related to stress and satisfaction with life in families of children with Down's syndrome. *Journal of Child Psychology and Psychiatry, 32*, 655–676.

Slusarek, M., Velling, S., Bunk, D., & Eggers, C. (2001). Motivational effects on inhibitory control in children with ADHD. *Journal of the American Academy of Child and Adolescent Psychiatry, 40*, 355–363.

Smith, D. W., & Brodzinsky, D. M. (2002). Coping with birthparent loss in adopted children. *Journal of Child Psychology and Psychiatry, 43*, 213–223.

Smith, G. T., & Goldman, M. S. (1994). Alcohol expectancy theory and the identification of high risk adolescents. *Journal of Research on Adolescence, 4*, 229–248.

Smith, G. T., Goldman, M. S., Greenbaum, P. E., and Christiansen, B. A. (1995). Expectancy for social facilitation from drinking: The divergent paths of high-expectancy and low-expectancy adolescents. *Journal of Abnormal Psychology, 104*, 32–40.

Smith, J., & Prior, M. (1995). Temperament and stress resilience in school-age children: A within-families study. *Journal of the American Academy of Child and Adolescent Psychiatry, 34*, 168–179.

Smith, J. L., Johnstone, S. J., & Barry, R. J. (2003). Aiding diagnosis of attention-deficit/hyperactivity disorder and its subtypes: Discriminant function analysis of event-related potential data. *Journal of Child Psychology and Psychiatry, 44*, 1067–1075.

Smith, P. K. (1988). Children's play and its role in early development: A re-evaluation of the "play ethos." In A. D. Pellegrini (Ed.), *Psychological bases for early education*. New York: Wiley.

Smith, P. K., Cowie, H., Olafsson, R. F., & Liefooghe, P. D. (2002). Definitions of bullying: A comparison of terms used, and age and gender differences, in a fourteen country international comparison. *Child Development, 73*, 1119–1133.

Smith, S. L. (1970). School refusal with anxiety: A review of 60 cases. *Canadian Psychiatric Association Journal, 15*, 257–264.

Smith, T. (1999, Spring). Outcome of early intervention for children with autism. *Clinical Psychology: Science and Practice, 6*, 33–49.

Smith, T., Groen, A., & Wynn, J. W. (2000). Randomized trial of intensive early intervention for children with pervasive developmental disorder. *American Journal on Mental Retardation, 104*, 269–285.

Smolak, L., & Murnen, S. K. (2002). A meta-analytic examination of the relationship between child sexual abuse and eating disorders. *International Journal of Eating Disorders, 31*, 136–150.

Smolak, L., & Murnen, S. K. (2004). A feminist approach to eating disorders. In J. K. Thompson (Ed.), *Handbook of eating disorders and obesity*. Hoboken, NJ: John Wiley.

Smolak, L., Murnen, S. K., & Ruble, A. E. (2000). Female athletes and eating problems: A meta-analysis. *International Journal of Eating Disorders, 27*, 371–380.

Smolak, L., & Striegel-Moore, R. H. (2001). Challenging the myth of the golden girl: Ethnicity and eating disorders. In R. H. Striegel-Moore & L. Smolak (Eds.), *Eating disorders*. Washington, DC: American Psychological Association.

Snider, L. A., & Swedo, S. E. (2003). Childhood-onset obsessive-compulsive disorder and tic disorders: Case report and literature review. *Journal of Child and Adolescent Psychopharmacology, 13*, S81-S88.

Snowling, M. J. (1991). Developmental reading disorders. *Journal of Child Psychology and Psychiatry, 32*, 49–77.

Snowling, M. J. (2000). Language and literacy skills: Who is at risk and why? In D. V. M. Bishop & L. B. Leonard (Eds.), *Speech and language impairments in children: Causes, characteristics, intervention and outcome*. Philadelphia: Taylor & Francis.

Snowling, M. J. (2002). Reading and other learning disabilities. In M. Rutter & E. Taylor (Eds.), *Child and adolescent psychiatry*. Oxford, UK: Blackwell Publishing.

Snowling, M., Bishop, D. V. M., & Stothard, S. E. (2000). Is pre-school language impairment a risk factor of dyslexia in adolescence? *Journal of Child Psychology and Psychiatry, 41*, 587–600.

Snowling, M. J., Gallagher, A., & Frith, U. (2003). Family risk of dyslexia is continuous: Individual differences in the precursors of reading skill. *Child Development, 74*, 358–373.

Snyder, J. (2002). Reinforcement and coercion mechanisms in the development of antisocial behavior: Peer relationships. In J. B. Reid, G. R. Patterson, & J. Snyder (Eds.), *Antisocial behavior in children and adolescents: A developmental analysis and model for intervention*. Washington, DC: American Psychological Association.

Sokolov, S., & Kutcher, S. (2001). Adolescent depression: Neuroendocrine aspects. In I. M. Goodyer (Ed.), *The depressed child and adolescent* (2nd ed.). Cambridge, UK: Cambridge University Press.

Solan, H. A., Larson, S., Shelley-Tremblay, J., Ficarra, A., & Silverman, M. (2001). Role of visual attention in cognitive control of oculomotor readiness in students with reading disabilities. *Journal of Learning Disabilities, 34*, 107–118.

Solanto, M. V., Abikoff, H., Sonuga-Barke, E., Schachar, R., Logan, G. D., Wigal, T. et al. (2001). The ecological validity of delay aversion and response inhibition as measures of impulsivity in AD/HD: A supplement to the NIMH Multimodal Treatment Study of AD/HD. *Journal of Abnormal Child Psychology, 29*, 215–228.

Soliday, E., Kool, E., & Lande, M. B. (2000). Psychosocial adjustment in children with kidney disease. *Journal of Pediatric Psychology, 25*, 93–103.

Sonuga-Barke, E. J. S. (1994). On dysfunction and function in psychological theories of childhood disorder. *Journal of Child Psychology and Psychiatry, 35*, 801–815.

Sonuga-Barke, E. J. S. (1998). Categorical models of childhood disorder: A conceptual and empirical analysis. *Journal of Child Psychology and Psychiatry, 39*, 115–133.

Sonuga-Barke, E. J. S., Dalen, L., & Remington, B. (2003). Do executive deficits and delay aversion make independent contributions to preschool attention-deficit/hyperactivity disorder? *Journal of the American Academy of Child and Adolescent Psychiatry, 42*, 1335–1342.

Sonuga-Barke, E. J. S., Daley, D., & Thompson, M. (2002). Does maternal ADHD reduce the effectiveness of parent training for preschool children's ADHD? *Journal of the American Academy of Child and Adolescent Psychiatry, 41*, 696–702.

Sonuga-Barke, E. J. S., Daley, D., Thompson, M., Laver-Bradbury, C., & Weeks, A. (2001). Parent-based therapies for attention-deficit/hyperactivity disorder: A randomized, controlled trial with a community sample. *Journal of the American Academy of Child and Adolescent Psychiatry, 40*, 402–408.

Sonuga-Barke, E. J. S., De Houwer, J., De Ruiter, K., Ajzenstzen, M., & Hollands, S. (2004). AD/HD and the capture of attention by briefly exposed delay-related cues: Evidence from a conditioning paradigm. *Journal of Child Psychology and Psychiatry, 45*, 274–283.

Sourander, A., Santalahti, P., Haavisto, A., Piha, J., Ikäheimo, K., & Helenius, H. (2004). Have there been changes in children's psychiatric symptoms and mental health service use? A 10-year comparison from Finland. *Journal of the American Academy of Child and Adolescent Psychiatry, 43*, 1134–1145.

Southam-Gerow, M. A., & Kendall, P. C. (2002). Emotion regulation and understanding: Implications for child psychopathology and therapy. *Clinical Psychology Review, 22*, 189–222.

Sowell, E. R., Thompson, P. M., Welcome, S. E., Henkenius, A. L., Toga, A, W., & Peterson, B. S. (2003). Cortical abnormalities in children and adolescents with attention-deficit hyperactivity disorder. *The Lancet, 362*, 1699–1707.

Spafford, P. A., von Baeyer, C. L., & Hicks, C. L. (2002). Expected and reported pain in children undergoing ear piercing: A randomized trial of preparation by parents. *Behaviour Research and Therapy, 40*, 37–50.

Spagna, M. E., Cantwell, D. P., & Baker, L. (2000a). Disorder of written expression. In B. J. Sadock & V. A. Sadock (Eds.), *Comprehensive textbook of psychiatry* (Vol. II). Philadelphia: Lippincott Williams & Wilkins.

Spagna, M. E., Cantwell, D. P., & Baker, L. (2000b). Mathematics disorder. In B. J. Sadock & V. A. Sadock (Eds.), *Comprehensive textbook of psychiatry* (Vol. II). Philadelphia: Lippincott Williams & Wilkins.

Spencer, T. J., Biederman, J., Wozniak, J., Faraone, S. V., Wilens, T. E., & Mick, E. (2001). Parsing pediatric bipolar disorder from its associated comorbidity with disruptive behavior disorders. *Biological Psychiatry, 49*, 1062–1070.

Spielberger, C. D. (1973). *Manual for the State-Trait Anxiety Inventory for Children*. Palo Alto, CA: Consulting Psychologists Press.

Spinath, F. M., Price, T. S., Dale, P. S., & Plomin, R. (2004). The genetic and environmental origins of language disability and ability. *Child Development, 75*, 445–454.

Spirito, A., Stark, L. J., & Tyc, V. L. (1994). Stressors and coping strategies described during hospitalization by chronically ill children. *Journal of Clinical Child Psychology, 23*, 314–322.

Spitz, R. A. (1946). Anaclitic depression. In *The psychoanalytic study of the child*, Vol. 2. New York: International Universities Press.

Spitzer, R. L., Gibbon, M., Skodol, A. E., Williams, J. B. W., & First, M. B. (2000). *DSM-IV-TR case book*. Washington, DC: American Psychiatric Publishing.

Spock, B. M., & Rothenberg, M. (1992). *Dr. Spock's baby and child care*. New York: Pocket Books.

Spomer, M. L., & Cowen, E. L. (2001). A comparison of the school mental health referral profiles of young ESL and English-speaking children. *Journal of Community Psychology, 29*, 69–82.

Sprich, S., Biederman, J., Crawford, M. H., Mundy, E., & Faraone, S. V. (2000). Adoptive and biological families of children and adolescents with ADHD. *Journal of the American Academy of Child and Adolescent Psychiatry, 39*, 1432–1437.

Spring, B., Chiodo, J., & Bowen, D. J. (1987). Carbohydrates, tryptophan, and behavior: A methodological review. *Psychological Bulletin, 102*, 234–256.

Sroufe, L. A. (1997). Psychopathology as an outcome of development. *Development and Psychopathology, 9*, 251–268.

Sroufe, L. A., & Rutter, M. (1984). The domain of developmental psychopathology. *Child Development, 55*, 17–29.

Sroufe, L. A., Carlson, A., Levy, A. K., & Egeland, B. (1999). Implications of attachment theory for developmental psychopathology. *Development and Psychopathology, 11*, 1–13.

Sroufe, L. A., Duggal, S., Weinfeld, N., & Carlson, E. (2000). Relationships, development, and psychopathology. In A. J. Sameroff, M. Lewis, & S. M. Miller (Eds.), *Handbook of developmental psychopathology* (2nd ed.). New York: Kluwer Academic/Plenum Publishers.

St. Pierre, R. G., & Layzer, J. I. (1998). Improving the life chances of children in poverty: Assumptions and what we have learned. *Social Policy Report. Society for Research in Child Development.* Vol. XII (4).

Stahl, A. (1991). Beliefs of Jewish-Oriental mothers regarding children who are mentally retarded. *Education and Training in Mental Retardation, 26*, 361–369.

Standart, S., & Le Couteur, A. (2003). The quiet child: A literature review of selective mutism. *Child and Adolescent Mental Health, 8*, 154–160.

Stanger, C., Achenbach, T. M., & Verhulst, F. C. (1997). Accelerated longitudinal comparisons of aggressive versus delinquent syndromes. *Development and Psychopathology, 9*, 43–58.

Stanger, C., MacDonald, V. V., McConaughy, S. H., & Achenbach, T. M. (1996). Predictors of cross-informant syndromes among children and youths referred for mental health services. *Journal of Abnormal Child Psychology. 24*, 597–614.

Stanley, L. (1980). Treatment of ritualistic behavior in an eight-year-old girl by response prevention: A case report. *Journal of Child Psychology and Psychiatry, 21*, 85–90.

Stanovich, K. E. (1989). Learning disabilities in broader context. *Journal of Learning Disabilities, 22*, 287–291, 297.

Stark, K. D., Rouse, L. W., & Kurowski, C. (1994). Psychological treatment approaches for depression in children. In W. M. Reynolds & H. F. Johnston (Eds.), *Handbook of depression in children and adolescents*. New York: Plenum Press.

Stark, K. D., Sander, J. B., Yancy, M. G., Bronik, M., & Hoke, J. A. (2000). Treatment of depression in childhood and adolescence: Cognitive-behavioral procedures for the individual and family. In P. C. Kendall (Ed.), *Child and adolescent therapy: Cognitive-behavioral procedures* (2nd ed.). New York: The Guilford Press.

Stark, K. D., Schmidt, K. L., & Joiner, T. E. (1996). Cognitive triad: Relationship to depressive symptoms, parents' cognitive triad, and perceived parental messages. *Journal of Abnormal Child Psychology, 24*, 615–631.

State of the World's Children (2000). UNICEF, United Nations. Online, unicef.org/sowc/stat_tab.htm. March 21, 2002.

Staub, D., & Peck, C. A. (January 1994/December 1995). What are the outcomes for nondisabled students? *Educational Leadership, 52*, 36–40.

Steele, C. M. (1997). A threat in the air: How stereotypes shape intellectual identity and performance. *American Psychologist, 52*, 613–629.

Steffenburg, S., Gillberg, C., Hellgren, L., Andersson, L., Gillberg, I. C., Jakobsson, G., & Bohman, M. (1989). A twin study of autism in Denmark, Finland, Iceland, Norway and Sweden. *Journal of Child Psychology and Psychiatry, 30*, 405–416.

Steil, J. M. (2001). Family forms and member well-being: A research agenda for the decade of the brain. *Psychology of Women Quarterly, 25*, 333–363.

Stein, M. B., & Seedat, S. (2004). Pharmacotherapy. In T. L. Morris & J. S. March (Eds.), *Anxiety disorders in children and adolescents*. New York: Guilford Press.

Steinberg, A. B., & Phares, V. (2001). Family functioning, body image, and eating disturbances. In J. K. Thompson & L. Smolak (Eds.), *Body image, eating disorders, and obesity in youth: Assessment, prevention, and treatment*. Washington, DC: American Psychological Association.

Steinberg, L., Lamborn, S. D., Darling, N., Mounts, N. S., & Dornbusch, S. M. (1994). Over-time changes in adjustment and competence among adolescents from authoritative, authoritarian, indulgent, and neglectful families. *Child Development, 65*, 754–770.

Steiner, H., & Lock, J. (1998). Anorexia nervosa and bulimia nervosa in children and adolescents: A review of the past 10 years. *Journal of the American Academy of Child and Adolescent Psychiatry, 37*, 352–359.

Steinhausen, H. C. (1997). Outcome of anorexia nervosa in the younger patient. *Journal of Child Psychology and Psychiatry, 38*, 271–276.

Sternberg, R. J., Wagner, R. K., Williams, W. M., & Horvath, J. A. (1995). Testing common sense. *American Psychologist, 50*, 912–927.

Stetson, E. G., & Stetson, R. (2001). Educational assessment. In C. E. Walker & M. C. Roberts (Eds.), *Handbook of clinical child psychology* (3rd ed.). New York: John Wiley & Sons.

Stevens, M. C., Fein, D. A. Dunn, M., Allen, D., Waterhouse, L. H., Feinstein, C., & Rapin, I. (2000). Subgroups of children with autism by cluster analysis: A longitudinal examination. *Journal of the American Academy of Child & Adolescent Psychiatry, 39*, 346–352.

Stevenson, J. (1996). Developmental changes in the mechanisms linking language disabilities and behavior disorders. In J. H. Beitchman, N. J. Cohen, M. M. Konstantareas, & R. Tannock (Eds.), *Language, learning, and behavior disorders*. New York: Cambridge University Press.

Stevenson, J., & Fredman, G. (1990). The social environmental correlates of reading ability. *Journal of Child Psychology and Psychiatry, 31*, 681–698.

Stewart, A. J., Steiman, M., Cauce, A. M., Cochran, B. N., Whitbeck, L. B., & Hoyt, D. R. (2004). Victimization and posttraumatic stress disorder among homeless adolescents. *Journal of the American Academy of Child and Adolescent Psychiatry, 43*, 325–331.

Stewart, S. M., Kennard, B. D., Lee, P. W. H., Hughes, C. W., Mayes, T. L., Emslie, G. J., & Lewinsohn, P. M. (2004). A cross-cultural investigation of cognitions and depressive symptoms in adolescents. *Journal of Abnormal Psychology, 113*, 248–257.

Stewart, T. M., & Williamson, D. A. (2004). Assessment of body image disturbances. In J. K. Thompson (Ed.), *Handbook of eating disorders and obesity*. Hoboken, NJ: John Wiley.

Stice, E., & Bearman, S. K. (2001). Body image and eating disturbances prospectively predict increases in depressive symptoms in adolescent girls: A growth curve analysis. *Developmental Psychology, 37*, 1–11.

Stock, S. L., Werry, J. S., McClellan, J. M. (2001). Pharmacological treatment of paediatric anxiety. In W. K. Silverman & P. D. A. Treffers (Eds.), *Anxiety disorders in children and adolescents: Research, assessment and intervention.* Cambridge, UK: Cambridge University Press.

Stone, W. L. (1997). Autism in infancy and early childhood. In D. J. Cohen & F. R. Volkmar (Eds.), *Handbook of autism and pervasive developmental disorders.* New York: John Wiley.

Stone, W. L., & LaGreca, A. M. (1990). The social status of children with learning disabilities: A reexamination. *Journal of Learning Disabilities, 23*, 23–37.

Stores, G. (1996). Assessment and treatment of sleep disorders in children and adolescents. *Journal of Child Psychology and Psychiatry, 37*, 907–925.

Stormont-Spurgin, M., & Zentall, S. S. (1995). Contributing factors in the manifestation of aggression in preschoolers with hyperactivity. *Journal of Child Psychology and Psychiatry, 36*, 491–509.

Stouthamer-Loeber, M., Loeber, R., Homish, D. L., & Wei, E. (2001). Maltreatment of boys and the development of disruptive and delinquent behavior. *Development and Psychopathology, 13*, 941–955.

Strauss, A., & Corbin, J. (1990). *Basics of qualitative research.* Newbury Park, CA: Sage.

Strauss, C. C. (1994). Overanxious disorder. In T. H. Ollendick, N. J. King, & W. Yule (Eds.), *International handbook of phobic and anxiety disorders in children and adolescents.* New York: Plenum Press.

Strauss, C. C., & Last, C. G. (1993). Social and simple phobias in children. *Journal of Anxiety Disorders, 7*, 141–152.

Strauss, C. C., Lease, C. A., Last, C. G., & Francis, G. (1988). Overanxious disorder: An examination of developmental differences. *Journal of Abnormal Child Psychology, 16*, 433–443.

Strauss, R. S., & Pollack, H. A. (2001). Epidemic increase in childhood overweight, 1986–1998. *Journal of the American Medical Association, 286*, 2845–2848.

Strein, W., Hoagwood, K., & Cohn, A. (2003). School psychology: A public health perspective I. Prevention, populations, and systems change. *School Psychology, 41*, 23–38.

Streisand, R., & Efron, L. A. (2003). Pediatric sleep disorders. In M. C. Roberts (Ed.), *Handbook of pediatric psychology* (3rd ed.). New York: Guilford Press.

Streissguth, A. P., Barr, H. M., Sampson, P. D., Darby, B. L., & Martin, D. C. (1989). IQ at age 4 in relation to maternal alcohol use and smoking during pregnancy. *Developmental Psychology, 25*, 3–11.

Streissguth, A. P., Bookstein, F. L., Sampson, P. D., & Barr, H. M. (1995). Attention: Prenatal alcohol and continuities of vigilance and attentional problems from 4 through 14 years. *Development and Psychopathology, 7*, 419–446.

Streissguth, A. P., Martin, D. C., Barr, H. M., Sandman, B. M., Kirchner, G. L., & Darby, D. L. (1984). Intrauterine alcohol and nicotine exposure: Attention and reaction time in 4-year-old children. *Developmental Psychology, 20*, 533–541.

Strickland, B. R. (2000). Misassumptions, misadventures, and the misuse of psychology. *American Psychologist, 55*, 331–338.

Strober, M., Freeman, R., Lampert, C., Diamond, J., & Kaye, W. (2000). Controlled family study of anorexia nervosa and bulimia nervosa: Evidence of shared liability and transmission of partial syndromes. *American Journal of Psychiatry, 157*, 393–401.

Strober, M., & Humphrey, L. (1987). Familial contributions to the etiology and course of anorexia nervosa and bulimia. *Journal of Consulting and Clinical Psychology, 55*, 654–659.

Stuber, J., Fairbrother, G., Galea, S. Pfefferbaum, B., Wilson-Genderson, M., & Vlahov, D. (2002). Determinants of counseling for children in Manhattan after the September 11 attacks. *Psychiatric Services, 53*, 815–822.

Stunkard, A. J., & Sobal, J. (1995). Psychosocial consequences of obesity. In K. D. Brownell & C. G. Fairburn (Eds.), *Eating disorders and obesity: A comprehensive handbook.* New York: Guilford Press.

Sue, S. (1999). Science, ethnicity, and bias. Where have we gone wrong? *American Psychologist, 54*, 1070–1077.

Sue, S. (2003). In defense of cultural competency in psychotherapy and treatment. *American Psychologist, 58*, 964–970.

Sullivan, P. F., Kendler, K. S., & Neale, M. C. (2003). Schizophrenia as a complex trait. *Archives of General Psychiatry, 60*, 1187–1192.

Sunohara, G. A., Roberts, W., Malone, M., Schaehar, R. J., Tannock, R., Basile, V. S. et al. (2000). Linkage of the dopamine D4 receptor gene and attention-deficit/hyperactivity disorder. *Journal of the American Academy of Child and Adolescent Psychiatry, 39*, 1537–1542.

Susman, E. J. (1993). Psychological, contextual, and psychobiological interactions: A developmental perspective on conduct disorder. *Development and Psychopathology, 5*, 181–189.

Sutcliffe, J. S., & Nurmi, E. L. (2003). Genetics of childhood disorders: XLVII. Autism, Part 6: Duplication and inherited susceptibility of chromosome 15q11-q13 genes in autism. *Journal of the American Academy of Child and Adolescent Psychiatry, 42*, 253–256.

Sutton, P. D. (2003). Births, marriages, divorces, and deaths: Provisional data for October–December 2002. *National Vital Statistics Reports* (Vol. 51). Hyattsville, MD: National Center for Health Statistics.

Swaab-Barneveld, H., de Sonneville, L., Cohen-Kettenis, P., Gielen, A., Buitelaar, J., & van Engeland, H. (2000). Visual sustained attention in a child psychiatric population. *Journal of the American Academy of Child and Adolescent Psychiatry, 39*, 651–659.

Swanson, H. L., & Hoskyn, M. (1998). Experimental intervention research on students with learning disabilities: A meta-analysis of treatment outcomes. *Review of Educational Research, 68*, 277–321.

Swanson, J., Gupta, S., Lam, A., Shoulson, I., Lerner, M., Modi, N. et al. (2003). Development of a new once-a-day formulation of methylphenidate for the treatment of attention-deficit/hyperactivity disorder. *Archives of General Psychiatry, 60*, 204–211.

Swanson, J. M., McBurnett, K., Christian, D. L., & Wigal, T. (1995). Stimulant medications and the treatment of children with ADHD. In T. H. Ollendick & R. J. Prinz (Eds.), *Advances in clinical child psychology*. New York: Plenum Press.

Swedo, S. E., Rapoport, J. L., Cheslow, D. L., Leonard, H. L., Ayoub, E. M., Hosier, D. M., & Wald, E. R. (1989b). High prevalence of obsessive-compulsive symptoms in patients with Sydenhams' Chorea. *American Journal of Psychiatry, 146*, 246–249.

Swedo, S. E., Rapoport, J. L., Leonard, H., Lenane, M., & Cheslow, D. (1989c). Obsessive-compulsive disorder in children and adolescents: Clinical phenomenology of 70 consecutive cases. *Archives of General Psychiatry, 46*, 335–341.

Swedo, S. E., Schapiro, M. B., Grady, C. L., Cheslow, D. L., Leonard, H. L., Kumar, A., Friedland, R., Rapoport, S. I., & Rapoport, J. L. (1989a). Cerebral glucose metabolism in childhood-onset obsessive-compulsive disorder. *Archives of General Psychiatry, 46*, 518–523.

Sykes, D. H., Hoy, E. A., Bill, J. M., McClure, B. G., Halliday, H. L., & Reid, M. M. (1997). Behavioural adjustment in school of very low birthweight children. *Journal of Child Psychology and Psychiatry, 38*, 315–325.

Sylva, K. (1994). School influences on children's development. *Journal of Child Psychology and Psychiatry, 35*, 135–170.

Szatmari, P. (2000). The classification of autism, Asperger's syndrome, and pervasive developmental disorder. *The Canadian Journal of Psychiatry, 45*, 731–738.

Szatmari, P., MacLean, J. E., Jones, M. B., Bryson, S. E., Zwaigenbaum, L., Bartolucci, G. et al. (2000). The familial aggregation of the lesser variant in biological and nonbiological relatives of PDD probands: A family history study. *Journal of Child Psychology and Psychiatry, 41*, 579–586.

Szatmari, P., Offord, D. R., & Boyle, M. H. (1989). Correlates, associated impairments, and patterns of service utilization of children with attention deficit disorders: Findings from the Ontario Child Health Study. *Journal of Child Psychology and Psychiatry, 30*, 205–217.

Szymanski, L. S., & Crocker, A. C. (1985). Mental retardation. In H. I. Kaplan & B. J. Sadock (Eds.), *Comprehensive textbook of psychiatry/IV*. Baltimore: Williams and Wilkins.

Szymanski, L., King, B. H. et al. (1999). Practice parameters for the assessment and treatment of children, adolescents, and adults with mental retardation and comorbid mental disorders. *Journal of the American Academy of Child and Adolescent Psychiatry, 38*, 5S–32S.

Tager-Flüsberg, H. (1993). What language reveals about the understanding of minds in children with autism. In S. Baron-Cohen, H. Tager-Flüsberg, & D. J. Cohen (Eds.), *Understanding other minds*. New York: Oxford.

Tager-Flüsberg, H. (1997). Perspectives on language and communication in autism. In D. J. Cohen & F. R. Volkmar (Eds.), *Handbook of autism and pervasive developmental disorders*. New York: John Wiley.

Tallal, P. (2000). Experimental studies of language learning impairments: From research to remediation. In D. V. M. Bishop & L. B. Leonard (Eds.), *Speech and language impairments in children: Causes, characteristics, intervention and outcome*. Philadelphia: Taylor & Francis.

Tallal, P., & Benasich, A. A. (2002). Developmental language learning impairments. *Development and Psychopathology, 14*, 559–579.

Tanguay, P. E. (2000). Pervasive developmental disorders: A 10-year review. *Journal of the American Academy of Child and Adolescent Psychiatry, 39*, 1079–1095.

Tannock, R. (1998). Attention deficit hyperactivity disorder: Advances in cognitive, neurobiological, and genetic research. *Journal of Child Psychology and Psychiatry, 39*, 65–99.

Tantleff-Dunn, S., Gokee-LaRose, J., & Peterson, R. D. (2004). Interpersonal psychotherapy for the treatment of anorexia nervosa, bulimia nervosa, and binge eating disorder. In J. K. Thompson (Ed.), *Handbook of eating disorders and obesity*. Hoboken, NJ: John Wiley.

Tao, K-T. (1992). Hyperactivity and attention deficit disorder syndrome in China. *Journal of the American Academy of Child and Adolescent Psychiatry, 31*, 1165–1166.

Taras, M. E., & Matese, M. (1990). Acquisition of self-help skills. In J. L. Matson (Ed.), *Handbook of behavior modification with the mentally retarded*. New York: Plenum.

Taylor, B., Miller, E., Farrington, C. P., Petropoulos, M-C., Favot-Mayaud, I., Li, J., & Waight, P. A. (1999). Autism and measles, mumps and rubella vaccine: No epidemiological evidence for a causal association. *Lancet, 353*, 2026–2029.

Taylor, E. (1994). Syndromes of attention deficit and hyperactivity. In M. Rutter, E. Taylor, & L. Hersov (Eds.), *Child and adolescent psychiatry: Modern approaches*. New York: Blackwell Scientific.

Taylor, E. (1995). Dysfunctions of attention. In D. Cicchetti & D. J. Cohen (Eds.), *Developmental psychopathology*. New York: John Wiley.

Taylor, H. G. (1988a). Learning disabilities. In E. J. Mash & L. G. Terdal (Eds.), *Behavioral assessment of childhood disorders* (2nd ed.). New York: Guilford.

Taylor, H. G. (1988b). Neuropsychological testing: Relevance for assessing children's learning disabilities. *Journal of Consulting and Clinical Psychology, 56*, 795–800.

Taylor, H. G. (1989). Learning disabilities. In E. J. Mash & R. A. Barkley (Eds.), *Treatment of childhood disorders*. New York: Guilford.

Taylor, J., Iacono, W. G., & McGue, M. (2000). Evidence for a genetic etiology of early-onset delinquency. *Journal of Abnormal Psychology, 109*, 634–643.

Temple, E., Deutsch, D. K., Poldrack, R. A., Miller, S. L., Tallal, P., Merzenich, M. M., & Gabrieli, J. D. E. (2003). Neural deficits in children with dyslexia ameliorated by behavioral remediation: Evidence from functional MRI. *Proceedings of the National Academy of Sciences, 100*, 2860–2865.

Tennant, C. (1988). Parental loss in childhood: Its effects in adult life. *Archives of General Psychiatry, 45*, 1045–1050.

Teodori, J. B. (1993). Neurological assessment. In T. H. Ollendick & M. Hersen (Eds.), *Handbook of child and adolescent assessment*. Boston: Allyn & Bacon.

Terr, L. (1979). Children of Chowchilla. *The Psychoanalytic Study of the Child, 34*, 522–563.

Terr, L. (1983). Chowchilla revisited: The effects of psychic trauma four years after a school-bus kidnapping. *American Journal of Psychiatry, 140*, 1543–1550.

Tesman, J. R., & Hills, A. (1994). Developmental effects of lead exposure in children. *Social Policy Report. Society for Research in Child Development, VIII (3)*, 1–16.

Thabet, A. A. M., Abed, Y., & Vostanis, P. (2004). Comorbidity of PTSD and depression among refugee children during war conflict. *Journal of Child Psychology and Psychiatry, 45,* 533–542.

Thapar, A., & McGuffin, P. (1995). Are anxiety symptoms in childhood heritable? *Journal of Child Psychology and Psychiatry, 36,* 439–447.

Thapar, A., & McGuffin, P. (1997). Anxiety and depressive symptoms in childhood: A genetic study of comorbidity. *Journal of Child Psychology and Psychiatry, 38,* 651–656.

Thapar, A., Gottesman, I. I., Owen, M. J., O'Donovan, M., & McGuffin, P. (1994). The genetics of mental retardation. *British Journal of Psychiatry, 164,* 747–758.

Thelen, E., & Adolph, K. E. (1992). Arnold L. Gessell: The paradox of nature and nuture. *Developmental Psychology, 28,* 368–380.

Thelen, M. H., Powell, A. L., Lawrence, C., & Kuhnert, M. E. (1992). Eating and body image concerns among children. *Journal of Consulting and Clinical Psychology, 21,* 41–46.

Them, M. A., Israel, A. C., Ivanova, M. Y., & Chalmers, S. M. (2003). *An investigation of the assessment and of and relationships between various aspects of family stability.* Boston, MA: Association for the Advancement of Behavior Therapy.

Thomas, A. M., Peterson, L., & Goldstein, D. (1997). Problem solving and diabetes regimen adherence by children and adolescents with IDDM in social pressure situations: A reflection on normal development. *Journal of Pediatric Psychology, 22,* 541–561.

Thompson, J. K., & Smolak, L. (2001). Body image, eating disorders, and obesity in youth—The future is now. In J. K. Thompson & L. Smolak (Eds.), *Body image, eating disorders, and obesity in youth: Assessment, prevention, and treatment.* Washington, DC: American Psychological Association.

Thompson, J. R., & McEvoy, M. A. (1992). Letters to the editor. Normalization—still relevant today. *Journal of Autism and Developmental Disorders, 22,* 666–671.

Thompson, L. A. (1997). Behavioral genetics and the classification of mental retardation. In W. E. MacLean (Ed.), *Ellis' handbook of mental deficiency, psychological theory and research.* Mahwah, NJ: Lawrence Erlbaum.

Thompson, R. A. (2000). The legacy of early attachments. *Child Development, 71,* 145–152.

Thompson, R. J., Jr., Gustafson, K. E., Bonner, M. J., & Ware, R. E. (2002). Neurocognitive development of young children with sickle cell disease through three years of age. *Journal of Pediatric Psychology, 27,* 235–244.

Thompson, R. J., Jr., Gustafson, K. E., Hamlett, K. W., & Spock, A. (1992). Stress, coping, and family functioning in the psychological adjustment of mothers and children with cystic fibrosis. *Journal of Pediatric Psychology, 17,* 573–585.

Thomson, G. O. B., Raab, G. M., Hepburn, W. S., Hunter, R., Fulton, M., & Laxen, D. P. H. (1989). Blood-lead levels and children's behaviour—results from the Edinburgh Lead Study. *Journal of Child Psychology and Psychiatry, 30,* 515–528.

Thornberry, T. P., Ireland, T. O., & Smith, C. A. (2001). The importance of timing: The varying impact of childhood and adolescent maltreatment on multiple problem outcomes. *Development and Psychopathology, 13,* 957–979.

Thorndike, E. L. (1905). *The elements of psychology.* New York: Seiler.

Thurber, C. A., & Sigman, M. D. (1998). Preliminary models of risk and protective factors for childhood homesickness: Review and empirical synthesis. *Child Development, 69,* 903–934.

Tienari, P., Lahti, I., Sorri, A., Naarala, M., Moring, J., Kaleva, M., Wahlberg, K-E., & Wynne, L. C. (1990). Adopted-away offspring of schizophrenics and controls: The Finnish adoptive family study of schizophrenia. In L. N. Robins & M. Rutter (Eds.), *Straight and devious pathways from childhood to adulthood.* New York: Cambridge University Press.

Tiggermann, M., & Anesbury, T. (2000). Negative stereotyping of obesity in children: The role of controllability beliefs. *Journal of Applied Social Psychology, 30,* 1997–1993.

Tiggerman, M., & Slater, A. (2004). Thin ideals in music television: A source of social comparison and body dissatisfaction. *International Journal of Eating Disorders, 35,* 48–58.

Tillman, R., Geller, B., Bolhofner, K., Craney, J. L., Williams, M., & Zimerman, B. (2003). Ages of onset and rates of syndromal and subsyndromal comorbid DSM-IV diagnosis in a prepubertal and early adolescent bipolar disorder phenotype. *Journal of the American Academy of Child and Adolescent Psychiatry, 42,* 1486–1493.

Timko, C., Baumgartner, M., Moos, R. H., & Miller, J. III (1993). Parental risk and resistance factors among children with juvenile rheumatic disease: A four-year predictive study. *Journal of Behavioral Medicine, 16,* 571–588.

Tolan, P. H. (2001). Emerging themes and challenges in understanding youth violence involvement. *Journal of Clinical Child Psychology, 30,* 233–239.

Tolan, P. H., & Thomas, P. (1995). The implications of age of onset for delinquency risk II: Longitudinal data. *Journal of Abnormal Child Psychology, 23,* 157–181.

Tomblin, J. B., Zhang, X., Buckwalter, P., & Catts, H. (2000). The association of reading disability, behavioral disorders, and language impairment among second-grade children. *Journal of Child Psychology and Psychiatry, 41,* 473–482.

Tomblin, J. B., Zhang, X., Buckwalter, P., & O'Brien, M. (2003). The stability of primary language disorder: Four years after kindergarten diagnosis. *Journal of Speech, Language, and Hearing Research, 46,* 1283–1296.

Tomporowski, P. D., & Tinsley, V. (1997). Attention in mentally retarded persons. In W. E. MacLean (Ed.), *Ellis' handbook of mental deficiency, psychological theory and research.* Mahwah, NJ: Lawrence Erlbaum.

Tonge, B. (1994). Separation anxiety disorder. In T. H. Ollendick, N. J. King, & W. Yule (Eds.), *International handbook of phobic and anxiety disorders in children and adolescents.* New York: Plenum Press.

Toppelberg, C. O., Medrano, L., Pena Morgens, L., & Nieto-Castanon, A. (2002). Bilingual children referred for psychiatric services: Associations of language disorders, language skills, and psychopathology. *Journal of the American Academy of Child and Adolescent Psychiatry, 41,* 712–722.

Toppelberg, C. O., & Shapiro, T. (2000). Language disorders: A 10-year research update review. *Journal of the American Academy of Child and Adolescent Psychiatry, 39,* 143–152.

Torbeyns, J., Verschaffel, L., & Ghesquière, P. (2004). Strategy development in children with mathematical disabilities: Insights from the choice/no-choice method and the chronological-age/ability-level-match design. *Journal of Learning Disabilities, 37,* 119–131.

Torgesen, J. K., Alexander, A. W., Wagner, R. K., Rashotte, C. A., Voeller, K. K. S., & Conway, T. (2001). Intensive remedial instruction for children with severe reading disabilities: Immediate and long-term outcomes from two instructional approaches. *Journal of Learning Disabilities, 34,* 33–58, 78.

Toro, P. A., Weissberg, R. P., Guare, J., & Liebenstein, N. L. (1990). A comparison of children with and without learning disabilities on social problem-solving skill, school behavior, and family background. *Journal of Learning Disabilities, 23,* 115–120.

Touyz, S. W., & Beumont, P. J. V. (1997). Behavioral treatment to promote weight gain in anorexia nervosa. In D. M. Garner & P. E. Garfinkel (Eds.), *Handbook of treatment for eating disorders* (2nd ed.). New York: Guilford Press.

Treatment for Adolescents with Depression Study (TADS) Team (2004). Fluoxetine, cognitive-behavioral therapy, and their combination for adolescents with depression: Treatment for Adolescents with Depression Study (TADS) randomized controlled trial. *Journal of the American Medical Association, 292,* 807–820.

Treatment for Adolescents with Depression Study (TADS) Team (2005). The Treatment for Adolescents with Depression Study (TADS): Demographic and clinical characteristics. *Journal of the American Academy of Child & Adolescent Psychiatry, 44,* 28–40.

Treffert, D. A. (1988). The idiot savant: A review of the syndrome. *American Journal of Psychiatry, 145,* 563–572.

Tremblay, G. C., & Israel, A. C. (1998). Children's adjustment to parental death. *Clinical Psychology: Science and Practice, 5,* 424–438.

Tremblay, G. C., & Peterson, L. (1999). Prevention of childhood injury: Clinical and public policy issues. *Clinical Psychology Review, 19,* 415–434.

Trevarthen, C., & Aitken, K. J. (2001). Infant intersubjectivity: Research, theory, and clinical applications. *Journal of Child Psychology and Psychiary, 42,* 3–48.

Trickett, P. K., Allen, L., Schellenbach, C. J., & Zigler, E. F. (1998). Integrating and advancing the knowledge base about violence against children: Implications for intervention and prevention. In P. K. Trickett & C. J. Schellenbach (Eds.), *Violence against children in the family and the community.* Washington, DC: American Psychological Association.

Trickett, P. K., McBride-Chang, C., & Putnam, F. W. (1994). The classroom performance and behavior of sexually abused females. *Development and Psychopathology, 6,* 183–194.

Trickett, P. K., Noll, J. G., Reiffman, A., & Putnam, F. W. (2001). Variants of intrafamilial sexual abuse experience: Implications for short- and long-term development. *Development and Psychopathology, 13,* 1001–1019.

Tripp, G., & Alsop, B. (2001). Sensitivity to reward delay in children with attention deficit hyperactivity disorder (ADHD). *Journal of Child and Adolescent Psychology, 42,* 691–698.

Tu, S. (2003). Developmental epidemiology: A review of three key measures of effect. *Journal of Clinical Child and Adolescent Psychology, 32,* 187–192.

Tuddenham, R. D. (1962). The nature and measurement of intelligence. In L. Postman (Ed.), *Psychology in the making.* New York: Knopf.

Tully, L. A., Arseneault, L., Caspi, A., Moffit, T. E., & Morgan, J. (2004). Does maternal warmth moderate the effects of birthweight on twins' Attention-Deficit/Hyperactivity Disorder (ADHD) symptoms and low IQ? *Journal of Consulting and Clinical Psychology, 72,* 218–226.

Tuma, R. S. (2001). Laying down the details: Clinical opportunities with growing use of imaging. *Brain Work: The Neuroscience Newsletter, 11(3),* 1–3.

Turnbull, A. P. (2004). President's address 2004: "Wearing two hats": Morphed perspectives on family quality of life. *Mental Retardation, 42,* 383–399.

Turner, M. (1999). Annotation: Repetitive behaviour in autism: A review of psychological research. *Journal of Child Psychology and Psychiatry, 40,* 839–849.

U.S. Bureau of the Census. (1998). *Statistical Abstract of the United States: 1998* (118th ed.). Washington, DC: U.S. Government Printing Office.

U.S. Bureau of the Census. (2001). *Statistical Abstract of the United States: 2001* (121st ed.). Washington, DC: U.S. Government Printing Office.

U.S. Bureau of the Census. (2003). *Statistical abstract of the United States: 2003* (123rd ed.). Washington, DC: U.S. Government Printing Office.

U.S. Bureau of the Census. (2004). *Current Population Survey, 2002 and 2003. Annual Social and Economic Supplements.* Retrieved March 2004 from www.census.gov.

U.S. Bureau of the Census (2004). *Statistical Abstract of the United States, 2004–2005: The National Data Book* (124th ed.). Washington, DC: U.S. Government Printing Office.

U.S. Bureau of the Census, Current Population Survey. (1999–2001). Census Bureau home page.

U.S. Department of Education. (2000). *Summary—Twenty-second Annual Report to Congress on the Implementation of the Individuals with Disabilities Education Act.* Retrieved August 16, 2004, from http://www.ed.gov.

U.S. Department of Education. (2003). *Executive Summary—Twenty-fourth Annual Report to Congress on the Implementation of the Individuals with Disabilities Education Act.* Retrieved August 16, 2004, from http://www.ed.gov.

U.S. Department of Health and Human Service, Administration on Children, Youth and Families. (2003). *Child maltreatment 2001.* Washington DC: U.S. Government Printing Office.

U.S. Office of Education. (1977). Definition and criteria for defining students as learning disabled. Federal Register, 42:250, p. 65083. Washington, DC: U.S. Government Printing Office.

Udwin, O., Boyle, S., Yule, W., Bolton, D., & O'Ryan, D. (2000). Risk factors for long-term psychological effects of a disaster experienced in adolescence: Predictors of Post Traumatic Stress Disorder. *Journal of Child Psychology and Psychiatry, 41,* 969–979.

Ullmann, L. P., & Krasner, L. (1975). *A psychological approach to abnormal behavior* (2nd ed.). Englewood Cliffs, NJ: Prentice Hall.

Ulloa, R. L. et al. (2000). Psychosis in a pediatric mood and anxiety disorders clinic: Phenomenology and correlates. *Journal of the American Academy of Child and Adolescent Psychiatry, 39*, 337–345.

Usiskin, S. I. et al. (1999). Velocardiofacial syndrome in childhood-onset schizophrenia. *Journal of the American Academy of Child and Adolescent Psychiatry, 38*, 1536–1543.

Valone, K., Goldstein, M. J., & Norton, J. P. (1984). Parental expressed emotion and psychophysiological reactivity in an adolescent sample at risk for schizophrenia spectrum disorder. *Journal of Abnormal Psychology, 93*, 448–457.

Van Acker, R. (1997). Rett's syndrome: A pervasive developmental disorder. In D. J. Cohen & F. R. Volkmar (Eds.), *Handbook of autism and pervasive developmental disorders*. New York: John Wiley.

van Balkom, A. J. L. M., van Oppen, P., Vermeulen, A. W. A., van Dyck, R., Nauta, M. C. E., & Vorst, H. C. M. (1994). A meta-analysis on the treatment of obsessive compulsive disorder: A comparison of antidepressants, behavior, and cognitive therapy. *Clinical Psychology Review, 14*, 359–381.

Vandell, D. L., & Shumow, L. (1999). After-school child care programs. *The Future of Children, 9(2)*, 64–80.

Vandereycken, W. (1995). The families of patients with an eating disorder. In K. D. Brownell & C. G. Fairburn (Eds.), *Eating disorders and obesity: A comprehensive handbook*. New York: Guilford Press.

Vannatta, K., & Gerhardt, C. A. (2003). Pediatric oncology. In M. C. Roberts (Ed.), *Handbook of pediatric psychology* (3rd ed.). New York: Guilford Press.

Varela, R. E., Vernberg, E. M., Sanchez-Sosa, J. J., Riveros, A., Mitchell, M., & Mashunkashey, J. (2004). Anxiety reporting and culturally associated interpretation biases and cognitive schema: A comparison of Mexican, Mexican American, and European American families. *Journal of Clinical Child and Adolescent Psychology, 33*, 237–247.

Varley, C. K., Vincent, J., Varley, P., & Calderon, R. (2001). Emergence of tics in children with attention deficits hyperactivity disorder treated with stimulant medications. *Comprehensive Psychiatry, 42*, 228–233.

Varni, J. W., Katz, E. R., Colegrove, J. R., & Dolgin, M. (1996). Family functioning predictors of adjustment of children with newly diagnosed cancer: A prospective analysis. *Journal of Child Pyschology and Psychiatry, 37*, 321–328.

Varni, J. W., Katz, E. R., & Waldron, S. A. (1993). Cognitive-behavioral treatment interventions in childhood cancer. *The Clinical Psychologist, 46*, 192–197.

Vasey, M. W., & Daleiden, E. L. (1994). Worry in children. In G. C. L. Davey & F. Tallis (Eds.), *Worrying: Perspectives on theory, assessment and treatment*. Chichester, England: Wiley.

Vasey, M. W., Dalgleish, T., & Silverman, W. K. (2003). Research on information-processing factors in child and adolescent psychopathology: A critical commentary. *Journal of Clinical Child and Adolescent Psychology, 32*, 81–93.

Vaughn, S., La Greca, A. M., & Kuttler, A. (1999). The why, who, and how of social skills. In W. N. Bender (Ed.), *Professional issues in learning disabilities*. Austin, TX: PRO-ED.

Veenstra-vanderweele, J., & Cook, E. H. (2003). Genetics of childhood disorders: XLVI. Autism, Part 5: Genetics of autism. *Journal of the American Academy of Child and Adolescent Psychiatry, 42*, 116–118.

Vellutino, F. R. (1979). *Dyslexia. Theory and research.* Cambridge MA: MIT Press.

Vellutino, F. R. (1987). Dyslexia, *Scientific American, 256*, 34–41.

Vellutino, F. R., Fletcher, J. M., Snowling M. J., & Scanlon, D. M. (2004). Specific reading disability (dyslexia): What have we learned in the past four decades? *Journal of Child Psychology and Psychiatry, 45*, 2–40.

Velosa, J. F., & Riddle, M. A. (2000). Pharmacologic treatment of anxiety disorders in children and adolescents. *Child and Adolescent Clinics of North America, 9*, 119–133.

Velting, O. N., & Albano, A. M. (2001). Current trends in the understanding and treatment of social phobia in youth. *Journal of Child Psychology and Psychiatry, 42*, 127–140.

Verduin, T. L., & Kendall, P. C. (2003). Differential occurrence of comorbidity within childhood anxiety disorders. *Journal of Clinical Child and Adolescent Psychology, 32*, 290–295.

Verhulst, F. C., & van der Ende, J. (1997). Factors associated with mental health service use in the community. *Journal of the American Academy of Child and Adolescent Psychiatry, 36*, 901–909.

Vernberg, E. M., & Vogel, J. M. (1993). Interventions with children after disasters. *Journal of Clinical Child Psychology, 22*, 485–498.

Vernick, J., & Karon, M. (1965). Who's afraid of death on a leukemia ward? *American Journal of Diseases of Children, 109*, 393–397.

Vernon, D. T. A., & Thompson, R. H. (1993). Research on the effects of experimental interventions on children's behavior after hospitalizations: A review and synthesis. *Developmental and Behavioral Pediatrics, 14*, 36–44.

Vickers, B., & Garralda, E. (2000). Hallucinations in nonpsychotic children. *Journal of the Academy of Child and Adolescent Psychiatry, 39*, 1073.

Viding, E., Spinath, F. M., Price, T. S., Bishop, D. V. M., Dale, P. S., & Plomin, R. (2004). Genetic and environmental influences on language impairment in 4-year-old same-sex and opposite-sex twins. *Journal of Child Psychology and Psychiatry, 45*, 315–325.

Vila, G., Nollet-Clemencon, C., de Blic, J., Mouren-Simeoni, M., & Scheinmann, P. (2000). Prevalence of DSM-IV anxiety and affective disorders in a pediatric population of asthmatic children and adolescents. *Journal of Affective Disorders, 58*, 223–231.

Vila, G., Nollet-Clemencon, C., Vera, M., Robert, J. J., de-Blic, J., Jouvent, R., Mouren-Simeoni, M. C., & Scheinmann, P. (1999). Prevalence of DSM-IV disorders in children and adolescents with asthma versus diabetes. *Canadian Journal of Psychiatry, 44*, 562–569.

Villani, S. (2001). Impact of media on children and adolescents: A 10-year review of the research. *Journal of the American Academy of Child and Adolescent Psychiatry, 40*, 392–401.

Visser, J. H., van der Ende, J., Koot, H. M., & Verhulst, F. C. (2003). Predicting change in psychopathology in youth referred to mental health services in childhood or adolescence. *Journal of Child Psychology and Psychiatry, 44*, 509–519.

Vitiello, B., Severe, J. B., Greenhill, L. L., Arnold, L. E., Abikoff, H. B., Bukstein, O. G. et al. (2001). Methlyphenidate dosage for children with ADHD over time under controlled conditions: Lessons from the MTA. *Journal of the American Academy of Child and Adolescent Psychiatry, 40,* 188–196.

Vitiello, B., & Swedo, S. (2004). Antidepressant medications in children. *New England Journal of Medicine, 350,* 1489–1491.

Volkmar, F. R. (1987). Annotation. Diagnostic issues in the pervasive developmental disorders. *Journal of Child Psychology and Psychiatry, 28,* 365–369.

Volkmar, F. R. (1991). Childhood schizophrenia. In M. Lewis (Ed.), *Child and adolescent psychiatry: A comprehensive textbook.* Baltimore: Williams & Wilkins.

Volkmar, F. R. (1996a). Autism and the pervasive developmental disorders. In M. Lewis (Ed.), *Child and adolescent psychiatry: A comprehensive textbook.* Baltimore: Williams & Wilkins.

Volkmar, F. R. (1996b). Childhood and adolescent psychosis: A review of the past 10 years. *Journal of the American Academy of Child and Adolescent Psychiatry, 35,* 843–851.

Volkmar, F. R. (2001). Pharmacological interventions in autism: Theoretical and practical issues. *Journal of Clinical Child Psychology, 30,* 80–87.

Volkmar, F. R., Becker, D. F., King, R. A., & McGlashan, T. H. (1995). Psychotic processes. In D. Cicchetti & D. J. Cohen (Eds.), *Developmental psychopathology.* New York: John Wiley.

Volkmar, F. R., Carter, A., Grossman, J., & Klin, A. (1997). Social development in autism. In D. J. Cohen & F. R. Volkmar (Eds.), *Handbook of autism and pervasive developmental disorders.* New York: John Wiley.

Volkmar, F. R., & Dykens, E. (2002). Mental retardation. In M. Rutter & E. Taylor (Eds.), *Child and adolescent psychiatry.* Oxford, UK: Blackwell Publishing.

Volkmar, F. R., & Klin, A. (2000). Pervasive developmental disorders. In B. J. Sadock & V. A. Sadock (Eds.), *Comprehensive textbook of psychiatry* (Vol. II). Philadelphia: Lippincott Williams & Wilkins.

Volkmar, F. R., Klin, A., Schultz, R. T., Rubin, E., & Bronen, R. (2000). Asperger's disorder. *American Journal of Psychiatry, 157,* 262–267.

Volkmar, F. R., Lord, C., Bailey, A., Schultz, R. T., & Klin, A. (2004). Autism and developmental pervasive disorders. *Journal of Child Psychology and Psychiatry, 45,* 135–170.

von Gonard, A., Backes, M., Laufersweiler-Plass, C., Wendland, C., Lehmkuhl, G., Zerres, K. et al. (2002). Psychopathology and familial stress—comparison of boys with fragile X syndrome and spinal muscular atrophy. *Journal of Child Psychology and Psychiatry, 43,* 949–957.

Votruba-Drzal, E., Coley, R. L., & Chase-Lansdale, P. L. (2004). Child care and low-income children's development: Direct and moderated effects. *Child Development, 75,* 296–312.

Wachsler-Felder, J. L., & Golden, C. J. (2002). Neuropsychological consequences of HIV in children: A review of current literature. *Clinical Psychology Review, 22,* 441–462.

Wade, T. J., Cairney, J., & Pevalin, D. J. (2002). Emergence of gender differences in depression during adolescence: National panel results from three countries. *Journal of the American Academy of Child and Adolescent Psychiatry, 2002, 41,* 190–198.

Wagner, B. M. (1997). Family risk factors for child and adolescent suicidal behavior. *Psychological Bulletin, 121,* 246–298.

Wagner, J. L., Chaney, J. M., Hommel, K. A., Page, M. C., Mullins, L. L., White, M. M., & Jarvis, J. N. (2003). The influence of parental distress on child depressive symptoms in juvenile rheumatic diseases: The moderating effect of illness intrusiveness. *Journal of Pediatric Psychology, 28,* 453–462.

Wagner, K. D., & Ambrosini, P. J. (2001). Childhood depression: Pharmacological therapy/treatment (pharmacotherapy of childhood depression). *Journal of Clinical Child Psychology, 30,* 88–97.

Wagner, K. D., Cook, E. H., Chung, H., & Messig, M. (2003). Remission status after long-term sertraline treatment of pediatric obsessive-compulsive disorder. *Journal of Child and Adolescent Psychopharmacology, 13,* S53–S60.

Wagner, W. G., Smith D., & Norris, W. R. (1988). The psychological adjustment of enuretic children: A comparison of two types. *Journal of Pediatric Psychology, 13,* 33–38.

Wahler, R. G., & Dumas, J. E. (1984). Changing the observational coding styles of insular and noninsular mothers: A step towards maintenance of parent training effects. In R. F. Dangel & R. A. Polster (Eds.), *Parent training: Foundations of research and practice.* New York: Guilford.

Wahler, R. G., & Dumas, J. E. (1989). Attentional problems in dysfunctional mother-child interactions: An interbehavioral model. *Psychological Bulletin, 105,* 116–130.

Wakefield, A. J. et al. (1998). Ileal-lymphoid-nodular hypoplasia, non-specific colitis, and pervasive developmental disorder in children. *Lancet, 351,* 637–641.

Walco, G. A., Sterling, C. N., Conte, P. M., & Engel, R. G. (1999). Empirically supported treatments in pediatric psychology: Disease-related pain. *Journal of Pediatric Psychology, 24,* 155–167.

Waldman, I. D., Lilienfeld, S. O., & Lahey, B. B. (1995). Toward construct validity in the childhood disruptive behavior disorders: Classification and diagnosis in DSM-IV and beyond. In T. H. Ollendick & R. J. Prinz (Eds.), *Advances in clinical child psychology.* Vol. 17. New York: Plenum Press.

Waldron, N. L., & McLeskey, J. (1998). The effects of an inclusive school program on students with mild and severe learning disabilities. *Exceptional Children, 64,* 395–405.

Walker, C. E. (2003). Elimination disorders: Enuresis and encopresis. In M. C. Roberts (Ed.), *Handbook of pediatric psychology* (3rd ed.). New York: Guilford Press.

Walkup, J. T., Labellarte, M. J., Riddle, M. A., Pine, D. S., Greenhill, L., Klein, R. et al. (2001). Fluvoxamine for the treatment of anxiety disorders in children and adolescents. *The New England Journal of Medicine, 344,* 1279–1285.

Wallace, T., Anderson, A. R., Bartholomay, T., & Hupp, S. (2002). An ecobehavioral examination of high school classrooms that include students with disabilities. *Exceptional Children, 68,* 345–359.

Wallander, J. L., Thompson, R. J., Jr., & Alriksson-Schmidt, A. (2003). Psychosocial adjustment of children with chronic physical conditions. In M. C. Roberts (Eds.), *Handbook of pediatric psychology* (3rd ed.). New York: Guilford Press.

Wallander, J. L., & Varni, J. W. (1998). Effects of pediatric chronic physical disorders on child and family adjustment. *Journal of Child Psychology and Psychiatry, 39,* 29–46.

Wallerstein, J. S. (1991). The long-term effects of divorce on children: A review. *Journal of the American Academy of Child and Adolescent Psychiatry, 30,* 349–360.

Warfield, M. E. (2001). Employment, parenting, and well-being among mothers of children with disabilities. *Mental Retardation, 39,* 297–309.

Warren, S. L., Gunnar, M. R., Kagan, J., Anders, T. F., Simmens, S. J., Rones, M., Wease, S., Aron, E., Dahl, R. E., & Sroufe, L. A. (2003). Maternal panic disorder: Infant temperament, neurophysiology, and parenting behaviors. *Journal of the American Academy of Child and Adolescent Psychiatry, 42,* 814–825.

Warren, S. L., Huston, L., Egeland, B., & Sroufe, L. A. (1997). Child and adolescent anxiety disorders and early attachment. *Journal of the American Academy of Child and Adolescent Psychiatry, 36,* 637–644.

Waschbusch, D. A. (2002). A meta-analytic examination of comorbid hyperactive-impulsive-attention problems and conduct problems. *Psychological Bulletin, 128,* 118–150.

Waterhouse, L., & Fein, D. (1997). Perspectives on social impairment. In D. J. Cohen & F. R. Volkmar (Eds.), *Handbook of autism and pervasive developmental disorders.* New York: John Wiley.

Watkins, C. E., Campbell, V. L., Nieberding, R., & Hallmark, R. (1995). Contemporary practice of psychological assessment by clinical psychologists. *Professional Psychology: Research and Practice, 26,* 54–60.

Watkins, J. M., Asarnow, R. F., & Tanguay, P. E. (1988). Symptom development in childhood onset schizophrenia. *Journal of Child Psychology and Psychiatry, 29,* 865–878.

Watson, J. B. (1913). Psychology as the behaviorist views it. *Psychological Review, 20,* 158–177.

Watson, J. B. (1930). *Behaviorism.* New York: Norton.

Watson, J. B., & Rayner, R. (1920). Conditioned emotional reactions. *Journal of Experimental Psychology, 3,* 1–14.

We the Children: Meeting the Promises of the World Summit for Children. (2001). Report of the U.N. Secretary General Kofi Annan. New York: United Nations.

Webster-Stratton, C. (1984). Randomized trial of two parent-training programs for families with conduct-disordered children. *Journal of Consulting and Clinical Psychology, 52,* 666–678.

Webster-Stratton, C. (1994). Advancing videotape parent training: A comparison study. *Journal of Consulting and Clinical Psychology, 62,* 583–593.

Webster-Stratton, C., & Hammond, M. (1997). Treating children with early-onset conduct problems: A comparison of child and parent training interventions. *Journal of Consulting and Clinical Psychology, 65,* 93–109.

Webster-Stratton, C., & Hancock, L. (1998). Parent training: Content, methods, and process. In E. Schaefer (Ed.), *Handbook of parent training* (2nd ed.). New York: Wiley.

Webster-Stratton, C., Hollinsworth, T., & Kolpacoff, M. (1989). The long-term effectiveness and clinical significance of three cost-effective training programs for families with conduct-problem children. *Journal of Consulting and Clinical Psychology, 57,* 550–553.

Webster-Stratton, C., & Hooven, C. (1998). Parent training for child conduct problems. In T. Ollendick (Ed.), *Comprehensive clinical psychology* (Vol. 5). Oxford, England: Elsevier Science.

Webster-Stratton, C., & Reid, M. J. (2003). The incredible years parents, teachers, and children training series: A multifaceted treatment approach for young children. In A. E. Kazdin & J. R. Weisz (Eds.), *Evidence-based psychotherapies for children and adolescents.* New York: Guilford Press.

Webster-Stratton, C., Reid, M. J., & Hammond, M. (2004). Treating children with early-onset conduct problems: Intervention outcomes for parent, child, and teacher training. *Journal of Clinical Child and Adolescent Psychology, 33,* 105–124.

Webster-Stratton, C., & Spitzer, A. (1991). Development, reliability, and validity of the Daily Telephone Discipline Interview. *Behavioral Assessment, 13,* 221–239.

Wechsler, D. (2002). *Wechsler Preschool and Primary Scale of Intelligence—Third Edition (WPPSI-III).* San Antonio, TX: Psychological Corporation.

Wechsler, D. (2003). *Wechsler Intelligence Scale for Children—Fourth Edition (WISC-IV).* San Antonio, TX: Psychological Corporation.

Weersing, V. R., & Brent, D. A. (2003). Cognitive-behavioral therapy for adolescent depression: Comparative efficacy, mediation, moderation, and effectiveness. In A. E. Kazdin & J. R. Weisz (Eds.), *Evidence-based psychotherapies for children and adolescents.* New York: Guilford Press.

Wehmeyer, M. L. (2003). Eugenics and sterilization in the heartland. *Mental Retardation, 41,* 57–60.

Weibe, D. J., Berg, C. A., Korbel, C., Palmer, D. L., Beveridge, R. M., Upchurch, R. et al. (2005). Children's appraisals of maternal involvement in coping with diabetes: Enhancing our understanding of adherence, metabolic control, and quality of life across adolescence. *Journal of Pediatric Psychology, 30,* 167–178.

Weinberger, D. R. (1987). Implications of normal brain development for the pathogenesis of schizophrenia. *Archives of General Psychiatry, 44,* 660–669.

Weinberger, D. R. (1994). Biological basis of schizophrenia: Structural/functional considerations relevant to potential for antipsychotic drug response. *Journal of Clinical Psychiatry Mongraph, 12:2,* 4–8.

Weinberger, D. R., & McClure, R. K. (2002). Neurotoxicity, neuroplasticity, and magnetic resonance imaging morphometry. *Archives of General Psychiatry, 59,* 553–558.

Weinrott, M. R., Jones, R. R., & Howard, J. R. (1982). Cost-effectiveness of teaching family programs for delinquents: Results of a national evauation. *Evaluation Review, 6,* 173–201.

Weiss, B., & Garber, J. (2003). Developmental differences in the phenomenology of depression. *Development and Psychopathology, 15,* 403–430.

Weiss, G., & Hechtman, L. T. (1986). *Hyperactive children grown up.* New York: Guilford.

Weiss, K. B., Gergen, P. J., Hodgson, T. A. (1992). An economic evaluation of asthma in the United States. *New England Journal of Medicine, 326,* 862–866.

Weissberg, R. P., Kumpfer, K. L., & Seligman, M. E. P. (2003). Prevention that works for children: An introduction. *American Psychologist, 58,* 425–432.

Weissman, M. M., Kidd, K. K., & Prusoff, B. A. (1982). Variability in rates of affective disorders in relatives of depressed and normal probands. *Archives of General Psychiatry, 39,* 1397–1403.

Weissman, M. M., Warner, V., Wickramarante, P., Moreau, D., & Olfson, M. (1997). Offspring of depressed parents: 10 years later. *Archives of General Psychiatry, 54*, 932–940.

Weissman, M. M., Warner, V., Wichramaratne, P., & Prusoff, B. A. (1988). Onset of major depression in adolescence and early adulthood: Findings from a family study of children. *Journal of Affective Disorders, 15*, 269–277.

Weist, M. D. (1997). Expanded school mental health services: A national movement in progress. In T. H. Ollendick & R. J. Prinz (Eds.), *Advances in clinical child psychology* (Vol. 19). New York: Plenum Press.

Weist, M. D., & Cooley-Quille, M. (2001). Advancing efforts to address youth violence involvement. *Journal of Clinical Child Psychology, 30*, 147–151.

Weist, M. D., Finney, J. W., Barnard, M. U., Davis, C. D., & Ollendick, T. H. (1993). Empirical selection of psychosocial treatment targets for children and adolescents with diabetes. *Journal of Pediatric Psychology, 18*, 11–28.

Weisz, J. R., Abidin, R. R., Campbell, S. B. et al. (2004). APA resolution on bullying among children and youth. *Clinical Child and Adolescent Psychology Newsletter, 19(3)*, 5, 7.

Weisz, J. R., Chaiyasit, W., Weiss, B., Eastman, K. L., & Jackson, E. W. (1995). A multimethod study of problem behavior among Thai and American children in school: Teacher reports versus direct observations. *Child Development, 66*, 402–415.

Weisz, J. R., & Kazdin, A. E. (2003). Concluding thoughts: Present and future of evidence-based psychotherapies for children and adolescents. In A. E. Kazdin & J. R. Weisz (Eds.), *Evidence-based psychotherapies for children and adolescents.* New York: Guilford Press.

Weisz, J. R., Sigman, M., Weiss, B., & Mosk, J. (1993a). Parent reports of behavioral and emotional problems among children in Kenya, Thailand, and the United States. *Child Development, 64*, 98–109.

Weisz, J. R., Southam-Gerow, M. A., Gordis, E. B., & Connor-Smith, J. (2003). Primary and secondary control enhancement training for youth depression. In A. E. Kazdin & J. R. Weisz (Eds.), *Evidence-based psychotherapies for children and adolescents.* New York: Guilford Press.

Weisz, J. R., Suwanlet, S., Chaiyasit, W., Weiss, B., Walter, B. R., & Anderson, W. W. (1988). Thai and American perspectives on over- and undercontrolled child behavior problems: Exploring the threshold model among parents, teachers, and psychologists. *Journal of Consulting and Clinical Psychology, 56*, 601–609.

Weisz, J. R., Sweeney, L., Proffitt, V., & Carr, T. (1993b). Control-related beliefs and self-reported depressive symptoms in late childhood. *Journal of Abnormal Psychology, 102*, 411–418.

Weithorn, L. A. (1987). Informed consent for prevention research involving children: Legal and ethical issues. In J. A. Steinberg & M. M. Silverman (Eds.), *Preventing mental disorders.* Rockville, MD: U.S. Department of Health and Human Services.

Weizman, Z. O., & Snow, C. E. (2001). Lexical input as related to children's vocabulary acquisition: Effects of sophisticated exposure and support for meaning. *Developmental Psychology, 37*, 265–279.

Wekerle, C., & Wolfe, D. A. (2003). Child maltreatment. In E. J. Mash & R. A. Barkley (Eds.), *Child psychopathology* (2nd ed.). New York: Guilford Press.

Wellman, H. M. (1993). Early understanding of mind: The normal case. In S. Baron-Cohen, H. Tager-Flüsberg, & D. J. Cohen (Eds.), *Understanding other minds.* New York: Oxford Press.

Wells, K. C., Forehand, R., & Griest, D. L. (1980). Generality of treatment effects from treated to untreated behaviors resulting from a parent training program. *Journal of Clinical Child Psychology, 9*, 217–219.

Wender, P. H., Kety, S. S., Rosenthal, D., Schulsinger, F., Ortmann, J., & Lunde, I. (1986). Psychiatric disorders in the biological and adoptive families of adopted individuals with affective disorders. *Archives of General Psychiatry, 43*, 923–929.

Wentz, E., Gillberg, C., Gillberg, I. C., & Rastam, M. (2001). Ten-year follow-up of adolescent-onset anorexia nervosa: Psychiatric disorders and overall functioning scales. *Journal of Child Psychology and Psychiatry, 42*, 613–622.

Werner, E., Dawson, G., Osterling, J., & Dinno, N. (2000). Brief report: Recognition of autism spectrum disorder before one year of age: A retrospective study based on home videotapes. *Journal of Autism and Developmental Disorders, 30*, 157–162.

Werner, E. E., & Smith, R. S. (1982). *Vulnerable but invincible.* New York: McGraw-Hill.

Werry, J. S. (1986). Physical illness, symptoms and allied disorders. In H. C. Quay & J. S. Werry (Eds.), *Psychopathological disorders of childhood*, 3rd ed. New York: Wiley.

Werry, J. S. (2001). Pharmacological treatments of autism, attention deficit hyperactivity disorder, oppositional defiant disorder, and depression in children and youth—commentary. *Journal of Clinical Child Psychology, 30*, 110–113.

Werry, J. S., & Aman, M. G. (1999). *Practitioner's guide to psychoactive drugs for children and adolescents* (2nd ed.). New York: Plenum Medical Book Company.

Wertheim, E. H., Paxton, S. J., & Blaney, S. (2004). Risks factors for the development of body image disturbances. In J. K. Thompson (Ed.), *Handbook of eating disorders and obesity.* Hoboken, NJ: John Wiley.

Wertlieb, D., Hauser, S. T., & Jacobson, A. M. (1986). Adaptation to diabetes: Behavior symptoms and family context. *Journal of Pediatric Psychology, 11*, 463–479.

West, M. O., & Prinz, R. J. (1987). Parental alcoholism and childhood psychopathology. *Psychological Bulletin, 102*, 204–218.

West, P., & Sweeting, H. (2003). Fifteen, female, and stressed: Changing patterns of psychological stress over time. *Journal of Child Psychology and Psychiatry, 44*, 399–411.

West, S. G., Sandler, I., Pillow, D. R., Baca, L., & Gersten, J. C. (1991). The use of structural equation modeling in generative research: Toward the design of a preventative intervention for bereaved children. *American Journal of Community Psychology, 19*, 459–480.

Westenberg, P. M., Drewes, M. J., Goedhart, A. W., Siebelink, B. M., & Treffers, P. D. A. (2004). A developmental analysis of self-reported fears in late childhood through mid-adolescence: Social-evaluative fears on the rise? *Journal of Child Psychology and Psychiatry, 45*, 481–495.

Western Psychological Services. (2004). *WPS 2004 catalogue.* Los Angeles: Western Psychological Services.

Wexler, A. (1995). *Mapping fate.* New York: Random House.

Whalen, C. K. (1989). Attention deficit and hyperactivity disorders. In T. H. Ollendick & M. Hersen (Eds.), *Handbook of child psychopathology.* New York: Plenum.

Whalen, C. K. (2001). ADHD treatment in the 21st century: Pushing the envelope. *Journal of Clinical Child Psychology, 30,* 136–140.

Whalen, C. K., & Henker, B. (1985). The social worlds of hyperactive (ADHD) children. *Clinical Psychology Review, 5,* 447–448.

Whalen, C. K., & Henker, B. (1998). Attention-deficit/hyperactivity disorders. In T. H. Ollendick & M. Hersen (Eds.), *Handbook of child psychopathology.* New York: Plenum Press.

Whalen, C. K., Henker, B., King, P. S., Jamner, L. D., & Levine, L. (2004). Adolescents react to the events of September 11, 2001: Focused versus ambient impact. *Journal of Abnormal Child Psychology, 32,* 1–11.

Whisman, M. (2000). Marital distress and depression: Findings from community and clinical studies. In S. R. H. Beach (Ed.), *Marital and family processes in depression: A scientific foundation for clinical practice.* Washington, DC: American Psychological Association.

Whitaker, A., Johnson, J., Shaffer, D., Rappoport, J., Kalikow, K., Walsh, B. T., Davies, M., Braiman, S., & Dolinsky, A. (1990). Uncommon troubles in young people: Prevalence estimates of selected psychiatric disorders in a nonreferred adolescent population. *Archives of General Psychiatry, 47,* 487–496.

White, H. R., Bates, M. E., & Buyske, S. (2001). Adolescence-limited delinquency: Extending Moffitt's hypothesis into adulthood. *Journal of Abnormal Psychology, 110,* 600–609.

White, H. R., Loeber, R., Stouthamer-Loeber, M., & Farrington, D. P. (1999). Developmental associations between substance use and violence. *Development and Psychopathology, 11,* 785–803.

White, J. L., Moffitt, T. E., & Silva, P. A. (1989). A prospective replication of the protective effects of IQ in subjects at high risk for juvenile delinquency. *Journal of Consulting and Clinical Psychology, 57,* 719–724.

White, K. J., & Kistner, J. (1992). The influence of teacher feedback on young children's peer preferences and perceptions. *Developmental Psychology, 28,* 933–940.

White, S. H. (1992). G. Stanley Hall: From philosophy to developmental psychology. *Developmental Psychology, 28,* 25–34.

White, T., Andreasen, N. C., Nopoulos, P., & Magnotta, V. (2003). Gyrification abnormalities in childhood- and adolescent-onset schizophrenia. *Biological Psychiatry, 54,* 418–426.

Whitehurst, G. J. (1982). Language development. In B. B. Wolman (Ed.), *Handbook of developmental psychology.* Upper Saddle River, NJ: Prentice Hall.

Whitehurst, G. J., & Fischel, J. E. (1994). Early developmental language delay: What, if anything, should the clinician do about it? *Journal of Child Psychology and Psychiatry, 35,* 613–648.

Whitman, T. L., Hantula, D. A., & Spence, B. H. (1990). Current issues in behavior modification with mentally retarded persons. In J. L. Matson (Ed.), *Handbook of behavior modification with the mentally retarded.* New York: Plenum.

Whittlesey, S. W., Allen, J. R., Bell, B. D., Lindsey, E. D., Speed, L. F., Lucas, A. F., Ware, M. M., Allen, S. F., Pfefferbaum, B. (1999). Avoidance in trauma: Conscious and unconscious defense, pathology, and health. *Psychiatry: Interpersonal and Biological Processes, 62,* 303–312.

Widiger, T. A., & Clark, L. A. (2000). Toward DSM-V and the classification of psychopathology. *Psychological Bulletin, 126,* 946–961.

Widiger, T. A., Frances, A. J., Pincus, H. A., Davis, W. W., & First, M. B. (1991). Toward an empirical classification for DSM-IV. *Journal of Abnormal Psychology, 100,* 280–288.

Wiebe, D. J., Alderfer, M. A., Palmer, S. C., Lindsay, R., & Jarrett, L. (1994). Behavioral self-regulation in adolescents with type I diabetes: Negative affectivity and blood glucose symptom perception. *Journal of Consulting and Clinical Psychology, 62,* 1204–1212.

Wight, R. G., Sepúlveda, J. E., & Aneshensel, C. S. (2004). Depressive symptoms: How do adolescents compare with adults? *Journal of Adolescent Health, 34,* 314–323.

Wilens, T. E., Faraone, S. V., Biederman, J., & Gunawardene, S. (2003). Does stimulant therapy of attention-deficit/hyperactivity disorder beget later substance abuse? A meta-analytic review of the literature. *Pediatrics, 111,* 175–185.

Wilfley, D. E., & Rodin, J. (1995). Cultural influences on eating disorders. In K. D. Brownell & C. G. Fairburn (Eds.), *Eating disorders and obesity: A comprehensive handbook.* New York: Guilford Press.

Wilkinson, G. S. (1993). *Wide Range Achievement Test—Revision 3.* Wilmington, DE: Jastak Associates.

Willcutt, E. G., & Pennington, B. F. (2000). Psychiatric comorbidity in children and adolescents with reading disability. *Journal of Child Psychology and Psychiatry, 41,* 1039–1048.

Willcutt, E. G., Pennington, B. F., Brada, R., Ogline, J. S., Tunick, R. A., Chhabildas, N. A., & Olson, R. K. (2001). A comparison of the cognitive deficits in reading disability and attention deficit/hyperactivity disorder. *Journal of Abnormal Psychology, 110,* 157–172.

Willemsen-Swinkels, S. H. N., Bakermans-Franenburg, M. J., Buitelaar, J. K., van IJzendoorn, M. H., & van Engeland, H. (2000). Insecure and disorganized attachment in children with a pervasive developmental disorder: Relationship with social interaction and heart rate. *Journal of Child Psychology and Psychiatry, 41,* 759–767.

Williams, S., & McGee, R. (1996). Reading in childhood and mental health in early adulthood. In J. H. Beitchman, N. J. Cohen, M. M. Konstantareas, & R. Tannock (Eds.), *Language learning, and behavior disorders.* New York: Cambridge University Press.

Willner, A. C., Braukmann, G. J., Kirigin, K. A., & Wolf, M. M. (1978). Achievement Place: A community model for youths in trouble. In D. Marholin (Ed.), *Child behavior therapy.* New York: Gardner.

Willoughby, M., Kupersmidt, J., & Bryant, D. (2001). Overt and covert dimensions of antisocial behavior in early childhood. *Journal of Abnormal Child Psychology, 29,* 177–187.

Willoughby, M. T. (2003). Developmental course of ADHD symptomatology during the transition from childhood to adolescence: A review with recommendations. *Journal of Child Psychology and Psychiatry, 44,* 88–106.

Willoughby, M. T., Curran, P. J., Costello, E. J., & Angold, A. (2000). Implications of early versus late onset of attention-deficit/hyperactivity disorder symptoms. *Journal of the American Academy of Child and Adolescent Psychiatry, 39,* 1512–1519.

Wills, T. A., & Dishion, T. J. (2004). Temperament and adolescent substance abuse: A transactional analysis of emerging self-control. *Journal of Clinical and Child and Adolescent Psychology, 33,* 69–81.

Wills, T. A., & Filer, M. (1996). Stress-coping model of adolescent substance use. In T. H. Ollendick & R. J. Prinz (Eds.), *Advances in clinical child psychology* (Vol. 18). New York: Plenum Press.

Wilson, A. M., & Lesaux, N. K. (2002). Persistence of phonological processing deficits in college students with dyslexia who have age-appropriate reading skills. *Journal of Learning Disabilities, 34,* 394–400.

Wilson, C. C., & Haynes, S. N. (1985). Sleep disorders. In P. H. Bornstein & A. E. Kazdin (Eds.), *Handbook of clinical behavior therapy with children.* Homewood, IL: Dorsey.

Wilson, G. T., Becker, C. B., & Heffernan, K. (2003). Eating disorders. In E. J. Mash & R. A. Barkley (Eds.), *Child psychopathology* (2nd ed.). New York: Guilford Press.

Wilson, G. T., & Fairburn, C. G. (2002). Eating disorders. In P. E. Nathan & J. M. Gorman (Eds.), *Treatments that work* (2nd ed.). New York: Oxford University Press.

Wilson, K. M., & Swanson, H. L. (2001). Are mathematics disabilities due to a domain-general or domain-specific working memory deficit? *Journal of Learning Disabilities, 34,* 237–248.

Windle, M. (1990). A longitudinal study of antisocial behaviors in early adolescence as predictors of late adolescent substance use: Gender and ethnic group differences. *Journal of Abnormal Psychology, 99,* 86–91.

Winett, R. A. (1995). A framework for health promotion and disease prevention programs. *American Psychologist, 50,* 341–350.

Wing, L. (1997). Syndromes of autism and atypical development. In D. J. Cohen & F. R. Volkmar (Eds.), *Handbook of autism and pervasive developmental disorders.* New York: John Wiley.

Wirt, R. D., Lachar, D., Klinedinst, J. E., Seat, P. D., & Broen, W. E. (2001). *Personality Inventory for Children Manual* (2nd ed.). Los Angeles: Western Psychological Services.

Wolf, L., Fisman, S., Ellison, D., & Freeman, T. (1998). Effect of sibling perception of differential parental treatment in sibling dyads with one disabled child. *Journal of the American Academy of Child and Adolescent Psychiatry, 37,* 1317–1325.

Wolf, M. M., Braukmann, C. J., & Ramp, K. A. (1987). Serious delinquent behavior as part of a significantly handicapping condition: Cures and supportive environments. *Journal of Applied Behavior Analysis, 20,* 347–359.

Wolfe, D. A., Scott, K., Wekerle, C., & Pittman, A. L. (2001). Child maltreatment: Risk of adjustment problems and dating violence in adolescence. *Journal of the American Academy of Child and Adolescent Psychiatry, 40,* 282–289.

Wolfe, J., Grier, H. E., Klar, N., Levin, S. B., Ellenbogen, J. M., Salem-Schatz, S. et al. (2000a). Symptoms and suffering at the end of life in children with cancer. *New England Journal of Medicine, 342,* 326–333.

Wolfe, J., Klar, N., Grier, H. E., Duncan, J., Salem-Schatz, S. Emanuel, E. J., Weeks, J. C. (2000b). Understanding of prognosis among parents of children who died of cancer: Impact on treatment goals and integration of palliative care. *Journal of the American Medical Association, 284,* 2469–2475.

Wolfe, V. V., & Birt, J. (1995). The psychological sequelae of child sexual abuse. In T. H. Ollendick & R. J. Prinz (Eds.), *Advances in clinical child psychology.* Vol. 17. New York: Plenum Press.

Wolfensberger, W. (1980). *The principle of normalization in human services.* Toronto: National Institute on Mental Retardation.

Wolke, D., Woods, S., Bloomfield, L., & Karstadt, L. (2000). The association between direct and relational bullying and behaviour problems among primary school children. *Journal of Child Psychology and Psychiatry, 41,* 989–1002.

Wolraich, M. L. (2003). Annotation: The use of psychotropic medications in children: An American view. *Journal of Child Psychology and Psychiatry, 44,* 159–168.

Wolraich, M., Wilson, D. B., & White, J. W. (1995). The effect of sugar on behavior or cognition in children. *Journal of the American Medical Association, 274,* 1617–1621.

Wonderlich, S., Crosby, R., Mitchell, J., Thompson, K., Redlin, J., Demuth, G., & Smyth, J. (2001). Pathways mediating sexual abuse and eating disturbance in children. *Journal of Eating Disorders, 13,* 25–34.

Wong, B. Y. L., Butler, D. L., Ficzere, S. A., & Kuperis, S. (1997). Teaching adolescents with learning disabilities and low achievers to plan, write, and revise compare-and-contrast essays. *Learning Disabilities Research & Practice, 12,* 2–15.

Wong, B. Y. L., Harris, K. R., Graham, S., & Butler, D. L. (2003). Cognitive strategies instruction research in learning disabilities. In H. L. Swanson, K. R. Harris & S. Graham (Eds.), *Handbook of learning disabilities.* New York: Guilford Press.

Wood, B. L. (1994). One articulation of the structural family therapy model: A biobehavioral family model of chronic illness in children. *Journal of Family Therapy, 16,* 53–72.

Wood, B., Watkins, J. B., Boyle, J. T., Noguiera, J., Aimand, E., & Carrol, L. (1989). The "psychosomatic family" model: An empirical analysis. *Family Process, 28,* 399–417.

Wood, J. J., McLeod, B. D., Sigman, M., Hwang, W. C., & Chu, B. C. (2003). Parenting and childhood anxiety: theory, empirical findings, and future directions. *Journal of Child Psychology and Psychiatry, 44,* 134–151.

Wood, M., & Valdez-Menchaca, M. C. (1996). The effect of a diagnostic label of language delay on adults' perceptions of preschool children. *Journal of Learning Disabilities, 29,* 582–588.

Woodcock, R. W. (1998). *Woodcock Reading Mastery Tests-Revised-Normative Update: Examiner's Manual, Forms G and H.* Circle Pines, MN: American Guidance Service.

Woodward, L. J., & Fergusson, D. M. (2000). Childhood peer relationship problems and later risks of educational underachievement and unemployment. *Journal of Child Psychology and Psychiatry, 41,* 191–201.

Woodward, L. J., Fergusson, D. M., & Horwood, L. J. (2000). Driving outcomes of young people with attentional difficulties in adolescence. *Journal of the American Academy of Child and Adolescent Psychiatry, 39,* 627–634.

Woodward, L., Taylor, E., & Dowdney, L. (1998). The parenting and family functioning of children with hyperactivity. *Journal of Child Psychology and Psychiatry, 39*, 161–169.

World Health Organization. (1992). *International classification of diseases: Tenth revision.* Chapter V. Mental and behavioural disorders. Diagnostic criteria for research. Geneva: Author.

Woznick, L. A., & Goodheart, C. D. (2002). *Living with childhood cancer: A practical guide to help families cope.* Washington, DC: American Psychological Association.

Wright, H. F. (1960). Observational child study. In P. H. Mussen (Ed.), *Handbook of research methods in child development.* New York: John Wiley.

Wysocki, T., Greco, P., & Buckloh, L. M. (2003). Childhood diabetes in psychological context. In M. C. Roberts (Ed.), *Handbook of pediatric psychology* (3rd ed.). New York: Guilford Press.

Yates, A. (1989). Current perspectives on the eating disorders: I. History, psychological and biological aspects. *Journal of the American Academy of Child and Adolescent Psychiatry, 28*, 813–828.

Yates, T. M. (2004). The developmental psychopathology of self-injurious behavior: Compensatory regulation in posttraumatic adaptation. *Clinical Psychology Review, 24*, 35–74.

Yeates, K. O., Taylor, H. G., Barry, C. T., Drotar, D., Wade, S. L., & Stancin, T. (2001). Neurobehavioral symptoms in childhood closed-head injuries: Changes in prevalence and correlates during the first year postinjury. *Journal of Pediatric Psychology, 26*, 79–91.

Yeates-Frederikx, M. H. M., Nijman, H., Logher, E., & Merckelbach, H. L. G. M. (2000). Birth patterns in mentally retarded autistic patients. *Journal of Autism and Developmental Disorders, 30*, 257–262.

Yeatts, K. B., & Shy, C. M. (2001). Prevalence and consequences of asthma and wheezing in African-American and White adolescents. *Journal of Adolescent Health, 29*, 314–319.

Yeganeh, R., Beidel, D. C., Turner, S. M., Pina, A. A., & Silverman, W. K. (2003). Clinical distinctions between selective mutism and social phobia: An investigation of childhood psychopathology. *Journal of the American Academy of Child and Adolescent Psychiatry, 42*, 1069–1075.

Yeh, M., Hough, R. L., McCabe, K., Lau, A., & Garland, A. (2004). Parental beliefs about the cause of child problems: Exploring racial/ethnic patterns. *Journal of the American Academy of Child and Adolescent Psychiatry, 43*, 605–612.

Yeo, R. A., Hill, D. E., Campbell, R. A., Vigil, J., Petropoulos, H., Hart, B. et al. (2003). Proton magnetic resonance spectroscopy investigation of the right frontal lobe in children with attention-deficit/hyperactivity disorder. *Journal of the American Academy of Child and Adolescent Psychiatry, 42*, 303–310.

Yirmiya, N., Erel, O., Shaked, M., & Solomonica-Levi, D. (1998). Meta-analysis comparing theory of mind abilities in individuals with autism, individuals with mental retardation, and normally developing individuals. *Psychological Bulletin, 124*, 283–307.

Youdin, M. B. H., & Riederer, P. (1997). Understanding Parkinson's disease. *Scientific American, 276*, 52–59.

Young, A. R., Beitchman, J. H., Johnson, C., Douglas, L., Atkinson, L., Escobar, M., & Wilson, B. (2002). Young adult academic outcomes in a longitudinal sample of early identified language impaired and control children. *Journal of Child Psychology and Psychiatry, 43*, 635–645.

Young, M. H., Brennan, L. C., Baker, R. D., & Baker, S. S. (1996). Functional encopresis. In R. S. Feldman (Ed.), *The psychology of adversity.* Amherst: University of Massachusetts Press.

Young, R. C., Biggs, J. T., Ziegler, V. E., & Meyer, D. A. (1978). A rating scale for mania: Reliability, validity, and sensitivity. *British Journal of Psychiatry, 133*, 429–435.

Youngblade, L. M. (2003). Peer and teacher ratings of third- and fourth-grade children's social behavior as a function of early maternal employment. *Journal of Child Psychology and Psychiatry, 44*, 477–488.

Youngstrom, E., Loeber, R., & Stouthamer-Loeber, M. (2000). Patterns and correlates of agreement between parent, teacher, and male adolescent ratings of externalizing and internalizing problems. *Journal of Consulting and Clinical Psychology, 68*, 1038–1050.

Youngstrom, E. A., Findling, R. L., Danielson, C. K., & Calabrese, J. R. (2001). Discriminative validity of parent report of hypomanic and depressive symptoms in the General Behavior Inventory. *Psychological Assessment, 13*, 267–276.

Youngstrom, E. A., Findling, R. L., & Feeny, N. (2004). Assessment of bipolar spectrum disorders in children and adolescents. In S. L. Johnson & R. L. Leahy (Eds.), *Psychological treatment of bipolar disorder.* New York: Guilford Press.

Yule, W. (1994). Posttraumatic stress disorder. In T. H. Ollendick, N. J. King, & W. Yule (Eds.), *International handbook of phobic and anxiety disorders in children and adolescents* (pp. 223–240). New York: Plenum Press.

Yule, W. (2000). Emanuel Miller Lecture: From pogroms to "ethnic cleansing": Meeting the needs of war affected children. *Journal of Child Psychology and Psychiatry, 41*, 695–702.

Yule, W., Udwin, O., & Murdoch, K. (1990). The "Jupiter" sinking: Effects on children's fears, depression and anxiety. *Journal of Child Psychology and Psychiatry, 31*, 1051–1061.

Zalecki, C. A., & Hinshaw, S. P. (2004). Overt and relational aggression in girls with attention deficit hyperactivity disorder. *Journal of Clinical Child and Adolescent Psychology, 33*, 125–137.

Zametkin, A. J., Ernst, M., & Silver, R. (1998). Laboratory and diagnostic testing in child and adolescent psychiatry: A review of the past 10 years. *Journal of the American Academy of Child and Adolescent Psychiatry, 37*, 464–472.

Zametkin, A. J., & Rapoport, J. L. (1986). The pathophysiology of attention deficit disorder with hyperactivity: A review. In B. B. Lahey & A. E. Kazdin (Eds.), *Advance in clinical child psychology.* Vol. 9. New York: Plenum.

Zametkin, A. J., Zoon, C. K., Klein, H. W., & Munson, S. (2004). Psychiatric aspects of child and adolescent obesity: A review of the past 10 years. *Journal of the American Academy of Child and Adolescent Psychiatry, 43*, 134–150.

Zax, M., & Cowen, E. L. (1967). Early identification and prevention of emotional disturbance in a public school. In E. L. Cowen, E. A. Gardner, & M. Zax (Eds.), *Emergent approaches to mental health problems.* New York: Appleton-Century-Crofts.

Zeanah, C. H., Anders, T. F., Seifer, R., & Stern, D. N. (1989). Implications of research on infant development for psychodynamic theory and practice. *Journal of the American Academy of Child and Adolescent Psychiatry, 28,* 657–668.

Zeanah, C. H., Nelson, C. A., Fox. N. A., Smyke, A. T., Marshall, P., Parker, S. W., & Koga, S. (2003). Designing research to study the effects of institutionalization on brain and behavioral development: The Bucharest Early Intervention Project. *Development and Psychopathology, 15,* 885–907.

Zero to Three/National Center for Clinical Infant Programs. (1995). *Diagnostic classification: 0–3.* Arlington, VA: Author.

Zigler, E. (1999). Comment: Head Start is not child care. *American Psychologist, 54,* 142.

Zigler, E., Balla, D., & Hodapp, R. (1984). On the definition and classification of mental retardation. *American Journal of Mental Deficiency, 89,* 215–230.

Zito, J. M., Safer, D. J., dos Reis, S., Gardner, J. F., Boles, M., & Lynch, F. (2000). Trends in the prescribing of psychotropic medications to preschoolers. *Journal of the American Medical Association, 283,* 1025–1031.

Zwaigenbaum, L., Szatmari, P., Mahoney, W., Bryson, S., Bartolucci, G., & MacLean, J. (2000). High functioning autism and childhood disintegrative disorder in half brothers. *Journal of Autism and Developmental Disorders, 30,* 121–126.

Credits

CHAPTER OPENER PHOTOS

Page 1   Shirley Zeiberg/Pearson Education/PH College.
Page 18   Silver Burdett Ginn.
Page 38   Laima Druskis/Pearson Education/PH College.
Page 72   Laima Druskis/Pearson Education/PH College.
Page 94   Ken Karp/Pearson Education/PH College.
Page 123   David Mager/Pearson Learning Photo Studio.
Page 161   Silver Burdett Ginn.
Page 194   Shirley Zeiberg/Pearson Education/PH College.
Page 240   Larry Fleming/Pearson Education/PH College.
Page 270   Ken Karp/Pearson Education/PH College.
Page 303   Laima Druskis/Pearson Education/PH College.
Page 335   Charles Gatewood/Pearson Education/PH College.
Page 369   George Dodson/Pearson Education/PH College.
Page 400   Charles Gatewood/Pearson Education/PH College.
Page 423   Ken Karp/Prentice Hall School Division.

CARTOONS

Page 22   © The New Yorker Collection 2002 Robert Weber from cartoonbank.com. All rights reserved.

Page 63   © The New Yorker Collection 2002 Bud Handelsman from cartoonbank.com. All rights reserved.

Page 75   © The New Yorker Collection 2003 Michael Shaw from cartoonbank.com. All rights reserved.

Page 134   © The New Yorker Collection 1989 Robert Weber from cartoonbank.com. All rights reserved.

Page 215   © The New Yorker Collection 2002 Harry Bliss from cartoonbank.com. All rights reserved.

Page 251   © The New Yorker Collection 1999 Robert Weber from cartoonbank.com. All rights reserved.

Page 386   © The New Yorker Collection 2001 Robert Weber from cartoonbank.com. All rights reserved.

CHAPTER 1

Page 8   Table 1–2 Based in part on Hartung & Widiger, 1998. Gender differences in the diagnosis of mental disorders: conclusions and controversies of the DSM-IV. *Psychological Bulletin* 123, pp. 260–278. © 1998 by the American Psychological Association. Reprinted with permission.

Page 11   "Little Hans" Kessler, 1966.

CHAPTER 2

Page 20   Figure 2–1 Adapted from Achenbach, T.M. (1990). Conceptualization of Developmental Psychopathology. In M. Lewis & S.M. Miller (eds.) *Handbook of Developmental Psychopathology.* Reprinted by permission from Springer Science and Business Media.

Page 22   Figure 2–2 Adapted from Buhs & Ladd, "Peer Rejection as an Antecedent of Young Children's School Adjustment: An Examination of Mediating Processes," *Developmental Psychology*, 2001, Vol. 37, No. 4, pp. 550–560. © 2001 American Psychological Association, Inc.

Page 23   Figure 2–3 Adapted from Compas, Hinden and Gerhardt (1995). Adolescent Development: Pathways and Processes of Risk and Resilience. Reprinted with permission from the *Annual Review of Psychology*, © 1995, volume 46, pp. 265–293. www.annual reviews. org

Page 25   Figure 2–5 Adapted from Grant et al., 2003.

Page 25   Table 2–1 Based in part on Coie et al., 1993

Page 27   "The Timing of Risky Experiences" Rutter, 1989b

Page 28   Table 2–2 From Masten, A.S. & Coatsworth, J.D. (1998). The Development of Competence in Favorable and Infavorable Environments: Lessons From Research on Successful Children. *American Psychologist*, 53, pp. 205–220. © 1998 by the American Psychological Association. Reprinted with permission.

Page 28   Table 2–3 From Masten, A.S. & Coatsworth, J.D. (1998). The Development of Competence in Favorable and Infavorable Environments: Lessons From Research on Successful Children. *American Psychologist*, 53, pp. 205–220. © 1998 by the American Psychological Association. Reprinted with permission.

Page 29   Table 2–4 Adapted from Rutter, M. (1987). Psychosocial Resilience and Protective Mechanisms. *American Journal of Orthopsychiatry*, 57, pp. 316–317. © 1987 by the American Psychological Association. Reprinted with permission.

Page 32   Table 2–5 Adapted from Lyons-Ruth, Zeanah & Benoit, 2003.

Page 33   "Carl: A Case of 'Goodness of Fit'" Chess & Thomas, 1977, pp. 220–221.

CHAPTER 3

Page 47   Table 3–1   Adapted from Plomin, 1994b.

Page 51   Figure 3–4   Based in part on Belsky (1980); Bronfenbrenner (1977); and Lynch & Cicchetti (1998).

Page 52   Figure 3–5   Based in part on Maccoby & Martin, 1983.

Page 54   Table 3–4   From English, 1998.

Page 54   Figure 3–6   Adapted from U.S. Census Bureau, *Statistical Abstract of the United States: 2003* (123rd Ed.) Washington, DC, 2003.

Page 57   Figure 3–7   Adapted from De Bellis, 2001.

Page 58   Figure 3–8   Adapted from U.S. Census Bureau, *Statistical Abstract of the United States: 1996* and *2003* (116th and 123rd eds.) Washington, DC, 1996, 2003.

Page 60   Figure 3–9   From Hetherington, Bridges and Insabella, 1998.

Page 62   "Delano: A Problematic Friendship" Hartup, 1996, p. 1.

Page 64   Figure 3–10   U.S. Bureau of the Census, Current Population Survey, 2002 and 2003.

Page 64   Table 3–5   Adapted from Brooks-Gunn, J. & Duncan, G. (1997, Summer/Fall). The effects of poverty on children. "The Future of Children," from *Children and Poverty*, Vol. 7, No. 2, pp. 55–71, © 1997 The Center for the Future of Children. Reprinted with the permission of the David and Lucille Packard Foundation.

Page 65   "Visit to East St. Louis" Jonathon Kozol, Savage Inequalities, 1991.

Page 66   Figure 3–11   From Evans, 2004.

Page 67   Figure 3–12   Based on Leventhal & Brooks-Gunn, 2000.

Page 68   Figure 3–13   From Garcia Coll et al., 1996.

CHAPTER 4

Page 80   Figure 4–1   From Ramey, C.T. & Campbell, F.A. (1984). Preventive Education for High-Risk Children: Cognitive Consequences of the Carolina Abecedarian Project. *American Journal of Mental Deficiency*, 88, pp. 515–523.

Page 83   Figure 4–4   From Koegel, O'Dell and Koegel (1987). A Natural Language Teaching Paradigm for Nonverbal Autistic Children. *Journal of Autism and Developmental Disorders*, 17, pp. 187–200. Reprinted by permission from Springer Science and Business Media.

Page 90   Table 4–3   Summarized from the Report from the Committee for Ethical Conduct in the Children Development Research. SRCD Newsletter (Winter 1990). Society for Research in Child Development, Inc.

CHAPTER 5

Page 97   Table 5–1   Reprinted with permission from the *Diagnostic and Statistical Manual of Mental Disorders*, Fourth Edition, Text Revision, Copyright 2000 American Psychiatric Association.

Page 101   Table 5–2   Adapted from Achenbach, T.M. & Rescorla, L.A. (2001). *Manual for the ASEBA School-Age Forms and Profiles*. Burlington, VT: University of Vermont, Research Center for Children, Youth and Families.

Page 106   Figure 5–2   Adapted from Achenbach, T.M. & Rescorla, L.A. (2001). *Manual for the ASEBA School-Age Forms and Profiles*. Burlington, VT: University of Vermont, Research Center for Children, Youth and Families.

CHAPTER 6

Page 125   Figure 6–1   From King, Ollier, Iacuone, Schuster, Bays, Gullone & Ollendick, 1989.

Page 126   Table 6–1   Adapted from Achenbach, T.M. & Rescorla, L.A. (2001). *Manual for the ASEBA School-Age Forms and Profiles*. Burlington, VT: University of Vermont, Research Center for Children, Youth and Families.

Page 127   Table 6–2   Reprinted with permission from the *Diagnostic and Statistical Manual of Mental Disorders*, Fourth Edition, Text Revision, Copyright 2000 American Psychiatric Association.

Page 128   Figure 6–2   Adapted from Ost, L. (1987). Age of Onset in Different Phobias. *Journal of Abnormal Psychology*, 96, pp. 123–145. © 1987 by the American Psychological Association. Reprinted with permission.

Page 128   Table 6–3   Reprinted with permission from the *Diagnostic and Statistical Manual of Mental Disorders*, Fourth Edition, Text Revision, Copyright 2000 American Psychiatric Association.

Page 129   Table 6–4   By permission of author Annette M. La Greca.

Page 132   Table 6–5   Reprinted with permission from the *Diagnostic and Statistical Manual of Mental Disorders*, Fourth Edition, Text Revision, Copyright 2000 American Psychiatric Association.

Page 137   Table 6–6   Reprinted with permission from the *Diagnostic and Statistical Manual of Mental Disorders*, Fourth Edition, Text Revision, Copyright 2000 American Psychiatric Association.

Page 138   Table 6–7   Reprinted with permission from the *Diagnostic and Statistical Manual of Mental Disorders*, Fourth Edition, Text Revision, Copyright 2000 American Psychiatric Association.

Page 139   Table 6–8   Reprinted with permission from the *Diagnostic and Statistical Manual of Mental Disorders*, Fourth Edition, Text Revision, Copyright 2000 American Psychiatric Association.

Page 141   Table 6–9   Reprinted with permission from the *Diagnostic and Statistical Manual of Mental Disorders*, Fourth Edition, Text Revision, Copyright 2000 American Psychiatric Association.

Page 143   Figure 6–3   Adapted from De Bellis, "Developmental Traumatology: The Psychobiological Development of Maltreated Children and Its Implications for Research, Treatment and Policy," *Development and Psychopathology*, 13 (2001), pp. 539–564 © 2001. Reprinted with the permission of Cambridge University Press.

Page 144   Table 6–10   Adapted from Fletcher, 2003

Page 146   Table 6–11   Reprinted with permission from the *Diagnostic and Statistical Manual of Mental Disorders*, Fourth Edition, Text Revision, Copyright 2000 American Psychiatric Association.

Page 147   Table 6–12   From tables by Johnny Johnson from the article "The Biology of Obsessions and Compulsions" by Judith L. Rapaport, March 1989. © 1989 Scientific American, Inc. All rights reserved.

Page 155   Table 6–13   Adapted from Kendall, P.C., Chu, B.C., Pimentel, S.S. & Choudhury, M. (2000).

CHAPTER 7

Page 163   Table 7–1   Adapted from Kazdin, A.E. (1989). Identifying Depression in Children: A Comparison of Alternative Selection Criteria. *Journal of Abnormal Child Psychology*, 17, pp. 437–454. Reprinted by permission from Springer Science and Business Media.

Page 164   Table 7–2   Reprinted with permission from the *Diagnostic and Statistical Manual of Mental Disorders*, Fourth Edition, Text Revision, Copyright 2000 American Psychiatric Association.

Page 164   Table 7–3   Reprinted with permission from the *Diagnostic and Statistical Manual of Mental Disorders*, Fourth Edition, Text Revision, Copyright 2000 American Psychiatric Association.

Page 166   Table 7–4   Reprinted with permission from the *Diagnostic and Statistical Manual of Mental Disorders*, Fourth Edition, Text Revision, Copyright 2000 American Psychiatric Association.

Page 167   Table 7–5   Adapted from Geller et al., 2003.

Page 169   Figure 7–1   From Hankin, Abramson, Moffitt, Silva, McGee & Angell (1998). Development of Depression from Preadolescence to Young Adulthood: Emerging Gender Differences in a 10-Year Longitudinal Study. *Journal of Abnormal Psychology*, 107, pp. 128–140. © 1998 by the American Psychological Association. Reprinted with permission.

Page 170   Figure 7–2   Adapted from Kistner, David & White, 2003.

Page 178   Table 7–6   Adapted from Weissman, Warner, Wickramaratne, Moreau & Olfsen (1997). Offspring of Depressed Parents: 10 Years Later. *Archives of General Psychiatry*, 54, pp. 932–940.

Page 180   Figure 7–4   Adapted from Murray, L. (1992). The Impact of Postnatal Depression on Infant Development. *Journal of Child Psychology and Psychiatry*, 33, pp. 543–561.

Page 183   Table 7–7   From Anderson & Smith, 2003.

Page 185   Figure 7–5   Adapted from Lewisohn, Rhode & Seeley (1996). Adolescent Suicidal Ideation and Attempts: Prevalence, Risk Factors and Clinical Implications. *Clinical Psychology: Science and Practice*, 3, pp. 25–46. Reprinted by permission of Oxford University Press.

Page 187   Table 7–8   From Lefkowitz, M., & Tesiny, E. (1980). Assessment of Childhood Depression. *Journal of Consulting and Clinical Psychology*, 48, pp. 43–50. © 1980 by the American Psychological Association. Reprinted with permission.

Page 187   Table 7–9   Adapted fom Garber & Kaminski, 2000. Laboratory and Performance-Based Measures of Depression in Children and Adolescents. *Journal of Clinical Child Psychology*, 2000, Vol. 29, No. 4, pp. 509–525.

Page 189   Figure 7–6   From Weisz, Thurber, Sweeney, Proffitt & LaGagnoux (1997). Brief Treatment of Mild-to-Moderate Child Depression Using Primary and Secondary Control Enhancement Training. *Journal of Consulting and Clinical Psychology*, 65, pp. 703–707. © 1997 by the American Psychological Association. Reprinted with permission.

Page 191   Figure 7–7   From Rosselló & Bernal, 1999. "The Efficacy of Cognitive-Behavioral and Interpersonal Treatments for Depression in Puerto Rican Adolescents," from the *Journal of Consulting and Clinical Psychology*, 1999, Vol. 67, No. 5 pp. 734–745. © 1999 by the American Psychological Association, Inc.

CHAPTER 8

Page 195   Table 8–1   Adapted from Achenbach, T.M. & Rescorla, L.A. (2001). *Manual for the ASEBA School-Age Forms and Profiles.* Burlington, VT: University of Vermont, Research Center for Children, Youth and Families.

Page 196   Figure 8–1   Adapted from Stanger, C. et al. (1997). Accelerated Longitudinal Comparisons of Aggressive vs. Delinquent Syndromes. *Development and Psychopathology*, 9, pp. 43–58. Reprinted with the permission of Cambridge University Press.

Page 197   Figure 8–2   From Frick, P.J. (1998). Conduct Disorders. In T.H. Ollendick & M. Hersen (eds.) *Handbook of Child Psychopathology* (3rd ed.). Reprinted by permission from Springer Science and Business Media.

Page 199   Table 8–2   Reprinted with permission from the *Diagnostic and Statistical Manual of Mental Disorders*, Fourth Edition, Text Revision, Copyright 2000 American Psychiatric Association.

Page 200   Table 8–3   Reprinted with permission from the *Diagnostic and Statistical Manual of Mental Disorders*, Fourth Edition, Text Revision, Copyright 2000 American Psychiatric Association.

Page 203   Table 8–4   From U.S. Bureau of the Census, *Statistical Abstract of the United States: 1998* (118th ed.), Washington, DC: U.S. Bureau of the Census, *Statistical Abstract of the United States: 2003* (123rd ed.). Washington, DC.

Page 207   Table 8–5   Reprinted with permission from the *Diagnostic and Statistical Manual of Mental Disorders*, Fourth Edition, Text Revision, Copyright 2000 American Psychiatric Association.

Page 207   Table 8–6   Reprinted with permission from the *Diagnostic and Statistical Manual of Mental Disorders*, Fourth Edition, Text Revision, Copyright 2000 American Psychiatric Association.

Page 208   Figure 8–3   Adapted from Johnston, O'Malley & Bachman, 2003.

Page 211   Figure 8–4   Adapted from Lynskey, M.T. et al. (1998). The Origins and Correlations Between Tobacco, Alcohol and Cannabis During Adolescence. *Journal of Child Psychology and Psychiatry*, 39, pp. 995–1005.

Page 212 Figure 8–5 Adapted from Maughan et al., 2004.

Page 217 Figure 8–6 Reprinted from Loeber, R., & Hay, D.F. (1994). Interaction Between Conduct Disorder and Its Comorbid Conditions: Effects of Age and Gender. *Clinical Psychology Review*, 14, pp. 497–623 with permission from Elsevier Science.

Page 218 Table 8–7 From Loeber & Farrington, 2000.

Page 221 Figure 8–7 From Patterson, Reid & Dishion, 1992. *Antisocial Boys*. Eugene, OR: Castalia Publishing Co.

Page 222 Figure 8–8 From Capaldi et al., 2002.

Page 226 Table 8–8 Adapted from Brendgen, Vitaro, Tremblay & Lavoie, "Reactive and Proactive Aggression: Predictions to Physical Violence in Different Contexts and Moderating Effects of Parental Monitoring and Caregiving Behavior." *Journal of Abnormal Psychology*, Vol. 29, No. 4, 2001, pp. 293–304.

Page 227 Figure 8–9 From Dishion, T.J. et al. (1995). The Development and Ecology of Antisocial Behavior. In D. Cicchetti & D.J. Cohen (eds.), *Developmental Psychopathology, Vol. 2: Risk, Disorder and Adaptation.* This material used by permission of John Wiley and Sons, Inc.

Page 231 Table 8–9 Adapted from Kazdin, 1997.

Page 232 Table 8–10 Adapted from Querido, Bearss & Eyberg, 2002.

Page 233 Table 8–11 Adapted from Kazdin, 1997.

Page 236 Figure 8–10 From Henggeler, S.W. et al. (1998). *Multisystematic Treatment of Antisocial Behavior in Children and Adolescents.* New York: Guilford Press. Reprinted with permission.

Page 237 Figure 8–11 Adapted from Henggeler, S.W. et al. (1992). Family Preservation Using Multisystematic Therapy: An Effective Alternative to Incarcerating Serious Juvenile Offenders. *Journal of Consulting and Clinical Psychology*, 60, pp. 953–961. © 1992 by the American Psychological Association. Reprinted with permission.

CHAPTER 9

Page 241 Table 9–1 Reprinted with permission from the *Diagnostic and Statistical Manual of Mental Disorders*, Fourth Edition, Text Revision, Copyright 2000 American Psychiatric Association.

Page 243 Figure 9–1 Adapted from Dane, Schachar & Tannock, 2000.

Page 254 Figure 9–2 From Barkley, R.A. (1997). Attention-Deficit/Hyperactivity Disorder. In E.J. Mash & L.G. Terdal (eds.) *Assessment of Childhood Disorders.* New York: Guilford Press. Reprinted with permission.

Page 256 Figure 9–3 Adapted with permission (from an illustration by Carol Donner) from Youdin and Riederer (1997). Understanding Parkinson's Disease. *Scientific American*, 276, pp. 52–59.

Page 259 Table 9–3 Reprinted with permission from Barkley, R. (1981). Hyperactivity in E.J. Mash & L.G. Terdal (eds.) *Behavioral Assessment of Childhood Disorders.* New York: Guilford Press. Reprinted with permission.

Page 260 Table 9–4 Adapted from Conners, Sitarenios, Parker & Epstein, 1998b. The Revised Conners' Parent Rating Scale (CPRS-R): Factor Structure, Reliability and Criterion Validity. *Journal of Abnormal Child Psychology*, 26, pp. 257–268. Reprinted by permission from Springer Science and Business Media.

Page 264 Table 9–6 Adapted from Anastopoulos & Farley, 2003.

Page 264 Table 9–7 From DuPaul, Guevrement and Barkley in *The Practice of Child Therapy*, 2e, Kratochwill Morris. Published by Allyn and Bacon, Boston, MA. Copyright © 1991 by Pearson Education. Adapted by permission of the publisher.

Page 267 Figure 9–4 Adapted from MTA Cooperative Group, 2004b.

CHAPTER 10

Page 271 Table 10–1 Based on Hallahan & Mock, 2003.

Page 274 Table 10–3 Based on Bryant 1997; Whitehurst, 1982.

Page 275 Table 10–6 Adapted from Young et al., 2002.

Page 282 Figure 10–1 Adapted from Snowling, Gallagher & Frith, 2003.

Page 283 Figure 10–2 From Taylor, 1988a.

Page 284 Figure 10–3 From Wong, Butler, Ficzere & Kuperis, 1997. Teaching Adolescents with Learning Disabilities and Low Achievers to Plan, Write and Revise Compare-and-Contrast Essays. *Learning Disabilities Research and Practice*, 12, pp. 2–15.

Page 285 Figure 10–4 From Taylor, H.G. (1988). Learning Disabilities. In E.J. Mash & L.G. Terdal (eds.) *Behavioral Assessment of Childhood Disorders.* 2nd ed. New York: Guilford Press. Reprinted with permission.

Page 287 Figure 10–5 Data from Stone and La Greca, 1990. The Social Status of Children with Learning Disabilities. A Reexamination. *Journal of Learning Disabilities*, 23, pp. 23–37. Copyright © Sage Publications, 1990, by permission of Sage Publications Ltd.

Page 288 Figure 10–6 From Willcutt and Pennington, 2000, "Psychiatric Comorbidity in Children and Adolescents with Reading Disability," *Journal of Child Psychology and Psychiatry*, Vol. 41, No. 8, pp. 1039–1048.

Page 290 Figure 10–8 Adapted from Shaywitz & Shaywitz, 2003.

Page 293 Figure 10–9 From Taylor, H.G. (1989). Learning Disabilities. In E.J. Mash & R.A. Bankley (eds.) *Treatment of Childhood Disorders.* New York: Guilford Press. Reprinted with permission.

Page 298 Figure 10–11 *Students With Learning Disabilities*, 5/E by Cecil D. Mercer © 1997. Reprinted by permission of Pearson Education, Inc. Upper Saddle River, NJ.

Page 299 Figure 10–12 Baumeister & Baumeister "Mental Retardation: Causes and Effects" from *Advanced Abnormal Child Psychology.* 2nd ed. Ed. Michael Hersen & Robert Ammerman. © 2000 Lawrence Erlbaum Associates, Publishers.

CHAPTER 11

Page 304 Figure 11–1 Luckasson et al., 2002.

Page 305 Table 11–1 Luckasson et al., 2002.

Page 305 Table 11–2 Adapted from Bromley & Blacher, 1991. Parental Reasons for Out-of-Home Placement of Children with Severe Handicaps. *Mental Retardation*, 29, pp. 275–280.

Page 307 Figure 11–3 From Kirk, Gallagher & Anastasiow, 2000.

Page 310 Table 11–4 American Psychiatric Association, 2000; and Singh, Oswald & Ellis, 1998.

Page 311 Figure 11–3 From Kirk, Gallagher & Anastasiow, 2000.

Page 312 Table 11–5 Adapted from King, Hodapp & Dykens, "Mental Retardation" from Kaplan & Saddock's *Comprehensive Textbook of Psychiatry*. © 2000 Lippincott, Williams and Wilkins.

Page 315 Table 11–6 Adapted from Hodapp & Dykens, 2003.

Page 315 Table 11–7 Adapted from King, Hodapp & Dykens, "Mental Retardation" from Kaplan & Saddock's *Comprehensive Textbook of Psychiatry*. © 2000 Lippincott, Williams and Wilkins.

Page 316 Table 11–8 From Aman, Hammer & Rojahn, 1993; Bailey et al., 2000; Capone, 2001; Karminoff-Smith & Thomas, 2003; Moldavsky et al., 2001; State, King & Dykens, 1997; Volkman & Dykens, 2003; Whitman, O'Callaghan & Sommer, 1997.

Page 317 Figure 11–4 Courtesy of the March of Dimes Birth Defects Foundation.

Page 318 Figure 11–5 Adapted from Rossen, Klima, Bellugi, Bihrle & Jones, 1996.

Page 321 Table 11–9 From Luckasson et al., 2002.

Page 322 Table 11–10 Adapted from Bromley & Blacher, 1991. Parental Reasons for Out-of-Home Placement of Children with Severe Handicaps. *Mental Retardation*, 29, pp. 275–280.

Page 323 Table 11–11 Adapted from Scorgie & Sobsey, *Mental Retardation*, Vol. 38, No. 3, pp. 105–206, June 2000.

Page 327 Figure 11–6 From Braddock, Rizzolo & Hemp, 2004.

Page 331 Figure 11–7 Adapted from Newsom, 1998. Autistic Disorder. In E.J. Mash & R.A. Barkley (eds.) *Treatment of Childhood Disorders*. New York: Guilford Press. Reprinted with permission.

Page 332 Figure 11–8 Durand, "Functional Communication Training Using Assistive Devices: Recruiting Natural Communities of Reinforcement," *Journal of Applied Behavior Analysis*, 1999, 32, pp. 247–267, Number 3, Fall 1999.

CHAPTER 12

Page 337 Table 12–1 Reprinted with permission from the *Diagnostic and Statistical Manual of Mental Disorders*, Fourth Edition, Text Revision, Copyright 2000 American Psychiatric Association.

Page 338 Figure 12–1 Adapted from Dissanayake and Crossley, 1996. Proximity and Social Behaviours in Autism: Evidence for Attachment. *Journal of Child Psychology and Psychiatry*, 27, pp. 149–156.

Page 343 Figure 12–2 Two theory of mind tasks. From Baron-Cohen et al., 1999.

Page 344 Figure 12–3 From Happé, Briskman & Frith, "Exploring the Cognitive Phenotype of Autism: Weak 'Central Coherence' in Parents and Siblings of Children with Autism: I. Experimental Test" *Journal of Child Psychology and Psychiatry*, Vol. 42, No. 3, pp. 299–307, 2001.

Page 347 Figure 12–4 From Madsen et al., 2003.

Page 348 Figure 12–5 Based on Szatmari et al., 2000.

Page 349 Table 12–2 Reprinted with permission from the *Diagnostic and Statistical Manual of Mental Disorders*, Fourth Edition, Text Revision, Copyright 2000 American Psychiatric Association.

Page 354 Table 12–3 Based on Koegel, Koegel & McNerney, 2001.

Page 354 Table 12–4 From Lovaas & Smith, 2003.

Page 355 Table 12–5 Adapted from Lovaas, 1987. Behavioral Treatment and Normal Educational and Intellectual Functioning in Young Autistic Children. *Journal of Consulting and Clinical Psychology*, 55, pp. 3–9. © 1987 by the American Psychological Association. Reprinted with permission.

Page 356 Table 12–6 Based on Schloper, 1997. Implementation of TEACCH Philosophy. In D.J. Cohen & F.R. Volkmar (eds.) *Handbook of Autism and Pervasive Developmental Disorders*. New York: John Wiley and Sons, Inc.

Page 357 Table 12–7 Reprinted with permission from the *Diagnostic and Statistical Manual of Mental Disorders*, Fourth Edition, Text Revision, Copyright 2000 American Psychiatric Association.

Page 358 Table 12–8 Adapted from Green et al. 1992; Russell et al. 1989; and Volkmar et al. 1991. Schizophrenia with Childhood Onset. A Phenomenological Study of 38 Cases. *Journal of American Academy of Child and Adolescent Psychiatry*, 31, pp. 968–976; and Russell, A.T. et al. 1989. The Phenomenology of Schizophrenia Occurring in Childhood. *Journal of the American Academy of Child and Adolescent Psychiatry*, 28, pp. 399–407; and Volkmar, F.R. 1991. Childhood Schizophrenia in M. Lewis (ed.) *Child and Adolescent Psychiatry: A Comprehensive Textbook*. Baltimore: Williams and Wilkins.

Page 358 Table 12–9 From Russell, Bott & Sammons, 1989.

Page 360 Table 12–10 Adapted from Green, Padron-Gayol, Hardesty & Bassin, 1992. Schizophrenia with Childhood Onset: A Phenomenological Study of 38 Cases. *Journal of American Academy of Child and Adolescent Psychiatry*, 31, pp. 968–976.

Page 366 Table 12–11 Adapted from Asarnow, Tompson & McGrath, 2003.

CHAPTER 13

Page 377 Table 13–1 Adapted from Wilson and Haynes, 1985. Sleep Disorders. In P.H. Bornstein & A.E. Kazdin (eds.) *Handbook of Clinical Behavior Therapy with Children*. Homewood, IL: Dorsey.

Page 378   Figure 13–2   Reprinted from Muris et al, Children's Nighttime Fears: Parent-Child Ratings of Frequency, Content, Origins, Coping Behaviors and Severity, *Behaviour Research and Therapy*, 39 (2001) pp. 13–28 with permission from Elsevier Science.

Page 383   Figure 13–3   Adapted from National Center for Health Statistics, 2001.

Page 384   Figure 13–4   Adapted from Israel & Shapiro, 1985. Behavior Problems of Obese Children Enrolling in a Weight Reduction Program. *Journal of Pediatric Psychology*, 10, pp. 449–460. Reprinted by permission of Oxford University Press.

Page 387   Figure 13–5   From Israel, A.C. et al. (1994). An Evaluation of Enhanced Self-Regulation Training in the Treatment of Childhood Obesity. *Journal of Pediatric Psychology*, 19, pp. 737–749. Reprinted by permission of Oxford University Press.

Page 388   Table 13–2   Reprinted with permission from the *Diagnostic and Statistical Manual of Mental Disorders*, Fourth Edition, Text Revision, Copyright 2000 American Psychiatric Association.

Page 389   Table 13–3   Reprinted with permission from the *Diagnostic and Statistical Manual of Mental Disorders*, Fourth Edition, Text Revision, Copyright 2000 American Psychiatric Association.

Page 394   Figure 13–6   Adapted from Collins, 1991. Body Figure Perceptions and Preferences Among Preadolescent Children. *International Journal of Eating Disorders*, 10, pp. 199–208. This material used by permission of John Wiley and Sons, Inc.

CHAPTER 14

Page 405   Figure 14–1   From Wallander and Varni, 1998. Effects of Pediatric Chronic Physical Disorders on Child and Family Adjustment. *Journal of Child Psychology and Psychiatry*, 39, pp. 29–46.

Page 407   Figure 14–2   Adapted from Bleil, Ramesh, Miller & Wood, 2000.

Page 411   Table 14–1   Adapted from Karoly & Bay, 1990.

Page 413   Figure 14–3   Adapted from Palmer et al., 2004.

Page 414   Table 14–2   Adapted from Thomas, Peterson & Goldstein, 1997. Problem Solving and Diabetes Regimen Adherence by Children and Adolescents with IDDM in Social Pressure Situations: A Reflection on Normal Development. *Journal of Pediatric Psychology*, 22, pp. 541–561. Reprinted by permission from Springer Science and Business Media.

Page 417   Table 14–3   Adapted from Dahlquist, 1992. Coping with Aversive Medical Treatments. In A.M. LaGreca, L.J. Siegal, J.L. Walander & C.E. Walker (eds.) *Stress and Coping in Child Health*. New York: Guilford Press. Reprinted with permission.

CHAPTER 15

Page 434   Figure 15–2   Urban Institute for Calculations from the 1987 National Survey of America's Families.

Page 437   Figure 15–3   From Allen & Bissell, 2004.

Page 441   Figure 15–4   Data from *The State of the World's Children*, 2000. UNICEF, United Nations.

Name Index

Subject Index